GREAT BRITAIN ROAD ATLAS

Journey Route Planning maps

Southern Britain......II-III

Northern Britain......IV-V

Mileage Chart..........2

Great Britain Road map section

Key to map pages inside front cover

Reference..................3

Road Maps..............4-173

Detailed Main Route maps

London.....................174-181

Birmingham..............182-183

Manchester...............184

City and Town centre maps

Plans of 80 principal cities and towns in Great Britain

Reference..................185-186

Cities and Towns......187-214

Sea Port & Channel Tunnel plans

Principal Sea Ports in Great Britain..............215

Folkestone and Calais Terminals..................276

Airport plans

Access maps to principal Airports in Great Britain
.................................216

Over 32,000 Index References

A
Abbas Combe. *Som* 4C **22**
Abberley. *Worc* 4B **60**
Abberley Common. *Worc* 4B **60**
Abberton. *Essx* 4D **54**
Abberton. *Worc* 5D **61**
Abberwick. *Nmbd* 3F **121**
Abbas Roding. Essy 4F 52

Including cities, towns, villages, hamlets and locations..............217-269

Index to Places of Interest

L
Lacock Abbey (SN15 2LG) ....
Lady Lever Art Gallery (CH62 5EQ) ......
Lady of the North (NE23 8AU) ....
Laing Art Gallery (NE1 8AG) ....New
Lake District Nat. Pk. (LA9 7RL) ....
Lakeside & Haverthwaite Railway (LA12 8AL)
Lamb House (TN31 7ES)

Full postcodes to easily locate over 1,700 selected places of interest on your SatNav...270-273

Motorway Junctions

M25

Junction 5
Clockwise: No exit to M26 Eastbound
Anti-clockwise: No access from M26 Westbound

Details of motorway junctions with limited interchange........274-275

Safety Camera Information

Details of Safety Camera symbols used on the maps, and the responsible use of camera information
.................inside back cover

EDITION 22 2015

Copyright © Geographers' A-Z Map Company Ltd.

Telephone: 01732 781000 (Enquiries & Trade Sales)
01732 783422 (Retail Sales)

  www./az.co.uk

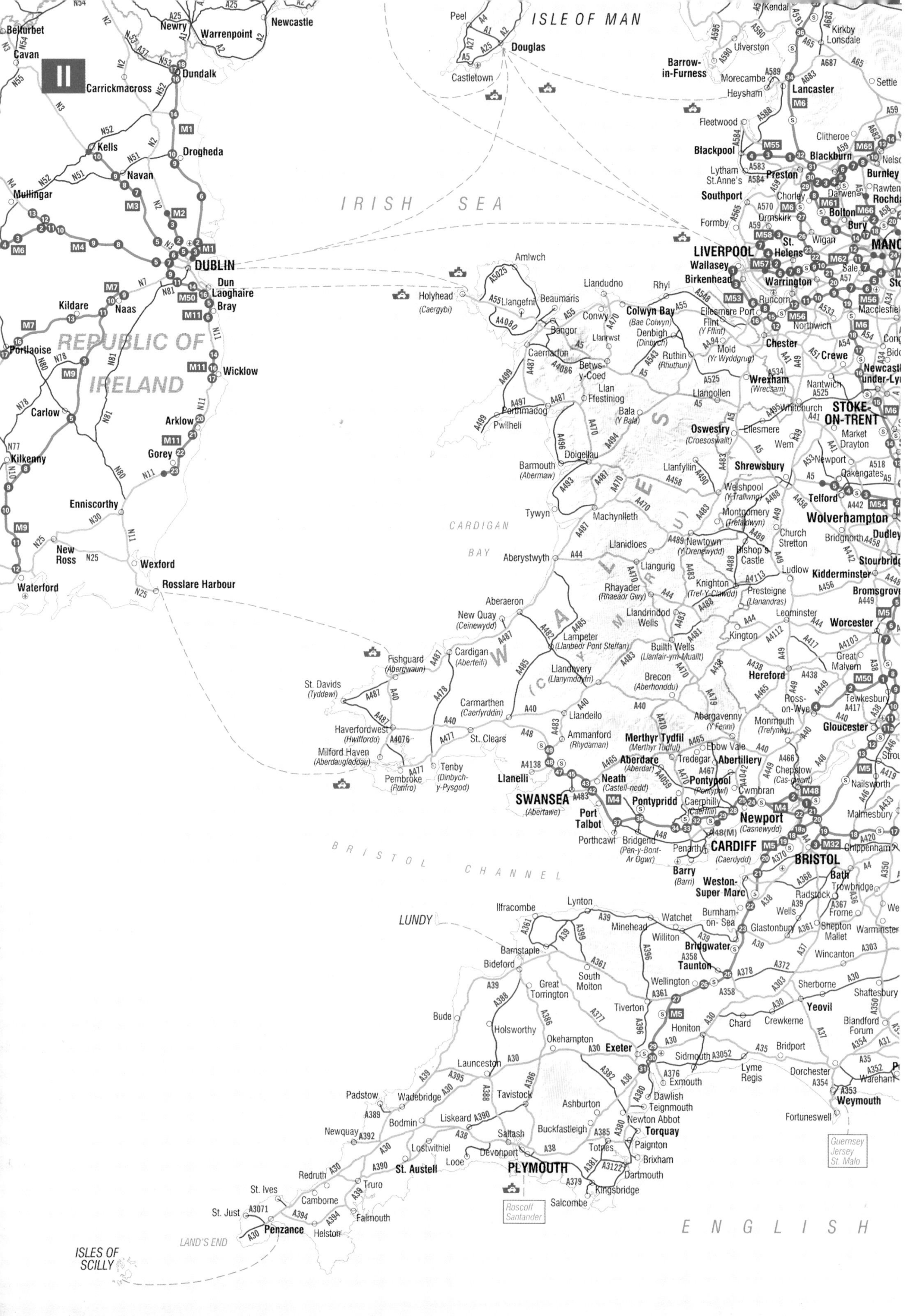
II
ISLE OF MAN
Peel
Douglas
Castletown
IRISH SEA
REPUBLIC OF IRELAND
Belturbet
Cavan
Newry
Warrenpoint
Newcastle
Carrickmacross
Dundalk
Kells
Drogheda
Navan
Mullingar
DUBLIN
Dun Laoghaire
Bray
Kildare
Naas
Portlaoise
Wicklow
Carlow
Arklow
Kilkenny
Gorey
Enniscorthy
New Ross
Wexford
Waterford
Rosslare Harbour
Kendal
Kirkby Lonsdale
Ulverston
Barrow-in-Furness
Morecambe
Heysham
Lancaster
Settle
Fleetwood
Blackpool
Clitheroe
Blackburn
Burnley
Lytham St.Anne's
Preston
Southport
Chorley
Darwen
Bolton
Bury
Ormskirk
Formby
Wigan
St. Helens
LIVERPOOL
Wallasey
Birkenhead
Warrington
Sale
Runcorn
Ellesmere Port
Northwich
Macclesfield
Amlwch
Holyhead
(Caergybi)
Llangefni
Beaumaris
Llandudno
Rhyl
Conwy
Colwyn Bay
(Bae Colwyn)
Flint
(Y Fflint)
Denbigh
(Dinbych)
Bangor
Llanrwst
Mold
(Yr Wyddgrug)
Chester
Crewe
Caernarfon
Betws-y-Coed
Ruthin
(Rhuthun)
Wrexham
(Wrecsam)
Nantwich
Llan Ffestiniog
Llangollen
Porthmadog
Pwllheli
Bala
(Y Bala)
Whitchurch
STOKE-ON-TRENT
Oswestry
(Croesoswallt)
Ellesmere
Wem
Market Drayton
Barmouth
(Abermaw)
Dolgellau
Llanfyllin
Shrewsbury
Newport
Telford
Welshpool
(Y Trallwng)
Tywyn
Machynlleth
Montgomery
(Trefaldwyn)
Wolverhampton
CARDIGAN BAY
Aberystwyth
Llanidloes
Newtown
(Y Drenewydd)
Church Stretton
Bridgnorth
Dudley
Llangurig
Bishop's Castle
Stourbridge
Ludlow
Kidderminster
Rhayader
(Rhaeadr Gwy)
Knighton
(Tref-Y-Clawdd)
Presteigne
(Llanandras)
Aberaeron
New Quay
(Ceinewydd)
Llandrindod Wells
Leominster
Worcester
WALES
(CYMRU)
Lampeter
(Llanbedr Pont Steffan)
Kington
Builth Wells
(Llanfair-ym-Muallt)
Great Malvern
Fishguard
(Abergwaun)
Cardigan
(Aberteifi)
Llandovery
(Llanymddyfri)
Hereford
St. Davids
(Tyddewi)
Brecon
(Aberhonddu)
Tewkesbury
Carmarthen
(Caerfyrddin)
Ross-on-Wye
Llandeilo
Abergavenny
(Y Fenni)
Monmouth
(Trefynwy)
Gloucester
Haverfordwest
(Hwlffordd)
St. Clears
Ammanford
(Rhydaman)
Merthyr Tydfil
(Merthyr Tudful)
Ebbw Vale
Milford Haven
(Aberdaugleddau)
Tredegar
Aberdare
(Aberdâr)
Abertillery
Chepstow
(Cas-gwent)
Pembroke
(Penfro)
Tenby
(Dinbych-y-Pysgod)
Llanelli
Neath
(Castell-nedd)
Pontypool
(Pontypŵl)
Cwmbran
Nailsworth
SWANSEA
(Abertawe)
Pontypridd
Caerphilly
(Caerffili)
Newport
(Casnewydd)
Malmesbury
Port Talbot
Porthcawl
Bridgend
(Pen-y-Bont-Ar Ogwr)
Penarth
CARDIFF
(Caerdydd)
BRISTOL
Chippenham
BRISTOL CHANNEL
Barry
(Barri)
Weston-Super Mare
Bath
Trowbridge
Radstock
Frome
Wells
LUNDY
Ilfracombe
Lynton
Minehead
Watchet
Burnham-on-Sea
Glastonbury
Shepton Mallet
Warminster
Williton
Bridgwater
Barnstaple
Bideford
Taunton
Wincanton
South Molton
Great Torrington
Wellington
Sherborne
Shaftesbury
Tiverton
Yeovil
Chard
Crewkerne
Bude
Holsworthy
Honiton
Blandford Forum
Okehampton
Exeter
Bridport
Sidmouth
Launceston
Lyme Regis
Dorchester
Exmouth
Wareham
Padstow
Wadebridge
Tavistock
Dawlish
Weymouth
Teignmouth
Ashburton
Newquay
Bodmin
Liskeard
Newton Abbot
Fortuneswell
Torquay
Buckfastleigh
Saltash
Lostwithiel
Paignton
Looe
Devonport
Totnes
Guernsey
Jersey
St. Malo
Brixham
Redruth
St. Austell
PLYMOUTH
Dartmouth
Truro
Kingsbridge
St. Ives
Camborne
Roscoff
Santander
Salcombe
St. Just
Falmouth
Penzance
Helston
LAND'S END
ENGLISH
ISLES OF SCILLY

REFERENCE

MOTORWAY WITH NUMBER	M4 (S) Service Area
MOTORWAY (Under Construction/Proposed)	– – – –
MOTORWAY JUNCTIONS	5 23a
PRIMARY ROUTE	A5
A ROAD	A272
NATIONAL BOUNDARY	————
TOWNS SHOWN IN THE MILEAGE CHART	NORWICH

SCALE

0   10   20   30   40 Miles

0   10   20   30   40   50   60 Kilometres

NORTH SEA

ENGLAND

CHANNEL

FRANCE

GUERNSEY
St. Peter Port

JERSEY
St. Helier

Jersey and Guernsey lie 85 miles south of Weymouth

ISLE OF WIGHT

THE WASH

Rotterdam Zeebrugge

Esbjerg Hook of Holland

Channel Tunnel

Bilbao
Caen
Cherbourg
Guernsey
Jersey
Le Havre
St. Malo
Santander

Cherbourg
Guernsey
Jersey
St. Malo

Dieppe

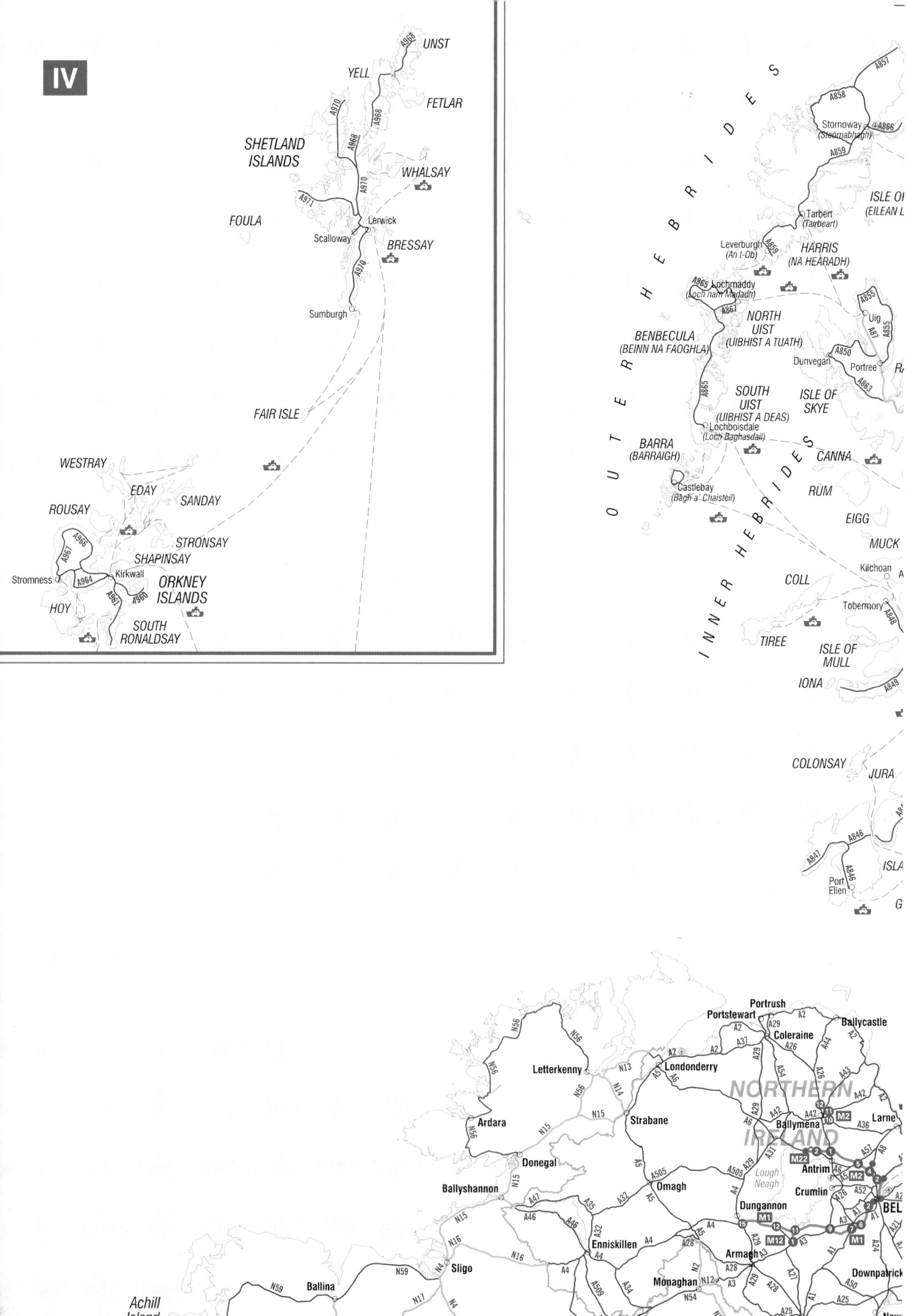
IV
UNST
YELL
FETLAR
SHETLAND ISLANDS
WHALSAY
FOULA
Lerwick
Scalloway
BRESSAY
Sumburgh
FAIR ISLE
WESTRAY
EDAY
SANDAY
ROUSAY
STRONSAY
SHAPINSAY
Stromness
Kirkwall
ORKNEY ISLANDS
HOY
SOUTH RONALDSAY
OUTER HEBRIDES
Stornoway (Steornabhagh)
ISLE OF LEWIS (EILEAN LEÒDHAIS)
Tarbert (Tairbeart)
Leverburgh (An t-Ob)
HARRIS (NA HEARADH)
Lochmaddy (Loch nam Madadh)
Uig
NORTH UIST (UIBHIST A TUATH)
BENBECULA (BEINN NA FAOGHLA)
Dunvegan
Portree
SOUTH UIST (UIBHIST A DEAS)
ISLE OF SKYE
Lochboisdale (Loch Baghasdail)
BARRA (BARRAIGH)
CANNA
Castlebay (Bagh a' Chaisteil)
RUM
EIGG
INNER HEBRIDES
MUCK
Kilchoan
COLL
Tobermory
TIREE
ISLE OF MULL
IONA
COLONSAY
JURA
Port Ellen
ISLAY
Portrush
Portstewart
Ballycastle
Coleraine
Letterkenny
Londonderry
NORTHERN IRELAND
Ardara
Strabane
Ballymena
Larne
Donegal
Antrim
Lough Neagh
Ballyshannon
Omagh
Crumlin
Dungannon
BELFAST
Enniskillen
Armagh
Sligo
Ballina
Monaghan
Downpatrick
Achill Island
Newry

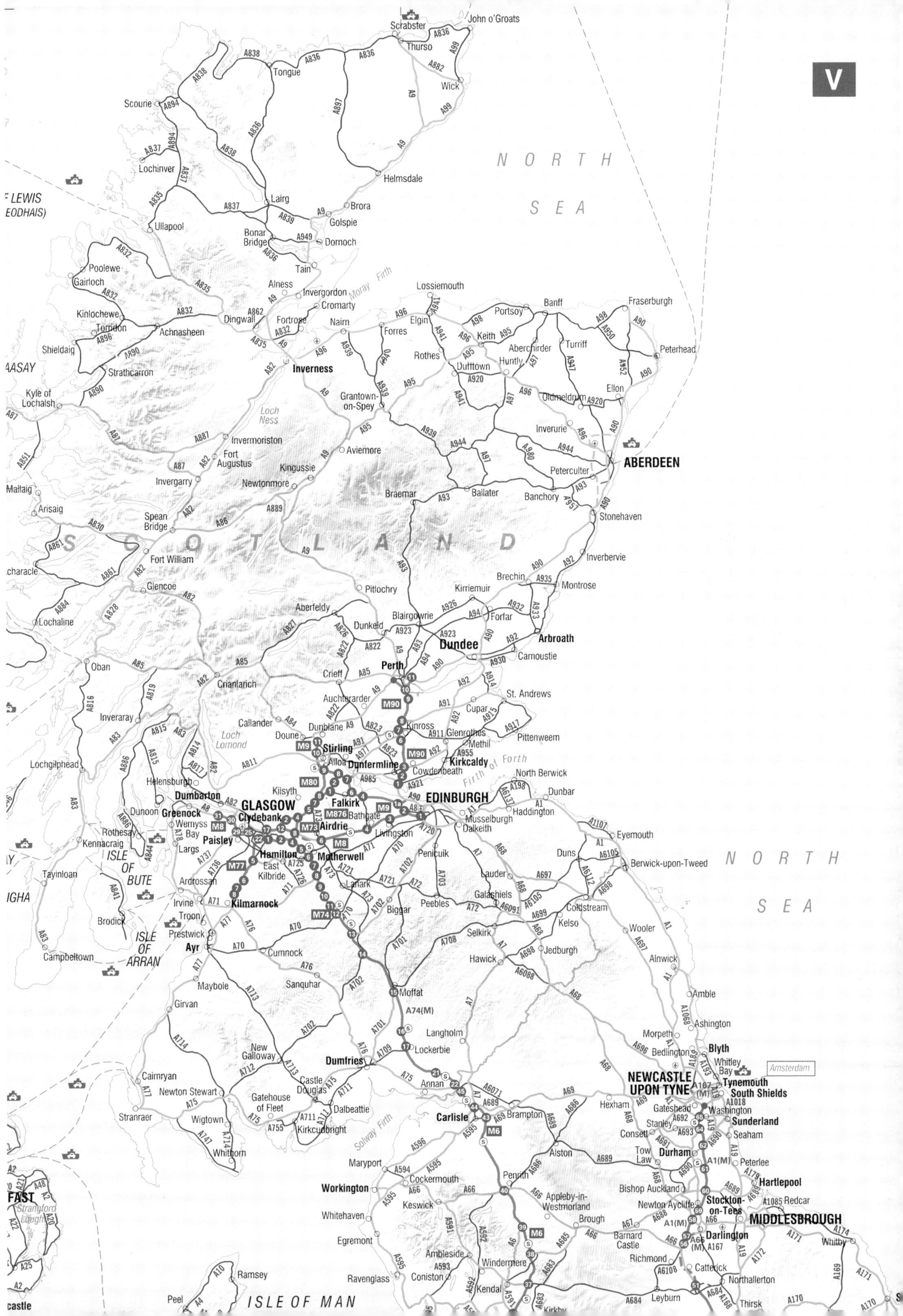

V

N O R T H   S E A

John o'Groats
Scrabster · Thurso
Tongue
Scourie
Lochinver
Lairg
Helmsdale
Ullapool
Bonar Bridge · Brora · Golspie
Dornoch · Tain
Poolewe
Gairloch
Kinlochewe
Torridon · Dingwall · Fortrose · Nairn
Shieldaig · Achnasheen
Strathcarron
Kyle of Lochalsh
Inverness
Invermoriston · Aviemore
Fort Augustus · Kingussie
Invergarry · Newtonmore
Spean Bridge
Fort William · Braemar · Ballater · Banchory
Glencoe · Stonehaven

Lossiemouth · Banff · Fraserburgh
Elgin · Portsoy · Peterhead
Forres · Keith · Turriff · Ellon
Rothes · Huntly · Oldmeldrum
Dufftown · Inverurie
ABERDEEN
Peterculter
Kirriemuir · Brechin · Montrose
Pitlochry · Forfar · Inverbervie
Aberfeldy · Blairgowrie · Arbroath
Dunkeld · Dundee · Carnoustie
Crieff · Perth
Auchterarder
Callander · Dunblane · Kinross · St. Andrews
Stirling · Glenrothes · Cupar · Pittenweem
Alloa · Dunfermline · Kirkcaldy · Methil
GLASGOW · Falkirk · Cowdenbeath · North Berwick
Clydebank · Bathgate · EDINBURGH · Dunbar
Paisley · Airdrie · Livingston · Haddington
Hamilton · Motherwell · Musselburgh · Dalkeith · Eyemouth
East Kilbride · Lanark · Penicuik · Lauder · Berwick-upon-Tweed
Kilmarnock · Biggar · Peebles · Galashiels · Duns
Irvine · Selkirk · Coldstream
Troon · Moffat · Hawick · Kelso · Wooler
Prestwick · Jedburgh · Alnwick
Ayr · Cumnock · Langholm · Amble
Maybole · Sanquhar · Lockerbie · Morpeth · Ashington
Girvan · Dumfries · Annan · Bedlington · Blyth
New Galloway · NEWCASTLE UPON TYNE · Whitley Bay
Cairnryan · Castle Douglas · Carlisle · Tynemouth · South Shields
Newton Stewart · Gatehouse of Fleet · Dalbeattie · Hexham · Washington · Sunderland
Stranraer · Wigtown · Kirkcudbright · Brampton · Stanley · Consett · Seaham
Whithorn · Maryport · Penrith · Durham · Peterlee
Workington · Cockermouth · Alston · Bishop Auckland · Hartlepool
Whitehaven · Keswick · Appleby-in-Westmorland · Newton Aycliffe · Stockton-on-Tees · Redcar
Egremont · Brough · Barnard Castle · Darlington · MIDDLESBROUGH
Ravenglass · Ambleside · Windermere · Richmond · Catterick · Whitby
Coniston · Kendal · Leyburn · Northallerton · Thirsk
ISLE OF MAN · Peel

ISLE OF BUTE · ISLE OF ARRAN · Brodick · Campbeltown

SCOTLAND
Loch Ness · Loch Lomond
Moray Firth · Firth of Forth · Solway Firth
NORTH SEA
Amsterdam

Mileage Chart and Journey Times

This chart shows the distance in miles and journey time between two cities or towns in Great Britain. Each route has been calculated using a combination of motorways, primary routes and other major roads. This is normally the quickest, though not always the shortest route.

Average journey times are calculated whilst driving at the maximum speed limit. These times are approximate and do not include traffic congestion or convenience breaks.

To find the distance and journey time between two cities or towns, follow a horizontal line and vertical column until they meet each other.

For example, the 285 mile journey from London to Penzance is approximately 4 hours and 59 minutes.

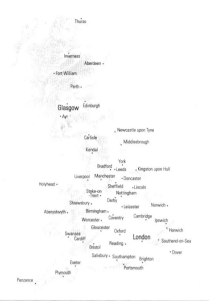

Britain

Journey times

	Aberystwyth	Ayr	Birmingham	Bradford	Brighton	Bristol	Cambridge	Cardiff	Carlisle	Coventry	Derby	Doncaster	Dover	Edinburgh	Exeter	Fort William	Glasgow	Gloucester	Harwich	Holyhead	Inverness	Ipswich	Kendal	Kingston upon Hull	Leeds	Leicester	Lincoln	Liverpool	Manchester	Middlesbrough	Newcastle upon Tyne	Norwich	Nottingham	Oxford	Penzance	Perth	Plymouth	Portsmouth	Reading	Salisbury	Sheffield	Shrewsbury	Southampton	Southend-on-Sea	Stoke-on-Trent	Swansea	Thurso	Worcester	York	London
Aberdeen	8:21	3:31	7:13	6:28	9:56	8:26	8:15	8:55	4:08	7:27	7:09	6:25	10:16	2:39	9:38	3:38	2:50	7:55	9:32	7:41	2:30	9:08	4:55	6:51	6:16	7:40	7:07	6:13	6:01	5:16	4:39	9:18	7:14	8:18	11:22	1:48	10:16	9:33	8:57	9:21	6:42	7:07	9:25	9:22	6:28	9:31	4:52	7:35	6:07	9:03
Aberystwyth		6:34	2:34	3:27	5:21	2:44	4:00	2:29	4:24	2:52	2:56	3:45	5:41	6:20	3:51	8:13	5:53	2:34	5:17	2:29	8:39	4:53	3:40	4:20	3:29	3:18	4:11	2:39	2:54	4:34	5:07	5:03	3:17	3:43	5:35	6:41	4:29	4:27	3:50	4:01	3:41	1:47	4:18	4:56	2:48	1:48	11:00	2:19	4:00	4:28
Ayr			5:28	4:28	8:11	6:42	6:31	7:10	2:24	5:43	5:25	4:41	8:32	1:48	7:54	3:03	0:48	6:11	7:48	5:56	3:51	7:24	3:10	5:06	4:32	5:55	5:22	4:29	4:16	3:56	3:28	7:34	5:29	6:34	9:37	1:53	8:31	7:49	7:13	7:37	4:57	5:23	7:40	7:37	4:43	7:46	6:12	5:50	4:22	7:16
Birmingham				2:15	3:04	1:41	1:43	2:09	3:16	0:36	1:01	1:40	3:25	5:12	2:53	7:05	4:45	1:10	3:01	2:59	7:31	2:37	2:32	2:21	2:05	1:01	1:55	1:49	1:46	2:55	3:28	2:46	1:08	1:27	4:36	5:33	3:30	2:42	2:06	2:39	1:36	0:59	2:33	2:39	1:02	2:44	9:52	0:49	2:21	2:11
Bradford					4:30	3:34	2:43	4:03	2:17	2:19	1:34	0:53	4:37	4:17	4:46	6:06	3:46	3:03	4:01	2:49	6:31	3:37	1:32	1:18	0:28	2:02	1:35	1:22	0:57	1:32	2:06	3:46	1:37	3:05	6:29	4:33	5:24	4:20	3:44	4:18	1:00	2:15	4:12	3:50	1:36	4:38	8:52	2:42	0:59	3:32
Brighton						2:49	2:09	3:26	6:00	2:42	3:15	3:53	1:53	7:53	3:41	9:49	7:29	2:47	2:19	5:39	10:14	2:20	5:15	4:35	4:19	2:57	3:43	4:32	4:29	5:08	5:42	3:05	3:21	1:58	5:24	8:16	4:18	1:14	1:39	1:54	3:49	3:45	1:35	1:41	3:45	4:01	12:35	3:07	4:35	1:27
Bristol							3:02	0:56	4:31	1:44	2:21	2:59	3:18	6:27	1:37	8:20	6:00	0:47	3:27	4:13	8:45	3:28	3:46	3:41	3:25	2:17	3:11	3:03	3:01	4:15	4:48	3:58	2:28	1:30	3:20	6:48	2:14	2:03	1:26	1:37	2:56	2:14	1:54	2:58	2:17	1:30	11:07	1:07	3:41	2:07
Cambridge								3:28	4:20	1:30	1:52	2:03	2:06	6:04	4:11	8:09	5:49	2:29	1:28	4:20	8:35	1:04	3:56	2:37	2:34	1:25	1:47	3:12	3:10	3:19	3:52	1:13	1:41	1:55	5:54	6:37	4:49	2:34	1:51	2:47	2:15	2:26	2:35	1:19	2:26	4:03	10:56	2:08	2:45	1:17
Cardiff									4:58	2:15	2:48	3:27	3:54	6:54	2:02	8:47	6:27	1:16	4:03	4:23	9:13	4:03	4:14	4:09	3:53	2:46	3:39	3:31	3:28	4:42	5:16	4:31	2:55	2:05	3:46	7:15	2:40	2:38	2:01	2:12	3:23	2:24	2:29	3:33	2:44	0:53	11:34	1:35	4:09	2:43
Carlisle										3:30	3:12	2:28	6:19	2:08	5:41	4:01	1:41	3:58	5:35	3:44	4:27	5:11	0:58	2:54	2:19	3:43	3:10	2:16	2:04	1:44	1:15	5:21	3:17	4:21	7:25	2:29	6:19	5:36	5:00	5:24	2:45	3:10	5:28	5:25	2:31	5:34	6:48	3:38	2:10	5:07
Coventry											1:03	1:41	3:05	5:29	2:55	7:22	5:02	1:12	2:49	3:13	7:48	2:21	2:49	2:23	2:06	0:45	1:39	2:06	2:03	2:56	3:30	2:31	1:09	1:04	4:38	5:50	3:32	2:19	1:43	2:17	1:37	1:18	2:11	2:20	1:19	2:49	10:09	0:56	2:22	1:53
Derby												0:57	3:33	4:58	3:31	7:02	4:42	1:48	3:09	2:52	7:27	2:45	2:28	1:39	1:23	0:49	1:24	1:45	1:42	2:13	2:46	2:55	0:33	1:51	5:14	5:29	4:08	3:06	2:30	3:04	0:54	1:21	2:58	2:48	0:53	3:22	9:49	1:27	1:39	2:19
Doncaster													3:58	4:13	4:12	6:19	3:59	2:30	3:21	3:17	6:44	2:57	2:16	0:56	0:43	1:27	0:55	1:48	1:25	1:28	2:02	3:07	1:02	2:30	5:56	4:46	4:50	3:45	3:09	3:43	0:30	2:13	3:36	3:11	1:44	4:04	9:05	2:09	0:54	2:57
Dover														7:56	4:14	10:08	7:48	3:16	2:16	5:59	10:34	2:17	5:35	4:29	4:26	3:14	3:40	4:52	4:49	5:11	5:45	3:02	3:34	2:27	5:57	8:36	4:51	2:23	2:08	2:50	4:06	4:05	2:38	1:37	4:05	4:29	12:55	3:36	4:38	1:34
Edinburgh															7:38	3:01	1:05	5:55	7:20	5:41	3:02	6:56	2:55	4:38	4:04	5:26	4:54	4:13	4:00	3:00	2:23	7:06	5:01	6:18	9:21	1:02	8:16	7:33	6:57	7:21	4:29	5:07	7:25	7:09	4:28	7:30	5:24	5:34	3:54	6:57
Exeter																9:31	7:11	1:58	4:36	5:24	9:56	4:37	4:57	4:52	4:36	3:28	4:22	4:14	4:12	5:26	5:59	5:07	3:39	2:46	1:54	7:59	0:53	2:38	2:43	1:55	4:07	3:25	2:27	4:02	3:28	2:37	12:18	2:18	4:52	3:16
Fort William																	2:26	7:49	9:26	7:35	1:32	9:02	4:49	6:44	6:10	7:34	7:00	6:07	5:54	5:34	5:06	9:12	7:07	8:12	11:15	2:09	10:10	9:27	8:51	9:15	6:35	7:01	9:19	9:16	6:22	9:24	4:04	7:28	6:01	8:56
Glasgow																		5:28	7:05	5:13	3:08	6:41	2:28	4:23	3:49	5:12	4:39	3:46	3:33	3:13	2:45	6:51	4:46	5:51	8:54	1:10	7:48	7:06	6:30	6:54	4:14	4:40	6:57	6:55	4:01	7:03	5:29	5:07	3:40	6:36
Gloucester																			3:25	3:42	8:14	3:22	3:15	3:10	2:54	1:46	2:39	2:32	2:29	3:43	4:17	3:31	1:56	1:11	3:39	6:16	2:33	2:00	1:24	1:42	2:24	1:42	1:52	2:56	1:45	1:49	10:35	0:36	3:10	2:05
Harwich																				5:38	9:53	0:42	5:13	3:55	3:52	2:43	3:05	4:30	4:28	4:37	5:10	1:32	2:59	2:26	6:20	7:55	5:14	2:49	2:17	3:12	3:33	3:44	3:01	1:09	3:44	4:38	12:14	3:26	4:03	1:42
Holyhead																					7:58	5:16	2:59	3:39	2:49	3:23	3:52	1:53	2:13	3:53	4:26	5:25	3:15	4:06	7:06	6:00	6:00	5:21	4:45	5:05	3:06	2:10	5:12	5:18	2:11	4:33	10:19	3:19	3:19	4:47
Inverness																						9:27	5:14	7:10	6:35	7:59	7:26	6:32	6:20	5:41	5:04	9:37	7:33	8:37	11:41	2:10	10:35	9:52	9:16	9:40	7:01	7:26	9:44	9:41	6:47	9:50	2:31	7:54	6:26	9:21
Ipswich																							4:50	3:31	3:28	2:20	2:41	4:06	4:04	4:13	4:46	1:08	2:35	2:27	6:21	7:31	5:15	2:50	2:18	3:13	3:09	3:20	3:02	1:10	3:20	4:39	11:50	3:02	3:39	1:43
Kendal																								2:44	1:53	3:02	3:00	1:36	1:23	1:38	1:59	5:00	2:54	3:41	6:44	3:13	5:38	4:56	4:20	4:44	2:22	2:30	4:47	4:53	1:50	4:53	7:32	2:57	2:04	4:22
Kingston upon Hull																									1:08	2:08	0:58	2:13	1:49	1:54	2:27	3:18	1:43	3:10	6:36	5:12	5:30	4:25	3:49	4:23	1:11	2:53	4:17	3:43	2:25	4:44	9:31	2:49	1:02	3:39
Leeds																										1:53	1:25	1:23	0:58	1:20	1:53	3:37	1:27	2:55	6:21	4:38	5:15	4:10	3:34	4:08	0:50	2:16	4:02	3:40	1:37	4:29	8:57	2:34	0:46	3:23
Leicester																											1:16	2:17	2:14	2:42	3:15	2:27	0:46	1:32	5:11	6:01	4:05	2:47	2:11	2:45	1:23	1:43	2:39	2:29	1:24	3:20	10:20	1:25	2:08	2:01
Lincoln																												2:31	2:02	2:11	2:44	2:20	0:59	2:28	6:07	5:29	5:01	3:43	3:07	3:41	1:07	2:33	3:34	2:54	2:10	4:16	9:48	2:21	1:35	2:51
Liverpool																													0:48	2:28	3:01	4:16	2:10	2:56	6:00	4:33	4:54	4:11	3:35	3:59	1:52	1:25	4:03	4:09	1:06	3:48	8:53	2:13	1:54	3:39
Manchester																														2:03	2:36	4:12	1:51	2:52	5:55	4:22	4:49	4:07	3:30	3:55	1:14	1:41	3:58	4:04	1:01	4:04	8:41	2:08	1:29	3:37
Middlesbrough																															0:55	4:20	2:15	3:43	7:09	3:40	6:03	4:58	4:22	4:56	1:43	3:20	4:50	4:24	2:40	5:17	8:02	3:22	1:05	4:12
Newcastle upon Tyne																																4:54	2:49	4:17	7:43	3:03	6:37	5:32	4:56	5:30	2:17	3:54	5:24	4:58	3:14	5:51	7:25	3:56	1:43	4:46
Norwich																																	2:44	2:58	6:51	7:40	5:45	3:31	2:48	3:43	3:18	3:29	3:32	2:00	3:28	5:06	11:59	3:10	3:48	2:13
Nottingham																																		1:57	5:23	5:34	4:17	3:12	2:36	3:10	0:57	1:44	3:04	2:49	1:18	3:31	9:53	1:36	1:42	2:25
Oxford																																			4:30	6:40	3:24	1:28	0:45	1:25	2:25	2:08	1:19	1:56	2:09	2:40	10:59	1:31	3:10	1:15
Penzance																																				9:43	1:41	4:22	4:27	3:39	5:51	5:09	4:11	5:46	5:12	4:20	14:02	4:02	6:36	4:59
Perth																																					8:37	7:54	7:18	7:42	5:03	5:28	7:46	7:43	4:49	7:52	4:30	5:55	4:28	7:24
Plymouth																																						3:16	3:20	2:32	4:44	4:02	3:04	4:39	4:05	3:14	12:55	2:55	5:29	3:54
Portsmouth																																							1:18	0:52	3:39	3:23	0:32	2:11	3:23	3:13	12:13	2:20	4:25	1:39
Reading																																								1:22	3:01	2:45	1:09	1:46	2:45	2:37	11:35	1:44	3:47	0:56
Salisbury																																									3:37	3:09	0:40	2:37	3:12	2:47	12:02	2:02	4:22	1:52
Sheffield																																										2:08	3:32	3:22	1:40	3:59	9:22	2:04	1:11	2:53
Shrewsbury																																											3:16	3:22	1:04	2:45	9:46	1:23	2:46	2:53
Southampton																																												2:26	3:15	3:05	12:05	2:12	4:16	1:40
Southend-on-Sea																																													3:21	4:09	12:02	3:03	3:51	1:07
Stoke-on-Trent																																														3:18	9:08	1:23	2:09	2:53
Swansea																																															12:11	2:10	4:44	3:18
Thurso																																																10:15	8:47	11:43
Worcester																																																	2:49	2:24
York																																																		3:39

Distance in miles

	Aberdeen	Aberystwyth	Ayr	Birmingham	Bradford	Brighton	Bristol	Cambridge	Cardiff	Carlisle	Coventry	Derby	Doncaster	Dover	Edinburgh	Exeter	Fort William	Glasgow	Gloucester	Harwich	Holyhead	Inverness	Ipswich	Kendal	Kingston upon Hull	Leeds	Leicester	Lincoln	Liverpool	Manchester	Middlesbrough	Newcastle upon Tyne	Norwich	Nottingham	Oxford	Penzance	Perth	Plymouth	Portsmouth	Reading	Salisbury	Sheffield	Shrewsbury	Southampton	Southend-on-Sea	Stoke-on-Trent	Swansea	Thurso	Worcester	York
Aberystwyth	471
Ayr	181	324
Birmingham	423	114	272
Bradford	377	159	196	124
Brighton	596	258	441	169	263
Bristol	505	122	375	88	215	129
Cambridge	487	198	366	102	156	117	167
Cardiff	525	106	377	106	233	168	42	201
Carlisle	229	232	89	183	107	345	286	256	288
Coventry	442	134	297	18	124	157	102	84	129	200
Derby	418	137	269	41	88	188	134	99	159	180	43
Doncaster	371	192	239	95	40	232	184	117	210	150	94	57
Dover	620	315	477	195	284	81	194	118	233	393	180	208	244
Edinburgh	126	340	75	284	198	466	377	326	379	91	303	266	212	444
Exeter	581	199	425	161	282	170	75	323	107	336	166	213	257	244	439
Fort William	159	430	136	391	305	568	478	456	486	198	415	387	345	591	131	549
Glasgow	146	322	36	291	203	468	378	355	384	96	313	282	245	491	46	449	100
Gloucester	473	109	317	53	171	152	35	132	53	228	59	93	149	189	331	107	435	324
Harwich	568	258	411	170	224	130	203	64	234	323	152	167	185	129	397	262	524	419	171
Holyhead	452	96	315	151	158	330	204	252	209	226	167	156	169	358	316	279	423	323	189	331
Inverness	105	492	198	449	353	620	536	490	558	260	458	421	369	601	157	607	63	162	496	554	481
Ipswich	538	268	420	156	210	125	206	54	240	311	138	155	171	127	381	264	510	409	177	21	307	538
Kendal	280	182	139	151	62	324	235	215	232	50	170	136	99	344	141	307	248	146	200	279	180	310	268
Kingston upon Hull	398	235	255	139	68	243	228	134	239	165	123	94	37	254	230	290	367	255	195	204	218	387	189	127
Leeds	359	171	198	119	9	256	209	144	226	111	117	74	32	275	190	279	309	208	167	217	162	345	197	72	60
Leicester	445	155	294	43	99	163	118	70	140	214	24	30	73	183	282	189	412	312	83	146	182	431	125	166	98	97
Lincoln	411	208	249	87	80	207	170	88	192	178	76	53	41	206	247	241	376	274	135	152	204	402	124	140	46	72	52
Liverpool	354	120	199	99	67	267	180	179	169	110	113	90	89	294	201	240	308	213	142	265	95	370	236	75	126	73	110	118
Manchester	349	128	204	87	37	252	167	159	188	117	99	58	51	273	208	239	315	215	132	230	120	363	211	72	96	42	95	87	34
Middlesbrough	289	233	181	174	69	316	265	196	287	92	175	130	84	316	147	337	279	192	230	266	226	306	253	77	88	64	154	127	134	106
Newcastle upon Tyne	252	266	146	209	98	345	300	232	312	58	209	165	115	350	104	369	237	153	263	207	257	263	207	88	130	98	188	153	167	136	40
Norwich	536	270	348	163	185	174	234	62	256	280	142	146	142	169	351	284	478	378	193	72	289	505	44	249	145	178	112	103	222	177	221	252
Nottingham	416	155	267	54	78	191	140	84	165	188	52	15	48	210	256	218	386	286	108	165	177	410	140	141	92	72	27	37	107	68	128	159	118
Oxford	497	151	335	68	167	106	73	92	106	267	57	101	138	142	358	151	465	365	47	134	208	515	128	223	175	162	76	123	168	157	218	253	159	104
Penzance	688	301	552	269	394	279	184	343	218	463	278	316	369	355	551	109	663	561	217	374	388	715	375	419	412	391	310	359	353	344	449	481	393	323	261
Perth	86	366	85	336	245	509	412	370	422	134	346	309	254	485	43	487	103	59	362	439	360	113	424	184	273	233	326	290	244	254	191	148	394	299	404	598
Plymouth	619	232	461	203	325	206	111	274	159	372	209	254	300	286	485	43	592	490	150	305	322	648	305	348	326	323	231	284	299	281	379	412	327	255	193	75	529
Portsmouth	579	231	440	147	274	50	95	132	138	357	132	184	231	137	448	127	555	455	114	161	303	603	158	308	268	245	166	209	254	237	315	360	200	191	83	235	486	170
Reading	538	180	399	103	213	79	77	90	112	309	90	138	184	115	402	141	506	406	75	129	264	554	126	263	209	207	113	168	193	197	264	295	152	129	25	251	445	184	60
Salisbury	538	178	383	121	245	82	53	140	101	312	113	159	207	158	400	91	510	408	73	177	262	569	177	265	251	230	132	187	213	208	287	318	200	162	65	201	443	132	43	57
Sheffield	390	173	235	79	40	225	163	121	193	154	75	35	21	268	230	245	352	250	139	185	164	387	176	102	66	33	68	46	74	40	102	133	144	37	137	361	273	293	228	160	203
Shrewsbury	419	73	260	47	100	216	116	140	107	171	64	67	114	249	262	175	369	267	77	215	104	424	195	125	163	102	79	123	59	67	166	203	196	86	105	286	309	218	195	147	150	85
Southampton	564	213	401	128	235	64	75	129	122	330	114	167	201	150	433	106	528	426	98	157	287	590	162	276	249	230	136	189	235	215	288	320	190	162	66	217	476	149	20	47	23	206	175
Southend-on-Sea	549	258	431	152	220	85	177	64	211	342	129	168	185	89	395	226	548	438	152	57	303	549	57	283	200	213	139	156	255	225	262	299	99	160	105	337	439	269	117	98	132	197	173	126
Stoke-on-Trent	381	108	243	47	75	217	127	137	140	150	64	36	74	236	241	202	348	248	95	201	122	410	179	121	117	78	55	87	56	36	142	173	171	55	118	311	287	241	201	147	168	50	35	183	199
Swansea	529	76	368	124	220	209	80	236	41	279	150	184	244	264	370	154	477	375	91	279	172	578	279	249	262	229	174	226	168	187	293	323	286	178	144	266	446	196	175	147	136	202	124	159	245	159
Thurso	212	584	304	557	461	728	644	589	640	352	552	529	475	706	262	715	169	268	604	657	589	108	654	402	492	453	544	510	463	471	410	367	613	519	621	823	220	758	709	662	664	506	523	682	659	502	631
Worcester	448	96	309	29	135	162	62	119	73	220	46	68	124	197	306	136	418	311	28	168	151	480	174	169	166	146	72	118	108	101	203	229	180	85	57	244	350	177	146	95	101	103	49	124	150	65	97	572
York	345	193	201	129	34	269	227	151	237	116	129	84	33	269	187	289	314	214	181	232	185	344	200	81	38	24	108	76	96	65	48	83	176	84	174	400	230	331	257	217	244	54	132	244	214	114	268	450	164
London	537	228	440	118	203	53	118	61	151	309	97	129	171	76	403	179	511	404	116	86	277	562	82	263	214	195	103	155	211	209	251	283	117	128	59	285	451	216	84	41	92	166	161	82	43	161	187	669	136	211

Scale to Map Pages

1:220,594 = 3.5 miles to 1 inch (2.54 cm) / 2.2 km to 1 cm

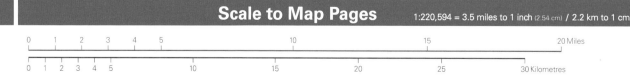

Motorway
Autoroute
Autobahn
M1

Motorway Under Construction
Autoroute en construction
Autobahn im Bau

Motorway Proposed
Autoroute prévue
Geplante Autobahn

Motorway Junctions with Numbers
Unlimited Interchange 4
Limited Interchange 5

Autoroute échangeur numéroté
Échangeur complet
Échangeur partiel

Autobahnanschlußstelle mit Nummer
Unbeschränkter Fahrtrichtungswechsel
Beschränkter Fahrtrichtungswechsel

Motorway Service Area (with fuel station)
with access from one carriageway only
Aire de services d'autoroute (avec station service)
accessible d'un seul côté
Rastplatz oder Raststätte (mit tankstelle)
Einbahn

Major Road Service Areas (with fuel station) with 24 hour facilities
Primary Route (S)   Class A Road (S)
Aire de services sur route prioritaire (avec station service) Ouverte 24h sur 24
Route à grande circulation   Route de type A
Raststätte (mit tankstelle) Durchgehend geöffnet
Hauptverkehrsstraße   A- Straße

Truckstop (selection of)
Sélection d'aire pour poids lourds
Auswahl von Fernfahrerrastplatz

Primary Route
Route à grande circulation
Hauptverkehrsstraße
A41

Primary Route Junction with Number
Échangeur numéroté
Hauptverkehrsstraßenkreuzung mit Nummer
5

Primary Route Destination
Route prioritaire, direction
Hauptverkehrsstraße Richtung
DOVER

Dual Carriageways (A & B roads)
Route à double chaussées séparées (route A & B)
Zweispurige Schnellstraße (A- und B- Straßen)

Class A Road
Route de type A
A-Straße
A129

Class B Road
Route de type B
B-Straße
B177

Narrow Major Road (passing places)
Route prioritaire étroite (possibilité de dépassement)
Schmale Hauptverkehrsstaße (mit Überholmöglichkeit)

Major Roads Under Construction
Route prioritaire en construction
Hauptverkehrsstraße im Bau

Major Roads Proposed
Route prioritaire prévue
Geplante Hauptverkehrsstraße

Safety Cameras with Speed Limits
Single Camera (30)
Multiple Cameras located along road (50)
Single & Multiple Variable Speed Cameras (V) (V)

Radars de contrôle de vitesse
Radar simple
Radars multiples situés le long de la route
Radars simples et multiples de contrôle de vitesse variable

Sicherheitskameras mit Tempolimit
Einzelne Kamera
Mehrere Kameras entlang der Straße
Einzelne und mehrere Kameras für variables Tempolimit

Fuel Station
Station service
Tankstelle

Gradient 1:5 (20%) **& steeper**
(ascent in direction of arrow)
Pente égale ou supérieure à 20% (dans le sens de la montée)
20% Steigung und steiler (in Pfeilrichtung)

Toll
Barrière de péage
Gebührenpflichtig
TOLL

Mileage between markers
Distance en miles entre les flèches
Strecke zwischen Markierungen in Meilen
8

Railway and Station
Voie ferrée et gare
Eisenbahnlinie und Bahnhof

Level Crossing and Tunnel
Passage à niveau et tunnel
Bahnübergang und Tunnel

River or Canal
Rivière ou canal
Fluß oder Kanal

County or Unitary Authority Boundary
Limite de comté ou de division administrative
Grafschafts- oder Verwaltungsbezirksgrenze

National Boundary
Frontière nationale
Landesgrenze

Built-up Area
Agglomération
Geschlossene Ortschaft

Village or Hamlet
Village ou hameau
Dorf oder Weiler

Wooded Area
Zone boisée
Waldgebiet

Spot Height in Feet
Altitude (en pieds)
Höhe in Fuß
· 813

Relief above 400' (122m)
Relief par estompage au-dessus de 400' (122m)
Reliefschattierung über 400' (122m)

National Grid Reference (kilometres)
Coordonnées géographiques nationales (Kilomètres)
Nationale geographische Koordinaten (Kilometer)
100

Page Continuation
Suite à la page indiquée
Seitenfortsetzung
48

Area covered by Main Route map
Répartition des cartes des principaux axes routiers
Von Karten mit Hauptverkehrsstrecken
MAIN ROUTE 180

Area covered by Town Plan
Ville ayant un plan à la page indiquée
Von Karten mit Stadtplänen erfaßter Bereich
SEE PAGE 194

Tourist Information Information Touristeninformationen

i

Airport
Aéroport
Flughafen
✈

Airfield
Terrain d'aviation
Flugplatz
✦

Heliport
Héliport
Hubschrauberlandeplatz

Battle Site and Date
Champ de bataille et date
Schlachtfeld und Datum
✕ 1066

Castle (open to public)
Château (ouvert au public)
Schloß / Burg (für die Öffentlichkeit zugänglich)

Castle with Garden (open to public)
Château avec parc (ouvert au public)
Schloß mit Garten (für die Öffentlichkeit zugänglich)

Cathedral, Abbey, Church, Friary, Priory
Cathédrale, abbaye, église, monastère, prieuré
Kathedrale, Abtei, Kirche, Mönchskloster, Kloster
✝

Country Park
Parc régional
Landschaftspark

Ferry (vehicular, sea)
(vehicular, river)
(foot only)
Bac (véhicules, mer)
(véhicules, rivière)
(piétons)
Fähre (auto, meer)
(auto, fluß)
(nur für Personen)

Garden (open to public)
Jardin (ouvert au public)
Garten (für die Öffentlichkeit zugänglich)
✳

Golf Course
(9 hole) ▶9   (18 hole) ▶18
Terrain de golf
(9 trous)   (18 trous)
Golfplatz
(9 Löcher)   (18 Löcher)

Historic Building (open to public)
Monument historique (ouvert au public)
Historisches Gebäude (für die Öffentlichkeit zugänglich)

Historic Building with Garden (open to public)
Monument historique avec jardin (ouvert au public)
Historisches Gebäude mit Garten (für die Öffentlichkeit zugänglich)

Horse Racecourse
Hippodrome
Pferderennbahn

Lighthouse
Phare
Leuchtturm

Motor Racing Circuit
Circuit Automobile
Automobilrennbahn

Museum, Art Gallery
Musée
Museum, Galerie

National Park
Parc national
Nationalpark

National Trust Property
(open) NT
(restricted opening) NT
(National Trust for Scotland) NTS NTS
National Trust Property
(ouvert)
(heures d'ouverture)
(National Trust for Scotland)
National Trust- Eigentum
(geöffnet)
(beschränkte Öffnungszeit)
(National Trust for Scotland)

Nature Reserve or Bird Sanctuary
Réserve naturelle botanique ou ornithologique
Natur- oder Vogelschutzgebiet

Nature Trail or Forest Walk
Chemin forestier, piste verte
Naturpfad oder Waldweg

Place of Interest
Site, curiosité
Sehenswürdigkeit
Monument •

Picnic Site
Lieu pour pique-nique
Picknickplatz

Railway, Steam or Narrow Gauge
Chemin de fer, à vapeur ou à voie étroite
Eisenbahn, Dampf- oder Schmalspurbahn

Theme Park
Centre de loisirs
Vergnügungspark

Tourist Information Centre
Syndicat d'initiative
Information

Viewpoint
(360 degrees)   (180 degrees)
Vue panoramique (360 degrés)   (180 degrés)
Aussichtspunkt   (360 Grade)   (180 Grade)

Visitor Information Centre
Centre d'information touristique
Besucherzentrum
V

Wildlife Park
Réserve de faune
Wildpark

Windmill
Moulin à vent
Windmühle

Zoo or Safari Park
Parc ou réserve zoologique
Zoo oder Safari-Park

Please note: symbols have been enlarged for clarity

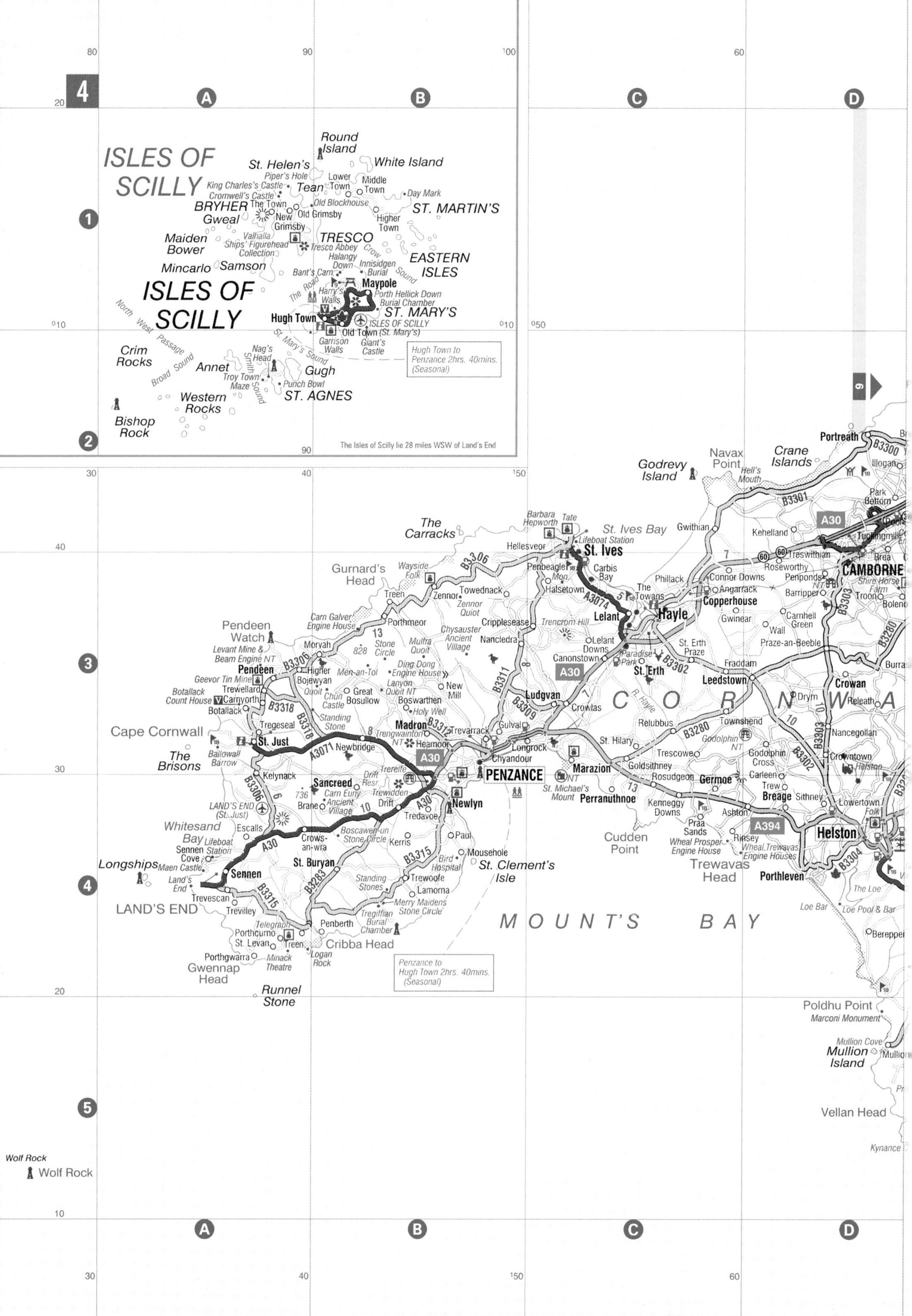
4
ISLES OF SCILLY
Round Island
St. Helen's
White Island
Piper's Hole
King Charles's Castle
Cromwell's Castle
Tean
Lower Town
Middle Town
Day Mark
BRYHER
The Town
Old Blockhouse
ST. MARTIN'S
Gweal
New Grimsby
Old Grimsby
Higher Town
Maiden Bower
Valhalla Ships' Figurehead Collection
TRESCO
Tresco Abbey
Crow Sound
EASTERN ISLES
Halangy Down
Innisidgen Burial
Mincarlo
Samson
Bant's Carn
Maypole
ISLES OF SCILLY
Harry's Walls
Porth Hellick Down Burial Chamber
ST. MARY'S
North West Passage
Hugh Town
ISLES OF SCILLY (St. Mary's)
Garrison Walls
Old Town
Giant's Castle
Crim Rocks
Nag's Head
St. Mary's Sound
Hugh Town to Penzance 2hrs. 40mins. (Seasonal)
Broad Sound
Annet
Smith Sound
Gugh
Troy Town Maze
Punch Bowl
Western Rocks
ST. AGNES
Bishop Rock
The Isles of Scilly lie 28 miles WSW of Land's End
Godrevy Island
Navax Point
Hell's Mouth
Crane Islands
Portreath
Illogan
Park Bottom
The Carracks
Barbara Hepworth
Tate
St. Ives Bay
Lifeboat Station
Gwithian
Kehelland
Hellesveor
St. Ives
Treswithian
Brea
CAMBORNE
Gurnard's Head
Wayside Folk
Penbeagle
Carbis Bay
Phillack
Connor Downs
Roseworthy
Penponds
Shire Horse Farm
Treen
Zennor
Towednack
Zennor Quoit
Halsetown
The Towans
Angarrack
Barripper
Troon
Carn Galver Engine House
Porthmeor
Cripplesease
Trencrom Hill
Lelant
Hayle
Copperhouse
Gwinear
Carnhell Green
Pendeen Watch
Chysauster Ancient Village
Mulfra Quoit
Nancledra
Lelant Downs
Wall
Praze-an-Beeble
Levant Mine & Beam Engine NT
Morvah
Stone Circle
St. Erth Praze
Ding Dong Engine House
Canonstown
Paradise Park
St. Erth
Fraddam
Geevor Tin Mine
Pendeen
Higher Bojewyan
Men-an-Tol
Lanyon Quoit NT
Leedstown
Crowan
Botallack Count House
Trewellard
Carnyorth
Botallack
Chun Castle
Great Bosullow
Boswarthen
New Mill
Ludgvan
Crowlas
CORNWALL
Drym
Releath
Holy Well
Standing Stone
Relubbus
Townshend
Cape Cornwall
Tregeseal
Madron
Trengwainton NT
Trevarrack
Gulval
Godolphin NT
Nancegollan
St. Just
Newbridge
Heamoor
St. Hilary
Ballowall Barrow
Long Rock
Trescowe
Godolphin Cross
Crowntown
The Brisons
Chyandour
PENZANCE
Marazion
Goldsithney
Kelynack
Sancreed
Drift Resr.
Trereife
Rosudgeon
Germoe
Carleen
Carn Euny Ancient Village
Trewidden
Newlyn
St. Michael's Mount NT
Perranuthnoe
Trew
Breage
Sithney
LAND'S END (St. Just)
Brane
Drift
Tredavoe
Kenneggy Downs
Lowertown
Whitesand Bay
Escalls
Boscawen-un Stone Circle
Paul
Cudden Point
Praa Sands
Ashton
Helston
Lifeboat Station
Sennen Cove
Crows-an-wra
Kerris
Mousehole
Wheal Prosper Engine House
Rinsey
Wheal Trewavas Engine Houses
Longships
Maen Castle
St. Buryan
Bird Hospital
St. Clement's Isle
Trewavas Head
Porthleven
Land's End
Sennen
Standing Stones
Trewoofe
Lamorna
The Loe
LAND'S END
Trevescan
Trevilley
Merry Maidens Stone Circle
MOUNT'S BAY
Loe Bar
Loe Pool & Bar
Telegraph
Porthcurno
Penberth
Tregiffian Burial Chamber
Berepper
St. Levan
Treen
Cribba Head
Porthgwarra
Minack Theatre
Logan Rock
Penzance to Hugh Town 2hrs. 40mins. (Seasonal)
Gwennap Head
Runnel Stone
Poldhu Point
Marconi Monument
Mullion Cove
Mullion Island
Vellan Head
Kynance
Wolf Rock
A30
A3071
A3074
A394
B3306
B3311
B3309
B3318
B3312
B3315
B3283
B3302
B3280
B3301
B3300
B3303
B3304
A B C D
1 2 3 4 5
9

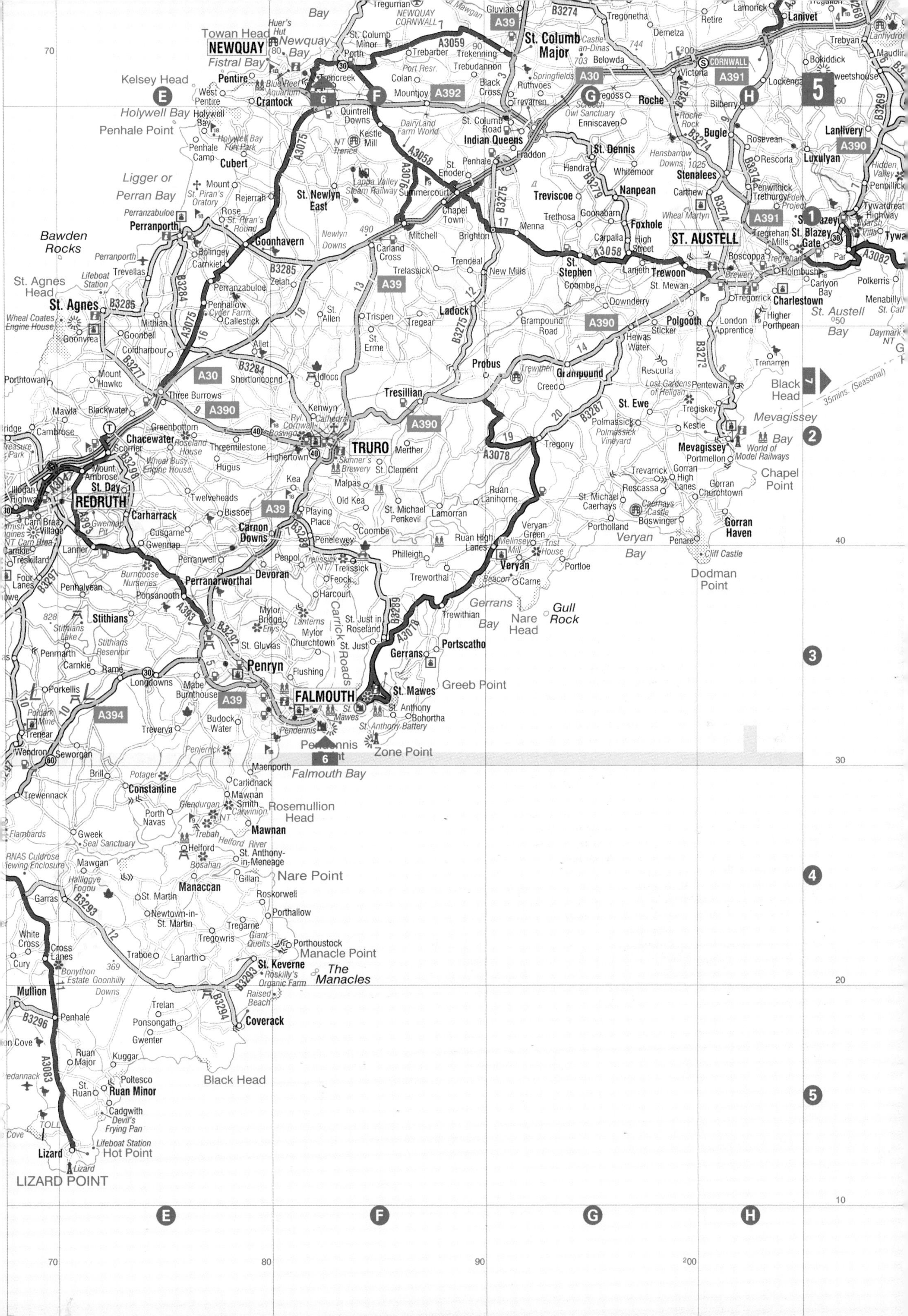

NEWQUAY
Towan Head
Fistral Bay
Kelsey Head
Pentire
Crantock
Holywell Bay
Penhale Point
Cubert
Ligger or
Perran Bay
Perranporth
Bawden
Rocks
St. Agnes
Head
St. Agnes
Goonhavern
St. Newlyn
East
Mitchell
Indian Queens
St. Columb
Major
Roche
St. Dennis
Bugle
Lanlivery
Luxulyan
Lanivet
ST. AUSTELL
St. Blazey
Par
Charlestown
St. Austell
Bay
St. Stephen
Grampound
Probus
Tresillian
Ladock
TRURO
Kenwyn
Three Burrows
Chacewater
REDRUTH
Carharrack
Stithians
Perranarworthal
Devoran
Carnon
Downs
Penryn
FALMOUTH
Falmouth Bay
Pendennis
Point
St. Mawes
Zone Point
Portscatho
Gerrans
Gerrans
Bay
Nare
Head
Gull
Rock
Veryan
Veryan
Bay
Tregony
Mevagissey
Mevagissey
Bay
Chapel
Point
Gorran
Haven
Dodman
Point
Black
Head
35mins. (Seasonal)
Constantine
Mawnan
Rosemullion
Head
Nare Point
Manaccan
St. Keverne
Manacle Point
The
Manacles
Coverack
Black Head
Mullion
Ruan Minor
Lizard
Hot Point
LIZARD POINT
A30
A39
A390
A391
A392
A394
A3058
A3059
A3075
A3076
A3078
A3082
A3083
E
F
G
H
5
70
80
90
200
10
20
30
40
50
60

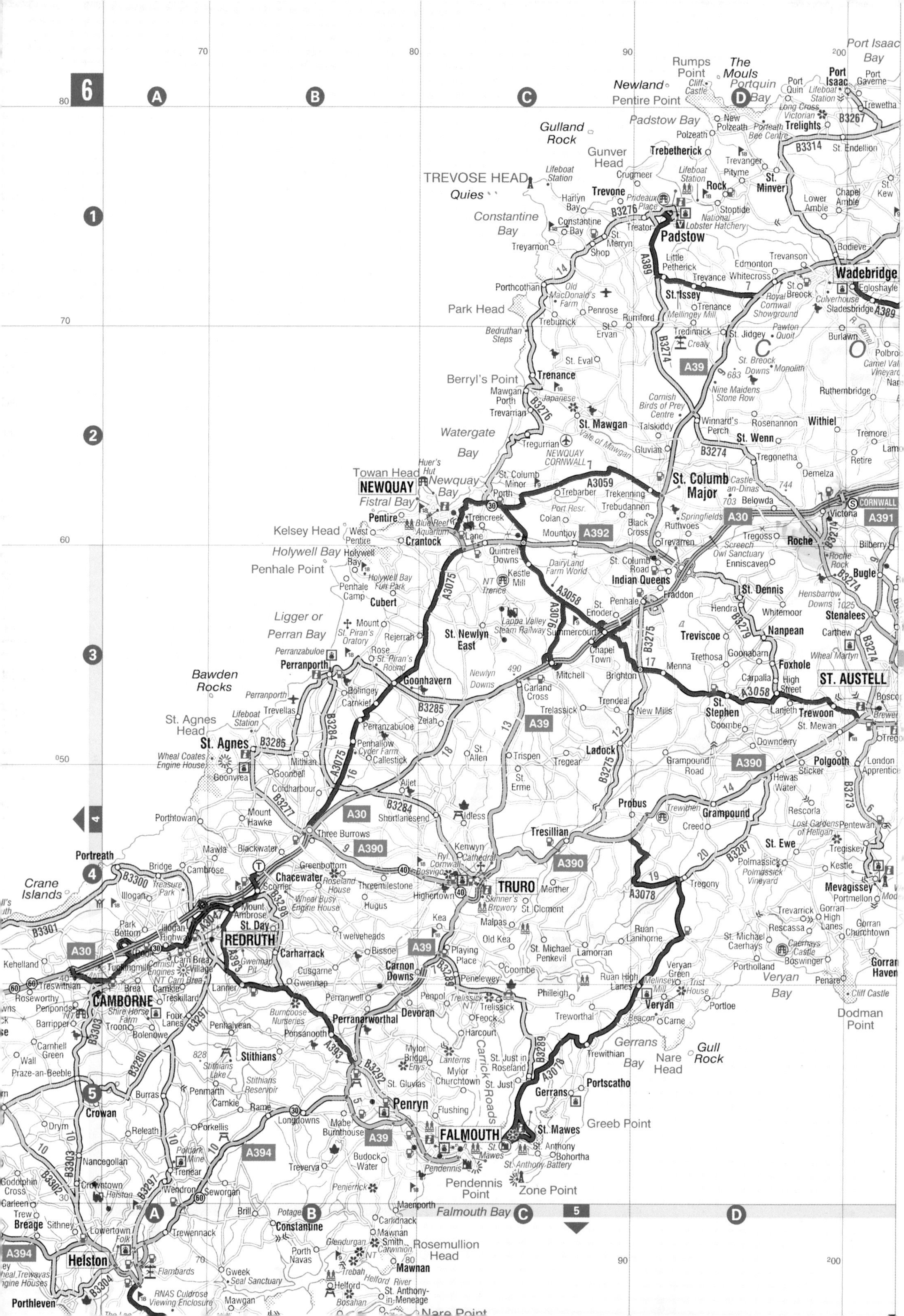
6
A
B
C
D
1
2
3
4
5
70
80
90
200
60
50
Port Isaac Bay
Rumps Point
The Mouls
Newland
Pentire Point
Portquin Bay
Port Quin
Port Isaac
Port Gaverne
Trewetha
Padstow Bay
Gulland Rock
New Polzeath
Polzeath
Trelights
B3267
B3314
St. Endellion
Gunver Head
Trebetherick
Trevanger
TREVOSE HEAD
Quies
Crugmeer
Pityme
St. Minver
Lifeboat Station
Trevone
Rock
Harlyn Bay
Prideaux Place
Stoptide
Lower Amble
Chapel Amble
St. Kew
Constantine Bay
B3276
Treator
Lobster Hatchery
Padstow
St. Merryn
Treyarnon
Shop
Bodieve
Little Petherick
Edmonton
Trevanson
Trevance
Whitecross
Wadebridge
Egloshayle
Porthcothan
St. Issey
Royal Cornwall Showground
St. Breock
Trenance
Sladesbridge
A389
Park Head
Penrose
Mellingey Mill
Rumford
Treburrick
St. Ervan
Tredinnick
St. Jidgey
Pawton Quoit
Burlawn
Bedruthan Steps
Crealy
B3274
A39
St. Eval
St. Breock Downs
Monolith
Camel Valley Vineyard
Berryl's Point
Trenance
683
Nine Maidens Stone Row
Ruthernbridge
Mawgan Porth
Japanese
Cornish Birds of Prey Centre
Trevarrian
St. Mawgan
Talskiddy
Winnard's Perch
Rosenannon
Withiel
Watergate Bay
Tregurrian
Vale of Mawgan
Gluvian
St. Wenn
Tremore
NEWQUAY CORNWALL
B3274
Tregonetha
Retire
Towan Head
Huer's Hut
St. Columb Minor
A3059
St. Columb Major
Castle-an-Dinas
Demelza
744
NEWQUAY
Newquay Bay
Porth
Trebarber
Trekenning
703
Belowda
Fistral Bay
Trebudannon
CORNWALL
Victoria
A391
Pentire
Blue Reef Aquarium
Trencreek
Port Resr.
Colan
Springfields
A30
Kelsey Head
West Pentire
Crantock
Lane
Mountjoy
A392
Black Cross
Ruthvoes
Tregoss
Roche
Bilberry
Holywell Bay
Quintrell Downs
Trevarren
Screech Owl Sanctuary
Roche Rock
Penhale Point
Holywell Bay Fun Park
Kestle Mill
DairyLand Farm World
St. Columb Road
Enniscaven
Bugle
Penhale Camp
Cubert
A3075
NT Trerice
Indian Queens
Fraddon
St. Dennis
Hensbarrow Downs
1025
A3058
Penhale
Hendra
Whitemoor
Stenalees
Ligger or Perran Bay
Mount
St. Piran's Oratory
Rejerrah
St. Newlyn East
Lappa Valley Steam Railway
A3076
Summercourt
St. Enoder
B3279
Treviscoe
Nanpean
Carthew
Perranzabuloe
Rose
St. Piran's Round
B3275
Chapel Town
Goonabarn
Wheal Martyn
Perranporth
Goonhavern
Newlyn Downs
490
17
Menna
Trethosa
Foxhole
Bawden Rocks
Bolingey
Mitchell
Brighton
Carpalla
High Street
ST. AUSTELL
Carnkief
Carland Cross
B3285
St. Stephen
Trewoon
Bosco
Trevellas
Trelassick
Trendeal
Lanjeth
St. Agnes Head
Zelah
New Mills
Coombe
St. Mewan
Lifeboat Station
St. Agnes
Perranzabuloe
13
A39
Downderry
Tregoney
Wheal Coates Engine House
B3284
Penhallow Cyder Farm
Callestick
St. Allen
Trispen
Tregear
Ladock
Grampound Road
A390
Polgooth
London Apprentice
Goonvrea
Goonbell
Mithian
St. Erme
Sticker
Coldharbour
Allet
Hewas Water
B3273
B3277
Probus
Trewithen
Grampound
Rescorla
Porthtowan
Mount Hawke
A30
Shortlanesend
Idless
Creed
Lost Gardens of Heligan
Pentewan
Three Burrows
Tresillian
Portreath
Mawla
Blackwater
Kenwyn
Cathedral
St. Ewe
Tregiskey
Crane Islands
Bridge
Cambrose
Greenbottom
A390
Polmassick Vineyard
Kestle
Treasure Park
Chacewater
Ryl. Cornwall Mus.
Bosvigo
TRURO
Merther
A3078
Tregony
Mevagissey
Portmellon
Illogan
Scorrier
Roseland House
Threemilestone
Skinner's Brewery
St. Clement
Trevarrick
Gorran High Lanes
Wheal Busy Engine House
Hugus
Highertown
Mount Ambrose
B3298
Malpas
Ruan Lanihorne
Gorran Churchtown
B3301
Park Bottom
Illogan Highway
St. Day
Twelveheads
Kea
Old Kea
St. Michael Caerhays
Caerhays Castle
A30
REDRUTH
Carharrack
Bissoe
A39
Playing Place
St. Michael Penkevil
Lamorran
Boswinger
Gorran Haven
Kehelland
Tuckingmill
Cornish Engines
Carn Brea Village
Gwennap Pit
Carnon Downs
Coombe
Portholland
Treswithian
Brea
NT Carn Brea
Cusgarne
Gwennap
Penelewey
Ruan High Lanes
Veryan Green
Melinsey Mill
Veryan Bay
Penare
Roseworthy
Carnkie
Lanner
Perranwell
Pennpol
Trelissick
Philleigh
Trist House
Cliff Castle
Penponds
CAMBORNE
Treskillard
Devoran
Veryan
Portloe
Dodman Point
Shire Horse Farm
Four Lanes
Perranarworthal
Burncoose Nurseries
Feock
Treworthal
Beacon
Carne
Barripper
Troon
B3297
Penhalvean
Ponsanooth
Harcourt
Bolenowe
Gerrans Bay
Carnhell Green
Stithians
Mylor Bridge
Enys
Lanterns
Mylor Churchtown
Carrick Roads
St. Just in Roseland
Trewithian
Nare Head
Gull Rock
Wall
Stithians Lake
828
Stithians Reservoir
Praze-an-Beeble
B3280
B3292
St. Gluvias
St. Just
A3078
Portscatho
Burras
Penmarth
Carnkie
Penryn
Flushing
Gerrans
Crowan
Rame
Longdowns
Mabe Burnthouse
FALMOUTH
St. Mawes
Greeb Point
Drym
Porkellis
Releath
A39
St. Mawes
St. Anthony
Bohortha
A394
Budock Water
Pendennis
St. Anthony Battery
Nancegollan
Poldark Mine
Trenear
Treverva
Pendennis Point
Zone Point
Godolphin Cross
Crowntown
Helston
Wendron
Seworgan
Penjerrick
Carleen
Maenporth
Falmouth Bay
Trew
Breage
Sithney
Brill
Potager
Constantine
Carlidnack
Lowertown
Trewennack
Mawnan Smith
Carwinion
Rosemullion Head
A394
Folk
Glendurgan
Porth Navas
Trebah
Helston
Flambards
Gweek
Seal Sanctuary
Helford River
Mawnan
Helford
Bosahan
St. Anthony-in-Meneage
Porthleven
RNAS Culdrose Viewing Enclosure
B3304
Nare Point

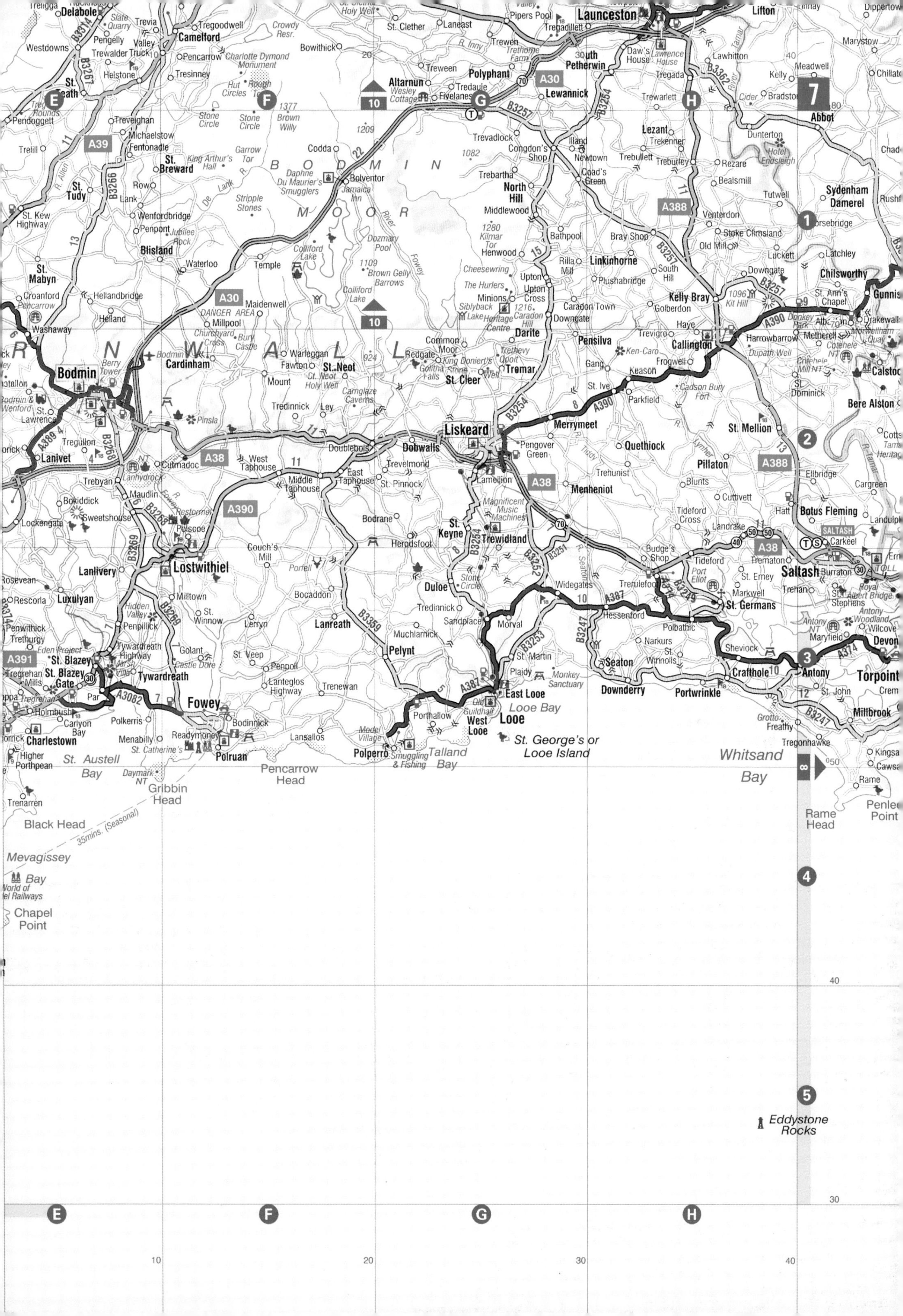

Delabole
Slate Quarry
Trevia
Tregoodwell
Camelford
Crowdy Resr.
Holy Well
St. Clether
Laneast
Pipers Pool
Launceston
Lifton
Dippertown
Westdowns
Pengelly
Valley
Trewalder
Truck
Pencarrow
Charlotte Dymond Monument
Bowithick
R. Inny
Trewen
Tregadillett
Trethorne Farm
South Petherwin
Daw's House
Lawrence House
Lawhitton
Marystow
Meadwell
St. Teath
Helstone
Tresinney
Hut Circles
Rough Tor
Treween
Altarnun
Wesley Cottage
Polyphant
Tredaule
Fivelanes
A30
Lewannick
Tregada
Kelly
Chillaton
Trewarlett
Cider
Bradstone
7
Pendoggett
Treveighan
1377 Brown Willy
Stone Circle
Stone Circle
B3257
Trevadlock
Lezant
Trekenner
Abbot
Michaelstow
A39
Fentonadle
1209
Codda
1082
Congdon's Shop
Illand
Newtown
Trebullett
Treburley
Dunterton
Hotel Endsleigh
Rezare
Chadd
Trelill
St. Breward
King Arthur's Hall
Garrow Tor
B O D M I N
Daphne Du Maurier's Smugglers
Bolventor
Jamaica Inn
Trebartha
Coad's Green
Bealsmill
St. Tudy
B3266
Row
Lank
De Lank
Stripple Stones
M O O R
North Hill
Middlewood
A388
Tutwell
Sydenham Damerel
Rushford
St. Kew Highway
Wenfordbridge
Penpont
Jubilee Rock
River Fowey
Dozmary Pool
1280 Kilmar Tor
Bathpool
Bray Shop
Venterdon
Horsebridge
Stoke Climsland
Colliford Lake
Henwood
Old Mill
Luckett
Latchley
Blisland
Waterloo
Temple
1109 Brown Gelly Barrows
Cheesewring
Rilla Mill
Linkinhorne
South Hill
Downgate
Chilsworthy
St. Mabyn
The Hurlers
Upton
Plushabridge
Croanford
Pencarrow
Hellandbridge
A30
Maidenwell
Colliford Lake
Minions
Upton Cross
1096 Kit Hill
Kelly Bray
St. Ann's Chapel
Gunnislake
Helland
Danger Area
Millpool
Siblyback Lake
Heritage Centre
1216 Caradon Hill
Caradon Town
Golberdon
Donkey Park
Drakewalls
Washaway
Churchyard Cross
Bury Castle
Darite
Downgate
Trevigro
Haye
Albaston
Morwellham Quay
C O R N W A L L
Bodmin
Berry Tower
Cardinham
Warleggan
Fawton
St. Neot
924
Redgate
Common Moor
Trethevy Quoit
Pensilva
Ken-Caro
Callington
Harrowbarrow
Metherell
Cotehele
Dupath Well
Cotehele Mill NT
Calstock
Nanstallon
Bodmin & Wenford
St. Lawrence
Mount
St. Neot Holy Well
Golitha Falls
King Doniert's Stone
Well
Tremar
St. Cleer
Gang
Keason
Frogwell
Cadson Bury Fort
St. Dominick
Bere Alston
Tredinnick
Ley
Carnglaze Caverns
St. Ive
Parkfield
Pinsla
A389
Lanivet
Treguddon
B3268
A38
Cutmadoc
West Taphouse
Doublebois
Dobwalls
Liskeard
Merrymeet
A390
Pengover Green
Quethiock
St. Mellion
Cotts
Tamar Heritage
Trebyan
Lanhydrock
Middle Taphouse
East Taphouse
Trevelmond
St. Pinnock
Lamellion
Menheniot
Trehunist
Pillaton
A388
Ellbridge
Cargreen
Maudlin
Bokiddick
Sweetshouse
Lockengate
B3268
Restormel
A390
Magnificent Music Machines
Blunts
Cuttivett
Botus Fleming
Hatt
Landulph
Polscoe
Bodrane
St. Keyne
Trewidland
Tideford Cross
Landrake
Saltash
Carkeel
B3269
Lostwithiel
Couch's Mill
Porfell
Herodsfoot
B3254
B3252
B3251
R. Seaton
Budge's Shop
Tideford
Port Eliot
Trematon
A38
Saltash
Burraton
Toll
Lanlivery
Rosevean
Duloe
Stone Circle
Widegates
Trerulefoot
B3249
St. Erney
Trehan
Royal Albert Bridge
Rescorla
Luxulyan
Milltown
Bocaddon
Tredinnick
Sandplace
A387
Hessenford
Markwell
St. Germans
St. Stephens
Antony Woodland
B3269
St. Winnow
Hidden Valley
Penpillick
Lerryn
Lanreath
B3359
Morval
Polbathic
Antony NT
Maryfield
Wilcove
Penwithick
Trethurgy
Eden Project
Tywardreath Highway
Golant
Castle Dore
St. Veep
Muchlarnick
Pelynt
B3253
B3247
Narkurs
St. Winnolls
Sheviock
Devonport
A391
St. Blazey
Marsh Villa
Penpoll
St. Martin
Seaton
Crafthole
Antony
A374
Torpoint
Tregrehan Mills
St. Blazey Gate
Tywardreath
Lanteglos Highway
Trenewan
Plaidy
Monkey Sanctuary
Downderry
Portwrinkle
St. John
Cremyll
Par
A3082
Fowey
East Looe
Looe Bay
Holmbush
Carlyon Bay
Polkerris
Bodinnick
Porthallow
Old Guildhall
West Looe
Looe
B3247
Millbrook
Charlestown
Menabilly
Readymoney
St. Catherine's
Polruan
Lansallos
Model Village
Polperro
Smuggling & Fishing
Talland Bay
St. George's or Looe Island
Grotto
Freathy
Tregonhawke
Whitsand Bay
Kingsand
Cawsand
Higher Porthpean
St. Austell Bay
Daymark NT
Pencarrow Head
Gribbin Head
8
Rame
Rame Head
Penlee Point
Trenarren
Black Head
35mins. (Seasonal)
Mevagissey
Bay
World of Model Railways
Chapel Point
Eddystone Rocks
E
F
G
H
1
2
3
4
5
10
20
30
40

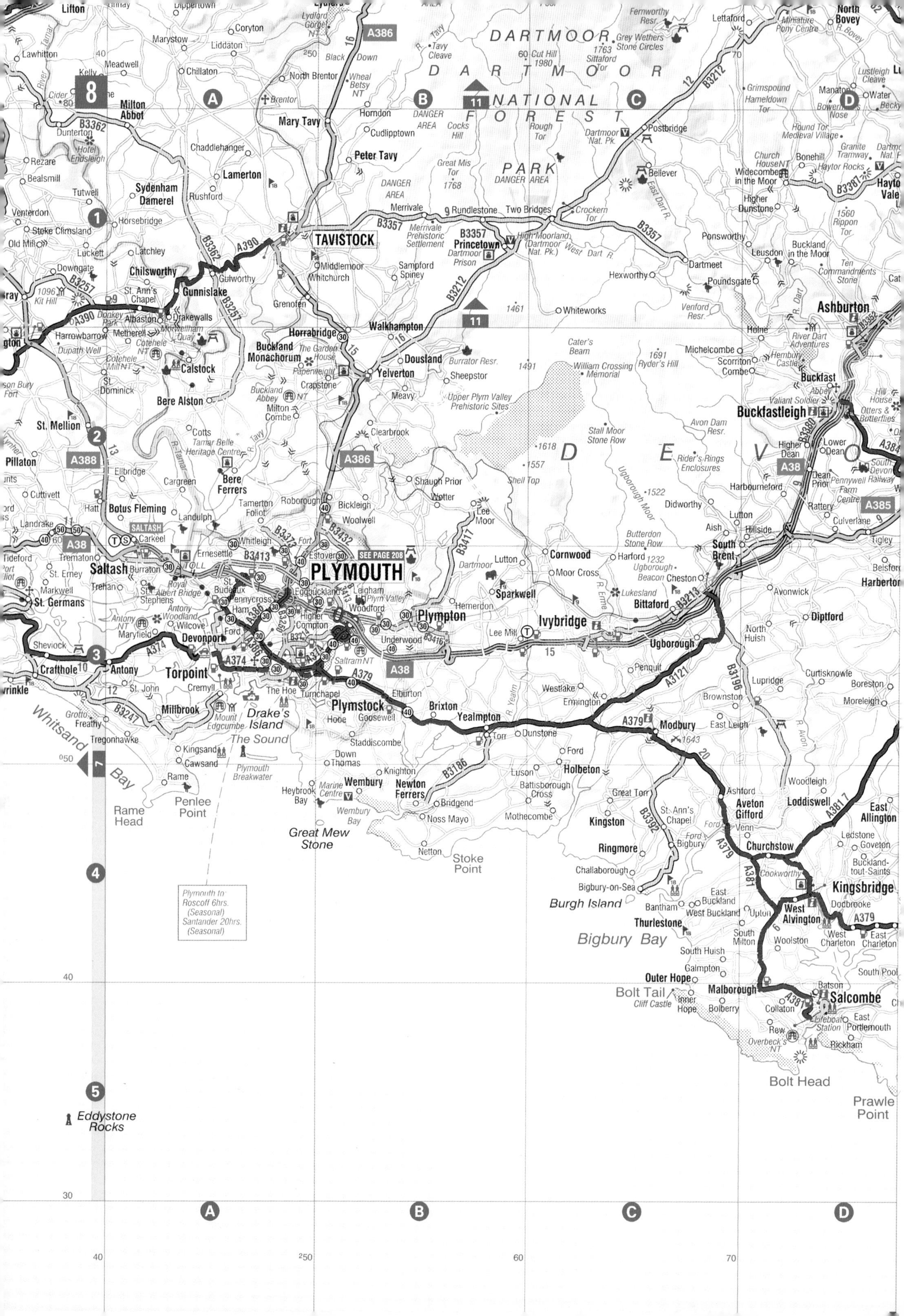
8
Lifton
Lawhitton
Marystow
Coryton
Liddaton
Chillaton
Meadwell
Kelly
Milton Abbot
Dunterton
B3362
Rezare
Bealsmill
Tutwell
Sydenham Damerel
Chaddlehanger
Lamerton
Rushford
Venterdon
Horsebridge
Stoke Climsland
Old Mill
Luckett
Latchley
Downgate
Chilsworthy
Gulworthy
B3257
Kit Hill
Gunnislake
St. Ann's Chapel
A390
Drakewalls
Albaston
Harrowbarrow
Metherell
Dupath Well
Cotehele
Calstock
St. Dominick
Bere Alston
St. Mellion
Pillaton
A388
Cotts
Tamar Belle Heritage Centre
Ellbridge
Cargreen
Bere Ferrers
Cuttivett
Hatt
Botus Fleming
Landulph
Landrake
SALTASH
Carkeel
A38
Trematon
Tideford
Saltash
Burraton
Ernesettle
St. Erney
Trehan
Markwell
St. Germans
Antony
Maryfield
Wilcove
Devonport
A374
Sheviock
Crafthole
Torpoint
St. John
Cremyll
Millbrook
B3247
Freathy
Tregonhawke
Whitsand Bay
Kingsand
Cawsand
Rame
Rame Head
Penlee Point
Mount Edgcumbe
Drake's Island
The Sound
Plymouth Breakwater
Plymouth to: Roscoff 6hrs. (Seasonal) Santander 20hrs. (Seasonal)
Eddystone Rocks
Lydford Gorge NT
A386
Black Down
North Brentor
Wheal Betsy NT
Brentor
Mary Tavy
Horndon
Cudlipptown
Peter Tavy
Tavy Cleave
TAVISTOCK
Middlemoor
Whitchurch
Grenofen
Horrabridge
Walkhampton
Buckland Monachorum
The Garden House
Dousland
Yelverton
Burrator Resr.
Sheepstor
Crapstone
Buckland Abbey
Milton Combe
Meavy
Clearbrook
Shaugh Prior
Wotter
Bickleigh
Woolwell
Roborough
Tamerton Foliot
Whitleigh
Estover
SEE PAGE 208
PLYMOUTH
Leigham
Plym Valley
Woodford
Plympton
Eggbuckland
St. Budeaux
Pennycross
Ham
Higher Compton
Ford
Underwood
A379
Saltram NT
The Hoe
Turnchapel
Plymstock
Hooe
Goosewell
Elburton
Staddiscombe
Down Thomas
Knighton
Wembury
Heybrook Bay
Wembury Bay
Great Mew Stone
Brixton
Yealmpton
Newton Ferrers
Bridgend
Noss Mayo
Netton
Stoke Point
DARTMOOR
DARTMOOR NATIONAL FOREST PARK
Cut Hill
Sittaford Tor
Fernworthy Resr.
Grey Wethers Stone Circles
Cocks Hill
Rough Tor
Great Mis Tor
DANGER AREA
Merrivale
Merrivale Prehistoric Settlement
Rundlestone
Two Bridges
Princetown
Dartmoor Prison
B3357
B3212
Sampford Spiney
Postbridge
Bellever
Crockern Tor
Dartmoor Nat. Pk.
Whiteworks
Cater's Beam
William Crossing Memorial
Ryder's Hill
Upper Plym Valley Prehistoric Sites
Stall Moor Stone Row
Shell Top
Ugborough Moor
Butterdon Stone Row
Lee Moor
Lutton
Cornwood
Moor Cross
Harford
Ugborough Beacon
Dartmoor
Sparkwell
Hemerdon
Lukesland
Ivybridge
Lee Mill
Bittaford
Cheston
Ugborough
Penquit
Westlake
Ermington
A3121
Modbury
Torr
Dunstone
Ford
Holbeton
Luson
Battisborough Cross
Mothecombe
Great Torr
Kingston
St. Ann's Chapel
Ringmore
Challaborough
Bigbury-on-Sea
Burgh Island
Bigbury Bay
Bantham
Thurlestone
South Huish
Galmpton
Outer Hope
Inner Hope
Bolt Tail
Cliff Castle
Malborough
Bolberry
Lettaford
North Bovey
Miniature Pony Centre
Grimspound
Hameldown Tor
Hound Tor Medieval Village
Manaton
Water
Church House NT
Widecombe in the Moor
Bonehill
Haytor Rocks
Higher Dunstone
Ponsworthy
Leusdon
Buckland in the Moor
Dartmeet
Hexworthy
Poundsgate
Venford Resr.
Ten Commandments Stone
Ashburton
Holne
River Dart Adventures
Michelcombe
Scorriton
Combe
Hembury Castle
Buckfast
Valiant Soldier
Buckfastleigh
Avon Dam Resr.
Rider's Rings Enclosures
Higher Dean
Lower Dean
Dean Prior
Pennywell Farm Centre
Harbourneford
Didworthy
Rattery
A385
Aish
Lutton
Hillside
Culverlane
South Brent
Avonwick
Diptford
Harberton
North Huish
B3196
Curtisknowle
Lupridge
Brownston
East Leigh
Boreston
Moreleigh
Woodleigh
Ashford
Aveton Gifford
Loddiswell
Venn
Ford
Bigbury
Churchstow
East Allington
A381
Ledstone
Goveton
Buckland-tout-Saints
Cookworthy
Kingsbridge
Dodbrooke
West Alvington
East Buckland
West Buckland
Upton
South Milton
Woolston
West Charleton
East Charleton
South Pool
Batson
Salcombe
Collaton
East Portlemouth
Rew
Lifeboat Station
Overbeck's NT
Rickham
Bolt Head
Prawle Point
A B C D
1 2 3 4 5

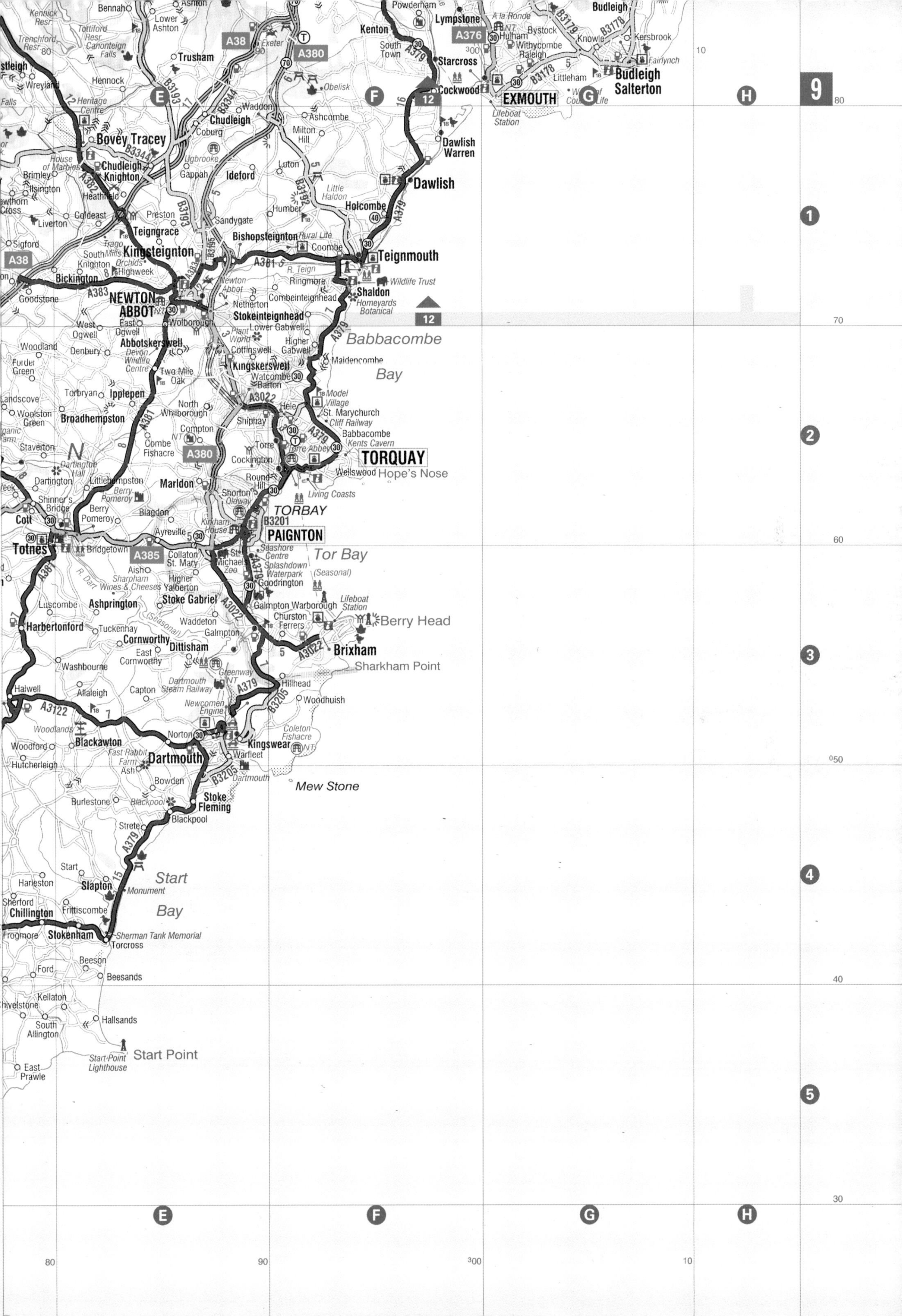

9
Exeter
Exmouth
Budleigh Salterton
Dawlish
Teignmouth
Newton Abbot
Kingsteignton
Bovey Tracey
Chudleigh
Torquay
Babbacombe Bay
Paignton
Torbay
Tor Bay
Brixham
Berry Head
Sharkham Point
Hope's Nose
Totnes
Dartmouth
Kingswear
Mew Stone
Stoke Fleming
Start Bay
Slapton
Stokenham
Torcross
Start Point
Start Point Lighthouse
E
F
G
H
1
2
3
4
5
80
70
60
50
40
30
90
300
10

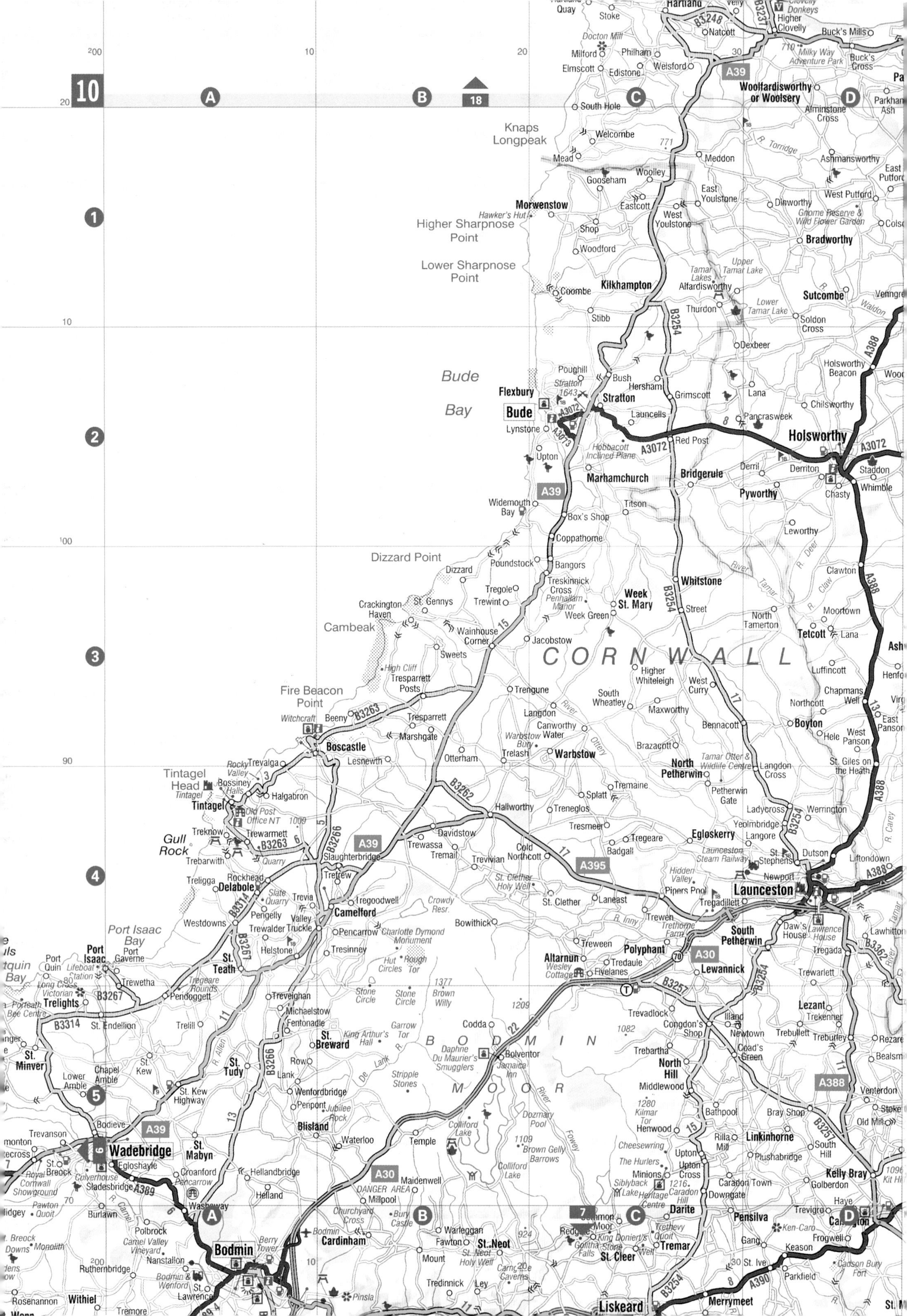

10
A
B
C
D
18
7
1
2
3
4
5
6
Hartland Quay
Stoke
Hartland
Higher Clovelly
Clovelly Donkeys
Natcott
Buck's Mills
Milky Way Adventure Park
Buck's Cross
Doctor Mill
Milford
Philham
Elmscott
Edistone
Welsford
Woolfardisworthy or Woolsery
Alminstone Cross
Parkham Ash
South Hole
Knaps Longpeak
Welcombe
Mead
Meddon
R. Torridge
Ashmansworthy
East Putford
Gooseham
Woolley
East Youlstone
Dinworthy
West Putford
Morwenstow
Hawker's Hut
Eastcott
West Youlstone
Gnome Reserve & Wild Flower Garden
Higher Sharpnose Point
Shop
Bradworthy
Woodford
Lower Sharpnose Point
Tamar Lakes
Upper Tamar Lake
Alfardisworthy
Kilkhampton
Coombe
Sutcombe
Thurdon
Lower Tamar Lake
Stibb
Soldon Cross
R. Waldon
Dexbeer
Bude Bay
Poughill
Stratton 1643
Bush
Hersham
Flexbury
Stratton
Grimscott
Lana
Holsworthy Beacon
Chilsworthy
Bude
Launcells
Pancrasweek
Lynstone
Red Post
Holsworthy
Hobbacott Inclined Plane
Upton
Derril
Derriton
Staddon
Whimble
Marhamchurch
Bridgerule
Pyworthy
Chasty
Widemouth Bay
Titson
Box's Shop
Leworthy
Coppathorne
Dizzard Point
Poundstock
Bangors
Dizzard
Clawton
Tregole
Treskinnick Cross
Whitstone
Trewint
Week St. Mary
Penhallam Manor
Crackington Haven
St. Gennys
Week Green
Street
Moortown
North Tamerton
Cambeak
Wainhouse Corner
Jacobstow
Tetcott
Sweets
CORNWALL
Higher Whiteleigh
Luffincott
High Cliff
Tresparrett Posts
West Curry
Fire Beacon Point
Trengune
South Wheatley
Chapmans Well
Maxworthy
Northcott
Witchcraft
Beeny
Langdon
Tresparrett
Canworthy Water
Bennacott
Boyton
Hele
West Panson
Marshgate
Warbstow Bury
Boscastle
Trelash
Warbstow
Brazacott
Lesnewth
Otterham
Tamar Otter & Wildlife Centre
Langdon Cross
St. Giles on the Heath
Tintagel Head
Rocky Valley
Trevalga
North Petherwin
Bossiney Halls
Tremaine
Petherwin Gate
Tintagel
Halgabron
Splatt
Hallworthy
Old Post Office NT
Treneglos
Ladycross
Werrington
Tresmeer
Yeolmbridge
Gull Rock
Treknow
Trewarmett
Slaughterbridge
Davidstow
Tregeare
Egloskerry
Langore
Trebarwith
Quarry
Trewassa
Tremail
Cold Northcott
Badgall
Launceston Steam Railway
St. Stephens
Dutson
Liftondown
Treligga
Rockhead
Tretrew
Trevivian
St. Clether Holy Well
Hidden Valley
Newport
Delabole
Slate Quarry
Trevia
Tregoodwell
Crowdy Resr.
Piper's Pool
Launceston
Pengelly
Valley Truckle
Camelford
St. Clether
Laneast
Tregadillett
Westdowns
Bowithick
R. Inny
Trewen
Trethorne Farm
Daw's House
Lawrence House
Lawhitton
Port Isaac Bay
Trewalder
Pencarrow
Charlotte Dymond Monument
South Petherwin
Port Isaac
Port Gaverne
Helstone
Tresinney
Treween
Tregada
St. Teath
Hut Circles
Rough Tor
Altarnun
Polyphant
Wesley Cottage
Tredaule
Lewannick
Port Quin
Lifeboat Station
Trewetha
Fivelanes
Trewarlett
Long Cross Victorian Garden
Tregeare Rounds
Stone Circle
1377 Brown Willy
Lezant
Trelights
Pendoggett
Treveighan
Trevadlock
Trekenner
Michaelstow
1209
Illand
Fentonadle
Congdon's Shop
Newtown
Trebullett
Treburley
B3314
St. Endellion
Trelill
Codda
1082
St. Breward
King Arthur's Hall
Garrow Tor
BODMIN
MOOR
Coad's Green
St. Minver
Row
Daphne Du Maurier's Smugglers
Bolventor
Trebartha
North Hill
Beals
Chapel Amble
St. Kew
St. Tudy
Jamaica Inn
Lower Amble
Lank
Stripple Stones
Middlewood
Venterdon
St. Kew Highway
Wenfordbridge
1280 Kilmar Tor
Bathpool
Bray Shop
Stoke
Penpont
Jubilee Rock
Dozmary Pool
Old Mill
Bodieve
Blisland
Colliford Lake
Henwood
Rilla Mill
Linkinhorne
South Hill
Trevanson
Wadebridge
St. Mabyn
Waterloo
Temple
1109 Brown Gelly Barrows
Cheesewring
Upton
Plushabridge
St. Breock
Egloshayle
The Hurlers
Upton Cross
Royal Cornwall Showground
Colverhouse
Croanford
Hellandbridge
Colliford Lake
Minions
Caradon Town
Kelly Bray
Golberdon
Sladesbridge
Pencarrow
Maidenwell
Sibly Lake
Heritage Centre
Caradon Hill
Pawton Quoit
Helland
DANGER AREA
Millpool
Downgate
Hayes
Burlawn
Washaway
Churchyard Cross
Bury Castle
Common Moor
Darite
Pensilva
Trevigro
Callington
Bodmin
Warleggan
Redgate
King Doniert's Stone
Trethevy Quoit
Ken-Caro
Polbrock
Cardinham
Golitha Falls
Tremar
Gang
Frogwell
St. Breock Downs Monolith
Camel Valley Vineyard
Berry Tower
Fawton
St. Neot
St. Cleer
Keason
Nanstallon
Mount
St. Neot Holy Well
Carnglaze Caverns
St. Ive
Cadson Bury Fort
Ruthernbridge
Bodmin & Wenford
St. Lawrence
Parkfield
Tredinnick
Ley
Rosenannon
Withiel
Pinsla
Liskeard
Merrymeet
Tremore
A39
B3248
B3237
A388
A3072
A3073
B3254
B3263
B3262
B3266
A395
B3314
B3267
A30
B3257
B3362
A389
A390

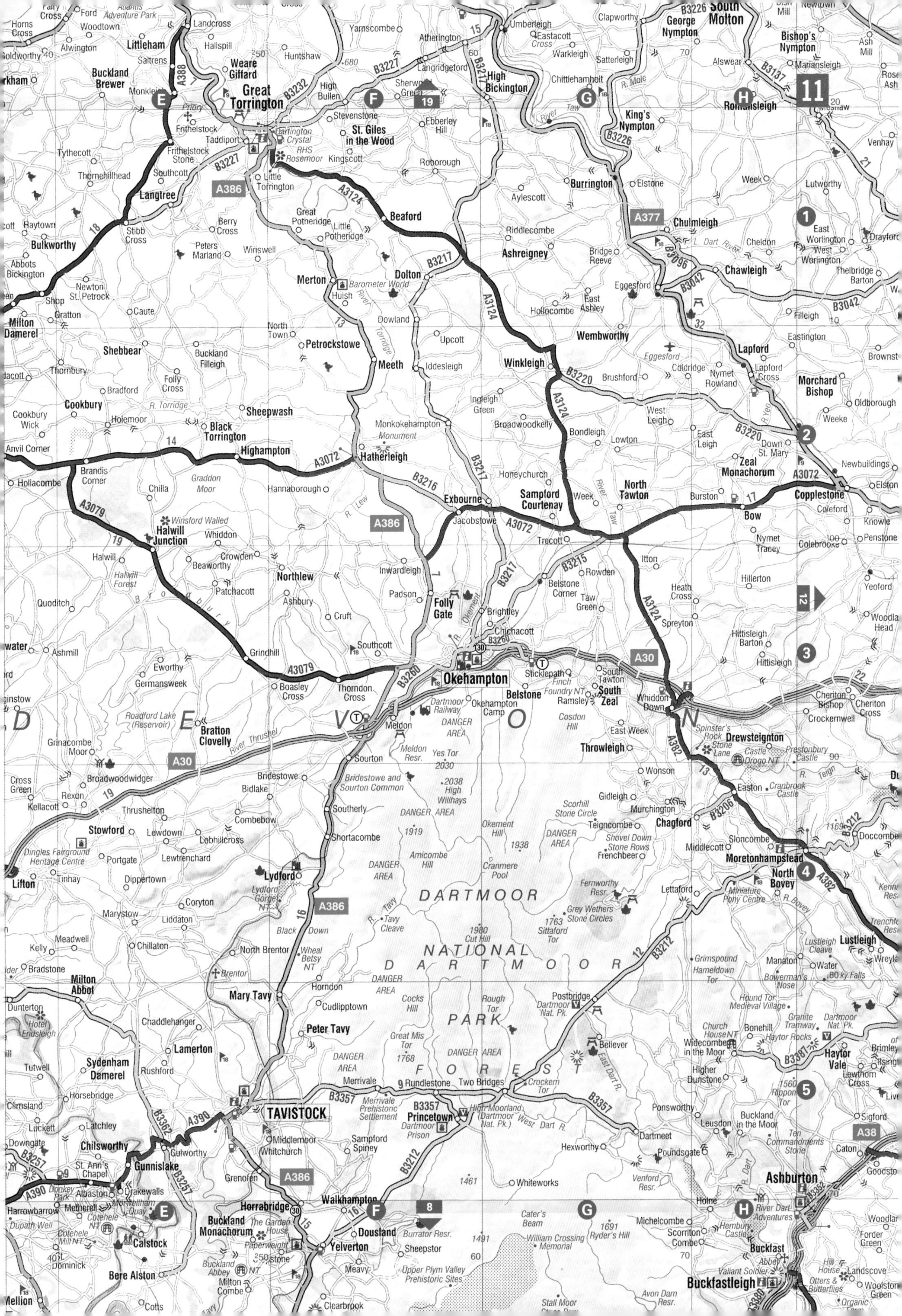

Great Torrington
South Molton
Okehampton
Tavistock
Hatherleigh
Chulmleigh
Winkleigh
Bow
Copplestone
Moretonhampstead
Chagford
Ashburton
Buckfastleigh
Princetown
Yelverton
Lydford
Lifton
Holsworthy
Dolton
Beaford
Burrington
Lapford
Morchard Bishop
North Tawton
Sampford Courtenay
Exbourne
Black Torrington
Highampton
Halwill Junction
Shebbear
Petrockstowe
Meeth
Merton
Langtree
Weare Giffard
High Bickington
St. Giles in the Wood
King's Nympton
George Nympton
Bishop's Nympton
Drewsteignton
Lustleigh
North Bovey
Widecombe in the Moor
Mary Tavy
Peter Tavy
Milton Abbot
Gunnislake
Calstock
Bere Alston
Horrabridge
Buckland Monachorum
Dousland
Walkhampton
DARTMOOR
DARTMOOR NATIONAL PARK
DARTMOOR FOREST
DEVON
A30
A386
A3124
A3072
A3079
A377
A382
A390
A388
A38
B3227
B3217
B3220
B3212
B3357
11
12
19
8

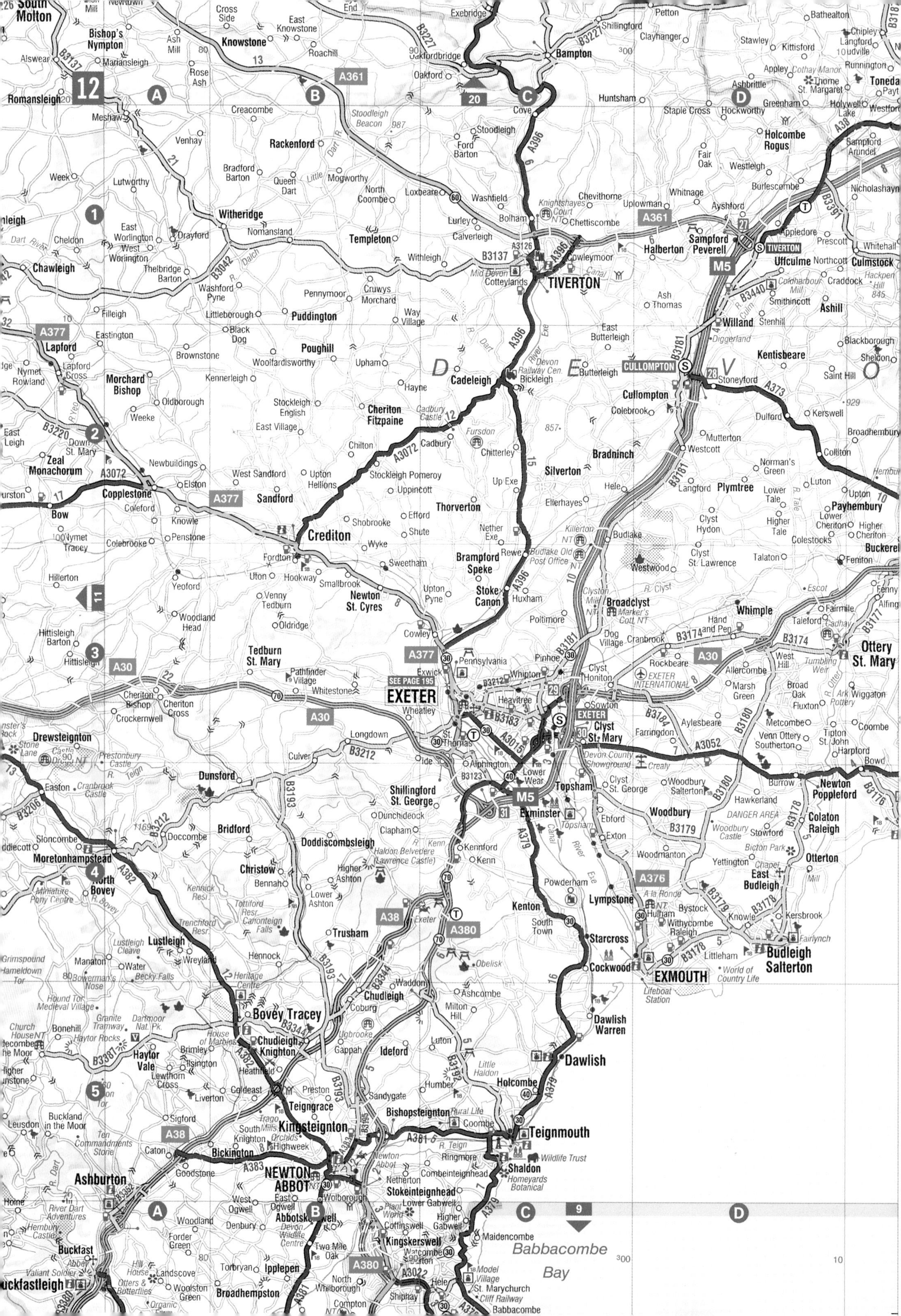

South Molton
Bishop's Nympton
Mariansleigh
Alswear
Romansleigh
12
A
B
C
D
Cross Side
East Knowstone
Knowstone
Roachill
Ash Mill
Rose Ash
Meshaw
Creacombe
A361
Exebridge
B3227
Oakfordbridge
Oakford
20
Bampton
Shillingford
Petton
Clayhanger
Bathealton
Stawley
Kittisford
Chipley
Langford Budville
Runnington
Appley
Cothay Manor
Thorne St. Margaret
Ashbrittle
Toneda
Huntsham
Cove
Staple Cross
Hockworthy
Greenham
Holywell Lake
Westford
Venhay
Stoodleigh Beacon
Rackenford
Stoodleigh
Ford Barton
Holcombe Rogus
Fair Oak
Westleigh
Sampford Arundel
Week
Lutworthy
Bradford Barton
Queen Dart
Mogworthy
North Coombe
Loxbeare
Washfield
Chevithorne
Uplowman
Whitnage
Ayshford
Burlescombe
Nicholashayne
Witheridge
Nomansland
Templeton
Lurley
Calverleigh
Bolham
Knightshayes Court NT
Chettiscombe
Halberton
Sampford Peverell
Appledore
Prescott
Whitehall
Cheldon
East Worlington
West Worlington
Drayford
Chawleigh
Thelbridge Barton
Withleigh
B3137
A3126
Cowleymoor
TIVERTON
M5
Uffculme
Northcott
Culmstock
Mid Devon
Cotteylands
Washford Pyne
Pennymoor
Cruwys Morchard
Way Village
Ash Thomas
Coldharbour Mill
Craddock
Smithincott
Ashill
Filleigh
Littleborough
Puddington
Willand
Stenhill
A377
Lapford
Eastington
Black Dog
Brownstone
Poughill
Diggerland
Blackborough
East Butterleigh
Nymet Rowland
Lapford Cross
Morchard Bishop
Woolfardisworthy
Upham
Cadeleigh
Devon Railway Cen.
Bickleigh
Butterleigh
CULLOMPTON
Stoneyford
Kentisbeare
Saint Hill
Sheldon
Kennerleigh
Hayne
A373
Oldborough
Stockleigh English
Cheriton Fitzpaine
Cadbury Castle
Cullompton
Colebrook
Dulford
Kerswell
Weeke
East Village
Fursdon
Mutterton
Broadhembury
East Leigh
B3220
Down St. Mary
Zeal Monachorum
A3072
Cadbury
Chilton
Chitterley
Westcott
Colliton
Bradninch
Newbuildings
West Sandford
Upton Hellions
Stockleigh Pomeroy
Silverton
Norman's Green
Elston
Uppincott
Up Exe
Hele
Langford
Plymtree
Lower Tale
Luton
Upton
Payhembury
Copplestone
Bow
Sandford
Thorverton
Ellerhayes
Coleford
Knowle
Efford
Shobrooke
Clyst Hydon
Higher Tale
Lower Cheriton
Higher Cheriton
Nymet Tracey
Colebrooke
Penstone
Crediton
Shute
Nether Exe
Killerton NT
Budlake
Colestocks
Wyke
Rewe
Budlake Old Post Office NT
Clyst St. Lawrence
Talaton
Buckerell
Fordton
Sweetham
Brampford Speke
Westwood
Feniton
Hillerton
Yeoford
Uton
Hookway
Smallbrook
Stoke Canon
Huxham
Clyston Mill NT
Broadclyst
Marker's Cott NT
R. Clyst
Escot
Fenny
Venny Tedburn
Newton St. Cyres
Upton Pyne
Whimple
Fairmile
Woodland Head
Oldridge
Cowley
Poltimore
Dog Village
Cranbrook
Hand and Pen
Talaford
Hittisleigh Barton
Hittisleigh
Tedburn St. Mary
Pathfinder Village
A30
Pennsylvania
Pinhoe
Clyst Honiton
B3174
Rockbeare
Ottery St. Mary
West Hill
Cheriton Bishop
Cheriton Cross
Whitestone
SEE PAGE 195
EXETER
Exwick
B3212
Whipton
Heavitree
EXETER INTERNATIONAL
Allercombe
Tumbling Weir
Broad Oak
Ark Wiggaton Pottery
Crockernwell
Wheatley
B3183
Sowton
Marsh Green
Fluxton
Drewsteignton
Stone Lane
Castle Drogo NT
Prestonbury Castle
Longdown
St. Thomas
A3015
Clyst St. Mary
B3184
Farringdon
Aylesbeare
B3180
Metcombe
Venn Ottery
Southerton
Tipton St. John
Coombe
Culver
Ide
Alphington
Devon County Showground
Crealy
A3052
Harpford
Bowd
Easton
Cranbrook Castle
Dunsford
B3193
B3123
Lower Wear
Topsham
Clyst St. George
Woodbury Salterton
Burrow
Newton Poppleford
B3206
Shillingford St. George
Dunchideock
Exminster
Ebford
Woodbury
Hawkerland
DANGER AREA
Colaton Raleigh
Slocombe
Bridford
Doccombe
Clapham
Exton
B3179
Woodbury Castle
Stowford
Moretonhampstead
Doddiscombsleigh
Haldon Belvedere (Lawrence Castle)
Kennford
Kenn
A379
Woodmanton
Bicton Park
Otterton
North Bovey
A382
Christow
Bennah
Higher Ashton
Powderham
Yettington
East Budleigh
Miniature Pony Centre
Kennick Resr.
Lower Ashton
A376
Lympstone
A la Ronde
Bystock
Tottiford Resr.
Canonteign Falls
Trenchford Resr.
A38
Exeter
A380
Kenton
South Town
Hulham
Withycombe Raleigh
Knowle
Kersbrook
Trusham
Starcross
B3178
Fairlynch
Lustleigh
Lustleigh Cleave
Manaton
Water
Wreyland
Hennock
Obelisk
Cockwood
Littleham
World of Country Life
Budleigh Salterton
EXMOUTH
Grimspound
Hameldown Tor
Bowerman's Nose
Becky Falls
Heritage Centre
Waddon
B3344
Chudleigh
Ashcombe
Lifeboat Station
Hound Tor Medieval Village
Bovey Tracey
Coburg
Milton Hill
Dawlish Warren
Church House NT
Widecombe in the Moor
Bonehill
Granite Tramway
Dartmoor Nat. Pk.
Haytor Rocks
House of Marbles
Chudleigh Knighton
Ugbrooke
Gappah
Ideford
Luton
Little Haldon
Dawlish
Haytor Vale
B3387
Brimley
Ilsington
Heathfield
Lewthorn Cross
Liverton
Coldeast
Preston
Humber
Holcombe
Teigngrace
Sandygate
Bishopsteignton
Rural Life
Coombe
Buckland in the Moor
Leusdon
Sigford
Ten Commandments Stone
South Knighton
Trago Mills
Kingsteignton
Orchids
Teignmouth
Wildlife Trust
Caton
Bickington
Highweek
A383
A381
R. Teign
Ringmore
Shaldon
Goodstone
NEWTON ABBOT
Newton Abbot
Netherton
Combeinteignhead
Homeyards Botanical
Ashburton
Stokeinteignhead
Holne
River Dart Adventures
Hembury Castle
West Ogwell
East Ogwell
Wolborough
Lower Gabwell
Woodland
Abbotskerswell
Plant World
Higher Gabwell
Denbury
Devon Wildlife Centre
Coffinswell
Kingskerswell
Maidencombe
Babbacombe Bay
9
Buckfast Abbey
Forder Green
Two Mile Oak
Watcombe
Hill House
Landscove
Torbryan
Ipplepen
Model Village
Valiant Soldier
Buckfastleigh
Otters & Butterflies
Woolston Green
Broadhempston
North Whilborough
A3022
Hele
St. Marychurch
Cliff Railway
Babbacombe
Shiphay
Compton

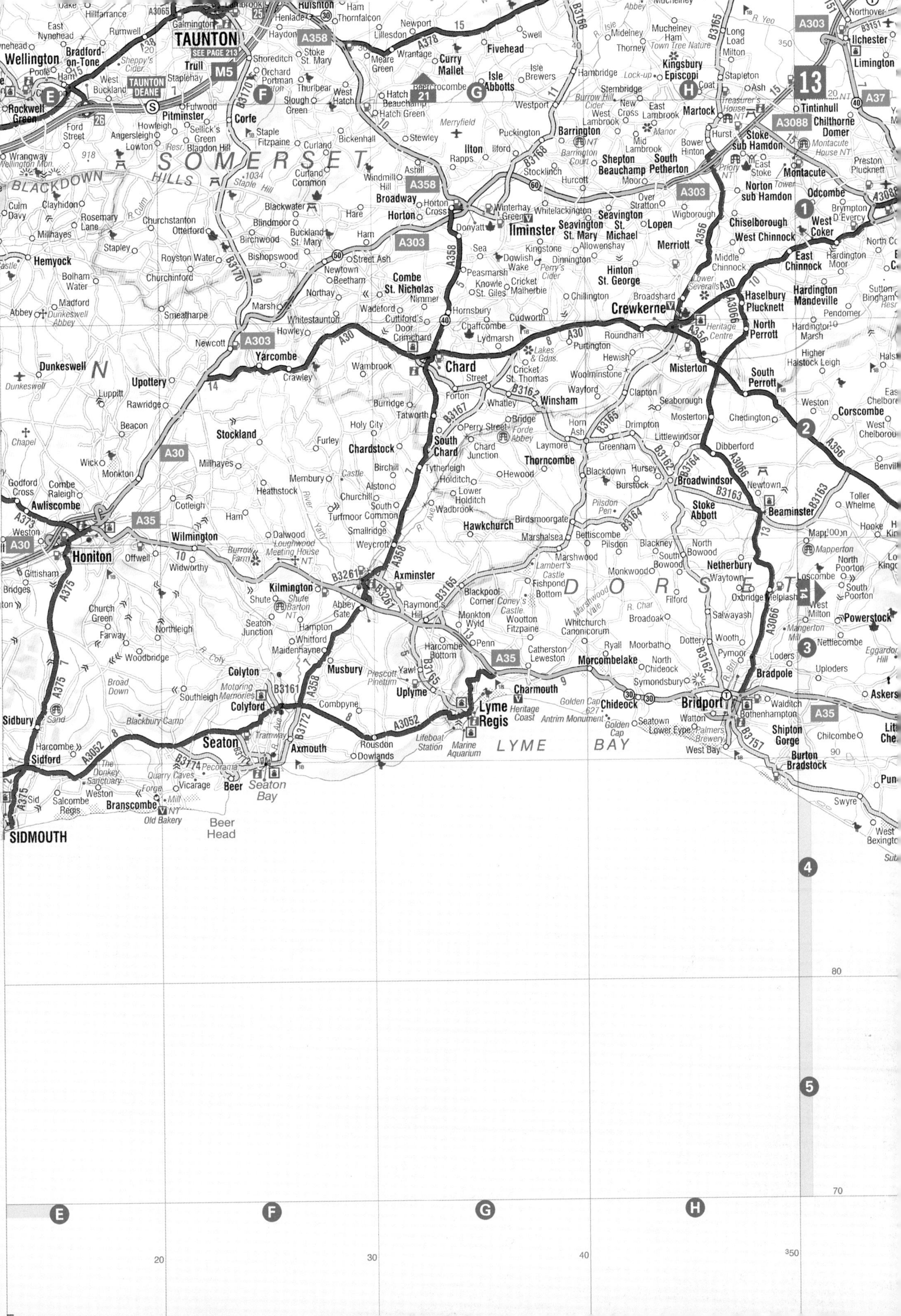
TAUNTON
SEE PAGE 213
Wellington
SOMERSET
BLACKDOWN HILLS
Chard
Ilminster
Crewkerne
Honiton
Axminster
Seaton
Colyford
Lyme Regis
Charmouth
Bridport
Beaminster
SIDMOUTH
LYME BAY
DORSET
Beer Head
13
14
A30
A303
A358
A35
A375
A3052
A356
A3066
M5
E
F
G
H
20
30
40
350
80
70
90

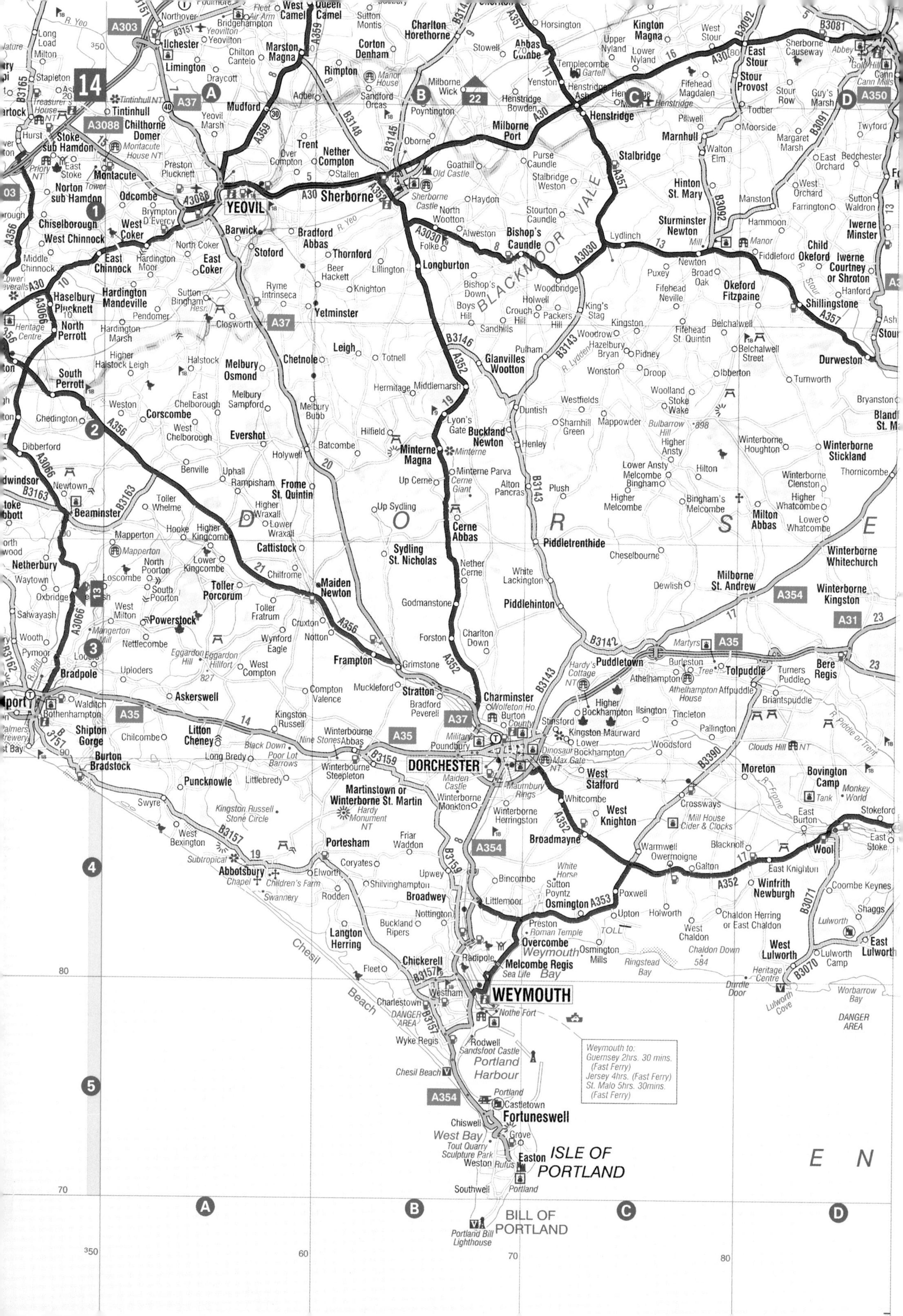14
A303
Ilchester
Limington
Yeovilton
Northover
Bridgehampton
Chilton Cantelo
Marston Magna
West Camel
Queen Camel
Sutton Montis
Corton Denham
Charlton Horethorne
Horsington
Kington Magna
Upper Nyland
Lower Nyland
West Stour
East Stour
Stour Provost
Sherborne Causeway
Abbas Combe
Templecombe
Stowell
Rimpton
Milborne Wick
Sandford Orcas
Adber
Mudford
Tintinhull
Chilthorne Domer
Stoke sub Hamdon
Montacute
Norton sub Hamdon
Odcombe
Brympton D'Evercy
YEOVIL
Preston Plucknett
Yeovil Marsh
Trent
Over Compton
Nether Compton
Stallen
Sherborne
Sherborne Castle
Oborne
Poyntington
Goathill
Old Castle
Henstridge Bowden
Henstridge Ash
Henstridge
Milborne Port
Yenston
Purse Caundle
Stalbridge
Stalbridge Weston
Fifehead Magdalen
Marnhull
Todber
Stour Row
Guy's Marsh
Margaret Marsh
Twyford
East Orchard
West Orchard
Bedchester
Walton Elm
Hinton St. Mary
Sturminster Newton
Manston
Hammoon
Farrington
Sutton Waldron
Iwerne Minster
Child Okeford
Iwerne Courtney or Shroton
Hanford
Shillingstone
Durweston
Okeford Fitzpaine
Fiddleford
Chiselborough
West Coker
West Chinnock
Middle Chinnock
East Chinnock
Hardington Moor
North Coker
East Coker
Barwick
Stoford
Bradford Abbas
Thornford
Beer Hackett
Lillington
Longburton
Haydon
North Wootton
Alweston
Folke
Bishop's Caundle
Stourton Caundle
BLACKMOOR VALE
Lydlinch
Newton
Broad Oak
Puxey
Fifehead Neville
Haselbury Plucknett
Hardington Mandeville
Sutton Bingham
Pendomer
Closworth
Ryme Intrinseca
Yetminster
Knighton
Bishop's Down
Boys Hill
Holwell
Crouch Hill
Packers Hill
Woodbridge
King's Stag
Sandhills
Pulham
Glanvilles Wootton
Woodrow
Hazelbury Bryan
Pidney
Kingston
Fifehead St. Quintin
Belchalwell
Belchalwell Street
Ibberton
Turnworth
Wonston
Droop
North Perrott
Hardington Marsh
Higher Halstock Leigh
Halstock
Melbury Osmond
Chetnole
Leigh
Totnell
South Perrott
Chedington
East Chelborough
West Chelborough
Melbury Sampford
Corscombe
Weston
Melbury Bubb
Hermitage
Middlemarsh
Lyon's Gate
Buckland Newton
Duntish
Westfields
Sharnhill Green
Mappowder
Woolland
Stoke Wake
Bulbarrow Hill
Bryanston
Blandford St. M
Dibberford
Evershot
Holywell
Batcombe
Hilfield
Minterne Magna
Minterne
Minterne Parva
Henley
Higher Ansty
Lower Ansty
Melcombe Bingham
Hilton
Winterborne Houghton
Winterborne Stickland
Thornicombe
Broadwindsor
Newtown
Benville
Uphall
Rampisham
Frome St. Quintin
Up Cerne
Cerne Giant
Alton Pancras
Plush
Higher Melcombe
Bingham's Melcombe
Winterborne Clenston
Higher Whatcombe
Lower Whatcombe
Milton Abbas
Beaminster
Toller Whelme
Hooke
Higher Kingcombe
Higher Wraxall
Lower Wraxall
Up Sydling
Cerne Abbas
Piddletrenthide
D O R S E
Mapperton
Netherbury
Waytown
Oxbridge
Salwayash
North Poorton
South Poorton
Loscombe
Lower Kingcombe
Cattistock
Chilfrome
Sydling St. Nicholas
Nether Cerne
White Lackington
Cheselbourne
Dewlish
Milborne St. Andrew
Winterborne Whitechurch
Winterborne Kingston
A354
A31
Toller Porcorum
Maiden Newton
Godmanstone
Piddlehinton
West Milton
Powerstock
Toller Fratrum
Wynford Eagle
Cruxton
Notton
Forston
Charlton Down
Mangerton Mill
Nettlecombe
Eggardon Hill
Eggardon Hillfort
Wooth
Pymore
Loders
Bradpole
Uploders
West Compton
Frampton
Grimstone
Stratton
Bradford Peverell
Muckleford
Compton Valence
Askerswell
Kingston Russell
Charminster
Wolfeton Ho.
Burton
Puddletown
Hardy's Cottage NT
Burleston
Tolpuddle
Athelhampton
Athelhampton House
Affpuddle
Turners Puddle
Bere Regis
Briantspuddle
Tincleton
Pallington
Higher Bockhampton
Ilsington
Stinsford
Kingston Maurward
Lower Bockhampton
Woodsford
Bridport
Walditch
Bothenhampton
Shipton Gorge
Chilcombe
Litton Cheney
Black Down
Poor Lot Barrows
Nine Stones
Winterbourne Abbas
Poundbury
DORCHESTER
Max Gate
Dinosaur
Burton Bradstock
Long Bredy
Littlebredy
Winterbourne Steepleton
Puncknowle
Maiden Castle
Maumbury Rings
West Stafford
Moreton
Bovington Camp
Tank
Monkey World
Clouds Hill NT
Swyre
Kingston Russell Stone Circle
Martinstown or Winterborne St. Martin
Hardy Monument NT
Winterborne Monkton
Winterborne Herringston
Whitcombe
West Knighton
Crossways
Mill House Cider & Clocks
East Burton
Stokeford
West Bexington
Subtropical
Abbotsbury
Chapel
Children's Farm
Swannery
Portesham
Friar Waddon
Coryates
Elworth
Shilvinghampton
Rodden
Upwey
Broadwey
Broadmayne
Warmwell
Owermoigne
Galton
Blacknoll
Wool
East Stoke
East Knighton
Winfrith Newburgh
Coombe Keynes
White Horse
Sutton Poyntz
Bincombe
Littlemoor
Osmington
Poxwell
Upton
Holworth
West Chaldon
Chaldon Herring or East Chaldon
Chaldon Down
Shaggs
Lulworth
East Lulworth
West Lulworth
Lulworth Camp
Nottington
Buckland Ripers
Langton Herring
Preston
Roman Temple
Overcombe
Weymouth Bay
Osmington Mills
Ringstead Bay
Chesil Beach
Fleet
Chickerell
Radipole
Melcombe Regis
Sea Life
Heritage Centre
Durdle Door
Lulworth Cove
Worbarrow Bay
DANGER AREA
WEYMOUTH
Westham
Charlestown
Nothe Fort
Wyke Regis
Rodwell
Sandsfoot Castle
Portland Harbour
Chesil Beach
Portland
Castletown
Chiswell
Fortuneswell
West Bay
Grove
Tout Quarry Sculpture Park
Weston
Rufus
Easton
ISLE OF PORTLAND
Southwell
BILL OF PORTLAND
Portland Bill Lighthouse
E N
Weymouth to:
Guernsey 2hrs. 30 mins. (Fast Ferry)
Jersey 4hrs. (Fast Ferry)
St. Malo 5hrs. 30mins. (Fast Ferry)
A30
A37
A35
A352
A356
A357
A359
A3030
A3066
A3088
A353
B3081
B3091
B3092
B3143
B3145
B3146
B3148
B3151
B3157
B3159
B3163
B3390
B3070
B3071
A B C D
1 2 3 4 5
350
60
70
80

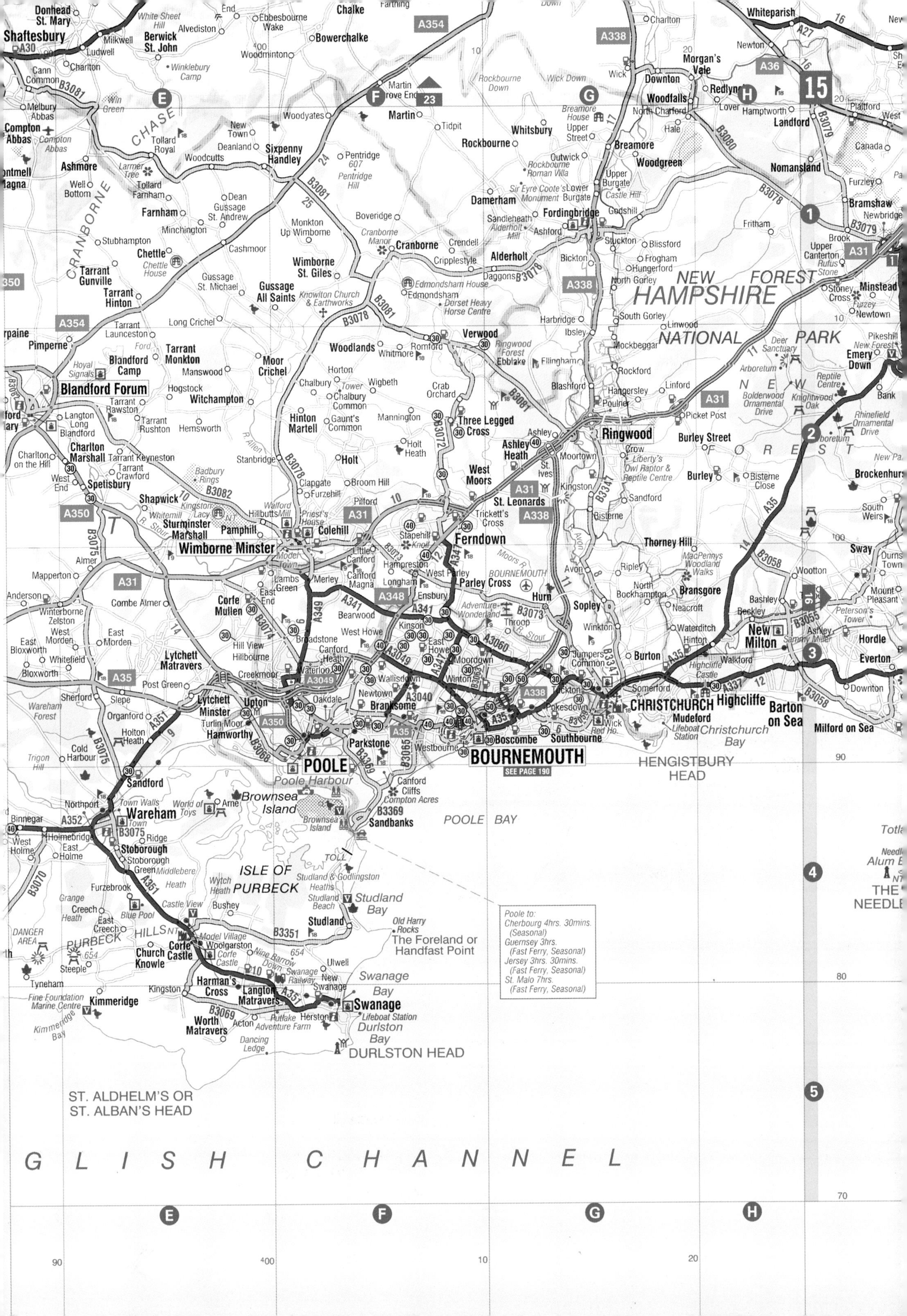

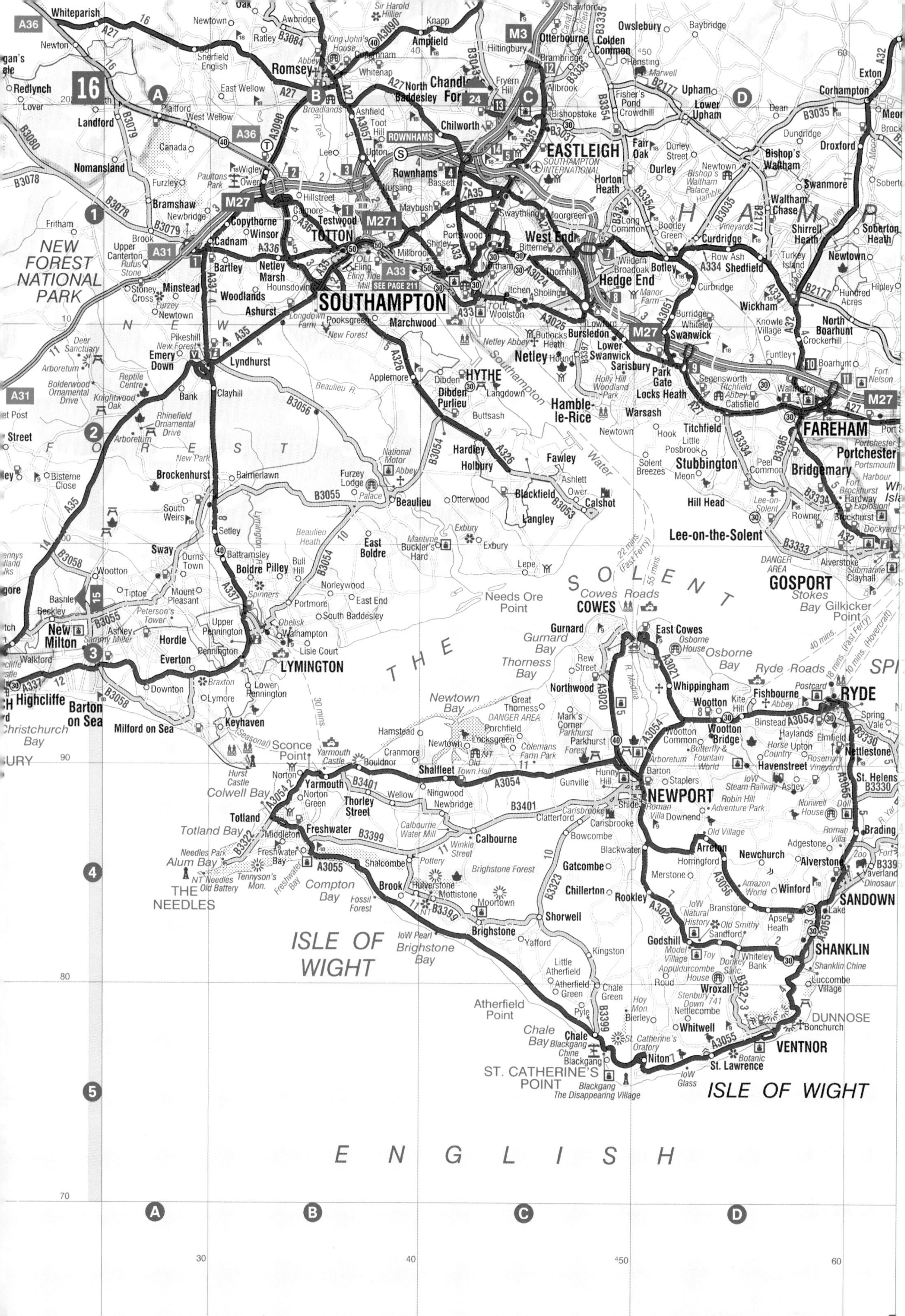

16
A36
Whiteparish
Newton
Redlynch
Lover
Landford
Plaitford
West Wellow
Nomansland
Canada
Sherfield English
Newtown
Awbridge
Ratley
Romsey
King John's House
Cupernham
Abbey
Whitenap
Broadlands
Knapp
Ampfield
Sir Harold Hillier
North Baddesley
Chandler's Ford
Hiltingbury
Fryern Hill
Otterbourne
Shawford
Colden Common
Owslebury
Baybridge
Hensting
Marwell
Brambridge
Allbrook
Bishopstoke
Fisher's Pond
Crowdhill
Upham
Lower Upham
Dean
Corhampton
Exton
Meonstoke
Dundridge
Droxford
Bishop's Waltham
Swanmore
Waltham Chase
Soberton
Soberton Heath
Shirrell Heath
Newtown
Curdridge
Durley
Durley Street
Fair Oak
Horton Heath
EASTLEIGH
SOUTHAMPTON INTERNATIONAL
Chilworth
Ashfield
Toot Hill
Upton
Lee
ROWNHAMS
Rownhams
Bassett
Nursling
Hillstreet
Calmore
Testwood
TOTTON
Wigley
Ower
Paultons Park
Furzley
Bramshaw
Newbridge
Copythorne
Winsor
Cadnam
Brook
Fritham
NEW FOREST NATIONAL PARK
Upper Canterton
Rufus Stone
Stoney Cross
Minstead
Furzey
Newtown
Bartley
Netley Marsh
Hounsdown
Woodlands
Ashurst
Eling
Eling Tide Mill
Millbrook
Shirley
Portswood
Maybush
Swaythling
Moorgreen
West End
Bitterne
Northam
Thornhill
Itchen
Sholing
Woolston
Wildern
Broadoak
Botley
Boorley Green
Long Common
Hedge End
Manor Farm
Row Ash
Shedfield
Turkey Island
Curbridge
Wickham
Hundred Acres
Hipley
Knowle Village
North Boarhunt
Crockerhill
Funtley
Boarhunt
Fort Nelson
Wallington
Fareham
FAREHAM
Portchester
Portchester Castle
Portsmouth Harbour
SOUTHAMPTON
SEE PAGE 211
Pooksgreen
Marchwood
Longdown Farm
New Forest
Bursledon
Lowford
Butlocks Heath
Netley
Netley Abbey
Hound
Lower Swanwick
Swanwick
Sarisbury
Park Gate
Holly Hill Woodland Park
Locks Heath
Segensworth
Titchfield
Titchfield Abbey
Catisfield
Warsash
Hook
Little Posbrook
Stubbington
Solent Breezes
Meon
Peel Common
Bridgemary
Fort Brockhurst
Hardway
Explosion!
Brockhurst
Rowner
Dockyard
Lee-on-Solent
Lee-on-the-Solent
Hill Head
Alverstoke
Submarine
Clayhall
GOSPORT
Stokes Bay
Gilkicker Point
DANGER AREA
Hamble-le-Rice
Newtown
Southampton Water
Fawley
Ashlett
Ower
Calshot
Blackfield
Langley
Hythe
HYTHE
Dibden
Langdown
Dibden Purlieu
Applemore
Buttsash
Hardley
Holbury
Pikeshill
Deer Sanctuary
Arboretum
Bolderwood Ornamental Drive
Knightwood Oak
Emery Down
Lyndhurst
Bank
Clayhill
Reptile Centre
Rhinefield Ornamental Drive
Arboretum
New Park
FOREST
Brockenhurst
Balmerlawn
Bisterne Close
South Weirs
Setley
Sway
Durns Town
Battramsley
Boldre
Pilley
Bull Hill
Wootton
Tiptoe
Mount Pleasant
Spinners
Bashley
Beckley
New Milton
Sammy Miller
Ashley
Peterson's Tower
Hordle
Upper Pennington
Pennington
Everton
Walkford
Highcliffe
Barton on Sea
Christchurch Bay
Downton
Braxton
Lymore
Lower Pennington
Keyhaven
Milford on Sea
Hurst Castle
LYMINGTON
Obelisk
Walhampton
Lisle Court
Portmore
South Baddesley
Norleywood
East End
East Boldre
Beaulieu Heath
Beaulieu
Palace
Furzey Lodge
National Motor Museum
Abbey
Otterwood
Buckler's Hard
Maritime
Exbury
Lepe
Needs Ore Point
THE SOLENT
Cowes Roads
COWES
East Cowes
Osborne House
Osborne Bay
Gurnard
Gurnard Bay
Thorness Bay
Rew Street
Northwood
Whippingham
Ryde Roads
RYDE
Spring Vale
Fishbourne
Kite Hill
Wootton
Wootton Bridge
Wootton Common
Binstead
Haylands
Elmfield
Upton
Horse Country
Rosemary Vineyard
Butterfly & Fountain World
Havenstreet
IoW Steam Railway
Ashey
Nettlestone
St. Helens
Newtown Bay
Great Thorness
Mark's Corner
Parkhurst
Parkhurst Forest
Porchfield
Locksgreen
Newtown
Colemans Farm Park
Hamstead
Cranmore
Bouldnor
Yarmouth
Yarmouth Castle
Sconce Point
Norton
Norton Green
Colwell Bay
Shalfleet
Ningwood
Newbridge
Wellow
Thorley Street
Gunville
Hunny Hill
NEWPORT
Shide
Roman Villa
Downend
Robin Hill Adventure Park
Carisbrooke
Clatterford
Calbourne
Calbourne Water Mill
Winkle Street
Totland
Totland Bay
Middleton
Freshwater
Freshwater Bay
Needles Park
Alum Bay
NT Needles Old Battery
Tennyson's Mon.
THE NEEDLES
Compton Bay
Fossil Forest
Shalcombe
Brook
Hulverstone
Mottistone
Pottery
Brighstone Forest
Moortown
Brighstone
IoW Pearl
Brighstone Bay
Yafford
Shorwell
Bowcombe
Gatcombe
Blackwater
Chillerton
Rookley
Arreton
Horringford
Merstone
Newchurch
Adgestone
Nunwell House
Brading
Roman Villa
Alverstone
Winford
Amazon World
Zoo
Fort
Yaverland
Dinosaur
SANDOWN
Lake
Apse Heath
Branstone
Old Smithy
IoW Natural History
Sandford
Godshill
Model Village
Toy
Donkey Sanc.
Whiteley Bank
SHANKLIN
Shanklin Chine
Luccombe Village
Appuldurcombe House
Roud
Wroxall
Stenbury Down
Nettlecombe
Whitwell
Kingston
Little Atherfield
Atherfield Green
Chale Green
Hoy Mon.
Bierley
Pyle
Atherfield Point
Chale
Chale Bay
Blackgang Chine
Blackgang
St. Catherine's Oratory
Niton
ST. CATHERINE'S POINT
Blackgang The Disappearing Village
IoW Glass
St. Lawrence
Botanic
VENTNOR
Bonchurch
DUNNOSE
ISLE OF WIGHT
ENGLISH
M27
M271
M3
A27
A31
A33
A35
A36
A326
A337
A3024
A3025
A3054
A3055
A3056
A3020
A3021
A32
A334
B3055
B3054
B3058
B3078
B3079
B3080
B3401
B3399
B3323
B3322
B3330
B3335
B3354
B3035
B2177
30 mins.
22 mins. (Fast Ferry)
55 mins.
40 mins.
18 mins. (Fast Ferry)
10 mins. (Hovercraft)
A
B
C
D
1
2
3
4
5
30
40
450
60
70
80
90

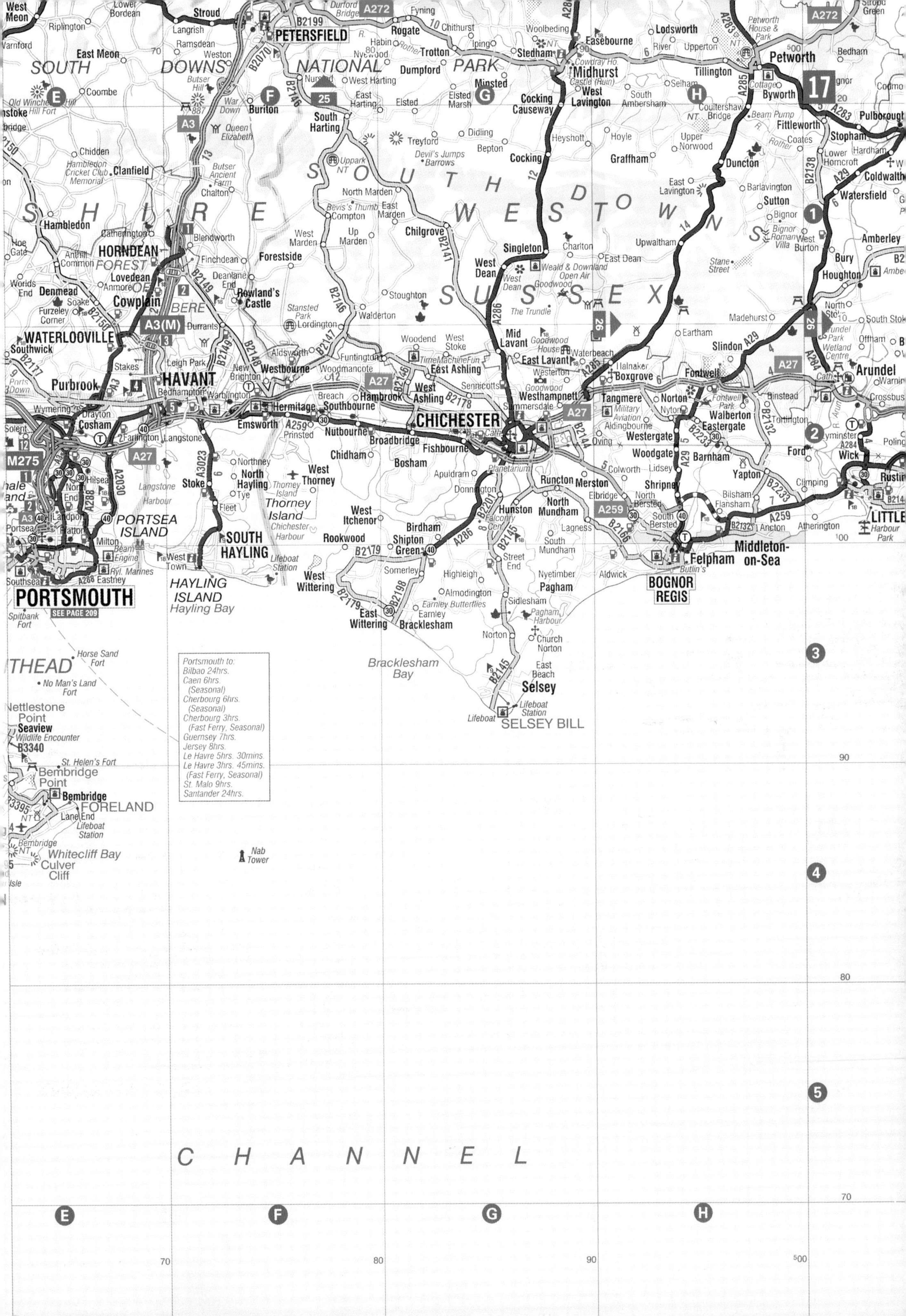

Portsmouth to:
Bilbao 24hrs.
Caen 6hrs. (Seasonal)
Cherbourg 6hrs. (Seasonal)
Cherbourg 3hrs. (Fast Ferry, Seasonal)
Guernsey 7hrs.
Jersey 8hrs.
Le Havre 5hrs. 30mins.
Le Havre 3hrs. 45mins. (Fast Ferry, Seasonal)
St. Malo 9hrs.
Santander 24hrs.

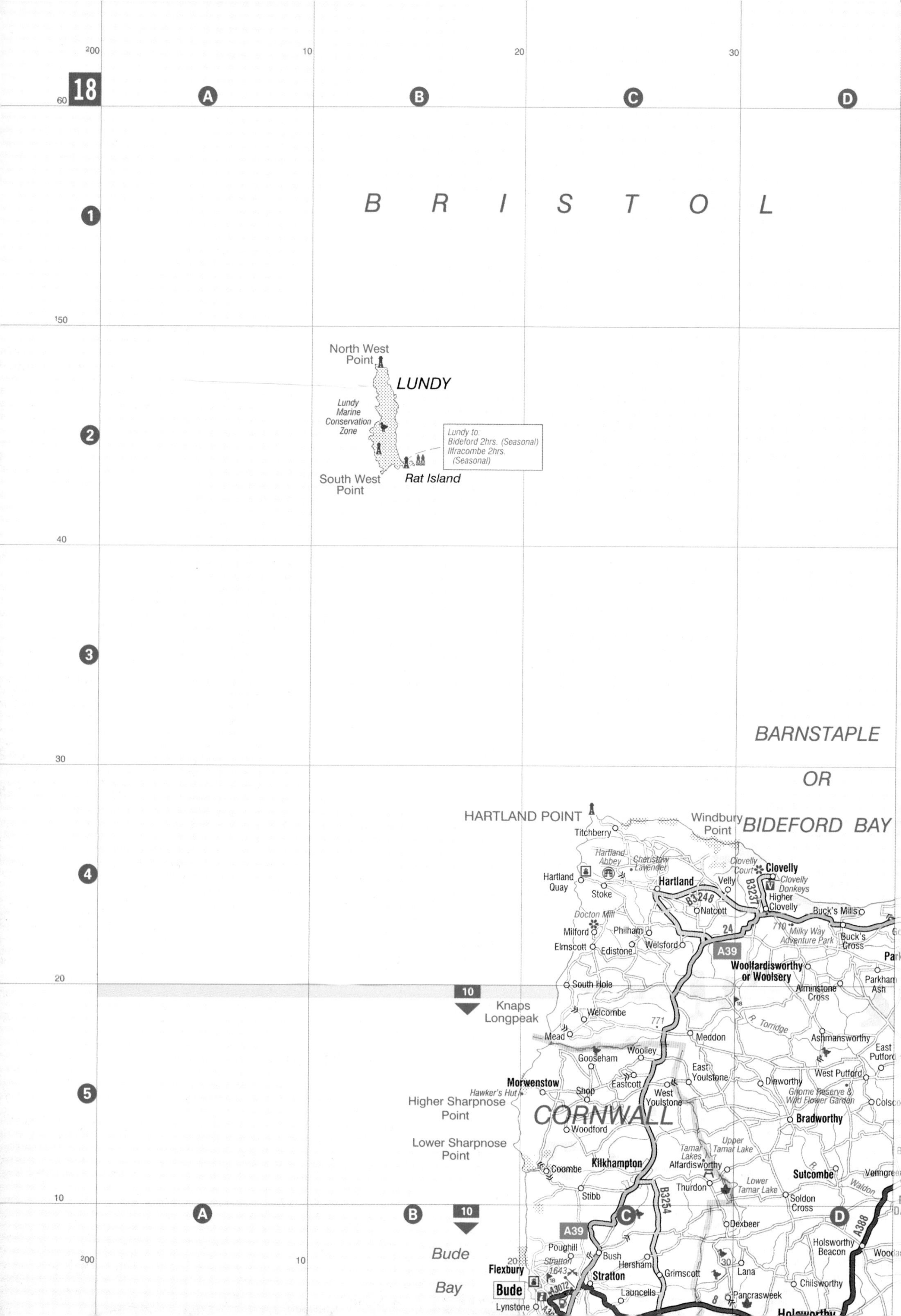

200   10   20   30

60

A   **B**   **C**   **D**

1

B R I S T O L

150

North West
Point

LUNDY

2

Lundy
Marine
Conservation
Zone

> Lundy to:
> Bideford 2hrs. (Seasonal)
> Ilfracombe 2hrs.
> (Seasonal)

South West
Point

Rat Island

40

3

BARNSTAPLE

30

OR

BIDEFORD BAY

HARTLAND POINT   Windbury
Point

Titchberry

*Hartland
Abbey*   *Cheristow
Lavender*   Clovelly
Court   **Clovelly**

4

Hartland
Quay   **Hartland**   Velly   *Clovelly
Donkeys*

Stoke   B3248   Higher
Clovelly

Natcott   B3237   Buck's Mills

Docton Mill   24   710   *Milky Way
Adventure Park*   Buck's
Cross

Milford   A39

Elmscott   Philham   **Woolfardisworthy
or Woolsery**   Par

Edistone   Welsford   Alminstone
Cross   Parkham
Ash

20

South Hole   *R. Torridge*   Ashmansworthy

10

Knaps
Longpeak   Welcombe   771   Meddon   West Putford   East
Putford

Mead   Gooseham   Woolley   East
Youlstone   Dinworthy   *Gnome Reserve &
Wild Flower Garden*   Colsc

5

Hawker's Hut   **Morwenstow**   Shop   Eastcott   West
Youlstone   **Bradworthy**

Higher Sharpnose
Point   *CORNWALL*   Woodford

Lower Sharpnose
Point   *Upper
Tamar Lake*   **Sutcombe**   Venngree

Coombe   **Kilkhampton**   *Tamar
Lakes*   Alfardisworthy   *Lower
Tamar Lake*   *Waldon*

10

Stibb   Thurdon   Soldon
Cross

A   **B**   **10**   **C**   B3254   Dexbeer   **D**

A39   Holsworthy
Beacon   Woodac

200   10

Bude   Poughill   Bush   A388

Flexbury   *Stratton
1643*   Hersham   Grimscott   Lana   Chilsworthy

Bay   **Bude**   **Stratton**

Lynstone   Launcells   8   Pancrasweek

Holsworthy

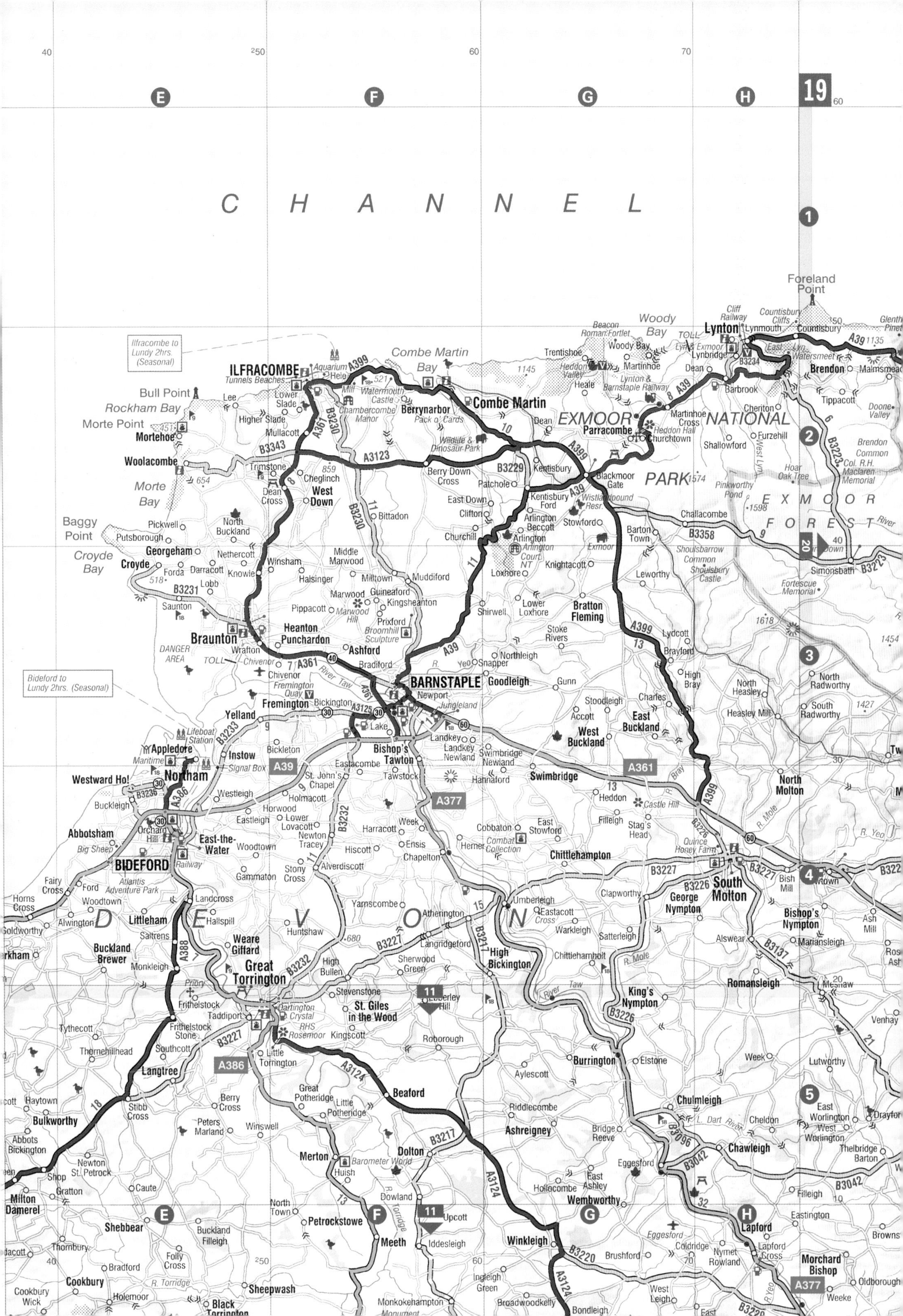
C H A N N E L
Foreland Point
Lynton
Lynmouth
Countisbury
Woody Bay
Ilfracombe to Lundy 2hrs. (Seasonal)
ILFRACOMBE
Tunnels Beaches
Combe Martin Bay
Combe Martin
Berrynarbor
Bull Point
Rockham Bay
Morte Point
Mortehoe
Woolacombe
Morte Bay
Baggy Point
Croyde Bay
Croyde
Georgeham
Braunton
EXMOOR NATIONAL PARK
Parracombe
Blackmoor Gate
Brendon
E X M O O R F O R E S T
Simonsbath
Challacombe
Arlington
Bratton Fleming
BARNSTAPLE
Goodleigh
Bideford to Lundy 2hrs. (Seasonal)
Fremington
Instow
Appledore
Northam
Westward Ho!
BIDEFORD
East-the-Water
Abbotsham
Bishop's Tawton
Swimbridge
West Buckland
East Buckland
Chittlehampton
South Molton
North Molton
George Nympton
Bishop's Nympton
D E V O N
Littleham
Weare Giffard
Great Torrington
High Bickington
King's Nympton
St. Giles in the Wood
Langtree
Bulkworthy
Beaford
Burrington
Chulmleigh
Chawleigh
Merton
Dolton
Ashreigney
Wembworthy
Winkleigh
Lapford
Morchard Bishop
Petrockstowe
Meeth
Shebbear
Cookbury
Black Torrington
Sheepwash
Milton Damerel
Romansleigh
A39
A361
A377
A386
A388
A399
A3124
A3123
B3230
B3232
B3227
B3226
B3217
B3220
B3042

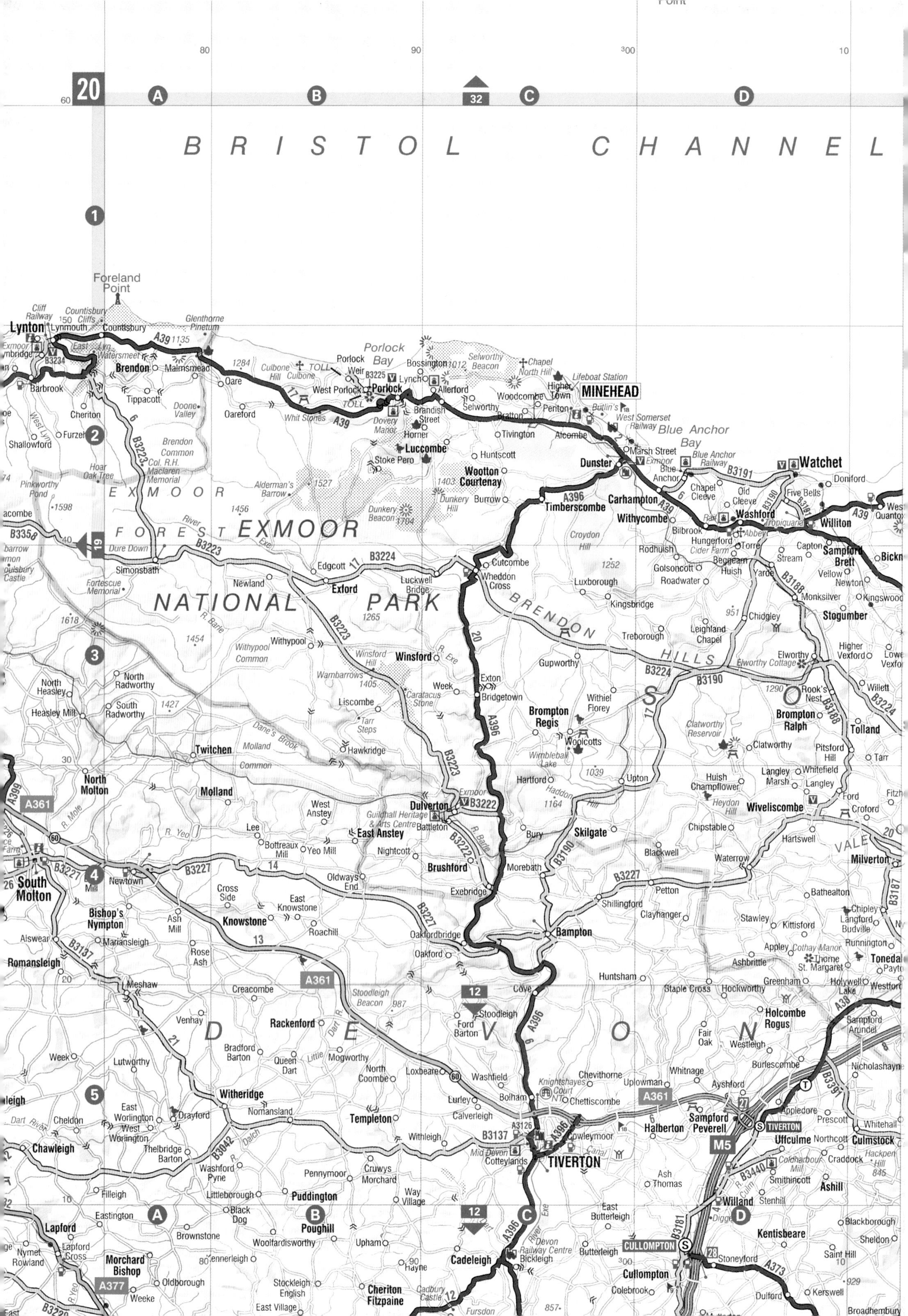
BRISTOL CHANNEL
Foreland Point
Lynton
Lynmouth
Countisbury
Brendon
Malmsmead
Oare
Porlock Bay
Porlock
Porlock Weir
West Porlock
Bossington
Allerford
Selworthy
Selworthy Beacon
MINEHEAD
Blue Anchor Bay
Dunster
Watchet
Williton
Luccombe
Wootton Courtenay
Dunkery Beacon
Timberscombe
Carhampton
Withycombe
EXMOOR FOREST
EXMOOR NATIONAL PARK
Simonsbath
Exford
Winsford
Withypool
Cutcombe
Wheddon Cross
BRENDON HILLS
Brompton Regis
Brompton Ralph
Wiveliscombe
Dulverton
Twitchen
North Molton
Molland
South Molton
East Anstey
Brushford
Skilgate
Bampton
Milverton
Knowstone
Oakfordbridge
Rackenford
Romansleigh
Bishop's Nympton
Witheridge
Templeton
Holcombe Rogus
Sampford Peverell
Halberton
TIVERTON
Uffculme
Culmstock
Willand
Cullompton
Cadeleigh
Puddington
Poughill
Morchard Bishop
Lapford
Chawleigh
Cheriton Fitzpaine
Kentisbeare
Ashill
DEVON
A39
A396
A361
A377
A373
A38
M5

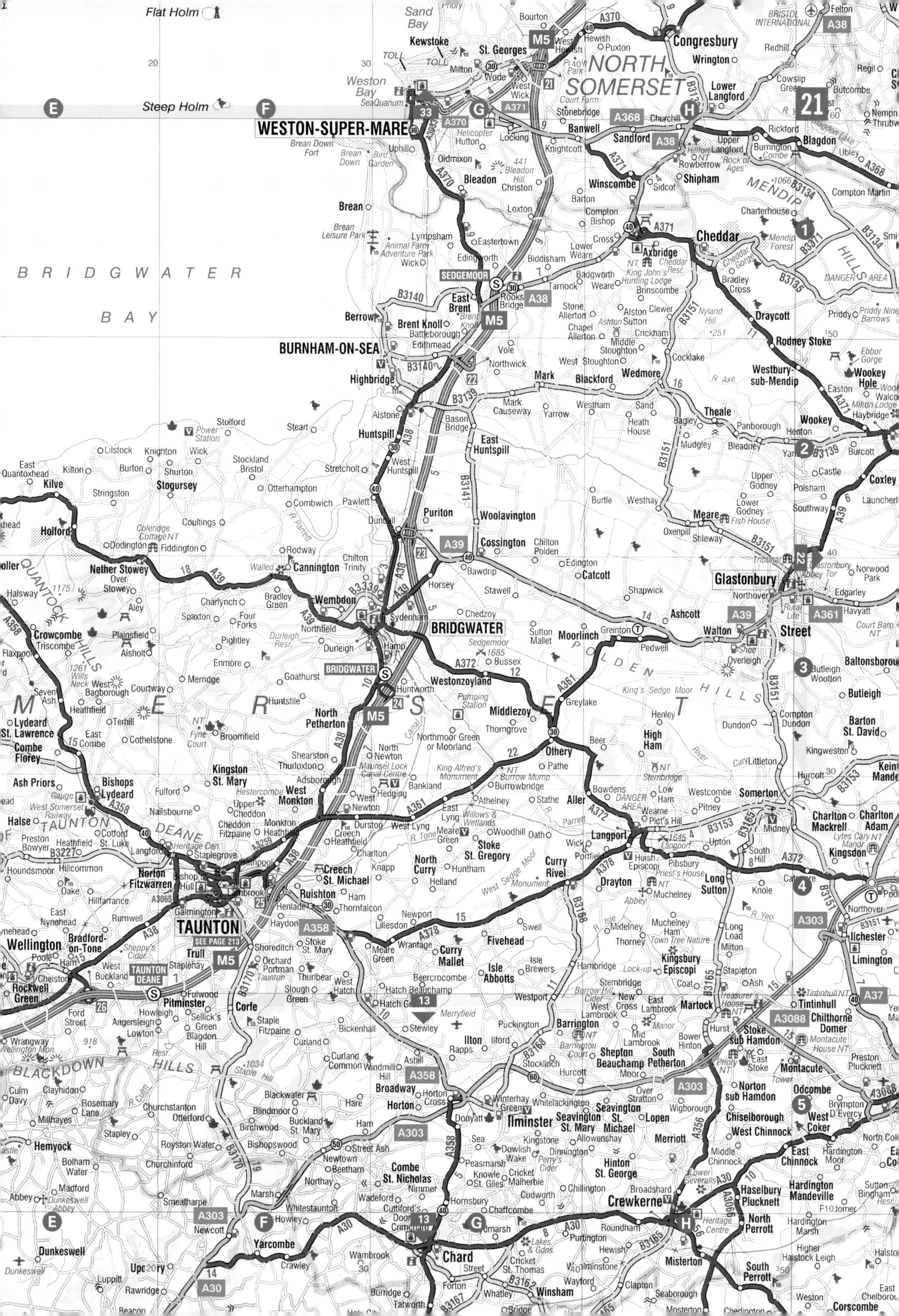

WESTON-SUPER-MARE
BURNHAM-ON-SEA
BRIDGWATER
TAUNTON
SEE PAGE 213
Glastonbury
Street
Cheddar
Congresbury
NORTH SOMERSET
BRIDGWATER BAY
MENDIP HILLS
QUANTOCK HILLS
BLACKDOWN HILLS
POLDEN HILLS
TAUNTON DEANE
Wellington
Chard
Crewkerne
Ilminster
Langport
Somerton
Ilchester
Yeovil
M5
A38
A39
A30
A303
A358
A370
A371
A372
A361
A368
A378
A3088
A37
21
22
23
24
25
26
13

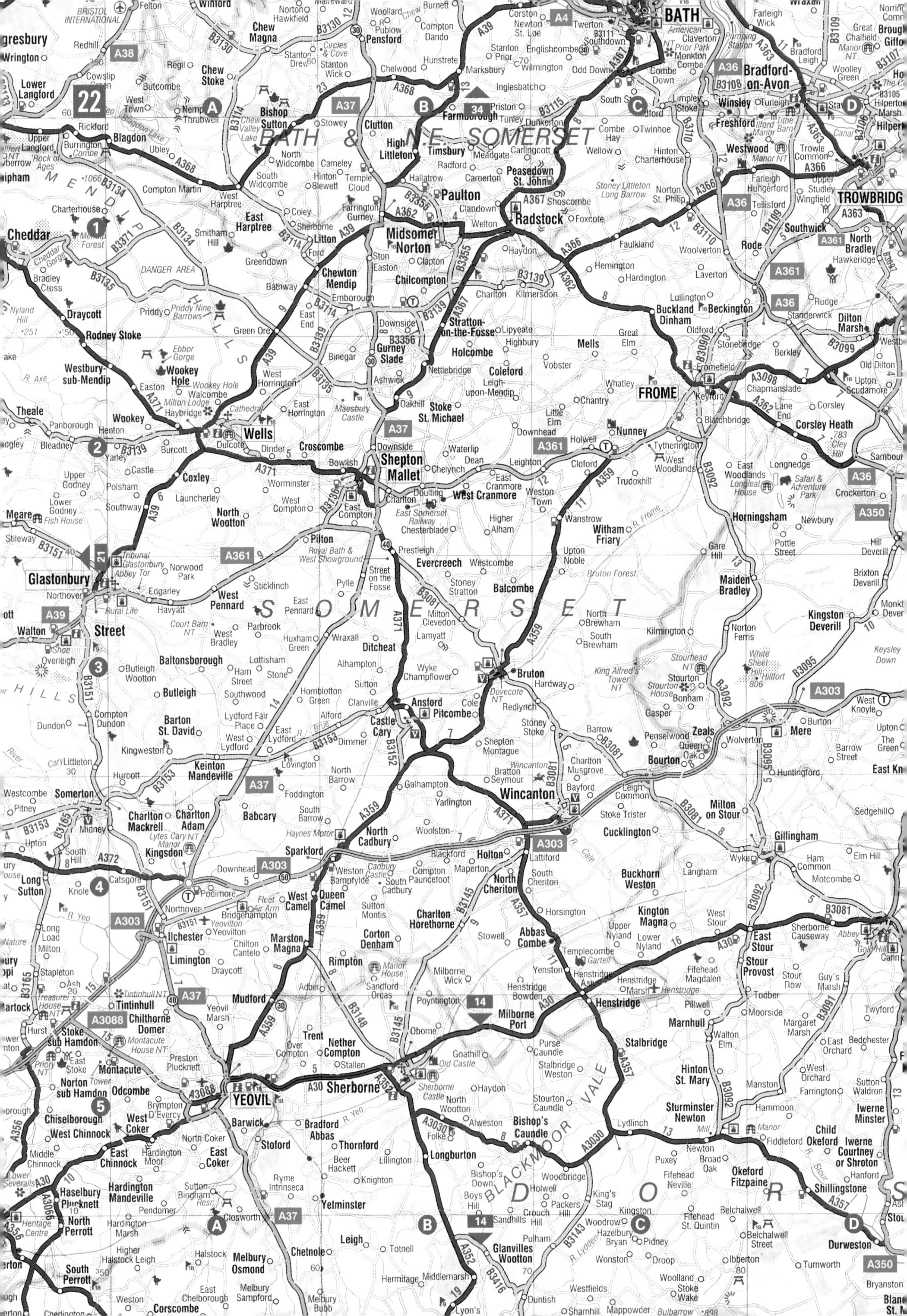

22
BRISTOL INTERNATIONAL
BATH
BATH & N.E. SOMERSET
SOMERSET
MENDIP HILLS
BLACKMOOR VALE
DORSET
Cheddar
Wells
Glastonbury
Street
Shepton Mallet
Frome
Radstock
Paulton
Midsomer Norton
Bradford-on-Avon
TROWBRIDGE
Wincanton
Bruton
Castle Cary
Somerton
Yeovil
Sherborne
Ilchester
Sturminster Newton
Stalbridge
Gillingham
Mere
Shillingstone
Chew Magna
Blagdon
Bishop Sutton
Timsbury
Westbury-sub-Mendip
Draycott
Rodney Stoke
Wookey Hole
Evercreech
Batcombe
Nunney
Beckington
Warminster
Corsley Heath
Horningsham
Maiden Bradley
Kingston Deverill
Zeals
Bourton
Milton on Stour
Templecombe
Henstridge
Milborne Port
Marston Magna
Queen Camel
Sparkford
North Cadbury
Babcary
Keinton Mandeville
Butleigh
Baltonsborough
Charlton Mackrell
Long Sutton
Martock
Stoke sub Hamdon
Montacute
Tintinhull
Chilthorne Domer
Odcombe
Norton sub Hamdon
West Coker
East Coker
Haselbury Plucknett
North Perrott
South Perrott
Yetminster
Melbury Osmond
Longburton
Bishop's Caundle
Okeford Fitzpaine
Child Okeford
Iwerne Minster
Durweston
A4
A36
A37
A38
A39
A303
A350
A357
A359
A361
A362
A366
A367
A368
A371
A372
A3030
A3088
B3081
B3092
B3135
B3139
B3151
B3153
14
21
34
A
B
C
D
1
2
3
4
5

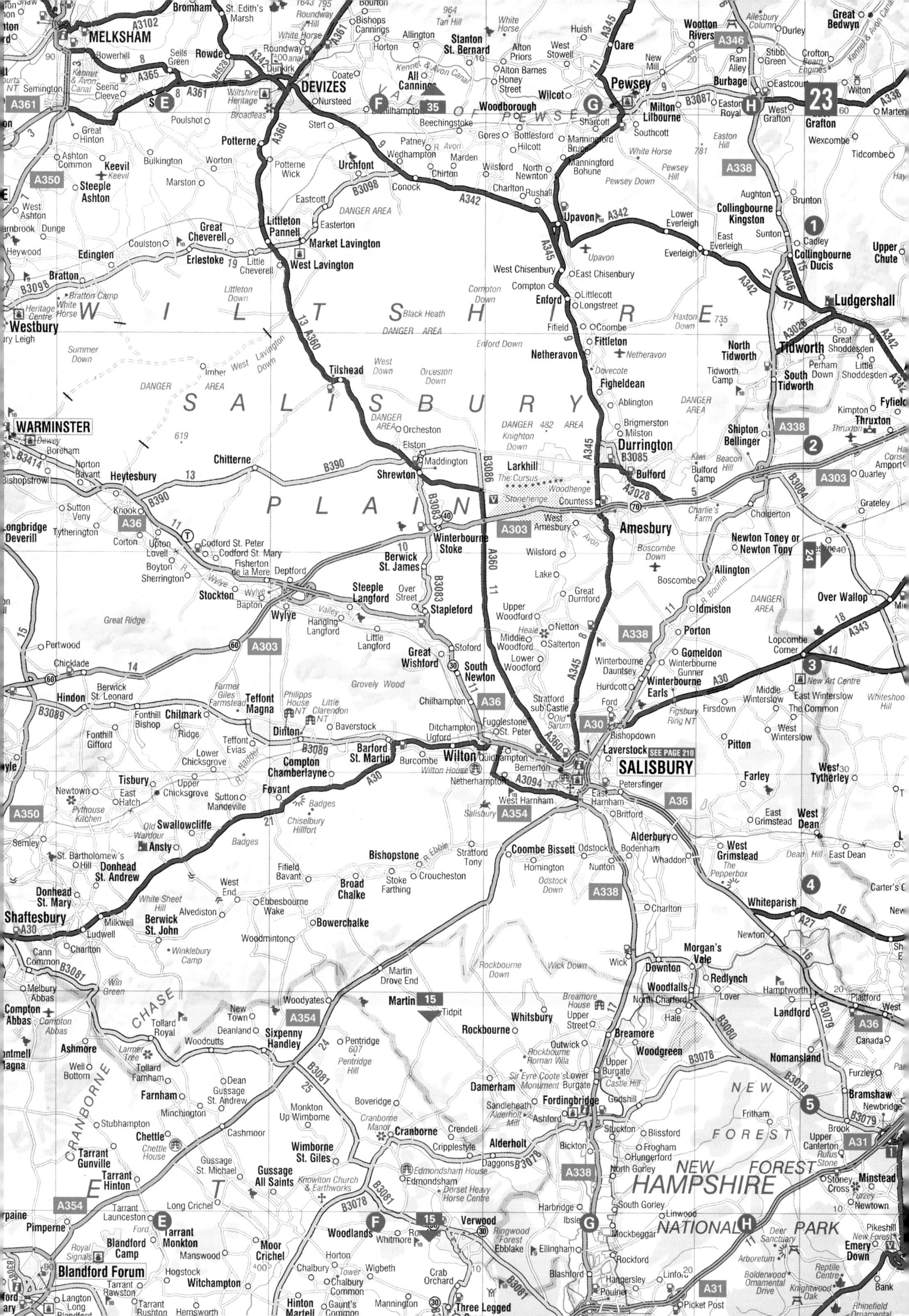

MELKSHAM
Bromham
St. Edith's Marsh
Roundway Hill
Bishops Cannings
Allington
Stanton St. Bernard
White Horse
Huish
Oare
Wootton Rivers
Aliesbury Column
Durley
Great Bedwyn
Bowerhill
Sells Green
Rowde
Roundway
Dunkirk
Horton
Alton Priors
West Stowell
New Mill
Ram Alley
Stibb Green
Crofton Beam Engines
Kennet & Avon Canal
Semington
Seend Cleeve
Wiltshire Heritage
DEVIZES
Coate
All Cannings
Alton Barnes
Honey Street
Wilcot
Pewsey
Burbage
Eastcourt
Wilton
Marten
Nursteed
Broadleas
Poulshot
Stert
Etchilhampton
Beechingstoke
Woodborough
VALE OF PEWSEY
Sharcott
Milton Lilbourne
Easton Royal
West Grafton
Grafton
Wexcombe
Great Hinton
Potterne
Patney
Gores
Bottlesford
Hilcott
Manningford Bruce
Southcott
White Horse
Easton Hill
Tidcombe
Ashton Common
Keevil
Bulkington
Worton
Potterne Wick
Urchfont
Wedhampton
Marden
Chirton
Wilsford
North Newnton
Manningford Bohune
Pewsey Hill
Pewsey Down
Steeple Ashton
Marston
Conock
Charlton
Rushall
Aughton
Brunton
Collingbourne Kingston
Eastcott
DANGER AREA
Upavon
Lower Everleigh
West Ashton
Littleton Pannell
Easterton
Market Lavington
Sunton
Cadley
Collingbourne Ducis
Upper Chute
Dunge
Great Cheverell
Coulston
Edington
Erlestoke
Little Cheverell
West Lavington
East Everleigh
Everleigh
Heywood
West Chisenbury
East Chisenbury
Bratton
Bratton Camp
Littleton Down
Compton Down
Compton
Enford
Littlecott
Longstreet
Ludgershall
Heritage Centre
White Horse
Westbury
Leigh
WILTSHIRE
Black Heath
DANGER AREA
Fifield
Coombe
Haxton Down
Tidworth
Great Shoddesden
Summer Down
Imber
West Lavington Down
Tilshead
West Down
Orcheston Down
Enford Down
Fittleton
Netheravon
North Tidworth
Tidworth Camp
Perham Down
South Tidworth
Little Shoddesden
DANGER AREA
SALISBURY
Dovecote
Figheldean
Ablington
Kimpton
Fyfield
Thruxton
WARMINSTER
Dewey
Boreham
DANGER AREA
Orcheston
Elston
DANGER AREA
Knighton Down
Brigmerston
Milston
Durrington
Shipton Bellinger
Norton Bavant
Heytesbury
Chitterne
Maddington
Shrewton
Larkhill
The Cursus
Woodhenge
Bulford
Kiwi
Beacon Hill
Bulford Camp
Quarley
Amport
Bishopstrow
Sutton Veny
Knook
PLAIN
Stonehenge
Countess
Grateley
Longbridge Deverill
Tytherington
Corton
Upton Lovell
Codford St. Peter
Codford St. Mary
Winterbourne Stoke
West Amesbury
Amesbury
Charlie's Farm
Cholderton
Boyton
Sherrington
Fisherton de la Mere
Deptford
Berwick St. James
Wilsford
Boscombe Down
Newton Toney or Newton Tony
Stockton
Wylye
Bapton
Steeple Langford
Over Street
Stapleford
Lake
Great Durnford
Boscombe
Allington
Idmiston
Over Wallop
Great Ridge
Hanging Langford
Little Langford
Upper Woodford
Heale
Netton
Middle Woodford
Salterton
Porton
Pertwood
Great Wishford
Stoford
Lower Woodford
Gomeldon
Winterbourne Dauntsey
Winterbourne Gunner
Lopcombe Corner
Chicklade
South Newton
Grovely Wood
Hurdcott
Winterbourne Earls
Middle Winterslow
East Winterslow
New Art Centre
Whiteshoot Hill
Hindon
Berwick St. Leonard
Farmer Giles Farmstead
Teffont Magna
Philipps House
Little Clarendon
Chilhampton
Stratford sub Castle
Ford
Firsdown
The Common
Fonthill Bishop
Chilmark
Dinton
Baverstock
Ditchampton
Ugford
Fugglestone St. Peter
Old Sarum
Figsbury Ring
West Winterslow
Fonthill Gifford
Ridge
Teffont Evias
Barford St. Martin
Burcombe
Wilton
Wilton House
Quidhampton
Bemerton
Bishopdown
Laverstock
SEE PAGE 210
SALISBURY
Pitton
Lower Chicksgrove
Compton Chamberlayne
Netherhampton
Petersfinger
Farley
West Tytherley
Tisbury
Upper Chicksgrove
Fovant
Newtown
East Hatch
Sutton Mandeville
Pythouse Kitchen
Badges
West Harnham
East Harnham
Britford
West Dean
East Grimstead
Chiselbury Hillfort
Old Wardour
Swallowcliffe
Ansty
Semley
Badges
Salisbury
Alderbury
Bodenham
St. Bartholomew's Hill
Donhead St. Andrew
Bishopstone
Stratford Tony
Coombe Bissett
Odstock
Homington
Nunton
Whaddon
West Grimstead
The Pepperbox
Dean Hill
East Dean
Fifield Bavant
Broad Chalke
Stoke Farthing
Croucheston
Odstock Down
Donhead St. Mary
West End
Ebbesbourne Wake
Charlton
Whiteparish
Carter's Clay
White Sheet Hill
Alvediston
Shaftesbury
Milkwell
Berwick St. John
Bowerchalke
Ludwell
Newton
Charlton
Woodminton
Winklebury Camp
Cann Common
Martin Drove End
Rockbourne Down
Wick Down
Morgan's Vale
Downton
Wick
Woodfalls
Redlynch
Hamptworth
Melbury Abbas
Win Green
Breamore House
Compton Abbas
CHASE
New Town
Woodyates
Martin
Tidpit
North Charford
Lover
Plaitford
West
Tollard Royal
Deanland
Sixpenny Handley
Rockbourne
Whitsbury
Upper Street
Hale
Landford
Ashmore
Larmer Tree
Woodcutts
Pentridge
Pentridge Hill
Breamore
Outwick
Rockbourne Roman Villa
Woodgreen
Canada
Well Bottom
Tollard Farnham
Dean
Gussage St. Andrew
Upper Burgate
Nomansland
Farnham
Boveridge
Sir Eyre Coote's Monument
Damerham
Lower Burgate
Castle Hill
NEW
Furzley
CRANBORNE
Minchington
Monkton Up Wimborne
Cranborne Manor
Sandleheath
Alderholt Mill
Fordingbridge
Godshill
Fritham
Bramshaw
Newbridge
Stubhampton
Cashmoor
Cranborne
Crendell
Ashford
Chettle
Chettle House
Wimborne St. Giles
Cripplestyle
Alderholt
Stuckton
Blissford
Frogham
FOREST
Brook
Upper Canterton
Rufus Stone
Tarrant Gunville
Gussage St. Michael
Gussage All Saints
Knowlton Church & Earthworks
Edmondsham House
Edmondsham
Daggons
Bickton
Hungerford
North Gorley
NEW FOREST
HAMPSHIRE
Stoney Cross
Minstead
Furzey
Newtown
Tarrant Hinton
Long Crichel
Dorset Heavy Horse Centre
Harbridge
South Gorley
Linwood
Ibsley
Mockbeggar
NATIONAL PARK
Deer Sanctuary
Pikeshill
New Forest
Emery Down
Tarrant Launceston
Tarrant Monkton
Pimperne
Woodlands
Whitmore
Verwood
Ringwood Forest
Ebblake
Ellingham
Rockford
Arboretum
Reptile Centre
Blandford Camp
Royal Signals
Blandford Forum
Manswood
Moor Crichel
Horton
Chalbury
Tower
Wigbeth
Chalbury Common
Crab Orchard
Blashford
Hangersley
Poulner
Linford
Bolderwood Ornamental Drive
Knightwood Oak
Bank
Hogstock
Witchampton
Tarrant Rawston
Tarrant Rushton
Langton Long
Hemsworth
Hinton Martell
Gaunt's Common
Mannington
Three Legged
Picket Post
Rhinefield Ornamental

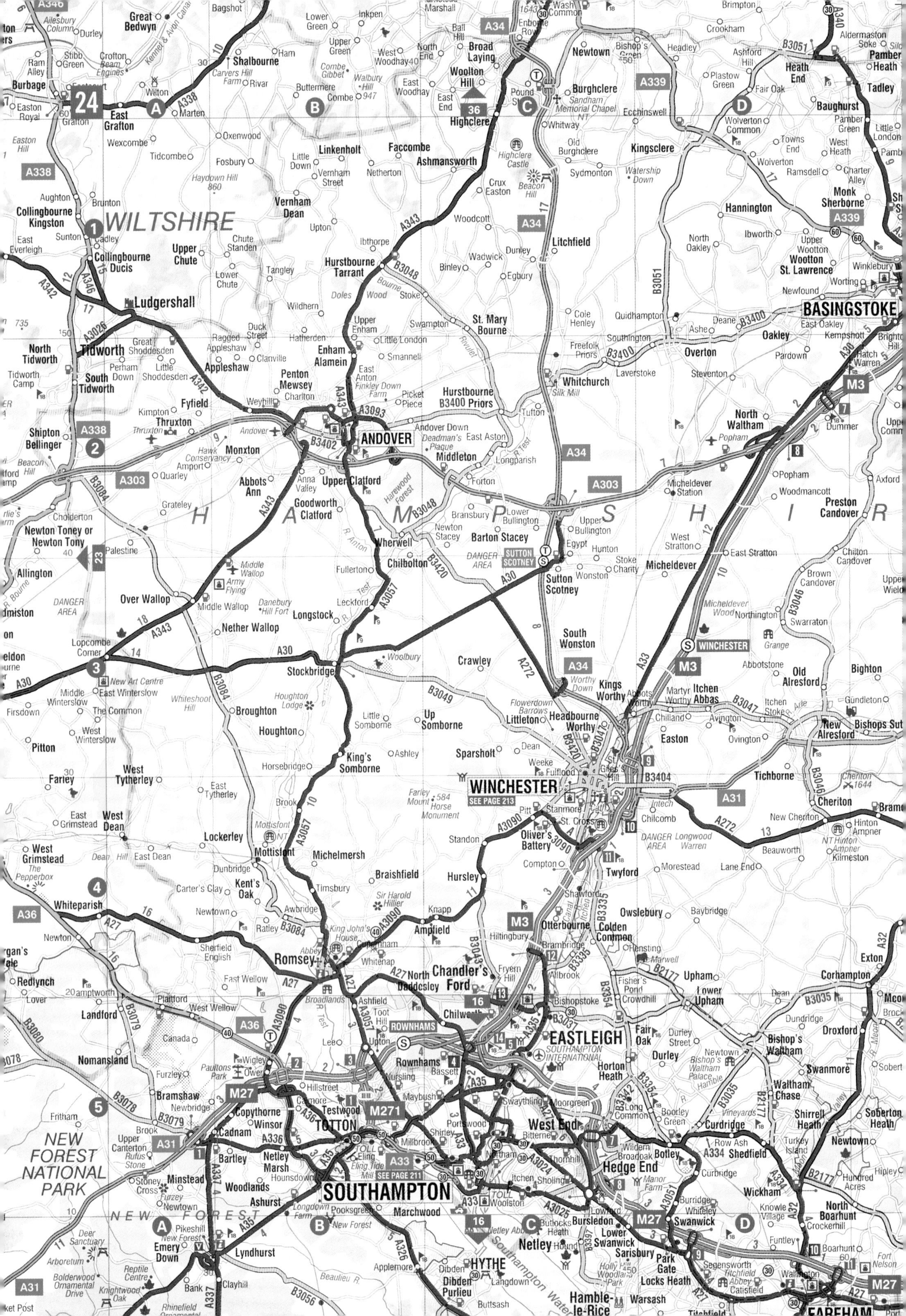

24
WILTSHIRE
Great Bedwyn
Bagshot
Shalbourne
Ham
East Grafton
Burbage
Marten
Wilton
Oxenwood
Wexcombe
Tidcombe
Fosbury
Haydown Hill 860
Linkenholt
Faccombe
Ashmansworth
Vernham Dean
Vernham Street
Netherton
Little Down
Upton
Ibthorpe
Hurstbourne Tarrant
Lower Green
Inkpen
Upper Green
Combe Gibbet
Walbury Hill 947
Combe
Buttermere
West Woodhay
East Woodhay
North End
Ball Hill
Broad Laying
Woolton Hill
East End
Highclere
36
Highclere Castle
Beacon Hill
Crux Easton
Woodcott
Dunley
Binley
Wadwick
Egbury
Litchfield
Pound Street
Burghclere
Sandham Memorial Chapel
Whitway
Old Burghclere
Sydmonton
Newtown
Bishop's Green
Headley
Ecchinswell
Kingsclere
Watership Down
Brimpton
Crookham
Aldermaston Soke
Ashford Hill
Plastow Green
Fair Oak
Heath End
Pamber Heath
Tadley
Baughurst
Pamber Green
Wolverton Common
Wolverton
Towns End
West Heath
Ramsdell
Charter Alley
Monk Sherborne
Hannington
Ibworth
North Oakley
Upper Wootton
Wootton St. Lawrence
Worting
Winklebury
Newfound
BASINGSTOKE
Quidhampton
Deane
Ashe
Oakley
East Oakley
Kempshott
Cole Henley
Freefolk Priors
Southington
Overton
Laverstoke
Steventon
Pardown
Whitchurch
Silk Mill
North Waltham
Popham
Dummer
Micheldever Station
Woodmancott
Preston Candover
Axford
Chilton Candover
Brown Candover
East Stratton
West Stratton
Micheldever
Northington
Swarraton
Grange
WINCHESTER
Abbotstone
Old Alresford
Bighton
Itchen Abbas
Martyr Worthy
Itchen Stoke
Gundleton
New Alresford
Bishops Sutton
Ovington
Avington
Chilland
Easton
Tichborne
Cheriton
Cheriton 1644
New Cheriton
Hinton Ampner
Kilmeston
Beauworth
Longwood Warren
DANGER AREA
Lane End
Morestead
Chilcomb
Ludgershall
Collingbourne Kingston
Collingbourne Ducis
Aughton
Brunton
Sunton
Cadley
East Everleigh
Upper Chute
Chute Standen
Lower Chute
Tangley
Doles Wood
Bourne
Stoke
Wildhern
Hatherden
Duck Street
Ragged Appleshaw
Appleshaw
Clanville
North Tidworth
Tidworth
South Tidworth
Tidworth Camp
Great Shoddesden
Little Shoddesden
Perham Down
Penton Mewsey
Charlton
Upper Enham
Enham Alamein
Little London
Smannell
East Anton
Finkley Down Farm
Picket Piece
Swampton
St. Mary Bourne
Hurstbourne Priors
Tufton
Kimpton
Thruxton
Fyfield
Weyhill
Shipton Bellinger
ANDOVER
Andover Down
Deadman's Plaque
East Aston
Middleton
Longparish
Monxton
Hawk Conservancy
Amport
Quarley
Abbots Ann
Anna Valley
Upper Clatford
Goodworth Clatford
Harewood Forest
Forton
Bransbury
Lower Bullington
Upper Bullington
Barton Stacey
Newton Stacey
Egypt
Hunton
Stoke Charity
Sutton Scotney
Wonston
South Wonston
Cholderton
Grateley
Newton Toney or Newton Tony
Palestine
Allington
Middle Wallop
Army Flying
Over Wallop
Danebury Hill Fort
Wherwell
Chilbolton
Fullerton
Leckford
Longstock
Nether Wallop
Lopcombe Corner
Stockbridge
Woolbury
Crawley
New Art Centre
East Winterslow
Middle Winterslow
The Common
West Winterslow
Firsdown
Pitton
Farley
West Tytherley
East Tytherley
Whiteshoot Hill
Broughton
Houghton Lodge
Houghton
Little Somborne
Up Somborne
King's Somborne
Ashley
Horsebridge
Sparsholt
Flowerdown Barrows
Littleton
Headbourne Worthy
Kings Worthy
Abbots Worthy
Worthy Down
Dean
Weeke
Fulflood
WINCHESTER
SEE PAGE 213
Stanmore
St. Cross
Pitt
Farley Mount 584
Horse Monument
Oliver's Battery
Standon
Compton
Twyford
Hursley
Shawford
Otterbourne
Colden Common
Owslebury
Baybridge
Brook
Mottisfont
Lockerley
East Grimstead
West Dean
West Grimstead
The Pepperbox
Dean Hill
East Dean
Dunbridge
Carter's Clay
Kent's Oak
Michelmersh
Timsbury
Braishfield
Sir Harold Hillier
Awbridge
Knapp
Ampfield
Hiltingbury
Whiteparish
Newton
Newtown
Ratley
King John's House
Cupernham
Whitenap
Romsey
Abbey
Sherfield English
Chandler's Ford
North Baddesley
Fryern Hill
Brambridge
Allbrook
Hensting
Marwell
Fisher's Pond
Crowdhill
Upham
Lower Upham
Corhampton
Exton
Redlynch
Lover
Hamptworth
Landford
Plaitford
West Wellow
Fast Wellow
Broadlands
Ashfield
Toot Hill
Nursling
Chilworth
ROWNHAMS
Rownhams
Bassett
Bishopstoke
EASTLEIGH
SOUTHAMPTON INTERNATIONAL
Fair Oak
Durley
Durley Street
Horton Heath
Bishop's Waltham
Bishop's Waltham Palace
Dundridge
Droxford
Swanmore
Sobert
Waltham Chase
Shirrell Heath
Soberton Heath
Newtown
Upton
Lee
Nomansland
Canada
Paultons Park
Wigley
Ower
Furzley
Bramshaw
Newbridge
Copythorne
Winsor
Cadnam
Hillstreet
Testwood
Calmore
TOTTON
Maybush
Shirley
Portswood
Swaythling
Moorgreen
West End
Bitterne
Long Common
Boorley Green
Curdridge
Vineyards
Row Ash
Shedfield
Turkey Island
Botley
Wildern
Broadoak
Hedge End
Manor Farm
Curbridge
Wickham
Hundred Acres
Hipley
Knowle Village
North Boarhunt
Crockerhill
Fritham
NEW FOREST NATIONAL PARK
Brook
Upper Canterton
Rufus Stone
Bartley
Netley Marsh
Eling
Eling Tide Mill
SEE PAGE 211
Millbrook
Northam
Itchen
Sholing
Thornhill
Woolston
Stoney Cross
Minstead
Furzey
Newtown
Woodlands
Ashurst
Hounsdown
Longdown Farm
Pooksgreen
Marchwood
New Forest
SOUTHAMPTON
NEW FOREST
Pikeshill
Deer Sanctuary
Emery Down
Lyndhurst
Arboretum
Reptile Centre
Bolderwood Ornamental Drive
Knightwood Oak
Rhinefield
Bank
Clayhill
Beaulieu R.
Applemore
Dibden
Dibden Purlieu
HYTHE
Langdown
Buttsash
Southampton Water
Netley Abbey
Netley
Butlocks Heath
Bursledon
Hound
Lowford
Lower Swanwick
Swanwick
Burridge
Whiteley
Sarisbury
Park Gate
Holly Hill Woodland Park
Locks Heath
Warsash
Hamble-le-Rice
Segensworth
Titchfield Abbey
Catisfield
Titchfield
Funtley
Boarhunt
Fort Nelson
Wallington
FAREHAM
A338
A346
A342
A3026
A303
A343
A3093
B3402
B3048
B3084
A30
A3057
B3420
A34
A272
A33
B3049
B3047
B3404
A31
B3046
M3
A3090
B3335
B3043
B3354
B3037
A335
A35
A27
B3084
A36
M27
M271
A3024
A3025
A326
A33
B3397
B3056
A337
A336
B3078
B3079
B3080
A32
B3035
B2177
A334
A3051
B3342
A339
B3051
B3400
A340
A30
B3035
B3079

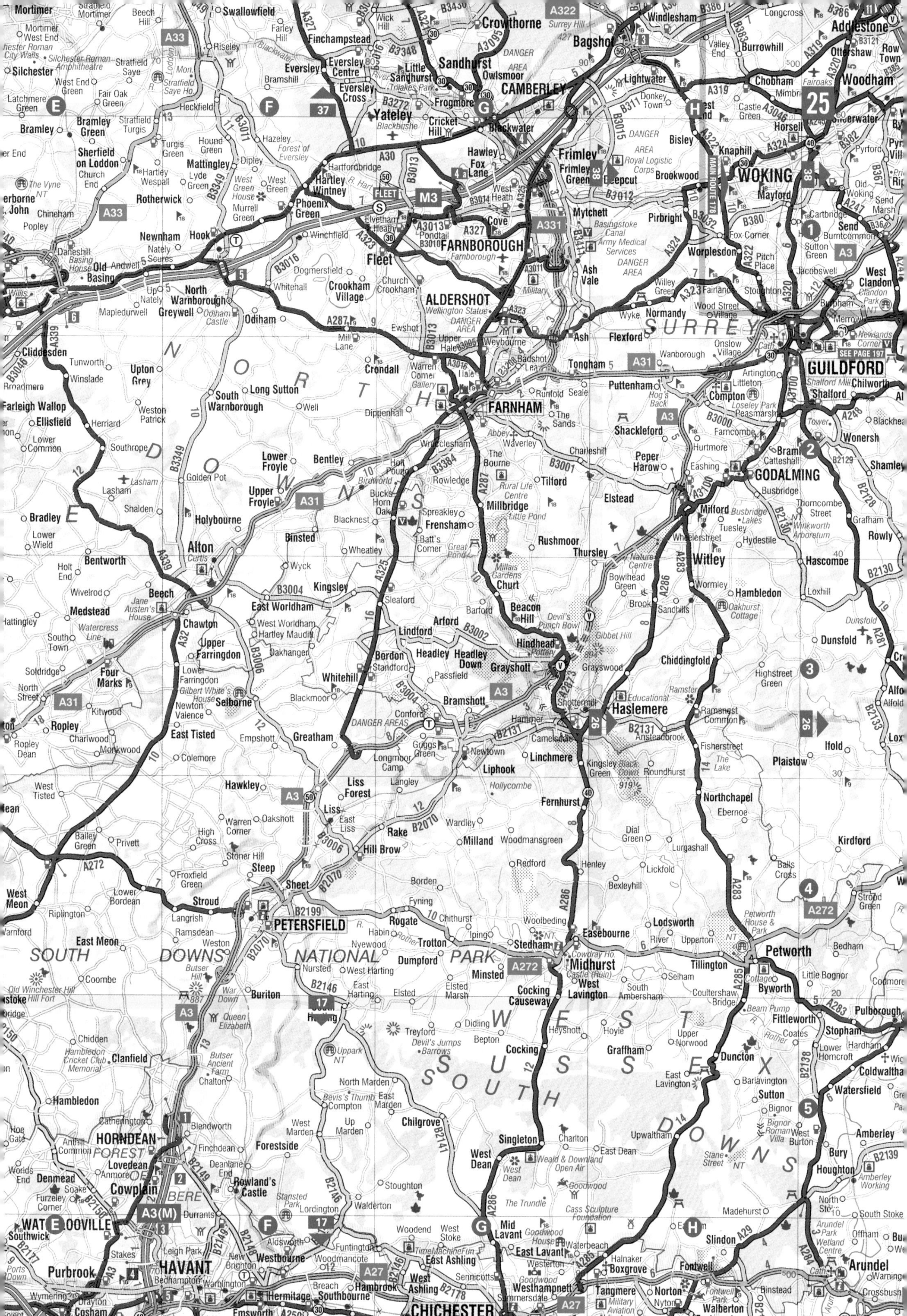
Mortimer
Swallowfield
Finchampstead
Crowthorne
Windlesham
Addlestone
Silchester
Stratfield Saye
Eversley
Sandhurst
Bagshot
Owlsmoor
CAMBERLEY
Lightwater
Chobham
Woodham
Ottershaw
Latchmere Green
Bramley
Bramley Green
Heckfield
Yateley
Frogmore
Cricket Hill
Blackwater
Bisley
Knaphill
Horsell
WOKING
Sherfield on Loddon
Hazeley
Hartley Wintney
Hartfordbridge
Hawley
Frimley
Frimley Green
Deepcut
Brookwood
Mayford
The Vyne
Rotherwick
Mattingley
Phoenix Green
FLEET
M3
Mytchett
Pirbright
Chineham
Popley
Newnham
Hook
Winchfield
Elvetham Heath
Cove
FARNBOROUGH
Worplesdon
Old Basing
Nately Scures
Fleet
Dogmersfield
Crookham Village
Church Crookham
ALDERSHOT
Ash Vale
Jacobswell
West Clandon
North Warnborough
Greywell
Odiham
Mapledurwell
Ewshot
Normandy
Wood Street Village
Cliddesden
Tunworth
Upton Grey
Crondall
Ash
Flexford
SURREY
GUILDFORD
Winslade
Long Sutton
South Warnborough
Tongham
Puttenham
Compton
Chilworth
Farleigh Wallop
Ellisfield
Herriard
Weston Patrick
Well
Dippenhall
FARNHAM
Runfold
Seale
The Sands
Shalford
NORTH DOWNS
Lower Froyle
Bentley
Wrecclesham
Waverley
Shackleford
Farncombe
Wonersh
Upper Froyle
Rowledge
Tilford
Peper Harow
Eashing
GODALMING
Shamley
Lasham
Golden Pot
Millbridge
Elstead
Busbridge
Bradley
Holybourne
Blacknest
Frensham
Milford
Tuesley
Grafham
Alton
Binsted
Wheatley
Rushmoor
Thursley
Witley
Hydestile
Rowly
Bentworth
Wyck
Churt
Hascombe
Beech
Kingsley
Medstead
East Worldham
Sleaford
Beacon Hill
Brook
Sandhills
Wormley
Hambledon
Chawton
West Worldham
Hartley Mauditt
Lindford
Arford
Barford
Hindhead
Dunsfold
Upper Farringdon
Oakhanger
Bordon
Headley
Headley Down
Grayshott
Grayswood
Chiddingfold
Four Marks
Lower Farringdon
Whitehill
Passfield
Highstreet Green
Selborne
Newton Valence
Blackmoor
Bramshott
Haslemere
Ropley
East Tisted
Empshott
Greatham
Conford
Hammer
Camelsdale
Ramsnest Common
Fisherstreet
Ifold
Colemore
Liphook
Linchmere
Plaistow
Kingsley Green
Roundhurst
Hawkley
Liss Forest
Liss
Hollycombe
Fernhurst
Northchapel
Ebernoe
Privett
Rake
Milland
Woodmansgreen
Dial Green
Lurgashall
Kirdford
Steep
Hill Brow
Redford
Henley
Lickfold
Sheet
Borden
Bexleyhill
West Meon
Stroud
PETERSFIELD
Rogate
Chithurst
Lodsworth
Easebourne
Midhurst
Petworth
Bedham
East Meon
SOUTH DOWNS
NATIONAL PARK
Trotton
Dumpford
Minsted
Stedham
Tillington
Byworth
Coombe
Buriton
Nursted
West Harting
East Harting
Elsted
Cocking Causeway
West Lavington
South Ambersham
Selham
Pulborough
Fittleworth
Stopham
Treyford
Didling
Bepton
Heyshott
Cocking
Graffham
Duncton
Chidden
Clanfield
Uppark
WEST SUSSEX
SOUTH DOWNS
North Marden
East Marden
Compton
Chilgrove
Upwaltham
Sutton
Bignor
Watersfield
Hambledon
Blendworth
HORNDEAN
Forestside
West Marden
Up Marden
Singleton
Charlton
East Dean
West Dean
Amberley
Lovedean
Cowplain
Rowland's Castle
Stoughton
Walderton
Bury
Houghton
WATERLOOVILLE
Lordington
Mid Lavant
East Lavant
Slindon
Arundel
Purbrook
HAVANT
Westbourne
Funtington
West Stoke
Woodend
East Ashling
Boxgrove
Fontwell
Tangmere
Westhampnett
Cosham
Emsworth
Southbourne
Hermitage
Hambrook
West Ashling
CHICHESTER
Norton
Walberton
Binstead

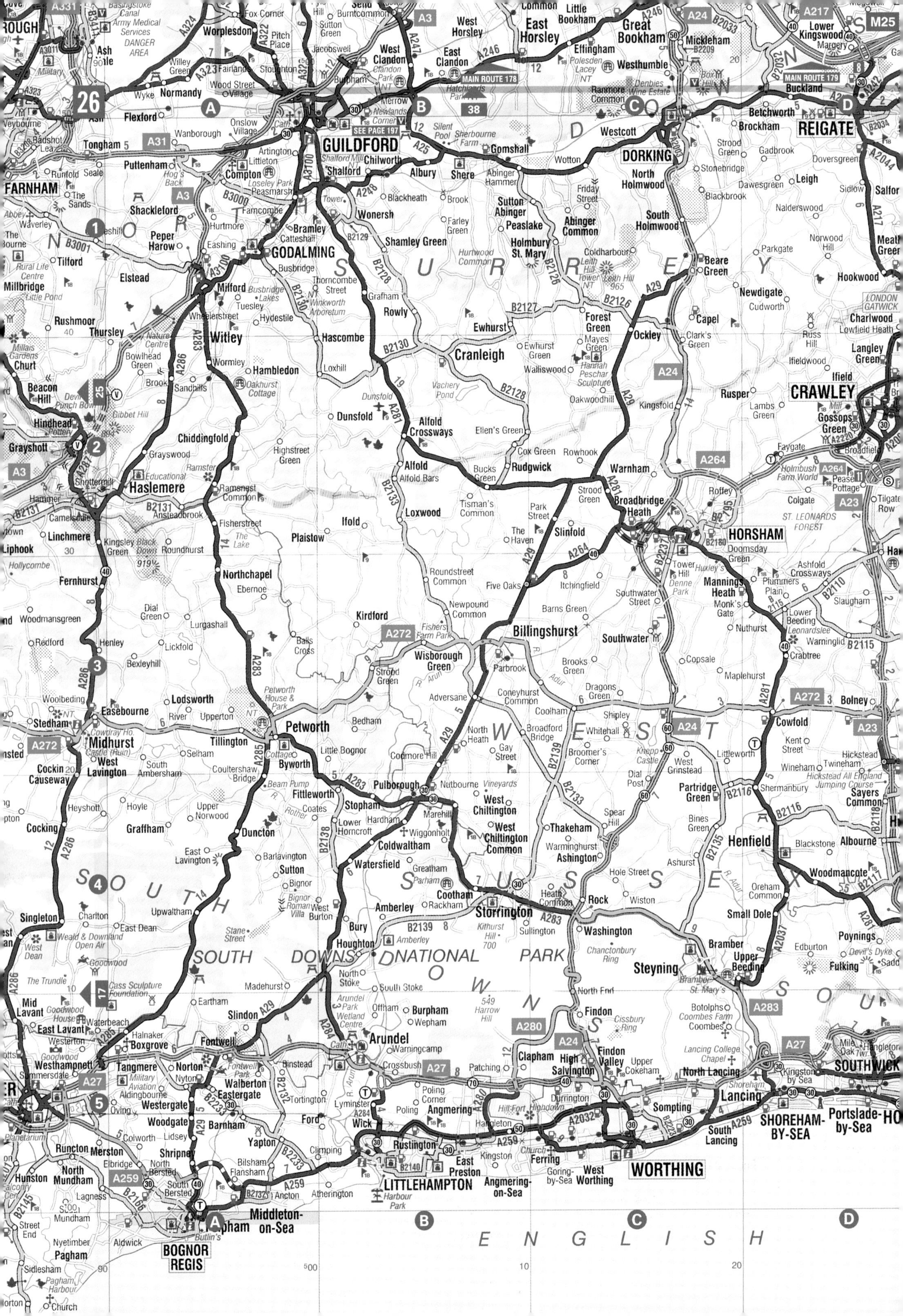

26
A
B
C
D
MAIN ROUTE 178
MAIN ROUTE 179
38
SEE PAGE 197
25
17
1
2
3
4
5
GUILDFORD
GODALMING
DORKING
REIGATE
CRAWLEY
HORSHAM
FARNHAM
Haslemere
Midhurst
Petworth
Billingshurst
Cranleigh
Pulborough
Storrington
Steyning
Henfield
Arundel
LITTLEHAMPTON
WORTHING
BOGNOR REGIS
SHOREHAM-BY-SEA
SOUTHWICK
Portslade-by-Sea
Lancing
Worplesdon
Normandy
Flexford
Tongham
Puttenham
Compton
Shalford
Chilworth
Albury
Shere
Gomshall
Wonersh
Bramley
Shamley Green
Milford
Witley
Elstead
Tilford
Thursley
Hindhead
Grayshott
Hambledon
Chiddingfold
Dunsfold
Alfold
Loxwood
Ewhurst
Rudgwick
Ockley
Capel
Beare Green
Newdigate
Rusper
Warnham
Slinfold
Broadbridge Heath
Kirdford
Plaistow
Wisborough Green
Northchapel
Fernhurst
Easebourne
Lodsworth
Tillington
Byworth
Fittleworth
Duncton
Graffham
Cocking
Singleton
Upwaltham
Slindon
Fontwell
Walberton
Barnham
Yapton
Westergate
Woodgate
Tangmere
Westhampnett
Boxgrove
Halnaker
Runcton
Merston
North Mundham
Hunston
Pagham
Nyetimber
Aldwick
Middleton-on-Sea
Felpham
Bersted
Shripney
Flansham
Climping
Ford
Rustington
East Preston
Angmering
Ferring
Goring-by-Sea
West Worthing
Findon
Washington
Ashington
Thakeham
West Chiltington
Bury
Amberley
Houghton
Cootham
Rock
Cowfold
Partridge Green
Bramber
Upper Beeding
Small Dole
Sompting
North Lancing
South Lancing
Poynings
Fulking
Edburton
Albourne
Bolney
Woodmancote
Shermanbury
Sayers Common
Mannings Heath
Colgate
Faygate
Ifield
Langley Green
Charlwood
Hookwood
Leigh
Buckland
Betchworth
Brockham
Westcott
Westhumble
Mickleham
Great Bookham
Little Bookham
Effingham
East Horsley
West Horsley
East Clandon
West Clandon
Merrow
Burpham
Ripley
Send
Jacobswell
Sutton Green
Pitch Place
Fox Corner
Ash
Wanborough
Seale
Runfold
The Sands
Shackleford
Peper Harow
Eashing
Hurtmore
Farncombe
Catteshall
Busbridge
Hascombe
Grafham
Rowly
Loxhill
Alfold Crossways
Ifold
Lurgashall
Henley
Linchmere
Camelsdale
Liphook
Rogate
Stedham
West Lavington
Heyshott
Selham
Coates
Sutton
Bignor
Barlavington
Stopham
Hardham
Coldwaltham
Watersfield
Greatham
Parham
Rackham
Sullington
Wiston
Ashurst
West Grinstead
Shipley
Coolham
Dial Post
Southwater
Itchingfield
Five Oaks
Barns Green
Adversane
Parbrook
Coneyhurst
Nutbourne
Marehill
Wiggonholt
Burpham
Wepham
Warningcamp
Crossbush
Poling
Lyminster
Wick
Patching
Clapham
High Salvington
Findon Valley
Durrington
Coombes
Botolphs
Kingston by Sea
Tortington
Binsted
Madehurst
Eartham
East Dean
Charlton
West Dean
Mid Lavant
East Lavant
Oving
Colworth
Lidsey
Elbridge
Lagness
Sidlesham
Chichester Harbour
SURREY
WEST SUSSEX
SOUTH DOWNS NATIONAL PARK
NORTH DOWNS
ENGLISH
A3
A31
A3100
A281
A283
A286
A272
A29
A24
A264
A23
A27
A259
A280
A284
A285
A2032
A2037
A25
A246
A247
A217
M25
B2128
B2130
B2133
B2139
B2116
B2135
Leith Hill 965
Gibbet Hill
Black Down 919
Chanctonbury Ring
Cissbury Ring
Harrow Hill 549
Kithurst Hill 700

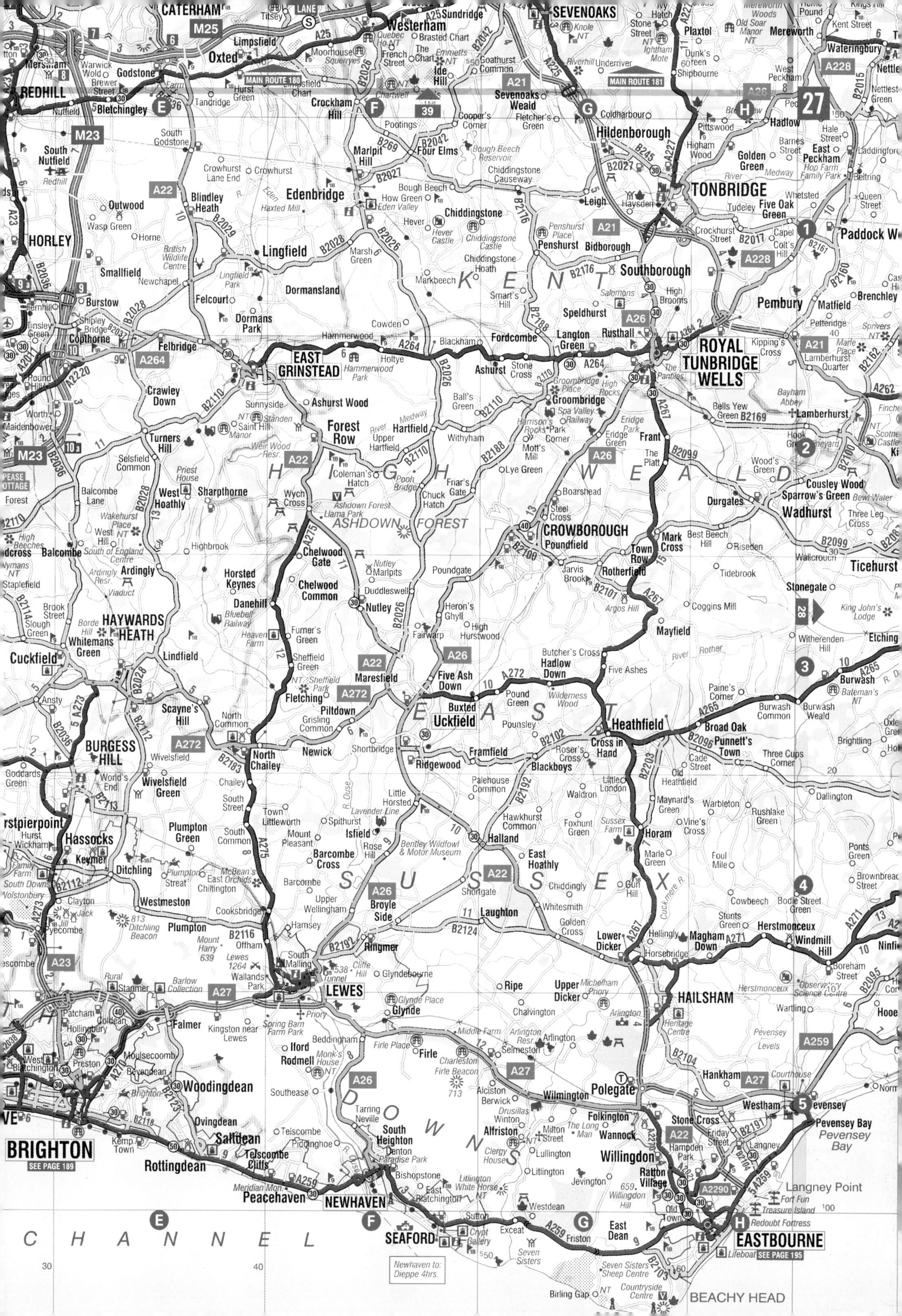

CATERHAM
M25
Westerham
SEVENOAKS
Oxted
Limpsfield
Godstone
REDHILL
Bletchingley
Crockham Hill
MAIN ROUTE 180
MAIN ROUTE 181
27
Sevenoaks Weald
Hildenborough
Tonbridge
Plaxtol
Mereworth
Wateringbury
Hadlow
East Peckham
South Nutfield
M23
Edenbridge
Four Elms
Chiddingstone
Leigh
Penshurst
Bidborough
Southborough
HORLEY
Lingfield
Smallfield
Dormansland
Burstow
Felbridge
EAST GRINSTEAD
Copthorne
Hammerwood
Fordcombe
Langton Green
Rusthall
ROYAL TUNBRIDGE WELLS
Pembury
Matfield
Brenchley
Paddock Wood
K E N T
Crawley Down
Ashurst Wood
Forest Row
Hartfield
Groombridge
Frant
Lamberhurst
Turners Hill
West Hoathly
Sharpthorne
H I G H   W E A L D
ASHDOWN FOREST
CROWBOROUGH
Wadhurst
Ticehurst
Balcombe
Ardingly
Chelwood Gate
Nutley
Rotherfield
Mayfield
Stonegate
Burwash
HAYWARDS HEATH
Cuckfield
Lindfield
Danehill
Maresfield
Fletching
Five Ash Down
Heathfield
Uckfield
Buxted
E A S T
BURGESS HILL
Wivelsfield Green
North Chailey
Newick
Framfield
Blackboys
Cross in Hand
Hassocks
Keymer
Ditchling
Plumpton Green
Isfield
Halland
Horam
East Hoathly
S U S S E X
Westmeston
Plumpton
Barcombe Cross
Broyle Side
Laughton
Lower Dicker
Magham Down
Herstmonceux
Windmill Hill
HAILSHAM
Ringmer
LEWES
Glynde
Firle
Falmer
Woodingdean
Polegate
Wilmington
Alfriston
Westham
Pevensey
Pevensey Bay
BRIGHTON
SEE PAGE 189
Saltdean
Rottingdean
Telscombe Cliffs
Peacehaven
NEWHAVEN
SEAFORD
D O W N S
Willingdon
EASTBOURNE
SEE PAGE 195
East Dean
Friston
Seven Sisters
Birling Gap
BEACHY HEAD
Langney Point
C H A N N E L
Newhaven to: Dieppe 4hrs.

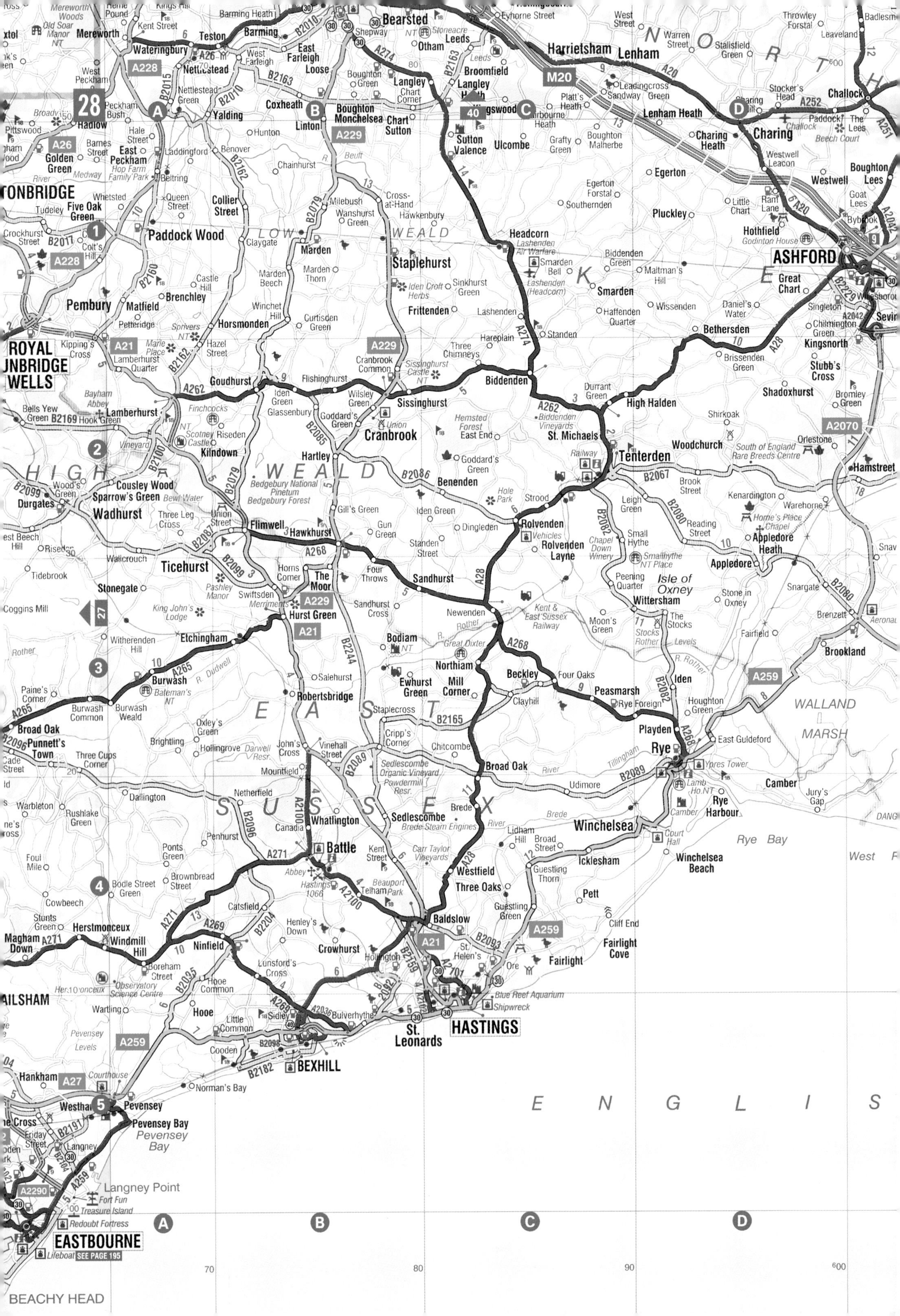

Mereworth Woods
Old Soar Manor NT
Mereworth
Kent Street
Barming Heath
Teston
Barming
Bearsted
Shepway
Stoneacre NT
Otham
Leeds
Eyhorne Street
West Street
Warren Street
Harrietsham
Lenham
Stalisfield Green
Throwley Forstal
Leaveland
Badlesmere
Wateringbury
West Farleigh
East Farleigh
Loose
Nettlestead
West Peckham
28
Nettlestead Green
Boughton Green
Langley
Chart Corner
Broomfield
Leeds
Langley Heath
Kingswood
M20
Platt's Heath
Leadingcross Green
Sandway
Lenham Heath
Stocker's Head
Charing Hill
Challock
Paddock
The Lees
Hadlow
Peckham Bush
Yalding
Coxheath
Boughton Monchelsea
Chart Sutton
Linton
Sutton Valence
Ulcombe
Grafty Green
Boughton Malherbe
Charing Heath
Charing
Chilham
Beech Court
Pittswood
Hale Street
East Peckham
Hunton
Laddingford
Benover
Golden Green
Hop Farm Family Park
Beltring
Chainhurst
Beult
Egerton
Westwell Leacon
Westwell
Boughton Lees
TONBRIDGE
Five Oak Green
Whetsted
Queen Street
Collier Street
Milebush
Wanshurst Green
Cross-at-Hand
Hawkenbury
Egerton Forstal
Southernden
Pluckley
Little Chart
Ram Lane
Goat Lees
Bybrook
Tudeley
Crockhurst Street
Colt's Hill
Paddock Wood
Claygate
LOW
WEALD
Marden
Headcorn
Lashenden Air Warfare
Biddenden Green
Maltman's Hill
Hothfield
Godinton House
ASHFORD
Staplehurst
Smarden Bell
Lashenden (Headcorn)
Smarden
Great Chart
Pembury
Matfield
Castle Hill
Brenchley
Marden Beech
Marden Thorn
Iden Croft Herbs
Sinkhurst Green
Frittenden
Lashenden
Haffenden Quarter
Wissenden
Daniel's Water
Singleton
Willesborough
Sevington
Petteridge
Horsmonden
Winchet Hill
Curtisden Green
Standen
Bethersden
Chilmington Green
ROYAL TUNBRIDGE WELLS
Kipping's Cross
Lamberhurst Quarter
Sprivers NT
Marle Place
Hazel Street
Cranbrook Common
Sissinghurst Castle NT
Three Chimneys
Hareplain
Brissenden Green
Kingsnorth
Stubb's Cross
Goudhurst
Flishinghurst
Biddenden
Durrant Green
High Halden
Shadoxhurst
Bromley Green
Bayham Abbey
Lamberhurst
Bells Yew Green
Hook Green
Finchcocks
Iden Green
Glassenbury
Wilsley Green
Goddard's Green
Sissinghurst
Union
Cranbrook
Hemsted Forest
East End
Biddenden Vineyards
St. Michaels
Shirkoak
Woodchurch
South of England Rare Breeds Centre
Orlestone
Hamstreet
Scotney Castle
Riseden
Kilndown
Vineyard
HIGH
WEALD
Hartley
Goddard's Green
Railway
Tenterden
Wood's Green
Cousley Wood
Sparrow's Green
Bewl Water
Durgates
Wadhurst
Bedgebury National Pinetum
Bedgebury Forest
Benenden
Hole Park
Strood
Leigh Green
Brook Street
Kenardington
Warehorne
Three Leg Cross
Union Street
Flimwell
Hawkhurst
Gill's Green
Gun Green
Iden Green
Dingleden
Rolvenden
Vehicles
Rolvenden Layne
Chapel Down Winery
Small Hythe
Smallhythe NT Place
Reading Street
Home's Place Chapel
Appledore Heath
Appledore
West Beech Hill
Riseden
Wallcrouch
Ticehurst
Standen Street
Four Throws
Sandhurst
Peening Quarter
Isle of Oxney
Snargate
Tidebrook
Stonegate
Pashley Manor
Horns Corner
The Moor
Swiftsden
Merriments
Hurst Green
Sandhurst Cross
Newenden
Kent & East Sussex Railway
Wittersham
Stone in Oxney
Brenzett
Coggins Mill
27
King John's Lodge
Moon's Green
The Stocks
Stocks
Rother Levels
Fairfield
Brookland
Etchingham
Witherenden Hill
Bodiam NT
Great Dixter
Northiam
Rother
Beckley
Four Oaks
Peasmarsh
Iden
Houghton Green
WALLAND
MARSH
Burwash
Bateman's NT
Salehurst
Robertsbridge
Ewhurst Green
Mill Corner
Clayhill
Rye Foreign
Playden
Paine's Corner
Burwash Common
Burwash Weald
Broad Oak
EAST
Staplecross
Punnett's Town
Oxley's Green
Brightling
Hollingrove
Darwell Resr.
John's Cross
Vinehall Street
Cripp's Corner
Chitcombe
Rye
East Guldeford
Cade Street
Three Cups Corner
Mountfield
Sedlescombe Organic Vineyard
Powdermill Resr.
Broad Oak
Udimore
Ypres Tower
Lamb Ho. NT
Camber
Jury's Gap
Warbleton
Dallington
Netherfield
Tillingham
Camber Castle
Rye Harbour
Rushlake Green
SUSSEX
Canadia
Whatlington
Sedlescombe
Brede Steam Engines
Brede
River
Winchelsea
Court Hall
Rye Bay
Penhurst
Ponts Green
Battle
Kent Street
Carr Taylor Vineyards
Lidham Hill
Broad Street
Icklesham
Winchelsea Beach
West
Foul Mile
Brownbread Street
Abbey
Hastings 1066
Beauport Park
Westfield
Guestling Thorn
Bodle Street Green
Telham
Three Oaks
Pett
Cowbeech
Catsfield
Guestling Green
Cliff End
Stunts Green
Herstmonceux
Henley's Down
Baldslow
Magham Down
Windmill Hill
Ninfield
Crowhurst
Hollington
St. Helen's
Fairlight Cove
Fairlight
Boreham Street
Lunsford's Cross
Ore
Herstmonceux
Observatory Science Centre
Hooe Common
Blue Reef Aquarium
Shipwreck
HAILSHAM
Wartling
Hooe
Little Common
Sidley
Bulverhythe
St. Leonards
HASTINGS
Pevensey Levels
Cooden
BEXHILL
Hankham
Courthouse
Norman's Bay
ENGLIS
Westham
Pevensey
Pevensey Bay
Friday Street
Langney
Langney Point
Fort Fun
Treasure Island
Redoubt Fortress
EASTBOURNE
Lifeboat
SEE PAGE 195
BEACHY HEAD
A
B
C
D
70
80
90
600

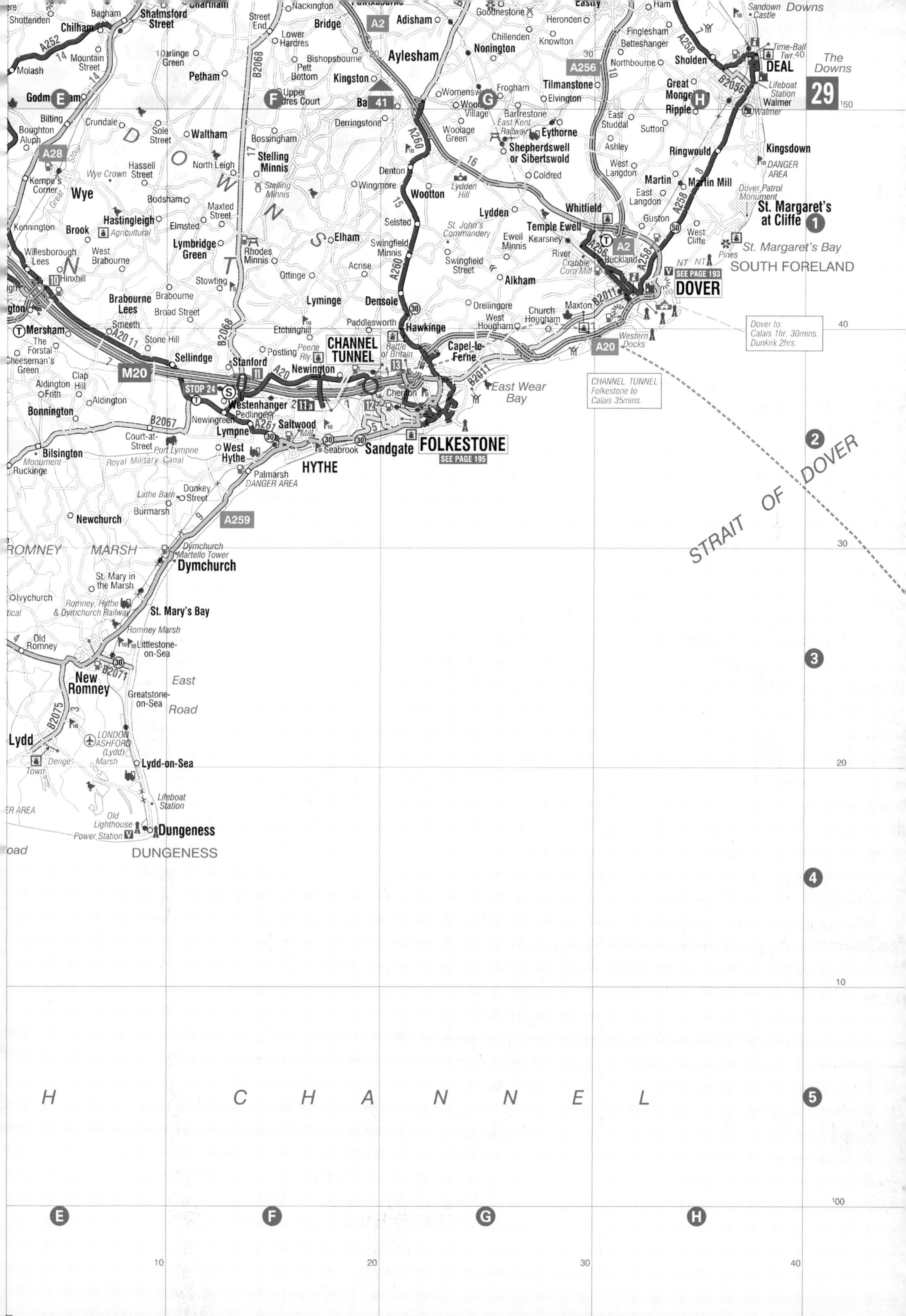

29
DEAL
DOVER
SEE PAGE 193
FOLKESTONE
SEE PAGE 195
CHANNEL TUNNEL
HYTHE
Aylesham
Dymchurch
New Romney
Lydd
Dungeness
DUNGENESS
St. Margaret's at Cliffe
SOUTH FORELAND
St. Margaret's Bay
STRAIT OF DOVER
The Downs
Sandown Castle
Dover to: Calais 1hr. 30mins. Dunkirk 2hrs.
CHANNEL TUNNEL Folkestone to Calais 35mins.
East Wear Bay
East Road
ROMNEY MARSH
Romney Marsh
Romney, Hythe & Dymchurch Railway
St. Mary's Bay
Littlestone-on-Sea
Greatstone-on-Sea
Lydd-on-Sea
LONDON ASHFORD (Lydd)
Denge Marsh
Lifeboat Station
Old Lighthouse
Power Station
Sandgate
Seabrook
Saltwood
Palmarsh
DANGER AREA
Royal Military Canal
Port Lympne
West Hythe
Lympne
Westenhanger
Newington
Cheriton
Capel-le-Ferne
Hawkinge
Sellindge
Stanford
Wye
Kingsdown
Walmer
Sholden
Ripple
Ringwould
Whitfield
Temple Ewell
Lydden
Alkham
Elham
Lyminge
Densole
Stelling Minnis
Waltham
Petham
Chilham
Hastingleigh
Brook
Mersham
Bilsington
Newchurch
Burmarsh
Bonnington
Brabourne Lees
M20
A20
A2
A256
A258
A259
A260
A28
A252
A261
B2068
B2067
B2011
B2071
B2075
H C H A N N E L
E
F
G
H
10
20
30
40

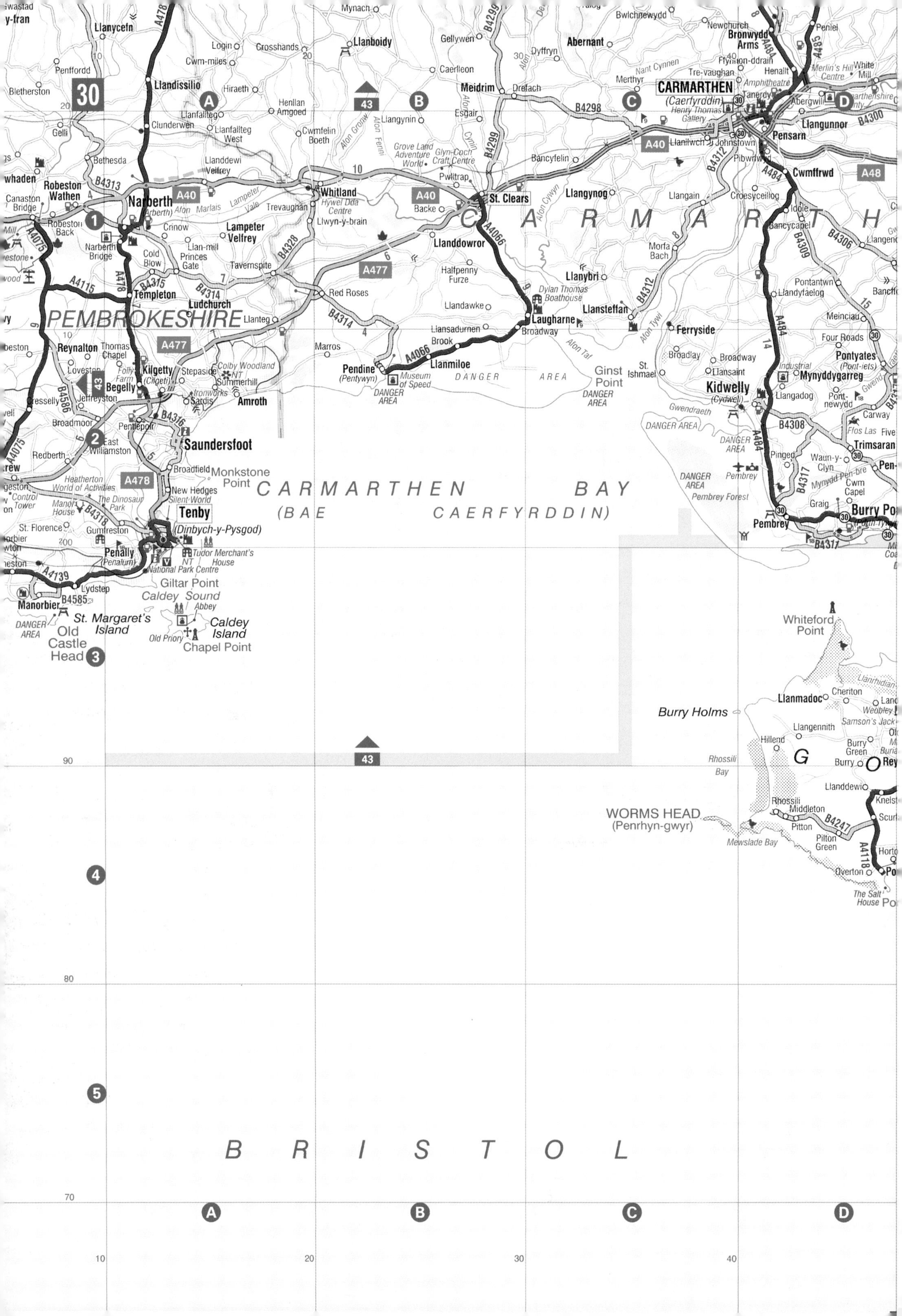
30
43
Llanycefn
A478
Login
Crosshands
Llanboidy
Mynachlog-ddu
Gellywen
B4299
Abernant
Bwlchnewydd
Newchurch
Bronwydd Arms
Peniel
Penffordd
Cwm-miles
Dyffryn
Nant Cynnen
Merthyr
Ffynnon-ddrain
Tre-vaughan
Henallt
Merlin's Hill Centre
White Mill
Bletherston
Llandissilio
Hiraeth
Caerlleon
Meidrim
Drefach
CARMARTHEN
(Caerfyrddin)
Henry Thomas Gallery
Amphitheatre
Abergwili
Carmarthenshire County Museum
Henllan Amgoed
B4298
Tanerdy
Llanfallteg
Clunderwen
Llanfallteg West
Llangynin
Esgair
Llangunnor
B4300
Gelli
Cwmfelin Boeth
Afon Gronw
Afon Fenni
Grove Land Adventure World
Glyn-Coch Craft Centre
Afon Cynin
A40
Llanllwch
Johnstown
Pensarn
Bethesda
Llanddewi Velfrey
Bancyfelin
Pibwrlwyd
A48
Robeston Wathen
B4313
Whitland
Hywel Dda Centre
Pwlltrap
B4312
Cwmffrwd
A484
Canaston Bridge
Narberth
(Arberth)
Afon Marlais
Lampeter Vale
Trevaughan
Llwyn-y-brain
Backe
St. Clears
Llangynog
Afon Cywyn
Llangain
Croesyceiliog
Idole
Robeston Back
A4075
Crinow
Lampeter Velfrey
C A R M A R T H
Bancycapel
B4309
B4306
Llangendeirne
Narberth Bridge
Llan-mill
Princes Gate
Cold Blow
B4328
Llanddowror
A4066
Morfa Bach
A4115
A478
Tavernspite
A477
Halfpenny Furze
Llanybri
Pontantwn
Llandyfaelog
Bancffosfelen
B4315
Templeton
B4314
Red Roses
Dylan Thomas Boathouse
PEMBROKESHIRE
Ludchurch
Llanteg
Llandawke
Laugharne
Llansteffan
Meinciau
Ferryside
Afon Tywi
Llansadurnen
Broadway
Reynalton
Thomas Chapel
Marros
Brook
Afon Taf
Four Roads
Pontyates
(Pont-iets)
Loveston
Kilgetty
(Cilgeti)
Stepaside
Colby Woodland
NT
Pendine
(Pentywyn)
Museum of Speed
Llanmiloe
Broadlay
Llansaint
Industrial Museum
Mynyddygarreg
Folly Farm
Begelly
Summerhill
DANGER AREA
Ginst Point
St. Ishmael
Kidwelly
(Cydweli)
Llangadog
Pont-newydd
B4586
Cresselly
Jeffreyston
Ironworks
Sardis
Amroth
Gwendraeth
Carway
Broadmoor
Pentlepoir
B4316
B4308
Ffos Las
Five Roads
East Williamson
Saundersfoot
Trimsaran
Redberth
Pinged
Waun-y-Clyn
Mynydd Pen-bre
Pen-y-groes
Carew
Heatherton World of Activities
Broadfield
Monkstone Point
C A R M A R T H E N   B A Y
Pembrey
Cwm Capel
Control Tower
Manor House
The Dinosaur Park
B4318
New Hedges
Silent World
Pembrey Forest
B4317
Graig
Burry Port
(Porth Tywyn)
(B A E   C A E R F Y R D D I N)
St. Florence
Gumfreston
Tenby
(Dinbych-y-Pysgod)
Manorbier
Penally
(Penalum)
Tudor Merchant's House
National Park Centre
A4139
Lydstep
Giltar Point
B4585
Caldey Sound
Abbey
St. Margaret's Island
Caldey Island
Old Priory
Chapel Point
Old Castle Head
Whiteford Point
Llanrhidian
Cheriton
Llanmadoc
Burry Holms
Weobley Castle
Samson's Jack
Llangennith
Hillend
Burry Green
Rhossili Bay
G
Burry
Reynoldston
Llanddewi
Knelston
Rhossili
Middleton
B4247
Scurlage
WORMS HEAD
(Penrhyn-gwyr)
Pitton
Mewslade Bay
Pitton Green
A4118
Horton
Port Eynon
Overton
The Salt House
B   R   I   S   T   O   L
A
B
C
D
1
2
3
4
5
10
20
30
40
70
80
90

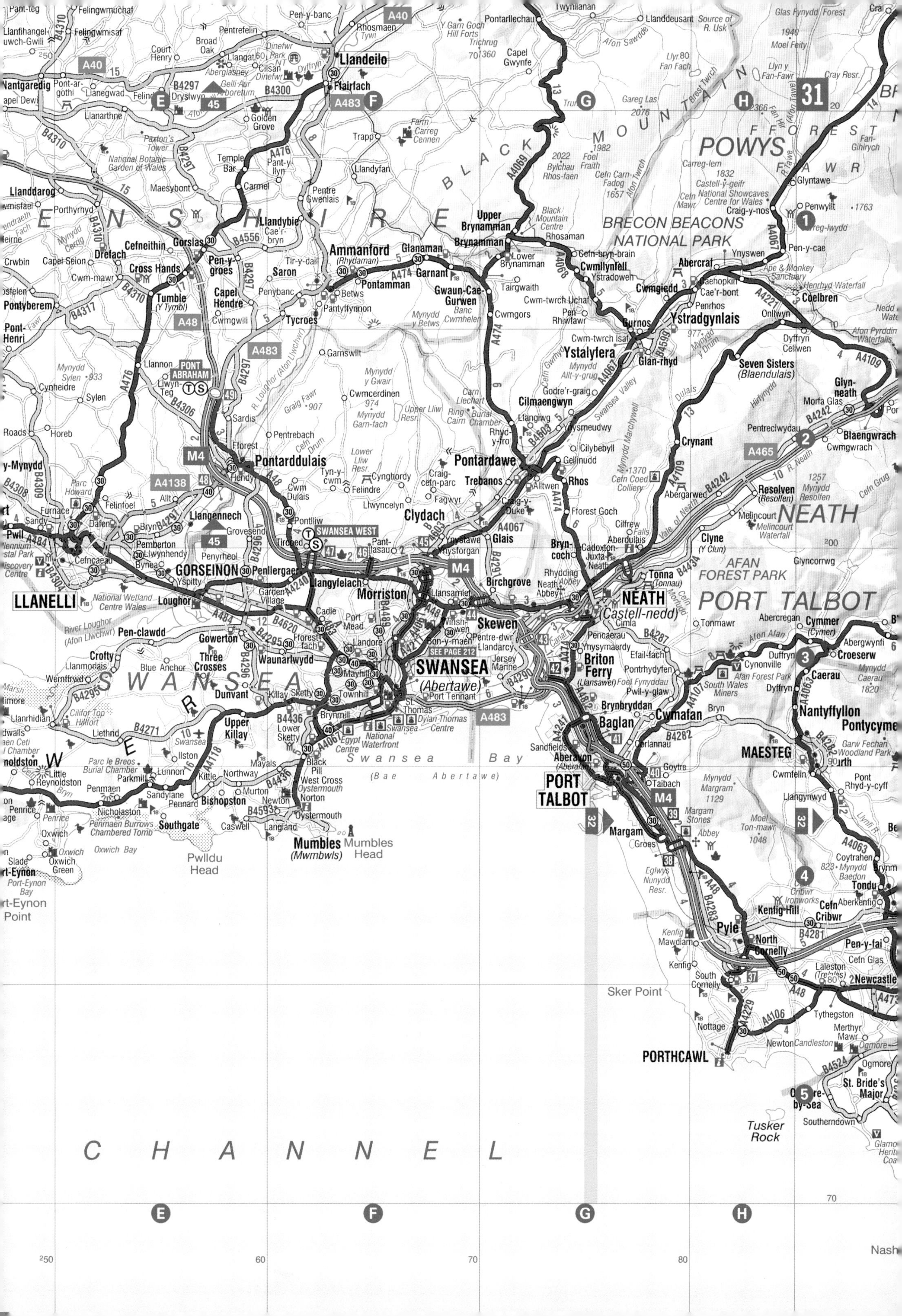

Felingwmuchaf
Llanfihangel-uwch-Gwili
Felingwmisaf
Pentrefelin
Pen-y-banc
Rhosmaen
A40
Y Garn Goch Hill Forts
Pontarllechau
Llanddeusant
Source of R. Usk
Glas Fynydd Forest
Court Henry
Broad Oak
Llangathen
Dinefwr Park
Llandeilo
Trichrug
Capel Gwynfe
Afon Sawdde
Fan Fach
Moel Feity
Nantgaredig
Pont-ar-gothi
Llanegwad
Felindre
Aberglasney
Cilsan
Dinefwr
Dyffryn
Cray Resr.
B4297
Dryslwyn
Gelli Aur Arboretum
45
B4300
Ffairfach
A483
Garreg Las
Fan Hir
Brest Twrch
31
Llanarthne
Golden Grove
Trapp
Farm
Carreg Cennen
BLACK MOUNTAIN
FFOREST FAWR
POWYS
Paxton's Tower
National Botanic Garden of Wales
Temple Bar
Pant-y-llyn
Llandyfan
Foel Fraith
Bylchau Rhos-faen
Cefn Carn-Fadog
Carreg-lem
Castell-y-geifr
National Showcaves Centre for Wales
Glyntawe
Penwyllt
Craig-y-nos
Llanddarog
Maesybont
Carmel
Pentre Gwenlais
Porthyrhyd
CARMARTHENSHIRE
Llandybie
Cae'r-bryn
Upper Brynamman
Black Mountain Centre
BRECON BEACONS NATIONAL PARK
Cefneithin
Gorslas
B4556
Drefach
Capel Seion
Cross Hands
Pen-y-groes
Ammanford (Rhydaman)
Tir-y-dail
Glanaman
Brynamman
Lower Brynamman
Rhosaman
Cefn-bryn-brain
Cwmllynfell
Ystradowen
Ynyswen
Abercraf
Penycae
Ape & Monkey Sanctuary
Henrhyd Waterfall
Coelbren
Cwm-mawr
Tumble (Y Tymbl)
Capel Hendre
Saron
Penybanc
Pontamman
Betws
Garnant
Gwaun-Cae-Gurwen
Tairgwaith
Cwm-twrch Uchaf
Cwmgiedd
Gaehopkin
Cae'r-bont
Penrhos
Ystradgynlais
Onllwyn
Pontyberem
B4317
A48
Cwmgwili
Tycroes
Pantyffynnon
Mynydd y Betws
Banc Cwmhelen
Cwmgors
Pen Rhiwfawr
Gurnos
Cwm-twrch Isaf
Glan-rhyd
Dyffryn Cellwen
Seven Sisters (Blaendulais)
Pont-Henri
Garnswllt
Ystalyfera
Glyn-neath
Llannon
PONT ABRAHAM
Llwyn-Teg
Mynydd Sylen
Cynheidre
Sylen
Mynydd y Gwair
Cwmcerdinen
Mynydd Garn-fach
Upper Lliw Resr.
Carn Llechart
Ring Cairn
Burial Chamber
Godre'r-graig
Cilmaengwyn
Swansea Valley
Morfa Glas
Pentreclwydau
Blaengwrach
Cwmgwrach
Horeb
Sardis
Pentrebach
Cefn Drum
Graig Fawr
Llangiwg
Rhyd-y-fro
Ynysmeudwy
Cilybebyll
Crynant
Roads
Fforest
Pontarddulais
Lower Lliw Resr.
Tyn-y-cwm
Cynghordy
Felindre
Craig-cefn-parc
Pontardawe
Trebanos
Gellinudd
Alltwen
Rhos
Cefn Coed Colliery
Abergarwed
Resolven
Mynydd Resolven
Cefn Grug
M4
A4138
Parc Howard
Furnace
Hendy
Cwm Dulais
Llwyncelyn
Fagwyr
Clydach
Craig-y-Duke
Forest Goch
Cilfrew
Melincourt
Melincourt Waterfall
NEATH
Felinfoel
Allt
Llangennech
Pontlliw
SWANSEA WEST
Ynystawe
Ynysforgan
Glais
A4067
Bryn-coch
Cadoxton-Juxta-Neath
Aberdulais
Falls
Clyne (Y Clun)
Sandy
Dafen
Bryn
Grovesend
Tircoed
Pant-lasau
Pwll
Millennium Coastal Park
Discovery Centre
Cefncaeau
Pemberton
Llwynhendy
Penyrheol
Bynea
GORSEINON
Penllergaer
Ysptty
Llangyfelach
Morriston
Birchgrove
Rhydding
Neath Abbey
Tonna (Tonnau)
AFAN FOREST PARK
Glyncorrwg
LLANELLI
National Wetland Centre Wales
Loughor
Garden Village
Llansamlet
PORT TALBOT
River Loughor (Afon Llwchwr)
Pen-clawdd
Gowerton
Cadle
Port Mead
Fforestfach
Landore
Winsh-wen
Skewen
Pentre-dwr
Llandarcy
Castell-nedd
Cimla
Tonmawr
Abercregan
Cymmer (Cymer)
Crofty
Llanmorlais
Three Crosses
Blue Anchor
Waunarlwydd
Bon-y-maen
Jersey Marine
Pencaerau
Ynysymaerdy
Briton Ferry (Llansawel)
Efail-fach
Pontrhydyfen
Afon Afan
Cynonville
Afan Forest Park
South Wales Miners
Duffryn
Abergwynfi
Croeserw
Caerau
Mynydd Caerau
Weernffrwd
SWANSEA
GOWER
Dunvant
Killay
Sketty
Mayhill
Townhill
SWANSEA (Abertawe)
Port Tennant
St. Thomas
Brynmill
Foel Fynyddau
Pwll-y-glaw
Cwmafan
Bryn
Dyffryn
Nantyffyllon
Pontycymer
Cilifor Top Hillfort
Llanrhidian
Llethrid
Upper Killay
Lower Sketty
Dylan Thomas Centre
National Waterfront
Egypt Centre
Brynbryddan
Baglan
Sandfields
Aberavon (Aberafan)
Corlannau
B4282
MAESTEG
Garw Fechan Woodland Park
Ilston
Parc le Breos Burial Chamber
Lunnon
Mayals
Black Pill
Swansea Bay (Bae Abertawe)
West Cross
Oystermouth
Goytre
Taibach
Cwmfelin
Pont Rhyd-y-cyff
Little Reynoldston
Penmaen
Parkmill
Kittle
Northway
Murton
Norton
Mynydd Margam
Margam Stones
Llangynwyd
Sandylane
Pennard
Bishopston
Newton
Penrice
Nicholaston
Penmaen Burrows Chambered Tomb
Southgate
Caswell
Langland
Oystermouth
Mumbles (Mwmbwls)
Mumbles Head
Margam
Abbey
Moel Ton-mawr
Oxwich
Oxwich Bay
Pwlldu Head
Groes
Coytrahen
Mynydd Baedon
Tondu
Slade
Oxwich Green
Port-Eynon
Port-Eynon Bay
Port-Eynon Point
Eglwys Nunydd Resr.
Cribwr Ironworks
Kenfig Hill
Cefn Cribwr
Aberkenfig
Pyle
North Cornelly
Kenfig
Mawdlam
Pen-y-fai
Cefn Glas
South Cornelly
Laleston (Trelales)
Newcastle
Sker Point
Tythegston
Nottage
Merthyr Mawr
Newton
Candleston
Ogmore
PORTHCAWL
Ogmore
St. Bride's Major
Ogmore-by-Sea
Southerndown
Tusker Rock
CHANNEL
Nash

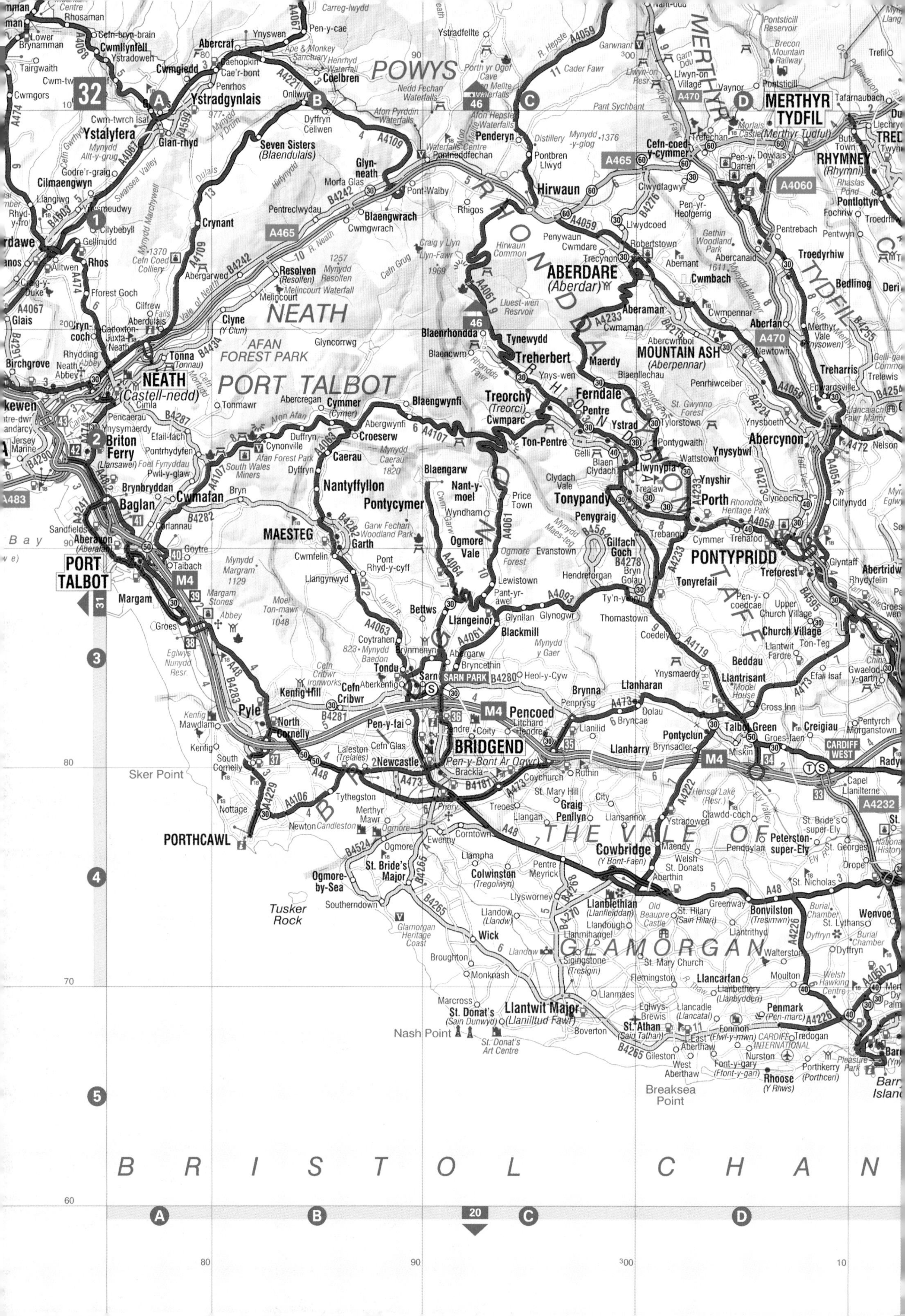

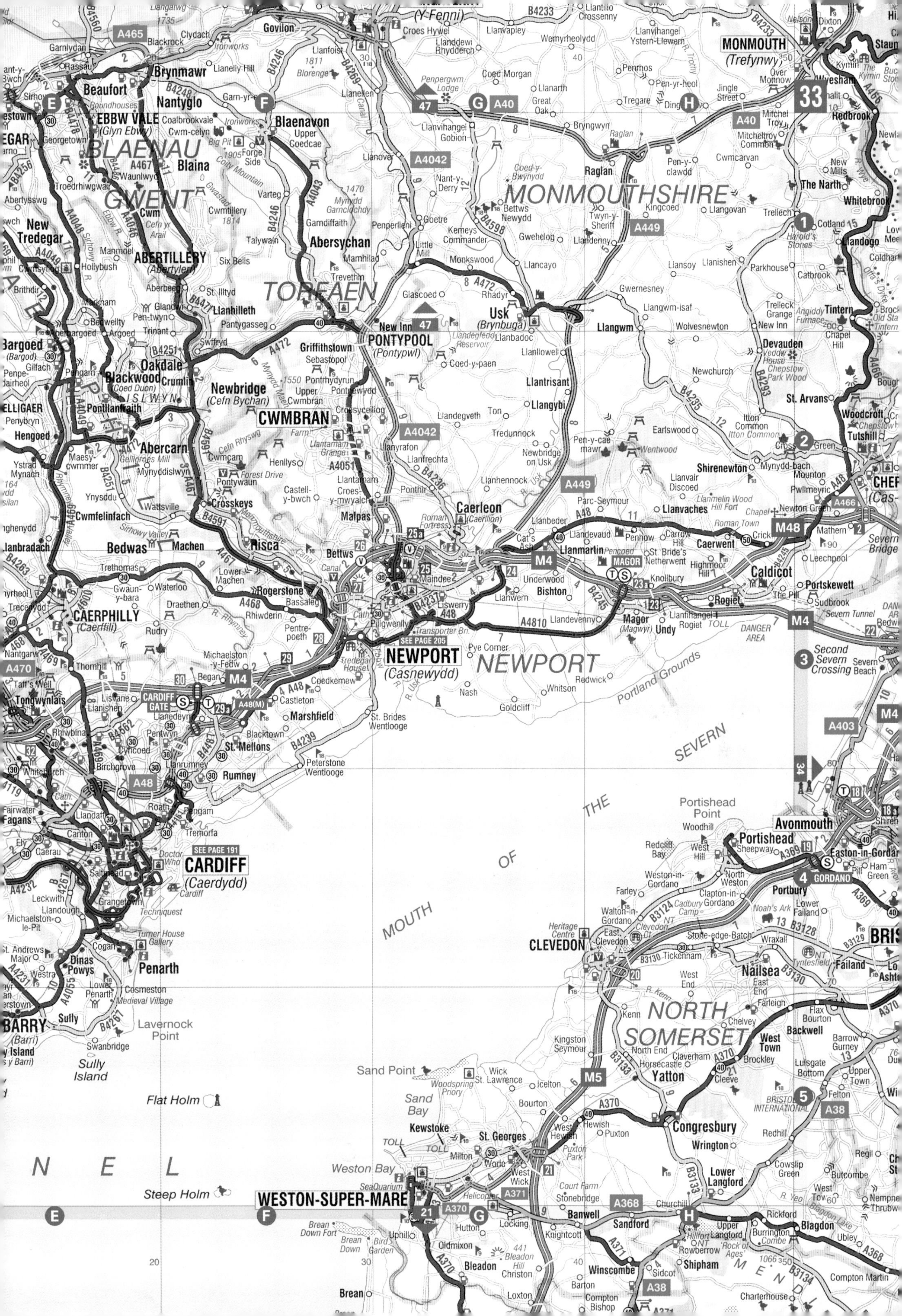

MONMOUTH
(Trefynwy)
33
Raglan
MONMOUTHSHIRE
Usk
(Brynbuga)
Abergavenny
(Y Fenni)
Govilon
Brynmawr
Beaufort
Nantyglo
Blaenavon
EBBW VALE
(Glyn Ebwy)
BLAENAU
GWENT
Blaina
Cwm
ABERTILLERY
(Abertyleri)
New Tredegar
Abersychan
TORFAEN
PONTYPOOL
(Pontypwl)
Griffithstown
Sebastopol
CWMBRAN
Newbridge
(Cefn Bychan)
Oakdale
Crumlin
Blackwood
(Coed Duon)
Pontllanfraith
Bargoed
(Bargod)
Hengoed
Abercarn
Crosskeys
Risca
Bedwas
Machen
CAERPHILLY
(Caerffili)
Rogerstone
Bassaleg
Caerleon
(Caerllion)
NEWPORT
(Casnewydd)
SEE PAGE 205
Llanmartin
Magor
(Magwyr)
Undy
Caerwent
Caldicot
Portskewett
Chepstow
Tintern
Devauden
St. Arvans
Shirenewton
Llangwm
Llantrisant
Llangybi
Marshfield
St. Mellons
Rumney
Castleton
St. Brides Wentlooge
Peterstone Wentlooge
Tongwynlais
Llanishen
Whitchurch
CARDIFF
(Caerdydd)
SEE PAGE 191
Penarth
Dinas Powys
Sully
BARRY
(Barri)
Lavernock Point
Sully Island
Flat Holm
Steep Holm
SEVERN
THE
OF
MOUTH
N E L
Portland Grounds
Second Severn Crossing
Severn Beach
Avonmouth
Portishead
Portishead Point
Portbury
CLEVEDON
Nailsea
NORTH
SOMERSET
Yatton
Congresbury
Wrington
Backwell
Kingston Seymour
Sand Point
Sand Bay
Kewstoke
St. Georges
Weston Bay
WESTON-SUPER-MARE
Worle
Locking
Banwell
Sandford
Churchill
Winscombe
Shipham
Blagdon
Bleadon
Uphill
Brean Down
Brean
M4
M48
M5
A40
A449
A4042
A48
A466
A48(M)
A470
A469
A403
A369
A370
A371
A368
A38
E
F
G
H
1
2
3
4
5

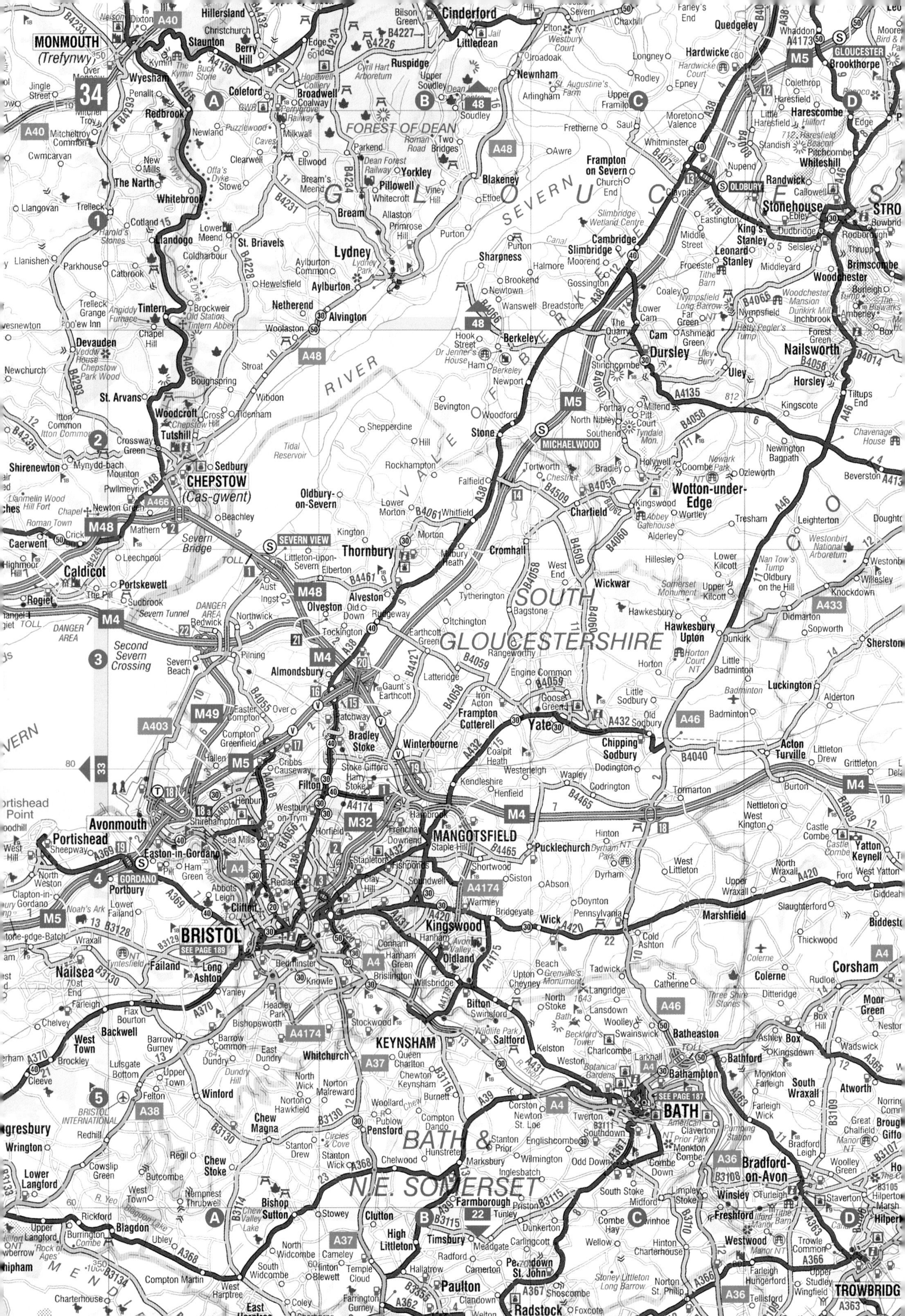

34
MONMOUTH
(Trefynwy)
Dixton
A40
Hillersland
Christchurch
Staunton
Berry Hill
Wyesham
Kymin
Jingle Street
Over Monnow
Penallt
Redbrook
A466
Coleford
Broadwell
Coalway
Mitchel Troy
Mitchel Troy Common
A40
Cwmcarvan
Newland
Puzzlewood
Clearwell
Milkwall
Ellwood
Parkend
Bream's Meend
Bream
New Mills
The North
Offa's Dyke
Stowe
Whitebrook
Llangovan
Trelleck
Harold's Stones
Cotland
Lower Meend
St. Briavels
Llandogo
Coldharbour
Llanishen
Parkhouse
Catbrook
Hewelsfield
Trelleck Grange
Tintern
Anniddy Furnace
Brockweir
Old Station
Tintern Abbey
Chapel Hill
Devauden
Veddw House
Chepstow Park Wood
Newchurch
Boughspring
Stroat
St. Arvans
Woodcroft
Tidenham
Tutshill
Itton Common
Crossway Green
Mynydd-bach
Mounton
Shirenewton
Sedbury
CHEPSTOW
(Cas-gwent)
Pwllmeyric
Newton Green
Mathern
Beachley
Llanmelin Wood Hill Fort
Chapel
Roman Town
Crick
Caerwent
M48
Caldicot
Portskewett
Leechpool
Sudbrook
The Pill
Rogiet
M4
Severn Tunnel
DANGER AREA
Second Severn Crossing
Severn Bridge
SEVERN VIEW
Aust
Ingst
Northwick
Redwick
Pilning
Severn Beach
Cinderford
Littledean
Bilson Green
Edge End
B4227
B4226
Ruspidge
Cyril Hart Arboretum
Hopewell Colliery
Perrygrove Railway
Upper Soudley
Soudley
Dean Heritage Centre
FOREST OF DEAN
Roman Road
Two Bridges
Dean Forest Railway
Yorkley
Pillowell
Whitecroft
Viney Hill
Allaston
Primrose Hill
Lydney
Lydney Park
Aylburton Common
Aylburton
Netherend
Alvington
Woolaston
A48
Blakeney
Etloe
Purton
Awre
Newnham
Arlingham
St. Augustine's Farm
Elton
Westbury Court
Broadoak
Chaxhill
Severn
Farley's End
Quedgeley
Longney
Hardwicke
Hardwicke Court
Rodley
Epney
Upper Framilode
Saul
Moreton Valence
Fretherne
Whitminster
Frampton on Severn
Church End
Slimbridge Wetland Centre
Cambridge
Slimbridge
Moorend
Purton
Sharpness
Halmore
Brookend
Newtown
Gossington
Wanswell
Breadstone
Berkeley
Hook Street
Dr Jenner's House
Ham
Berkeley
Newport
RIVER SEVERN
Bevington
Woodford
Shepperdine
Stone
Hill
Tidal Reservoir
Rockhampton
Oldbury-on-Severn
Falfield
Lower Morton
Whitfield
Kington
Morton
Thornbury
Littleton-upon-Severn
Elberton
Alveston
Olveston
Old Down
Rudgeway
Tockington
Almondsbury
Over
Easter Compton
Compton Greenfield
Hallen
Cribbs Causeway
Patchway
Bradley Stoke
Stoke Gifford
Harry Stoke
Filton
Gaunt's Earthcott
Earthcott Green
Tytherington
Itchington
Latteridge
Iron Acton
Frampton Cotterell
Winterbourne
Coalpit Heath
Westerleigh
Kendleshire
Henfield
Yate
Rangeworthy
Engine Common
Goose Green
Bagstone
Cromhall
Milbury Heath
Tortworth
Chestnut
MICHAELWOOD
Charfield
M5
Whaddon
A4173
Moorend
Bird & Hey
GLOUCESTER
Brookthorpe
Colethrop
Haresfield
Little Haresfield
Harescombe
Edge
Standish
Haresfield Beacon
Pitchcombe
Whiteshill
Nupend
Randwick
Callowell
OLDBURY
Claypits
Eastington
Stonehouse
Ebley
Dudbridge
Rodborough
STROUD
Bowbridge
Thrupp
Brimscombe
King's Stanley
Selsley
Middle Street
Leonard Stanley
Frocester
Tithe Barn
Middleyard
Woodchester
Burleigh
The Bulwarks
Amberley
Woodchester Mansion
Dunkirk Mill
Inchbrook
Nympsfield
Nympsfield Long Barrow
Coaley
Far Green
Lower Cam
Cam
The Quarry
Ashmead Green
Dursley
Uley Bury
Uley
Hetty Pegler's Tump
Forest Green
Nailsworth
Box
Horsley
Stinchcombe
Tiltups End
Kingscote
Forthay
Millend
Pitt Court
North Nibley
Tyndale Mon.
Southend
Newington Bagpath
Chavenage House
Beverston
Bradley
Holywell
Coombe
Newark Park
Ozleworth
Wotton-under-Edge
Kingswood
Abbey Gatehouse
Wortley
Alderley
Tresham
Leighterton
Doughton
Westonbirt National Arboretum
Hillesley
Lower Kilcott
Upper Kilcott
Somerset Monument
Nan Tow's Tump
Oldbury on the Hill
Knockdown
Westonbirt
Willesley
West End
Wickwar
Hawkesbury
Hawkesbury Upton
Horton Court NT
Horton
Didmarton
Sopworth
Dunkirk
Sherston
Little Badminton
Badminton
Luckington
Alderton
Little Sodbury
Old Sodbury
Chipping Sodbury
Dodington
Codrington
Wapley
Acton Turville
Littleton Drew
Grittleton
Tormarton
Burton
SOUTH GLOUCESTERSHIRE
GLOUCESTERSHIRE
Portishead Point
Portishead
Sheepway
Avonmouth
Shirehampton
Sea Mills
Henbury
Westbury on Trym
Horfield
Easton-in-Gordano
Pill
Ham Green
GORDANO
North Weston
Clapton-in-Gordano
Portbury
Lower Failand
Noah's Ark
Abbots Leigh
Clifton
BRISTOL
SEE PAGE 189
Wraxall
Tyntesfield
Failand
Nailsea
Long Ashton
Bedminster
Knowle
Brislington
Redland
Stapleton
Fishponds
Frenchay
Downend
Hambrook
MANGOTSFIELD
Staple Hill
Shortwood
Soundwell
Clay Hill
Kingswood
Hanham
Conham
Hanham Green
Avon Valley
Oldland
Willsbridge
Warmley
Bridgeyate
Siston
Pucklechurch
Dyrham Park
Dyrham
Hinton
Abson
Doynton
Pennsylvania
Wick
Cold Ashton
West Littleton
Marshfield
Upper Wraxall
North Wraxall
Nettleton
West Kington
Castle Combe
Yatton Keynell
West Yatton
Ford
Slaughterford
Giddeahall
Biddestone
Thickwood
Colerne
Corsham
Rudloe
St. Catherine
Three Shire Stones
Ditteridge
Box
Box Hill
Moor Green
Neston
Ashley
Kingsdown
Wadswick
Tadwick
Beach
Upton Cheyney
Grenville's Monument
North Stoke
Langridge
Lansdown
Woolley
Bath
Beckford's Tower
Swainswick
Batheaston
Charlcombe
Larkhall
Bathford
Bathampton
Monkton Farleigh
South Wraxall
Atworth
Farleigh Wick
Kelston
Weston
Botanical Gardens
Saltford
Bitton
Swineford
Wildlife Park
KEYNSHAM
Queen Charlton
Chewton Keynsham
Burnett
Whitchurch
East Dundry
Dundry
Bishopsworth
Headley Park
Stockwood
Yanley
Flax Bourton
Farleigh
Backwell
Barrow Gurney
Barrow Common
West Town
Chelvey
Brockley
Cleeve
Lulsgate Bottom
Upper Town
Felton
Winford
BRISTOL INTERNATIONAL
Redhill
Wrington
Regil
Chew Magna
North Wick
Norton Malreward
Norton Hawkfield
Woollard
Compton Dando
Publow
Pensford
Stanton Drew
Circles & Cove
Stanton Wick
Chelwood
Lower Langford
Cowslip Green
Butcombe
Chew Stoke
West Town
Nempnett Thrubwell
Bishop Sutton
Chew Valley Lake
Stowey
Blagdon
Upper Langford
Burrington Combe
Rickford
Ubley
Rock of Ages
Compton Martin
West Harptree
East Harptree
North Widcombe
South Widcombe
Cameley
Hinton Blewett
Temple Cloud
Clutton
High Littleton
Hallatrow
Timsbury
Farrington Gurney
Paulton
Clandown
Radstock
Welton
Camerton
Peasedown St. John
Shoscombe
Foxcote
Carlingcott
Meadgate
Radford
Farmborough
Priston
Tunley
Dunkerton
Marksbury
Hunstrete
Stanton Prior
Englishcombe
Wilmington
Inglesbatch
Newton St. Loe
Corston
Twerton
Southdown
Odd Down
BATH
SEE PAGE 187
Claverton
Prior Park
Monkton Combe
Combe Down
South Stoke
Midford
Limpley Stoke
Combe Hay
Wellow
Hinton Charterhouse
Stoney Littleton Long Barrow
Norton St. Philip
Winsley
Turleigh
Freshford
Iford Manor
Westwood
Farleigh Hungerford
Tellisford
Bradford-on-Avon
Staverton
Hilperton
Trowle Common
Upper Studley
Wingfield
TROWBRIDGE
Great Chalfield
Broughton Gifford
Bradford Leigh
Woolley Green
BATH & N.E. SOMERSET
Charterhouse
MENDIP
West Hill
Shipham

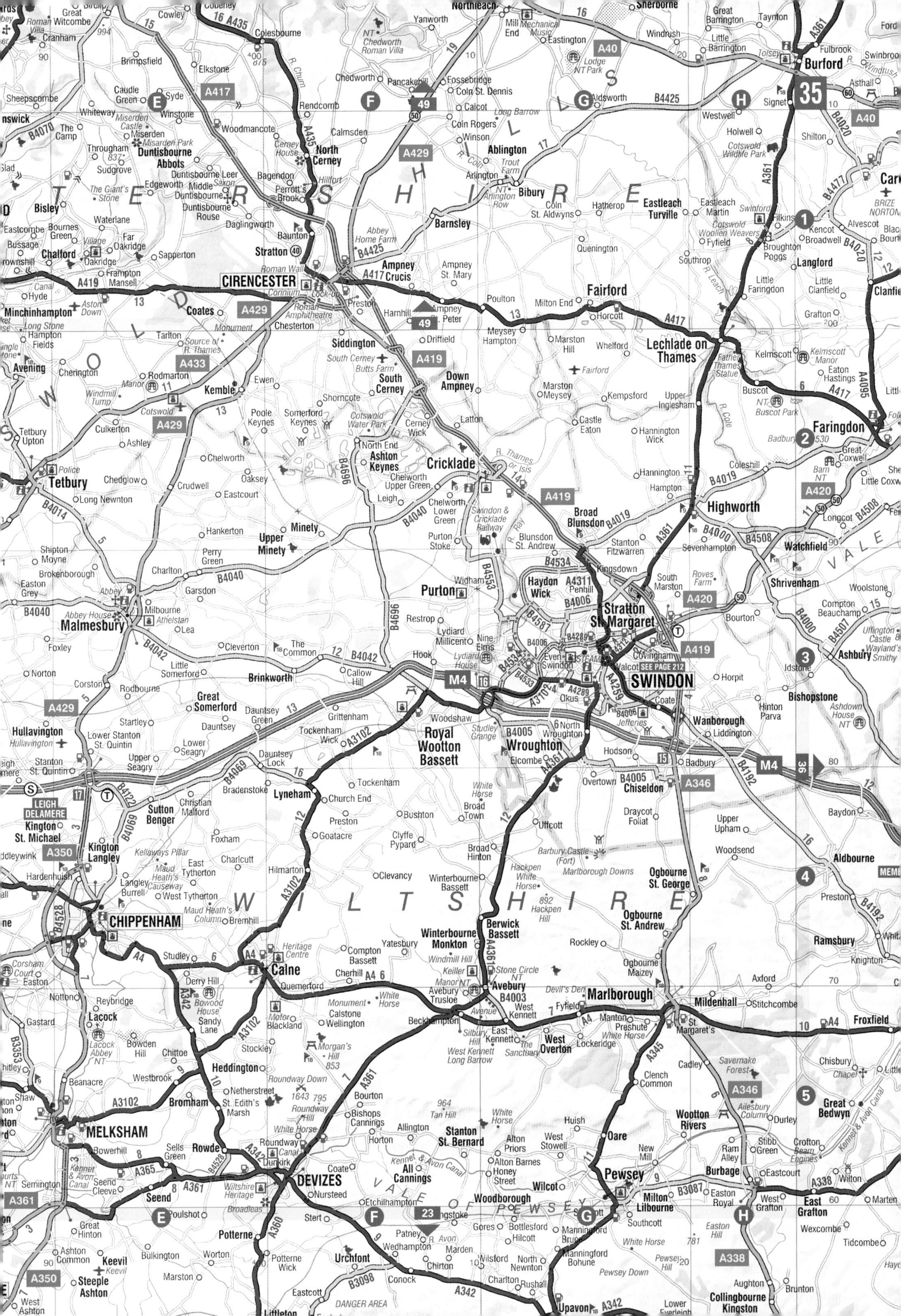

Cirencester
Swindon
See page 212
Chippenham
Melksham
Devizes
Malmesbury
Tetbury
Cricklade
Fairford
Lechlade on Thames
Burford
Faringdon
Highworth
Marlborough
Pewsey
Calne
Royal Wootton Bassett
Wroughton
Purton
Stratton St. Margaret
Chalford
Bisley
Minchinhampton
Avening
Kemble
Coates
Siddington
South Cerney
Ashton Keynes
Down Ampney
Latton
Minety
Upper Minety
Brinkworth
Great Somerfield
Lyneham
Sutton Benger
Kington Langley
Kington St. Michael
Lacock
Bromham
Rowde
Seend
Potterne
Urchfont
All Cannings
Stanton St. Bernard
Woodborough
Wilcot
Oare
Milton Lilbourne
Burbage
East Grafton
Great Bedwyn
Wootton Rivers
Froxfield
Ramsbury
Aldbourne
Chiseldon
Wanborough
Bishopstone
Ashbury
Shrivenham
Watchfield
Ogbourne St. George
Ogbourne St. Andrew
Avebury
Winterbourne Monkton
Berwick Bassett
West Overton
Mildenhall
Heddington
Bibury
Barnsley
Ablington
Ampney Crucis
North Cerney
Duntisbourne Abbots
Eastleach Turville
Langford
Collingbourne Kingston
Upavon
Steeple Ashton
Keevil
Cotswolds
Wiltshire
Vale of Pewsey
Vale
M4
A419
A417
A429
A433
A4
A346
A338
A350
A361
A3102
A420
A40
A342
A345
A360
A365
B4040
B4042
B4005
B4019
B4000
B4508
B4425

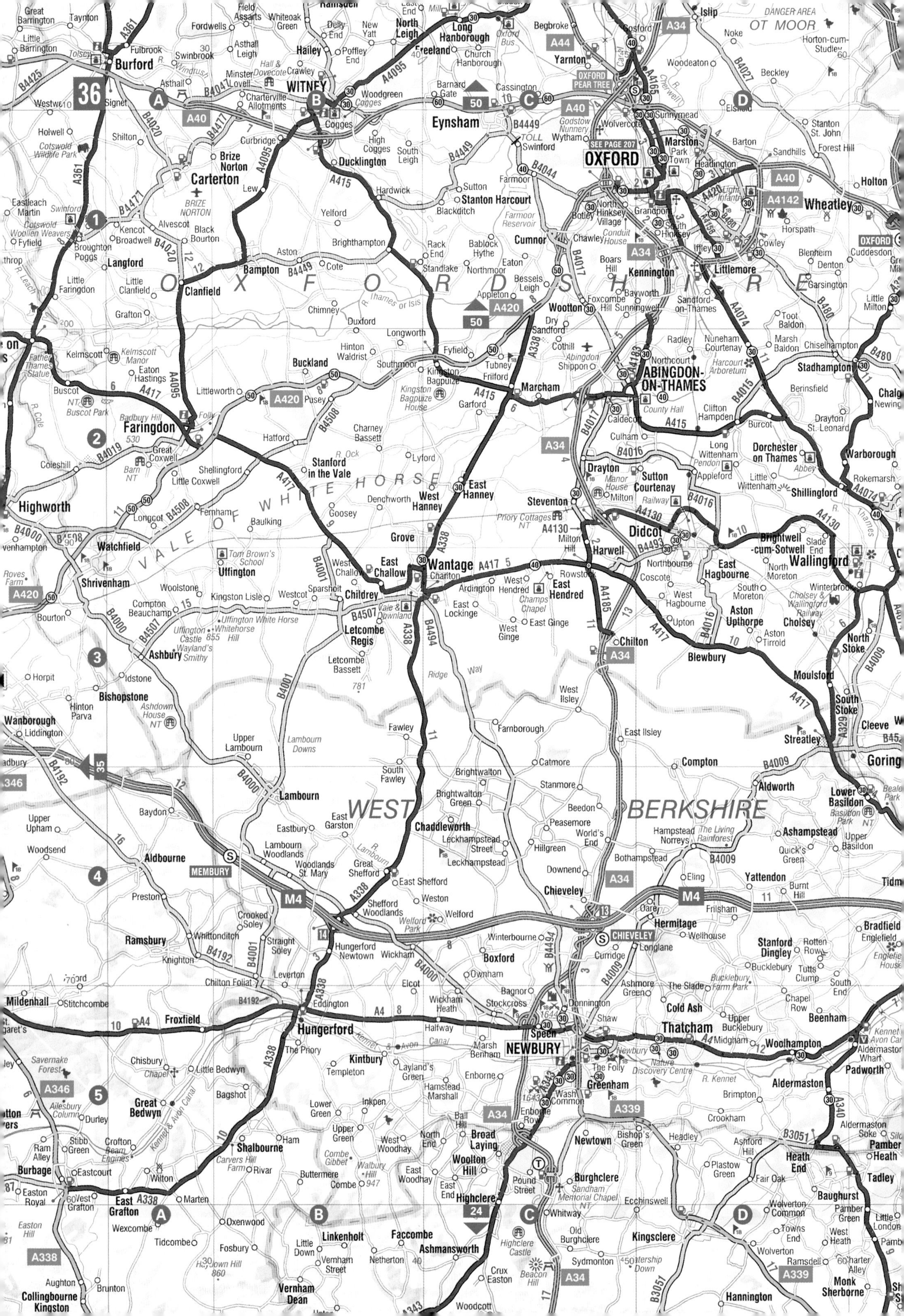
36
Great Barrington
Taynton
Little Barrington
Burford
Fulbrook
Fordwells
Field Assarts
Whiteoak Green
Swinbrook
Asthall Leigh
Asthall
Minster Lovell
Hall & Dovecote
Crawley
Hailey
Delly End
Poffley End
New Yatt
North Leigh
Long Hanborough
Freeland
Church Hanborough
Oxford Bus
Begbroke
Yarnton
Islip
Gosford
DANGER AREA
OT MOOR
Noke
Horton-cum-Studley
Woodeaton
Beckley
Charterville Allotments
WITNEY
Cogges
Woodgreen
Barnard Gate
Cassington
Eynsham
OXFORD PEAR TREE
Cherwell
Elsfield
Stanton St. John
Forest Hill
Westwell
Signet
Holwell
Shilton
Cotswold Wildlife Park
Curbridge
Brize Norton
Carterton
BRIZE NORTON
High Cogges
South Leigh
Ducklington
Godstow Nunnery
Wolvercote
Sunnymead
Wytham
TOLL
Swinford
SEE PAGE 207
OXFORD
Marston
Park Town
Barton
Sandhills
Headington
Holton
Wheatley
Horspath
Eastleach Martin
Swinford
Cotswold Woollen Weavers
Fyfield
Broughton Poggs
Kencot
Broadwell
Alvescot
Black Bourton
Lew
Hardwick
Sutton
Stanton Harcourt
Blackditch
Yelford
Farmoor
Farmoor Reservoir
North Hinksey Village
Botley
Grandpont
South Hinksey
Light Infantry
Cowley
Iffley
Littlemore
Cuddesdon
Blenheim
Denton
Garsington
Langford
Aston
Brighthampton
Rack End
Standlake
Bablock Hythe
Northmoor
Cumnor
Chawley
Conduit House
Eaton
Bessels Leigh
Boars Hill
Kennington
Little Faringdon
Little Clanfield
Bampton
Cote
Clanfield
OXFORDSHIRE
Appleton
Foxcombe Hill
Sunningwell
Bayworth
Sandford-on-Thames
Grafton
Chimney
Thames or Isis
Duxford
Wootton
Dry Sandford
Toot Baldon
Little Milton
Kelmscott
Kelmscott Manor
Eaton Hastings
Father Thames Statue
Hinton Waldrist
Longworth
Southmoor
Fyfield
Tubney
Frilford
Cothill
Abingdon
Shippon
Radley
Northcourt
Nuneham Courtenay
Harcourt Arboretum
Marsh Baldon
Chiselhampton
Stadhampton
Buckland
Kingston Bagpuize
Kingston Bagpuize House
Marcham
ABINGDON-ON-THAMES
Berinsfield
Buscot
Buscot Park
Littleworth
Pusey
Garford
County Hall
Caldecott
Clifton Hampden
Burcot
Drayton St. Leonard
Badbury Hill
Faringdon
Folly
Charney Bassett
Culham
Long Wittenham
Pendon
Dorchester on Thames
Abbey
Warborough
Coleshill
Great Coxwell
Barn
Hatford
Stanford in the Vale
Lyford
Drayton
Manor House
Milton
Sutton Courtenay
Appleford
Little Wittenham
Rokemarsh
Shillingford
Shellingford
Little Coxwell
East Hanney
West Hanney
VALE OF WHITE HORSE
Denchworth
Goosey
Highworth
Longcot
Fernham
Baulking
Steventon
Priory Cottages
Railway
Didcot
Watchfield
Shrivenham
Tom Brown's School
Uffington
Grove
East Challow
West Challow
Wantage
Charlton
Milton Hill
Harwell
Brightwell-cum-Sotwell
Slade End
Wallingford
East Hagbourne
North Moreton
Northbourne
Rowstock
Coscote
Roves Farm
Woolstone
Kingston Lisle
Westcot
Sparsholt
Childrey
Ardington
West Hendred
East Hendred
Champs Chapel
West Hagbourne
South Moreton
Winterbrook
Cholsey & Wallingford Railway
Compton Beauchamp
Bourton
Uffington White Horse
Uffington Castle
Whitehorse Hill
Wayland's Smithy
Vale & Downland
Letcombe Regis
East Lockinge
East Ginge
West Ginge
Upton
Aston Upthorpe
Cholsey
Aston Tirrold
North Stoke
Ashbury
Letcombe Bassett
Chilton
Blewbury
Horpit
Idstone
Bishopstone
Ridge Way
Moulsford
West Ilsley
South Stoke
Cleeve
Hinton Parva
Ashdown House
Wanborough
Liddington
Upper Lambourn
Lambourn Downs
Fawley
Farnborough
East Ilsley
Streatley
Goring
South Fawley
Catmore
Compton
Aldworth
Brightwalton
Stanmore
Lambourn
Brightwalton Green
Beedon
Lower Basildon
Basildon Park
Baydon
Upper Upham
WEST BERKSHIRE
East Garston
Eastbury
Chaddleworth
Peasemore
World's End
Hampstead Norreys
The Living Rainforest
Ashampstead
Upper Basildon
Quick's Green
Woodsend
Aldbourne
MEMBURY
Lambourn Woodlands
Woodlands St. Mary
Great Shefford
Leckhampstead Street
Leckhampstead
Hillgreen
Bothampstead
Downend
Eling
Yattendon
Burnt Hill
East Shefford
Weston
Chieveley
Preston
Shefford Woodlands
Welford Park
Welford
Crooked Soley
Oare
Hermitage
Frilsham
Bradfield
Englefield
Englefield House
Ramsbury
Whittonditch
Straight Soley
Hungerford Newtown
Wickham
Winterbourne
CHIEVELEY
Wellhouse
Longlane
Curridge
Stanford Dingley
Rotten Row
Bucklebury
Tutts Clump
South End
Knighton
Chilton Foliat
Leverton
Elcot
Boxford
Ownham
Bagnor
Ashmore Green
The Slade
Bucklebury Farm Park
Chapel Row
Cold Ash
Beenham
Mildenhall
Stitchcombe
Froxfield
Eddington
Hungerford
Wickham Heath
Halfway
Stockcross
Speen
Donnington
Shaw
Upper Bucklebury
Thatcham
Midgham
Woolhampton
Kennet & Avon Canal
Aldermaston Wharf
Savernake Forest
Chisbury
Chapel
Little Bedwyn
The Priory
Kintbury
Layland's Green
Templeton
Marsh Benham
Enborne
NEWBURY
Newbury
The Folly
Nature Discovery Centre
Greenham
R. Kennet
Brimpton
Padworth
Aldermaston
Great Bedwyn
Aylesbury Column
Durley
Bagshot
Lower Green
Inkpen
Hamstead Marshall
Wash Common
Enborne Row
Ball Hill
Crookham
Stibb Green
Crofton Beam Engines
Shalbourne
Ham
Upper Green
West Woodhay
North End
Broad Laying
Newtown
Bishop's Green
Headley
Ashford Hill
Aldermaston Soke
Pamber Heath
Ram Alley
Carvers Hill Farm
Rivar
Combe Gibbet
Walbury Hill
Woolton Hill
Plastow Green
Heath End
Burbage
Eastcourt
Wilton
Buttermere
Combe
East Woodhay
Pound Street
Burghclere
Sandham Memorial Chapel
Fair Oak
Tadley
Easton Royal
Vest Grafton
East Grafton
Marten
East End
Highclere
Ecchinswell
Baughurst
Wolverton Common
Pamber Green
Little London
Wexcombe
Oxenwood
Linkenholt
Faccombe
Whitway
Old Burghclere
Kingsclere
Towns End
West Heath
Easton Hill
Tidcombe
Fosbury
Little Down
Vernham Street
Netherton
Ashmansworth
Highclere Castle
Sydmonton
Watership Down
Wolverton
Ramsdell
Charter Alley
Haydown Hill
Beacon Hill
Aughton
Brunton
Collingbourne Kingston
Vernham Dean
Crux Easton
Woodcott
Hannington
Monk Sherborne
A40
A44
A34
A4142
A420
A415
A417
A338
A4130
A4185
A4074
A329
M4
A4
A346
A339
A343
A340
A361
A4095
A4165
B4020
B4047
B4477
B4449
B4044
B4017
B4016
B4493
B4009
B4001
B4000
B4507
B4508
B4019
B4192
B4494
B3051
B480
B4015
B4027
B4425
B4471
A4158
A4183
A420
A4
530
855
781
947
860
S
A
B
C
D
1
2
3
4
5
35
50
24
13
14
12
9
8

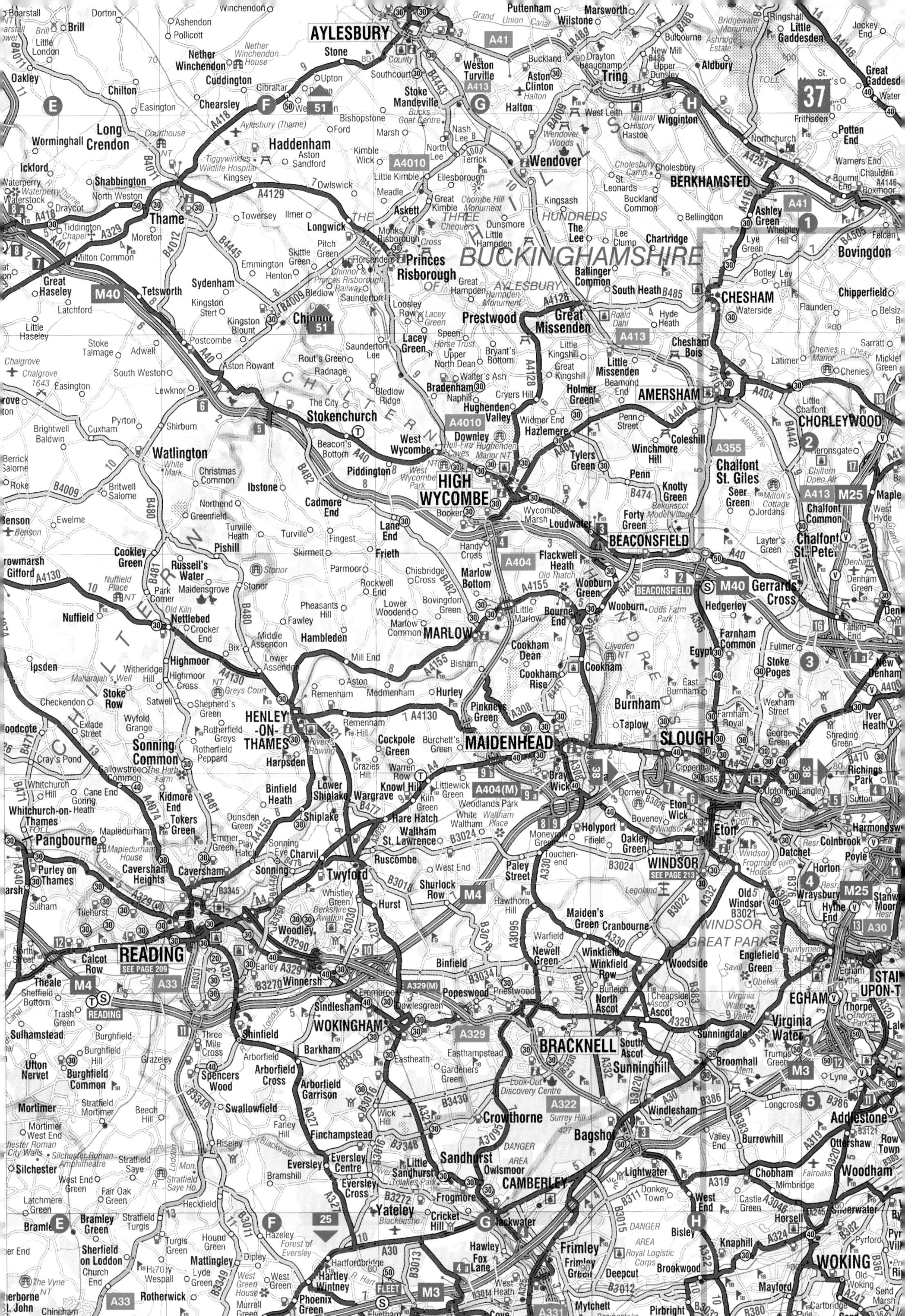
AYLESBURY
Stone
Upton
Southcourt
Stoke Mandeville
Weston Turville
Aston Clinton
Halton
Buckland
Drayton Beauchamp
Tring
Puttenham
Marsworth
Wilstone
Bulbourne
New Mill
Aldbury
Wigginton
Little Gaddesden
Ringshall
Jockey End
Great Gaddesden
Frithsden
Potten End
Northchurch
BERKHAMSTED
Warners End
Bourne End
Boxmoor
Wendover
Halton
Bishopstone
Ford
Marsh
Kimble Wick
Little Kimble
Ellesborough
Terrick
Nash Lee
Great Kimble
Askett
Monks Risborough
Princes Risborough
Longwick
Ilmer
Owlswick
Meadle
Kingsey
Haddenham
Aston Sandford
Chearsley
Cuddington
Nether Winchendon
Gibraltar
Dinton
Ashendon
Pollicott
Winchendon
Brill
Boarstall
Dorton
Little London
Oakley
Chilton
Easington
Long Crendon
Worminghall
Ickford
Shabbington
North Weston
Waterperry
Waterstock
Thame
Moreton
Towersey
Tiddington
Draycot
Milton Common
Great Haseley
Latchford
Little Haseley
Tetsworth
Sydenham
Emmington
Henton
Horsenden
Pitch Green
Skittle Green
Bledlow
Saunderton
Chinnor
Kingston Stert
Kingston Blount
Postcombe
Stoke Talmage
Adwell
Aston Rowant
Chalgrove
Easington
South Weston
Lewknor
Pyrton
Cuxham
Brightwell Baldwin
Watlington
Shirburn
Christmas Common
Britwell Salome
Berrick Salome
Roke
Benson
Ewelme
Northend
Greenfield
Turville Heath
Turville
Ibstone
Pishill
Cookley Green
Russell's Water
Maidensgrove
Stonor
Park Corner
Nuffield
Nettlebed
Crocker End
Bix
Highmoor
Highmoor Cross
Witheridge Hill
Ipsden
Checkendon
Stoke Row
Satwell
Shepherd's Green
Wyfold Grange
Rotherfield Greys
Rotherfield Peppard
Exlade Street
Cray's Pond
Sonning Common
Gallowstree Common
Whitchurch Hill
Whitchurch-on-Thames
Cane End
Goring Heath
Kidmore End
Tokers Green
Mapledurham
Pangbourne
Purley on Thames
Caversham Heights
Caversham
Emmer Green
Dunsden Green
Play Hatch
Sonning Eye
Sonning
Charvil
Twyford
Shiplake
Lower Shiplake
Binfield Heath
Harpsden
HENLEY-ON-THAMES
Middle Assendon
Lower Assendon
Remenham
Remenham Hill
Aston
Medmenham
Hurley
Hambleden
Mill End
Fawley
Pheasants Hill
Parmoor
Skirmett
Fingest
Frieth
Lane End
Rockwell End
Lower Woodend
Marlow Common
Bovingdon Green
Chisbridge Cross
MARLOW
Little Marlow
Bisham
Cookham Dean
Cookham Rise
Cookham
Bourne End
Wooburn Green
Wooburn
Flackwell Heath
Marlow Bottom
Handy Cross
Booker
HIGH WYCOMBE
Downley
West Wycombe
Piddington
Stokenchurch
Beacon's Bottom
Cadmore End
Radnage
The City
Bledlow Ridge
Rout's Green
Saunderton Lee
Lacey Green
Loosley Row
Speen
Bradenham
Naphill
Walter's Ash
Upper North Dean
Hughenden Valley
Cryers Hill
Bryant's Bottom
Great Hampden
Prestwood
Great Missenden
Little Kingshill
Great Kingshill
Widmer End
Hazlemere
Penn Street
Tylers Green
Penn
Winchmore Hill
Coleshill
Knotty Green
Forty Green
Loudwater
Wycombe Marsh
BEACONSFIELD
Holmer Green
Little Missenden
Beamond End
AMERSHAM
Hyde Heath
South Heath
Ballinger Common
The Lee
Lee Clump
Chartridge
Kingsash
Dunsmore
Little Hampden
Cholesbury
St. Leonards
Buckland Common
Bellingdon
Ashley Green
Whelpley Hill
Lye Green
Botley
Ley Hill
CHESHAM
Waterside
Chesham Bois
Bovingdon
Felden
Chipperfield
Flaunden
Belsize
Sarratt
Latimer
Chenies
Mickleffield Green
Little Chalfont
CHORLEYWOOD
Heronsgate
Chalfont St. Giles
Seer Green
Jordans
Chalfont Common
Chalfont St. Peter
Layter's Green
West Hyde
Maple Cross
Gerrards Cross
Denham
Denham Green
Hedgerley
Farnham Common
Fulmer
Tatling End
Stoke Poges
Egypt
East Burnham
Burnham
Farnham Royal
Wexham Street
Iver Heath
New Denham
George Green
Shreding Green
Taplow
SLOUGH
Cippenham
Upton
Langley
Richings Park
Sutton
Dorney
Boveney
Eton Wick
Eton
WINDSOR
Datchet
Harmondsworth
Colnbrook
Poyle
Horton
Wraysbury
Old Windsor
Stanwell Moor
Hythe End
Englefield Green
Egham Hythe
EGHAM
STAINES-UPON-THAMES
Thorpe
Virginia Water
Sunningdale
Trumps Green
Lyne
Longcross
Addlestone
Ottershaw
Row Town
Chobham
Fairoaks
Woodham
Mimbridge
Castle Green
Sheerwater
Horsell
Pyrford
WOKING
Knaphill
Old Woking
Mayford
Send Marsh
Cartbridge
Bisley
West End
Brookwood
Pirbright
Donkey Town
Lightwater
Bagshot
Windlesham
Broomhall
Sunninghill
South Ascot
Ascot
North Ascot
Cheapside
Woodside
Winkfield
Winkfield Row
Cranbourne
Maiden's Green
Warfield
Newell Green
BRACKNELL
Easthampstead
Priestwood
Popeswood
Binfield
Crowthorne
Gardeners Green
Sandhurst
Owlsmoor
Little Sandhurst
College Town
CAMBERLEY
Frimley
Frimley Green
Deepcut
Mytchett
Blackwater
Hawley
Fox Lane
Cove
West Heath
Frogmore
Cricket Hill
Yateley
Eversley Cross
Eversley Centre
Eversley
Finchampstead
Arborfield Garrison
Arborfield Cross
Arborfield
Barkham
WOKINGHAM
Sindlesham
Emmbrook
Bowlesgreen
Winnersh
Earley
Woodley
Hurst
Whistley Green
Shurlock Row
West End
Ruscombe
Waltham St. Lawrence
White Waltham
Woodlands Park
Littlewick Green
Kiln Green
Hare Hatch
Knowl Hill
Warren Row
Crazies Hill
Cockpole Green
Burchett's Green
Wargrave
MAIDENHEAD
Pinkneys Green
Bray
Bray Wick
Holyport
Fifield
Oakley Green
Moneyrow Green
Touchen-end
Paley Street
Hawthorn Hill
READING
Tilehurst
Calcot Row
Theale
Sulham
North Street
Sheffield Bottom
Trash Green
Sulhamstead
Burghfield
Burghfield Hill
Burghfield Common
Ufton Nervet
Three Mile Cross
Shinfield
Grazeley
Spencers Wood
Swallowfield
Riseley
Farley Hill
Bramshill
Mortimer
Mortimer West End
Stratfield Mortimer
Beech Hill
Silchester
Stratfield Saye
West End Green
Fair Oak Green
Heckfield
Latchmere Green
Bramley
Bramley Green
Stratfield Turgis
Turgis Green
Sherfield on Loddon
Church End
Hound Green
Mattingley
Lyde Green
Hazeley
Dipley
West Green
Hartley Wintney
Hartfordbridge
Phoenix Green
Rotherwick
Hartley Wespall
Sherborne St. John
Chineham
Elvetham
FLEET
BUCKINGHAMSHIRE
CHILTERN HILLS
37
25
51
38
SEE PAGE 209
SEE PAGE 213
M40
M4
M25
M3
A41
A413
A404
A355
A329
A30
A33
A322
A4010

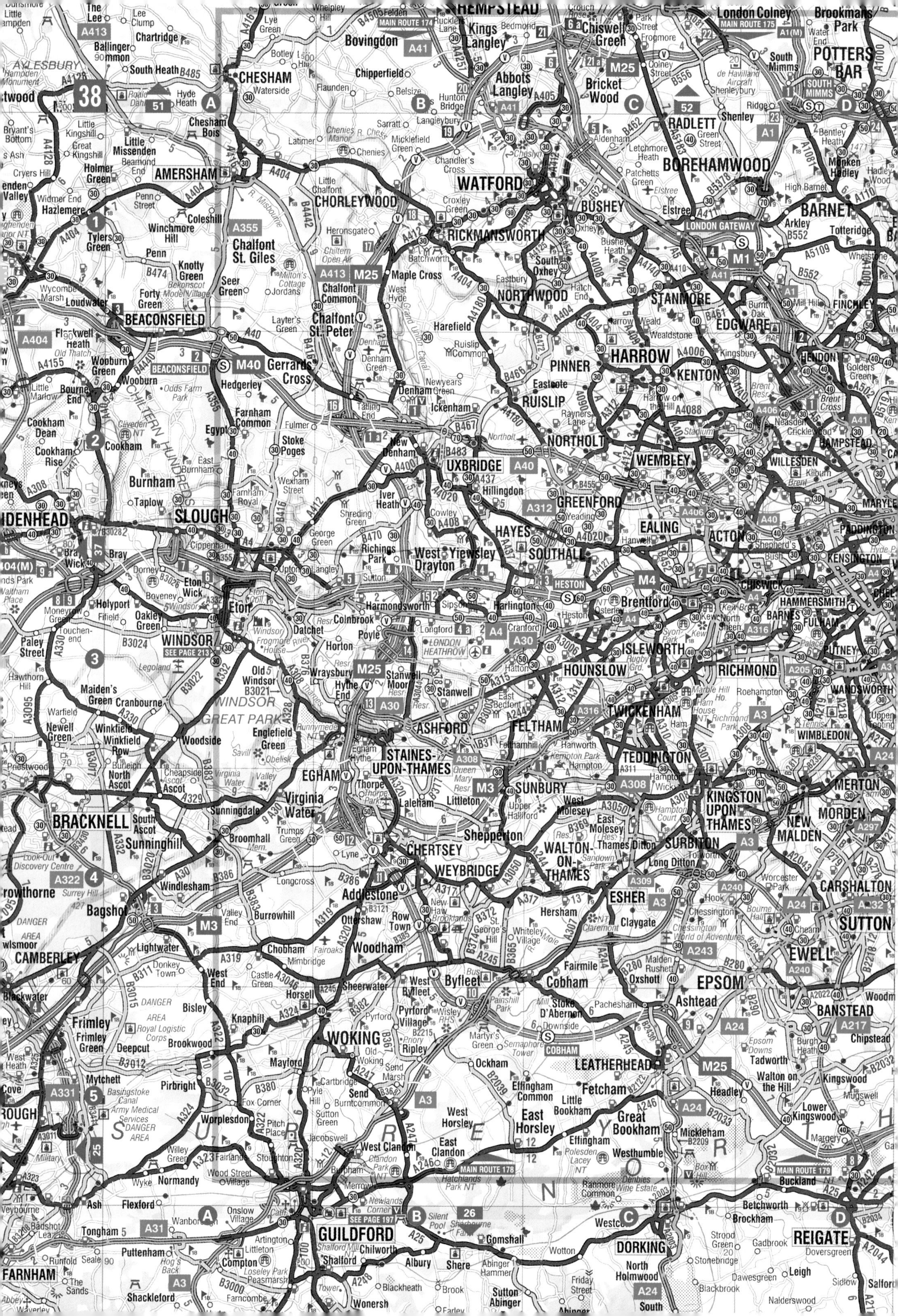

38
HEMPSTEAD
Kings Langley
Chiswell Green
London Colney
Brookmans Park
POTTERS BAR
MAIN ROUTE 174
MAIN ROUTE 175
Bovingdon
Chesham
AYLESBURY
Abbots Langley
Bricket Wood
South Mimms
Chartridge
Ballinger Common
South Heath
Hyde Heath
Chipperfield
Belsize
Hunton Bridge
Radlett
Shenley
Borehamwood
Amersham
Chesham Bois
Little Missenden
Latimer
Chenies
Sarratt
Watford
Bushey
Elstree
Barnet
Arkley
Totteridge
Chorleywood
Rickmansworth
Croxley Green
London Gateway
Hazlemere
Tylers Green
Penn
Chalfont St. Giles
Maple Cross
Northwood
Stanmore
Edgware
Finchley
Beaconsfield
Loudwater
Knotty Green
Seer Green
Chalfont Common
Chalfont St. Peter
Harefield
Ruislip Common
Pinner
Harrow
Kenton
Hendon
Wooburn Green
Bourne End
Gerrards Cross
Denham
Ruislip
Northolt
Wembley
Willesden
Hampstead
Cookham
Burnham
Farnham Common
Stoke Poges
Uxbridge
Hillingdon
Greenford
Ealing
Acton
Paddington
Maidenhead
Slough
Taplow
Iver Heath
Hayes
Southall
Yiewsley
West Drayton
Kensington
Bray
Eton
Windsor
Datchet
Colnbrook
Harmondsworth
Heston
Brentford
Chiswick
Hammersmith
Fulham
Holyport
Oakley Green
Horton
Poyle
London Heathrow
Cranford
Isleworth
Hounslow
Richmond
Putney
Wandsworth
Wraysbury
Stanwell
Ashford
Feltham
Twickenham
Wimbledon
Winkfield
Englefield Green
Staines-upon-Thames
Egham
Teddington
Kingston upon Thames
Merton
Morden
New Malden
Bracknell
Ascot
Sunningdale
Virginia Water
Laleham
Littleton
Sunbury
Shepperton
Chertsey
Walton-on-Thames
Surbiton
Weybridge
Esher
Crowthorne
Windlesham
Bagshot
Addlestone
Chessington
Worcester Park
Carshalton
Sutton
Ewell
Camberley
Lightwater
Chobham
Woodham
Byfleet
Cobham
Claygate
Epsom
Banstead
Frimley
Bisley
Knaphill
Woking
Pyrford
Ripley
Ockham
Leatherhead
Ashtead
Tadworth
Chipstead
Kingswood
Pirbright
Worplesdon
Send
West Horsley
East Horsley
Effingham
Fetcham
Great Bookham
Mickleham
Normandy
West Clandon
East Clandon
MAIN ROUTE 178
MAIN ROUTE 179
Buckland
Ash
Flexford
Guildford
Shalford
Chilworth
Albury
Shere
Gomshall
Dorking
Reigate
Betchworth
Brockham
Farnham
Puttenham
Compton
Wonersh
SEE PAGE 213
SEE PAGE 197

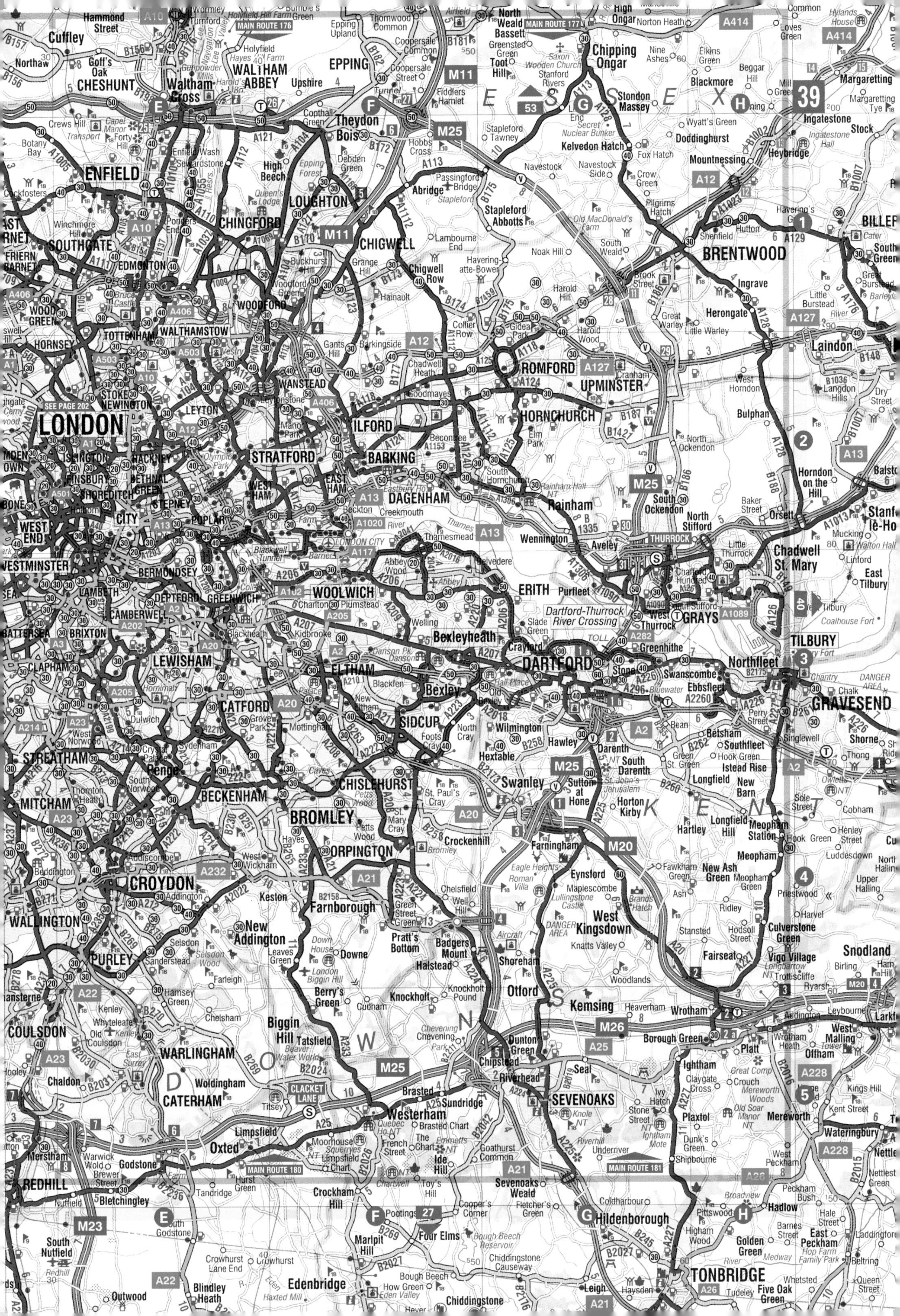

Cuffley
Hammond Street
Northaw
Goff's Oak
CHESHUNT
Waltham Cross
WALTHAM ABBEY
EPPING
MAIN ROUTE 176
MAIN ROUTE 177
North Weald Bassett
Chipping Ongar
High Ongar
Norton Heath
Upshire
Theydon Bois
M11
M25
Stondon Massey
Kelvedon Hatch
Doddinghurst
Mountnessing
Margaretting
Ingatestone
Stock
39
ESSEX
Crews Hill
Botany Bay
ENFIELD
Cockfosters
High Beech
LOUGHTON
CHINGFORD
CHIGWELL
Abridge
Passingford Bridge
Stapleford Abbotts
Navestock
Lambourne End
Havering-atte-Bower
Noak Hill
South Weald
BRENTWOOD
Shenfield
Hutton
Ingrave
Herongate
Billericay
Winchmore Hill
SOUTHGATE
FRIERN BARNET
EDMONTON
WOOD GREEN
WOODFORD
Grange Hill
Chigwell Row
Hainault
Collier Row
Gidea Park
Harold Wood
Harold Hill
Brook Street
Great Warley
Little Warley
Laindon
HORNSEY
TOTTENHAM
WALTHAMSTOW
Barkingside
Chadwell Heath
ROMFORD
UPMINSTER
Cranham
West Horndon
Bulphan
Langdon Hills
STOKE NEWINGTON
LEYTON
WANSTEAD
Goodmayes
Leytonstone
ILFORD
HORNCHURCH
Elm Park
North Ockendon
LONDON
SEE PAGE 202
ISLINGTON
HACKNEY
STRATFORD
BARKING
Becontree
DAGENHAM
South Hornchurch
Rainham
South Ockendon
North Stifford
Horndon on the Hill
Orsett
FINSBURY
BETHNAL GREEN
SHOREDITCH
STEPNEY
WEST HAM
EAST HAM
Beckton
Creekmouth
Wennington
Aveley
Baker Street
WEST END
CITY
POPLAR
LONDON CITY
Thamesmead
THURROCK
Little Thurrock
Chadwell St. Mary
Mucking
Linford
East Tilbury
WESTMINSTER
BERMONDSEY
Belvedere
ERITH
Purfleet
Dartford-Thurrock River Crossing
West Thurrock
GRAYS
Tilbury
LAMBETH
DEPTFORD
GREENWICH
WOOLWICH
Abbey Wood
Charlton
Plumstead
CAMBERWELL
BATTERSEA
BRIXTON
Blackheath
Kidbrooke
Welling
Bexleyheath
Slade Green
Crayford
DARTFORD
Greenhithe
Stone
Swanscombe
TILBURY
Northfleet
GRAVESEND
CLAPHAM
LEWISHAM
ELTHAM
Blackfen
Bexley
Ebbsfleet
Chalk
Shorne
CATFORD
Mottingham
New Eltham
SIDCUP
North Cray
Wilmington
Hawley
Darenth
Bean
Betsham
Southfleet
Perry Street
Singlewell
Thong
Dulwich
Grove Park
Sydenham
STREATHAM
Penge
South Norwood
Crystal Palace
Foots Cray
Hextable
South Darenth
Hook Green
Istead Rise
Longfield
New Barn
MITCHAM
Thornton Heath
BECKENHAM
CHISLEHURST
St. Paul's Cray
Swanley
Sutton at Hone
Horton Kirby
Hartley
Longfield Hill
Sole Street
Cobham
BROMLEY
Hayes
Petts Wood
ORPINGTON
St. Mary Cray
Crockenhill
Farningham
Meopham Station
Meopham
Luddesdown
KENT
Beddington
Addiscombe
CROYDON
West Wickham
Keston
Farnborough
Chelsfield
Eynsford
Fawkham Green
New Ash Green
Ash
WALLINGTON
Addington
New Addington
Green Street Green
Pratt's Bottom
Badgers Mount
Halstead
Shoreham
West Kingsdown
Knatts Valley
Ridley
Culverstone Green
Vigo Village
Stansted
Fairseat
Trottiscliffe
Snodland
Birling
Ryarsh
PURLEY
Sanderstead
Selsdon
Leaves Green
Downe
Farleigh
Berry's Green
Cudham
Knockholt
Knockholt Pound
Otford
Kemsing
Woodlands
Heaverham
Wrotham
Addington
Leybourne
Larkfield
COULSDON
Kenley
Whyteleafe
Old Coulsdon
Chelsham
Biggin Hill
Tatsfield
Chevening
Dunton Green
Chipstead
Riverhead
Seal
M26
Borough Green
Platt
Wrotham Heath
West Malling
Offham
Chaldon
WARLINGHAM
Woldingham
CATERHAM
CLACKET LANE
Titsey
Westerham
Brasted
Sundridge
Brasted Chart
SEVENOAKS
Ightham
Ivy Hatch
Stone Street
Plaxtol
Kings Hill
Mereworth
Wateringbury
Merstham
Godstone
Oxted
Limpsfield
Limpsfield Chart
French Street
The Chart
Ide Hill
Goathurst Common
Underriver
Dunk's Green
Shipbourne
West Peckham
REDHILL
Bletchingley
Tandridge
Hurst Green
Crockham Hill
Toy's Hill
Sevenoaks Weald
MAIN ROUTE 180
MAIN ROUTE 181
Hadlow
Nutfield
South Nutfield
M23
South Godstone
Pootings
Cooper's Corner
Four Elms
Fletcher's Green
Hildenborough
Marlpit Hill
Chiddingstone Causeway
Crowhurst
Crowhurst Lane End
Edenbridge
Bough Beech
Blindley Heath
Outwood
Leigh
Haysden
TONBRIDGE
Golden Green
East Peckham
Five Oak Green
Tudeley
Whetsted
Chiddingstone
Hever

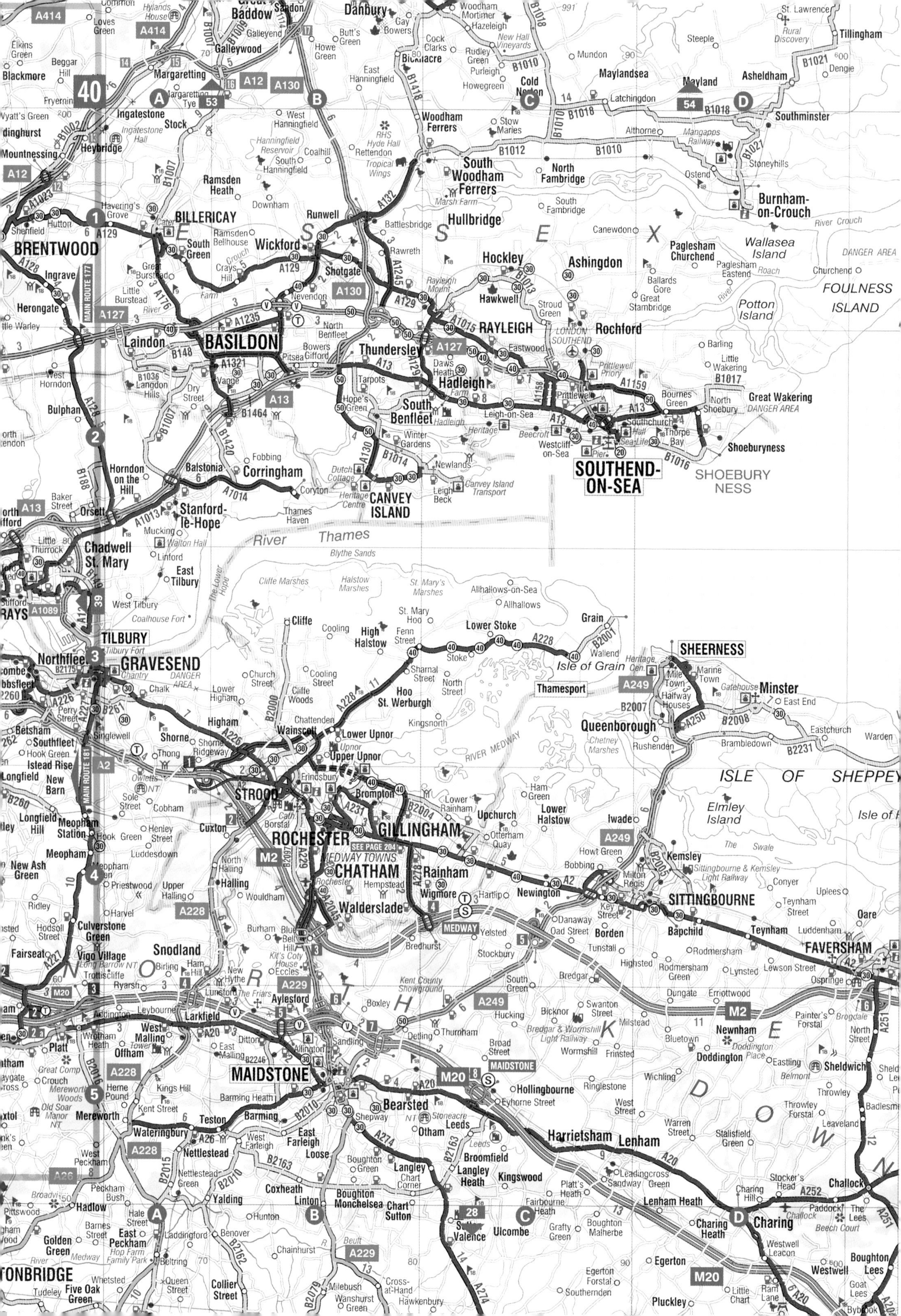
40
A414
Loves Green
Hylands House
Great Baddow
Sandon
Danbury
Woodham Mortimer
Hazeleigh
B1018
St. Lawrence
Rural Discovery
Tillingham
Elkins Green
Beggar Hill
Blackmore
Margaretting
Margaretting Tye
Galleywood
Galleyend
Butt's Green
Howe Green
Gay Bowers
Cock Clarks
Bicknacre
East Hanningfield
Rudley Green
Purleigh
Howegreen
New Hall Vineyards
B1010
Cold Norton
Mundon
Maylandsea
Steeple
Mayland
Asheldham
Dengie
B1021
A12
A130
53
54
Fryerning
Ingatestone
Ingatestone Hall
Stock
West Hanningfield
Woodham Ferrers
Stow Maries
Latchingdon
B1018
Southminster
Althorne
Mangapps Railway
Mountnessing
Heybridge
Hanningfield Reservoir
South Hanningfield
Coalhill
RHS Hyde Hall
Rettendon
Tropical Wings
South Woodham Ferrers
Marsh Farm
B1012
North Fambridge
Stoneyhills
Ostend
Burnham-on-Crouch
River Crouch
Ramsden Heath
Downham
Runwell
A132
Havering's Grove
Hutton
Shenfield
BRENTWOOD
A129
BILLERICAY
Ramsden Bellhouse
South Green
Wickford
Battlesbridge
Hullbridge
South Fambridge
Canewdon
Wallasea Island
DANGER AREA
Paglesham Churchend
Paglesham Eastend
Churchend
FOULNESS ISLAND
Potton Island
Ingrave
Herongate
Great Burstead
Crays Hill
Little Burstead
Rawreth
A1245
Shotgate
Nevendon
A130
Rayleigh Mount
Hockley
Hawkwell
Ashingdon
Ballards Gore
Great Stambridge
Stroud Green
B1013
A127
MAIN ROUTE 177
A1235
BASILDON
Laindon
Bowers Gifford
Pitsea
North Benfleet
Thundersley
A1015
RAYLEIGH
Eastwood
LONDON SOUTHEND
Rochford
Barling
Little Wakering
West Horndon
B148
A1321
Langdon Hills
Dry Street
Vange
A13
Tarpots
Hope's Green
Daws Heath
Hadleigh
Prittlewell Priory
A1159
B1017
Great Wakering
Bournes Green
North Shoebury
Bulphan
A128
B1464
B1007
South Benfleet
Hadleigh Farm
Leigh-on-Sea
Prittlewell
Southchurch
Thorpe Bay
Shoeburyness
Winter Gardens
Heritage
Beecroft
Westcliff-on-Sea
Sea Life
Pier
B1016
B1420
Fobbing
Corringham
Balstonia
Horndon on the Hill
B188
Dutch Cottage
B1014
Newlands
Canvey Island Transport
SOUTHEND-ON-SEA
SHOEBURY NESS
Baker Street
Orsett
A7014
Coryton
Leigh Beck
Heritage Centre
CANVEY ISLAND
A1013
Stanford-le-Hope
Thames Haven
A13
Mucking
Walton Hall
Little Thurrock
Chadwell St. Mary
River Thames
Blythe Sands
Linford
East Tilbury
The Lower Hope
Cliffe Marshes
Halstow Marshes
St. Mary's Marshes
Allhallows-on-Sea
Allhallows
39
West Tilbury
A1089
Coalhouse Fort
Cliffe
St. Mary Hoo
Cooling
High Halstow
Fenn Street
Lower Stoke
Grain
TILBURY
Tilbury Fort
A228
B2001
Stoke
Wallend
Isle of Grain
SHEERNESS
Heritage Cen.
Marine Town
Northfleet
GRAVESEND
Chantry
DANGER AREA
B2175
Church Street
Cooling Street
Sharnal Street
North Street
Thamesport
A249
Mile Town
Halfway Houses
Minster
Gatehouse
East End
Chalk
Lower Higham
Cliffe Woods
Hoo St. Werburgh
B2007
B2008
Queenborough
Chetney Marshes
Rushenden
Eastchurch
Brambledown
Warden
A226
B261
Perry Street
Betsham
Southfleet
Singlewell
Hook Green
Istead Rise
A2
MAIN ROUTE 181
Longfield
New Barn
B260
Higham
Shorne
Shorne Ridgeway
Thong
Owletts NT
Sole Street
Cobham
B2000
Chattenden
Wainscott
Lower Upnor
Upnor
Upper Upnor
Kingsnorth
RIVER MEDWAY
B2231
ISLE OF SHEPPEY
A250
Frindsbury
STROOD
Brompton
A231
B2004
Lower Rainham
Ham Green
Lower Halstow
Iwade
Elmley Island
Isle of
Longfield Hill
Meopham Station
Meopham
Henley Street
Cuxton
Luddesdown
Borstal
ROCHESTER
GILLINGHAM
SEE PAGE 204
MEDWAY TOWNS
Upchurch
Otterham Quay
The Swale
A249
Howt Green
Kemsley
Sittingbourne & Kemsley Light Railway
B2005
M2
New Ash Green
North Halling
Halling
A229
CHATHAM
Hempstead
A278
Rainham
Bobbing
Milton Regis
Conyer
Priestwood
Upper Halling
Wouldham
Rochester
Wigmore
Hartlip
Newington
A2
SITTINGBOURNE
Uplees
Teynham Street
Ridgley
Harvel
A2045
Walderslade
Danaway
Key Street
Oad Street
Borden
Bapchild
Teynham
Oare
Luddenham
Hodsoll Street
Culverstone Green
A228
Burham
Blue Bell Hill
MEDWAY
Yelsted
Bredhurst
Stockbury
Tunstall
Rodmersham
FAVERSHAM
Fairseat
Vigo Village
Long Barrow NT
Trottiscliffe
Snodland
Birling
Ham Hill
New Hythe
Kit's Coty House
Eccles
Highsted
Rodmersham Green
Lynsted
Lewson Street
Ospringe
Ryarsh
Lunsford
The Friars
Aylesford
Kent County Showground
South Green
Boxley
Bredgar
Dungate
Erriottwood
M20
Addington
Leybourne
Larkfield
A249
Hucking
Bicknor
Swanton Street
Bredgar & Wormshill Light Railway
Milstead
Painter's Forstal
Brogdale
Platt
Wrotham Heath
West Malling
Tower
Offham
A20
East Malling
Ditton
Allington
Sandling
Detling
Thurnham
Broad Street
Wormshill
Frinsted
Bluetown
Newnham
Doddington Place
North Street
A251
Great Comp
Crouch
Mereworth Woods
Old Soar Manor NT
Mereworth
B2016
A228
Herne Pound
Kings Hill
Kent Street
MAIDSTONE
B2246
Barming Heath
B2010
Bearsted
MAIDSTONE
Hollingbourne
Eyhorne Street
Ringlestone
Wichling
Doddington
Eastling
Belmont
Sheldwich
Throwley
Teston
Barming
Wateringbury
A26
Nettlestead
West Peckham
A228
East Farleigh
West Farleigh
Loose
Shepway
Stoneacre NT
Otham
Leeds
Leeds
A274
B2163
Broomfield
Harrietsham
Lenham
West Street
Warren Street
Stalisfield Green
Throwley Forstal
Leaveland
Badlesmere
Nettlestead Green
B2015
B2010
B2163
Boughton Green
Langley
Langley Heath
Chart Corner
Kingswood
Platt's Heath
Leadingcross Green
Sandway
Stocker's Head
Charing Hill
A252
Challock
A26
Peckham Bush
Hadlow
Broadwater
Pittswood
Hale Street
Barnes Street
East Peckham
Hop Farm Family Park
Yalding
Coxheath
Linton
Boughton Monchelsea
Chart Sutton
Hunton
Sutton Valence
Ulcombe
Fairbourne Heath
Grafty Green
Boughton Malherbe
Lenham Heath
Charing Heath
Charing
Paddock
The Lees
Beech Court
Golden Green
River Medway
Laddingford
Benover
B2162
Chainhurst
Beult
A229
Egerton
Westwell Leacon
Westwell
Boughton Lees
TONBRIDGE
Whetsted
Tudeley
Five Oak Green
Beltring
Queen Street
Collier Street
Milebush
Wanshurst Green
Cross-at-Hand
Hawkenbury
Egerton Forstal
Southernden
Pluckley
M20
Little Chart
Ram Lane
Goat Lees
Bybrook
B2079
A274
A20
Mill Street

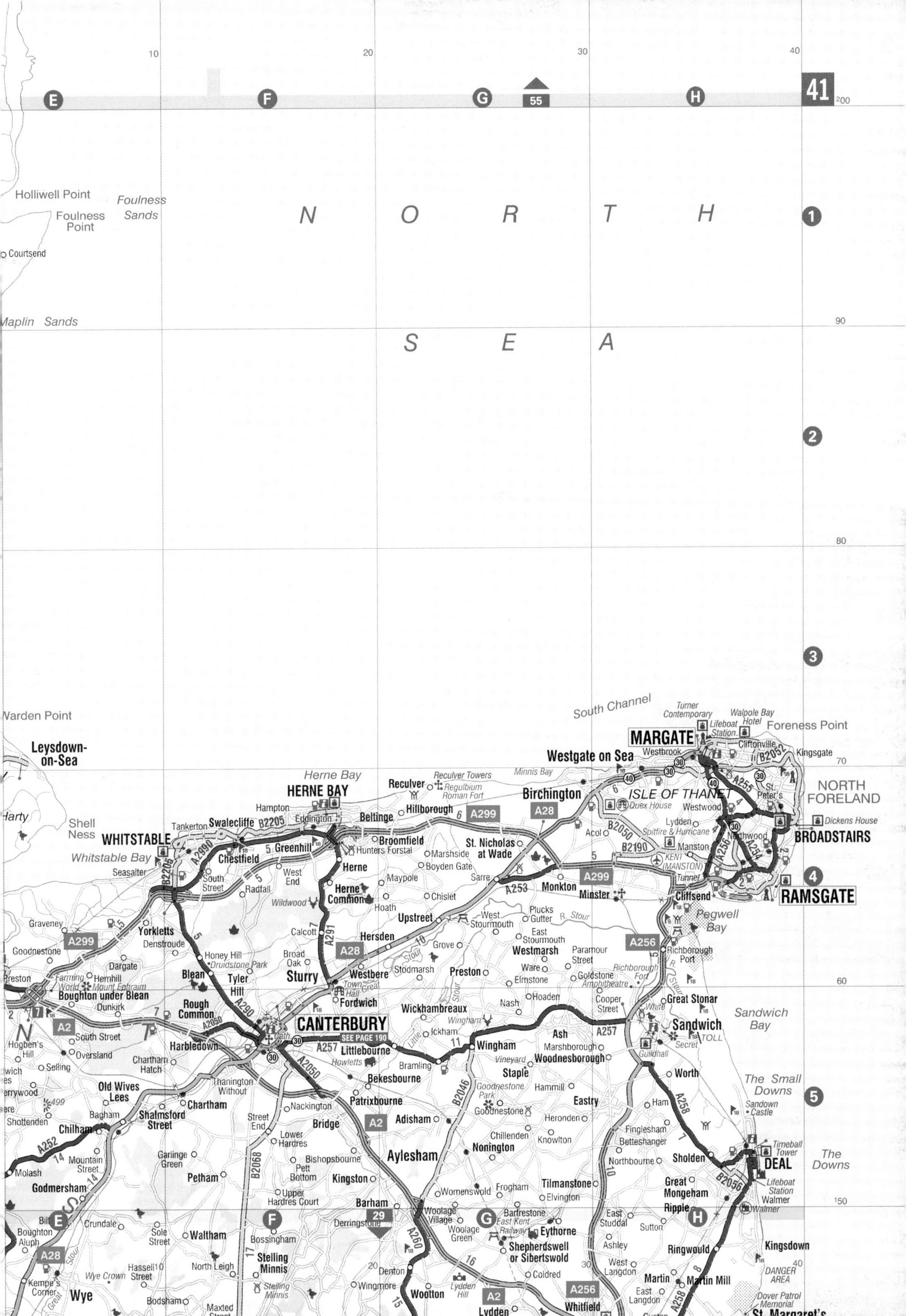

10
20
30
40
41
200
E
F
G
55
H
Holliwell Point
Foulness Sands
Foulness Point
Courtsend
N O R T H
S E A
Maplin Sands
90
1
2
80
3
Warden Point
Leysdown-on-Sea
Harty
Shell Ness
WHITSTABLE
Whitstable Bay
Seasalter
Tankerton
Swalecliffe
B2205
Chestfield
Greenhill
South Street
Radfall
West End
Herne Bay
HERNE BAY
Hampton
Eddington
Beltinge
Reculver
Reculver Towers
Regulbium Roman Fort
Hillborough
Broomfield
Hunters Forstal
Herne
Herne Common
Maypole
Hoath
Wildwood
Marshside
Boyden Gate
Chislet
St. Nicholas at Wade
Sarre
A299
A28
Birchington
Minnis Bay
Westgate on Sea
South Channel
MARGATE
Westbrook
Turner Contemporary
Lifeboat Station
Walpole Bay Hotel
Foreness Point
Cliftonville
B2052
Kingsgate
ISLE OF THANET
Quex House
Westwood
St. Peter's
NORTH FORELAND
A255
A254
A256
Acol
B2050
Lydden
Spitfire & Hurricane
Dickens House
BROADSTAIRS
Northwood
Manston
B2190
KENT (MANSTON)
Tunnel
Monkton
Minster
A253
Cliffsend
RAMSGATE
4
Pegwell Bay
Richborough Port
Plucks Gutter
R. Stour
West Stourmouth
East Stourmouth
Upstreet
Grove
Westmarsh
Paramour Street
Ware
Elmstone
Goldstone
Richborough Fort Amphitheatre
Graveney
Yorkletts
Denstroude
Goodnestone
Dargate
Calcott
Broad Oak
A291
Hersden
Stodmarsh
Preston
Westbere
Sturry
Honey Hill
Druidstone Park
Farming World
Hernhill
Mount Ephraim
Boughton under Blean
Dunkirk
Blean
Tyler Hill
Rough Common
A2050
A290
Fordwich
Town Hall
Great Stour
CANTERBURY
SEE PAGE 190
Wickhambreaux
Ickham
Wingham
Little Stour
Nash
Hoaden
Cooper Street
Ash
A257
Great Stonar
Sandwich
Sandwich Bay
Secret
TOLL
Guildhall
A2
South Street
Hogben's Hill
Oversland
Selling
Chartham Hatch
Harbledown
Littlebourne
Howletts
Bramling
Marshborough
Woodnesborough
Vineyard
Staple
Worth
Thanington Without
Bekesbourne
Old Wives Lees
Chartham
Patrixbourne
Nackington
Goodnestone Park
Hammill
Eastry
Ham
A258
The Small Downs
Sandown Castle
5
Bagham
Shalmsford Street
Street End
Bridge
Adisham
B2046
Heronden
Chilham
Shottenden
A252
Molash
Mountain Street
Godmersham
Garinge Green
Lower Hardres
Bishopsbourne
Pett Bottom
Kingston
Aylesham
Nonington
Chillenden
Knowlton
Finglesham
Betteshanger
Northbourne
Sholden
DEAL
Timeball Tower
The Downs
Lifeboat Station
Walmer
Petham
B2068
Upper Hardres Court
Barham
Womenswold
Frogham
Tilmanstone
Elvington
Great Mongeham
Ripple
B2056
150
Boughton Aluph
Crundale
Sole Street
Waltham
Bossingham
Derringstone
29
Woolage Village
Woolage Green
Barfrestone
East Kent Railway
Eythorne
East Studdal
Sutton
Ringwould
Kingsdown
A28
Kempe's Corner
Wye
Wye Crown
Hassell Street
North Leigh
Stelling Minnis
Denton
A260
Shepherdswell or Sibertswold
Coldred
Ashley
West Langdon
Martin
Martin Mill
DANGER AREA
Dover Patrol Memorial
Bodsham
Maxted Street
Wingmore
Wootton
Lydden Hill
Lydden
A256
Whitfield
East Langdon
St Margaret's

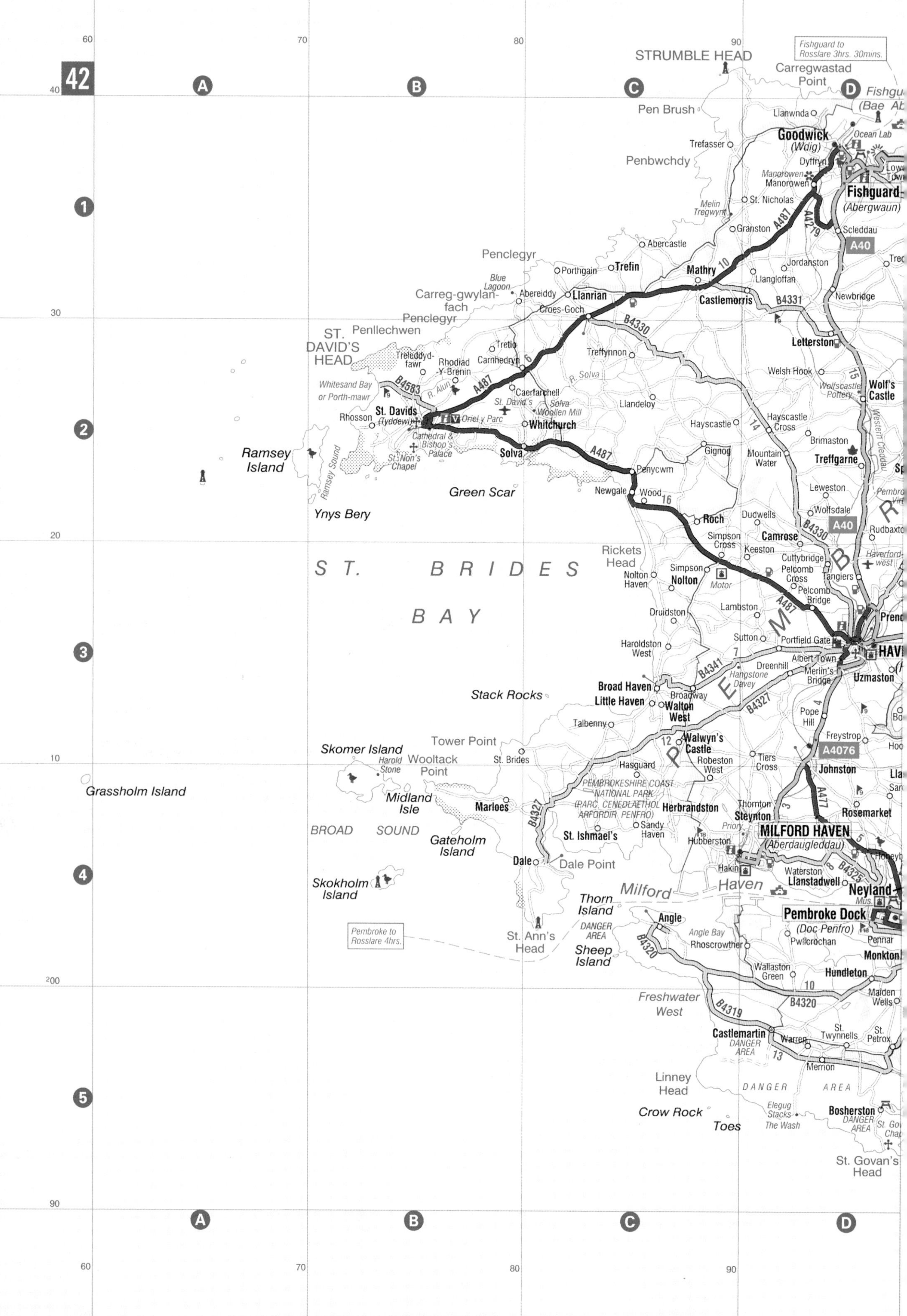
Fishguard to Rosslare 3hrs. 30mins.
STRUMBLE HEAD
Carregwastad Point
Fishguard (Bae Abergwaun)
Pen Brush
Llanwnda
Goodwick (Wdig)
Ocean Lab
Trefasser
Penbwchdy
Dyffryn
Manorowen
Fishguard (Abergwaun)
Lower Town
St. Nicholas
Melin Tregwynt
Granston
A487
A4219
Scleddau
A40
Abercastle
Penclegyr
Porthgain
Trefin
Mathry
Jordanston
Llangloffan
Blue Lagoon
Abereiddy
Llanrian
Castlemorris
B4331
Newbridge
Carreg-gwylan-fach
Croes-Goch
Penclegyr
ST. DAVID'S HEAD
Penllechwen
B4330
Letterston
Treffynnon
Tretio
Treleddyd-fawr
Rhodiad Y-Brenin
Carnhedryn
R. Solva
Welsh Hook
Whitesand Bay or Porth-mawr
B4583
R. Alun
A487
Caerfarchell
Wolfscastle Pottery
Wolf's Castle
Llandeloy
St. David's
Solva Woollen Mill
Rhosson
St. Davids (Tyddewi)
Oriel y Parc
Whitchurch
Hayscastle
Hayscastle Cross
Western Cleddau
Cathedral & Bishop's Palace
Brimaston
St. Non's Chapel
Solva
Gignog
Mountain Water
Treffgarne
Ramsey Island
Ramsey Sound
Penycwm
Leweston
Green Scar
Newgale
Wood
Wolfsdale
Ynys Bery
Roch
Dudwells
A40
Rudbaxton
Simpson Cross
Camrose
Keeston
Rickets Head
Cuttybridge
Haverfordwest
ST. BRIDES BAY
Simpson
Nolton Haven
Nolton
Motor
Pelcomb Cross
Tangiers
Pelcomb Bridge
Lambston
Druidston
Sutton
Portfield Gate
Haroldston West
HAVERFORDWEST
Dreenhill
Albert Town
Merlin's Bridge
B4341
Hangstone Davey
Uzmaston
Broad Haven
Stack Rocks
Broadway
Little Haven
Walton West
B4327
Pope Hill
Talbenny
PEMBROKE
Freystrop
Walwyn's Castle
Skomer Island
Tower Point
Harold Stone
Wooltack Point
St. Brides
Robeston West
Tiers Cross
A4076
Hasguard
Johnston
Grassholm Island
PEMBROKESHIRE COAST NATIONAL PARK (PARC CENEDLAETHOL ARFORDIR PENFRO)
Midland Isle
Marloes
B4327
Herbrandston
Thornton
Rosemarket
BROAD SOUND
St. Ishmael's
Sandy Haven
Steynton
Priory
MILFORD HAVEN (Aberdaugleddau)
A477
Gateholm Island
Hubberston
Dale
Dale Point
Hakin
Waterston
Llanstadwell
B4325
Neyland
Skokholm Island
Milford Haven
Thorn Island
Pembroke Dock (Doc Penfro)
Angle
DANGER AREA
Pembroke to Rosslare 4hrs.
St. Ann's Head
Angle Bay
Rhoscrowther
Pwllcrochan
Pennar
Sheep Island
B4320
Monkton
Wallaston Green
Hundleton
B4320
Freshwater West
B4319
Maiden Wells
Castlemartin
DANGER AREA
Warren
St. Twynnells
St. Petrox
Merrion
Linney Head
DANGER AREA
Crow Rock
Toes
Elegug Stacks
The Wash
Bosherston
St. Govan's Chapel
St. Govan's Head
A
B
C
D
1
2
3
4
5
60
70
80
90
40
30
20
10
200
90

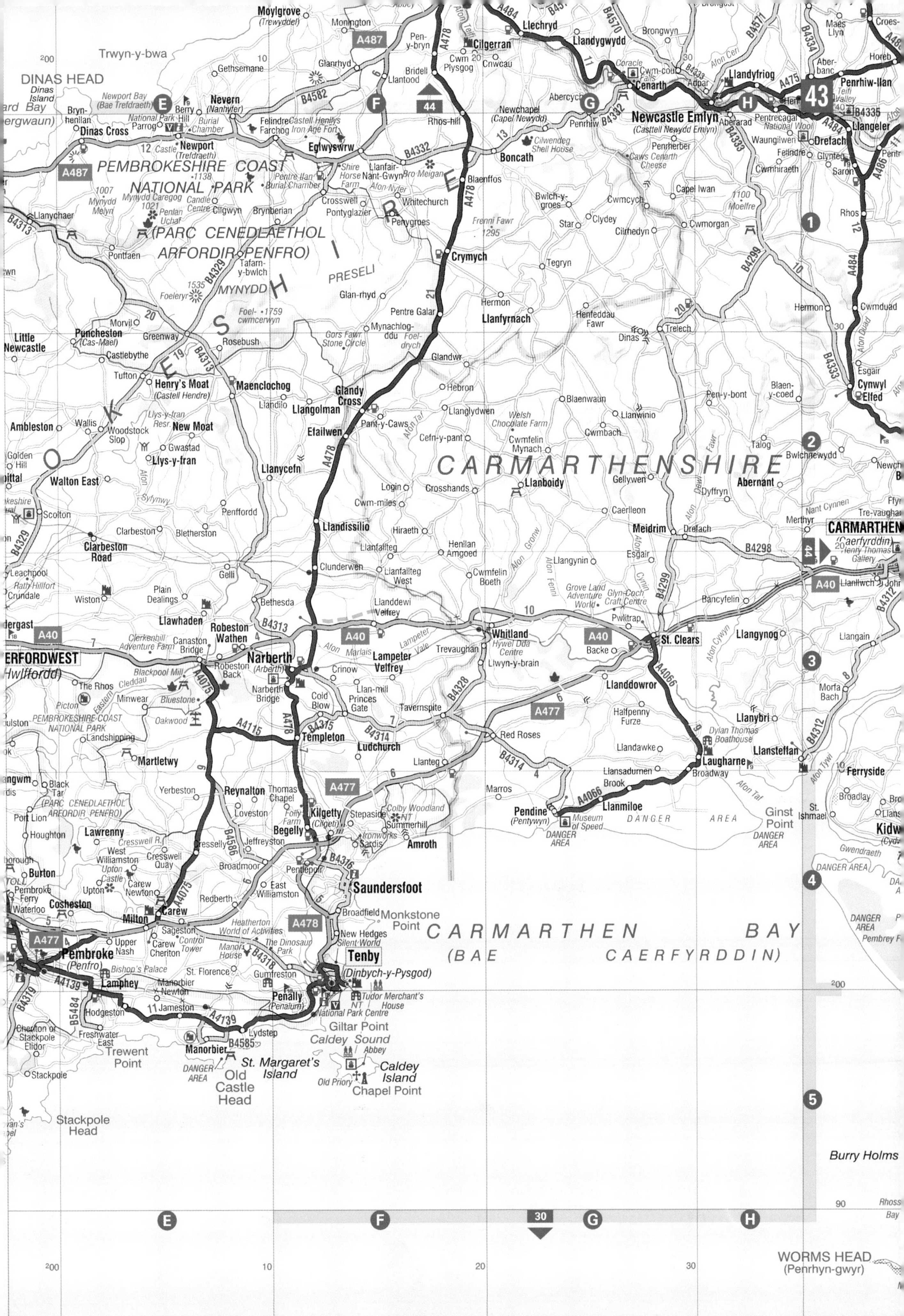

Moylgrove
(Trewyddel)
Monington
A487
Pen-y-bryn
A478
Cilgerran
Llechryd
Llandygwydd
Brongwyn
B4570
B4571
B4334
Maes Llyn
Cwm Plysgog
Cnwcau
Trwyn-y-bwa
Gethsemane
Glanrhyd
Bridell
Llantood
44
DINAS HEAD
Dinas Island
Newport Bay
(Bae Trefdraeth)
Nevern
(Nanhyfer)
Berry Hill
National Park
Burial Chamber
Parrog
Bryn-henllan
Dinas Cross
Newport
(Trefdraeth)
Castle
Felindre Farchog
Castell Henllys Iron Age Fort
Eglwyswrw
B4582
Rhos-hill
Newchapel
(Capel Newydd)
Abercych
Penrhiw
B4332
Coracle
Cwm-cou
Falls
Cenarth
Adpar
Llandyfriog
Newcastle Emlyn
(Castell Newydd Emlyn)
Aberarad
Pentrecagal
National Wool
Waungilwen
Drefach
Llangeler
Penrhiw-llan
Aber-banc
Horeb
Cres-
43
Teifi Valley
B4335
A484
A475
B4333
Cilwendeg Shell House
Boncath
Penrherber
Caws Cenarth Cheese
Felindre
Glynteg
Saron
Cwmhiraeth
A486
A487
PEMBROKESHIRE COAST
NATIONAL PARK
(PARC CENEDLAETHOL
ARFORDIR PENFRO)
1007
Mynydd Melyn
Mynydd Carregog
1021
Candle Centre
Cilgwyn
Penlan Uchaf
1138
Brynberian
Pentre Ifan Burial Chamber
Shire Horse Farm
Llanfair-Nant-Gwyn
Bro Meigan
Afon Nyfer
Crosswell
Pontyglazier
Whitechurch
Penygroes
Blaenffos
Bwlch-y-groes
Cwmcych
Capel Iwan
1100 Moelfre
Star
Clydey
Cilrhedyn
Cwmorgan
Rhos
Fenni Fawr
1295
B4313
Llanychaer
Pontfaen
B4329
Tafarn-y-bwlch
MYNYDD
PRESELI
Crymych
Tegryn
B4299
A484
1535
Foelcwmcerwyn
Foel-cwmcerwyn
• 1759
Glan-rhyd
Pentre Galar
21
Hermon
Llanfyrnach
Henfeddau Fawr
Dinas
Trelech
Hermon
Cwmduad
Afon Duad
Morvil
Little Newcastle
Puncheston
(Cas-Mael)
Greenway
Rosebush
Castlebythe
Gors Fawr Stone Circle
Mynachlog-ddu
Foel-drych
Glandwr
B4333
Esgair
Cynwyl Elfed
Tufton
Henry's Moat
(Castell Hendre)
Maenclochog
Llandilo
Llangolman
Glandy Cross
Hebron
Blaenwaun
Pen-y-bont
Blaen-y-coed
Llys-y-fran Resr.
Ambleston
Wallis
Woodstock Slop
New Moat
Efailwen
Pant-y-Caws
Llanglydwen
Welsh Chocolate Farm
Llanwinio
Cwmfelin Mynach
Cwmbach
Cefn-y-pant
Talog
Bwlchnewydd
Gwastad
Llys-y-fran
Golden Hill
Walton East
Llanycefn
A478
CARMARTHENSHIRE
Gellywen
Abernant
Login
Crosshands
Llanboidy
Dyffryn
Cwm-miles
Caerlleon
Nant Cynnen
Tre-vaughan
Scolton
Penffordd
Merthyr
Clarbeston
Bletherston
Llandissilio
Hiraeth
Meidrim
Drefach
CARMARTHEN
(Caerfyrddin)
Henry Thomas Gallery
Clarbeston Road
Llanfallteg
Henllan Amgoed
Esgair
B4298
Leachpool
Rath Hillfort
Crundale
Gelli
Clunderwen
Llanfallteg West
Cwmfelin Boeth
Llangynin
Afon Gronw
Afon Fenni
Grove Land Adventure World
Glyn-Coch Craft Centre
B4299
A40
Llanllwch
B4312
Wiston
Plain Dealings
Bethesda
Llanddewi Velfrey
Bancyfelin
Llawhaden
Robeston Wathen
B4313
10
Pwlltrap
A40
Clerkenhill Adventure Farm
Canaston Bridge
Lampeter Vale
Whitland
Hywel Dda Centre
Backe
St. Clears
Llangynog
Llangain
HAVERFORDWEST
(Hwlffordd)
Narberth
(Arberth)
Crinow
Lampeter Velfrey
Trevaughan
Llwyn-y-brain
Blackpool Mill
Robeston Back
Afon Marlais
The Rhos
Cleddau
Picton
Minwear
Bluestone
Narberth Bridge
Llan-mill
Princes Gate
Cold Blow
B4328
Tavernspite
Llanddowror
A4066
Morfa Bach
PEMBROKESHIRE COAST NATIONAL PARK
Oakwood
A4075
A4115
A478
B4315
Templeton
B4314
A477
Red Roses
Halfpenny Furze
Llanybri
Landshipping
Dylan Thomas Boathouse
Ludchurch
Llandawke
Laugharne
Broadway
Llansteffan
Martletwy
Llanteg
B4314
Llansadurnen
Brook
Ferryside
Black Tar
Yerbeston
Reynalton
Thomas Chapel
A477
Marros
Afon Taf
Broadlay
(PARC CENEDLAETHOL ARFORDIR PENFRO)
Loveston
Folly Farm
Kilgetty
(Cilgeti)
Stepaside
Colby Woodland
NT
Summerhill
Pendine
(Pentywyn)
Museum of Speed
A4066
Llanmiloe
DANGER AREA
Ginst Point
St. Ishmael
Kidw
Port Lion
Houghton
Lawrenny
Cresswell R.
West Williamston
Cresswell Quay
Begelly
Jeffreyston
Cresselly
B4586
Ironworks
Sardis
Amroth
DANGER AREA
Gwendraeth
Burton
Upton Castle
Carew Newton
Broadmoor
Pentlepoir
B4316
Saundersfoot
DANGER AREA
Pembroke Ferry
Waterloo
Cosheston
Upton
Milton
Carew
A4075
Redberth
East Williamston
A478
Broadfield
Monkstone Point
DANGER AREA
Pembrey
A477
Pembroke
(Penfro)
Upper Nash
Carew Cheriton
Sageston
Control Tower
Heatherton World of Activities
The Dinosaur Park
New Hedges
Silent World
Tenby
(Dinbych-y-Pysgod)
CARMARTHEN BAY
(BAE CAERFYRDDIN)
Bishop's Palace
Manor House
B4318
St. Florence
Gumfreston
Lamphey
Manorbier Newton
A4139
Jameston
A4139
Penally
(Penalum)
Tudor Merchant's House
NT
National Park Centre
B4319
B5484
Hodgeston
Freshwater East
Lydstep
Giltar Point
Caldey Sound
Abbey
Cheriton or Stackpole Elidor
Trewent Point
Manorbier
B4585
DANGER AREA
St. Margaret's Island
Old Castle Head
Caldey Island
Old Priory
Chapel Point
Stackpole
Stackpole Head
Burry Holms
Rhossili Bay
WORMS HEAD
(Penrhyn-gwyr)
E
F
G
H
30
1
2
3
4
5
200
10
20
30
90

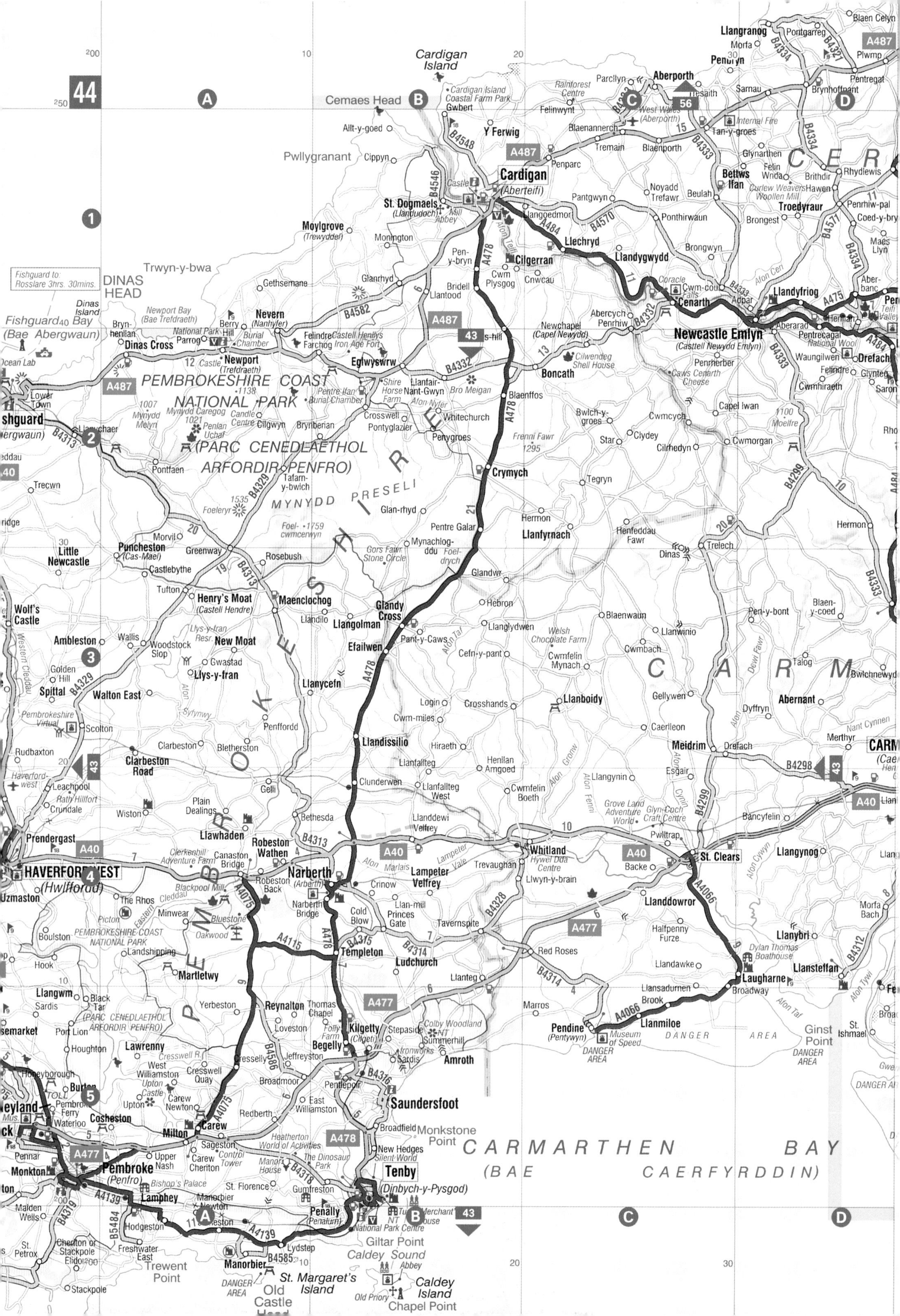
44
A
B
C
D
1
2
3
4
5
Cardigan Island
Cemaes Head
Cardigan Island Coastal Farm Park
Gwbert
Y Ferwig
Rainforest Centre
Felinwynt
Parcllyn
Aberporth
West Wales (Aberporth)
Tresaith
56
Blaenannerch
Sarnau
Llangranog
Morfa
Penbryn
Pontgarreg
Blaen Celyn
Plwmp
Pentregat
Brynhoffnant
A487
Internal Fire
Tan-y-groes
Glynarthen
Felin Wnda
Brithdir
Rhydlewis
Curlew Weavers Woollen Mill
Hawen
Troedyraur
Penrhiw-pal
Coed-y-bryn
Maes Llyn
Aber-banc
CER
Alt-y-goed
Pwllygranant
Cippyn
Tremain
Blaenporth
Penparc
Cardigan
(Aberteifi)
Castle
St. Dogmaels
(Llandudoch)
Mill
Abbey
Pantgwyn
Noyadd Trefawr
Beulah
Bettws Ifan
Brongest
Llangoedmor
Ponthirwaun
Llechryd
Llandygwydd
Brongwyn
Moylgrove
(Trewyddel)
Monington
Pen-y-bryn
Cilgerran
Cwm Plysgog
Cnwcau
Glanrhyd
Bridell
Llantood
Coracle
Cwm-cou
Falls
Cenarth
Adpar
Llandyfriog
Henllan
Teifi Valley
Aberarad
Newcastle Emlyn
(Castell Newydd Emlyn)
Pentrecagal
National Wool
Drefach
Trwyn-y-bwa
Fishguard to: Rosslare 3hrs. 30mins.
DINAS HEAD
Dinas Island
Fishguard Bay
(Bae Abergwaun)
Newport Bay
(Bae Trefdraeth)
Gethsemane
Nevern
(Nanhyfer)
Berry Hill
Bryn-henllan
Dinas Cross
National Park
Parrog
Burial Chamber
Felindre Farchog
Castell Henllys Iron Age Fort
Eglwyswrw
Newport
(Trefdraeth)
Castle
Abercych
Penrhiw
Newchapel
(Capel Newydd)
Cilwendeg Shell House
Boncath
Penrherber
Caws Cenarth Cheese
Waungilwen
Felindre
Glynteg
Cwmhiraeth
Saron
Ocean Lab
Lower Town
Fishguard
(Abergwaun)
A487
PEMBROKESHIRE COAST
NATIONAL PARK
(PARC CENEDLAETHOL
ARFORDIR PENFRO)
1007 Mynydd Melyn
Mynydd Carregog
1021
Penlan Uchaf
Candle Centre
Cilgwyn
Brynberian
Pentre Ifan Burial Chamber
Shire Horse Farm
Llanfair-Nant-Gwyn
Bro Meigan
Afon Nyfer
Crosswell
Pontyglazier
Whitechurch
Penygroes
Blaenffos
Bwlch-y-groes
Cwmcych
Capel Iwan
1100 Moelfre
Llanychaer
Star
Clydey
Cilrhedyn
Cwmorgan
Frenni Fawr 1295
Pontfaen
Tafarn-y-bwlch
Crymych
Tegryn
Trecwn
MYNYDD PRESELI
1535 Foeleryr
Glan-rhyd
Foel-cwmcerwyn 1759
Pentre Galar
Hermon
Llanfyrnach
Henfeddau Fawr
Hermon
Little Newcastle
Puncheston
(Cas-Mael)
Morvil
Greenway
Mynachlog-ddu
Foel-drych
Gors Fawr Stone Circle
Dinas
Trelech
Castlebythe
Rosebush
Glandwr
Tufton
Henry's Moat
(Castell Hendre)
Maenclochog
Hebron
Blaen-y-coed
Pen-y-bont
Wolf's Castle
Llandilo
Llangolman
Glandy Cross
Blaenwaun
Llanglydwen
Welsh Chocolate Farm
Llanwinio
Ambleston
Wallis
Woodstock Slop
Llys-y-fran Resr.
New Moat
Pant-y-Caws
Efailwen
Cefn-y-pant
Cwmbach
Cwmfelin Mynach
Talog
Bwlchnewydd
Golden Hill
Spittal
Gwastad
Llys-y-fran
Walton East
Llanycefn
C A R M
Western Cleddau
Login
Crosshands
Llanboidy
Gellywen
Abernant
Pembrokeshire Virtual
Scolton
Penffordd
Cwm-miles
Dyffryn
Caerlleon
Nant Cynnen
Merthyr
Rudbaxton
Clarbeston
Bletherston
Llandissilio
Hiraeth
Meidrim
Drefach
CARM
Clarbeston Road
Llanfallteg
Henllan Amgoed
Esgair
B4298
Haverfordwest
Leachpool
Rath Hillfort
Crundale
Gelli
Clunderwen
Llanfallteg West
Cwmfelin Boeth
Llangynin
Grove Land Adventure World
Glyn-Coch Craft Centre
Wiston
Plain Dealings
Bethesda
Llanddewi Velfrey
Bancyfelin
A40
Prendergast
Llawhaden
Robeston Wathen
Pwlltrap
Whitland
Hywel Dda Centre
St. Clears
Llangynog
HAVERFORDWEST
(Hwlffordd)
Clerkenhill Adventure Farm
Canaston Bridge
Narberth
(Arberth)
Lampeter Velfrey
Trevaughan
Llwyn-y-brain
Backe
Uzmaston
The Rhos
Blackpool Mill
Robeston Back
Crinow
Llanddowror
Picton
Minwear
Bluestone
Narberth Bridge
Cold Blow
Llan-mill
Princes Gate
Boulston
PEMBROKESHIRE COAST NATIONAL PARK
Oakwood
Tavernspite
A477
Halfpenny Furze
Llanybri
Morfa Bach
Landshipping
A4115
Templeton
Red Roses
Dylan Thomas Boathouse
Hook
Martletwy
Ludchurch
Llandawke
Laugharne
Llansteffan
Llanteg
Llansadurnen
Broadway
Llangwm
Black Tar
Sardis
Yerbeston
Reynalton
Thomas Chapel
Brook
Marros
Llanmiloe
Pendine
(Pentywyn)
Museum of Speed
DANGER AREA
Ginst Point
St. Ishmael
(PARC CENEDLAETHOL ARFORDIR PENFRO)
Port Lion
Loveston
Folly Farm
Kilgetty
(Cilgeti)
Stepaside
Colby Woodland
NT
Summerhill
Houghton
Lawrenny
Cresswell R.
Begelly
Jeffreyston
Ironworks
Sardis
Amroth
Honeyborough
West Williamston
Cresswell Quay
Burton
Upton Castle
Broadmoor
Pentlepoir
Saundersfoot
Neyland
Pembroke Ferry
Waterloo
Carew Newton
Upton
Redberth
East Williamston
Cosheston
Carew
Milton
Broadfield
Monkstone Point
Heatherton World of Activities
Sageston
Carew Cheriton
Control Tower
The Dinosaur Park
New Hedges
Silent World
CARMARTHEN BAY
(BAE CAERFYRDDIN)
Pennar
Upper Nash
Manor House
Tenby
(Dinbych-y-Pysgod)
Monkton
Pembroke
(Penfro)
St. Florence
Gumfreston
Bishop's Palace
Lamphey
Manorbier Newton
Penally
(Penalun)
Tudor Merchant's House
National Park Centre
Jameston
Hodgeston
Malden Wells
Gilter Point
Caldey Sound
Lydstep
Freshwater East
Cheriton or Stackpole Elidor
St. Petrox
Manorbier
Trewent Point
St. Margaret's Island
Abbey
Caldey Island
Old Priory
Chapel Point
Old Castle Head
Stackpole
43
DANGER AREA

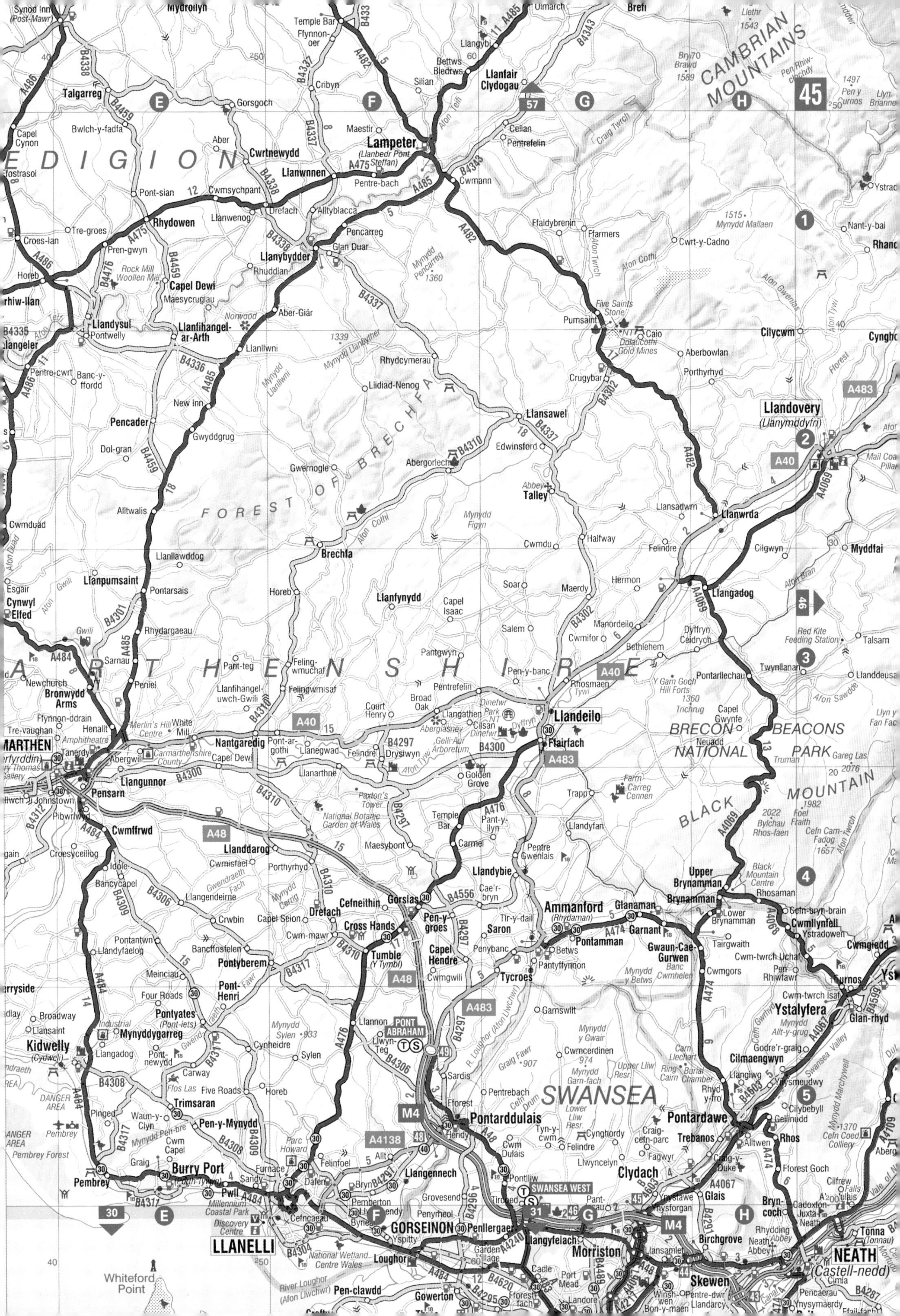
45
CAMBRIAN MOUNTAINS
CEREDIGION
FOREST OF BRECHFA
CARMARTHENSHIRE
BRECON BEACONS NATIONAL PARK
BLACK MOUNTAIN
SWANSEA
Synod Inn (Post-Mawr)
Mydroilyn
Temple Bar
Ffynnon-oer
Ulmarch
Llangybi
Betws Bledrws
Silian
Llanfair Clydogau
Llethr 1543
Bryn Brawd 1589
Pen Rhiw-ciochdy
1497 Pen y Cumos
Llyn Brianne
Talgarreg
Bwlch-y-fadfa
Gorsgoch
Cribyn
Maestir
Lampeter (Llanbedr Pont Steffan)
Cellan
Pentrefelin
Craig Twrch
Capel Cynon
Aber
Cwrtnewydd
Llanwnnen
Pentre-bach
Cwmann
Afon Teifi
Pont-sian
Cwmsychpant
Drefach
Alltyblacca
Rhydowen
Llanwenog
Pencarreg
Tre-groes
Croes-lan
Pren-gwyn
Llanybydder
Glan Duar
Rhuddlan
Rock Mill Woollen Mill
Capel Dewi
Maesycrugiau
Horeb
Rhiw-llan
Llandysul
Pontwelly
Llangeler
Norwood
Llanfihangel-ar-Arth
Aber-Giâr
Llanllwni
Mynydd Llanybyther
Mynydd Pencarreg 1360
Mynydd Llanllwni
1339
Ffaldybrenin
Ffarmers
Cwrt-y-Cadno
Afon Cothi
Afon Twrch
1515 Mynydd Mallaen
Nant-y-bai
Rhandirmwyn
Afon Gwenlais
Five Saints Stone
Pumsaint
NT Dolaucothi Gold Mines
Caio
Aberbowlan
Cilycwm
Afon Tywi
Porthyrhyd
Crugybar
Rhydcymerau
Llidiad-Nenog
Pentre-cwrt
Banc-y-ffordd
New Inn
Pencader
Gwyddgrug
Dol-gran
Llansawel
Edwinsford
Abergorlech
Gwernogle
Abbey
Talley
Mynydd Figyn
Llandovery (Llanymddyfri)
Mail Coach Pillar
Llansadwrn
Llanwrda
Cwmdu
Halfway
Felindre
Cilgwyn
Myddfai
Hermon
Llangadog
Alltwalis
Cwmduad
Brechfa
Afon Cothi
Llanllawddog
Esgair
Afon Gwili
Llanpumsaint
Pontarsais
Horeb
Cynwyl Elfed
Llanfynydd
Capel Isaac
Soar
Maerdy
Manordeilo
Dyffryn Ceidrych
Red Kite Feeding Station
Talsarn
Rhydargaeau
Gwili
Salem
Cwmifor
Bethlehem
Pantgwyn
Twynllanan
Llanddeusant
Sarnau
Pant-teg
Feling-wmuchaf
Felingwmisaf
Newchurch
Bronwydd Arms
Peniel
Llanfihangel-uwch-Gwili
Pentrefelin
Pen-y-banc
Rhosmaen
Y Garn Goch Hill Forts 1360
Trichrug
Capel Gwynfe
Pontarllechau
Afon Sawdde
Llyn y Fan Fach
Ffynnon-ddrain
Tre-vaughan
Henallt
Merlin's Hill Centre
White Mill
Court Henry
Broad Oak
Llangathen
Aberglasney
Dinefwr Park NT
Cilsan
Dinefwr
Dryslwyn
Llandeilo
Ffairfach
Neuadd
Truman
Gareg Las 2076
Carmarthen (Caerfyrddin)
Amphitheatre
Tanerdy
Abergwili
Carmarthenshire County
Capel Dewi
Nantgaredig
Pont-ar-gothi
Llanegwad
Felindre
Gelli Aur Arboretum
Afon Tywi
Llangunnor
Llanarthne
Golden Grove
Farm Carreg Cennen
Trapp
Pensarn
Johnstown
Paxton's Tower
National Botanic Garden of Wales
Temple Bar
Pant-y-llyn
Llandyfan
2022 Bylchau Rhos-faen
1982 Foel Fraith
Cefn Cam-Fadog 1657
Afon Twrch
Pibwrlwyd
Cwmffrwd
Llanddarog
Carmel
Maesybont
Pentre Gwenlais
Black Mountain Centre
Croesyceiliog
Cwmisfael
Porthyrhyd
Gwendraeth Fach
Mynydd Cerrig
Llandybie
Upper Brynamman
Brynamman
Rhosaman
Idole
Bancycapel
Llangendeirne
Drefach
Cefneithin
Gorslas
Cae'r-bryn
Crwbin
Capel Seion
Cross Hands
Pen-y-groes
Tir-y-dail
Saron
Ammanford (Rhydaman)
Glanaman
Garnant
Lower Brynamman
Cefn-bryn-brain
Cwmllynfell
Ystradowen
Cwmgiedd
Pontantwn
Llandyfaelog
Bancffosfelen
Cwm-mawr
Pontyberem
Tumble (Y Tymbl)
Capel Hendre
Cwmgwili
Betws
Pontamman
Pantyffynnon
Gwaun-Cae-Gurwen
Banc Cwmhelen
Mynydd y Betws
Tairgwaith
Cwm-twrch Uchaf
Pen Rhiwfawr
Cwmgors
Meinciau
Pont-Henri
Four Roads
Pontyates (Pont-iets)
Tycroes
Garnswllt
Cwm-twrch Isaf
Ystalyfera
Glan-rhyd
Abercraf
Broadway
Llansaint
Kidwelly (Cydweli)
Industrial Mynyddygarreg
Llangadog
Pont-newydd
Mynydd Sylen 933
Sylen
Cynheidre
Llannon
Pont Abraham
Llwyn-Teg
Mynydd y Gwair
Cwmcerdinen 974
Mynydd Garn-fach
Upper Lliw Resr
Carn Llechart
Ring Cairn
Burial Chamber
Rhyd-y-fro
Godre'r-graig
Cilmaengwyn
Llangiwg
Ynysmeudwy
Swansea Valley
Mynydd Marchywel
Cilybebyll
Gellinudd
Carway
Ffos Las
Five Roads
Horeb
Sardis
Graig Fawr 907
Pentrebach
Cefn Drum
Lower Lliw Resr
Pontardawe
Trebanos
Alltwen
Rhos
1370 Cefn Coed Colliery
Aberdulais
DANGER AREA
Pinged
Trimsaran
Waun-y-Clyn
Mynydd Pen-bre
Pen-y-Mynydd
Cwm Capel
Parc Howard
Fforest
Pontarddulais
Hendy
Tyn-y-cwm
Cwmdulais
Felindre
Cynghordy
Craig-cefn-parc
Fagwyr
Craig-y-Duke
Fforest Goch
Cilfrew
Aberdulais Falls
Pembrey
Pembrey Forest
Graig
Burry Port (Porth Tywyn)
Pwll
Sandy
Furnace
Felinfoel
Dafen
Allt
Bryn
Llangennech
Llwyncelyn
Clydach
Pontlliw
SWANSEA WEST
Tircoed
Pant-lasau
Ynystawe
Glais
Ynysforgan
Bryn-coch
Cadoxton-Juxta-Neath
Millennium Coastal Park
Discovery Centre
LLANELLI
Cefncaeau
Pemberton
Llwynhendy
Bynea
Penyrheol
Grovesend
GORSEINON
Penllergaer
Llangyfelach
Morriston
Birchgrove
Rhydding
Neath Abbey
Tonna (Tonnau)
NEATH (Castell-nedd)
National Wetland Centre Wales
Loughor
Ysgitty
Garden Village
Llansamlet
Skewen
Whiteford Point
River Loughor (Afon Llwchwr)
Pen-clawdd
Gowerton
Cadle
Port Mead
Fforestfach
Landore
Winsh-wen
Bon-y-maen
Pentre-dwr
Llandarcy
Cimla
Pencaerau
Ynysymaerdy
A486
A475
A485
A482
A483
A40
A4069
A484
A48
A476
A474
A4067
A4068
A4109
A4138
A4240
M4
B4459
B4338
B4337
B4343
B4476
B4335
B4336
B4302
B4310
B4301
B4300
B4297
B4312
B4309
B4306
B4317
B4308
B4556
B4306
B4297
B4296
B4603
B4291
B4599
46
30

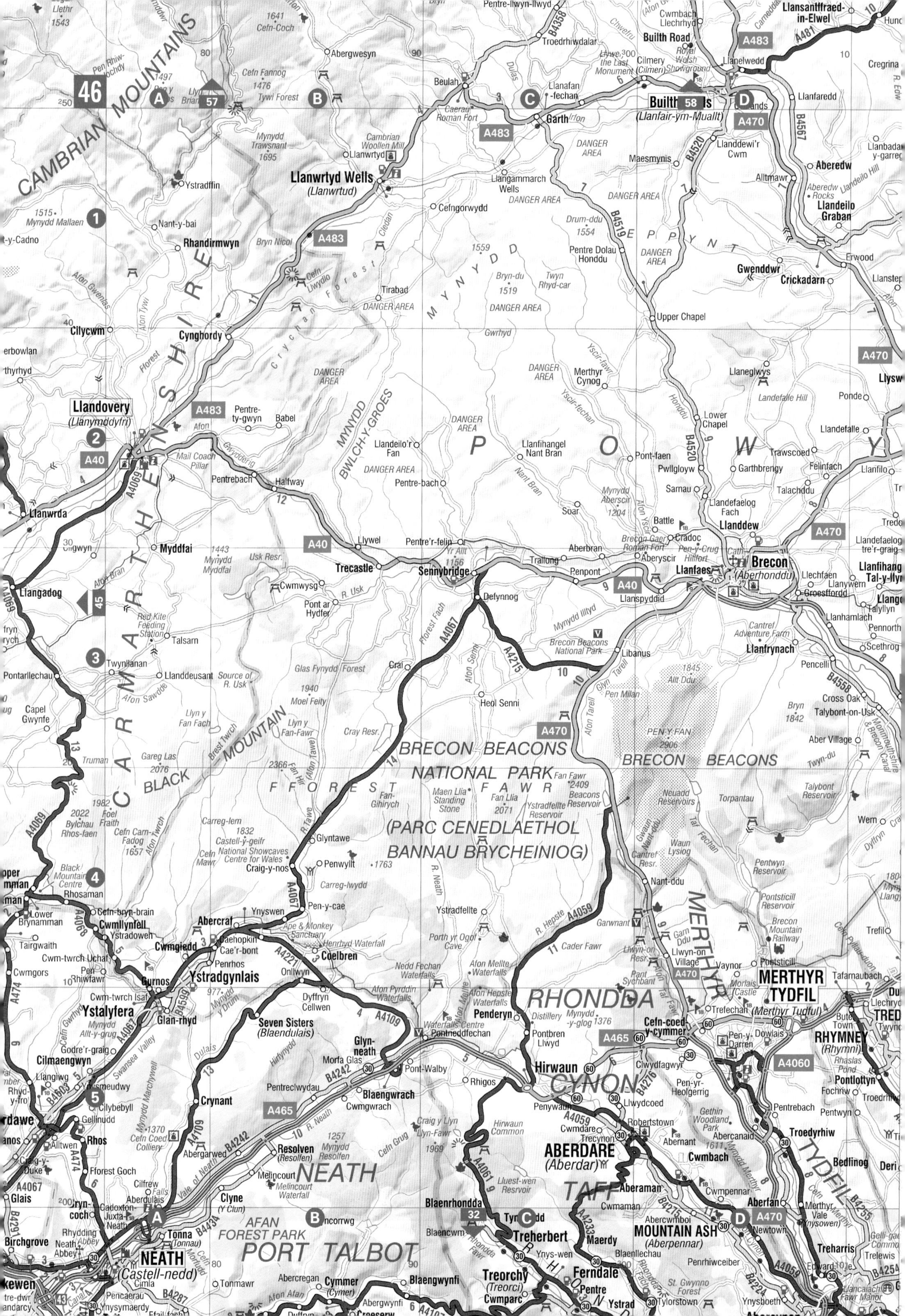

46
CAMBRIAN MOUNTAINS
Llethr
1543
1641
Cefn-Coch
Pen Rhiw-wchdy
1497
Pen y Garn
Llyn Brianne
57
Cefn Fannog
1476
Tywi Forest
Abergwesyn
Pentre-llwyn-llwyd
B4358
Troedrhiwdalar
Chwefru
Cwmbach Llechrhyd
Builth Road
Royal Welsh Showground
Llansantffraed-in-Elwel
A483
A481
Llyn-y-the Last Monument (Cilmeri)
Cilmery
Beulah
Caerau Roman Fort
Llanafan-fechan
Garth
Builth Wells
58
(Llanfair-ym-Muallt)
Llanelwedd
Llanfaredd
Cregrina
A470
B4567
B4520
Llanddewi'r Cwm
Maesmynis
Aberedw
Llanbadarn-y-garreg
Aberedw Rocks
Alltmawr
Llandeilo Graban
Llandeilo Hill
Erwood
Llanstephan
Mynydd Trawsnant
1695
Cambrian Woollen Mill
Llanwrtyd
Llanwrtyd Wells
(Llanwrtud)
Llangammarch Wells
DANGER AREA
Cefngorwydd
Ystradffin
1515
Mynydd Mallaen
Nant-y-bai
Rhandirmwyn
Bryn Nicol
A483
Cefn Llwydlo
Crychan Forest
Tirabad
Drum-ddu
1554
B4519
E P P Y N T
Pentre Dolau Honddu
Gwenddwr
Crickadarn
1559
MYNYDD
Bryn-du
1519
Twyn Rhyd-car
Afon Gwenlas
Afon Tywi
Cilycwm
Cynghordy
Upper Chapel
Gwrhyd
Yscir-fawr
Merthyr Cynog
Yscir-fechan
Llaneglwys
Landefalle Hill
Ponde
A470
Llandovery
(Llanymddyfri)
A483
Pentre-ty-gwyn
Babel
MYNYDD BWLCH-Y-GROES
Honddu
Lower Chapel
Llandefalle
A40
Mail Coach Pillar
Gwydderig
Llandeilo'r Fan
P O W Y S
Llanfihangel Nant Bran
Nant Bran
Pont-faen
Pwllgloyw
Garthbrengy
Trawscoed
Felinfach
Llanfilo
Talachddu
Pentrebach
Halfway
Pentre-bach
Sarnau
Mynydd Aberscir
1204
Soar
Llandefaelog Fach
Battle
Llanddew
A470
A4069
Llanwrda
Myddfai
1443
Mynydd Myddfai
Usk Resr.
A40
Llywel
Trecastle
Pentre'r-felin
Yr Allt
1156
Sennybridge
Aberbran
Trallong
Penpont
Brecon Gaer Roman Fort
Aberyscir
Pen-y-Crug Hillfort
Llanfaes
Brecon
(Aberhonddu)
Llechfaen
Llanywern
Llanfihangel Tal-y-llyn
Groesffordd
Llangadog
45
Cwmwysg
Pont ar Hydfer
R. Usk
Defynnog
A40
Llanspyddid
Mynydd Illtyd
Llanhamlach
Red Kite Feeding Station
Talsarn
Forest Fach
A4067
Brecon Beacons National Park
Libanus
Cantref Adventure Farm
Llanfrynach
Scethrog
Twynllanan
Llanddeusant
Source of R. Usk
Glas Fynydd Forest
Crai
A4215
Afon Senni
Afon Tarell
1845
Allt Ddu
Pencelli
Pontarllechau
Afon Sawdde
1940
Moel Feity
Heol Senni
Glyn Tarell
Pen Milan
B4558
Cross Oak
Talybont-on-Usk
Bryn
1842
Capel Gwynfe
Llyn y Fan Fach
Llyn y Fan-Fawr
Cray Resr.
A470
PEN Y FAN
2906
Aber Village
Monmouthshire & Brecon Canal
Truman
Garreg Las
2076
BLACK MOUNTAIN
Brest Twrch
BRECON BEACONS
NATIONAL PARK
BRECON BEACONS
Twyn-du
2366
Fan Hir
Afon Tawe
FFOREST FAWR
Fan Fawr
2409
Beacons Reservoir
Neuadd Reservoirs
Talybont Reservoir
Fan-Gihirych
Maen Llia Standing Stone
Fan Llia
2071
Ystradfellte Reservoir
Torpantau
1982
Foel Fraith
2022
Bylchau Rhos-faen
Cefn Carn-Fadog
1657
Carreg-lem
1832
Castell-y-geifr
National Showcaves Centre for Wales
Cefn Mawr
(PARC CENEDLAETHOL BANNAU BRYCHEINIOG)
Glyntawe
Penwyllt
1763
Craig-y-nos
Gwaun Nant-ddu
Taf Fechan
Waun Lysiog
Cantref Resr.
Pentwyn Reservoir
Black Mountain Centre
A4069
Rhosaman
A4067
Carreg-lwydd
R. Neath
Nant-ddu
MERTHYR
Pontsticill Reservoir
Brecon Mountain Railway
Lower Brynamman
A4068
Cefn-bryn-brain
Cwmllynfell
Ystradowen
Abercraf
Ynyswen
Pen-y-cae
Ape & Monkey Sanctuary
Ystradfellte
R. Hepste
A4059
Garwnant
Garn Ddu
Llwyn-on Resr.
Llwyn-on Village
Trefil
Tairgwaith
Cwm-twrch Uchaf
Cwmgiedd
Caehopkin
Cae'r-bont
Henrhyd Waterfall
Coelbren
Porth yr Ogof Cave
Cader Fawr
Vaynor
Pontsticill
Cwmgors
Pen Rhiwfawr
Gurnos
Penrhos
Ystradgynlais
A4221
Onllwyn
Nedd Fechan Waterfalls
Afon Mellte Waterfalls
Pant Sychbant
A470
Morlais Castle
MERTHYR TYDFIL
Tafarnaubach
Cwm-twrch Isaf
977
Mynydd y Drum
Dyffryn Cellwen
Afon Pyrddin Waterfalls
Afon Hepste Waterfalls
RHONDDA
Distillery
Mynydd-y-glog
1376
Trefechan
(Merthyr Tudful)
Ystalyfera
B4599
Glan-rhyd
Seven Sisters
(Blaendulais)
A4109
Waterfalls Centre
Pontneddfechan
Penderyn
Pontbren Llwyd
A465
Cefn-coed-y-cymmer
Pen-y-Darren
Dowlais
RHYMNEY
(Rhymni)
Mynydd Allt-y-grug
Cefn Gwrhyd
Godre'r-graig
Cilmaengwyn
Swansea Valley
Dulais
Hirfynydd
Glyn-neath
Morfa Glas
B4242
Pont-Walby
Hirwaun
CYNON
Clwydfagwyr
A4060
Rhaslas Pond
Pontlottyn
Llangiwg
Ynysmeudwy
Mynydd Marchywel
Pentreclwydau
Blaengwrach
Cwmgwrach
Rhigos
Penywaun
Pen-yr-Heolgerrig
Fochriw
Troedrhiw
Pentrebach
Pentwyn
Clydach
Clebybell
Gellinudd
Crynant
A465
R. Neath
Llwydcoed
Gethin Woodland Park
Robertstown
Cwmdare
Trecynon
Abernant
Abercanaid
Troedyrhiw
Rhos
Alltwen
1370
Cefn Coed Colliery
A4109
Abergarwed
Resolven
(Resolfen)
1257
Mynydd Resolfen
Cefn Grug
Craig y Llyn
Llyn-Fawr
1969
Hirwaun Common
A4059
ABERDARE
(Aberdar)
Cwmbach
Mynydd Merthyr
Bedlinog
Craig-y-Duke
Fforest Goch
A474
Melincourt
Melincourt Waterfall
NEATH
A4061
Lluest-wen Resrvoir
TAFF
Aberaman
Cwmpennar
A4067
Glais
Cilfrew
Aberdulais Falls
Vale of Neath
Clyne
(Y Clun)
Blaenrhondda
Cwmaman
B4275
Aberfan
Merthyr Vale
(Ynysowen)
TYDFIL
B4255
Bryn-coch
Cadoxton-Juxta-Neath
AFAN FOREST PARK
Blaencwm
32
Tynewydd
Treherbert
A4233
Abercwmboi
MOUNTAIN ASH
(Aberpennar)
A470
Newtown
Birchgrove
Rhydding
Neath Abbey
Tonna
(Tonnau)
B4434
PORT TALBOT
Ynys-wen
Maerdy
Blaenllechau
Penrhiwceiber
Treharris
Trelewis
NEATH
(Castell-nedd)
Cimla
Tonmawr
Abercregan
Cymmer
(Cymer)
Blaengwynfi
Treorchy
(Treorci)
Cwmparc
Ferndale
Pentre
Ystrad
St. Gwynno Forest
Tylorstown
Ynysboeth
A4059
B4254
Edwardsville
Llancaiach Fawr Manor
Pencaerau
Ynysymaerdy
B4287
Afon Afan
Abergwynfi
Croeserw

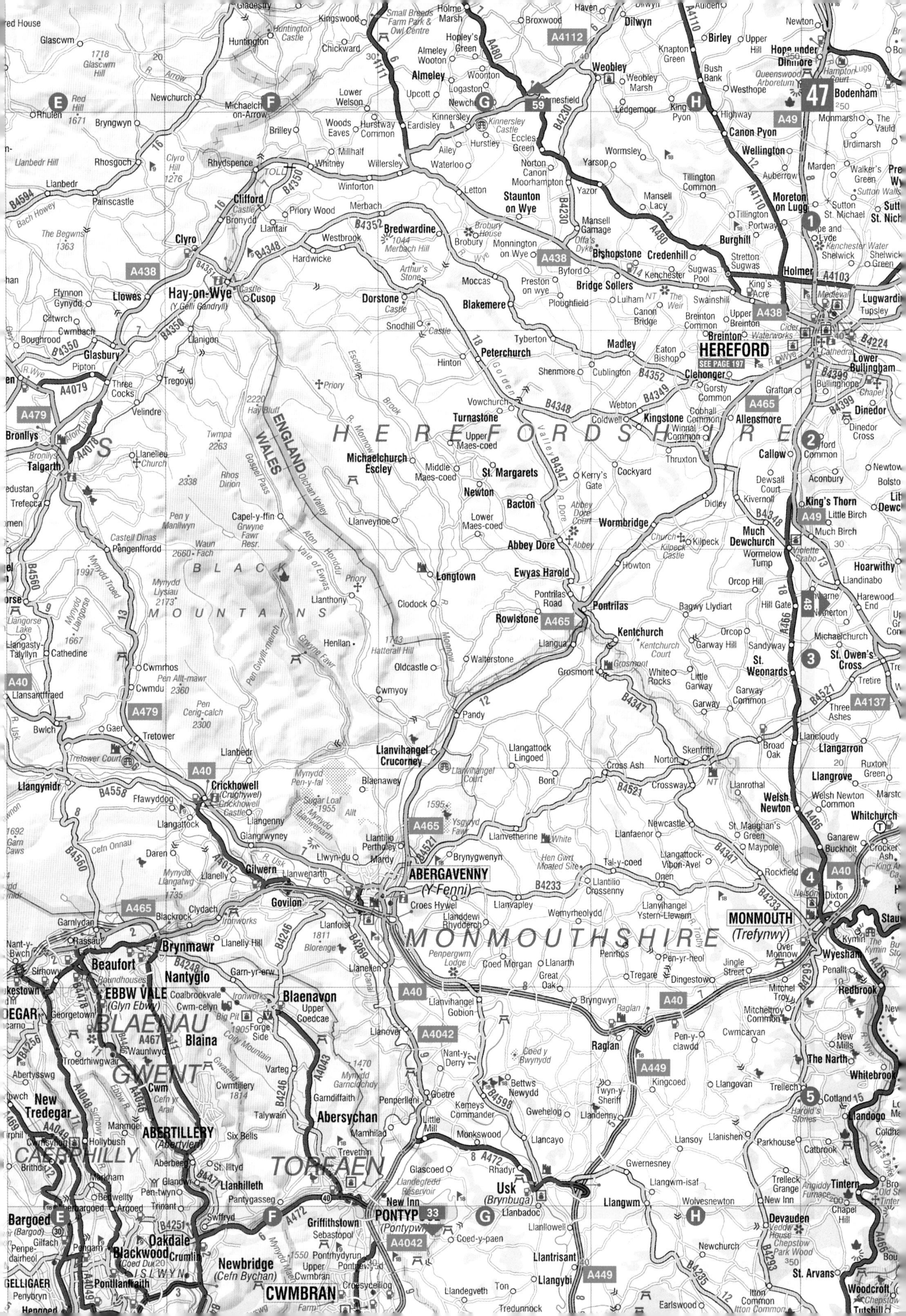

HEREFORDSHIRE
MONMOUTHSHIRE
BLAENAU GWENT
TORFAEN
CAERPHILLY
BLACK MOUNTAINS
ENGLAND
WALES
47
48
59
33
HEREFORD
SEE PAGE 197
MONMOUTH
(Trefynwy)
ABERGAVENNY
(Y Fenni)
Hay-on-Wye
(Y Gelli Gandryll)
Crickhowell
(Crughywel)
EBBW VALE
(Glyn Ebwy)
ABERTILLERY
(Abertyleri)
PONTYPOOL
(Pontypwl)
CWMBRAN
Usk
(Brynbuga)
Newbridge
(Cefn Bychan)
Blackwood
Bargoed
(Bargod)
New Tredegar
Glascwm
Huntington
Kingswood
Small Breeds Farm Park & Owl Centre
Holme Marsh
Broxwood
Dilwyn
Birley
Upper Hill
Hope under Dinmore
Newton
Almeley
Almeley Wooton
Hopley's Green
Woonton
Weobley
Weobley Marsh
Knapton Green
Bush Bank
Westhope
Bodenham
Queenswood Arboretum
Hampton Court
Upcott
Logaston
Newchurch
Sarnesfield
Ledgemoor
King Pyon
Highway
Canon Pyon
Monmarsh
The Vauld
Urdimarsh
Lower Welson
Michaelchurch-on-Arrow
Woods Eaves
Hurstway Common
Eardisley
Kinnersley
Kinnersley Castle
Eccles Green
Hurstley
Red Hill
Rhulen
Bryngwyn
Brilley
Millhalf
Whitney
Willersley
Ailey
Waterloo
Norton Canon
Moorhampton
Wormsley
Yarsop
Wellington
Marden
Walker's Green
Rhosgoch
Rhydspence
Clyro Hill
Llanbedr Hill
Llanbedr
Painscastle
Bach Howey
The Begwns
Winforton
Letton
Tillington Common
Auberrow
Sutton Walls
Clifford
Castle
Bronydd
Priory Wood
Merbach
Staunton on Wye
Yazor
Mansell Lacy
Tillington
Moreton on Lugg
Sutton St. Michael
Sutton St. Nicholas
Llanfair
Westbrook
Bredwardine
Merbach Hill
Brobury
Brobury House
Monnington on Wye
Mansell Gamage
Offa's Dyke
Bishopstone
Credenhill
Burghill
Portway
Stretton Sugwas
Lyde
Kenchester Water
Shelwick
Shelwick Green
Clyro
Hardwicke
Arthur's Stone
Byford
Kenchester
Sugwas Pool
Holmer
Llowes
Cusop
Moccas
Preston on Wye
Bridge Sollers
King's Acre
Lugwardine
Tupsley
Ffynnon Gynydd
Ciltwrch
Cwmbach
Boughrood
Glasbury
Pipton
Dorstone
Blakemere
Ploughfield
Lulham
The Weir
Canon Bridge
Swainshill
Upper Breinton
Breinton Common
Breinton
Cider
Waterworks
Cathedral
Medieval
Snodhill
Castle
Tyberton
Madley
Eaton Bishop
Lower Bullingham
Bullinghope
Llanigon
Hinton
Peterchurch
Golden Valley
Shenmore
Cublington
Clehonger
Gorsty Common
Grafton
Three Cocks
Tregoyd
Velindre
Priory
Hay Bluff
Escley Brook
R. Monnow
Vowchurch
Turnastone
Webton
Coldwell
Kingstone
Cobhall Common
Allensmore
Winnal Common
Dinedor
Dinedor Cross
Bronllys
Talgarth
Llanelieu
Church
Twmpa
Gospel Pass
Olchon Valley
Michaelchurch Escley
Upper Maes-coed
Middle Maes-coed
St. Margarets
Kerry's Gate
Cockyard
Thruxton
Callow
Aconbury
Newton
Rhos Dirion
Newton
Bacton
Abbey Dore Court
R. Dore
Wormbridge
Dewsall Court
Kivernoll
Didley
King's Thorn
Little Birch
Much Birch
Much Dewchurch
Trefecca
Capel-y-ffin
Llanveynoe
Lower Maes-coed
Abbey Dore
Abbey
Church
Kilpeck
Kilpeck Castle
Wormelow Tump
Violette Strabo
Pen y Manllwyn
Grwyne Fawr Resr.
Castell Dinas
Pengenffordd
Waun Fach
Mynydd Troed
Mynydd Llysiau
Vale of Ewyas
Afon Honddu
Longtown
Ewyas Harold
Howton
Hoarwithy
Llandinabo
Orcop Hill
Hill Gate
Harewood End
Llangorse
Llangorse Lake
Mynydd Llangorse
Llanthony
Clodock
Pontrilas Road
Pontrilas
Rowlstone
Bagwy Llydiart
Kentchurch
Kentchurch Court
Orcop
Garway Hill
Sandyway
St. Weonards
Llangasty-Talyllyn
Cathedine
Henllan
Hatterall Hill
Llangua
Michaelchurch
St. Owen's Cross
Tretire
Cwmrhos
Pen Allt-mawr
Walterstone
Oldcastle
Grosmont
White Rocks
Little Garway
Garway
Garway Common
Three Ashes
Llansantffraed
Cwmdu
Pen Cerig-calch
Cwmyoy
Pandy
Bwlch
Gaer
Tretower
Tretower Court
Llanbedr
Llanvihangel Crucorney
Llanvihangel Court
Llangattock Lingoed
Skenfrith
Broad Oak
Llancloudy
Llangarron
Ruxton Green
Llangynidr
Mynydd Pen-y-fal
Sugar Loaf
Blaenawey
Bont
Cross Ash
Norton
Crossway
Llanrothal
Llangrove
Welsh Newton
Welsh Newton Common
Marstow
Whitchurch
Ffawyddog
Crickhowell Castle
Llangattock
Llangenny
Glangrwyney
Allt
Mynydd Llanwenarth
Ysgyryd Fawr
Llanvetherine
White
Llanfaenor
Newcastle
St. Maughan's Green
Maypole
Ganarew
Buckholt
Crocker's Ash
Garn Caws
Cefn Onnau
Daren
Llantilio Pertholey
Mardy
Llwyn-du
Brynygwenyn
Hen Gwrt Moated Site
Tal-y-coed
Llangattock-Vibon-Avel
Onen
Rockfield
Dixton
Mynydd Llangatwg
Gilwern
Llanelly
Llanwenarth
R. Usk
Llantilio Crossenny
Llanvapley
Llanvihangel Ystern-Llewern
Wernyrheolydd
Nelson
Staunton
Garnlydan
Clydach
Blackrock
Ironworks
Govilon
Croes Hywel
Llanddewi Rhydderch
Kymin
The Kymin
Nant-y-Bwch
Rassau
Brynmawr
Llanelly Hill
Llanfoist
Blorenge
Penpergwm Lodge
Coed Morgan
Llanarth
Great Oak
Penrhos
Pen-yr-heol
Tregare
Dingestow
Jingle Street
Over Monnow
Wyesham
Penallt
Redbrook
Sirhowy
Beaufort
Roundhouses
Nantyglo
Garn-yr-erw
Blaenavon
Llanellen
Canal
Llanvihangel Gobion
Bryngwyn
Raglan
Mitchel Troy
Mitchel Troy Common
Tredegar
Georgetown
Coalbrookvale
Cwm-celyn
Ironworks
Big Pit
Forge Side
Upper Coedcae
Blaina
Coity Mountain
Llanover
Nant-y-Derry
Coed y Bwynydd
Pen-y-clawdd
Cwmcarvan
New Mills
The Narth
Waunlwyd
Troedrhiwgwair
Gwastad Mawr
Varteg
Mynydd Garnclochdy
Bettws Newydd
Twyn-y-Sheriff
Kingcoed
Llangovan
Trellech
Whitebrook
Harold's Stones
Cotland
Llandogo
Abertysswg
Cwm
Cefn yr Arail
Cwmtillery
Garndiffaith
Penperlleni
Goetre
Kemeys Commander
Gwehelog
Llandenny
Abersychan
Mamhilad
Little Mill
Monkswood
Llancayo
Llansoy
Llanishen
Parkhouse
Catbrook
Coldharbour
Ebbw R.
Sirhowy
Manmoel
Hollybush
Six Bells
Talywain
Trevethin
Glascoed
Llandegfedd Reservoir
Rhadyr
Gwernesney
Trelleck Grange
Anchor Furnace
Tintern
Old Station
Brithdir
Aberbeeg
St. Illtyd
Llanhilleth
Llangwm
Llangwm-isaf
New Inn
Chapel Hill
Markham
Llangynidr
Bedwellty
Argoed
Pant-twyn
Trinant
Pantygasseg
Swffryd
Oakdale
Crumlin
Griffithstown
Sebastopol
Llanbadoc
Llanllowell
Wolvesnewton
Devauden
Veddw House
Chepstow Park Wood
Aberbargoed
Pengam
Gilfach
Penpedairheol
Coed Duon
ISLWYN
Pontrhydyrun
Upper Cwmbran
Pontnewydd
Coed-y-paen
Llantrisant
Newchurch
St. Arvans
GELLIGAER
Penybryn
Hengoed
Pontllanfraith
Croesyceiliog
Llandegveth
Ton
Tredunnock
Llangybi
Earlswood
Itton Common
Woodcroft
Tutshill
Chepstow
Greenmeadow Farm
A4112
A49
A480
A438
A4110
A4103
A465
A479
A4078
A4079
A40
A4077
A4137
A466
A4042
A4043
A449
A472
A467
A4046
A4048
A4049
B4594
B4350
B4351
B4348
B4352
B4349
B4399
B4224
B4230
B4347
B4348
B4560
B4558
B4521
B4233
B4246
B4248
B4269
B4598
B4235
B4293
B4251
B4256

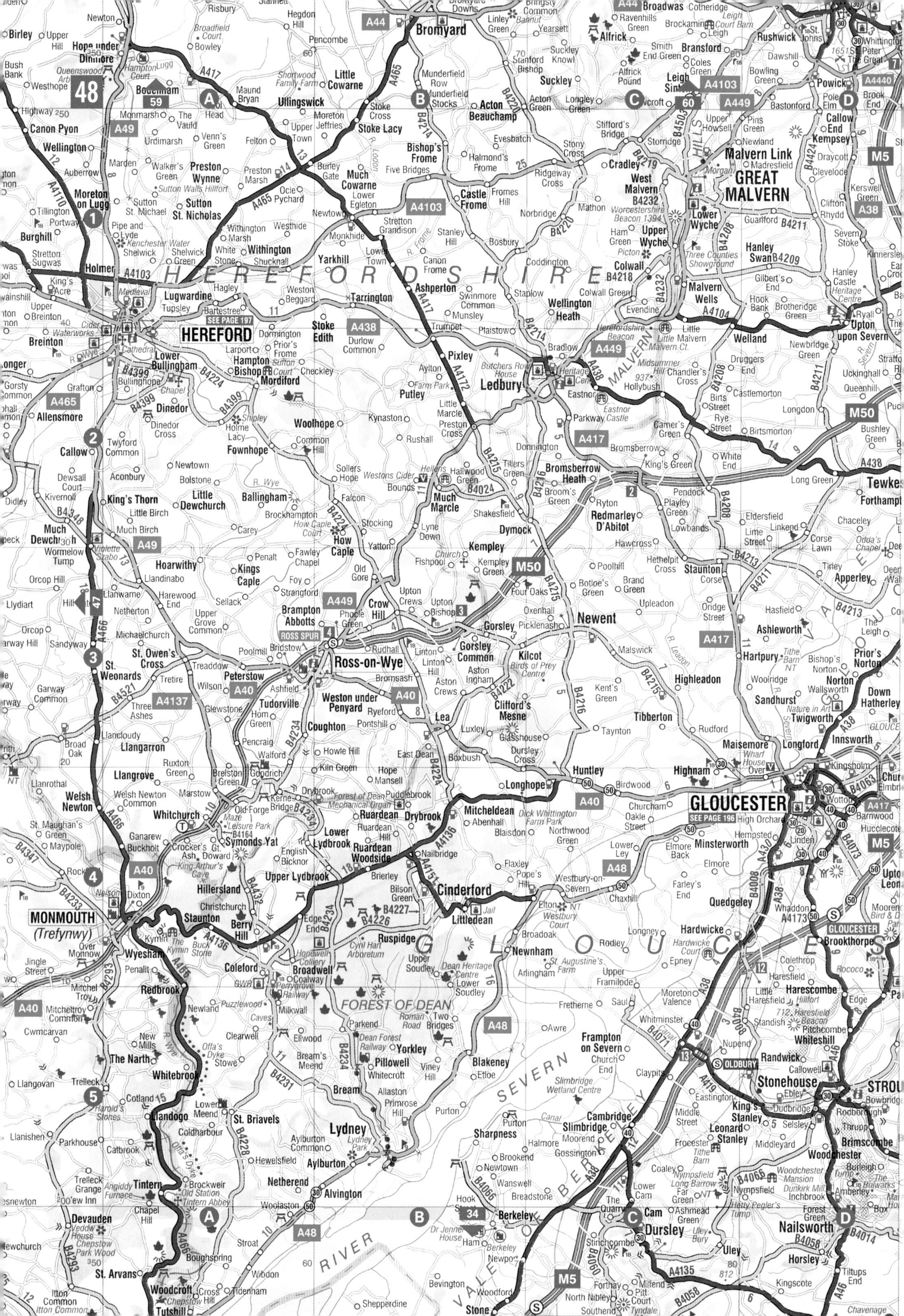
48
HEREFORDSHIRE
HEREFORD
SEE PAGE 197
Bromyard
Ledbury
GREAT MALVERN
Malvern Link
Malvern Wells
Upton upon Severn
Ross-on-Wye
ROSS SPUR
Newent
GLOUCESTER
SEE PAGE 196
MONMOUTH
(Trefynwy)
Cinderford
Coleford
Lydney
FOREST OF DEAN
Dursley
Stonehouse
Nailsworth
Berkeley
Sharpness
Tintern
Chepstow
Mitcheldean
Much Marcle
Dymock
Kempley
Highnam
Huntley
Longhope
Lydbrook
Symonds Yat
Goodrich
Whitchurch
Kilcot
Gorsley
Redmarley D'Abitot
Staunton
Hartpury
Maisemore
Quedgeley
Hardwicke
Frampton on Severn
Slimbridge
Cam
Uley
Blakeney
Newnham
Yorkley
Bream
St. Briavels
Llandogo
Whitebrook
Redbrook
Wyesham
Welsh Newton
Much Dewchurch
Callow
Allensmore
Mordiford
Fownhope
Woolhope
How Caple
Kings Caple
Hoarwithy
Peterstow
Weston under Penyard
Upton Bishop
Bosbury
Colwall
Wellington Heath
Cradley
West Malvern
Upper Wyche
Bromsberrow Heath
Eastnor
Withington
Lugwardine
Tarrington
Stoke Edith
Ashperton
Much Cowarne
Stoke Lacy
Acton Beauchamp
Suckley
Leigh Sinton
Alfrick
Wellington
Canon Pyon
Moreton on Lugg
Burghill
Holmer
Sutton St. Nicholas
Preston Wynne
Bodenham
Ullingswick
Little Cowarne
A4103
A465
A49
A438
A417
A449
A40
A48
A38
A466
A4136
A4137
M50
M5
RIVER SEVERN
MALVERN HILLS
VALE OF BERKELEY
A
B
C
D
1
2
3
4
5

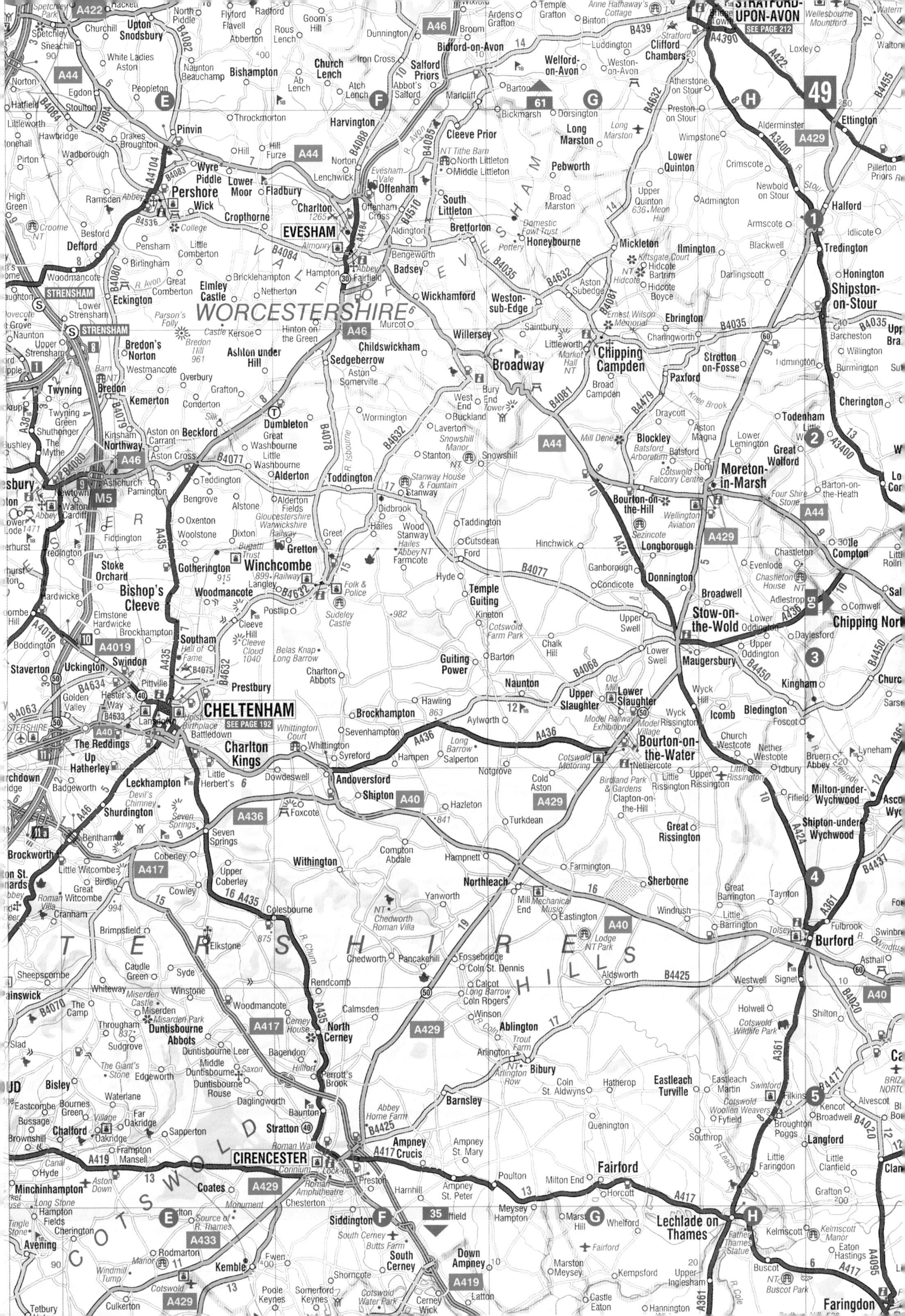

Spetchley Park
A422
Churchill
Upton Snodsbury
North Piddle
Flyford Flavell
Radford
Abberton
Rous Lench
Goom's Hill
Dunnington
A46
Broom
Ardens Grafton
Temple Grafton
Binton
Anne Hathaway's Cottage
STRATFORD-UPON-AVON
SEE PAGE 212
Wellesbourne Mountford
Spetchley
Sneachill
White Ladies Aston
Naunton Beauchamp
Bishampton
Church Lench
Iron Cross
Ab Lench
Atch Lench
Salford Priors
Abbot's Salford
Bidford-on-Avon
Welford-on-Avon
Weston-on-Avon
Luddington
B439
Clifford Chambers
Stratford
A4390
A422
Loxley
Walton
A44
Norton
Egdon
Peopleton
E
F
Marlcliff
Barton
61
G
Atherstone on Stour
H
49
B4455
Hatfield
Stoulton
B4084
Littleworth
Throckmorton
Harvington
Cleeve Prior
Bickmarsh
Dorsington
B4632
Preston on Stour
Ettington
Hawbridge
Drakes Broughton
Pinvin
B4088
B4085
Long Marston
Alderminster
A429
Wimpstone
A3400
Pirton
Wadborough
Hill
Hill Furze
A44
Norton
R. Avon
NT Tithe Barn
North Littleton
Middle Littleton
Long Marston
Lower Quinton
Crimscote
Pillerton Priors
A4104
B4083
Wyre Piddle
Lower Moor
Fladbury
Lenchwick
Evesham Vale
Offenham
Pebworth
High Green
Ramsden
Abbey
Pershore
Wick
Charlton
Offenham Cross
South Littleton
Broad Marston
Upper Quinton
Meon Hill
Admington
Newbold on Stour
R. Stour
Halford
Croome NT
Besford
B4536
College
Cropthorne
EVESHAM
A4184
B4510
Aldington
Bretforton
Domestic Fowl Trust
Honeybourne
Mickleton
Armscote
Idlicote
Defford
Pensham
Little Comberton
Almonry
Bengeworth
Pottery
Ilmington
Blackwell
Tredington
Birlingham
B4084
Badsey
B4035
Kiftsgate Court
Hidcote Bartrim
Darlingscott
Woodmancote
B4080
R. Avon
Great Comberton
Bricklehampton
Hampton
Abbey
Fairfield
Aston Subedge
NT Hidcote
Hidcote Boyce
Honington
STRENSHAM
Eckington
Elmley Castle
Netherton
Wickhamford
Weston-sub-Edge
B4081
Shipston-on-Stour
Lower Strensham
WORCESTERSHIRE
VALE OF EVESHAM
Murcot
Ernest Wilson Memorial
Ebrington
B4035
Parson's Folly
Saintbury
Upper Brailes
Naunton
Upper Strensham
STRENSHAM
Castle
Kersoe
Hinton on the Green
A46
Willersey
Littleworth
Charingworth
Barcheston
Bredon's Norton
Bredon Hill 961
Ashton under Hill
Childswickham
Markot Hall NT
Chipping Campden
Stretton on-Fosse
Willington
Westmancote
Sedgeberrow
Broadway
Ilmington
Burmington
Barn NT
Bredon
Overbury
Aston Somerville
Broad Campden
Paxford
Twyning
Kemerton
Grafton
Conderton
Dumbleton
West End
Bury End
Buckland
Tower
B4081
B4479
Knee Brook
Cherington
Twyning Green
Shuthonger
B4079
Silk
Great Washbourne
Wormington
Laverton
Snowshill Manor
Draycott
Aston Magna
Todenham
The Mythe
Kinsham
Northway
Aston on Carrant
Beckford
Little Washbourne
B4078
R. Isbourne
B4632
Mill Dene
Blockley
Lower Lemington
A44
Batsford Arboretum
Batsford
Great Wolford
Aston Cross
B4077
Alderton
Toddington
Stanton
Snowshill
Cotswold Falconry Centre
Moreton-in-Marsh
A46
Ashchurch
Pamington
Teddington
Stanway House & Fountain
Stanway
Barton-on-the-Heath
Newtown
Walton Cardiff
M5
Bengrove
Alstone
Alderton Fields
Didbrook
Bourton-on-the-Hill
Four Shire Stone
A44
Abbey
Oxenton
Gloucestershire Warwickshire Railway
Wood Stanway
Hailes
Taddington
Wellington Aviation
Fiddington
A435
Woolstone
Dixton
Greet
Hailes Abbey NT
Cutsdean
Hinchwick
Sezincote
A429
Tredington
Bugatti Trust
Gretton
Farmcote
Ford
A424
Longborough
Chastleton
Little Compton
Stoke Orchard
Gotherington
Winchcombe
899 Railway
B4077
Ganborough
Evenlode
Chastleton House NT
915
Langley
Folk & Police
Hyde
Condicote
Donnington
Bishop's Cleeve
Woodmancote
B4632
Temple Guiting
Broadwell
Adlestrop
Cornwell
Hardwicke
Elmstone Hardwicke
Postlip
Sudeley Castle
982
Kineton
Stow-on-the-Wold
Lower Oddington
A436
50
Chipping Norton
Brockhampton
Cleeve Hill
Cleeve Cloud 1040
Cotswold Farm Park
Upper Swell
Daylesford
Boddington
A4019
10
A4019
Southam
Hall of Fame
Belas Knap Long Barrow
Chalk Hill
Lower Swell
Upper Oddington
Staverton
Uckington
Swindon
A435
B4075
B4632
Guiting Power
Barton
B4068
Maugersbury
B4450
3
Kingham
Churchill
Golden Valley
B4634
Hester's Way
Pittville
Prestbury
Charlton Abbots
Naunton
Old Mill
Lower Slaughter
Upper Slaughter
Wyck Hill
B4063
CHELTENHAM
SEE PAGE 192
Holst Birthplace
Brockhampton
Hawling 863
Aylworth
Model Railway Exhibition
Model Village
Wyck Rissington
Icomb
Bledington
Foscot
Sarsden
A40
B4633
Lansdown
Battledown
Whittington Court
Sevenhampton
A436
A436
Bourton-on-the-Water
Church Westcote
Nether Westcote
Lyneham
The Reddings
Up Hatherley
Charlton Kings
Whittington
Syreford
Hampen
Long Barrow
Salperton
Cotswold Motoring
Nethercote
Bruern Abbey
Idbury
Churchdown
Badgeworth
Leckhampton
Little Herbert's
Dowdeswell
Andoversford
Notgrove
Cold Aston
Birdland Park & Gardens
Little Rissington
Upper Rissington
Little Rissington
Fifield
Milton-under-Wychwood
Devil's Chimney
Shipton
A40
Hazleton
A429
Clapton-on-the-Hill
A424
Shurdington
A436
Foxcote
841
Turkdean
Great Rissington
Shipton-under-Wychwood
Seven Springs
A46
Bentham
Seven Springs
Brockworth
Coberley
A417
Compton Abdale
Hampnett
Farmington
Withington
Little Witcombe
Upper Coberley
Northleach
Sherborne
Great Barrington
Taynton
Birdlip
Great Witcombe
Roman Villa
Cowley
A435
Yanworth
Mill End
Mechanical Music
16
Windrush
Cranham
994
Colesbourne
NT Chedworth Roman Villa
Eastington
Lodge NT Park
A40
Little Barrington
Tolsey
Fulbrook
Burford
Brimpsfield
Elkstone
875
R. Churn
GLOUCESTERSHIRE
Chedworth
Pancakehill
Fossebridge
Coln St. Dennis
Aldsworth
B4425
Westwell
Signet
Asthall
Caudle Green
Syde
COTSWOLD HILLS
A40
B4020
Sheepscombe
Rendcomb
Calcot
Long Barrow
Coln Rogers
Winson
Painswick
Whiteway
Miserden Castle
Miserden
Winstone
Woodmancote
Calmsden
Holwell
Shilton
B4070
The Camp
Througham
Misarden Park
Duntisbourne Abbots
A417
Cerney House
North Cerney
A429
R. Coln
Ablington
Trout Farm
Cotswold Wildlife Park
A361
Slad
Sudgrove
Duntisbourne Leer
Bagendon
Arlington
Bibury
NT Arlington Row
The Giant's Stone
Edgeworth
Middle Duntisbourne
Saxon
Hillfort
Perrott's Brook
Coln St. Aldwyns
Hatherop
Eastleach Turville
Eastleach Martin
Swinford
Filkins
B4477
Alvescot
Bisley
Waterlane
Duntisbourne Rouse
Daglingworth
Barnsley
Cotswold Woollen Weavers
Kencot
Broadwell
Eastcombe
Bournes Green
Far Oakridge
Baunton
Abbey Home Farm
Quenington
Fyfield
Broughton Poggs
B4020
Bussage
Village
Oakridge
Sapperton
Stratton
B4425
Ampney Crucis
Ampney St. Mary
Southrop
Langford
Brownshill
Chalford
Frampton Mansell
Roman Wall
Canal
A419
CIRENCESTER
Corinium
Lock-up
A417
Little Faringdon
Little Clanfield
Hyde
13
Aston Down
Coates
A429
Roman Amphitheatre
Preston
Harnhill
Ampney St. Peter
Poulton
Milton End
Fairford
Horcott
A417
Grafton
Minchinhampton
Long Stone
Monument
Chesterton
Hampton Fields
Tingle Stone
Cherington
E
Source of R. Thames
A433
Siddington
F
35
Driffield
Meysey Hampton
Marston Hill
G
Whelford
Lechlade on Thames
H
Kelmscott
Kelmscott Manor
Father Thames Statue
Avening
South Cerney
Butts Farm
Fairford
Eaton Hastings
Rodmarton
Manor
Ewen
South Cerney
Down Ampney
A417
A4095
Windmill Tump
Kemble
Marston Meysey
Kempsford
Upper Inglesham
R. Cole
Buscot
NT Buscot Park
Cotswold
A429
Poole Keynes
Somerford Keynes
Shorncote
Cotswold Water Park
A419
Cerney Wick
Latton
Castle Eaton
Hannington
A361
Faringdon
Tetbury
Culkerton

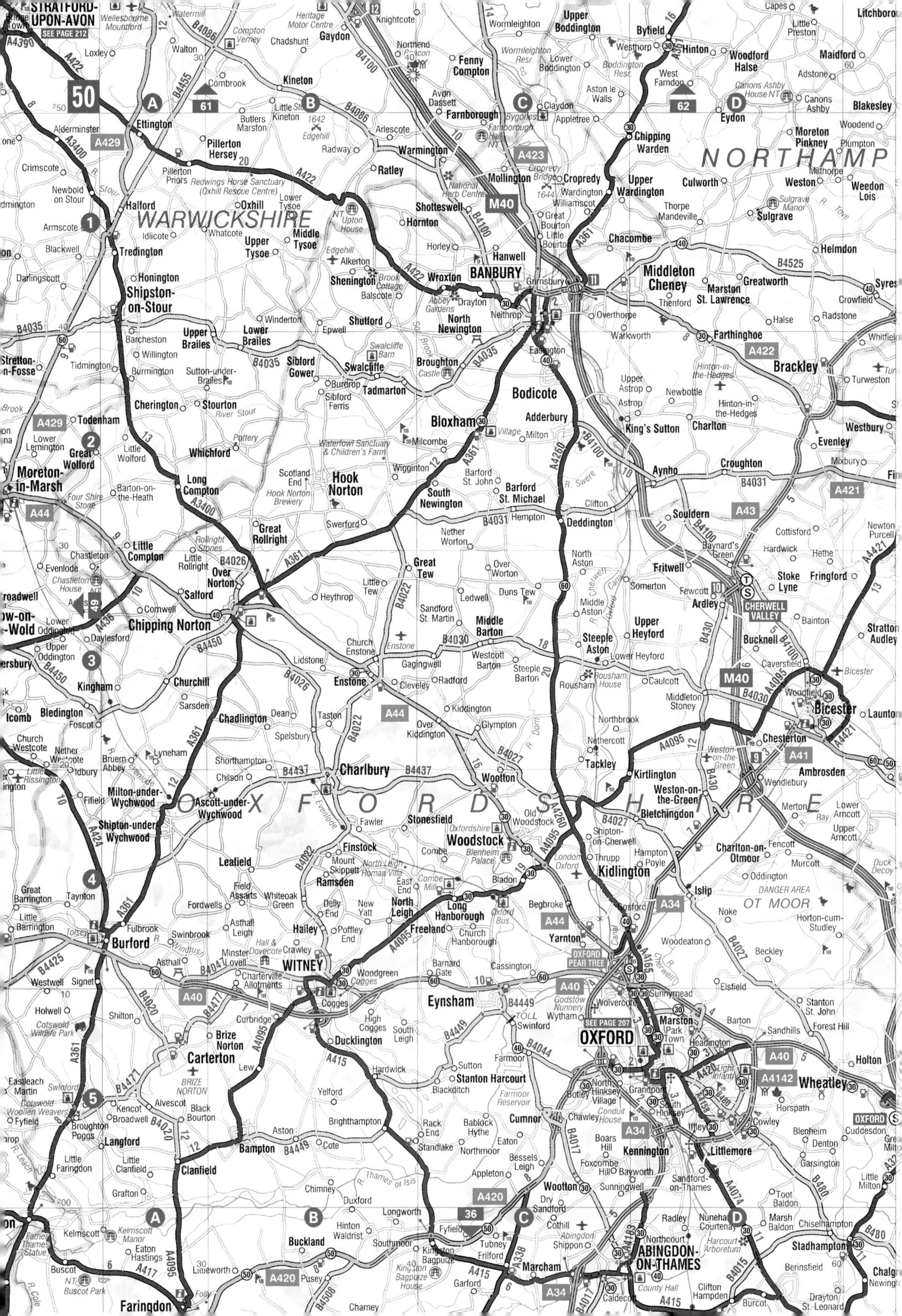

STRATFORD-UPON-AVON
SEE PAGE 212
50
A
B
C
D
61
62
Wellesbourne Mountford
Watermill
Compton Verney
Heritage Motor Centre
Gaydon
Knightcote
Wormleighton
Upper Boddington
Byfield
Capes
Litchborough
Little Preston
Loxley
Walton
Chadshunt
Northend
Fenny Compton
Wormleighton Resr.
Lower Boddington
Boddington Resr.
Westhorp
Hinton
Woodford Halse
Maidford
Combrook
Kineton
Avon Dassett
Aston le Walls
West Farndon
Canons Ashby House NT
Adstone
Canons Ashby
Little Kineton
1642 Edgehill
Farnborough
Farnborough Hall NT
Bygones
Claydon
Appletree
Eydon
Blakesley
Alderminster
Ettington
Butlers Marston
Arlescote
Woodend
Pillerton Hersey
Radway
Warmington
Chipping Warden
Moreton Pinkney
Plumpton
Crimscote
Pillerton Priors
Redwings Horse Sanctuary (Oxhill Rescue Centre)
Ratley
National Herb Centre
Mollington
Cropredy Bridge 1644
Cropredy
Wardington
Upper Wardington
Culworth
NORTHAMP
Newbold on Stour
Halford
Oxhill
Lower Tysoe
Upton House NT
M40
Shotteswell
Williamscot
Great Bourton
Little Bourton
Thorpe Mandeville
Sulgrave Manor
Sulgrave
Weston
Weedon Lois
WARWICKSHIRE
Armscote
Idlicote
Whatcote
Upper Tysoe
Middle Tysoe
Hornton
Chacombe
Helmdon
Blackwell
Tredington
Edgehill
Alkerton
Horley
Hanwell
Middleton Cheney
Marston St. Lawrence
Greatworth
Darlingscott
Honington
Shenington
Brook Cottage
Balscote
Wroxton
Abbey Gardens
Drayton
BANBURY
Grimsbury
Neithrop
Thenford
Crowfield
Syresham
Shipston-on-Stour
Winderton
Epwell
Shutford
North Newington
Overthorpe
Halse
Radstone
Barcheston
Upper Brailes
Lower Brailes
Warkworth
Farthinghoe
Whitfield
Stretton-on-Fosse
Willington
Sibford Gower
Swalcliffe Barn
Swalcliffe
Broughton Castle
Broughton
Easington
Hinton-in-the-Hedges
Brackley
Tidmington
Burmington
Sutton-under-Brailes
Burdrop
Sibford Ferris
Tadmarton
Bodicote
Upper Astrop
Newbottle
Turweston
Cherington
Stourton
River Stour
Adderbury
Astrop
Hinton-in-the-Hedges
Todenham
Bloxham
Village
Milton
King's Sutton
Charlton
Westbury
Lower Lemington
Great Wolford
Little Wolford
Pottery
Waterfowl Sanctuary & Children's Farm
Milcombe
Whichford
Evenley
Moreton-in-Marsh
Long Compton
Scotland End
Hook Norton
Wigginton
Barford St. John
Barford St. Michael
Aynho
Croughton
Mixbury
Barton-on-the-Heath
Four Shire Stone
Hook Norton Brewery
South Newington
R. Swere
B4031
A421
A44
Clifton
Hempton
Deddington
Souldern
A43
Cottisford
Newton Purcell
Great Rollright
Swerford
Nether Worton
Baynard's Green
Hardwick
Hethe
Little Compton
Chastleton
Rollright Stones
Little Rollright
Great Tew
Over Worton
North Aston
Fritwell
Stoke Lyne
Fringford
Evenlode
Chastleton House
Over Norton
Little Tew
Ledwell
Duns Tew
Somerton
Fewcott
Ardley
Broadwell
Salford
Heythrop
Sandford St. Martin
Middle Aston
CHERWELL VALLEY
Bainton
Cornwell
Lower Oddington
Chipping Norton
Middle Barton
Upper Heyford
Stratton Audley
Daylesford
Church Enstone
Enstone
Westcott Barton
Steeple Aston
Lower Heyford
Bucknell
Upper Oddington
Lidstone
Gagingwell
Radford
Steeple Barton
Rousham House
Rousham
Caulcott
Caversfield
Bicester
Kingham
Churchill
Cleveley
Middleton Stoney
Woodfield
Launton
Bledington
Sarsden
Chadlington
Dean
Taston
Kiddington
Glympton
Northbrook
Foscot
Spelsbury
Over Kiddington
Nethercott
Chesterton
Church Westcote
Nether Westcote
Lyneham
Bruern Abbey
Shorthampton
Wootton
Tackley
Kirtlington
Weston-on-the-Green
Ambrosden
Idbury
Chilson
Charlbury
Wendlebury
Fifield
Milton-under-Wychwood
Ascott-under-Wychwood
OXFORDSHIRE
Old Woodstock
Weston-on-the-Green
Bletchingdon
Merton
Lower Arncott
Shipton-under-Wychwood
Fawler
Stonesfield
Oxfordshire Museum
Woodstock
Blenheim Palace
Shipton-on-Cherwell
Thrupp
Hampton Poyle
Upper Arncott
Charlton-on-Otmoor
Fencott
Finstock
Leafield
Mount Skippett
North Leigh Roman Villa
Combe
London Oxford
Kidlington
Murcott
Duck Decoy
Ramsden
East End
Combe Mill
Bladon
Oddington
DANGER AREA
OT MOOR
Great Barrington
Taynton
Field Assarts
Whiteoak Green
Delly End
New Yatt
North Leigh
Long Hanborough
Oxford Bus
Begbroke
Islip
Noke
Fordwells
Asthall Leigh
Freeland
Church Hanborough
Gosford
Horton-cum-Studley
Little Barrington
Fulbrook
Burford
Swinbrook
Hailey
Poffley End
Yarnton
Woodeaton
Beckley
Minster Lovell
Hall & Dovecote
Crawley
Asthall
Charterville Allotments
WITNEY
Woodgreen
Cogges
Barnard Gate
Cassington
OXFORD PEAR TREE
Elsfield
Westwell
Signet
Eynsham
Godstow Nunnery
Wytham
Wolvercote
Sunnymead
Stanton St. John
Holwell
Shilton
Curbridge
High Cogges
South Leigh
Swinford
TOLL
SEE PAGE 207
Marston
Barton
Forest Hill
Cotswold Wildlife Park
Brize Norton
Ducklington
OXFORD
Park Town
Headington
Sandhills
Carterton
Farmoor
BRIZE NORTON
Lew
Hardwick
Sutton
Stanton Harcourt
Holton
Botley
North Hinksey Village
Grandpont
Light Infantry
Wheatley
Eastleach Martin
Swinford
Alvescot
Black Bourton
Yelford
Blackditch
Farmoor Reservoir
Cumnor
Chawley
Conduit House
South Hinksey
Horspath
Cotswold Woollen Weavers
Kencot
Broadwell
Brighthampton
Rack End
Bablock Hythe
Iffley
Cowley
Blenheim
Cuddesdon
Fyfield
Broughton Poggs
Langford
Aston
Bampton
Cote
Standlake
Eaton
Northmoor
Boars Hill
Kennington
Littlemore
Denton
Little Faringdon
Little Clanfield
Clanfield
Bessels Leigh
Foxcombe Hill
Bayworth
Garsington
Chimney
Thames or Isis
Appleton
Sunningwell
Sandford-on-Thames
Little Milton
Grafton
Duxford
Wootton
Toot Baldon
Kelmscott
Kelmscott Manor
Hinton Waldrist
Longworth
Fyfield
Dry Sandford
Cothill
Abingdon Airfield
Radley
Nuneham Courtenay
Marsh Baldon
Chiselhampton
Father Thames Statue
Buckland
Southmoor
Tubney
Frilford
Shippon
Northcourt
Harcourt Arboretum
Stadhampton
Eaton Hastings
Kingston Bagpuize
ABINGDON-ON-THAMES
Berinsfield
Buscot
Buscot Park NT
Littleworth
Pusey
Kingston Bagpuize House
Marcham
County Hall
Clifton Hampden
Chalgrove
Newington
Garford
Caldecott
Burcot
Drayton St. Leonard
Faringdon
Folly
Charney
A4390
A422
A429
A3400
B4455
B4086
B4100
A423
A361
B4525
B4035
A4260
A436
B4450
B4026
B4022
B4030
B4027
A4095
A41
A4421
M40
A44
B4437
B4020
A424
B4425
B4047
B4477
A40
A415
B4449
B4044
A34
A4142
B4017
A420
A338
A417
B4508
A4183
A4074
B4015
B480
B4471

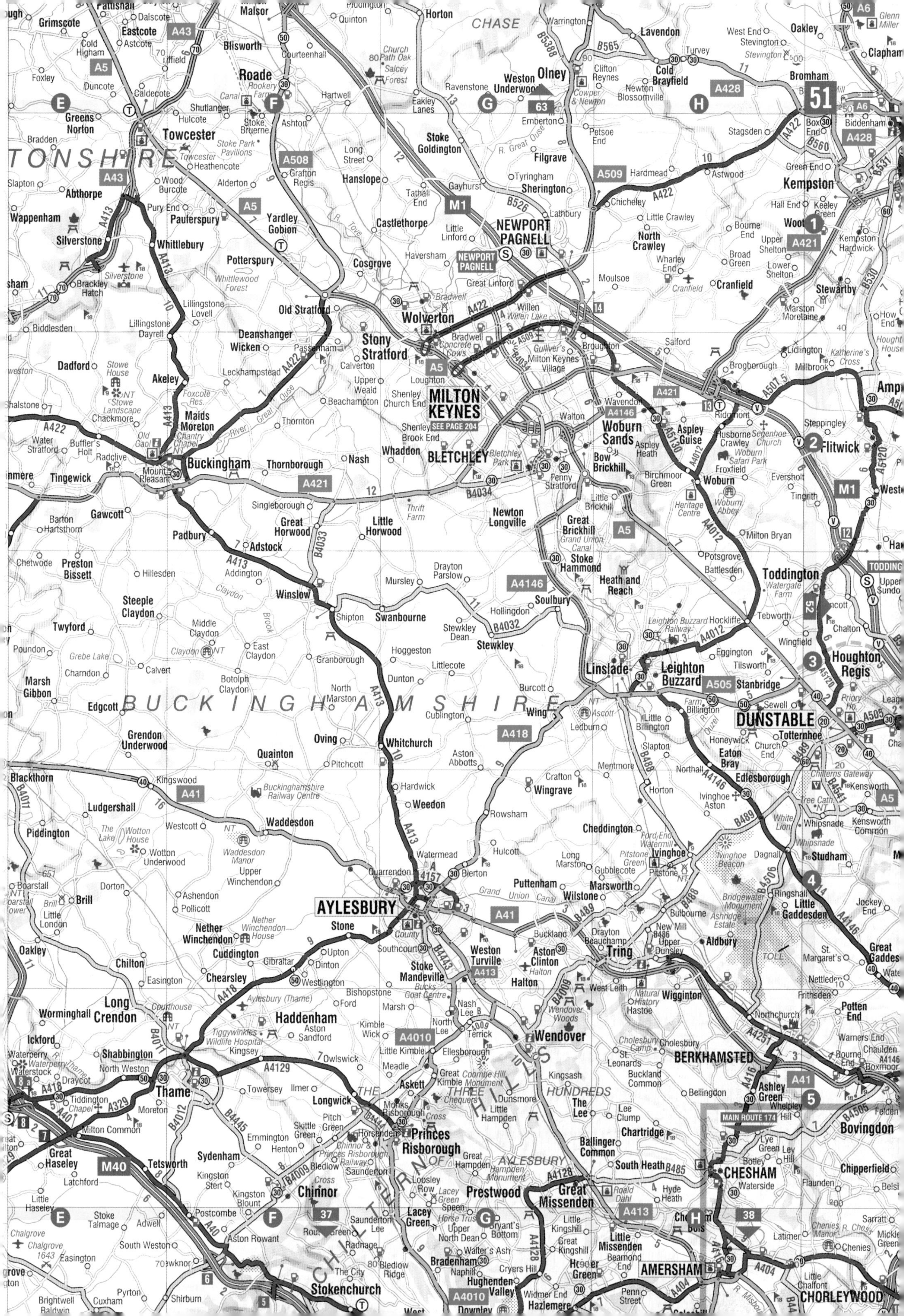

Grimscote
Dalscote
Eastcote
Astcote
Malsor
Quinton
Horton
CHASE
Warrington
Lavendon
West End
Oakley
A6
Cold Higham
A43
Blisworth
Courteenhall
Church Path Oak
Salcey Forest
B5388
B565
Turvey
Stevington
Clapham
Foxley
A5
Duncote
Roade
Rookery Farm
Hartwell
Ravenstone
Weston Underwood
Olney
Clifton Reynes
Cold Brayfield
Newton Blossomville
A428
Bromham
51
Caldecote
Canal
Eakley Lanes
Cowper & Newton
63
E
F
G
H
Greens Norton
Shutlanger
Hulcote
Stoke Bruerne
Ashton
Emberton
Petsoe End
Stagsden
Box End
Biddenham
Bradden
Towcester
Stoke Park Pavilions
Stoke Goldington
R. Great Ouse
Filgrave
B560
TONSHIRE
Towcester
Heathencote
A508
Grafton Regis
Long Street
Hardmead
Astwood
Green End
Slapton
Abthorpe
A43
Wood Burcote
Alderton
Hanslope
Tyringham
Sherington
A509
A422
Kempston
Pury End
Paulerspury
A5
Yardley Gobion
Tathall End
Gayhurst
Chicheley
Little Crawley
Hall End
Keeley Green
Wappenham
Silverstone
Whittlebury
Potterspury
Castlethorpe
M1
B526
Lathbury
NEWPORT PAGNELL
North Crawley
Bourne End
Wootton
A421
Upper Shelton
Kempston Hardwick
Whittlewood Forest
Haversham
Little Linford
NEWPORT PAGNELL
Broad Green
Wharley End
Lower Shelton
Cosgrove
Moulsoe
Cranfield
Brackley Hatch
Silverstone
Great Linford
Stewartby
A413
Lillingstone Lovell
Old Stratford
Bradwell
Willen
Willen Lake
Marston Moretaine
B530
Biddlesden
Lillingstone Dayrell
Wolverton
A422
14
How End
Deanshanger
Wicken
Passenham
Stony Stratford
Bradwell
Concrete Cows
A509
Gulliver's
Milton Keynes Village
Broughton
Salford
Lidlington
Katherine's Cross
Houghton House
Dadford
Stowe House
Calverton
A5
Brogborough
Millbrook
Akeley
Leckhampstead
Upper Weald
Loughton
A507
Ampthill
NT Stowe Landscape
Foxcote Res.
Beachampton
Shenley Church End
MILTON KEYNES
SEE PAGE 204
A421
Wavendon
A4146
13
Ridgmont
Chackmore
Maids Moreton
Thornton
Walton
Woburn Sands
Aspley Guise
Husborne Crawley
Segenhoe Church
Steppingley
A422
Water Stratford
Buffler's Holt
Old Gaol
Chantry Chapel
River Great Ouse
Shenley Brook End
Whaddon
Bletchley Park
Aspley Heath
Woburn Safari Park
Flitwick
Radclive
BLETCHLEY
Bow Brickhill
A5130
A4012
Froxfield
Eversholt
Tingewick
Mount Pleasant
Buckingham
Thornborough
Nash
Fenny Stratford
Birchmoor Green
Woburn
A5120
Westoning
A421
12
B4034
Woburn Abbey
Heritage Centre
Tingrith
M1
Gawcott
Singleborough
Thrift Farm
Newton Longville
Little Brickhill
Barton Hartshorn
Padbury
Great Horwood
Little Horwood
Great Brickhill
Grand Union Canal
A5
A4012
Milton Bryan
12
Adstock
B4033
Potsgrove
Battlesden
Chetwode
Preston Bissett
A413
Addington
Drayton Parslow
A4146
Stoke Hammond
Heath and Reach
Toddington
Watergate Farm
TODDINGTON
Hillesden
Mursley
Claydon
Winslow
Steeple Claydon
Middle Claydon
Brook
Shipton
Swanbourne
Hollingdon
Soulbury
Leighton Buzzard Railway
Hockliffe
Tebworth
Twyford
Stewkley Dean
B4032
Stewkley
Claydon NT
East Claydon
Hoggeston
A4012
Eggington
Chalton
Wingfield
Poundon
Grebe Lake
Littlecote
Tilsworth
Houghton Regis
Calvert
Granborough
Linslade
Leighton Buzzard
Charndon
Dunton
A505
Stanbridge
Marsh Gibbon
Botolph Claydon
North Marston
Burcott
Farm
Billington
Sewell
Edgcott
BUCKINGHAMSHIRE
Cublington
Wing
Ascott
Little Billington
DUNSTABLE
Ledburn
Grendon Underwood
Oving
A418
Totternhoe
Honeywick
Church End
Whitchurch
Slapton
Eaton Bray
Quainton
Pitchcott
Aston Abbotts
Mentmore
B488
Northall
Edlesborough
Blackthorn
Kingswood
Crafton
Wingrave
A41
Hardwick
Horton
Chilterns Gateway
Kensworth
B4011
Buckinghamshire Railway Centre
A4146
Ivinghoe Aston
A5
Ludgershall
Weedon
Rowsham
Tree Cathedral
Waddesdon
Westcott
B489
White Lion
Whipsnade
Kensworth Common
Piddington
The Lake
Wotton House
Waddesdon Manor
Cheddington
Ford End
Wotton Underwood
A413
Hulcott
Long Marston
Pitstone Green
Ivinghoe
Ivinghoe Beacon
Dagnall
Studham
Upper Winchendon
Watermead
Bierton
Gubblecote
Pitstone
Boarstall
Dorton
Quarrendon
A4157
Puttenham
Marsworth
B4506
Ringshall
Little Gaddesden
Jockey End
Brill
Ashendon
AYLESBURY
Grand Union Canal
Wilstone
Bridgewater Monument
Ashridge Estate
A4146
Little London
Pollicott
A41
B488
Bulbourne
Nether Winchendon
Nether Winchendon House
Stone
County
Buckland
Drayton Beauchamp
New Mill
B486
Aldbury
Oakley
Cuddington
Upton
Southcourt
B4443
Weston Turville
Aston Clinton
Tring
Upper Dunsley
TOLL
St. Margaret's
Great Gaddesden
Chilton
Easington
Gibraltar
Dinton
Westlington
Stoke Mandeville
A413
Halton
Chearsley
Long Crendon
A418
Courthouse
Aylesbury (Thame)
Bishopstone
Bucks Goat Centre
Nash Lee
B4009
Wendover Woods
West Leith
Natural History
Hastoe
Wigginton
Nettleden
Frithsden
Worminghall
Crendon
Haddenham
Aston Sandford
Ford
Marsh
Kimble Wick
North Lee
A4010
Terrick
Wendover
Northchurch
Potten End
Tiggywinkles Wildlife Hospital
Ickford
Waterperry
Shabbington
Kingsey
A4129
Little Kimble
Ellesborough
Cholesbury Camp
Cholesbury
A4251
Warners End
Chaulden
Waterstock
North Weston
Owlswick
Meadle
St. Leonards
BERKHAMSTED
Bourne End
Boxmoor
Draycot
Thame
Towersey
Ilmer
Askett
Great Kimble
Coombe Hill
Monument
Kingsash
Buckland Common
Ashley Green
A41
Tiddington
A329
Moreton
B4445
Longwick
Monks Risborough
Chequers
THREE HUNDREDS
Dunsmore
Bellingdon
Whelpley Hill
B4505
Felden
A418
A40
Milton Common
B4012
Skittle Green
Pitch Green
Horsenden
Cross
Little Hampden
The Lee
Lee Clump
MAIN ROUTE 174
Bovingdon
Great Haseley
M40
Tetsworth
Emmington
Henton
Chinnor & Princes Risborough Railway
Princes Risborough
Great Hampden
Hampden Monument
AYLESBURY
Chartridge
Ballinger Common
Lye Green
Ley Hill
Botley
Latchford
Sydenham
Kingston Stert
Saunderton
Loosley Row
Lacey Green
Speen
A4128
Prestwood
Great Missenden
South Heath
B485
CHESHAM
Waterside
Chipperfield
Little Haseley
B4009
Chinnor
Roald Dahl
Hyde Heath
Flaunden
Stoke Talmage
Adwell
Kingston Blount
Postcombe
37
Saunderton Lee
Horse Trust
Bryant's Bottom
Upper North Dean
A413
Little Kingshill
Chesham Bois
38
Sarratt
Chalgrove
Chalgrove 1643
Aston Rowant
Rout Green
Radnage
Great Kingshill
Little Missenden
Latimer
Chenies Manor
Chenies
R. Chess
Easington
South Weston
A40
Bledlow Ridge
Walter's Ash
Bradenham
Naphill
Beamond End
Holmer Green
AMERSHAM
A404
A416
Little Chalfont
Pyrton
Wheatley
The City
Cryers Hill
Hughenden Valley
Widmer End
Hazlemere
Penn Street
R. Misbourne
Brightwell Baldwin
Cuxham
Shirburn
Stokenchurch
A4010
Downley
CHORLEYWOOD

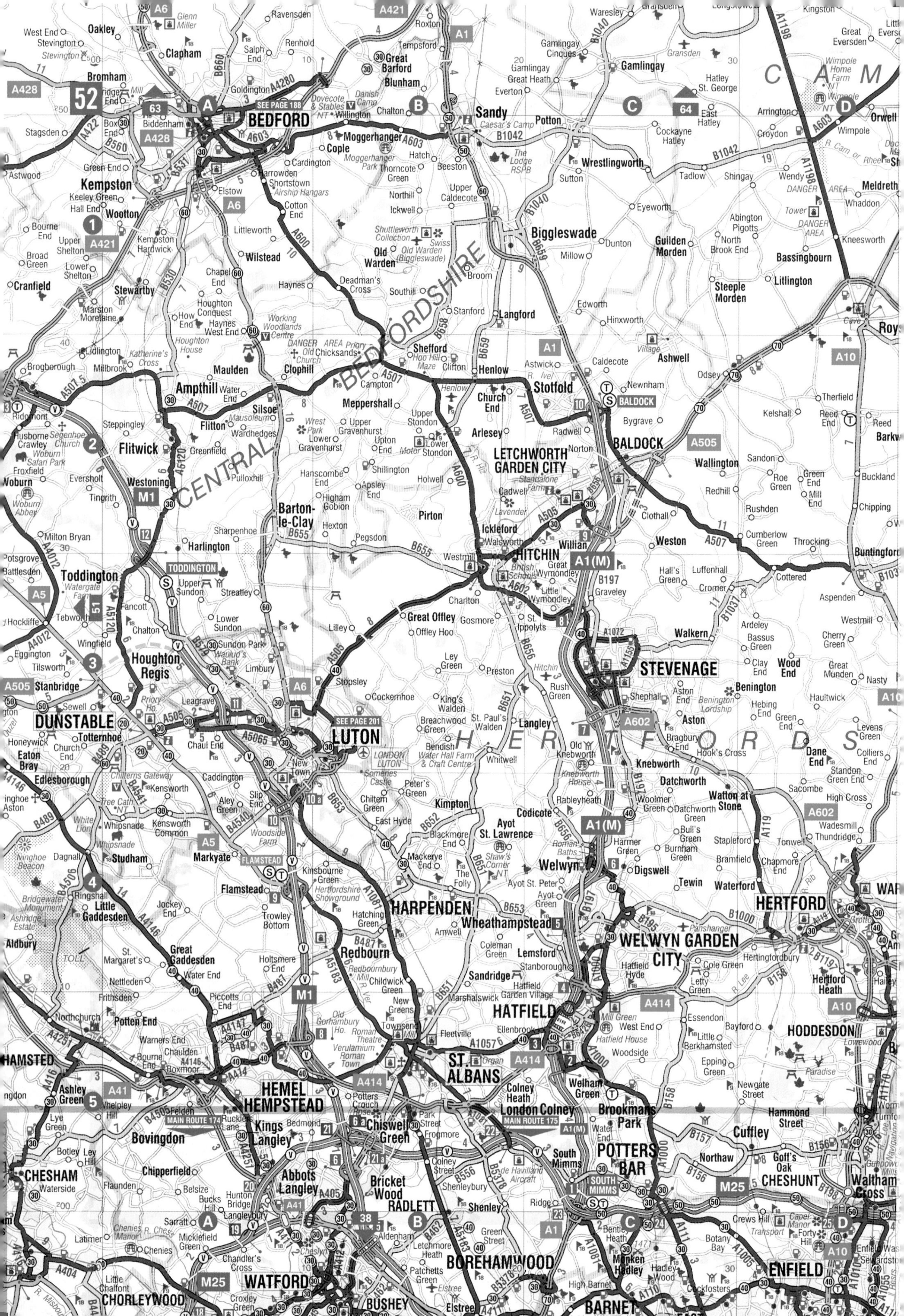

52
53
BEDFORD
SEE PAGE 188
Kempston
Oakley
Clapham
Bromham
Biddenham
Wootton
Cranfield
Stewartby
Marston Moretaine
Lidlington
Ampthill
Flitwick
Westoning
Toddington
Houghton Regis
DUNSTABLE
LUTON
SEE PAGE 201
Barton-le-Clay
Harlington
Sundon Park
Stopsley
Great Offley
HITCHIN
LETCHWORTH GARDEN CITY
BALDOCK
Stotfold
Arlesey
Henlow
Shefford
Biggleswade
Sandy
Potton
Gamlingay
Wrestlingworth
Guilden Morden
Steeple Morden
Ashwell
Royston
STEVENAGE
Knebworth
Welwyn
WELWYN GARDEN CITY
HERTFORD
Harpenden
Wheathampstead
Redbourn
HATFIELD
ST. ALBANS
HEMEL HEMPSTEAD
Kings Langley
Abbots Langley
WATFORD
CHORLEYWOOD
CHESHAM
BUSHEY
RADLETT
BOREHAMWOOD
Shenley
London Colney
POTTERS BAR
Brookmans Park
Cuffley
CHESHUNT
Waltham Cross
ENFIELD
BARNET
HODDESDON
Ware
Edlesborough
Studham
Markyate
Flamstead
Kensworth
Little Gaddesden
Great Gaddesden
Berkhamsted
Bovingdon
Chipperfield
Sarratt
Chenies
Kimpton
Codicote
Ayot St. Lawrence
Watton at Stone
Datchworth
BEDFORDSHIRE
CENTRAL
HERTFORDS
CAM
MAIN ROUTE 174
MAIN ROUTE 175
M1
A1(M)
M25
A1
A6
A5
A10
A505
A507
A600
A602
A414
A41
A428
A421
A603

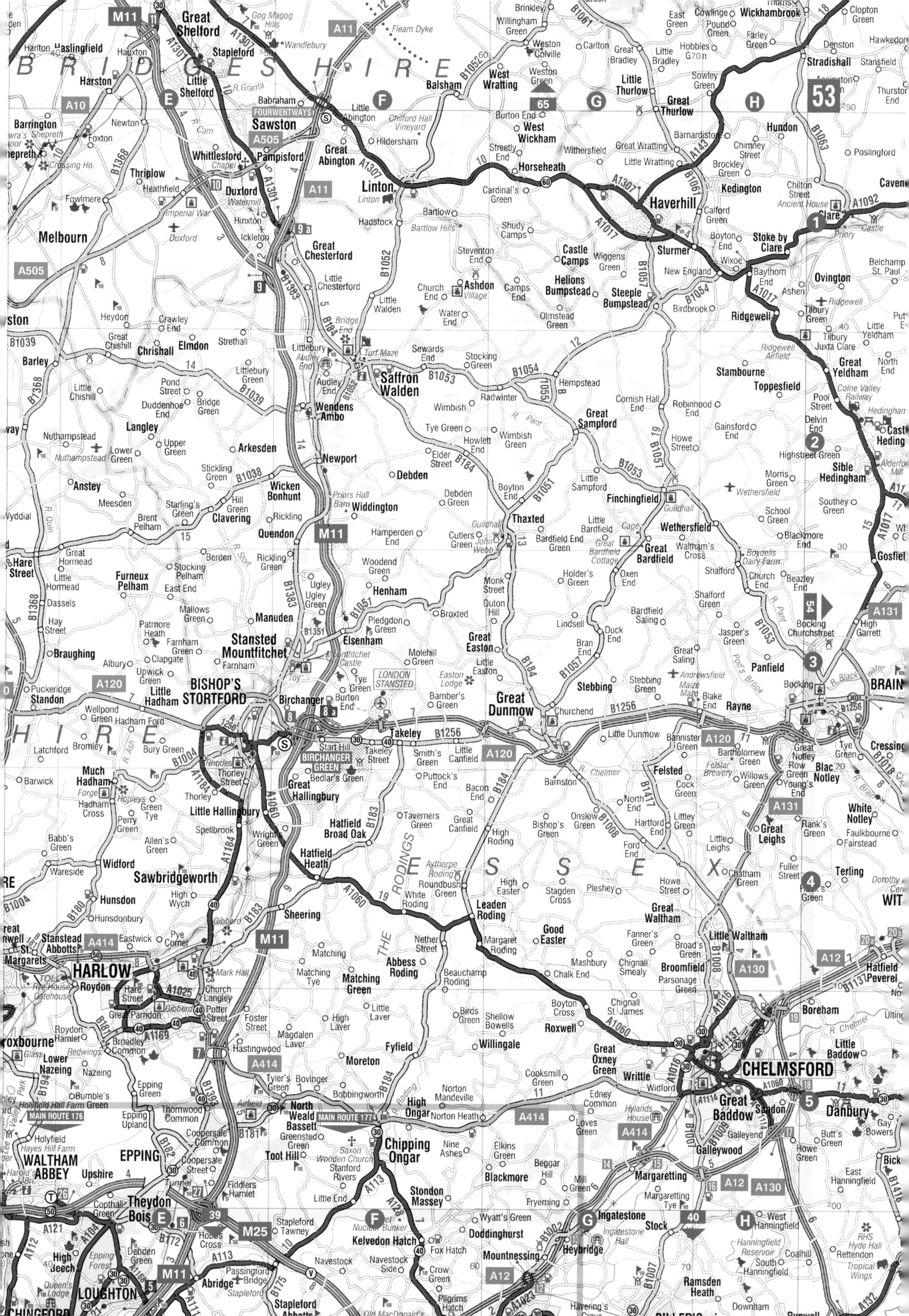

M11
Great Shelford
Gog Magog Hills
Wandlebury
A1307
Stapleford
A11
Fleam Dyke
Brinkley
Willingham Green
B1061
Carlton
Weston Colville
Weston Green
West Wratting
Balsham
B1052
Great Bradley
Little Bradley
Little Thurlow
Great Thurlow
East Green
Cowlinge
Pound Green
Farley Green
Hobbles Green
Sowley Green
Wickhambrook
Clopton Green
Denston
Hawkedon
Stradishall
Stansfield
Thurston End
53
Harlton
Haslingfield
Hauxton
CAMBRIDGESHIRE
Harston
Little Shelford
R. Granta
Babraham
Little Abington
Sawston
FOURWENTWAYS
A505
A10
Barrington
Shepreth
Foxton
Newton
Crossing Ho.
Whittlesford
Pampisford
Great Abington
Hildersham
Chilford Hall Vineyard
Burton End
West Wickham
65
Withersfield
Great Wratting
Little Wratting
Barnardiston
Chimney Street
Hundon
Poslingford
B1063
Thriplow
Heathfield
Duxford
Chapel
Linton
Horseheath
Streetly End
Cardinal's Green
A1017
A1307
Haverhill
Brockley Green
Kedington
Chilton Street
Ancient House
Clare
A1092
Cavendish
Fowlmere
Watermill
Imperial War Museum
Hinxton
Ickleton
Melbourn
Duxford
Hadstock
Bartlow
Bartlow Hills
Shudy Camps
Calford Green
Boyton End
Stoke by Clare
Priory
Castle
Great Chesterford
Steventon End
Castle Camps
Wiggens Green
Sturmer
New England
Wixoe
Baythorn End
Belchamp St. Paul
A505
Little Chesterford
B1383
B1052
Little Walden
Church End
Ashdon
Ashdon Village
Camps End
Helions Bumpstead
Steeple Bumpstead
Birdbrook
B1054
Ovington
Ashen
Ridgewell
Tilbury Green
Tilbury Juxta Clare
Little Yeldham
Heydon
Crawley End
Great Chishill
Chrishall
Elmdon
Strethall
Littlebury
Audley End
Bridge End
Turf Maze
Sewards End
Water End
Olmstead Green
Stocking Green
Hempstead
Ridgewell Airfield
Great Yeldham
North End
Barley
B1039
Little Chishill
Pond Street
Littlebury Green
Duddenhoe End
Bridge Green
Saffron Walden
B1053
B1054
Radwinter
Wimbish
Wimbish Green
Wendens Ambo
Great Sampford
Cornish Hall End
Robinhood End
Stambourne
Toppesfield
Pool Street
Colne Valley Railway
Hedingham
Langley
Upper Green
Arkesden
Tye Green
Howlett End
Elder Street
Nuthampstead
Lower Green
Newport
Debden
Little Sampford
Howe Street
Gainsford End
Delvin End
Highstreet Green
Sible Hedingham
Castle Hedingham
Stickling Green
B1038
Wicken Bonhunt
Anstey
Meesden
Starling's Green
Hill Green
Clavering
Priors Hall Barn
Widdington
Debden Green
Boyton End
Finchingfield
Guildhall
Morris Green
Wethersfield
Southey Green
Wyddial
Brent Pelham
Rickling
Quendon
Hamperden End
Cutlers Green
John Webb's
Thaxted
Bardfield End Green
Little Bardfield
Great Bardfield
Wethersfield
Waltham's Cross
Boydells Dairy Farm
School Green
Blackmore End
Hare Street
Great Hormead
Little Hormead
Furneux Pelham
Berden
Stocking Pelham
East End
Rickling Green
Woodend Green
Henham
Monk Street
Holder's Green
Oxen End
Shalford
Church End
Beazley End
Gosfield
Dassels
Hay Street
Ugley
Ugley Green
Mallows Green
Manuden
Broxted
Duton Hill
Lindsell
Bardfield Saling
Shalford Green
Bocking Churchstreet
High Garrett
A131
Braughing
Patmore Heath
Farnham Green
Clapgate
Stansted Mountfitchet
Piedgdon Green
Elsenham
Molehill Green
Great Easton
Little Easton
Duck End
Bran End
Jasper's Green
Great Saling
Panfield
Puckeridge
Standon
Albury
Upwick Green
Little Hadham
Farnham
BISHOP'S STORTFORD
Mountfitchet Castle
Toy Museum
Birchanger
Tye Green
Burton End
LONDON STANSTED
Easton Lodge
Bamber's Green
Great Dunmow
Churchend
Stebbing
Stebbing Green
Andrewsfield
Maize Maze
Blake End
Rayne
Bocking
BRAINTREE
A120
Wellpond Green
Hadham Ford
Latchford
Bromley
Bury Green
B1004
Start Hill
Takeley
Takeley Street
B1256
Smith's Green
Little Canfield
A120
Little Dunmow
Bannister Green
Felsted
Bartholomew Green
Great Notley
Black Notley
Cressing
Barwick
Much Hadham
Forge
Hopleys
Hadham Cross
Thorley Street
Thorley
BIRCHANGER GREEN
Bedlar's Green
Great Hallingbury
Puttock's End
Bacon End
Barnston
R. Chelmer
Felstar Brewery
Willows Green
Cock Green
Young's End
White Notley
Little Hallingbury
Perry Green
Green Tye
Spellbrook
Wright's Green
Hatfield Broad Oak
Taverners Green
Great Canfield
High Roding
Bishop's Green
Onslow Green
North End
Hartford End
Littley Green
Great Leighs
Rank's Green
Faulkbourne
Fairstead
Babb's Green
Allen's Green
Widford
Wareside
Sawbridgeworth
Hatfield Heath
Aythorpe Roding
THE RODINGS
ESSEX
High Easter
Stagden Cross
Pleshey
Ford End
Little Leighs
Chatham Green
Howe Street
Fuller Street
Terling
Hunsdon
High Wych
Hunsdonbury
Gibberd Garden
Sheering
White Roding
Roundbush Green
Leaden Roding
Great Waltham
Hawk's Green
Stanstead Abbotts
St. Margarets
Eastwick
Pye Corner
M11
Matching
Nether Street
Good Easter
Margaret Roding
Fanner's Green
Chignall Smealy
Broad's Green
Little Waltham
A130
A12
Hatfield Peverel
HARLOW
Roydon
Rye House Gatehouse
Hare Street
Church Langley
Mark Hall
Matching Tye
Matching Green
Abbess Roding
Beauchamp Roding
Mashbury
Chalk End
Broomfield
Parsonage Green
Boreham
Great Parndon
Potter Street
Foster Street
Little Laver
High Laver
Birds Green
Shellow Bowells
Boyton Cross
Chignall St. James
Roxwell
Hoddesdon
Roydon Hamlet
Broadley Common
Lower Nazeing
Nazeing
Hastingwood
Magdalen Laver
Moreton
Fyfield
Willingale
Great Oxney Green
Writtle
CHELMSFORD
Little Baddow
Glass
Epping Green
Bumble's Green
A414
Tyler's Green
Bovinger
Bobbingworth
Norton Mandeville
Cooksmill Green
Widford
Great Baddow
Sandon
Danbury
Gay Bowers
Holyfield
Hayes Hill Farm
Holyfield Hall Farm
MAIN ROUTE 176
Epping Upland
Thornwood Common
North Weald Bassett
MAIN ROUTE 177
High Ongar
Norton Heath
A414
Edney Common
Hylands House
Galleyend
Butt's Green
Howe Green
WALTHAM ABBEY
EPPING
Coopersale Common
Coopersale Street
Greensted Green
Toot Hill
Saxon Wooden Church
Stanford Rivers
Chipping Ongar
Nine Ashes
Elkins Green
Loves Green
Galleywood
Upshire
Theydon Bois
Fiddlers Hamlet
Little End
Stondon Massey
Blackmore
Beggar Hill
Mill Green
Fryerning
Margaretting
Margaretting Tye
East Hanningfield
Copthall Green
Hobbs Cross
M25
Stapleford Tawney
Nuclear Bunker
Kelvedon Hatch
Wyatt's Green
Doddinghurst
Ingatestone
Ingatestone Hall
Stock
West Hanningfield
Hanningfield Reservoir
RHS Hyde Hall
Rettendon
High Beech
Epping Forest
Debden Green
Abridge
Passingford Bridge
Stapleford
Navestock
Navestock Side
Fox Hatch
Crow Green
Mountnessing
Heybridge
Coalhill
South Hanningfield
Tropical Wings
Queen's Lodge
LOUGHTON
CHINGFORD
Stapleford Abbotts
Pilgrims Hatch
Havering's Grove
Ramsden Heath
Downham

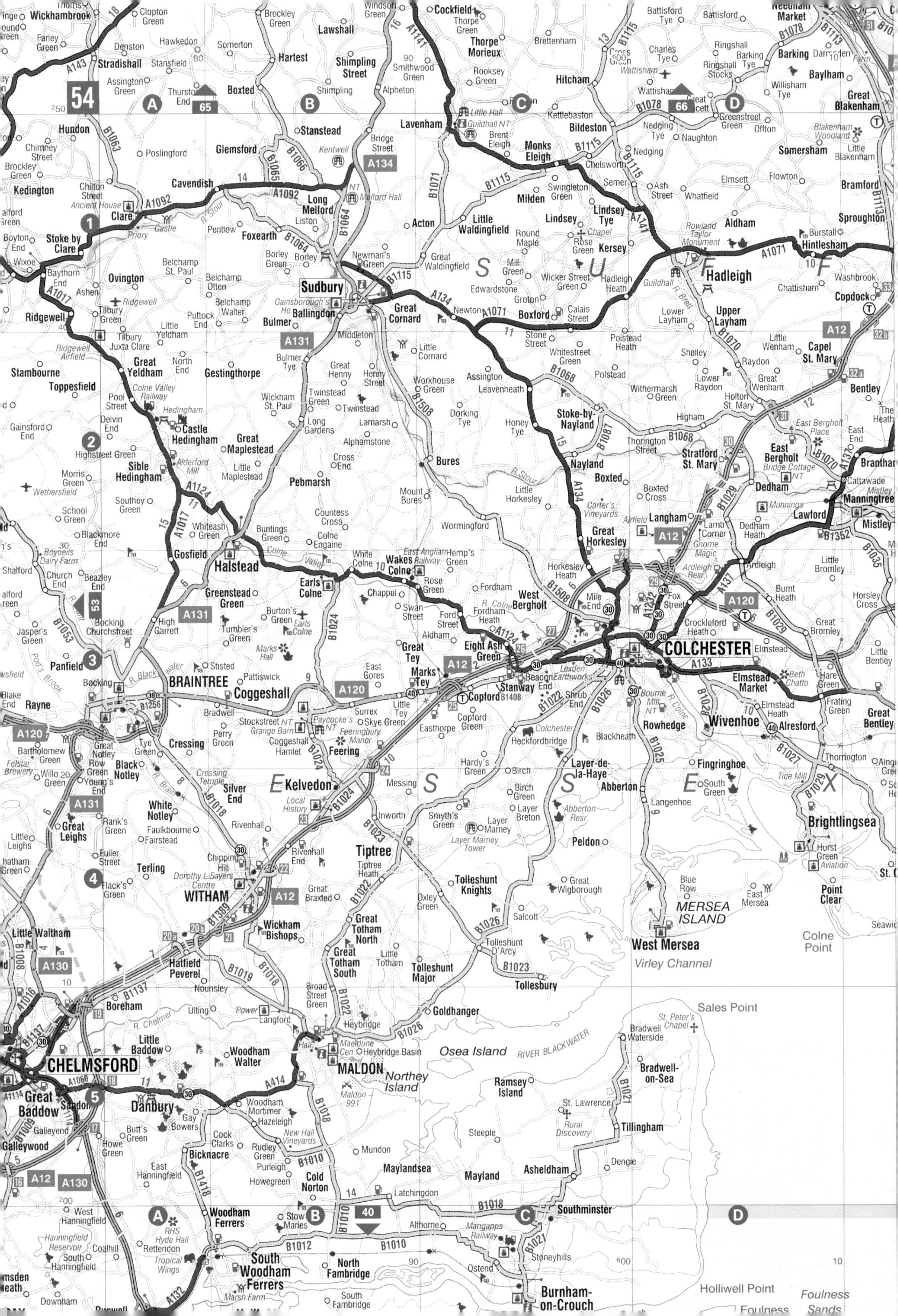
54
Wickhambrook
Clopton Green
Brockley Green
Lawshall
Cockfield
Thorpe Green
Thorpe Morieux
Battisford Tye
Battisford
Needham Market
Farley Green
Denston
Hawkedon
Somerton
Hartest
Shimpling Street
Smithwood Green
Brettenham
Cross Green
Charles Tye
Ringshall
Barking Tye
Barking
Darmsden
Stradishall
Stansfield
Assington Green
Thurston End
Boxted
Shimpling
Alpheton
Rooksey Green
Hitcham
Wattisham
Ringshall Stocks
Willisham Tye
Baylham
Great Blakenham
65
66
A
B
C
D
Little Hall
Guildhall NT
Kettlebaston
Great Bricett
Greenstreet Green
Offton
Blakenham Woodland
Little Blakenham
Hundon
Stanstead
Lavenham
Bridge Street
Brent Eleigh
Bildeston
Nedging Tye
Naughton
Somersham
Chimney Street
Poslingford
Glemsford
Kentwell
Monks Eleigh
Nedging
Chelsworth
Brockley Green
Kedington
Chilton Street
Ancient House
Clare
Cavendish
Long Melford
Melford Hall
Liston
Milden
Swingleton Green
Semer
Ash Street
Whatfield
Elmsett
Flowton
Bramford
Castle
Priory
R. Stour
Pentlow
Foxearth
Acton
Little Waldingfield
Lindsey
Lindsey Tye
Round Maple
Chapel
Rowland Taylor Monument
Aldham
Sproughton
Stoke by Clare
Boyton End
Wixoe
Baythorn End
Ashen
Ovington
Belchamp St. Paul
Belchamp Otten
Borley Green
Borley
Newman's Green
Great Waldingfield
Mill Green
Rose Green
Kersey
Wicker Street Green
Hadleigh Heath
Hadleigh
Guildhall
Hintlesham
Burstall
Washbrook
Chattisham
Copdock
Ridgewell
Tilbury Green
Belchamp Walter
Sudbury
Gainsborough's Ho.
Ballingdon
Bulmer
Great Cornard
Newton
Edwardstone
Groton
Boxford
Calais Street
Lower Layham
Upper Layham
Tilbury Juxta Clare
Little Yeldham
Puttock End
Middleton
Little Cornard
Stone Street
Whitestreet Green
Polstead Heath
Shelley
Little Wenham
Capel St. Mary
Ridgewell Airfield
Great Yeldham
North End
Gestingthorpe
Bulmer Tye
Great Henny
Henny Street
Assington
Leavenheath
Polstead
Raydon
Great Wenham
Lower Raydon
Holton St. Mary
Withermarsh Green
Bentley
Stambourne
Toppesfield
Pool Street
Colne Valley Railway
Hedingham
Wickham St. Paul
Twinstead Green
Twinstead
Workhouse Green
Dorking Tye
Honey Tye
Stoke-by-Nayland
Higham
East Bergholt Place
East End
The Heath
Gainsford End
Delvin End
Castle Hedingham
Great Maplestead
Long Gardens
Lamarsh
Alphamstone
Bures
Thorington Street
Stratford St. Mary
East Bergholt
Bridge Cottage NT
Brantham
Highstreet Green
Alderford Mill
Little Maplestead
Cross End
Nayland
Boxted
Boxted Cross
Dedham
Cattawade
Mistley Heath
Manningtree
Morris Green
Wethersfield
Sible Hedingham
Pebmarsh
Mount Bures
R. Stour
Little Horkesley
Carter's Vineyards
Munnings
Southey Green
School Green
Whiteash Green
Buntings Green
Countess Cross
Colne Engaine
Wormingford
Airfield
Langham
Lamb Corner
Dedham Heath
Lawford
Mistley
Blackmore End
Boyceis Dairy Farm
Shalford
Church End
Beazley End
Gosfield
Halstead
White Colne
Wakes Colne
East Anglian Railway
Hemp's Green
Great Horkesley
Gnome Magic
Ardleigh Resr.
Ardleigh
Little Bromley
Horkesley Heath
Earls Colne
Chappel
Rose Green
Fordham
West Bergholt
Mile End
Fox Street
Burnt Heath
Horsley Cross
Alford Green
53
Greenstead Green
Burton's Green
Swan Street
Ford Street
Fordham Heath
R. Colne
Crockleford Heath
Great Bromley
Jasper's Green
Bocking Churchstreet
High Garrett
Tumbler's Green
Earls Colne
Marks Hall
Aldham
Eight Ash Green
Great Tey
COLCHESTER
Elmstead
Little Bentley
Panfield
Stisted
Pattiswick
East Gores
Marks Tey
Beacon End
Lexden Earthworks
Stanway
Beth Chatto
Elmstead Market
Hare Green
Bocking
BRAINTREE
Coggeshall
Little Tey
Copford
Shrub End
Bourne Mill NT
Frating Green
Great Bentley
Blake End
Rayne
Bradwell
Stockstreet NT Grange Barn
Paycocke's NT
Surrex
Skye Green
Easthorpe
Copford Green
Colchester Zoo
Rowhedge
Wivenhoe
Elmstead Heath
Alresford
Bartholomew Green
Felsted Brewery
Great Notley
Black Notley
Tye Green
Cressing
Perry Green
Coggeshall Hamlet
Feeringbury Manor
Feering
Heckfordbridge
Blackheath
Thorrington
Willo Green
Young's End
Row Green
Cressing Temple
R. Brain
Silver End
Kelvedon
Local History
Messing
Hardy's Green
Birch
Layer-de-la-Haye
Abberton
Fingringhoe
South Green
Tide Mill
Great Leighs
White Notley
Rank's Green
Faulkbourne
Fairstead
Rivenhall
Inworth
Smyth's Green
Layer Marney
Layer Marney Tower
Birch Green
Layer Breton
Abberton Resr.
Peldon
Langenhoe
Brightlingsea
Little Leighs
Fuller Street
Terling
Chipping Hill
Rivenhall End
Tiptree
Tiptree Heath
Hurst Green
Aviation
Flack's Green
Dorothy L Sayers Centre
WITHAM
Great Braxted
Oxley Green
Tolleshunt Knights
Great Wigborough
Blue Row
East Mersea
MERSEA ISLAND
Point Clear
Little Waltham
Wickham Bishops
Great Totham North
Great Totham South
Little Totham
Salcott
Tolleshunt D'Arcy
Tolleshunt Major
West Mersea
Virley Channel
Colne Point
Seawick
Hatfield Peverel
Nounsley
Broad Street Green
Tollesbury
Boreham
Ulting
Power
Langford
Heybridge
Goldhanger
Sales Point
R. Chelmer
Little Baddow
Woodham Walter
Maeldune Cen.
Heybridge Basin
Osea Island
RIVER BLACKWATER
St. Peter's Chapel
Bradwell Waterside
CHELMSFORD
MALDON
Northey Island
Maldon
Bradwell-on-Sea
Great Baddow
Sandon
Danbury
Gay Bowers
Woodham Mortimer
Hazeleigh
Ramsey Island
St. Lawrence
Rural Discovery
Tillingham
Galleyend
Galleywood
Butt's Green
Howe Green
Cock Clarks
Bicknacre
Rudley Green
New Hall Vineyards
Purleigh
Steeple
Mundon
Dengie
East Hanningfield
Howegreen
Cold Norton
Maylandsea
Mayland
Asheldham
Latchingdon
Southminster
West Hanningfield
Woodham Ferrers
Stow Maries
Althorne
Mangapps Railway
Hanningfield Reservoir
RHS Hyde Hall
Rettendon
Coalhill
South Hanningfield
Tropical Wings
South Woodham Ferrers
North Fambridge
Ostend
Stoneyhills
Burnham-on-Crouch
Holliwell Point
Foulness Sands
Downham
Marsh Farm
South Fambridge
Ramsden Heath
40
A12
A120
A130
A131
A133
A134
A137
A143
A414
A1017
A1071
A1092
A1124
A1141
B1018
B1019
B1023
B1024
B1026
B1027
B1029
B1063
B1064
B1068
B1070
B1071
B1078
B1087
B1115
B1352
B1508

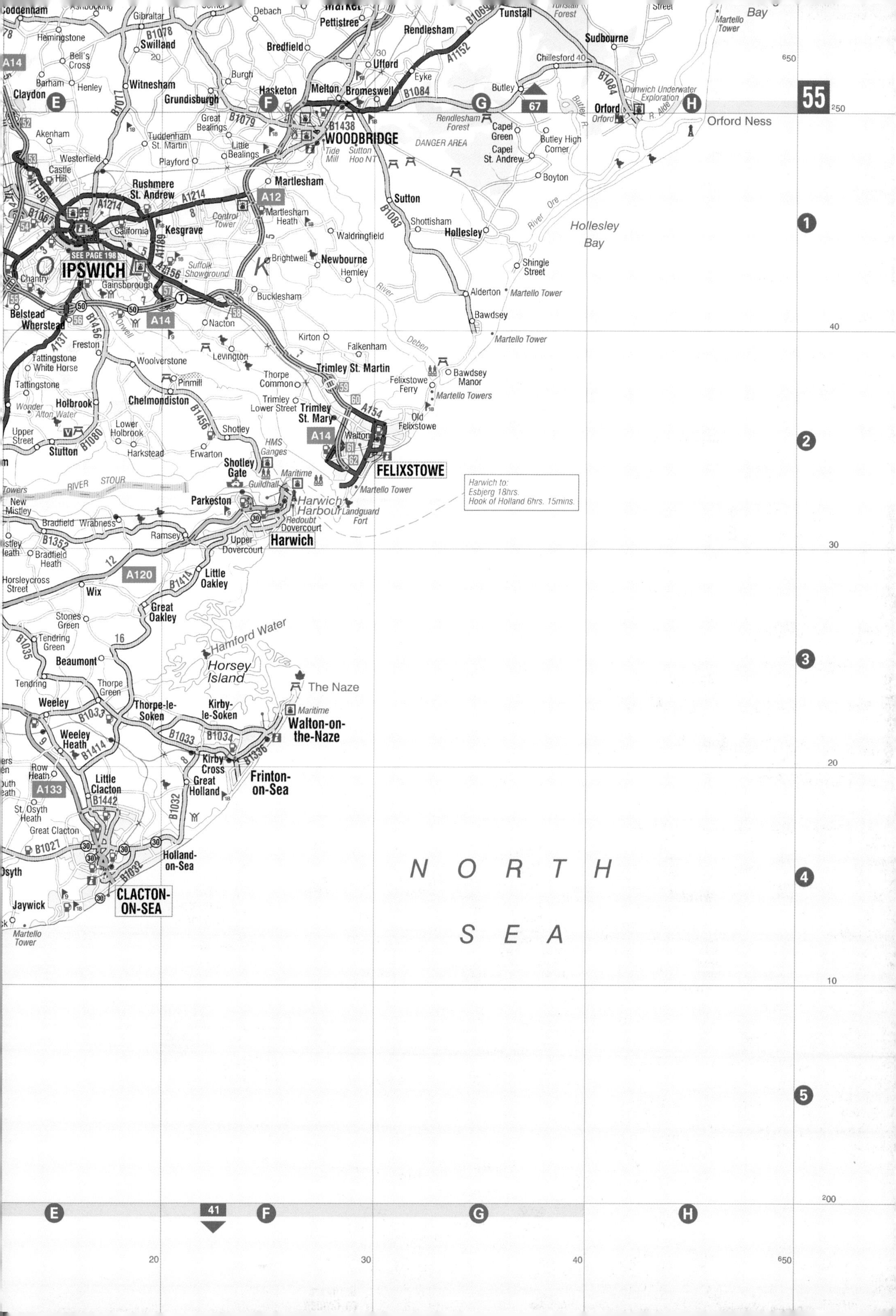
55
Tunstall
Sudbourne
Pettistree
Rendlesham
Bredfield
Gibraltar
Swilland
Hemingstone
Bell's Cross
Ufford
Eyke
Chillesford
Orford
Orford Ness
Dunwich Underwater Exploration
Butley
Claydon
Barham
Henley
Witnesham
Grundisburgh
Burgh
Hasketon
Melton
Bromeswell
Rendlesham Forest
Capel Green
Butley High Corner
Capel St. Andrew
Boyton
DANGER AREA
Great Bealings
Little Bealings
WOODBRIDGE
Tide Mill
Sutton Hoo NT
Akenham
Tuddenham St. Martin
Westerfield
Playford
Castle Hill
Martlesham
Rushmere St. Andrew
Sutton
Martlesham Heath
Control Tower
Kesgrave
California
Shottisham
Hollesley
Hollesley Bay
River Ore
Waldringfield
SEE PAGE 198
IPSWICH
Chantry
Gainsborough
Brightwell
Newbourne
Hemley
Suffolk Showground
Shingle Street
Alderton
Martello Tower
Bawdsey
Bucklesham
Belstead
Wherstead
Nacton
Kirton
Falkenham
River Deben
Freston
Levington
Tattingstone White Horse
Woolverstone
Trimley St. Martin
Bawdsey Manor
Felixstowe Ferry
Martello Towers
Tattingstone
Pinmill
Thorpe Common
Chelmondiston
Trimley Lower Street
Trimley St. Mary
Wonder
Holbrook
Alton Water
Old Felixstowe
Walton
Upper Street
Lower Holbrook
Shotley
Stutton
Harkstead
Erwarton
HMS Ganges
FELIXSTOWE
Shotley Gate
Maritime
Guildhall
Harwich to:
Esbjerg 18hrs.
Hook of Holland 6hrs. 15mins.
RIVER STOUR
Parkeston
Harwich Harbour
Landguard Fort
New Mistley
Bradfield
Wrabness
Redoubt
Dovercourt
Ramsey
Upper Dovercourt
Harwich
Bradfield Heath
Little Oakley
Horsleycross Street
Wix
Stones Green
Great Oakley
Tendring Green
Hamford Water
Beaumont
Horsey Island
The Naze
Tendring
Thorpe Green
Weeley
Thorpe-le-Soken
Kirby-le-Soken
Walton-on-the-Naze
Weeley Heath
Kirby Cross
Frinton-on-Sea
Row Heath
Little Clacton
Great Holland
St. Osyth Heath
Great Clacton
Holland-on-Sea
Jaywick
CLACTON-ON-SEA
NORTH SEA
A14
A12
A120
A133
A154
A1214
A1189
A1156
A1152
A137
B1078
B1077
B1079
B1084
B1069
B1438
B1083
B1456
B1080
B1352
B1414
B1035
B1033
B1034
B1336
B1442
B1032
B1027
41
67
E
F
G
H
1
2
3
4
5
10
20
30
40
200
250
650

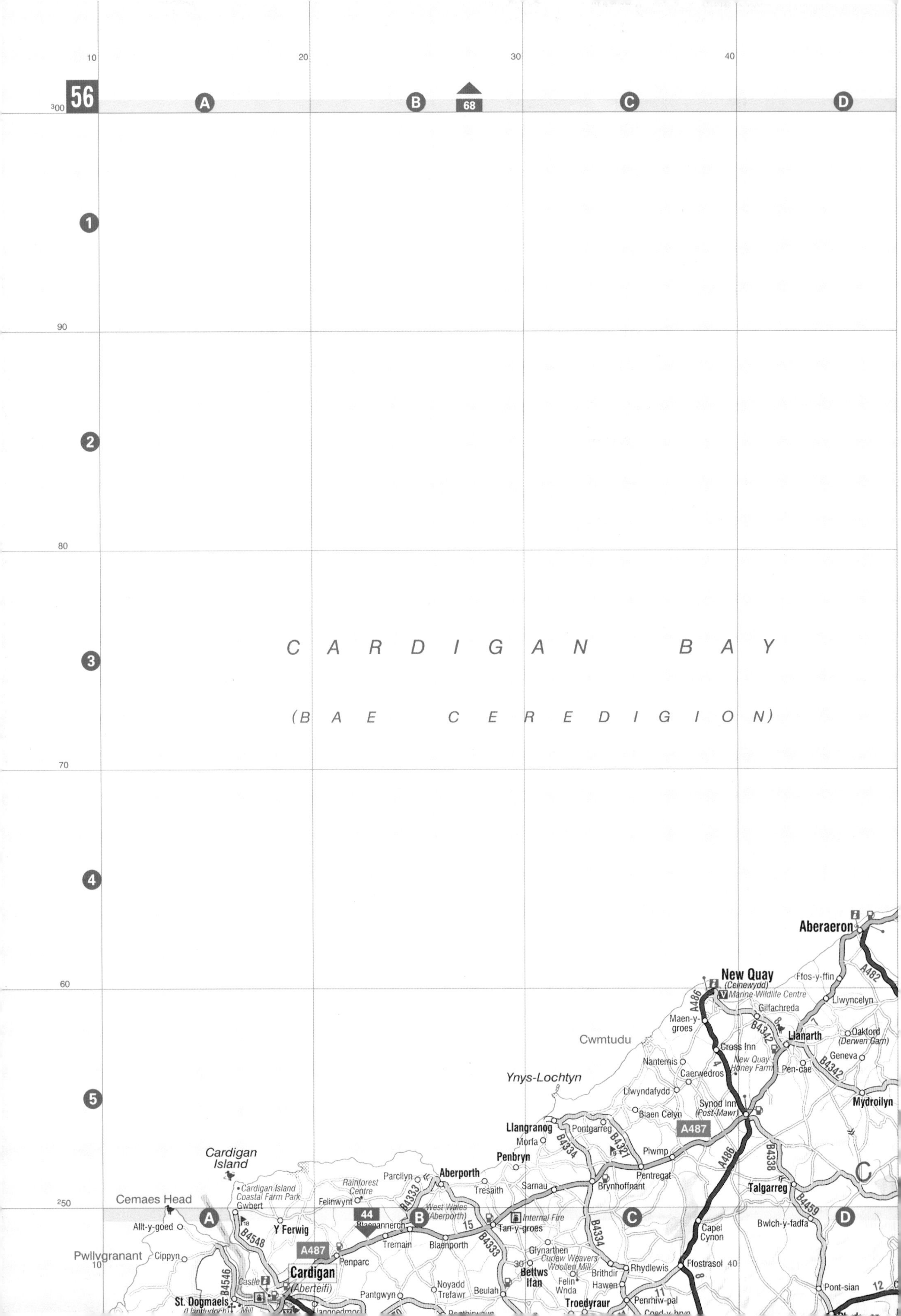
68
CARDIGAN BAY
(BAE CEREDIGION)
Aberaeron
New Quay
(Ceinewydd)
Marine Wildlife Centre
Ffos-y-ffin
Llwyncelyn
Gilfachreda
Maen-y-groes
Cwmtudu
Cross Inn
Llanarth
Oakford
(Derwen Gam)
Nanternis
New Quay Honey Farm
Geneva
Caerwedros
Pen-cae
Ynys-Lochtyn
Llwyndafydd
Synod Inn
(Post-Mawr)
Mydroilyn
Blaen Celyn
Llangranog
Pontgarreg
Morfa
Plwmp
Penbryn
Pentregat
Cardigan Island
Aberporth
Tresaith
Sarnau
Brynhoffnant
Talgarreg
Cardigan Island Coastal Farm Park
Parcllyn
Rainforest Centre
Gwbert
Felinwynt
West Wales (Aberporth)
Cemaes Head
Allt-y-goed
Y Ferwig
Blaenannerch
Tremain
Blaenporth
Tan-y-groes
Internal Fire
Capel Cynon
Bwlch-y-fadfa
Glynarthen
Curlew Weavers Woollen Mill
Pwllygranant
Cippyn
Penparc
Beulah
Cardigan
(Aberteifi)
Castle
Noyadd Trefawr
Beltws Ifan
Felin Wnda
Brithdir
Hawen
Rhydlewis
Ffostrasol
Pont-sian
St. Dogmaels
Pantgwyn
Troedyraur
Penrhiw-pal
A486
A482
B4342
A487
B4321
B4334
B4338
B4459
B4333
B4548
B4546
44
A
B
C
D
1
2
3
4
5

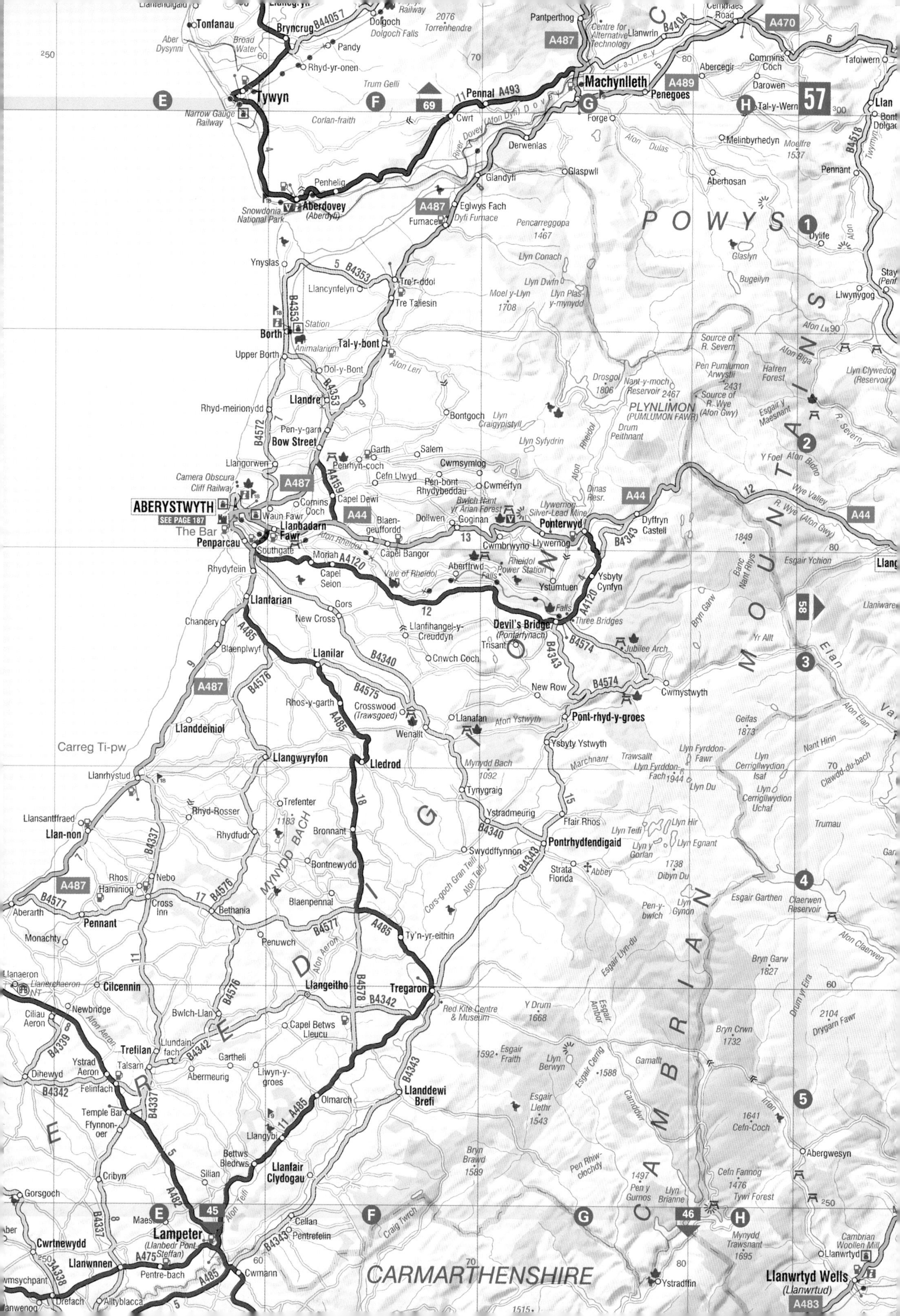

Tywyn
Machynlleth
Aberdovey
(Aberdyfi)
Borth
ABERYSTWYTH
SEE PAGE 187
POWYS
PLYNLIMON
(PUMLUMON FAWR)
CAMBRIAN MOUNTAINS
CEREDIGION
Devil's Bridge
(Pontarfynach)
Ponterwyd
Tregaron
Lampeter
(Llanbedr Pont Steffan)
Llanwrtyd Wells
(Llanwrtud)
CARMARTHENSHIRE
Pontrhydfendigaid
Strata Florida
Llangeitho
Llanon
Aberarth
Llanrhystud
Carreg Ti-pw
A487
A44
A485
A4120
A470
A489
A493
A482
A475
A483
57
58
69
45
46

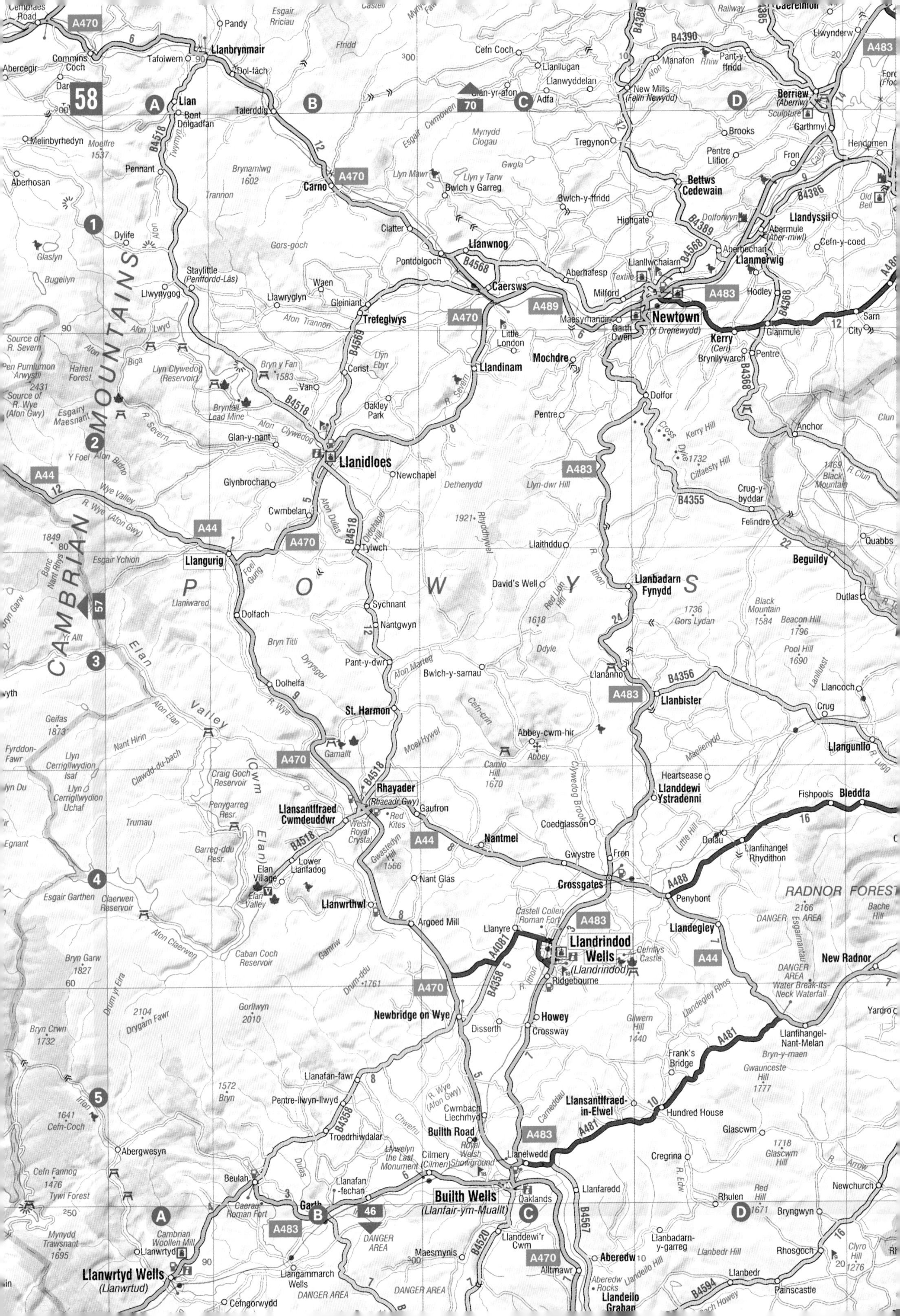
58
A470
Pandy
Llanbrynmair
Tafolwern
Commins Coch
Abercegir
Dol-fâch
Llan
Bont Dolgadfan
Talerddig
Melinbyrhedyn
Moelfre 1537
Pennant
Aberhosan
Brynamlwg 1602
Trannon
Carno
Dylife
Glaslyn
Bugeilyn
Gors-goch
Staylittle (Penffordd-Lâs)
Llwynygog
Waen
Llawryglyn
Gleiniant
Trefeglwys
Afon Trannon
CAMBRIAN MOUNTAINS
Source of R. Severn
Pen Pumlumon Arwystli 2431
Hafren Forest
Source of R. Wye (Afon Gwy)
Esgairy Maesnant
Llyn Clywedog (Reservoir)
Bryn y Fan 1583
Van
Cerist
Llyn Ebyr
Bryntail Lead Mine
Glan-y-nant
Oakley Park
Y Foel
A44
Glynbrochan
Llanidloes
Newchapel
Cwmbelan
Wye Valley
A470
B4518
Tylwch
1849
Banc Nant Rhys
Esgair Ychion
Llangurig
POWYS
Llaniwared
Dolfach
Sychnant
Nantgwyn
Bryn Titli
Pant-y-dwr
Yr Allt
Elan Valley
Dolhelfa
St. Harmon
Geifas 1873
Nant Hirin
Fyrddon-Fawr
Llyn Cerrigllwydion Isaf
Llyn Cerrigllwydion Uchaf
Clawdd-du-bach
Craig Goch Reservoir
Penygarreg Resr.
Gamallt
Rhayader
(Rhaeadr Gwy)
Llansantffraed Cwmdeuddwr
Welsh Royal Crystal
Red Kites
Gaufron
Trumau
Garreg-ddu Resr.
Lower Llanfadog
Gwastedyn Hill 1566
Elan Village
Elan Valley
Esgair Garthen
Claerwen Reservoir
Llanwrthwl
Nant Glas
Argoed Mill
Afon Claerwen
Caban Coch Reservoir
Bryn Garw 1827
Drum yr Eira
Drum-ddu 1761
2104 Drygarn Fawr
Gorllwyn 2010
Newbridge on Wye
Bryn Crwn 1732
Llanafan-fawr
1572 Bryn
Pentre-llwyn-llwyd
1641 Cefn-Coch
Irfon
Abergwesyn
Troedrhiwdalar
Cefn Fannog 1476
Tywi Forest
Beulah
Caerau Roman Fort
Garth
B4358
A483
46
DANGER AREA
Mynydd Trawsnant 1695
Cambrian Woollen Mill
Llanwrtyd
Llanwrtyd Wells (Llanwrtud)
Llangammarch Wells
DANGER AREA
Cefngorwydd
Llanafan -fechan
Cilmery (Cilmeri)
Llywelyn the Last Monument
Builth Road
Royal Welsh Showground
Builth Wells (Llanfair-ym-Muallt)
Maesmynis
DANGER AREA
B4520
Llanddewi'r Cwm
Oaklands
Cwmbach Llechrhyd
R. Wye (Afon Gwy)
Chwefru
Disserth
Howey
Crossway
Cefn Coch
Llanllugan
Llanwyddelan
Glan-yr-afon
Adfa
70
Mynydd Clogau
Gwgla
Llyn Mawr
Llyn y Tarw
Bwlch y Garreg
Clatter
Llanwnog
Pontdolgoch
B4568
Caersws
A489
Little London
Llandinam
Mochdre
Dethenydd
Llyn-dwr Hill
1921
Llaithddu
David's Well
Red Lion Hill
1618
Ddyle
Bwlch-y-sarnau
Cefn-crin
Abbey-cwm-hir
Abbey
Camlo Hill 1670
Moel Hywel
Clywedog Brook
Nantmel
Gwystre
Crossgates
Coedglasson
Castell Collen Roman Fort
Llanyre
A4081
Llandrindod Wells
(Llandrindod)
Ridgebourne
Cefnllys Castle
Gilwern Hill 1440
Llansantffraed-in-Elwel
Hundred House
Llanelwedd
A481
Cregrina
Llanfaredd
B4567
Aberedw
Aberedw Rocks
Llandeilo Graban
Llandeilo Hill
Alltmawr
B4389
B4390
Manafon
Pant-y-ffridd
New Mills (Felin Newydd)
Tregynon
Bwlch-y-ffridd
Highgate
Bettws Cedewain
Dolforwyn
Aberhafesp
Llanllwchaiarn
Textile
Milford
Maesyrhandir
Garth Owen
Newtown (Y Drenewydd)
Dolfor
Pentre
Kerry Hill
Cross Dyke
1732
Cilfaesty Hill
B4355
A483
Llanbadarn Fynydd
Llananno
Llanbister
B4356
1736 Gors Lydan
Black Mountain 1584
Beacon Hill 1796
Pool Hill 1690
Maelienydd
Heartsease
Llanddewi Ystradenni
Little Hill
Fron
A488
Penybont
Llandegley
Llandegley Rhos
Frank's Bridge
Glascwm
1718 Glascwm Hill
Rhulen
Red Hill 1671
Llanbadarn-y-garreg
Llanbedr Hill
Railway
Caereinion
Llwynderw
Berriew (Aberriw)
Sculpture
Garthmyl
Brooks
Pentre Llifior
Fron
Hendomen
B4386
Old Bell
Llandyssil
Abermule (Aber-miwl)
Aberbechan
Cefn-y-coed
Llanmerwig
Hodley
B4368
Kerry (Ceri)
Brynllywarch
Glanmule
Sarn
City
Pentre
Anchor
Clun
1469 Black Mountain
R. Clun
Crug-y-byddar
Felindre
Quabbs
Beguildy
Dutlas
Llancoch
Crug
Llangunllo
R. Lugg
Fishpools
Bleddfa
Dolau
Llanfihangel Rhydithon
RADNOR FOREST
2166 AREA
DANGER
Bache Hill
New Radnor
DANGER AREA
Water Break-its-Neck Waterfall
Yardro
Llanfihangel-Nant-Melan
Bryn-y-maen
Gwaunceste Hill 1777
Arrow
Newchurch
Bryngwyn
Rhosgoch
Clyro Hill 1276
Llanbedr
Painscastle
B4594

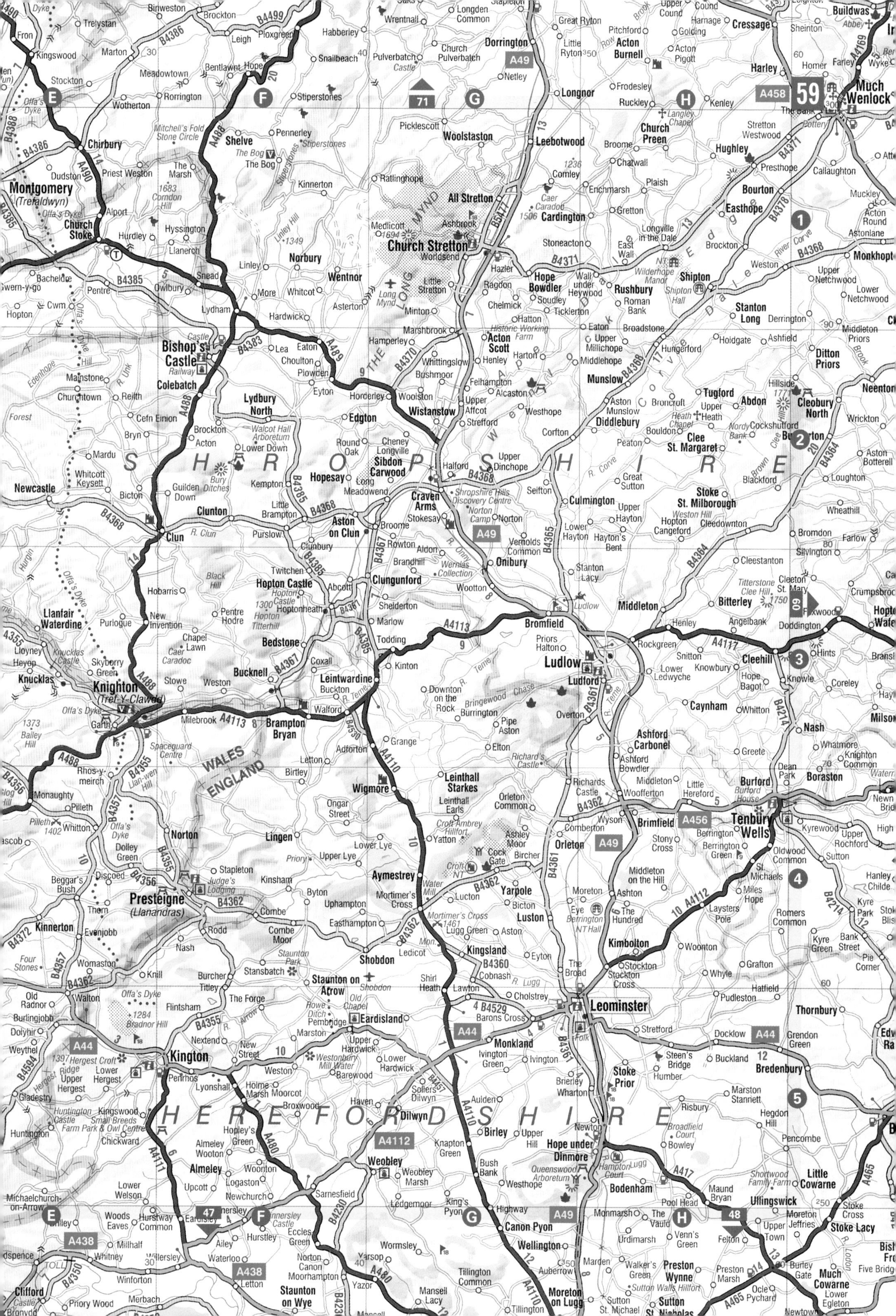

59
60
71
47
48
SHROPSHIRE
HEREFORDSHIRE
WALES
ENGLAND
Binweston
Brockton
B4499
Trelystan
Wrentnall
Longden Common
Dorrington
Great Ryton
Pitchford
Acton Burnell
Acton Pigott
Cound
Harnage
Golding
Cressage
Sheinton
Buildwas
Much Wenlock
Fron
Kingswood
Marton
B4386
Leigh
Ploxgreen
Habberley
Snailbeach
Pulverbatch Castle
Church Pulverbatch
Little Ryton
A49
Netley
Longnor
Frodesley
Ruckley
Kenley
Harley
Homer
Farley
Wyke
A458
A4169
Stockton
Meadowtown
Bentlawnt
Hope
Rorrington
Wotherton
Stiperstones
Picklescott
Woolstaston
Leebotwood
Church Preen
Stretton Westwood
Hughley
Presthope
Callaughton
Offa's Dyke
Mitchell's Fold Stone Circle
Shelve
Pennerley
The Bog
Chirbury
B4386
A490
A488
Dudston
Priest Weston
The Marsh
Broome
Chatwall
Comley
Plaish
Bourton
Montgomery
(Trefaldwyn)
Corndon Hill
Kinnerton
Ratlinghope
LONG MYND
All Stretton
Caer Caradoc
Cardington
Enchmarsh
Gretton
Easthope
B4371
B4378
Muckley
Acton Round
Astonlane
Church Stoke
Alport
Hurdley
Hyssington
Llanerch
Linley Hill
Norbury
Medlicott
Ashbrook
Church Stretton
Worldsend
Stoneacton
East Wall
Longville in the Dale
Brockton
B4368
Monkhopton
Weston
River Corve
Bacheldre
Pentre
B4385
Owlbury
Snead
Linley
Wentnor
Whitcot
More
Asterton
Long Mynd
Little Stretton
Hazler
Ragdon
Hope Bowdler
Soudley
Wall under Heywood
Rushbury
Wilderhope Manor
Shipton
Shipton Hall
Upper Netchwood
Lower Netchwood
Hopton
Cwm
Lydham
Hardwick
Minton
Chelmick
Ticklerton
Roman Bank
Stanton Long
Derrington
Middleton Priors
Bishop's Castle
Castle
Railway
B4383
Lea
Eaton
Choulton
A489
Plowden
Marshbrook
Hamperley
Whittingslow
Bushmoor
Acton Scott
Henley
Hatton
Harton
Eaton
Upper Millichope
Middlehope
Broadstone
Hungerford
Holdgate
Ashfield
Ditton Priors
Mainstone
Churchtown
Reilth
Colebatch
Lydbury North
Eyton
Horderley
Woolston
Wistanstow
Felhampton
Alcaston
Munslow
Aston Munslow
Diddlebury
Broncroft
Tugford
Abdon
Upper Heath
Heath Chapel
Nordy Bank
Cockshutford
Cleobury North
Neenton
Wrickton
Forest
Cefn Einion
Bryn
Brockton
Acton
Walcot Hall Arboretum
Lower Down
Edgton
Upper Affcot
Strefford
Westhope
Corfton
Peaton
Bouldon
Clee St. Margaret
Burwarton
Aston Botterell
Mardu
Whitcott Keysett
Newcastle
Bury Ditches
Round Oak
Cheney Longville
Sibdon Carwood
Hopesay
Long Meadowend
Halford
Upper Dinchope
B4368
Shropshire Hills Discovery Centre
Great Sutton
Brown Clee
Blackford
Loughton
Bicton
Guilden Down
Kempton
Little Brampton
Aston on Clun
Craven Arms
Stokesay
Norton Camp
Norton
Seifton
Culmington
Upper Hayton
Stoke St. Milborough
Weston Hill
Hopton Cangeford
Cleedownton
Wheathill
Clunton
Clun
R. Clun
Purslow
Clunbury
B4367
B4385
Rowton
Aldon
Brandhill
R. Onny
Wernlas Collection
Vernolds Common
Onibury
B4365
Lower Hayton
Hayton's Bent
Bromdon
Farlow
Silvington
Cleestanton
Twitchen
Black Hill
Hopton Castle
Hoptonheath
Abcott
Clungunford
Shelderton
Wootton
Stanton Lacy
Titterstone Clee Hill
Cleeton St. Mary
Crumpsbrook
Hobarris
Llanfair Waterdine
Purlogue
New Invention
Pentre Hodre
Hopton Titterhill
Marlow
A4113
Bromfield
Ludlow
Middleton
Bitterley
Henley
Angelbank
Doddington
Foxwood
Llwyney
Heyop
Knucklas
Knucklas Castle
Skyborry Green
Chapel Lawn
Caer Caradoc
Bedstone
Todding
Kinton
Priors Halton
Rockgreen
A4117
Cleehill
Hints
Snitton
Knowbury
Lower Ledwyche
Hope Bagot
Knowle
Coreley
Knighton
(Tref-Y-Clawdd)
Stowe
Weston
Bucknell
Coxall
Leintwardine
Buckton
R. Teme
Downton on the Rock
Burrington
Bringewood Chase
Ludford
Overton
B4361
Caynham
Whitton
B4214
Nash
Offa's Dyke
Garth
Bailey Hill
Milebrook
Brampton Bryan
Walford
B4530
Pipe Aston
Grange
Elton
Adforton
A4110
Richard's Castle
Ashford Carbonel
Ashford Bowdler
Greete
Whatmore
Knighton Common
Spaceguard Centre
Letton
Birtley
Rhos-y-meirch
Llan-wen Hill
B4355
B4357
Monaughty
Pilleth
Whitton
Pilleth 1402
Wigmore
Leinthall Starkes
Leinthall Earls
Orleton Common
Middleton
Little Hereford
Richards Castle
Woofferton
Burford
Burford House
Dean Park
Boraston
Ongar Street
Lingen
Croft Ambrey Hillfort
Yatton
Ashley Moor
Bircher
Wyson
Brimfield
A456
B4362
Comberton
Orleton
Stony Cross
Tenbury Wells
Berrington
Berrington Green
Kyrewood
Upper Rochford
Oldwood Common
Sutton
Norton
Dolley Green
Offa's Dyke
Priory
Upper Lye
Lower Lye
Aymestrey
Water Mill
Croft
Cock Gate
Yarpole
Moreton
Eye
Berrington NT Hall
Middleton on the Hill
St. Michaels
Miles Hope
A4112
Hanley Childe
Beggar's Bush
Discoed
Stapleton
Judge's Lodging
Kinsham
Byton
Uphampton
Mortimer's Cross
Lucton
Bicton
Luston
Ashton
The Hundred
Laysters Pole
Romers Common
Kyre Park
Presteigne
(Llanandras)
B4356
B4362
Thorn
Combe
Easthampton
Mortimer's Cross 1461
Lugg Green
Aston
Kimbolton
Woonton
Kyre Green
Bank Street
Kinnerton
Evenjobb
Rodd
Nash
Combe Moor
Staunton Park
Shobdon
Ledicot
Kingsland
B4360
Cobnash
Eyton
The Broad
Stockton
Stockton Cross
Grafton
Whyle
Pie Corner
Four Stones
Womaston
Knill
Stansbatch
Staunton on Arrow
Shobdon
Burcher
Titley
The Forge
Shirl Heath
Lawton
Cholstrey
R. Lugg
Hatfield
Pudleston
Old Radnor
Walton
Offa's Dyke
Bradnor Hill
Flintsham
Rowe Ditch
Old Chapel
Pembridge
Eardisland
B4529
Barons Cross
Leominster
Thornbury
Burlingjobb
Dolyhir
Weythel
A44
B4355
Nextend
Marston
Upper Hardwick
Monkland
Stretford
Docklow
Grendon Green
Kington
Hergest Croft
Lower Hergest
Upper Hergest
New Street
Westonbury Mill Water
Lower Hardwick
Ivington Green
Ivington
Steen's Bridge
Humber
Buckland
Bredenbury
Penrhos
Lyonshall
Weston
Barewood
B4457
Brierley
Wharton
Stoke Prior
Gladestry
Holme Marsh
Moorcot
Broxwood
Haven
Sollers Dilwyn
Aulden
Marston Stannett
Huntington Castle
Kingswood
Small Breeds Farm Park & Owl Centre
Dilwyn
Birley
Upper Hill
Newton
Risbury
Broadfield Court
Hegdon Hill
Huntington
Chickward
Hopley's Green
A480
A4112
Knapton Green
Hope under Dinmore
Bowley
Pencombe
Almeley Wooton
Almeley
Woonton
Weobley
Weobley Marsh
Bush Bank
Queenswood Arboretum
Hampton Court
Lugg
A417
Shortwood Family Farm
Little Cowarne
A4111
Lower Welson
Upcott
Logaston
Newchurch
Sarnesfield
Westhope
Bodenham
Maund Bryan
Ullingswick
Michaelchurch-on-Arrow
Woods Eaves
Hurstway Common
Eardisley
Kinnersley
Kinnersley Castle
Hurstley
B4230
Ledgemoor
King's Pyon
Highway
Canon Pyon
Monmarsh
The Vauld
Pool Head
Felton
Upper Town
Moreton Jeffries
Stoke Cross
Stoke Lacy
A465
A438
Millhalf
Whitney
Willersley
Ailey
Eccles Green
Norton Canon
Wormsley
Urdimarsh
Venn's Green
Wellington
Marden
Walker's Green
Preston Wynne
Sutton Walls Hillfort
Preston Marsh
Burley Gate
Much Cowarne
Five Bridges
Clifford
Winforton
Waterloo
Letton
Moorhampton
Yarsop
Yazor
Tillington Common
Auberrow
Moreton on Lugg
Sutton St. Michael
Sutton St. Nicholas
Ocle Pychard
Lower Egleton
Newtown
Priory Wood
Merbach
Staunton on Wye
Mansell Lacy
Tillington
A4110
A465

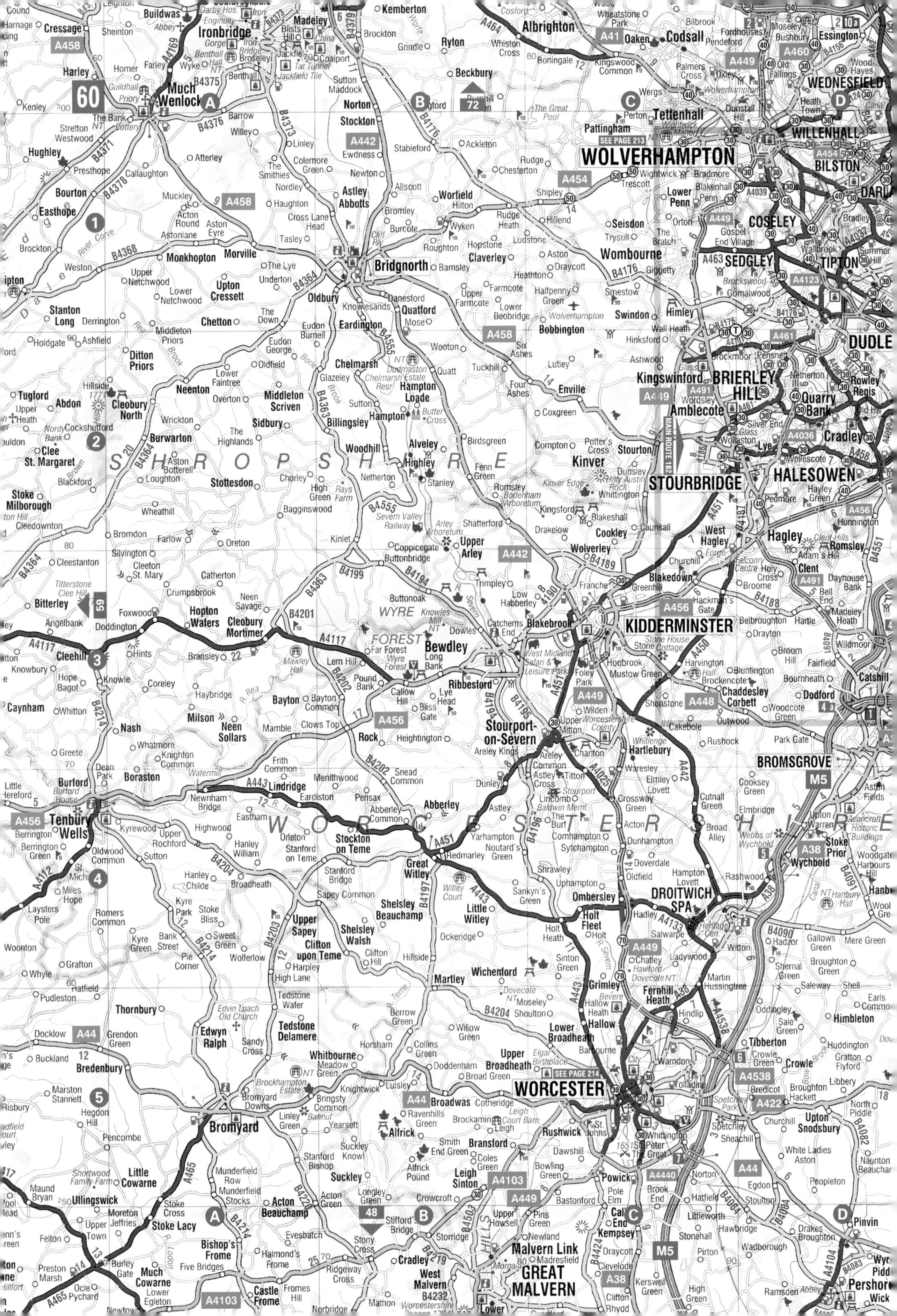

60
Cressage
A458
Buildwas
Ironbridge
Madeley
Kemberton
Albrighton
A41
Oaken
Codsall
Bilbrook
Essington
Harley
Much Wenlock
Broseley
Coalport
Sutton Maddock
Brockton
Ryton
Beckbury
72
Tettenhall
WEDNESFIELD
WILLENHALL
Norton
Stockton
A442
Pattingham
SEE PAGE 213
WOLVERHAMPTON
BILSTON
Hughley
Presthope
Bourton
Easthope
Atterley
Callaughton
Worfield
A454
Lower Penn
Astley Abbotts
Muckley
A458
Monkhopton
Morville
Bridgnorth
Claverley
Wombourne
Seisdon
COSELEY
SEDGLEY
TIPTON
Upton Cressett
Oldbury
Quatford
Eardington
Himley
Swindon
Bobbington
Stanton Long
Chetton
Ditton Priors
Neenton
Chelmarsh
Hampton Loade
A458
Kingswinford
BRIERLEY HILL
DUDLEY
Middleton Scriven
Sidbury
Cleobury North
Abdon
Tugford
Burwarton
Billingsley
Hampton
Enville
Amblecote
Quarry Bank
Rowley Regis
Cradley
Clee St. Margaret
SHROPSHIRE
Highley
Alveley
Kinver
Stourton
STOURBRIDGE
HALESOWEN
Stottesdon
Woodhill
Stoke Milborough
Kinlet
Upper Arley
A442
Cookley
Wolverley
West Hagley
Hagley
Romsley
Clent
Bitterley
Hopton Wafers
Cleobury Mortimer
WYRE FOREST
Bewdley
Blakebrook
KIDDERMINSTER
A456
A4117
Cleehill
Caynham
Nash
Milson
Neen Sollars
Bayton
Rock
Ribbesford
Stourport-on-Severn
A449
Hartlebury
Chaddesley Corbett
A448
BROMSGROVE
M5
Burford
Tenbury Wells
A456
Boraston
Lindridge
Eardiston
Abberley
WORCESTERSHIRE
Stockton on Teme
Great Witley
A451
Ombersley
Holt Fleet
DROITWICH SPA
Stoke Prior
Wychbold
A38
Shelsley Beauchamp
Little Witley
Upper Sapey
Shelsley Walsh
Clifton upon Teme
Martley
Wichenford
Grimley
Fernhill Heath
Thornbury
Edwyn Ralph
Tedstone Delamere
Whitbourne
A44
Bredenbury
Upper Broadheath
Lower Broadheath
SEE PAGE 214
WORCESTER
A4538
A422
Tibberton
Crowle
Bromyard
Broadwas
Alfrick
Bransford
Rushwick
Upton Snodsbury
Little Cowarne
Ullingswick
Stoke Lacy
Suckley
Acton Beauchamp
Leigh Sinton
A4103
A449
Powick
Kempsey
M5
A44
Pinvin
48
Bishop's Frome
Cradley
Malvern Link
GREAT MALVERN
A38
Much Cowarne
West Malvern
Castle Frome
A4103
Pershore

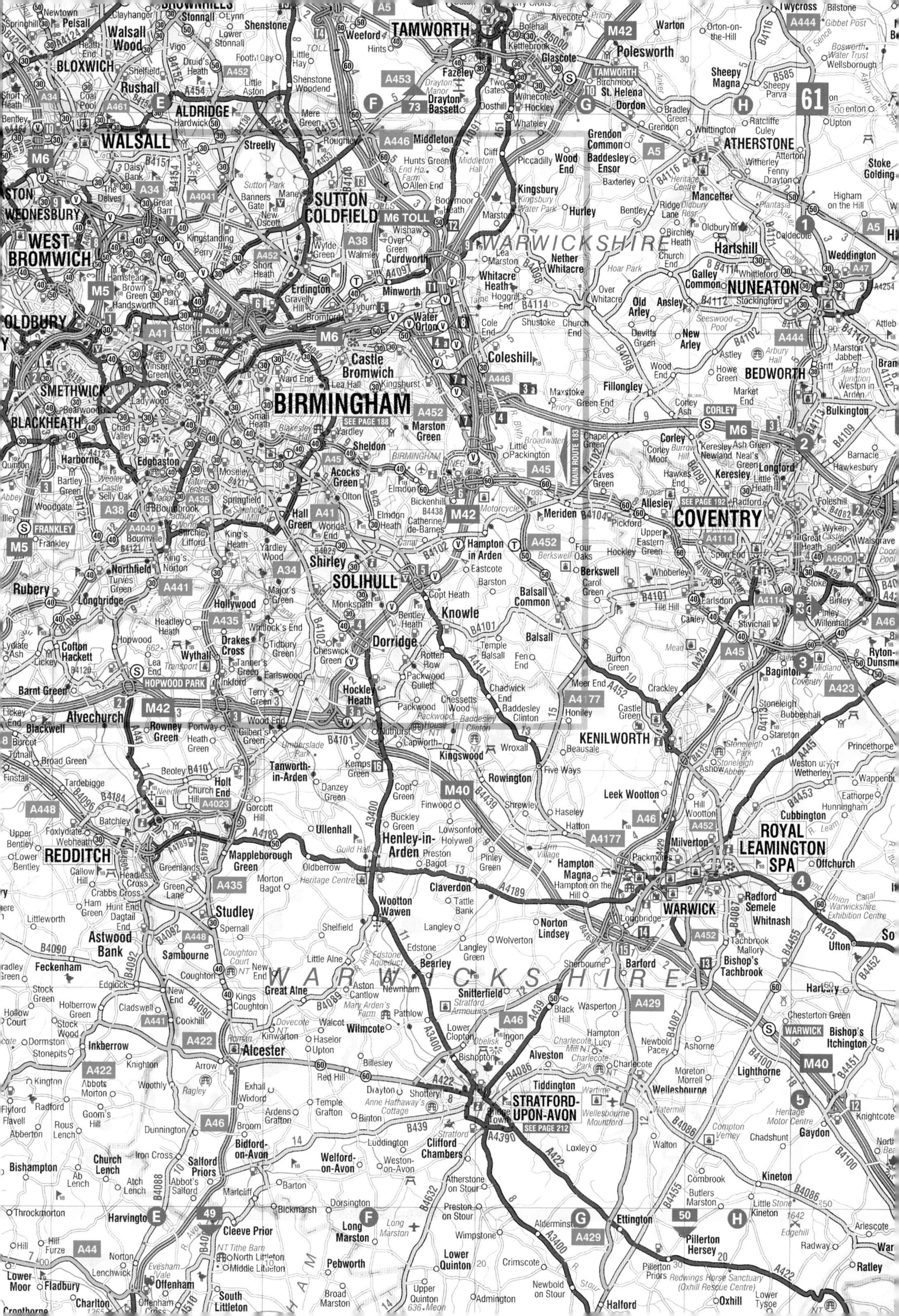

TAMWORTH
Polesworth
Warton
Orton-on-the-Hill
Twycross
Bilstone
Gibbet Post
Bosworth Water Trust
Wellsborough
Sheepy Magna
Sheepy Parva
61
Newtown
Pelsall
Clayhanger
Brownhills
Stonnall
Lynn
Shenstone
Weeford
Hints
Walsall Wood
BLOXWICH
Rushall
ALDRIDGE
WALSALL
Streetly
Little Hay
Shenstone Woodend
Mere Green
Roughley
Middleton
Drayton Manor
Drayton Bassett
Fazeley
Glascote
Kettlebrook
Bolehall
Wilnecote
Hockley
Dosthill
Two Gates
Whateley
TAMWORTH
St. Helena
Dordon
Grendon
Grendon Common
Baddesley Ensor
Baxterley
ATHERSTONE
Mancetter
Ratcliffe Culey
Witherley
Atterton
Fenny Drayton
Stoke Golding
Higham on the Hill
Upton
Hunts Green
Allen End
Bodymoor Heath
Middleton Hall
Cliff
Piccadilly
Wood End
Kingsbury
Kingsbury Water Park
Hurley
Bentley
Ridge Lane
Oldbury
Hartshill
Caldecote
Weddington
NUNEATON
Galley Common
Stockingford
Ansley
Old Arley
New Arley
Devitts Green
Hoar Park
Over Whitacre
Nether Whitacre
Whitacre Heath
Hoggrill's End
Lea Marston
Marston
WARWICKSHIRE
SUTTON COLDFIELD
M6 TOLL
Wishaw
Over Green
Curdworth
Walmley
Wylde Green
Minworth
Erdington
Gravelly Hill
Tyburn
Bromford
Water Orton
Castle Bromwich
Kingshurst
Coleshill
Cole End
Shustoke
Church End
Maxstoke
Green End
Fillongley
Wood End
Astley
Arbury Hall
BEDWORTH
Marston Jabbett
Bulkington
Weston in Arden
Corley
Corley Ash
Corley Moor
Keresley
Keresley Newland
Ash Green
Neal's Green
Longford
Little Heath
Hawkesbury
Barnacle
WEDNESBURY
WEST BROMWICH
OLDBURY
SMETHWICK
BLACKHEATH
Harborne
Edgbaston
Quinton
Bartley Green
Woodgate
Selly Oak
Bournbrook
Stirchley
Bournville
Lifford
King's Norton
Northfield
Rubery
Longbridge
Frankley
Great Barr
Perry Barr
Handsworth
Aston
Winson Green
Ladywood
Chad Valley
Moseley
Sparkhill
Springfield
Hall Green
Small Heath
BIRMINGHAM
SEE PAGE 188
Ward End
Lea Hall
Yardley
Sheldon
Marston Green
Acocks Green
Olton
Elmdon
Elmdon Heath
Bickenhill
Catherine-de-Barnes
Little Packington
Hampton in Arden
Meriden
Eastcote
Barston
Four Oaks
Berkswell
Balsall Common
Carol Green
Pickford
Allesley
Eaves Green
Chapel Green
COVENTRY
SEE PAGE 192
Radford
Foleshill
Wyken
Walsgrave
Upper Eastern Green
Hockley
Whoberley
Spon End
Earlsdon
Tile Hill
Canley
Stivichall
Stoke
Binley
Willenhall
Ryton-on-Dunsmore
Baginton
Bubbenhall
Stoneleigh
Stareton
Princethorpe
Shirley
SOLIHULL
Monkspath
Major's Green
Hollywood
Yardley Wood
King's Heath
Kings Norton
Wythall
Drakes Cross
Tidbury Green
Cheswick Green
Dorridge
Knowle
Bentley Heath
Copt Heath
Temple Balsall
Balsall
Fen End
Rotten Row
Packwood Gullett
Hockley Heath
Chadwick End
Chessetts Wood
Packwood
Baddesley Clinton
Meer End
Honiley
Burton Green
Crackley
Castle Green
KENILWORTH
Beausale
Wroxall
Lapworth
Kingswood
Rowington
Five Ways
Shrewley
Haseley
Hatton
Leek Wootton
Hill Wootton
Milverton
ROYAL LEAMINGTON SPA
Cubbington
Hunningham
Weston under Wetherley
Eathorpe
Offchurch
Cofton Hackett
Hopwood
Lea End
Earlswood
Terry's Green
Inkford
HOPWOOD PARK
Barnt Green
Alvechurch
Lickey
Blackwell
Rowney Green
Portway
Wood End
Heath Green
Gilbert's End
Nuthurst
Umberslade Park
Tanworth-in-Arden
Kemps Green
Danzey Green
Copt Green
Finwood
Buckley Green
Lowsonford
Holywell
Henley-in-Arden
Preston Bagot
Pinley Green
Claverdon
Tattle Bank
Hampton Magna
Hampton on the Hill
Packmores
WARWICK
Longbridge
Radford Semele
Whitnash
Bishop's Tachbrook
Tachbrook Mallory
Ufton
Harbury
Chesterton Green
Bishop's Itchington
Lighthorne
Gaydon
Knightcote
Tardebigge
Batchley
REDDITCH
Webheath
Foxlydiate
Upper Bentley
Lower Bentley
Callow Hill
Headless Cross
Crabbs Cross
Hunt End
Ham Green
Dagtail End
Greenlands
Green Lane
Beoley
Holt End
Church Hill
Gorcott Hill
Mappleborough Green
Oldberrow
Ullenhall
Morton Bagot
Studley
Spernall
Sambourne
Coughton
Coughton Court
Kings Coughton
New End
Astwood Bank
Feckenham
Littleworth
Edgiock
Cladswell
Cookhill
Inkberrow
Alcester
Arrow
Ragley
Exhall
Wixford
Great Alne
Little Alne
Aston Cantlow
Wootton Wawen
Shelfield
Edstone
Bearley
Langley
Wolverton
Norton Lindsey
Snitterfield
Wilmcote
Pathlow
Mary Arden's Farm
Kinwarton
Haselor
Upton
Walcot
Billesley
Drayton
Shottery
Anne Hathaway's Cottage
Temple Grafton
Binton
Ardens Grafton
Broom
Bidford-on-Avon
Welford-on-Avon
Weston-on-Avon
Luddington
Clifford Chambers
STRATFORD-UPON-AVON
SEE PAGE 212
Tiddington
Alveston
Charlecote
Charlecote Park
Hampton Lucy
Wasperton
Barford
Sherbourne
Newbold Pacey
Ashorne
Moreton Morrell
Wellesbourne
Wellesbourne Mountford
Walton
Loxley
Compton Verney
Chadshunt
Kineton
Little Kineton
Combrook
Butlers Marston
Ettington
Pillerton Hersey
Pillerton Priors
Alderminster
Atherstone on Stour
Preston on Stour
Wimpstone
Lower Quinton
Upper Quinton
Admington
Crimscote
Newbold on Stour
Halford
Oxhill
Lower Tysoe
Ratley
Radway
Edgehill
Arlescote
Dorsington
Long Marston
Pebworth
Barton
Bickmarsh
Marlcliff
Cleeve Prior
Salford Priors
Abbot's Salford
Harvington
Iron Cross
Dunnington
Church Lench
Atch Lench
Ab Lench
Rous Lench
Radford
Abbots Morton
Goom's Hill
Flyford Flavell
Abberton
Bishampton
Throckmorton
Hill Furze
Lower Moor
Fladbury
Norton
Lenchwick
Offenham
Evesham
Charlton
South Littleton
North Littleton
Middle Littleton
Cropthorne
WARWICKSHIRE
M6
M5
M42
M40
A5
A38
A41
A45
A34
A435
A452
A46
A422
A3400
A4189
A429
A444
A446
A47
A441
A448
A44
A439
A4177
A425
A423
A426

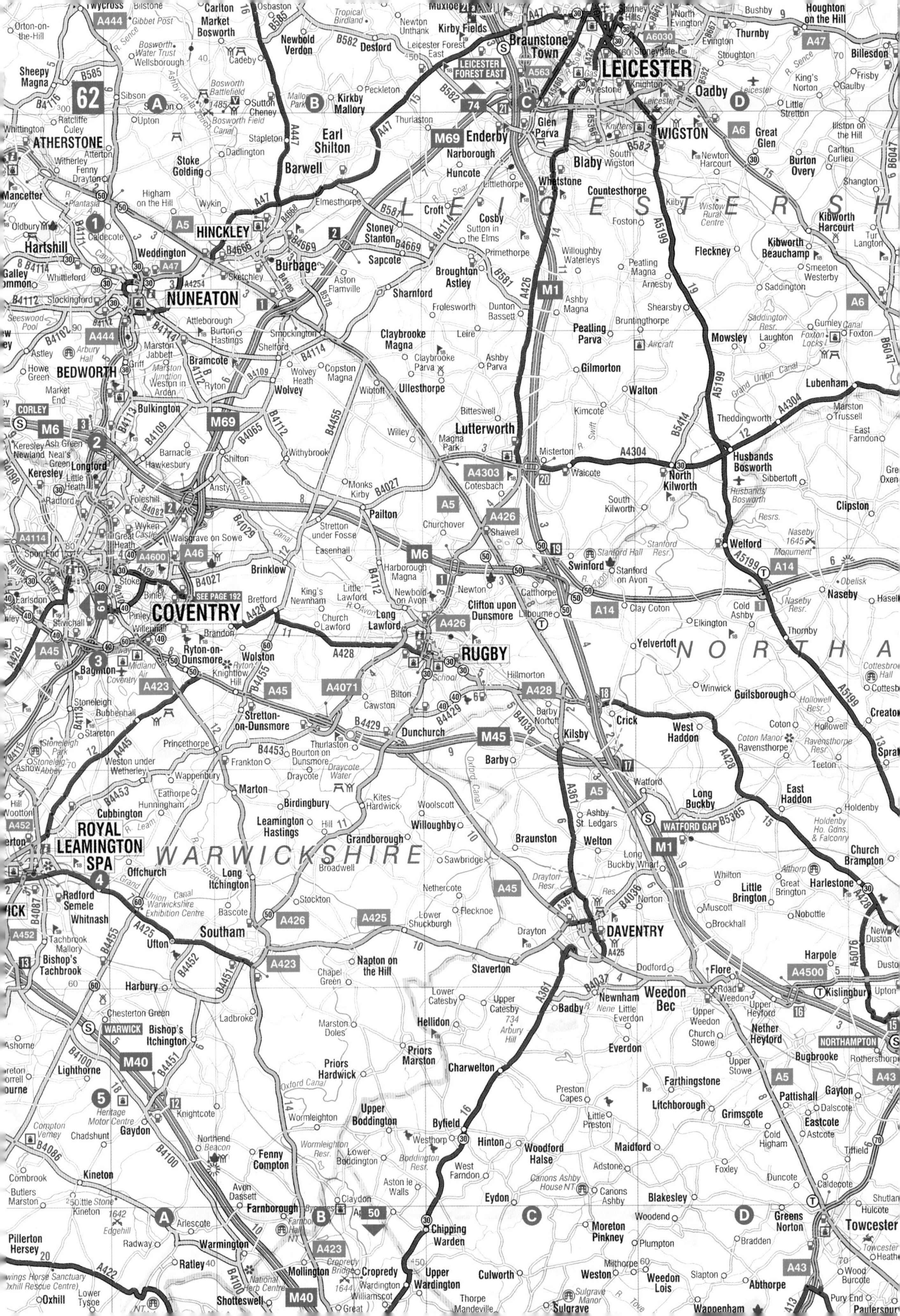
62
LEICESTER
Braunstone Town
Oadby
Wigston
South Wigston
Blaby
Glen Parva
Enderby
Narborough
Huncote
Whetstone
Countesthorpe
Leicester Forest East
Kirby Muxloe
Kirby Fields
Thurnby
Houghton on the Hill
Bushby
Billesdon
Evington
Stoughton
Great Glen
Kibworth Harcourt
Kibworth Beauchamp
Fleckney
Arnesby
Peatling Magna
Peatling Parva
Shearsby
Bruntingthorpe
Saddington
Mowsley
Laughton
Foxton
Lubenham
Theddingworth
Husbands Bosworth
North Kilworth
South Kilworth
Walcote
Misterton
Lutterworth
Gilmorton
Walton
Kimcote
Ashby Magna
Dunton Bassett
Broughton Astley
Cosby
Croft
Sapcote
Stoney Stanton
Sharnford
Frolesworth
Leire
Claybrooke Magna
Ullesthorpe
Ashby Parva
Bitteswell
Magna Park
Cotesbach
Shawell
Swinford
Stanford on Avon
Catthorpe
Lilbourne
Clay Coton
Welford
Naseby
Clipston
Sibbertoft
Cold Ashby
Thornby
Elkington
Yelvertoft
Crick
West Haddon
Guilsborough
Winwick
Ravensthorpe
Coton
Hollowell
Teeton
Holdenby
East Haddon
Long Buckby
Watford
Kilsby
Barby
Ashby St. Ledgers
Welton
Braunston
Daventry
Norton
Whilton
Church Brampton
Harlestone
Little Brington
Great Brington
Nobottle
Muscott
Brockhall
Flore
Dodford
Weedon Bec
Upper Weedon
Kislingbury
Upper Heyford
Nether Heyford
Bugbrooke
Rothersthorpe
NORTHAMPTON
Church Stowe
Upper Stowe
Farthingstone
Litchborough
Pattishall
Gayton
Grimscote
Eastcote
Astcote
Cold Higham
Tiffield
Maidford
Adstone
Foxley
Blakesley
Woodend
Greens Norton
Towcester
Duncote
Caldecote
Bradden
Slapton
Abthorpe
Wappenham
Weston
Weedon Lois
Plumpton
Moreton Pinkney
Canons Ashby
Eydon
Woodford Halse
Hinton
Byfield
Charwelton
Preston Capes
Little Preston
Everdon
Little Everdon
Newnham
Badby
Staverton
Drayton
Upper Catesby
Lower Catesby
Hellidon
Priors Marston
Priors Hardwick
Upper Boddington
Lower Boddington
Aston le Walls
West Farndon
Chipping Warden
Upper Wardington
Culworth
Thorpe Mandeville
Sulgrave
Cropredy
Wardington
Williamscot
Claydon
Farnborough
Avon Dassett
Fenny Compton
Wormleighton
Northend
Mollington
Shotteswell
Warmington
Ratley
Arlescote
Radway
Edgehill
Kineton
Little Kineton
Butlers Marston
Combrook
Pillerton Hersey
Oxhill
Lower Tysoe
Gaydon
Chadshunt
Knightcote
Lighthorne
Chesterton Green
Bishop's Itchington
Ladbroke
Harbury
Bishop's Tachbrook
Tachbrook Mallory
Whitnash
Radford Semele
Ufton
Southam
Long Itchington
Offchurch
Napton on the Hill
Stockton
Lower Shuckburgh
Flecknoe
Sawbridge
Nethercote
Grandborough
Willoughby
Woolscott
Kites Hardwick
Birdingbury
Leamington Hastings
Marton
Frankton
Eathorpe
Hunningham
Wappenbury
Cubbington
ROYAL LEAMINGTON SPA
WARWICKSHIRE
Weston under Wetherley
Princethorpe
Bourton on Dunsmore
Draycote
Thurlaston
Dunchurch
Stretton-on-Dunsmore
Ryton-on-Dunsmore
Wolston
Brandon
Baginton
Stoneleigh
Bubbenhall
Stareton
Ashow
COVENTRY
Binley
Willenhall
Stivichall
Earlsdon
Walsgrave on Sowe
Wyken
Foleshill
Radford
Keresley
Longford
Ansty
Shilton
Barnacle
Hawkesbury
Brinklow
Easenhall
Stretton under Fosse
Monks Kirby
Pailton
Withybrook
Willey
Churchover
Harborough Magna
Little Lawford
Long Lawford
Church Lawford
King's Newnham
Newbold on Avon
Newton
Clifton upon Dunsmore
RUGBY
Hillmorton
Bilton
Cawston
Wolvey
Wolvey Heath
Copston Magna
Wibtoft
Bramcote
Burton Hastings
Attleborough
Marston Jabbett
Bulkington
Ryton
Weston in Arden
BEDWORTH
NUNEATON
Stockingford
Whittleford
Weddington
Caldecote
Hartshill
Oldbury
Galley Common
Mancetter
ATHERSTONE
Witherley
Fenny Drayton
Atterton
Ratcliffe Culey
Sibson
Sheepy Magna
Orton-on-the-Hill
Twycross
Bilstone
Gibbet Post
Bosworth Water Trust
Wellsborough
Market Bosworth
Carlton
Cadeby
Bosworth Battlefield 1485
Bosworth Field
Sutton Cheney
Upton
Stapleton
Dadlington
Stoke Golding
Higham on the Hill
Wykin
HINCKLEY
Burbage
Sketchley
Aston Flamville
Smockington
Barwell
Earl Shilton
Kirkby Mallory
Peckleton
Newbold Verdon
Desford
Osbaston
Thurlaston
Elmesthorpe
Newton Unthank
Tropical Birdland
M1
M6
M69
M45
M40
A5
A47
A426
A428
A45
A46
A423
A425
A361
A14
A4304
A5199
A6
A444
A4303
A4071
A452
A43
A4500
A5076
LEICESTER FOREST EAST
WATFORD GAP
CORLEY
WARWICK
NORTHAMPTON
SEE PAGE 192
50
LEICESTERSHIRE
NORTHA

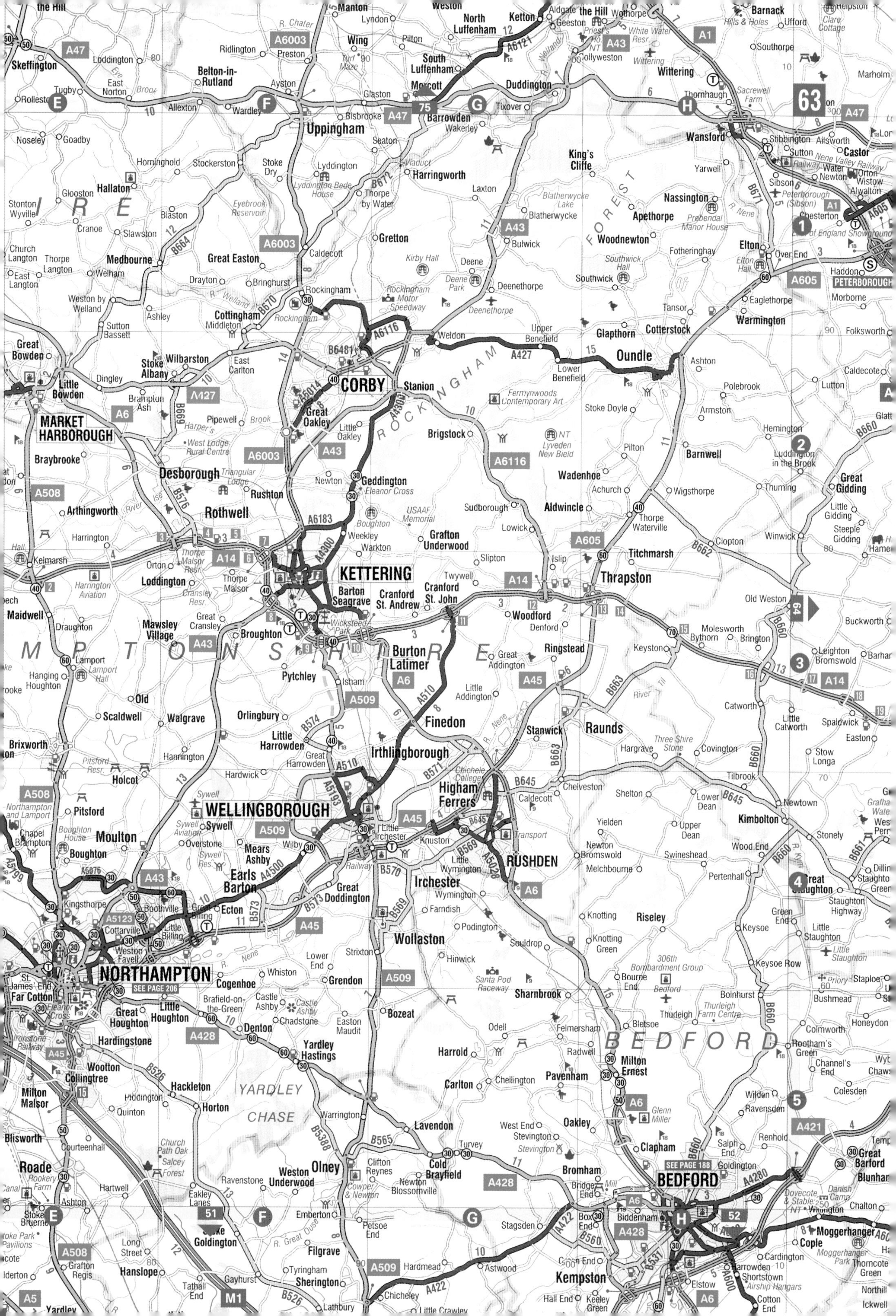

63
64
SEE PAGE 206
SEE PAGE 188
51
52
Skeffington
Loddington
East Norton
Tugby
Rolleston
Ridlington
Belton-in-Rutland
Allexton
Wardley
Ayston
Preston
Wing
Manton
Lyndon
Pilton
North Luffenham
South Luffenham
Ketton
Geeston
Aldgate
the Hill
Wothorpe
Collyweston
Barnack
Hills & Holes
Ufford
Southorpe
Wittering
Thornhaugh
Sacrewell Farm
Marholm
Morcott
Glaston
Bisbrooke
Uppingham
Seaton
Barrowden
Wakerley
Duddington
Tixover
Wansford
Stibbington
Ailsworth
Sutton
Castor
Nene Valley Railway
Water Newton
Orton
Wistow
Alwalton
Yarwell
Sibson
Peterborough (Sibson)
Chesterton
East of England Showground
Noseley
Goadby
Horninghold
Stockerston
Stoke Dry
Lyddington
Lyddington Bede House
Thorpe by Water
Viaduct
Harringworth
Laxton
King's Cliffe
Nassington
Apethorpe
Prebendal Manor House
Blatherwycke
Blatherwycke Lake
Woodnewton
Fotheringhay
Elton
Elton Hall
Over End
Haddon
PETERBOROUGH
Glooston
Hallaton
Stonton Wyville
Cranoe
Blaston
Slawston
Eyebrook Reservoir
Church Langton
Thorpe Langton
East Langton
Medbourne
Welham
Great Easton
Drayton
Bringhurst
Caldecott
Gretton
Kirby Hall
Deene
Deene Park
Bulwick
Southwick Hall
Southwick
Tansor
Eaglethorpe
Warmington
Morborne
Weston by Welland
Ashley
Sutton Bassett
Cottingham
Middleton
Rockingham
Rockingham Motor Speedway
Deenethorpe
Weldon
Upper Benefield
Lower Benefield
Glapthorn
Cotterstock
Oundle
Ashton
Folksworth
Caldecote
Great Bowden
Little Bowden
Dingley
Stoke Albany
Wilbarston
East Carlton
Brampton Ash
CORBY
Stanion
Great Oakley
Little Oakley
ROCKINGHAM FOREST
Fermynwoods Contemporary Art
Stoke Doyle
Polebrook
Armston
Lutton
MARKET HARBOROUGH
Braybrooke
Pipewell
West Lodge Rural Centre
Brigstock
Lyveden New Bield
Pilton
Barnwell
Hemington
Luddington in the Brook
Desborough
Triangular Lodge
Rushton
Newton
Geddington
Eleanor Cross
Wadenhoe
Achurch
Thurning
Great Gidding
Little Gidding
Steeple Gidding
Arthingworth
Rothwell
Sudborough
Aldwincle
Wigsthorpe
Thorpe Waterville
Boughton
USAAF Memorial
Lowick
Harrington
Weekley
Warkton
Grafton Underwood
Clopton
Winwick
Kelmarsh
Orton
Thorpe Malsor
Thorpe Malsor Resr.
Loddington
KETTERING
Slipton
Islip
Titchmarsh
Thrapston
Harrington Aviation
Cransley Resr.
Barton Seagrave
Cranford St. Andrew
Cranford St. John
Twywell
Woodford
Denford
Old Weston
Buckworth
Maidwell
Draughton
Mawsley Village
Great Cransley
Broughton
Wicksteed Park
Burton Latimer
Great Addington
Ringstead
Molesworth
Bythorn
Brington
Keyston
Leighton Bromswold
Lamport
Lamport Hall
Hanging Houghton
Pytchley
Isham
Little Addington
Catworth
Little Catworth
Spaldwick
Easton
Old
Scaldwell
Walgrave
Orlingbury
Finedon
Stanwick
Raunds
Brixworth
Pitsford Resr.
Little Harrowden
Great Harrowden
Irthlingborough
Hargrave
Three Shire Stone
Covington
Stow Longa
Holcot
Hannington
Hardwick
Chichele College
Higham Ferrers
Chelveston
Caldecott
Shelton
Lower Dean
Upper Dean
Tilbrook
Newtown
Kimbolton
Stonely
Pitsford
Northampton and Lamport Railway
Sywell
Sywell Aviation
WELLINGBOROUGH
Yielden
Chapel Brampton
Boughton House
Moulton
Boughton
Overstone
Sywell Res.
Mears Ashby
Wilby
Little Irchester
Knuston
Transport
RUSHDEN
Newton Bromswold
Melchbourne
Swineshead
Pertenhall
Wood End
Great Staughton
Staughton Highway
Kingsthorpe
Boothville
Great Billing
Ecton
Earls Barton
Great Doddington
Little Wymington
Irchester
Wymington
Farndish
Podington
Knotting
Riseley
Knotting Green
Keysoe
Green End
Little Staughton
Keysoe Row
Cottarville
Little Billing
Weston Favell
Strixton
Wollaston
Hinwick
Souldrop
306th Bombardment Group
Santa Pod Raceway
Bourne End
Bedford
NORTHAMPTON
St. James End
Far Cotton
Eleanor Cross
Cogenhoe
Whiston
Lower End
Grendon
Brafield-on-the-Green
Castle Ashby
Chadstone
Easton Maudit
Bozeat
Sharnbrook
Thurleigh Farm Centre
Bolnhurst
Priory
Bushmead
Staploe
Great Houghton
Little Houghton
Denton
Hardingstone
Yardley Hastings
Odell
Felmersham
Bletsoe
Thurleigh
Colmworth
Honeydon
BEDFORD
Radwell
Rootham's Green
Wooton
Collingtree
Harrold
Milton Ernest
Channel's End
Hackleton
Carlton
Chellington
Pavenham
Colesden
Milton Malsor
Piddington
Quinton
Horton
YARDLEY CHASE
Warrington
Wilden
Ravensden
Blisworth
Courteenhall
Lavendon
West End
Stevington
Oakley
Glenn Miller
Renhold
Salph End
Church Path Oak
Salcey Forest
Roade
Rookery Farm
Hartwell
Ashton
Eakley Lanes
Ravenstone
Weston Underwood
Olney
Clifton Reynes
Cold Brayfield
Newton Blossomville
Turvey
Stevington
Bromham
Bridge End
Mill
Clapham
Goldington
Great Barford
Blunham
Danish Camp
Stoke Bruerne
Stoke Park Pavilions
Goldington
Cowper & Newton
Emberton
Petsoe End
Stagsden
Box End
Biddenham
Dovecote & Stable
Willington
Chalton
Moggerhanger
Moggerhanger Park
Cople
Cardington
Long Street
Hanslope
Grafton Regis
Filgrave
Tyringham
Sherington
Gayhurst
Tathall End
Hardmead
Astwood
Cotton End
Kempston
Elstow
Harrowden
Shortstown
Airship Hangars
Thorncote Green
Northill
Ickwell
Cotton End
Yardley
Chicheley
Little Crawley
Lathbury
Hall End
Keeley Green
A47
A6003
A1
A43
A6121
A605
B664
B670
B672
A6116
B6481
A5014
A4300
A427
A6003
A43
A508
B576
A6183
A14
A4500
A6
A509
B574
A510
B663
B660
B662
B645
B571
A5193
A45
B569
A5028
B570
B573
A5123
A5076
A5199
A428
B526
B5388
B565
A422
B560
A4280
B531
A421
A600
A5
M1
A603
A509
BEDFORD

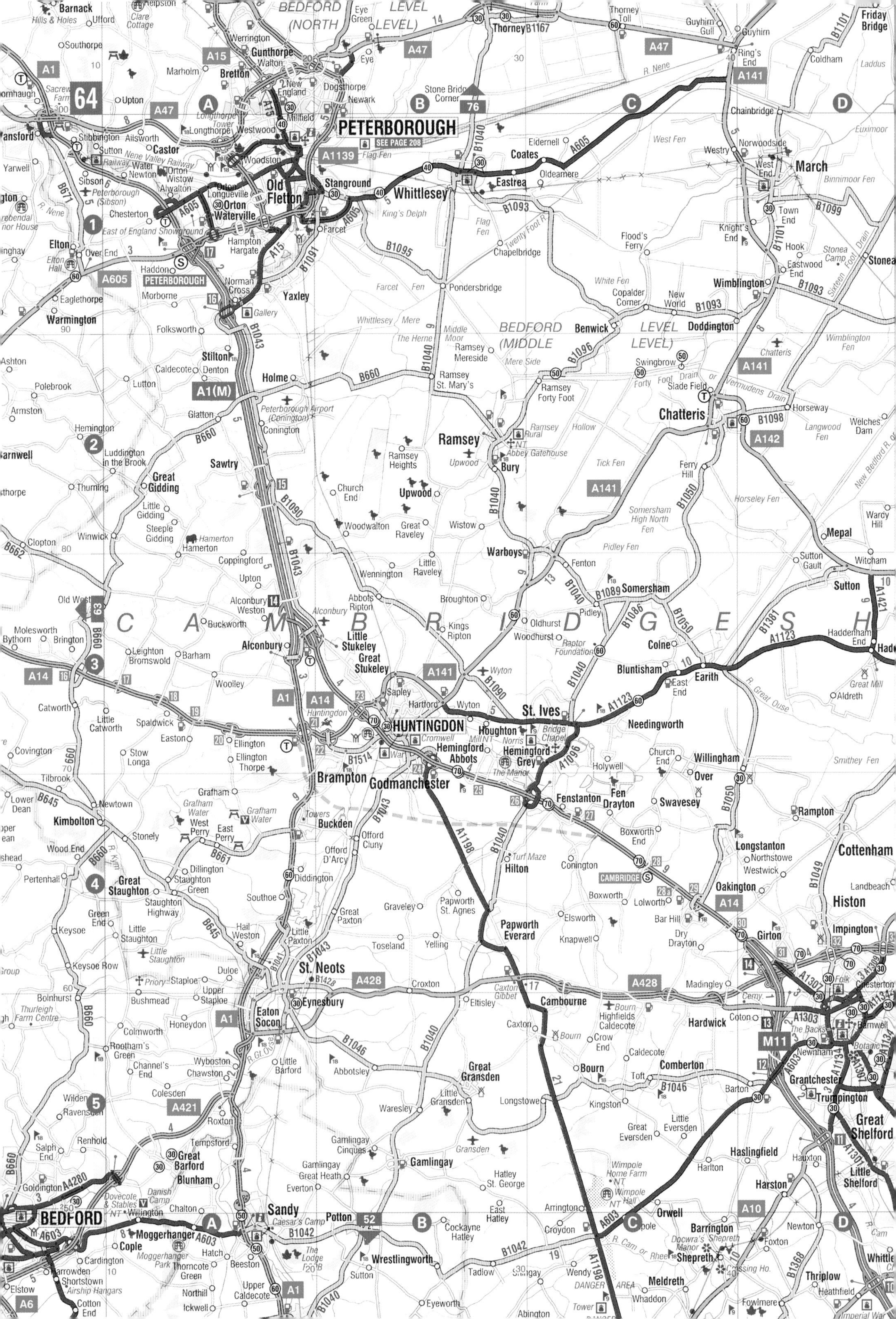

64
76
63
52
PETERBOROUGH
SEE PAGE 208
BEDFORD (NORTH LEVEL)
BEDFORD (MIDDLE LEVEL)
CAMBRIDGESHIRE
Barnack
Hills & Holes
Ufford
Clare Cottage
Werrington
Gunthorpe
Walton
Eye
Eye Green
Thorney
Thorney Toll
Guyhirn
Guyhirn Gull
Ring's End
Friday Bridge
Coldham
Southorpe
Marholm
Bretton
New England
Dogsthorpe
Newark
Stone Bridge Corner
Upton
Longthorpe
Millfield
Stibbington
Ailsworth
Castor
Sutton
Westwood
Woodston
Nene Valley Railway
Water Newton
Orton Wistow
Alwalton
Orton Longueville
Orton Waterville
Old Fletton
Stanground
Whittlesey
King's Delph
Farcet
Flag Fen
Eldernell
Coates
Eastrea
Oldeamere
Chainbridge
Norwoodside
Westry
March
West Fen
Binnimoor Fen
Town End
Knight's End
Hook
Eastwood End
Stonea Camp
Stonea
Wimblington
Sibson
Peterborough (Sibson)
Chesterton
East of England Showground
Elton
Elton Hall
Over End
Haddon
Hampton Hargate
Norman Cross
Morborne
Yaxley
Gallery
Eaglethorpe
Warmington
Folksworth
Chapelbridge
Pondersbridge
Farcet Fen
Flood's Ferry
White Fen
Copalder Corner
New World
Benwick
Doddington
Whittlesey Mere
The Herne
Middle Moor
Ramsey Mereside
Mere Side
Ramsey St. Mary's
Ramsey Forty Foot
Swingbrow
Forty Foot Drain
Slade Field
Vermuden's Drain
Chatteris
Horseway
Langwood Fen
Welches Dam
Wimblington Fen
Stilton
Caldecote
Denton
Holme
Ashton
Polebrook
Lutton
Armston
Glatton
Peterborough Airport (Conington)
Conington
Hemington
Luddington in the Brook
Barnwell
Sawtry
Great Gidding
Thurning
Little Gidding
Steeple Gidding
Hamerton
Winwick
Clopton
Coppingford
Upton
Alconbury Weston
Old Weston
Buckworth
Alconbury
Leighton Bromswold
Barham
Woolley
Molesworth
Bythorn
Brington
Ramsey
Ramsey Heights
Upwood
Church End
Woodwalton
Great Raveley
Little Raveley
Wistow
Warboys
Bury
Ramsey Rural
Abbey Gatehouse
Tick Fen
Somersham High North Fen
Pidley Fen
Ferry Hill
Horseley Fen
Mepal
Wardy Hill
Sutton Gault
Witcham
Sutton
Fenton
Somersham
Pidley
Oldhurst
Woodhurst
Raptor Foundation
Colne
Bluntisham
Earith
East End
Haddenham End
Great Mill
Aldreth
Wennington
Abbots Ripton
Broughton
Kings Ripton
Little Stukeley
Great Stukeley
Wyton
Sapley
Hartford
HUNTINGDON
Houghton
Mill NT
Bridge Chapel
St. Ives
Needingworth
Holywell
Church End
Willingham
Over
Swavesey
Fen Drayton
Fenstanton
Hemingford Abbots
Hemingford Grey
The Manor
Godmanchester
Brampton
Huntingdon
Cromwell
Ellington
Ellington Thorpe
Easton
Spaldwick
Catworth
Little Catworth
Stow Longa
Covington
Tilbrook
Lower Dean
Kimbolton
Newtown
Grafham
Grafham Water
West Perry
East Perry
Stonely
Wood End
Buckden
Offord Cluny
Offord D'Arcy
Diddington
Southoe
Great Staughton
Dillington
Staughton Green
Staughton Highway
Pertenhall
Green End
Little Staughton
Keysoe
Keysoe Row
Hail Weston
Little Paxton
Great Paxton
St. Neots
Eynesbury
Eaton Socon
Toseland
Yelling
Graveley
Papworth St. Agnes
Papworth Everard
Hilton
Turf Maze
Conington
Elsworth
Knapwell
Boxworth
Boxworth End
Lolworth
Bar Hill
Dry Drayton
Longstanton
Northstowe
Westwick
Oakington
Girton
Cottenham
Landbeach
Histon
Impington
Rampton
Smithey Fen
CAMBRIDGE
Croxton
Eltisley
Caxton Gibbet
Cambourne
Caxton
Bourn
Highfields Caldecote
Crow End
Caldecote
Hardwick
Madingley
Coton
Chesterton
Barnwell
Newnham
Grantchester
Trumpington
Great Shelford
Little Shelford
Comberton
Toft
Barton
Kingston
Little Eversden
Great Eversden
Haslingfield
Harlton
Hauxton
Harston
Longstowe
Great Gransden
Little Gransden
Abbotsley
Waresley
Gamlingay
Gamlingay Cinques
Gamlingay Great Heath
Hatley St. George
East Hatley
Everton
Sandy
Potton
Cockayne Hatley
Wrestlingworth
Tadlow
Croydon
Arrington
Wimpole Home Farm
Wimpole Hall
Orwell
Barrington
Shepreth
Foxton
Newton
Thriplow
Heathfield
Meldreth
Whaddon
Wendy
Abington
Fowlmere
Eyeworth
Sutton
Upper Caldecote
Northill
Ickwell
Beeston
Hatch
Thorncote Green
Moggerhanger
Moggerhanger Park
Chalton
Blunham
Great Barford
Tempsford
Roxton
Little Barford
Wyboston
Chawston
Channel's End
Colesden
Rootham's Green
Colmworth
Honeydon
Upper Staploe
Staploe
Duloe
Bushmead
Priory
Bolnhurst
Thurleigh Farm Centre
Wilden
Ravensden
Renhold
Salph End
Goldington
Willington
Dovecote & Stables
Danish Camp
BEDFORD
Cople
Cardington
Harrowden
Shortstown
Airship Hangars
Elstow
Cotton End
A1 A1(M) A14 A15 A47 A141 A142 A605 A1139 A1123 A1096 A1198 A421 A428 A4280 A603 A6 A10 M11
B1040 B1043 B1090 B1091 B1093 B1095 B1096 B1098 B1099 B1101 B1167 B660 B662 B645 B661 B671 B1514 B1041 B1428 B1046 B1042 B1050 B1086 B1089 B1381 B1049 B1368

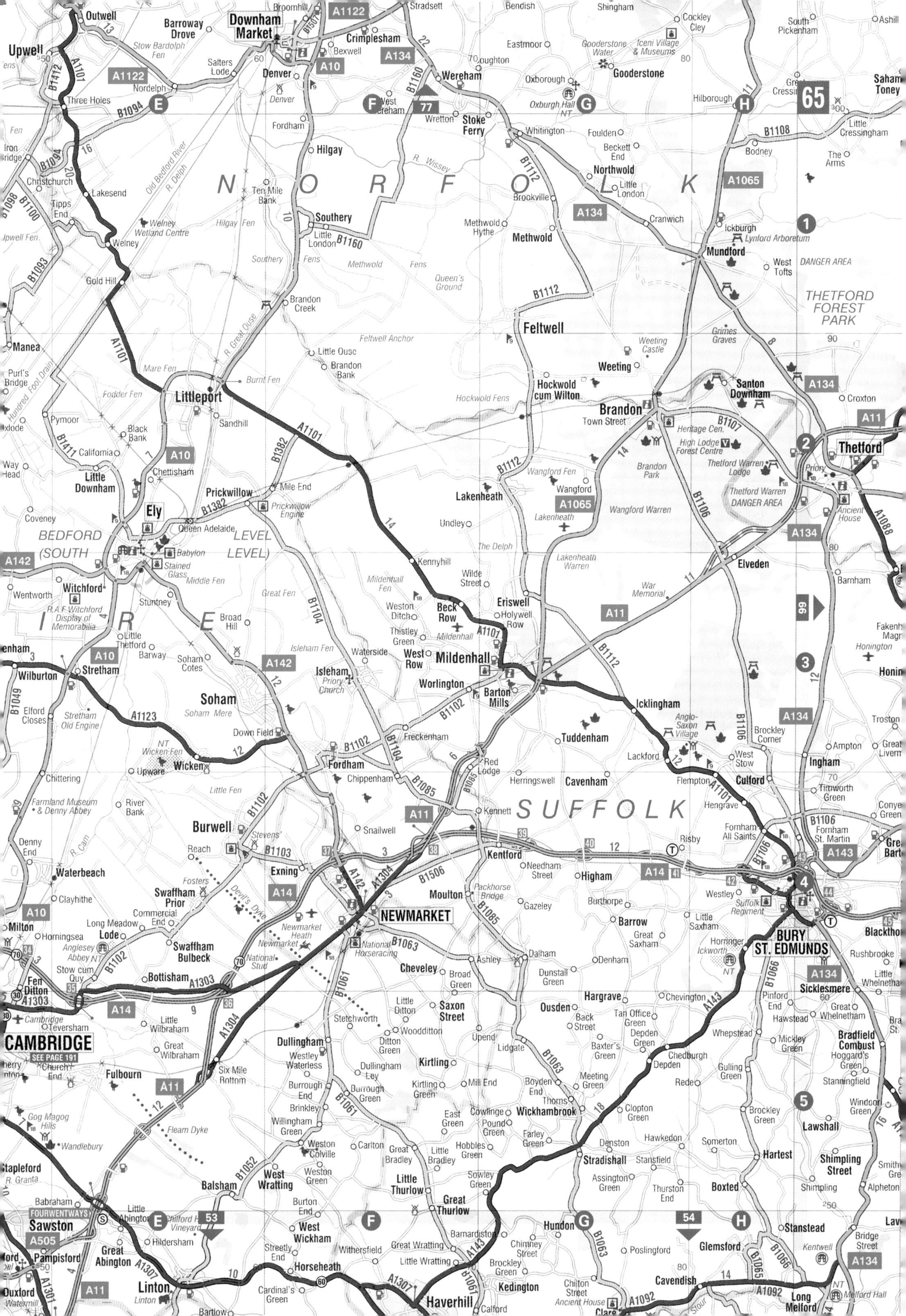

65
99
77
53
54
N O R F O L K
S U F F O L K
BEDFORD (SOUTH LEVEL)
Outwell
Upwell
Barroway Drove
Downham Market
Broomhill
A1122
Stradsett
Bendish
Shingham
Cockley Cley
South Pickenham
Ashill
Crimplesham
Bexwell
A134
A10
Stow Bardolph Fen
Salters Lode
Nordelph
A1101
B1412
Three Holes
B1094
Denver
Wereham
West Dereham
Eastmoor
Gooderstone Water
Iceni Village & Museums
Gooderstone
Oxborough
Oxburgh Hall NT
Hilborough
Great Cressingham
Saham Toney
Little Cressingham
Wretton
Stoke Ferry
Whitington
Foulden
Beckett End
Northwold
Little London
Bodney
The Arms
B1108
A1065
Fordham
Hilgay
Fen
Iron Bridge
Christchurch
Lakesend
Old Bedford River
R. Delph
Ten Mile Bank
R. Wissey
Brookville
Methwold Hythe
Methwold
Cranwich
Ickburgh
Lynford Arboretum
Mundford
West Tofts
DANGER AREA
Tipps End
Welney
Welney Wetland Centre
Hilgay Fen
Southery
Little London
B1160
Upwell Fen
B1093
Gold Hill
Southery Fens
Methwold Fens
Queen's Ground
THETFORD FOREST PARK
Brandon Creek
B1112
Feltwell
Grimes Graves
Manea
R. Great Ouse
Feltwell Anchor
Little Ouse
Brandon Bank
Weeting Castle
Weeting
Purl's Bridge
Hundred Foot Drain
Mare Fen
Burnt Fen
Littleport
Hockwold cum Wilton
Hockwold Fens
Brandon
Town Street
Santon Downham
Croxton
Fodder Fen
Pymoor
Sandhill
Black Bank
B1382
B1411
California
Little Downham
Chettisham
Prickwillow
Mile End
Prickwillow Engine
Heritage Cen.
High Lodge Forest Centre
Thetford Warren Lodge
Brandon Park
B1107
Thetford
Priory
Thetford Warren
A1088
Way Head
Coveney
Ely
Queen Adelaide
Babylon
Stained Glass
Middle Fen
Great Fen
Wangford Fen
Wangford
Lakenheath
Lakenheath Warren
Wangford Warren
B1106
Ancient House
Undley
The Delph
Kennyhill
Elveden
Barnham
A142
Witchford
R.A.F. Witchford Display of Memorabilia
Wentworth
Stuntney
Broad Hill
Mildenhall Fen
Weston Ditch
Beck Row
Wilde Street
Eriswell
Holywell Row
War Memorial
A11
Fakenham Magna
Honington
Little Thetford
Barway
Soham Cotes
Isleham Fen
Thistley Green
Mildenhall
Waterside
Isleham
Priory Church
West Row
Worlington
Barton Mills
Wilburton
Stretham
A1123
Soham
Soham Mere
Stretham Old Engine
Elford Closes
B1049
B1104
B1102
Icklingham
Anglo-Saxon Village
Tuddenham
Brockley Corner
Troston
Ampton
Great Livermere
Ingham
Down Field
Freckenham
NT Wicken Fen
Upware
Wicken
Fordham
Chippenham
Red Lodge
Lackford
West Stow
Culford
Flempton
Herringswell
Cavenham
Timworth Green
Chittering
Little Fen
Farmland Museum & Denny Abbey
River Bank
B1085
Kennett
Hengrave
Conyers Green
Denny End
Burwell
Stevens'
Reach
Snailwell
Fornham All Saints
Fornham St. Martin
Risby
B1103
Exning
Kentford
Needham Street
Higham
A14
A143
R. Cam
Waterbeach
Fosters
Devil's Dyke
Swaffham Prior
B1506
Moulton
Packhorse Bridge
Gazeley
Burthorpe
Barrow
Westley
Suffolk Regiment
Clayhithe
Commercial End
Newmarket Heath
NEWMARKET
Little Saxham
Great Saxham
BURY ST. EDMUNDS
Blackthorpe
Milton
Horningsea
Long Meadow
Lode
Anglesey Abbey NT
Swaffham Bulbeck
National Stud
B1063
National Horseracing
Ashley
Dalham
Denham
Horringer
Ickworth NT
Rushbrooke
Stow cum Quy
Bottisham
A1303
B1061
Cheveley
Broad Green
Dunstall Green
Fen Ditton
A1303
Little Ditton
Saxon Street
Ousden
Hargrave
Chevington
Pinford End
Sicklesmere
Great Whelnetham
Little Whelnetham
Cambridge
Teversham
Little Wilbraham
Stetchworth
Woodditton
Back Street
Tan Office Green
Hawstead
Bradfield Combust
CAMBRIDGE
SEE PAGE 191
Cherry Hinton
Church End
Great Wilbraham
A1304
Dullingham
Ditton Green
Upend
Lidgate
Depden Green
Baxter's Green
Whepstead
Mickley Green
Hoggard's Green
Fulbourn
Six Mile Bottom
Westley Waterless
Dullingham Ley
Kirtling
Chedburgh
Depden
Gulling Green
Stanningfield
Gog Magog Hills
Burrough End
Burrough Green
Kirtling Green
Mill End
Boyden End
Thorns
Meeting Green
Rede
Fleam Dyke
Brinkley
East Green
Cowlinge
Wickhambrook
Clopton Green
Brockley Green
Lawshall
Windolf Green
Wandlebury
Willingham Green
Pound Green
Farley Green
Denston
Hawkedon
Somerton
Hartest
Shimpling Street
Weston Colville
Carlton
Great Bradley
Little Bradley
Hobbles Green
Stradishall
Stansfield
Stapleford
R. Granta
B1052
West Wratting
Weston Green
Sowley Green
Assington Green
Thurston End
Boxted
Shimpling
Smithwood Green
Alpheton
Balsham
Little Thurlow
Great Thurlow
Babraham
FOURWENTWAYS
Little Abington
Chilford Hall Vineyard
Burton End
West Wickham
Barnardiston
Hundon
Stanstead
Bridge Street
Sawston
A505
Hildersham
Great Wratting
Chimney Street
Poslingford
Glemsford
Kentwell
Pampisford
Great Abington
A1307
Streetly End
Horseheath
Withersfield
Little Wratting
Brockley Green
Cavendish
Duxford
Linton
Cardinal's Green
Haverhill
Kedington
Chilton Street
Ancient House
A1092
Long Melford
Melford Hall
A1301
Bartlow
Calford
Clare
Stour
B1065
B1066

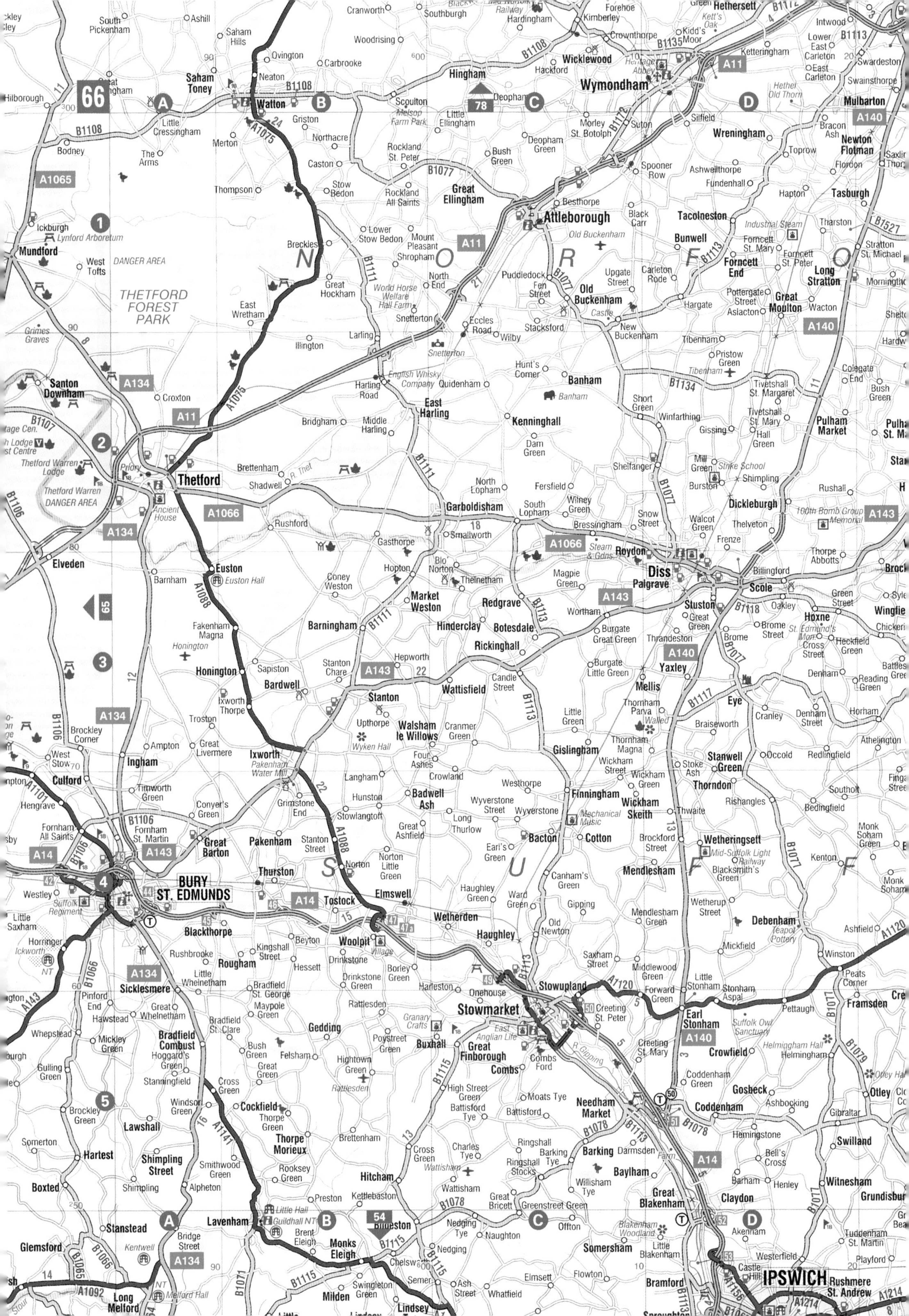

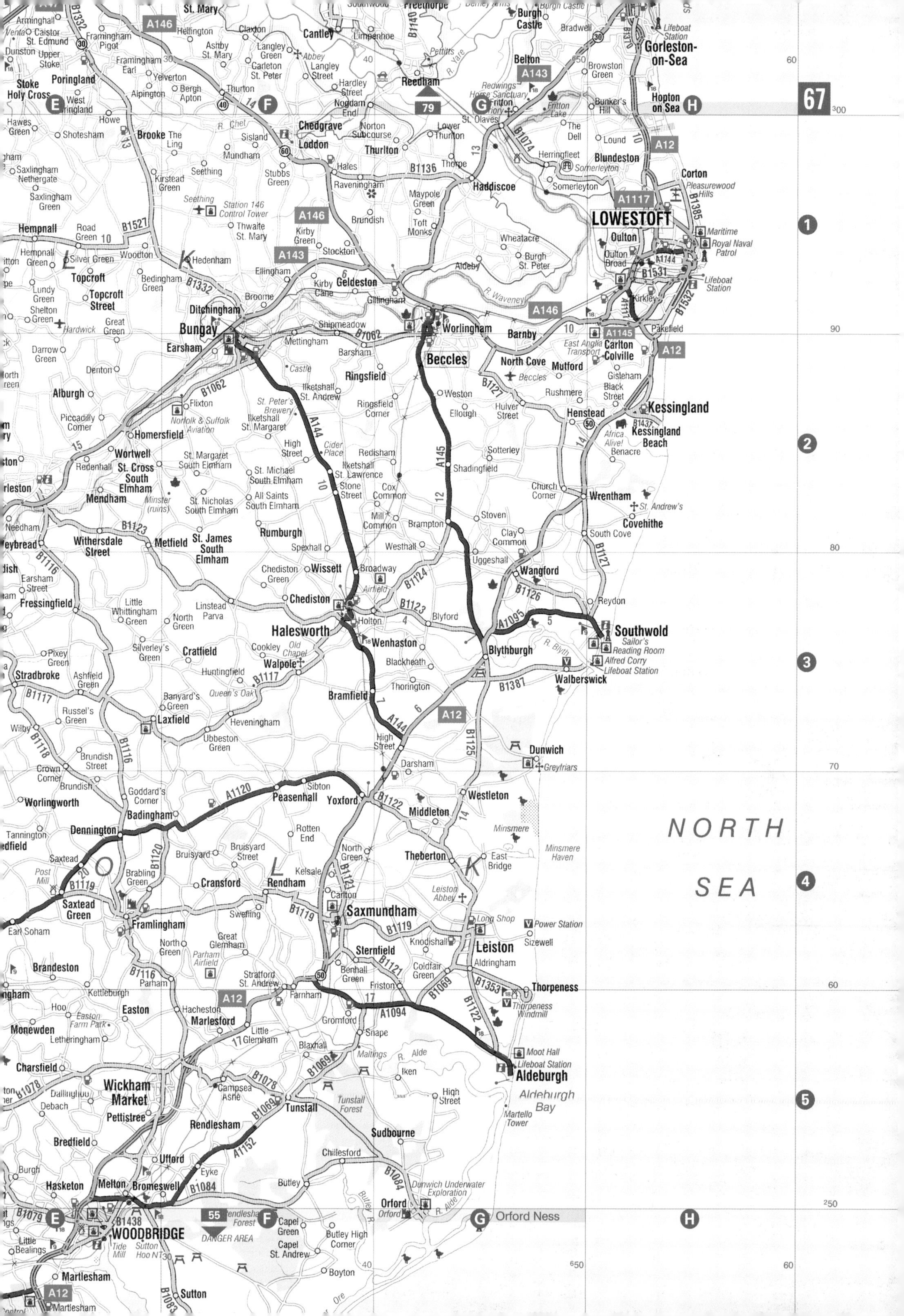
67
St. Mary
Cantley
Limpenhoe
Freethorpe
Burgh Castle
Bradwell
Gorleston-on-Sea
Lifeboat Station
Arminghall
Venta Caistor St. Edmund
Framingham Pigot
Dunston
Upper Stoke
Framingham Earl
Hellington
Claxton
Ashby St. Mary
Langley Green
Carleton St. Peter
Langley Abbey
Langley Street
Hardley Street
Nogdam End
Reedham
Pettitts
R. Yare
Belton
Browston Green
Redwings Horse Sanctuary
Fritton
Fritton Lake
Bunker's Hill
Hopton on Sea
Stoke Holy Cross
Poringland
West Poringland
Yelverton
Alpington
Bergh Apton
Thurton
Howe
Hawes Green
Shotesham
Brooke
The Ling
R. Chet
Sisland
Chedgrave
Loddon
Mundham
Norton Subcourse
Thurlton
Lower Thurlton
St. Olaves
The Dell
Lound
Herringfleet
Somerleyton
Blundeston
Corton
Pleasurewood Hills
Saxlingham Nethergate
Saxlingham Green
Kirstead Green
Seething
Stubbs Green
Hales
Raveningham
Thorpe
Haddiscoe
Maypole Green
Somerleyton
Station 146 Control Tower
Thwaite St. Mary
Kirby Green
Brundish
Toft Monks
LOWESTOFT
Oulton
Oulton Broad
Maritime
Royal Naval Patrol
Hempnall
Road Green
Hempnall Green
Silver Green
Woodton
Hedenham
Stockton
Wheatacre
Burgh St. Peter
Aldeby
Topcroft
Topcroft Street
Lundy Green
Bedingham Green
Ellingham
Kirby Cane
Geldeston
Gillingham
R. Waveney
Lifeboat Station
Kirkley
Shelton Green
Hardwick
Great Green
Ditchingham
Broome
Bungay
Earsham
Shipmeadow
Mettingham
Barsham
Worlingham
Barnby
East Anglia Transport
Carlton Colville
Pakefield
Darrow Green
Denton
Castle
Ringsfield
Beccles
North Cove
Mutford
Gisleham
Black Street
Alburgh
Ilketshall St. Andrew
Weston
Ellough
Hulver Street
Rushmere
Henstead
Kessingland
Kessingland Beach
Flixton
Norfolk & Suffolk Aviation
Piccadilly Corner
St. Peter's Brewery
Ilketshall St. Margaret
Ringsfield Corner
Africa Alive!
Benacre
Homersfield
Wortwell
Redenhall
St. Cross South Elmham
St. Margaret South Elmham
High Street
Cider Place
Redisham
Ilketshall St. Lawrence
Shadingfield
Sotterley
St. Michael South Elmham
Stone Street
Cox Common
Church Corner
Wrentham
St. Andrew's
Covehithe
Mendham
Minster (ruins)
St. Nicholas South Elmham
All Saints South Elmham
Mill Common
Brampton
Stoven
South Cove
Needham
Withersdale Street
Metfield
St. James South Elmham
Rumburgh
Spexhall
Westhall
Clay Common
Uggeshall
Earsham Street
Fressingfield
Chediston Green
Wissett
Broadway
Airfield
Wangford
Little Whittingham Green
North Green
Linstead Parva
Chediston
Blyford
Reydon
Southwold
Sailor's Reading Room
Alfred Corry Lifeboat Station
Halesworth
Holton
Wenhaston
Blythburgh
R. Blyth
Walberswick
Pixey Green
Silverley's Green
Cratfield
Cookley
Old Chapel
Walpole
Blackheath
Stradbroke
Ashfield Green
Huntingfield
Queen's Oak
Thorington
Bramfield
Russel's Green
Banyard's Green
Laxfield
Heveningham
Wilby
Brundish Street
Ubbeston Green
High Street
Darsham
Dunwich
Greyfriars
Crown Corner
Brundish
Goddard's Corner
Sibton
Peasenhall
Yoxford
Middleton
Westleton
Worlingworth
Badingham
Minsmere
Tannington
Dennington
Rotten End
NORTH
SEA
Saxtead
Bruisyard
Bruisyard Street
North Green
Theberton
East Bridge
Minsmere Haven
Post Mill
Brabling Green
Cransford
Rendham
Kelsale
Saxtead Green
Carlton
Leiston Abbey
Framlingham
Swefling
Saxmundham
Long Shop
Power Station
Earl Soham
Great Glemham
North Green
Parham Airfield
Knodishall
Leiston
Sizewell
Brandeston
Sternfield
Coldfair Green
Aldringham
Benhall Green
Friston
Thorpeness
Kettleburgh
Parham
Stratford St. Andrew
Farnham
Thorpeness Windmill
Hoo
Easton Farm Park
Easton
Hacheston
Marlesford
Gromford
Snape
Monewden
Letheringham
Little Glemham
Blaxhall
Maltings
R. Alde
Iken
Moot Hall
Lifeboat Station
Aldeburgh
Charsfield
Campsea Ashe
Aldeburgh Bay
Wickham Market
Dallinghoo
Debach
Pettistree
Tunstall
Tunstall Forest
High Street
Martello Tower
Rendlesham
Bredfield
Sudbourne
Chillesford
Burgh
Ufford
Eyke
Butley
Hasketon
Melton
Bromeswell
Dunwich Underwater Exploration
Orford
Orford Castle
Orford Ness
Rendlesham Forest
DANGER AREA
Butley R.
WOODBRIDGE
Capel Green
Butley High Corner
Little Bealings
Tide Mill
Sutton Hoo NT
Capel St. Andrew
Boyton
Martlesham
Sutton
Martlesham
Ore

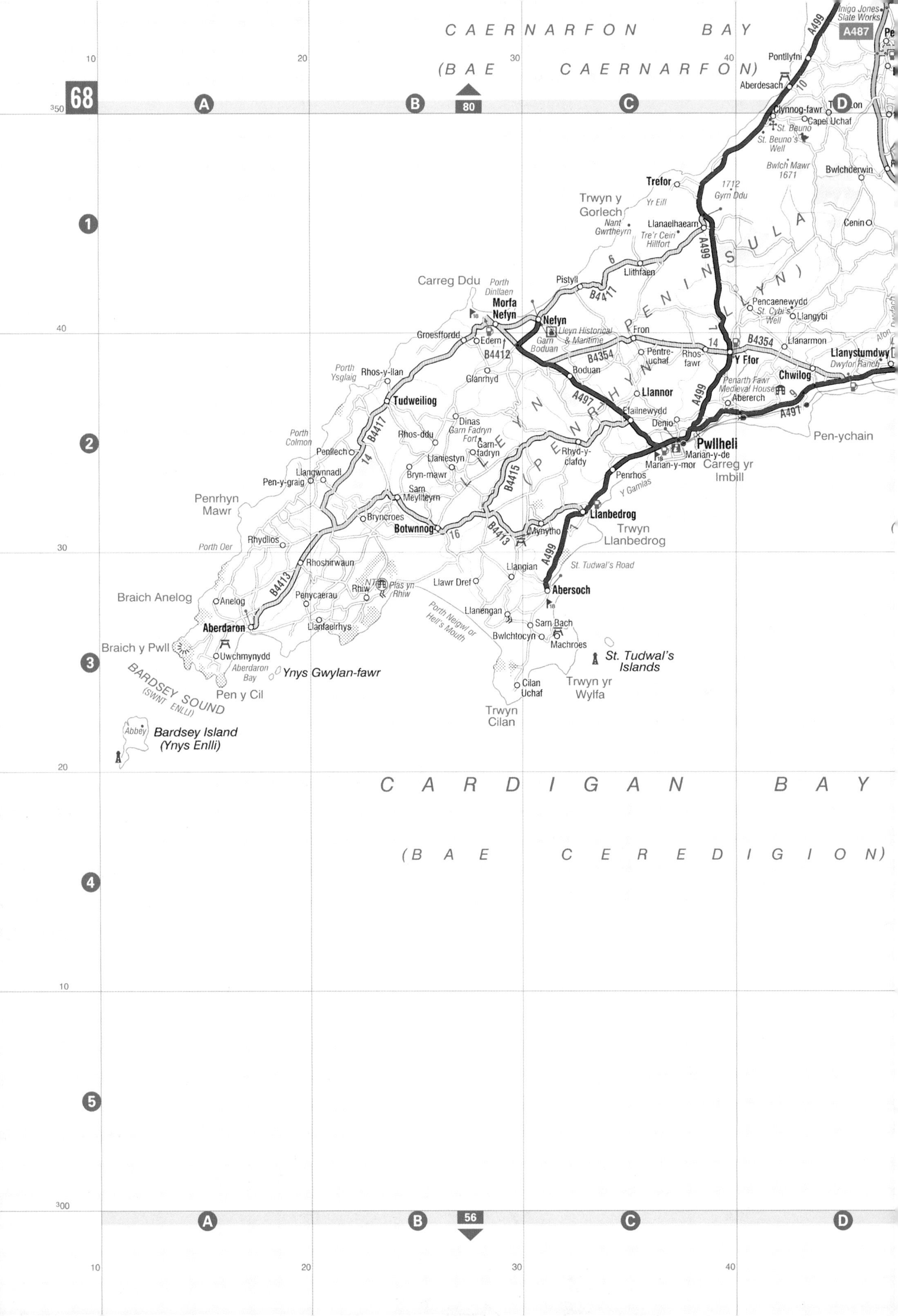
CAERNARFON BAY
(BAE CAERNARFON)
CARDIGAN BAY
(BAE CEREDIGION)
LLEYN PENINSULA
(PENRHYN LLYN)
80
56
A
B
C
D
Inigo Jones Slate Works
A487
A499
A497
Pontllyfni
Aberdesach
Clynnog-fawr
Capel Uchaf
St. Beuno
St. Beuno's Well
Bwlch Mawr 1671
Bwlchderwin
Trefor
1712
Gyrn Ddu
Yr Eifl
Trwyn y Gorlech
Nant Gwrtheyrn
Llanaelhaearn
Tre'r Ceiri Hillfort
Cenin
Llithfaen
Pistyll
B4417
Carreg Ddu
Porth Dinllaen
Morfa Nefyn
Nefyn
Lleyn Historical & Maritime
Garn Boduan
Fron
Pencaenewydd
St. Cybi's Well
Llangybi
Llanarmon
B4354
Llanystumdwy
Dwyfor Ranch
Groesffordd
Edern
B4412
Pentre-uchaf
Rhos-fawr
Y Ffor
Boduan
Porth Ysglaig
Rhos-y-llan
Glanrhyd
Chwilog
Penarth Fawr Medieval House
Llannor
Abererch
Tudweiliog
Efailnewydd
Denio
Pwllheli
Dinas
Garn Fadryn Fort
Garn-fadryn
Rhos-ddu
Porth Colmon
Penllech
Llaniestyn
Rhyd-y-clafdy
Marian-y-de
Marian-y-mor
Carreg yr Imbill
Pen-ychain
Llangwnnadl
Pen-y-graig
Bryn-mawr
Penrhos
Y Gamlas
Penrhyn Mawr
Sarn Meyllteyrn
Bryncroes
B4415
Llanbedrog
Trwyn Llanbedrog
Botwnnog
Mynytho
B4413
Rhydlios
Porth Oer
Rhoshirwaun
Llangian
St. Tudwal's Road
Braich Anelog
Anelog
Penycaerau
Rhiw
Plas yn Rhiw
Llawr Dref
Abersoch
Aberdaron
Llanfaelrhys
Porth Neigwl or Hell's Mouth
Llanengan
Sarn Bach
Bwlchtocyn
Machroes
Braich y Pwll
Uwchmynydd
Aberdaron Bay
Ynys Gwylan-fawr
St. Tudwal's Islands
BARDSEY SOUND
(SWNT ENLLI)
Pen y Cil
Cilan Uchaf
Trwyn yr Wylfa
Trwyn Cilan
Abbey
Bardsey Island
(Ynys Enlli)
1
2
3
4
5
10
20
30
40
350
300

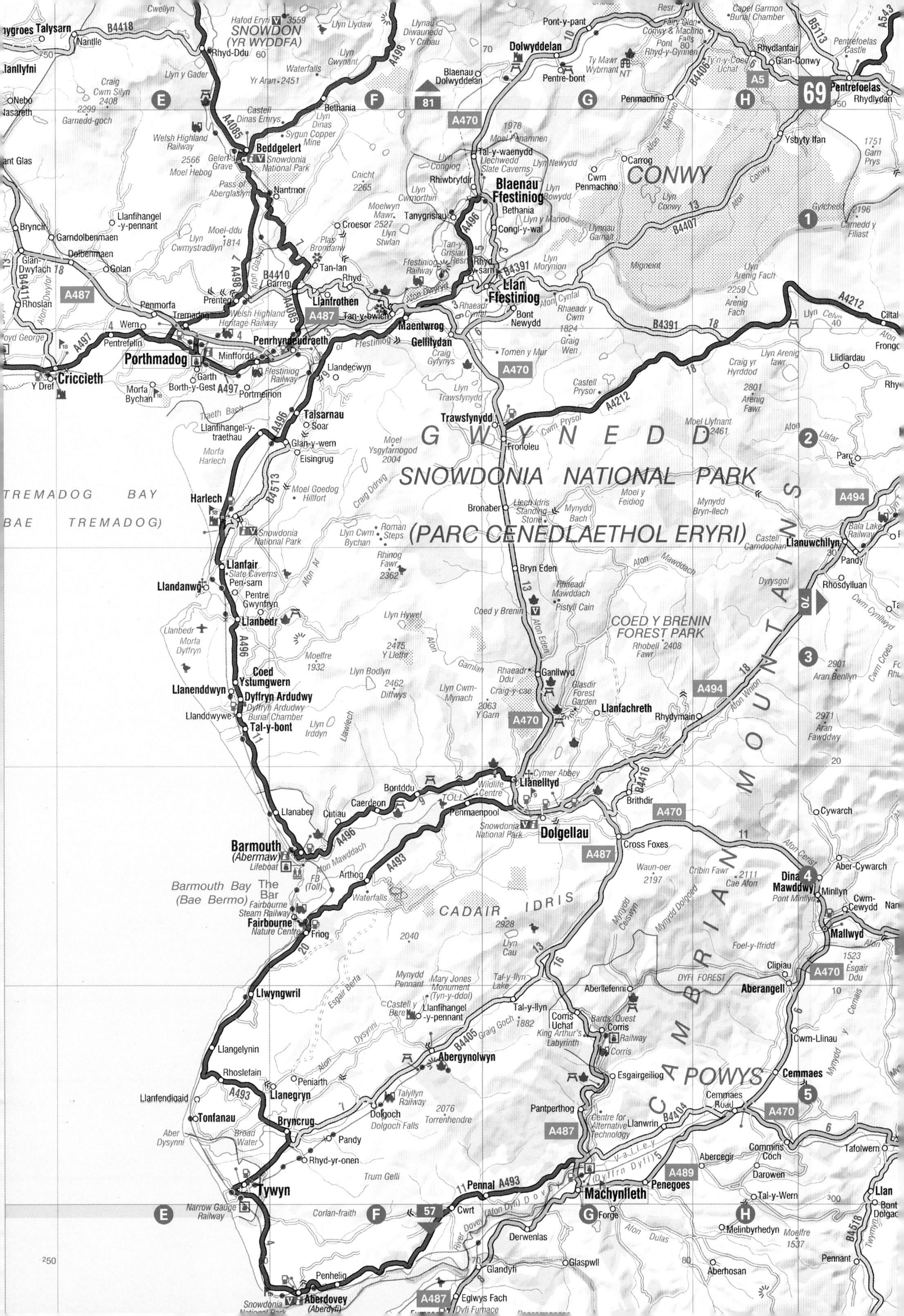

69
GWYNEDD
SNOWDONIA NATIONAL PARK
(PARC CENEDLAETHOL ERYRI)
CONWY
POWYS
CAMBRIAN MOUNTAINS
TREMADOG BAY
(BAE TREMADOG)
Barmouth Bay
(Bae Bermo)
SNOWDON
(YR WYDDFA)
CADAIR IDRIS
COED Y BRENIN
FOREST PARK
Porthmadog
Criccieth
Beddgelert
Blaenau Ffestiniog
Llan Ffestiniog
Penrhyndeudraeth
Harlech
Barmouth
(Abermaw)
Dolgellau
Tywyn
Aberdovey
(Aberdyfi)
Machynlleth
Dolwyddelan
Trawsfynydd
Fairbourne
Llanelltyd
Dinas Mawddwy
Mallwyd
Cemmaes
Corris
Abergynolwyn
Talsarnau
Maentwrog
Llanbedr
A487
A470
A493
A496
A494
A4212
A497
A498
A4085
B4391
B4407
B4410
B4405
B4404
A489
A5
81
57
70

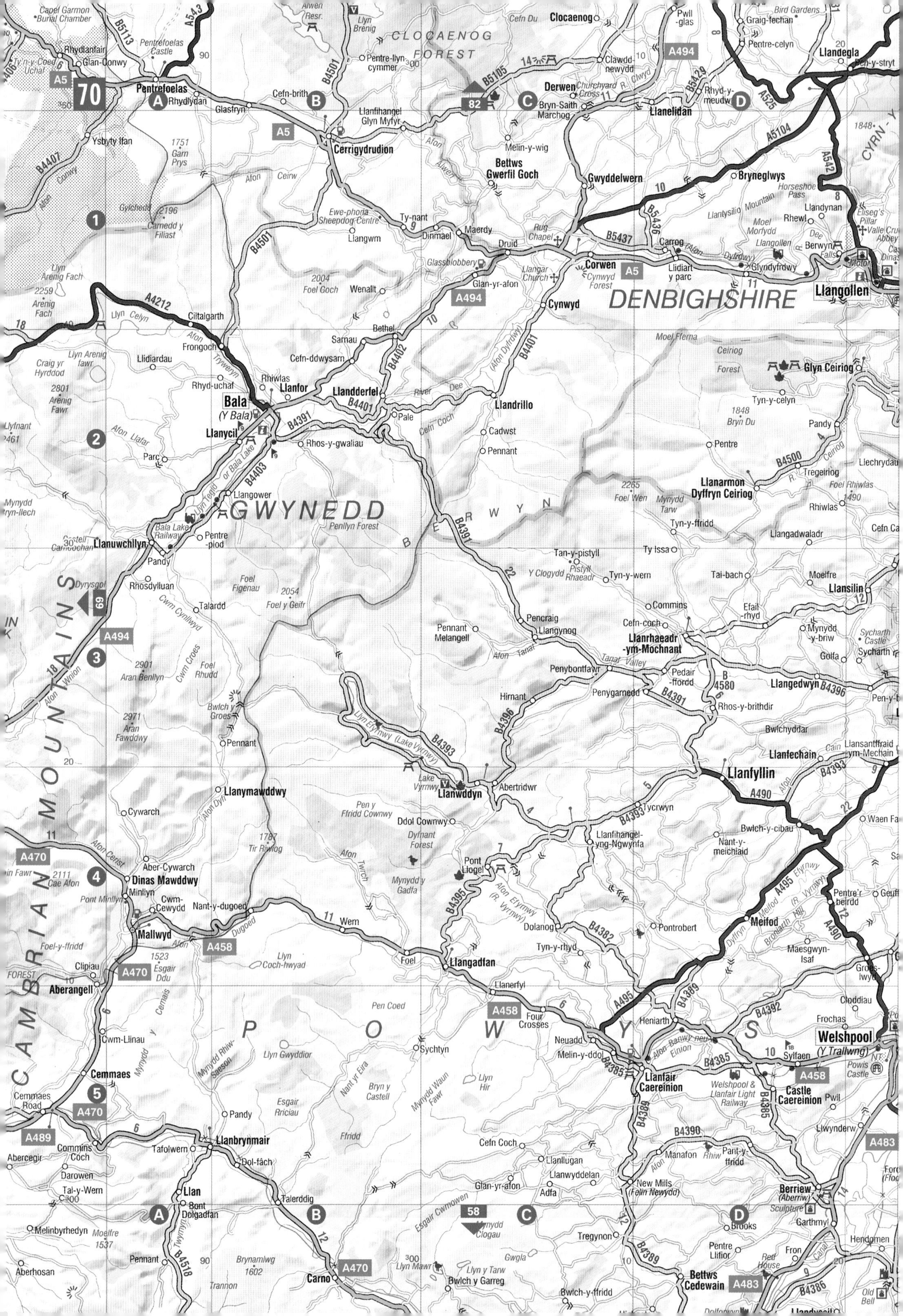

70
Capel Garmon Burial Chamber
Rhydlanfair
Glan-Conwy
Ty-n-y-Coed Uchaf
Pentrefoelas Castle
Pentrefoelas
Rhydlydan
Glasfryn
Ysbyty Ifan
1751 Garn Prys
Gylchedd
2196 Carnedd y Filiast
Alwen Resr.
Llyn Brenig
CLOCAENOG FOREST
Pentre-llyn-cymmer
Cefn-brith
Llanfihangel Glyn Myfyr
Cerrigydrudion
Ewe-phoria Sheepdog Centre
Ty-nant
Llangwm
Dinmael
Maerdy
Cefn Du
Clocaenog
Clawdd-newydd
Derwen
Churchyard Cross
Bryn-Saith Marchog
Melin-y-wig
Bettws Gwerfil Goch
Pwll-glas
Llanelidan
Rhyd-y-meudwy
Graig-fechan
Pentre-celyn
Bird Gardens
Llandegla
Pen-y-stryt
Gwyddelwern
Bryneglwys
Horseshoe Pass
Llantysilio Mountain
Moel Morfydd
Llandynan
Rhewl
Eliseg's Pillar
Valle Crucis Abbey
Llangollen
Berwyn
Glyndyfrdwy
Carrog
Rug Chapel
Druid
Corwen
Llidiart y parc
Glassblobbery
Llangar Church
Cynwyd Forest
Glan-yr-afon
Cynwyd
DENBIGHSHIRE
Llyn Arenig Fach
2259 Arenig Fach
2004 Foel Goch
Wenallt
Llyn Celyn
Ciltalgarth
Frongoch
Llyn Arenig fawr
Craig yr Hyrddod
Llidiardau
2801 Arenig Fawr
Rhyd-uchaf
Rhiwlas
Llanfor
Bethel
Sarnau
Cefn-ddwysarn
Llandderfel
Bala
(Y Bala)
Llanycil
Pale
Rhos-y-gwaliau
Llandrillo
Cadwst
Pennant
Moel Fferna
Ceiriog Forest
Glyn Ceiriog
Tyn-y-celyn
1848 Bryn Du
Pandy
Pentre
Llechrydau
Tregeiriog
Llanarmon Dyffryn Ceiriog
Foel Rhiwlas
Rhiwlas
Parc
Llangower
GWYNEDD
Bala Lake Railway
Pentre-piod
Llanuwchllyn
Pandy
Rhosdylluan
Penllyn Forest
BERWYN
2265 Foel Wen
Mynydd Tarw
Tyn-y-ffridd
Llangadwaladr
Tan-y-pistyll
Pistyll Rhaeadr
Y Clogydd
Tyn-y-wern
Ty Issa
Tai-bach
Moelfre
Llansilin
Foel Figenau
2054 Foel y Geifr
Talardd
Cwm Cynllwyd
Dyrysgol
69
Pennant Melangell
Pencraig
Llangynog
Commins
Cefn-coch
Llanrhaeadr-ym-Mochnant
Efail-rhyd
Mynydd-y-briw
Sycharth Castle
Sycharth
Golfa
Tanat Valley
Penybontfawr
Pedair-ffordd
Penygarnedd
Llangedwyn
Rhos-y-brithdir
Bwlchyddar
2901 Aran Benllyn
Cwm Croes
Foel Rhudd
2971 Aran Fawddwy
Bwlch y Groes
Pennant
Hirnant
Llyn Efyrnwy (Lake Vyrnwy)
Lake Vyrnwy
Llanwddyn
Abertridwr
Llanfechain
Llansantffraid-ym-Mechain
Llanfyllin
Llanymawddwy
Cywarch
Pen y Ffridd Cownwy
Ddol Cownwy
Dyfnant Forest
Tycrwyn
Llanfihangel-yng-Ngwynfa
Bwlch-y-cibau
Nant-y-meichiaid
Waen Fach
1787 Tir Rhiwiog
Aber-Cywarch
Dinas Mawddwy
2111 Cae Afon
Pont Minllyn
Minllyn
Cwm-Cewydd
Nant-y-dugoed
Mallwyd
Mynydd y Gadfa
Pont Llogel
Dolanog
Pontrobert
Meifod
Pentre'r beirdd
Wern
Foel
Llangadfan
Tyn-y-rhyd
Maesgwyn-Isaf
Foel-y-ffridd
Clipiau
1523 Esgair Ddu
Llyn Coch-hwyad
Aberangell
Llanerfyl
Pen Coed
Four Crosses
Heniarth
Cloddiau
Frochas
Welshpool
(Y Trallwng)
Powis Castle
Sylfaen
Cwm-Llinau
Mynydd y Cemais
Mynydd Rhiw-Saeson
Llyn Gwyddior
Sychtyn
Llyn Hir
Neuadd
Melin-y-ddol
Llanfair Caereinion
Welshpool & Llanfair Light Railway
Castle Caereinion
Pwll
Cemmaes
Cemmaes Road
Nant yr Eira
Bryn y Castell
Esgair Rriciau
Mynydd Waun Fawr
Pandy
Ffridd
Llanbrynmair
Tafolwern
Abercegir
Commins Coch
Darowen
Tal-y-Wern
Dol-fâch
Llan
Bont Dolgadfan
Talerddig
Cefn Coch
Llanllugan
Llanwyddelan
Glan-yr-afon
Adfa
Manafon
Pant-y-ffridd
New Mills (Felin Newydd)
Llwynderw
Berriew (Aberriw)
Sculpture
Garthmyl
Esgair Cwmowen
58
Mynydd Clogau
Tregynon
Brooks
Pentre Llifior
Fron
Hendomen
Melinbyrhedyn
Moelfre 1537
Pennant
Aberhosan
Brynamlwg 1602
Trannon
Carno
Llyn Mawr
Llyn y Tarw
Bwlch y Garreg
Gwgla
Bwlch-y-ffridd
Bettws Cedewain
Red House
Old Bell
CAMBRIAN MOUNTAINS
POWYS
A5
A543
B5113
B4501
B5105
A494
B5429
A525
A5104
A542
B4407
A4212
B5436
B5437
B4402
B4401
B4391
B4403
B4500
B4580
B4396
B4393
B4395
B4382
A490
A495
B4389
B4392
B4385
A458
A470
A489
A483
B4390
B4518
B4386

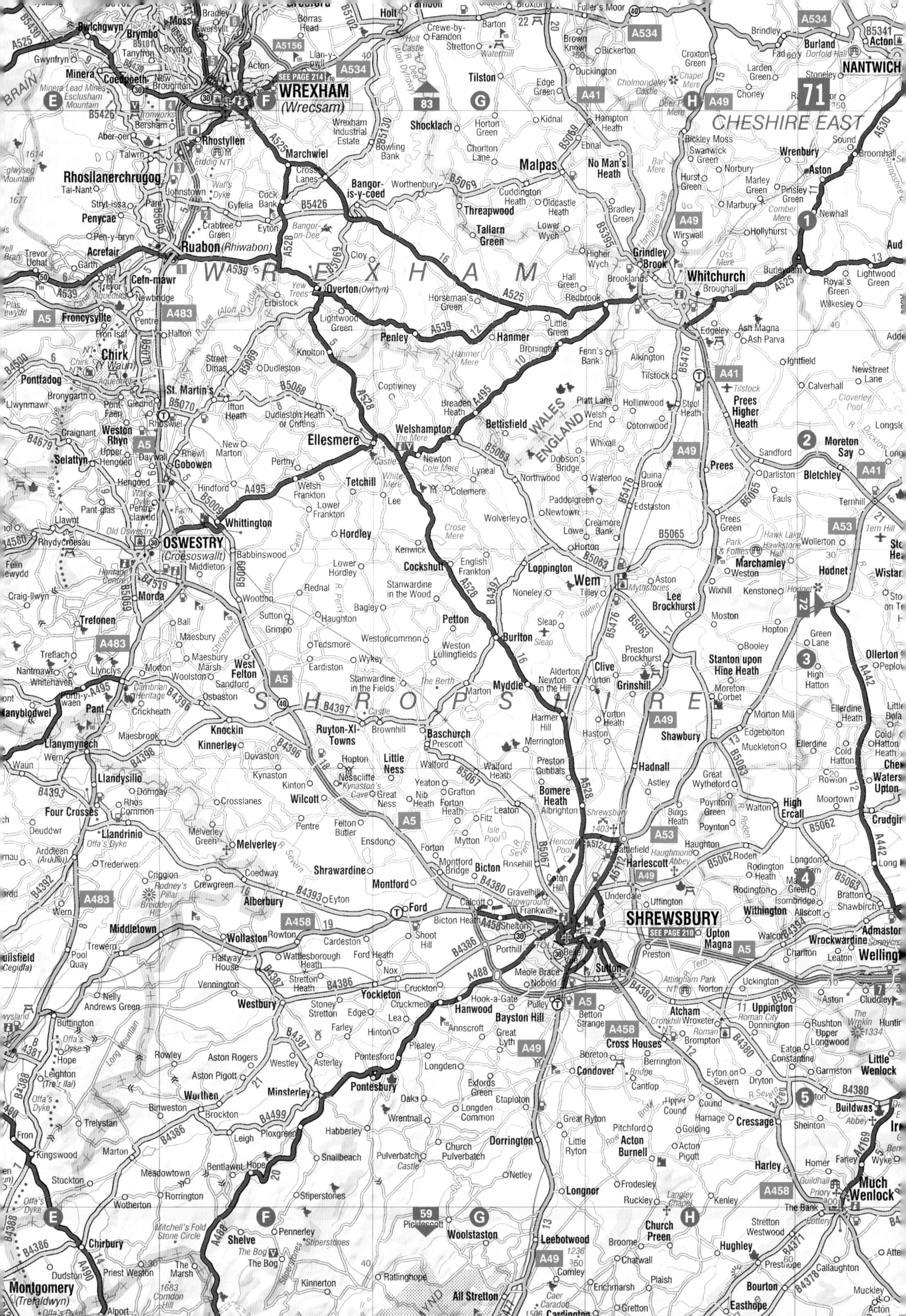

WREXHAM
(Wrecsam)
SEE PAGE 214
NANTWICH
71
CHESHIRE EAST
W R E X H A M
S H R O P S H I R E
WALES
ENGLAND
Bwlchgwyn
Brymbo
Moss
Gwersyllt
Holt
Farndon
Barton
Fuller's Moor
Broxton
Brindley
Burland
Acton
Minera
Coedpoeth
New Broughton
Tanyfron
Acton
Crewe-by-Farndon
Stretton
Tilston
Brown Knowl
Bickerton
Duckington
Edge Green
Croxton Green
Larden Green
Chorley
Stoneley
Cholmondeley Castle
Chapel Mere
Deer Park Mere
Bersham
Aber-oer
Rhostyllen
Erddig NT
Wrexham Industrial Estate
Bowling Bank
Shocklach
Horton Green
Kidnal
Hampton Heath
Ebnal
Chorlton Lane
Malpas
No Man's Heath
Bickley Moss
Swanwick Green
Norbury
Hurst Green
Marley Green
Pinsley Green
Sound
Wrenbury
Broomhall
Aston
Newhall
Talwrn
Rhosllanerchrugog
Tai-Nant
Johnstown
Marchwiel
Cross Lanes
Bangor-is-y-coed
Worthenbury
Cuddington Heath
Oldcastle Heath
Threapwood
Tallarn Green
Lower Wych
Bradley Green
Marbury
Comber Mere
Wirswall
Hollyhurst
Stryt-issa
Pant
Gyfelia
Cock Bank
Penycae
Pen-y-bryn
Crabtree Green
Eyton
Bangor-on-Dee
Acrefair
Ruabon (Rhiwabon)
Cloy
Higher Wych
Grindley Brook
Oss Mere
Whitchurch
Burleydam
Lightwood Green
Royal's Green
Wilkesley
Trevor Uchaf
Garth
Trevor
Cefn-mawr
Newbridge
Erbistock
Overton (Owrtyn)
Yew Trees
Horseman's Green
Hall Green
Redbrook
Brooklands
Broughall
Froncysyllte
Pentre
Halton
Lightwood Green
Penley
Hanmer
Little Green
Bronington
Edgeley
Ash Magna
Ash Parva
Chirk (Y Waun)
Fron Isaf
Knolton
Hanmer Mere
Fenn's Bank
Alkington
Ightfield
Newstreet Lane
Pontfadog
Bronygarth
Street Dinas
Dudleston
Tilstock
Calverhall
Cloverley Pool
St. Martin's
Coptiviney
Llwynmawr
Pont-Faen
Gledrid
Rhoswiel
Ifton Heath
Dudleston Heath or Criftins
Breaden Heath
Platt Lane
Hollinwood
Stool Heath
Prees Higher Heath
Craignant
Weston Rhyn
Welshampton
The Mere
Bettisfield
Welsh End
Cotonwood
Ellesmere
Newton
Cole Mere
Whixall
Moreton Say
Sandford
Selattyn
Upper Hengoed
Daywall
Rhewl
New Marton
Gobowen
Perthy
Castle
Lyneal
Dobson's Bridge
Waterloo
Quina Brook
Prees
Darliston
Bletchley
Hengoed
Wat's Dyke
Hindford
Welsh Frankton
Tetchill
White Mere
Colemere
Northwood
Edstaston
Fauls
Ternhill
Pant-glas
Pentre-clawdd
Whittington
Lower Frankton
Lee
Paddolgreen
Newtown
Wolverley
Creamore Bank
Prees Green
Tern Hill
Llawnt
Old Oswestry
Hordley
Crose Mere
Lowe
Horton
Hawk Lake
Hawkstone Hall
Park & Follies
Wollerton
Rhydycroesau
OSWESTRY
(Croesoswallt)
Babbinswood
Kenwick
Cockshutt
English Frankton
Loppington
Wem
Aston
Marchamley
Weston
Hodnet
Felin Newydd
Middleton
Lower Hordley
Mythstories
Heritage Centre
Rednal
Stanwardine in the Wood
Noneley
Tilley
Lee Brockhurst
Wixhill
Kenstone
Hodnet Hall
Craig-llwyn
Morda
Wootton
Bagley
Sleap
Moston
Hopton
Trefonen
Ball
Sutton
Grimpo
Haughton
Petton
Burlton
Green Lane
Booley
Maesbury
Westoncommon
Weston Lullingfields
Preston Brockhurst
Stanton upon Hine Heath
High Hatton
Ollerton
Treflach
Maesbury Marsh
West Felton
Tedsmore
Wykey
Eardiston
Alderton
Clive
Yorton
Grinshill
Moreton Corbet
Nantmawr
Whitehaven
Llynclys
Morton
Woolston
Sandford
Stanwardine in the Fields
The Berth
Marton
Myddle
Newton on the Hill
Morton Mill
Ellerdine Heath
Porth-y-waen
Pant
Crickheath
Cambrian Heritage
Osbaston
Ruyton-XI-Towns
Brownhill
Baschurch
Prescott
Harmer Hill
Yorton Heath
Haston
Shawbury
Edgebolton
Muckleton
Ellerdine
Cold Hatton
Cold Hatton Heath
Llanyblodwel
Llanymynech
Maesbrook
Knockin
Kinnerley
Dovaston
Wern
Hopton
Little Ness
Walford
Walford Heath
Merrington
Preston Gubbals
Hadnall
Waun
Llandysilio
Domgay
Kynaston
Nesscliffe
Kynaston's Cave
Yeaton
Grafton
Astley
Great Wytheford
Rowton
Waters Upton
Four Crosses
Rhos Common
Kinton
Wilcott
Great Ness
Nib Heath
Forton Heath
Bomere Heath
Albrighton
Poynton
Poynton Green
Walton
High Ercall
Moortown
Crudgington
Deuddwr
Llandrinio
Crosslanes
Melverley Green
Melverley
Pentre
Felton Butler
Leaton
Fitz
Isle Pool
Shrewsbury
Bings Heath
Arddleen (Arddlîn)
Offa's Dyke
Trederwen
Ensdon
Mytton
Forton
Battlefield
Haughmond Abbey
Haughton
Roden
Longdon on Tern
Criggion
Coedway
Shrawardine
Montford Bridge
Bicton
Rosehill
Hencott Pool
Harlescott
Rodington
Rodington Heath
Rodney's Pillar
Breidden Hill
Crewgreen
Alberbury
Montford
Gravelhill
Coton Hill
Underdale
Uffington
Isombridge
Bratton
Shawbirch
Eyton
Calcott
Showground
Frankwell
SHREWSBURY
SEE PAGE 210
Withington
Allscott
Admaston
Middletown
Ford
Bicton Heath
Shelton
Upton Magna
Walcot
Wrockwardine
Wellington
Trewern
Pool Quay
Wollaston
Rowton
Cardeston
Shoot Hill
Porthill
Belle Vue
Preston
Charlton
Leaton
Halfway House
Wattlesborough Heath
Ford Heath
Nox
Meole Brace
Nobold
Sutton
Tern
Uckington
Vennington
Stretton Heath
Cruckton
Attingham Park NT
Norton
Aston
Cluddley
Nelly Andrews Green
Westbury
Yockleton
Stoney Stretton
Cruckmeole
Hook-a-Gate
Hanwood
Pulley
Bayston Hill
Betton Strange
Atcham
Wroxeter
Uppington
Donnington
Roman City
The Wrekin
Buttington
Long Mountain
Edge
Farley
Lea
Hinton
Annscroft
Great Lyth
Cronkhill NT
Brompton
Rushton
Upper Longwood
Hope
Rowley
Aston Rogers
Westley
Asterley
Pontesford
Pleaeley
Longden
Cross Houses
Berrington
Eaton Constantine
Garmston
Little Wenlock
Leighton (Tre'r llai)
Aston Pigott
Worthen
Minsterley
Pontesbury
Oaks
Exfords Green
Boreton
Condover
Bridge
Cantlop
Eyton on Severn
Dryton
Binweston
Brockton
Wrentnall
Longden Common
Great Ryton
Upper Cound
Cound
Harnage
Golding
Cressage
Sheinton
Buildwas
Abbey
Trelystan
Habberley
Ploxgreen
Leigh
Marton
Snailbeach
Pulverbatch Castle
Church Pulverbatch
Dorrington
Little Ryton
Pitchford
Acton Burnell
Acton Pigott
Harley
Homer
Farley
Wyke
Fron
Kingswood
Meadowtown
Bentlawnt
Hope
Netley
Frodesley
Ruckley
Langley Chapel
Kenley
Guildhall
Priory
Much Wenlock
The Bank
Stockton
Rorrington
Stiperstones
Longnor
Wotherton
Chirbury
Mitchell's Fold Stone Circle
Shelve
Pennerley
Stiperstones
Pickleescott
Woolstaston
Leebotwood
Church Preen
Stretton Westwood
Montgomery (Trefaldwyn)
Priest Weston
The Bog
The Marsh
Corndon Hill
Ratlinghope
Broome
Chatwall
Hughley
Presthope
Callaughton
Dudston
Kinnerton
All Stretton
Comley
Enchmarsh
Plaish
Bourton
Easthope
Muckley
Alport
Cardington
Gretton
A5
A483
A525
A539
A528
A495
A41
A49
A534
A5156
A53
A442
A458
A488
A490
A5112
A5124
A4169
B5426
B5069
B5070
B5130
B5063
B5065
B5476
B4397
B4396
B4393
B4386
B4380
B4387
B4499
B5062
B5067
B5009
B4579
B4580
B4679
B4392
B4381
B4388
B4371
B4378
B4394
B5061
B5060
B5341
B5605
B5101
B5395
B5089
B5068
B5069
B4500
83
59

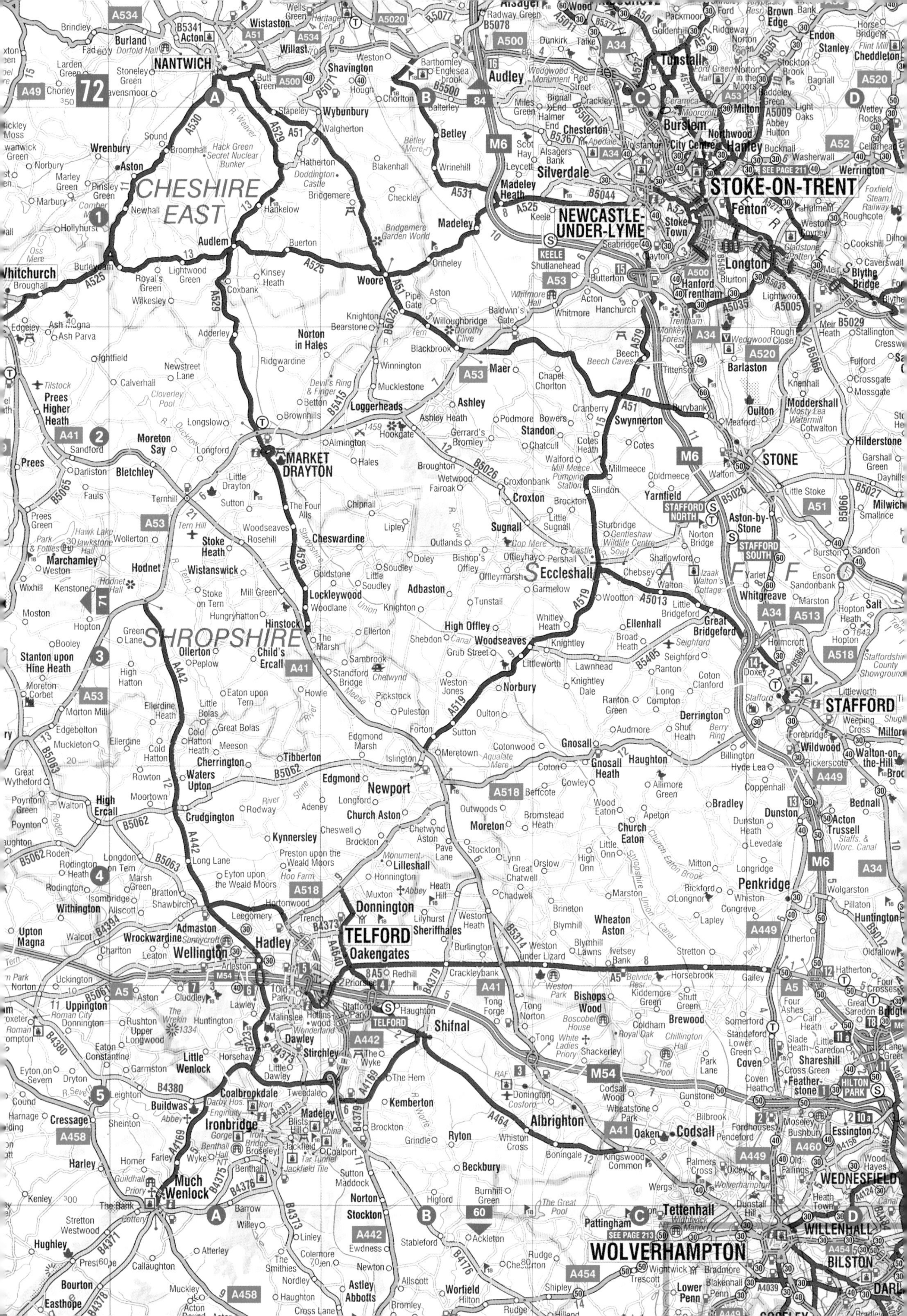

72
NANTWICH
CHESHIRE EAST
Wistaston
Willaston
Shavington
Wybunbury
Audley
Madeley Heath
Madeley
Betley
Audlem
Woore
Whitchurch
Wrenbury
Aston
Hankelow
Norton in Hales
Loggerheads
MARKET DRAYTON
Hodnet
SHROPSHIRE
Prees
Moreton Say
Bletchley
Marchamley
Wistanswick
Stoke Heath
Cheswardine
Lockleywood
Hinstock
Child's Ercall
Ollerton
Adbaston
High Offley
Woodseaves
Norbury
Eccleshall
Sugnall
Croxton
Standon
Ashley
Maer
Swynnerton
Yarnfield
Slindon
Cotes
NEWCASTLE-UNDER-LYME
STOKE-ON-TRENT
Silverdale
Tunstall
Burslem
Hanley
Fenton
Longton
Stoke Town
Trentham
Barlaston
STONE
Moddershall
Hilderstone
Milwich
STAFFORD NORTH
STAFFORD SOUTH
STAFFORD
Aston-by-Stone
Great Bridgeford
Seighford
Derrington
Gnosall
Gnosall Heath
Haughton
Church Eaton
Bradley
Dunston
Acton Trussell
Penkridge
Bednall
Wheaton Aston
Newport
Edgmond
Church Aston
Lilleshall
Donnington
TELFORD
Oakengates
Hadley
Wellington
Admaston
Wrockwardine
Shifnal
Dawley
Madeley
Ironbridge
Coalbrookdale
Much Wenlock
Broseley
Albrighton
Codsall
Tettenhall
WOLVERHAMPTON
WILLENHALL
WEDNESFIELD
BILSTON
Brewood
Bishops Wood
Coven
Shareshill
Essington
Cannock
High Ercall
Crudgington
Waters Upton
Withington
Upton Magna
Cressage
Harley
Stockton
Norton
Beckbury
Ryton
Kemberton
Worfield
Pattingham
SEE PAGE 211
SEE PAGE 213
KEELE
HILTON PARK
M6
M54
A34
A51
A53
A41
A442
A518
A519
A529
A5
A449
A458
A500
A525
A530
60
71
84

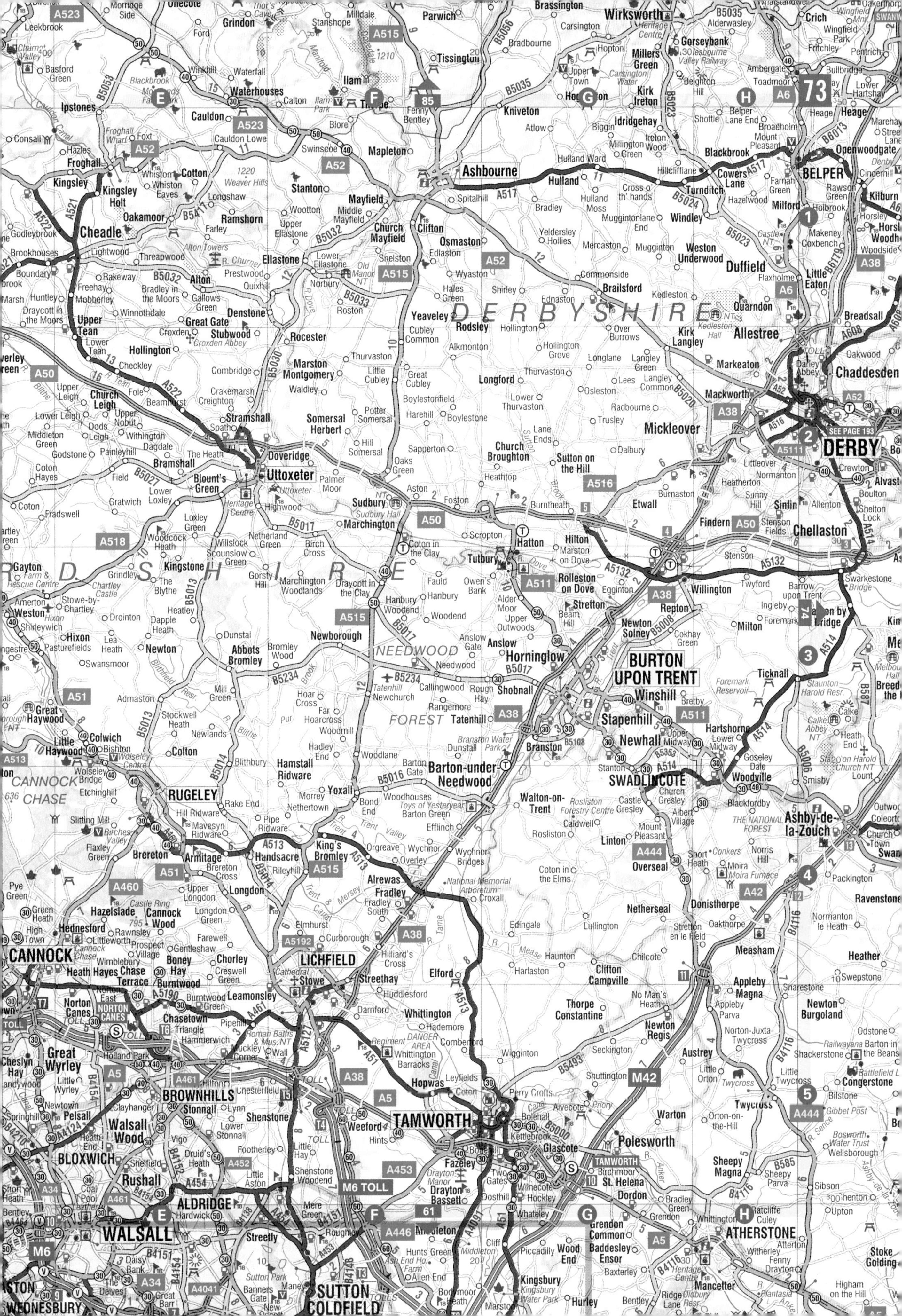

DERBYSHIRE
STAFFORDSHIRE
NEEDWOOD FOREST
CANNOCK CHASE
THE NATIONAL FOREST
73
74
SEE PAGE 193
DERBY
BELPER
Ashbourne
Wirksworth
Brassington
Parwich
Tissington
Crich
Heage
Kilburn
Duffield
Allestree
Chaddesden
Mickleover
Mackworth
Chellaston
Melbourne
Ticknall
Ashby-de-la-Zouch
Measham
Cheadle
Kingsley
Froghall
Ipstones
Cauldon
Waterhouses
Grindon
Ilam
Mayfield
Ellastone
Rocester
Denstone
Alton
Uttoxeter
Doveridge
Sudbury
Marchington
Tutbury
Hatton
Hilton
Etwall
Findern
Willington
Repton
Swarkestone
BURTON UPON TRENT
Winshill
Stapenhill
Newhall
SWADLINCOTE
Woodville
Branston
Barton-under-Needwood
Walton-on-Trent
Abbots Bromley
Newborough
Yoxall
Kingstone
Great Haywood
Little Haywood
RUGELEY
Armitage
Handsacre
Brereton
Alrewas
Fradley
LICHFIELD
Whittington
Elford
Hednesford
CANNOCK
Great Wyrley
Cheslyn Hay
Norton Canes
BROWNHILLS
Walsall Wood
Pelsall
BLOXWICH
Rushall
ALDRIDGE
WALSALL
WEDNESBURY
Streetly
SUTTON COLDFIELD
Shenstone
TAMWORTH
Fazeley
Polesworth
ATHERSTONE
Twycross
Appleby Magna
Netherseal
Overseal
Donisthorpe
Kingsbury
Hurley
Wood End
Grendon
Dordon
A523
A515
A52
A50
A522
A521
A518
A51
A513
A460
A5
A38
A516
A511
A514
A444
A453
A446
A5127
A5192
A6
A517
A5132
A42
M42
M6
M6 TOLL
B5035
B5032
B5033
B5030
B5027
B5017
B5234
B5013
B5014
B5016
B5008

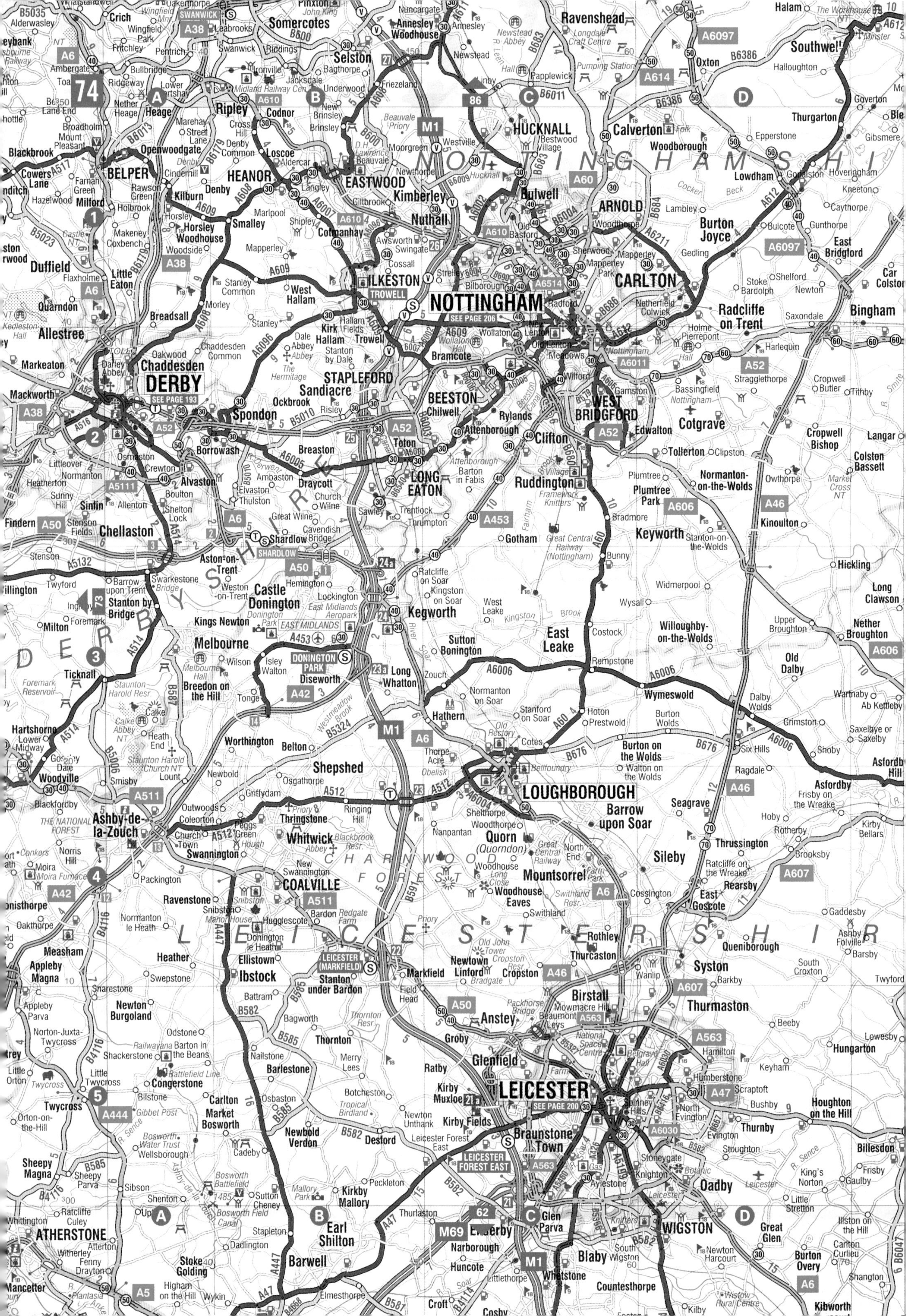

74
Crich
Somercotes
Annesley Woodhouse
Ravenshead
Halam
Southwell
Alderwasley
Ambergate
Selston
Newstead Abbey
Newstead
Oxton
Heage
Ripley
Codnor
Underwood
Papplewick
Linby
Hucknall
Calverton
Thurgarton
Nether Heage
Belper
Openwoodgate
Heanor
Eastwood
Kimberley
Nuthall
Bulwell
Arnold
Woodborough
Lowdham
Epperstone
Gonalston
Hoveringham
Duffield
Kilburn
Denby
Horsley Woodhouse
Smalley
Mapperley
Cossall
Ilkeston
Trowell
Nottingham
See page 206
Carlton
Burton Joyce
Gedling
Stoke Bardolph
Shelford
East Bridgford
Radcliffe on Trent
Bingham
Allestree
Chaddesden
Derby
See page 193
Spondon
Stanley
West Hallam
Kirk Hallam
Stapleford
Sandiacre
Beeston
Chilwell
Wollaton
Lenton
Bramcote
West Bridgford
Clifton
Cotgrave
Edwalton
Ruddington
Tollerton
Long Eaton
Toton
Attenborough
Breaston
Draycott
Borrowash
Alvaston
Sinfin
Chellaston
Shardlow
Aston-on-Trent
Castle Donington
Kegworth
Gotham
Keyworth
Normanton-on-the-Wolds
Plumtree
Melbourne
Kings Newton
East Leake
Sutton Bonington
Willoughby-on-the-Wolds
Long Whatton
Diseworth
Hathern
Wymeswold
Ticknall
Breedon on the Hill
Isley Walton
Donington Park
Stanton by Bridge
Hartshorne
Woodville
Worthington
Belton
Shepshed
Loughborough
Barrow upon Soar
Ashby-de-la-Zouch
Coleorton
Thringstone
Whitwick
Coalville
Quorn
(Quorndon)
Mountsorrel
Sileby
Seagrave
Thrussington
Rearsby
East Goscote
Woodhouse Eaves
Charnwood Forest
Leicestershire
Derbyshire
Nottinghamshire
Measham
Appleby Magna
Ibstock
Markfield
Newtown Linford
Anstey
Rothley
Thurcaston
Syston
Birstall
Thurmaston
Newton Burgoland
Barlestone
Groby
Glenfield
Leicester
See page 200
Braunstone Town
Oadby
Wigston
Kirby Muxloe
Desford
Newbold Verdon
Market Bosworth
Carlton
Congerstone
Twycross
Sheepy Magna
Atherstone
Earl Shilton
Kirby Mallory
Barwell
Stoke Golding
Blaby
Countesthorpe
Narborough
Enderby
Whetstone
Glen Parva
Houghton on the Hill
Thurnby
Evington
Billesdon
Burton Overy
Great Glen
Kibworth
M1
M69
A6
A38
A52
A60
A42
A46
A47
A50
A511
A6097
A614
A610
A453
A606
A607
A563
A444
A5

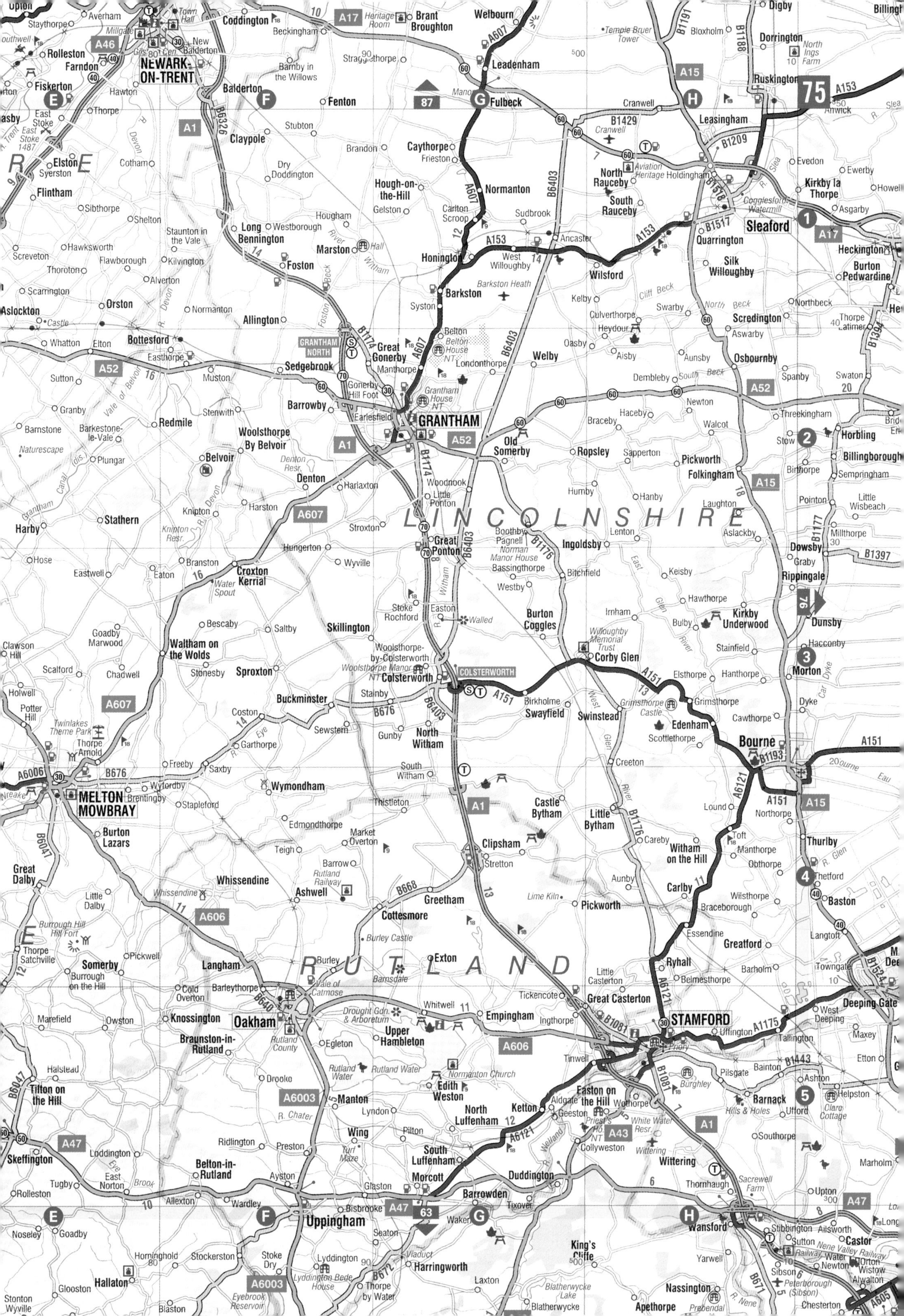

Upton
Staythorpe
Averham
Town Hall
Coddington
Beckingham
A17
Heritage Room
Brant Broughton
Welbourn
Temple Bruer Tower
B1191
Bloxholm
B1188
Digby
Dorrington
North Ings Farm
Rolleston
A46
Millgate
NEWARK-ON-TRENT
New Balderton
Barnby in the Willows
Stragglethorpe
A607
Leadenham
Farndon
Fiskerton
Hawton
Balderton
F
Fenton
87
Manor
G
Fulbeck
Cranwell
B1429
H
Leasingham
Ruskington
75
A153
Anwick
A15
East Stoke
Thorpe
A1
B6326
Claypole
Stubton
Brandon
Caythorpe
Frieston
B6403
Aviation Heritage
North Rauceby
B1209
Evedon
Ewerby
Elston
Syerston
Cotham
Dry Doddington
Hough-on-the-Hill
Normanton
Holdingham
Kirkby la Thorpe
Howell
Flintham
Gelston
Carlton Scroop
South Rauceby
Sudbrook
Cogglesford Watermill
Asgarby
Sibthorpe
Shelton
Hougham
Long Bennington
Westborough
Staunton in the Vale
Marston
Hall
Honington
A153
West Willoughby
Ancaster
B1517
Quarrington
Sleaford
1
A17
Heckington
Hawksworth
Screveton
Flawborough
Kilvington
Thoroton
Foston
Wilsford
Silk Willoughby
Burton Pedwardine
Alverton
Barkston Heath
Barkston
Scarrington
Orston
Syston
Kelby
Cliff Beck
Swarby
North Beck
Northbeck
Aslockton
Normanton
Allington
Culverthorpe
Heydour
Scredington
Thorpe Latimer
Castle
Belton
Belton House NT
Aswarby
B1394
Whatton
Elton
Bottesford
GRANTHAM NORTH
B1174
Great Gonerby
Oasby
Welby
Aisby
Aunsby
Osbournby
Spanby
Easthorpe
Manthorpe
Londonthorpe
Swaton
A52
Sutton
Muston
Sedgebrook
Dembleby
South Beck
Gonerby Hill Foot
Grantham House NT
Barrowby
Newton
A52
Granby
Stenwith
Earlesfield
GRANTHAM
Haceby
Threekingham
Barnstone
Barkestone-le-Vale
Redmile
Woolsthorpe By Belvoir
A1
A52
Old Somerby
Braceby
Walcot
Horbling
Naturescape
Plungar
Belvoir
Ropsley
Sapperton
Pickworth
Stow
2
Billingborough
Denton Resr.
Denton
Harlaxton
Woodnook
Folkingham
A15
Birthorpe
Sempringham
Grantham Canal
Knipton
Harston
Little Ponton
Humby
Hanby
Laughton
Pointon
Little Wisbeach
Stathern
A607
LINCOLNSHIRE
Harby
Knipton Resr.
Stroxton
Great Ponton
Boothby Pagnell
Lenton
Aslackby
Millthorpe
Hungerton
B6403
Norman Manor House
B1176
Ingoldsby
Dowsby
B1177
Graby
B1397
Hose
Eastwell
Eaton
Branston
Croxton Kerrial
Wyville
Bassingthorpe
Bitchfield
Rippingale
Water Spout
Westby
Keisby
Stoke Rochford
Easton
Walled
Burton Coggles
Irnham
Hawthorpe
76
Goadby Marwood
Bescaby
Saltby
Skillington
Bulby
Kirkby Underwood
Dunsby
Clawson Hill
Waltham on the Wolds
Woolsthorpe-by-Colsterworth
Willoughby Memorial Trust
Corby Glen
Stainfield
Hacconby
3
Scalford
Chadwell
Stonesby
Sproxton
Woolsthorpe Manor NT
Colsterworth
COLSTERWORTH
A151
Elsthorpe
Hanthorpe
Morton
Holwell
A607
Buckminster
Stainby
Birkholme
Swayfield
Swinstead
Grimsthorpe
Grimsthorpe Castle
Dyke
Potter Hill
Twinlakes Theme Park
Thorpe Arnold
Coston
B676
Sewstern
Gunby
North Witham
Edenham
Scottlethorpe
Cawthorpe
Bourne
B1193
A151
Garthorpe
Freeby
Saxby
South Witham
Creeton
A6006
B676
Wyfordby
Brentingby
MELTON MOWBRAY
Wymondham
Stapleford
Thistleton
Castle Bytham
Little Bytham
Lound
A151
Northorpe
A15
A1
Burton Lazars
Edmondthorpe
Market Overton
B1176
Toft
Thurlby
Teigh
Clipsham
Stretton
Careby
Witham on the Hill
Manthorpe
Obthorpe
Great Dalby
Barrow
Rutland Railway
Thetford
4
Whissendine
Ashwell
Aunby
Carlby
Baston
Little Dalby
Whissendine
A606
B668
Greetham
Lime Kiln
Pickworth
Wilsthorpe
Braceborough
Cottesmore
Burrough Hill Hill Fort
Burley Castle
Essendine
Greatford
Langtoft
Thorpe Satchville
Pickwell
Somerby
Burrough on the Hill
Langham
Burley
Exton
RUTLAND
Ryhall
Barholm
Towngate
Little Casterton
Belmesthorpe
A6121
Vale of Catmose
Barnsdale
Cold Overton
Barleythorpe
B640
Whitwell
Tickencote
Great Casterton
Deeping Gate
West Deeping
Marefield
Owston
Knossington
Oakham
Drought Gdn. & Arboretum
Empingham
Ingthorpe
STAMFORD
Uffington
A1175
Maxey
Braunston-in-Rutland
Rutland County
Egleton
Upper Hambleton
A606
Tinwell
Tallington
Etton
Halstead
Rutland Water
Normanton Church
Burghley
Pilsgate
Bainton
B1443
Ashton
Tilton on the Hill
Brooke
Edith Weston
Easton on the Hill
Wothorpe
Barnack
5
Helpston
B6047
A6003
Manton
Lyndon
North Luffenham
Ketton
Aldgate
Geeston
Priest's Ho. NT
White Water Resr.
Hills & Holes
Ufford
Claro Cottage
R. Chater
A43
A1
Wing
Pilton
Collyweston
Wittering
Southorpe
Skeffington
A47
Loddington
Ridlington
Preston
South Luffenham
Wittering
Marholm
East Norton
Belton-in-Rutland
Ayston
Morcott
Duddington
Thornhaugh
Sacrewell Farm
Upton
Tugby
Rolleston
Allexton
Wardley
Glaston
Barrowden
A47
Bisbrooke
A47
63
Tixover
E
F
G
H
Uppingham
Wakerley
Wansford
Noseley
Goadby
Seaton
Stibbington
Ailsworth
Castor
Sutton
Nene Valley Railway
Horninghold
Stockerston
Stoke Dry
Lyddington
Viaduct
Harringworth
King's Cliffe
Yarwell
Sibson
Water Newton
Orton Wistow
Alwalton
Hallaton
Lyddington Bede House
B672
Thorpe by Water
Laxton
Blatherwycke Lake
Nassington
Peterborough (Sibson)
Glooston
A6003
Eyebrook Reservoir
Stonton Wyville
Blaston
Blatherwycke
Apethorpe
Prebendal
B671
Chesterton
A605

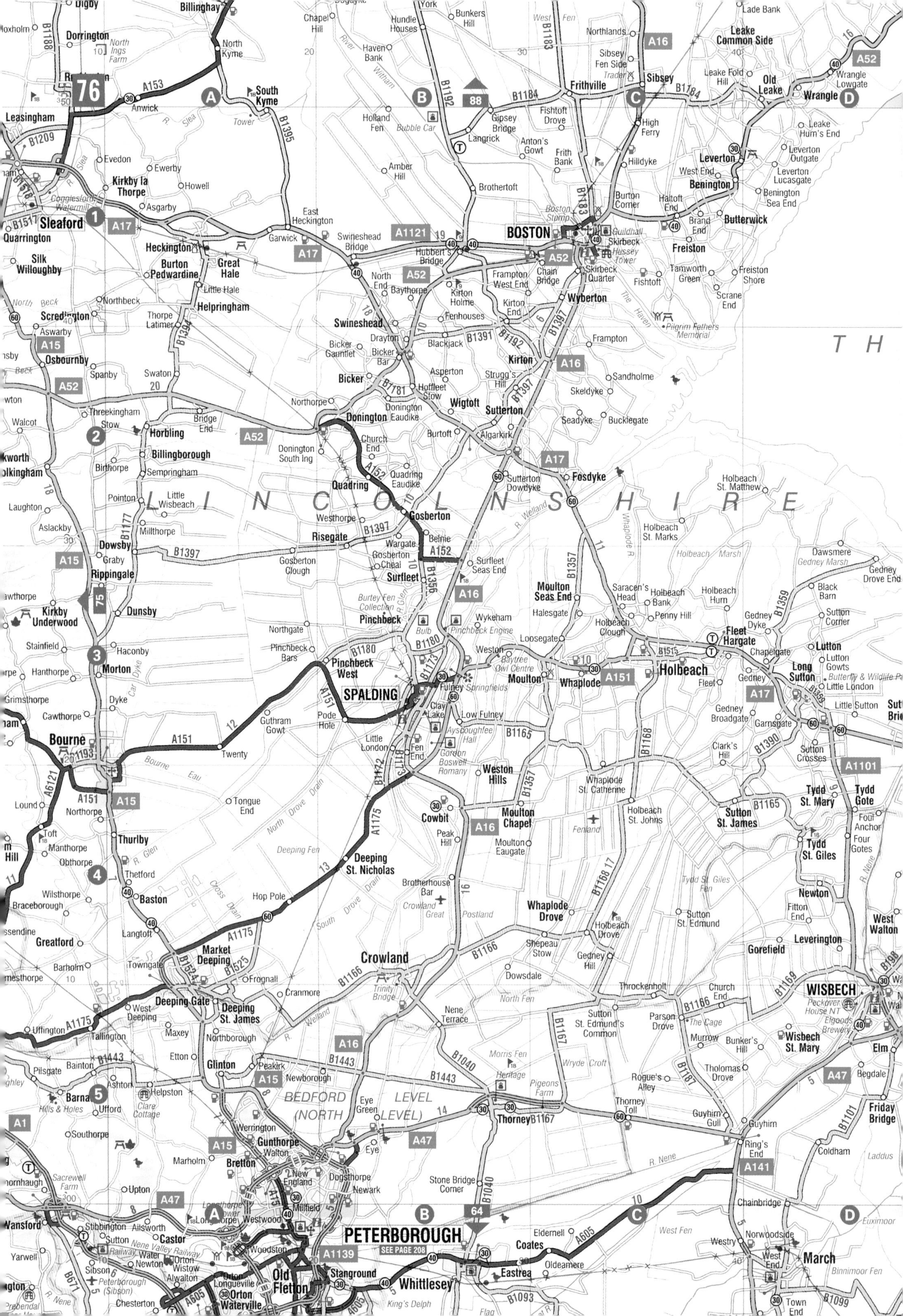

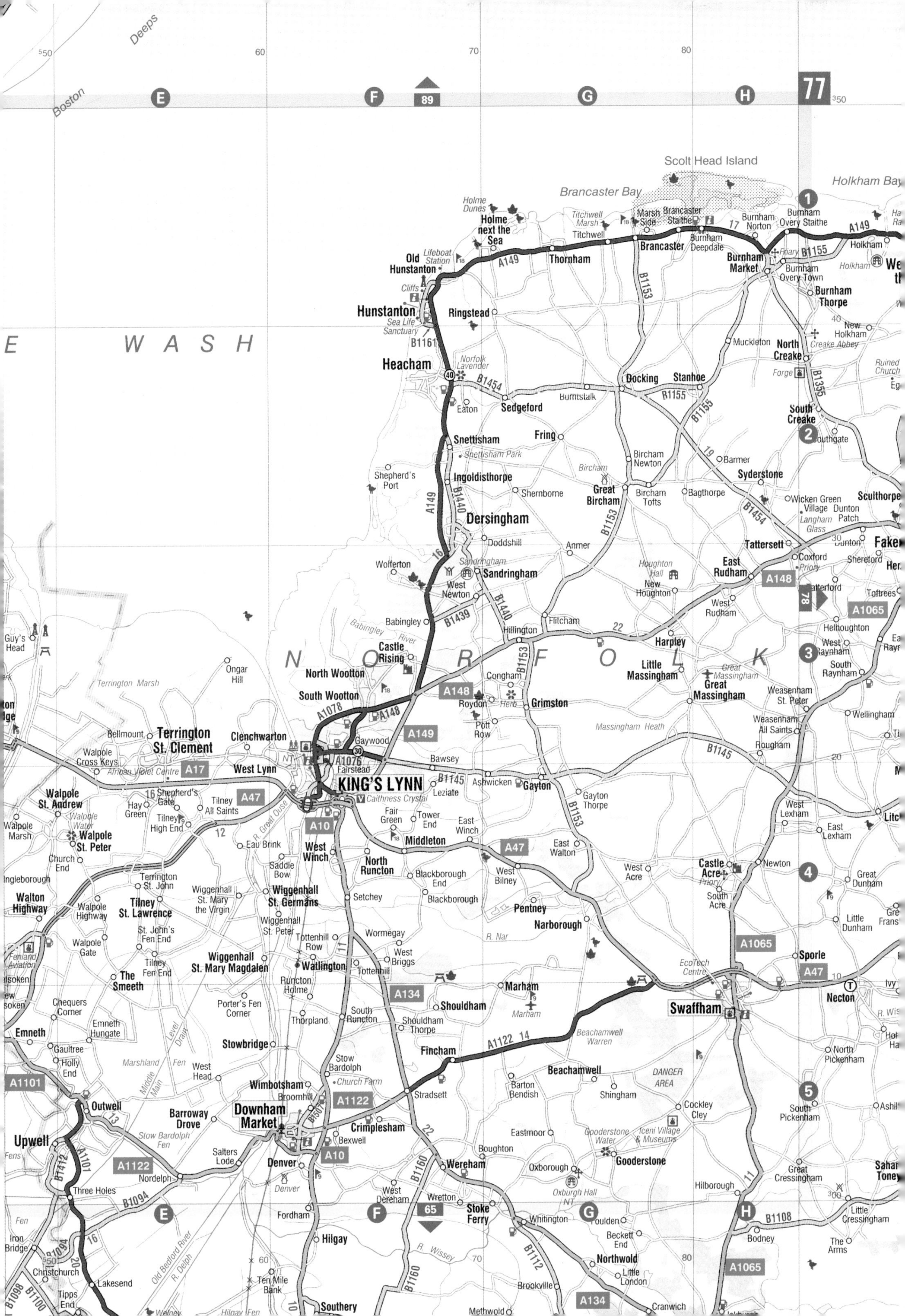
77
Deeps
Boston
550
60
70
80
350
E
F
G
H
89
Scolt Head Island
Brancaster Bay
Holkham Bay
1
Holme Dunes
Holme next the Sea
Titchwell Marsh
Titchwell
Marsh Side
Brancaster Staithe
Burnham Norton
Burnham Overy Staithe
A149
Holkham
Old Hunstanton
Lifeboat Station
Thornham
Brancaster
Burnham Deepdale
Burnham Market
Friary
B1155
Burnham Overy Town
Burnham Thorpe
Cliffs
Hunstanton
Sea Life Sanctuary
B1161
Ringstead
B1153
THE WASH
Heacham
Norfolk Lavender
B1454
Eaton
Sedgeford
Burnt Stalk
Docking
Stanhoe
B1155
Muckleton
North Creake
Creake Abbey
New Holkham
Forge
B1355
South Creake
Southgate
2
Ruined Church
Snettisham
Snettisham Park
Fring
Bircham Newton
Barmer
Syderstone
Shepherd's Port
Ingoldisthorpe
Bircham
Great Bircham
Bircham Tofts
Bagthorpe
Shernborne
Wicken Green Village
Sculthorpe
Dunton Patch
Langham Glass
B1440
A149
Dersingham
B1153
B1454
Doddshill
Anmer
Tattersett
Coxford Priory
Dunton
Shereford
Fakenham
Wolferton
Sandringham
Houghton Hall
East Rudham
A148
New Houghton
West Newton
B1440
West Rudham
Tatterford
Toftrees
A1065
78
Babingley
B1439
Flitcham
Hillington
22
Helhoughton
Babingley River
Castle Rising
Harpley
West Raynham
3
N O R F O L K
North Wootton
Little Massingham
Great Massingham
South Raynham
Ongar Hill
Terrington Marsh
Congham
A148
Roydon
Herb
Grimston
Weasenham St. Peter
South Wootton
A1078
A148
Pott Row
Weasenham All Saints
Wellingham
Massingham Heath
Bellmount
Terrington St. Clement
Clenchwarton
Gaywood
A149
Rougham
B1145
Walpole Cross Keys
African Violet Centre
A17
West Lynn
A1076
30
Fairstead
Bawsey
KING'S LYNN
B1145
Leziate
Ashwicken
Gayton
Caithness Crystal
Walpole St. Andrew
Shepherd's Gate
Tilney All Saints
A47
Gayton Thorpe
West Lexham
Hay Green
Walpole Water
Tilney High End
12
R. Great Ouse
A10
Fair Green
Tower End
East Winch
B1153
East Lexham
Walpole Marsh
Walpole St. Peter
Eau Brink
West Winch
Middleton
A47
East Walton
Church End
Saddle Bow
North Runcton
West Acre
Castle Acre Priory
Newton
4
Ingleborough
Terrington St. John
Blackborough End
West Bilney
South Acre
Great Dunham
Walton Highway
Walpole Highway
Tilney St. Lawrence
Wiggenhall St. Mary the Virgin
Wiggenhall St. Germans
Setchey
Blackborough
Pentney
Wiggenhall St. Peter
Narborough
Little Dunham
St. John's Fen End
Tottenhill Row
Wormegay
R. Nar
A1065
Walpole Gate
West Briggs
Sporle
Fenland Aviation
Tilney Fen End
Wiggenhall St. Mary Magdalen
Watlington
Tottenhill
EcoTech Centre
A47
The Smeeth
Runcton Holme
A134
Marham
Necton
Chequers Corner
Porter's Fen Corner
Shouldham
Swaffham
Emneth Hungate
Thorpland
South Runcton
Shouldham Thorpe
Marham
Emneth
Level Drain
Beachamwell Warren
North Pickenham
Gaultree
Stowbridge
A1122 14
Holly End
Marshland Fen
West Head
Fincham
Stow Bardolph
Beachamwell
DANGER AREA
A1101
Middle Level Main
Wimbotsham
Church Farm
Barton Bendish
Outwell
Broomhill
A1122
Stradsett
Shingham
5
Barroway Drove
Downham Market
Crimplesham
Cockley Cley
South Pickenham
Upwell
Stow Bardolph Fen
Bexwell
Eastmoor
Gooderstone Water
Iceni Village & Museums
Salters Lode
A10
Boughton
Gooderstone
A1122
Denver
B1160
Wereham
Oxborough
Great Cressingham
Fens
Nordelph
Three Holes
B1094
Denver
West Dereham
Wretton
Oxburgh Hall NT
Hilborough
Fordham
Stoke Ferry
Whitington
Foulden
B1108
Little Cressingham
Fen
65
Iron Bridge
Hilgay
Beckett End
Bodney
The Arms
R. Wissey
Christchurch
Old Bedford River
R. Delph
Northwold
Little London
A1065
Lakesend
Ten Mile Bank
Tipps End
Southery
Brookville
A134
Welney
Hilgay Fen
Methwold
Cranwich

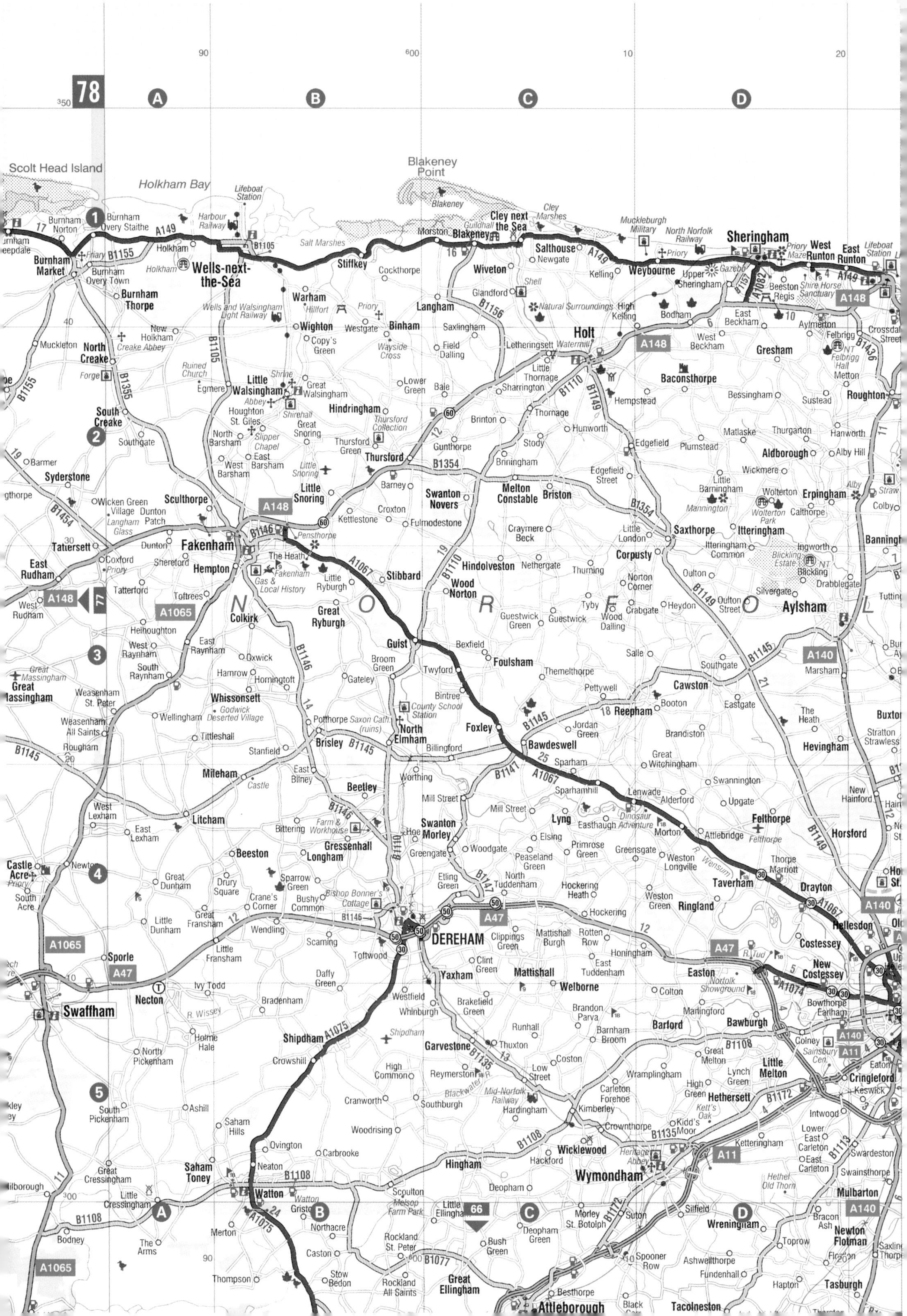

90   600   10   20

350

A   B   C   D

Scolt Head Island
Holkham Bay
Blakeney Point

Blakeney

Burnham Norton
Burnham Overy Staithe
Harbour Railway
Lifeboat Station
Burnham Deepdale
17
Burnham Market
Friary B1155
Burnham Overy Town
Holkham
Wells-next-the-Sea
Burnham Thorpe
Wells and Walsingham Light Railway
New Holkham
Muckleton
North Creake
Forge
South Creake
Southgate
Barmer
Syderstone
Wicken Green Village
Dunton Patch
Langham Glass
Sculthorpe
Tattersett
East Rudham
West Rudham
Coxford Priory
Shereford
Hempton
Tatterford
Toftrees
Helhoughton
Colkirk
Fakenham
Gas & Local History
Fakenham
The Heath
Pensthorpe
Little Ryburgh
Great Ryburgh
Stibbard
Guist
Broom Green
Twyford
Bintree
County School Station
North Elmham
Billingford
Foxley
Bawdeswell
Sparham
Sparhamhill
Lenwade
Alderford
Morton
Attlebridge
Felthorpe
Taverham
Drayton
Hellesdon
Costessey
New Costessey
Colney
Bowthorpe
Earlham
Little Melton
Cringleford
Keswick
Hethersett
Wreningham
Newton Flotman
Mulbarton

Salt Marshes
Stiffkey
Cockthorpe
Warham
Hillfort
Wighton
Westgate
Copy's Green
Binham
Priory
Langham
Saxlingham
Field Dalling
Bale
Lower Green
Hindringham
Thursford Collection
Thursford Green
Thursford
Barney
Croxton
Kettlestone
Little Snoring
Fulmodestone
Swanton Novers
Melton Constable
Briston
Stody
Brinton
Gunthorpe
Wood Norton
Hindolveston
Guestwick Green
Guestwick
Wood Dalling
Salle
Reepham
Booton
Cawston
Eastgate
Brandiston
Great Witchingham
Swannington
Upgate
Ringland

Morston
Cley next the Sea
Guildhall
Blakeney
Wiveton
Glandford
Shell
Newgate
Kelling
Weybourne
Upper Sheringham
Holt
Watermill
Letheringsett
Little Thornage
Sharrington
Thornage
Hunworth
Edgefield
Hempstead
Baconsthorpe
Plumstead
Matlaske
Thurgarton
Aldborough
Saxthorpe
Itteringham
Corpusty
Heydon
Crabgate
Oulton Street
Oulton
Aylsham
Marsham

Cley Marshes
Muckleburgh Military
North Norfolk Railway
Sheringham
West Runton
East Runton
Lifeboat Station
Priory Maze
Beeston Regis
Shire Horse Sanctuary
Gazebo
East Beckham
West Beckham
Gresham
Bodham
High Kelling
Natural Surroundings
Sustead
Roughton
Metton
Felbrigg
Felbrigg Hall
Crossdale Street
Aylmerton
Bessingham
Little Barningham
Wickmere
Thurgarton
Hanworth
Alby Hill
Colby
Erpingham
Wolterton Park
Calthorpe
Ingworth
Blickling Estate
Drabblegate
Silvergate
Banningham
Tuttington

NORFOLK

Great Massingham
Weasenham St. Peter
Weasenham All Saints
Rougham
West Lexham
East Lexham
Litcham
Mileham
Stanfield
Tittleshall
Wellingham
Godwick Deserted Village
Potthorpe
Brisley
Beetley
East Bilney
Worthing
Mill Street
Hoe
Swanton Morley
Gressenhall
Beeston
Great Dunham
Little Dunham
Sparrow Green
Crane's Corner
Bushy Common
Bishop Bonner's Cottage
Dereham
Toftwood
Scaming
Wendling
Little Fransham
Great Fransham
Daffy Green
Bradenham
Westfield
Whinburgh
Yaxham
Clint Green
Mattishall
Mattishall Burgh
Welborne
Honingham
East Tuddenham
North Tuddenham
Hockering
Hockering Heath
Weston Green
Honingham
Easton
Norfolk Showground
Marlingford
Colton
Barford
Brandon Parva
Runhall
Coston
Barnham Broom
Wramplingham
Great Melton
Kimberley
Carleton Forehoe
Crownthorpe
Hackford
Wicklewood
Deopham
Morley St. Botolph
Wymondham
Suton
Silfield
Spooner Row
Ashwellthorpe
Fundenhall
Hapton
Tasburgh

Castle Acre
Priory
South Acre
Newton
Swaffham
Necton
Ivy Todd
Holme Hale
North Pickenham
Sporle
Shipdham
Crowshill
Garvestone
Reymerston
Low Street
Thuxton
High Common
Cranworth
Southburgh
Letton
Woodrising
Hardingham
Hingham
Deopham
Scoulton
Melsop Farm Park
Little Ellingham
Rockland St. Peter
Deopham Green
Bush Green
Great Ellingham
Attleborough
Tacolneston

South Pickenham
Ashill
Saham Hills
Saham Toney
Ovington
Carbrooke
Neaton
Watton
Griston
Northacre
Caston
Merton
Thompson
Stow Bedon
Rockland All Saints
The Arms
Bodney
Little Cressingham
Great Cressingham

A149 A148 A1065 A47 A1075 A1067 A1075 B1108 B1110 B1145 B1146 B1147 B1149 B1108 B1135 B1172 A11 A140 A1074 A1067 A1078 B1077 B1354 B1156 B1149 B1354 B1145

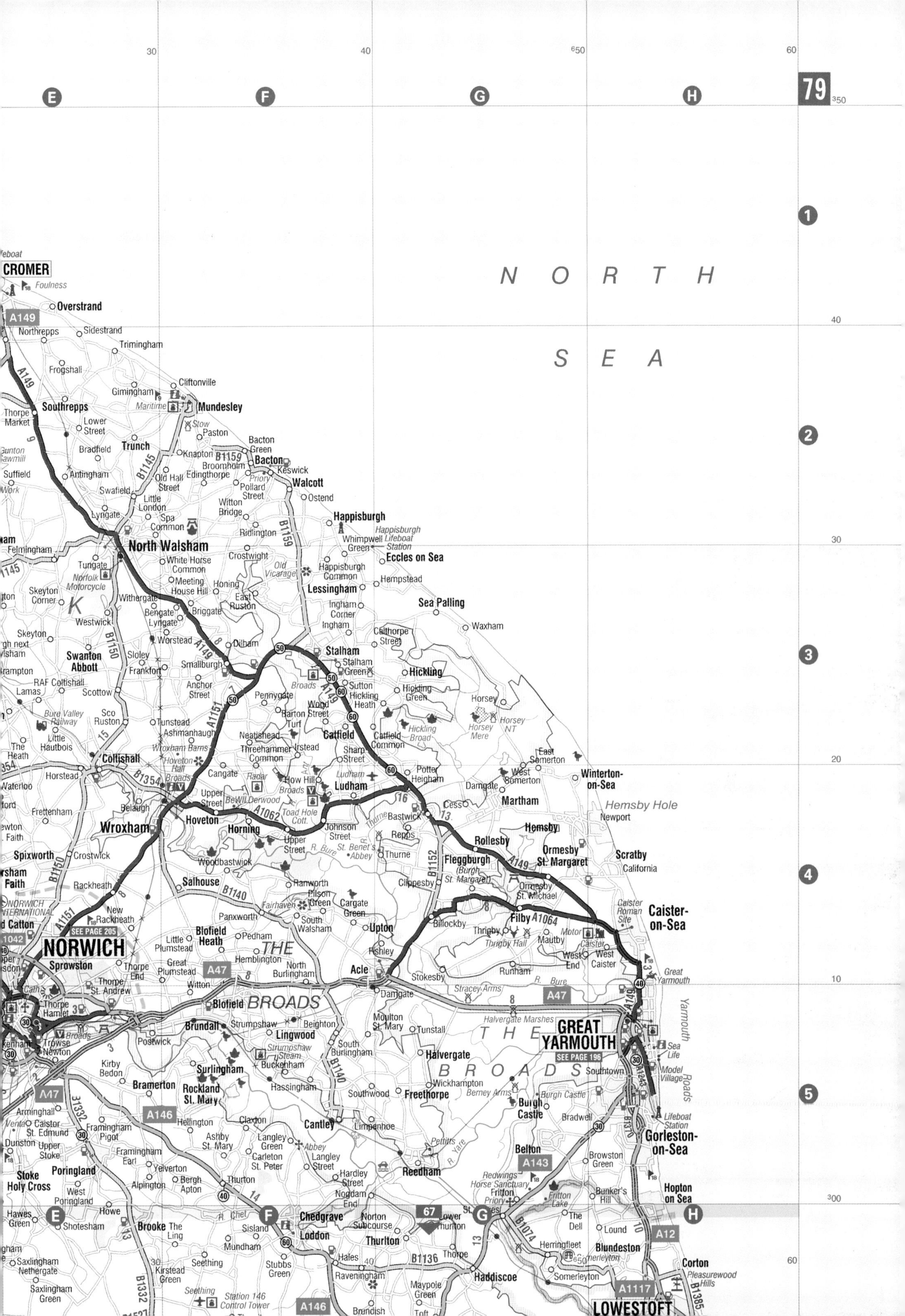
30
40
650
60
E
F
G
H
350
1
2
3
4
5
40
30
20
10
300
60
NORTH
SEA
CROMER
Foulness
Overstrand
A149
Northrepps
Sidestrand
Trimingham
Frogshall
Cliftonville
Gimingham
Maritime
Mundesley
Southrepps
Thorpe Market
Lower Street
Stow
Paston
Bacton Green
Bradfield
Trunch
Knapton
B1159
Bacton
Broomholm
Keswick
Gunton Sawmill
Suffield
Antingham
B1145
Old Hall Street
Edingthorpe
Priory
Pollard Street
Walcott
Ostend
Swafield
Little London
Witton Bridge
Lyngate
Spa Common
Ridlington
B1159
Happisburgh
Happisburgh Lifeboat Station
Whimpwell Green
North Walsham
Felmingham
Crostwight
Eccles on Sea
Tungate
White Horse Common
Old Vicarage
Happisburgh Common
Norfolk Motorcycle
Meeting House Hill
Honing
Hempstead
Skeyton Corner
Witheregate
East Ruston
Lessingham
Sea Palling
Bengate
Briggate
Ingham Corner
Westwick
Lyngate
Ingham
Waxham
Skeyton
Worstead
Calthorpe Street
B1150
Dilham
Swanton Abbott
Sloley
Stalham
Stalham Green
Frankfort
Smallburgh
Hickling
RAF Coltishall
Anchor Street
Broads
Sutton
Hickling Green
Lamas
Scottow
Pennygate
Hickling Heath
Horsey
Bure Valley Railway
Sco Ruston
A1151
Barton Turf
Wood Street
Tunstead
Catfield
Hickling Broad
Horsey Mere
Horsey NT
Little Hautbois
Ashmanhaugh
Neatishead
Catfield Common
The Heath
Wroxham Barns
Threehammer Common
Irstead
Sharp Street
East Somerton
Coltishall
Hoveton Hall
Cangate
Radar
Potter Heigham
West Somerton
Winterton-on-Sea
Horstead
B1354
How Hill
Ludham
Dam gate
Martham
Waterloo
Upper Street
BeWILDerwood
Ludham
Hemsby Hole
Belaugh
A1062
Toad Hole Cott.
Cess
Bastwick
Newport
Frettenham
Hoveton
Horning
Johnson Street
Thurne
Repps
Hemsby
Wroxham
Upper Street
R. Bure
St. Benet's Abbey
Rollesby
Crostwick
Thurne
Ormesby St. Margaret
Scratby
Spixworth
B1152
Fleggburgh
California
Woodbastwick
Burgh St. Margaret
B1150
Salhouse
Ranworth
Clippesby
Ormesby St. Michael
Rackheath
B1140
Pilson Green
Cargate Green
Caister Roman Site
Caister-on-Sea
NORWICH INTERNATIONAL
Fairhaven
Filby
A1064
New Rackheath
Panxworth
South Walsham
Billockby
Catton
SEE PAGE 205
Little Plumstead
Blofield Heath
Pedham
Upton
Thrigby
Thrigby Hall
Mautby
Motor
Caister
THE
Fishley
West End
West Caister
NORWICH
Sprowston
Hemblington
Great Plumstead
A47
Thorpe End
North Burlingham
Acle
Runham
Great Yarmouth
Thorpe St. Andrew
Witton
Stokesby
R. Bure
Yarmouth
Damgate
Stracey Arms
A47
Thorpe Hamlet
Blofield
BROADS
Halvergate Marshes
Brundall
Strumpshaw
Beighton
Moulton St. Mary
Tunstall
GREAT YARMOUTH
Broads
Trowse Newton
Lingwood
Postwick
THE
Strumpshaw Steam
South Burlingham
SEE PAGE 196
Sea Life
Kirby Bedon
Buckenham
Halvergate
BROADS
Southtown
Model Village
Surlingham
B1140
Bramerton
Hassingham
Wickhampton
Yarmouth Roads
Rockland St. Mary
Southwood
Freethorpe
Berney Arms
Burgh Castle
A47
Arminghall
A146
Burgh Castle
Lifeboat Station
Caistor St. Edmund
Hellington
Claxton
Cantley
Limpenhoe
Bradwell
Framingham Pigot
Gorleston-on-Sea
Dunston
Upper Stoke
Ashby St. Mary
Langley Green
Abbey
Carleton St. Peter
Pettitts
Framingham Earl
Langley Street
R. Yare
Belton
A143
Browston Green
Stoke Holy Cross
Poringland
Yelverton
Hardley Street
Reedham
Redwings Horse Sanctuary
Alpington
Bergh Apton
Thurton
Fritton
Priory
Fritton Lake
Bunker's Hill
Hopton on Sea
West Poringland
Nogdam End
Howe
R. Chet
67
Lower Thurlton
Hawes Green
Shotesham
Brooke
The Ling
Chedgrave
Norton Subcourse
St. Olaves
The Dell
Lound
Loddon
Sisland
Thurlton
B1074
A12
Mundham
Herringfleet
Blundeston
Somerleyton
Saxlingham Nethergate
Seething
Hales
B1136
Thorpe
Corton
Pleasurewood Hills
Kirstead Green
Stubbs Green
Raveningham
Haddiscoe
Somerleyton
Saxlingham Green
B1332
Seething
Station 146 Control Tower
Maypole Green
A1117
A146
Brundish
Toft
LOWESTOFT
B1385

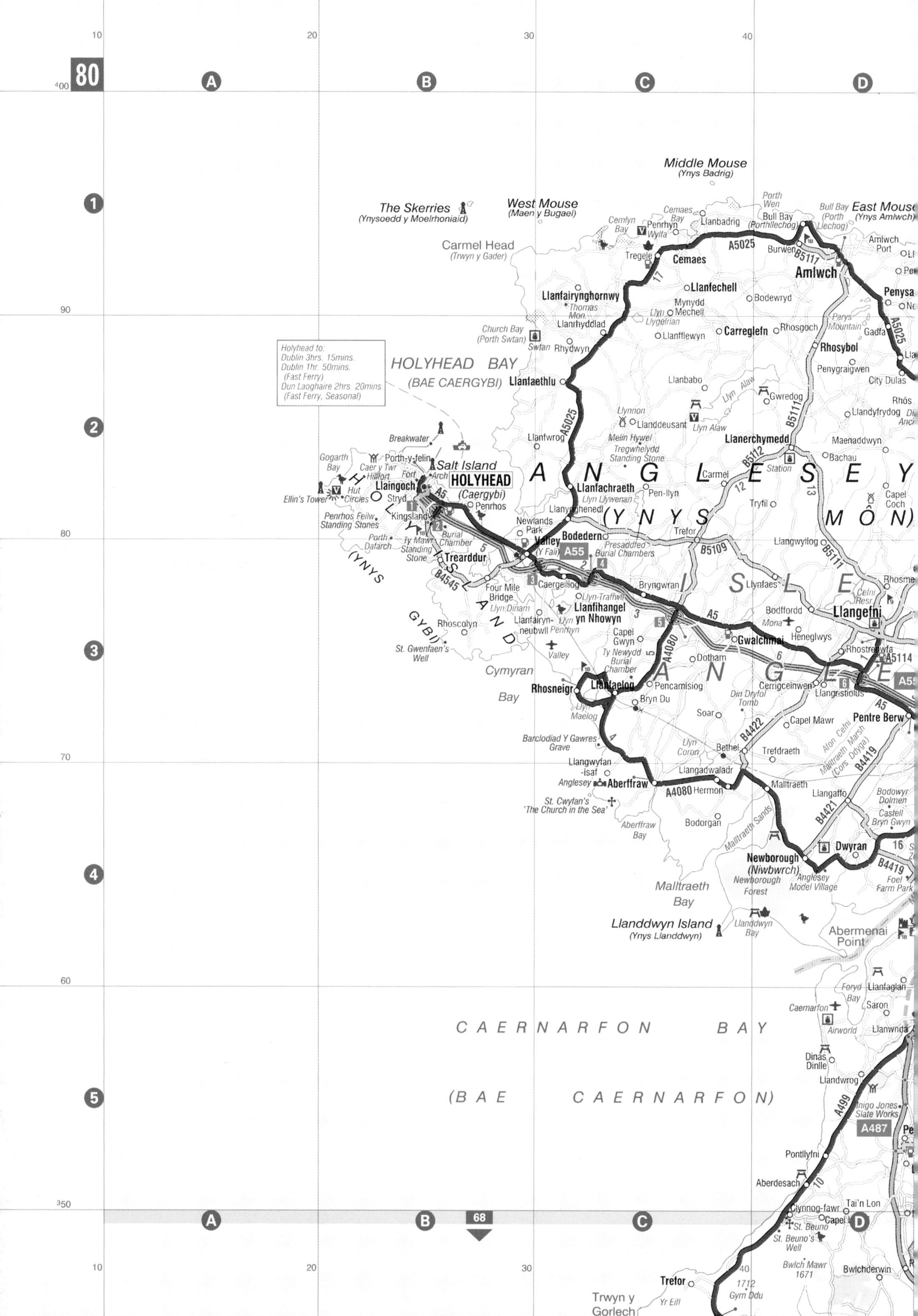

80
A
B
C
D
10
20
30
40
400
90
80
70
60
350
1
2
3
4
5
Middle Mouse
(Ynys Badrig)
The Skerries
(Ynysoedd y Moelrhoniaid)
West Mouse
(Maen y Bugael)
East Mouse
(Ynys Amlwch)
Carmel Head
(Trwyn y Gader)
Cemlyn Bay
Cemaes Bay
Porth Wen
Bull Bay
(Porthllechog)
Bull Bay
(Porth Llechog)
Penrhyn
Wylfa
Llanbadrig
A5025
Tregele
Cemaes
Burwen
B5111
Amlwch
Amlwch Port
Llanfechell
Llanfairynghornwy
Thomas Mon.
Mynydd Mechell
Bodewryd
Llyn Llygeirian
Llanrhyddlad
Church Bay
(Porth Swtan)
Swtan
Rhydwyn
Llanfflewyn
Carreglefn
Rhosgoch
Parys Mountain
Gadfa
Penysa
Rhosybol
Penygraigwen
City Dulas
Rhôs
Llandyfrydog
Holyhead to:
Dublin 3hrs. 15mins.
Dublin 1hr. 50mins.
(Fast Ferry)
Dun Laoghaire 2hrs. 20mins
(Fast Ferry, Seasonal)
HOLYHEAD BAY
(BAE CAERGYBI)
Llanfaethlu
Llanbabo
Llyn Alaw
Gwredog
B5111
Llynnon
Llanddeusant
Maenaddwyn
Llanfwrog
Melin Hywel
Tregwehelydd Standing Stone
Llanerchymedd
Bachau
Breakwater
Gogarth Bay
Porth-y-felin
Salt Island
Caer y Twr Hillfort
Fort
Arch
HOLYHEAD
(Caergybi)
Llaingoch
Hut Circles
Ellin's Tower
Stryd
Penrhos
Kingsland
Penrhos Feilw Standing Stones
Porth Dafarch
Ty Mawr Standing Stone
Burial Chamber
Trearddur
ANGLESEY
(YNYS MÔN)
Llanfachraeth
Pen-llyn
Carmel
Station
Capel Coch
Tryfil
Llanynghenedl
Newlands Park
Valley
(Y Fali)
A55
Bodedern
Presaddfed Burial Chambers
Trefor
B5109
Llangwyllog
HOLY ISLAND
(YNYS GYBI)
B4545
Four Mile Bridge
Llyn Dinam
Caergeiliog
Llyn Traffwll
Llanfihangel yn Nhowyn
Bryngwran
Llynfaes
Rhosmeirch
Cefni Resr.
Bodffordd
Llangefni
Mona
Heneglwys
Rhoscolyn
St. Gwenfaen's Well
Llanfairyn-neubwll
Llyn Penrhyn
Capel Gwyn
A4080
Gwalchmai
A5
Rhostrehwfa
A5114
Valley
Ty Newydd Burial Chamber
Dotham
Cymyran Bay
Rhosneigr
Llanfaelog
Pencarnisiog
Cerrigceinwen
Llangristiolus
Llyn Maelog
Bryn Du
Din Dryfol Tomb
Soar
Capel Mawr
Pentre Berw
Barclodiad Y Gawres Grave
Llyn Coron
Bethel
B4422
Trefdraeth
Afon Cefni
Malltraeth Marsh
(Cors Ddyga)
B4419
Llangwyfan-isaf
Anglesey
Aberffraw
A4080
Hermon
Llangadwaladr
Malltraeth
Llangaffo
Bodowyr Dolmen
Castell Bryn Gwyn
St. Cwyfan's
'The Church in the Sea'
Aberffraw Bay
Bodorgan
Malltraeth Sands
B4421
Dwyran
Newborough
(Niwbwrch)
Newborough Forest
Anglesey Model Village
B4419
Foel Farm Park
Malltraeth Bay
Llanddwyn Island
(Ynys Llanddwyn)
Llanddwyn Bay
Abermenai Point
Foryd Bay
Llanfaglan
Caernarfon
Saron
Airworld
Llanwnda
CAERNARFON BAY
(BAE CAERNARFON)
Dinas Dinlle
Llandwrog
Inigo Jones Slate Works
A499
A487
Pontllyfni
Aberdesach
Clynnog-fawr
Tai'n Lon
St. Beuno
Capel
St. Beuno's Well
68
Bwlch Mawr 1671
Bwlchderwin
Trefor
1712 Gyrn Ddu
Yr Eifl
Trwyn y Gorlech

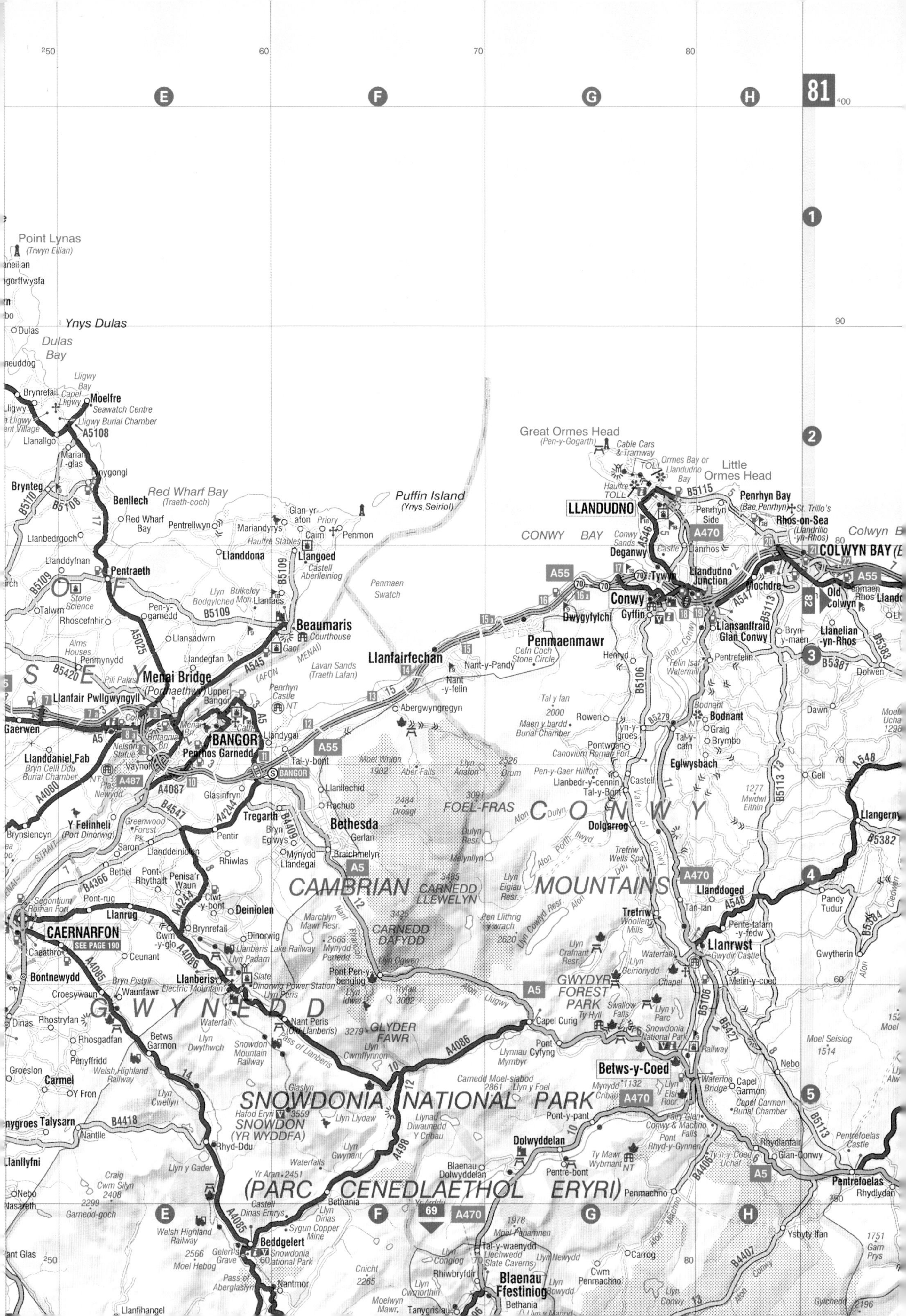
E
F
G
H
1
2
3
4
5
Point Lynas
(Trwyn Eilian)
Ynys Dulas
Dulas
Dulas Bay
Ligwy Bay
Brynrefail
Capel Lligwy
Moelfre
Seawatch Centre
Lligwy Burial Chamber
A5108
Llanallgo
Marian-glas
Tynygongl
Brynteg
Benllech
Red Wharf Bay
(Traeth-coch)
Red Wharf Bay
Pentrellwyn
Llanbedrgoch
Llanddyfnan
Pentraeth
Mariandyrys
Glan-yr-afon
Priory
Caim
Penmon
Puffin Island
(Ynys Seiriol)
Haulfre Stables
Llanddona
Llangoed
Castell Aberlleiniog
Penmaen Swatch
Stone Science
Talwrn
Rhoscefnhir
Pen-y-garnedd
Llyn Bodgylched
Bulkeley Mon.
Llanfaes
B5109
Beaumaris
Courthouse
Gaol
Llansadwrn
Alms Houses
Penmynydd
Llandegfan
A5025
A545
Lavan Sands
(Traeth Lafan)
Llanfairfechan
Menai Bridge
(Porthaethwy)
Pili Palas
Llanfair Pwllgwyngyll
Upper Bangor
Penrhyn Castle
NT
Gaerwen
Nelson Statue
Britannia Br.
BANGOR
Penrhos Garnedd
Llandygai
A55
Tal-y-bont
Llanddaniel Fab
Bryn Celli Ddu Burial Chamber
Vaynol
A487
A4087
Plas Newydd
A4080
Glasinfryn
B4547
A4244
Tregarth
Llanllechid
Rachub
Bethesda
Gerlan
Bryn Eglwys
Mynydd Llandegai
Braichmelyn
Y Felinheli
(Port Dinorwig)
Greenwood Forest Pk.
Brynsiencyn
Saron
Llanddeiniolen
Pentir
Rhiwlas
Bethel
Pont-Rhythallt
Penisa'r Waun
Clwt-y-bont
Deiniolen
B4366
Pont-rug
Segontium Roman Fort
Llanrug
CAERNARFON
SEE PAGE 190
Caeathro
Cwm-y-glo
Brynrefail
Dinorwig
Llanberis Lake Railway
Llyn Padarn
Ceunant
A4086
Bontnewydd
A4085
Bryn Pistyll
Waunfawr
Electric Mountain
Llanberis
Slate
Dinorwig Power Station
Croesywaun
Llyn Peris
Dinas
Rhostryfan
GWYNEDD
Nant Peris
(Old Llanberis)
Waterfall
Rhosgadfan
Betws Garmon
Llyn Dwythwch
Snowdon Mountain Railway
Pass of Llanberis
Penyffridd
Groeslon
Carmel
Y Fron
Welsh Highland Railway
Llyn Cwellyn
Glaslyn
SNOWDONIA NATIONAL PARK
Hafod Eryri
3559
SNOWDON
(YR WYDDFA)
Llyn Llydaw
Talysarn
B4418
Nantlle
Rhyd-Ddu
Llanllyfni
Llyn y Gader
Waterfalls
Llyn Gwynant
Craig Cwm Silyn
2408
Yr Aran
2451
(PARC CENEDLAETHOL ERYRI)
Nebo
Nasareth
2299
Garnedd-goch
Castell Dinas Emrys
Bethania
Llyn Dinas
Sygun Copper Mine
Welsh Highland Railway
Beddgelert
Snowdonia National Park
2566
Moel Hebog
Gelert's Grave
Pass of Aberglaslyn
Nantmor
Llanfihangel
Cnicht
2265
Moelwyn Mawr
Tanygrisiau
Llyn Cwmorthin
Llyn Conglog
Rhiwbryfdir
Blaenau Ffestiniog
Bethania
Tal-y-waenydd
Llechwedd Slate Caverns
Llyn Newydd
Llyn Bowydd
Moel Penamnen
1978
Cwm Penmachno
Carrog
Llyn Conwy
Penmachno
69
A470
Blaenau Dolwyddelan
Pentre-bont
Dolwyddelan
Ty Mawr Wybrnant
NT
Pont Rhyd-y-Gynnen
Fairy Glen
Conwy & Machno Falls
Ty-n-y-Coed Uchaf
B4406
Carnedd Moel-siabod
2861
Llyn y Foel
Mynydd Cribau
1132
Llynau Diwaunedd
Y Cribau
Pont-y-pant
A498
Tryfan
3002
Llyn Idwal
Glyder Fawr
3279
Llyn Cwmffynnon
Llynnau Mymbyr
Pont Cyfyng
Capel Curig
A4086
A5
Afon Llugwy
Llyn Ogwen
Pont Pen-y-benglog
Marchlyn Mawr Resr.
Mynydd Perfedd
2665
Carnedd Dafydd
3425
Carnedd Llewelyn
3485
CAMBRIAN MOUNTAINS
Nant Ffrancon
Moel Wnion
1902
Aber Falls
Drosgl
2484
Llyn Anafon
2526
Drum
FOEL-FRAS
3091
Dulyn Resr.
Melynllyn
Llyn Eigiau Resr.
Pen Llithrig y wrach
2620
Llyn Cowlyd Resr.
Llyn Crafnant Resr.
GWYDYR FOREST PARK
Ty Hyll
Swallow Falls
Llyn y Parc
Llyn Geirionydd
Waterfall
Chapel
Snowdonia National Park
Betws-y-Coed
Railway
Llyn Elsi
Waterloo Bridge
Capel Garmon
Capel Garmon Burial Chamber
Rhydlanfair
Glan-Conwy
A5
B5113
Pentrefoelas Castle
Pentrefoelas
Rhydlydan
Ysbyty Ifan
1751 Garn Prys
Glyn Clwyd
2196
B4407
Nebo
Moel Seisiog
1514
Melin-y-coed
Gwydir Castle
Llanrwst
Pente-tafarn-y-fedw
Tan-lan
A548
Llanddoged
Pandy Tudur
Gwytherin
Llangernyw
B5382
B5384
Gell
1277
Mwdwl Eithin
Eglwysbach
Bodnant
NT
Bodnant
Graig
Brymbo
Tal-y-cafn
Trefriw
Woollen Mills
Trefriw Wells Spa
Dolgarrog
CONWY
Vale of Conwy
Afon Dulyn
Afon Porth-llwyd
Tal-y-Bont
Castell
Llanbedr-y-cennin
Pen-y-Gaer Hillfort
Canovium Roman Fort
Pontwgan
Tyn-y-groes
Rowen
Maen y bardd
Burial Chamber
Tal y fan
2000
Abergwyngregyn
Nant-y-felin
Nant-y-Pandy
Cefn Coch Stone Circle
Penmaenmawr
Henryd
Felin Isaf Watermill
Pentrefelin
Llansanffraid Glan Conwy
Bryn-y-maen
Llanelian-yn-Rhos
Dawn
Dolwen
B5381
B5383
Dwygyfylchi
Gyffin
Conwy
A55
Tywyn
Llandudno Junction
Mochdre
A547
Old Colwyn
Penmaen Rhos
B5113
COLWYN BAY
A470
Llanrhos
Deganwy
Conwy Sands
CONWY BAY
LLANDUDNO
Castle
A546
Penrhyn Side
Penrhyn Bay
(Bae Penrhyn)
St. Trillo's
Rhos-on-Sea
(Llandrillo-yn-Rhos)
Colwyn Bay
Great Ormes Head
(Pen-y-Gogarth)
Cable Cars & Tramway
Ormes Bay or Llandudno Bay
Little Ormes Head
TOLL
Haulfre
B5115
60
70
80
90
400
380
250

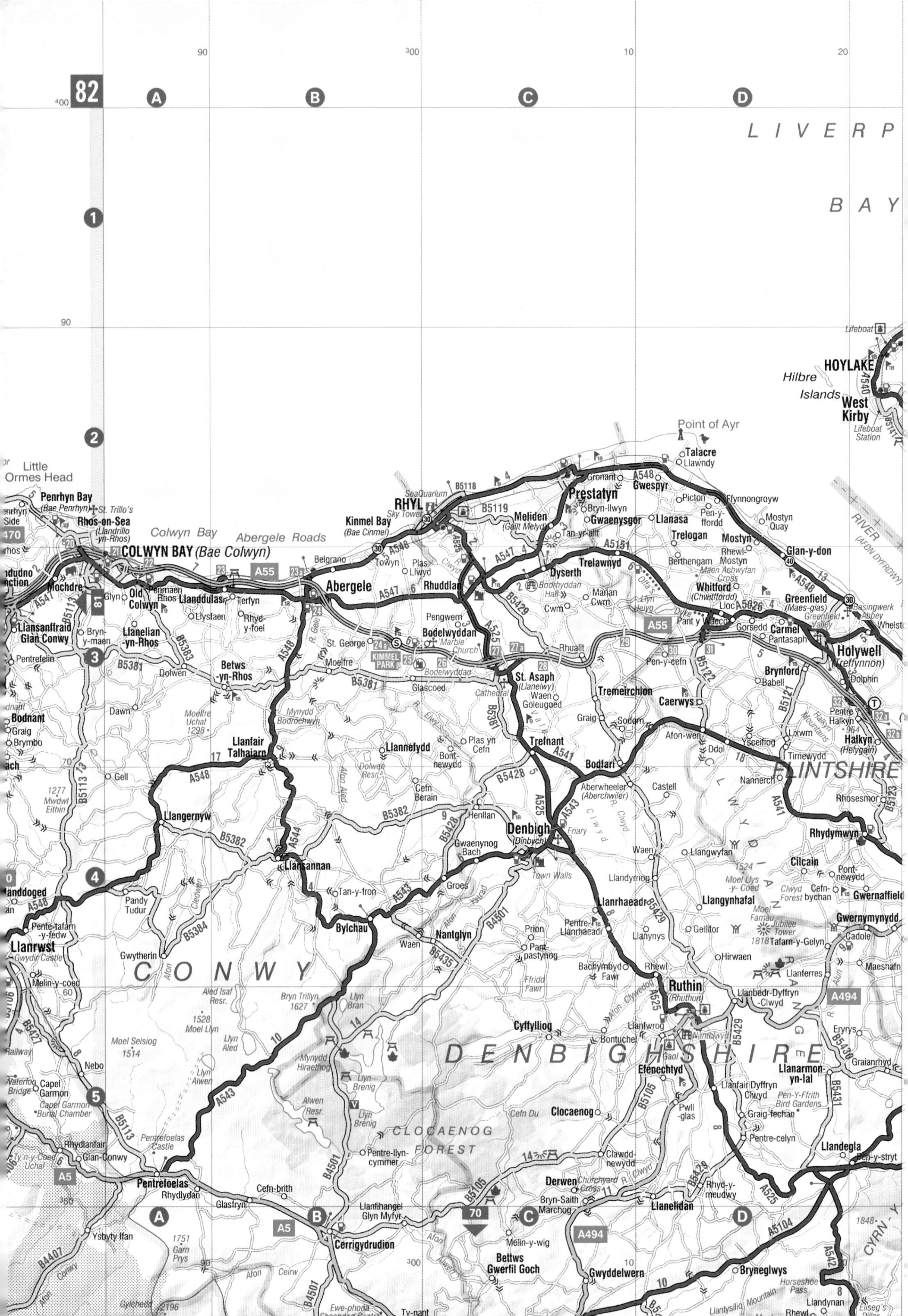
A
B
C
D
1
2
3
4
5
90
300
10
20
400
380
LIVERP
BAY
Little Ormes Head
Penrhyn Bay (Bae Penrhyn)
St. Trillo's
Rhos-on-Sea (Llandrillo -yn-Rhos)
Colwyn Bay
Abergele Roads
COLWYN BAY (Bae Colwyn)
Mochdre
Glyn
Old Colwyn
Penmaen Rhos
Llanddulas
Terfyn
Llysfaen
Rhyd-y-foel
Llansanffraid Glan Conwy
Bryn-y-maen
Llanelian -yn-Rhos
Pentrefelin
Dolwen
Betws -yn-Rhos
Dawn
Bodnant
Graig
Brymbo
Moelfre Uchaf 1298
Llanfair Talhaiarn
Gell
1277 Mwdwl Eithin
Llangernyw
Llansannan
Pandy Tudur
Llanddoged
Pente-tafarn -y-fedw
Llanrwst
Gwydir Castle
Gwytherin
CONWY
Melin-y-coed
Aled Isaf Resr.
1528 Moel Llyn
Llyn Aled
Moel Seisiog 1514
Llyn Alwen
Nebo
Capel Garmon
Capel Garmon Burial Chamber
Waterloo Bridge
Railway
Rhydlanfair
Glan-Conwy
Pentrefoelas Castle
Pentrefoelas
Rhydlydan
Glasfryn
Cefn-brith
Ysbyty Ifan
1751 Garn Prys
Afon Conwy
Gylchedd
Belgrano
Towyn
Abergele
Kinmel Bay (Bae Cinmel)
RHYL
SeaQuarium
Sky Tower
Plas Llwyd
Rhuddlan
Pengwern
Bodelwyddan
'Marble' Church
St. George
KIMMEL PARK
Moelfre
Glascoed
Bodelwyddan
Mynydd Bodrochwyn
Llannefydd
Plas yn Cefn
Bont-newydd
Dolwen Resr.
Afon Aled
Cefn Berain
Henllan
Gwaenynog Bach
Tan-y-fron
Groes
Bylchau
Nantglyn
Waen
Bryn Trillyn 1627
Llyn Bran
Mynydd Hiraethog
Llyn Brenig
Alwen Resr.
CLOCAENOG FOREST
Pentre-llyn-cymmer
Llanfihangel Glyn Myfyr
Cerrigydrudion
Ceirw
Ewe-phorla
Ty-nant
Melin-y-wig
Bettws Gwerfil Goch
B5118
B5119
Meliden (Gallt Melyd)
Prestatyn
Gronant
Gwespyr
Talacre
Llawndy
Point of Ayr
Bryn-llwyn
Gwaenysgor
Llanasa
Tan-yr-allt
Picton
Pen-y-ffordd
Ffynnongroyw
Mostyn Quay
Trelogan
Mostyn
Rhewl-Mostyn
Berthengam
Maen Achwyfan Cross
Dyserth
Trelawnyd
Bodrhyddan Hall
Marian Cwm
Cwm
Llyn Helyg
Whitford (Chwitffordd)
Lloc
Pant y Waco
Gorsedd
Carmel
Pantasaph
Greenfield (Maes-glas)
Greenfield Valley
Basingwerk Abbey
Holywell (Treffynnon)
Rhuallt
St. Asaph (Llanelwy)
Cathedral
Waen
Goleugoed
Tremeirchion
Pen-y-cefn
Caerwys
Graig
Sodom
Brynford
Babell
Trefnant
Afon-wen
Ddol
Ysceifiog
Lixwm
Bodfari
Aberwheeler (Aberchwiler)
Castell
Denbigh (Dinbych)
Friary
Town Walls
Waen
Llangwyfan
Llandyrnog
Llanrhaeadr
Pentre-Llanrhaeadr
Prion
Pant-pastynog
Llanynys
Gellifor
Bachymbyd Fawr
Rhewl
Ruthin (Rhuthun)
Ffridd Fawr
Cyffylliog
Llanfwrog
Bontuchel
Nantclwyd
Gaol
Efenechtyd
DENBIGHSHIRE
Cefn Du
Clocaenog
Pwll-glas
Clawdd-newydd
Derwen
Churchyard Cross
Bryn-Saith Marchog
Llanelidan
Rhyd-y-meudwy
Gwyddelwern
Lifeboat
HOYLAKE
Hilbre Islands
West Kirby
Lifeboat Station
RIVER (AFON DYFRDWY)
Glan-y-don
Whelston
Dolphin
Pentre Halkyn
Halkyn Mountains
964
Halkyn (Helygain)
Tirnewydd
Nannerch
FLINTSHIRE
Rhosesmor
CLWYDIAN RANGE
Rhydymwyn
Cilcain
1524
Moel Llys -y- Coed
Pont-newydd
Clwyd Forest
Cefn-bychan
Gwernaffield
Llangynhafal
Moel Famau
Jubilee Tower
1818
Tafarn-y-Gelyn
Gwernymynydd
Cadole
Hirwaen
Llanferres
Maeshafn
Llanbedr-Dyffryn -Clwyd
Eryrys
Graianrhyd
Llanarmon-yn-Ial
Llanfair Dyffryn Clwyd
Pen-Y-Ffrith Bird Gardens
Graig-fechan
Pentre-celyn
Llandegla
Pen-y-stryt
1848
Bryneglwys
Horseshoe Pass
Llantysilio Mountain
Llandynan
Rhewl
Eliseg's
A55
A5
A494
A548
A547
A543
A544
A525
A541
A5151
A5026
A5104
A542
B5381
B5382
B5383
B5384
B5113
B5428
B5429
B5435
B4501
B5105
B5122
B5121
B5123
B5430
B5431
70
81

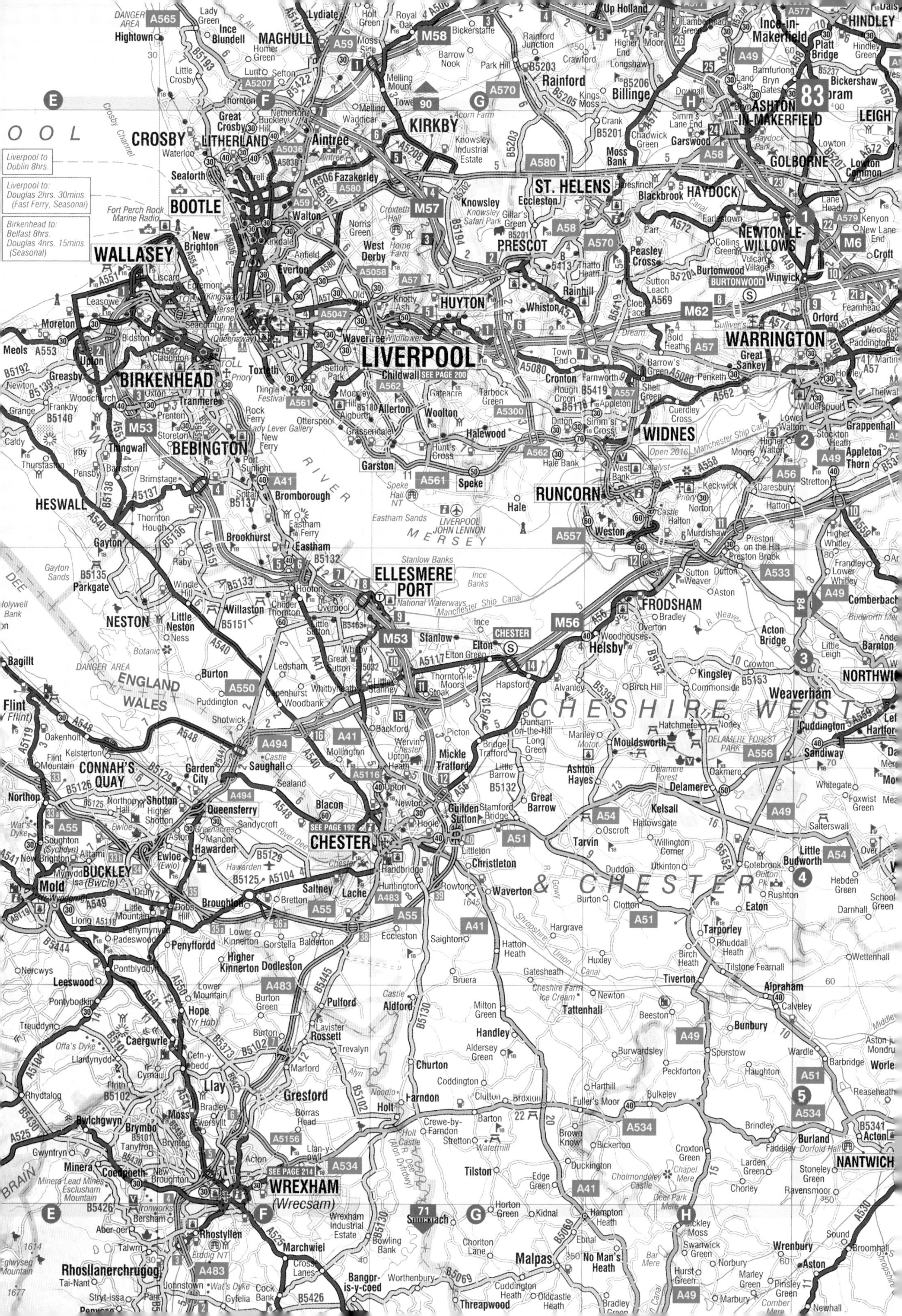

83
Liverpool to Dublin 8hrs.
Liverpool to: Douglas 2hrs. 30mins. (Fast Ferry, Seasonal)
Birkenhead to: Belfast 8hrs. Douglas 4hrs. 15mins. (Seasonal)
SEE PAGE 200
SEE PAGE 192
SEE PAGE 214
90
84
71
Open 2016
Hightown
Lady Green
Ince Blundell
MAGHULL
Lydiate
Holt Green
Royal Oak
Bickerstaffe
Up Holland
Lamberhead Green
Ince-in-Makerfield
HINDLEY
Platt Bridge
Hindley Green
Bickershaw
Bamfurlong
Land Gate
Bryn Gates
Rainford Junction
Rainford
Crawford
Higher End
Far Moor
Longshaw
Billinge
Downall Green
Barrow Nook
Park Hill
Kings Moss
Melling Mount
Melling
Tower Hill
Waddicar
Homer Green
Lunt
Sefton
Little Crosby
Thornton
Netherton
Great Crosby
Buckley Hill
CROSBY
LITHERLAND
Aintree
KIRKBY
Knowsley Industrial Estate
Crank
Chadwick Green
Simm's Lane End
Garswood
ASHTON-IN-MAKERFIELD
GOLBORNE
LEIGH
Lowton
Lowton Common
Haydock Park
Moss Bank
Waterloo
Seaforth
BOOTLE
Fazakerley
Fort Perch Rock Marine Radio
New Brighton
Orrell
Walton
Kirkdale
Anfield
Everton
Croxteth Hall
Norris Green
West Derby
Knowsley
Knowsley Safari Park
Eccleston
Gillar's Green
ST. HELENS
Haresfinch
Blackbrook
HAYDOCK
Earlestown
NEWTON-LE-WILLOWS
Lane Head
Kenyon
New Lane End
Croft
WALLASEY
Liscard
Egremont
Leasowe
Moreton
Meols
Seacombe
Bidston
Upton
Claughton
Greasby
Newton
BIRKENHEAD
Woodchurch
Frankby
Grange
Caldy
Irby
Thurstaston
Pensby
Oxton
Tranmere
Prenton
Storeton
Barnston
Thingwall
BEBINGTON
Brimstage
HESWALL
Home Farm
Old Swan
Knotty Ash
HUYTON
PRESCOT
Thatto Heath
Rainhill
Whiston
Peasley Cross
Sutton Leach
Clock Face
Collins Green
Vulcan Village
Burtonwood
BURTONWOOD
Winwick
Orford
Fearnhead
Woolston
Paddington
WARRINGTON
Great Sankey
Martinscroft
Hollins Green
Thelwall
Wilderspool
Grappenhall
Stockton Heath
Appleton Thorn
Lower Walton
Higher Walton
Moore
Daresbury
Hatton
Stretton
Wavertree
LIVERPOOL
Childwall
Sefton Park
Toxteth
Dingle
Festival
Mossley Hill
Gateacre
Tarbock Green
Allerton
Aigburth
Woolton
Halewood
Otterspool
Grassendale
Hunt's Cross
Garston
Speke
Speke Hall NT
Hale
Hale Bank
Town End
Cronton
Farnworth
Hough Green
Appleton
Ditton
Simm's Cross
WIDNES
Barrow's Green
Penketh
Cuerdley Cross
Bold Heath
Shell Green
West Bank
Catalyst
RUNCORN
Weston
Halton
Norton
Murdishaw
Keckwick
Preston on the Hill
Preston Brook
Dutton
Aston
Sutton Weaver
Rock Ferry
Lady Lever Gallery
New Ferry
Port Sunlight
Spital
Bromborough
Eastham
Eastham Ferry
Eastham Sands
LIVERPOOL JOHN LENNON
RIVER MERSEY
Manchester Ship Canal
Thornton Hough
Brookhurst
Raby
Gayton
Gayton Sands
Parkgate
Neston
Little Neston
Ness
Botanic
Windle Hill
Willaston
Hooton
Childer Thornton
Overpool
ELLESMERE PORT
National Waterways
Stanlow Banks
Ince Banks
Ince
Stanlow
Elton
Elton Green
Little Sutton
Great Sutton
Whitby
Ledsham
Capenhurst
Woodbank
Whitbyheath
Little Stanney
Thornton-le-Moors
Stoak
Hapsford
Helsby
FRODSHAM
Bradley
Overton
Woodhouses
Alvanley
Birch Hill
Kingsley
Commonside
Crowton
Acton Bridge
Little Leigh
Barnton
NORTHWICH
Weaverham
Cuddington
Hartford
Sandiway
Whitegate
Foxwist Green
Salterswall
Comberbach
Frandley
Lower Whitley
Higher Whitley
Budworth Mere
CHESHIRE WEST & CHESTER
DANGER AREA
ENGLAND
WALES
DEE
Holywell
Bagillt
Flint
Fflint
Oakenholt
Flint Mountain
Kelsterton
CONNAH'S QUAY
Northop
Northop Hall
Shotton
Higher Shotton
Queensferry
Sandycroft
Mancot
Hawarden
Ewloe
Garden City
Saughall
Sealand
Puddington
Burton
Shotwick
Backford
Wervin
Mollington
Upton Heath
Picton
Mickle Trafford
Bridge Trafford
Dunham-on-the-Hill
Long Green
Manley
Mouldsworth
Hatchmere
Norley
DELAMERE FOREST PARK
Delamere
Oakmere
Ashton Hayes
Kelsall
Great Barrow
Little Barrow
Blacon
Newton
Hoole
Guilden Sutton
Stamford Bridge
CHESTER
Handbridge
Christleton
Littleton
Rowton
Waverton
Hallowsgate
Willington Corner
Utkinton
Oscroft
Tarvin
Duddon
Burton
Clotton
Little Budworth
Cotebrook
Oulton Pk.
Rushton
Eaton
Hebden Green
School Green
Darnhall
Over
Tarporley
Rhuddall Heath
Birch Heath
Tilstone Fearnall
Tiverton
Alpraham
Calveley
Wettenhall
Wat's Dyke
Soughton
Sychdyn
Alltami
New Brighton
Mynydd Isa
Bwcle
BUCKLEY
Mold
Yr Wyddgrug
Drury
Dobs Hill
Broughton
Bretton
Saltney
Lache
Huntington
Little Mountain
Llong
Penymynydd
Padeswood
Penyffordd
Lower Kinnerton
Higher Kinnerton
Gorstella
Balderton
Dodleston
Eccleston
Saighton
Hatton Heath
Hargrave
Huxley
Gatesheath
Newton
Tattenhall
Beeston
Bunbury
Spurstow
Wardle
Barbridge
Haughton
Peckforton
Bulkeley
Burwardsley
Nercwys
Leeswood
Pontblyddyn
Pontybodkin
Lower Mountain
Hope
Yr Hob
Burton Green
Pulford
Aldford
Bruera
Milton Green
Handley
Aldersey Green
Churton
Coddington
Clutton
Broxton
Harthill
Fuller's Moor
Treuddyn
Offa's Dyke
Caergwrle
Llanfynydd
Cymau
Ffrith
Cefn-y-bedd
Llay
Bradley
Gwersyllt
Burton
Lavister
Rossett
Trevalyn
Marford
Gresford
Borras Head
Holt
Farndon
Crewe-by-Farndon
Barton
Stretton
Watermill
Brown Knowl
Bickerton
Duckington
Tilston
Edge Green
Rhydtalog
Bwlchgwyn
Brymbo
Tanyfron
Moss
Gwynfryn
Minera
Coedpoeth
Minera Lead Mines
Esclusham Mountain
New Broughton
Acton
Llan-y-pwll
WREXHAM
Wrecsam
Wrexham Industrial Estate
Sutton
Marchwiel
Bowling Bank
Horton Green
Kidnal
Hampton Heath
Malpas
No Man's Heath
Ebnal
Cholmondeley Castle
Chapel Mere
Deer Park Mere
Croxton Green
Larden Green
Chorley
Brindley
Faddiley
Dorfold Hall
Burland
Acton
NANTWICH
Stoneley Green
Ravensmoor
Reaseheath
Wrenbury
Broomhall
Aston
Sound
Newhall
Pinsley Green
Marley Green
Norbury
Marbury
Swanwick Green
Hurst Green
Bickley Moss
Bar Mere
Cuddington Heath
Oldcastle Heath
Threapwood
Worthenbury
Bangor-is-y-coed
Cross Lanes
Cock Bank
Gyfelia
Johnstown
Wat's Dyke
Rhosllanerchrugog
Tai-Nant
Stryt-issa
Penycae
Talwrn
Eglwyseg Mountain
Aber-oer
Bersham
Ironworks
Rhostyllen
Erddig NT
BRAIN
Crosby Channel
OOL

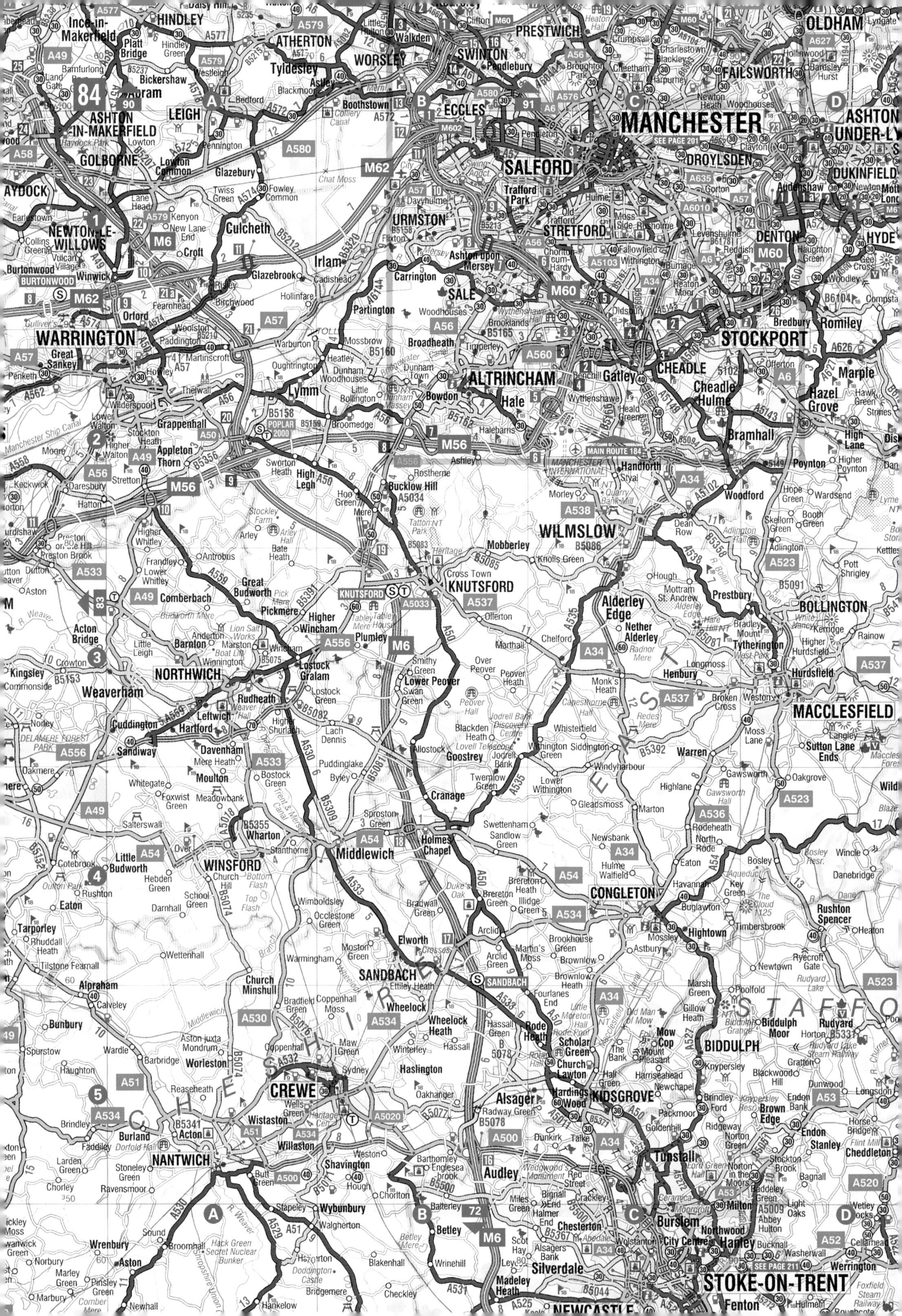

84
83
90
91
72
SEE PAGE 201
SEE PAGE 211
MAIN ROUTE 184
Ince-in-Makerfield
HINDLEY
ATHERTON
Tyldesley
WORSLEY
Walkden
SWINTON
Pendlebury
PRESTWICH
OLDHAM
FAILSWORTH
MANCHESTER
ASHTON-UNDER-LYNE
DROYLSDEN
DUKINFIELD
SALFORD
ECCLES
Trafford Park
Platt Bridge
Bickershaw
Abram
ASHTON-IN-MAKERFIELD
LEIGH
GOLBORNE
Lowton Common
Glazebury
Culcheth
NEWTON-LE-WILLOWS
HAYDOCK
Irlam
Cadishead
URMSTON
Flixton
STRETFORD
Ashton upon Mersey
SALE
DENTON
HYDE
Carrington
Partington
Glazebrook
Risley
Birchwood
Winwick
Burtonwood
Orford
WARRINGTON
Great Sankey
Penketh
Lymm
ALTRINCHAM
Timperley
Broadheath
Hale
Bowdon
Gatley
CHEADLE
Cheadle Hulme
STOCKPORT
Bredbury
Romiley
Marple
Hazel Grove
Bramhall
Poynton
Handforth
Wythenshawe
Didsbury
MANCHESTER INTERNATIONAL
Woodford
WILMSLOW
Mobberley
KNUTSFORD
Alderley Edge
Prestbury
BOLLINGTON
MACCLESFIELD
Grappenhall
Appleton Thorn
Stretton
High Legh
Rostherne
Ashley
Tatton Park
Great Budworth
Comberbach
Pickmere
NORTHWICH
Barnton
Weaverham
Acton Bridge
Cuddington
Hartford
Sandiway
Rudheath
Lostock Gralam
Plumley
Lower Peover
Goostrey
Cranage
Holmes Chapel
Chelford
Henbury
Warren
Middlewich
WINSFORD
Little Budworth
Tarporley
Eaton
CONGLETON
Biddulph
Sandbach
Elworth
Wheelock
Alsager
KIDSGROVE
CREWE
Haslington
Church Minshull
Alpraham
Bunbury
Wistaston
NANTWICH
Acton
Willaston
Shavington
Audley
Wybunbury
Betley
Wrenbury
Aston
Tunstall
Burslem
Hanley
STOKE-ON-TRENT
NEWCASTLE
Silverdale
Chesterton
Madeley Heath
Endon
Stanley
Cheddleton
Rudyard
Rushton Spencer
Bosley
Hightown
Mow Cop
Brown Edge
Milton
Werrington
Fenton
CHESHIRE
STAFFORDSHIRE
M6
M56
M60
M62
M602
A556
A50
A34
A54
A533
A530
A51
A49
A537
A523
A500
A534

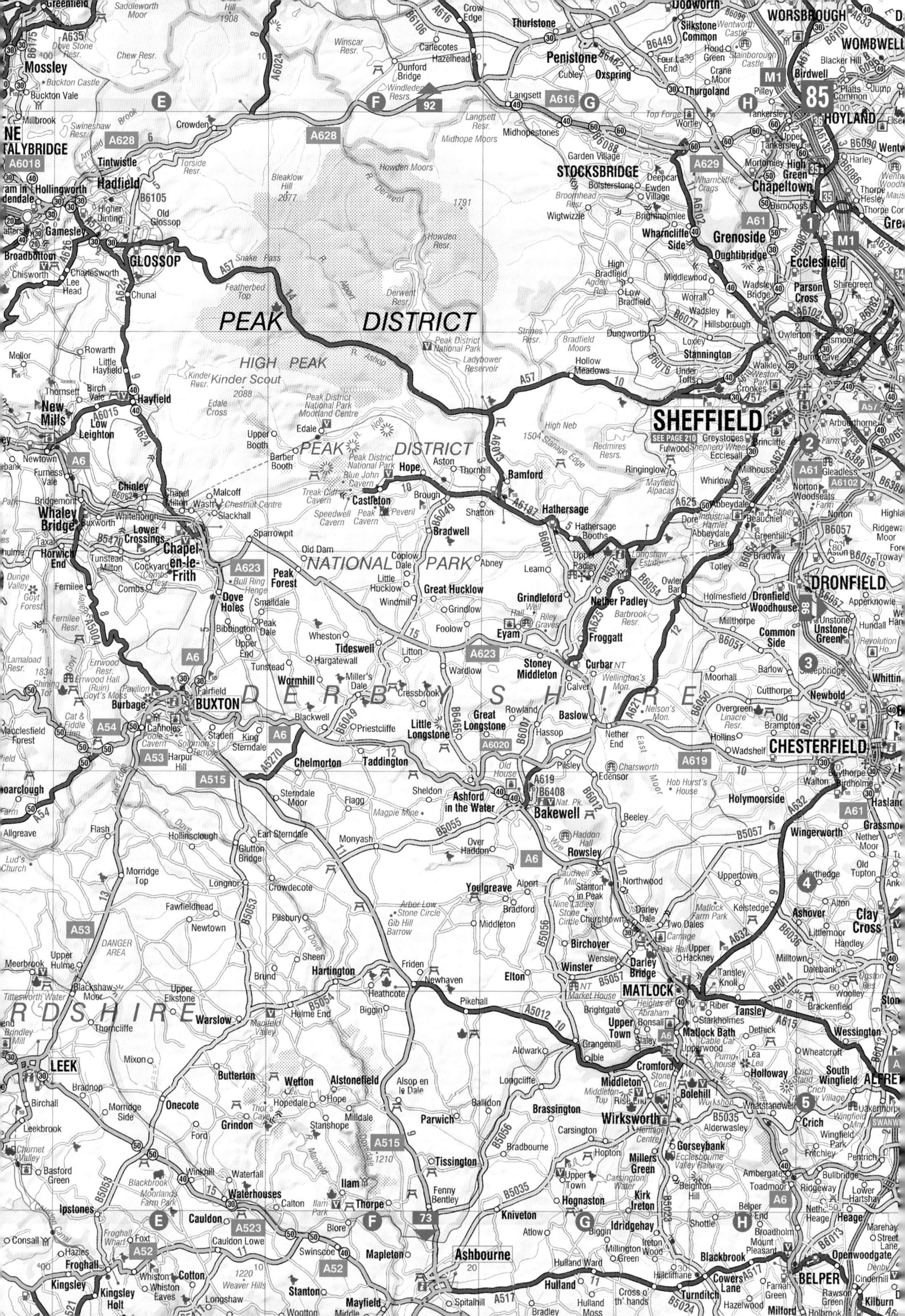

PEAK DISTRICT
HIGH PEAK
PEAK DISTRICT NATIONAL PARK
D E R B Y S H I R E
R D S H I R E
Greenfield
Saddleworth Moor
Mossley
Dove Stone Resr.
Chew Resr.
Buckton Castle
Buckton Vale
Millbrook
STALYBRIDGE
A6018
A635
A628
Tintwistle
Hadfield
Hollingworth
Mottram in Longdendale
Gamesley
Broadbottom
Charlesworth
Chisworth
Lee Head
Hadfield
Higher Dinting
Old Glossop
GLOSSOP
Chunal
B6105
Crowden
Torside Resr.
Swineshaw Resr.
Arnfield
Bleaklow Hill 2077
Featherbed Top
Snake Pass
A57
Howden Moors
Howden Resr.
Derwent Resr.
Alport
R. Derwent
1791
Langsett Resr.
Midhope Moors
Winscar Resr.
Dunford Bridge
Windleden Resrs.
Carlecotes
Hazelhead
Crow Edge
A616
A6024
A6106
92
Thurlstone
Penistone
Oxspring
Cubley
Langsett
Midhopestones
Silkstone Common
Dodworth
Four Lane End
Hood Green
Crane Moor
Thurgoland
Top Forge
Wortley
Stainborough Castle
Wentworth Castle
WORSBROUGH
WOMBWELL
Blacker Hill
Birdwell
Pilley
Tankersley
Upper Tankersley
HOYLAND
Platts Common
Jump
Harley
Wentworth
Mortomley
High Green
Chapeltown
Burncross
Thorpe Hesley
Thorpe Common
M1
85
35
36
1
2
3
4
5
Garden Village
STOCKSBRIDGE
Deepcar
Bolsterstone
Ewden Village
Broomhead Resr.
Wigtwizzle
Brightholmlee
Wharncliffe Crags
Wharncliffe Side
A629
A6102
A61
Grenoside
Oughtibridge
Ecclesfield
Shiregreen
Parson Cross
Wadsley Bridge
Wadsley
Middlewood
Worrall
Hillsborough
High Bradfield
Low Bradfield
Agden Res.
Dungworth
Strines Resr.
Bradfield Moors
Loxley
Stannington
Owlerton
Pitsmoor
Burngreave
Walkley
Crookes
Under Tofts
Hollow Meadows
Ladybower Reservoir
Peak District National Park
SHEFFIELD
SEE PAGE 210
Greystones
Shepherd Wheel
Fulwood
Ecclesall
Brincliffe
Arbourthorne
Redmires Resrs.
High Neb
Stanage Edge
1504
Ringinglow
Mayfield Alpacas
Whirlow
Millhouses
Gleadless
Norton Woodseats
Norton
Abbeydale
Beauchief
Dore
Abbeydale Industrial Hamlet
Abbeydale Park
Greenhill
Bradway
Totley
Highlane
Ridgeway Moor
Troway
Longshaw Estate
Owler Bar
Holmesfield
Dronfield Woodhouse
DRONFIELD
Apperknowle
Unstone
Unstone Green
Hundall
Millthorpe
Common Side
Barlow
Sheepbridge
Revolution Ho.
Moorhall
Cutthorpe
Whittington
Newbold
Overgreen
Linacre Resr.
Old Brampton
Hollins
Wadshelf
CHESTERFIELD
Boythorpe
Birdholme
Walton
Hasland
Holymoorside
Grassmoor
Wingerworth
Nether Moor
Old Tupton
Northedge
Alton
Ashover
Clay Cross
Littlemoor
Handley
Milltown
Dalebank
Ogston Res.
Woolley
Brackenfield
Wessington
Wheatcroft
South Wingfield
ALFRETON
Crich
Wingfield Park
Fritchley
Pentrich
Bullbridge
Ambergate
Toadmoor
Ridgeway
Lower Hartshay
Nether Heage
Heage
Belper Lane End
Shottle
Broadholm
Mount Pleasant
Openwoodgate
BELPER
Cinderhill
Blackbrook
Cowers Lane
Farnah Green
Rawson Green
Kilburn
Milford
Hazelwood
Turnditch
Hulland
Hulland Ward
Cross o' th' hands
Bradley
Hulland Moss
Kinder Scout 2088
Kinder Resr.
Edale Cross
Peak District National Park Moorland Centre
Edale
Upper Booth
Barber Booth
Hope
Aston
Thornhill
Bamford
Castleton
Peak Cavern
Peveril
Speedwell Cavern
Treak Cliff Cavern
Blue John Cavern
Brough
Shatton
Hathersage
Hathersage Booths
Upper Padley
Nether Padley
Grindleford
Bradwell
Abney
Leam
Barbrook Resr.
Froggatt
Curbar
Calver
Stoney Middleton
Eyam
Riley Graves
Foolow
Grindlow
Great Hucklow
Little Hucklow
Windmill
Coplow Dale
Old Dam
Sparrowpit
Peak Forest
Dove Holes
Bull Ring Henge
Smalldale
Peak Dale
Bibbington
Upper End
Tunstead
Wormhill
Miller's Dale
Tideswell
Hargatewall
Wheston
Litton
Wardlow
Cressbrook
Blackwell
Priestcliffe
Little Longstone
Great Longstone
Rowland
Hassop
Baslow
Nether End
Nelson's Mon.
Wellington's Mon.
East Moor
Chatsworth
Edensor
Pilsley
Hob Hurst's House
Beeley
Bakewell
Old House
Ashford in the Water
Sheldon
Taddington
Chelmorton
Flagg
Magpie Mine
Monyash
Over Haddon
Haddon Hall
Rowsley
Caudwell's Mill
Stanton in Peak
Nine Ladies Stone Circle
Northwood
Darley Dale
Two Dales
Churchtown
Birchover
Winster
Wensley
Darley Bridge
Elton
Alport
Youlgreave
Bradford
Middleton
Arbor Low Stone Circle
Gib Hill Barrow
Peak Rail
Upper Hackney
Tansley Knoll
Tansley
MATLOCK
Riber
Starkholmes
Matlock Bath
Heights of Abraham
Bonsall
Upper Town
Slaley
Brightgate
Cable Car
Upperwood
Dethick
Lea
Holloway
Whatstandwell
Cromford
Grangemill
Ible
Aldwark
Middleton
Middleton Top
Bolehill
Wirksworth
Alderwasley
Gorseybank
Ecclesbourne Valley Railway
Brassington
Carsington
Carsington Water
Hopton
Millers Green
Kirk Ireton
Hognaston
Idridgehay
Ireton Wood
Biggin
Atlow
Kniveton
Millington Green
Hillcliffane
Chinley
Chapel Milton
Malcoff
Wash
Chestnut Centre
Slackhall
Chapel-en-le-Frith
Combs
Combs Resr.
Cockyard
Tunstead Milton
Whitehough
Buxworth
Lower Crossings
Bridgemont
Whaley Bridge
Horwich End
Taxal
Furness Vale
Newtown
New Mills
Thornsett
Birch Vale
Hayfield
Little Hayfield
Rowarth
Mellor
Low Leighton
Fernilee
Fernilee Resr.
Goyt Forest
Errwood Resr.
Errwood Hall (Ruin)
Goyt's Moss
Shining Tor
Lamaload Resr.
Macclesfield Forest
Cat & Fiddle Inn
Burbage
Fairfield
BUXTON
Cannoles
Poole's Cavern
Solomon's Temple
Staden
King Sterndale
Harpur Hill
Sterndale Moor
Earl Sterndale
Glutton Bridge
Hollinsclough
Flash
Allgreave
Lud's Church
Morridge Top
Longnor
Crowdecote
Fawfieldhead
Newtown
Pilsbury
Sheen
Hartington
Friden
Newhaven
Heathcote
Biggin
Pikehall
Hulme End
Manifold Valley
Warslow
Upper Elkstone
Brund
Thorncliffe
Mixon
Blackshaw Moor
Upper Hulme
Meerbrook
Tittesworth Water
Danger Area
Bradnop
LEEK
Birchall
Leekbrook
Morridge Side
Onecote
Butterton
Wetton
Alstonefield
Hopedale
Hope
Milldale
Stanshope
Grindon
Thor's Cave
Dovedale
Alsop en le Dale
Parwich
Ballidon
Longcliffe
Tissington
Fenny Bentley
Bradbourne
Thorpe
Ilam
Ilam Park
Blore
Calton
Waterhouses
Waterfall
Winkhill
Ford
Blackbrook Moorlands Farm Park
Basford Green
Cheddleton
Ipstones
Cauldon
Cauldon Lowe
Froghall Wharf
Foxt
Consall
Hazles
Froghall
Kingsley
Kingsley Holt
Whiston
Whiston Eaves
Cotton
Weaver Hills
Longshaw
Swinscoe
Stanton
Mapleton
Mayfield
Ashbourne
Spitalhill
Wootton
A6
A623
A6187
A6013
A625
A621
A6020
A619
B6408
A6012
A5012
A515
A5270
A53
A54
A5004
A624
A6015
B5470
B6049
B6465
B6001
B6012
B5055
B5056
B5057
B5053
B5054
B5035
B5023
B5024
A632
A615
A61
A517
A523
A52
A50
73
E
F
G
H

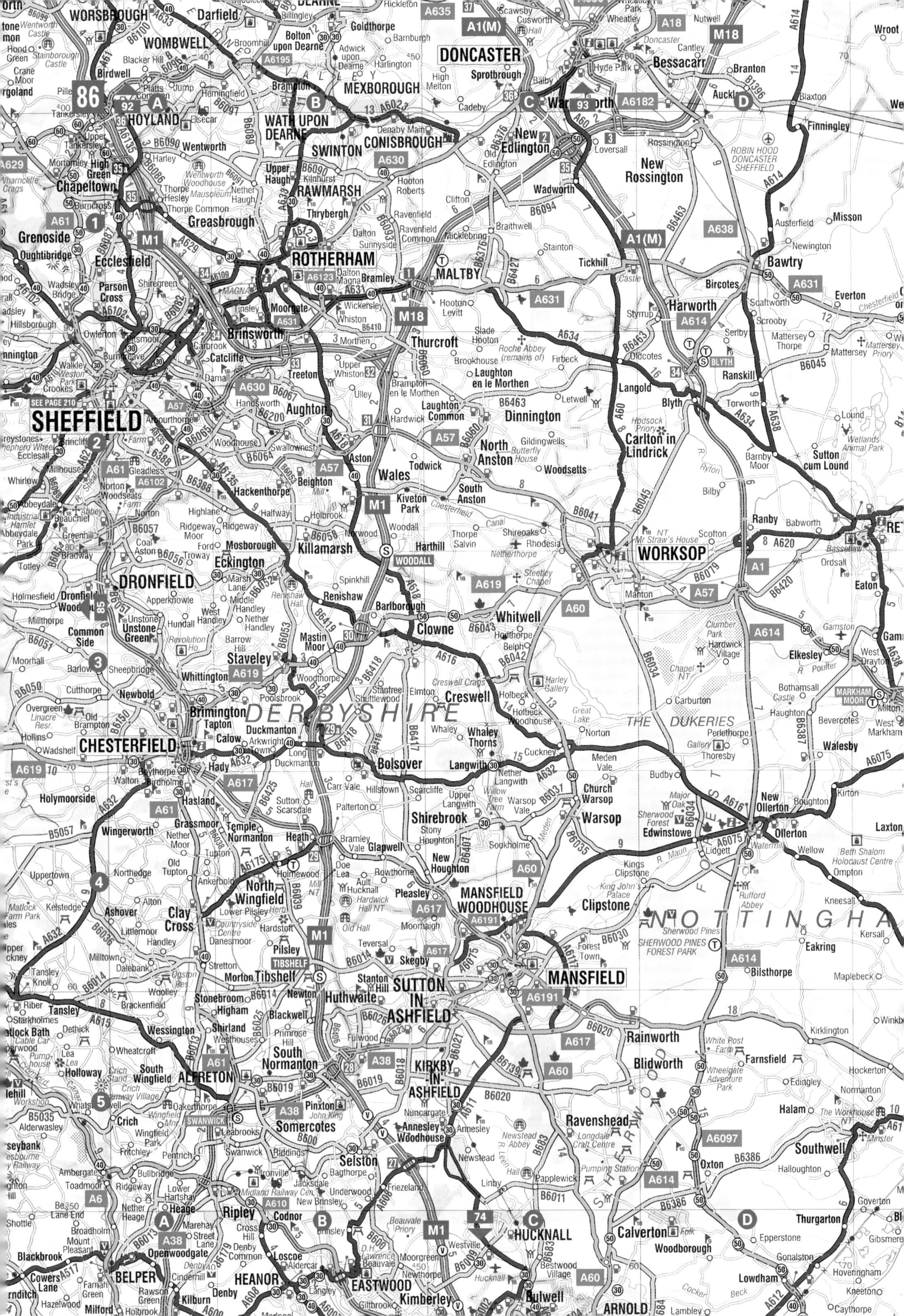
86
WORSBROUGH
Darfield
WOMBWELL
Goldthorpe
Bolton upon Dearne
DONCASTER
Sprotbrough
Bessacarr
Branton
Cantley
A1(M)
M18
Birdwell
HOYLAND
Elsecar
Hemingfield
WATH UPON DEARNE
MEXBOROUGH
SWINTON
CONISBROUGH
Warmsworth
New Edlington
Auckley
Finningley
ROBIN HOOD DONCASTER SHEFFIELD
Tankersley
Wentworth
Chapeltown
High Green
Upper Haugh
RAWMARSH
Thrybergh
Greasbrough
New Rossington
Rossington
Loversall
Wadworth
Grenoside
Oughtibridge
Ecclesfield
ROTHERHAM
Dalton Magna
Bramley
MALTBY
Tickhill
Bawtry
Austerfield
Misson
Parson Cross
Brinsworth
Catcliffe
Treeton
Thurcroft
Harworth
Bircotes
Everton
Scrooby
Ranskill
SHEFFIELD
SEE PAGE 210
Aughton
Laughton en le Morthen
Dinnington
Langold
Carlton in Lindrick
Blyth
Oldcotes
Hackenthorpe
Beighton
Wales
Kiveton Park
North Anston
South Anston
Todwick
Woodsetts
Killamarsh
Mosborough
Eckington
Harthill
WOODALL
WORKSOP
Ranby
Babworth
RETFORD
DRONFIELD
Renishaw
Barlborough
Clowne
Whitwell
Staveley
Whittington
Newbold
Brimington
Tapton
CHESTERFIELD
DERBYSHIRE
Creswell
Bolsover
Cuckney
Langwith
Elkesley
THE DUKERIES
Walesby
New Ollerton
Ollerton
Boughton
Edwinstowe
Church Warsop
Warsop
Shirebrook
Hasland
Grassmoor
Temple Normanton
Heath
Glapwell
Clay Cross
North Wingfield
MANSFIELD WOODHOUSE
Clipstone
NOTTINGHA
Sherwood Pines Forest Park
Pilsley
TIBSHELF
Tibshelf
SUTTON IN ASHFIELD
Huthwaite
Skegby
MANSFIELD
Rainworth
Blidworth
Farnsfield
Bilsthorpe
Eakring
Tansley
Wessington
South Normanton
KIRKBY-IN-ASHFIELD
ALFRETON
South Wingfield
Somercotes
Pinxton
Selston
Annesley Woodhouse
Ravenshead
Southwell
Crich
SWANWICK
Ripley
Codnor
Heage
HUCKNALL
Calverton
Woodborough
Thurgarton
Lowdham
Epperstone
Belper
Heanor
Eastwood
Kimberley
Bulwell
ARNOLD
Denby
Kilburn
Milford
Cowers Lane
Blackbrook
A B C D
1 2 3 4 5
74
M1
A1
A60
A614
A617
A38

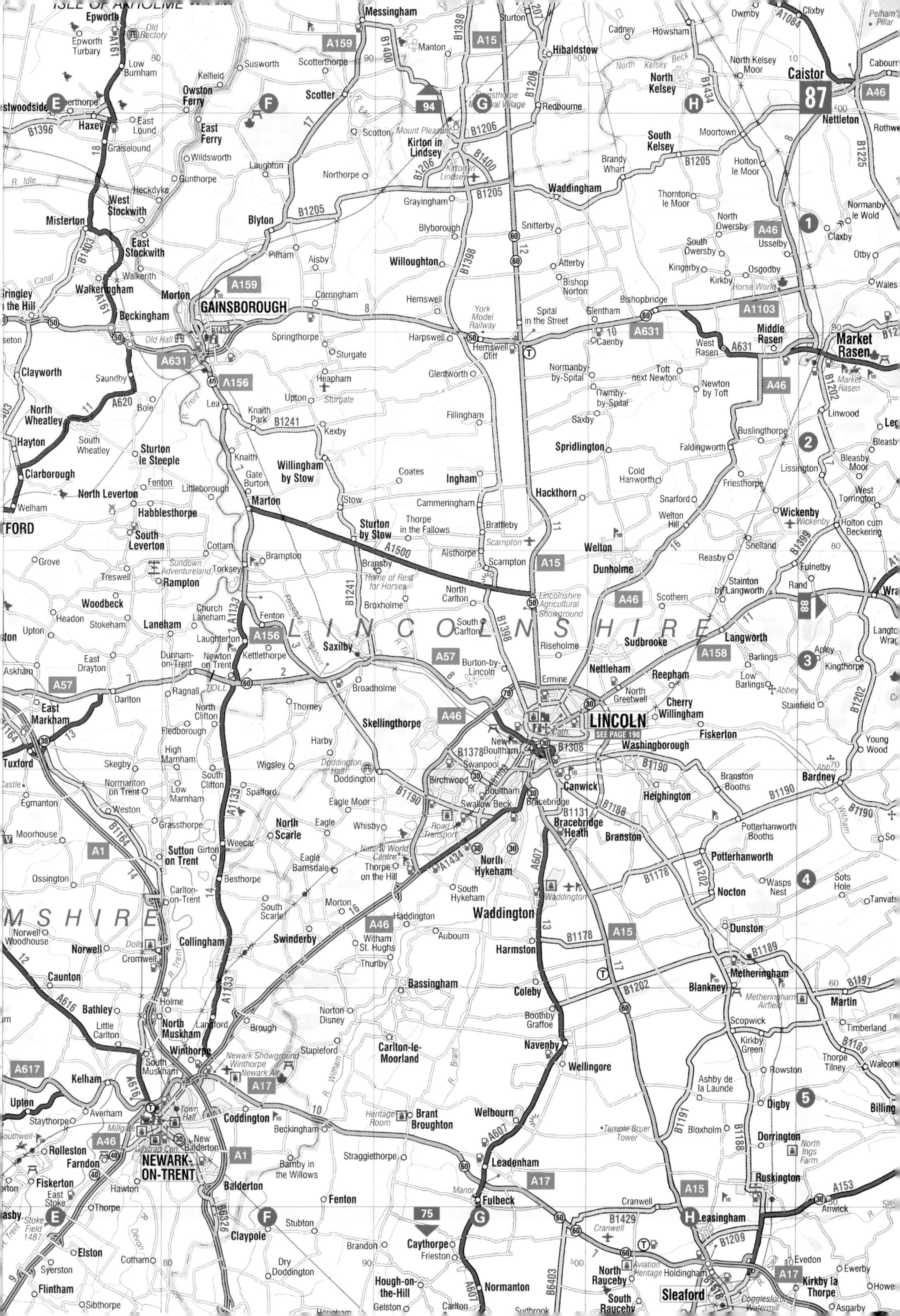
ISLE OF AXHOLME
Epworth
Old Rectory
Epworth Turbary
A161
Low Burnham
Messingham
Sturton
Owmby
Clixby
Pelham's Pillar
A159
Manton
B1398
A15
Cadney
Howsham
A1084
Cabourne
Scotterthorpe
B1400
Hibaldstow
North Kelsey Beck
North Kelsey Moor
Caistor
87
Susworth
Kelfield
Owston Ferry
Scotter
94
Gainsthorpe Medieval Village
Redbourne
B1206
North Kelsey
B1434
A46
Nettleton
Rothwell
E
F
G
H
Westwoodside
Haxey
East Lound
East Ferry
Scotton
Mount Pleasant
Kirton in Lindsey
B1206
Moortown
South Kelsey
B1225
B1396
Graiseland
Wildsworth
Laughton
B1400
Kirton in Lindsey
Brandy Wharf
B1205
Holton le Moor
R. Idle
Heckdyke
Gunthorpe
Northorpe
Grayingham
B1205
Waddingham
Thornton le Moor
Normanby le Wold
West Stockwith
Misterton
Blyton
B1205
Blyborough
Snitterby
North Owersby
A46
Usselby
Claxby
East Stockwith
B1403
Pilham
Aisby
Willoughton
B1398
Atterby
South Owersby
Kingerby
Osgodby
Otby
Canal
Walkerith
Walkeringham
A161
Morton
A159
Corringham
Bishop Norton
Kirkby
Horse World
Walesby
Gringley on the Hill
GAINSBOROUGH
Hemswell
York Model Railway
Glentham
Bishopbridge
A1103
Beckingham
Springthorpe
Harpswell
Hemswell Cliff
Spital in the Street
Caenby
A631
Middle Rasen
West Rasen
A631
Market Rasen
Old Hall
Sturgate
Normanby-by-Spital
Toft next Newton
Newton by Toft
Market Rasen
B1202
A46
Clayworth
Saundby
A631
A156
Heapham
Glentworth
Owmby-by-Spital
Linwood
A620
Bole
Lea
Upton
Sturgate
Knaith Park
B1241
Kexby
Fillingham
Saxby
Buslingthorpe
North Wheatley
Hayton
South Wheatley
Sturton le Steeple
Knaith
Spridlington
Faldingworth
Bleasby Moor
Lissington
Willingham by Stow
Coates
Ingham
Cold Hanworth
Clarborough
Gate Burton
Fenton
Littleborough
Marton
Stow
Cammeringham
Hackthorn
Friesthorpe
Snarford
West Torrington
North Leverton
Welham
Habblesthorpe
Sturton by Stow
Thorpe in the Fallows
Brattleby
Welton Hill
Wickenby
Holton cum Beckering
RETFORD
South Leverton
A1500
Scampton
Welton
Snelland
B1399
Cottam
Aisthorpe
Scampton
A15
Dunholme
Reasby
Grove
Sundown Adventureland
Torksey
Brampton
Bransby
Home of Rest for Horses
Fulnetby
Treswell
Rampton
Stainton by Langworth
Rand
Woodbeck
Church Laneham
Fenton
North Carlton
Lincolnshire Agricultural Showground
A46
Scothern
Headon
Laneham
B1241
Broxholme
South Carlton
88
Upton
Stokeham
Laughterton
A156
LINCOLNSHIRE
Fossdyke Navigation
B1398
Langworth
Langton by Wragby
Dunham-on-Trent
Newton on Trent
Kettlethorpe
Saxilby
Riseholme
Sudbrooke
A158
Apley
East Drayton
A57
Burton-by-Lincoln
Nettleham
Barlings
Kingthorpe
Askham
A57
Darlton
Ragnall
TOLL
Broadholme
Ermine
Reepham
Low Barlings
Abbey
East Markham
North Clifton
Thorney
North Greetwell
Cherry Willingham
Stainfield
Tuxford
Fledborough
Skellingthorpe
A46
LINCOLN
SEE PAGE 198
Fiskerton
B1202
High Marnham
Harby
New Boultham
B1308
Washingborough
Young Wood
Skegby
South Clifton
Wigsley
Doddington Hall
B1378
Swanpool
Doddington
Birchwood
Boultham
B1190
Canwick
Branston Booths
Bardney
Normanton on Trent
Low Marnham
Spalford
A1133
B1190
Swallow Beck
Bracebridge
B1131
B1188
Heighington
B1190
Egmanton
Weston
Eagle Moor
Bracebridge Heath
Branston
Potterhanworth Booths
Moorhouse
Grassthorpe
North Scarle
Eagle
Whisby
Road Transport
A1
Sutton on Trent
Girton
Weecar
Natural World Centre
Thorpe on the Hill
Eagle Barnsdale
A1434
North Hykeham
A607
Potterhanworth
B1178
B1202
Nocton
Wasps Nest
Sots Hole
Ossington
Besthorpe
Carlton-on-Trent
South Hykeham
Waddington
Tanvats
South Scarle
Morton
Haddington
Waddington
Norwell Woodhouse
MSHIRE
A46
Witham St. Hughs
B1178
A15
Dunston
Norwell
Dolls
Collingham
Swinderby
Auborn
Harmston
B1189
Cromwell
Thurlby
Metheringham
Caunton
Bassingham
Coleby
B1202
Blankney
Metheringham Airfield
Martin
B1191
A616
Bathley
Holme
Norton Disney
Boothby Graffoe
Scopwick
Little Carlton
North Muskham
Langford
Brough
Timberland
Kirkby Green
Winthorpe
Newark Showground
Winthorpe
Newark Air
Stapleford
Carlton-le-Moorland
Navenby
Wellingore
Thorpe Tilney
Walcott
A617
Kelham
South Muskham
A17
Brant
Rowston
Ashby de la Launde
Upton
Averham
Town Hall
Coddington
Heritage Room
Brant Broughton
Welbourn
Digby
Billinghay
Staythorpe
Millgate
R. Witham
B1191
Southwell
A46
New Balderton
Beckingham
Temple Bruer Tower
Bloxholm
B1188
Dorrington
North Ings Farm
Rolleston
Farndon
NEWARK-ON-TRENT
A1
A607
Leadenham
Barnby in the Willows
Stragglethorpe
Ruskington
Fiskerton
Hawton
Balderton
A17
A15
A153
East Stoke
Thorpe
Fenton
Manor
Fulbeck
Cranwell
Anwick
B6326
Claypole
Stubton
75
B1429
Cranwell
Leasingham
Stoke Field 1487
Devon
Brandon
Caythorpe
Frieston
B1209
Evedon
Elston
Cotham
Dry Doddington
Aviation Heritage
North Rauceby
Holdingham
Ewerby
Syerston
A607
B6403
A17
Kirkby la Thorpe
Flintham
Sibthorpe
Hough-on-the-Hill
Gelston
Carlton
Normanton
South Rauceby
Sleaford
Cogglesford Watermill
Howell
Asgarby
Sudbrook

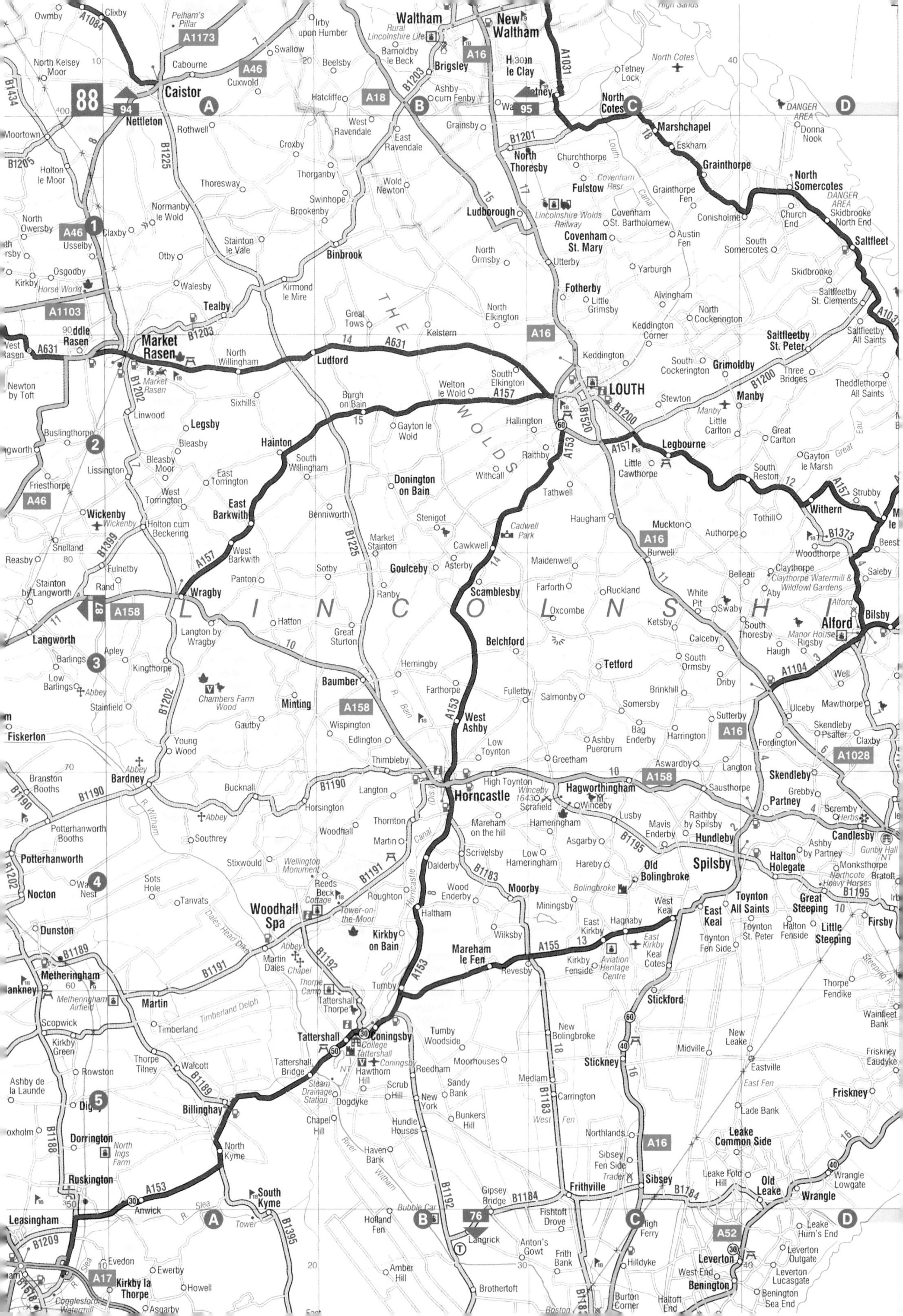
88
Owmby
Clixby
A1084
Pelham's Pillar
A1173
Irby upon Humber
Waltham
Rural Lincolnshire Life
Barnoldby le Beck
New Waltham
High Sands
North Kelsey Moor
Swallow
Cabourne
A46
Cuxwold
Beelsby
Brigsley
A16
Humberston
Holton le Clay
A1031
North Cotes
Tetney Lock
B1434
Caistor
94
Nettleton
Hatcliffe
A18
B1203
Ashby cum Fenby
Tetney
95
Waithe
North Cotes
DANGER AREA
Donna Nook
Marshchapel
Eskham
Moortown
Rothwell
West Ravendale
East Ravendale
Grainsby
B1201
North Thoresby
Churchthorpe
Grainthorpe
B1205
Holton le Moor
B1225
Croxby
Thorganby
Fulstow
Covenham Resr
Grainthorpe Fen
North Somercotes
Thoresway
Wold Newton
Swinhope
Brookenby
Ludborough
Lincolnshire Wolds Railway
Covenham St. Bartholomew
Conisholme
DANGER AREA
Skidbrooke North End
Church End
North Owersby
Normanby le Wold
A46
Usselby
Claxby
Stainton le Vale
Binbrook
North Ormsby
Covenham St. Mary
Austin Fen
South Somercotes
Saltfleet
Osgodby
Otby
Utterby
Yarburgh
Kirkby
Horse World
Walesby
Kirmond le Mire
Fotherby
Little Grimsby
Alvingham
Skidbrooke
Saltfleetby St. Clements
A1103
Tealby
THE WOLDS
Great Tows
North Elkington
North Cockerington
Keddington Corner
Middle Rasen
Market Rasen
B1203
Kelstern
A16
Saltfleetby St. Peter
Saltfleetby All Saints
A1031
West Rasen
A631
North Willingham
Ludford
A631
Keddington
South Cockerington
Grimoldby
Three Bridges
Theddlethorpe All Saints
Newton by Toft
Market Rasen
B1202
Sixhills
Burgh on Bain
Welton le Wold
South Elkington
A157
LOUTH
Stewton
B1200
Manby
Linwood
Gayton le Wold
Hallington
B1520
Manby
Little Carlton
Great Carlton
Buslingthorpe
Legsby
Bleasby
Hainton
South Willingham
A153
Raithby
A157
Legbourne
Gayton le Marsh
Friesthorpe
Lissington
Bleasby Moor
East Torrington
West Torrington
Donington on Bain
Withcall
Little Cawthorpe
Tathwell
South Reston
Strubby
A46
Wickenby
Holton cum Beckering
East Barkwith
Benniworth
Stenigot
Haugham
Muckton
Authorpe
Tothill
Withern
B1373
Snelland
B1399
West Barkwith
Market Stainton
Cadwell Park
Cawkwell
A16
Burwell
Woodthorpe
Reasby
Fulnetby
A157
Sotby
Goulceby
Asterby
Maidenwell
Claythorpe
Claythorpe Watermill & Wildfowl Gardens
Belleau
Saleby
Stainton by Langworth
Rand
Panton
Farforth
Ruckland
Aby
87
A158
Wragby
Ranby
Scamblesby
White Pit
Swaby
Alford
Bilsby
LINCOLNSHIRE
Langworth
Langton by Wragby
Hatton
Great Sturton
Oxcombe
Ketsby
South Thoresby
Manor House
Rigsby
Barlings
Apley
Kingthorpe
Belchford
Calceby
Haugh
Low Barlings
Abbey
Chambers Farm Wood
Hemingby
Tetford
South Ormsby
Driby
A1104
Well
Stainfield
Baumber
Farthorpe
Fulletby
Salmonby
Brinkhill
Ulceby
Mawthorpe
B1202
Minting
A158
A153
Somersby
Sutterby
Skendleby Psalter
Fiskerton
Gautby
Wispington
West Ashby
Bag Enderby
Harrington
Skendleby
Claxby
Young Wood
Edlington
Low Toynton
Ashby Puerorum
A16
Fordington
A1028
Thimbleby
Greetham
Aswardby
Langton
Branston Booths
Bardney
Abbey
B1190
Bucknall
Langton
High Toynton
Winceby 1643
Scrafield
Hagworthingham
A158
Sausthorpe
Skendleby
Grebby
B1190
Horsington
Horncastle
Winceby
Partney
Scremby
Herbs
Abbey
Thornton
Mareham on the hill
Hameringham
Lusby
Mavis Enderby
Raithby by Spilsby
Candlesby
Potterhanworth Booths
Southrey
Woodhall
Asgarby
Hundleby
Ashby by Partney
Gunby Hall NT
Potterhanworth
Stixwould
Wellington Monument
Martin
Scrivelsby
Low Hameringham
Hareby
Old Bolingbroke
Spilsby
Halton Holegate
Monksthorpe
B1202
Reeds Beck
Cottage
B1191
Dalderby
B1183
Bolingbroke
Northcote Heavy Horses
Bratoft
Nocton
Washingborough Nest
Sots Hole
Roughton
Wood Enderby
Moorby
Miningsby
West Keal
Toynton All Saints
Great Steeping
B1195
Irby
Tanvats
Woodhall Spa
Tower-on-the-Moor
Haltham
Hagnaby
East Keal
Toynton St. Peter
Halton Fenside
Little Steeping
Firsby
Dunston
Dales Head Dike
Kirkby on Bain
Wilksby
East Kirkby
East Kirkby
Toynton Fen Side
B1189
Martin Dales
Abbey
Chapel
B1192
Mareham le Fen
A155
Kirkby Fenside
Aviation Heritage Centre
Keal Cotes
Metheringham
B1191
Thorpe Camp
A153
Tumby
Revesby
Thorpe Fendike
Metheringham Airfield
Martin
Tattershall Thorpe
Stickford
Timberland Delph
Wainfleet Bank
Nocton
Scopwick
Timberland
Tattershall
Coningsby
Tumby Woodside
New Bolingbroke
New Leake
Kirkby Green
Thorpe Tilney
Walcott
Tattershall Bridge
College
Tattershall
Coningsby
Moorhouses
Midville
Friskney Eaudyke
Rowston
B1189
Steam Drainage Station
Hawthorn Hill
Reedham
Stickney
Eastville
Ashby de la Launde
Scrub Hill
Sandy Bank
Medlam
B1183
Carrington
East Fen
Friskney
Digby
Billinghay
Dogdyke
New York
Bunkers Hill
West Fen
Lade Bank
Oxholm
B1188
Dorrington
North Ings Farm
Chapel Hill
Hundle Houses
Northlands
A16
Leake Common Side
North Kyme
River Witham
Haven Bank
Sibsey Fen Side
Trader
Leake Fold Hill
Wrangle Lowgate
Ruskington
A153
South Kyme
B1192
Gipsey Bridge
B1184
Frithville
Sibsey
B1184
Old Leake
Wrangle
Leasingham
Anwick
Slea
Tower
B1395
Holland Fen
Bubble Car
76
Langrick
Fishtoft Drove
High Ferry
A52
Leake Hurn's End
B1209
Evedon
Amber Hill
Anton's Gowt
Frith Bank
Hilldyke
Leverton
Leverton Outgate
A17
Ewerby
Kirkby la Thorpe
Howell
Brothertoft
West End
Benington
Leverton Lucasgate
Cogglesford Watermill
Asgarby
B1518
Boston
B1183
Burton Corner
Haltoft End
Benington Sea End

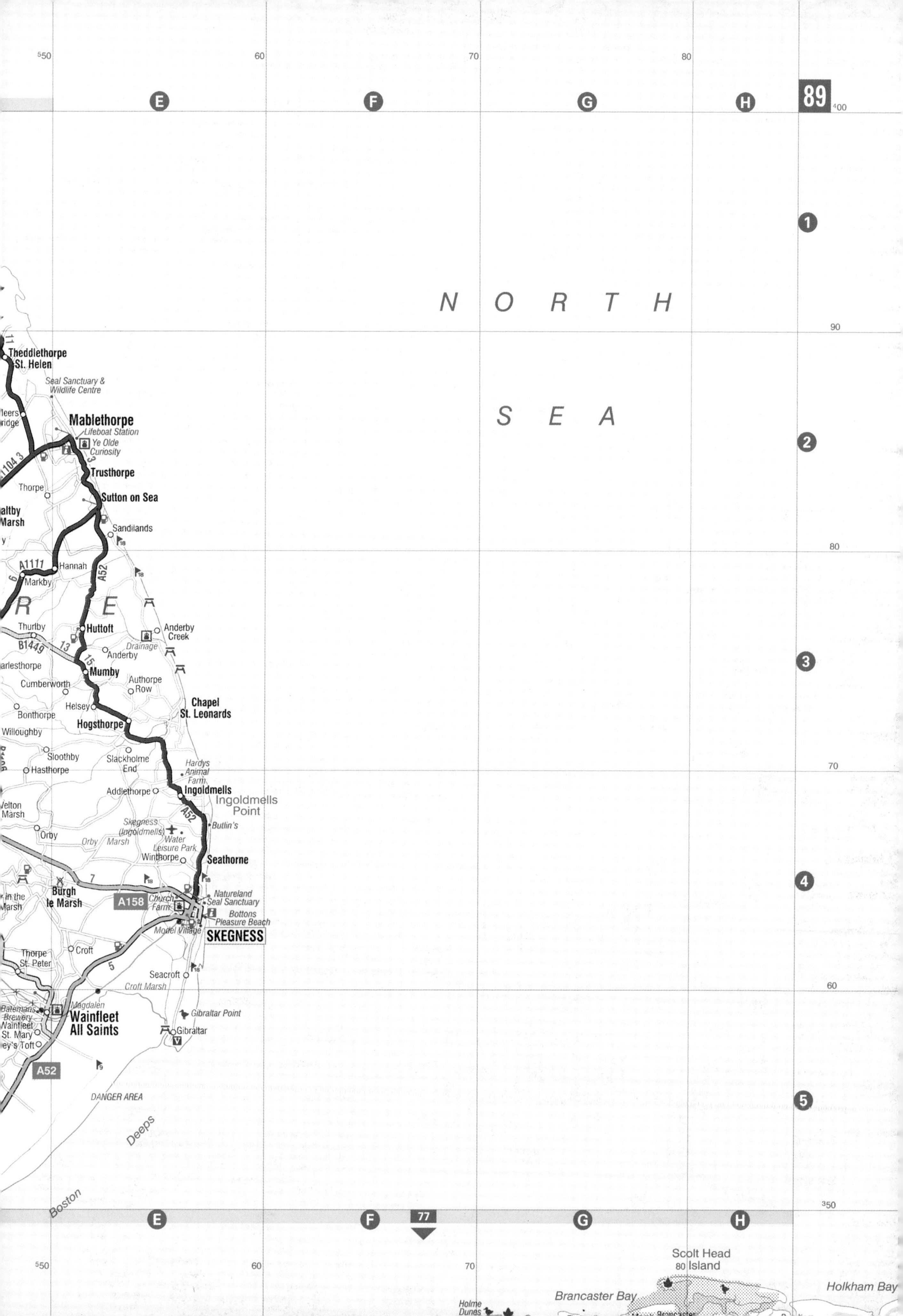

N O R T H

S E A

Theddlethorpe
St. Helen

Seal Sanctuary &
Wildlife Centre

Mablethorpe
Lifeboat Station
Ye Olde
Curiosity

Thorpe

Trusthorpe

Sutton on Sea

Sandilands

Hannah

Markby

Thurlby

Huttoft

Anderby
Creek

Drainage

Anderby

Mumby

Authorpe
Row

Chapel
St. Leonards

Cumberworth

Helsey

Hogsthorpe

Willoughby

Sloothby

Slackholme
End

Hasthorpe

Hardys
Animal
Farm

Addlethorpe

Ingoldmells

Ingoldmells
Point

Skegness
(Ingoldmells)

Butlin's

Orby

Orby
Marsh

Water
Leisure Park

Winthorpe

Seathorne

Burgh
le Marsh

A158

Natureland
Seal Sanctuary

Church
Farm

Bottons
Pleasure Beach

Model Village

SKEGNESS

Thorpe
St. Peter

Croft

Seacroft

Croft Marsh

Batemans
Brewery
Nainfleet
St. Mary
ey's Toft

Magdalen

Wainfleet
All Saints

Gibraltar Point

Gibraltar

A52

DANGER AREA

Deeps

Boston

Scolt Head
Island

Brancaster Bay

Holme
Dunes

Holkham Bay

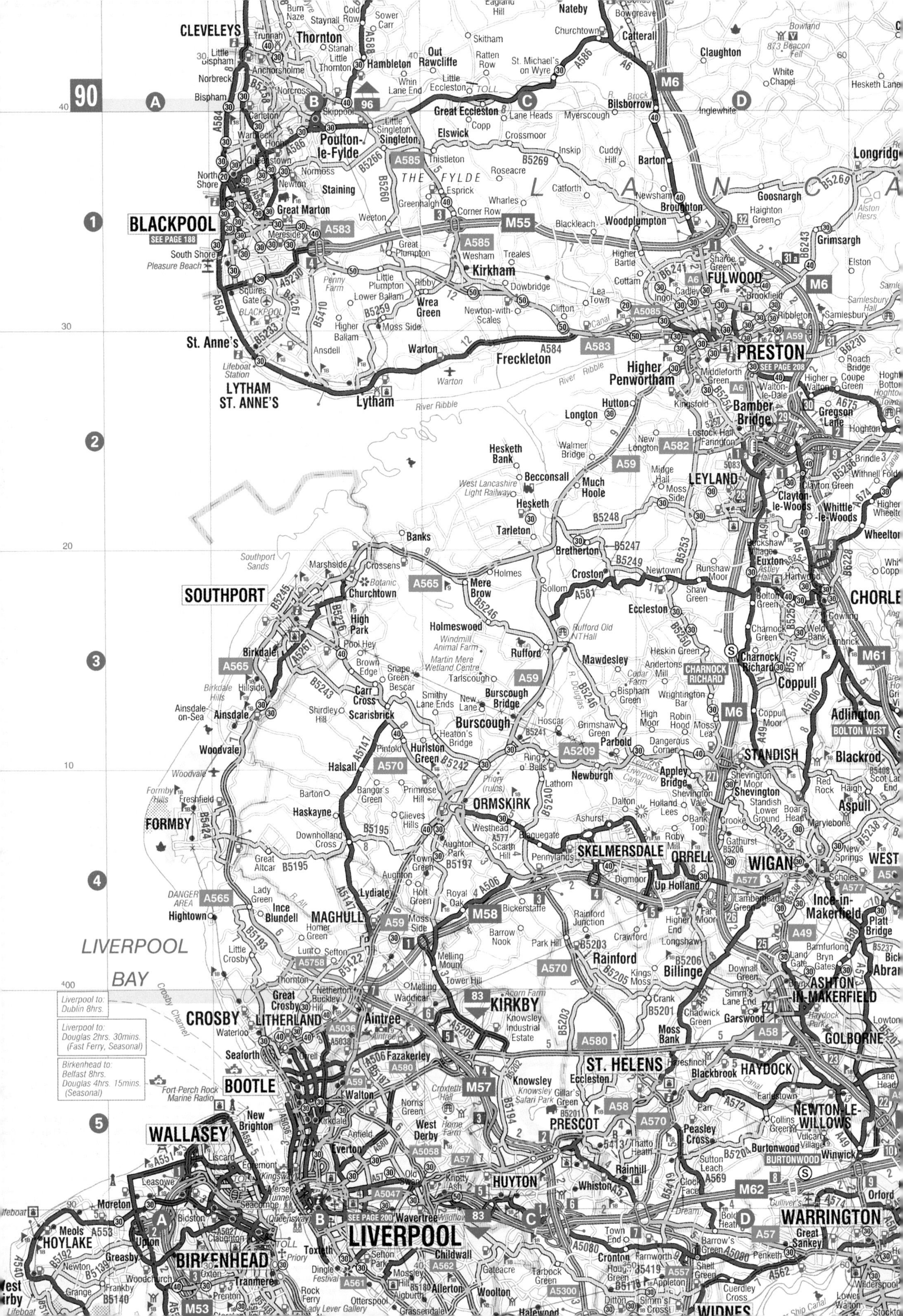

90
96
A
B
C
D
1
2
3
4
5
40
30
20
10
400
CLEVELEYS
Thornton
Hambleton
Out Rawcliffe
Nateby
Churchtown
Catterall
Claughton
Bowland
Bilsborrow
Great Eccleston
St. Michael's on Wyre
Poulton-le-Fylde
Singleton
Elswick
THE FYLDE
LANCASHIRE
Longridge
Goosnargh
Grimsargh
BLACKPOOL
SEE PAGE 188
South Shore
Pleasure Beach
Great Marton
Staining
Kirkham
Wrea Green
Warton
Freckleton
St. Anne's
LYTHAM ST. ANNE'S
Lytham
River Ribble
FULWOOD
PRESTON
SEE PAGE 208
Higher Penwortham
Bamber Bridge
LEYLAND
Hesketh Bank
Becconsall
West Lancashire Light Railway
Much Hoole
Hesketh
Tarleton
Banks
Southport Sands
SOUTHPORT
Crossens
Churchtown
Mere Brow
Croston
Eccleston
CHORLEY
Birkdale
Ainsdale
Rufford
Rufford Old NT Hall
Martin Mere Wetland Centre
Mawdesley
Charnock Richard
CHARNOCK RICHARD
Coppull
Adlington
BOLTON WEST
Scarisbrick
Burscough
Burscough Bridge
Parbold
Woodvale
Halsall
ORMSKIRK
Newburgh
Appley Bridge
STANDISH
Blackrod
FORMBY
SKELMERSDALE
ORRELL
WIGAN
Up Holland
Ince-in-Makerfield
Hightown
MAGHULL
Lydiate
LIVERPOOL BAY
Liverpool to: Dublin 8hrs.
Liverpool to: Douglas 2hrs. 30mins. (Fast Ferry, Seasonal)
Birkenhead to: Belfast 8hrs. Douglas 4hrs. 15mins. (Seasonal)
CROSBY
LITHERLAND
Aintree
KIRKBY
Rainford
Billinge
ASHTON-IN-MAKERFIELD
GOLBORNE
Bootle
BOOTLE
ST. HELENS
HAYDOCK
Knowsley
Knowsley Safari Park
PRESCOT
NEWTON-LE-WILLOWS
WALLASEY
New Brighton
HUYTON
BURTONWOOD
WARRINGTON
HOYLAKE
BIRKENHEAD
LIVERPOOL
SEE PAGE 200
Wavertree
Childwall
Woolton
Allerton
WIDNES
West Kirby
M6
M55
M58
M57
M62
M53
M61
A583
A585
A565
A59
A570
A580
A5209
A58
A57
A49

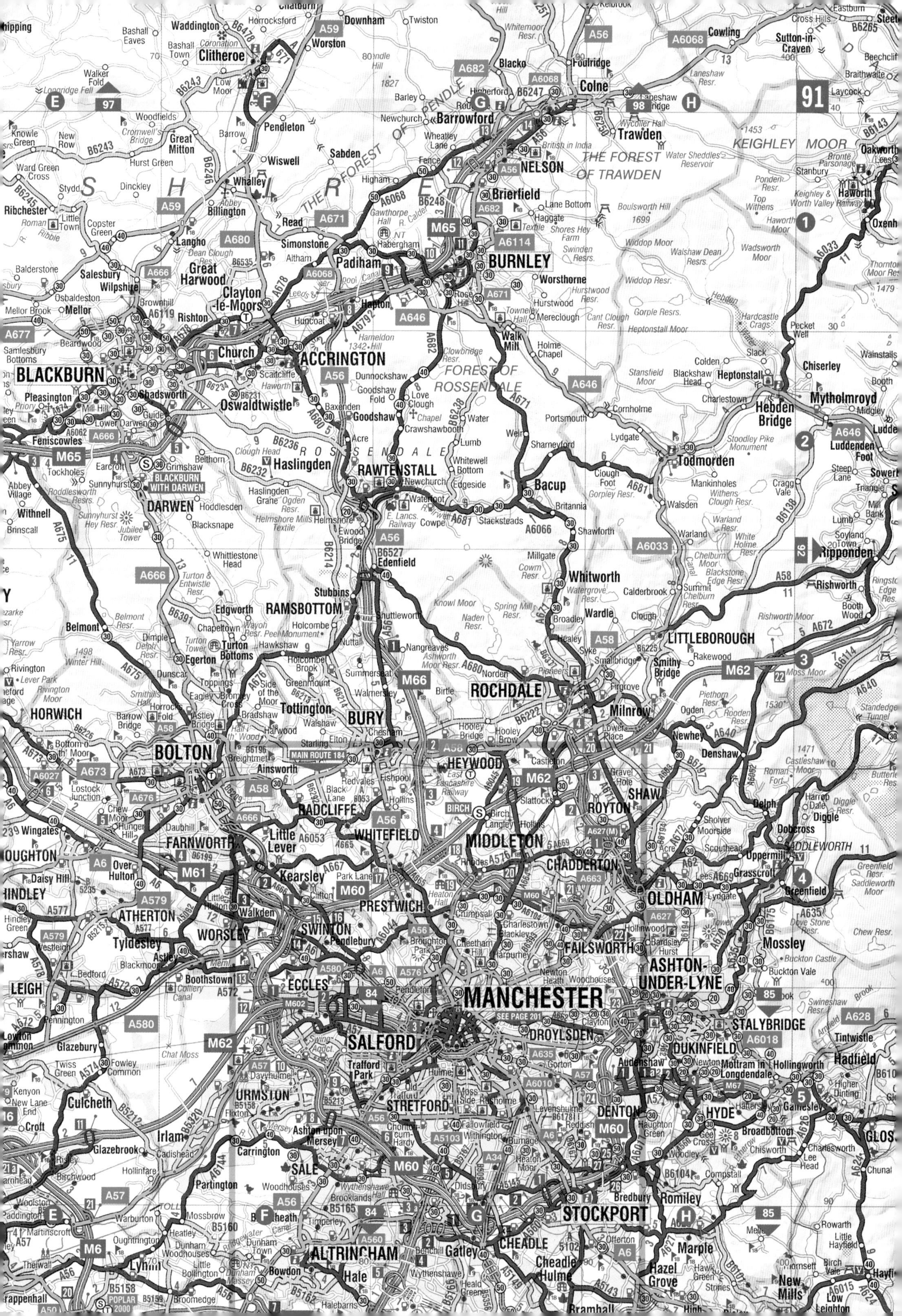

91
97
98
84
85
Clitheroe
Waddington
Downham
Twiston
Worston
Chatburn
Bashall Eaves
Bashall Town
Low Moor
Walker Fold
Longridge Fell
Woodfields
Pendleton
Great Mitton
Knowle Green
New Row
Hurst Green
Ward Green Cross
Stydd
Dinckley
Whalley
Abbey Village
Billington
Ribchester
Little Town
Copster Green
Langho
Great Harwood
Balderstone
Salesbury
Wilpshire
Osbaldeston
Mellor Brook
Mellor
Clayton-le-Moors
Rishton
Brownhill
Beardwood
Samlesbury Bottoms
BLACKBURN
Church
ACCRINGTON
Oswaldtwistle
Shadsworth
Pleasington
Feniscowles
Lower Darwen
Guide
Tockholes
Earcroft
Grimshaw
BLACKBURN WITH DARWEN
DARWEN
Sunnyhurst
Hoddlesden
Blacksnape
Withnell
Brinscall
Abbey Village
Roddlesworth Resrs.
Haslingden
Haslingden Grane
Helmshore
RAWTENSTALL
Newchurch
Waterfoot
Cowpe
Stacksteads
Bacup
Britannia
Shawforth
Whitworth
Edenfield
Stubbins
RAMSBOTTOM
Shuttleworth
Holcombe
Nangreaves
Edgworth
Chapeltown
Turton Bottoms
Egerton
Belmont
Rivington
HORWICH
Dunscar
Toppings
Eagley
Bromley Cross
Tottington
BURY
Greenmount
Walmersley
Summerseat
Birtle
ROCHDALE
Norden
Wardle
Littleborough
LITTLEBOROUGH
Smithy Bridge
Milnrow
Newhey
Denshaw
Delph
Diggle
Dobcross
Uppermill
Grasscroft
Greenfield
Mossley
SADDLEWORTH
BOLTON
Lostock Junction
Chew Moor
Hunger Hill
Daubhill
FARNWORTH
Little Lever
Kearsley
Radcliffe
RADCLIFFE
Ainsworth
Breightmet
Harwood
Starling
Elton
Chesham
HEYWOOD
Hooley Bridge
Hooley Brow
Castleton
WHITEFIELD
PRESTWICH
MIDDLETON
Rhodes
CHADDERTON
ROYTON
SHAW
OLDHAM
Lees
Springhead
Lydgate
Moorside
Sholver
Wingates
WESTHOUGHTON
Over Hulton
Daisy Hill
HINDLEY
ATHERTON
Tyldesley
Astley
WORSLEY
Walkden
Little Hulton
SWINTON
Pendlebury
Clifton
Prestwich
Crumpsall
Cheetham Hill
Harpurhey
Blackley
Charlestown
FAILSWORTH
ASHTON-UNDER-LYNE
Hollinwood
Bardsley
Stalybridge
STALYBRIDGE
DUKINFIELD
Hadfield
Tintwistle
Hollingworth
Mottram in Longdendale
HYDE
Gamesley
GLOSSOP
LEIGH
Boothstown
ECCLES
MANCHESTER
SEE PAGE 201
SALFORD
DROYLSDEN
Gorton
Audenshaw
DENTON
Haughton Green
Trafford Park
STRETFORD
URMSTON
Davyhulme
Flixton
Irlam
Cadishead
Culcheth
Glazebury
Glazebrook
Fowley Common
Twiss Green
Kenyon
New Lane End
Croft
Risley
Birchwood
Partington
Carrington
SALE
Ashton upon Mersey
Chorlton-cum-Hardy
Fallowfield
Withington
Burnage
Didsbury
Heaton Moor
Reddish
Levenshulme
Rusholme
Moss Side
Hulme
Brooklands
Timperley
ALTRINCHAM
Hale
Bowdon
Dunham Town
Little Bollington
Gatley
CHEADLE
Cheadle Hulme
STOCKPORT
Bredbury
Romiley
Woodley
Marple
Hazel Grove
New Mills
Lymm
Warburton
Heatley
Oughtrington
Thelwall
Padgate
Martinscroft
Woolston
Grappenhall
Higher
Broadbottom
Charlesworth
Chisworth
Compstall
Mellor
Rowarth
Little Hayfield
Hayfield
Birch Vale
Low Leighton
Chunal
Whalley
Read
Simonstone
Padiham
Higham
Sabden
Wiswell
Barrow
Hapton
Huncoat
Altham
Fence
Barley
Newchurch
Barrowford
Wheatley Lane
Roughlee
Higherford
Blacko
Foulridge
Colne
NELSON
Brierfield
BURNLEY
Worsthorne
Hurstwood
Mereclough
Walk Mill
Holme Chapel
Cliviger
Rose Hill
Laneshaw Bridge
Trawden
THE FOREST OF TRAWDEN
THE FOREST OF PENDLE
FOREST OF ROSSENDALE
ROSSENDALE
KEIGHLEY MOOR
Cowling
Cross Hills
Sutton-in-Craven
Laycock
Oakworth
Haworth
Oxenhope
Stanbury
Wainstalls
Pecket Well
Heptonstall
Hebden Bridge
Mytholmroyd
Luddenden Foot
Todmorden
Walsden
Cornholme
Portsmouth
Sharneyford
Lydgate
Ripponden
Rishworth
Cragg Vale
Sowerby
Soyland Town
Calderbrook
Clough
Smallbridge
Firgrove
A59
A56
A6068
A682
A671
A680
A666
A646
A6114
A677
A58
A673
A6027
A676
A6
A579
A577
A580
A57
M65
M66
M62
M60
M61
M6
M67
A627(M)
A663
A576
A635
A6018
A628
A34
A5103
A560
A523
A6010
A6033
A640
A672
A670
MAIN ROUTE 184
POPLAR 2000

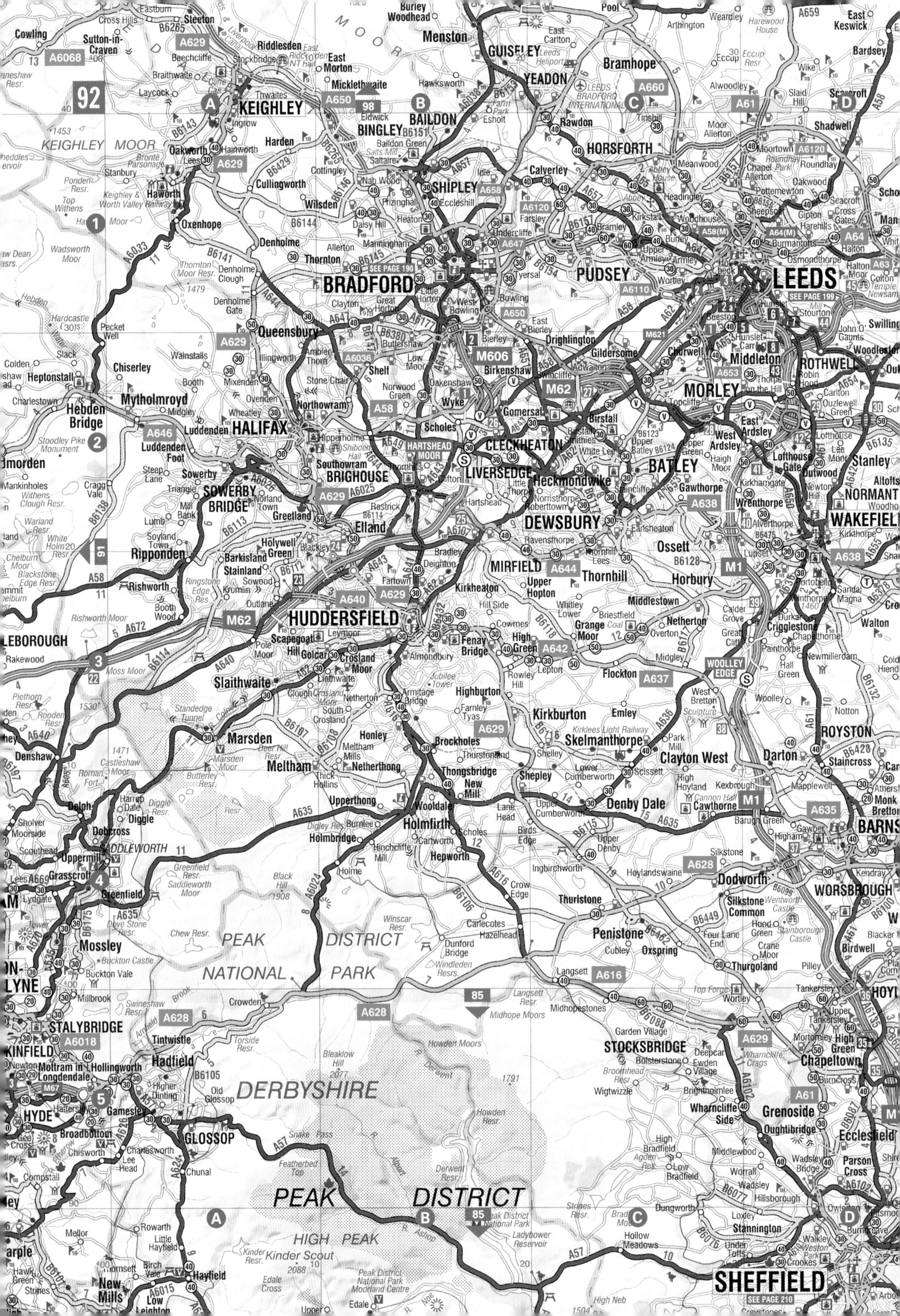
92
KEIGHLEY
BINGLEY
BAILDON
GUISELEY
YEADON
Menston
Bramhope
HORSFORTH
SHIPLEY
Calverley
PUDSEY
BRADFORD
SEE PAGE 190
LEEDS
SEE PAGE 199
Oxenhope
Haworth
Denholme
Thornton
Queensbury
HALIFAX
Mytholmroyd
Hebden Bridge
Heptonstall
Todmorden
SOWERBY BRIDGE
Ripponden
BRIGHOUSE
Elland
Greetland
CLECKHEATON
LIVERSEDGE
Heckmondwike
Birstall
BATLEY
MORLEY
Middleton
ROTHWELL
DEWSBURY
Ossett
Horbury
WAKEFIELD
MIRFIELD
HUDDERSFIELD
Slaithwaite
Marsden
Meltham
Honley
Holmfirth
Kirkburton
Skelmanthorpe
Clayton West
Denby Dale
Darton
ROYSTON
BARNSLEY
Penistone
Dodworth
WORSBROUGH
STOCKSBRIDGE
Chapeltown
Grenoside
Ecclesfield
SHEFFIELD
SEE PAGE 210
Stannington
GLOSSOP
Hadfield
Tintwistle
STALYBRIDGE
Mossley
HYDE
Hayfield
New Mills
Diggle
Delph
Uppermill
Greenfield
SADDLEWORTH
PEAK DISTRICT NATIONAL PARK
DERBYSHIRE
PEAK DISTRICT
HIGH PEAK
Kinder Scout
KEIGHLEY MOOR
HARTSHEAD MOOR
WOOLLEY EDGE
M62
M1
M606
M621
A629
A58
A616
A628
A635
A57
A61
85
98
91

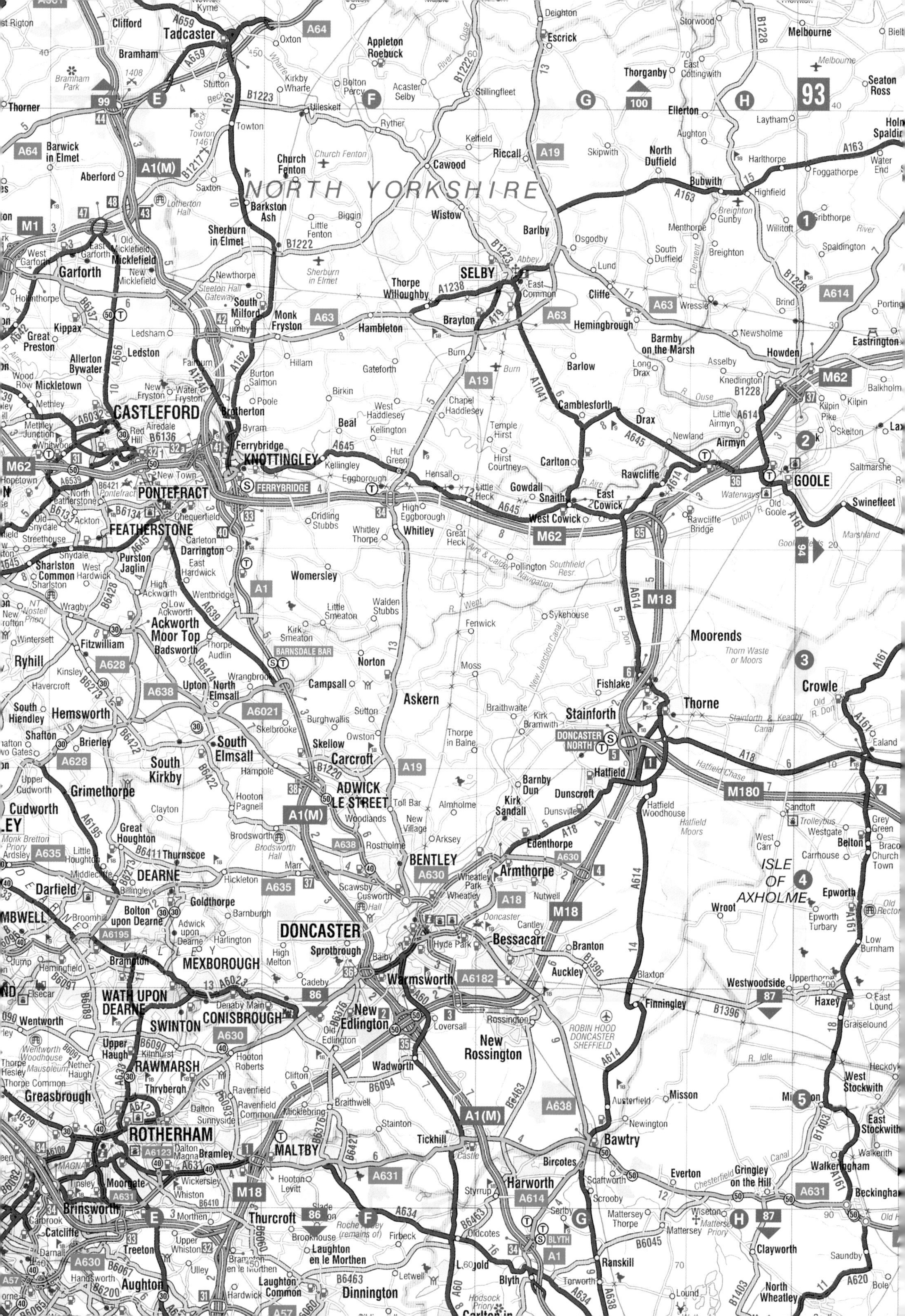

Clifford
Tadcaster
A659
A64
Oxton
Appleton Roebuck
Deighton
Escrick
Storwood
B1228
Melbourne
Bramham
Bramham Park
1408
Stutton
Kirkby Wharfe
Bolton Percy
Acaster Selby
Stillingfleet
Thorganby
East Cottingwith
Seaton Ross
93
Thorner
99
E
F
G
100
H
B1223
Ulleskelf
Ellerton
Laytham
Towton
Towton 1461
Ryther
Aughton
Barwick in Elmet
A64
A1(M)
Church Fenton
Kelfield
Riccall
A19
Skipwith
North Duffield
Harlthorpe
A163
Water End
Aberford
B1217
Saxton
Cawood
Bubwith
Foggathorpe
Highfield
NORTH YORKSHIRE
Lotherton Hall
Barkston Ash
Biggin
Wistow
Breighton
Gunby
Gribthorpe
M1
Little Fenton
Barlby
Menthorpe
Willitoft
River
Sherburn in Elmet
B1222
Osgodby
South Duffield
Breighton
Spaldington
West Garforth
East Garforth
Old Micklefield
Micklefield
New Micklefield
Abbey
Lund
Garforth
Newthorpe
SELBY
Sherburn in Elmet
Thorpe Willoughby
A1238
East Common
Cliffe
A63
Wressle
Brind
A614
Holmthorpe
B6137
Steeton Hall Gateway
South Milford
Monk Fryston
A63
Hambleton
Brayton
A63
Hemingbrough
Portington
Kippax
Great Preston
Ledsham
Lumby
Newsholme
Barmby on the Marsh
Eastrington
Burn
Howden
Allerton Bywater
Ledston
Fairburn
Hillam
Gateforth
Burn
Barlow
Long Drax
Asselby
Knedlington
M62
Balkholm
Burton Salmon
Wood Row
Mickletown
A656
New Fryston
Water Fryston
Birkin
A19
B1228
Poole
A1041
Chapel Haddlesey
Camblesforth
Kilpin
Kilpin Pike
Methley
CASTLEFORD
Brotherton
West Haddlesey
Beal
Temple Hirst
Drax
Little Airmyn
Skelton
Methley Junction
Airedale
Byram
Kellington
Newland
Airmyn
Whitwood
Red Hill
B6136
Ferrybridge
A645
Hirst Courtney
Carlton
Saltmarshe
M62
Hopetown
New Town
KNOTTINGLEY
Kellingley
Hut Green
Hensall
Rawcliffe
GOOLE
A6539
B6421
Pontefract
PONTEFRACT
FERRYBRIDGE
Eggborough
Little Heck
Gowdall
Snaith
East Cowick
Waterways
Old Goole
Swinefleet
North Featherstone
B6134
Chequerfield
High Eggborough
A645
West Cowick
Rawcliffe Bridge
Dutch R.
Ackton
FEATHERSTONE
Cridling Stubbs
Whitley Thorpe
Whitley
Great Heck
M62
Marshland
Snydale
Streethouse
Carleton
Darrington
Aire & Calder Navigation
Pollington
Southfield Resr.
Goole
94
Sharlston
Sharlston Common
West Hardwick
Purston Jaglin
East Hardwick
Womersley
A614
M18
Nostell Priory
High Ackworth
Low Ackworth
Wentbridge
A1
A639
Little Smeaton
Walden Stubbs
R. Went
Sykehouse
Wragby
B6428
Ackworth Moor Top
Fenwick
Moorends
Thorn Waste or Moors
Wintersett
Fitzwilliam
Badsworth
Thorpe Audlin
Kirk Smeaton
BARNSDALE BAR
Norton
Moss
3
Crowle
Ryhill
A628
Kinsley
B6474
Wrangbrook
Campsall
Fishlake
A161
Havercroft
B6273
Upton
North Elmsall
Askern
Braithwaite
Stainforth
Thorne
Old R. Don
South Hiendley
Hemsworth
A638
A6021
Skelbrooke
Sutton
Kirk Bramwith
Stainforth & Keadby Canal
Burghwallis
New Junction Canal
Shafton
Brierley
South Elmsall
Owston
Thorpe in Balne
DONCASTER NORTH
Eaton
B6422
Skellow
Carcroft
A18
A628
South Kirkby
Hampole
B1220
A19
Hatfield
Hatfield Chase
Upper Cudworth
Grimethorpe
Hooton Pagnell
ADWICK LE STREET
Barnby Dun
Dunscroft
M180
Cudworth
Clayton
A1(M)
Toll Bar
Almholme
Kirk Sandall
Dunsville
Hatfield Woodhouse
Sandtoft
Trolleybus
Grey Green
Monk Bretton Priory
A6195
Great Houghton
Woodlands
New Village
Hatfield Moors
Westgate
Ardsley
A635
Little Houghton
B6411
Thurnscoe
Brodsworth
Brodsworth Hall
Rostholme
Arksey
Edenthorpe
West Carr
Belton
Middlecliffe
B6273
DEARNE
Marr
A638
BENTLEY
A630
Carrhouse
ISLE OF AXHOLME
Church Town
Darfield
Billingley
Hickleton
A635
Scawsby
A630
Armthorpe
Wheatley Park
Wheatley
Cusworth
Hall
A18
Nutwell
M18
Goldthorpe
Barnburgh
Epworth
Wroot
Epworth Turbary
A161
Old Rectory
WOMBWELL
Broomhill
Bolton upon Dearne
Adwick upon Dearne
DONCASTER
Doncaster
Cantley
A6195
Harlington
Hyde Park
Bessacarr
Branton
Low Burnham
High Melton
Sprotbrough
MEXBOROUGH
Balby
B1396
Jump
Hemingfield
Brampton
Cadeby
Warmsworth
A6182
Auckley
Blaxton
Westwoodside
Upperthorpe
Elsecar
B6097
WATH UPON DEARNE
A6023
Denaby Main
86
B6376
New Edlington
Old Edlington
A60
Finningley
B1396
87
Haxey
East Lound
Wentworth
CONISBROUGH
A630
Loversall
Rossington
ROBIN HOOD DONCASTER SHEFFIELD
Graiselound
SWINTON
Wentworth Woodhouse
Upper Haugh
B6090
Kilnhurst
Hooton Roberts
New Rossington
A614
R. Idle
Thorpe Hesley
Mausoleum
Nether Haugh
RAWMARSH
Clifton
Wadworth
Heckdyke
Thorpe Common
A633
Thrybergh
Ravenfield
B6094
B6463
Misson
West Stockwith
Greasbrough
Ravenfield Common
Micklebring
Braithwell
A1(M)
A638
Austerfield
A629
A6123
Dalton
Sunnyside
Stainton
Tickhill
Newington
East Stockwith
ROTHERHAM
Dalton Magna
Bramley
MALTBY
B6427
Castle
Bawtry
B1403
Walkerith
MAGNA
A631
A6123
Wickersley
Hooton Levitt
A631
Bircotes
Everton
Gringley on the Hill
Chesterfield Canal
Walkeringham
Tinsley
Moorgate
Whiston
M18
Styrrup
Harworth
Scaftworth
A631
Beckingham
Brinsworth
B6410
Slade Hooton
A614
Scrooby
Wiseton
Mattersey Priory
Canklow
Catcliffe
E
Morthen
Thurcroft
86
F
Roche Abbey (remains of)
A634
Serlby
G
Mattersey Thorpe
H
87
Upper Whiston
Brookhouse
Firbeck
B6463
Oldcotes
BLYTH
Mattersey
Clayworth
Darnall
Treeton
Laughton en le Morthen
Ranskill
B6045
A630
B6067
Brampton en le Morthen
A1
Saundby
Ulley
Letwell
Handsworth
Aughton
Laughton Common
B6463
Dinnington
Blyth
Torworth
A60
Hodsock Priory
A634
A638
Lound
B1403
North Wheatley
A620
Bole

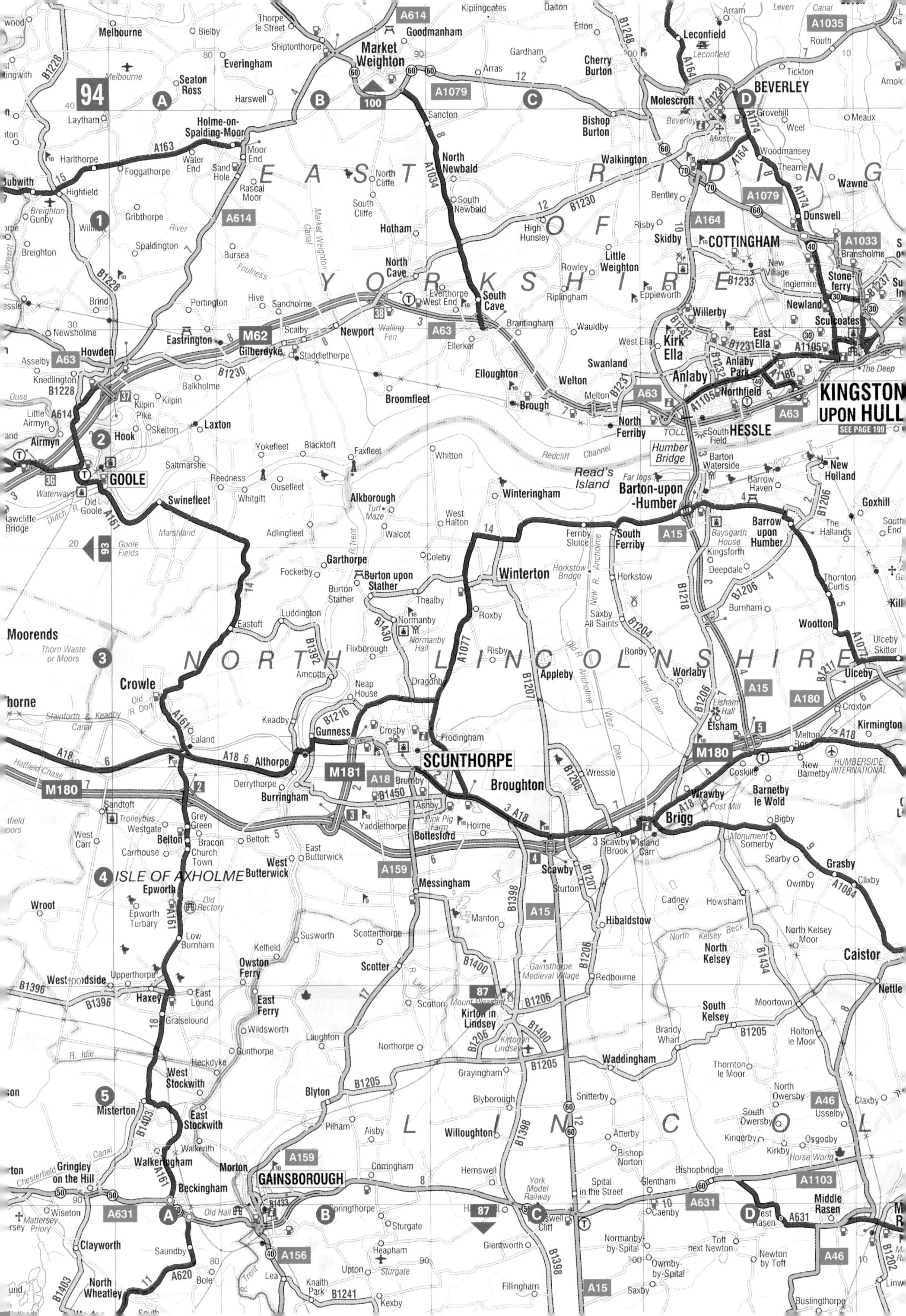

Melbourne
Bielby
Thorpe le Street
A614
Goodmanham
Kiplingcotes
Dalton
Etton
B1248
Arram
Leven
Canal
Leconfield
A1035
Routh
94
Seaton Ross
Everingham
Shiptonthorpe
Market Weighton
Gardham
Cherry Burton
Tickton
Beverley
Arnold
Harswell
A
B
C
D
100
A1079
Arras
Sancton
Molescroft
Grovehill
Weel
Meaux
Laytham
Holme-on-Spalding-Moor
Bishop Burton
Minster
Woodmansey
Harlthorpe
A163
Foggathorpe
Water End
Moor End
Sand Hole
Rascal Moor
North Cliffe
North Newbald
A1034
Walkington
Thearne
Bubwith
Highfield
Breighton
Gunby
EAST RIDING OF YORKSHIRE
South Newbald
B1230
Bentley
A164
A1174
Wawne
1
Willitoft
Gribthorpe
River
A614
South Cliffe
Hotham
High Hunsley
Risby
Skidby
COTTINGHAM
Dunswell
A1033
Breighton
Spaldington
Bursea
Foulness
Market Weighton Canal
North Cave
Little Weighton
Rowley
Riplingham
Eppleworth
New Village
Bransholme
Inglemire
Stoneferry
B1233
Brind
B1228
Hive
Portington
Sandholme
Everthorpe
West End
South Cave
Willerby
Newland
Sculcoates
Newsholme
Eastrington
M62
Scalby
Newport
Walling Fen
A63
Brantingham
Wauldby
Kirk Ella
East Ella
A1105
Asselby
Howden
Gilberdyke
Staddlethorpe
Ellerker
West Ella
B1231
Anlaby Park
The Deep
Knedlington
B1228
B1230
Balkholme
Broomfleet
Elloughton
Swanland
Welton
Anlaby
Northfield
A1166
KINGSTON UPON HULL
SEE PAGE 199
Ouse
Little Airmyn
A614
Kilpin Pike
Kilpin
Brough
Melton
North Ferriby
HESSLE
South Field
Airmyn
2
Hook
Skelton
Laxton
Yokefleet
Blacktoft
Faxfleet
Whitton
Redcliff
Channel
Humber Bridge
Barton Waterside
New Holland
Saltmarshe
Reedness
Read's Island
Far Ings
Barton-upon-Humber
Barrow Haven
GOOLE
Waterways
Old Goole
Whitgift
Ousefleet
Alkborough
Turf Maze
Winteringham
Goxhill
Rawcliffe Bridge
Dutch R.
A161
Swinefleet
Marshland
West Halton
Walcot
Ferriby Sluice
South Ferriby
A15
Barrow upon Humber
The Hallands
South End
93
Goole Fields
Adlingfleet
Baysgarth House
Kingsforth
Garthorpe
Coleby
Winterton
Horkstow Bridge
Horkstow
Deepdale
Thornton Curtis
Fockerby
Burton upon Stather
Burton Stather
Thealby
Normanby
Normanby Hall
Roxby
Saxby All Saints
B1206
Burnham
Luddington
Eastoft
B1430
B1204
B1218
Wootton
Moorends
Thorn Waste or Moors
3
NORTH LINCOLNSHIRE
Flixborough
Risby
Bonby
Ulceby Skitter
Crowle
Old R. Don
B1392
Amcotts
A1077
Appleby
B1207
Worlaby
Ulceby
Neap House
Dragonby
Elsham
Elsham Hall
A180
Croxton
Thorne
Stainforth & Keadby Canal
Keadby
B1216
Gunness
Crosby
Frodingham
Kirmington
A161
Ealand
A18
Melton Ross
HUMBERSIDE INTERNATIONAL
Hatfield Chase
Althorpe
SCUNTHORPE
M180
Wressle
New Barnetby
M181
Brumby
Broughton
B1208
Coskills
Barnetby le Wold
Derrythorpe
Burringham
B1450
Ashby
Wrawby
Post Mill
Sandtoft
Trolleybus
Grey Green
Westgate
Yaddlethorpe
Pink Pig Farm
Holme
Brigg
Bigby
West Carr
Belton
Bracon
Church Town
Beltoft
Bottesford
Scawby Brook
Island Carr
Monument
Somerby
Carrhouse
East Butterwick
West Butterwick
A159
Scawby
B1207
Searby
Grasby
4
ISLE OF AXHOLME
Messingham
Sturton
Clixby
Epworth
Old Rectory
Cadney
Howsham
Owmby
A1084
Wroot
Epworth Turbary
Manton
B1398
Hibaldstow
North Kelsey Moor
Low Burnham
Susworth
Scotterthorpe
North Kelsey
Kelsey Beck
Caistor
Kelfield
Owston Ferry
Scotter
B1400
Gainsthorpe Medieval Village
Redbourne
B1434
West Woodside
Upperthorpe
Nettle
B1396
Haxey
East Lound
East Ferry
87
Scotton
Kirton in Lindsey
B1206
South Kelsey
Moortown
Graiselound
Wildsworth
B1400
Brandy Wharf
B1205
Holton le Moor
Laughton
Northorpe
R. Idle
Heckdyke
Gunthorpe
Kirton in Lindsey
Waddingham
Thornton le Moor
West Stockwith
Grayingham
B1205
5
Misterton
Blyton
B1205
Snitterby
North Owersby
A46
Claxby
East Stockwith
Blyborough
Usselby
South Owersby
B1403
Pilham
Aisby
Willoughton
Atterby
Kingerby
Osgodby
Walkerith
Kirkby
Horse World
Canal
Gringley on the Hill
Walkeringham
Morton
Corringham
Hemswell
Bishop Norton
Bishopbridge
A1103
Chesterfield
Beckingham
GAINSBOROUGH
York Model Railway
Spital in the Street
Glentham
Middle Rasen
A631
Wiseton
Old Hall
B1433
Springthorpe
Hemswell Cliff
Caenby
West Rasen
Mattersey Priory
Sturgate
Normanby-by-Spital
Toft next Newton
Clayworth
Saundby
Heapham
Glentworth
Owmby-by-Spital
Newton by Toft
A156
A620
Upton
Sturgate
Bole
Lea
Fillingham
Saxby
North Wheatley
Knaith Park
B1241
Kexby
Buslingthorpe
B1202
Linwood

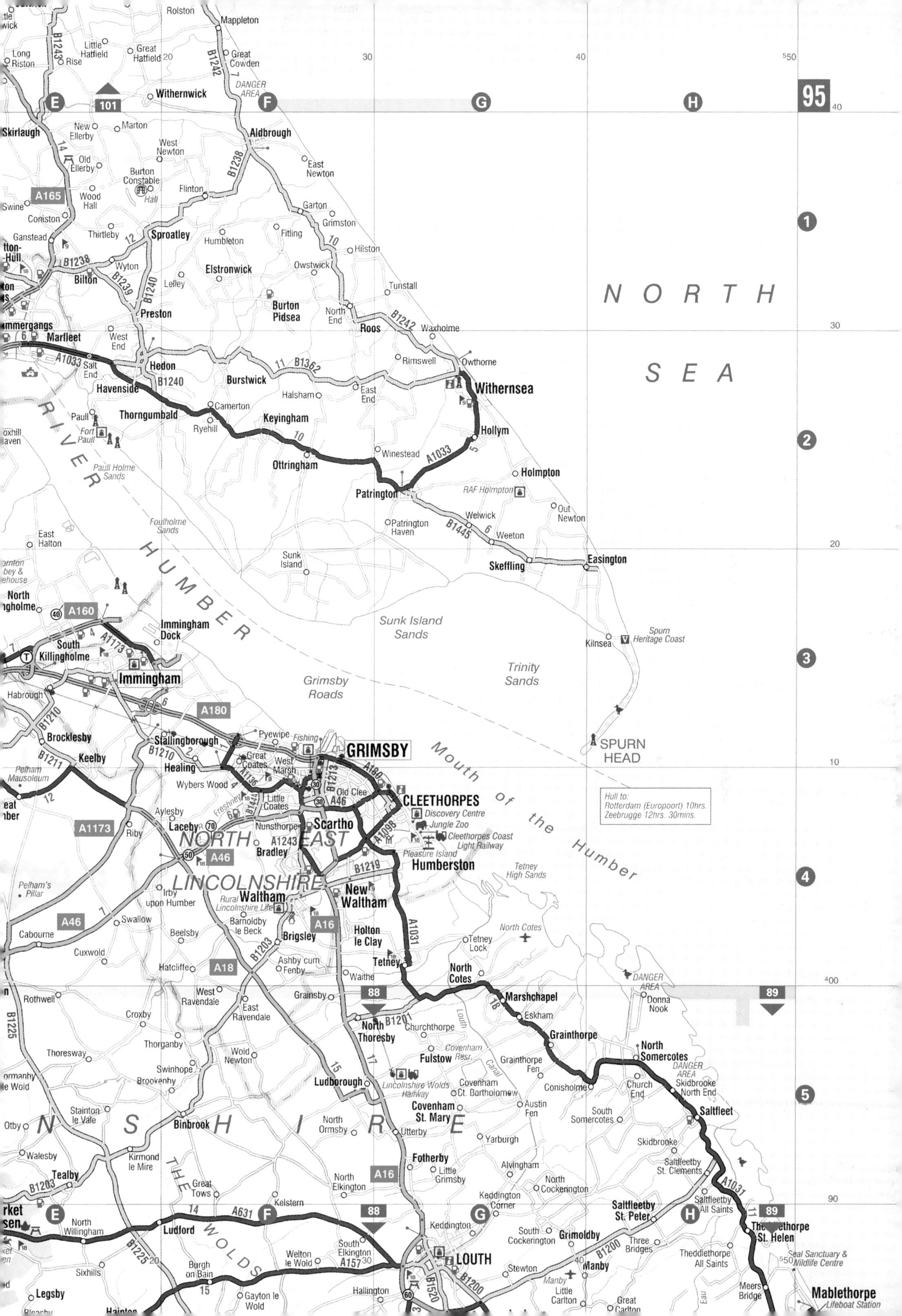
95
Rolston
Mappleton
Long Riston
Little Hatfield
Rise
Great Hatfield
Great Cowden
DANGER AREA
Withernwick
101
Skirlaugh
New Ellerby
Marton
Aldbrough
West Newton
Old Ellerby
Burton Constable
Hall
East Newton
Flinton
A165
Wood Hall
Swine
Coniston
Garton
Grimston
Ganstead
Thirtleby
Sproatley
Humbleton
Fitling
Hilston
Wyton
Elstronwick
Owstwick
Bilton
Lelley
Tunstall
Burton Pidsea
North End
Roos
Waxholme
Preston
West End
Marfleet
NORTH
SEA
Salt End
Hedon
Rimswell
Owthorne
Burstwick
Withernsea
Havenside
Halsham
East End
Thorngumbald
Camerton
Paull
Fort Paull
Ryehill
Keyingham
Hollym
RIVER
Winestead
Paull Holme Sands
Ottringham
Holmpton
Patrington
RAF Holmpton
Out Newton
Foulholme Sands
Welwick
Patrington Haven
Weeton
East Halton
HUMBER
Sunk Island
Skeffling
Easington
North Killingholme
A160
Sunk Island Sands
Immingham Dock
Kilnsea
Spurn Heritage Coast
South Killingholme
Trinity Sands
Immingham
Grimsby Roads
Habrough
A180
SPURN HEAD
Brocklesby
Pyewipe
Fishing
Stallingborough
GRIMSBY
Keelby
Great Coates
West Marsh
Healing
Mouth of the Humber
Pelham Mausoleum
Wybers Wood
Old Clee
Little Coates
CLEETHORPES
Hull to:
Rotterdam (Europoort) 10hrs.
Zeebrugge 12hrs. 30mins.
Aylesby
Discovery Centre
Jungle Zoo
Laceby
Nunsthorpe
Scartho
Cleethorpes Coast Light Railway
A1173
Riby
NORTH EAST
Bradley
A46
Pleasure Island
Humberston
Tetney High Sands
Pelham's Pillar
LINCOLNSHIRE
New Waltham
Irby upon Humber
Rural Lincolnshire Life
Waltham
Swallow
Barnoldby le Beck
A16
Cabourne
Beelsby
Brigsley
Holton le Clay
North Cotes
Tetney Lock
Cuxwold
Ashby cum Fenby
Tetney
Hatcliffe
A18
North Cotes
Waithe
DANGER AREA
Rothwell
West Ravendale
Grainsby
88
89
Marshchapel
East Ravendale
Donna Nook
Croxby
North Thoresby
Churchthorpe
Eskham
Thorganby
Covenham Resr.
Grainthorpe
Thoresway
Wold Newton
Fulstow
Grainthorpe Fen
North Somercotes
Swinhope
DANGER AREA
Brookenby
Ludborough
Lincolnshire Wolds Railway
Covenham St. Bartholomew
Conisholme
Church End
Skidbrooke North End
Stainton le Vale
Covenham St. Mary
Austin Fen
South Somercotes
Saltfleet
Binbrook
North Ormsby
Utterby
Otby
Yarburgh
Skidbrooke
Walesby
Kirmond le Mire
Fotherby
Little Grimsby
Alvingham
Saltfleetby St. Clements
Tealby
Great Tows
North Elkington
Keddington Corner
North Cockerington
Saltfleetby St. Peter
Saltfleetby All Saints
Kelstern
North Willingham
Ludford
A631
Keddington
South Cockerington
Grimoldby
Three Bridges
Theddlethorpe St. Helen
South Elkington
LOUTH
Theddlethorpe All Saints
Seal Sanctuary & Wildlife Centre
Sixhills
Burgh on Bain
Welton le Wold
Stewton
Manby
THE WOLDS
Legsby
Gayton le Wold
Hallington
Little Carlton
Great Carlton
Meers Bridge
Mablethorpe
Lifeboat Station

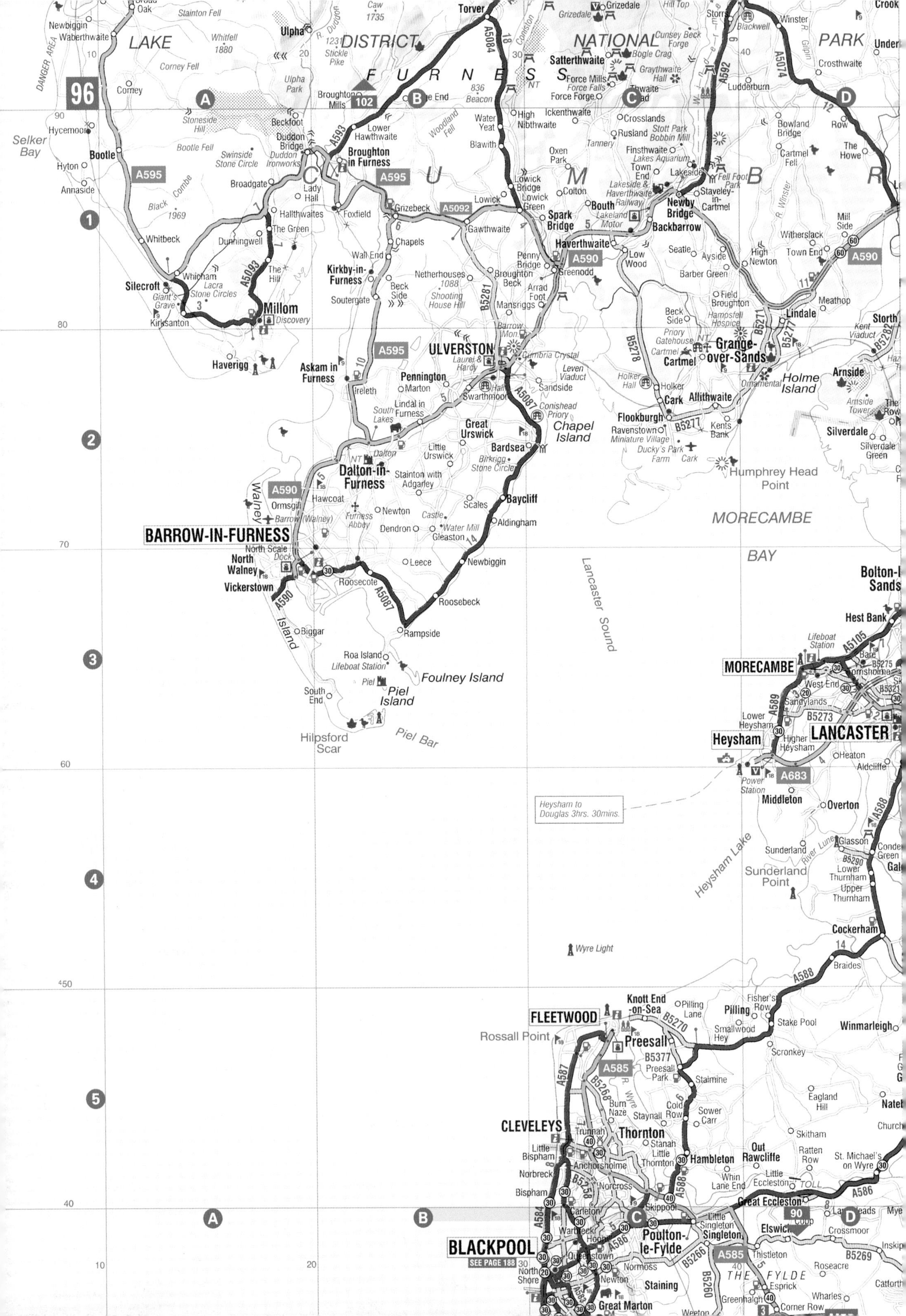

96
LAKE
DISTRICT
NATIONAL
PARK
FURNESS
CUMBRIA
Ulpha
Torver
Grizedale
Hill Top
Storrs
Blackwell
Winster
Crook
Newbiggin
Waberthwaite
Corney
Bootle
Hycemoor
Selker Bay
Hyton
Annaside
Broughton in Furness
Broughton Mills
Duddon Bridge
Beckfoot
Lower Hawthwaite
Broadgate
Lady Hall
Foxfield
Hallthwaites
The Green
Dunningwell
The Hill
Whicham
Whitbeck
Silecroft
Kirksanton
Millom
Haverigg
Askam in Furness
Ireleth
Kirkby-in-Furness
Grizebeck
Chapels
Wall End
Soutergate
Beck Side
Gawthwaite
Lowick
Lowick Bridge
Lowick Green
Spark Bridge
Bouth
Colton
Oxen Park
Rusland
Crosslands
Satterthwaite
Force Mills
Force Forge
Thwaite Head
Ickenthwaite
High Nibthwaite
Water Yeat
Blawith
Finsthwaite
Lakeside
Newby Bridge
Backbarrow
Haverthwaite
Low Wood
Greenodd
Penny Bridge
Arrad Foot
Mansriggs
Broughton Beck
Netherhouses
ULVERSTON
Pennington
Marton
Lindal in Furness
Swarthmoor
Sandside
Great Urswick
Little Urswick
Bardsea
Dalton-in-Furness
Stainton with Adgarley
Hawcoat
Ormsgill
Newton
Dendron
Scales
Baycliff
Aldingham
Gleaston
Leece
Newbiggin
Roosebeck
Rampside
Roosecote
BARROW-IN-FURNESS
North Scale
North Walney
Vickerstown
Walney Island
Biggar
Roa Island
Foulney Island
Piel Island
South End
Hilpsford Scar
Piel Bar
Chapel Island
Leven Viaduct
Conishead Priory
Holker
Cark
Flookburgh
Allithwaite
Cartmel
Grange-over-Sands
Kents Bank
Humphrey Head Point
Field Broughton
Beck Side
Seatle
Ayside
Barber Green
High Newton
Lindale
Meathop
Witherslack
Town End
Mill Side
Staveley-in-Cartmel
Bowland Bridge
Cartmel Fell
Row
The Howe
Crosthwaite
Ludderburn
Storth
Arnside
Silverdale
Silverdale Green
Holme Island
MORECAMBE BAY
Lancaster Sound
Bolton-le-Sands
Hest Bank
MORECAMBE
West End
Torrisholme
Bare
Sandylands
LANCASTER
Heysham
Lower Heysham
Higher Heysham
Heaton
Aldcliffe
Middleton
Overton
Heysham to Douglas 3hrs. 30mins.
Heysham Lake
Sunderland
Sunderland Point
Glasson
Lower Thurnham
Upper Thurnham
Cockerham
Braides
Wyre Light
FLEETWOOD
Knott End-on-Sea
Pilling Lane
Pilling
Fisher's Row
Stake Pool
Smallwood Hey
Winmarleigh
Scronkey
Rossall Point
Preesall
Preesall Park
Stalmine
Eagland Hill
Burn Naze
Staynall
Cold Row
Sower Carr
CLEVELEYS
Thornton
Stanah
Little Thornton
Hambleton
Out Rawcliffe
Ratten Row
Skitham
St. Michael's on Wyre
Little Bispham
Anchorsholme
Norbreck
Norcross
Bispham
Whin Lane End
Little Eccleston
Great Eccleston
Carleton
Skippool
Poulton-le-Fylde
Little Singleton
Singleton
Elswick
Crossmoor
BLACKPOOL
SEE PAGE 188
North Shore
Normoss
Newton
Staining
Great Marton
Thistleton
Roseacre
Esprick
Greenhalgh
Corner Row
THE FYLDE
A595
A5092
A590
A593
A5084
A592
A5074
A5281
A5087
A589
A5105
A683
A588
A585
A587
A586
A584
B5277
B5278
B5271
B5282
B5273
B5290
B5270
B5377
B5268
B5266
B5269
90
102

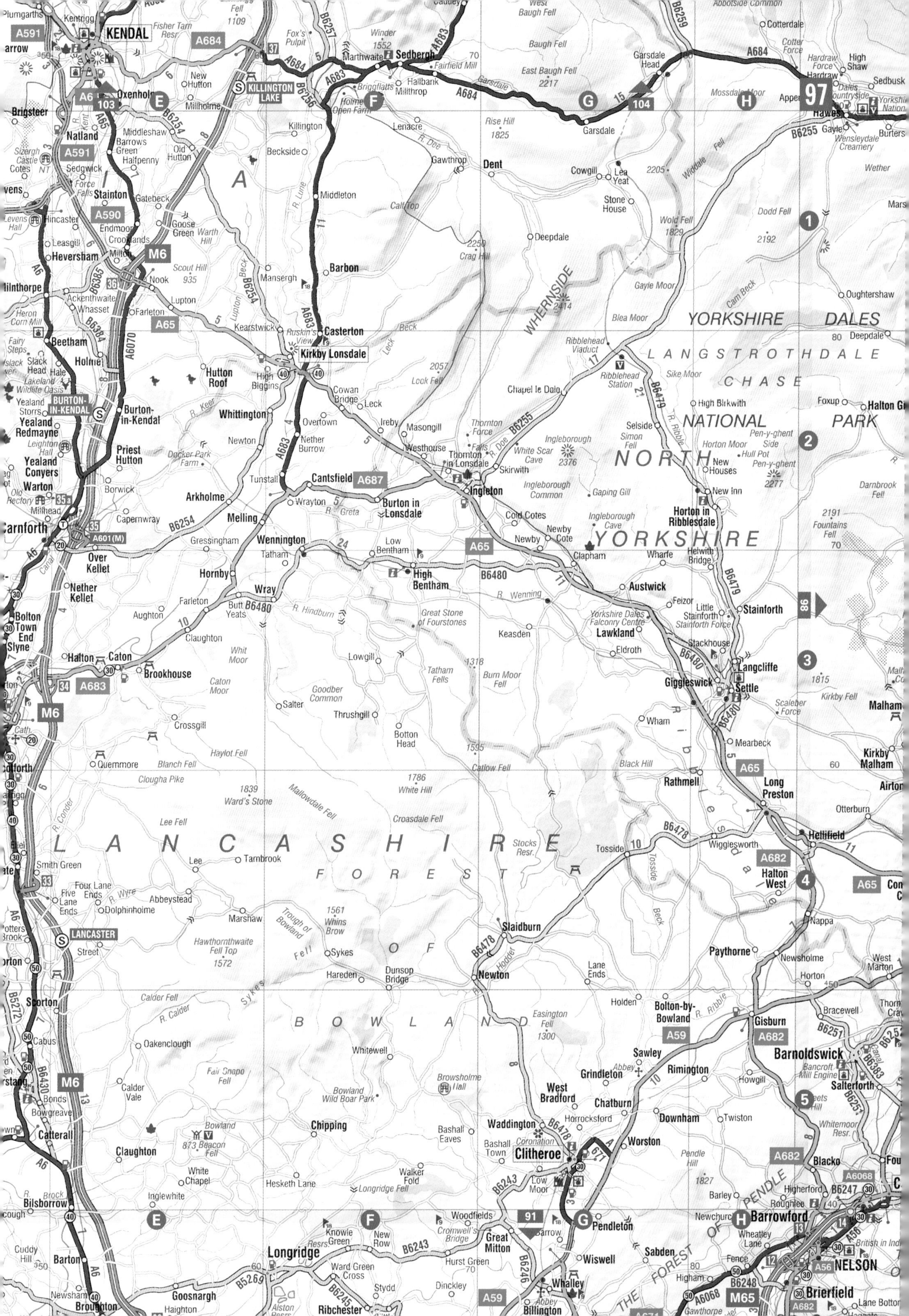

KENDAL
A591
A684
A6
103
Oxenholme
Fisher Tarn Resr
37
KILLINGTON LAKE
New Hutton
Millholme
Brigsteer
Natland
Sizergh Castle
Sedgwick
Stainton
A590
Levens Hall
Hincaster
Heversham
Endmoor
Crooklands
Milton
M6
36
Nook
Milnthorpe
Ackenthwaite
Whasset
Heron Corn Mill
B6385
B6384
A6070
Farleton
Lupton
A65
Beetham
Fairy Steps
Slack Head
Hale
Holme
Lakeland Wildlife Oasis
Yealand Storrs
BURTON-IN-KENDAL
Burton-in-Kendal
Yealand Redmayne
Leighton Hall
Yealand Conyers
Priest Hutton
Warton
Borwick
35a
Millhead
Capernwray
Carnforth
35
A601(M)
Over Kellet
Nether Kellet
Bolton Town End
Slyne
Halton
Caton
Brookhouse
34
A683
Aughton
Claughton
Quernmore
Crossgill
Clougha Pike
Blanch Fell
Haylot Fell
Lee Fell
Ward's Stone
1839
L A N C A S H I R E
F O R E S T
O F
B O W L A N D
Smith Green
Four Lane Ends
Five Lane Ends
Abbeystead
Dolphinholme
Lee
Tarnbrook
Marshaw
Trough of Bowland
LANCASTER
Street
Hawthornthwaite Fell Top 1572
Scorton
Cabus
Calder Fell
R. Calder
Oakenclough
Calder Vale
Bonds
Bowgreave
Garstang
B6430
Catterall
Claughton
Bowland Beacon Fell
White Chapel
Inglewhite
E
Bilsborrow
Barton
Cuddy Hill
Newsham
Broughton
Goosnargh
Haighton
Longridge
B5269
Knowle Green
New Row
F
Ward Green Cross
Stydd
Ribchester
B6245
B6243
Woodfields
Cromwell's Bridge
Hurst Green
Dinckley
Great Mitton
91
Barrow
Whalley
Billington
A59
G
Pendleton
Wiswell
Sabden
Newchurch
H
Barrowford
Wheatley Lane
Fence
Higham
M65
NELSON
Brierfield
A56
A6068
B6248
Gawthorpe
Lane Bottom
THE FOREST OF PENDLE
Roughlee
Higherford
B6247
Barley
Blacko
A682
A6068
1827
Pendle Hill
Worston
Clitheroe
Low Moor
Coronation
Bashall Town
Bashall Eaves
Waddington
B6478
West Bradford
Grindleton
Chatburn
Horrocksford
Downham
Twiston
Rimington
Sawley
Abbey
Browsholme Hall
Chipping
Bowland Wild Boar Park
Whitewell
Walker Fold
Hesketh Lane
Longridge Fell
Fair Snape Fell
Dunsop Bridge
Hareden
Sykes
Whins Brow 1561
Newton
Slaidburn
Easington Fell 1300
Holden
Bolton-by-Bowland
Lane Ends
A59
Gisburn
A682
Barnoldswick
Bancroft Mill Engine
Salterforth
B6251
B6383
Howgill
Weets Hill
Whitemoor Resr.
5
Bracewell
West Marton
Horton
Newsholme
Paythorne
Nappa
Halton West
4
A65
A682
Hellifield
Otterburn
Wigglesworth
Tosside
B6478
Stocks Resr.
Croasdale Fell
White Hill 1786
Mallowdale Fell
Catlow Fell
1595
Black Hill
Rathmell
Long Preston
Airton
Kirkby Malham
Mearbeck
Wham
Giggleswick
Settle
B6480
Scaleber Force
Kirkby Fell
Malham
1815
3
Langcliffe
Stackhouse
Stainforth
Little Stainforth
Stainforth Force
Feizor
Yorkshire Dales Falconry Centre
Lawkland
Eldroth
Austwick
Keasden
R. Wenning
Clapham
Newby Cote
Newby
Wharfe
Helwith Bridge
B6479
86
YORKSHIRE
NORTH
NATIONAL
PARK
YORKSHIRE DALES
Horton in Ribblesdale
New Inn
New Houses
Horton Moor
Hull Pot
Pen-y-ghent Side
Pen-y-ghent 2277
2
Darnbrook Fell
Fountains Fell 2191
Gaping Gill
Ingleborough Cave
Ingleborough Common
Ingleborough 2376
White Scar Cave
Selside
Simon Fell
High Birkwith
Foxup
Halton Gill
L A N G S T R O T H D A L E
C H A S E
Sike Moor
Ribblehead Station
Ribblehead Viaduct
Blea Moor
Chapel le Dale
B6255
Thornton Force
Thornton in Lonsdale
Skirwith
Ingleton
Cold Cotes
A65
High Bentham
B6480
Low Bentham
Burton in Lonsdale
Wrayton
Cantsfield
A687
Tunstall
Westhouse
Masongill
Ireby
Nether Burrow
Overtown
Leck
Cowan Bridge
Lock Fell 2057
Kirkby Lonsdale
Casterton
Ruskin's View
High Biggins
Hutton Roof
Whittington
Newton
Docker Park Farm
Arkholme
Melling
Gressingham
B6254
Hornby
Wennington
Tatham
Wray
Butt Yeats
Farleton
R. Hindburn
Great Stone of Fourstones
Lowgill
Tatham Fells
Burn Moor Fell
1318
Goodber Common
Salter
Thrushgill
Botton Head
Whit Moor
Caton Moor
Kearstwick
Mansergh
Barbon
Scout Hill 935
Goose Green
Warth Hill
Gatebeck
Old Hutton
Middleshaw
Barrows Green
Halfpenny
B6254
Beckside
Killington
Middleton
A683
B6256
B6257
Fox's Pulpit
Winder 1552
Marthwaite
Sedbergh
Briggflatts
Holme Open Farm
Hallbank
Millthrop
Fairfield Mill
A684
Lenacre
R. Dee
Gawthrop
Dent
Calf Top
Crag Hill 2250
Deepdale
WHERNSIDE 2414
Rise Hill 1825
East Baugh Fell 2217
Baugh Fell
West Baugh Fell
Garsdale
Garsdale Head
104
Cowgill
Lea Yeat
Stone House
Wold Fell 1829
Gayle Moor
Cam Beck
Dodd Fell
2192
1
Oughtershaw
Deepdale
Widdale Fell
2205
Mossdale Moor
Hawes
Gayle
Wensleydale Creamery
Burtens
Wether
B6255
97
Hardraw
Hardraw Force
High Shaw
Sedbusk
Dales Countryside
Cotter Force
Cotterdale
Abbotside Common
B6259

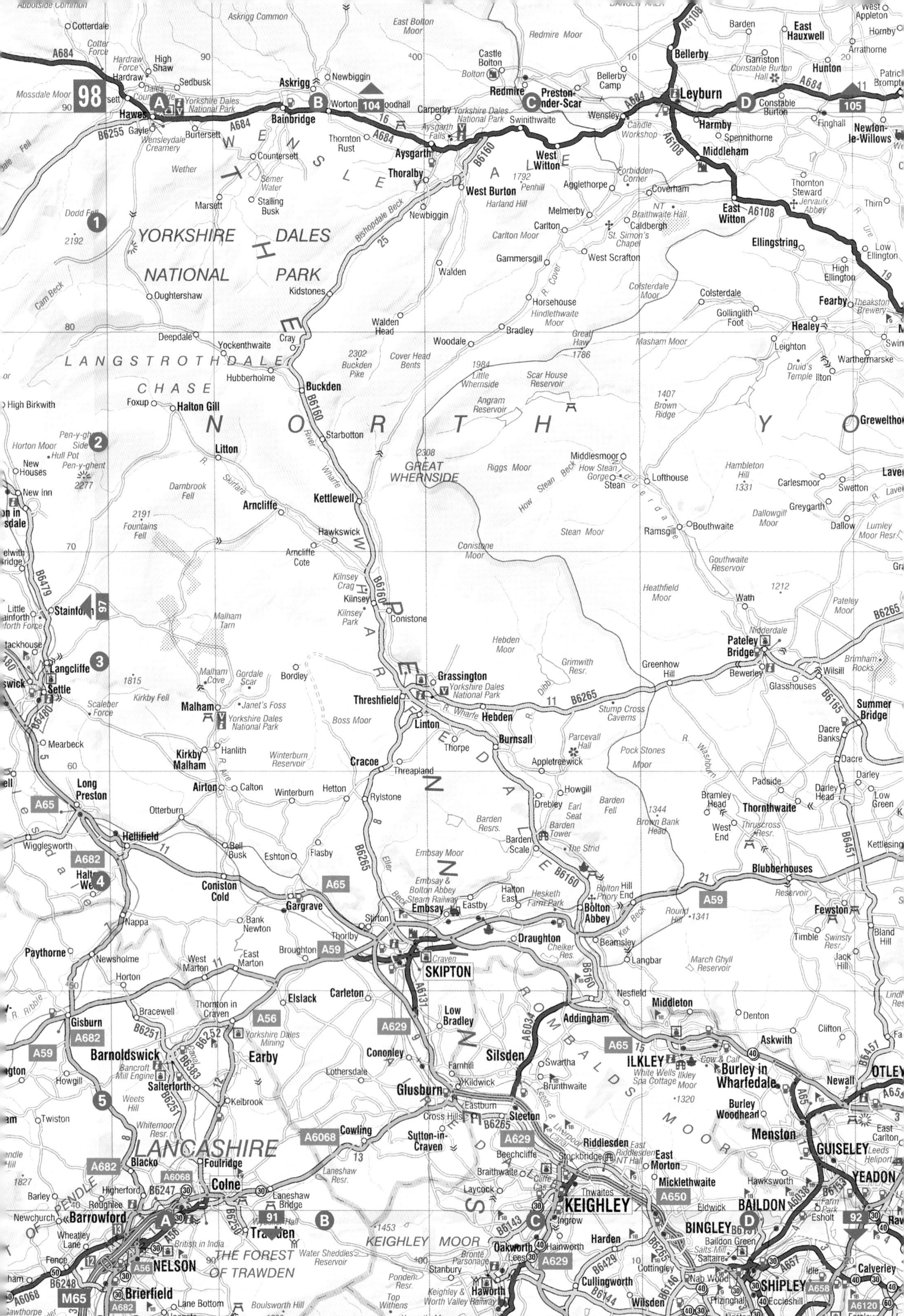
98
104
105
97
91
92
A
B
C
D
1
2
3
4
5
Cotterdale
Askrigg Common
East Bolton Moor
Redmire Moor
Barden
East Hauxwell
West Appleton
Hornby
Arrathorne
Cotter Force
A684
Hardraw Force
Hardraw
High Shaw
Sedbusk
Askrigg
Newbiggin
Castle Bolton
Bolton
Bellerby
Bellerby Camp
Garriston
Constable Burton Hall
Hunton
Patrick Brompton
Mossdale Moor
Hawes
Yorkshire Dales National Park
Bainbridge
Worton
Carperby
Redmire
Preston-under-Scar
Leyburn
Constable Burton
Wensley
Finghall
Newton-le-Willows
Gayle
B6255
Burtersett
Wensleydale Creamery
Aysgarth Falls
Swinithwaite
Candle Workshop
Harmby
Spennithorne
Thornton Rust
Aysgarth
A6108
Middleham
Countersett
Thoralby
West Witton
Wether
Semer Water
Stalling Busk
Marsett
West Burton
Penhill
Agglethorpe
Forbidden Corner
Coverham
East Witton
Thornton Steward
Jervaulx Abbey
Thirn
Dodd Fell
Bishopdale Beck
Newbiggin
Harland Hill
Melmerby
NT
Braithwaite Hall
Carlton
Caldbergh
YORKSHIRE DALES
NATIONAL PARK
Carlton Moor
St. Simon's Chapel
Ellingstring
Low Ellington
High Ellington
Gammersgill
West Scrafton
Walden
R. Cover
Cam Beck
Oughtershaw
Kidstones
Colsterdale Moor
Horsehouse
Colsterdale
Hindlethwaite Moor
Fearby
Theakston Brewery
Gollinglith Foot
Healey
Walden Head
Bradley
Deepdale
Yockenthwaite
Cray
Woodale
Great Haw
Masham Moor
Leighton
LANGSTROTHDALE
CHASE
Buckden Pike
Cover Head Bents
Little Whernside
Scar House Reservoir
Druid's Temple
Ilton
Warthermarske
Hubberholme
Buckden
Angram Reservoir
Brown Ridge
High Birkwith
Foxup
Halton Gill
B6160
Pen-y-ghent Side
Horton Moor
Hull Pot
Pen-y-ghent
New Houses
New Inn
Starbotton
River Wharfe
N O R T H   Y O
Grewelthorpe
Litton
GREAT WHERNSIDE
Riggs Moor
Middlesmoor
How Stean Gorge
Stean
Lofthouse
Hambleton Hill
Carlesmoor
Swetton
Darnbrook Fell
R. Skirfare
Kettlewell
Arncliffe
How Stean Beck
Greygarth
Dallowgill Moor
Dallow
Lumley Moor Resr.
Fountains Fell
Hawkswick
Stean Moor
Ramsgill
Bouthwaite
Arncliffe Cote
Conistone Moor
Gouthwaite Reservoir
B6479
Kilnsey Crag
Kilnsey
Kilnsey Park
Conistone
Heathfield Moor
Wath
Pateley Moor
B6265
Stainforth
Little Stainforth
Stainforth Force
Malham Tarn
Hebden Moor
Nidderdale
Pateley Bridge
Brimham Rocks
Langcliffe
Malham Cove
Gordale Scar
Bordley
Grimwith Resr.
Greenhow Hill
Bewerley
Wilsill
Glasshouses
Settle
Kirkby Fell
Janet's Foss
Grassington
Threshfield
R. Wharfe
Hebden
Stump Cross Caverns
Summer Bridge
B6165
Scaleber Force
Malham
Boss Moor
Linton
Burnsall
Parcevall Hall
Dacre Banks
B6480
Mearbeck
Hanlith
Thorpe
Pock Stones Moor
R. Washburn
Dacre
Kirkby Malham
R. Aire
Winterburn Reservoir
Cracoe
Threapland
Appletreewick
Darley
Long Preston
Airton
Calton
Winterburn
Hetton
Rylstone
Howgill
Padside
Darley Head
Low Green
Drebley
Earl Seat
Barden Fell
Bramley Head
Thornthwaite
A65
Otterburn
Barden Resrs.
Barden Tower
Brown Bank Head
West End
Thruscross Resr.
B6451
Hellifield
Wigglesworth
A682
Bell Busk
Eshton
Flasby
Barden Scale
The Strid
Kettlesing
Embsay Moor
Halton West
Coniston Cold
Gargrave
Embsay & Bolton Abbey Steam Railway
Halton East
Hesketh Farm Park
Bolton Abbey
Bolton Priory
Hill End
Blubberhouses
A59
Reservoir
Fewston
Nappa
Bank Newton
Stirton
Embsay
Eastby
Round Hill
Kex Beck
Thorlby
Draughton
Beamsley
Chelker Res.
Timble
Swinsty Resr.
Bland Hill
Paythorne
Broughton
Craven
SKIPTON
Langbar
Jack Hill
March Ghyll Reservoir
Newsholme
West Marton
East Marton
Horton
A6131
Nesfield
Elslack
Carleton
Low Bradley
Middleton
Denton
R. Ribble
Gisburn
Bracewell
Thornton in Craven
A56
Yorkshire Dales Mining
A629
Addingham
Clifton
A6034
RUMBALDS MOOR
Askwith
Barnoldswick
Bancroft Mill Engine
B6252
B6383
B6251
Earby
Cononley
Silsden
ILKLEY
Cow & Calf
White Wells Spa Cottage
Ilkley Moor
Burley in Wharfedale
OTLEY
Newall
Howgill
Salterforth
Lothersdale
Farnhill
Kildwick
Swartha
Brunthwaite
Glusburn
Kelbrook
Weets Hill
Eastburn
Steeton
Burley Woodhead
Twiston
Whitemoor Resr.
Cross Hills
B6265
Menston
East Carlton
A6068
Cowling
Sutton-in-Craven
Riddlesden
East Riddlesden NT Hall
Stockbridge
GUISELEY
Leeds Bradford Heliport
LANCASHIRE
Blacko
Foulridge
Laneshaw Resr.
Beechcliffe
East Morton
YEADON
Barley
Higherford
B6247
Colne
Laneshaw Bridge
Braithwaite
Micklethwaite
Hawksworth
Roughlee
Laycock
Thwaites
A650
Newchurch
Barrowford
Wycoller Hall
KEIGHLEY
Ingrow
Eldwick
BAILDON
Esholt
Wheatley Lane
Trawden
KEIGHLEY MOOR
B6143
Harden
BINGLEY
Baildon Green
British in India
THE FOREST OF TRAWDEN
Water Sheddles Reservoir
Oakworth
Hainworth
Salts Mill
Saltaire
Fence
NELSON
A56
Brontë Parsonage
Lees
B6429
Cottingley
Idle
Calverley
B6248
Stanbury
Ponden Resr.
Cullingworth
Nab Wood
SHIPLEY
A658
Brierfield
Keighley & Worth Valley Railway
Haworth
Top Withens
Boulsworth Hill
Wilsden
Frizinghall
Eccleshill
M65
Lane Bottom
B6144
B6146
A6120

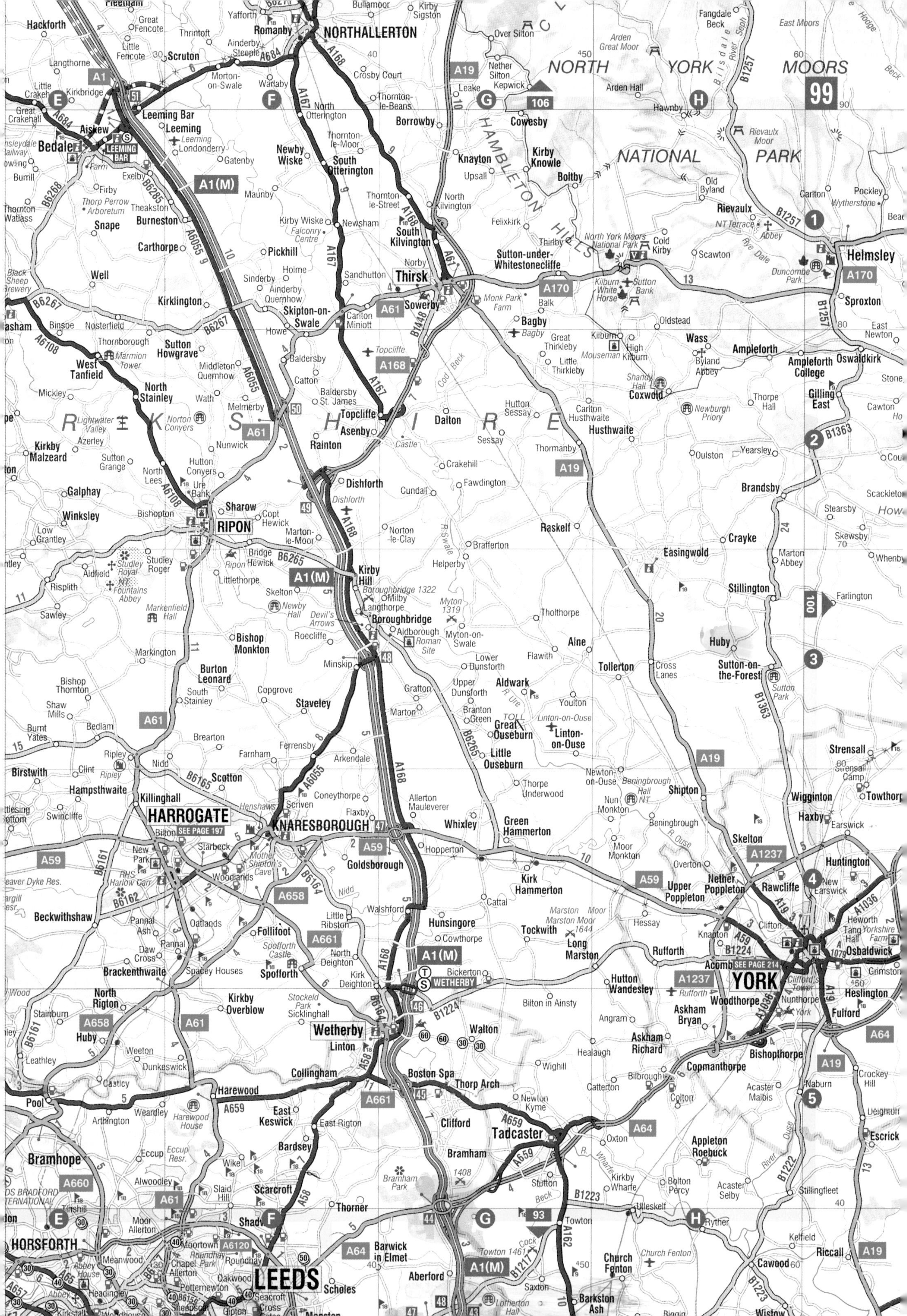

NORTHALLERTON
NORTH YORK MOORS
NATIONAL PARK
HAMBLETON HILLS
99
100
A1
A1(M)
A19
A61
A168
A167
A170
A6055
A6108
A684
A59
A658
A661
A64
A659
A660
A1237
A1036
A162
B1257
B1363
B1448
B6265
B6267
B6268
B6285
B6161
B6162
B6164
B6165
B1224
B1222
B1223
B1217
Hackforth
Great Fencote
Thrintoft
Yafforth
Romanby
Bullamoor
Kirby Sigston
Ainderby Steeple
Scruton
Langthorne
Little Fencote
Morton-on-Swale
Warlaby
Crosby Court
Thornton-le-Beans
North Otterington
Thornton-le-Moor
South Otterington
Newby Wiske
Borrowby
Over Silton
Nether Silton
Kepwick
Leake
Cowesby
Knayton
Kirby Knowle
Upsall
Boltby
Arden Great Moor
Arden Hall
Hawnby
Fangdale Beck
East Moors
Rievaulx Moor
Old Byland
Rievaulx
NT Terrace
Abbey
Carlton
Pockley
Wytherstone
Helmsley
Duncombe Park
Sproxton
Little Crakehall
Kirkbridge
Great Crakehall
Aiskew
Bedale
Leeming Bar
Leeming
Leeming
Londonderry
LEEMING BAR
Gatenby
Exelby
Burrill
Firby
Thorp Perrow Arboretum
Theakston
Thornton Watlass
Snape
Burneston
Carthorpe
Well
Black Sheep Brewery
Kirklington
Maunby
Kirby Wiske
Falconry Centre
Newsham
Pickhill
Holme
Sinderby
Ainderby Quernhow
Thornton-le-Street
North Kilvington
South Kilvington
Norby
Thirsk
Sowerby
Sandhutton
Carlton Miniott
Skipton-on-Swale
Felixkirk
Thirlby
North York Moors National Park
Cold Kirby
Scawton
Sutton-under-Whitestonecliffe
Kilburn White Horse
Sutton Bank
Monk Park Farm
Balk
Bagby
Great Thirkleby
Little Thirkleby
Kilburn
High Kilburn
Mouseman
Oldstead
Wass
Byland Abbey
Ampleforth
Ampleforth College
Oswaldkirk
Shandy Hall
Coxwold
Newburgh Priory
Gilling East
Thorpe Hall
Cawton
Stonegrave
East Newton
Binsoe
Nosterfield
Thornborough
West Tanfield
Marmion Tower
Sutton Howgrave
Middleton Quernhow
Howe
Baldersby
Topcliffe
Catton
Baldersby St. James
North Stainley
Mickley
Wath
Melmerby
Lightwater Valley
Norton Conyers
Azerley
Kirkby Malzeard
Sutton Grange
Nunwick
Hutton Conyers
North Lees
Ure Bank
Asenby
Rainton
Dalton
Castle
Hutton Sessay
Sessay
Carlton Husthwaite
Husthwaite
Thormanby
Oulston
Yearsley
Brandsby
Crakehill
Fawdington
Dishforth
Cundall
Galphay
Winksley
Sharow
Bishopton
Copt Hewick
RIPON
Low Grantley
Marton-le-Moor
Norton-le-Clay
Brafferton
Raskelf
Crayke
Easingwold
Stearsby
Skewsby
Marton Abbey
Whenby
Scackleton
Studley Royal
Studley Roger
NT Fountains Abbey
Aldfield
Risplith
Sawley
Ripon
Bridge Hewick
Littlethorpe
Kirby Hill
Skelton
Newby Hall
Boroughbridge 1322
Milby
Langthorpe
Boroughbridge
Devil's Arrows
Aldborough
Roman Site
Helperby
Myton 1319
Myton-on-Swale
Tholthorpe
Stillington
Farlington
Markenfield Hall
Bishop Monkton
Roecliffe
Markington
Burton Leonard
Minskip
Lower Dunsforth
Flawith
Alne
Tollerton
Cross Lanes
Huby
Sutton-on-the-Forest
Sutton Park
Bishop Thornton
Shaw Mills
South Stainley
Copgrove
Staveley
Grafton
Upper Dunsforth
Aldwark
Youlton
Linton-on-Ouse
Burnt Yates
Bedlam
Marton
Branton Green
Great Ouseburn
Little Ouseburn
Brearton
Ferrensby
Farnham
Arkendale
Ripley
Nidd
Birstwith
Clint
Hampsthwaite
Scotton
Killinghall
HARROGATE
SEE PAGE 197
Bilton
Henshaws
Scriven
Coneythorpe
KNARESBOROUGH
Flaxby
Allerton Mauleverer
Whixley
Green Hammerton
Thorpe Underwood
Newton-on-Ouse
Beningbrough Hall
NT
Nun Monkton
Beningbrough
Shipton
Strensall
Strensall Camp
Towthorpe
Wigginton
Haxby
Earswick
Swincliffe
New Park
Starbeck
Mother Shipton's Cave
Goldsborough
Hopperton
Kirk Hammerton
Moor Monkton
Skelton
Overton
Nether Poppleton
Upper Poppleton
Rawcliffe
Huntington
New Earswick
RHS Harlow Carr
Woodlands
Beaver Dyke Res.
Beckwithshaw
Pannal Ash
Oatlands
Pannal
Follifoot
Little Ribston
Walshford
Cattal
Hunsingore
Cowthorpe
Tockwith
Marston Moor
Marston Moor 1644
Long Marston
Hessay
Knapton
Clifton
Heworth
Tang Hall
Yorkshire Farm
Osbaldwick
Acomb
SEE PAGE 214
YORK
Rufforth
Clifford's Tower
Grimston
Dunnington
Daw Cross
Brackenthwaite
Spacey Houses
Spofforth Castle
Spofforth
North Deighton
Kirk Deighton
Bickerton
WETHERBY
Hutton Wandesley
Askham Bryan
Woodthorpe
Nunthorpe
Heslington
Fulford
North Rigton
Stainburn
Huby
Kirkby Overblow
Stockeld Park
Sicklinghall
Wetherby
Linton
Walton
Bilton in Ainsty
Angram
Askham Richard
Bishopthorpe
Weeton
Leathley
Dunkeswick
Collingham
Boston Spa
Thorp Arch
Healaugh
Wighill
Bilbrough
Copmanthorpe
Catterton
Colton
Acaster Malbis
Naburn
Crockey Hill
Castley
Pool
Harewood
Weardley
Arthington
Harewood House
A659
East Keswick
East Rigton
Clifford
Newton Kyme
Tadcaster
Bramham
Oxton
Appleton Roebuck
Escrick
Bramhope
Eccup
Eccup Resr.
Wike
Bardsey
Alwoodley
Slaid Hill
Bramham Park
Kirkby Wharfe
Bolton Percy
Acaster Selby
Stillingfleet
Stutton
Scarcroft
Thorner
Ulleskelf
Ryther
Kelfield
Riccall
Tinshill
Moor Allerton
Shadwell
Towton
HORSFORTH
Meanwood
Moortown
Roundhay Park
Roundhay
Chapel Allerton
Barwick in Elmet
Towton 1461
Church Fenton
Cawood
Headingley
Potternewton
Oakwood
LEEDS
Scholes
Aberford
Saxton
Barkston Ash
Seacroft
Cross Gates
Gipton
Sheepscar
Kirkstall
Abbey
Lotherton Hall

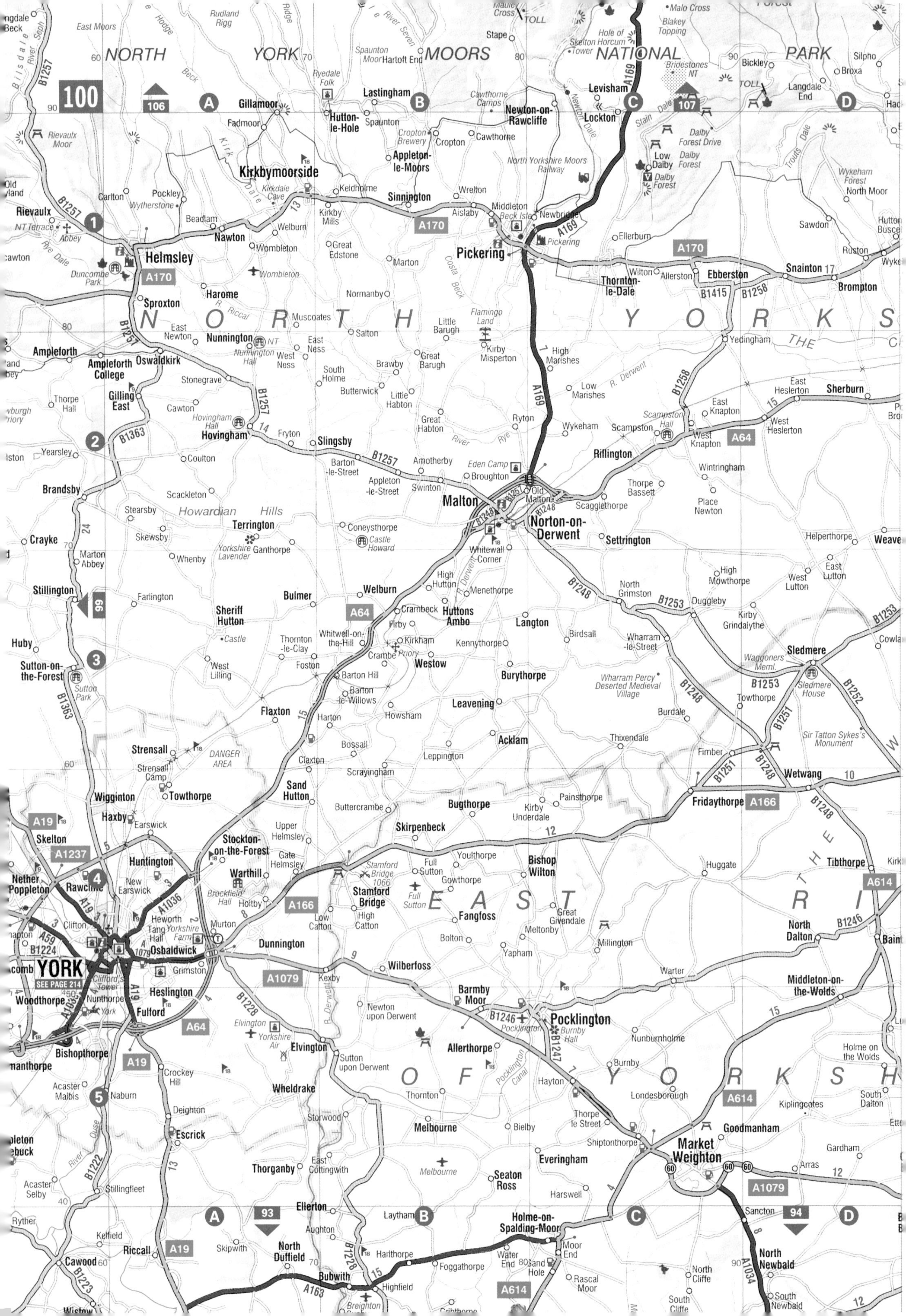
100
106
107
99
93
94
NORTH YORK MOORS NATIONAL PARK
NORTH YORKS
THE
EAST RI
OF YORKSH
Bilsdale
East Moors
Rudland Rigg
Spaunton Moor
Hartoft End
Malo Cross
Blakey Topping
Hole of Horcum
Saltergate
Skelton Tower
Levisham
Lockton
Bridestones NT
Bickley
Broxa
Silpho
Langdale End
Hackness
Stape
Gillamoor
Fadmoor
Lastingham
Ryedale Folk
Hutton-le-Hole
Spaunton
Cropton Brewery
Cropton
Cawthorne Camps
Cawthorne
Newton-on-Rawcliffe
Appleton-le-Moors
North Yorkshire Moors Railway
Low Dalby
Dalby Forest
Dalby Forest Drive
Wykeham Forest
North Moor
Rievaulx Moor
Kirkbymoorside
Kirkdale Cave
Keldholme
Sinnington
Wrelton
Middleton
Beck Isle
Newbridge
Pickering
Aislaby
Kirkby Mills
Carlton
Pockley
Wytherstone
Rievaulx
NT Terrace
Abbey
Beadlam
Nawton
Welburn
Wombleton
Great Edstone
Marton
Ellerburn
Thornton-le-Dale
Wilton
Allerston
Ebberston
Snainton
Brompton
Sawdon
Ruston
Wykeham
Hutton Buscel
Scawton
Helmsley
Duncombe Park
Sproxton
Harome
Normanby
Costa Beck
Muscoates
Salton
Little Barugh
Great Barugh
Flamingo Land
Kirby Misperton
High Marishes
Low Marishes
Yedingham
East Heslerton
Sherburn
East Knapton
Scampston Hall
Scampston
West Knapton
West Heslerton
Rillington
Wintringham
Thorpe Bassett
Place Newton
Scagglethorpe
East Newton
Nunnington
NT Nunnington Hall
East Ness
West Ness
South Holme
Butterwick
Brawby
Little Habton
Great Habton
Ryton
Wykeham
Ampleforth
Ampleforth College
Oswaldkirk
Stonegrave
Gilling East
Thorpe Hall
Newburgh Priory
Cawton
Hovingham Hall
Hovingham
Fryton
Slingsby
Barton-le-Street
Appleton-le-Street
Swinton
Amotherby
Broughton
Eden Camp
Malton
Old Malton
Norton-on-Derwent
Settrington
Yearsley
Coulton
Brandsby
Scackleton
Stearsby
Howardian Hills
Terrington
Skewsby
Yorkshire Lavender
Ganthorpe
Whenby
Coneysthorpe
Castle Howard
Whitewall Corner
Crayke
Marton Abbey
Stillington
Farlington
Sheriff Hutton
Castle
Bulmer
Welburn
High Hutton
Menethorpe
Crambeck
Huttons Ambo
Firby
Kirkham
Kirkham Priory
Crambe
Westow
Langton
Kennythorpe
Birdsall
North Grimston
Duggleby
Kirby Grindalythe
High Mowthorpe
West Lutton
East Lutton
Helperthorpe
Weaverthorpe
Wharram-le-Street
Wharram Percy Deserted Medieval Village
Sledmere
Sledmere House
Waggoners Meml.
Cowlam
Huby
Sutton-on-the-Forest
Sutton Park
West Lilling
Thornton-le-Clay
Whitwell-on-the-Hill
Foston
Barton Hill
Barton-le-Willows
Howsham
Harton
Flaxton
Burythorpe
Leavening
Acklam
Burdale
Thixendale
Towthorpe
Sir Tatton Sykes's Monument
Fimber
Wetwang
Fridaythorpe
Strensall
Strensall Camp
DANGER AREA
Towthorpe
Bossall
Claxton
Scrayingham
Leppington
Sand Hutton
Buttercrambe
Bugthorpe
Kirby Underdale
Painsthorpe
Wigginton
Haxby
Earswick
Skelton
Upper Helmsley
Gate Helmsley
Skirpenbeck
Youlthorpe
Bishop Wilton
Huggate
Tibthorpe
Nether Poppleton
Rawcliffe
Huntington
New Earswick
Stockton-on-the-Forest
Warthill
Brockfield Hall
Holtby
Stamford Bridge 1066
Stamford Bridge
Full Sutton
Gowthorpe
Fangfoss
Great Givendale
Meltonby
Millington
North Dalton
Bainton
Clifton
Heworth
Tang Hall
Yorkshire Farm
Murton
Low Catton
High Catton
Bolton
Yapham
Osbaldwick
Dunnington
Acomb
YORK
SEE PAGE 214
Grimston
Clifford's Tower
Kexby
Wilberfoss
Warter
Middleton-on-the-Wolds
Woodthorpe
Nunthorpe
Heslington
Fulford
Elvington
Yorkshire Air
Newton upon Derwent
Barmby Moor
Pocklington
Burnby Hall
Nunburnholme
Dringhouses
Bishopthorpe
Allerthorpe
Pocklington Canal
Burnby
Holme on the Wolds
Copmanthorpe
Crockey Hill
Sutton upon Derwent
Hayton
Londesborough
South Dalton
Acaster Malbis
Naburn
Wheldrake
Thornton
Kiplingcotes
Deighton
Storwood
Melbourne
Bielby
Thorpe le Street
Goodmanham
Shiptonthorpe
Market Weighton
Everingham
Escrick
Appleton Roebuck
Gardham
Arras
Thorganby
East Cottingwith
Seaton Ross
Acaster Selby
Stillingfleet
Harswell
Ryther
Ellerton
Laytham
Holme-on-Spalding-Moor
Sancton
Aughton
Kelfield
Riccall
Skipwith
North Duffield
Harlthorpe
Moor End
North Newbald
Cawood
Foggathorpe
Water End
Sand Hole
Rascal Moor
North Cliffe
Bubwith
Highfield
South Newbald
Breighton
South Cliffe
Wistow
A169
A170
A64
A166
A19
A1237
A1036
A1079
A59
B1224
B1222
B1223
B1228
B1246
B1247
A614
A163
A1034
B1257
B1251
B1363
B1248
B1253
B1252
B1258
B1415
B1249
A

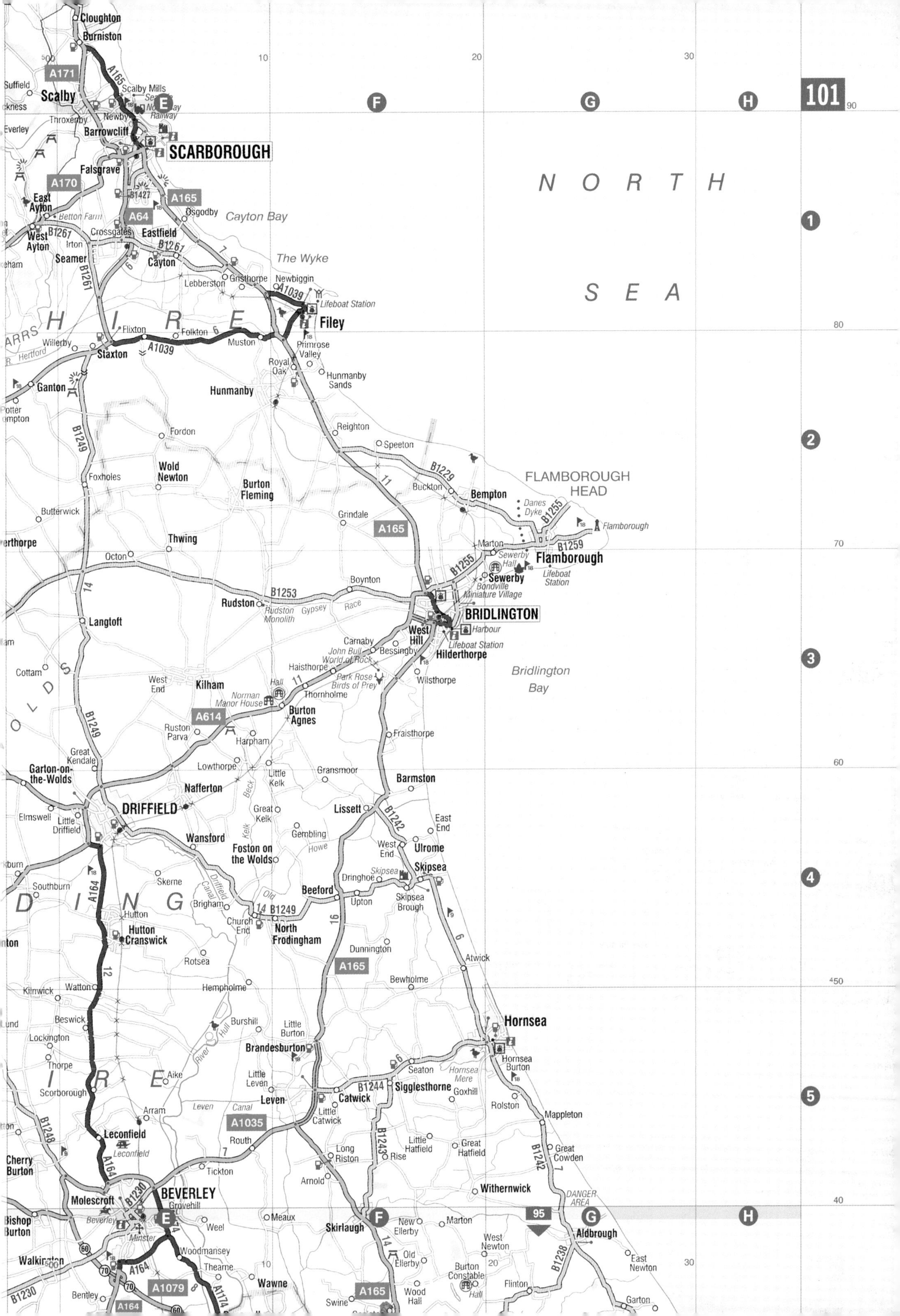
101
NORTH SEA
SCARBOROUGH
Cloughton
Burniston
Scalby
Scalby Mills
Newby
Barrowcliff
Throxenby
Everley
Suffield
Falsgrave
East Ayton
West Ayton
Irton
Seamer
Crossgates
Eastfield
Osgodby
Cayton
Cayton Bay
The Wyke
Lebberston
Gristhorpe
Newbiggin
Lifeboat Station
Filey
Flixton
Folkton
Muston
Primrose Valley
Willerby
Staxton
Ganton
Royal Oak
Hunmanby Sands
Hunmanby
Fordon
Reighton
Speeton
Foxholes
Wold Newton
Burton Fleming
Buckton
Bempton
FLAMBOROUGH HEAD
Danes Dyke
Flamborough
Butterwick
Grindale
Thwing
Octon
Marton
Sewerby Hall
Sewerby
Bondville Miniature Village
Lifeboat Station
Boynton
Rudston
Rudston Monolith
Gypsey Race
BRIDLINGTON
Harbour
Langtoft
West Hill
Carnaby
John Bull World of Rock
Bessingby
Hilderthorpe
Cottam
Haisthorpe
Park Rose Birds of Prey
Wilsthorpe
Bridlington Bay
West End
Kilham
Norman Manor House
Thornholme
Burton Agnes
Ruston Parva
Harpham
Fraisthorpe
Great Kendale
Garton-on-the-Wolds
Lowthorpe
Little Kelk
Gransmoor
Barmston
Nafferton
DRIFFIELD
Elmswell
Little Driffield
Great Kelk
Lissett
East End
Wansford
Foston on the Wolds
Gembling
West End
Ulrome
Skipsea
Southburn
Skerne
Dringhoe
Beeford
Upton
Skipsea Brough
Hutton
Brigham
Church End
North Frodingham
Hutton Cranswick
Dunnington
Rotsea
Atwick
Bewholme
Kilnwick
Watton
Hempholme
Hornsea
Beswick
Burshill
Little Burton
Lockington
Brandesburton
Hornsea Burton
Hornsea Mere
Seaton
Thorpe
Aike
Little Leven
Sigglesthorne
Goxhill
Scorborough
Leven
Catwick
Rolston
Arram
Little Catwick
Mappleton
Leconfield
Routh
Long Riston
Little Hatfield
Great Hatfield
Great Cowden
Rise
Cherry Burton
Tickton
Arnold
Withernwick
BEVERLEY
Molescroft
Grovehill
DANGER AREA
Bishop Burton
Beverley
Minster
Weel
Meaux
Skirlaugh
New Ellerby
Marton
Aldbrough
West Newton
Walkington
Woodmansey
Old Ellerby
East Newton
Thearne
Burton Constable Hall
Wawne
Bentley
Flinton
Swine
Wood Hall
Garton
A171
A165
A170
A64
B1427
B1261
A1039
B1249
B1229
B1255
B1259
B1253
A614
B1242
A164
A1035
B1244
B1243
B1248
B1230
A1079
A1174
B1238
95
10
20
30
40
50
60
70
80
90

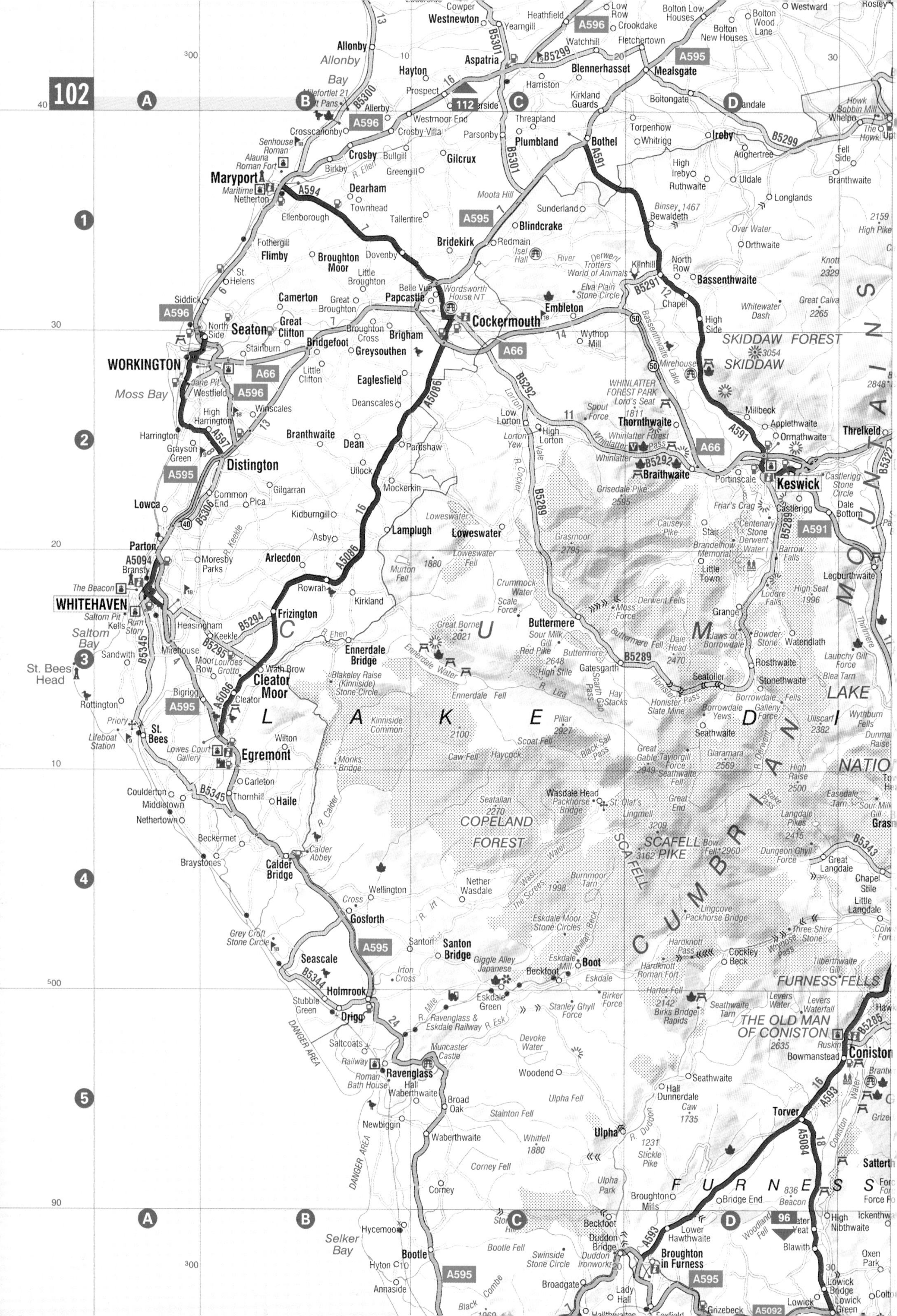
Cowper
Westnewton
Yearngill
Heathfield
Low Row
A596
Crookdake
Bolton Low Houses
Bolton Wood Lane
Westward
Bolton New Houses
Allonby
Allonby Bay
Hayton
Aspatria
B5299
Watchhill
Fletchertown
A595
Blennerhasset
Mealsgate
Prospect
Harriston
Kirkland Guards
Boltongate
Milefortlet 21
B5300
Allerby
112
C
D
A
B
Westmoor End
Threapland
Howk Bobbin Mill
Whelpo
A596
Crosscanonby
Crosby Villa
Parsonby
Plumbland
Torpenhow
Ireby
B5299
The Howk
Senhouse Roman Museum
Alauna Roman Fort
Crosby
Bullgill
Gilcrux
B5301
Bothel
Whitrigg
Aughertree
Fell Side
Birkby
R. Ellen
Greengill
A591
High Ireby
Maryport
Maritime
Netherton
A594
Dearham
Ruthwaite
Uldale
Branthwaite
Moota Hill
Sunderland
Longlands
Townhead
Ellenborough
Tallentire
A595
Blindcrake
Binsey 1467
Bewaldeth
2159
High Pike
1
Fothergill
Flimby
Broughton Moor
Dovenby
Bridekirk
Redmain
Isel Hall
River Derwent
Trotters World of Animals
Kilnhill
North Row
Over Water
Orthwaite
Knott 2329
St. Helens
Little Broughton
Belle Vue
Elva Plain Stone Circle
Bassenthwaite
B5291
Siddick
Camerton
Great Broughton
Papcastle
Wordsworth House NT
Cockermouth
Embleton
Chapel
Whitewater Dash
Great Calva 2265
A596
Seaton
North Side
Great Clifton
Broughton Cross
Brigham
Wythop Mill
High Side
Stainburn
Bridgefoot
Greysouthen
A66
SKIDDAW FOREST
Bassenthwaite Lake
Mirehouse
SKIDDAW
3054
WORKINGTON
A66
Little Clifton
Eaglesfield
B5292
Lorton
WHINLATTER FOREST PARK
Lord's Seat 1811
Moss Bay
Westfield
A596
Jane Pit
Deanscales
A5086
Low Lorton
Spout Force
Thornthwaite
Millbeck
Applethwaite
Threlkeld
High Harrington
Winscales
13
A597
High Lorton
Whinlatter Forest
Ormathwaite
Harrington
2
Branthwaite
Dean
Pardshaw
Lorton Yew
Whinlatter Pass
A66
A591
Grayson Green
Distington
A595
Ullock
B5292
Braithwaite
Portinscale
Keswick
Castlerigg Stone Circle
Common End
Gilgarran
Mockerkin
Grisedale Pike 2595
Friar's Crag
Dale Bottom
Lowca
Pica
Castlerigg
B5306
Kidburngill
Loweswater
Causey Pike
Centenary Stone
A591
Asby
Lamplugh
Loweswater
Grasmoor 2795
Stair
Derwent Water
Parton
R. Keekle
Brandelhow Memorial
Barrow Falls
A5094
Bransty
Moresby Parks
Arlecdon
Loweswater Fell
Murton Fell 1880
Little Town
Legburthwaite
The Beacon
Rowrah
Crummock Water
Lodore Falls
High Seat 1996
WHITEHAVEN
Kirkland
Scale Force
Derwent Fells
Grange
Saltom Pit
Kells
Rum Story
Frizington
Moss Force
Buttermere
Jaws of Borrowdale
Saltom Bay
Hensingham
B5294
Great Borne 2021
Sour Milk Gill
Bowder Stone
Watendlath
Keekle
Red Pike
Buttermere Fell
Dale Head 2470
Launchy Gill Force
B5345
Mirehouse
B5295
R. Ehen
Ennerdale Bridge
High Stile 2648
Buttermere
B5289
Rosthwaite
St. Bees Head
Sandwith
3
Moor Row
Lourdes Grotto
Wath Brow
Ennerdale Water
Gatesgarth
Blea Tarn
Cleator Moor
Blakeley Raise (Kinniside) Stone Circle
R. Liza
Honister Pass
Seatoller
Stonethwaite
Bigrigg
Cleator
Ennerdale Fell
Scarth Gap Pass
Hay Stacks
Honister Slate Mine
Borrowdale Fells
LAKE
Rottington
A595
A5086
Borrowdale Yews
Galleny Force
Wythburn Fells
L A K E D I
Kinniside Common
Pillar 2927
Seathwaite
Ullscarf 2382
Dunmail Raise
Priory
St. Bees
Lifeboat Station
Wilton
2100
Scoat Fell
Black Sail Pass
Lowes Court Gallery
Egremont
Caw Fell
Haycock
Great Gable 2949
Taylorgill Force
Glaramara 2569
High Raise 2500
NATIO
Monks Bridge
Seathwaite Fell
Carleton
Coulderton
B5345
Thornhill
Haile
Seatallan 2270
Wasdale Head
Packhorse Bridge
St. Olaf's
Great End
Easedale Tarn
Middletown
COPELAND
Lingmell
Langdale Pikes 2415
Sour Milk Gill
Nethertown
R. Calder
3209
Beckermet
FOREST
SCAFELL PIKE
Bow Fell 2960
Dungeon Ghyll Force
B5343
Calder Abbey
3162
SCA FELL
Braystones
Calder Bridge
Great Langdale
4
Burnmoor Tarn
Chapel Stile
Nether Wasdale
Wast Water
The Screes 1998
Little Langdale
Wellington
Cross
Gosforth
R. Irt
Lingcove Packhorse Bridge
Eskdale Moor Stone Circles
Whillan Beck
Three Shire Stone
Grey Croft Stone Circle
A595
Santon
Santon Bridge
Hardknott Pass
Cockley Beck
Wrynose Pass
Seascale
Giggle Alley Japanese
Eskdale Mill
Boot
Hardknott Roman Fort
Tilberthwaite Gill
B5344
Irton Cross
Beckfoot
Eskdale
FURNESS FELLS
Holmrook
Eskdale Green
Birker Force
Harter Fell 2142
Birks Bridge Rapids
Seathwaite Tarn
Levers Water
Levers Waterfall
Stubble Green
Drigg
R. Mite
Ravenglass & Eskdale Railway
R. Esk
Stanley Ghyll Force
THE OLD MAN OF CONISTON 2635
Ruskin
B5285
DANGER AREA
Saltcoats
Muncaster Castle
Devoke Water
Coniston
Railway
Bowmanstead
Roman Bath House
Ravenglass
Woodend
Seathwaite
Brantwood
Hall Waberthwaite
Hall Dunnerdale
5
Broad Oak
Ulpha Fell
Caw 1735
Torver
Stainton Fell
A593
Newbiggin
R. Duddon
Ulpha
Waberthwaite
Whitfell 1880
1231
A5084
Coniston Water
DANGER AREA
Stickle Pike
Corney Fell
Ulpha Park
Satterth
Corney
F U R N E S S
836 Beacon
Broughton Mills
Bridge End
Force Forge
A
B
C
D
96
High Nibthwaite
Ickenthwaite
Hycemoor
Stoneside Hill
Beckfoot
Lower Hawthwaite
Woodland Fell
Selker Bay
Bootle Fell
Duddon Bridge
Blawith
Bootle
Swinside Stone Circle
Duddon Ironworks
A593
Broughton in Furness
Hyton
Oxen Park
A595
Broadgate
Annaside
Lady Hall
Lowick Bridge
Lowick Green
Black Combe
Grizebeck
A5092
Lowick
300
10
20
30
40
30
20
10
500
90
300

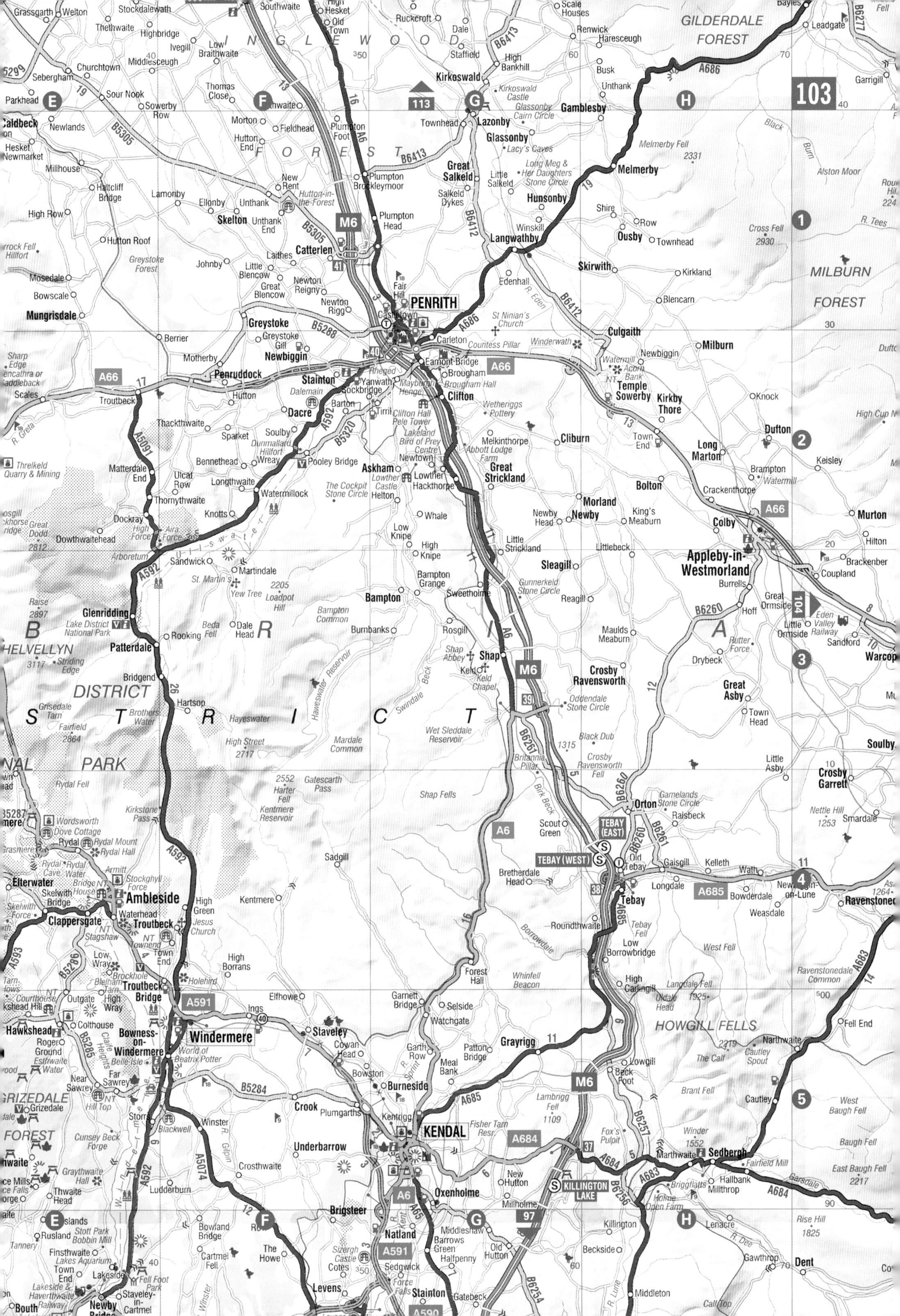

103
104
113
97
E
F
G
H
1
2
3
4
5
I N G L E W O O D
F O R E S T
GILDERDALE
FOREST
MILBURN
FOREST
Alston Moor
Black Burn
Melmerby Fell
2331
Cross Fell
2930
R. Tees
L A K E
D I S T R I C T
N A T I O N A L
P A R K
HELVELLYN
3117
Striding Edge
Lake District National Park
HOWGILL FELLS
Shap Fells
GRIZEDALE FOREST
PENRITH
KENDAL
Appleby-in-Westmorland
Ambleside
Windermere
Bowness-on-Windermere
Sedbergh
Tebay
Shap
Orton
Kirkoswald
Lazonby
Glassonby
Gamblesby
Melmerby
Hunsonby
Langwathby
Great Salkeld
Little Salkeld
Salkeld Dykes
Plumpton
Plumpton Head
Plumpton Foot
Catterlen
Greystoke
Newbiggin
Penruddock
Stainton
Dacre
Pooley Bridge
Askham
Lowther
Hackthorpe
Clifton
Eamont Bridge
Brougham
Carleton
Temple Sowerby
Kirkby Thore
Long Marton
Dufton
Knock
Milburn
Culgaith
Skirwith
Ousby
Kirkland
Blencarn
Great Strickland
Little Strickland
Cliburn
Bolton
Morland
Newby
King's Meaburn
Colby
Murton
Hilton
Brackenber
Coupland
Great Ormside
Little Ormside
Sandford
Warcop
Burrells
Hoff
Drybeck
Great Asby
Crosby Ravensworth
Maulds Meaburn
Bampton
Bampton Grange
Burnbanks
Rosgill
Sleagill
Reagill
Patterdale
Glenridding
Hartsop
Watermillock
Matterdale End
Troutbeck
Troutbeck Bridge
Staveley
Burneside
Grayrigg
Oxenholme
Natland
Levens
Crook
Underbarrow
Hawkshead
Coniston
Clappersgate
Skelwith Bridge
Elterwater
Rydal
Grasmere
Kirkstone Pass
Raisbeck
Gaisgill
Kelleth
Newbiggin-on-Lune
Ravenstonedale
Killington
Middleton
Dent
Garsdale
Cautley
Lowgill
Beck Foot
Crosby Garrett
Soulby
Smardale
Little Asby
Killington Lake
TEBAY (EAST)
TEBAY (WEST)
M6
A6
A66
A591
A592
A593
A684
A685
A683
A686
A5091
A5074
A590
A65
B5288
B5305
B5320
B6260
B6261
B6412
B6413
B5284
B5285
B5286
B6254
B6256
B6257
B6277

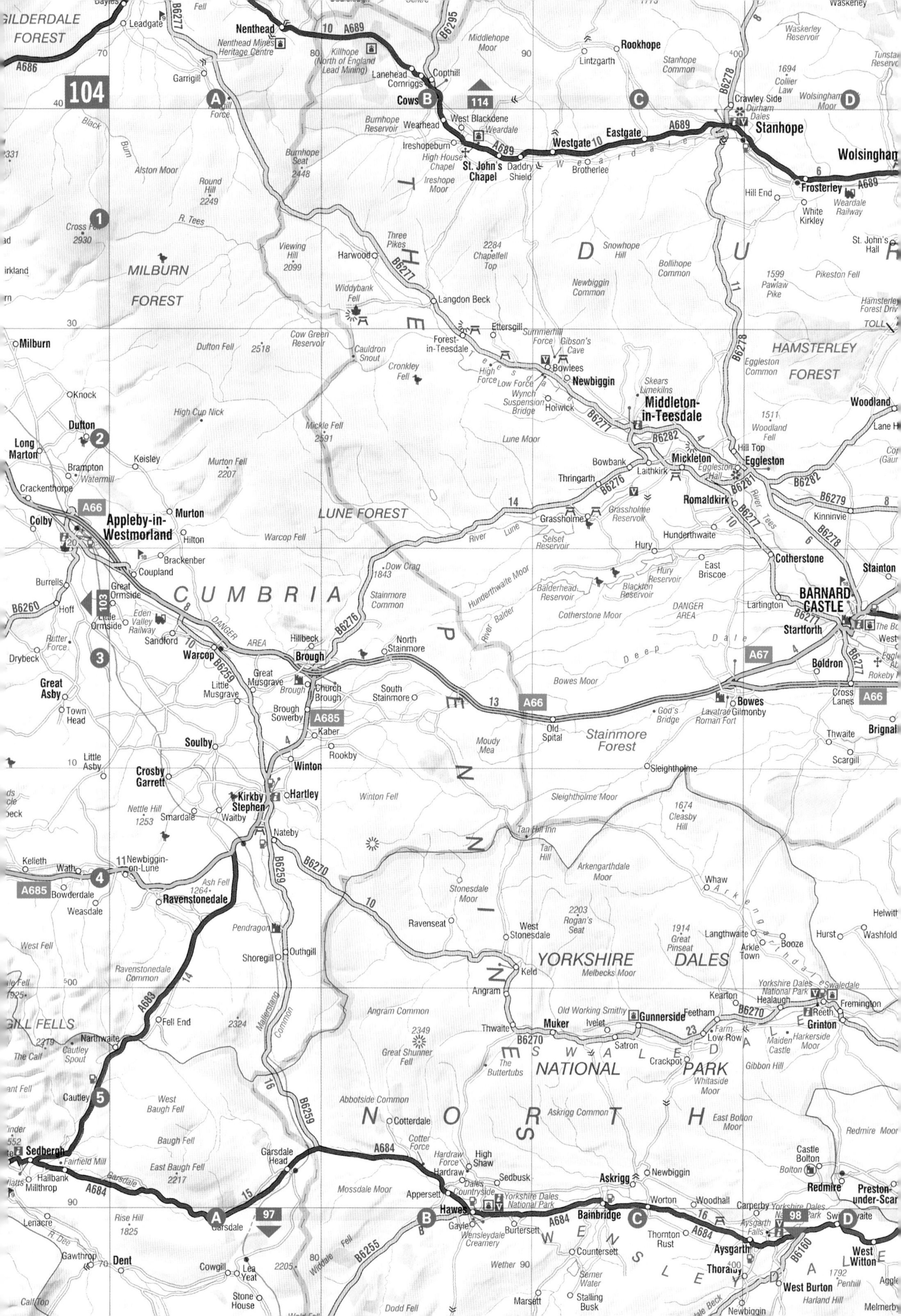
104
114
103
97
98
CUMBRIA
PENNINE
NORTH
YORKSHIRE DALES NATIONAL PARK
WENSLEYDALE
Nenthead
Alston Moor
MILBURN FOREST
Appleby-in-Westmorland
Brough
Kirkby Stephen
Sedbergh
Middleton-in-Teesdale
Stanhope
Wolsingham
BARNARD CASTLE
Hawes
Askrigg
Bainbridge
Aysgarth
Reeth
Muker
Keld
Gunnerside
Cotherstone
Eggleston
Romaldkirk
Mickleton
Bowes
Warcop
Ravenstonedale
Garsdale
Dent
Redmire
West Witton
LUNE FOREST
HAMSTERLEY FOREST
Stainmore Forest

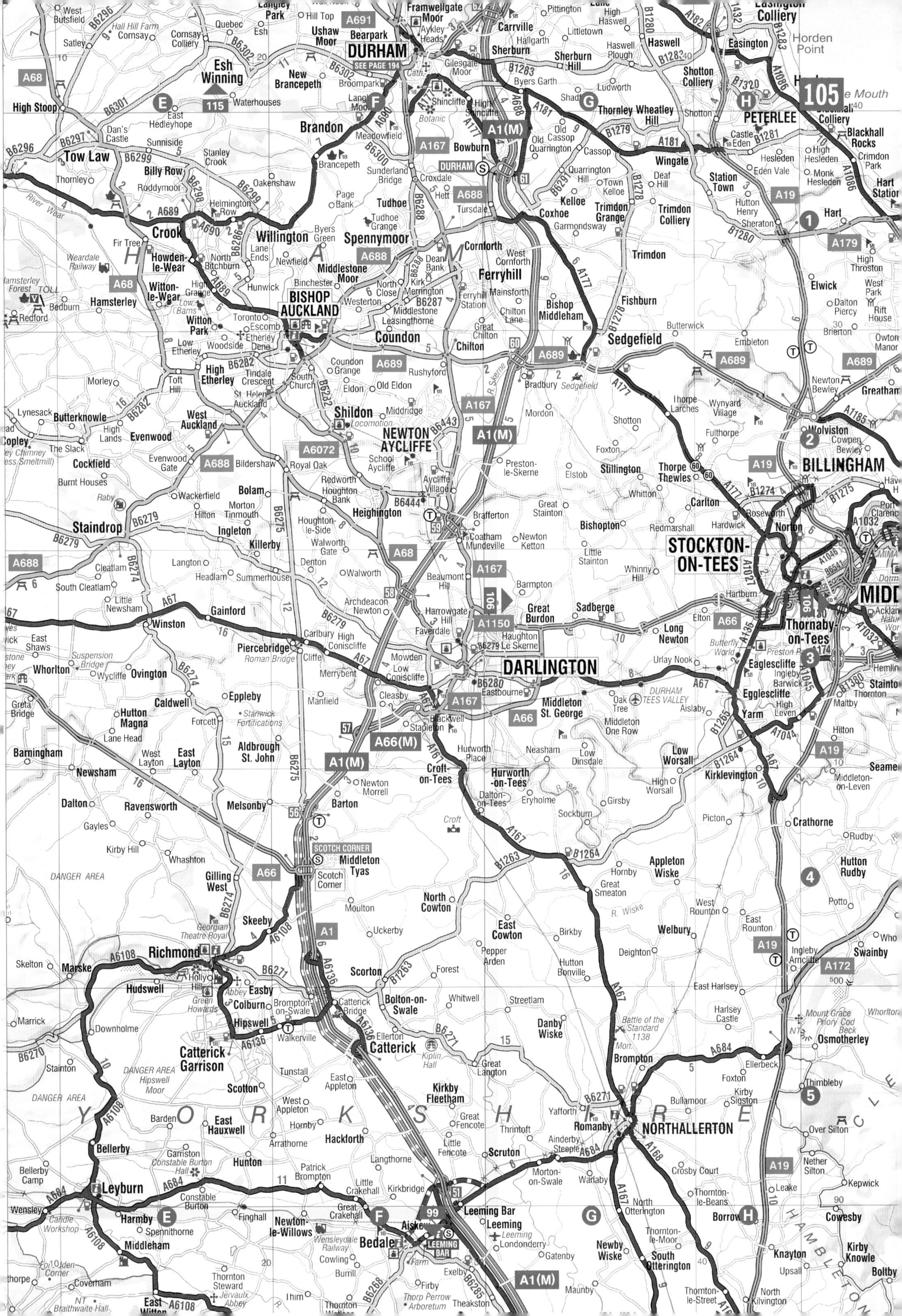

West Butsfield
Hall Hill Farm
Cornsay
Quebec
Esh
Langley Park
Hill Top
Ushaw Moor
Framwellgate Moor
Aykley Heads
Bearpark
DURHAM
SEE PAGE 194
Pittington
High Haswell
Easington Colliery
Horden Point
Satley
Cornsay Colliery
Esh Winning
115
New Brancepeth
Broompark
Carrville
Hallgarth
Littletown
Sherburn
Sherburn Hill
Haswell
Haswell Plough
Easington
Shotton Colliery
105
Gilesgate Moor
Byers Garth
Ludworth
Shadforth
Thornley
Wheatley Hill
Shotton
PETERLEE
Blackhall Colliery
Blackhall Rocks
High Stoop
Waterhouses
East Hedleyhope
Langley Moor
Brandon
Shincliffe
High Shincliffe
Botanic
A1(M)
Old Cassop
Cassop
Castle Eden
Crimdon Park
Dan's Castle
Sunniside
Tow Law
Stanley Crook
Meadowfield
Brancepeth
Bowburn
Old Quarrington
Wingate
High Hesleden
Hesleden
Monk Hesleden
Eden Vale
Hart Station
Billy Row
Thornley
Roddymoor
Oakenshaw
Sunderland Bridge
Croxdale
Page Bank
Quarrington Hill
Town Kelloe
Deaf Hill
Station Town
Hutton Henry
Sheraton
Hart
Helmington Row
Hett
Tursdale
Kelloe
Coxhoe
Trimdon Grange
Trimdon Colliery
Garmondsway
River Wear
Crook
Fir Tree
Willington
Byers Green
Tudhoe
Tudhoe Grange
Spennymoor
Cornforth
West Cornforth
Ferryhill
Trimdon
High Throston
Elwick
West Park
Weardale Railway
Howden-le-Wear
North Bitchburn
Lane Ends
Newfield
Middlestone Moor
Dean Bank
Kirk Merrington
Hamsterley Forest
TOLL
Hamsterley
Witton-le-Wear
High Grange
Hunwick
Binchester
BISHOP AUCKLAND
Westerton
North Close
Middlestone
Leasingthorne
Ferryhill Station
Mainsforth
Chilton Lane
Bishop Middleham
Fishburn
Dalton Piercy
Rift House
Bedburn
Redford
Low Barns
Witton Park
Toronto
Escomb
Etherley Dene
Coundon
Great Chilton
Chilton
Butterwick
Sedgefield
Brierton
Embleton
Owton Manor
Low Etherley
Woodside
High Etherley
Tindale Crescent
South Church
Coundon Grange
Rushyford
Bradbury
Sedgefield
Newton Bewley
Greatham
Morley
Toft Hill
St. Helen Auckland
Eldon
Old Eldon
Mordon
Thorpe Larches
Wynyard Village
Lynesack
Butterknowle
West Auckland
Shildon
Locomotion
Middridge
Shotton
Wolviston
Cowpen Bewley
Copley
High Lands
Evenwood
NEWTON AYCLIFFE
Fulthorpe
Foxton
BILLINGHAM
Hamsterley Chimney
The Slack
Evenwood Gate
Bildershaw
Royal Oak
School Aycliffe
Preston-le-Skerne
Elstob
Stillington
Thorpe Thewles
Cockfield
Burnt Houses
Redworth
Houghton Bank
Aycliffe Village
Whitton
Carlton
Raby
Wackerfield
Bolam
Morton Tinmouth
Hilton
Heighington
Brafferton
Great Stainton
Bishopton
Redmarshall
Hardwick
Roseworth
Norton
Port Clarence
Staindrop
Ingleton
Houghton-le-Side
Coatham Mundeville
Newton Ketton
STOCKTON-ON-TEES
Killerby
Walworth Gate
Little Stainton
Whinny Hill
Langton
Cleatham
Headlam
Summerhouse
Denton
Walworth
Beaumont Hill
Barmpton
South Cleatham
Little Newsham
Archdeacon Newton
Harrowgate Hill
Great Burdon
Sadberge
Hartburn
MIDDLESBROUGH
Gainford
Winston
Faverdale
Haughton Le Skerne
Long Newton
Elton
Thornaby-on-Tees
East Shaws
Piercebridge
Roman Bridge
Carlbury
High Coniscliffe
Cliffe
Suspension Bridge
Mowden
Low Coniscliffe
DARLINGTON
Urlay Nook
Butterfly World
Preston Park
Eaglescliffe
Ingleby Barwick
Hemlington
Whorlton
Wycliffe
Ovington
Merrybent
Eastbourne
Egglescliffe
Stainton
Thornton
Eppleby
Cleasby
Manfield
Middleton St. George
Oak Tree
DURHAM TEES VALLEY
Aislaby
Yarm
High Leven
Maltby
Greta Bridge
Caldwell
Hutton Magna
Stanwick Fortifications
Forcett
Stapleton
Blackwell
Middleton One Row
Hilton
Lane Head
Aldbrough St. John
A66(M)
Hurworth Place
Neasham
Low Dinsdale
Low Worsall
Barningham
West Layton
East Layton
Croft-on-Tees
Hurworth-on-Tees
High Worsall
Kirklevington
Seamer
Middleton-on-Leven
Newsham
Newton Morrell
Dalton-on-Tees
Eryholme
Girsby
Dalton
Ravensworth
Melsonby
Barton
Sockburn
Picton
Crathorne
Rudby
Gayles
Croft
Kirby Hill
Whashton
Scotch Corner
Middleton Tyas
Hornby
Appleton Wiske
Hutton Rudby
DANGER AREA
Gilling West
Great Smeaton
Moulton
North Cowton
West Rounton
East Rounton
Potto
Skeeby
Georgian Theatre Royal
R. Wiske
Uckerby
East Cowton
Birkby
Welbury
Whorlton
Swainby
Ingleby Arncliffe
Skelton
Marske
Richmond
Pepper Arden
Deighton
Hutton Bonville
Scorton
Forest
Hudswell
Holly Hill
Easby
Abbey
Green Howards
Brompton-on-Swale
Colburn
Catterick Bridge
Bolton-on-Swale
Whitwell
Streetlam
East Harlsey
Harlsey Castle
Mount Grace Priory
Cod Beck
Marrick
Downholme
Hipswell
Walkerville
Ellerton
Danby Wiske
Battle of the Standard 1138
Osmotherley
Catterick Garrison
Catterick
Kiplin Hall
Great Langton
Brompton
Ellerbeck
Stainton
DANGER AREA
Hipswell Moor
Tunstall
Scotton
East Appleton
Foxton
Thimbleby
Kirby Sigston
Kirkby Fleetham
Great Fencote
Yafforth
Bullamoor
YORKSHIRE
Barden
East Hauxwell
West Appleton
Hornby
Hackforth
Little Fencote
Thrintoft
Romanby
NORTHALLERTON
Over Silton
Bellerby
Garriston
Constable Burton Hall
Hunton
Arrathorne
Langthorne
Scruton
Ainderby Steeple
Crosby Court
Nether Silton
Bellerby Camp
Leyburn
Constable Burton
Patrick Brompton
Little Crakehall
Kirkbridge
Morton-on-Swale
Warlaby
Thornton-le-Beans
Leake
Kepwick
Wensley
Candle Workshop
Harmby
Spennithorne
Finghall
Great Crakehall
Newton-le-Willows
Aiskew
Leeming Bar
Leeming
North Otterington
Borrowby
Cowesby
Middleham
Wensleydale Railway
Bedale
Leeming Bar
Londonderry
Newby Wiske
Thornton-le-Moor
South Otterington
Knayton
Kirby Knowle
Cowling
Burrill
Farm
Exelby
Gatenby
Upsall
Boltby
Coverham
Thornton Steward
Jervaulx Abbey
Firby
Thorp Perrow Arboretum
Theakston
Maunby
Thornton-le-Street
North Kilvington
Braithwaite Hall
East Witton
Ilton
Thornton Watlass
HAMBLETON

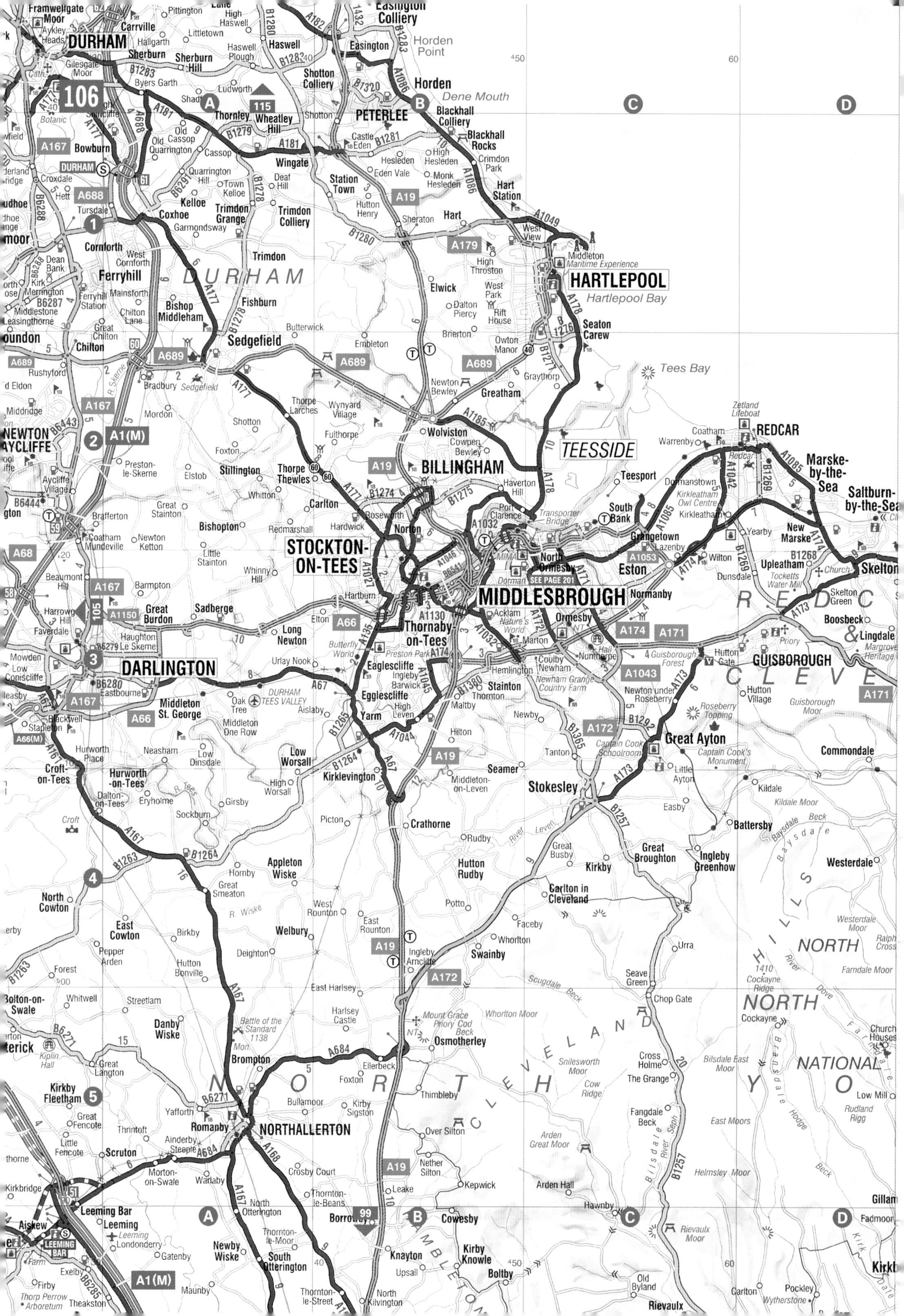

Framwellgate Moor
Aykley Heads
DURHAM
Pittington
Carrville
High Haswell
Littletown
Hallgarth
Sherburn
Sherburn Hill
Haswell
Haswell Plough
Haswell
Easington Colliery
Easington
Horden Point
Horden
Dene Mouth
Gilesgate Moor
106
Byers Garth
Ludworth
115
Shadforth
Thornley
Wheatley Hill
Shotton Colliery
Shotton
PETERLEE
Blackhall Colliery
Blackhall Rocks
Castle Eden
Hesleden
High Hesleden
Crimdon Park
Eden Vale
Monk Hesleden
Hart Station
Botanic
Old Cassop
Old Quarrington
Cassop
Bowburn
Wingate
Quarrington Hill
Town Kelloe
Deaf Hill
Station Town
Hutton Henry
Croxdale
Hett
Kelloe
Trimdon Grange
Trimdon Colliery
Tursdale
Coxhoe
Garmondsway
Sheraton
Hart
West View
Middleton
Maritime Experience
HARTLEPOOL
Hartlepool Bay
Cornforth
West Cornforth
Trimdon
DURHAM
Ferryhill
Dean Bank
Kirk Merrington
Ferryhill Station
Mainsforth
Middlestone
Leasingthorne
Chilton Lane
Great Chilton
Chilton
Bishop Middleham
Fishburn
Sedgefield
Butterwick
High Throston
Elwick
West Park
Dalton Piercy
Rift House
Brierton
Seaton Carew
Embleton
Owton Manor
Graythorp
Greatham
Tees Bay
Rushyford
Eldon
Bradbury
Sedgefield
Newton Bewley
Thorpe Larches
Wynyard Village
Middridge
Mordon
Shotton
Fulthorpe
Wolviston
Cowpen Bewley
TEESSIDE
NEWTON AYCLIFFE
Preston-le-Skerne
Foxton
Elstob
Stillington
Thorpe Thewles
Whitton
BILLINGHAM
Haverton Hill
Teesport
Aycliffe Village
Great Stainton
Carlton
Port Clarence
Transporter Bridge
South Bank
Grangetown
Dormanstown
Kirkleatham Owl Centre
Kirkleatham
Coatham
Warrenby
Zetland Lifeboat
REDCAR
Marske-by-the-Sea
Saltburn-by-the-Sea
New Marske
Yearby
Brafferton
Bishopton
Redmarshall
Hardwick
Bosewoth
Norton
Coatham Mundeville
Newton Ketton
Little Stainton
STOCKTON-ON-TEES
North Ormesby
SEE PAGE 201
Eston
Lazenby
Wilton
Upleatham
Church
Skelton
Beaumont Hill
Barmpton
Whinny Hill
Dorman
MIDDLESBROUGH
Normanby
Dunsdale
Tocketts Water Mill
Skelton Green
REDCAR
Harrowgate Hill
Great Burdon
Sadberge
Hartburn
Elton
Acklam
Nature's World
Ormesby
Boosbeck
Lingdale
Faverdale
Haughton Le Skerne
Long Newton
Thornaby-on-Tees
Marton
Hall
Nunthorpe
Priory
Margrove Heritage
Mowden
DARLINGTON
Urlay Nook
Butterfly World
Preston Park
Coulby Newham
Guisborough Forest
Hutton Gate
GUISBOROUGH
Low Coniscliffe
Eastbourne
Eaglescliffe
Ingleby Barwick
Hemlington
Newham Grange Country Farm
Newton under Roseberry
CLEVELAND
Blackwell
Middleton St. George
Oak Tree
DURHAM TEES VALLEY
Aislaby
Egglescliffe
Stainton
Thornton
Maltby
Hutton Village
Guisborough Moor
Stapleton
Middleton One Row
Yarm
High Leven
Newby
Roseberry Topping
Hurworth Place
Neasham
Low Dinsdale
Low Worsall
Hilton
Tanton
Captain Cook Schoolroom
Great Ayton
Captain Cook's Monument
Commondale
Croft-on-Tees
Hurworth-on-Tees
High Worsall
Kirklevington
Seamer
Middleton-on-Leven
Stokesley
Little Ayton
Kildale
Dalton-on-Tees
Eryholme
Girsby
Kildale Moor
Croft
Sockburn
Picton
Crathorne
Rudby
River Leven
Easby
Battersby
Baysdale Beck
Great Busby
Great Broughton
Hornby
Appleton Wiske
Hutton Rudby
Kirkby
Ingleby Greenhow
Westerdale
North Cowton
Great Smeaton
Carlton in Cleveland
R. Wiske
West Rounton
Potto
East Cowton
Birkby
East Rounton
Faceby
Westerdale Moor
Welbury
Whorlton
Ralph Cross
Pepper Arden
Deighton
Ingleby Arncliffe
Swainby
Urra
NORTH
Forest
Hutton Bonville
Scugdale Beck
Seave Green
1410 Cockayne Ridge
Farndale Moor
Bolton-on-Swale
Whitwell
Streetlam
East Harlsey
Chop Gate
Harlsey Castle
Mount Grace Priory
Cod Beck
Whorlton Moor
NORTH
Danby Wiske
Battle of the Standard 1138
Osmotherley
Cockayne
Church Houses
Catterick
Kiplin Hall
Great Langton
Brompton
Ellerbeck
Snilesworth Moor
Cross Holme
The Grange
Bilsdale East Moor
NATIONAL
Foxton
Cow Ridge
Low Mill
Kirkby Fleetham
Yafforth
Bullamoor
Kirby Sigston
Thimbleby
Rudland Rigg
Great Fencote
Thrintoft
Romanby
NORTHALLERTON
Fangdale Beck
East Moors
Little Fencote
Ainderby Steeple
Over Silton
Arden Great Moor
Scruton
Crosby Court
Nether Silton
Morton-on-Swale
Warlaby
Thornton-le-Beans
Kepwick
Arden Hall
Helmsley Moor
Kirkbridge
North Otterington
Leeming Bar
Aiskew
Leeming
Londonderry
Borrowby
Leake
Cowesby
Hawnby
Rievaulx Moor
Gillam
Fadmoor
Thornton-le-Moor
Newby Wiske
South Otterington
Knayton
Kirby Knowle
Gatenby
Exelby
Upsall
Boltby
Old Byland
Firby
Thorp Perrow Arboretum
Theakston
Maunby
Thornton-le-Street
North Kilvington
Carlton
Pockley
Wytherstone
Rievaulx
Kirkby
HAMBLETON
CLEVELAND
Bilsdale
NORTH YORK
A1(M)
A19
A167
A168
A172
A173
A174
A171
A1043
A1053
A179
A689
A688
A66
A66(M)
A67
A684
A1150
A177
A181
A182
A1086
A1085
A1042
A1032
A1130
A1027
A1045
A1044
A1046
A135
A1185
A178
A1049
B1283
B1279
B1281
B1280
B1278
B6291
B6288
B6287
B6443
B6444
B1274
B1275
B1276
B1277
B1269
B1268
B6280
B6279
B1380
B1365
B1292
B1265
B1264
B1263
B1257
B6271
B6285
99
105
61
60
59
58
57
51
450
1
2
3
4
5
A
B
C
D

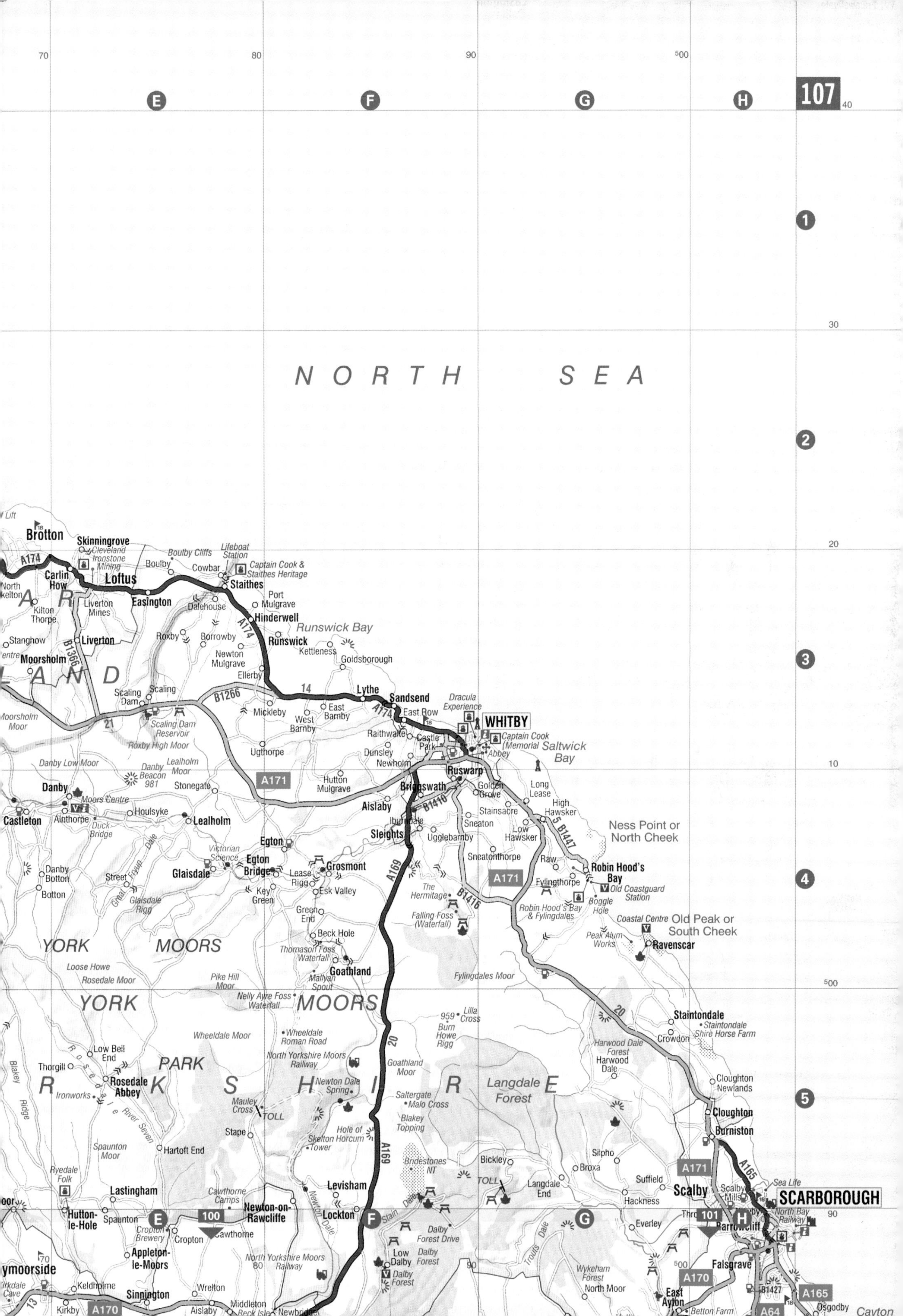

NORTH SEA

Brotton
Skinningrove
Cleveland
Ironstone
Mining
Boulby Cliffs
Boulby
Lifeboat Station
Captain Cook &
Staithes Heritage
Carlin How
Loftus
Cowbar
Staithes
North
Skelton
A174
Easington
Liverton Mines
Dalehouse
Port Mulgrave
Hinderwell
Kilton Thorpe
Stanghow
Liverton
Roxby
Borrowby
Runswick
Runswick Bay
Centre
Moorsholm
Newton Mulgrave
Kettleness
Goldsborough
Ellerby
Scaling Dam
Scaling
B1266
14
Lythe
Sandsend
Dracula Experience
D
Mickleby
East Barnby
A174
East Row
WHITBY
Moorsholm Moor
21
West Barnby
Raithwaite
Captain Cook (Memorial
Saltwick Bay
Scaling Dam Reservoir
Ugthorpe
Dunsley
Castle Park
Abbey
Roxby High Moor
Newholm
A171
Hutton Mulgrave
Briggswath
Ruswarp
Danby Low Moor
Danby Beacon 981
Lealholm Moor
Stonegate
Golden Grove
Long Lease
Danby
Moors Centre
Houlsyke
Lealholm
Aislaby
B1416
Stainsacre
High Hawsker
Ness Point or North Cheek
Castleton
Ainthorpe
Duck Bridge
Iburndale
Sneaton
Low Hawsker
Victorian Science
Sleights
Ugglebarnby
Danby Botton
Egton
Sneatonthorpe
Botton
Street
Egton Bridge
Lease Rigg
Grosmont
A169
Raw
Robin Hood's Bay
Glaisdale
Key Green
Esk Valley
Fylingthorpe
A171
Old Coastguard Station
Glaisdale Rigg
Green End
The Hermitage
B1416
Robin Hood's Bay & Fylingdales
Boggle Hole
Beck Hole
Falling Foss (Waterfall)
Coastal Centre
Old Peak or South Cheek
YORK
MOORS
Loose Howe
Thomason Foss Waterfall
Peak Alum Works
Ravenscar
Rosedale Moor
Pike Hill Moor
Goathland
Mallyan Spout
Fylingdales Moor
YORK
MOORS
Nelly Ayre Foss Waterfall
Wheeldale Moor
Wheeldale Roman Road
Lilla Cross
Burn Howe Rigg
Staintondale
Staintondale Shire Horse Farm
Crowdon
Thorgill
Low Bell End
PARK
North Yorkshire Moors Railway
Goathland Moor
Langdale Forest
Harwood Dale Forest
Harwood Dale
Cloughton Newlands
Rosedale Abbey
Mauley Cross
Newton Dale Spring
Saltergate
Malo Cross
A171
Cloughton
Ironworks
SHIRE
Stape
Hole of Skelton Horcum
Tower
Blakey Topping
Bickley
Broxa
Silpho
Burniston
A165
Spaunton Moor
Hartoft End
Bridestones NT
Langdale End
Suffield
Sea Life
Ryedale Folk
Lastingham
Levisham
TOLL
Scalby
Scalby Mills
SCARBOROUGH
Hutton-le-Hole
Spaunton
Cawthorne Camps
Newton-on-Rawcliffe
Lockton
Stain
Hackness
Everley
North Bay Railway
Cropton Brewery
Cawthorne
Dalby Forest Drive
Low Dalby
Dalby Forest
G
Wykeham Forest
North Moor
101
Barrowcliff
Appleton-le-Moors
North Yorkshire Moors Railway
Falsgrave
Keldholme
Sinnington
Middleton
Aislaby
Beck Isle
Newbridge
East Ayton
A170
Betton Farm
B1427
A165
Osgodby
Cayton
A64

A170

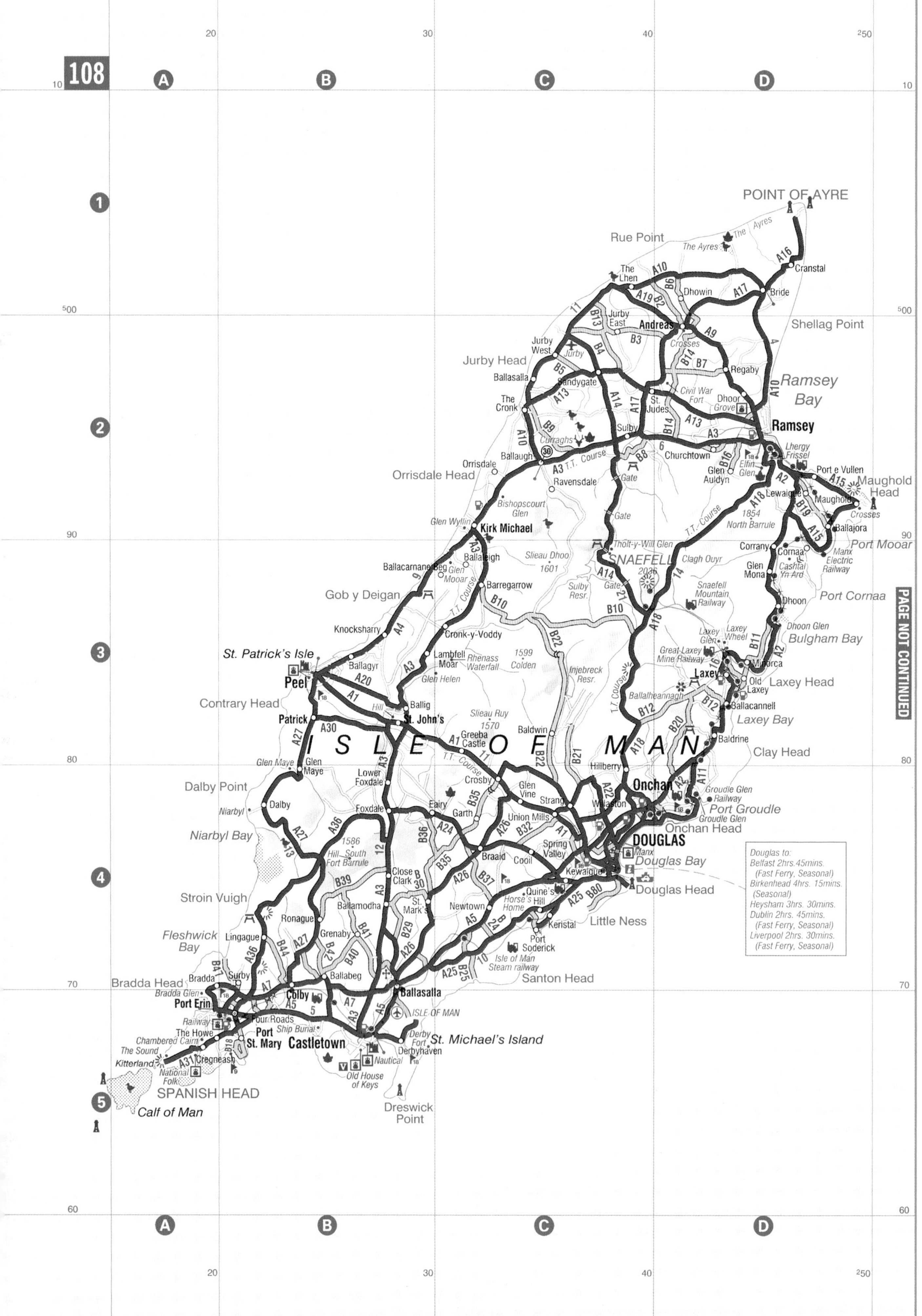

POINT OF AYRE

Rue Point

The Ayres

Cranstal

The Lhen

Dhowin

Bride

Shellag Point

Jurby West

Jurby East

Andreas

Crosses

Regaby

Ramsey Bay

Jurby Head

Jurby

Ballasalla

Sandygate

St. Judes

Civil War Fort

Dhoor Grove

Ramsey

The Cronk

Sulby

Lhergy Frissel

Port e Vullen

Maughold Head

Orrisdale

Ballaugh

Churchtown

Glen Auldyn

Elfin Glen

Lewaigue

Maughold

Orrisdale Head

Curraghs

Gate

T.T. Course

1854

North Barrule

A18

Crosses

Ballajora

Port Mooar

Bishopscourt Glen

Ravensdale

Glen Wyllin

Kirk Michael

Tholt-y-Will Glen

SNAEFELL

1601

Slieu Dhoo

Clagh Ouyr

Corrany

Glen Mona

Cornaa

Cashtal Yn Ard

Manx Electric Railway

Port Cornaa

Ballacarnane Beg

Ballaleigh

Barregarrow

Sulby Resr.

Gate

2036

Snaefell Mountain Railway

Dhoon

Gob y Deigan

Glen Mooar

Knocksharry

Cronk-y-Voddy

Lambfell Moar

Rhenass Waterfall

Colden

1599

Injebreck Resr.

Laxey Glen

Laxey Wheel

Great-Laxey Mine Railway

Dhoon Glen

Bulgham Bay

St. Patrick's Isle

Ballagyr

Peel

Ballig

Glen Helen

Slieau Ruy

1570

Baldwin

Ballaheannagh

Minorca

Old Laxey

Laxey Head

Contrary Head

Patrick

St. John's

Greeba Castle

T.T. Course

Laxey

Ballacannell

Laxey Bay

I S L E   O F   M A N

Baldrine

Clay Head

Glen Maye

Glen Maye

Lower Foxdale

Crosby

Glen Vine

Strang

Hillberry

Onchan

Baldrine

Dalby Point

Niarbyl

Eairy

Garth

Union Mills

Wilaston

Groudle Glen Railway

Port Groudle

Niarbyl Bay

Dalby

Foxdale

1586

Hill South Fort Barrule

Braaid

Cooil

Spring Valley

DOUGLAS

Onchan Head

Groudle Glen

Stroin Vuigh

Ballamodha

St. Mark's

Newtown

Quine's Hill

Kewaigue

Manx

Douglas Bay

Douglas Head

Fleshwick Bay

Lingague

Ronague

Grenaby

Horse's Home

Keristal

Little Ness

Kirstal

Bradda Head

Bradda

Surby

Ballabeg

Port Soderick

Bradda Glen

Port Erin

Colby

Ballasalla

Isle of Man Steam railway

Santon Head

Railway

The Howe

Four Roads

Ship Buria

ISLE OF MAN

Chambered Cairn

Port St. Mary

Castletown

Derby Fort

Derbyhaven

St. Michael's Island

The Sound

Kitterland

Cregneash

Nautical

National Folk

Old House of Keys

SPANISH HEAD

Calf of Man

Dreswick Point

PAGE NOT CONTINUED

Douglas to:
Belfast 2hrs.45mins.
(Fast Ferry, Seasonal)
Birkenhead 4hrs. 15mins.
(Seasonal)
Heysham 3hrs. 30mins.
Dublin 2hrs. 45mins.
(Fast Ferry, Seasonal)
Liverpool 2hrs. 30mins.
(Fast Ferry, Seasonal)

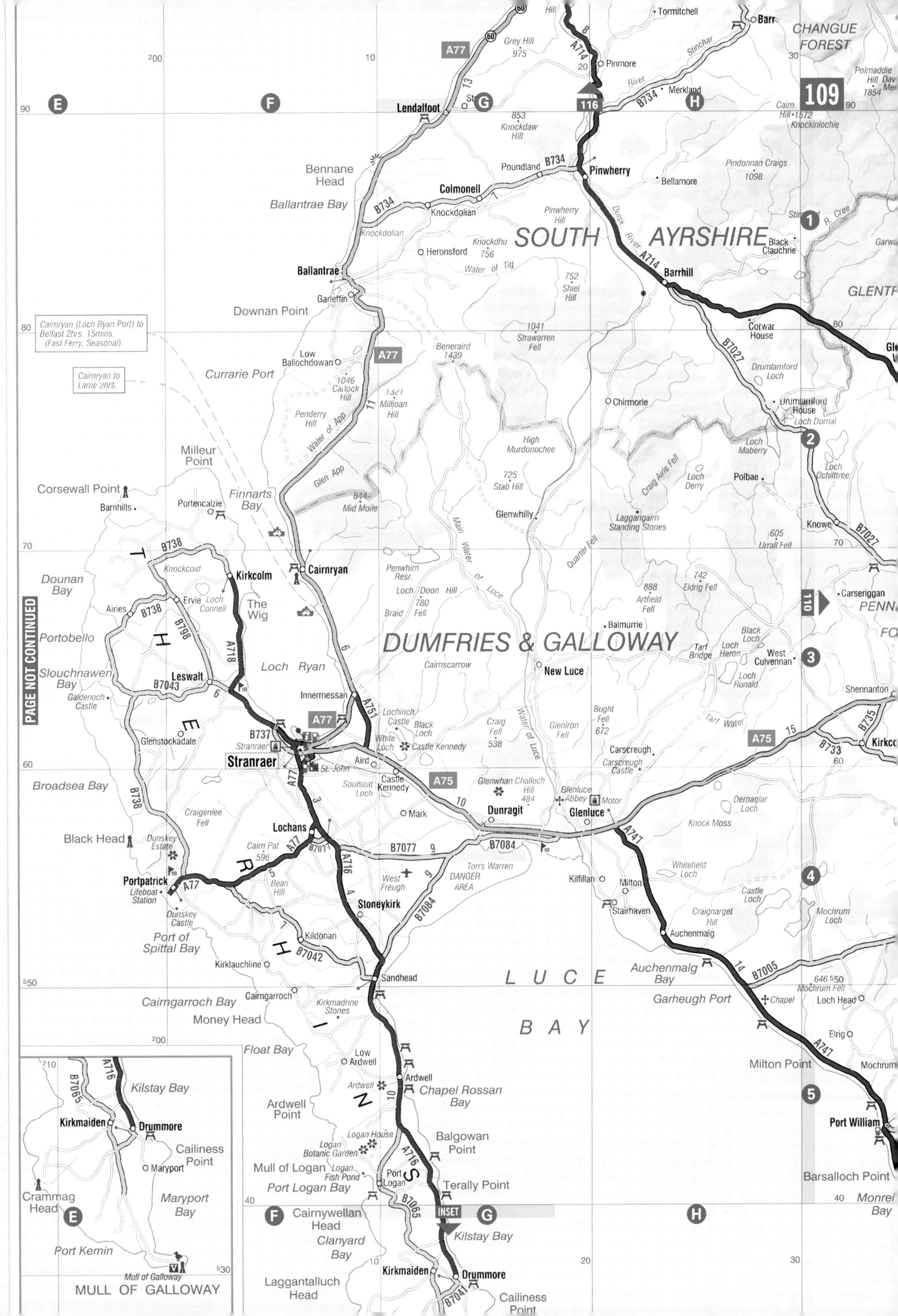

CHANGUE FOREST

• Tormitchell
• Barr

Polmaddie Hill Dav 1854

Cairn Hill 1572
Knockinlochie

Grey Hill 975

• Pinmore
River Stinchar
• Merkland

A77
60

A714
20

116

Lendalfoot
G
St

853 Knockdaw Hill

Poundland **B734**
• Pinwherry

Bennane Head

Colmonell
Knockdolian

Pinwherry Hill
• Bellamore

Pindonnan Craigs 1098

Ballantrae Bay

B734
Knockdolian

Heronsford

Knockdhu 756

SOUTH AYRSHIRE

Black Clauchrie

Garwa

1
R. Cree

Dusk River **A714**
• Barrhill

Ballantrae
Garleffin
Water of Tig

752 Shiel Hill

Corwar House

GLENTRE

Downan Point

Beneraird 1439

1041 Strawarren Fell

80
B7027

Cairnryan (Loch Ryan Port) to Belfast 2hrs. 15mins. (Fast Ferry, Seasonal)

Low Ballochdowan

A77

Drumlamford Loch

Drumlamford House

Cairnryan to Larne 2hrs.

Currarie Port

1046 Carlock Hill

1321 Milljoan Hill

• Chirmorie

Loch Dornal

2

Milleur Point

Penderry Hill
Water of App

High Murdonochee

Loch Maberry

Corsewall Point

Portencalzie
Finnarts Bay

Glen App

844 Mid Moile

725 Stab Hill

Glenwhilly

Craig Airie Fell

Loch Derry

Polbae

Loch Ochiltree

Knowe

B7027

Barnhills

T
Knockcoid
B738

Quarter Fell

Laggangairn Standing Stones

605 Urrall Fell

70

Dounan Bay

Airies
Ervie
Loch Connell

Kirkcolm
Cairnryan

742 Eldrig Fell

110
Carseriggan

PENN

Portobello

B738
B798

The Wig

Penwhirn Resr.

Loch Doon Hill

Main Water of Luce

888 Artfield Fell

Black Loch

West Culvennan

FO

Slouchnawen Bay

A718

Loch Ryan

780 Braid Fell

DUMFRIES & GALLOWAY

Tarf Bridge

Loch Heron

3

Galdenoch Castle

Leswalt
B7043

Cairnscarrow

• Balmurrie

Loch Ronald

Shennanton

PAGE NOT CONTINUED

E

Innermessan

• New Luce

A75

B735

Glenstockadale

A77

Lochinch Castle

Black Loch

Craig Fell 538

Gleniron Fell

Bught Fell 672

Carscreugh

Dernaglar Loch

A75
15

B733
Kirkc

60

B737
Stranraer

White Loch

Castle Kennedy

Carscreugh Castle

Stranraer
St John
Aird

60

Broadsea Bay

B738

Craigenlee Fell

A77

Soulseat Loch

Castle Kennedy

A75
10

Glenwhan Gardens

Challoch Hill 484

Glenluce Abbey
Motor

Knock Moss

Whitefield Loch

Castle Loch

4

Black Head

Dunskey Estate

Lochans

A77
B701

B7077
9

B7084

Dunragit

Glenluce

A747

Mochrum Loch

Portpatrick

Cairn Pat 596

Mark

Glenwhan

DANGER AREA

Kilfillan

Milton

Craignarget Hill

Auchenmalg

Lifeboat Station
A77

A716
4

West Freugh

Torrs Warren

Stairhaven

5
B7005

Dunskey Castle

Bean Hill

Stoneykirk

B7084

Auchenmalg Bay

646 Mochrum Fell

50

Port of Spittal Bay

Kildonan

B7042

Kirklauchline

Sandhead

L U C E

Garheugh Port

Loch Head

A747

50

Cairngarroch Bay

Cairngarroch

Kirkmadrine Stones

B A Y

14
Elrig

Money Head

I

Float Bay

Low Ardwell

Ardwell

Milton Point

Mochrum

Ardwell Point

Z
10
Ardwell

Chapel Rossan Bay

Chapel

Balgowan Point

5

Port William

Logan Botanic Garden

Logan House

A716

Mull of Logan
Logan Fish Pond

Port Logan

Terally Point

Barsalloch Point

Port Logan Bay

B1065

S

INSET
G

Monrei Bay

40

F
Cairnywellan Head

Clanyard Bay

Kilstay Bay

H

Laggantalluch Head

B7041

Kirkmaiden
Drummore

Cailiness Point

INSET (bottom left):

210
B7065
A716

Kilstay Bay

Kirkmaiden
Drummore

Cailiness Point

Maryport

Crammag Head
E

Maryport Bay

Port Kemin

Mull of Galloway

MULL OF GALLOWAY

30

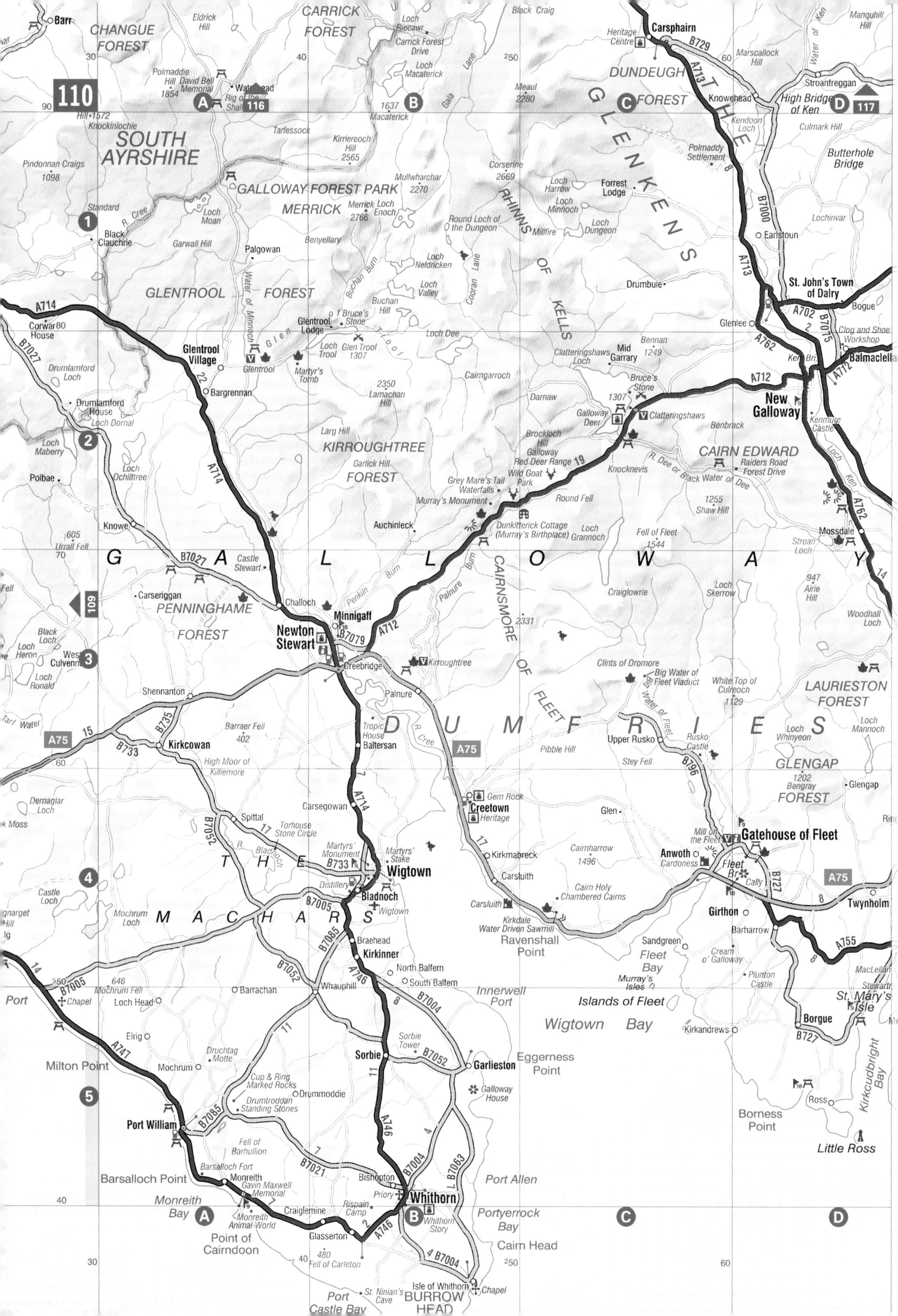

110
Barr
CHANGUE FOREST
Eldrick Hill
CARRICK FOREST
Loch Riecawr
Carrick Forest Drive
Loch Macaterick
Black Craig
Carsphairn
Heritage Centre
B729
Manquhill Hill
Water of Ken
Marscalloch Hill
Polmaddie Hill 1854
David Bell Memorial
Waterhead
Rig of the Shalloch
116
1637
Macaterick
Gala Lane
Meaul 2280
DUNDEUGH FOREST
A713
THE GLENKENS
Knowehead
Stroanfreggan
High Bridge of Ken
117
Hill 1572
Knockinlochie
Tarfessock
Kirriereoch Hill 2565
Kendoon Loch
Culmark Hill
SOUTH AYRSHIRE
Pindonnan Craigs 1098
Corserine 2669
Polmaddy Settlement
Butterhole Bridge
GALLOWAY FOREST PARK
Mullwharchar 2270
Loch Harrow
Forrest Lodge
MERRICK
Merrick 2766
Loch Enoch
Loch Minnoch
Standard
R. Cree
Loch Moan
Round Loch of the Dungeon
Millfire
Loch Dungeon
B7000
Lochinvar
Black Clauchrie
Garwall Hill
RHINNS OF KELLS
Earlstoun
Palgowan
Benyellary
Loch Neldricken
Buchan Burn
Cooran Lane
Loch Valley
GLENTROOL FOREST
Water of Minnoch
Drumbuie
St. John's Town of Dalry
A714
Corwar House
80
Buchan Hill
Glentrool Lodge
Bruce's Stone
Glen Trool
Loch Dee
Glenlee
A702
B7075
Bogue
B7027
Glentrool Village
Loch Trool
Glen Trool 1307
Clatteringshaws Loch
Mid Garrary
Bennan 1249
A762
Clog and Shoe Workshop
Drumlamford Loch
Glentrool
Martyr's Tomb
Cairngarroch
Ken Bri.
Balmaclellan
A712
Bargrennan
22
Drumlamford House
Loch Dornal
2350 Lamachan Hill
Darnaw
1307
Bruce's Stone
New Galloway
Galloway Deer
Clatteringshaws
Kenmure Castle
Loch Maberry
Larg Hill
KIRROUGHTREE FOREST
Brockloch Hill
Galloway Red Deer Range
Benbrack
CAIRN EDWARD
Raiders Road Forest Drive
Loch Ochiltree
Garlick Hill
Wild Goat Park
19
Knocknevis
R. Dee or Black Water of Dee
Polbae
Grey Mare's Tail Waterfalls
Murray's Monument
Round Fell
1255 Shaw Hill
Loch Ken
Knowe
Auchinleck
Dunkitterick Cottage (Murray's Birthplace)
Loch Grannoch
Fell of Fleet 1544
Mossdale
605 Urrall Fell
70
GALLOWAY
Castle Stewart
CAIRNSMORE OF FLEET
Stroan Loch
B7027
Penkiln Burn
Palnure Burn
Loch Skerrow
947 Airie Hill
Carseriggan
PENNINGHAME FOREST
109
Challoch
Minnigaff
Craiglowrie
2331
Woodhall Loch
Black Loch
Loch Heron
West Culvennan
Newton Stewart
B7079
A712
Loch Ronald
Creebridge
Kirroughtree
Clints of Dromore
Big Water of Fleet Viaduct
White Top of Culreoch 1129
LAURIESTON FOREST
Shennanton
Palnure
Tarf Water
B735
Barraer Fell 402
Tropic House
DUMFRIES
Rusko Castle
Loch Whinyeon
Loch Mannoch
A75
15
B733
Kirkcowan
Baltersan
R. Cree
A75
Upper Rusko
Pibble Hill
Stey Fell
B796
GLENGAP FOREST
High Moor of Killiemore
60
1202 Bengray
Glengap
Dernaglar Loch
Gem Rock
Creetown
Heritage
Carsegowan
Glen
Moss
Spittal
Torhouse Stone Circle
A714
17
Mill on the Fleet
Gatehouse of Fleet
B7052
R. Bladnoch
Martyrs' Monument
Martyrs' Stake
B733
Wigtown
Kirkmabreck
Cairnharrow 1496
Anwoth
Cardoness
Fleet Br.
Cally
B727
A75
THE MACHARS
Castle Loch
Distillery
Bladnoch
Carsluith
Cairn Holy Chambered Cairns
Girthon
Twynholm
B7005
Wigtown
Carsluith
Kirkdale Water Driven Sawmill
Mochrum Loch
Braehead
Ravenshall Point
Barharrow
A755
B7085
Kirkinner
Sandgreen
Fleet Bay
Cream o' Galloway
14
550
B7005
646
Mochrum Fell
B7052
North Balfern
South Balfern
A746
Murray's Isles
Plunton Castle
MacLellan
Port
Chapel
Loch Head
Barrachan
Whauphill
Innerwell Port
Islands of Fleet
St. Mary's Isle
B7004
Wigtown Bay
Borgue
Kirkandrews
B727
Elrig
Sorbie Tower
Druchtag Motte
Sorbie
B7052
Garlieston
Eggerness Point
Milton Point
A747
Mochrum
Cup & Ring Marked Rocks
Drummoddie
Galloway House
Kirkcudbright Bay
Port William
B7085
Drumtroddan Standing Stones
A746
Ross
Borness Point
Fell of Barhullion
B7021
B7004
B7063
Little Ross
Barsalloch Point
Barsalloch Fort
Monreith
Gavin Maxwell Memorial
Bishopton
Port Allen
Priory
Whithorn
Monreith Bay
Monreith Animal World
Craiglemine
Rispain Camp
Whithorn Story
Portyerrock Bay
Point of Cairndoon
Glasserton
Cairn Head
480 Fell of Carleton
B7004
Isle of Whithorn
Chapel
Port Castle Bay
St. Ninian's Cave
BURROW HEAD

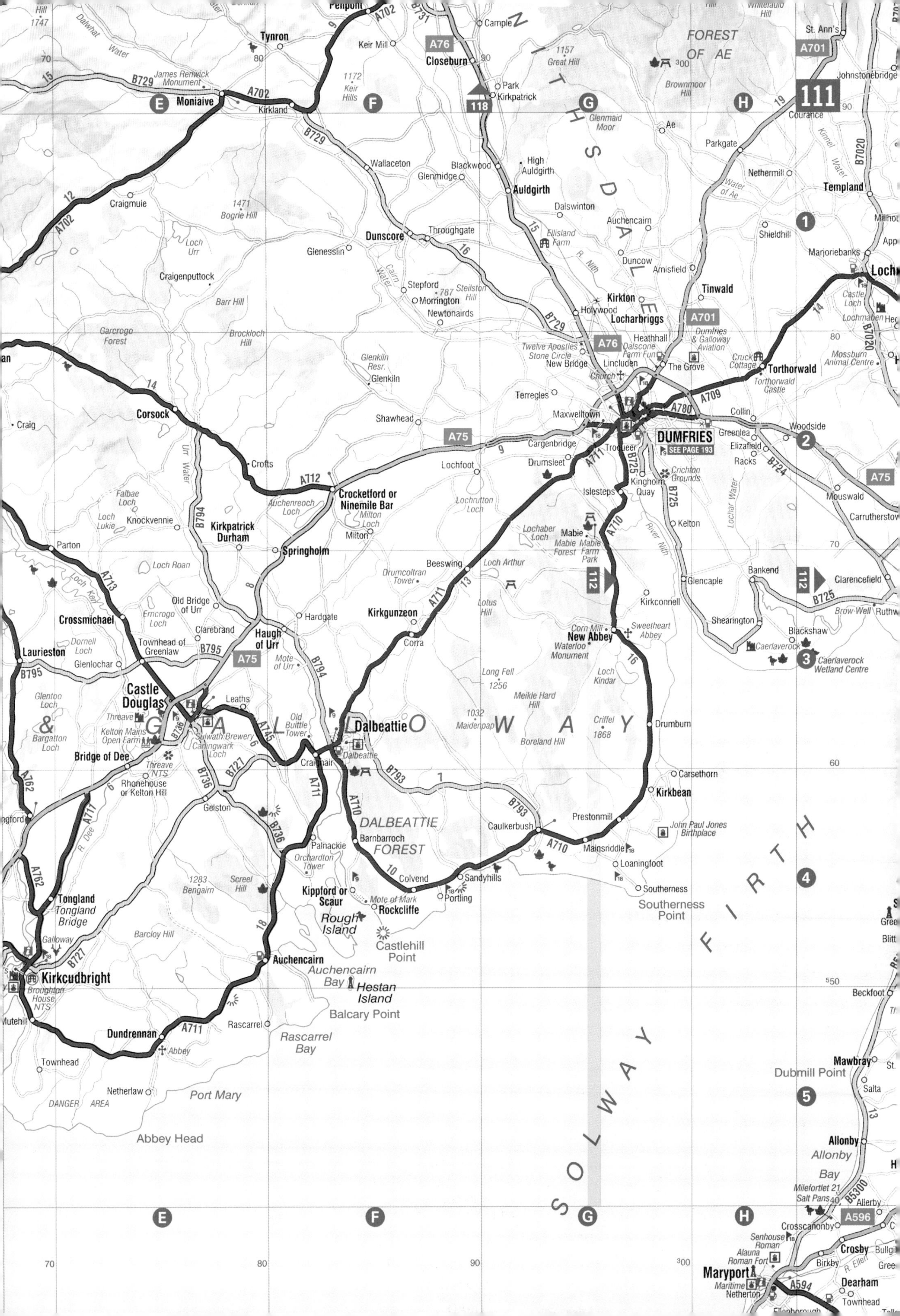
Penpont
A702
B731
Campleton
NITHSDALE
FOREST OF AE
St. Ann's
A701
Tynron
Keir Mill
A76
Closeburn
1157 Great Hill
Johnstonebridge
Dalwhat Water
James Renwick Monument
B729
Moniaive
A702
Kirkland
1172 Keir Hills
Park
Kirkpatrick
118
Brownmoor Hill
111
Courance
E
F
G
H
Glenmaid Moor
Ae
Parkgate
B7020
Kinnel Water
B729
Wallaceton
Blackwood
High Auldgirth
Glenmidge
Auldgirth
Nethermill
Water of Ae
Templand
A702
Craigmuie
1471 Bogrie Hill
Dalswinton
Auchencairn
Millhousebridge
1
Shieldhill
Loch Urr
Dunscore
Throughgate
Ellisland Farm
Glenesslin
Duncow
Amisfield
Marjoriebanks
Lochmaben
Cairn Water
Craigenputtock
Stepford
787 Steilston Hill
Morrington
R. Nith
Kirkton
Tinwald
Castle Loch
Barr Hill
Newtonairds
B729
Holywood
Locharbriggs
A701
Garcrogo Forest
Brockloch Hill
Twelve Apostles Stone Circle
A76
Heathhall
Dumfries & Galloway Aviation
Dalscone Farm Fun
Cruck Cottage
Torthorwald
Torthorwald Castle
Lochmaben
Mossburn Animal Centre
Glenkiln Resr.
Glenkiln
New Bridge
Lincluden
The Grove
Church
A709
Terregles
A780
14
Corsock
Shawhead
Maxwelltown
Collin
Craig
A75
Cargenbridge
DUMFRIES
SEE PAGE 193
Greenlea
Woodside
2
Elizafield
Drumsleet
Troqueer
Lochfoot
B725
Racks
Crofts
A711
B724
A75
Urr Water
A712
Crichton Grounds
Kingholm Quay
Falbae Loch
Crocketford or Ninemile Bar
Lochrutton Loch
Islesteps
Lochar Water
Mouswald
Auchenreoch Loch
Milton Loch
Milton
B794
B725
Carrutherstown
Loch Lukie
Knockvennie
Kirkpatrick Durham
Lochaber Loch
Mabie
Mabie Forest
Mabie Farm Park
A710
River Nith
Kelton
Parton
Springholm
Loch Roan
Beeswing
Loch Arthur
112
Bankend
112
Clarencefield
Drumcoltran Tower
Glencaple
Loch Ken
A713
Old Bridge of Urr
Lotus Hill
B725
Kirkconnell
Brow Well
Ruthwell
Crossmichael
Erncrogo Loch
Hardgate
Kirkgunzeon
Corra
Shearington
Clarebrand
Haugh of Urr
Corn Mill
New Abbey
Sweetheart Abbey
Blackshaw
Laurieston
Dornell Loch
Townhead of Greenlaw
B795
A75
Waterloo Monument
Caerlaverock
3
Caerlaverock Wetland Centre
Glenlochar
Mote of Urr
Long Fell 1256
Loch Kindar
B795
Castle Douglas
Leaths
B794
Meikle Hard Hill
Glentoo Loch
Threave
GALLOWAY
Old Buittle Tower
Dalbeattie
1032 Maidenpap
Criffel 1868
Drumburn
Kelton Mains Open Farm
Sulwath Brewery
Carlingwark Loch
Boreland Hill
Bargatton Loch
Bridge of Dee
Threave NTS
Craignair
Dalbeattie
B793
Carsethorn
Rhonehouse or Kelton Hill
B736
B727
A711
60
A762
Gelston
A710
B793
Kirkbean
A711
R. Dee
B736
DALBEATTIE FOREST
Caulkerbush
Prestonmill
Barnbarroch
John Paul Jones Birthplace
Palnackie
A710
Mainsriddle
A762
Orchardton Tower
1283 Bengairn
Screel Hill
Colvend
Sandyhills
Loaningfoot
4
Tongland
Tongland Bridge
Kippford or Scaur
Mote of Mark
Portling
Southerness
Rockcliffe
Southerness Point
Rough Island
Galloway
Barcloy Hill
Castlehill Point
SOLWAY FIRTH
B727
Auchencairn
Kirkcudbright
Auchencairn Bay
Hestan Island
Broughton House NTS
Balcary Point
Beckfoot
Mutehill
Rascarrel
Dundrennan
A711
Abbey
Rascarrel Bay
Townhead
Mawbray
Dubmill Point
Salta
5
Netherlaw
Port Mary
DANGER AREA
Abbey Head
Allonby
Allonby Bay
Milefortlet 21 Salt Pans
B5300
Allerby
A596
E
F
G
H
Crosscanonby
Senhouse Roman Museum
Alauna Roman Fort
Crosby
Bullgill
Birkby
R. Ellen
Maryport
Maritime Museum
Netherton
A594
Dearham
Townhead
70
80
90
300
Ellenborough

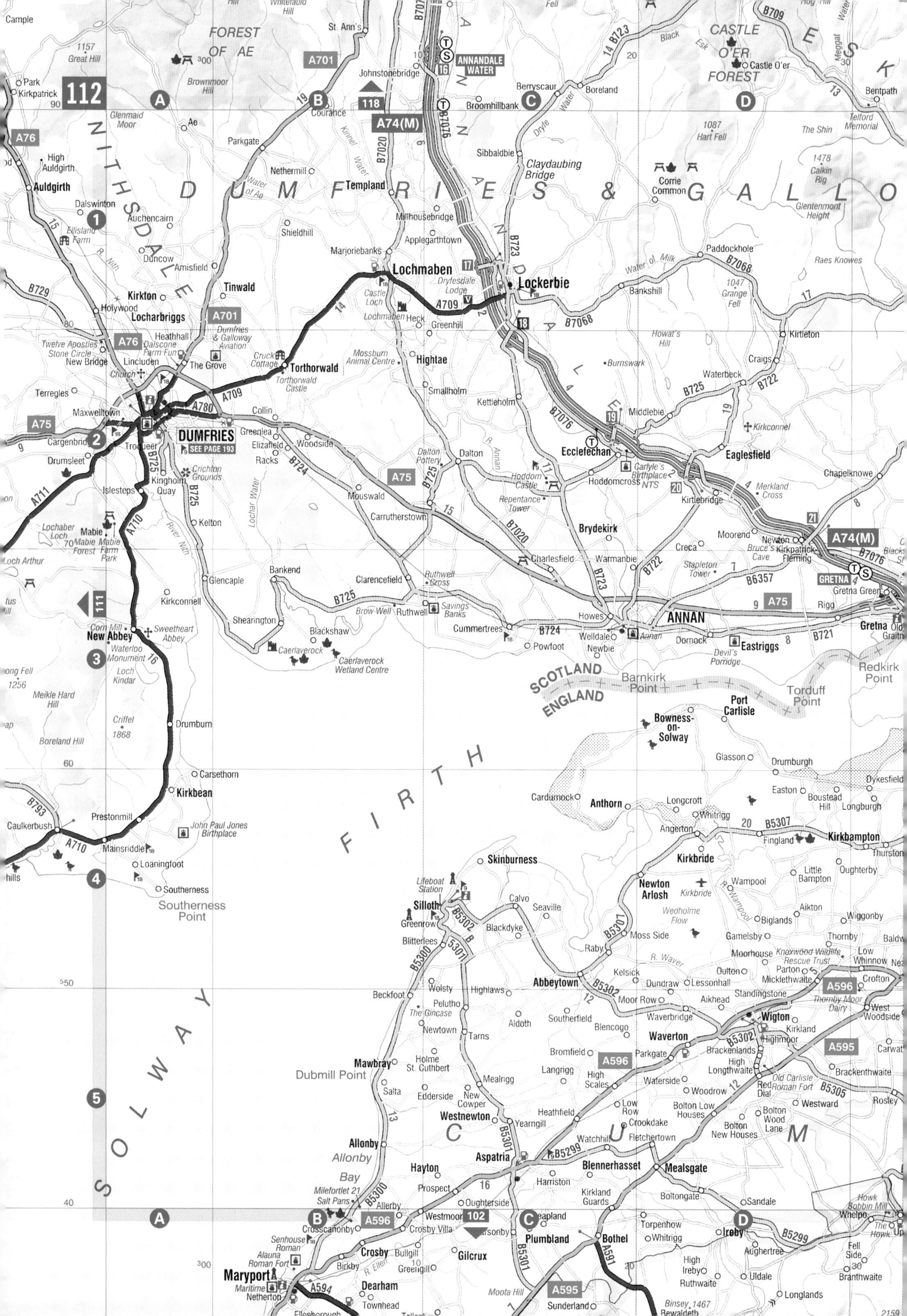

112
A
B
C
D
1
2
3
4
5
118
111
102
DUMFRIES & GALLOWAY
NITHSDALE
ANNANDALE
CUMBRIA
SOLWAY FIRTH
SCOTLAND
ENGLAND
FOREST OF AE
CASTLE O'ER FOREST
ESK
Cample
Park
Kirkpatrick
1157 Great Hill
Brownmoor Hill
Glenmaid Moor
Ae
Water of Ae
Parkgate
Courance
St. Ann's
Johnstonebridge
ANNANDALE WATER
Kinnel Water
Berryscaur
Boreland
Broomhillbank
Castle O'er
Black Esk
Bentpath
Telford Memorial
The Shin
1087 Hart Fell
1478 Calkin Rig
Glenkenmont Height
High Auldgirth
Auldgirth
Dalswinton
Ellisland Farm
Auchencairn
Nethermill
Shieldhill
Templand
Millhousebridge
Applegarthtown
Marjoriebanks
Sibbaldbie
Claydaubing Bridge
Dryfe Water
Corrie Common
Paddockhole
Water of Milk
Raes Knowes
1047 Grange Fell
Duncow
Amisfield
R. Nith
Lochmaben
Dryfesdale Lodge
Castle Loch
Lochmaben
Heck
Lockerbie
Bankshill
Kirkton
Tinwald
Holywood
Locharbriggs
Twelve Apostles Stone Circle
New Bridge
Heathhall
Dalscone Farm Fun
Dumfries & Galloway Aviation
Lincluden
Church
The Grove
Cruck Cottage
Torthorwald
Torthorwald Castle
Mossburn Animal Centre
Greenhill
Hightae
Smallholm
Howat's Hill
Burnswark
Kirtleton
Craigs
Waterbeck
Terregles
Maxwelltown
Collin
Kettleholm
Middlebie
Kirkconnel
Cargenbridge
Troqueer
DUMFRIES
SEE PAGE 193
Greenlea
Elizafield
Woodside
Racks
Dalton
Dalton Pottery
Ecclefechan
Carlyle's Birthplace NTS
Eaglesfield
Chapelknowe
Drumsleet
Kingholm Quay
Crichton Grounds
Hoddom Castle
Hoddomcross
Kirtlebridge
Merkland Cross
Islesteps
Mouswald
Carruthers town
Repentance Tower
Brydekirk
Moorend
Newton
Bruce's Cave
Kirkpatrick-Fleming
Lochaber Loch
Mabie
Mabie Forest
Mabie Farm Park
Kelton
River Nith
Lochar Water
Charlesfield
Warmanbie
Creca
Stapleton Tower
GRETNA
Gretna Green
Loch Arthur
Glencaple
Bankend
Clarencefield
Ruthwell Cross
Brow Well
Ruthwell
Savings Banks
Howes
ANNAN
Rigg
Gretna
Kirkconnell
Shearington
Cummertrees
Powfoot
Welldale
Newbie
Annan
Dornock
Eastriggs
Devil's Porridge
Redkirk Point
Corn Mill
New Abbey
Sweetheart Abbey
Waterloo Monument
Loch Kindar
Blackshaw
Caerlaverock
Caerlaverock Wetland Centre
Barnkirk Point
Torduff Point
Port Carlisle
Bowness-on-Solway
Long Fell 1256
Meikle Hard Hill
Criffel 1868
Boreland Hill
Drumburn
Glasson
Drumburgh
Dykesfield
Carsethorn
Kirkbean
Cardurnock
Anthorn
Longcroft
Whitrigg
Easton
Boustead Hill
Longburgh
Caulkerbush
Prestonmill
John Paul Jones Birthplace
Angerton
Fingland
Kirkbampton
Thurston
Mainsriddle
Loaningfoot
Southerness
Southerness Point
Skinburness
Kirkbride
Little Bampton
Oughterby
Lifeboat Station
Silloth
Greenrow
Calvo
Seaville
Newton Arlosh
Wampool
Wedholme Flow
Biglands
Aikton
Wiggonby
Blitterlees
Blackdyke
Moss Side
Gamelsby
Thornby
Raby
R. Waver
Moorhouse
Knoxwood Wildlife Rescue Trust
Low Whinnow
Kelsick
Oulton
Parton
Micklethwaite
Crofton
Wolsty
Abbeytown
Dundraw
Lessonhall
Beckfoot
Highlaws
Pelutho
The Gincase
Moor Row
Aikhead
Standingstone
Thornby Moor Dairy
Wigton
West Woodside
Newtown
Aldoth
Southerfield
Waverbridge
Kirkland
Tarns
Blencogo
Waverton
Highmoor
Carwath
Bromfield
Parkgate
Brackenlands
Mawbray
Holme St. Cuthbert
Langrigg
High Scales
High Longthwaite
Old Carlisle Roman Fort
Brackenthwaite
Dubmill Point
Salta
Mealrigg
Waterside
Woodrow
Red Dial
Westward
Rosley
Edderside
New Cowper
Low Row
Bolton Low Houses
Bolton Wood Lane
Westnewton
Heathfield
Yearngill
Crookdake
Bolton New Houses
Allonby
Allonby Bay
Watchhill
Fletchertown
Aspatria
Hayton
Blennerhasset
Mealsgate
Prospect
Harriston
Milefortlet 21 Salt Pans
Oughterside
Kirkland Guards
Boltongate
Sandale
Allerby
Westmoor
Crosscanonby
Crosby Villa
Parsonby
Plumbland
Bothel
Torpenhow
Whitrigg
Ireby
Aughertree
Whelpo
Howk Bobbin Mill
The Howk
Senhouse Roman Museum
Alauna Roman Fort
Crosby
Bullgill
Greengill
Gilcrux
High Ireby
Ruthwaite
Fell Side
Branthwaite
Maryport
Maritime Museum
Netherton
Birkby
R. Ellen
Dearham
Townhead
Moota Hill
Sunderland
Binsey 1467
Bewaldeth
Uldale
Longlands
A76
A701
A74(M)
A709
A780
A75
A711
A710
A724
B7020
B7076
B723
B7068
B725
B724
B722
B6357
B721
B729
B793
B5307
B5302
B5300
B5301
B5299
A596
A595
A594
A591
B5305
B709
B723

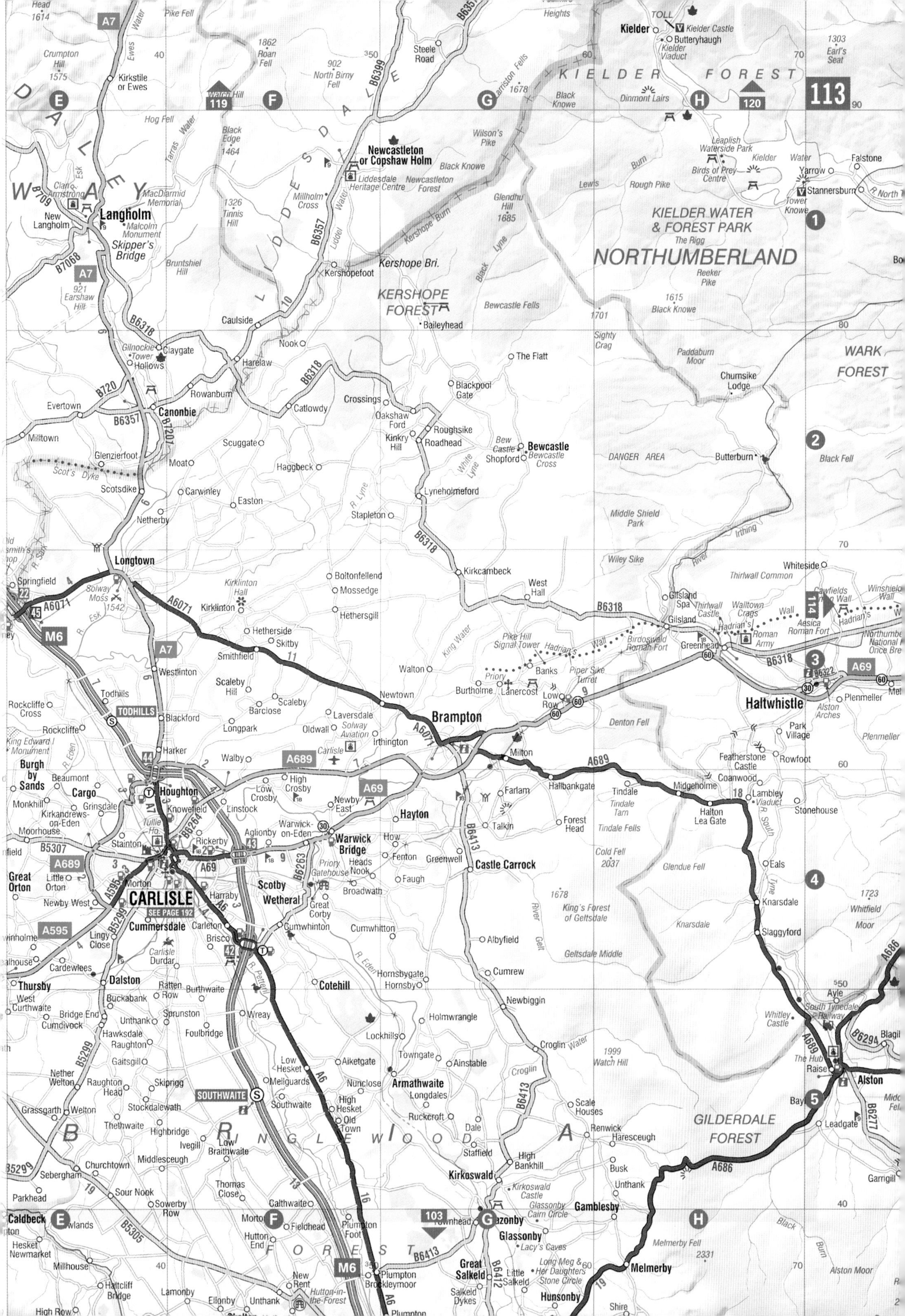

113
Head 1614
A7
Pike Fell
Heights
B6357
TOLL
Kielder
Kielder Castle
Butteryhaugh
Kielder Viaduct
1303 Earl's Seat
Crumpton Hill 1575
Ewes Water
1862 Roan Fell
Steele Road
902 North Birny Fell
B6399
Kirkstile or Ewes
KIELDER FOREST
Watch Hill 119
Garriston Fells 1678
Black Knowe
Dinmont Lairs
120
E
F
G
H
Hog Fell
Tarras Water
Black Edge 1464
Wilson's Pike
Newcastleton or Copshaw Holm
Leaplish Waterside Park
Kielder Water
Falstone
Yarrow
Birds of Prey Centre
Stannersburn
R. North Tyne
Tower Knowe
Black Knowe
Rough Pike
Lewis Burn
B709
Clan Armstrong
MacDiarmid Memorial
Liddesdale Heritage Centre
Newcastleton Forest
Millholm Cross
Glendhu Hill 1685
KIELDER WATER & FOREST PARK
The Rigg
1
New Langholm
Langholm
Malcolm Monument
1326 Tinnis Hill
Kershope Burn
Liddel Water
B6357
Skipper's Bridge
B7068
A7
Bruntshiel Hill
Kershope Bri.
Kershopefoot
NORTHUMBERLAND
Reeker Pike
921 Earshaw Hill
Black Lyne
KERSHOPE FOREST
Bewcastle Fells
1615 Black Knowe
Baileyhead
1701
Sighty Crag
80
B6318
Caulside
Claygate
Gilnockie Tower
Hollows
Nook
Harelaw
B6318
The Flatt
Paddaburn Moor
WARK FOREST
B720
Rowanburn
Blackpool Gate
Chirnsike Lodge
Evertown
Canonbie
Catlowdy
Crossings
Oakshaw Ford
Roughsike
B6357
B7201
Kinkry Hill
Roadhead
2
Milltown
Scuggate
Bew Castle
Bewcastle
Bewcastle Cross
Shopford
DANGER AREA
Butterburn
Black Fell
Glenzierfoot
Moat
Haggbeck
White Lyne
Scot's Dyke
Scotsdike
Carwinley
Easton
Lyneholmeford
Netherby
R. Lyne
Stapleton
Middle Shield Park
Irthing
B6318
70
Longtown
Springfield
Boltonfellend
Wiley Sike
Whiteside
Thirlwall Common
Solway Moss 1542
Kirklinton Hall
Mossedge
West Hall
Gilsland Spa
Thirlwall Castle
Walltown Crags
Cawfields
Wall
Winshields Wall
114
A6071
Kirklinton
Hethersgill
B6318
Gilsland
Hadrian's Wall
Aesica Roman Fort
Hadrian's
M6
R. Esk
Hetherside
Skitby
Pike Hill Signal Tower
Birdoswald Roman Fort
Greenhead
Roman Army
Northumberland National Park
Once Brewed
A7
Smithfield
King Water
B6318
3
A69
Westlinton
Walton
Banks
Piper Sike Turret
B6322
Haltwhistle
Plenmeller
Rockcliffe Cross
Todhills
Scaleby Hill
Scaleby
Newtown
Priory
Burtholme
Lanercost
Low Row
Alston Arches
TODHILLS
Barclose
Laversdale
Brampton
Denton Fell
Park Village
Plenmeller
Rockcliffe
Blackford
Longpark
Oldwall
Solway Aviation
Irthington
King Edward I Monument
R. Eden
Harker
Walby
A689
Carlisle
A6071
Milton
Featherstone Castle
Rowfoot
60
Burgh by Sands
Beaumont
Houghton
High Crosby
Low Crosby
A69
Farlam
Hallbankgate
Tindale
Coanwood
Midgeholme
Lambley
Lambley Viaduct
Cargo
Grinsdale
Knowefield
Linstock
Newby East
Hayton
Tindale Tarn
Halton Lea Gate
Monkhill
Kirkandrews-on-Eden
Tullie Ho.
B6264
Warwick-on-Eden
Talkin
Forest Head
Tindale Fells
Stonehouse
R. South Tyne
Moorhouse
Stainton
Rickerby
Aglionby
Warwick Bridge
How
B6413
Cold Fell 2037
B5307
A689
Priory Gatehouse
Heads Nook
Fenton
Greenwell
Castle Carrock
Glendue Fell
Eals
4
Great Orton
Little Orton
A595
Morton
CARLISLE
SEE PAGE 192
Harraby
A69
Scotby
Wetheral
Broadwath
Faugh
B6263
Newby West
Great Corby
1678
King's Forest of Geltsdale
Knarsdale
1723 Whitfield Moor
A595
Cummersdale
Carleton
Brisco
Cumwhinton
Cumwhitton
River Gelt
Knarsdale
Slaggyford
Lingy Close
B5299
Carlisle Durdar
Albyfield
Geltsdale Middle
A686
Cardewlees
Dalston
Ratten Row
Burthwaite
R. Petteril
Hornsbygate
Hornsby
Cotehill
Cumrew
R. Eden
550
Ayle
Thursby
West Curthwaite
Buckabank
Newbiggin
South Tynedale Railway
Bridge End
Cumdivock
Unthank
Sprunston
Wreay
Holmwrangle
Whitley Castle
Hawksdale
Foulbridge
Raughton
Lockhills
Croglin Water
B6294
Blagill
B5299
Gaitsgill
Aiketgate
Towngate
Ainstable
1999 Watch Hill
A689
The Hub
Raise
Alston
Nether Welton
Raughton Head
Skiprigg
Low Hesket
Mellguards
A6
Nunclose
Armathwaite
Longdales
Croglin
B6413
SOUTHWAITE
Southwaite
High Hesket
Scale Houses
Bayles
5
B6277
Grassgarth
Welton
Stockdalewath
Old Town
Ruckcroft
Dale
Renwick
GILDERDALE FOREST
Leadgate
Thethwaite
Highbridge
Harescough
Ivegill
Low Braithwaite
INGLEWOOD
Staffield
High Bankhill
Busk
Middlesceugh
Churchtown
Sebergham
Kirkoswald
Kirkoswald Castle
Unthank
A686
Garrigill
Parkhead
Sour Nook
Thomas Close
Sowerby Row
Calthwaite
Glassonby Cairn Circle
Gamblesby
40
Caldbeck
Rowlands
B5305
Morton
Fieldhead
Plumpton Foot
103
Townhead
Lazonby
Glassonby
Black Burn
Hesket Newmarket
Hutton End
FOREST
B6413
Lacy's Caves
Melmerby Fell 2331
Millhouse
M6
Great Salkeld
B6412
Little Salkeld
Long Meg & Her Daughters Stone Circle
Melmerby
Alston Moor
Plumpton
Brockleymoor
New Rent
Hutton-in-the-Forest
Haltcliff Bridge
Lamonby
Ellonby
Unthank
Salkeld Dykes
Hunsonby
High Row
Shire
Plumpton
A6

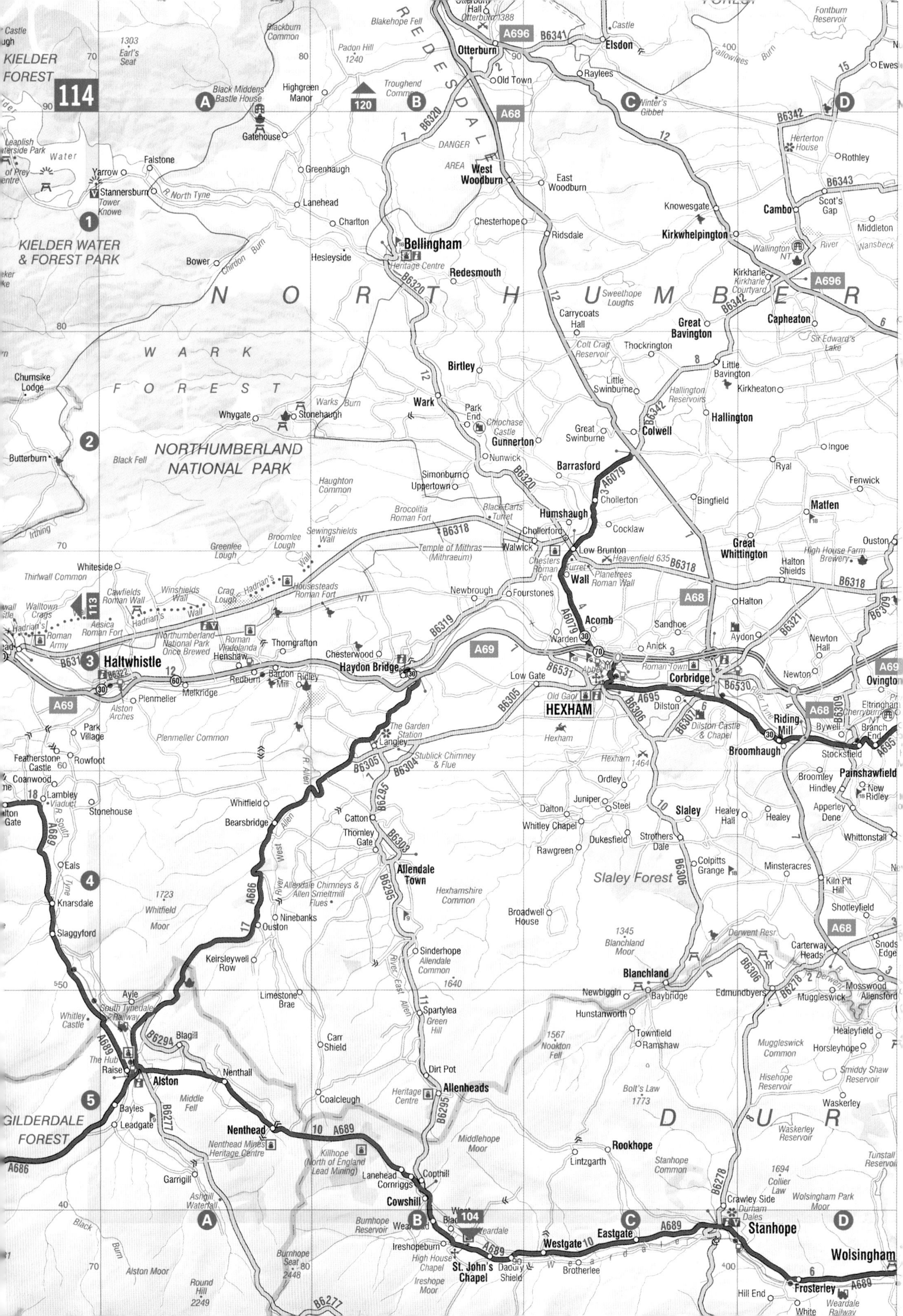

KIELDER FOREST
114
Blackburn Common
Blakehope Fell
Otterburn
A696
B6341
Elsdon
Castle
Fontburn Reservoir
Padon Hill 1240
Earl's Seat
Black Middens Bastle House
Highgreen Manor
Troughend Common
120
Old Town
Raylees
Winter's Gibbet
A68
Ewesley
B6342
Herterton House
Rothley
Gatehouse
Falstone
Yarrow
Stannersburn
Tower Knowe
R. North Tyne
Greenhaugh
Lanehead
Charlton
West Woodburn
East Woodburn
DANGER AREA
REDESDALE
B6320
B6343
Cambo
Scot's Gap
Knowesgate
Kirkwhelpington
Middleton
Wallington NT
Chesterhope
Ridsdale
KIELDER WATER & FOREST PARK
Bower
Hesleyside
Bellingham
Heritage Centre
Redesmouth
Kirkharle Courtyard
A696
Capheaton
N O R T H U M B E R
Sweethope Loughs
Carrycoats Hall
Great Bavington
Colt Crag Reservoir
Thockrington
Sir Edward's Lake
W A R K
F O R E S T
Chirnsike Lodge
Birtley
Little Bavington
Kirkheaton
Little Swinburne
Hallington Reservoirs
Wark
Park End
Chipchase Castle
Gunnerton
Whygate
Stonehaugh
Warks Burn
Great Swinburne
Colwell
Hallington
Butterburn
Black Fell
NORTHUMBERLAND NATIONAL PARK
Nunwick
Barrasford
Ingoe
Ryal
Simonburn
Uppertown
Haughton Common
A6079
Chollerton
Bingfield
Fenwick
Matfen
Brocolitia Roman Fort
Black Carts Turret
Humshaugh
Chollerford
Cocklaw
Irthing
Broomlee Lough
Sewingshields Wall
B6318
Greenlee Lough
Temple of Mithras (Mithraeum)
Walwick
Low Brunton
Great Whittington
Ouston
High House Farm Brewery
Whiteside
Thirlwall Common
Housesteads Roman Fort
Chesters Roman Fort
Heavenfield 635
Wall
Planetrees Roman Wall
Halton Shields
Cawfields Roman Wall
Winshields Wall
Crag Lough
Hadrian's Wall
113
Walltown Crags
Aesica Roman Fort
Roman Army
Newbrough
Fourstones
A68
Halton
Northumberland National Park Once Brewed
Roman Vindolanda
Thorngrafton
Henshaw
B6319
Acomb
Sandhoe
Aydon
Newton Hall
Haltwhistle
Chesterwood
Haydon Bridge
A69
Warden
Anick
Roman Town
Corbridge
Newton
Ovington
Redburn
Bardon Mill
Ridley
Melkridge
Plenmeller
Low Gate
B6531
Old Gaol
HEXHAM
A695
Dilston
B6530
Riding Mill
Eltringham
Bywell
Alston Arches
Park Village
Plenmeller Common
The Garden Station
Langley
B6305
Dilston Castle & Chapel
Hexham
Broomhaugh
Stocksfield
Featherstone Castle
Rowfoot
Stublick Chimney & Flue
B6304
Hexham 1464
Coanwood
Lambley Viaduct
Ordley
Broomley
Hindley
Painshawfield
New Ridley
Stonehouse
Whitfield
Bearsbridge
R. Allen
Catton
B6295
Juniper
Steel
Dalton
Whitley Chapel
Slaley
Healey Hall
Healey
Apperley Dene
A689
Thornley Gate
B6303
Rawgreen
Dukesfield
Strothers Dale
Whittonstall
Eals
West Allen
Allendale Town
Colpitts Grange
Allendale Chimneys & Allen Smeltmill Flues
Slaley Forest
B6306
Minsteracres
Knarsdale
1723 Whitfield Moor
A686
River
Hexhamshire Common
Kiln Pit Hill
Shotleyfield
Ninebanks
Broadwell House
Slaggyford
Ouston
1345 Blanchland Moor
Derwent Resr
A68
Keirsleywell Row
Sinderhope
Allendale Common
1640
River East Allen
Carterway Heads
Snods Edge
Blanchland
Mosswood
Allensford
Ayle
South Tynedale Railway
Whitley Castle
Limestone Brae
Newbiggin
Baybridge
Edmundbyers
Muggleswick
Spartylea
Green Hill
Hunstanworth
Healeyfield
Blagill
B6294
Carr Shield
1567 Nookton Fell
Townfield
Ramshaw
Muggleswick Common
Horsleyhope
The Hub
Raise
Alston
Nenthall
Dirt Pot
Smiddy Shaw Reservoir
Hisehope Reservoir
Middle Fell
Coalcleugh
Heritage Centre
Allenheads
Bolt's Law 1773
Waskerley
Bayles
Leadgate
B6277
GILDERDALE FOREST
Nenthead
Nenthead Mines Heritage Centre
A689
D U R
Waskerley Reservoir
Killhope (North of England Lead Mining)
Middlehope Moor
Rookhope
Linztgarth
Stanhope Common
Tunstall Reservoir
A686
Garrigill
Lanehead
Cornriggs
Copthill
1694 Collier Law
Ashgill Waterfall
Cowshill
Crawley Side
Wolsingham Park Moor
B6278
Durham Dales
Burnhope Reservoir
Wearhead
104
Weardale
Eastgate
Stanhope
Westgate
Ireshopeburn
High House Chapel
Brotherlee
Wolsingham
Black Burn
Alston Moor
Burnhope Seat 2448
St. John's Chapel
Daddry Shield
Ireshope Moor
Round Hill 2249
B6277
Frosterley
Hill End
Weardale Railway
White

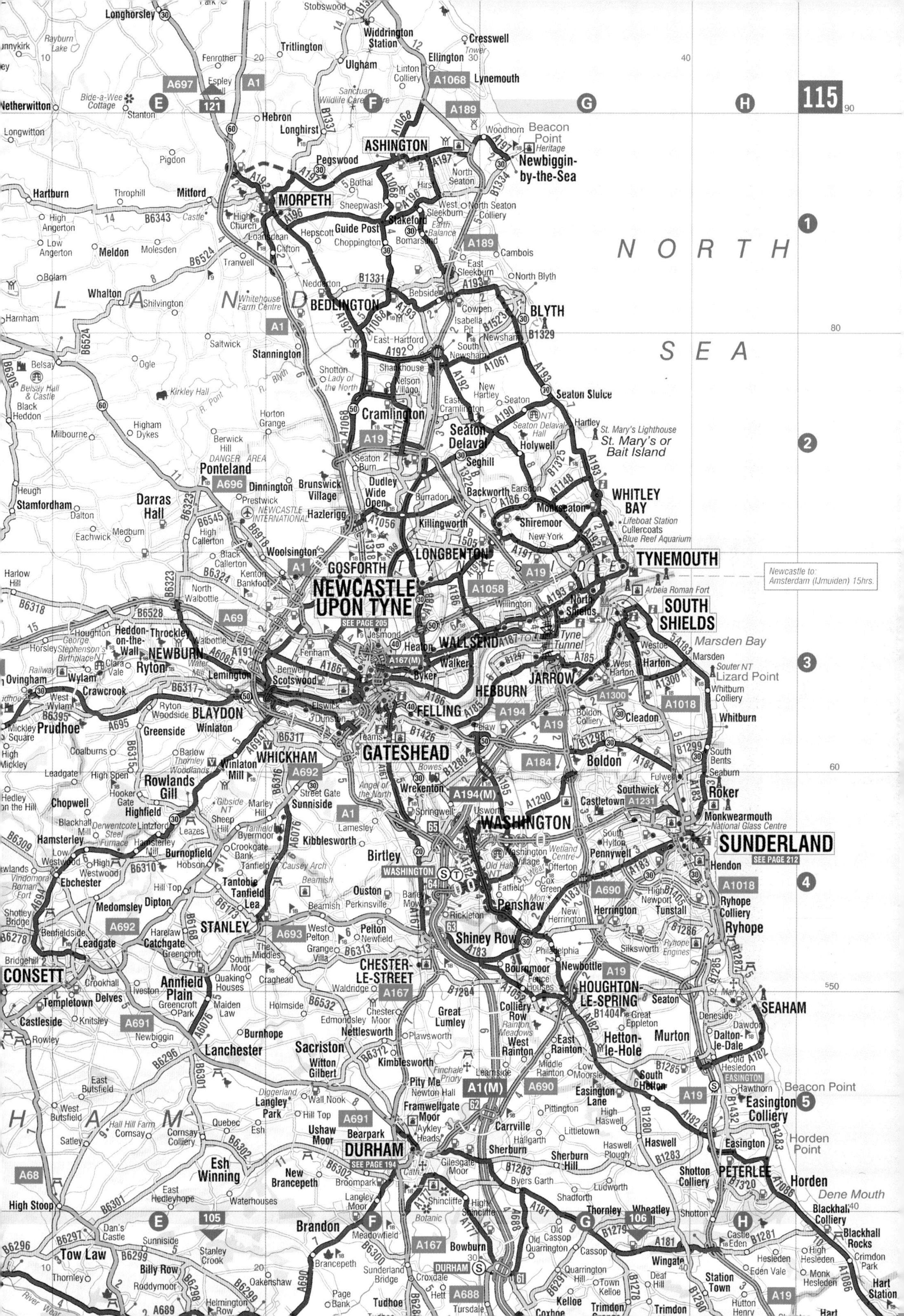
115
NORTH SEA
Longhorsley
Stobswood
Widdrington Station
Tritlington
Cresswell
Ellington
Ulgham
Linton Colliery
Lynemouth
Fenrother
Espley
Bide-a-Wee Cottage
Stanton
Netherwitton
Sanctuary Wildlife Care Centre
Hebron
Longhirst
Longwitton
Woodhorn
Beacon Point
Heritage
Ashington
Pegswood
Pigdon
Newbiggin-by-the-Sea
North Seaton
Bothal
Sheepwash
Hartburn
Throphill
Mitford
Morpeth
West Sleekburn
North Seaton Colliery
High Angerton
Low Angerton
Meldon
Molesden
High Church
Loansdean
Hepscott
Guide Post
Stakeford
Choppington
Bomarsund
Earth Balance
Cambois
Clifton
Tranwell
Bolam
East Sleekburn
North Blyth
Whalton
Shilvington
Whitehouse Farm Centre
Nedderton
Bebside
Bedlington
Cowpen
Blyth
Isabella Pit
Harnham
East Hartford
South Newsham
Newsham
Saltwick
Stannington
Belsay
Belsay Hall & Castle
Ogle
Shotton
Lady of the North
Shankhouse
Nelson Village
New Hartley
Seaton Sluice
Black Heddon
Kirkley Hall
East Cramlington
Seaton
Horton Grange
Cramlington
Seaton Delaval
Hartley
St. Mary's Lighthouse
St. Mary's or Bait Island
Milbourne
Higham Dykes
Seaton Delaval Hall
Berwick Hill
Holywell
DANGER AREA
Seaton Burn
Seghill
Ponteland
Dinnington
Brunswick Village
Dudley
Wide Open
Burradon
Backworth
Earsdon
Whitley Bay
Heugh
Stamfordham
Darras Hall
Prestwick
Newcastle International
Hazlerigg
Killingworth
Monkseaton
Shiremoor
Lifeboat Station
Cullercoats
Blue Reef Aquarium
New York
Dalton
Eachwick
Medburn
High Callerton
Black Callerton
Woolsington
Longbenton
Tynemouth
Gosforth
Harlow Hill
Kenton Bankfoot
Newcastle upon Tyne
SEE PAGE 205
North Walbottle
Willington
Arbeia Roman Fort
North Shields
South Shields
Newcastle to: Amsterdam (IJmuiden) 15hrs.
Jesmond
Heaton
Wallsend
Tyne Tunnel
Marsden Bay
Houghton
Heddon-on-the-Wall
Throckley
Walbottle
Horsley
George Stephenson's Birthplace
Newburn
Walker
Westoe
Harton
Marsden
Souter
Lizard Point
Clara Vale
Ryton
Water Mill
Lemington
Fenham
Benwell
Scotswood
Byker
Jarrow
West Harton
Whitburn Colliery
Ovingham
Wylam
Crawcrook
Hebburn
Whitburn
West Wylam
Ryton Woodside
Blaydon
Winlaton
Elswick
Dunston
Felling
Boldon Colliery
Cleadon
Mickley Square
Prudhoe
Greenside
Teams
Gateshead
Boldon
South Bents
High Mickley
Coalburns
Barlow
Thornley Woodlands
Winlaton Mill
Whickham
Bowes
Wrekenton
Seaburn
Fulwell
Leadgate
High Spen
Hooker Gate
Rowlands Gill
Street Gate
Sunniside
Angel of the North
Southwick
Castletown
Roker
Hedley on the Hill
Chopwell
Gibside
Highfield
Marley Hill
Springwell
Usworth
Washington
Monkwearmouth
National Glass Centre
Blackhall Mill
Derwentcote Steel Furnace
Lintzford
Sheep Hill
Tanfield Byermoor
Lamesley
Kibblesworth
South Hylton
Pennywell
Sunderland
SEE PAGE 212
Hamsterley
Low Westwood
High Westwood
Hamsterley Mill
Burnopfield
Crookgate Bank
Hobson
Tanfield
Causey Arch
Birtley
Washington Village
Wetland Centre
Offerton
Hendon
Vindomora Roman Fort
Ebchester
Hill Top
Tantobie
Tanfield Lea
Beamish
Ouston
Barley Mow
Fatfield
Cox Green
Penshaw
Penshaw Mon.
High Newport
Tunstall
Ryhope Colliery
Ryhope
Shotley Bridge
Medomsley
Dipton
Perkinsville
Rickleton
New Herrington
Herrington
Benfieldside
Leadgate
Harelaw
Catchgate
Stanley
West Pelton
Pelton
Newfield
Grange Villa
Shiney Row
Philadelphia
Silksworth
Ryhope Engines
Bridgehill
Consett
Greencroft
South Moor
The Middles
Craghead
Chester-le-Street
Bournmoor
Fence Houses
Newbottle
Houghton-le-Spring
Seaton
Crookhall
Iveston
Annfield Plain
Quaking Houses
Waldridge
Templetown
Delves
Greencroft Park
Maiden Law
Holmside
Chester Moor
Edmondsley
Great Lumley
Colliery Row
Rainton Meadows
Great Eppleton
Deneside
Seaham
Castleside
Knitsley
Newbiggin
Burnhope
Nettlesworth
Plawsworth
West Rainton
East Rainton
Hetton-le-Hole
Murton
Dawdon
Dalton-le-Dale
Rowley
Lanchester
Sacriston
Witton Gilbert
Kimblesworth
Middle Rainton
Low Moorsley
Cold Hesledon
South Hetton
East Butsfield
Pity Me
Finchale Priory
Newton Hall
Leamside
Easington Lane
Hawthorn
Beacon Point
Easington Colliery
West Butsfield
Diggerland
Langley Park
Wall Nook
Framwellgate Moor
Pittington
High Haswell
Hall Hill Farm
Cornsay
Hill Top
Aykley Heads
Carrville
Littletown
Satley
Cornsay Colliery
Quebec
Esh
Ushaw Moor
Bearpark
Durham
SEE PAGE 194
Hallgarth
Sherburn
Sherburn Hill
Haswell Plough
Haswell
Easington
Horden Point
Esh Winning
New Brancepeth
Broompark
Cath.
Gilesgate Moor
Byers Garth
Ludworth
Shotton Colliery
Peterlee
Horden
Dene Mouth
High Stoop
East Hedleyhope
Waterhouses
Langley Moor
Shincliffe
High Shincliffe
Botanic
Shadforth
Thornley
Wheatley Hill
Shotton
Blackhall Colliery
Dan's Castle
Sunniside
Brandon
Meadowfield
Old Cassop
Old Quarrington
Cassop
Castle Eden
Blackhall Rocks
Tow Law
Stanley Crook
Bowburn
Wingate
High Hesleden
Hesleden
Crimdon Park
Billy Row
Brancepeth
Sunderland Bridge
Croxdale
Quarrington Hill
Town Kelloe
Deaf Hill
Station Town
Eden Vale
Monk Hesleden
Thornley
Roddymoor
Oakenshaw
Hett
Tursdale
Kelloe
Trimdon
Hutton Henry
Hart Station
Hart
Helmington Row
Page Bank
Tudhoe
Coxhoe
Trimdon Grange
River Wear
WASHINGTON
DURHAM
EASINGTON
LANDA
HAM
TYNE SIDE
NT
A1
A1(M)
A19
A68
A69
A167
A167(M)
A181
A182
A183
A184
A185
A186
A187
A189
A191
A192
A193
A194
A194(M)
A195
A196
A197
A688
A689
A690
A691
A692
A693
A694
A695
A696
A697
A1018
A1056
A1058
A1061
A1068
A1086
A1231
A1290
A1300
B1331
B1337
B1329
B1523
B6343
B6524
B6318
B6323
B6528
B6545
B6324
B6317
B6395
B6315
B6309
B6310
B6173
B6168
B6313
B6532
B6312
B6301
B6302
B6296
B6297
B6299
B6298
B6300
B1284
B1285
B1286
B1287
B1283
B1279
B1281
B1280
B1278
B1404
B1405
B1426
B1288
B1298
B1299
B1320
B1432
121
105
106
E
F
G
H
1
2
3
4
5
40
60
80
90
50
20
14
8
11
15

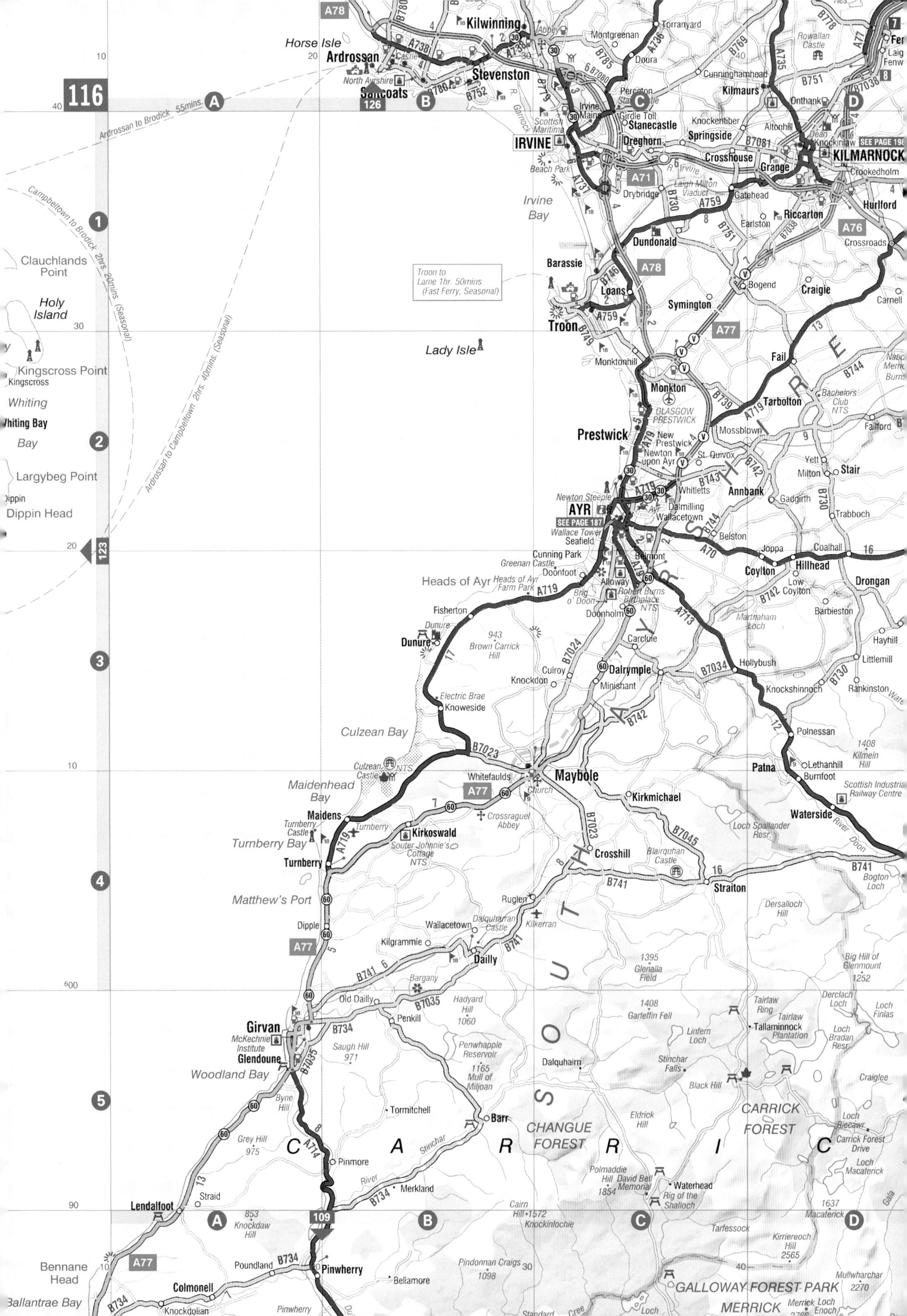
116
A78
Horse Isle
Ardrossan
North Ayrshire
Saltcoats
126
Kilwinning
Stevenston
Montgreenan
Torranyard
Doura
Cunninghamhead
Kilmaurs
Rowallan Castle
Fenwick
Laigh Fenwick
B751
Onthank
Perceton
Irvine Mains
Girdle Toll
Stanecastle
Knockentiber
Springside
Altonhill
Knockinlaw
SEE PAGE 198
KILMARNOCK
IRVINE
Scottish Maritime
Dreghorn
Crosshouse
Grange
Crookedholm
Beach Park
R. Irvine
Laigh Milton Viaduct
A71
Drybridge
Gatehead
A759
Hurlford
Irvine Bay
Earlston
Riccarton
A76
Crossroads
Ardrossan to Brodick 55mins.
Campbeltown to Brodick 2hrs. 20mins. (Seasonal)
Ardrossan to Campbeltown 2hrs. 40mins. (Seasonal)
Clauchlands Point
Holy Island
Kingscross Point
Kingscross
Whiting Bay
Largybeg Point
Dippin Head
Dundonald
Barassie
A78
Troon to Larne 1hr. 50mins. (Fast Ferry, Seasonal)
Loans
Symington
Bogend
Craigie
Carnell
Troon
A759
A77
Lady Isle
Monktonhill
Fail
Monkton
GLASGOW PRESTWICK
Tarbolton
Bachelors' Club NTS
Prestwick
New Prestwick
Newton upon Ayr
Mossblown
St. Quivox
Failford
Yett
Milton
Stair
Newton Steeple
AYR
SEE PAGE 187
Whitletts
Dalmilling
Wallacetown
Annbank
Gadgirth
Trabboch
Wallace Tower
Seafield
Belston
Joppa
Coalhall
123
Cunning Park
Greenan Castle
Doonfoot
Belmont
A70
Coylton
Hillhead
Drongan
Heads of Ayr
Heads of Ayr Farm Park
A719
Alloway
Robert Burns Birthplace NTS
Brig o' Doon
Low Coylton
B742
Doonholm
Martnaham Loch
Barbieston
Fisherton
A713
Dunure
943 Brown Carrick Hill
Carclue
Hayhill
Culroy
Dalrymple
Hollybush
Littlemill
Knockdon
Minishant
B7034
Knockshinnoch
Rankinston
Electric Brae
Knoweside
Culzean Bay
Polnessan
1408 Kilmein Hill
B7023
Culzean Castle NTS
Whitefaulds
Maybole
Patna
Lethanhill
Burnfoot
Maidenhead Bay
A77
Kirkmichael
Scottish Industrial Railway Centre
Maidens
Crossraguel Abbey
Waterside
Turnberry Castle
Kirkoswald
Souter Johnnie's Cottage NTS
Loch Spallander Resr.
Turnberry Bay
Turnberry
B7045
River Doon
Crosshill
Blairquhan Castle
B741
Bogton Loch
Straiton
Matthew's Port
Ruglen
Dersalloch Hill
Kilkerran
Dipple
Wallacetown
Dalquharran Castle
A77
Kilgrammie
Dailly
1395 Glenalla Field
Big Hill of Glenmount 1252
Bargany
Old Dailly
Hadyard Hill 1060
1408 Garleffin Fell
Tairlaw Ring
Derclach Loch
Loch Finlas
Penkill
Tallaminnock Plantation
Girvan
McKechnie Institute
Glendoune
Saugh Hill 971
Penwhapple Reservoir
Linfern Loch
Loch Bradan Resr.
Woodland Bay
Dalquhairn
Stinchar Falls
1165 Mull of Miljoan
Black Hill
Craiglee
Byne Hill
Tormitchell
Barr
Eldrick Hill
CARRICK FOREST
Loch Riecawr
Carrick Forest Drive
CHANGUE FOREST
Grey Hill 975
Pinmore
River Stinchar
Loch Macaterick
Polmaddie Hill
David Bell Memorial
1854
Waterhead
Rig of the Shalloch
Merkland
Lendalfoot
Straid
109
Cairn Hill 1572
Knockinlochie
Macaterick
1637
853 Knockdaw Hill
Tarfessock
Kirriereoch Hill 2565
Bennane Head
Poundland
Pinwherry
Pindonnan Craigs
1098
Bellamore
GALLOWAY FOREST PARK
Mullwharchar 2270
Colmonell
Ballantrae Bay
Knockdolian
MERRICK
Merrick
Loch Enoch
SOUTH AYRSHIRE
CARRICK

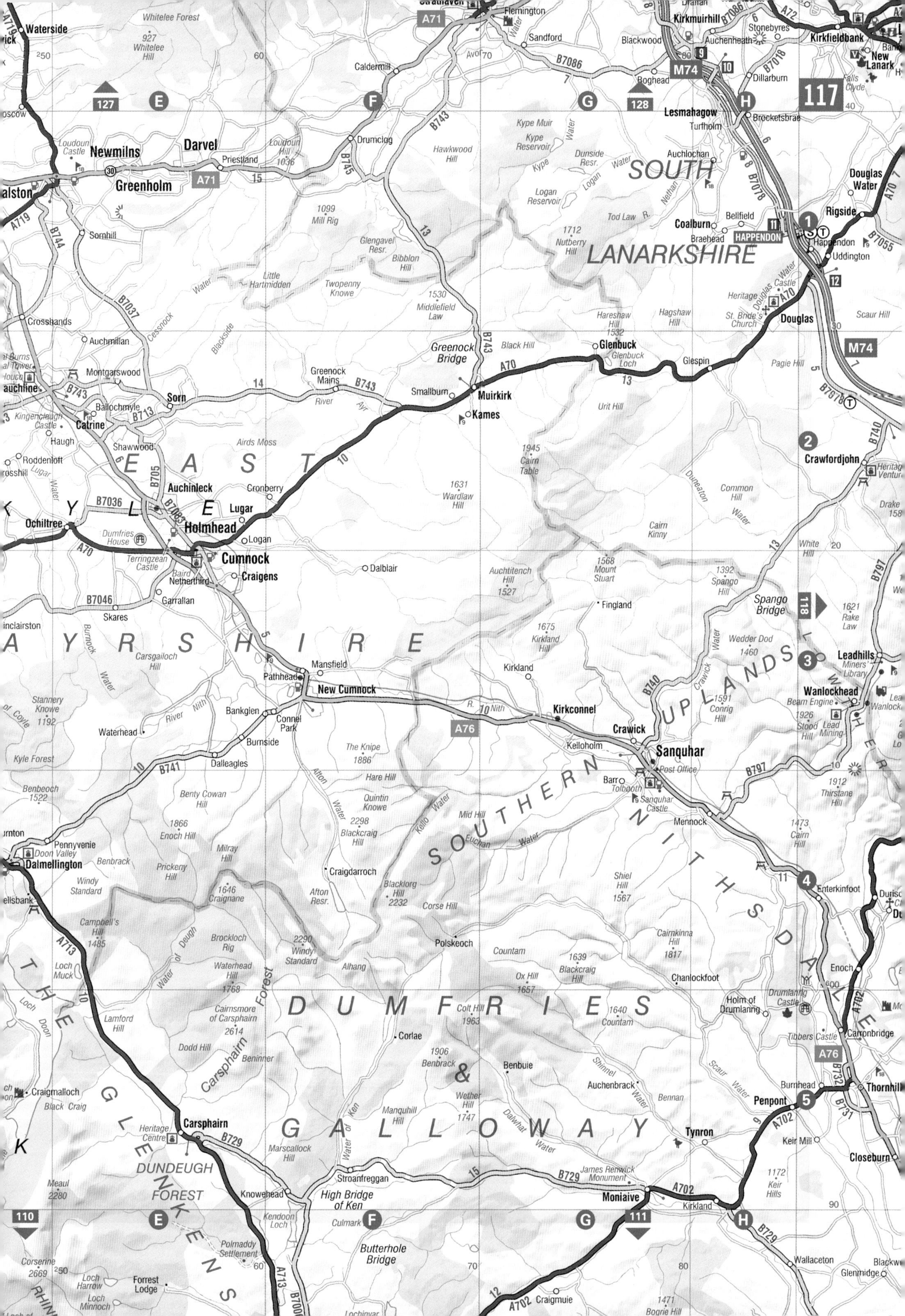
117
127
128
118
110
111
E
F
G
H
SOUTH
LANARKSHIRE
EAST
AYRSHIRE
KYLE
DUMFRIES
&
GALLOWAY
SOUTHERN UPLANDS
NITHSDALE
LOWTHER
THE GLENKENS
DUNDEUGH FOREST
Carsphairn Forest
Kyle Forest
Whitelee Forest
Waterside
927 Whitelee Hill
Flemington
Sandford
Caldermill
Blackwood
Kirkmuirhill
Auchenheath
Stonebyres
Kirkfieldbank
New Lanark
Boghead
Dillarburn
Lesmahagow
Brocketsbrae
Turfholm
Auchlochan
Douglas Water
Coalburn
Bellfield
Braehead
Rigside
HAPPENDON
Happendon
Uddington
Douglas Castle
Heritage
St. Bride's Church
Douglas
Scaur Hill
Pagie Hill
Glespin
Glenbuck
Glenbuck Loch
Hareshaw Hill 1532
Hagshaw Hill
Black Hill
Kype Muir
Kype Reservoir
Dunside Resr.
Logan Reservoir
Tod Law
1712 Nutberry Hill
Hawkwood Hill
Loudoun Castle
Newmilns
Darvel
Priestland
Loudoun Hill 1036
Drumclog
Greenholm
Galston
Sornhill
1099 Mill Rig
Glengavel Resr.
Bibblon Hill
Little Hartmidden
Twopenny Knowe
1530 Middlefield Law
Greenock Bridge
Crosshands
Auchmillan
Montgarswood
Mauchline
Greenock Mains
Smallburn
Muirkirk
Kames
Ballochmyle
Catrine
Sorn
Kingencleugh Castle
Haugh
Shawwood
Roddenloft
Airds Moss
Urit Hill
1945 Cairn Table
1631 Wardlaw Hill
Crawfordjohn
Heritage Venture
Common Hill
Cairn Kinny
Auchinleck
Cronberry
Lugar
Holmhead
Ochiltree
Dumfries House
Logan
Terringzean Castle
Cumnock
Craigens
Baird
Netherthird
Dalblair
Auchtitench Hill 1527
1568 Mount Stuart
1392 Spango Hill
White Hill
Spango Bridge
1621 Rake Law
Garrallan
Skares
Sinclairston
Fingland
Carsgailoch Hill
Mansfield
Pathhead
New Cumnock
1675 Kirkland Hill
Kirkland
Wedder Dod 1460
Leadhills
Miners' Library
Wanlockhead
Beam Engine
1926 Stood Hill
Lead Mining
1591 Conrig Hill
Stannery Knowe 1192
Bankglen
Connel Park
Waterhead
Burnside
Dalleagles
Kirkconnel
Crawick
Kelloholm
Sanquhar
Post Office
Barr
Tolbooth
Sanquhar Castle
Mennock
The Knipe 1886
Hare Hill
1912 Thirstane Hill
Benbeoch 1522
Benty Cowan Hill
Quintin Knowe
2298 Blackcraig Hill
Mid Hill
1866 Enoch Hill
1473 Cairn Hill
Pennyvenie
Doon Valley
Dalmellington
Benbrack
Milray Hill
Prickeny Hill
Craigdarroch
Blacklorg Hill 2232
Shiel Hill 1567
Enterkinfoot
Windy Standard
1646 Craignane
Afton Resr.
Corse Hill
Campbell's Hill 1485
Brockloch Rig
2290 Windy Standard
Polskeoch
Cairnkinna Hill 1817
Loch Muck
Waterhead Hill 1768
Alhang
Countam
1639 Blackcraig Hill
Ox Hill 1657
Chanlockfoot
Enoch
Loch Doon
Lamford Hill
Cairnsmore of Carsphairn 2614
Colt Hill 1963
1640 Countam
Holm of Drumlanrig
Drumlanrig Castle
Corlae
Tibbers Castle
Carronbridge
Dodd Hill
Beninner
1906 Benbrack
Benbuie
Auchenbrack
Craigmalloch
Black Craig
Wether Hill 1747
Manquhill Hill
Bennan
Burnhead
Thornhill
Penpont
Carsphairn
Heritage Centre
Marscallock Hill
Tynron
Keir Mill
Closeburn
Stroanfreggan
James Renwick Monument
1172 Keir Hills
Meaul 2280
Knowehead
High Bridge of Ken
Moniaive
Kirkland
Kendoon Loch
Culmark
Polmaddy Settlement
Butterhole Bridge
Wallaceton
Glenmidge
Corserine 2669
Loch Harrow
Forrest Lodge
Loch Minnoch
Craigmuie
1471 Bogrie Hill
A71
A719
A70
A76
A713
A702
M74
B7086
B7018
B743
B745
B7078
B7055
B740
B744
B7037
B713
B705
B7036
B7083
B7046
B741
B797
B729
B732
B731

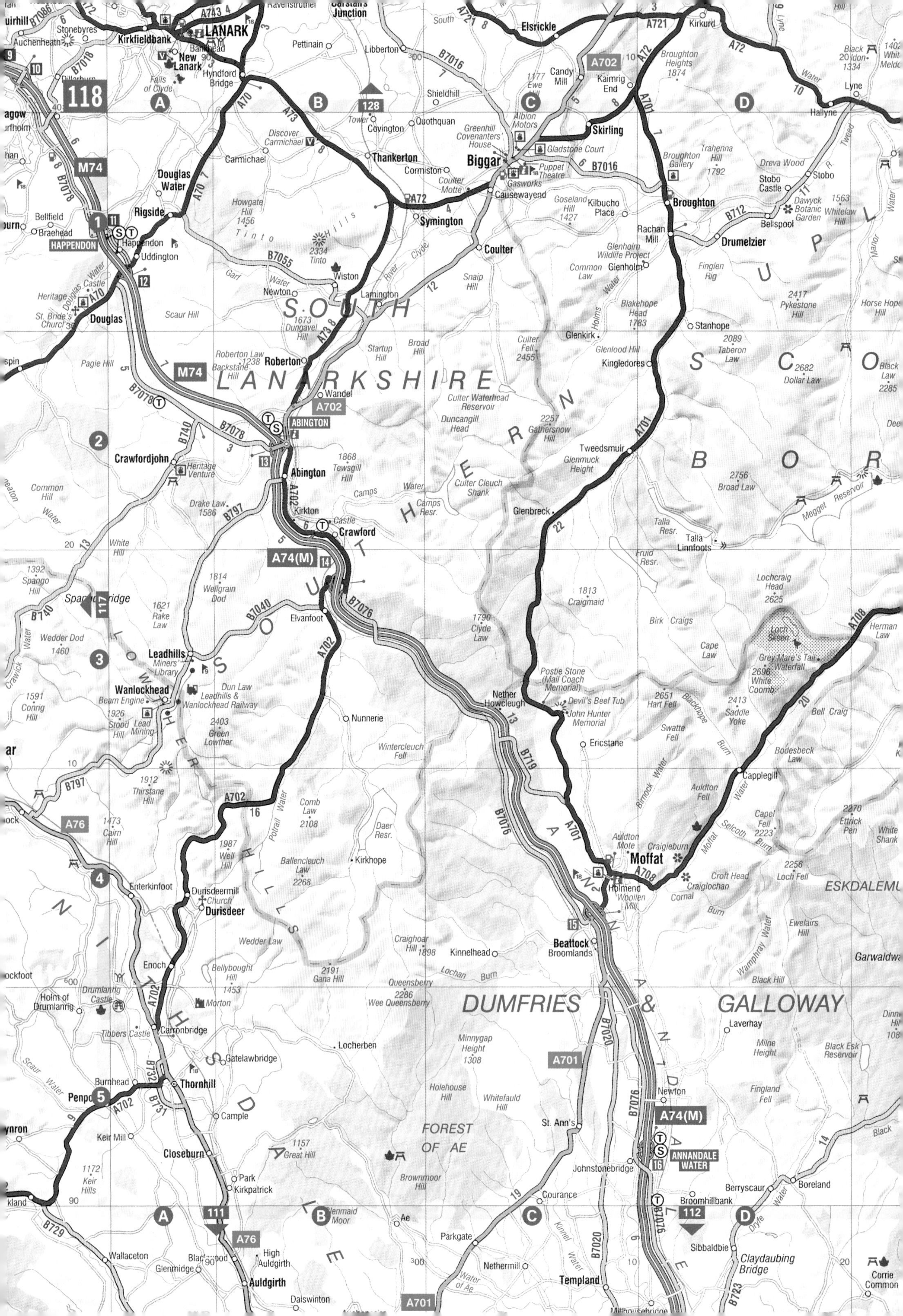

LANARK
New Lanark
Kirkfieldbank
Hyndford Bridge
Biggar
Skirling
Elsrickle
Kirkurd
Broughton
Symington
Thankerton
Covington
Coulter
Lamington
Wiston
Douglas
Douglas Water
Rigside
Happendon
HAPPENDON
Roberton
Wandel
Abington
ABINGTON
Crawford
Crawfordjohn
Elvanfoot
Leadhills
Wanlockhead
Durisdeer
Carronbridge
Thornhill
Penpont
Closeburn
Kirkpatrick
Auldgirth
Moffat
Beattock
Tweedsmuir
Drumelzier
Stobo
Lyne
Johnstonebridge
ANNANDALE WATER
SOUTH LANARKSHIRE
SOUTHERN UPLANDS
LOWTHER HILLS
NITHSDALE
ANNANDALE
DUMFRIES & GALLOWAY
FOREST OF AE
SCOTTISH BORDERS
Tinto 2334
Culter Fell 2455
Broad Law 2756
Green Lowther 2403
Grey Mare's Tail Waterfall
Devil's Beef Tub
M74
A74(M)
A702
A701
A708
A72
A76
118
128
117
111
112

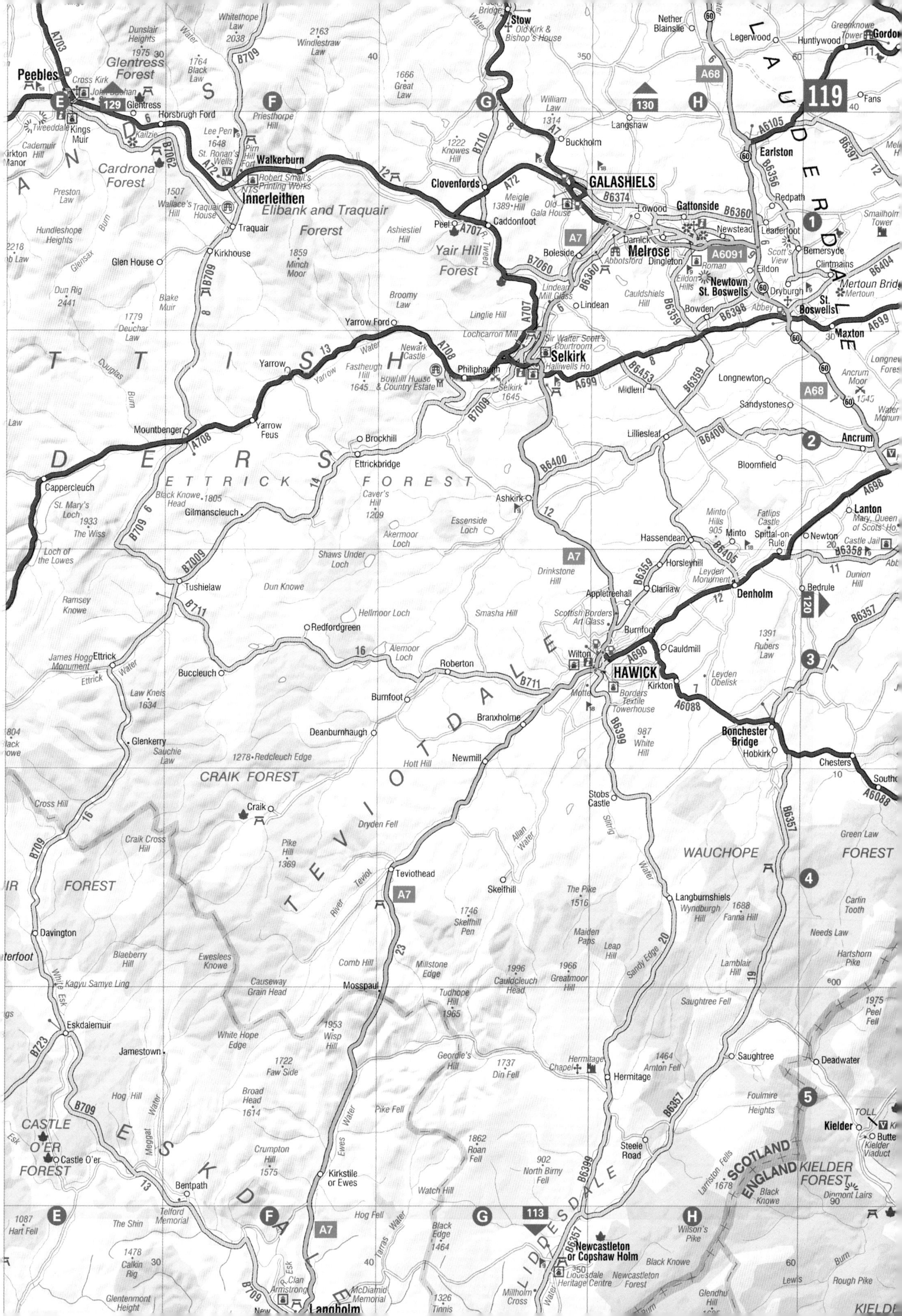

Stow
Old Kirk & Bishop's House
Nether Blainslie
Legerwood
Huntlywood
Greenknowe Tower
Gordon
Dunslair Heights
1975
Whitehope Law
2038
2163 Windlestraw Law
Glentress Forest
1764 Black Law
B709
1666 Great Law
Peebles
Cross Kirk
John Buchan
129
Glentress
Horsbrugh Ford
Priesthorpe Hill
William Law 1314
130
Langshaw
A68
119
Fans
Tweeddale
Kings Muir
Kailzie
Lee Pen 1648
St. Ronan's Wells
Pirn Hill Fort
1222 Knowes Hill
B710
Buckholm
A6105
Earlston
B6397
Cademuir Hill
Kirkton Manor
Cardrona Forest
B7062
A72
Walkerburn
Robert Smail's Printing Works
NTS
Clovenfords
GALASHIELS
B6356
Redpath
Preston Law
1507 Wallace's Hill
Traquair House
Innerleithen
Elibank and Traquair
Forrest
Meigle 1389 Hill
Old Gala House
B6374
Lowood
Gattonside
B6360
Smailholm Tower
Hundleshope Heights
Traquair
Ashiestiel Hill
Peel
A707
Caddonfoot
Newstead
Leaderfoot
Kirkhouse
Yair Hill
Forest
Boleside
A7
Darnick
Melrose
Abbotsford
Dingleton
A6091
Scott's View
Bemersyde
2218
Glen House
1859 Minch Moor
B7060
Roman
Eildon
Clintmains
B6404
Eildon Hills
Newtown St. Boswells
Dryburgh
Mertoun Bridge
Mertoun
Dun Rig 2441
Blake Muir
Broomy Law
Lindean Mill Glass
Lindean
Cauldshields Hill
B6359
Bowden
B6398
Abbey
St. Boswells
Maxton
A699
1779 Deuchar Law
Linglie Hill
Yarrow Ford
Lochcarron Mill
Sir Walter Scott's Courtroom
Newark Castle
A708
Fastheugh Hill 1645
Bowhill House & Country Estate
Philiphaugh
Selkirk
Halliwells Ho.
Selkirk 1645
B6453
Yarrow
Midlem
Longnewton
Ancrum Moor
A68
Sandystones
Mountbenger
Yarrow Feus
Brockhill
B7009
Lilliesleaf
B6400
Ancrum
Ettrickbridge
Bloomfield
Cappercleuch
ETTRICK FOREST
Black Knowe 1805 Head
Caver's Hill 1209
Ashkirk
St. Mary's Loch
1933 The Wiss
Gilmanscleuch
Essenside Loch
Akermoor Loch
Minto Hills 905
Minto
Fatlips Castle
Spittal-on-Rule
Lanton
Mary, Queen of Scots' Ho.
Newton
Castle Jail
B6358
Loch of the Lowes
Shaws Under Loch
Hassendean
Horsleyhill
B6405
Drinkstone Hill
Leyden Monument
Bedrule
Dunion Hill
Tushielaw
Dun Knowe
Appletreehall
Clarilaw
Denholm
120
B6357
Ramsey Knowe
B711
Hellmoor Loch
Smasha Hill
Scottish Borders Art Glass
Redfordgreen
Burnfoot
1391 Rubers Law
James Hogg Monument
Ettrick
Alemoor Loch
Wilton
Cauldmill
Buccleuch
Roberton
HAWICK
A698
Kirkton
Leyden Obelisk
Law Kneis 1634
Burnfoot
Motte
Borders Textile Towerhouse
A6088
Bonchester Bridge
Hobkirk
Deanburnhaugh
Branxholme
987 White Hill
Glenkerry
Sauchie Law
1278 Redcleuch Edge
Hott Hill
Newmill
Chesters
CRAIK FOREST
TEVIOTDALE
Stobs Castle
Cross Hill
Craik
Dryden Fell
Green Law
B709
Craik Cross Hill
Pike Hill 1369
Allan Water
WAUCHOPE
FOREST
Teviothead
Skelfhill
The Pike 1516
B6357
River Teviot
FOREST
Langburnshiels
Wyndburgh Hill
1688 Fanna Hill
Carlin Tooth
1746 Skelfhill Pen
Maiden Paps
Needs Law
Davington
Leap Hill
Sandy Edge
Hartshorn Pike
Blaeberry Hill
Eweslees Knowe
Comb Hill
Millstone Edge
1996 Cauldcleuch Head
1966 Greatmoor Hill
Lamblair Hill
Causeway Grain Head
Mosspaul
Tudhope Hill 1965
Kagyu Samye Ling
White Esk
Saughtree Fell
1975 Peel Fell
Eskdalemuir
1953 Wisp Hill
White Hope Edge
Jamestown
B723
1722 Faw Side
Geordie's Hill
1737 Din Fell
Hermitage Chapel
Hermitage
1464 Arnton Fell
Saughtree
Deadwater
Hog Hill
Broad Head 1614
Pike Fell
Foulmire Heights
CASTLE O'ER FOREST
Castle O'er
Meggat Water
Crumpton Hill 1575
Kirkstile or Ewes
1862 Roan Fell
902 North Birny Fell
Steele Road
SCOTLAND
ENGLAND
KIELDER FOREST
Kielder
TOLL
Butteroburn
Kielder Viaduct
Bentpath
Watch Hill
B6399
Larriston Fells
1678
Black Knowe
Dinmont Lairs
ESKDALE
LIDDESDALE
Telford Memorial
1087 Hart Fell
The Shin
Hog Fell
Tarras Water
Black Edge 1464
113
Wilson's Pike
1478 Calkin Rig
Newcastleton or Copshaw Holm
Black Knowe
Liddesdale Heritage Centre
Newcastleton Forest
Lewis
Rough Pike
Clan Armstrong
McDiarmid Memorial
Glentenmont Height
Langholm
1326 Tinnis
Millholm Cross
Glendhu Hill
KIELDER

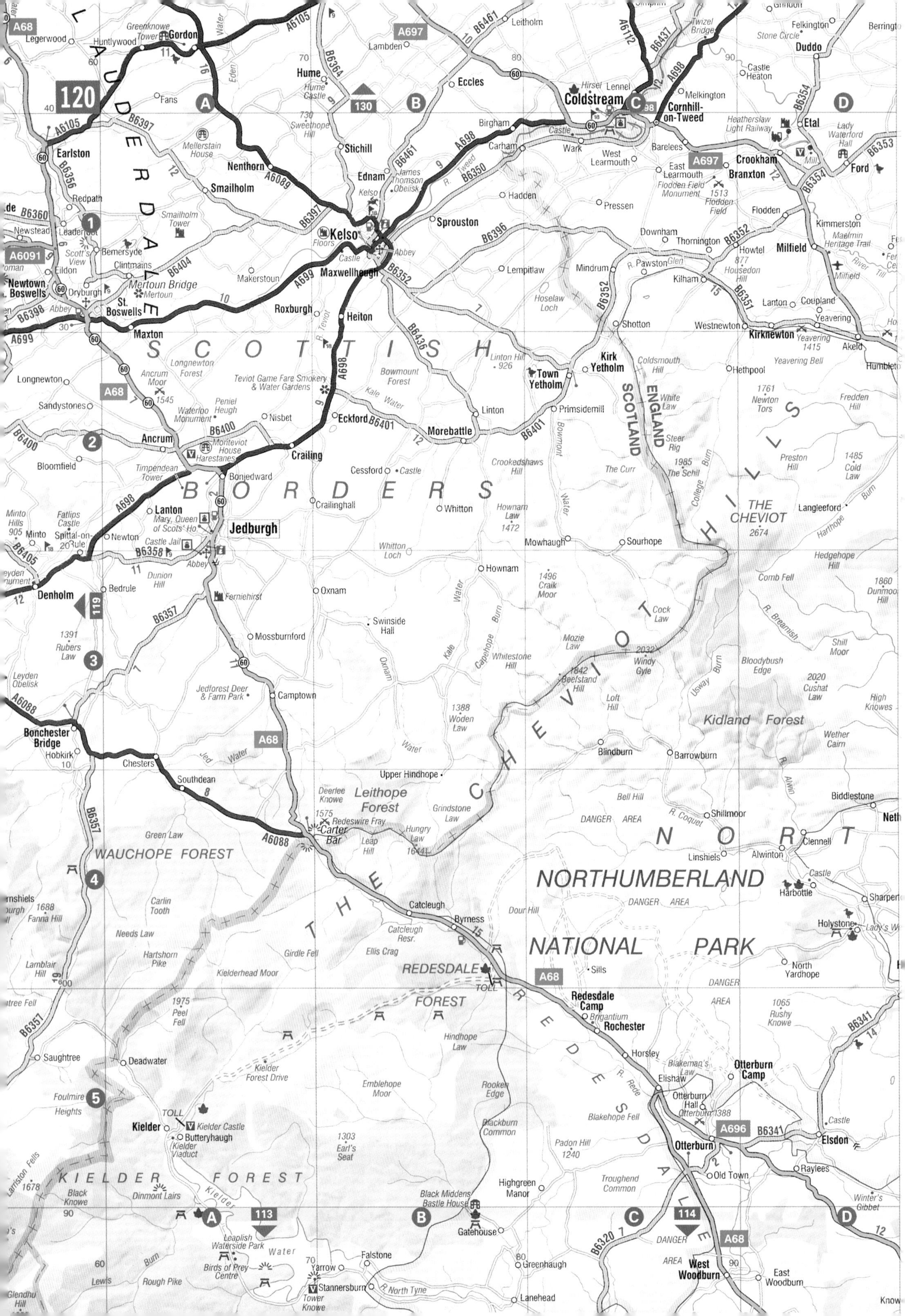
120
130
119
113
114
LAUDERDALE
SCOTTISH BORDERS
THE CHEVIOT HILLS
NORTHUMBERLAND NATIONAL PARK
REDESDALE
KIELDER FOREST
WAUCHOPE FOREST
REDESDALE FOREST
SCOTLAND
ENGLAND
Legerwood
Huntlywood
Greenknowe Tower
Gordon
Fans
Mellerstain House
Nenthorn
Smailholm
Smailholm Tower
Earlston
Redpath
Leaderfoot
Newstead
Scott's View
Bemersyde
Clintmains
Eildon
Newtown St. Boswells
Dryburgh
Abbey
St. Boswells
Mertoun Bridge
Mertoun
Makerstoun
Maxton
Longnewton
Longnewton Forest
Sandystones
Ancrum Moor 1545
Waterloo Monument
Peniel Heugh
Ancrum
Monteviot House
Harestanes
Bloomfield
Timpendean Tower
Bonjedward
Lanton
Mary, Queen of Scots' Ho.
Jedburgh
Castle Jail
Minto Hills 905
Minto
Fatlips Castle
Spittal-on-Rule
Newton
Leyden Monument
Denholm
Dunion Hill
Bedrule
Ferniehirst
1391 Rubers Law
Leyden Obelisk
Bonchester Bridge
Hobkirk
Chesters
Southdean
Green Law
Hume
Hume Castle
Lambden
Sweethope Hill
Stichill
Ednam
James Thomson Obelisk
Kelso
Floors Castle
Abbey
Maxwellheugh
Roxburgh
Heiton
Teviot Game Fare Smokery & Water Gardens
Nisbet
Eckford
Crailing
Crailinghall
Cessford
Castle
Bowmount Forest
Kale Water
Morebattle
Linton
Linton Hill 926
Whitton
Whitton Loch
Oxnam
Swinside Hall
Mossburnford
Jedforest Deer & Farm Park
Camptown
Leitholm
Eccles
Birgham
Carham
Sprouston
Lempitlaw
Hadden
Hoselaw Loch
Mindrum
Town Yetholm
Kirk Yetholm
Primsidemill
Crookedshaws Hill
Hownam Law 1472
Mowhaugh
Hownam
1496 Craik Moor
Sourhope
Coldstream
Hirsel
Lennel
Wark
Castle
West Learmouth
East Learmouth
Flodden Field Monument
1513 Flodden Field
Pressen
Downham
Thornington
Pawston
Shotton
Coldsmouth Hill
White Law
Steer Rig
The Curr
1985 The Schil
Cornhill-on-Tweed
Twizel Bridge
Melkington
Barelees
Crookham
Branxton
Flodden
Howtel
877 Housedon Hill
Kilham
Westnewton
Kirknewton
Yeavering 1415
Yeavering Bell
Hethpool
1761 Newton Tors
Preston Hill
Grindon
Felkington
Duddo
Stone Circle
Castle Heaton
Heatherslaw Light Railway
Etal
Lady Waterford Hall
Mill
Ford
Kimmerston
Maelmin Heritage Trail
Milfield
Lanton
Coupland
Yeavering
Akeld
Humbleton
Fredden Hill
1485 Cold Law
THE CHEVIOT 2674
Langleeford
Hedgehope Hill
Comb Fell
1860 Dunmoor Hill
R. Breamish
Shill Moor
Bloodybush Edge
2020 Cushat Law
High Knowes
Kidland Forest
Wether Cairn
Cock Law
Mozie Law
2032 Windy Gyle
1842 Beefstand Hill
Whitestone Hill
Loft Hill
1388 Woden Law
Blindburn
Barrowburn
Upper Hindhope
Deerlee Knowe
Leithope Forest
1575 Redeswire Fray
Carter Bar
Leap Hill
Hungry Law 1644
Grindstone Law
Bell Hill
DANGER AREA
R. Coquet
Shillmoor
Linshiels
Alwinton
Clennell
Biddlestone
Castle
Harbottle
Sharperton
Holystone
Lady's Well
North Yardhope
Catcleugh
Byrness
Catcleugh Resr.
Dour Hill
Sills
Ellis Crag
Girdle Fell
Carlin Tooth
1688 Fanna Hill
Needs Law
Hartshorn Pike
Kielderhead Moor
Lamblair Hill
1975 Peel Fell
Saughtree
Deadwater
Kielder Forest Drive
Foulmire Heights
Kielder
Kielder Castle
Butteryhaugh
Kielder Viaduct
TOLL
Larriston Fells
1678 Black Knowe
Dinmont Lairs
Emblehope Moor
1303 Earl's Seat
Hindhope Law
Rooken Edge
Blackburn Common
Black Middens Bastle House
Gatehouse
Leaplish Waterside Park
Birds of Prey Centre
Rough Pike
Lewis
Glendhu Hill
Yarrow
Falstone
Stannersburn
Tower Knowe
R. North Tyne
Greenhaugh
Lanehead
Highgreen Manor
Redesdale Camp
Bremenium
Rochester
Horsley
Blakeman's Law
Otterburn Camp
Elishaw
Otterburn Hall
Otterburn 1388
Blakehope Fell
Padon Hill 1240
Troughend Common
Otterburn
Old Town
Elsdon
Castle
Raylees
1065 Rushy Knowe
Winter's Gibbet
West Woodburn
East Woodburn
A68
A697
A698
A699
A6105
A6089
A6088
A6091
A6112
A696
B6461
B6364
B6397
B6350
B6437
B6354
B6353
B6352
B6351
B6396
B6436
B6401
B6400
B6404
B6397
B6356
B6360
B6398
B6405
B6358
B6357
B6341
B6320

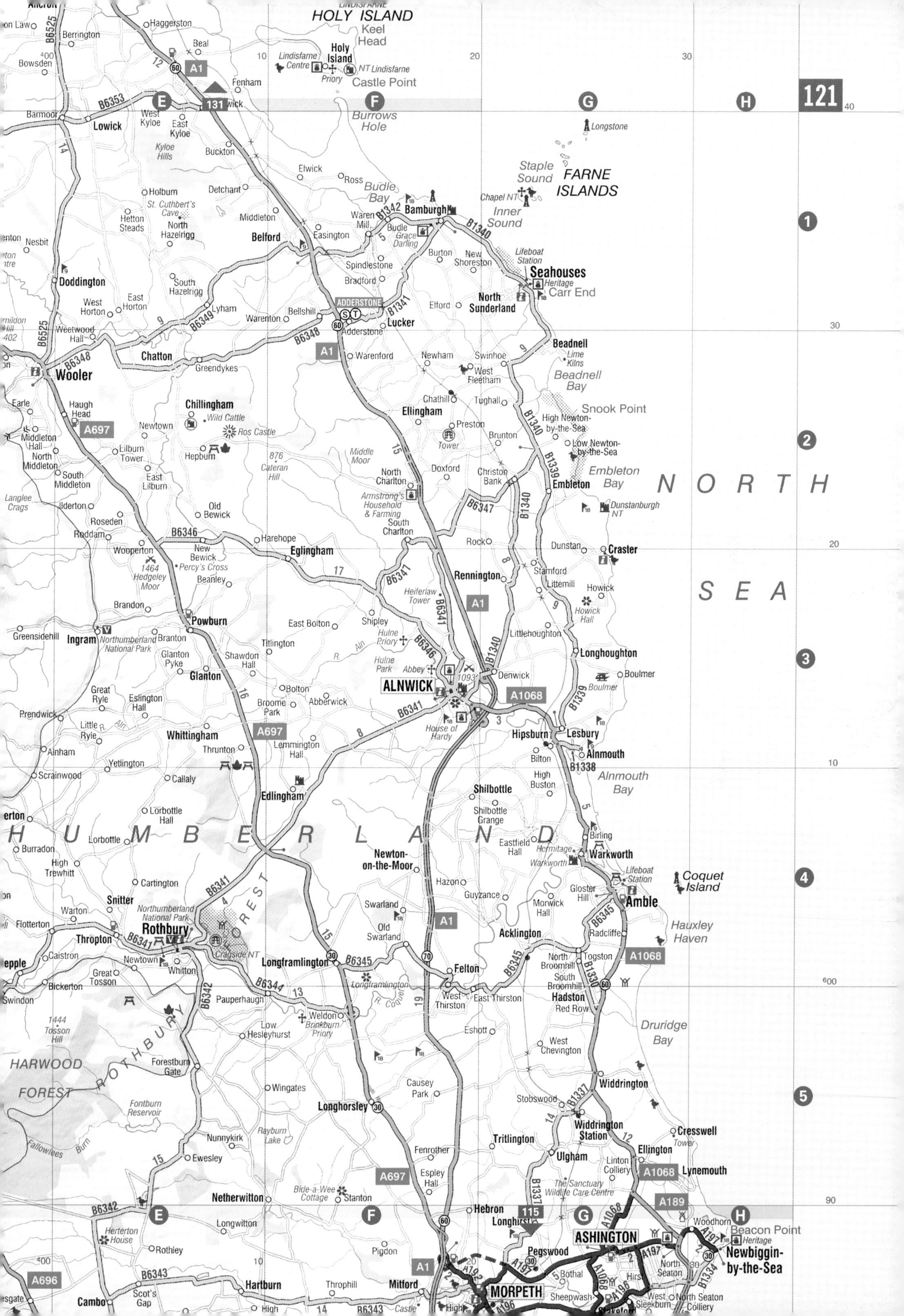
121
HOLY ISLAND
Keel Head
Holy Island
Lindisfarne Centre
NT Lindisfarne Priory
Castle Point
Burrows Hole
Haggerston
Berrington
Beal
Bowsden
Fenham
Barmoor
Lowick
West Kyloe
East Kyloe
Kyloe Hills
Buckton
Longstone
Staple Sound
FARNE ISLANDS
Chapel NT
Inner Sound
Elwick
Ross
Budle Bay
Holburn
Detchant
St. Cuthbert's Cave
Hetton Steads
North Hazelrigg
Middleton
Belford
Easington
Waren Mill
Budle
Bamburgh
Grace Darling
Nesbit
Burton
New Shoreston
Lifeboat Station
Seahouses
Heritage
Carr End
Spindlestone
Bradford
Doddington
South Hazelrigg
West Horton
East Horton
Lyham
Bellshill
ADDERSTONE
Adderstone
Warenton
Elford
North Sunderland
Lucker
Weetwood Hall
Beadnell
Lime Kilns
Beadnell Bay
Wooler
Chatton
Greendykes
Warenford
Newham
Swinhoe
West Fleetham
Earle
Haugh Head
Chillingham
Wild Cattle
Ros Castle
Chathill
Ellingham
Tughall
Snook Point
High Newton-by-the-Sea
Low Newton-by-the-Sea
Middleton Hall
North Middleton
Newtown
Lilburn Tower
Hepburn
876 Cateran Hill
Middle Moor
Preston
Tower
Brunton
Embleton Bay
Embleton
South Middleton
East Lilburn
North Charlton
Doxford
Christon Bank
NORTH SEA
Langlee Crags
Ilderton
Roseden
Roddam
Old Bewick
Armstrong's Household & Farming
South Charlton
Dunstanburgh NT
Wooperton
1464 Hedgeley Moor
New Bewick
Percy's Cross
Beanley
Harehope
Eglingham
Rock
Dunstan
Craster
Rennington
Stamford
Littemill
Howick
Howick Hall
Brandon
Heiferlaw Tower
Powburn
East Bolton
Shipley
Greensidehill
Ingram
Northumberland National Park
Branton
Tittington
Hulne Priory
Littlehoughton
Longhoughton
Boulmer
Glanton Pyke
Shawdon Hall
Hulne Park
Abbey
ALNWICK
Denwick
Glanton
Great Ryle
Eslington Hall
Bolton
Broome Park
Abberwick
House of Hardy
Hipsburn
Lesbury
Alnmouth
Prendwick
Little Ryle
Whittingham
Lemmington Hall
Bilton
Alnham
Thrunton
Yetlington
High Buston
Alnmouth Bay
Scrainwood
Callaly
Edlingham
Shilbottle
Shilbottle Grange
Lorbottle Hall
NORTHUMBERLAND
Lorbottle
Birling
Burradon
Newton-on-the-Moor
Eastfield Hall
Hermitage
Warkworth
High Trewhitt
Cartington
Hazon
Guyzance
Coquet Island
Gloster Hill
Amble
Snitter
Warton
Northumberland National Park
Swarland
Morwick Hall
Hauxley Haven
Flotterton
Thropton
Rothbury
Cragside NT
Old Swarland
Acklington
Radcliffe
Caistron
Newtown
Whitton
Longframlington
Felton
North Broomhill
Togston
South Broomhill
Great Tosson
Bickerton
Pauperhaugh
West Thirston
East Thirston
Hadston
Red Row
Swindon
1444 Tosson Hill
Weldon
Brinkburn Priory
Low Hesleyhurst
Eshott
Druridge Bay
West Chevington
HARWOOD FOREST
ROTHBURY FOREST
Forestburn Gate
Fontburn Reservoir
Wingates
Causey Park
Widdrington
Longhorsley
Stobswood
Widdrington Station
Cresswell
Tower
Fallowlees Burn
Nunnykirk
Rayburn Lake
Tritlington
Ulgham
Ellington
Ewesley
Fenrother
Linton Colliery
Lynemouth
Espley Hall
The Sanctuary Wildlife Care Centre
Bide-a-Wee Cottage
Stanton
Netherwitton
Hebron
Longhirst
Woodhorn
Beacon Point
Herterton House
Longwitton
ASHINGTON
Heritage
Newbiggin-by-the-Sea
Rothley
Pigdon
Pegswood
Bothal
North Seaton
Hartburn
Throphill
Mitford
MORPETH
Sheepwash
West Sleekburn
North Seaton Colliery
Cambo
Scot's Gap
High
Castle
A1
A697
A1068
A189
A197
A196
A192
A696
B6525
B6353
B6348
B6349
B6341
B6346
B6347
B1340
B1339
B1342
B1338
B6345
B6344
B6342
B6343
B1337
B1330
B1334
30
20
10
600
90
40

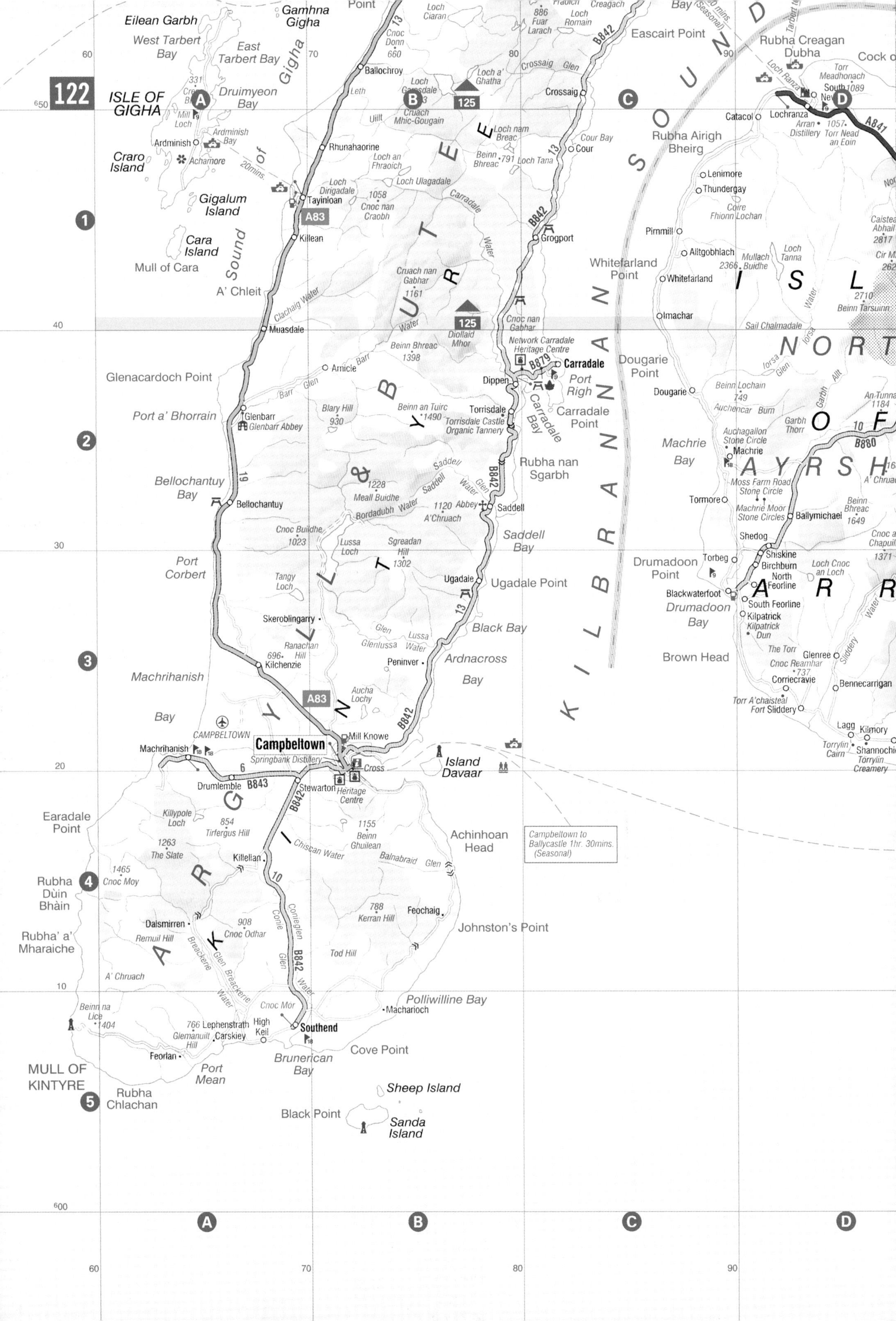
ISLE OF GIGHA
Eilean Garbh
Gamhna Gigha
West Tarbert Bay
East Tarbert Bay
Druimyeon Bay
Ardminish
Ardminish Bay
Achamore
Craro Island
Gigalum Island
Cara Island
Mull of Cara
Sound of Gigha
A' Chleit
Ballochroy
Rhunahaorine
Tayinloan
A83
Killean
Muasdale
Clachaig Water
Glenacardoch Point
Amicle
Port a' Bhorrain
Glenbarr
Glenbarr Abbey
Bellochantuy Bay
Bellochantuy
Port Corbert
Skeroblingarry
Kilchenzie
Machrihanish Bay
CAMPBELTOWN
Machrihanish
Campbeltown
Springbank Distillery
Drumlemble
B843
Stewarton
Heritage Centre
Mill Knowe
Cross
Island Davaar
Earadale Point
Killypole Loch
Tirfergus Hill
The Slate
Cnoc Moy
Killellan
Chiscan Water
Balnabraid Glen
Beinn Ghuilean
Achinhoan Head
Rubha Dùin Bhàin
Dalsmirren
Remuil Hill
Cnoc Odhar
Kerran Hill
Feochaig
Johnston's Point
Rubha' a' Mharaiche
A' Chruach
Conie Glen
Tod Hill
Polliwilline Bay
Machariochh
Beinn na Lice
Lephenstrath
Glemanuilt Hill
Carskiey
High Keil
Southend
Cnoc Mor
Feorlan
Port Mean
Brunerican Bay
Cove Point
MULL OF KINTYRE
Rubha Chlachan
Sheep Island
Black Point
Sanda Island
ARGYLL & BUTE
Loch Ciaran
Cnoc Donn
Fuar Larach
Loch Romain
Crossaig Glen
Crossaig
Loch a' Ghatha
Loch Garasdale
Cruach Mhic-Gougain
Uillt
Loch nam Breac
Loch an Fhraoich
Loch Ulagadale
Loch Dirigadale
Cnoc nan Craobh
Beinn Bhreac
Loch Tana
Cour Bay
Cour
Carradale Water
Grogport
Cruach nan Gabhar
Diollaid Mhor
Cnoc nan Gabhar
Network Carradale Heritage Centre
Carradale
B879
Dippen
Port Righ
Carradale Bay
Carradale Point
Torrisdale
Torrisdale Castle Organic Tannery
Blary Hill
Beinn an Tuirc
Barr Glen
Rubha nan Sgarbh
Meall Buidhe
Saddell Water
Bordadubh Water
Abbey
Saddell
A'Chruach
Saddell Bay
Cnoc Buidhe
Lussa Loch
Sgreadan Hill
Tangy Loch
Ugadale
Ugadale Point
Black Bay
Ranachan Hill
Glenlussa Water
Peninver
Ardnacross Bay
Aucha Lochy
B842
KILBRANNAN SOUND
Eascairt Point
Rubha Creagan Dubha
Cock of
Torr Meadhonach
Lochranza
Catacol
Arran Distillery
Torr Nead an Eoin
A841
Rubha Airigh Bheirg
Lenimore
Thundergay
Coire Fhionn Lochan
Pirnmill
Alltgobhlach
Mullach Buidhe
Loch Tanna
Whitefarland Point
Whitefarland
Imachar
Sail Chalmadale
Beinn Tarsuinn
Dougarie Point
Dougarie
Beinn Lochain
Auchencar Burn
An Tunna
Machrie Bay
Auchagallon Stone Circle
Machrie
Garbh Thorr
B880
Moss Farm Road Stone Circle
Tormore
Machrie Moor Stone Circles
Ballymichael
Beinn Bhreac
Shedog
Shiskine
Birchburn
Drumadoon Point
Torbeg
Loch Cnoc an Loch
North Feorline
Blackwaterfoot
South Feorline
Drumadoon Bay
Kilpatrick
Kilpatrick Dun
Brown Head
The Torr
Glenree
Sliddery
Cnoc Reamhar
Corriecravie
Bennecarrigan
Torr A'chaisteal Fort
Sliddery
Lagg
Kilmory
Torrylin Cairn
Shannochie
Torrylin Creamery
ISLE OF ARRAN
NORTH AYRSHIRE
Campbeltown to Ballycastle 1hr. 30mins. (Seasonal)
125
A
B
C
D
1
2
3
4
5
60
70
80
90
40
30
20
10
600
650

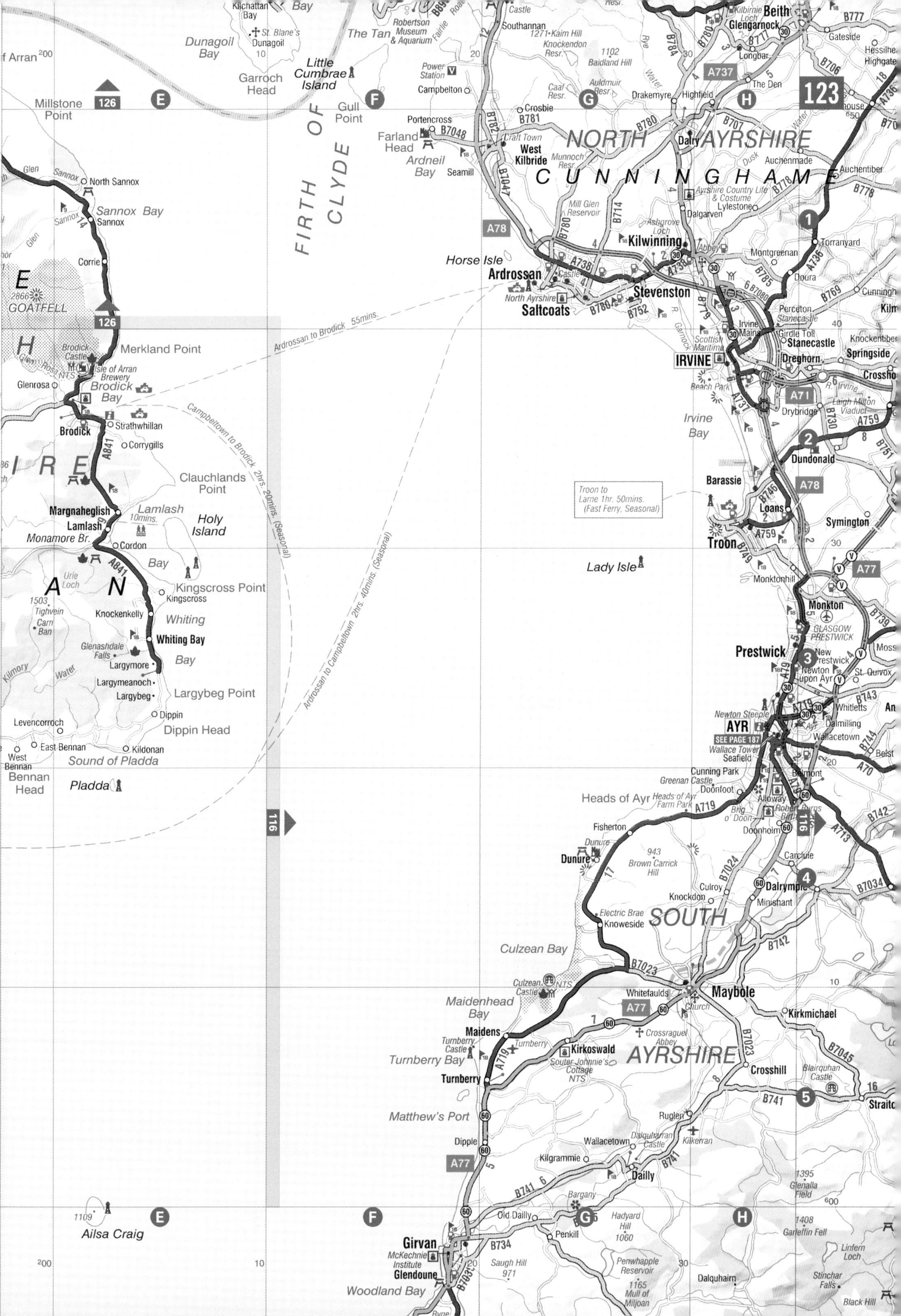

123
126
116
SEE PAGE 187
NORTH AYRSHIRE
CUNNINGHAME
SOUTH AYRSHIRE
FIRTH OF CLYDE
Troon to Larne 1hr. 50mins. (Fast Ferry, Seasonal)
Ardrossan to Brodick 55mins.
Campbeltown to Brodick 2hrs. 20mins. (Seasonal)
Ardrossan to Campbeltown 2hrs. 40mins. (Seasonal)
Kilchattan Bay
St. Blane's
Dunagoil
Dunagoil Bay
Garroch Head
Little Cumbrae Island
The Tan
Robertson Museum & Aquarium
Millstone Point
Gull Point
Power Station
Campbelton
Portencross
Farland Head
Ardneil Bay
Seamill
West Kilbride
Crosbie
Craft Town
Castle
Southannan
Kaim Hill
Knockendon Resr.
Baidland Hill
Caaf Resr.
Auldmuir Resr.
Munnoch Resr.
Kilbirnie Loch
Beith
Glengarnock
Longbar
Gateside
Hessilhead
Highgate
The Den
Drakemyre
Highfield
Dalry
Auchenmade
Auchentiber
Ayrshire Country Life & Costume
Lylestone
Dalgarven
Mill Glen Reservoir
Ashgrove Loch
Kilwinning
Abbey
Montgreenan
Torranyard
Doura
Horse Isle
Ardrossan
Saltcoats
North Ayrshire
Stevenston
Perceton
Stanecastle
Girdle Toll
Irvine Mains
Scottish Maritime
IRVINE
Beach Park
Dreghorn
Springside
Knockentiber
Drybridge
Laigh Milton Viaduct
Irvine Bay
Dundonald
Barassie
Loans
Symington
Troon
Lady Isle
Monktonhill
Monkton
GLASGOW PRESTWICK
Prestwick
New Prestwick
Newton upon Ayr
St. Quivox
Newton Steeple
AYR
Whitletts
Dalmilling
Wallacetown
Wallace Tower
Seafield
Cunning Park
Greenan Castle
Doonfoot
Belmont
Heads of Ayr
Heads of Ayr Farm Park
Alloway
Brig o' Doon
Robert Burns
Doonholm
Fisherton
Dunure
Brown Carrick Hill
Carcluie
Dalrymple
Culroy
Knockdon
Minishant
Electric Brae
Knoweside
Culzean Bay
Culzean Castle
Maidenhead Bay
Maidens
Whitefaulds
Maybole
Church
Kirkmichael
Crossraguel Abbey
Turnberry Castle
Turnberry Bay
Turnberry
Kirkoswald
Souter Johnnie's Cottage
Crosshill
Blairquhan Castle
Straiton
Matthew's Port
Ruglen
Kilkerran
Dipple
Wallacetown
Dalquharran Castle
Kilgrammie
Dailly
Glenalla Field
Bargany
Old Dailly
Hadyard Hill
Penkill
Garleffin Fell
Linfern Loch
Girvan
McKechnie Institute
Glendoune
Saugh Hill
Penwhapple Reservoir
Mull of Miljoan
Dalquhairn
Stinchar Falls
Black Hill
Woodland Bay
Ailsa Craig
Arran
North Sannox
Sannox Bay
Sannox
Corrie
GOATFELL
Merkland Point
Brodick Castle
Isle of Arran Brewery
Brodick Bay
Glenrosa
Brodick
Strathwhillan
Corrygills
Clauchlands Point
Margnaheglish
Lamlash
Holy Island
Monamore Br.
Cordon
Urie Loch
Kingscross Point
Kingscross
Tighvein
Knockenkelly
Whiting Bay
Glenashdale Falls
Largymore
Largymeanoch
Largybeg
Largybeg Point
Dippin
Dippin Head
Levencorroch
East Bennan
West Bennan
Kildonan
Sound of Pladda
Bennan Head
Pladda

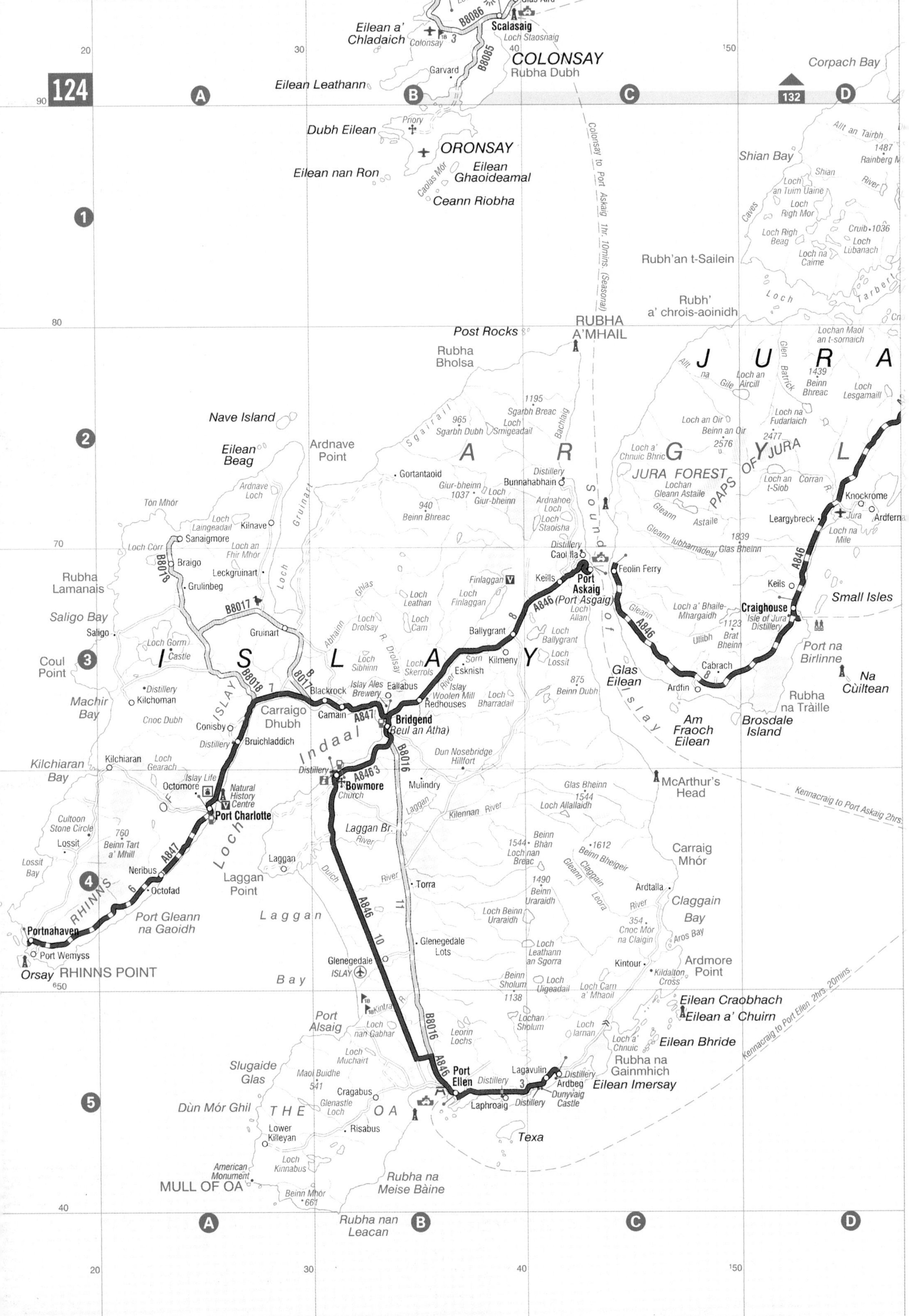
124
132
A
B
C
D
1
2
3
4
5
Glas Aird
Scalasaig
Loch Staosnaig
Eilean a' Chladaich
Colonsay
COLONSAY
Rubha Dubh
Garvard
Eilean Leathann
Corpach Bay
Dubh Eilean
Priory
ORONSAY
Eilean Ghaoideamal
Eilean nan Ron
Caolas Mòr
Ceann Riobha
Colonsay to Port Askaig 1hr. 10mins. (Seasonal)
Shian Bay
Allt an Tairbh
1487
Rainberg Mòr
Loch an Tuim Uaine
Loch Righ Mor
Loch Righ Beag
Loch na Caime
Loch Lubanach
Cruib
1036
Rubh'an t-Sailein
Rubh' a' chrois-aoinidh
Post Rocks
RUBHA A'MHAIL
Rubha Bholsa
Lochan Maol an t-sornaich
J U R A
Loch an Aircill
1439
Beinn Bhreac
Loch Lesgamaill
1195
Sgarbh Breac
965
Sgarbh Dubh
Loch Smigeadail
Nave Island
Loch an Oir
Beinn an Oir
2576
2477
Loch na Fudarlaich
Eilean Beag
Ardnave Point
A R G Y L L
JURA FOREST
PAPS OF JURA
Ardnave Loch
Tòn Mhòr
Gortantaoid
Giur-bheinn
1037
Loch Giur-bheinn
Distillery
Bunnahabhain
Ardnahoe Loch
Loch Staoisha
Lochan Gleann Astaile
Loch an t-Siob
Corran
Knockrome
Leargybreck
Jura
Ardfernal
Loch na Mile
940
Beinn Bhreac
Loch Laingeadail
Kilnave
Sanaigmore
Loch Corr
Loch an Fhir Mhoir
Sound of Islay
1839
Glas Bheinn
Caol Ila
Feolin Ferry
Rubha Lamanais
Braigo
Leckgruinart
Grulinbeg
Finlaggan
Loch Finlaggan
Keills
Port Askaig
A846 (Port Asgaig)
Loch Allan
Keils
Small Isles
Saligo Bay
Saligo
Loch Leathan
Loch Drolsay
Loch Cam
Ballygrant
Loch Ballygrant
Loch a' Bhaile-Mhargaidh
Craighouse
Isle of Jura Distillery
1123
Brat Bheinn
Ullibh
Port na Birlinne
Loch Gorm
Castle
Gruinart
I S L A Y
Coul Point
Loch Sibhinn
Loch Skerrols
Sorn
Esknish
Kilmeny
Loch Lossit
Glas Eilean
Cabrach
Na Cùiltean
Machir Bay
Distillery
Kilchoman
Islay Ales Brewery
Eallabus
Blackrock
Islay Woolen Mill
Redhouses
Loch Bharradail
875
Beinn Dubh
Ardfin
Rubha na Tràille
Carraigo Dhubh
Cnoc Dubh
Conisby
Camain
Bridgend
(Beul an Atha)
Am Fraoch Eilean
Brosdale Island
Distillery
Bruichladdich
Dun Nosebridge Hillfort
Kilchiaran Bay
Kilchiaran
Loch Gearach
Loch Indaal
Islay Life
Octomore
Natural History Centre
Port Charlotte
Bowmore
Church
Mulindry
Glas Bheinn
1544
Loch Allallaidh
McArthur's Head
Kennacraig to Port Askaig 2hrs.
Cultoon Stone Circle
760
Beinn Tart a' Mhill
Lossit
Lossit Bay
Laggan Br.
Kilennan River
Beinn Bhàn
Loch nan Breac
1612
Beinn Bheigeir
Carraig Mhòr
Neribus
Octofad
Laggan
Laggan Point
Torra
1490
Beinn Uraraidh
Ardtalla
Claggain Bay
RHINNS OF ISLAY
Port Gleann na Gaoidh
Laggan Bay
Loch Beinn Uraraidh
354
Cnoc Mòr na Claigin
Aros Bay
Portnahaven
Port Wemyss
Orsay
RHINNS POINT
Glenegedale
Glenegedale Lots
ISLAY
Loch Leathann an Sgorra
Kintour
Kildalton Cross
Ardmore Point
Beinn Sholum
1138
Loch Uigeadail
Loch Carn a' Mhaoil
Eilean Craobhach
Eilean a' Chuirn
Kennacraig to Port Ellen 2hrs. 20mins.
Port Alsaig
Kintra
Loch nan Gabhar
Leorin Lochs
Lochan Sholum
Loch Iarnan
Loch a' Chnuic
Eilean Bhride
Rubha na Gainmhich
Slugaide Glas
Loch Muichairt
Maol Buidhe
541
Port Ellen
Distillery
Lagavulin
Distillery
Ardbeg
Eilean Imersay
Dunyvaig Castle
Cragabus
Glenastle Loch
Dùn Mòr Ghil
THE OA
Laphroaig
Distillery
Risabus
Lower Killeyan
Texa
Loch Kinnabus
American Monument
MULL OF OA
Beinn Mhòr
661
Rubha na Meise Bàine
Rubha nan Leacan
A846
A847
A8463
B8016
B8017
B8018
B8078
B8085
B8086
20
30
40
150
90
80
70
650
40

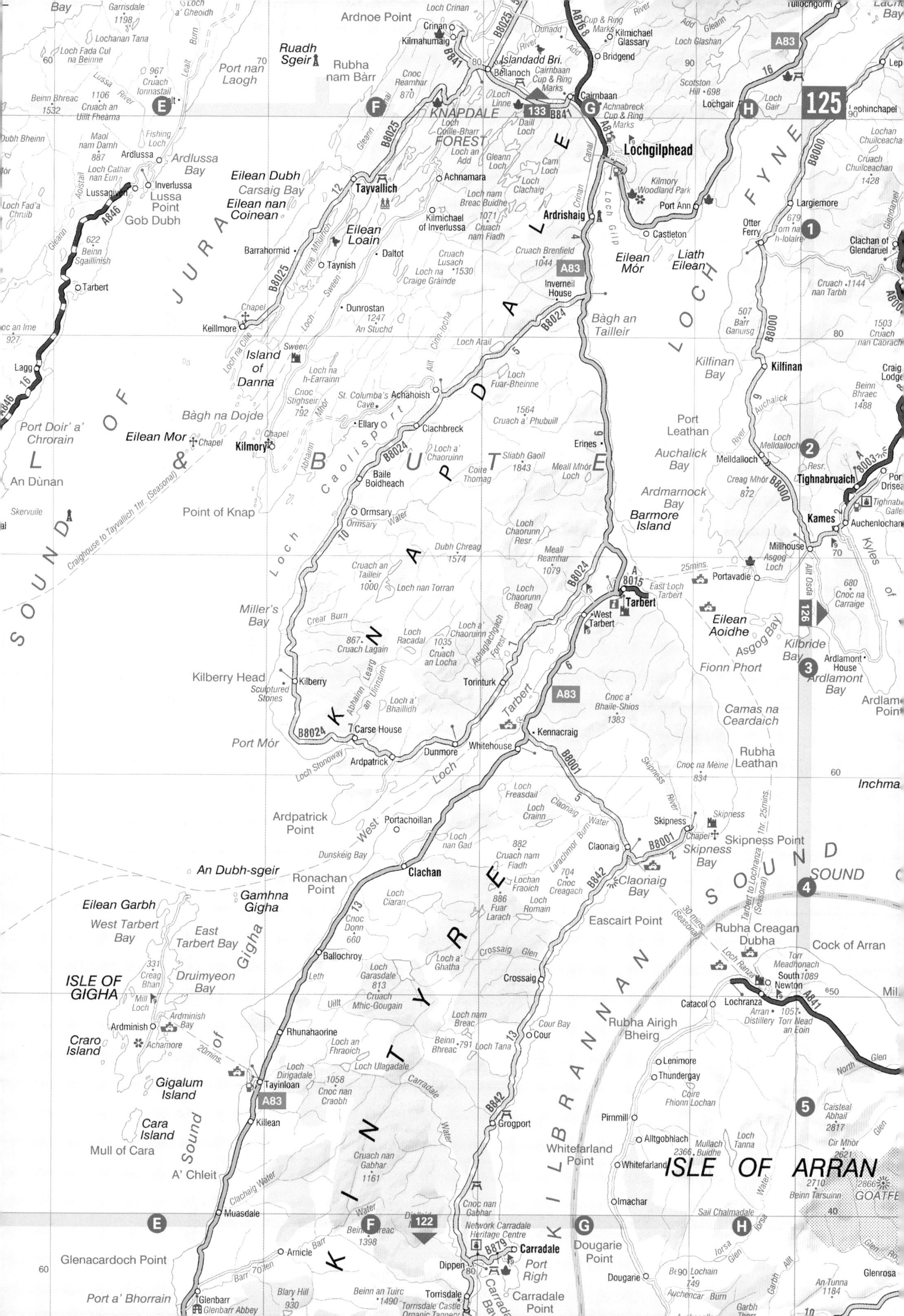

125
Ardnoe Point
Loch Crinan
Crinan
Kilmahumaig
Ruadh Sgeir
Rubha nam Bàrr
Port nan Laogh
Islandadd Bri.
Bellanoch
Dunadd
Kilmichael Glassary
Bridgend
Cairnbaan
Loch Glashan
Scotston Hill 698
Lochgair
Loch Gair
Lephinchapel
KNAPDALE FOREST
Lochgilphead
Kilmory Woodland Park
Port Ann
Castleton
Ardrishaig
Loch Gilp
Eilean Mór
Liath Eilean
Inverneil House
Bàgh an Tailleir
Tayvallich
Achnamara
Eilean Dubh
Carsaig Bay
Eilean nan Coinean
Eilean Loain
Barrahormid
Taynish
Daltot
Kilmichael of Inverlussa
Dunrostan
Keillmore
Island of Danna
Sween
Loch Arail
Achahoish
Ellary
Clachbreck
Bàgh na Dojde
Eilean Mor
Kilmory
Point of Knap
Baile Boidheach
Ormsary
Erines
Barmore Island
Ardmarnock Bay
Auchalick Bay
Port Leathan
Kilfinan Bay
Kilfinan
Otter Ferry
Largiemore
Clachan of Glendaruel
Melldalloch
Tighnabruaich
Kames
Auchenlochan
Millhouse
Asgog Loch
Portavadie
Tarbert
West Tarbert
East Loch Tarbert
Eilean Aoidhe
Asgog Bay
Kilbride Bay
Ardlamont House
Ardlamont Bay
Fionn Phort
Camas na Ceardaich
Rubha Leathan
Miller's Bay
Kilberry Head
Kilberry
Sculptured Stones
Torinturk
Carse House
Port Mór
Ardpatrick
Dunmore
Whitehouse
Kennacraig
West Loch Tarbert
Ardpatrick Point
Portachoillan
Skipness
Skipness Point
Skipness Bay
Claonaig
Claonaig Bay
Eascairt Point
Rubha Creagan Dubha
Cock of Arran
Lochranza
Catacol
Rubha Airigh Bheirg
An Dubh-sgeir
Ronachan Point
Clachan
Gamhna Gigha
Eilean Garbh
West Tarbert Bay
East Tarbert Bay
ISLE OF GIGHA
Druimyeon Bay
Ardminish
Achamore
Craro Island
Gigalum Island
Cara Island
Mull of Cara
Ballochroy
Rhunahaorine
Tayinloan
Killean
A' Chleit
Muasdale
Crossaig
Cour
Grogport
Lenimore
Thundergay
Pirnmill
Alltgobhlach
Whitefarland Point
Whitefarland
Imachar
ISLE OF ARRAN
Glenacardoch Point
Amicle
Glenbarr
Glenbarr Abbey
Port a' Bhorrain
Carradale
Network Carradale Heritage Centre
Dippen
Torrisdale
Port Righ
Carradale Point
Dougarie Point
Dougarie
Glenrosa
SOUND OF JURA
LOCH FYNE
KNAPDALE
KINTYRE
KILBRANNAN SOUND
Lussagiven
Inverlussa
Ardlussa
Lussa Point
Gob Dubh
Tarbert
Lagg
Port Doir' a' Chrorain
An Dùnan
Skervuile
Craighouse to Tayvallich 1hr. (Seasonal)
Tarbert to Lochranza 1hr. 25mins.
122
126

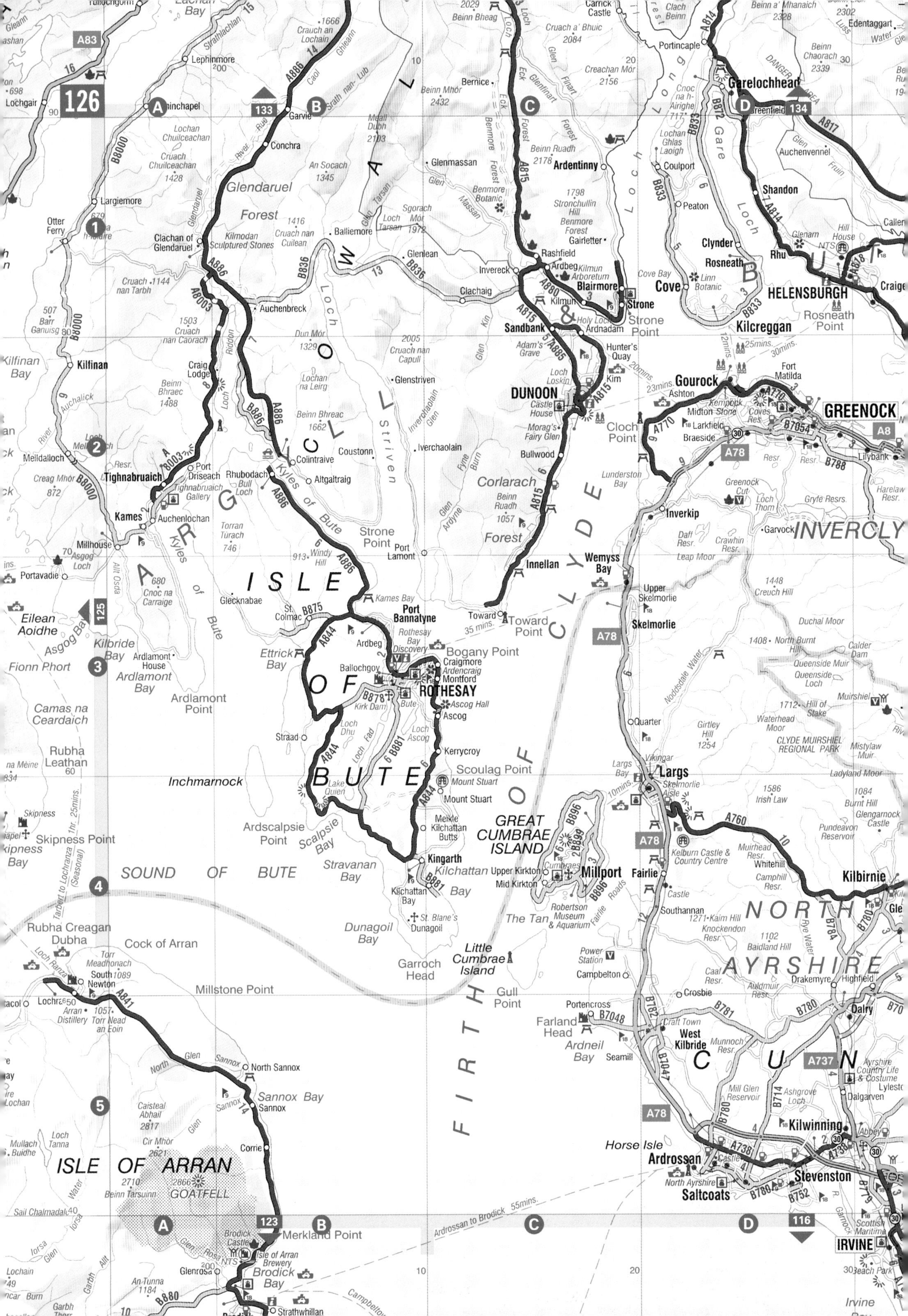
126
A83
Lochgair
Lephinmore
Strathlachlan
Crauch an Lochain
1666
Caol Ghleann
A886
Beinn Bheag
2029
Carrick Castle
Cruach a' Bhuic 2084
Clach Beinn
Beinn a' Mhanaich 2328
Edentaggart
Portincaple
A814
Beinn Chaorach 2339
Garelochhead
Greenfield
134
A817
Glen Auchenvennel
133
Garvie
Srath nan Lub
Beinn Mhòr 2432
Bernice
Eck
Glenfinart
Creachan Mòr 2156
Cnoc na h-Airighe 717
Lochan Ghlas Laoigh
B872
B833
Gare Loch
Coulport
Peaton
Shandon
Lochan Chuilceachan
Cruach Chuilceachan 1428
Conchra
Meall Dubh 2103
An Socach 1345
Glenmassan
Benmore Forest
Benmore Botanic
Beinn Ruadh 2178
Ardentinny
1798 Stronchullin Hill
Benmore Forest
Gairletter
Glendaruel Forest
B8000
Largiemore
Otter Ferry
Clachan of Glendaruel
Kilmodan Sculptured Stones
Balliemore
Sgorach Mòr 1972
Loch Tarsan
Glen Tarsan
Cruach nan Cuilean 1416
Glenlean
B836
Inverneck
Rashfield
Ardbeg
Kilmun Arboretum
Blairmore
Strone
Strone Point
Clynder
Rosneath
Linn Botanic
Cove
Rhu
Glenarn
Hill House NTS
HELENSBURGH
Kilcreggan
Rosneath Point
B833
Cruach nan Tarbh 1144
A8003
Auchenbreck
Clachaig
Kilmun
Holy Loch
Ardnadam
Sandbank
A815
A885
Adam's Grave
Hunter's Quay
Kim
Barr Ganuisg 507
Cruach nan Caorach 1503
Dun Mòr 1329
Cruach nan Capull 2005
Glenstriven
Kilfinan
Kilfinan Bay
Craig Lodge
Beinn Bhreac 1488
Lochan na Leirg
Beinn Bhreac 1662
Loch Striven
Inverchaolain Glen
DUNOON
Castle House
Morag's Fairy Glen
Loch Loskin
Gourock
Ashton
Fort Matilda
Kempock
Midton Stone
Coves Res
Larkfield
Braeside
GREENOCK
A770
B7054
A8
A78
Lilybank
Cloch Point
Melldalloch
Creag Mhòr 872
Tighnabruaich
Port Driseach
Tighnabruaich Gallery
Rhubodach
Bull Loch
Colintraive
Altgaltraig
Coustonn
Iverchaolain
Bullwood
Corlarach
Beinn Ruadh 1057
Corlarach Forest
Lunderston Bay
Greenock Cut
Loch Thom
Gryfe Resrs.
Harelaw Resr.
Inverkip
Garvock
INVERCLYDE
Kames
Auchenlochan
Millhouse
Asgog Loch
Torran Tùrach 746
Kyles of Bute
Windy Hill 913
Strone Point
Port Lamont
Innellan
Wemyss Bay
Daff Resr.
Crawhin Resr.
Leap Moor
Portavadie
ARGYLL
Cnoc na Carraige 680
ISLE OF BUTE
Glecknabae
St. Colmac
B875
Kames Bay
Port Bannatyne
Toward
Toward Point
35 mins.
FIRTH OF CLYDE
Upper Skelmorlie
Skelmorlie
1448 Creuch Hill
Duchal Moor
Eilean Aoidhe
125
Asgog Bay
Kilbride Bay
Ardlamont House
Ardlamont Bay
Ardlamont Point
Fionn Phort
Camas na Ceardaich
Ettrick Bay
A844
Ardbeg
Rothesay Bay Discovery
Bogany Point
Craigmore
Ardencraig
Montford
Ballochgoy
ROTHESAY
B878
Kirk Dam
Ascog Hall
Ascog
Loch Ascog
Loch Dhu
Loch Fad
B881
Straad
Kerrycroy
Scoulag Point
Mount Stuart
Noddsdale Water
1408 North Burnt Hill
Calder Dam
Queenside Muir
Queenside Loch
Muirshiel
1712 Hill of Stake
Waterhead Moor
Girtley Hill 1254
CLYDE MUIRSHIEL REGIONAL PARK
Mistylaw Muir
Quarter
Rubha Leathan
Inchmarnock
Lake Quien
Meikle Kilchattan Butts
Vikingar
Largs Bay
Largs
Skelmorlie Aisle
Ladyland Moor
1586 Irish Law
1084 Burnt Hill
Glengarnock Castle
Skipness
Skipness Point
Skipness Bay
Tarbert to Lochranza 1hr. 25mins. (Seasonal)
Ardscalpsie Point
Scalpsie Bay
Stravanan Bay
Kingarth
Kilchattan Bay
GREAT CUMBRAE ISLAND
B896
B899
Upper Kirkton
Mid Kirkton
Cumbraes
Millport
Fairlie
A760
Kelburn Castle & Country Centre
Muirhead Resr.
Whitehill
Camphill Resr.
Pundeavon Reservoir
Kilbirnie
SOUND OF BUTE
Rubha Creagan Dubha
Cock of Arran
Dunagoil Bay
St. Blane's
Dunagoil
The Tan
Robertson Museum & Aquarium
Fairlie Roads
Castle
Southannan
1271 Kaim Hill
Knockendon Resr.
1102 Baidland Hill
NORTH AYRSHIRE
Rye Water
B784
B780
Loch Ranza
Torr Meadhonach
South Newton 1089
Lochranza
Arran Distillery
Torr Nead an Eoin 1057
A841
Millstone Point
Garroch Head
Little Cumbrae Island
Power Station
Campbelton
Caaf Resr.
Auldmuir Resr.
Drakemyre
Highfield
Dalry
Gull Point
Crosbie
Portencross
Farland Head
B7048
Ardneil Bay
Seamill
B781
Craft Town
West Kilbride
Munnoch Resr.
B782
B7047
A737
Ayrshire Country Life & Costume
Lylestone
Dalgarven
North Glen Sannox
North Sannox
Sannox Bay
Sannox
Caisteal Abhail 2817
Cir Mhòr 2621
Loch Tanna
Mullach Buidhe
Corrie
ISLE OF ARRAN
GOATFELL
2866
2710
Beinn Tarsuinn
Sail Chalmadale
Mill Glen Reservoir
Ashgrove Loch
B714
A78
Kilwinning
Abbey
Horse Isle
Ardrossan
Castle
A738
Stevenston
North Ayrshire
Saltcoats
B752
B780
B714
123
Merkland Point
Ardrossan to Brodick 55mins.
116
Brodick Castle
Isle of Arran Brewery
Glen Rosa
Glenrosa
Brodick Bay
An Tunna 1184
B880
Strathwhillan
Scottish Maritime
IRVINE
Beach Park
Irvine
Lochain
Garbh

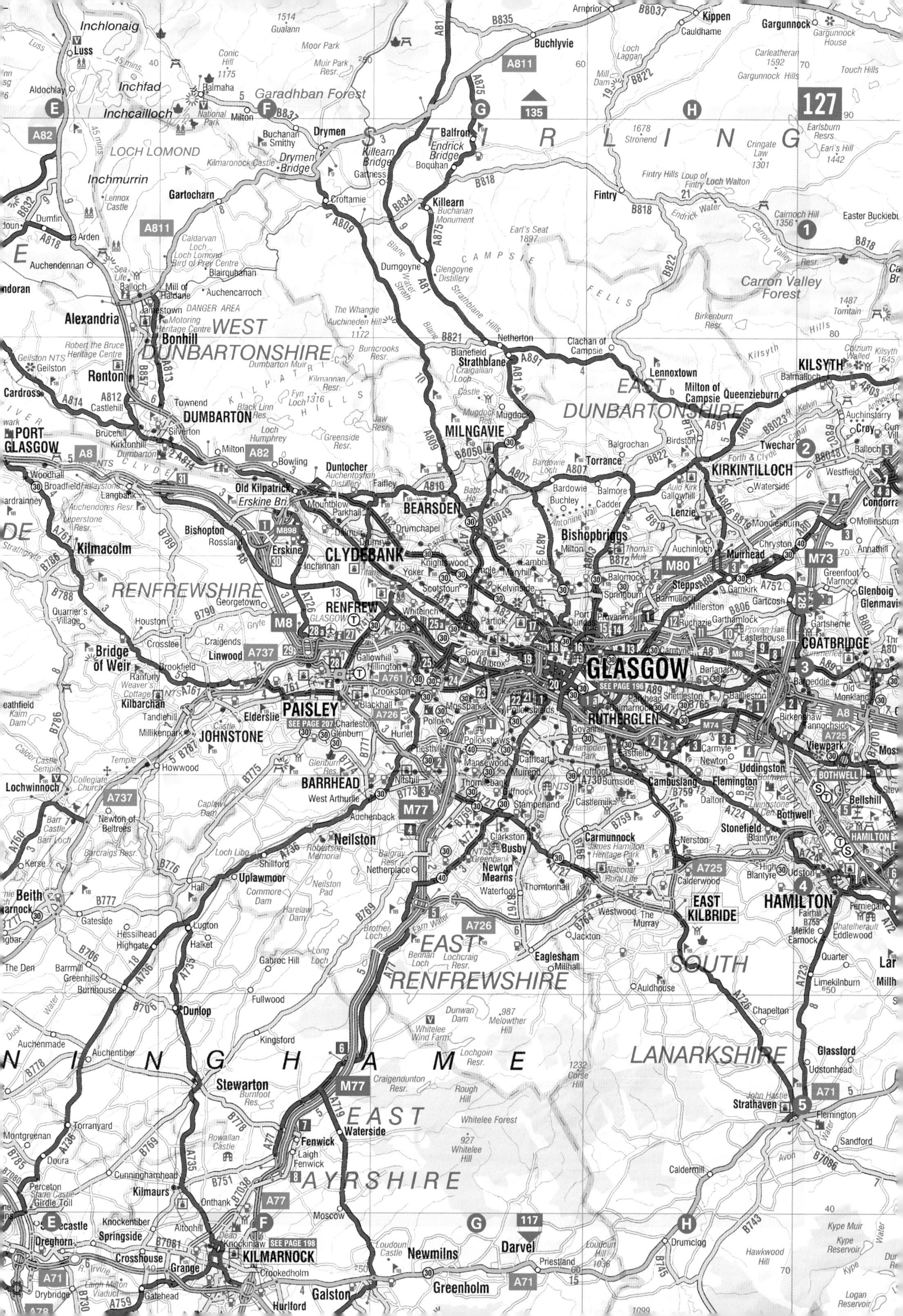
Inchlonaig
Luss
Inchfad
Inchcailloch
Balmaha
Conic Hill 1175
Garadhban Forest
Milton
1514 Gualann
Moor Park
Muir Park Resr.
Arnprior
B8037
Kippen
Cauldhame
Gargunnock
Gargunnock House
Buchlyvie
B835
A811
Loch Laggan
Mill Dam
B822
Carleatheran 1592
Gargunnock Hills
Touch Hills
135
127
Aldochlay
A82
Drymen
Buchanan Smithy
Drymen Bridge
Killearn Bridge
Balfron
Endrick Bridge
Boquhan
Gartness
LOCH LOMOND
Kilmaronock Castle
Inchmurrin
Lennox Castle
Gartocharn
S T I R L I N G
1678 Stronend
Cringate Law 1301
Earlsburn Resrs.
Earl's Hill 1442
Fintry Hills
Loup of Fintry
Loch Walton
Fintry
B818
Croftamie
Killearn
Buchanan Monument
B834
A809
A875
Endrick Water
Cairnoch Hill 1356
Easter Buckieburn
Carron Valley Resr.
Carron Valley Forest
Dumfin
Arden
A818
A811
Auchendennan
Caldarvan Loch
Loch Lomond Bird of Prey Centre
Blairquhanan
Earl's Seat 1897
C A M P S I E
F E L L S
Dumgoyne
Glengoyne Distillery
Blane Water
Strathblane Hills
B822
Birkenburn Resr.
1487 Tomtain
Sea Life
Balloch
Mill of Haldane
Auchencarroch
Jamestown
DANGER AREA
Motoring Heritage Centre
Alexandria
Bonhill
WEST DUNBARTONSHIRE
The Whangie
Auchineden Hill 1172
Burncrooks Resr.
Robert the Bruce Heritage Centre
Geilston NTS
Geilston
Renton
Dumbarton Muir
Kilmannan Resr.
B821
Netherton
Blanefield
Strathblane
Craigallian Loch
Clachan of Campsie
A891
Lennoxtown
Kilsyth Hills
KILSYTH
Colzium Walled Garden
Kilsyth 1645
Banknock
Cardross
A814
A812
Castlehill
Townend
DUMBARTON
Fyn Loch 1316
K I L P A T R I C K H I L L S
Black Linn Res.
Jaw Resr.
Mugdock Castle
Mugdock Res
Mugdock
EAST DUNBARTONSHIRE
Milton of Campsie
Queenzieburn
Kelvin
Auchinstarry
Croy
Brucehill
Kirktonhill
Silverton
Loch Humphrey
Greenside Resr.
MILNGAVIE
PORT GLASGOW
Dumbarton
Milton
Bowling
Balgrochan
Birdston
Twechar
Forth & Clyde Canal
Balloch
Woodhall
Broadfield
Finlaystone
Langbank
Auchendores Resr.
Leperstone Resr.
Duntocher
Auchentoshan Distillery
Old Kilpatrick
Erskine Bri.
Faifley
Bearsden
Torrance
Bardowie Loch
Bardowie
Balmore
Buchley
Cadder
Antonine Wall
KIRKINTILLOCH
Auld Kirk
Gallowhill
Waterside
Lenzie
Westfield
Condorrat
Moodiesburn
Mollinsburn
Bishopton
Rossland
Erskine
Mountblow
Parkhall
Dalmuir
Drumchapel
M898
Kilmacolm
CLYDEBANK
Inchinnan
Knightswood
Yoker
Scotstoun
Temple
Maryhill
Kelvinside
BISHOPBRIGGS
Milton
Lambhill
Thomas Muir
Balornock
Springburn
Auchinloch
Muirhead
Chryston
Annathill
Stepps
Garnkirk
Greenfoot
Marnock
Glenboig
Glenmavis
RENFREWSHIRE
Georgetown
RENFREW
GLASGOW
Whiteinch
Partick
Port Dundas
Provanmill
Millerston
Barmulloch
Ruchazie
Garthamlock
Provan Hall
Easterhouse
Gartcosh
Gartsherrie
Quarrier's Village
Houston
Gryfe
Crosslee
Craigends
Linwood
A737
M8
Bridge of Weir
Brookfield
Ranfurly
Weaver's Cottage NTS
Kilbarchan
Tandlehill
Millikenpark
Castle Semple
Gallowhill
Hillington
Crookston
Govan
Ibrox
GLASGOW
SEE PAGE 196
Carntyne
Barlanark
Shettleston
Parkhead
Baillieston
COATBRIDGE
Bargeddie
Summerlee
Old Monkland
PAISLEY
SEE PAGE 207
Elderslie
JOHNSTONE
Charleston
Glenburn
Blackhall
Hurlet
Pollok
Mosspark
Pollokshields
Pollokshaws
Dalmarnock
RUTHERGLEN
Govanhill
Eastfield
Carmyle
Newton
Birkenshaw
Tannochside
Viewpark
Calder Castle
Semple
Temple
Howwood
Collegiate Church
Lochwinnoch
Glenburn Res.
Priesthill
Mansewood
Cathcart
Hampden Park
Croftfoot
Burnside
Cambuslang
Flemington
Uddingston
BOTHWELL
BARRHEAD
West Arthurlie
Nitshill
Thornliebank
Giffnock
Muirend
Stamperland
Castlemilk
Dalton
Bothwell
Bellshill
Auchenback
M77
Newton of Beltrees
Barr Castle
Barr Loch
Caplaw Dam
Neilston
Robertson Memorial
Balgray Resr.
Netherplace
Clarkston
Busby
Greenbank NTS
Carmunnock
James Hamilton Heritage Park
Nerston
Stonefield
Blantyre
Livingstone Cen.
HAMILTON
Barcraigs Resr.
Loch Libo
Shillford
Uplawmoor
Newton Mearns
National Rural Life
A725
High Blantyre
Udston
Kerse
Beith
Commore Dam
Neilston Pad
Waterfoot
Thorntonhall
Calderwood
EAST KILBRIDE
HAMILTON
Gateside
Hessilhead
Highgate
Lugton
Halket
Harelaw Dam
Brother Loch
Earn Water
A726
Westwood
The Murray
Jackton
Fairhill
Meikle Earnock
Ferniegair
Chatelherault
Eddlewood
The Den
Barrmill
Greenhills
Burnhouse
Gabroc Hill
Long Loch
EAST RENFREWSHIRE
Bennan Loch
Lochcraig Resr.
Eaglesham
Millhall
SOUTH
Quarter
Limekilnburn
Dunlop
Fullwood
Auldhouse
Chapelton
Dusk Water
Auchenmade
Auchentiber
Kingsford
Dunwan Dam
987 Melowther Hill
Whitelee Wind Farm
Lochgoin Resr.
LANARKSHIRE
Glassford
Udstonhead
N I N G H A M E
Stewarton
Burnfoot Res.
Craigendunton Resr.
Rough Hill
1232 Corse Hill
Strathaven
John Hastie
A71
Flemington
Torranyard
EAST
Whitelee Forest
Sandford
Montgreenan
Rowallan Castle
Fenwick
Waterside
927 Whitelee Hill
Laigh Fenwick
Doura
Cunninghamhead
Caldermill
Avon
Perceton
Stane Castle
Girdle Toll
Kilmaurs
AYRSHIRE
Onthank
A77
Moscow
Kype Muir
Kype Reservoir
Hawkwood Hill
Springside
Knockentiber
Altonhill
Dean Castle
Knockinlaw
SEE PAGE 198
Dreghorn
Crosshouse
Grange
KILMARNOCK
117
Darvel
Drumclog
Newmilns
Loudoun Castle
Loudoun Hill 1036
Priestland
Irvine
Laigh Milton Viaduct
Crookedholm
Greenholm
Galston
Drybridge
Gatehead
Hurlford
Logan Reservoir
1099

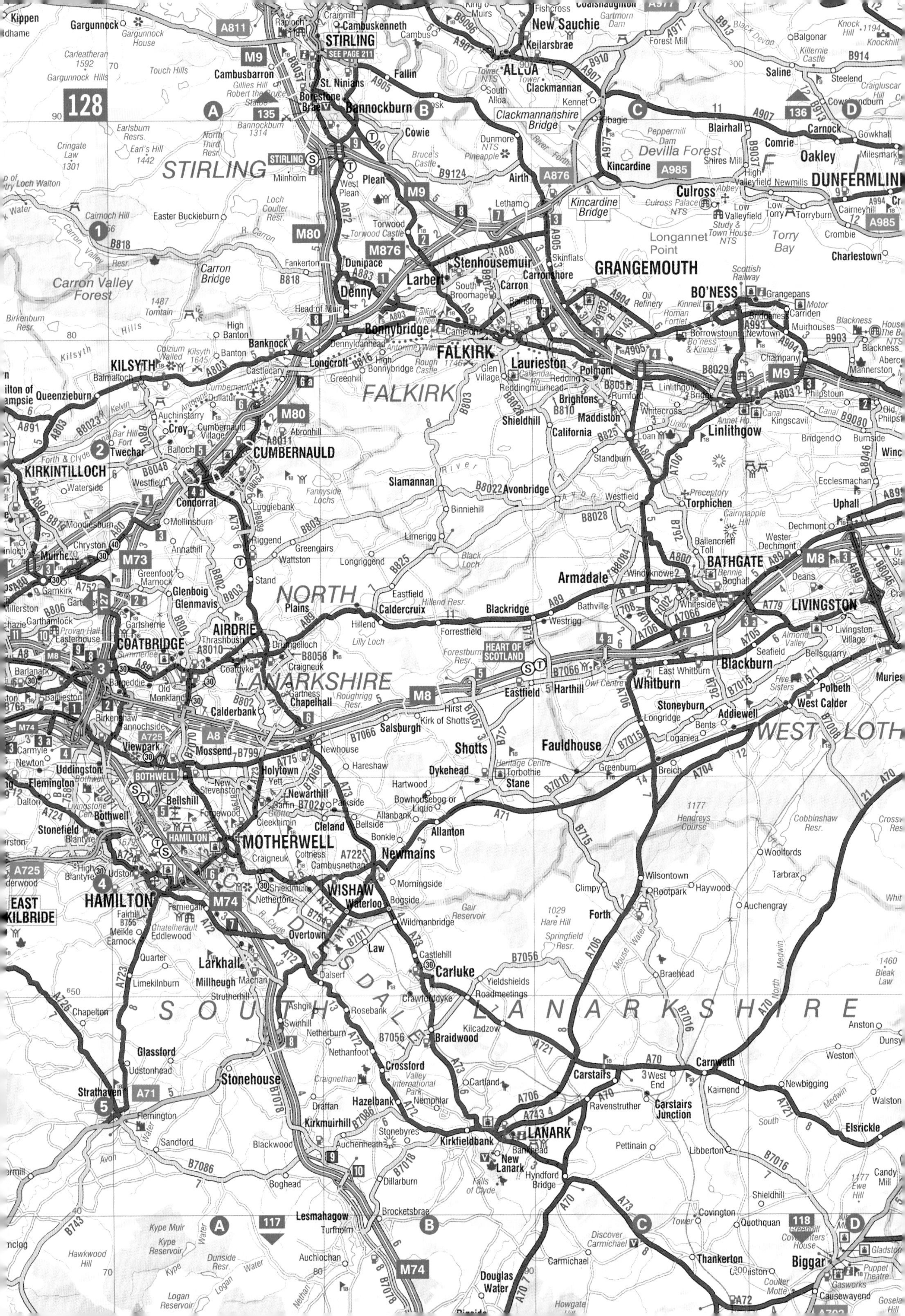

128
135
136
117
118
STIRLING
SEE PAGE 211
Kippen
Gargunnock
Gargunnock House
Cambusbarron
Cambuskenneth
Raploch
Craigmill
Cambus
St. Ninians
Borestone Brae
Bannockburn
Fallin
Cowie
Plean
West Plean
Torwood
Torwood Castle
Dunipace
Denny
Larbert
Stenhousemuir
Carron
Carronshore
Skinflats
Airth
Letham
Dunmore
Pineapple
Bruce's Castle
Milnholm
Touch Hills
Gargunnock Hills
Carleatheran
Gillies Hill
Bannockburn
North Third Resr.
Earlsburn Resrs.
Earl's Hill
Cringate Law
Loch Walton
Cairnoch Hill
Loch Coulter Resr.
Easter Buckieburn
Carron Valley Resr.
Carron Valley Forest
Carron Bridge
Fankerton
Tomtain
Birkenburn Resr.
Kilsyth Hills
High Banton
Banknock
Banton
KILSYTH
Kilsyth 1645
Colzium Walled Garden
Queenzieburn
Balmalloch
Castlecary
Longcroft
Dennyloanhead
Head of Muir
Bonnybridge
High Bonnybridge
Rough Castle
Greenhill
Antonine Wall
FALKIRK
Falkirk Wheel
Camelon
Glen Village
Laurieston
Polmont
Redding
Reddingmuirhead
Brightons
Rumford
Maddiston
Shieldhill
California
Standburn
Avonbridge
Slamannan
Binniehill
Limerigg
Black Loch
Longriggend
Wattston
Greengairs
Riggend
Stand
Plains
Eastfield
Caldercruix
Hillend Resr.
Hillend
Lilly Loch
Forrestfield
Blackridge
Westrigg
Armadale
Bathville
Whiteside
Windyknowe
BATHGATE
Ballencrieff Toll
Torphichen
Westfield
Cairnpapple Hill
Wester Dechmont
Dechmont
Uphall
Ecclesmachan
LIVINGSTON
Livingston Village
Deans
Almond Valley
Seafield
Bellsquarry
Blackburn
East Whitburn
Whitburn
Harthill
Eastfield
Owl Centre
HEART OF SCOTLAND
Stoneyburn
Longridge
Addiewell
Bents
Loganlea
Five Sisters
Polbeth
West Calder
WEST LOTH
Breich
Greenburn
Fauldhouse
Shotts
Torbothie
Stane
Heritage Centre
Dykehead
Kirk of Shotts
Hirst
Salsburgh
Forestburn Resr.
Roughrigg Resr.
NORTH LANARKSHIRE
AIRDRIE
Thrashbush
Drumgelloch
Craigneuk
Chapelhall
Gartness
Calderbank
Coatdyke
COATBRIDGE
Gartsherrie
Glenmavis
Glenboig
Greenfoot
Marnock
Garnkirk
Gartcosh
Garthamlock
Easterhouse
Provan Hall
Barlanark
Baillieston
Birkenshaw
Tannochside
Viewpark
Old Monkland
Bargeddie
Mossend
Newhouse
Holytown
New Stevenston
Bellshill
Yett
Newarthill
Carfin
Cleekhimin
Parkside
Bellside
Cleland
Hareshaw
Hartwood
Bowhousebog or Liquo
Allanbank
Allanton
Bonkle
Newmains
Coltness
Cambusnethan
Craigneuk
MOTHERWELL
Forgewood
WISHAW
Waterloo
Shieldmuir
Netherton
Bogside
Morningside
Wildmanbridge
Gair Reservoir
Overtown
Law
Castlehill
Carluke
Yieldshields
Roadmeetings
Crawforddyke
CUMBERNAULD
Cumbernauld Village
Abronhill
Condorrat
Luggiebank
Mollinsburn
Dullatur
Croy
Auchinstarry
Twechar
KIRKINTILLOCH
Waterside
Westfield
Moodiesburn
Chryston
Muirhead
Annathill
Kelvin
Forth & Clyde Canal
Bar Hill Fort
Balloch
Fannyside Lochs
Uddingston
BOTHWELL
Bothwell
Flemington
Dalton
Stonefield
Blantyre
High Blantyre
Udston
HAMILTON
EAST KILBRIDE
Fairhill
Meikle Earnock
Chatelherault
Eddlewood
Ferniegair
Quarter
Limekilnburn
Larkhall
Millheugh
Machan
Strutherhill
Chapelton
Ashgill
Swinhill
Dalserf
Rosebank
Netherburn
Nethanfoot
Glassford
Udstonhead
Stonehouse
Strathaven
Flemington
Sandford
Blackwood
Kirkmuirhill
Draffan
Hazelbank
Crossford
Craignethan Castle
Valley International Park
Nemphlar
Stonebyres
Auchenheath
Boghead
Dillarburn
Kirkfieldbank
LANARK
Bankhead
New Lanark
Falls of Clyde
Hyndford Bridge
Brocketsbrae
Lesmahagow
Turfholm
Auchlochan
Douglas Water
Carmichael
Discover Carmichael
Kype Muir
Kype Reservoir
Dunside Resr.
Logan Reservoir
Hawkwood Hill
SOUTH LANARKSHIRE
CLYDESDALE
Braidwood
Kilcadzow
Cartland
Carstairs
Ravenstruther
Carstairs Junction
West End
Pettinain
Carnwath
Kaimend
Newbigging
Walston
Elsrickle
Libberton
Shieldhill
Covington
Quothquan
Thankerton
Biggar
Gladstone Court
Puppet Theatre
Gasworks
Causewayend
Coulter Motte
Candy Mill
Ewe Hill
Dunsyre
Weston
Anston
Bleak Law
Woolfords
Tarbrax
Cobbinshaw Resr.
Auchengray
Haywood
Rootpark
Wilsontown
Climpy
Forth
Braehead
Hare Hill
Springfield Resr.
Hendreys Course
Mouse Water
North Medwin
New Sauchie
Fishcross
Keilarsbrae
ALLOA
Tower
South Alloa
Clackmannan
Kennet
Kilbagie
Clackmannanshire Bridge
River Forth
Kincardine
Kincardine Bridge
Devilla Forest
Peppermill Dam
Blairhall
Forest Mill
Balgonar
Knock Hill
Knockhill
Killernie Castle
Saline
Steelend
Craigluscar Hill
Cowstrandburn
Carnock
Gowkhall
Comrie
Oakley
Milesmark
Shires Mill
High Valleyfield
Newmills
DUNFERMLINE
Culross
Culross Palace
Low Valleyfield
Low Torry
Torryburn
Cairneyhill
Crombie
Charlestown
Torry Bay
Longannet Point
Study & Town House
GRANGEMOUTH
Oil Refinery
Scottish Railway
BO'NESS
Kinneil
Grangepans
Motor Museum
Carriden
Bridgeness
Blackness
Muirhouses
Borrowstoun
Newtown
Bo'ness & Kinneil
Roman Fortlet
Champany
Mannerston
Philpstoun
Linlithgow Bridge
Linlithgow
Annet Ho.
Kingscavil
Bridgend
Burnside
Whitecross
Union Canal
Loan
Preceptory
Bainsford
Callendar Ho.
South Broomage
Gartmorn Dam
Black Devon
Devilla Forest
Keilarsbrae
Fallin
Forth & Clyde Canal

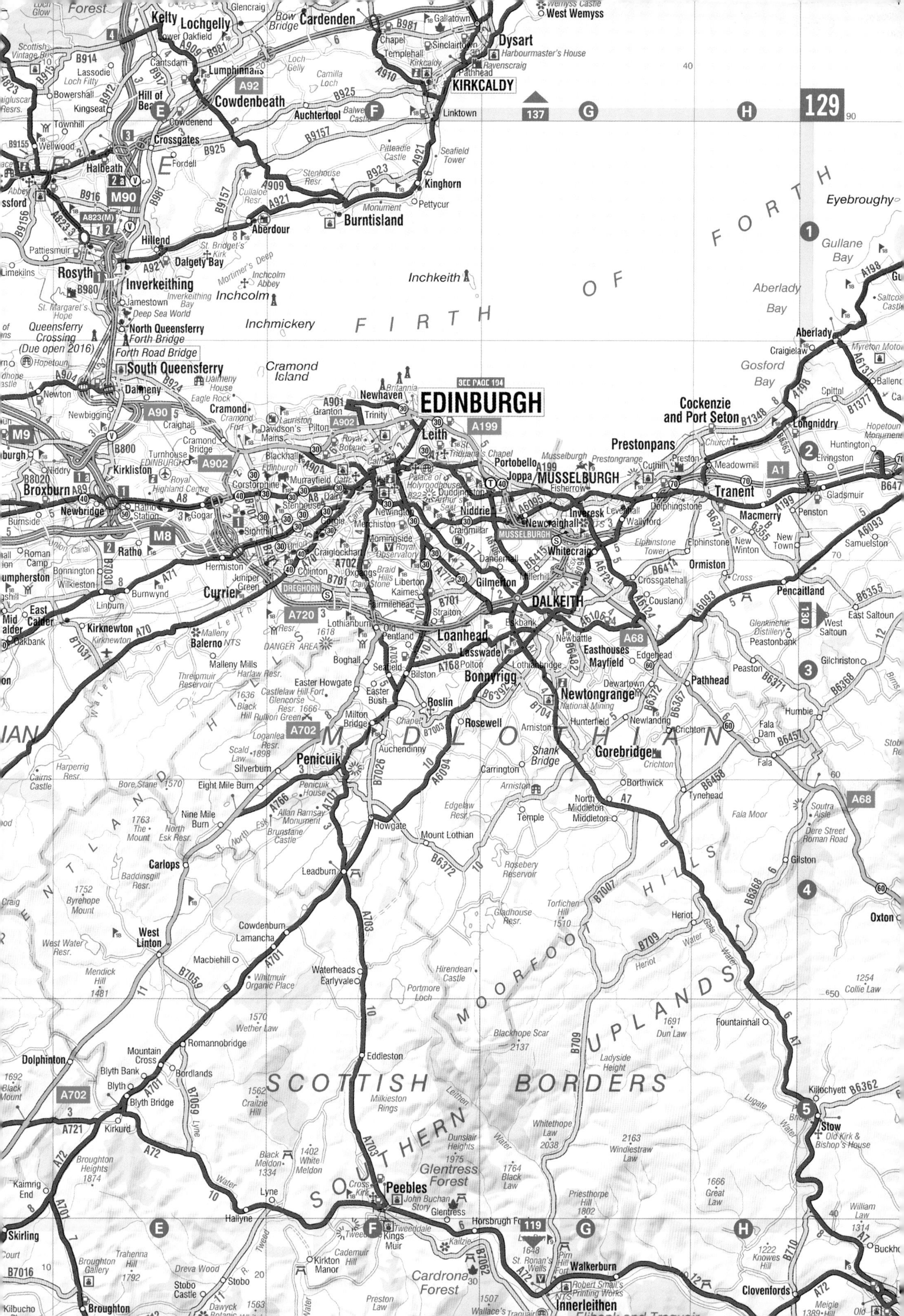
129
137
130
119
SEE PAGE 194
EDINBURGH
FIRTH OF FORTH
MIDLOTHIAN
SCOTTISH BORDERS
SOUTHERN UPLANDS
MOORFOOT HILLS
PENTLAND HILLS
Kelty
Lochgelly
Cardenden
Bow Bridge
Glencraig
Gallatown
West Wemyss
Wemyss Castle
Dysart
Harbourmaster's House
Ravenscraig
Chapel
Sinclairtown
Templehall
Kirkcaldy
Pathhead
KIRKCALDY
Linktown
Lower Oakfield
Lumphinnans
Cantsdam
Loch Gelly
Camilla Loch
Cowdenbeath
Hill of Beath
Auchtertool
Balwearie Castle
Lassodie
Loch Fitty
Bowershall
Kingseat
Townhill
Wellwood
Cowdenend
Crossgates
Fordell
Halbeath
Pitteadie Castle
Seafield Tower
Kinghorn
Pettycur
Stenhouse Resr.
Cullaloe Resr.
Monument
Burntisland
Aberdour
Hillend
St. Bridget's Kirk
Dalgety Bay
Mortimer's Deep
Inchcolm Abbey
Inchcolm
Inchkeith
Inchmickery
Rosyth
Limekilns
Pattiesmuir
Inverkeithing
Inverkeithing Bay
Jamestown
Deep Sea World
St. Margaret's Hope
Queensferry Crossing (Due open 2016)
North Queensferry
Forth Bridge
Forth Road Bridge
Hopetoun
South Queensferry
Dalmeny House
Dalmeny
Cramond Island
Eagle Rock
Cramond
Cramond Fort
Craighall
Cramond Bridge
Newton
Newbigging
Turnhouse
EDINBURGH
Kirkliston
Royal Highland Centre
Niddry
Broxburn
Newbridge
Ratho Station
Gogar
Ratho
Hermiston
Bonnington
Wilkieston
Burnwynd
Currie
Juniper Green
Linburn
East Calder
Kirknewton
Oakbank
Malleny
Balerno
Malleny Mills
Harlaw Resr.
Threipmuir Reservoir
Newhaven
Britannia
Granton
Trinity
Laurieston
Pilton
Davidson's Mains
Royal Botanic
Leith
St. Triduana's Chapel
Blackhall
Edinburgh
Murrayfield
Corstorphine
Stenhouse
Dalry
Gorgie
Sighthill
Union Canal
Palace of Holyroodhouse
Arthur's Seat
Duddingston
Newington
Merchiston
Morningside
Royal Observatory
Craiglockhart
Oxgangs
Braid Hills
Colinton
DREGHORN
Caiy Stone
Liberton
Kaimes
Fairmilehead
Straiton
Lothianburn
Old Pentland
Loanhead
Portobello
Joppa
Niddrie
Craigmillar
Danderhall
Gilmerton
Millerhill
MUSSELBURGH
Fisherrow
Musselburgh
Prestongrange
Inveresk
Levenhall
Wallyford
Newcraighall
Whitecraig
Elphinstone Tower
Elphinstone
DALKEITH
Eskbank
Newbattle
Easthouses
Mayfield
Lasswade
Polton
Bonnyrigg
Lothianbridge
Newtongrange
National Mining
Dewartown
Edgehead
Pathhead
Arniston
Hunterfield
Newlandrig
Crichton
Gorebridge
Shank Bridge
Carrington
Rosewell
Roslin
Bilston
Seafield
Boghall
Easter Howgate
Castlelaw Hill Fort
Glencorse Resr.
Easter Bush
Milton Bridge
Chapel
Auchendinny
Penicuik
Penicuik House
Allan Ramsay Monument
Brunstane Castle
Loganlea Resr.
Scald Law
Silverburn
Eight Mile Burn
Bore Stane
Harperrig Resr.
Cairns Castle
Nine Mile Burn
The Mount
North Esk Resr.
Carlops
Baddinsgill Resr.
Byrehope Mount
West Linton
West Water Resr.
Mendick Hill
Macbiehill
Howgate
Mount Lothian
Leadburn
Cowdenburn
Lamancha
Whitmuir Organic Place
Waterheads
Earlyvale
Portmore Loch
Rosebery Reservoir
Gladhouse Resr.
Hirendean Castle
Torfichen Hill
Heriot
Gala Water
Blackhope Scar
Dun Law
Ladyside Height
Fountainhall
Collie Law
Cockenzie and Port Seton
Prestonpans
Preston
Cuthill
Meadowmill
Tranent
Dolphingstone
Macmerry
Penston
Gladsmuir
New Winton
New Town
Samuelston
Ormiston
Crossgatehall
Cousland
Cross
Pencaitland
East Saltoun
West Saltoun
Glenkinchie Distillery
Peastonbank
Peaston
Gilchriston
Humbie
Fala Dam
Fala
Borthwick
Tynehead
North Middleton
Middleton
Temple
Fala Moor
Soutra Aisle
Dere Street Roman Road
Gilston
Oxton
Longniddry
Hopetoun Monument
Huntington
Elvington
Spittal
Ballencrieff
Craigielaw
Aberlady
Aberlady Bay
Gosford Bay
Myreton Motor
Gullane Bay
Eyebroughy
Saltcoats Castle
Dolphinton
Romannobridge
Mountain Cross
Bordlands
Blyth Bank
Blyth
Blyth Bridge
Kirkurd
Broughton Heights
Kaimrig End
Skirling
Broughton Gallery
Trahenna Hill
Dreva Wood
Stobo Castle
Stobo
Broughton
Kilbucho
Dawyck Botanic
Lyne
Hallyne
Black Meldon
White Meldon
Milkieston Rings
Eddleston
Cross Kirk
Peebles
John Buchan Story
Glentress
Glentress Forest
Dunslair Heights
Kings Muir
Tweeddale
Kailzie
Cademuir Hill
Kirkton Manor
Cardrona Forest
Horsburgh Ford
St. Ronan's Wells
Walkerburn
Robert Smail's Printing Works
Innerleithen
Preston Law
Whitehope Law
Windlestraw Law
Black Law
Priesthorpe Hill
Great Law
Knowes Hill
Clovenfords
William Law
Killochyett
Stow
Old Kirk & Bishop's House
Lugate Water
Buckholm
Meigle Hill

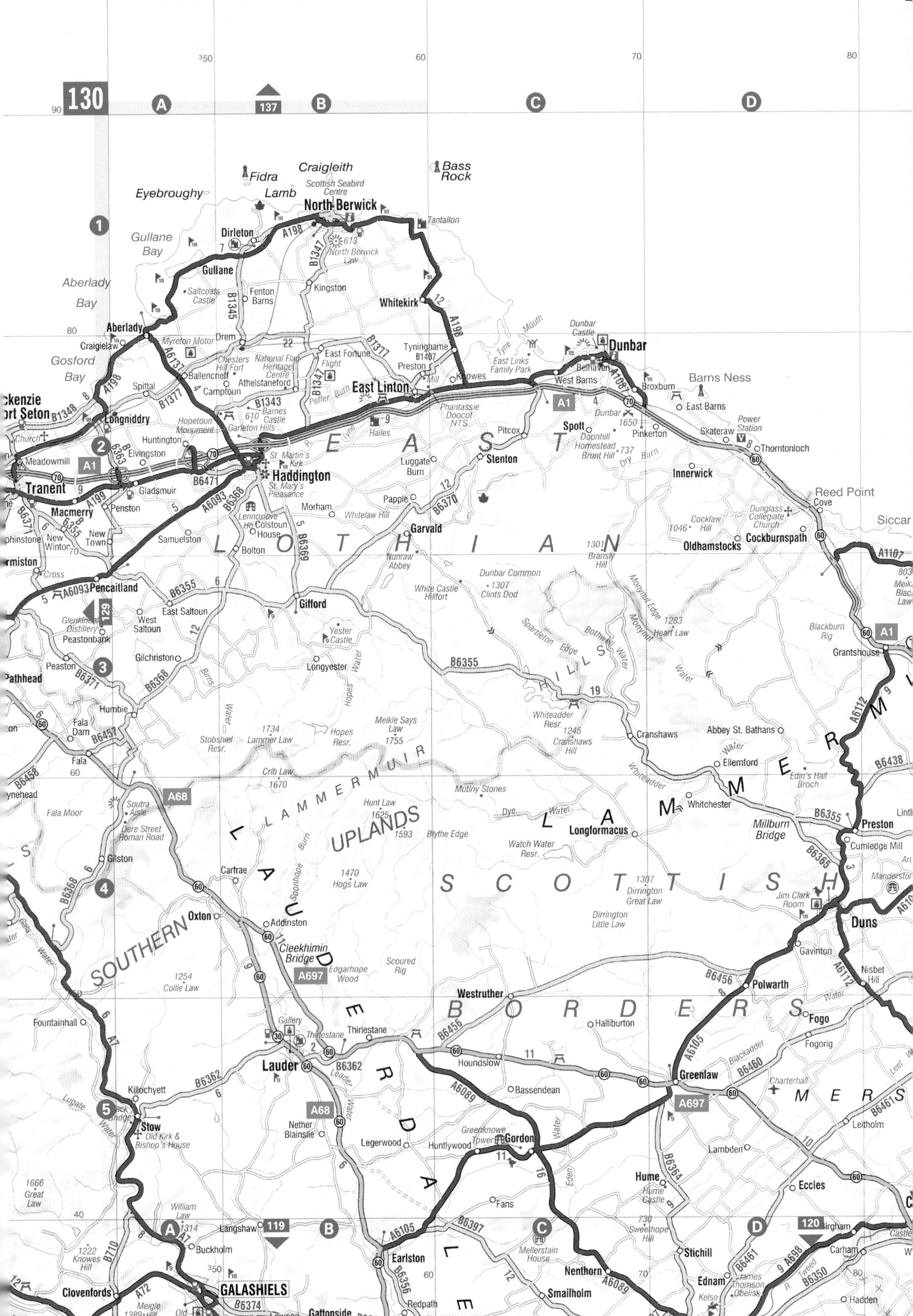

137
119
120
129
Fidra
Craigleith
Bass Rock
Eyebroughy
Lamb
Scottish Seabird Centre
North Berwick
Tantallon
Dirleton
Gullane Bay
North Berwick Law
Gullane
Aberlady Bay
Saltcoats Castle
Fenton Barns
Kingston
Whitekirk
Aberlady
Craigielaw
Gosford Bay
Myreton Motor
Drem
Chesters Hill Fort
National Flag Heritage Centre
East Fortune
Flight
Tyninghame
Preston
Knowes
Tyne Mouth
East Links Family Park
Dunbar Castle
Dunbar
Belhaven
West Barns
Broxburn
Barns Ness
East Barns
Ballencrieff
Camptoun
Athelstaneford
Spittal
East Linton
Mill
Phantassie Doocot NTS
Cockenzie
Port Seton
Longniddry
Hopetoun Monument
Garleton Hills
Barnes Castle
Hailes
Church
Huntington
Elvingston
Meadowmill
St. Martin's Kirk
Haddington
St. Mary's Pleasance
Luggate Burn
Pitcox
Stenton
Spott
Doonhill Homestead
Brunt Hill
Dunbar
Pinkerton
Skateraw
Power Station
Thorntonloch
Innerwick
Tranent
Gladsmuir
Penston
Macmerry
New Winton
New Town
Samuelston
Lennoxlove Ho
Colstoun House
Morham
Whitelaw Hill
Papple
Garvald
Nunraw Abbey
Reed Point
Cove
Siccar
Dunglass Collegiate Church
Cocklaw Hill
Cockburnspath
Oldhamstocks
EAST LOTHIAN
Bolton
Cross
Pencaitland
Glenkinchie Distillery
Peastonbank
West Saltoun
East Saltoun
Gifford
Dunbar Common
Clints Dod
White Castle Hillfort
Bransly Hill
Monynut Edge
Heart Law
Blackburn Rig
Grantshouse
Yester Castle
Longyester
Gilchriston
Peaston
Pathhead
Humbie
Spartleton Edge
Bothwell Water
Whiteadder Resr.
Cranshaws Hill
Cranshaws
Abbey St. Bathans
Ellemford
Fala Dam
Fala
Fala Moor
Stobshiel Resr.
Lammer Law
Hopes Resr.
Meikle Says Law
Crib Law
Edin's Hall Broch
Soutra Aisle
Dere Street Roman Road
Mutiny Stones
Hunt Law
Blythe Edge
Watch Water Resr.
Longformacus
Whitchester
Millburn Bridge
Preston
Cumledge Mill
Manderston
LAMMERMUIR
LAMMERMUIR HILLS
UPLANDS
SOUTHERN
LAUDERDALE
SCOTTISH BORDERS
Gilston
Carfrae
Hogs Law
Dirrington Great Law
Dirrington Little Law
Jim Clark Room
Duns
Oxton
Addinston
Cleekhimin Bridge
Edgarhope Wood
Scoured Rig
Gavinton
Nisbet Hill
Collie Law
Westruther
Polwarth
Fountainhall
Gallery
Thirlestane
Halliburton
Fogo
Fogorig
Lauder
Houndslow
Greenlaw
Charterhall
Killochyett
Bassendean
Stow
Old Kirk & Bishop's House
Nether Blainslie
Legerwood
Greenknowe Tower
Gordon
Huntlywood
Lambden
Leitholm
Hume
Hume Castle
Eccles
Great Law
William Law
Langshaw
Fans
Sweethope Hill
Knowes Hill
Buckholm
Earlston
Mellerstain House
Stichill
Birgham
Carham
Clovenfords
GALASHIELS
Meigle Hill
Old
Lowood
Gattonside
Redpath
Nenthorn
Smailholm
Ednam
James Thomson Obelisk
Kelso
Hadden

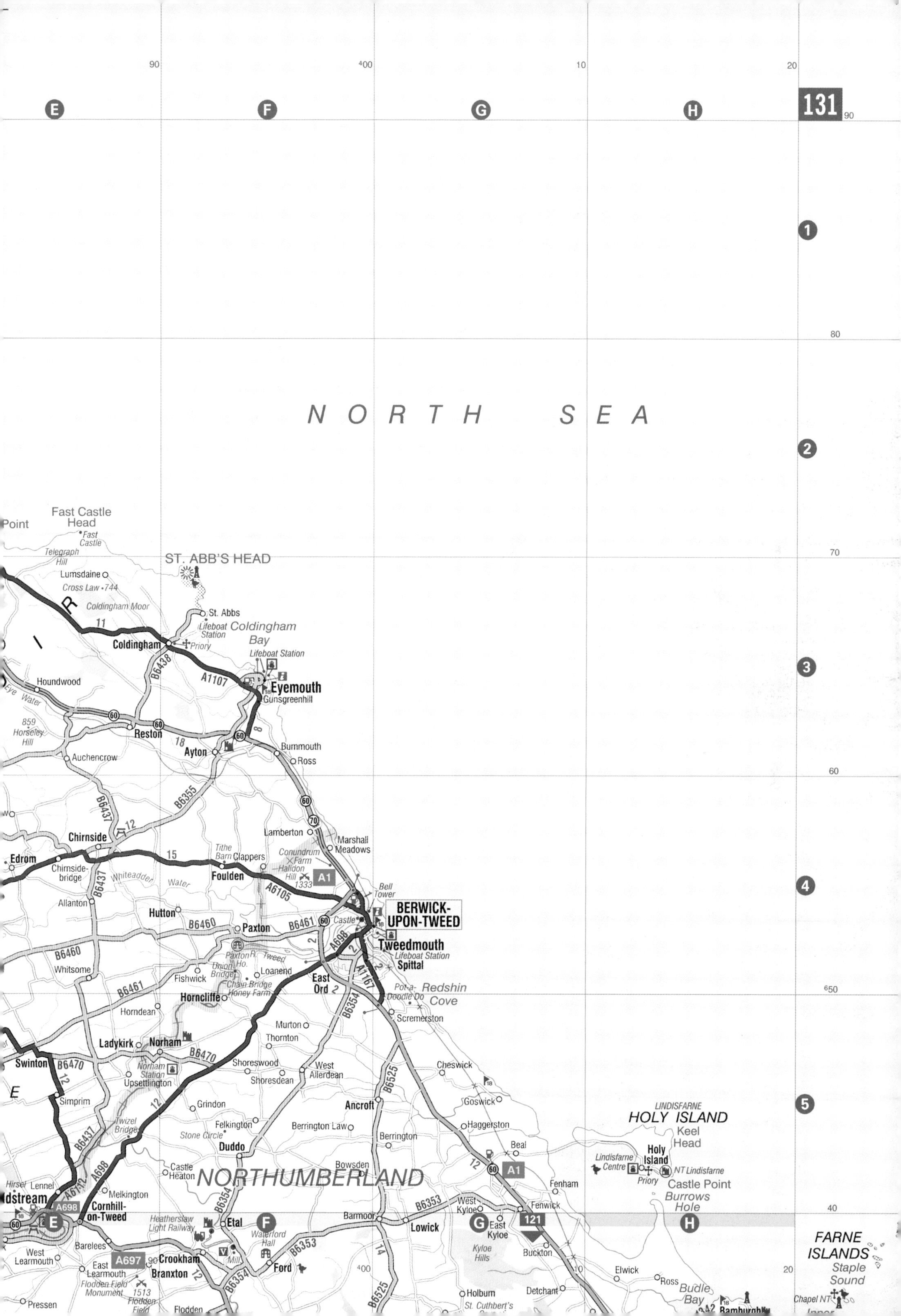

NORTH SEA

Fast Castle Head
Point
Fast Castle
Telegraph Hill
Lumsdaine
Cross Law •744
Coldingham Moor
11
Houndwood
ST. ABB'S HEAD
St. Abbs
Lifeboat Station
Coldingham Bay
Priory
Lifeboat Station
Coldingham
B6438
A1107
Eyemouth
Gunsgreenhill
Eye Water
859
Horseley Hill
Reston
18
Ayton
Burnmouth
Ross
Auchencrow
B6355
B6437
12
Chirnside
Lamberton
60
70
Edrom
15
Tithe Barn
Clappers
Marshall Meadows
Chirnside-bridge
B6437
Whiteadder
Water
Foulden
Conundrum Farm
Halidon Hill 1333
A6105
Bell Tower
Allanton
A1
Hutton
B6460
Paxton
B6461
Castle
BERWICK-UPON-TWEED
Whitsome
Paxton Ho.
Tweed
A698
Tweedmouth
Lifeboat Station
Spittal
B6460
Fishwick
Union Bridge
Loanend
B6461
Chain Bridge
Honey Farm
East Ord 2
Pot-a-Doodle Do
Redshin Cove
Horncliffe
Horndean
Murton
Scremerston
Thornton
Ladykirk
Norham
Shoreswood
Cheswick
Swinton
B6470
Norham Station
West Allerdean
B6525
Goswick
Upsettlington
Shoresdean
LINDISFARNE
HOLY ISLAND
Simprim
Grindon
Felkington
Ancroft
Haggerston
Keel Head
Twizel Bridge
Stone Circle
Berrington Law
Berrington
Beal
Lindisfarne
Holy Island
Duddo
Bowsden
Lindisfarne Centre
NT Lindisfarne
Castle Heaton
Priory
Castle Point
Hirsel
Lennel
NORTHUMBERLAND
Burrows Hole
Melkington
West Kyloe
Fenwick
dstream
A698
Cornhill-on-Tweed
Heatherslaw Light Railway
Etal
Barmoor
B6353
Lowick
East Kyloe
121
FARNE ISLANDS
West Learmouth
A697
Crookham
Waterford Hall
Buckton
Staple Sound
East Learmouth
Mill
Ford
Kyloe Hills
Branxton
Flodden Field Monument 1513
B6354
Elwick
Ross
Budle Bay
Pressen
Flodden Field
B6525
Holburn
St. Cuthbert's
Detchant
Chapel NT
Bamburgh

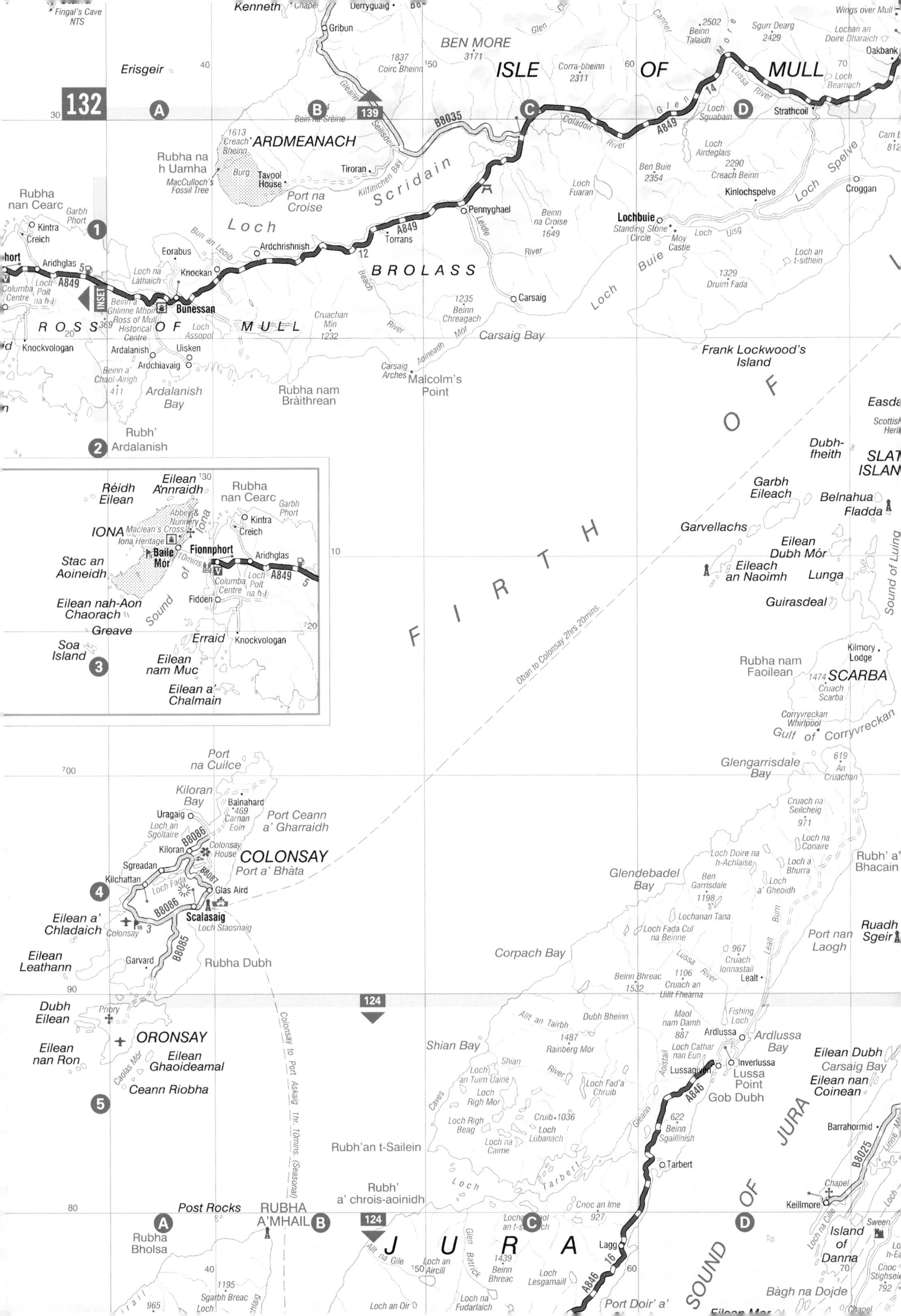

132
ISLE OF MULL
BEN MORE
3171
ARDMEANACH
Loch Scridain
BROLASS
ROSS OF MULL
Bunessan
Fionnphort
IONA
Baile Mòr
FIRTH OF LORN
Oban to Colonsay 2hrs 20mins.
COLONSAY
Scalasaig
ORONSAY
JURA
SOUND OF JURA
SCARBA
Gulf of Corryvreckan
Garvellachs
Lochbuie
Pennyghael
Carsaig
Carsaig Bay
Frank Lockwood's Island
Kiloran
Kiloran Bay
Port a' Bhàta
Glendebadel Bay
Corpach Bay
Shian Bay
Ardlussa
Inverlussa
Tarbert
Lagg
Colonsay to Port Askaig 1hr. 10mins. (Seasonal)
A849
A846
B8086
B8085
B8025
139
124

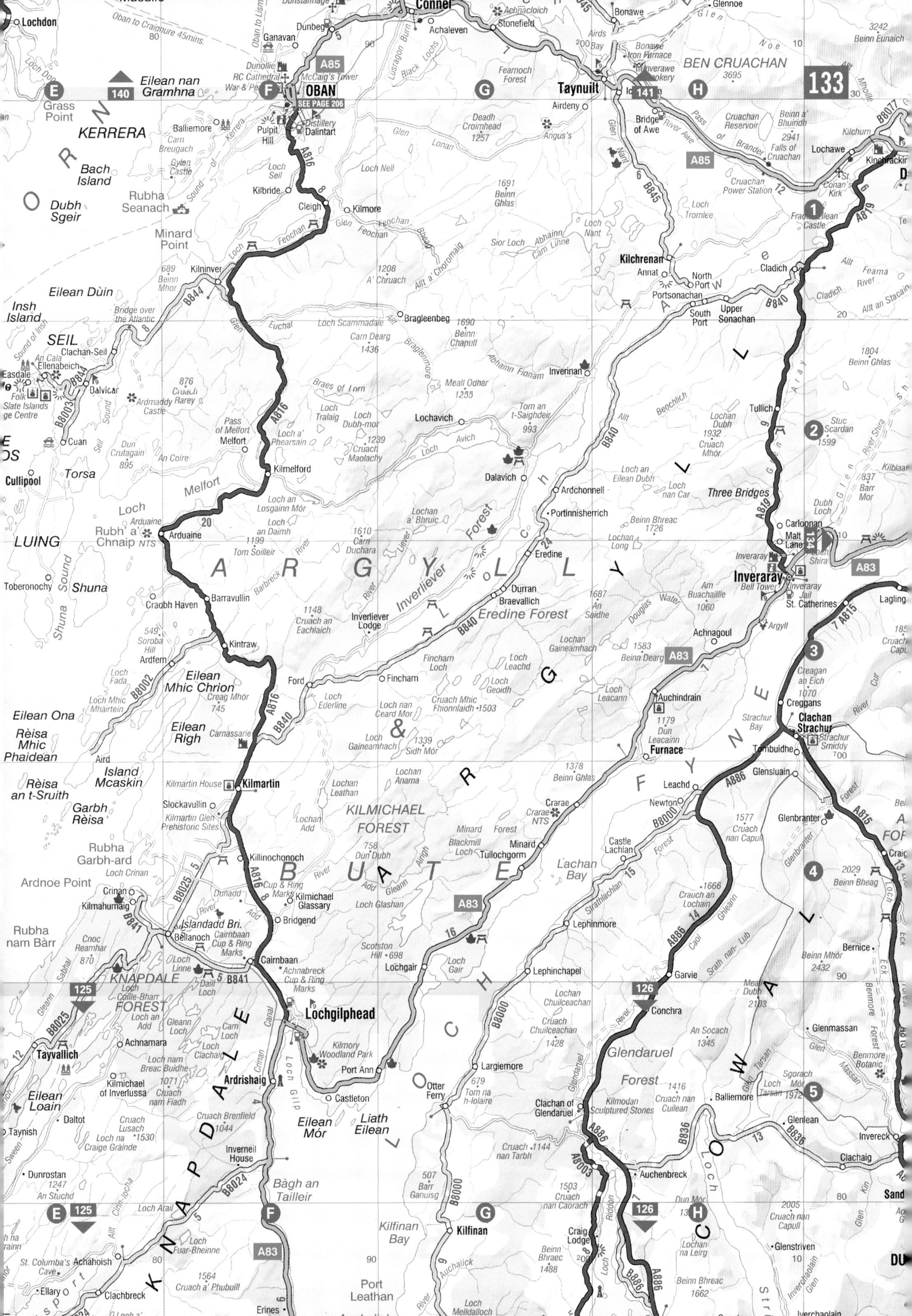
Lochdon
Oban to Craignure 45mins.
Dunstaffnage
Connel
Dunbeg
Ganavan
Achaleven
Achnacloich
Stonefield
Bonawe
Glennoe
Airds Bay
Bonawe Iron Furnace
Inverawe Smokery
BEN CRUACHAN
3695
3242
Beinn Eunaich
Eilean nan Gramhna
Dunollie
RC Cathedral
War & Peace
McCaig's Tower
OBAN
SEE PAGE 206
Fearnoch Forest
Taynuilt
Grass Point
KERRERA
Balliemore
Pulpit Hill
Distillery
Dalintart
Airdeny
Bridge of Awe
River Awe
Pass of Brander
Cruachan Reservoir
Beinn a' Bhuiridh
2941
Falls of Cruachan
Kilchurn
Lochawe
Kinglrackin
Carn Breugach
Gylen Castle
Bach Island
Deadh Croimhead
1257
Angus's
Glen Lonan
Loch Seil
Loch Nell
Kilbride
Dubh Sgeir
Rubha Seanach
Sound of Kerrera
Cleigh
Kilmore
1691
Beinn Ghlas
Cruachan Power Station
St. Conan's Kirk
Loch Tromlee
Fraoch Eilean Castle
Minard Point
Glen Feochan
Loch Feochan
Sior Loch
Abhainn Cam Linne
Loch Nant
Kilchrenan
Annat
North Port
Portsonachan
Cladich
Carloonan
689
Beinn Mhor
Kilninver
1208
A' Chruach
Allt a' Choromaig
Eilean Dùin
Insh Island
Bridge over the Atlantic
Sound of Insh
SEIL
Clachan-Seil
An Cala
Ellenabeich
Easdale
Folk
Slate Islands
Heritage Centre
Dalvicar
Cuan
Euchar
Loch Scammadale
Bragleenbeg
1690
Beinn Chapull
Carn Dearg
1436
Bragleenmore
Abhainn Fionam
Inverinan
South Port
Upper Sonachan
Allt an Stacain
Cladich River
Fearna River
1804
Beinn Ghlas
876
Cruach Rarey
Ardmaddy Castle
Braes of Lorn
Meall Odhar
1255
Loch Tralaig
Loch Dubh-mor
Pass of Melfort
Melfort
Loch a' Phearsain
1239
Cruach Maolachy
Lochavich
Loch Avich
Tom an t-Saighdeir
993
Beochlich
Lochan Dubh
1932
Cruach Mhór
Tullich
Stuc Scardan
1599
River Shira
Dun Crutagain
895
An Coire
Torsa
Cullipool
Kilmelford
Dalavich
Ardchonnell
Loch an Eilean Dubh
Loch nan Car
Three Bridges
Kilblaan
837
Barr Mor
Dubh Loch
Glen Shira
Loch Melfort
Loch an Losgainn Mór
Loch an Daimh
Lochan a' Bhruic
Portinnisherrich
Beinn Bhreac
1726
Carloonan
Malt Lane
Arduaine
Rubh' a' Chnaip
NTS
LUING
1199
Tom Soilleir
1610
Carn Duchara
Barbreck River
River Liever
Inverliever Forest
Eredine
Lochan Long
Inveraray
Inveraray Bell Tower
Inveraray Jail
Inveraray Castle
St. Catherines
Lagling
ARGYLL
Toberonochy
Shuna
Shuna Sound
Craobh Haven
Barravullin
1148
Cruach an Eachlaich
Inverliever Lodge
Durran
Braevallich
Eredine Forest
1687
An Suidhe
Douglas Water
Am Buachaille
1060
549
Soroba Hill
Ardfern
Kintraw
Lochan Gaineamhach
1583
Beinn Dearg
Achnagoul
Argyll
Creagan an Eich
1070
Loch Fada
Loch Mhic Mhairtein
Eilean Mhic Chrion
Creag Mhór
745
Ford
Fincharn
Fincharn Loch
Loch Leachd
Loch Geoidh
Loch Leacann
Auchindrain
Creggans
Clachan Strachur
Strachur Smiddy
Strachur Bay
Eilean Ona
Eilean Righ
Carnassarie
Loch Ederline
Cruach Mhic Fhionnlaidh
1503
Loch nan Ceard Mor
Loch Gaineamhach
1339
Sidh Mór
1179
Dun Leacainn
Furnace
Tombuidhe
700
Rèisa Mhic Phaidean
Aird
Island Mcaskin
Rèisa an t-Sruith
Kilmartin House
Kilmartin
Lochan Leathan
Lochan Anama
1378
Beinn Ghlas
Leachd
Glensluain
Newton
Glenbranter
Crarae
NTS
Loch Fyne
Garbh Rèisa
Slockavullin
Kilmartin Glen Prehistoric Sites
Lochan Add
KILMICHAEL FOREST
Minard Forest
1577
Cruach nan Capull
Rubha Garbh-ard
Loch Crinan
Killinochonoch
Blackmill Loch
758
Dùn Dubh
Minard
Tullochgorm
Castle Lachlan
Lachan Bay
Strathlachlan
2029
Beinn Bheag
Ardnoe Point
Crinan
Kilmahumaig
Dunadd
Cup & Ring Marks
Kilmichael Glassary
River Add
Gleann Airigh
Loch Glashan
1666
Cruach an Lochain
Gleann Ghlieann
Rubha nam Bàrr
Cnoc Reamhar
870
Islandadd Bri.
Bellanoch
Cairnbaan Cup & Ring Marks
Bridgend
Scotston Hill
698
Lochgair
Loch Gair
Lephinmore
Bernice
Beinn Mhór
2432
Loch Linne
Cairnbaan
Achnabreck Cup & Ring Marks
Daill Loch
KNAPDALE FOREST
Loch Coille-Bharr
Loch an Add
Lephinchapel
Garvie
Srath nan Lub
Meall Dubh
2103
Benmore Forest
Gleann Sabhal
Lochgilphead
Lochan Chuilceachan
Cruach Chuilceachan
1428
Conchra
Glenmassan
Tayvallich
Achnamara
Gleann Loch
Cam Loch
Loch Clachaig
Kilmory Woodland Park
Loch Gilp
Ardrishaig
Crinan Canal
An Socach
1345
Glendaruel Forest
Benmore Botanic
Glen Massan
Loch nam Breac Buidhe
1071
Cruach nam Fiadh
Kilmichael of Inverlussa
Port Ann
Castleton
Largiemore
Otter Ferry
679
Tom na h-Iolaire
Eilean Loain
Daltot
Taynish
Cruach Lusach
1530
Loch na Craige Gràinde
Cruach Brenfield
1044
Eilean Mór
Liath Eilean
Loch Fyne
Clachan of Glendaruel
Kilmodan Sculptured Stones
1416
Cruach nan Cuilean
Balliemore
Glen Tarsan
Loch Tarsan
Sgorach Mór
1972
Glenlean
Invereck
Clachaig
Dunrostan
1247
An Stùchd
Inverneil House
Bàgh an Tailleir
507
Barr Ganuisg
Cruach
1144
nan Tarbh
1503
Cruach nan Caorach
Auchenbreck
Loch Striven
COWAL
Sand
Loch Arail
Kilfinan Bay
Kilfinan
Craig Lodge
River Riddon
Dun Mor
2005
Cruach nan Capull
St. Columba's Cave
Achahoish
Loch Fuar-Bheinne
Beinn Bhreac
1488
Lochan na Leirg
Glenstriven
Ellary
Clachbreck
1564
Cruach a' Phubuill
Port Leathan
Auchalick
Loch Melldalloch
Erines
Beinn Bhreac
1662
Inverchaolain Glen
Iverchaolain
Loch Eck
A85
A816
B844
B8003
B8002
B840
A819
A83
A815
B8025
B841
B8000
A886
B836
B8024
B845
B8077
140
141
125
126
134
206

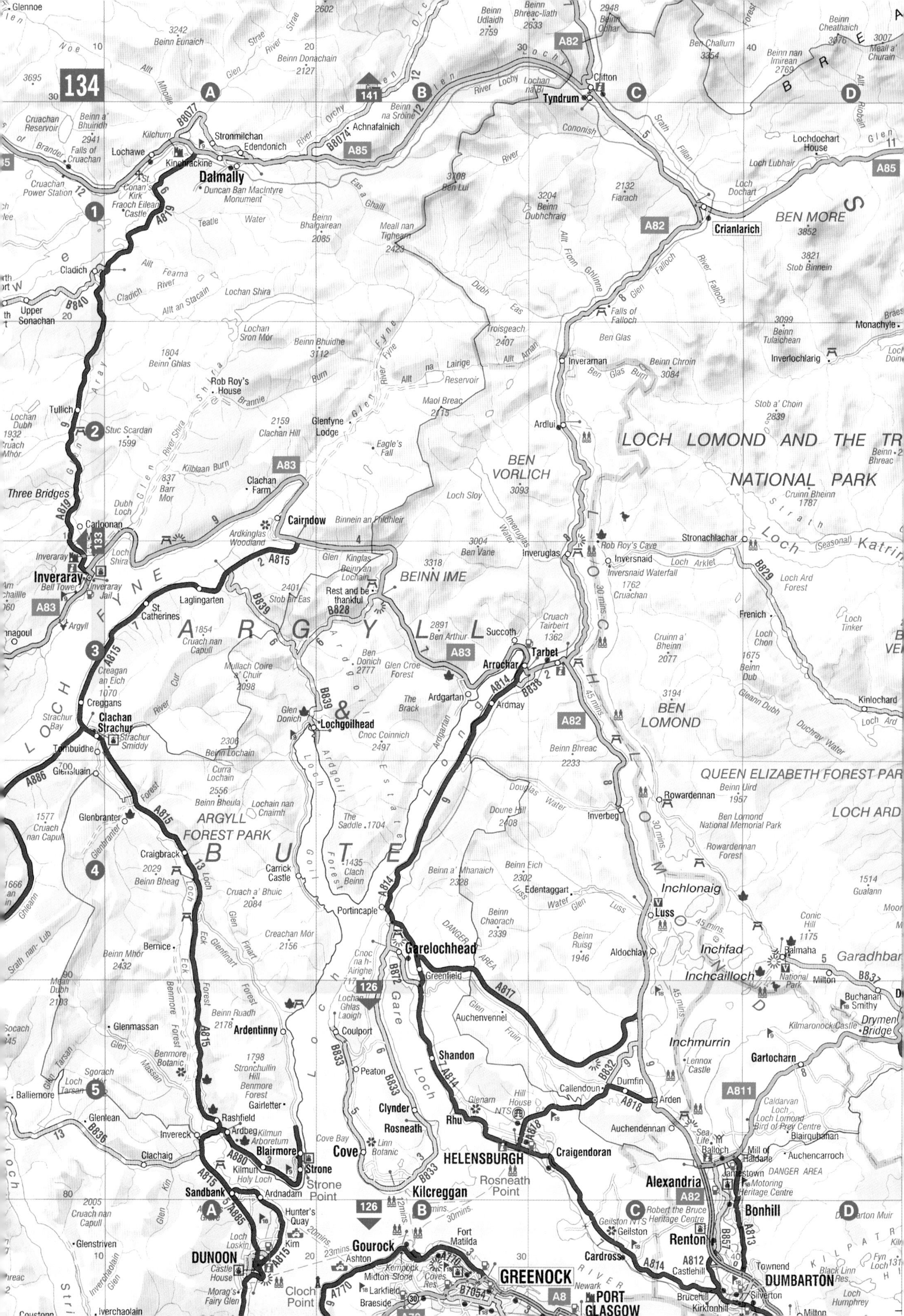

134
141
133
126
A
B
C
D
1
2
3
4
5
Glennoe
Beinn Eunaich
3242
Beinn Donachain
2127
Beinn Udlaidh
2759
Beinn Bhreac-liath
2633
Beinn Odhar
2948
Beinn Challum
3354
Beinn Cheathaich
Beinn nan Imirean
2769
Meall a' Churain
3007
BREADALBANE
Cruachan Reservoir
Beinn a' Bhuiridh
2941
Falls of Cruachan
Cruachan Power Station
Kilchurn
Lochawe
Stronmilchan
Edendonich
Kinchrackine
Dalmally
Duncan Ban MacIntyre Monument
St. Conan's Kirk
Fraoch Eilean Castle
Achnafalnich
Beinn na Sròine
River Orchy
River Lochy
Lochan na Bi
Clifton
Tyndrum
Cononish
Strath Fillan
Lochdochart House
Loch Lubhair
Loch Dochart
Crianlarich
BEN MORE
3852
3821
Stob Binnein
3708
Ben Lui
3204
Beinn Dubhchraig
2132
Fiarach
Beinn Bhalgairean
2085
Meall nan Tighearn
2423
Teatle Water
Cladich
Upper Sonachan
Lochan Shira
Allt an Stacain
Lochan Sròn Mòr
Beinn Bhuidhe
3112
1804
Beinn Ghlas
Rob Roy's House
Glen Shira
Tullich
Stuc Scardan
1599
2159
Clachan Hill
Glenfyne Lodge
Eagle's Fall
Maol Breac
2115
Lairige Reservoir
Troisgeach
2407
Falls of Falloch
Ben Glas
Inverarnan
Beinn Chroin
3084
3099
Beinn Tulaichean
Monachyle
Inverlochlarig
Stob a' Choin
2839
Ardlui
LOCH LOMOND AND THE TROSSACHS NATIONAL PARK
BEN VORLICH
3093
Loch Sloy
Cruinn Bheinn
1787
Three Bridges
837
Barr Mor
Kilblaan Burn
Clachan Farm
Dubh Loch
Carloonan
Cairndow
Binnein an Fhidhleir
Ardkinglas Woodland
3004
Ben Vane
Inveruglas
Rob Roy's Cave
Inversnaid
Inversnaid Waterfall
Stronachlachar
Loch Arklet
Loch Katrine
1762
Cruachan
Loch Ard Forest
Inveraray
Bell Tower
Inveraray Jail
Loch Shira
Glen Kinglas
Beinn an Lochain
3318
BEINN IME
Rest and be thankful
2401
Stob an Eas
Laglingarten
St. Catherines
ARGYLL
1854
Cruach nan Capull
2891
Ben Arthur
Succoth
Cruach Tairbeirt
1362
Frenich
Loch Chon
Loch Tinker
Cruinn a' Bheinn
2077
1675
Beinn Dub
Tarbet
Arrochar
Ben Donich
2777
Glen Croe Forest
Mullach Coire a' Chuir
2098
Creagan an Eich
1070
Creggans
Strachur Bay
Clachan Strachur
Strachur Smiddy
Tornbuidhe
Glensluain
LOCH FYNE
Glen Donich
Lochgoilhead
The Brack
Ardgartan
Ardmay
3194
BEN LOMOND
Kinlochard
Loch Ard
Cnoc Coinnich
2497
2306
Beinn Lochain
Curra Lochain
2556
Beinn Bheula
Lochain nan Cnaimh
Beinn Bhreac
2233
QUEEN ELIZABETH FOREST PARK
Beinn Uird
1957
LOCH ARD
Rowardennan
Glenbranter
1577
Cruach nan Capull
ARGYLL FOREST PARK
The Saddle 1704
Doune Hill
2408
Douglas Water
Inverbeg
Ben Lomond National Memorial Park
Rowardennan Forest
BUTE
Craigbrack
2029
Beinn Bheag
Carrick Castle
1435
Clach Beinn
Beinn a' Mhanaich
2328
Beinn Eich
2302
Edentaggart
Inchlonaig
1514
Gualann
Cruach a' Bhuic
2084
Portincaple
Beinn Chaorach
2339
Luss
Conic Hill
1175
Creachan Mòr
2156
Beinn Ruisg
1946
Aldochlay
Inchfad
Balmaha
Garadhban
Bernice
Beinn Mhòr
2432
Garelochhead
Greenfield
Inchcailloch
National Park
Milton
Cnoc na h-Airighe
717
Meall Dubh
2103
Lochan Ghlas Laoigh
DANGER AREA
Buchanan Smithy
Drymen Bridge
Kilmaronock Castle
Beinn Ruadh
2178
Ardentinny
Coulport
Auchenvennel
Glenmassan
Benmore Botanic
Shandon
Inchmurrin
1798
Stronchullin Hill
Benmore Forest
Peaton
Lennox Castle
Gartocharn
Sgorach
Loch Tarsan
Balliemore
Gairletter
Clynder
Hill House NTS
Glenarn
Callendoun
Dumfin
Arden
Caldarvan Loch
Loch Lomond Bird of Prey Centre
Glenlean
Rashfield
Rosneath
Rhu
Auchendennan
Sea Life
Balloch
Mill of Haldane
Blairquhanan
Invereck
Ardbeg
Kilmun Arboretum
Blairmore
Cove Bay
Cove
Linn Botanic
HELENSBURGH
Craigendoran
Auchencarroch
Clachaig
Kilmun
Holy Loch
Strone
Strone Point
Jamestown
Motoring Heritage Centre
DANGER AREA
Alexandria
Sandbank
Ardnadam
Kilcreggan
Rosneath Point
2005
Cruach nan Capull
Hunter's Quay
Robert the Bruce Heritage Centre
Geilston NTS
Geilston
Bonhill
Dalnottar Muir
Glenstriven
Loch Loskin
Kim
Fort Matilda
Renton
Gourock
Ashton
Cardross
Castlehill
Townend
DUMBARTON
Black Linn Res.
Fyn Loch
DUNOON
Castle House
Kempock
Midton
Larkfield
Braeside
Cloch Point
GREENOCK
Newark
RIVER CLYDE
PORT GLASGOW
Brucehill
Kirktonhill
Silverton
Milton
Loch Humphrey
Morag's Fairy Glen
Coustonn
Iverchaolain
A82
A85
A819
B8077
B8074
B840
A83
A815
B839
B828
A814
B838
A886
B836
A880
A885
B833
B872
A817
B832
A818
A811
B837
B829
A812
A813
B857
A8
A770
B7054
30 mins
45 mins
20 mins
23 mins
12 mins

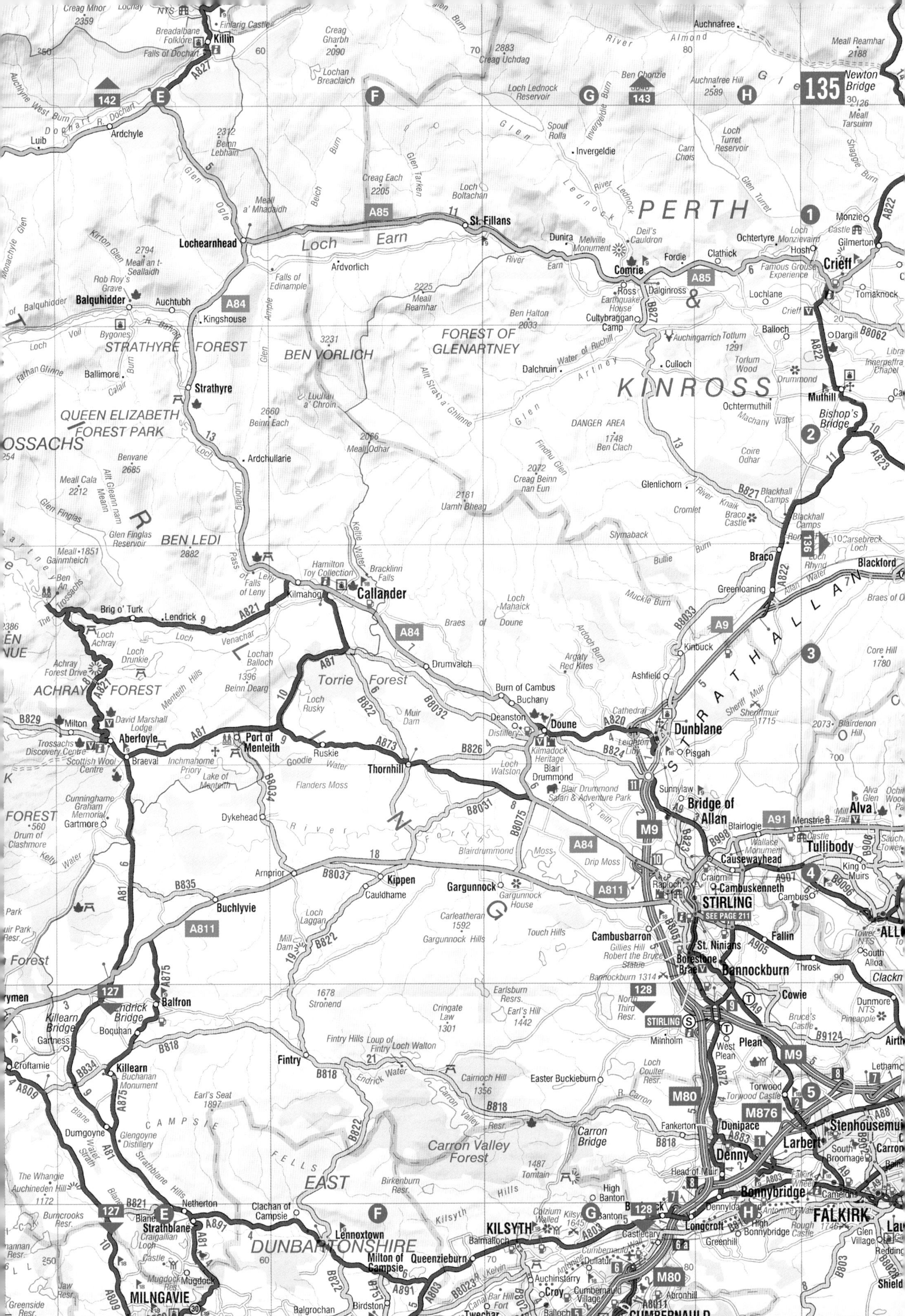

Creag Mhor
2359
Killin
Finlarig Castle
Breadalbane Folklore
Falls of Dochart
A827
60
142
E
Auchlyne West Burn
Dochart
R. Dochart
Luib
Ardchyle
2312
Beinn Lebhain
Glen Ogle
Creag Gharbh
2090
Lochan Breaclaich
F
Beich Burn
Glen Tarken
Creag Each
2205
70
2883
Creag Uchdag
Loch Lednock Reservoir
G
Ben Chonzie
3048
143
Spout Rolla
Invergeldie Burn
Invergeldie
Auchnafree
River Almond
80
Auchnafree Hill
2589
H
Glen Almond
135
Newton Bridge
Meall Reamhar
2188
2126
Meall Tarsuinn
Loch Turret Reservoir
Carn Chois
Glen Turret
Shaggie Burn
Monachyle Glen
Kirkton Glen
2794
Meall an t-Seallaidh
Meall a' Mhadaidh
Lochearnhead
Loch Boltachan
A85
11
St. Fillans
Loch Earn
Ardvorlich
River Lednock
PERTH
Dunira
Melville Monument
Deil's Cauldron
Fordle
Clathick
Loch Monzievaird
Ochtertyre
Hosh
Monzie
Castle
Gilmerton
Crieff
1
River Earn
Comrie
Ross
Earthquake House
Dalginross
A85
&
Famous Grouse Experience
Lochlane
Tomaknock
Cultybraggan Camp
B827
Crieff
Balloch
Dargill
B8062
Rob Roy's Grave
Balquhidder
Auchtubh
A84
Kingshouse
Falls of Edinample
2225
Meall Reamhar
Ben Halton
2033
FOREST OF GLENARTNEY
Auchingarrich
Totlum
1291
Torlum Wood
Drummond
A822
Innerpeffray Chapel
Bygones
Loch Voil
STRATHYRE FOREST
3231
BEN VORLICH
Glen Ample
Dalchruin
Water of Ruchill
Glen Artney
Culloch
KINROSS
Muthill
Fathan Glinne
Ballimore
Calair Burn
Strathyre
Lochan a' Chroin
Allt Srath a' Ghlinne
Ochtermuthill
Machany Water
Bishop's Bridge
QUEEN ELIZABETH FOREST PARK
2660
Beinn Each
DANGER AREA
1748
Ben Clach
2
TROSSACHS
13
Loch Lubnaig
Ardchullarie
2066
Meall Odhar
Findhu Glen
Coire Odhar
10
A823
Benvane
2685
Meall Cala
2212
Allt Gleann nam Meann
2072
Creag Beinn nan Eun
Glenlichorn
River Knaik
B827
Blackhall Camps
11
Glen Finglas
2181
Uamh Bheag
Cromlet
Braco Castle
Glen Finglas Reservoir
R
BEN LEDI
2882
Slymaback
Blackhall Camps
136
Carsebreck Loch
Meall Gainmheich
1851
Ben An
Pass of Leny
Falls of Leny
Hamilton Toy Collection
Keltie Water
Bracklinn Falls
Bullie Burn
Braco
Loch Rhynd
Blackford
The Trossachs
Kilmahog
Callander
Loch Mahaick
Muckle Burn
Greenloaning
Allan Water
A822
Braes of Ogilvie
Brig o' Turk
Lendrick
A821
Braes of Doune
B8033
A9
STRATHALLAN
Loch Achray
Loch Venachar
A84
Lochan Balloch
Ardoch Burn
Kinbuck
3
Core Hill
1780
Achray Forest Drive
Loch Drunkie
1396
Beinn Dearg
A81
Torrie Forest
Drumvaich
Argaty Red Kites
Ashfield
ACHRAY FOREST
Menteith Hills
10
Loch Rusky
B822
B8032
Burn of Cambus
Buchany
Cathedral
Sheriff Muir
Sheriffmuir
1715
B829
Milton
David Marshall Lodge
Aberfoyle
Muir Dam
Deanston Distillery
Doune
A820
Dunblane
2073
Blairdenon Hill
Trossachs Discovery Centre
Scottish Wool Centre
Braeval
Port of Menteith
Inchmahome Priory
Lake of Menteith
Ruskie
Goodie Water
A873
Thornhill
B826
Kilmadock Heritage
Loch Watson
Blair Drummond
Leighton Liby
B824
Pisgah
700
Flanders Moss
B8034
Blair Drummond Safari & Adventure Park
Sunnylaw
Bridge of Allan
Alva Glen
Alva
Mill Trail
Cunninghame Graham Memorial
Gartmore
FOREST
560
Drum of Clashmore
Dykehead
River Forth
B8031
8
B8075
R. Teith
M9
Blairlogie
A91
Menstrie
Wallace Monument
Tullibody
Kelty Water
A81
18
Blairdrummond Moss
A84
Drip Moss
10
Causewayhead
B998
B823
Arnprior
B8037
Kippen
Gargunnock
Gargunnock House
A811
Raploch
Craigmill
Cambuskenneth
A907
4
King o' Muirs
B9096
Cambus
B835
Buchlyvie
Cauldhame
Loch Laggan
Carleatheran
1592
Gargunnock Hills
STIRLING
SEE PAGE 211
A811
Mill Dam
B822
Touch Hills
Cambusbarron
Gillies Hill
Robert the Bruce Statue
B8051
St. Ninians
A905
Fallin
Tower NTS
South Alloa
ALLOA
Forest
A875
1678
Stronend
Earlsburn Resrs.
Bannockburn 1314
Borestone Brae
Bannockburn
Throsk
90
Clackmannan
127
Drymen
Killearn Bridge
Endrick Bridge
Balfron
Boquhan
Cringate Law
1301
Earl's Hill
1442
North Third Resr.
128
STIRLING
Cowie
Dunmore
NTS Pineapple
Bruce's Castle
B9124
Gartness
B818
Fintry Hills
Loup of Fintry
Loch Walton
Milnholm
West Plean
Plean
M9
Airth
Croftamie
B834
Killearn
Buchanan Monument
Fintry
21
B818
Endrick Water
Cairnoch Hill
1356
Easter Buckieburn
Loch Coulter Resr.
A872
Letham
A809
A875
Earl's Seat
1897
R. Carron
Carron Valley
B818
M80
Torwood
Torwood Castle
5
M876
Dumgoyne
Blane Water
CAMPSIE
Glengoyne Distillery
Carron Valley Resr.
Carron Bridge
Fankerton
Dunipace
A883
Stenhousemuir
Larbert
South Broomage
Carron
B822
Strathblane Hills
Carron Valley Forest
B818
Denny
The Whangie
Auchineden Hill
1172
FELLS
EAST
1487
Tomtain
Head of Muir
Bonnybridge
Falkirk Wheel
Camelon
Birkenburn Resr.
High Banton
Burncrooks Resr.
127
B821
E
Netherton
Clachan of Campsie
F
Kilsyth Hills
Colzium Walled
Kilsyth
1645
G
Banton
Banknock
128
Longcroft
Dennyloanhead
H
High Bonnybridge
Antonine Wall
Rough Castle
1746
FALKIRK
Blanefield
Strathblane
Craigallian Loch
A891
4
Lennoxtown
DUNBARTONSHIRE
KILSYTH
Balmalloch
A803
Castlecary
Greenhill
Glen Village
Redding
Castle
Mugdock Res.
Mugdock
250
Milton of Campsie
Queenzieburn
70
60
Kelvin
Dullatur
Cumbernauld
M80
80
B803
Shieldhill
Jaw Resr.
Greenside Resr.
A809
MILNGAVIE
30
Balgrochan
B822
B757
A891
Birdston
A803
B8023
Bar Hill Fort
Croy
Auchinstarry
Cumbernauld Village
Abronhill
A8011
Twechar
Balloch
CUMBERNAULD

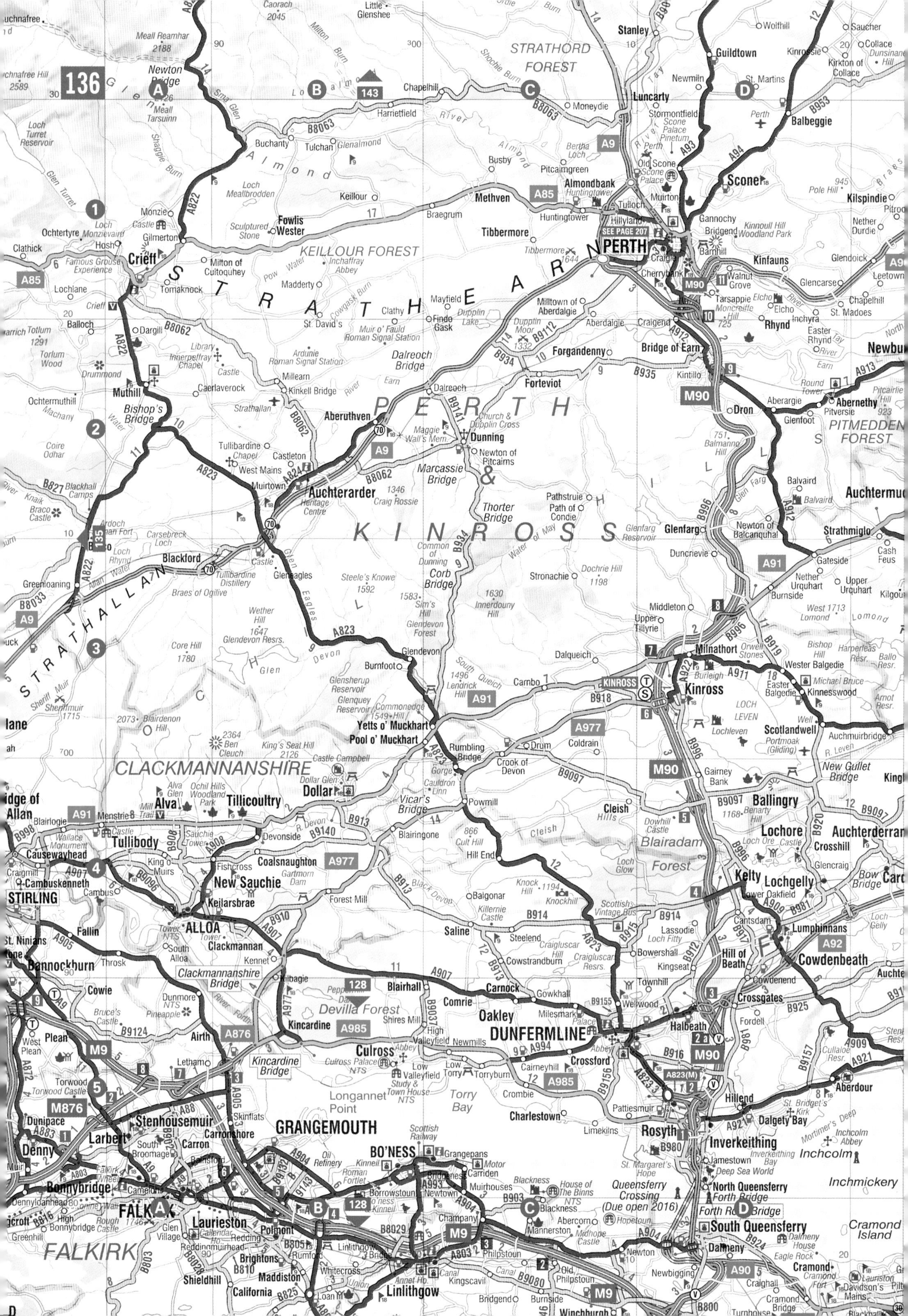

136
Meall Reamhar 2188
Newton Bridge
Glen Almond
Caorach 2045
Little Glenshee
143
Chapelhill
Harrietfield
STRATHORD FOREST
Stanley
Guildtown
Wolfhill
Saucher
Collace
Kinrossie
Kirkton of Collace
Loch Turret Reservoir
Buchanty
Tulchan
Glenalmond
B8063
Moneydie
Luncarty
Stormontfield
Scone Palace Pinetum
Newmiln
St. Martins
Balbeggie
Busby
Bertha Loch
Pitcairngreen
Almondbank
Huntingtower
A9
A85
A93
A94
Scone
Old Scone
Loch Mealbrodden
Keillour
Methven
Braegrum
Tullochy
Muirton
Gannochy
Bridgend
Kinnoull Hill Woodland Park
Kilspindie
Pole Hill 945
Monzie
Monzie Castle
Ochtertyre
Fowlis Wester
Sculptured Stone
Tibbermore
Hillyland
SEE PAGE 207
PERTH
Craigie
Barnhill
Kinfauns
Glendoick
Nether Durdie
Clathick
Gilmerton
Hosh
KEILLOUR FOREST
Inchaffray Abbey
Tibbermore 1644
Cherrybank
Walnut Grove
Glencarse
Leetown
Crieff
Famous Grouse Experience
Milton of Cultoquhey
Madderty
A85
Lochlane
Tomaknock
STRATHEARN
Mayfield
Findo Gask
Dupplin Lake
Milltown of Aberdalgie
M90
Tarsappie
Moncreiffe Hill
Elcho
Rhynd
Chapelhill
St. Madoes
Balloch
Dargill
B8062
St. David's
Clathy
Muir o' Fauld Roman Signal Station
Dupplin Moor 1332
B9112
Aberdalgie
Craigend
A912
Inchyra
Easter Rhynd
Totlum 1291
Torlum Wood
Drummond
Library
Innerpeffray Chapel
Castle
Ardunie Roman Signal Station
Dalreoch Bridge
B934
Forgandenny
Bridge of Earn
Newburgh
Muthill
Millearn
Kinkell Bridge
Forteviot
B935
Kintillo
M90
A913
Ochtermuthill
Machany
Bishop's Bridge
Caerlaverock
Strathallan
Aberuthven
Dalreoch
B9141
PERTH
Dron
Aberargie
Abernethy
Pitversie
Glenfoot
Pitcairlie Hill 923
PITMEDDEN FOREST
Coire Odhar
Tullibardine
Tullibardine Chapel
West Mains
Castleton
A823
B8062
Maggie Wall's Mem.
Church & Dupplin Cross
Dunning
Newton of Pitcairns
751 Balmanno Hill
Muirtown
A824
Auchterarder
Heritage Centre
Marcassie Bridge
1346 Craig Rossie
B827
Blackhall Camps
Knaik
Braco Castle
Pathstruie
Path of Condie
Thorter Bridge
Balvaird
Auchtermuchty
Ardoch Roman Fort
Carsebreck Loch
Braco
135
KINROSS
Glenfarg Reservoir
Glenfarg
B996
Newton of Balcanquhal
Strathmiglo
Loch Rhynd
A822
Blackford
Tullibardine Distillery
Castle
Gleneagles
Glen Eagles
Common of Dunning
Water of May
Duncrievie
Gateside
Cash Feus
Greenloaning
Allan Water
Braes of Ogilvie
Steele's Knowe 1592
Corb Bridge
Stronachie
Dochrie Hill 1198
A91
Nether Urquhart
Upper Urquhart
Burnside
Kilgour
B8033
A9
STRATHALLAN
Wether Hill 1647
1583 Sim's Hill
Glendevon Forest
1630 Innerdouny Hill
Middleton
Upper Tillyrie
West Lomond 1713
Lomond
Core Hill 1780
Glendevon Resrs.
A823
Glendevon
Dalqueich
Milnathort
Orwell Stones
Bishop Hill
B919
Harperleas Resr.
Ballo Resr.
Glen Devon
Burnfoot
South Queich
1496 Lendrick Hill
Carnbo
KINROSS
B918
A922
Burleigh
A911
Wester Balgedie
Easter Balgedie
Michael Bruce
Kinnesswood
Sheriff Muir
Sheriffmuir 1715
Glensherup Reservoir
Glenquey Reservoir
Commonedge 1549 Hill
A91
Kinross
LOCH LEVEN
Arnot Resr.
2073 Blairdenon Hill
2364 Ben Cleuch
King's Seat Hill 2126
Yetts o' Muckhart
Pool o' Muckhart
Castle Campbell
Rumbling Bridge
Drum
Coldrain
A977
Lochleven
Scotlandwell
Portmoak (Gliding)
Auchmuirbridge
R. Leven
CLACKMANNANSHIRE
Gorge
Crook of Devon
B9097
M90
Gairney Bank
New Gullet Bridge
Kinglassie
Alva
Alva Glen
Ochil Hills Woodland Park
Mill Trail
Tillicoultry
Dollar Glen
Dollar
Cauldron Linn
Vicar's Bridge
Powmill
Cleish
Cleish Hills
B9097
Ballingry
1168 Benarty Hill
B9097
Bridge of Allan
Blairlogie
A91
Menstrie
Castle
Wallace Monument
B998
Tullibody
Sauchie Tower
B908
A908
Devonside
B9140
R. Devon
B913
Blairingone
866 Cult Hill
Dowhill Castle
Blairadam Forest
Lochore
Loch Ore Castle
B920
Auchterderran
Crosshill
Causewayhead
Craigmill
A907
Cambuskenneth
STIRLING
King o' Muirs
B9096
Cambus
Fishcross
New Sauchie
Coalsnaughton
Gartmorn Dam
A977
Hill End
Loch Glow
Kelty
Lochgelly
Lower Oakfield
B981
B909
Glencraig
Bow Bridge
Cardenden
Keilarsbrae
Forest Mill
Black Devon
B913
Balgonar
Knock Hill 1194
Knockhill
Scottish Vintage Bus
Killernie Castle
B914
B914
Lassodie
Loch Fitty
Cantsdam
Lumphinnans
Loch Gelly
St. Ninians
Fallin
A905
ALLOA
Tower NTS
Clackmannan Tower
Clackmannan
South Alloa
Kennet
B910
A907
Saline
Steelend
Craigluscar Hill
Craigluscar Resrs.
A823
B915
Bowershall
Kingseat
B912
B917
Hill of Beath
Cowdenbeath
A92
Bannockburn
Throsk
Clackmannanshire Bridge
River Forth
Kilbagie
A977
128
11
A907
Cowstrandburn
B913
Townhill
Cowdenend
Auchtertool
Cowie
Dunmore NTS
Pineapple
Peppermill Dam
Devilla Forest
Blairhall
B9037
Comrie
Carnock
Gowkhall
Wellwood
B9155
Crossgates
B925
Bruce's Castle
B9124
Airth
A876
Kincardine
A985
Shires Mill
High Valleyfield
Newmills
Oakley
Milesmark
DUNFERMLINE
Abbey
Palace
Halbeath
Fordell
Plean
West Plean
M9
A872
Letham
Kincardine Bridge
Culross
Culross Palace NTS
Abbey
A994
Crossford
B916
M90
Cullaloe Resr.
B9157
B981
Torwood
Torwood Castle
M876
A88
A905
Low Valleyfield
Low Torry
Torryburn
Cairneyhill
A985
B9156
A823(M)
A921
A909
Aberdour
Dunipace
A883
Stenhousemuir
Carronshore
Carron
Skinflats
GRANGEMOUTH
Longannet Point
Torry Bay
Study & Town House NTS
Crombie
Charlestown
Patiesmuir
Rosyth
Hillend
St. Bridget's Kirk
Dalgety Bay
Denny
Larbert
South Broomage
B902
Bainsford
Scottish Railway
Oil Refinery
BO'NESS
Grangepans
Limekilns
B980
Inverkeithing
Mortimer's Deep
Inchcolm Abbey
Inchcolm
Falkirk Wheel
Camelon
A803
Bonnybridge
Kinneil
Roman Fortlet
Carriden
Motor
Bridgeness
A993
Borrowstoun
Newtown
A904
Muirhouses
Blackness
House of The Binns NTS
Queensferry Crossing (Due open 2016)
St. Margaret's Hope
Jamestown
Inverkeithing Bay
Deep Sea World
North Queensferry
Forth Rd Bridge
Forth Bridge
Inchmickery
Dennyloanhead
FALKIRK
High Bonnybridge
Rough Castle
Laurieston
Callendar
Polmont
B9132
128
Champany
Blackness Castle
Abercorn
Hopetoun
Mannerston
Midhope Castle
South Queensferry
Dalmeny House
Cramond Island
Greenhill
FALKIRK
Glen Village
Redding
Reddingmuirhead
B8028
B803
Brightons
Rumford
B805
B810
Linlithgow
Philpstoun
A803
A904
Newton
Dalmeny
B924
Eagle Rock
Cramond
Shieldhill
Maddiston
Whitecross
Union Canal
Annet Ho.
Kingscavil
B9080
Old Philpstoun
Newbigging
A90
Craighall
Cramond Fort
Lauriston
Davidson's Mains
California
B825
Loan
Linlithgow
Bridgend
Burnside
M9
Winchburgh
B800
Turnhouse
Cramond Bridge

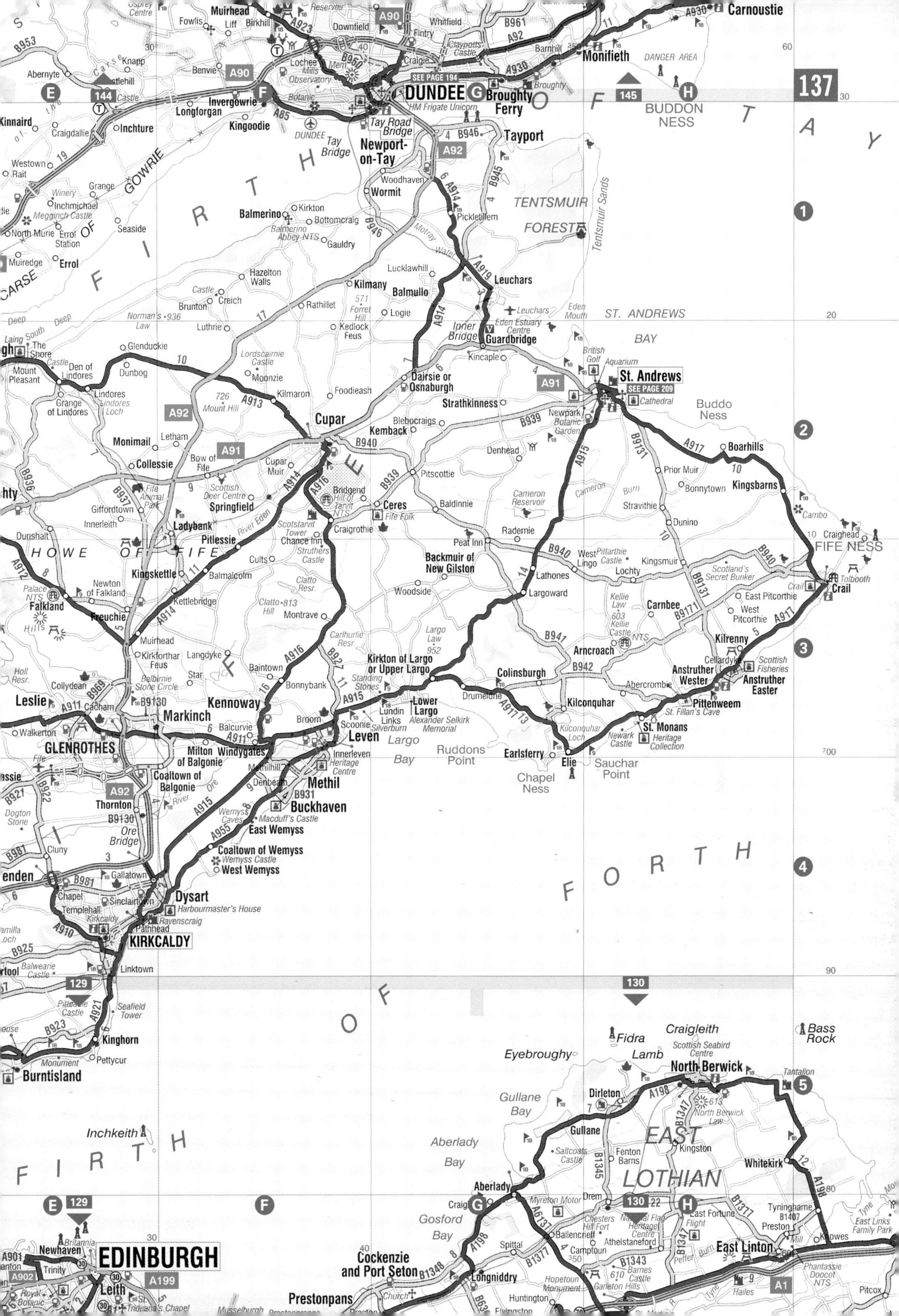
137
DUNDEE
Broughty Ferry
Monifieth
Carnoustie
BUDDON NESS
Tayport
Newport-on-Tay
Wormit
FIRTH OF TAY
TENTSMUIR FOREST
Leuchars
Guardbridge
St. Andrews
ST. ANDREWS BAY
Cupar
Dairsie or Osnaburgh
Strathkinness
Ceres
Ladybank
Springfield
HOWE OF FIFE
Falkland
Freuchie
Kingskettle
Boarhills
Kingsbarns
FIFE NESS
Crail
Anstruther Wester
Anstruther Easter
Pittenweem
St. Monans
Elie
Earlsferry
Kilconquhar
Colinsburgh
Largoward
Kirkton of Largo or Upper Largo
Lower Largo
Leven
Largo Bay
Methil
Buckhaven
Kennoway
Markinch
GLENROTHES
Leslie
Thornton
East Wemyss
Coaltown of Wemyss
West Wemyss
Dysart
KIRKCALDY
Kinghorn
Burntisland
FIRTH OF FORTH
North Berwick
Dirleton
Gullane
Aberlady
EAST LOTHIAN
East Linton
Longniddry
Cockenzie and Port Seton
Prestonpans
EDINBURGH
Leith
Newhaven
Bass Rock
Fidra
Inchkeith
SEE PAGE 194
SEE PAGE 209
129
130
144
145

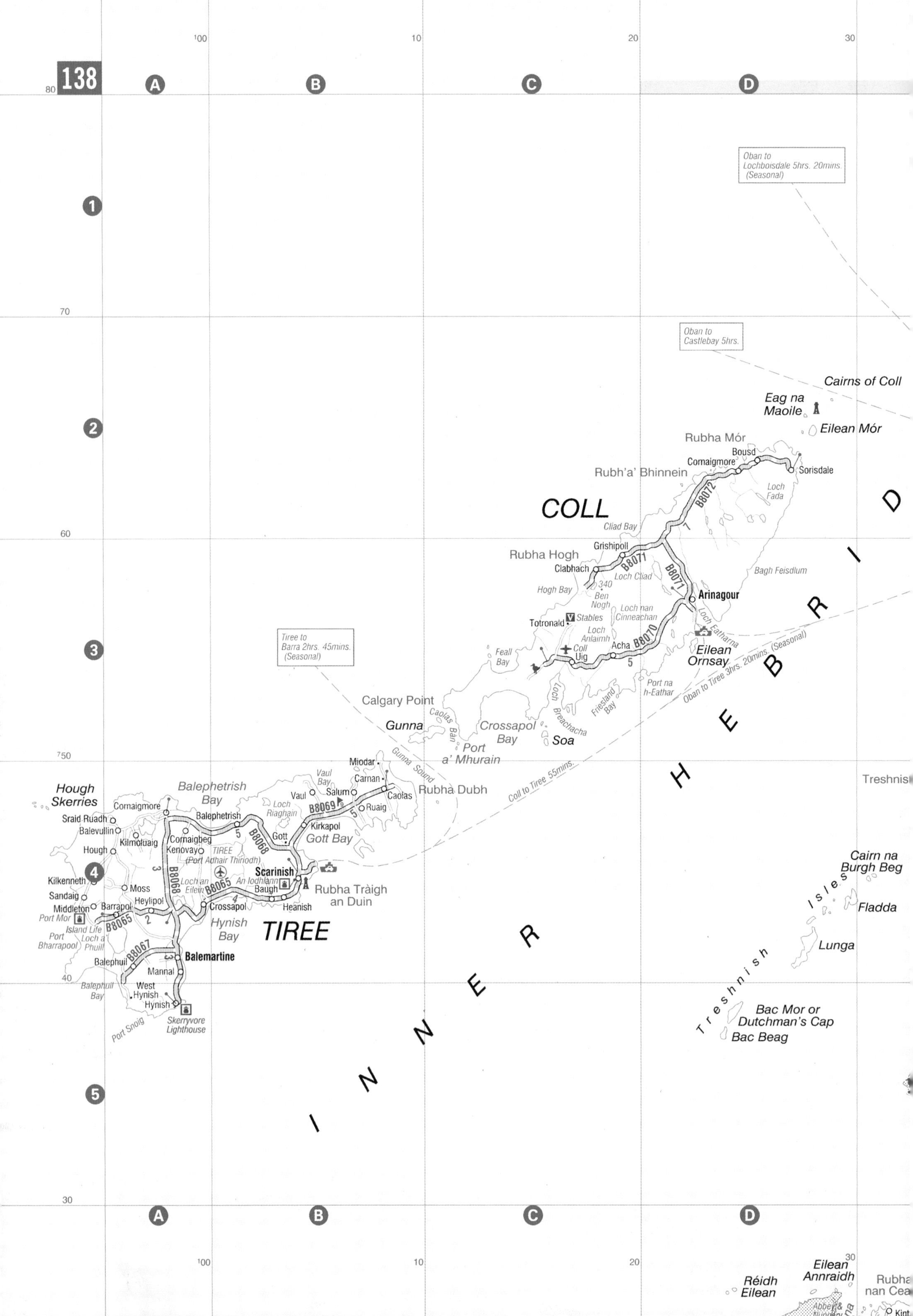

80

100   10   20   30

A   **B**   **C**   **D**

70

*Oban to
Lochboisdale 5hrs. 20mins.
(Seasonal)*

1

*Oban to
Castlebay 5hrs.*

60

Cairns of Coll

2

*Eag na
Maoile*

Eilean Mór

Rubha Mór

Bousd

Rubh'a' Bhinnein   Cornaigmore   Sorisdale

B8072

*Loch
Fada*

COLL

Cliad Bay

Grishipoll

Rubha Hogh   Clabhach   B8071   *Bagh Feisdlum*

Loch Cliad

Hogh Bay   340
Ben
Nogh   B8071

*Loch nan
Cinneachan*   Arinagour

Totronald   **V** Stables

*Loch
Anlaimh*   B8070

Feall
Bay   Coll   Acha   *Loch Eatharna*

Uig   5   *Eilean
Ornsay*

*Port na
h-Eathar*

*Tiree to
Barra 2hrs. 45mins.
(Seasonal)*

Oban to Tiree 3hrs. 20mins. (Seasonal)

3

*Loch
Breachacha*

*Friesland
Bay*

Calgary Point

Gunna   *Caolas Ban*   *Crossapol
Bay*   *Soa*

Coll to Tiree 55mins.

Treshnis

Port
a' Mhurain

Gunna Sound

Miodar

Vaul
Bay   Carnan

70 50   *Hough
Skerries*   Balephetrish
Bay   Vaul   Salum   Caolas   *Rubha Dubh*   *Cairn na
Burgh Beg*

Cornaigmore   B8069   Ruaig

Sraid Ruadh   Balephetrish   Kirkapol

Balevullin   Cornaigbeg   5   Gott   *Gott Bay*   *Fladda*

Kilmoluaig   Kenovay   B8068   *TIREE
(Port Adhair Thiriodh)*   Kirkapol

Hough   3   An Iodhlann   *Treshnish   Isles*

4   B8065   **Scarinish**   *Lunga*

Kilkenneth   Moss   Baugh

Sandaig   Heylipol   Crossapol   Heanish   Rubha Tràigh
an Duin

Port Mor   Middleton   Barrapol

Island Life   B8065   2   *Hynish
Bay*   **TIREE**

*Port
Bharrapool*   *Loch a'
Phuill*

B8067   *Bac Mor or
Dutchman's Cap*

Balephuil   3   *Bac Beag*

40   Mannal

*Balephuil
Bay*   West
Hynish   **Balemartine**

Hynish

Port Snoig   *Skerryvore
Lighthouse*

5

30

A   **B**   **C**   **D**

100   10   20   30

*Eilean
Annraidh*

*Réidh
Eilean*   *Rubha
nan Cea*

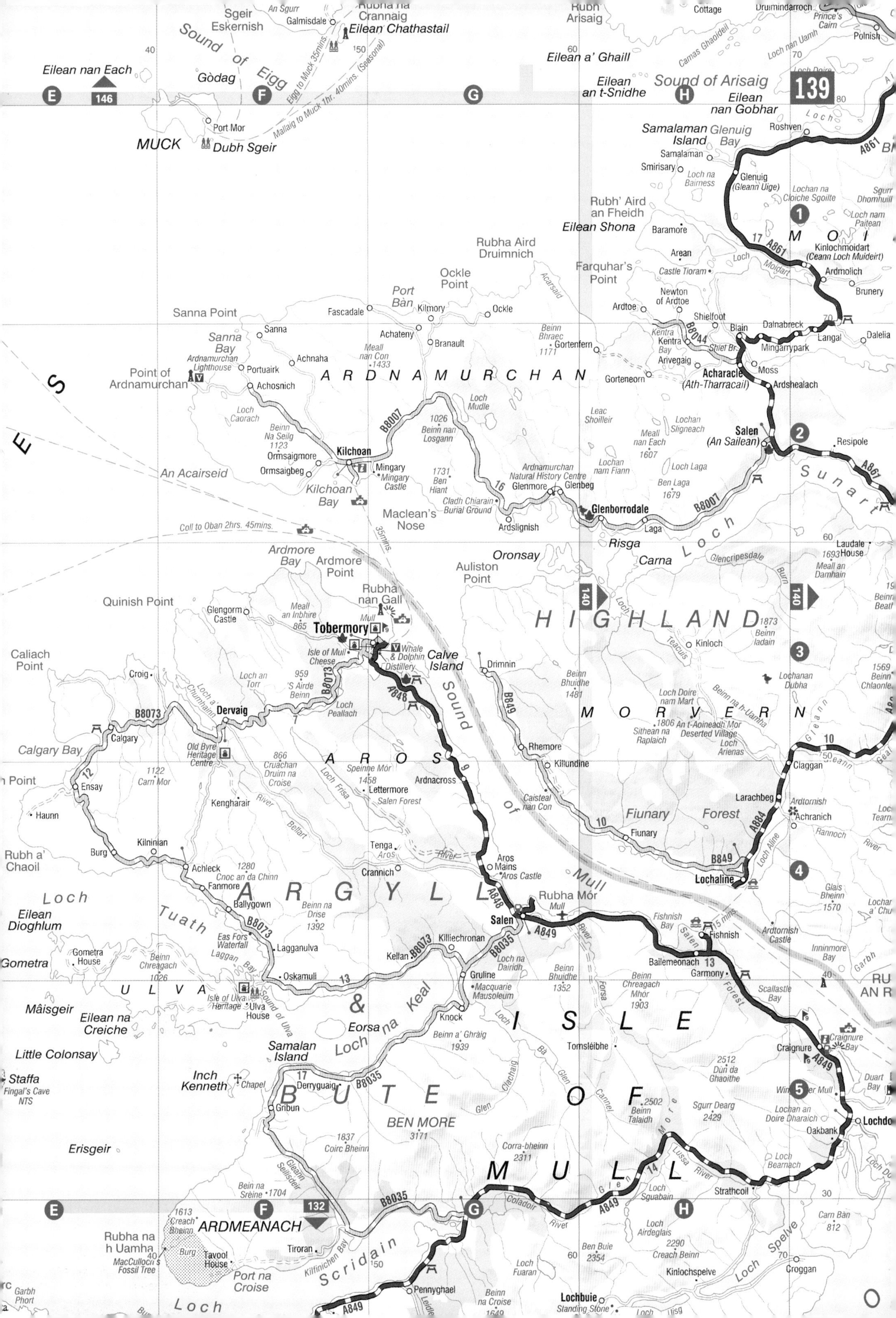

Sgeir Eskernish
An Sgurr
Galmisdale
Rubha na Crannaig
Eilean Chathastail
Sound of Eigg
Gòdag
Eilean nan Each
40
146
E
F
G
H
150
Eigg to Muck 35mins.
Mallaig to Muck 1hr. 40mins. (Seasonal)
Rubh Arisaig
60
Eilean a' Ghaill
Camas Ghaoideil
Eilean an t-Snidhe
Sound of Arisaig
Cottage
Druimindarroch
Prince's Cairn
Polnish
Loch nan Uamh
70
139
80
Eilean nan Gobhar
Loch
Port Mor
MUCK
Dubh Sgeir
Samalaman Island
Glenuig Bay
Roshven
A861
Samalaman
Smirisary
Loch na Bairness
Glenuig (Gleann Uige)
Lochan na Cloiche Sgoilte
Sgurr Dhomhuill
Loch nam Paitean
Rubh' Aird an Fheidh
Eilean Shona
Baramore
1
MOI
17
A861
Kinlochmoidart (Ceann Loch Muideirt)
Rubha Aird Druimnich
Arean
Loch Moidart
Castle Tioram
Farquhar's Point
Ardmolich
Brunery
Ockle Point
Acarsaid
Newton of Ardtoe
Ardtoe
Port Bàn
Kilmory
Ockle
Fascadale
Shielfoot
Blain
Dalnabreck
Sanna Point
Sanna
Sanna Bay
Achateny
Beinn Bhraec 1171
Gortenfern
Kentra Bay
Kentra
B8044
Shiel Br.
Mingarrypark
Langal
Dalelia
Meall nan Con 1433
Branault
Ardnamurchan Lighthouse
Portuairk
Achnaha
Arivegaig
Point of Ardnamurchan
ARDNAMURCHAN
Gorteneorn
Acharacle (Ath-Tharracail)
Moss
Ardshealach
Achosnich
Loch Mudle
Leac Shoilleir
Lochan Sligneach
Loch Caorach
B8007
1026 Beinn nan Losgann
Meall nan Each 1607
Salen (An Sailean)
2
Resipole
Beinn Na Seilg 1123
Kilchoan
Ormsaigmore
Ormsaigbeg
Mingary
Mingary Castle
Lochan nam Fiann
Loch Laga
An Acairseid
1731 Ben Hiant
Ardnamurchan Natural History Centre
Glenmore
Glenbeg
Ben Laga 1679
A861
Sunart
Kilchoan Bay
16
Cladh Chiarain Burial Ground
Glenborrodale
B8007
Maclean's Nose
Ardslignish
Laga
Loch
Coll to Oban 2hrs. 45mins.
35mins.
Risga
60
Laudale House
1693
Meall an Damhain
Ardmore Bay
Ardmore Point
Oronsay
Carna
Glencripesdale
Burn
Auliston Point
Rubha nan Gall
Quinish Point
140
Loch
140
Glengorm Castle
Meall an Inbhire 865
Mull
Tobermory
HIGHLAND
1873 Beinn Iadain
Caliach Point
Isle of Mull Cheese
Whale & Dolphin Distillery
Calve Island
Kinloch
Teacuis
3
Loch an Torr
959 'S Airde Beinn
B8073
Drimnin
Croig
Loch a' Chumhainn
A848
Sound
Beinn Bhuidhe 1481
Loch Doire nam Mart
Lochanan Dubha
1569 Beinn Chlaonleud
Dervaig
Loch Peallach
7
B849
MORVERN
Beinn na h-Uamha
B8073
Calgary
1806 Sithean na Raplaich
An t-Aoineadh Mòr Deserted Village
Loch Arienas
Calgary Bay
Old Byre Heritage Centre
AROS
Rhemore
Killundine
10
Gleann
Claggan
12
866 Cruachan Druim na Croise
Speinne Mòr 1458
Loch Frisa
Lettermore
Salen Forest
9
Ardnacross
Point
1122 Carn Mòr
Ensay
Kengharair
River
Bellart
of
Caisteal nan Con
Larachbeg
Ardtornish
Achranich
Haunn
10
Fiunary
Fiunary Forest
A884
Rannoch
River
Kilninian
Tenga
Aros
River
Loch Aline
Rubh a' Chaoil
Burg
Aros Mains
Aros Castle
B849
Lochaline
4
Achleck
1280 Cnoc an da Chinn
Crannich
Glais Bheinn 1570
Loch Tuath
Fanmore
ARGYLL
A848
Mull
Rubha Mòr
Eilean Dioghlum
Ballygown
Beinn na Drise 1392
Salen
Mull
A849
Fishnish Bay
Fishnish
15 mins.
Ardtornish Castle
B8073
Eas Fors Waterfall
River
Salen
Gometra House
Lagganulva
Killiechronan
B8035
Kellan
B8073
Loch na Dairidh
Ballemeonach
13
Garmony
Inninmore Bay
Garbh
Gometra
Beinn Chreagach 1026
Laggan Bay
Oskamull
13
Gruline
Beinn Bhuidhe 1352
Forsa
Beinn Chreagach Mhor 1903
Scallastle Bay
Forest
40
RU
AN R
ULVA
Isle of Ulva Heritage
Ulva House
Sound of Ulva
Macquarie Mausoleum
Knock
&
Loch na Keal
Màisgeir
Eilean na Creiche
Eorsa
Beinn a' Ghràig 1939
Loch
ISLE
Craignure
Craignure Bay
A849
Little Colonsay
Samalan Island
Ba
Tomsléibhe
2512 Dùn da Ghaoithe
Staffa
Fingal's Cave NTS
Inch Kenneth
Chapel
17
Derryguaig
B8035
BUTE
Clachaig
Glen
Glen Cannel
OF
2502 Beinn Talaidh
Sgurr Dearg 2429
Duart Bay
5
Lochan an Doire Dharaich
Gribun
BEN MORE 3171
Glen More
Oakbank
Lochdon
Erisgeir
1837 Coirc Bheinn
Corra-bheinn 2311
Gleann Seilisdeir
MULL
14
Lussa River
Loch Bearnach
Loch Don
Bein na Srèine 1704
Glen
A849
Loch Sguabain
Strathcoil
30
132
B8035
1613 Creach Bheinn
ARDMEANACH
Coladoir River
Loch Airdeglais
Carn Ban 812
Rubha na h Uamha
40
Burg
Tavool House
MacCulloch's Fossil Tree
Tiroran
Kilfinichen Bay
Loch Scridain
150
Ben Buie 2354
2290 Creach Beinn
Loch Spelve
70
Croggan
Garbh Phort
Port na Croise
Loch Fuaran
Kinlochspelve
Loch
Pennyghael
Leidle
Beinn na Croise 1649
Lochbuie
Standing Stone
Uisg
A849
O

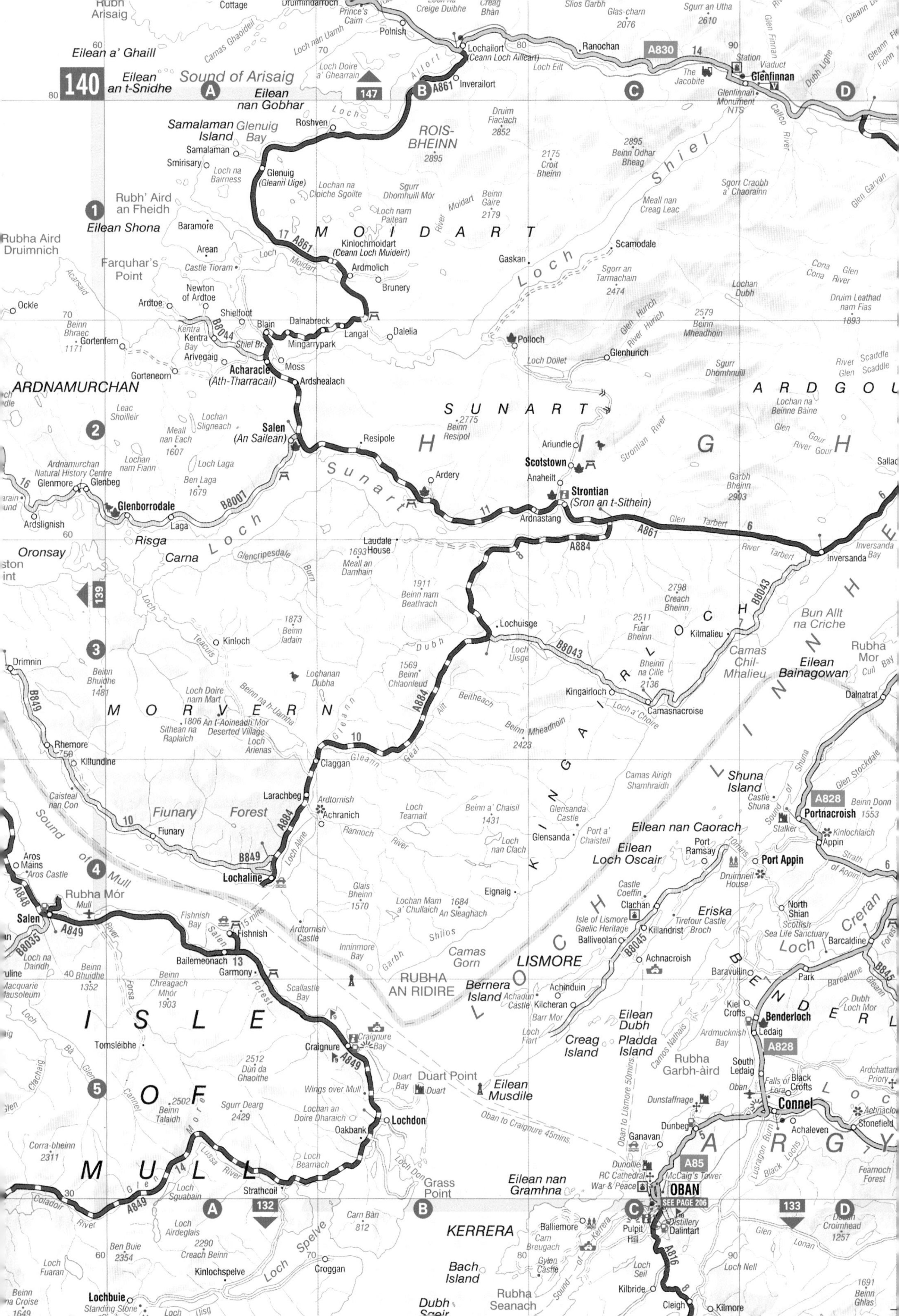

140
Rubh Arisaig
Cottage
Prince's Cairn
Polnish
Creige Duibhe
Creag Bhàn
Slios Garbh
Glas-charn 2076
Sgurr an Utha 2610
Eilean a' Ghaill
Camas Ghaoideil
Loch nan Uamh
Lochailort (Ceann Loch Ailleart)
Ranochan
A830
Station
Viaduct
Glen Finnan
Glenfinnan
Eilean an t-Snidhe
Sound of Arisaig
Loch Doire a' Ghearrain
147
Ailort
Inverailort
Loch Eilt
The Jacobite
Glenfinnan Monument NTS
Dubh Lighe
Eilean nan Gobhar
Samalaman Island
Glenuig Bay
Roshven
Druim Fiaclach 2852
ROIS-BHEINN 2895
Samalaman
Smirisary
Loch na Bairness
Glenuig (Gleann Uige)
Lochan na Cloiche Sgoilte
Sgurr Dhomhuill Mòr
2895 Beinn Odhar Bheag
2175 Croit Bheinn
Shiel
Callop River
Sgorr Craobh a' Chaorainn
Glen Garvan
Rubh' Aird an Fheidh
Eilean Shona
Baramore
Loch nam Paitean
River Moidart
Beinn Gàire 2179
Meall nan Creag Leac
Rubha Aird Druimnich
M O I D A R T
A861
Kinlochmoidart (Ceann Loch Muideirt)
Arean
Farquhar's Point
Castle Tioram
Loch Moidart
Ardmolich
Brunery
Gaskan
Scamodale
Sgorr an Tarmachain 2474
Cona Glen
Cona River
Lochan Dubh
Druim Leathad nam Fias 1893
Acarsaid
Ockle
Newton of Ardtoe
Ardtoe
Shielfoot
Beinn Bhraec 1171
Gortenfern
Kentra Bay
Kentra
B8044
Blain
Shiel Br.
Dalnabreck
Mingarrypark
Langal
Dalelia
Polloch
Glen Hurich
River Hurich
2579 Beinn Mheadhoin
Arivegaig
Gorteneorn
Acharacle (Ath-Tharracail)
Moss
Ardshealach
Loch Doilet
Glenhurich
Sgurr Dhomhnuill
River Scaddle
Glen Scaddle
ARDNAMURCHAN
A R D G O U
Lochan na Beinne Bàine
Leac Shoilleir
Lochan Sligneach
Meall nan Each 1607
Salen (An Sailean)
Resipole
S U N A R T
2775 Beinn Resipol
Ariundle
Strontian River
Glen Gour
River Gour
Ardnamurchan Natural History Centre
Lochan nam Fiann
Loch Laga
Ben Laga 1679
Sunart
Ardery
Scotstown
Anaheilt
Strontian (Sron an t-Sithein)
Garbh Bheinn 2903
Sallac
Glenmore
Glenbeg
Glenborrodale
B8007
Ardslignish
Laga
Risga
Carna
Loch
Ardnastang
Glen Tarbert
A861
Oronsay
Glencripesdale
Laudale House
1693
Meall an Damhain
A884
River Tarbert
Inversanda
Inversanda Bay
139
1911 Beinn nam Beathrach
2798 Creach Bheinn
B8043
Bun Allt na Criche
1873 Beinn Iadain
Lochuisge
2511 Fuar Bheinn
Kilmalieu
Loch Teacuis
Kinloch
Dubh
Loch Uisge
Camas Chil-Mhalieu
Rubha Mor
Cuil Bay
Drimnin
Beinn Bhuidhe 1481
1569 Beinn Chlaonleud
Lochanan Dubha
Bheinn na Cille 2136
Eilean Bainagowan
B849
Loch Doire nam Mart
Beinn na h-Uamha
Beitheach
Kingairloch
Dalnatrat
M O R V E R N
1806 An t-Aoineadh Mòr Deserted Village
Sithean na Raplaich
Loch Arienas
Gleann
Allt
Loch a' Choire
Camasnacroise
Beinn Mheadhoin 2423
Rhemore
750
Killundine
10
Claggan
Gleann Geal
Camas Airigh Shamhraidh
Shuna Island
Glen Stockdale
Caisteal nan Con
Fiunary Forest
Larachbeg
Ardtornish
Achranich
Loch Tearnait
Beinn a' Chaisil 1431
Glensanda Castle
Castle Shuna
A828
Beinn Donn 1553
Portnacroish
Sound of Mull
Rannoch River
Loch nan Clach
Glensanda
Port a' Chaisteil
Eilean nan Caorach
Kinlochlaich
Appin
Strath of Appin
Aros Mains
Aros Castle
Fiunary
Lochaline
Port Ramsay
Eilean Loch Oscair
Port Appin
Rubha Mór
Mull
Glais Bheinn 1570
Eignaig
Druimneil House
Salen
A848
A849
B8035
Fishnish Bay
15 mins
Fishnish
Lochan Mam a' Chullaich
1684 An Sleaghach
Castle Coeffin
Clachan
Isle of Lismore Gaelic Heritage
Eriska
Tirefour Castle
Broch
North Shian
Scottish Sea Life Sanctuary
Loch Creran
Barcaldine
Loch na Dairidh
Beinn Bhuidhe 1352
Ardtornish Castle
Shlios
Camas Gorn
Killandrist
Balliveolan
B8045
Bailemeonach
13
Garmony
Beinn Chreagach Mhòr 1903
Forsa
Inninmore Bay
Garbh
LISMORE
Achnacroish
Baravullin
Park
B845
Macquarie Mausoleum
Scallastle Bay
RUBHA AN RIDIRE
Bernera Island
Achadun Castle
Achinduin
Kilcheran
Barr Mor
Dubh Loch Mor
I S L E
Benderloch
Kiel Crofts
Ledaig
Ardmucknish Bay
Tomsléibhe
Craignure
Craignure Bay
Loch Fiart
Creag Island
Eilean Dubh
Pladda Island
Camas Nathais
Rubha Garbh-àird
South Ledaig
Falls of Lora
Black Crofts
Ardchattan Priory
2512 Dùn da Ghaoithe
Duart Bay
Duart Point
Duart
Eilean Musdile
Oban
O F
2502 Beinn Talaidh
Sgurr Dearg 2429
Wings over Mull
Lochan an Doire Dharaich
Oban to Craignure 45mins
Oban to Lismore 50mins
Dunstaffnage
Connel
Achnacloich
Stonefield
Achaleven
Lochdon
Oakbank
Dunbeg
Ganavan
Corra-bheinn 2311
Lussa River
Loch Beanach
Loch Don
Dunollie
RC Cathedral
War & Peace
McCaig's Tower
A85
Lusragan Burn
Black Lochs
Fearnoch Forest
M U L L
Glen
30
Coladoir River
Loch Sguabain
Strathcoil
Grass Point
Eilean nan Gramhna
OBAN
SEE PAGE 206
133
Dun Croimhead 1257
132
Carn Ban 812
KERRERA
Balliemore
Carn Breugach
Pulpit Hill
Distillery
Dalintart
Glen Lonan
Loch Airdeglais
2290 Creach Beinn
Ben Buie 2354
Loch Spelve
Croggan
Gylen Castle
Sound of Kerrera
Loch Seil
Loch Nell
Kinlochspelve
Bach Island
A816
Kilbride
1691 Beinn Ghlas
Loch Fuaran
Rubha Aird na Croise 1649
Lochbuie
Standing Stone
Dubh Sgeir
Rubha Seanach
Cleigh
Kilmore

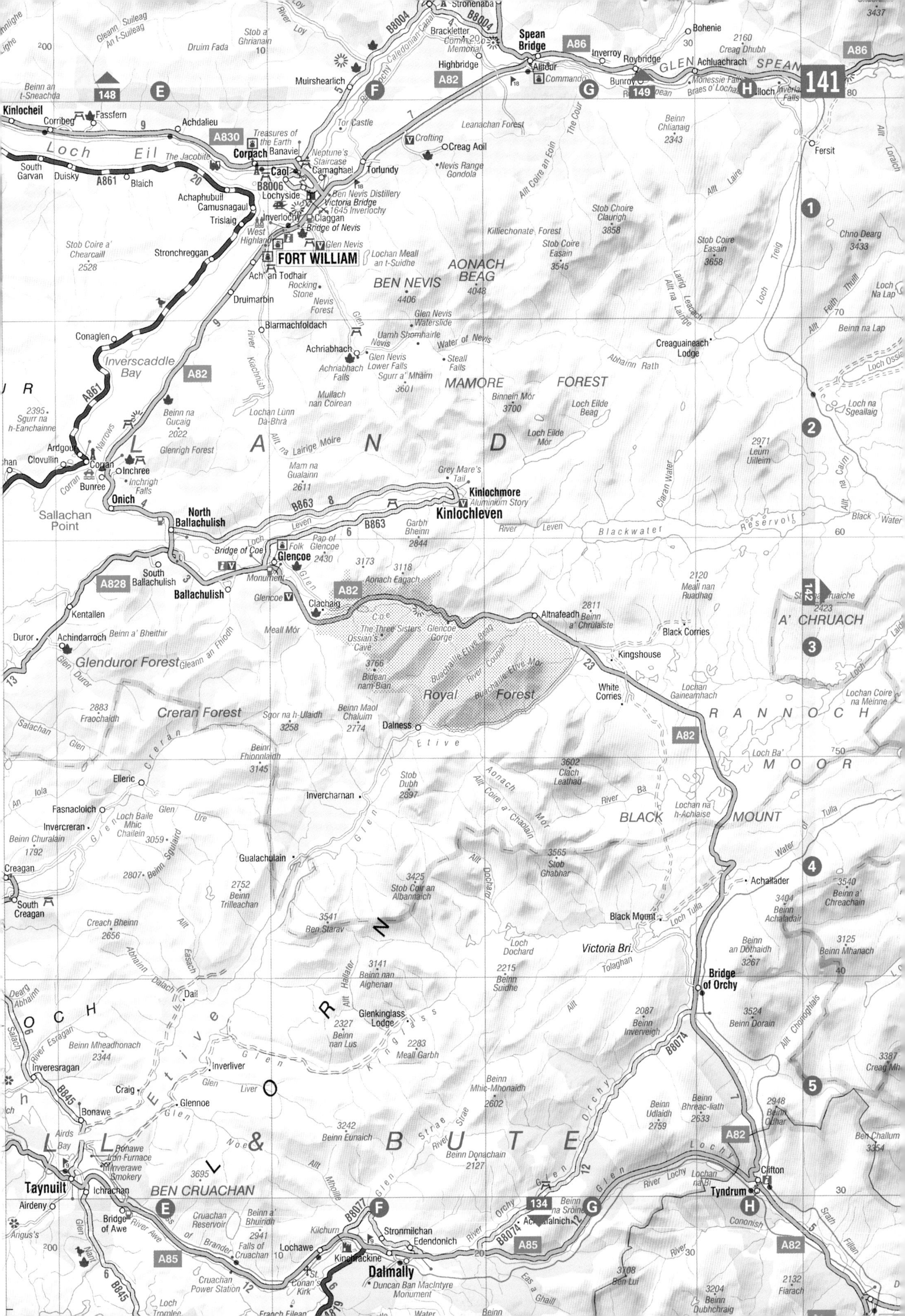

141
148
149
142
134
Spean Bridge
A86
Inverroy
Roybridge
Bohenie
Glen Spean
Achluachrach
Creag Dhubh
Bunroy
Monessie Falls
Braes o' Lochaber
Inverlair Falls
Stronenaba
B8004
Brackletter
Commando Memorial
Highbridge
A82
Alltour
Commando
Muirshearlich
Caledonian Canal
Stob a' Ghrianain
Druim Fada
Gleann Suileag
Beinn an t-Sneachda
Kinlocheil
Corribeg
Fassfern
Achdalieu
Loch Eil
A830
Treasures of the Earth
Corpach
Banavie
Neptune's Staircase
Caol
Camaghael
Torlundy
Tor Castle
Crofting
Creag Aoil
Nevis Range Gondola
Leanachan Forest
South Garvan
Duisky
A861
Blaich
The Jacobite
B8006
Lochyside
Ben Nevis Distillery
Victoria Bridge
1645 Inverlochy
Claggan
Achaphubuil
Camusnagaul
Trislaig
Inverlochy
West Highland
Bridge of Nevis
Glen Nevis
FORT WILLIAM
Lochan Meall an t-Suidhe
Stob Coire a' Chearcaill 2528
Stronchreggan
Ach' an Todhair
Rocking Stone
Nevis Forest
Druimarbin
BEN NEVIS 4406
AONACH BEAG 4048
Killiechonate Forest
Stob Coire Easain 3545
Stob Choire Claurigh 3858
Stob Coire Easain 3658
Beinn Chlianaig 2343
Fersit
Chno Dearg 3433
Loch Treig
Lairig Leacach
Loch Na Lap
Beinn na Lap
Allt Coire an Eoin
The Cour
Allt Laire
Blarmachfoldach
Glen Nevis Waterslide
Uamh Shomhairle
Water of Nevis
Steall Falls
Achriabhach
Achriabhach Falls
Glen Nevis Lower Falls
Sgurr a' Mhaim 3601
Conaglen
Inverscaddle Bay
A82
River Kiachnish
Mullach nan Coirean
MAMORE FOREST
Binnein Mòr 3700
Loch Eilde Beag
Loch Eilde Mòr
Creaguainneach Lodge
Abhainn Rath
Loch Ossian
Loch na Sgeallaig
2395 Sgurr na h-Eanchainne
Beinn na Gucaig 2022
Glenrigh Forest
Lochan Lùnn Da-Bhrà
Allt na Lairige Mòire
L A N D
Leum Uilleim 2971
Ardgour
Clovullin
Corran
Corran Narrows
Inchree
Inchree Falls
Bunree
Mam na Gualainn 2611
Grey Mare's Tail
Kinlochmore
Aluminium Story
Kinlochleven
Ciaran Water
Allt na Caim
Onich
Sallachan Point
North Ballachulish
B863
Loch Leven
River Leven
Blackwater Reservoir
Black Water
Garbh Bheinn 2844
Bridge of Coe
Folk
Glencoe
Pap of Glencoe 2430
3173
3118
Aonach Eagach
Glen Coe
South Ballachulish
A828
Ballachulish
Monument
Glencoe
Clachaig
Meall nan Ruadhag 2120
A' CHRUACH
Stob na Cruaiche 2423
Kentallen
Duror
Achindarroch
Beinn a' Bheithir
Meall Mòr
The Three Sisters
Ossian's Cave
Glencoe Gorge
Altnafeadh
Beinn a' Chrùlaiste 2811
Black Corries
Kingshouse
Glen Duror
Glendurror Forest
Gleann an Fhiodh
Bidean nam Bian 3766
Buachaille Etive Beag
River Coupall
Buachaille Etive Mòr
Royal Forest
White Corries
Lochan Gaineamhach
Lochan Coire na Meinne
Fraochaidh 2883
Creran Forest
Sgor na h-Ulaidh 3258
Beinn Maol Chaluim 2774
Dalness
Glen Etive
RANNOCH MOOR
Loch Ba'
Salachan Glen
Beinn Fhionnlaidh 3145
Elleric
Glen Creran
Inverchernan
Stob Dubh 2897
Aonach Mòr
Allt Coire a' Chaolain
3602 Clach Leathad
River Bà
Lochan na h-Achlaise
BLACK MOUNT
Water of Tulla
Fasnacloich
Invercreran
Loch Baile Mhic Chailein
Glen Ure
Beinn Churalain 1792
3059
Beinn Sguliaird
Gualachulain
Allt Dochard
3565 Stob Ghabhar
Achallader
3540 Beinn a' Chreachain
3404 Beinn Achaladair
Creagan
South Creagan
2807
2752 Beinn Trilleachan
3425 Stob Coir an Albannaich
Black Mount
Loch Tulla
Creach Bheinn 2656
3541 Ben Starav
Loch Dochard
Victoria Bri.
Tolaghan
Beinn an Dothaidh 3267
3125 Beinn Mhanach
Abhainn Dalach
Allt Easach
Allt Hallater
3141 Beinn nan Aighenan
2215 Beinn Suidhe
Bridge of Orchy
Dail
Glenkinglass Lodge
2327 Beinn nan Lus
2087 Beinn Inverveigh
3524 Beinn Dorain
Allt Chonoghlais
Abhainn Dearg
Loch Etive
River Esragan
Beinn Mheadhonach 2344
Glen Kinglass
2283 Meall Garbh
B8074
Inveresragan
Inverliver
Glen Liver
Beinn Mhic-Mhonaidh 2602
Glen Orchy
3387 Creag Mhor
B845
Craig
Glennoe
Bonawe
Beinn Udlaidh 2759
Beinn Bhreac-liath 2633
2948 Beinn Odhar
Ben Challum 3354
Airds Bay
Bonawe Iron Furnace
Inverawe Smokery
Glen Noe
3242 Beinn Eunaich
ARGYLL & BUTE
River Strae
Glen Strae
Beinn Donachain 2127
River Lochy
Glen Lochy
Lochan na Bi
Clifton
Tyndrum
Taynuilt
Ichrachan
3695
BEN CRUACHAN
Allt Mhoille
Airdeny
Bridge of Awe
River Awe
Pass of Brander
Cruachan Reservoir
Beinn a' Bhuiridh 2941
Falls of Cruachan
B8077
Stronmilchan
Kilchurn
Edendonich
River Orchy
B8074
Achallalnich
Beinn na Sroine
A85
Cononish
Strath Fillan
A82
Angus's
Glen Nant
Lochawe
Kinchrackine
Dalmally
Duncan Ban MacIntyre Monument
St. Conan's Kirk
Cruachan Power Station
Loch Tromlee
Fraoch Eilean
3708 Ben Lui
Eas a Ghaill
3204 Beinn Dubhchraig
2132 Fiarach
B819
A85
B845

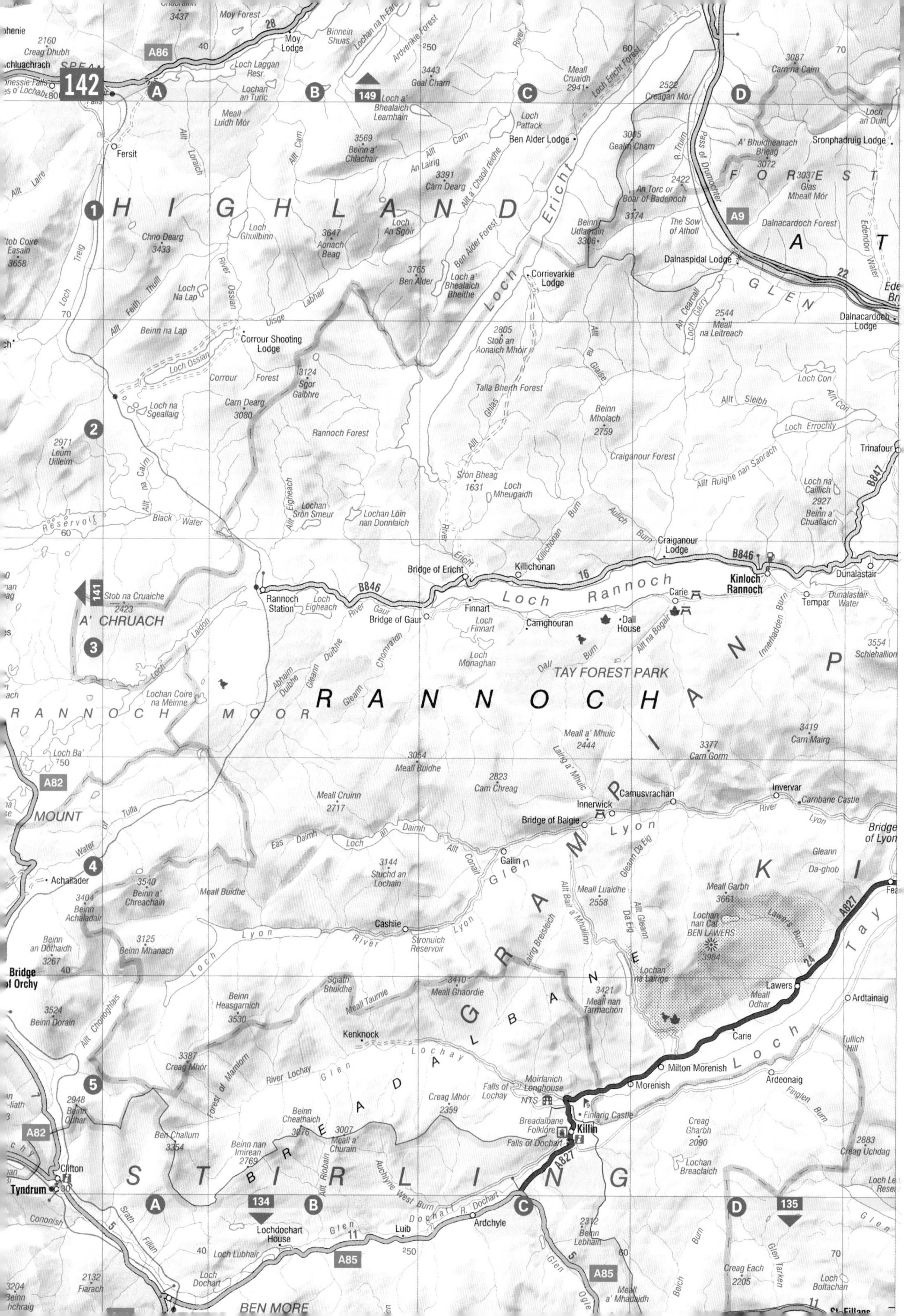

142
149
141
134
135
A
B
C
D
1
2
3
4
5
HIGHLAND
RANNOCH
GRAMPIAN
BREADALBANE
STIRLING
RANNOCH MOOR
A' CHRUACH
TAY FOREST PARK
Moy Forest
Moy Lodge
Loch Laggan Resr.
Lochan an Turic
Binnein Shuas
Lochan na h-Earba
Ardverikie Forest
3443 Geal Charn
Loch a' Bhealaich Leamhain
Meall Cruaidh 2941
Loch Ericht Forest
2522 Creagan Mór
3087 Carn na Caim
Loch an Duin
Sronphadruig Lodge
A' Bhuidheanach Bheag 3072
3037 Glas Mheall Mór
Fersit
Meall Luidh Mór
Allt Loraich
3569 Beinn a' Chlachair
Loch Pattack
Ben Alder Lodge
3005 Geal Charn
Pass of Drumochter
An Lairig
3391 Carn Dearg
Allt a' Chaoil-réidhe
An Torc or Boar of Badenoch
2422
3174
The Sow of Atholl
Beinn Udlamain 3306
Dalnacardoch Forest
A9
Dalnaspidal Lodge
Edendon Water
Chno Dearg 3433
Loch Ghuilbinn
3647 Aonach Beag
Loch An Sgòir
3765 Ben Alder
Ben Alder Forest
Loch a' Bhealaich Bheithe
Loch Ericht
Corrievarkie Lodge
Loch Treig
Loch Na Lap
Beinn na Lap
Corrour Shooting Lodge
Loch Ossian
Corrour Forest
3124 Sgor Gaibhre
Loch na Sgeallaig
Carn Dearg 3080
2805 Stob an Aonaich Mhóir
Talla Bheith Forest
Allt na Glaise
2544 Meall na Leitreach
Loch Garry
An Cearcall
Dalnacardoch Lodge
Loch Con
Allt Sleibh
2971 Leum Uilleim
Rannoch Forest
Beinn Mholach 2759
Loch Errochty
Trinafour
Craiganour Forest
Sron Bheag 1631
Loch Mheugaidh
Allt Ruighe nan Saorach
Loch na Caillich 2927
Beinn a' Chuallaich
B847
Lochan Sron Smeur
Lochan Loin nan Donnlaich
Allt Eigheach
Black Water
Reservoir
Craiganour Lodge
Killichonan Burn
Aulich Burn
Bridge of Ericht
Killichonan
B846
Kinloch Rannoch
Dunalastair
Stob na Cruaiche 2423
Rannoch Station
Loch Eigheach
River Gaur
Bridge of Gaur
Finnart
Loch Finnart
Loch Rannoch
Carie
Tempar
Dunalastair Water
Camghouran
Dall House
Allt na Bogair
Inverhadden Burn
3554 Schiehallion
Loch Monaghan
Dall Burn
Lochan Coire na Mèinne
Loch Laidon
Abhainn Duibhe
Gleann Duibhe
Gleann Chomraidh
Meall a' Mhuic 2444
3419 Carn Mairg
3377 Carn Gorm
Loch Ba'
A82
3054 Meall Buidhe
2823 Cam Chreag
Lairig a' Mhuic
Camusvrachan
Innerwick
Inverar
Carnbane Castle
MOUNT
Meall Cruinn 2717
Bridge of Balgie
River Lyon
Bridge of Lyon
Water of Tulla
Eas Daimh
Loch an Daimh
Allt Conait
Gallin
Glen Lyon
Gleann Da Eig
Gleann Da-ghob
Achallader
3540 Beinn a' Chreachain
Meall Buidhe
3144 Stuchd an Lochain
Allt Bail a' Mhuilinn
Meall Luaidhe 2558
Meall Garbh 3661
Lochan nan Cat
BEN LAWERS 3984
Lawers Burn
A827
3404 Beinn Achaladair
Cashlie
Stronuich Reservoir
Allt Gleann Da Eig
Lairig Breisleich
Beinn an Dòthaidh 3267
3125 Beinn Mhanach
Loch Lyon
Lochan na Lairige
Lawers
Meall Odhar
Ardtainaig
Bridge of Orchy
Allt Chonoghlais
Sgiath Bhuidhe
3410 Meall Ghaordie
3421 Meall nan Tarmachan
Loch Tay
Tullich Hill
3524 Beinn Dorain
Beinn Heasgarnich 3530
Meall Taurnie
Kenknock
Carie
Milton Morenish
Ardeonaig
3387 Creag Mhór
Forest of Mamlorn
River Lochay
Glen Lochay
Falls of Lochay
Moirlanich Longhouse
NTS
Morenish
Finglen Burn
2948 Beinn Odhar
Creag Mhór 2359
Finlarig Castle
Beinn Cheathaich 3076
3007 Meall a' Churain
Breadalbane Folklore
Killin
Creag Gharbh 2090
Ben Challum 3354
Beinn nan Imirean 2769
Falls of Dochart
2883 Creag Uchdag
Clifton
Tyndrum
Allt Riobain
Auchlyne West Burn
Lochan Breaclaich
Loch Lednock Reservoir
Cononish
Strath Fillan
R. Dochart
Glen Dochart
Ardchyle
Lochdochart House
Luib
2312 Beinn Lebhain
Glen Ogle
Beich Burn
Glen Tarken
Loch Lubhair
A85
Creag Each 2205
Loch Boltachan
2132 Fiarach
Loch Dochart
Meall a' Mhadaidh
3204 Beinn Chabhair
BEN MORE
St Fillans
A86
Spean
Loch Pattack
Glen Garry
Glen Lednock

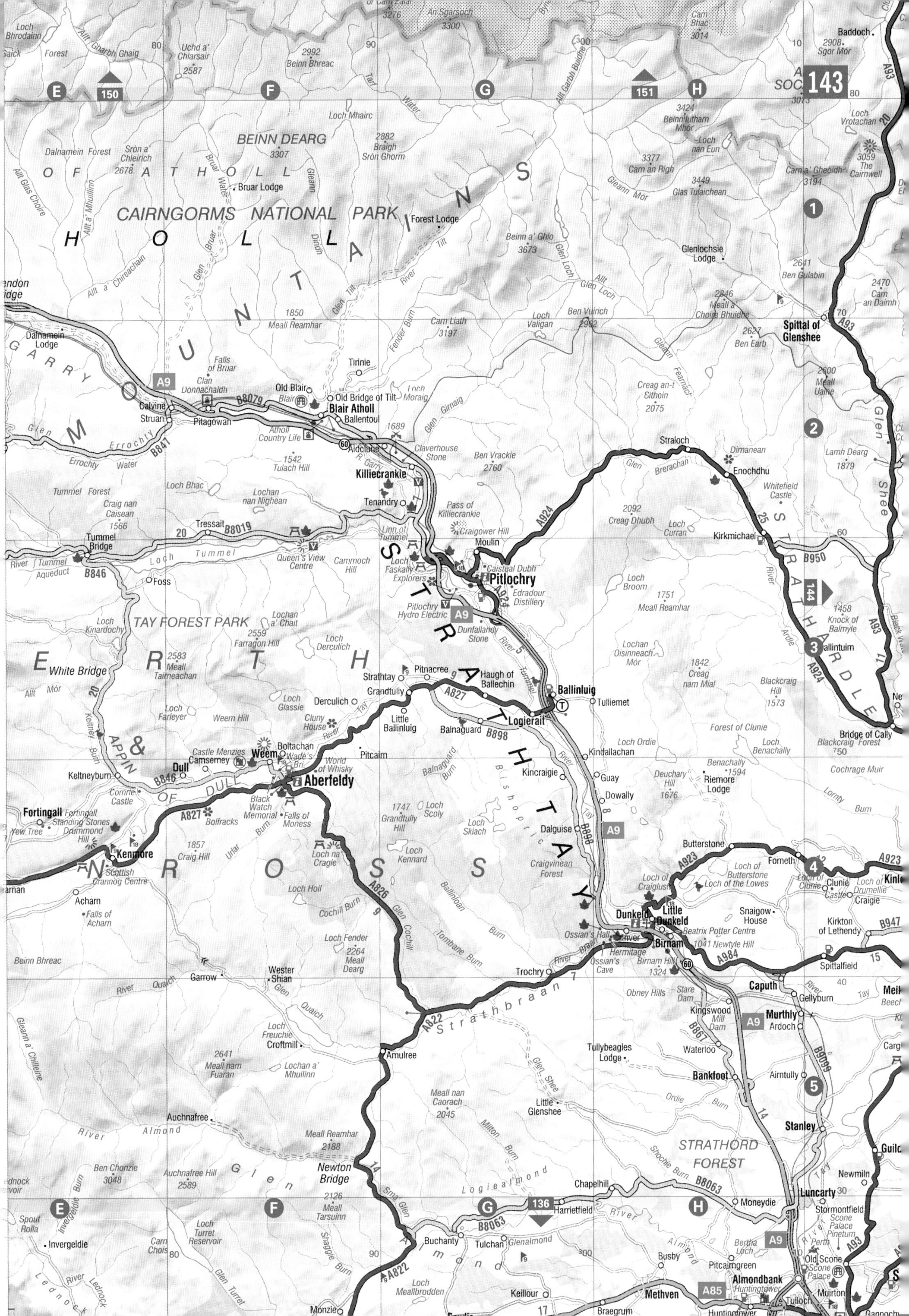
143
150
151
144
136
CAIRNGORMS NATIONAL PARK
HOLL OF ATHOLL
MOUNTAINS
TAY FOREST PARK
PERTH & KINROSS
STRATH TAY
STRATHARDLE
STRATHORD FOREST
Blair Atholl
Killiecrankie
Pitlochry
Ballinluig
Logierait
Aberfeldy
Weem
Dull
Kenmore
Fortingall
Dunkeld
Little Dunkeld
Birnam
Spittal of Glenshee
Kirkmichael
Bridge of Cally
Amulree
Caputh
Murthly
Bankfoot
Stanley
Luncarty
Almondbank
Methven
Newton Bridge
Tummel Bridge
Beinn Dearg 3307
Beinn a' Ghlo 3673
Ben Vrackie 2760
Schiehallion
Loch Tummel
River Tay
River Almond
Glen Shee
A9
A93
A924
A827
A826
A822
A923
A984
A85
B8079
B8019
B846
B847
B898
B950
B867
B8063
B9099
B947

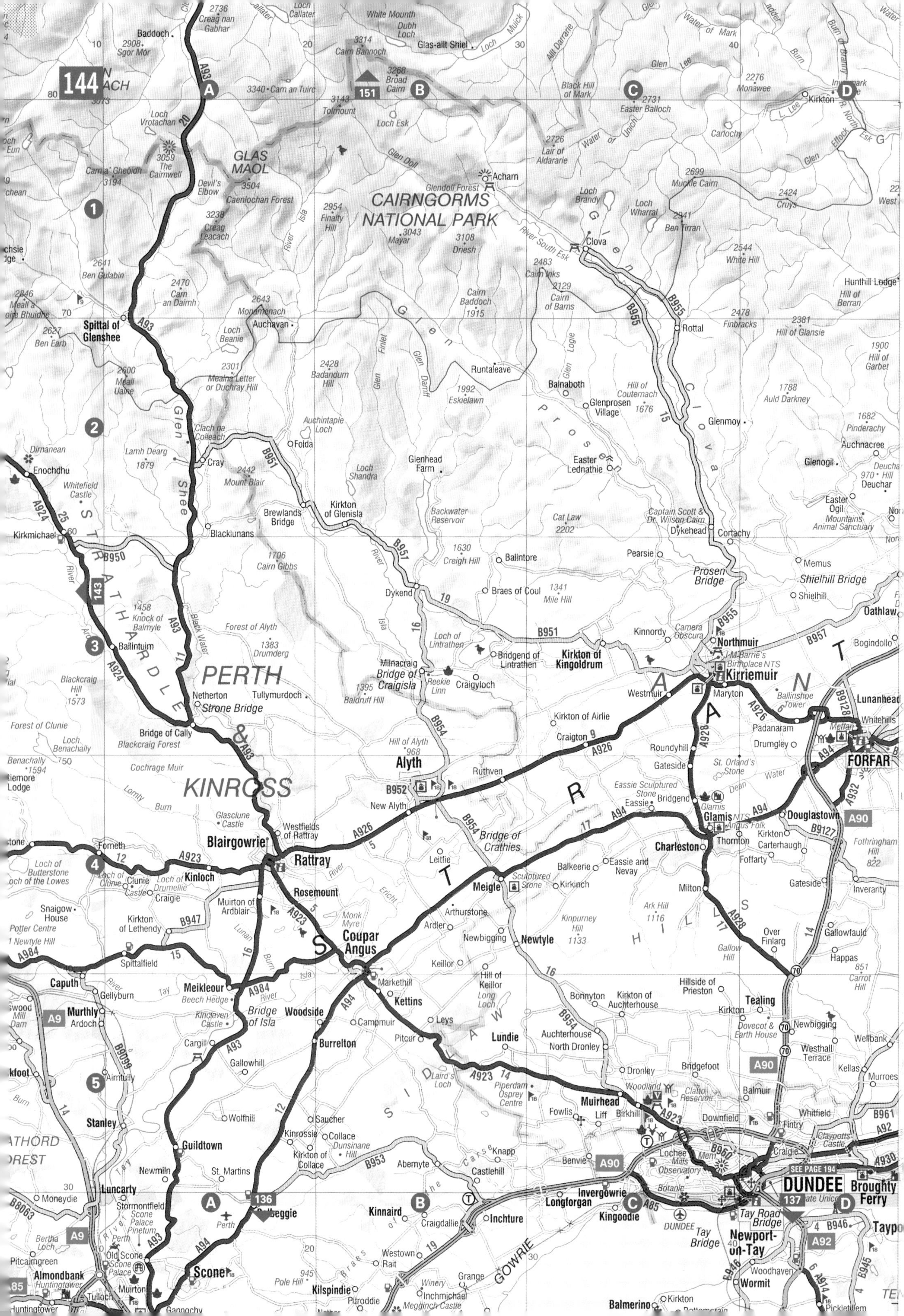

144
151
143
136
137
SEE PAGE 194
A
B
C
D
1
2
3
4
5
CAIRNGORMS
NATIONAL PARK
GLAS
MAOL
PERTH
&
KINROSS
A N G U S
S T R A T H A R D L E
S I D L A W
H I L L S
Baddoch
Creag nan Gabhar
Sgor Mòr
Loch Callater
White Mounth
Dubh Loch
Glas-allt Shiel
Loch Muick
Cairn Bannoch
Broad Cairn
Cairn an Tuirc
Tolmount
Loch Esk
Loch Vrotachan
The Cairnwell
Carn a' Gheoidh
Devil's Elbow
Caenlochan Forest
Creag Leacach
Glen Doll
Acharn
Glendoll Forest
Finalty Hill
Mayar
Driesh
Black Hill of Mark
Easter Balloch
Lair of Aldararie
Water of Unich
Water of Mark
Glen Lee
Monawee
Kirkton
Carlochy
Glen Effock
Muckle Cairn
Cruys
Loch Brandy
Loch Wharral
Ben Tirran
White Hill
Clova
River South Esk
Cairn Inks
Cairn of Barns
Cairn Baddoch
Ben Gulabin
Carn an Daimh
Monamenach
Auchavan
Spittal of Glenshee
Ben Earb
Loch Beanie
Meall Uaine
Mealna Letter or Duchray Hill
Badandum Hill
Glen Finlet
Glen Damff
Runtaleave
Eskielawn
Balnaboth
Glenprosen Village
Hill of Couternach
Glen Prosen
Glen Clova
Rottal
Finbracks
Hill of Glansie
Hunthill Lodge
Hill of Berran
Hill of Garbet
Auld Darkney
Pinderachy
Glenmoy
Auchnacree
Glenogil
Deuchar
Easter Ogil
Mountains Animal Sanctuary
Clach na Coileach
Auchintaple Loch
Folda
Dirnanean
Enochdhu
Lamh Dearg
Cray
Mount Blair
Glen Shee
Whitefield Castle
Loch Shandra
Glenhead Farm
Easter Lednathie
Backwater Reservoir
Cat Law
Captain Scott & Dr. Wilson Cairn
Dykehead
Cortachy
Kirkmichael
Blacklunans
Brewlands Bridge
Kirkton of Glenisla
Creigh Hill
Balintore
Pearsie
Prosen Bridge
Memus
Shielhill Bridge
Shielhill
Cairn Gibbs
Dykend
Braes of Coul
Mile Hill
Knock of Balmyle
Black Water
Forest of Alyth
Drumderg
Loch of Lintrathen
Bridgend of Lintrathen
Kirkton of Kingoldrum
Kinnordy
Camera Obscura
Northmuir
J.M. Barrie's Birthplace NTS
Kirriemuir
Oathlaw
Bogindollo
Ballintuim
Blackcraig Hill
Netherton
Strone Bridge
Tullymurdoch
Milnacraig
Bridge of Craigisla
Reekie Linn
Craigyloch
Baldruff Hill
Westmuir
Maryton
Ballinshoe Tower
Lunanhead
Padanaram
Whitehills
Forest of Clunie
Loch Benachally
Bridge of Cally
Blackcraig Forest
Hill of Alyth
Kirkton of Airlie
Craigton
Roundyhill
Drumgley
Benachally
Riemore Lodge
Cochrage Muir
Lornty Burn
Alyth
Ruthven
Gateside
St. Orland's Stone
Dean Water
FORFAR
Glasclune Castle
Westfields of Rattray
Blairgowrie
Rattray
New Alyth
Eassie Sculptured Stone
Eassie
Bridgend
Glamis
Angus Folk
Douglastown
Kirkton
Carterhaugh
Foffarty
Fothringham Hill
Forneth
Loch of Butterstone
Loch of the Lowes
Loch of Clunie
Clunie
Castle
Kinloch
Loch of Drumellie
Craigie
Rosemount
Leitfie
Bridge of Crathies
Charleston
Thornton
Balkeerie
Eassie and Nevay
Meigle
Sculptured Stone
Kirkinch
Milton
Inverarity
Snaigow House
Potter Centre
Newtyle Hill
Kirkton of Lethendy
Muirton of Ardblair
Monk Myre
Coupar Angus
Arthurstone
Ardler
Newbigging
Newtyle
Kinpurney Hill
Ark Hill
Over Finlarg
Gallowfauld
Gallow Hill
Happas
Carrot Hill
Spittalfield
Caputh
Gellyburn
Meikleour
Beech Hedge
Bridge of Isla
Murthly
Ardoch
Kinclaven Castle
Woodside
Markethill
Kettins
Keillor
Hill of Keillor
Long Loch
Bonnyton
Kirkton of Auchterhouse
Hillside of Prieston
Tealing
Kirkton
Dovecot & Earth House
Newbigging
Wellbank
Westhall Terrace
Kellas
Murroes
Cargill
Campmuir
Leys
Pitcur
Burrelton
Lundie
Auchterhouse
North Dronley
Dronley
Bridgefoot
Balmuir
Airntully
Gallowhill
Laird's Loch
Piperdam Osprey Centre
Muirhead
Woodland
Clatto Reservoir
Whitfield
Stanley
Wolfhill
Saucher
Fowlis
Liff
Birkhill
Downfield
Fintry
Claypotts Castle
Kinrossie
Collace
Dunsinane Hill
Kirkton of Collace
Lochee
Mem
Mills Observatory
Craigie
Guildtown
Newmiln
St. Martins
Abernyte
Knapp
Castlehill
Benvie
Carse of Gowrie
DUNDEE
Broughty Ferry
Luncarty
Moneydie
Stormontfield
Scone Palace Pinetum
Balbeggie
Perth
Kinnaird
Craigdallie
Inchture
Longforgan
Invergowrie
Kingoodie
Botanic
Tay Road Bridge
Tay Bridge
Newport-on-Tay
Tayport
Bertha Loch
Pitcairngreen
Almondbank
Huntingtower
Old Scone
Scone Palace
Scone
Muirton
Tulloch
Gannochy
Pole Hill
Kilspindie
Westown
Rait
Pitroddie
Braes of the Carse
Grange
Winery
Inchmichael
Megginch Castle
GOWRIE
Woodhaven
Wormit
Balmerino
Kirkton
Pickletillem
Caputh
Stanley
Tay
River Isla
River Ericht
Lunan Burn
River Tay
A93
A924
A926
A923
A928
A94
A984
A90
A9
A92
A85
A930
A914
A932
B955
B951
B950
B952
B954
B947
B953
B9099
B960
B957
B9128
B9127
B961
B946
B945
B8063
Lunan
Burn
Isla
River
Tay

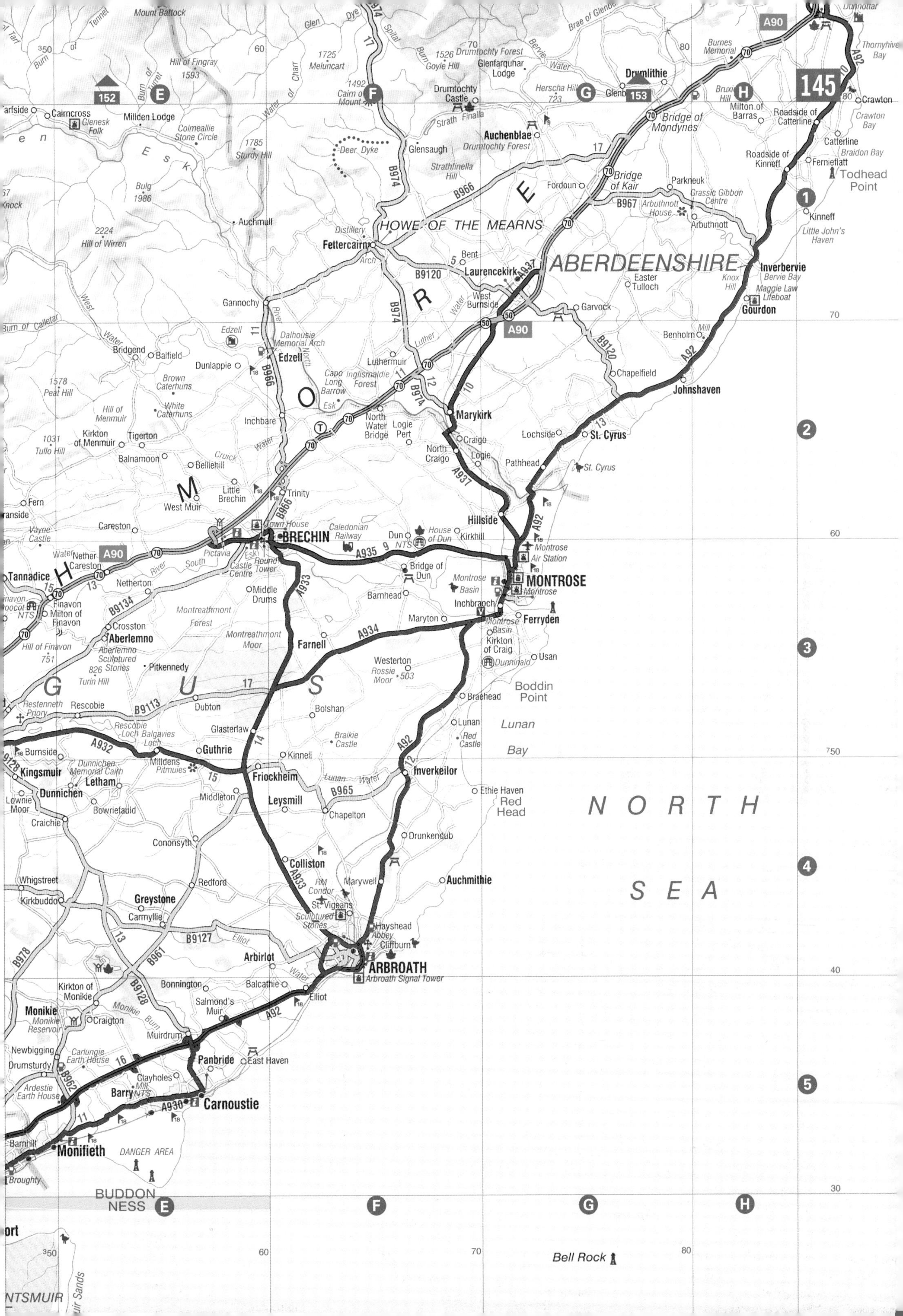
145
NORTH SEA
ABERDEENSHIRE
HOWE OF THE MEARNS
MONTROSE
BRECHIN
ARBROATH
Carnoustie
Monifieth
Inverbervie
Gourdon
Johnshaven
St. Cyrus
Laurencekirk
Fettercairn
Edzell
Auchenblae
Drumlithie
Marykirk
Hillside
Ferryden
Friockheim
Inverkeilor
Auchmithie
Letham
Kingsmuir
Dunnichen
Monikie
Panbride
Barry
Aberlemno
Tannadice
Lunan Bay
Boddin Point
Red Head
Todhead Point
Buddon Ness
Bell Rock

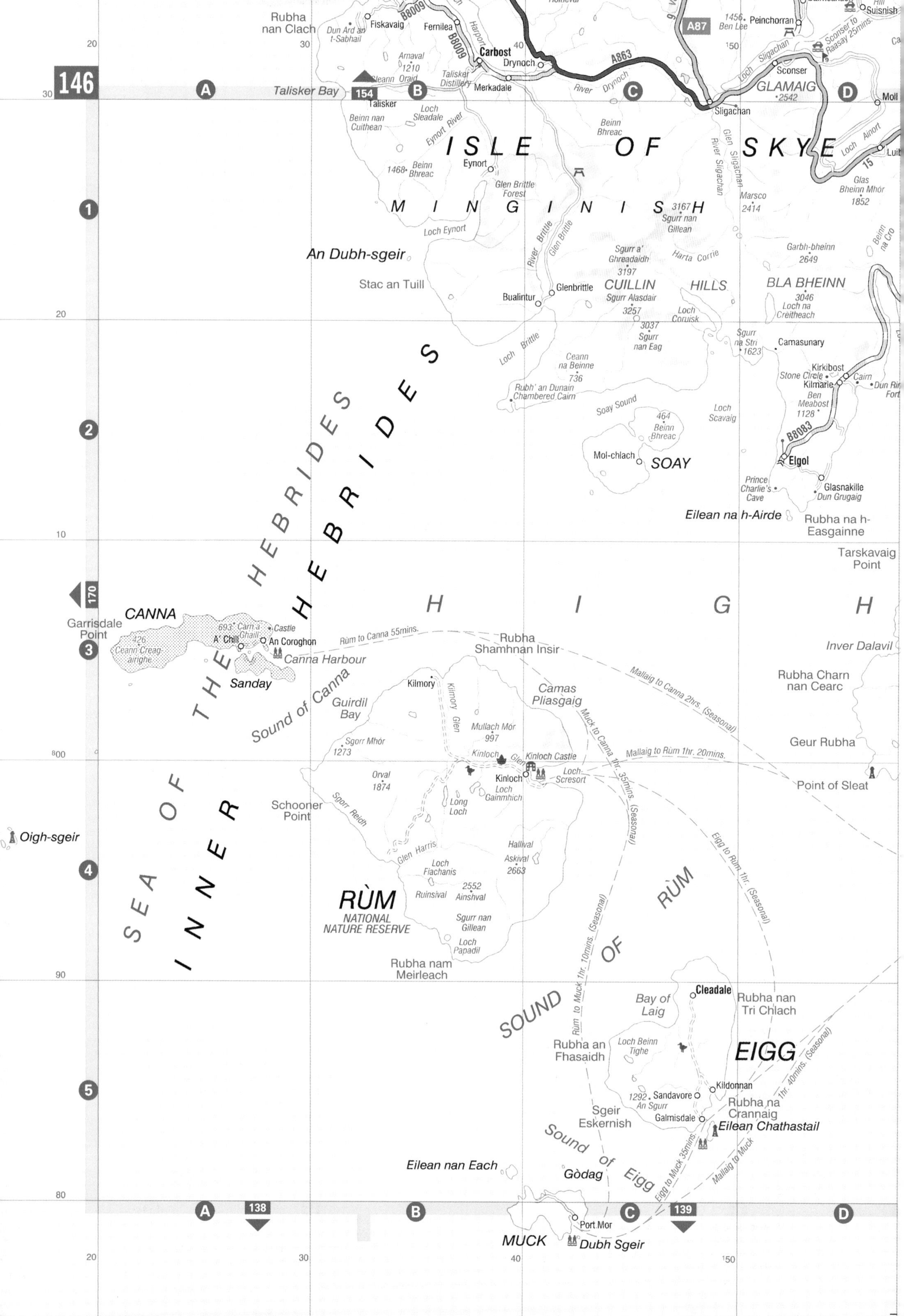
Rubha nan Clach
Dun Ard an t-Sabhail
Fiskavaig
B8009
Fernilea
Harport
Carbost
Drynoch
A863
A87
1456 Ben Lee
Peinchorran
Sconser to Raasay 25mins.
Suisnish
Arnaval 1210
Talisker Distillery
Merkadale
Loch Sligachan
Sconser
Glen Oraid
Talisker Bay
154
Talisker
River Drynoch
GLAMAIG 2542
Sligachan
Moll
Beinn nan Cuithean
Loch Sleadale
Eynort River
Beinn Bhreac
Glen Sligachan
River Sligachan
ISLE OF SKYE
Loch Ainort
15
1468 Beinn Bhreac
Eynort
Glen Brittle Forest
Glas Bheinn Mhór 1852
MINGINISH
3167 Sgurr nan Gillean
Marsco 2414
Loch Eynort
River Brittle
Glen Brittle
Sgurr a' Ghreadaidh 3197
Harta Corrie
Garbh-bheinn 2649
Beinn na Cro
An Dubh-sgeir
Stac an Tuill
Glenbrittle
Bualintur
CUILLIN HILLS
Sgurr Alasdair 3257
BLA BHEINN 3046
Loch na Creitheach
Loch Coruisk
3037 Sgurr nan Eag
Sgurr na Stri 1623
Camasunary
Loch Brittle
Ceann na Beinne 736
Kirkibost
Stone Circle
Kilmarie
Cairn
Dun Ringill Fort
Rubh' an Dunain Chambered Cairn
Soay Sound
464 Beinn Bhreac
Loch Scavaig
Ben Meabost 1128
B8083
Mol-chlach
SOAY
Elgol
Prince Charlie's Cave
Glasnakille
Dun Grugaig
Eilean na h-Airde
Rubha na h-Easgainne
Tarskavaig Point
THE HEBRIDES
HEBRIDES
HIGH
170
CANNA
Garrisdale Point
693 Carn a' Ghaill
Castle
426 Ceann Creag airighe
A' Chill
An Coroghon
Rùm to Canna 55mins.
Rubha Shamhnan Insir
Inver Dalavil
Canna Harbour
Sanday
Mallaig to Canna 2hrs. (Seasonal)
Rubha Charn nan Cearc
Kilmory
Camas Pliasgaig
Sound of Canna
Guirdil Bay
Kilmory Glen
Mullach Mór 997
Muck to Canna 1hr. 35mins. (Seasonal)
Sgorr Mhór 1273
Geur Rubha
Kinloch Glen
Kinloch Castle
Mallaig to Rùm 1hr. 20mins.
Orval 1874
Kinloch
Loch Scresort
Loch Gainmhich
Point of Sleat
Schooner Point
Sgorr Reidh
Long Loch
SEA OF
INNER
Oigh-sgeir
Eigg to Rùm 1hr. (Seasonal)
Hallival
Askival 2663
Glen Harris
Loch Fiachanis
2552 Ainshval
Ruinsival
RÙM
NATIONAL NATURE RESERVE
Sgurr nan Gillean
Loch Papadil
OF
RÙM
Rubha nam Meirleach
Rùm to Muck 1hr. 10mins. (Seasonal)
SOUND
Bay of Laig
Cleadale
Rubha nan Tri Chlach
Rubha an Fhasaidh
Loch Beinn Tighe
EIGG
Kildonnan
1292 An Sgurr
Sandavore
Rubha na Crannaig
1hr. 40mins. (Seasonal)
Sgeir Eskernish
Galmisdale
Eilean Chathastail
Sound of Eigg
Eigg to Muck 35mins.
Mallaig to Muck
Eilean nan Each
Gòdag
138
139
Port Mor
MUCK
Dubh Sgeir
A
B
C
D
1
2
3
4
5
20
30
40
150
10
800
90
80

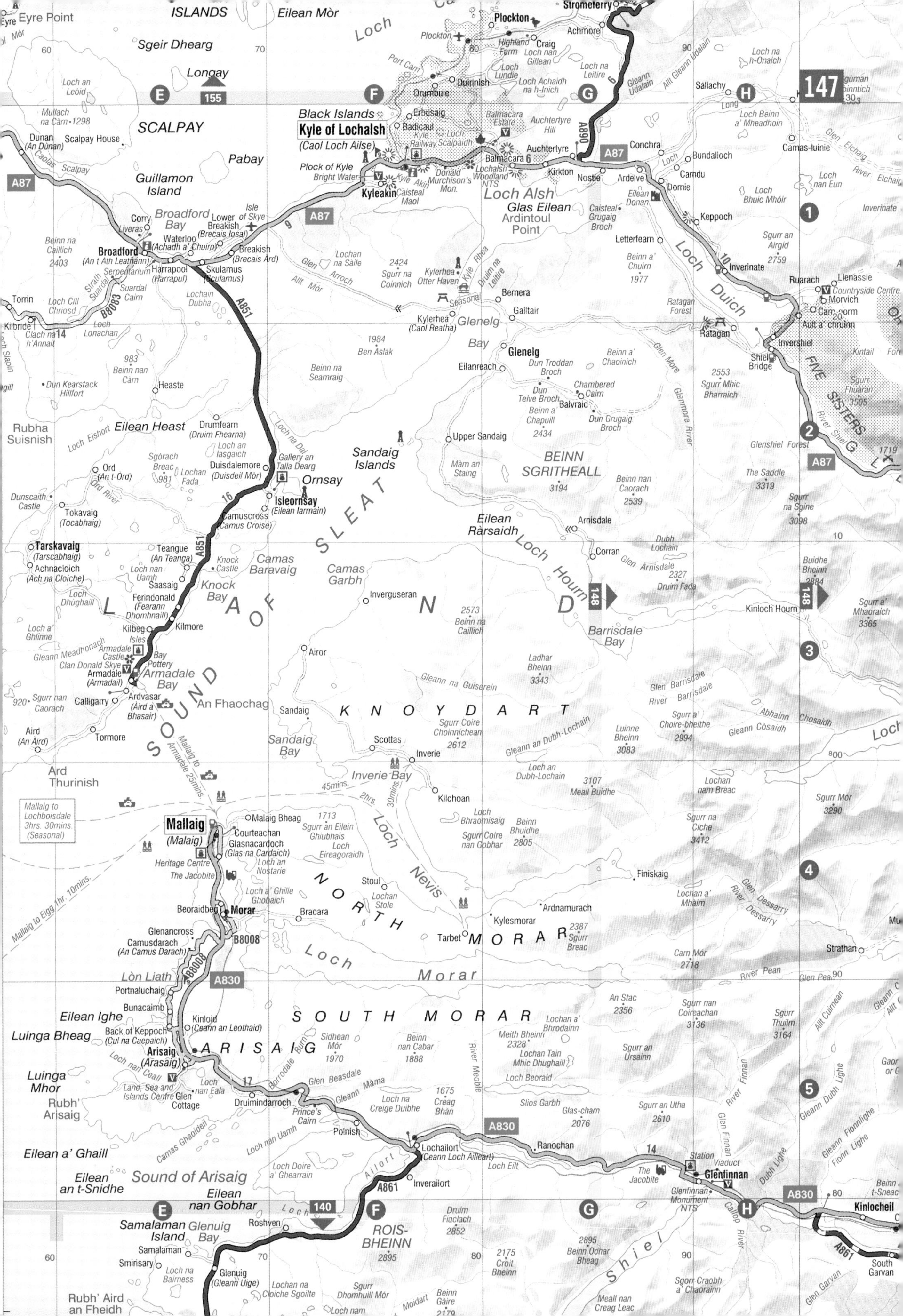

147
155
148
148
140
Eyre Point
ISLANDS
Eilean Mòr
Sgeir Dhearg
Longay
Loch
Stromeferry
Plockton
Plockton
Achmore
Highland Farm
Craig
Loch nan Gillean
Port Cam
Loch Lundie
Loch na Leitire
Duirinish
Drumbuie
Loch Achaidh na h-Inich
Gleann Udalain
Allt Gleann Udalain
Loch na h-Oraich
Sallachy
Loch Beinn a' Mheadhoin
Mullach na Càrn 1298
Loch an Leòid
SCALPAY
Black Islands
Kyle of Lochalsh
(Caol Loch Ailse)
Erbusaig
Badicaul
Balmacara Estate
Auchtertyre Hill
Dunan
(An Dùnan)
Scalpay House
Caolas Scalpay
Pabay
Plock of Kyle
Bright Water
Kyleakin
Caisteal Maol
Kyle Akin
Donald Murchison's Mon.
Lochalsh Woodland NTS
Balmacara
Auchtertyre
Kirkton
Conchra
A87
A890
Nostie
Ardelve
Bundalloch
Carndu
Dornie
Camas-luinie
Glen Elchaig
River Elchaig
Loch nan Eun
Guillamon Island
Loch Alsh
Glas Eilean
Ardintoul Point
Caisteal Grugaig Broch
Eilean Donan
Loch Bhuic Mhòir
Keppoch
Invérinate
Corry
Liveras
Broadford Bay
Lower Breakish
(Breacais Ìosal)
Isle of Skye
Waterloo
(Achadh a' Chuirn)
Breakish
(Brecais Àrd)
Beinn na Caillich 2403
Broadford
(An t Àth Leathann)
Harrapool
(Harrapul)
Skulamus
(Sculamus)
Serpentarium
Strath Suardal
Suardal Cairn
Lochan na Sàile
Glen Arroch
Allt Mòr
2424 Sgurr na Coinnich
Kylerhea Otter Haven
Kyle Rhea
Druim na Leitire
Letterfearn
Beinn a' Chuirn 1977
Loch Duich
Sgurr an Airgid 2759
Inverinate
Ruarach
Lienassie
Morvich
Countryside Centre
Carn-gorm
Ault a' chruinn
Torrin
Loch Cill Chriosd
B8083
Lochain Dubha
A851
Seasonal
Bernera
Galltair
Ratagan Forest
Ratagan
Invershiel
Shiel Bridge
Kilbride
Clach na h'Annait
Loch Lonachan
Kylerhea
(Caol Reatha)
Glenelg Bay
1984 Ben Aslak
Glenelg
Eilanreach
Dun Troddan Broch
Beinn a' Chaoinich
Glen More
2553 Sgurr Mhic Bharraich
Kintail
Sgurr Fhuaran 3505
FIVE SISTERS
983 Beinn nan Càrn
Beinn na Seamraig
Dun Telve Broch
Chambered Cairn
Balvraid
Beinn a Chapuill 2434
Dun Grugaig Broch
Glenmore River
Dun Kearstack Hillfort
Heaste
Rubha Suisnish
Eilean Heast
Loch Eishort
Drumfearn
(Druim Fhearna)
Loch na Dal
Upper Sandaig
River Shiel
Glenshiel Forest
A87
1719
Sgòrach Breac 981
Loch an Iasgaich
Lochan Fada
Duisdalemore
(Duisdeil Mòr)
Gallery an Talla Dearg
Sandaig Islands
Màm an Staing
BEINN SGRITHEALL 3194
Beinn nan Caorach 2539
The Saddle 3319
Ord
(An t-Òrd)
Ord River
Ornsay
Isleornsay
(Eilean Iarmain)
Dunscaith Castle
Tokavaig
(Tocabhaig)
Camuscross
(Camus Croise)
SOUND OF SLEAT
Eilean Ràrsaidh
Arnisdale
Sgurr na Sgine 3098
Tarskavaig
(Tarscabhaig)
Achnacloich
(Ach na Cloiche)
Teangue
(An Teanga)
Loch nan Uamh
Knock Castle
Camas Baravaig
Camas Garbh
Loch Hourn
Corran
Dubh Lochain
Glen Arnisdale
2327 Druim Fada
Buidhe Bheinn 2884
Saasaig
Knock Bay
Loch Dhughaill
Ferindonald
(Fearann Dhomhnaill)
Inverguseran
2573 Beinn na Caillich
Kinloch Hourn
Sgurr a' Mhaoraich 3365
Loch a' Ghlinne
Kilbeg
Isles
Kilmore
Barrisdale Bay
Gleann Meadhonach
Armadale Castle
Clan Donald Skye
Armadale
(Armadail)
Bay Pottery
Armadale Bay
Airor
Ladhar Bheinn 3343
Gleann na Guiserein
Glen Barrisdale
River Barrisdale
920
Sgurr nan Caorach
Calligarry
Ardvasar
(Àird a Bhasair)
An Fhaochag
Sandaig
KNOYDART
Sgurr Coire Choinnichean 2612
Gleann an Dubh-Lochain
Luinne Bheinn 3083
Sgurr a' Choire-bheithe 2994
Gleann Cosaidh
Abhainn Chosaidh
Aird
(An Àird)
Tormore
Mallaig to Armadale 25mins.
Sandaig Bay
Scottas
Inverie
Loch an Dubh-Lochain
3107 Meall Buidhe
Lochan nam Breac
Sgurr Mòr 3290
Ard Thurinish
Inverie Bay
Kilchoan
45mins.
2hrs.
30mins.
Mallaig to Lochboisdale 3hrs. 30mins. (Seasonal)
Mallaig
(Malaig)
Malaig Bheag
Courteachan
Glasnacardoch
(Glas na Cardaich)
1713 Sgurr an Eilein Ghiubhais
Loch Eireagoraidh
Loch Nevis
Loch Bhraomisaig
Beinn Bhuidhe 2805
Sgurr Coire nan Gobhar
Sgurr na Ciche 3412
Heritage Centre
The Jacobite
Loch an Nostarie
Loch a' Ghille Ghobaich
Stoul
Lochan Stole
Finiskaig
Lochan a' Mhaim
Glen Dessarry
River Dessarry
Mallaig to Eigg 1hr. 10mins.
Beoraidbeg
Morar
Bracara
NORTH MORAR
Kylesmorar
Ardnamurach
Glenancross
Camusdarach
(An Camus Darach)
B8008
Tarbet
2387 Sgurr Breac
Carn Mòr 2718
Strathan
Loch Morar
Lòn Liath
A830
River Pean
Glen Pean
Portnaluchaig
Bunacaimb
Eilean Ighe
Kinloid
(Ceann an Leothaid)
SOUTH MORAR
An Stac 2356
Sgurr nan Coireachan 3136
Lochan a' Bhrodainn
Sgurr Thuilm 3164
Allt Cuirnean
Luinga Bheag
Back of Keppoch
(Cul na Caepaich)
Arisaig
(Arasaig)
ARISAIG
Sidhean Mòr 1970
Beinn nan Cabar 1888
Meith Bheinn 2328
Lochan Tain Mhic Dhughaill
River Meoble
Sgurr an Ursainn
Loch nan Ceall
Luinga Mhor
Loch nan Eala
Borrodale Burn
Glen Beasdale
Loch Beoraid
River Finnan
Gleann Dubh Lighe
Land, Sea and Islands Centre
Glen Cottage
Rubh' Arisaig
Druimindarroch
Prince's Cairn
Gleann Màma
Loch na Creige Duibhe
1675 Creag Bhàn
Slios Garbh
Glas-charn 2076
Sgurr an Utha 2610
Glen Finnan
Gleann Fionnlighe
Eilean a' Ghaill
Camas Ghaoideil
Loch nan Uamh
Polnish
Lochailort
(Ceann Loch Ailleart)
Ranochan
Station
Viaduct
Glenfinnan
Dubh Lighe
Eilean an t-Snidhe
Sound of Arisaig
Loch Doire a' Ghearrain
Loch Eilt
The Jacobite
Glenfinnan Monument NTS
A830
Kinlocheil
Eilean nan Gobhar
Loch Ailort
A861
Inverailort
Samalaman Island
Glenuig Bay
Roshven
ROIS-BHEINN 2895
Druim Fiaclach 2852
2175 Croit Bheinn
2895 Beinn Odhar Bheag
Shiel
Callop River
A861
South Garvan
Samalaman
Smirisary
Loch na Bairness
Glenuig
(Gleann Uige)
Lochan na Cloiche Sgoilte
Sgurr Dhomhnuill Mòr
Moidart
Beinn Gàire 2179
Loch nam
Sgorr Craobh a' Chaorainn
Meall nan Creag Leac
Glen Garvan
Rubh' Aird an Fheidh

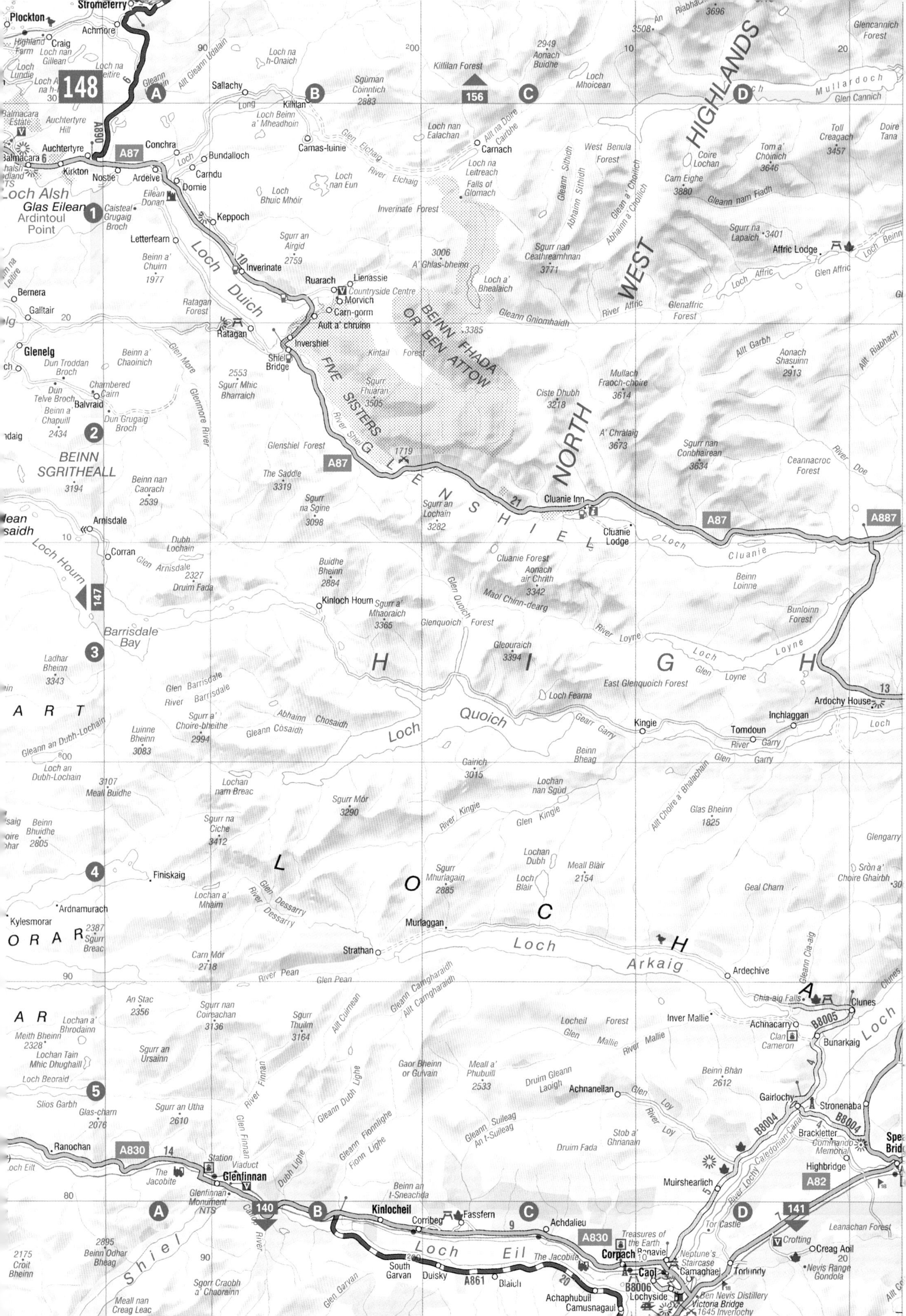

Stromeferry
Plockton
Achmore
Highland Farm
Craig
Loch nan Gillean
Loch Lundie
Loch na Leitire
Loch a' Mhuillin
148
Allt Gleann Udalain
Gleann Udalain
A
Sallachy
B
Loch na h-Onaich
Sgùman Coinntich
2883
Killilan Forest
156
C
2949
Aonach Buidhe
Loch Mhoicean
An Riabhachan
3508
3696
HIGHLANDS
D
Loch Mullardoch
Glencannich Forest
Glen Cannich
Balmacara Estate
Auchtertyre Hill
A890
Long
Killilan
Loch Beinn a' Mheadhoin
Loch nan Ealachan
Allt na Doire Cairbhe
Carnach
Toll Creagach
3457
Doire Tana
Balmacara
Auchtertyre
Kirkton
Nostie
A87
Conchra
Bundalloch
Camas-luinie
Glen Elchaig
River Elchaig
West Benula Forest
Coire Lochan
Tom a' Chòinich
3646
Loch Alsh
Glas Eilean
Ardintoul Point
1
Ardelve
Carndu
Dornie
Eilean Donan
Caisteal Grugaig Broch
Keppoch
Loch nan Eun
Loch Bhuic Mhòir
Loch na Leitreach
Falls of Glomach
Inverinate Forest
Gleann Sithidh
Abhainn Sithidh
Glean a' Choilich
Abhainn a' Choilich
Carn Eighe
3880
Gleann nam Fiadh
Sgurr na Lapaich
3401
Affric Lodge
Loch Beinn a' Mheadhoin
Letterfearn
Beinn a' Chuirn
1977
Loch Duich
Inverinate
Sgurr an Airgid
2759
3006
A' Ghlas-bheinn
Sgurr nan Ceathreamhnan
3771
Loch a' Bhealaich
WEST
Loch Affric
Glen Affric
Bernera
Galltair
Ratagan Forest
Ratagan
Ruarach
Lienassie
Countryside Centre
Morvich
Carn-gorm
Ault a' chruinn
River Affric
Glenaffric Forest
Gleann Gniomhaidh
Glenelg
Dun Troddan Broch
Dun Telve Broch
Chambered Cairn
Balvraid
Beinn a' Chaoinich
Glen More
Invershiel
Shiel Bridge
Kintail Forest
BEINN FHADA OR BEN ATTOW
3385
FIVE SISTERS
Allt Garbh
Aonach Shasuinn
2913
Allt Riabhach
2553
Sgurr Mhic Bharraich
Glenmore River
Sgurr Fhuaran
3505
Mullach Fraoch-choire
3614
Ciste Dhubh
3218
Beinn a' Chapuill
2434
Dun Grugaig Broch
2
BEINN SGRITHEALL
3194
Glenshiel Forest
River Shiel
1719
A87
NORTH
A' Chralaig
3673
Sgurr nan Conbhairean
3634
River Doe
Ceannacroc Forest
The Saddle
3319
Beinn nan Caorach
2539
Sgurr na Sgine
3098
Sgurr an Lochain
3282
GLEN SHIEL
21
Cluanie Inn
A87
A887
Arnisdale
Corran
Dubh Lochain
Glen Arnisdale
Loch Hourn
Cluanie Lodge
Loch Cluanie
2327
Druim Fada
Buidhe Bheinn
2884
Cluanie Forest
Aonach air Chrith
3342
Maol Chinn-dearg
Glen Quoich
Beinn Loinne
147
Kinloch Hourn
Sgurr a' Mhaoraich
3365
Glenquoich Forest
Bunloinn Forest
Barrisdale Bay
River Loyne
3
Ladhar Bheinn
3343
H
Gleouraich
3394
I
G
H
Loch Loyne
Glen Loyne
East Glenquoich Forest
Loch Fearna
13
Ardochy House
Glen Barrisdale
River Barrisdale
A R T
Sgurr a' Choire-bheithe
2994
Abhainn Chosaidh
Gleann Cosaidh
Loch Quoich
Gearr Garry
Kingie
Inchlaggan
Tomdoun
Loch
River Garry
Gleann an Dubh-Lochain
Luinne Bheinn
3083
Glen Garry
Beinn Bheag
Loch an Dubh-Lochain
3107
Meall Buidhe
Lochan nam Breac
Gairich
3015
Lochan nan Sgùd
Sgurr Mòr
3290
River Kingie
Glen Kingie
Allt Choire a' Bhalachain
Glas Bheinn
1825
Beinn Bhuidhe
2805
Sgurr na Ciche
3412
Glengarry
4
Finiskaig
L
Lochan Dubh
Meall Blàir
2154
Loch Blàir
Sròn a' Choire Ghairbh
Sgurr Mhurlagain
2885
O
Geal Charn
Ardnamurach
Lochan a' Mhaim
Glen Dessarry
River Dessarry
C
Kylesmorar
2387
Sgurr Breac
MORAR
Murlaggan
Strathan
Loch Arkaig
H
Carn Mòr
2718
Ardechive
90
River Pean
Glen Pean
Gleann Cia-aig
A
Chia-aig Falls
Clunes
An Stac
2356
Sgurr nan Coireachan
3136
Sgurr Thuilm
3164
Allt Cuirnean
Gleann Camgharaidh
Allt Camgharaidh
Locheil Forest
Glen Mallie
River Mallie
Inver Mallie
Achnacarry
Clan Cameron
B8005
Bunarkaig
Loch Lochy
Lochan a' Bhrodainn
Meith Bheinn
2328
Lochan Tain Mhic Dhughaill
Sgurr an Ursainn
Gaor Bheinn or Gulvain
Meall a' Phubuill
2533
Beinn Bhàn
2612
Loch Beoraid
5
Achnanellan
Druim Gleann Laoigh
Glen Loy
River Loy
Gairlochy
Stronenaba
Slios Garbh
Glas-charn
2076
Sgurr an Utha
2610
River Finnan
Gleann Dubh Lighe
Gleann Fionnlighe
Fionn Lighe
Gleann Suileag
An t-Suileag
Stob a' Ghrianain
Druim Fada
B8004
Caledonian Canal
Brackletter
Commando Memorial
Spean Bridge
Ranochan
A830
14
Loch Eilt
Glen Finnan
Station
Viaduct
Glenfinnan
The Jacobite
Dubh Lighe
Muirshearlich
Highbridge
A82
80
Glenfinnan Monument NTS
Beinn an t-Sneachda
A
140
B
Kinlocheil
Corribeg
Fassfern
C
9
Achdalieu
D
141
Tor Castle
River Lochy
Leanachan Forest
2895
Beinn Odhar Bheag
2175
Croit Bheinn
Loch Shiel
90
Callop River
Loch Eil
A830
The Jacobite
Corpach
Treasures of the Earth
Banavie
Neptune's Staircase
Caol
Camaghael
Crofting
Torlundy
Creag Aoil
Nevis Range Gondola
20
South Garvan
Duisky
A861
Blaich
20
B8006
Lochyside
Ben Nevis Distillery
Victoria Bridge
Inverlochy
Sgorr Craobh a' Chaorainn
Glen Garvan
Meall nan Creag Leac
Achaphubuil
Camusnagaul

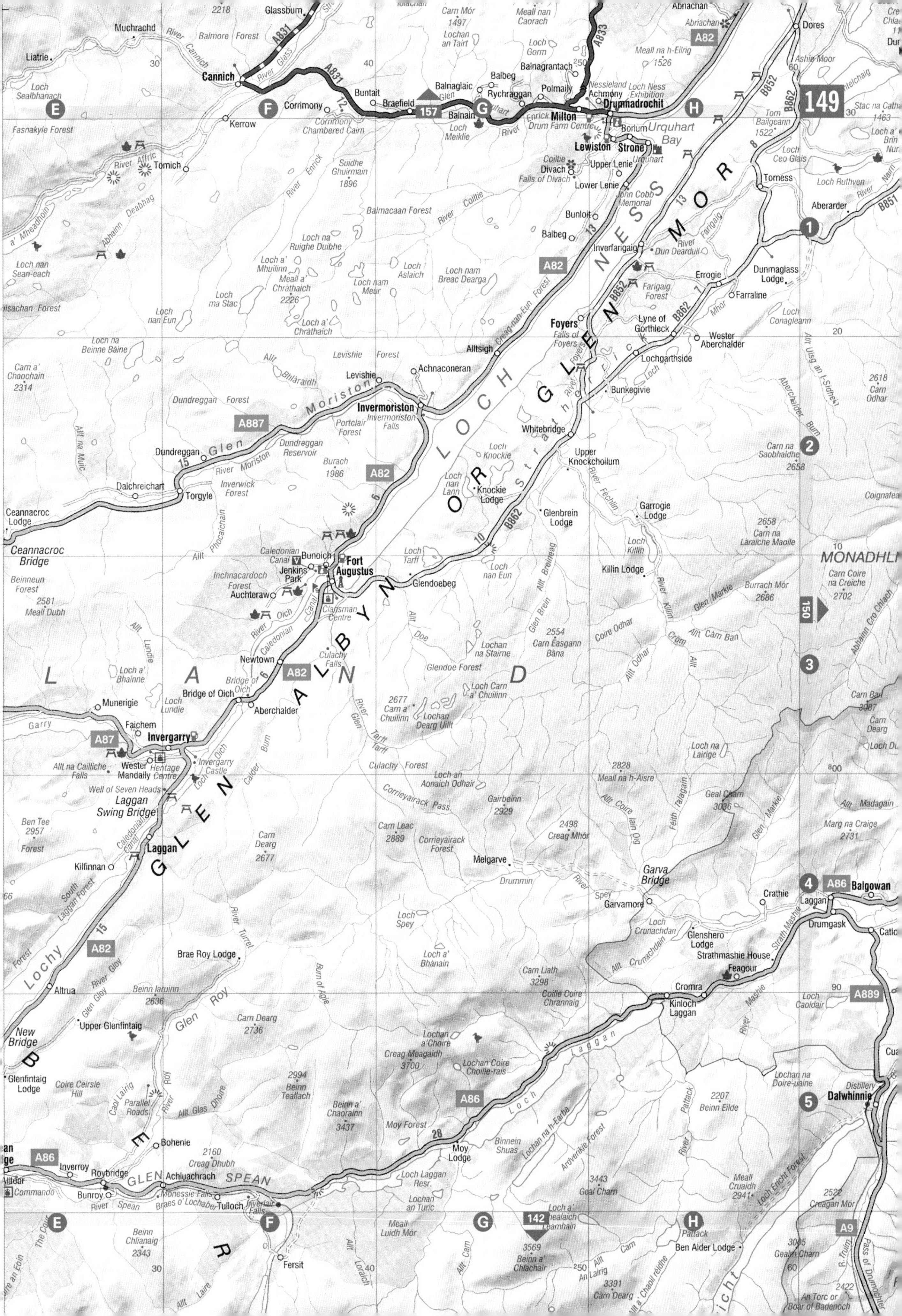

149
Glassburn
Muchrachd
Balmore Forest
Liatrie
River Cannich
Cannich
River Glass
A831
A833
Carn Mór 1497
Lochan an Tairt
Meall nan Caorach
Loch Gorm
Balnagrantach
Abriachan
Dores
Meall na h-Eilrig 1526
A82
Ashie Moor
Loch Sealbhanach
Buntait
Braefield
Balnaglaic
Balbeg
Rychraggan
Polmaily
Nessieland
Loch Ness Exhibition
Achmony
Drumnadrochit
Milton
Drum Farm Centre
Corrimony
Corrimony Chambered Cairn
157
Balnain
Loch Meiklie
River Enrick
Borlum
Urquhart Bay
Lewiston
Strone
Urquhart
B852
B862
Tom Bailgeann 1522
Stac na Cath 1463
Fasnakyle Forest
Kerrow
River Affric
Tomich
Suidhe Ghuirmain 1896
Coiltie
Divach
Falls of Divach
Upper Lenie
Lower Lenie
John Cobb Memorial
Torness
Loch Ceo Glais
Loch Ruthven
Aberarder
River Nairn
B851
Abhainn Deabhag
Balmacaan Forest
River Coiltie
Bunloit
Balbeg
Loch na Ruighe Duibhe
Inverfarigaig
Dun Deardail
River Farigaig
Loch nan Sean-each
Loch a' Mhuilinn
Meall a' Chràthaich 2226
Loch Aslaich
Loch nam Breac Dearga
Loch nam Meur
Errogie
Dunmaglass Lodge
Farigaig Forest
Farraline
Loch ma Stac
Loch nan Eun
Loch a' Chràthaich
Creag-nan-Eun Forest
Foyers
Falls of Foyers
Lyne of Gorthleck
Wester Aberchalder
Loch Conagleann
Loch na Beinne Bàine
Levishie Forest
Alltsigh
Lochgarthside
Carn a' Chaochain 2314
Allt Bhlàraidh
Levishie
Achnaconeran
Bunkegivie
Allt Uisg an t-Sidhein
2618 Carn Odhar
Dundreggan Forest
Glen Moriston
Invermoriston
Invermoriston Falls
Portclair Forest
A887
LOCH NESS
Whitebridge
Aberchalder Burn
Carn na Saobhaidhe 2658
Dundreggan
Dundreggan Reservoir
River Moriston
Burach 1986
Loch Knockie
Upper Knockchoilum
A82
Loch nan Lann
Knockie Lodge
Strath Errick
River Fechlin
Dalchreichart
Torgyle
Inverwick Forest
Coignafearn
Ceannacroc Lodge
Glenbrein Lodge
Garrogie Lodge
2658 Carn na Laraiche Maoile
Ceannacroc Bridge
Allt Phocaichain
Loch Killin
Caledonian Canal
Bunoich
Fort Augustus
Jenkins Park
Loch Tarff
Loch nan Eun
MONADHLIATH
Carn Coire na Creiche 2702
Beinneun Forest
Inchnacardoch Forest
Auchteraw
Glendoebeg
Allt Breineag
Killin Lodge
2581 Meall Dubh
Clansman Centre
River Oich
Glen Markie
Burrach Mór 2686
150
Allt Lundie
Allt Doe
Glen Brein
2554 Carn Easgann Bàna
Coire Odhar
Lochan na Stairne
River Killin
Allt Cam Ban
Abhainn Cro Chlach
Loch a' Bhainne
Newtown
Culachy Falls
Glendoe Forest
Allt Odhar
LAND
Bridge of Oich
Loch Carn a' Chuilinn
Carn Ban 3087
Munerigie
Loch Lundie
Aberchalder
2677 Carn a' Chuilinn
Lochan Dearg Uillt
Carn Dearg
Garry
Faichem
A87
Invergarry
Invergarry Castle
River Tarff
Loch na Lairige
Allt na Cailliche Falls
Wester Mandally
Heritage Centre
Culachy Forest
Calder Burn
Loch Oich
2828 Meall na h-Aisre
Well of Seven Heads
Laggan Swing Bridge
Loch an Aonaich Odhair
Corrieyairack Pass
Gairbeinn 2929
Allt Coire Iain Òig
Fèith Talagain
Geal Charn 3036
Allt Madagain
Ben Tee 2957
Forest
Caledonian Canal
Carn Dearg 2677
Carn Leac 2889
Corrieyairack Forest
2498 Creag Mhór
Marg na Craige 2731
Laggan
Kilfinnan
Melgarve
Drummin
River Spey
Garva Bridge
Garvamore
Crathie
A86
Balgowan
GLEN ALBYN OR GLEN MOR
South Laggan Forest
River Turret
Loch Spey
Loch Crunachdan
Glenshero Lodge
Drumgask
Strath Mashie
Catlodge
A82
Brae Roy Lodge
Loch a' Bhànain
Allt Crunachdain
Strathmashie House
Feagour
Loch Lochy
Forest
Altrua
River Gloy
Glen Gloy
Beinn Iaruinn 2636
Burn of Agie
Carn Liath 3298
Coille Coire Chrannaig
Cromra
Kinloch Laggan
Loch Caoldair
A889
River Mashie
New Bridge
Upper Glenfintaig
Glen Roy
Carn Dearg 2736
Lochan a'Choire
Creag Meagaidh 3700
Lochan Coire Choille-rais
Loch Laggan
Lochan na Doire-uaine
Glenfintaig Lodge
Coire Ceirsle Hill
Caol Lairig
Parallel Roads
River Roy
Allt Glas Dhoire
2994 Beinn Teallach
Beinn a' Chaorainn 3437
A86
Moy Forest
Lochan na h-Earba
Ardverikie Forest
Pattack
2207 Beinn Eilde
Distillery
Dalwhinnie
Bohenie
2160 Creag Dhubh
28
Moy Lodge
Binnein Shuas
River Pattack
Loch Ericht Forest
A86
Inverroy
Roybridge
Glen Spean
Achluachrach
Monessie Falls
Braes o' Lochaber
Tulloch
Inverlair Falls
Loch Laggan Resr.
Lochan an Turic
3443 Geal Charn
Meall Cruaidh 2941
2522 Creagan Mór
Bunroy
River Spean
Commando
Loch a' Bhealaich Leamhain
142
A9
Beinn Chlianaig 2343
Meall Luidh Mór
Pattack
Ben Alder Lodge
3005 Gealm Charn
R. Truim
Pass of Drumochter
Fersit
Allt Loraich
3569 Beinn a' Chlachair
Allt Cam
Allt An Lairig
3391 Carn Dearg
Allt a' Chaoil-reidhe
Allt Laire
An Torc or Boar of Badenoch 2422
E
F
G
H
1
2
3
4
5

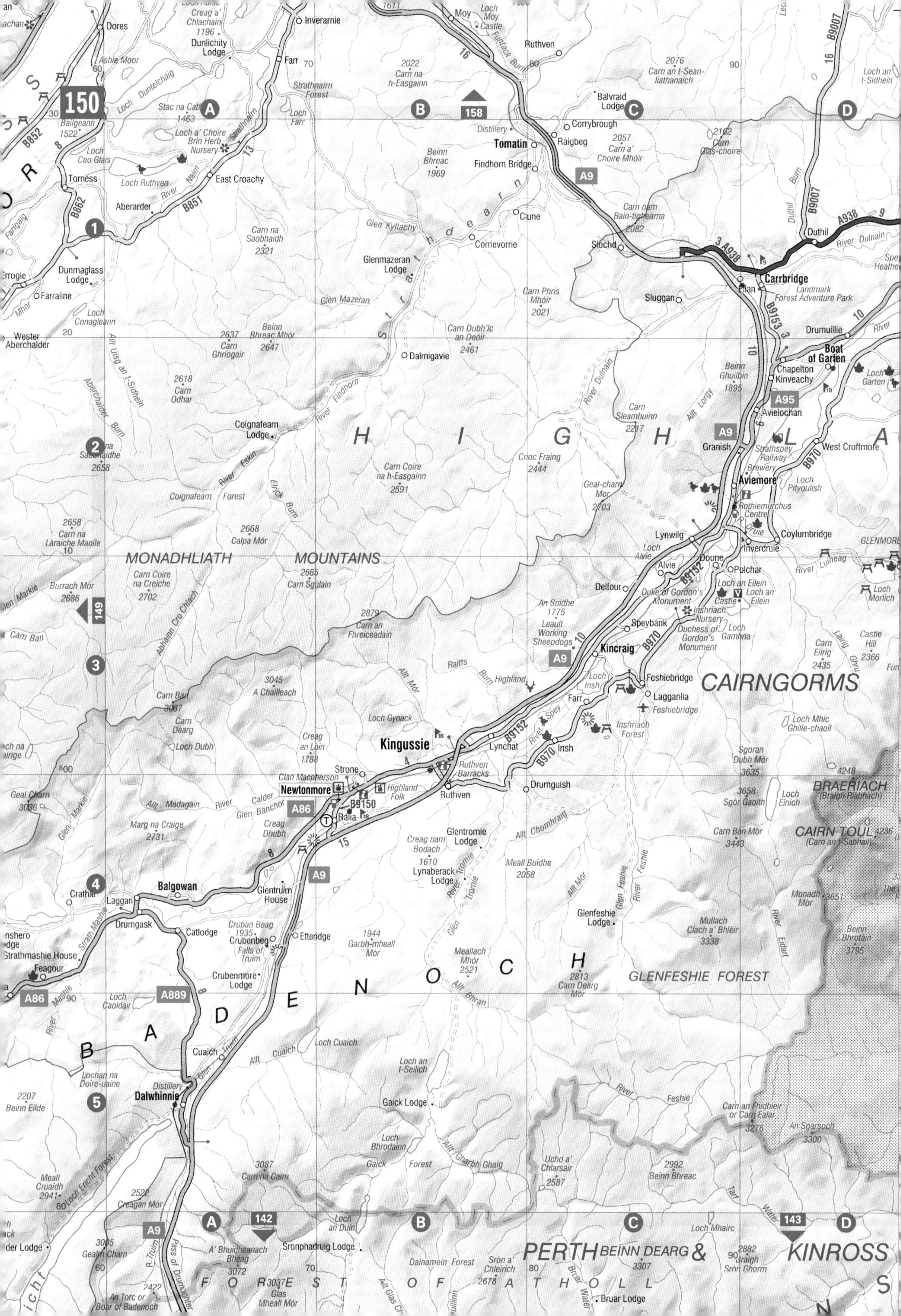
150
Dores
Inverarnie
Creag a' Chlachain 1196
Dunlichity Lodge
Ashie Moor
Farr
Loch Duntelchaig
Stac na Cath 1463
Bailgeann 1522
B852
Loch a' Choire
Brin Herb Nursery
Strathnairn
Strathnairn Forest
Loch Farr
Loch Ceo Glais
Torness
Loch Ruthven
East Croachy
River Nairn
B851
Aberarder
B862
Farigaig
Errogie
Dunmaglass Lodge
Farraline
Loch Conagleann
Wester Aberchalder
Moy
Loch Moy
Castle
Funtack Burn
Ruthven
2022 Carn na h-Easgainn
158
Distillery
Tomatin
Corrybrough
Raigbeg
Findhorn Bridge
Beinn Bhreac 1969
Balvraid Lodge
2076 Carn an t-Sean-liathanaich
2057 Carn a' Choire Mhóir
2162 Carn Glas-choire
Loch an t-Sidhein
B9007
A9
Clune
Corrievorrie
Glen Kyllachy
Carn nam Bain-tighearna 2082
Slochd
Duthil
Duthil Burn
A938
River Dulnain
Carrbridge
Ellan
Landmark Forest Adventure Park
Sluggan
Carn na Saobhaidh 2321
Glenmazeran Lodge
Glen Mazeran
Carn Phris Mhóir 2021
Carn Dubh'Ic an Deòir 2461
Dalmigavie
Strathdearn
B9153
Drumuillie
Boat of Garten
Chapelton
Kinveachy
Loch Garten
Beinn Ghuilbin 1895
A95
Avielochan
2637 Carn Ghriogair
Beinn Bhreac Mhór 2647
Allt Uisg an t-Sidhein
Aberchalder Burn
2618 Carn Odhar
Coignafearn Lodge
River Findhorn
River Dulnain
Carn Sleamhuinn 2217
Allt Lorgy
H I G H L A
Granish
Strathspey Railway
West Croftmore
Brewery
B970
Aviemore
Loch Pityoulish
Rothiemurchus Centre
Coylumbridge
Inverdruie
GLENMORE
Carn na Saobhaidhe 2658
River Eskin
Coignafearn Forest
Elrick Burn
Carn Coire na h-Easgainn 2591
Cnoc Fraing 2444
Geal-charn Mor 2703
2658 Carn na Laraiche Maoile
2668 Calpa Mór
Lynwilg
Loch Alvie
Alvie
Doune
Polchar
River Luineag
MONADHLIATH MOUNTAINS
2665 Carn Sgulain
Carn Coire na Creiche 2702
Burrach Mór 2686
Glen Markie
149
Abhainn Cro Chlach
2879 Carn an Fhreiceadain
Delfour
Duke of Gordon's Monument
B9152
Loch an Eilein
Castle
Loch Morlich
An Suidhe 1775
Inshriach Nursery
Speybank
Leault Working Sheepdogs
Duchess of Gordon's Monument
Loch Gamhna
Kincraig
Càrn Ban
Allt Mór
Raitts Burn
Highland
Carn Eilrig 2435
Castle Hill 2366
Lairig Ghru
3045 A Chailleach
Carn Ban 3087
Carn Dearg
Loch Dubh
Loch Gynack
Creag an Loin 1788
Kingussie
Loch Insh
Feshiebridge
Lagganlia
Feshiebridge
CAIRNGORMS
Farr
Lynchat
River Spey
Insh
Inshriach Forest
Loch Mhic Ghille-chaoil
Geal Charn 3036
Strone
Clan Macpherson
Newtonmore
Highland Folk
Ruthven Barracks
Ruthven
Drumguish
Sgoran Dubh Mór 3635
3658 Sgòr Gaoith
Loch Einich
4248 BRAERIACH (Braigh Riabhach)
Allt Madagain
River Calder
Glen Banchor
A86
B9150
Ralia
Marg na Craige 2731
Creag Dhubh
Creag nam Bodach 1610
Glentromie Lodge
Allt Chomhraig
Meall Buidhe 2058
Carn Ban Mór 3443
CAIRN TOUL 4236 (Carn an t-Sabhail)
Lynaberack Lodge
River Tromie
Glen Tromie
Glen Feshie
River Feshie
Allt Mór
Crathie
Laggan
Balgowan
Glentruim House
Drumgask
Catlodge
Strath Mashie
Strathmashie House
Feagour
Cruban Beag 1935
Crubenbeg
Falls of Truim
Etteridge
1944 Garbh-mheall Mór
Glenfeshie Lodge
Mullach Clach a' Bhlèir 3338
River Eidart
Monadh Mór 3651
Beinn Bhrotain 3795
Crubenmore Lodge
Meallach Mhór 2521
2813 Carn Dearg Mór
GLENFESHIE FOREST
A86
River Mashie
Loch Caoldair
A889
B A D E N O C H
Allt Bhran
Cuaich
Loch Cuaich
Allt Cuaich
Loch an t-Seilich
Lochan na Doire-uaine
Distillery
Dalwhinnie
2207 Beinn Eilde
Glen Truim
Gaick Lodge
River Feshie
Carn an Fhidhleir or Carn Ealar 3276
An Sgarsoch 3300
Loch Bhrodainn
Allt Gharbh Ghaig
Uchd a' Chlarsair 2587
2992 Beinn Bhreac
Tarf Water
Meall Cruaidh 2941
Loch Ericht Forest
3087 Carn na Caim
Gaick Forest
2522 Creagan Mór
A9
142
Loch an Duin
143
Loch Mhairc
3005 Geal Charn
A' Bhuidheanach Bheag 3072
Sronphadruig Lodge
PERTH & KINROSS
BEINN DEARG 3307
2882 Bràigh Sròn Ghorm
Dalnamein Forest
Sron a' Chleirich 2678
River Truim
Pass of Drumochter
FOREST OF ATHOLL
3037 Glas Mheall Mór
Allt Glas Choire
Bruar Water
Bruar Lodge
2422 An Torc or Boar of Badenoch
der Lodge

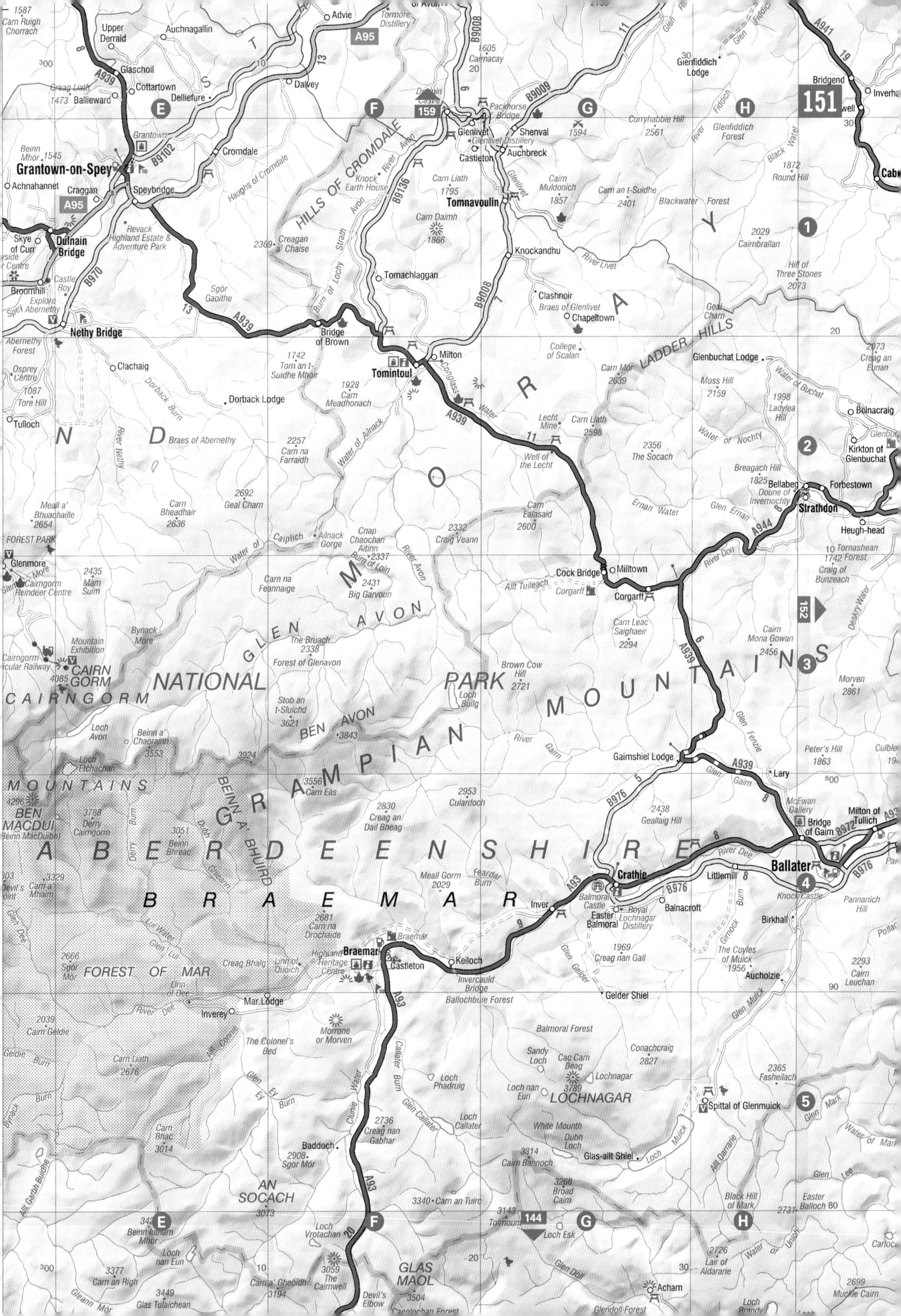
151
152
159
144
Grantown-on-Spey
Upper Derraid
Auchnagallin
Advie
Tormore Distillery
A95
B9008
Glaschoil
Cottartown
Dellifure
Dalvey
Greag Liath 1473
Ballieward
Grantown
Beinn Mhòr 1545
Cromdale
B9102
Achnahannet
Craggan
Speybridge
Haughs of Cromdale
HILLS OF CROMDALE
Knock Earth House
Revack Highland Estate & Adventure Park
Skye of Curr
Dulnain Bridge
Broomhill
Castle Roy
Explore Abernethy
B970
Nethy Bridge
Abernethy Forest
Osprey Centre
1087 Tore Hill
Tulloch
Sgòr Gaoithe
A939
Creagan a' Chaise 2369
Burn of Lochy
Strath Avon
River Avon
B9136
Bridge of Brown
Tomachlaggan
Drumin Castle
Packhorse Bridge
Glenlivet
Glenlivet Distillery
Castleton
Auchbreck
Shenval
1594
Carn Liath 1795
Tomnavoulin
Carn Daimh 1866
Knockandhu
River Livet
Clashnoir
Braes of Glenlivet
Chapeltown
Cairn Muldonich 1857
Carn an t-Suidhe 2401
Blackwater Forest
Corryhabbie Hill 2561
Glenfiddich Forest
Glenfiddich Lodge
Bridgend
Inverharroch
Cabrach
1872 Round Hill
2029 Cairnbrallan
Hill of Three Stones 2073
Geal Charn
LADDER HILLS
Glenbuchat Lodge
Moss Hill 2159
Water of Buchat
1998 Ladylea Hill
Belnacraig
Kirkton of Glenbuchat
Water of Nochty
2356 The Socach
Breagach Hill 1825
Bellabeg
Doune of Invernochty
Forbestown
Strathdon
Heugh-head
Glen Ernan
Ernan Water
A944
River Don
Tornashean Forest 1742
Craig of Bunzeach
Tomintoul
Milton
Conglass Water
Clachaig
Dorback Lodge
Dorback Burn
Tom an t-Suidhe Mhòr 1742
1928 Carn Meadhonach
College of Scalan
Carn Mòr 2639
Lecht Mine
Carn Liath 2598
Well of the Lecht
Braes of Abernethy
River Nethy
2257 Carn na Farraidh
Water of Ailnack
2692 Geal Charn
Carn Bheadhair 2636
Meall a' Bhuachaille 2654
FOREST PARK
Glenmore
Glenmore Cairngorm Reindeer Centre
2435 Meall Suim
Water of Caiplich
Ailnack Gorge
Cnap Chaochan Aitinn 2337
Burn of Loin
2332 Craig Veann
Carn Ealasaid 2600
Cock Bridge
Milltown
Allt Tuileach
Corgarff
Carn na Feannaige
2431 Big Garvoun
GLEN AVON
The Bruach 2338
Forest of Glenavon
Carn Leac Saighaeir 2294
Cairn Mona Gowan 2456
Morven 2861
Bynack More
Mountain Exhibition
Cairngorm Funicular Railway
CAIRN GORM 4085
CAIRNGORM
NATIONAL PARK
Brown Cow Hill 2721
Loch Builg
Stob an t-Sluichd 3621
BEN AVON
3843
Loch Avon
Beinn a' Chaorainn 3553
3924
Loch Etchachan
GRAMPIAN MOUNTAINS
MOUNTAINS
River Gairn
Glen Fenzie
Gairnshiel Lodge
Glen Gairn
Lary
Peter's Hill 1863
McEwan Gallery
Bridge of Gairn
Milton of Tullich
B972
BEN MACDUI 4296
3788 Derry Cairngorm
BEINN A' BHUIRD
3556 Carn Eas
2953 Culardoch
2830 Creag an Dail Bheag
B976
2438 Geallaig Hill
3051 Beinn Bhreac
ABERDEENSHIRE
Derry Burn
Dubh Ghleann
River Dee
Crathie
Littlemill
Ballater
3329 Carn a' Mhaim
Devil's Point
Meall Gorm 2029
Feardar Burn
BRAEMAR
Inver
Balmoral Castle
Royal Lochnagar Distillery
Balnacroft
Knock Castle
Pannanich Hill
Easter Balmoral
Birkhall
Glen Dee
Lui Water
Glen Lui
2681 Carn na Drochaide
Braemar
Highland Heritage Centre
Castleton
Keiloch
Invercauld Bridge
Ballochbuie Forest
1969 Creag nan Gall
Glen Gelder
The Coyles of Muick 1956
Aucholzie
2293 Cairn Leuchan
2666 Sgor Mòr
FOREST OF MAR
Creag Bhalg
Linn of Quoich
Linn of Dee
Mar Lodge
Inverey
Gelder Shiel
Glen Muick
2039 Cairn Geldie
Morrone or Morven
The Colonel's Bed
Balmoral Forest
Conachcraig 2827
Carn Liath 2676
Geldie Burn
Glen Ey
Callater Burn
Clunie Water
Loch Phadruig
Sandy Loch
Cac Carn Beag 3789
Lochnagar
LOCHNAGAR
Loch nan Eun
2365 Fasheilach
Spittal of Glenmuick
Glen Mark
Carn Bhac 3014
2736 Creag nan Gabhar
Glen Callater
Loch Callater
White Mounth
Dubh Loch
Glas-allt Shiel
Loch Muick
Allt Darrarie
Baddoch
2908 Sgor Mòr
Cairn Bannoch 3314
3268 Broad Cairn
AN SOCACH 3073
3340 Carn an Tuirc
Black Hill of Mark
Easter Balloch
3143 Tolmount
Loch Esk
Beinn Iutharn Mhor
Loch Vrotachan
Loch nan Eun
3377 Carn an Righ
3059 The Cairnwell
Carn a' Gheoidh 3194
GLAS MAOL 3504
Devil's Elbow
Glen Doll
Lair of Aldararie 2726
Acharn
2699 Muckle Cairn
3449 Glas Tulaichean
Glendoll Forest
Loch Brandy
Allt Garbh Buidhe
Water of Unich
A93
A941
A939

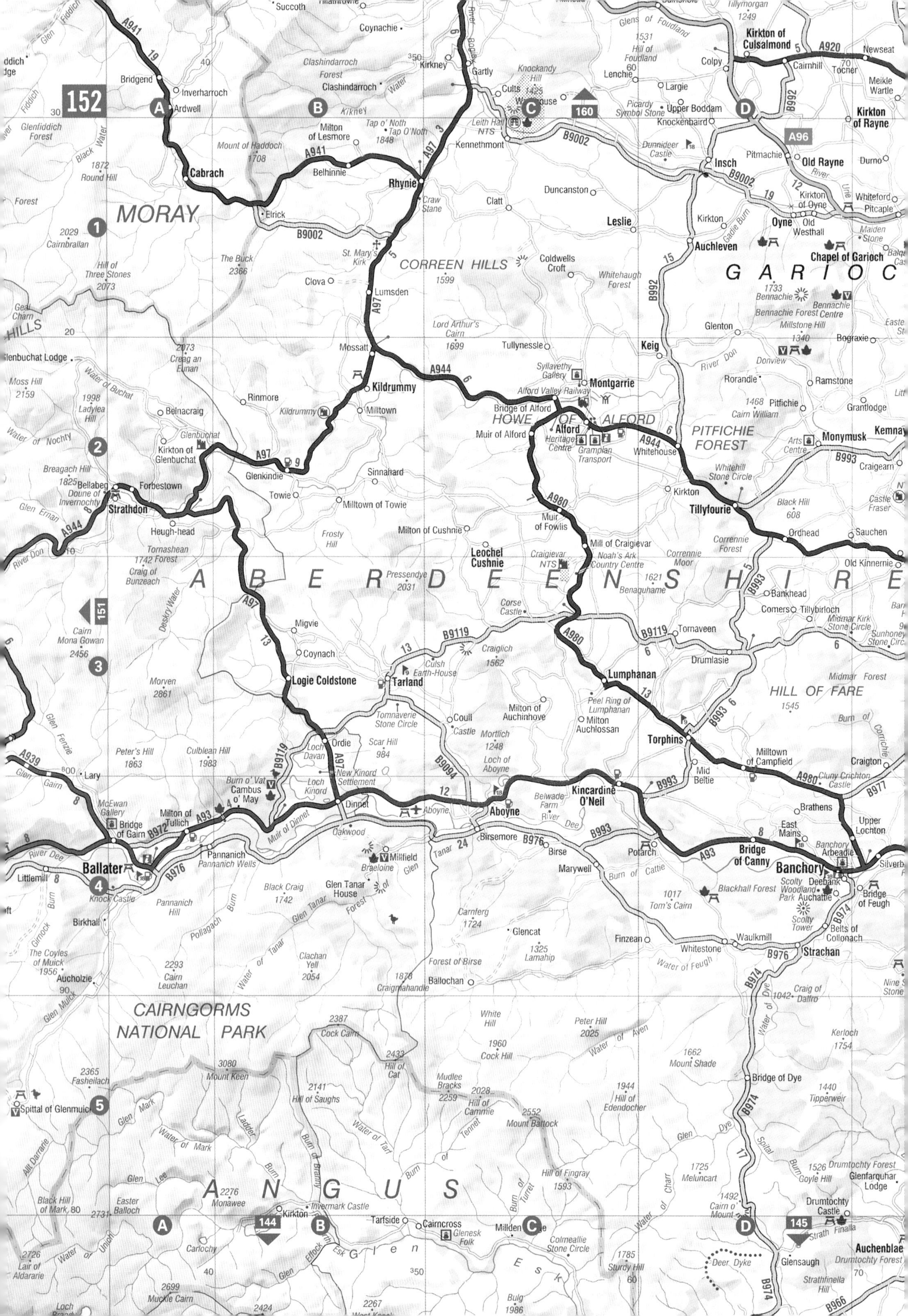
152
160
151
144
145
MORAY
ABERDEENSHIRE
GARIOC
ANGUS
CAIRNGORMS NATIONAL PARK
CORREEN HILLS
HOWE OF ALFORD
PITFICHIE FOREST
HILL OF FARE
A941
A97
A944
A980
A93
A939
A920
A96
B9002
B9119
B9094
B993
B976
B974
B977
B966
B992
B972
Succoth
Coynachie
Clashindarroch Forest
Clashindarroch
Kirkney
Gartly
Cults
Knockandy Hill 1425
Leith Hall NTS
Kennethmont
Glens of Foudland
Hill of Foudland 1531
Lenchie
Largie
Picardy Symbol Stone
Upper Boddam
Knockenbaird
Dunnideer Castle
Insch
Colpy
Kirkton of Culsalmond
Newseat
Cairnhill
Tocher
Meikle Wartle
Kirkton of Rayne
Old Rayne
Pitmachie
Durno
Tillymorgan 1249
Bridgend
Inverharroch
Ardwell
Glenfiddich Forest
Black Water
Round Hill 1872
Cabrach
Mount of Haddoch 1708
Milton of Lesmore
Tap o' Noth 1848
Belhinnie
Rhynie
Craw Stane
Elrick
Clatt
Duncanston
Leslie
Kirkton
Kirkton of Oyne
Oyne
Old Westhall
Whiteford
Pitcaple
Maiden Stone
Auchleven
Chapel of Garioch
Cairnbrallan 2029
Hill of Three Stones 2073
The Buck 2366
St. Mary's Kirk
Clova
Lumsden
Coldwells Croft
Whitehaugh Forest
Bennachie 1733
Bennachie Forest Centre
Millstone Hill 1340
Bograxie
Glenton
Keig
Lord Arthur's Cairn 1699
Tullynessle
Mossatt
Creag an Eunan 2073
Glenbuchat Lodge
Moss Hill 2159
Ladylea Hill 1998
Water of Buchat
Belnacraig
Rinmore
Kildrummy
Milltown
Syllavethy Gallery
Montgarrie
Alford Valley Railway
Bridge of Alford
Alford
Muir of Alford
Heritage Centre
Grampian Transport
Whitehouse
Rorandle
Ramstone
Donview
Pitfichie
Cairn William
Grantlodge
Monymusk
Kemnay
Arts Centre
Craigearn
Castle Fraser
Water of Nochty
Kirkton of Glenbuchat
Glenkindie
Sinnahard
Breagach Hill 1825
Bellabeg
Forbestown
Doune of Invernochty
Strathdon
Heugh-head
Towie
Milltown of Towie
Milton of Cushnie
Muir of Fowlis
Kirkton
Tillyfourie
Whitehill Stone Circle
Black Hill 608
Ordhead
Sauchen
Tornashean Forest 1742
Craig of Bunzeach
Frosty Hill
Leochel Cushnie
Mill of Craigievar
Craigievar NTS
Noah's Ark Country Centre
Correnie Moor
Corrennie Forest
Old Kinnernie
Pressendye 2031
Benaquhame 1621
Bankhead
Comers
Tillybirloch
Midmar Kirk Stone Circle
Sunhoney Stone Circle
Corse Castle
Cairn Mona Gowan 2456
Migvie
Coynach
Craiglich 1562
Tornaveen
Drumlasie
Culsh Earth-House
Tarland
Logie Coldstone
Morven 2861
Lumphanan
Peel Ring of Lumphanan
Milton of Auchinhove
Milton Auchlossan
Midmar Forest
Tomnaverie Stone Circle
Coull Castle
Mortlich 1248
Loch of Aboyne
Torphins
Milltown of Campfield
Craigton
Cluny Crichton Castle
Mid Beltie
Peter's Hill 1863
Culblean Hill 1983
Scar Hill 984
Ordie
Loch Davan
Loch Kinord
New Kinord Settlement
Burn o' Vat
Cambus o' May
Lary
Glen Gairn
McEwan Gallery
Bridge of Gairn
Milton of Tullich
Muir of Dinnet
Dinnet
Aboyne
Kincardine O'Neil
Belwade Farm
Brathens
East Mains
Upper Lochton
Banchory
Arbeadie
Silverb
Bridge of Canny
Oakwood
Birsemore
Birse
Marywell
Potarch
Ballater
Pannanich
Pannanich Wells
Millfield
Braeloine
Glen Tanar House
Littlemill
Knock Castle
Pannanich Hill
Black Craig 1742
Tom's Cairn 1017
Blackhall Forest
Scolty Woodland Park
Auchattie
Deebank
Bridge of Feugh
Scolty Tower
Belts of Collonach
Birkhall
Carnferg 1724
Glencat
Finzean
Waulkmill
Whitestone
Strachan
Lamahip 1325
Water of Feugh
The Coyles of Muick 1956
Cairn Leuchan 2293
Clachan Yell 2054
Forest of Birse
Ballochan
Craigmahandle 1878
Aucholzie
Craig of Dalfro 1042
Kerloch 1754
Nine Stone
Glen Muick
Cock Cairn 2387
White Hill
Peter Hill 2025
Water of Aven
Cock Hill 1960
Mount Shade 1662
Fasheilach 2365
Mount Keen 3080
Hill of Cat 2433
Mudlee Bracks 2259
Hill of Saughs 2141
Hill of Cammie 2028
Mount Battock 2552
Hill of Edendocher 1944
Bridge of Dye
Tipperweir 1440
Spittal of Glenmuick
Glen Mark
Water of Mark
Water of Tarf
Hill of Fingray 1593
Meluncart 1725
Drumtochty Forest 1526
Goyle Hill
Glenfarquhar Lodge
Alltl Darrarie
Monawee 2276
Black Hill of Mark 2731
Easter Balloch
Kirkton
Invermark Castle
Tarfside
Cairncross
Glenesk Folk
Millden
Colmeallie Stone Circle
Water of Charr
Cairn o' Mount 1492
Drumtochty Castle
Strath Finalla
Auchenblae
Drumtochty Forest
Carlochy
Lair of Aldararie 2726
Water of Unich
Glen Esk
Sturdy Hill 1785
Deer Dyke
Glensaugh
Strathfinella Hill
Muckle Cairn 2699
Bulg 1986
River Dee
River Don
River Bogie

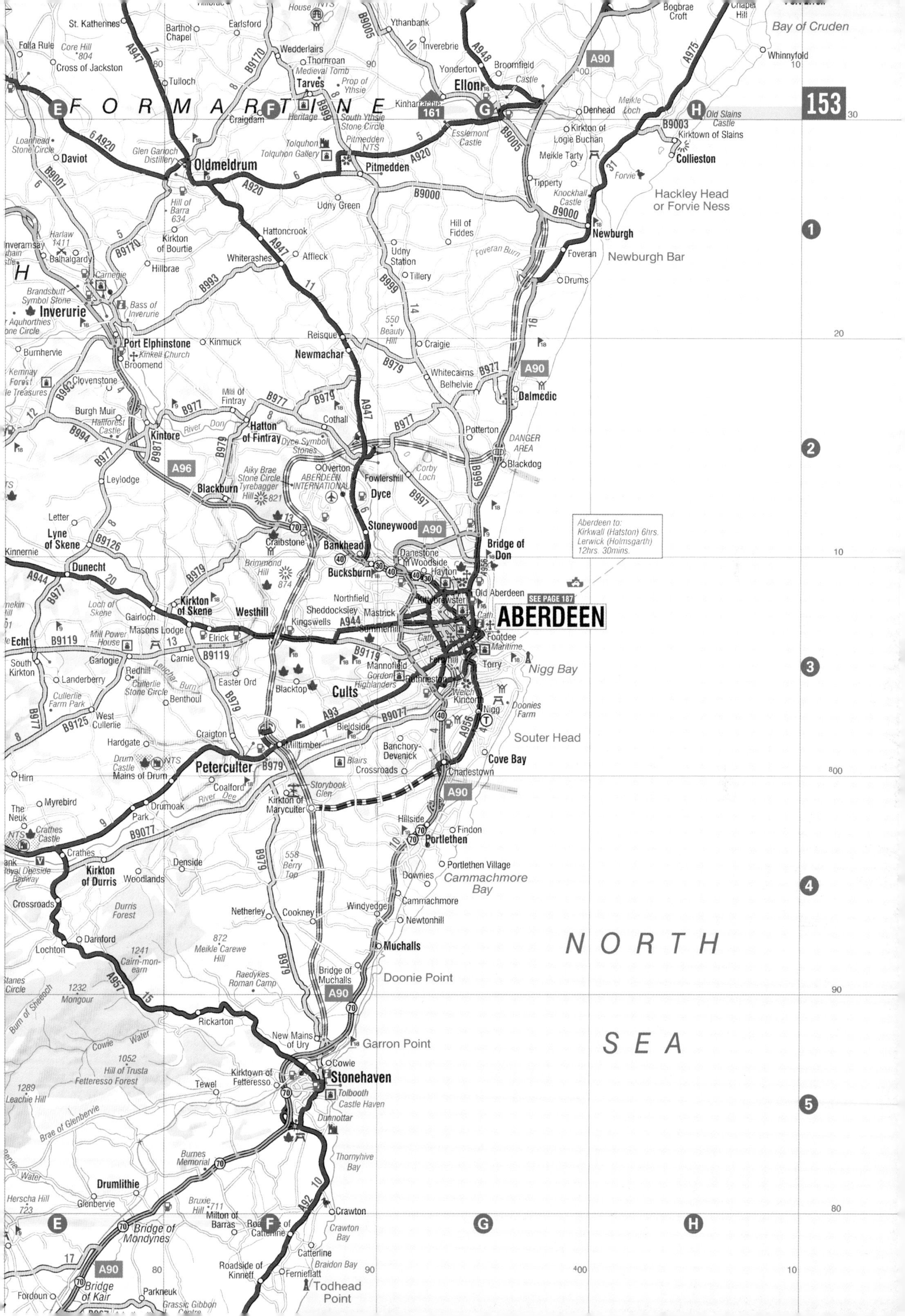

153
Bay of Cruden
Bogbrae Croft
Whinnyfold
St. Katherines
Barthol Chapel
Earlsford
Ythanbank
Inverebrie
Folla Rule
Core Hill 804
Cross of Jackston
Wedderlairs
Thornroan
Medieval Tomb
Prop of Ythsie
Yonderton
Broomfield
Ellon
Castle
Tulloch
Tarves
A947
A948
A975
A90
B9005
B9170
F O R M A R T I N E
Kinharrachie
161
Craigdam
Heritage
South Ythsie Stone Circle
Pitmedden NTS
Tolquhon
Tolquhon Gallery
Esslemont Castle
Denhead
Meikle Loch
Old Slains Castle
Kirkton of Logie Buchan
B9003
Kirktown of Slains
Collieston
Meikle Tarty
Loanhead Stone Circle
Daviot
Glen Garioch Distillery
Oldmeldrum
Pitmedden
A920
B9001
Forvie
Hackley Head or Forvie Ness
Tipperty
Knockhall Castle
Udny Green
B9000
Hill of Barra 634
Hill of Fiddes
Newburgh
Harlaw 1411
Inveramsay
Balhalgardy
Kirkton of Bourtie
Hattoncrook
Udny Station
Foveran Burn
Foveran
Newburgh Bar
Whiterashes
Affleck
Hillbrae
Carnegie
Tillery
Drums
B9170
B993
B999
Brandsbutt Symbol Stone
Bass of Inverurie
Inverurie
Aquhorthies Stone Circle
Reisque
550 Beauty Hill
Craigie
Port Elphinstone
Kinmuck
Kinkell Church
Broomend
Burnhervie
Newmachar
B979
Whitecairns
Belhelvie
B977
Kemnay Forest
Clovenstone
Mill of Fintray
Burgh Muir
Hallforest Castle
Kintore
River Don
Hatton of Fintray
Cothall
Dalmadie
Potterton
DANGER AREA
Blackdog
B994
B987
A96
Leylodge
Dyce Symbol Stones
Overton
Aiky Brae Stone Circle
Tyrebagger Hill 821
Blackburn
ABERDEEN INTERNATIONAL
Fowlershill
Corby Loch
Dyce
B997
Letter
Lyne of Skene
B9126
Craibstone
Stoneywood
Bankhead
Danestone
Woodside
Bridge of Don
Hayton
Aberdeen to:
Kirkwall (Hatston) 6hrs.
Lerwick (Holmsgarth) 12hrs. 30mins.
Kinnernie
Dunecht
A944
Brimmond Hill 874
Bucksburn
B977
Loch of Skene
Gairloch
Kirkton of Skene
Westhill
Northfield
Sheddocksley
Mastrick
Kingswells
Kittybrewster
Old Aberdeen
SEE PAGE 187
ABERDEEN
Summerhill
Cath
Footdee
Maritime
Mill Power House
Masons Lodge
Elrick
Echt
B9119
South Kirkton
Carnie
Garlogie
Landerberry
Redhill
Cullerlie Stone Circle
Leuchar Burn
Easter Ord
Blacktop
Cults
Mannofield
Gordon Highlanders
Ruthrieston
Torry
Nigg Bay
Cullerlie Farm Park
West Cullerlie
B9125
Benthoul
Welch
Kincorth
Nigg
Doonies Farm
A93
B9077
A956
Hardgate
Craigton
Bieldside
Banchory-Devenick
Souter Head
Drum Castle
Mains of Drum
NTS
Peterculter
Milltimber
Blairs
Crossroads
Cove Bay
Charlestown
Hirn
Coalford
River Dee
Storybook Glen
Kirkton of Maryculter
Myrebird
Drumoak
The Neuk
Park
Crathes Castle
Crathes
Royal Deeside Railway
Hillside
Findon
Portlethen
Kirkton of Durris
Woodlands
Denside
558 Berry Top
Portlethen Village
Downies
Cammachmore Bay
Crossroads
Durris Forest
Cammachmore
Netherley
Cookney
Windyedge
Newtonhill
Darnford
Lochton
872 Meikle Carewe Hill
1241 Cairn-mon-earn
Muchalls
NORTH
Raedykes Roman Camp
Bridge of Muchalls
Doonie Point
Stanes Circle
1232 Mongour
A957
Burn of Sheeoch
Rickarton
Cowie Water
New Mains of Ury
Garron Point
SEA
1052 Hill of Trusta
Fetteresso Forest
Cowie
Kirktown of Fetteresso
Stonehaven
1289 Leachie Hill
Tewel
Tolbooth
Castle Haven
Brae of Glenbervie
Dunnottar
Burnes Memorial
Thornyhive Bay
Bervie Water
Drumlithie
A92
Herscha Hill 723
Glenbervie
Bruxie Hill 711
Milton of Barras
Roadside of Catterline
Crawton
Crawton Bay
Bridge of Mondynes
Catterline
Braidon Bay
Roadside of Kinneff
Fernieflatt
Todhead Point
A90
Bridge of Kair
Fordoun
Parkneuk
Grassic Gibbon Centre

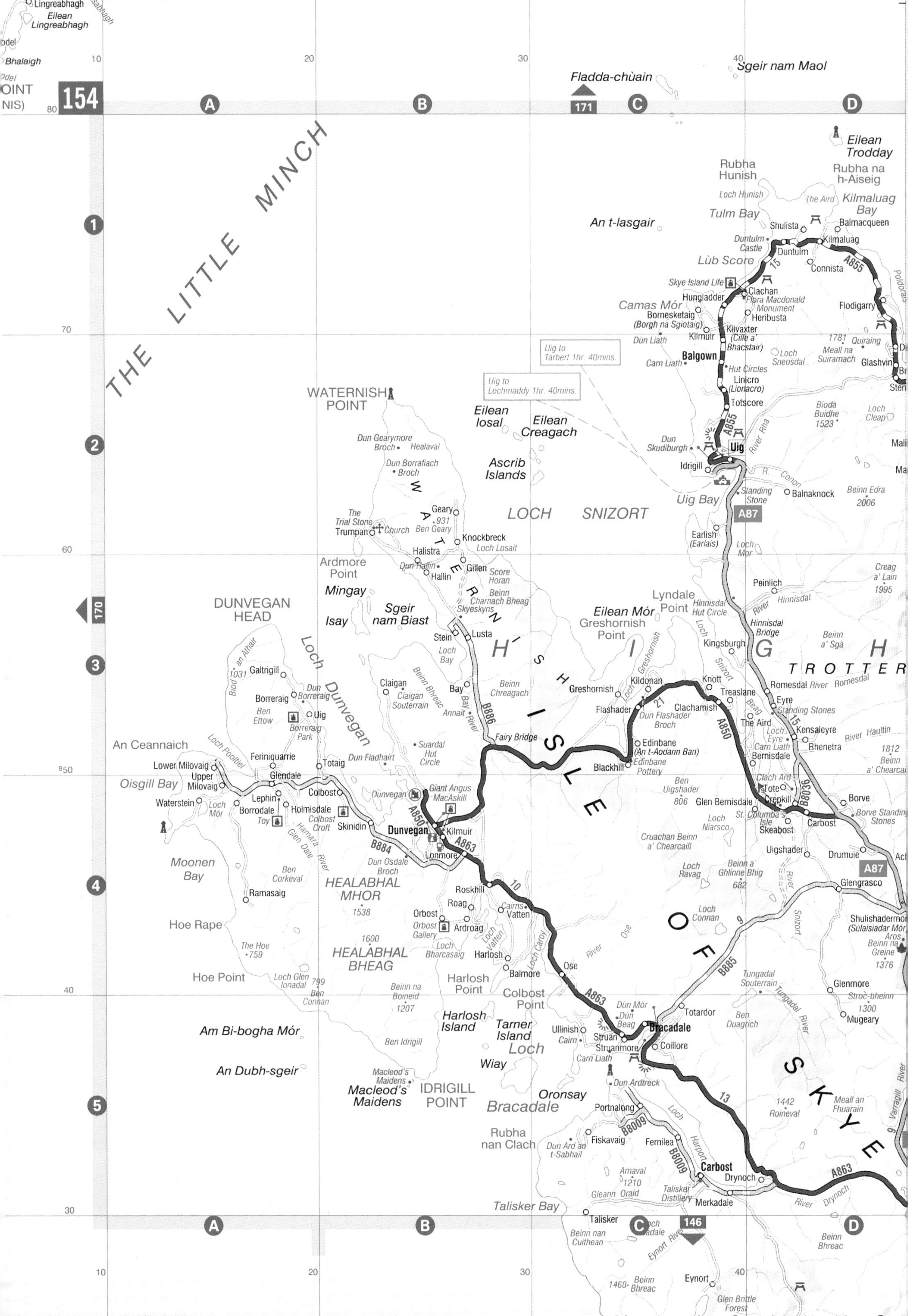

154
171
146
170
A
B
C
D
1
2
3
4
5
10
20
30
40
80
70
60
50
THE LITTLE MINCH
Lingreabhagh
Eilean Lingreabhagh
Bhalaigh
Fladda-chùain
Sgeir nam Maol
Eilean Trodday
Rubha Hunish
Rubha na h-Aiseig
Loch Hunish
The Aird
Kilmaluag Bay
Tulm Bay
An t-Iasgair
Shulista
Balmacqueen
Duntulm Castle
Duntulm
Kilmaluag
Lùb Score
Connista
A855
15
Skye Island Life
Clachan
Flora Macdonald Monument
Hungladder
Camas Mór
Bornesketaig (Borgh na Sgiotaig)
Heribusta
Kilvaxter (Cille a' Bhacstair)
Kilmuir
Dùn Liath
Flodigarry
Quiraing
1781
Meall na Suiramach
Glashvin
Uig to Tarbert 1hr. 40mins.
Uig to Lochmaddy 1hr. 40mins.
Balgown
Carn Liath
Loch Sneosdal
Hut Circles
Linicro (Lionacro)
Totscore
Bioda Buidhe 1523
Loch Cleap
WATERNISH POINT
Eilean Iosal
Eilean Creagach
Dun Skudiburgh
Uig
Idrigill
River Rha
R. Conon
Dun Gearymore Broch
Healaval
Dun Borrafiach Broch
Ascrib Islands
Standing Stone
Balnaknock
Beinn Edra 2006
Uig Bay
A87
LOCH SNIZORT
The Trial Stone
Trumpan
Church
Geary
931 Ben Geary
Knockbreck
Loch Losait
Halistra
Earlish (Earlais)
Loch Mor
Ardmore Point
Dun Hallin
Hallin
Gillen
Score Horan
Beinn Charnach Bheag
Skyeskyns
Peinlich
Hinnisdal
Creag a' Lain 1995
Mingay
Isay
Sgeir nam Biast
DUNVEGAN HEAD
Lyndale Point
Hinnisdal Hut Circle
Eilean Mór
Greshornish Point
River Hinnisdal Bridge
Beinn a' Sgà
Stein
Lusta
Loch Bay
Kingsburgh
Loch Greshornish
Loch Snizort Beag
TROTTERNISH
Loch Dunvegan
Biod an Athair
1031
Galtrigill
Dun Borreraig
Borreraig
Ben Ettow
Uig
Borreraig Park
Claigan
Claigan Souterrain
Beinn Bhreac
Bay
Annait
Bay River
B886
Beinn Chreagach
Greshornish
Kildonan
Knott
Treaslane
Romesdal River
Romesdal
Eyre
Standing Stones
Flashader
Dun Flashader Broch
21
Clachamish
A850
The Aird
Kensaleyre
Eyre
Loch Eyre
Rhenetra
River Haultin
An Ceannaich
Loch Pooltiel
Fairy Bridge
Suardal Hut Circle
Edinbane (An t-Aodann Ban)
Edinbane Pottery
Carn Liath
Bernisdale
1812 Beinn a' Chearcall
Lower Milovaig
Upper Milovaig
Feriniquarrie
Glendale
Totaig
Dun Fiadhairt
Blackhill
Oisgill Bay
Colbost
Dunvegan
Giant Angus MacAskill
Ben Uigshader 806
Glen Bernisdale
Clach Ard
Tote
Skeabost
Borve
Borve Standing Stones
Waterstein
Loch Mór
Lephin
Borrodale
Holmisdale
Colbost Croft
Toy
Glen Dale
Hamara River
Skinidin
A850
Kilmuir
A863
Lonmore
St. Columba's Isle
Skeabost
Carbost
B8036
Loch Niarsco
Cruachan Beinn a' Chearcall
Uigshader
Drumuie
B884
Dun Osdale Broch
Moonen Bay
Ben Corkeval
HEALABHAL MHOR 1538
Roskhill
10
Roag
Loch Ravag
Beinn a' Ghlinne Bhig 682
River Snizort
Glengrasco
Ramasaig
Orbost
Orbost Gallery
Ardroag
Cairns
Vatten
Loch Vatten
Loch Connan
Shulishadermor (Sùlaisiadar Mòr)
Aros
Beinn na Greine 1376
Hoe Rape
The Hoe 759
1600
HEALABHAL BHEAG
Loch Bharcasaig
Harlosh
Loch Caroy
River Ose
Ose
B885
9
Hoe Point
Loch Glen Ionadal
799
Ben Connan
Beinn na Boineid 1207
Harlosh Point
Balmore
Colbost Point
Tungadal Souterrain
Tungadal River
Glenmore
Stroc-bheinn 1300
Mugeary
Am Bi-bogha Mór
Harlosh Island
Tarner Island
Dùn Mór
Dùn Beag
Totardor
Ben Duagrich
Bracadale
Ullinish
Cairn
Struan
Struanmore
Coillore
Ben Idrigill
Loch Wiay
Carn Liath
An Dubh-sgeir
Macleod's Maidens
IDRIGILL POINT
Dun Ardtreck
Oronsay
13
Loch Bracadale
Portnalong
Loch Harport
1442 Roineval
Meall an Fhuarain
SKYE
ISLE OF
B8009
Rubha nan Clach
Dun Ard an t-Sabhail
Fiskavaig
Fernilea
Carbost
Drynoch
A863
Arnaval 1210
Gleann Oraid
Talisker Distillery
Merkadale
River Drynoch
Talisker Bay
Talisker
Loch Eynort
Eynort River
Beinn nan Cuithean
Beinn Bhreac
1460 Beinn Bhreac
Eynort
Glen Brittle Forest
Varragill River

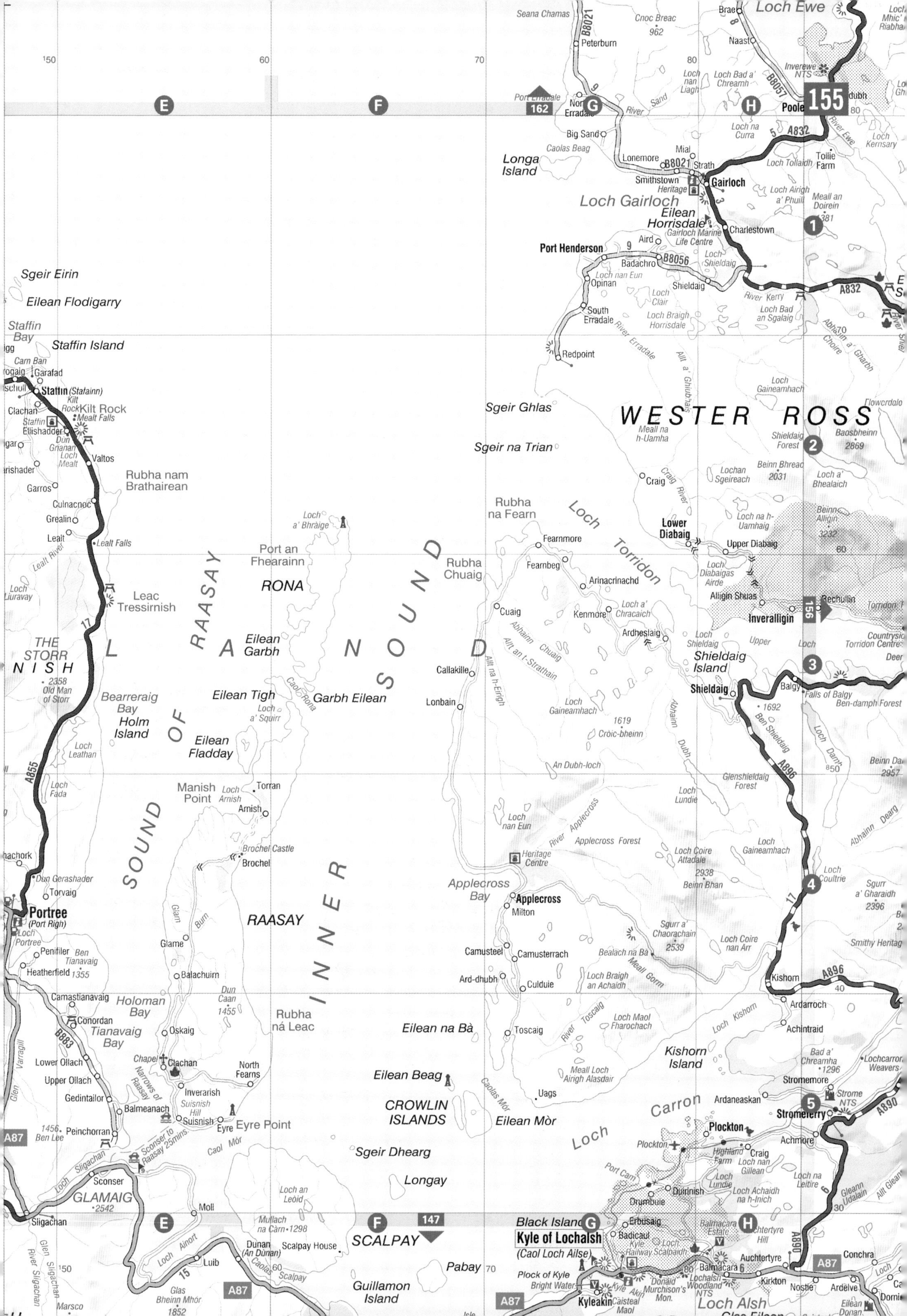

162

156

147

Loch Ewe

Loch Mhic' Riabha

Brae

Cnoc Breac
962

B8021

Peterburn

Naast

Inverewe
NTS

80

Poolewe

Loch Bad a' Chreamh

Loch na Curra

A832

River Ewe

Loch Kernsary

Loch dubh

Port Erradale

Nor
Erradale

G

River Sand

Big Sand

Loch nan Liagh

Toilie Farm

Caolas Beag

Mial

Lonemore

Strath

Tollie

H

Longa
Island

B8021

Smithstown

Gairloch

Loch Tollaidh

Loch Gairloch

Heritage

Loch Airigh a' Phuill

Eilean
Horrisdale

Meall an
Doirein
381

1

Port Henderson

Aird

Gairloch Marine
Life Centre

Charlestown

B8056

Loch-
Shieldaig

A832

ES

Badachro

Loch nan Eun

Shieldaig

River Kerry

Opinan

Loch Clair

Loch Bad an Sgalaig

Abhuinn a' Gharbh Choire

South
Erradale

Loch Braigh
Horrisdale

River Erradale

River Snel

Redpoint

WESTER ROSS

Sgeir Eirin

Staffin
Bay

Eilean Flodigarry

Sgeir Ghlas

Meall na h-Uamha

Shieldaig
Forest

Baosbheinn
2869

Flowerdale

Staffin Island

Sgeir na Trian

Craig River

Lochan Sgeireach

Beinn Bhreac
2031

Loch a' Bhealaich

2

igg

Carn Ban

Garafad

Craig

Beinn
Alligin
3232

Loch na h-Uamhaig

60

rogaig

choll

Staffin (Stafainn)

Kilt
Rock

Kilt Rock

Rubha na Fearn

Loch Torridon

Lower
Diabaig

Upper Diabaig

Clachan

Mealt Falls

Fearnmore

Loch
Diabaigas
Airde

Garros

Staffin

Ellishadder

Dun
Gnanan

Loch
Mealt

Valtos

Fearnbeg

Arinacrinachd

Alligin Shuas

Bechullin

Torridon F

 rishader

Grealin

Rubha nam
Brathairean

Kenmore

Loch a' Chracaich

Inveralligin

156

Countryside
Torridon Centre

Lealt

Lealt Falls

Port an
Fhearainn

Ardheslaig

Upper
Loch
Shieldaig

Upper
Loch

Deer

Loch
Liuravay

Lealt River

Leac
Tressirnish

RONA

Rubha
Chuaig

Cuaig

Abhainn Chuaig

Shieldaig
Island

Shieldaig

3

THE
STORR

2358
Old Man
of Storr

Eilean
Garbh

Port an
Fhearainn

Callakille

Allt an t-Srathain

Balgy

Falls of Balgy

Ben-damph Forest

NISH

Bearreraig
Bay

Holm
Island

Eilean Tigh

Garbh Eilean

Loch
a' Squirr

Lonbain

Loch
Gaineamhach

An Dubh-loch

1619
Croic-bheinn

1692

Ben Shieldaig
850

Beinn Da
2957

Eilean
Fladday

Loch
Leathan

Loch
Fada

Manish
Point

Loch
Arnish

Torran

Arnish

A896

Glenshieldaig
Forest

Loch
Lundie

Abhainn Dearg

Beinn Dearg
2995

Portree
(Port Righ)

Loch
Portree

Dun Gerashader

Torvaig

Brochel Castle

Brochel

SOUND OF RAASAY

RAASAY

INNER SOUND

River Applecross

Applecross Forest

Loch Coire
Attadale

Loch
Gaineamhach

2938
Beinn Bhan

Loch
Coultrie

Sgurr a' Gharaidh
2396

Smithy Heritag

4

17

40

Penifiler

Ben
Tianavaig
1355

Heatherfield

Camastianavaig

Holoman
Bay

Dun
Caan
1455

Applecross
Bay

Heritage
Centre

Applecross

Milton

Sgurr a'
Chaorachain
2539

Loch Coire
nan Àrr

Kishorn

A896

Tianavaig
Bay

Conordan

B883

Oskaig

Glame

Balachuirn

Rubha
ná Leac

Camusteel

Camusterrach

Bealach na Ba

Meall Gorm

Loch Braigh
an Achaidh

Ardarroch

Achintraid

Lower Ollach

Gedintailor

Balmeanach

Chapel

Clachan

North
Fearns

Eilean na Bà

Ard-dhubh

Culduie

Toscaig

River Toscaig

Loch Maol
Fharochach

Loch Kishorn

Kishorn
Island

Bad a'
Chreamha
1296

Lochcarron
Weavers

Upper Ollach

Inverarish

Suisnish
Hill

A87

Peinchorran

1456
Ben Lee

Loch
Varragill

Balmeanach

Suisnish

Eyre Point

Eyre Mòr

Eilean Beag

Eilean na Bà

Meall Loch
Airigh Alasdair

Uags

Stromemore

Ardaneaskan

Strome
NTS

5

Loch Carron

Plockton

Plockton

Ardaneaskan

Stromeferry

A890

GLAMAIG
2542

Sconser

Sconser to
Raasay 25mins

Caol Mòr

CROWLIN
ISLANDS

Eilean Mòr

Port Cam

Highland
Farm

Craig

Loch na
Gillean

Loch na
Leitire

Achmore

Sligachan

Moll

Sgeir Dhearg

Black Island

Drumbuie

Loch
Lundie

Loch Achaidh
na h-Inich

Gleann
Udalain

30

Glen Sligachan

Luib

Mullach
na Càrn 1298

Longay

G

Kyle of Lochalsh
(Caol Loch Ailse)

Badicaul

Balmacara
Estate

Balmacara

H

chtertyre

Auchtertyre

A87

River Sligachan

150

15

60

Dunan
(An Dunan)

Scalpay House

SCALPAY

Pabay

70

Guillamon
Island

Kyle
Railway

Plock of Kyle
Bright Water

Loch
Scalpaidh

V

Donald
Murchison's
Mon.

Highland
Woodland
NTS

Kirkton

Nostie

Ardelve

A87

Marsco

Glas
Bheinn Mhòr
1852

Kyleakin

Kyle
Akin

Caisteal
Maol

Loch Alsh

Loch
Duich

Eilean Ellen

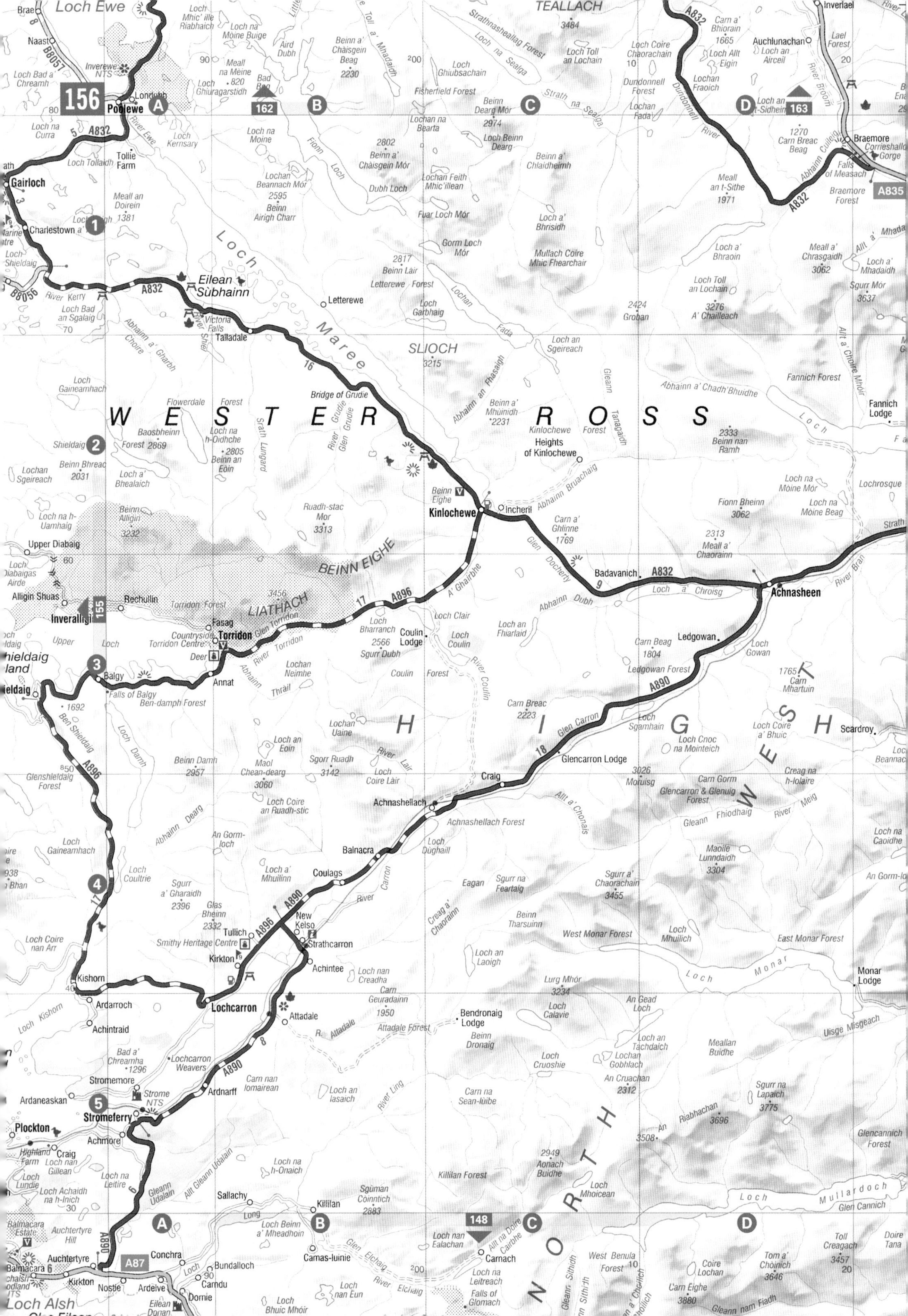

Loch Ewe
Brae
Naast
B8057
Inverewe NTS
156
Poolewe
Londubh
A
Loch Mhic' ille Riabhaich
Loch na Mòine Buige
Aird Dubh
Loch Bad a' Chreamh
Meall na Meine 820
Loch Ghiuragarstidh
Bad Bea
162
B
Beinn a' Chàisgein Beag 2230
TEALLACH
3484
Strathnasheallag Forest
Loch na Sealga
Loch Toll an Lochain
Loch Ghiubsachain
Fisherfield Forest
Beinn Dearg Mòr 2974
C
Strath na Sealga
Loch Coire Chaorachain
Dundonnell Forest
Loch Fada
A832
Carn a' Bhiorain 1665
Loch Allt Eigin
Lochan Fraoich
Dundonnell River
Auchlunachan
Loch an Airceil
Inverlael
Lael Forest
D
Loch an t-Sidheim
163
River Broom
1270 Carn Breac Beag
Braemore
Corrieshalloch Gorge
Falls of Measach
Braemore Forest
A835
Meall an t-Sithe 1971
Loch na Curra
A832
Loch Kernsary
Loch na Moine
Tollie Farm
Loch Tollaidh
Gairloch
Lochan na Bearta
2802 Beinn a' Chàisgein Mòr
Loch Beinn Dearg
Beinn a' Chlaidheimh
Lochan Beannach Mòr 2595
Beinn Airigh Charr
Fionn Loch
Dubh Loch
Lochan Feith Mhic'illean
Fuar Loch Mòr
Meall an Doirein 1381
Charlestown
1
Loch a' Bhrisidh
Gorm Loch Mòr
Mullach Coire Mhic Fhearchair
Loch a' Bhraoin
Meall a' Chrasgaidh 3062
Loch a' Mhadaidh
Sgurr Mòr 3637
Loch Shieldaig
Loch Maree
2817 Beinn Làir
Letterewe Forest
Eilean Sùbhainn
A832
River Kerry
B8056
Loch Bad an Sgalaig
Letterewe
Loch Garbhaig
Lochan Fada
2424 Groban
Loch Toll an Lochain
3276 A' Chailleach
Victoria Falls
Talladale
River Sheil
Abhainn a' Gharbh Choire
SLIOCH 3215
Loch an Sgeireach
Fannich Forest
Loch Gaineamhach
16
Bridge of Grudie
Abhainn an Fhasaigh
Abhainn a' Chadh'Bhuidhe
Fannich Lodge
Flowerdale Forest
WESTER ROSS
Beinn a' Mhùinidh 2231
Kinlochewe Forest
Gleann Tanagaidh
Shieldaig
2
Baosbheinn 2669
Loch na h-Oidhche
2805 Beinn an Eòin
Strath Lungard
River Grudie
Glen Grudie
Heights of Kinlochewe
2333 Beinn nan Ramh
Lochan Sgeireach
Beinn Bhreac 2031
Loch a' Bhealaich
Abhainn Bruachaig
Loch na Mòine Mòr
Lochrosque
Beinn Eighe
Incheril
Kinlochewe
Ruadh-stac Mor 3313
Fionn Bheinn 3062
Loch na Mòine Beag
Loch na h-Uamhaig
Beinn Alligin 3232
Carn a' Ghlinne 1769
2313 Meall a' Chaorainn
Upper Diabaig
Loch Diabaigas Airde
BEINN EIGHE
Glen Docherty
Badavanich
A832
9
Alligin Shuas
155
Inveralligin
Rechullin
Torridon Forest
3456 LIATHACH
17
A896
A' Ghairbhe
Loch a' Chroisg
Achnasheen
Abhainn Dubh
Fasag
Torridon
Countryside Torridon Centre
Glen Torridon
Loch Bharranch
Coulin Lodge
Loch Clair
Loch Coulin
Loch an Fhiarlaid
Carn Beag 1804
Ledgowan
Loch Gowan
Upper Loch Torridon
2566 Sgurr Dubh
Deer
River Torridon
Lochan Neimhe
Coulin Forest
River Coulin
Ledgowan Forest
3
Balgy
Annat
Abhainn Thrail
1765 Carn Mhartuin
Shieldaig
Falls of Balgy
Ben-damph Forest
A890
1692
Ben Shieldaig
Loch Damh
Carn Breac 2223
Glen Carron
Loch Sgamhain
Loch Coire a' Bhuic
Scardroy
Lochan Uaine
Loch an Eoin
River Lair
HIGHLANDS
Loch Cnoc na Mointeich
850
A896
Beinn Damh 2957
Maol Chean-dearg 3060
Sgorr Ruadh 3142
Loch Coire Làir
18
Glencarron Lodge
Craig
Glenshieldaig Forest
Loch Coire an Ruadh-stic
Achnashellach
3026 Moruisg
Carn Gorm
Glencarron & Glenuig Forest
Creag na h-Iolaire
Abhainn Dearg
An Gorm-loch
Achnashellach Forest
Allt a' Chonais
Gleann Fhiodhaig
River Meig
Loch Gaineamhach
Balnacra
Loch Dùghaill
Maoile Lunndaidh 3304
Loch na Caoidhe
Loch Coultrie
Loch a' Mhuilinn
Coulags
River Carron
Eagan
Sgurr na Feartaig
Sgurr a' Chaorachain 3455
An Gorm-loch
4
Sgurr a' Gharaidh 2396
A890
Glas Bheinn 2332
New Kelso
Beinn Tharsuinn
Creag a' Chaorainn
West Monar Forest
Loch Mhuilich
East Monar Forest
Tullich
A896
Smithy Heritage Centre
Strathcarron
Loch Coire nan Arr
Kirkton
Achintee
Loch an Laoigh
Loch nan Creadha
Loch Monar
Monar Lodge
Kishorn
Lochcarron
Carn Geuradainn 1950
Lurg Mhòr 3234
An Gead Loch
Ardarroch
Loch Kishorn
Achintraid
Attadale
Bendronaig Lodge
Attadale Forest
Beinn Dronaig
Loch Calavie
Uisge Misgeach
Loch an Tachdaich
Meallan Buidhe
Bad a' Chreamha 1296
Lochcarron Weavers
A890
8
Lochan Gobhlach
Loch Cruoshie
Stromemore
Carn nan Iomairean
An Cruachan 2312
Ardaneaskan
Strome NTS
Ardnarff
Loch an Iasaich
Carn na Sean-luibe
River Ling
Sgurr na Lapaich 3775
5
Stromeferry
An Riabhachan 3696
Plockton
Achmore
3508
Highland Farm
Craig
Loch nan Gillean
NORTH WEST
Glencannich Forest
Loch Lundie
Loch na Leitire
Loch na h-Onaich
Killilan Forest
2949 Aonach Buidhe
Loch Achaidh na h-Inich
Gleann Udalain
Allt Gleann Udalain
Sgùman Coinntich 2883
Loch Mhoicean
Loch Mullardoch
Glen Cannich
Sallachy
Killilan
A
Balmacara Estate
Auchtertyre Hill
Long
Loch Beinn a' Mheadhoin
B
148
C
D
Loch nan Ealachan
Allt na Doire Gairbhe
Toll Creagach 3457
Doire Tana
A890
Auchtertyre
Conchra
Camas-luinie
Carnach
West Benula Forest
Tom a' Chòinich 3646
Balmacara
A87
Kirkton
Nostie
Ardelve
Bundalloch
Carndu
Glen Elchaig
River Elchaig
Loch na Leitreach
Coire Lochan
Carn Eighe 3880
Loch Alsh
Dornie
Eilean Donan
Loch Bhuic Mhòir
Loch nan Eun
Falls of Glomach
Gleann nam Fiadh

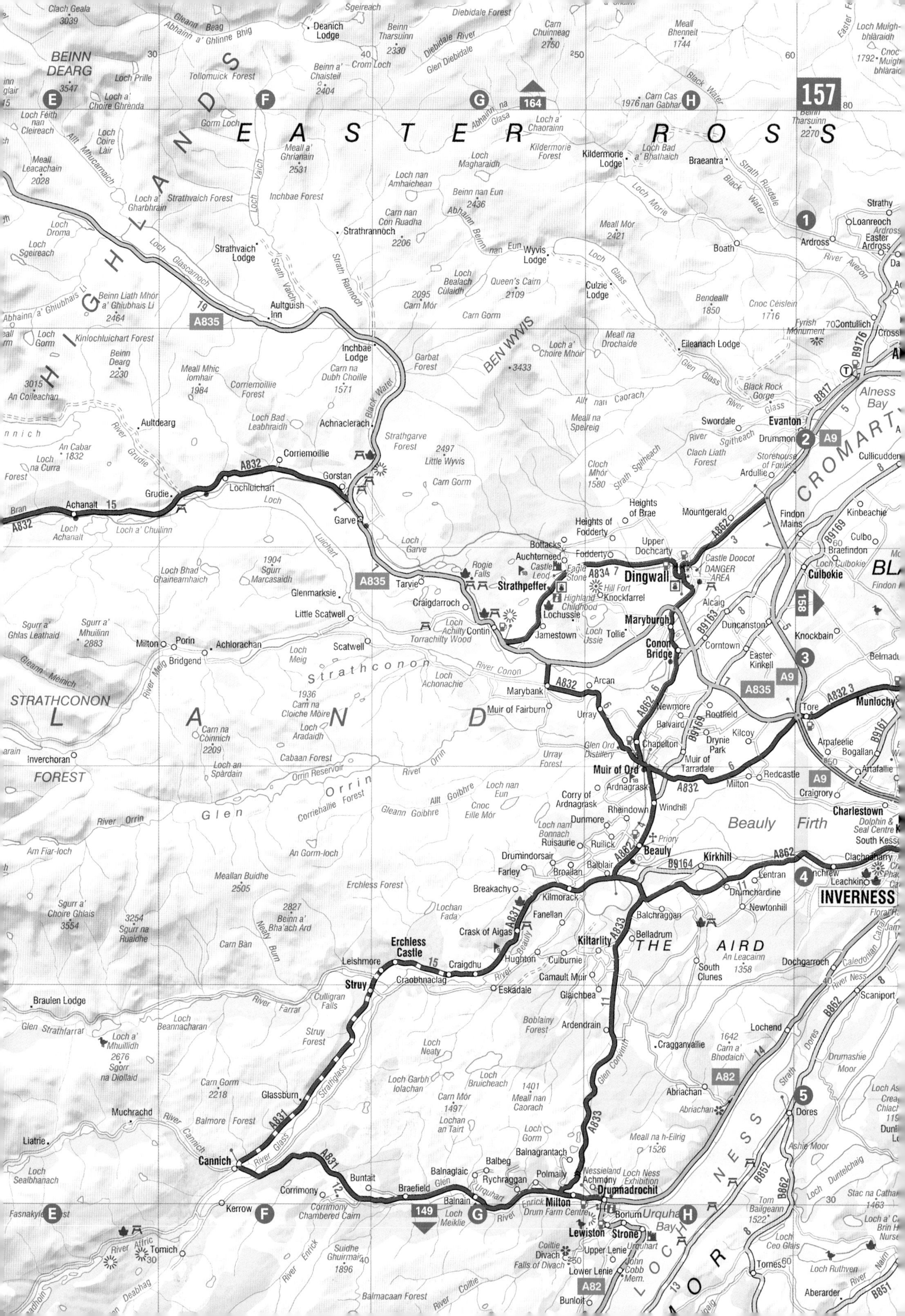

157
164
149
HIGHLANDS
EASTER ROSS
LAND
CROMARTY
Clach Geala 3039
Sgeireach
Diebidale Forest
Gleann Beag
Abhainn a' Ghlinne Bhig
Deanich Lodge
Beinn Tharsuinn 2330
Diebidale River
Glen Diebidale
Carn Chuinneag 2750
Meall Bhenneit 1744
Loch Mugh-bhlàraidh
BEINN DEARG 3547
Loch Prille
Tollomuick Forest
Beinn a' Chaisteil 2404
Crom Loch
Black Water
Loch a' Choire Ghrènda
Carn Cas nan Gabhar 1976
Beinn Tharsuinn 2270
Loch Féith nan Cleireach
Allt Mhucarnaich
Gorm Loch
Abhainn na Glasa
Loch a' Chaorainn
Loch Coire Làir
Meall a' Ghrianain 2531
Kildermorie Forest
Kildermorie Lodge
Loch Bad a' Bhathaich
Braeantra
Strath Rusdale
Meall Leacachain 2028
Loch Vaich
Loch Magharaidh
Loch nan Amhaichean
Loch a' Gharbhrain
Strathvaich Forest
Inchbae Forest
Beinn nan Eun 2436
Loch Morie
Black Water
Strathy
Loanreoch
Easter Ardross
Ardross
Loch Droma
Carn nan Con Ruadha 2206
Abhainn Beinn nan Eun
Strathrannoch
Meall Mòr 2421
Loch Sgeireach
Strathvaich Lodge
Wyvis Lodge
Boath
River Averon
Loch Glascarnoch
Strath Vaich
Strath Rannoch
Loch Bealach Cùlaidh
Queen's Cairn 2109
Loch Glass
Culzie Lodge
Beinn Liath Mhór a' Ghiubhais Li 2464
2095 Carn Mór
Carn Gorm
Bendeallt 1850
Cnoc Céislein 1716
Abhainn a' Ghiubhais Li
Aultguish Inn
A835
Fyrish Monument
Contullich
Loch Gorm
Kinlochluichart Forest
Inchbae Lodge
Carn na Dubh Choille 1571
Garbat Forest
BEN WYVIS 3433
Loch a' Choire Mhóir
Meall na Drochaide
Eileanach Lodge
Glen Glass
Beinn Dearg 2230
Meall Mhic Iomhair 1984
Corriemoillie Forest
Black Water
B9176
B817
Alness Bay
Black Rock Gorge
River Glass
3015 An Coileachan
Allt nan Caorach
Loch Bad Leabhraidh
Achnaclerach
Meall na Speireig
Swordale
Evanton
Aultdearg
River Grudie
Strathgarve Forest
River Sgitheach
Drummond
A9
An Cabar 1832
2497 Little Wyvis
Clach Liath Forest
Storehouse of Foulis
Cullicudden
Loch na Curra
Forest
Corriemoillie
A832
Carn Gorm
Cloch Mhór 1580
Strath Sgitheach
Ardullie
Gorstan
Grudie
Lochluichart
Loch
Heights of Brae
Mountgerald
Findon Mains
Kinbeachie
Achanalt
Bran
Garve
Heights of Fodderty
A862
B9169
Culbo
Loch Achanalt
Loch a' Chuilinn
Loch Luichart
Loch Garve
Bottacks
Upper Dochcarty
Braefindon
Auchterneed
Fodderty
Loch Culbokie
Rogie Falls
Castle Leod
Eagle Stone
Castle Doocot
DANGER AREA
Culbokie
1904 Sgurr Marcasaidh
Loch Bhad Ghaineamhaich
A835
Tarvie
Strathpeffer
A834
Hill Fort
Dingwall
Findon
Glenmarksie
Craigdarroch
Highland Childhood
Knockfarrel
Alcaig
Lochussie
Little Scatwell
Maryburgh
B9163
Duncanston
Sgurr a' Ghlas Leathaid
Sgurr a' Mhuilinn 2883
Loch Achilty
Contin
Torrachilty Wood
Jamestown
Loch Ussie
Tollie
Knockbain
Milton
Porin
Achlorachan
Scatwell
Conon Bridge
Corntown
Loch Meig
Bridgend
River Meig
Easter Kinkell
Belmaduthy
Gleann Meinich
Strathconon
River Conon
Loch Achonachie
STRATHCONON
Marybank
A832
Arcan
A835
Tore
A832
Munlochy
1936 Carn na Cloiche Mòire
Muir of Fairburn
Urray
Newmore
Rootfield
Carn na Coinnich 2209
Loch Aradaidh
Balvaird
Drynie Park
Kilcoy
Arpafeelie
Bogallan
B9161
Invercharan
Loch an Spàrdain
Cabaan Forest
Glen Ord Distillery
Urray Forest
Chapelton
Muir of Tarradale
Artafallie
FOREST
Orrin Reservoir
River Orrin
Muir of Ord
Redcastle
Milton
A9
Craigrory
Orrin
Corriehallie Forest
Allt Goibhre
Loch nan Eun
Ardnagrask
Corry of Ardnagrask
Charlestown
River Orrin
Glen
Gleann Goibhre
Cnoc Eille Mòr
Rheindown
Windhill
Beauly Firth
Dolphin & Seal Centre
South Kessock
Loch nam Bonnach
Dunmore
Ruisaurie
Ruilick
Priory
Am Fiar-loch
An Gorm-loch
Beauly
Kirkhill
A862
Clachnaharry
Drumindorsair
Farley
Broallan
Balblair
B9164
Lentran
Inchrew
Leachkin
Meallan Buidhe 2505
Erchless Forest
Breakachy
Kilmorack
Drumchardine
INVERNESS
Sgurr a' Choire Ghlais 3554
3254 Sgurr na Ruaidhe
2827 Beinn a' Bha'ach Ard
Lochan Fada
Fanellan
Newtonhill
Balchraggan
Carn Bàn
Neaty Burn
Crask of Aigas
A831
Belladrum
THE AIRD
Kiltarlity
A833
An Leacainn 1358
Erchless Castle
Leishmore
Craigdhu
Hughton
Culburnie
South Clunes
Dochgarroch
Caledonian Canal
Struy
Craobhnaclag
River Beauly
Camault Muir
Eskadale
Glaichbea
River Ness
Scaniport
Braulen Lodge
River Farrar
Culligran Falls
Loch Beannacharan
Glen Strathfarrar
Struy Forest
Boblainy Forest
Ardendrain
Lochend
B862
Loch a' Mhuillidh
2676 Sgorr na Diollaid
Loch Neaty
Cragganvallie
1642 Carn a' Bhodaich
Dores
Drumashie Moor
Glen Convinth
Loch Bruicheach
Carn Gorm 2218
Loch Garbh Iolachan
Glassburn
Strathglass
1401 Meall nan Caorach
A82
Abriachan
Carn Mór 1497
Muchrachd
River Cannich
Balmore Forest
Lochan an Tairt
Liatrie
Loch Gorm
Strath Dores
Dores
Meall na h-Eilrig 1526
Ashie Moor
River Glass
Cannich
Balnagrantach
LOCH NESS
Loch Sealbhanach
Balbeg
Rychraggan
Polmaily
Nessieland
Achmony
Loch Ness Exhibition
B852
Loch Duntelchaig
Buntait
Corrimony
Braefield
Glen Urquhart
Drumnadrochit
Fasnakyle Forest
Kerrow
Corrimony Chambered Cairn
Balnain
Loch Meiklie
River Enrick
Milton
Drum Farm Centre
Borlum
Urquhart Bay
Tom Bailgeann 1522
Stac na Cathaig 1463
River Affric
Tomich
Lewiston
Strone
Urquhart Castle
Loch a' Chaorainn
Suidhe Ghuirmain 1896
Coiltie
Divach
Falls of Divach
Upper Lenie
Lower Lenie
John Cobb Mem.
Loch Ceo Glais
Torness
Loch Ruthven
River Nairn
River Enrick
River Coiltie
Deabhag
Balmacaan Forest
Bunloit
A82
Aberarder
B851

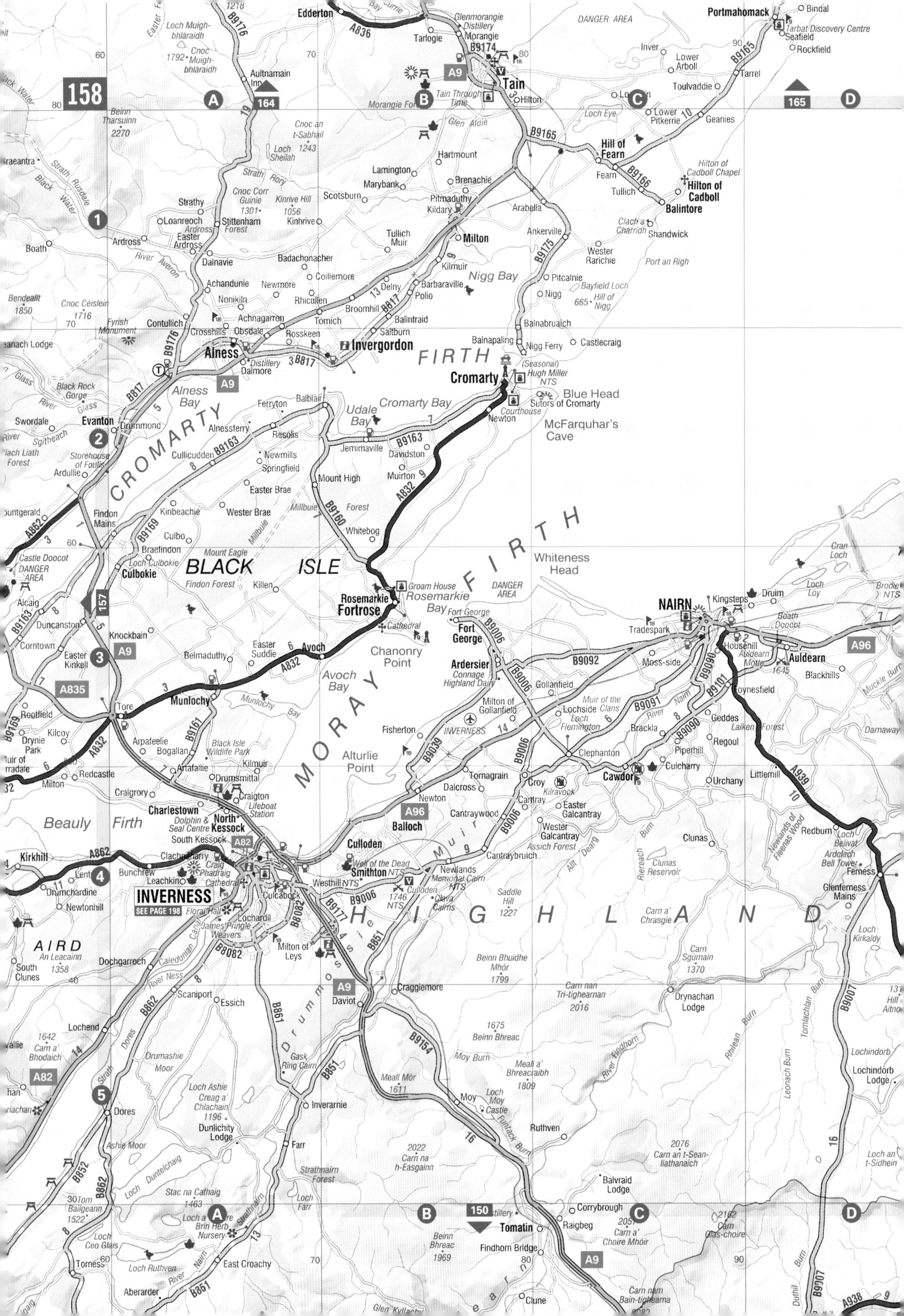
158
Edderton
Glenmorangie Distillery
Morangie
Tarlogie
B9174
A836
A9
Tain
Tain Through Time
Hilton
Morangie Forest
Glen Aldie
DANGER AREA
Portmahomack
Bindal
Tarbat Discovery Centre
Seafield
Rockfield
Inver
Lower Arbol
Tarrel
Toulvaddie
B9165
Loch Eye
Lower Pitkerrie
Geanies
165
164
Loch Muigh-bhlàraidh
Cnoc Muigh-bhlàraidh
1792
Aultnamain Inn
B9176
Beinn Tharsuinn
2270
Cnoc an t-Sabhail
1243
Loch Sheilah
Strath Rory
Hartmount
Hill of Fearn
Fearn
B9166
Hilton of Cadboll Chapel
Hilton of Cadboll
Tullich
Balintore
Lamington
Marybank
Brenachie
Scotsburn
Pitmaduthy
Kildary
Arabella
Strathy
Loanreoch
Stittenham Forest
Cnoc Corr Guinie
1301
Kinrive Hill
1056
Kinhrive
Ardross
Easter Ardross
Strath Rusdale
Black Water
Boath
River Averon
Dalnavie
Tullich Muir
Milton
Ankerville
Clach a' Charridh
Shandwick
Wester Rarichie
Port an Righ
B9175
Badachonacher
Coillemore
Kilmuir
Nigg Bay
Barbaraville
Polio
Delny
Achandunie
Newmore
Rhicullen
Nonikiln
Pitcalnie
Bayfield Loch
Nigg
Hill of Nigg
665
Bendeallt
1850
Cnoc Céislein
1716
Fyrish Monument
Contullich
Achnagarron
Broomhill
Balintraid
Tomich
Saltburn
Balnabruaich
Crosshills
Obsdale
Rosskeen
Invergordon
Balnapaling
Nigg Ferry
Castlecraig
Alness
Distillery
Dalmore
B817
B9176
FIRTH
Cromarty
Hugh Miller NTS
Blue Head
Sutors of Cromarty
Courthouse
Newton
McFarquhar's Cave
Black Rock Gorge
River Glass
Alness Bay
Balblair
Ferryton
Udale Bay
Cromarty Bay
Swordale
Evanton
Drummond
Alnessferry
Resolis
Jemimaville
B9163
Davidston
Storehouse of Foulis
Cullicudden
Newmills
Springfield
Mount High
Muirton
A832
Ardullie
CROMARTY
Easter Brae
Millbuie Forest
B9160
Findon Mains
Kinbeachie
Wester Brae
Whitebog
A862
B9169
Culbo
Braefindon
Mount Eagle
Castle Doocot DANGER AREA
Loch Culbokie
Culbokie
BLACK ISLE
Findon Forest
Killen
Groam House
Rosemarkie
Fortrose
Rosemarkie Bay
MORAY FIRTH
Whiteness Head
DANGER AREA
Fort George
Cathedral
Alcaig
Duncanston
Cornton
Knockbain
Easter Kinkell
157
A9
A835
Belmaduthy
Easter Suddie
Avoch
Chanonry Point
Avoch Bay
Ardersier
Connage Highland Dairy
B9006
Tore
Munlochy
Munlochy Bay
Rootfield
Kilcoy
Drynie Park
Muir of Ord
Redcastle
Milton
Arpafeelie
Bogallan
B9161
Black Isle Wildlife Park
Artafallie
Kilmuir
Drumsmittal
Craigton Lifeboat Station
Fisherton
Alturlie Point
Craigrory
Charlestown
Dolphin & Seal Centre
North Kessock
South Kessock
Beauly Firth
Kirkhill
Clachnaharry
Craig Phadraig
Bunchrew
Leachkin
Lentran
Drumchardine
Newtonhill
INVERNESS
SEE PAGE 198
Cathedral
Floral Hall
Culcabock
Lochardil
James Pringle Weavers
B8082
Milton of Leys
B9177
AIRD
An Leacainn
1358
South Clunes
Dochgarroch
Caledonian Canal
River Ness
Scaniport
Essich
B862
B861
Drummossie Muir
A82
Lochend
Carn a' Bhodaich
1642
Drumashie Moor
Dores
Strath Dores
Loch Ashie
Creag a' Chlachain
1196
Dunlichity Lodge
Ashie Moor
Loch Duntelchaig
Stac na Cathaig
1463
Brin Herb Nursery
B852
Tom Bailgeann
1522
Loch Ceo Glais
Torness
Loch Ruthven
River Nairn
East Croachy
Aberarder
Gask Ring Cairn
Inverarnie
Farr
Strathnairn Forest
Loch Farr
Strathnairn
Culloden
Balloch
Smithton
Well of the Dead
Westhill
Culloden NTS
Clava Cairns
1746 NTS
Newlands Memorial Cairn NTS
B9006
B851
A96
Dalcross
Tornagrain
Cantraywood
Cantraybruich
Newton
INVERNESS
B9039
Milton of Gollanfield
Gollanfield
B9092
Lochside
Loch Flemington
Muir of the Clans
Clephanton
Croy
Cantray
Kilravock
Easter Galcantray
Wester Galcantray
Assich Forest
Allt Dearg
Saddle Hill
1227
NAIRN
Tradespark
Kingsteps
Druim
Loch Loy
Cran Loch
Brodie NTS
Beath Doocot
Househill
Auldearn Motte
Auldearn
Blackhills
Muckle Burn
Moss-side
B9090
B9091
B9101
Boath
Foynesfield
Brackla
Geddes
Laiken Forest
Darnaway
Regoul
Piperhill
Cawdor
Culcharry
Urchany
Littlemill
A939
Redburn
Loch Belivat
Ardclach Bell Tower
Ferness
Newlands of Fleenas Wood
Clunas
Clunas Reservoir
Riereach Burn
Carn a' Chrasgie
HIGHLAND
Glenferness Mains
Loch Kirkaldy
Carn Sgùmain
1370
Beinn Bhuidhe Mhòr
1799
Carn nan Tri-tighearnan
2016
Drynachan Lodge
Craggiemore
Daviot
B9154
1675 Beinn Bhreac
Moy Burn
River Findhorn
Rhilean Burn
Tomlachlan Burn
Leonach Burn
B9007
Meall a' Bhreacraibh
1809
Meall Mòr
1611
Moy
Loch Moy
Castle
Funtack Burn
Ruthven
Lochindorb
Lochindorb Lodge
2022 Carn na h-Easgainn
2076 Carn an t-Sean-liathanaich
Loch an t-Sidhein
Balvraid Lodge
Corrybrough
Raigbeg
Carn a' Choire Mhòir
2051
Carn Glas-choire
2162
150
Tomatin
Findhorn Bridge
Beinn Bhreac
1969
Clune
Carn nam Bain-tighearna
Dulnain Burn
A938
Glen Kyllachy
A9
A B C D

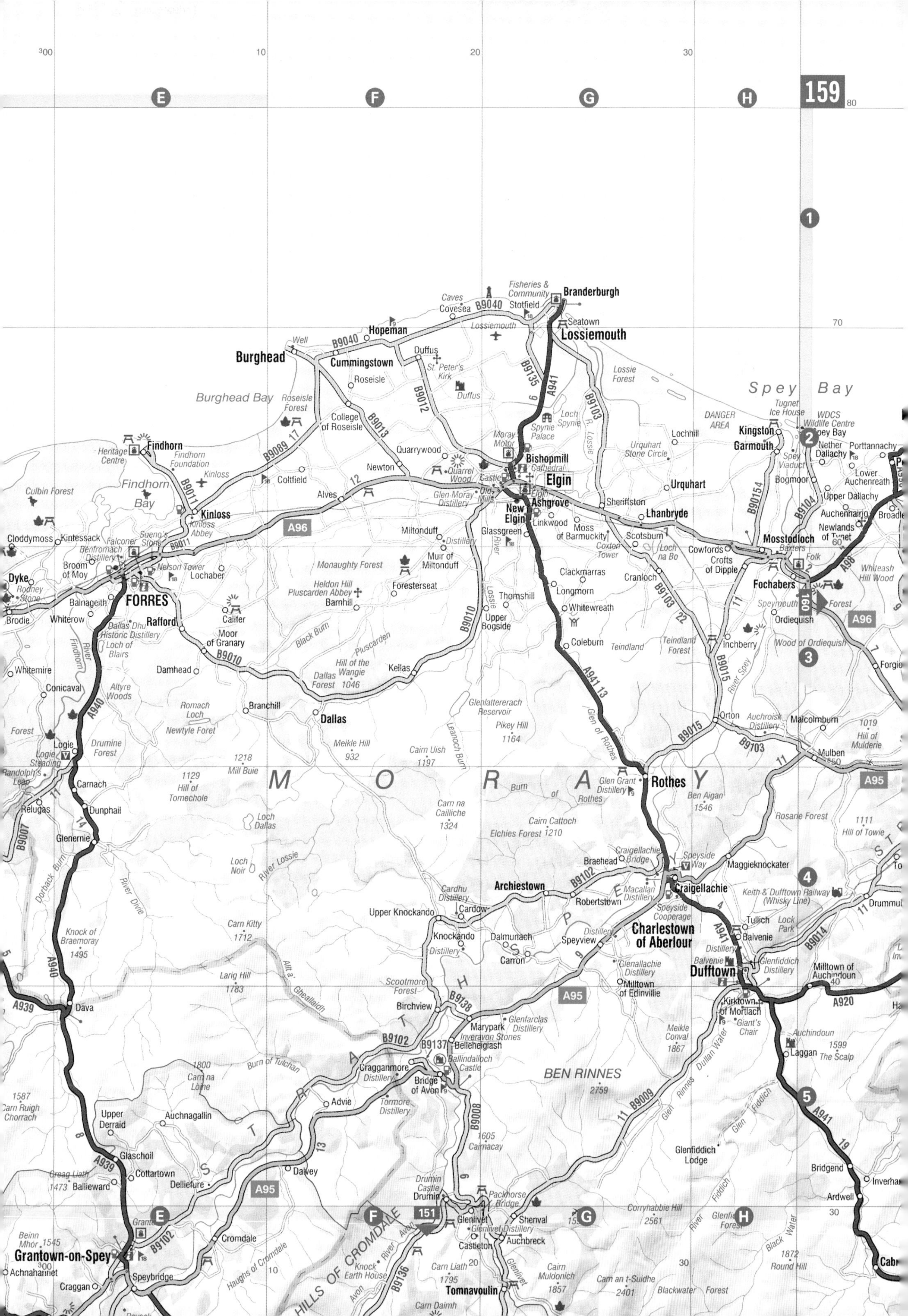

159
300
10
20
30
80
70
E
F
G
H
1
2
3
4
5
Branderburgh
Fisheries & Community
Caves
Covesea
B9040
Stotfield
Seatown
Lossiemouth
Hopeman
Well
Burghead
Cummingstown
Duffus
St. Peter's Kirk
Roseisle
Lossie Forest
Spey Bay
Burghead Bay
Roseisle Forest
College of Roseisle
B9013
B9012
Duffus
B9135
A941
B9103
Loch Spynie
Spynie Palace
DANGER AREA
Tugnet Ice House
WDCS Wildlife Centre
Kingston
Lochhill
Urquhart Stone Circle
Findhorn
Heritage Centre
Findhorn Foundation
Kinloss
Quarrywood
Moray Motor
Bishopmill
Cathedral
Garmouth
Spey Viaduct
Nether Dallachy
Porttannachy
Lower Auchenreath
Bogmoor
Newton
Quarrel Wood
Castle
Elgin
Urquhart
Culbin Forest
Findhorn Bay
B9011
Coltfield
Alves
Glen Moray Distillery
Old Mills
Ashgrove
New Elgin
Linkwood
Sheriffston
Lhanbryde
B90154
B9104
Upper Dallachy
Auchenhairig
Broadley
Kinloss Abbey
A96
Miltonduff
Glassgreen
Moss of Barmuckity
Scotsburn
Coxton Tower
Loch na Bo
Cowfords
Mosstodloch
Baxters
Newlands of Tynet
Cloddymoss
Kintessack
Falconer
Sueno's Stone
Benromach Distillery
Broom of Moy
Nelson Tower
Lochaber
Monaughty Forest
Muir of Miltonduff
Distillery
Crofts of Dipple
Folk
Fochabers
Whiteash Hill Wood
Dyke
Rodney Stone
Bainageith
FORRES
Heldon Hill
Pluscarden Abbey
Barnhill
Foresterseat
Clackmarras
Cranloch
Longmorn
Thornshill
Lossie
Speymouth
Ordiequish
Forest
A98
160
Brodie
Whiterow
Dallas Dhu Historic Distillery
Rafford
Califer
Upper Bogside
B9010
Whitewreath
Moor of Granary
Loch of Blairs
River Findhorn
Black Burn
Pluscarden
Coleburn
Teindland
Teindland Forest
Inchberry
Wood of Ordiequish
Forgie
Whitemire
Damhead
Hill of the Wangie
Kellas
Dallas Forest
1046
Conicaval
Altyre Woods
A941 13
B9015
River Spey
A940
Romach Loch
Branchill
Newtyle Forest
Dallas
Glenlatterach Reservoir
Pikey Hill
1164
Leanoch Burn
Glen of Rothes
Orton
Auchroisk Distillery
Malcolmburn
1019
Hill of Mulderie
Forest
Logie
Logie Steading
Drumine Forest
1218
Mill Buie
Meikle Hill
932
Cairn Uish
1197
B9103
Mulben
A95
Randolph's Leap
Carnach
1129
Hill of Tomechole
M O R A Y
Burn of Rothes
Glen Grant Distillery
Rothes
Ben Aigan
1546
Relugas
Dunphail
Loch Dallas
Carn na Cailliche
1324
Cairn Cattoch
Elchies Forest
1210
Rosarie Forest
1111
Hill of Towie
Glenernie
B9007
Dorback Burn
Loch Noir
River Lossie
River Divie
Braehead
Craigellachie Bridge
Speyside Way
Maggieknockater
Archiestown
B9102
Cardhu Distillery
Robertstown
Macallan Distillery
Craigellachie
Speyside Cooperage
Keith & Dufftown Railway (Whisky Line)
Upper Knockando
Cardow
Knockando Distillery
Dalmunach
Carron
Speyview
Distillery
Charlestown of Aberlour
A941
Tullich
Lock Park
Balvenie
B9014
Carn Kitty
1712
Knock of Braemoray
1495
Glenallachie Distillery
Distillery
Balvenie
Glenfiddich Distillery
Dufftown
Milltown of Auchindoun
Larig Hill
1783
Allt a' Ghealleidh
Scootmore Forest
Milltown of Edinvillie
A95
A920
A939
Dava
Birchview
B9138
Kirktown of Mortlach
Giant's Chair
Glenfarclas Distillery
Marypark
Inveravon Stones
B9102
B9137
Belleheiglash
Meikle Conval
1867
Dullan Water
Auchindoun
1599
The Scalp
Laggan
Burn of Tulchan
1800
Carn na Loine
Cragganmore Distillery
Ballindalloch Castle
Bridge of Avon
BEN RINNES
2759
1587
Carn Ruigh Chorrach
Advie
Tormore Distillery
B9009
Glen Rinnes
Glen Fiddich
A941
Upper Derraid
Auchnagallin
B9008
1605
Carnacay
Glenfiddich Lodge
Glaschoil
Cottartown
Dalvey
Bridgend
Creag Liath
1473
Ballieward
Dellefure
A95
Drumin Castle
Drumin
Packhorse Bridge
Corryhabbie Hill
2561
River Fiddich
Ardwell
151
Glenlivet
Shenval
Glenfiddich Forest
Beinn Mhor
1545
Cromdale
Glenlivet Distillery
Castleton
Auchbreck
Grantown-on-Spey
B9102
Haughs of Cromdale
HILLS OF CROMDALE
Knock Earth House
River Avon
Carn Liath
1795
Cairn Muldonich
1857
Carn an t-Suidhe
2401
Black Water
1872
Round Hill
Achnahannet
Speybridge
Craggan
B9136
Tomnavoulin
Carn Daimh
Blackwater Forest
Glenlivet

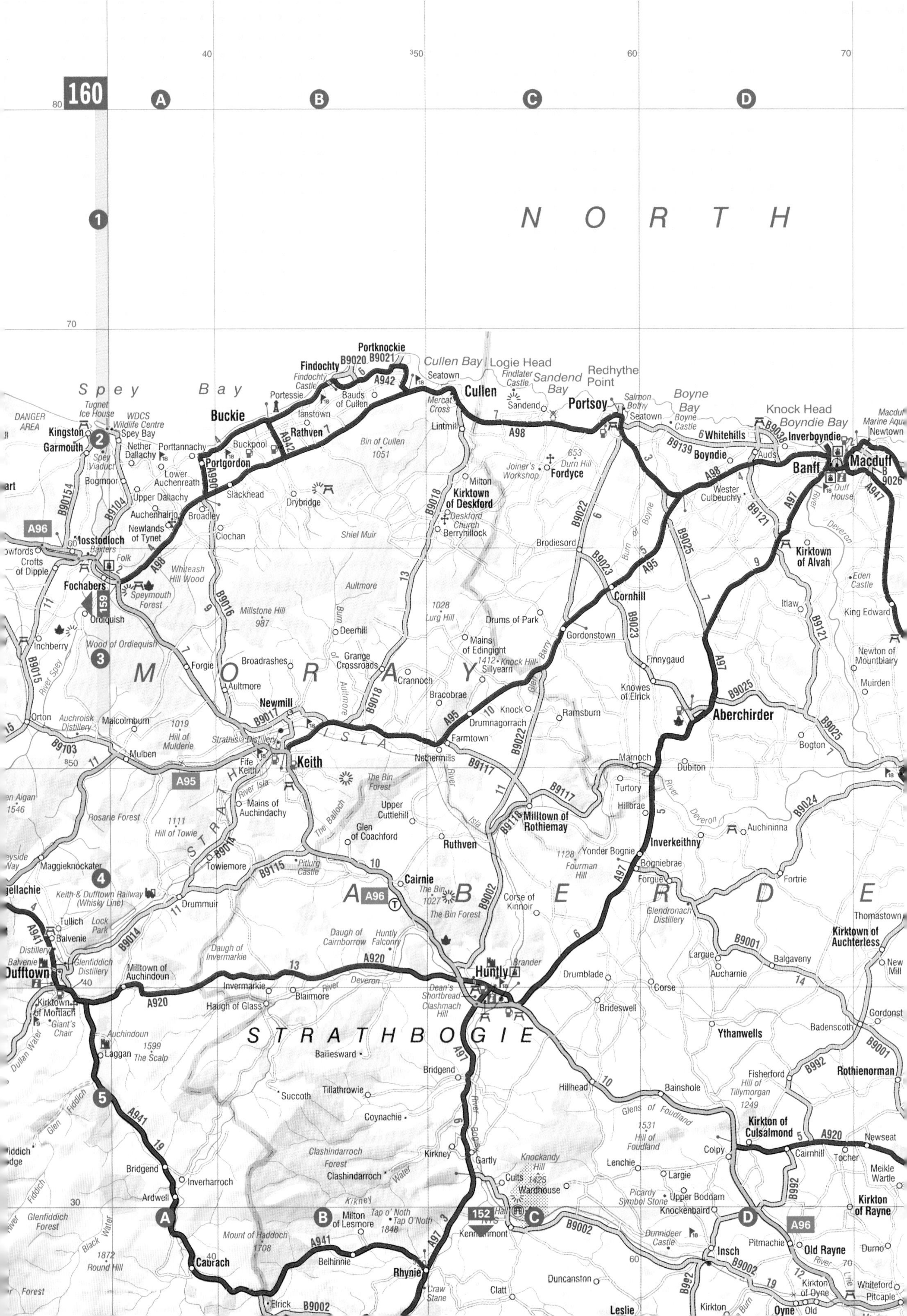

160
A
B
C
D
NORTH
Spey Bay
Tugnet Ice House
WDCS Wildlife Centre
Spey Bay
DANGER AREA
Kingston
Garmouth
Buckie
Portessie
Findochty
Findochty Castle
Portknockie
Bauds of Cullen
Ianstown
Rathven
Buckpool
Portgordon
Porttannachy
Nether Dallachy
Lower Auchenreath
Upper Dallachy
Slackhead
Spey Viaduct
Bogmoor
Auchenhalrig
Broadley
Newlands of Tynet
Clochan
Mosstodloch
Baxters
Folk
Crofts of Dipple
Fochabers
Ordiquish
Speymouth Forest
Whiteash Hill Wood
Inchberry
Wood of Ordiequish
Millstone Hill 987
Drybridge
Bin of Cullen 1051
Shiel Muir
Aultmore
Deerhill
Grange Crossroads
Broadrashes
Forgie
Aultmore
MORAY
Cullen Bay
Seatown
Cullen
Mercat Cross
Lintmill
Logie Head
Findlater Castle
Sandend Bay
Sandend
Redhythe Point
Portsoy
Salmon Bothy
Seatown
Boyne Bay
Boyne Castle
Knock Head
Boyndie Bay
Whitehills
Inverboyndie
Boyndie
Banff
Macduff
Marine Aqua
Newtown
Duff House
Auds
Wester Culbeuchly
Joiner's Workshop
Fordyce
653 Durn Hill
Milton
Kirktown of Deskford
Deskford Church
Berryhillock
Brodiesord
Kirktown of Alvah
Eden Castle
King Edward
Itlaw
1028 Lurg Hill
Drums of Park
Gordonstown
Cornhill
Mains of Edingight
1412 Knock Hill
Sillyearn
Cranoch
Bracobrae
Finnygaud
Knowes of Elrick
Newton of Mountblairy
Muirden
Knock
Drumnagorrach
Ramsburn
Aberchirder
Bogton
Newmill
Strathisla Distillery
Farmtown
Nethermills
Keith
Fife Keith
Mulben
1019 Hill of Mulderie
Orton
Auchroisk Distillery
Malcolmburn
The Bin Forest
Marnoch
Dubiton
Turtory
Hillbrae
Auchininna
Mains of Auchindachy
River Isla
Upper Cuttlehill
Glen of Coachford
Ruthven
Milltown of Rothiemay
Inverkeithny
Yonder Bognie
1128 Fourman Hill
Bogniebrae
Forgue
Fortrie
Glendronach Distillery
Rosarie Forest
1111 Hill of Towie
Towiemore
Maggieknockater
Pitlurg Castle
Cairnie
The Bin 1027
The Bin Forest
Corse of Kinnoir
ABERDEEN
Thomastown
Kirktown of Auchterless
Keith & Dufftown Railway (Whisky Line)
Drummuir
Tullich
Lock Park
Balvenie
Daugh of Cairnborrow
Huntly Falconry
Daugh of Invermarkie
Glenfiddich Distillery
Balvenie
Dufftown
Milltown of Auchindoun
Invermarkie
Blairmore
River Deveron
Huntly
Brander
Dean's Shortbread
Clashmach Hill
Drumblade
Largue
Aucharnie
Balgaveny
New Mill
Corse
Brideswell
Gordonst
Kirktown of Mortlach
Giant's Chair
Haugh of Glass
STRATHBOGIE
Auchindoun
1599 The Scalp
Laggan
Dullan Water
Bailiesward
Bridgend
Ythanwells
Badenscoth
Rothienorman
Hillhead
Bainshole
Fisherford
Hill of Tillymorgan 1249
Glens of Foudland
1531 Hill of Foudland
Tillathrowie
Succoth
Coynachie
Glen Fiddich
Clashindarroch Forest
Clashindarroch
Kirkney
Gartly
Knockandy Hill 1425
Cults
Wardhouse
Lenchie
Largie
Picardy Symbol Stone
Upper Boddam
Knockenbaird
Kirkton of Culsalmond
Colpy
Cairnhill
Tocher
Newseat
Meikle Wartle
Kirkton of Rayne
Bridgend
Inverharroch
Ardwell
Glenfiddich Forest
Black Water
1872 Round Hill
Milton of Lesmore
Tap o' Noth
Tap O'Noth 1848
Kirkney Water
Mount of Haddoch 1708
Belhinnie
Cabrach
Rhynie
Craw Stane
Elrick
152
Kennethmont
Hall
Dunnideer Castle
Insch
Pitmachie
Old Rayne
Durno
Duncanston
Clatt
Leslie
Kirkton
Kirkton of Oyne
Oyne
Old
Whiteford
Pitcaple
Forest
A96
A98
A942
A990
A95
A97
A947
A920
A941
B9002
B9020
B9021
B9038
B9139
B9121
B9026
B9025
B9022
B9023
B9018
B9016
B9104
B90154
B9015
B9703
B9017
B9014
B9115
B9117
B9118
B9024
B9001
B992

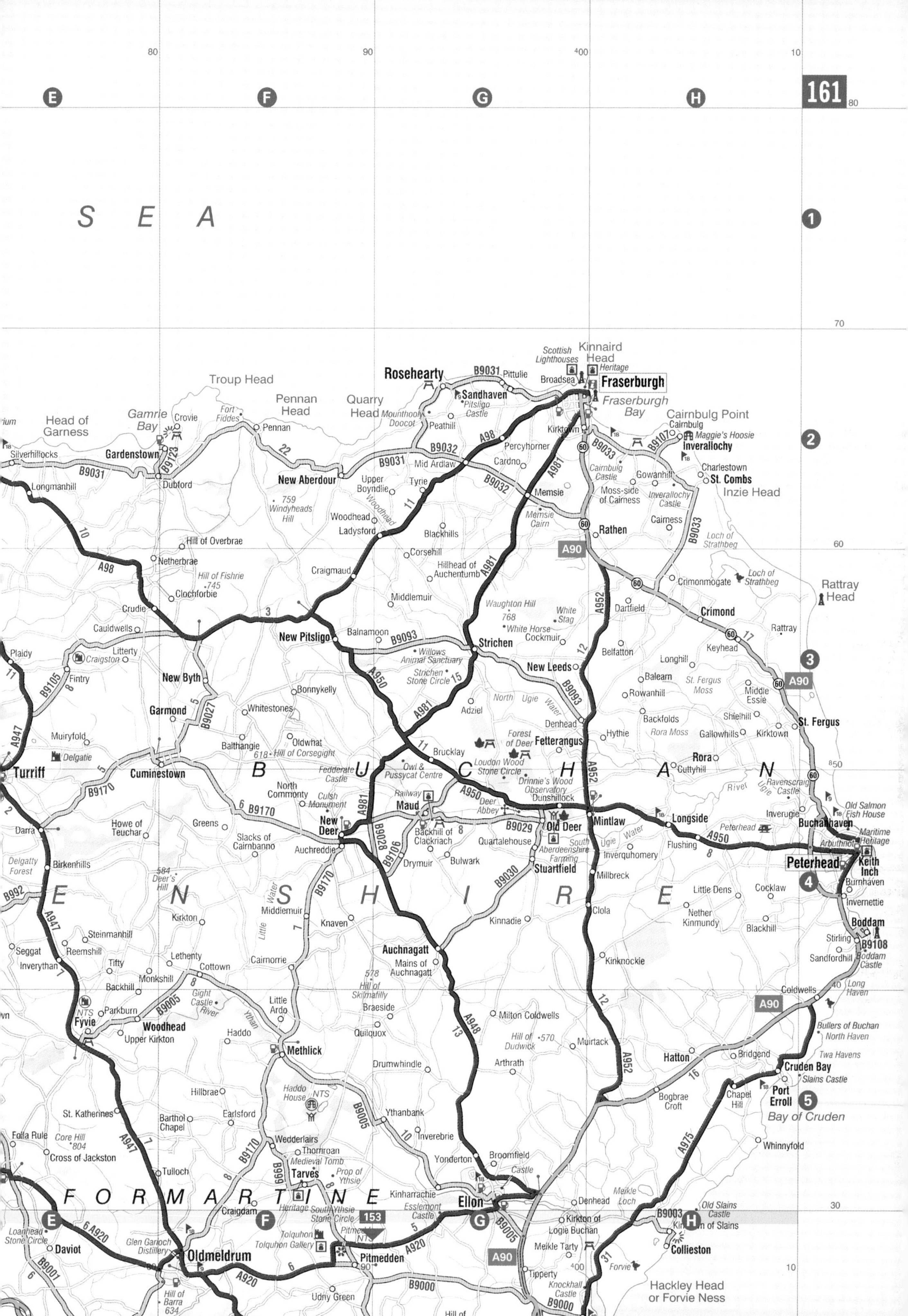
SEA
Troup Head
Pennan Head
Quarry Head
Head of Garness
Gamrie Bay
Crovie
Fort Fiddes
Pennan
Silverhillocks
Gardenstown
Dubford
Longmanhill
Rosehearty
Pittulie
Sandhaven
Pitsligo Castle
Mounthooly Doocot
Peathill
Scottish Lighthouses
Kinnaird Head
Heritage
Broadsea
Fraserburgh
Fraserburgh Bay
Cairnbulg Point
Cairnbulg
Maggie's Hoosie
Inverallochy
Charlestown
St. Combs
Inzie Head
Kirktown
Percyhorner
Cardno
Mid Ardlaw
New Aberdour
Upper Boyndlie
Tyrie
Memsie
Memsie Cairn
Cairnbulg Castle
Gowanhill
Moss-side of Cairness
Inverallochy Castle
Cairness
Rathen
Loch of Strathbeg
Windyheads Hill
Woodhead
Ladysford
Blackhills
Hill of Overbrae
Netherbrae
Corsehill
Hillhead of Auchentumb
Hill of Fishrie
Clochforbie
Craigmaud
Crimonmogate
Loch of Strathbeg
Rattray Head
Middlemuir
Waughton Hill
White Stag
White Horse
Dartfield
Crimond
Rattray
Crudie
Cauldwells
New Pitsligo
Balnamoon
Strichen
Cockmuir
Belfatton
Keyhead
Plaidy
Litterty
Craigston
Willows Animal Sanctuary
Strichen Stone Circle
New Leeds
Longhill
Balearn
St. Fergus Moss
Middle Essie
Fintry
New Byth
Bonnykelly
Rowanhill
Garmond
Whitestones
North Ugie Water
Adziel
Denhead
Backfolds
Rora Moss
Shielhill
Gallowhills
Kirktown
St. Fergus
Muiryfold
Delgatie
Balthangie
Oldwhat
Hill of Corsegight
Bruckley
Forest of Deer
Fetterangus
Hythie
Rora
Cuttyhill
Turriff
Cuminestown
Fedderate Castle
Owl & Pussycat Centre
Loudon Wood Stone Circle
Drinnie's Wood Observatory
Ravenscraig Castle
River Ugie
BUCHAN
North Commonty
Culsh Monument
Railway
Maud
Deer Abbey
Dunshillock
Longside
Inverugie
Old Salmon Fish House
Buchanhaven
Maritime Heritage
Howe of Teuchar
Greens
Darra
New Deer
Backhill of Clackriach
Old Deer
Mintlaw
Peterhead
Arbuthnot
Keith Inch
Slacks of Cairnbanno
Auchreddie
Quartalehouse
South Aberdeenshire Farming
Ugie Water
Inverquhomery
Flushing
Delgatty Forest
Birkenhills
Drymuir
Bulwark
Stuartfield
Millbreck
Burnhaven
Deer's Hill
Little Dens
Cocklaw
Invernettie
ABERDEENSHIRE
Middlemuir
Little Water
Clola
Nether Kinmundy
Blackhill
Boddam
Kirkton
Knaven
Kinnadie
Stirling
Steinmanhill
Seggat
Reemshill
Auchnagatt
Mains of Auchnagatt
Kinknockie
Sandfordhill
Boddam Castle
Inverythan
Tifty
Lethenty
Cottown
Cairnorrie
Hill of Skilmafilly
Coldwells
Long Haven
Backhill
Monkshill
Gight Castle
River Ythan
Little Ardo
Braeside
Milton Coldwells
NTS Fyvie
Parkburn
Woodhead
Upper Kirkton
Haddo
Methlick
Quilquox
Hill of Dudwick
Muirtack
Bullers of Buchan
North Haven
Twa Havens
Drumwhindle
Arthrath
Hatton
Bridgend
Cruden Bay
Slains Castle
Hillbrae
Haddo House NTS
Port Erroll
Chapel Hill
Bogbrae Croft
Bay of Cruden
St. Katherines
Barthol Chapel
Earlsford
Ythanbank
Fofla Rule
Core Hill
Cross of Jackston
Wedderlairs
Inverebrie
Whinnyfold
Thornroan
Medieval Tomb
Prop of Ythsie
Tulloch
Yonderton
Broomfield
Tarves
Castle
FORMARTINE
Kinharrachie
Meikle Loch
Heritage
Esslemont Castle
Ellon
Denhead
Old Slains Castle
Kirkton of Slains
Craigdam
South Ythsie Stone Circle
Kirkton of Logie Buchan
Loanhead Stone Circle
Glen Garioch Distillery
Tolquhon
Tolquhon Gallery
Pitmedden NTS
Collieston
Daviot
Oldmeldrum
Pitmedden
Meikle Tarty
Tipperty
Forvie
Hill of Barra
Udny Green
Knockhall Castle
Hackley Head or Forvie Ness
Hill of
A98
A981
A90
A952
A950
A947
A948
A920
A975
B9031
B9032
B9033
B9107
B9123
B9093
B9105
B9027
B9170
B9028
B9106
B9029
B9030
B9005
B9000
B9001
B992
B999
B9003
B9108
153
E F G H
1 2 3 4 5
80 90 400 10
70 60 50 40 30

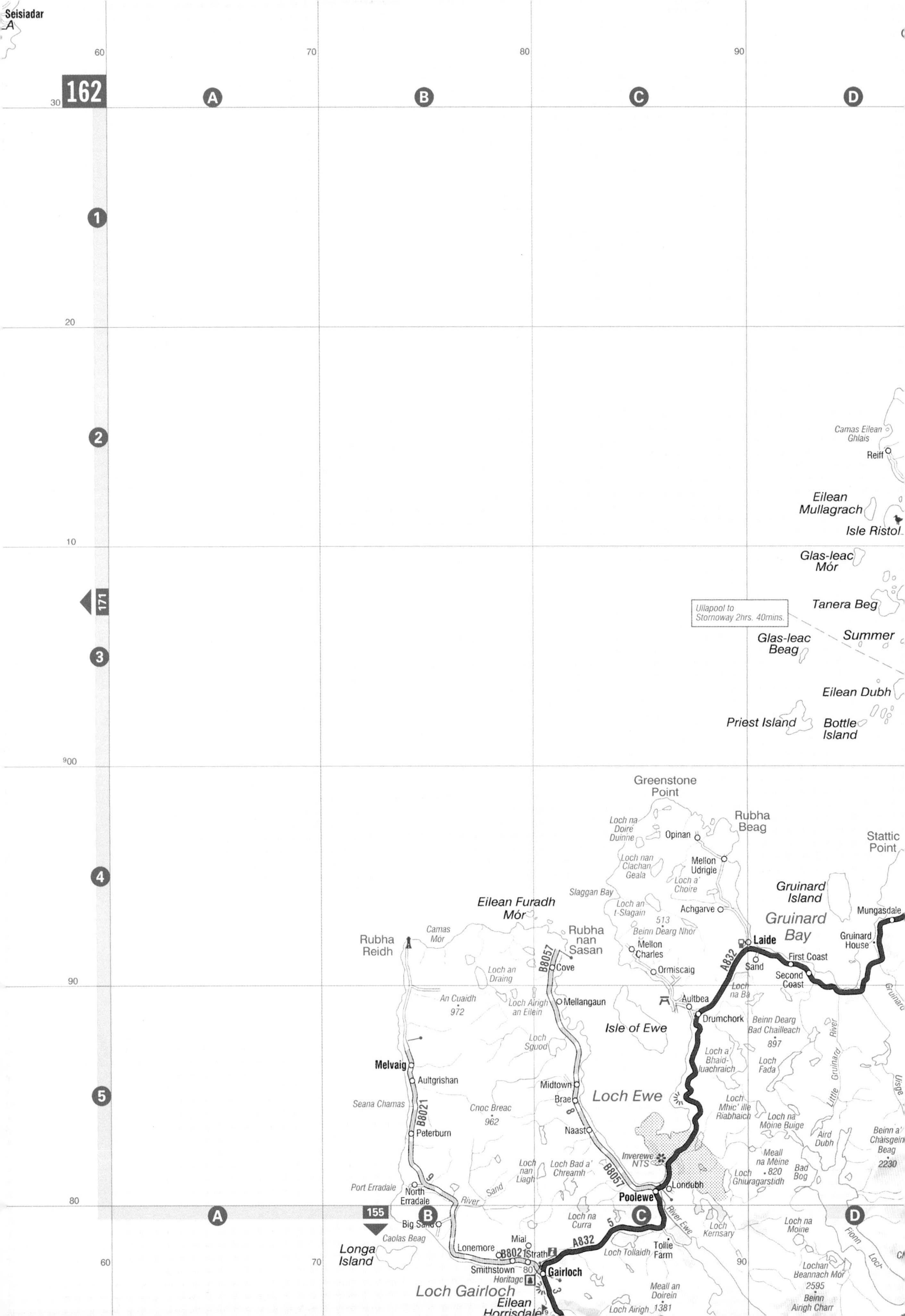

Seisiadar
A
Camas Eilean Ghlais
Reiff
Eilean Mullagrach
Isle Ristol
Glas-leac Mór
Tanera Beg
Ullapool to Stornoway 2hrs. 40mins.
Summer
Glas-leac Beag
Eilean Dubh
Priest Island
Bottle Island
Greenstone Point
Loch na Doire Duinne
Opinan
Rubha Beag
Stattic Point
Loch nan Clachan Geala
Mellon Udrigle
Loch a' Choire
Gruinard Island
Slaggan Bay
Eilean Furadh Mór
Loch an t-Slagain
Achgarve
Gruinard Bay
Mungasdale
513
Beinn Dearg Nhor
Camas Mór
Rubha nan Sasan
Rubha Reidh
Mellon Charles
Laide
Gruinard House
Sand
First Coast
Loch an Draing
B8057
Cove
Ormiscaig
A832
Second Coast
An Cuaidh 972
Loch Airigh an Eilein
Mellangaun
Aultbea
Loch na Ba
Drumchork
Beinn Dearg Bad Chailleach 897
Isle of Ewe
Loch Sguod
Loch a' Bhaid-luachraich
Loch Fada
Melvaig
Aultgrishan
Midtown
Loch Ewe
Seana Chamas
B8021
Cnoc Breac 962
Brae
Loch Mhic' ille Riabhaich
Loch na Moine Buige
Little Gruinard River
Peterburn
Naast
Aird Dubh
Beinn a' Chàisgein Beag 2230
Inverewe NTS
Meall na Mèine 820
Loch nan Liagh
Loch Bad a' Chreamh
Loch Ghiuragarstidh
Bad Bog
Port Erradale
North Erradale
Sand
River
Londubh
Poolewe
Big Sand
Caolas Beag
Loch na Curra
River Ewe
Loch Kernsary
Loch na Moine
Fionn Loch
Longa Island
Lonemore
Mial
B8021
Strath
A832
Loch Tollaidh
Tollie Farm
Smithstown
Heritage
Gairloch
Lochan Beannach Mór 2595
Loch Gairloch
Eilean Horrisdale
Meall an Doirein
Loch Airigh 1381
Beinn Airigh Charr

171
155

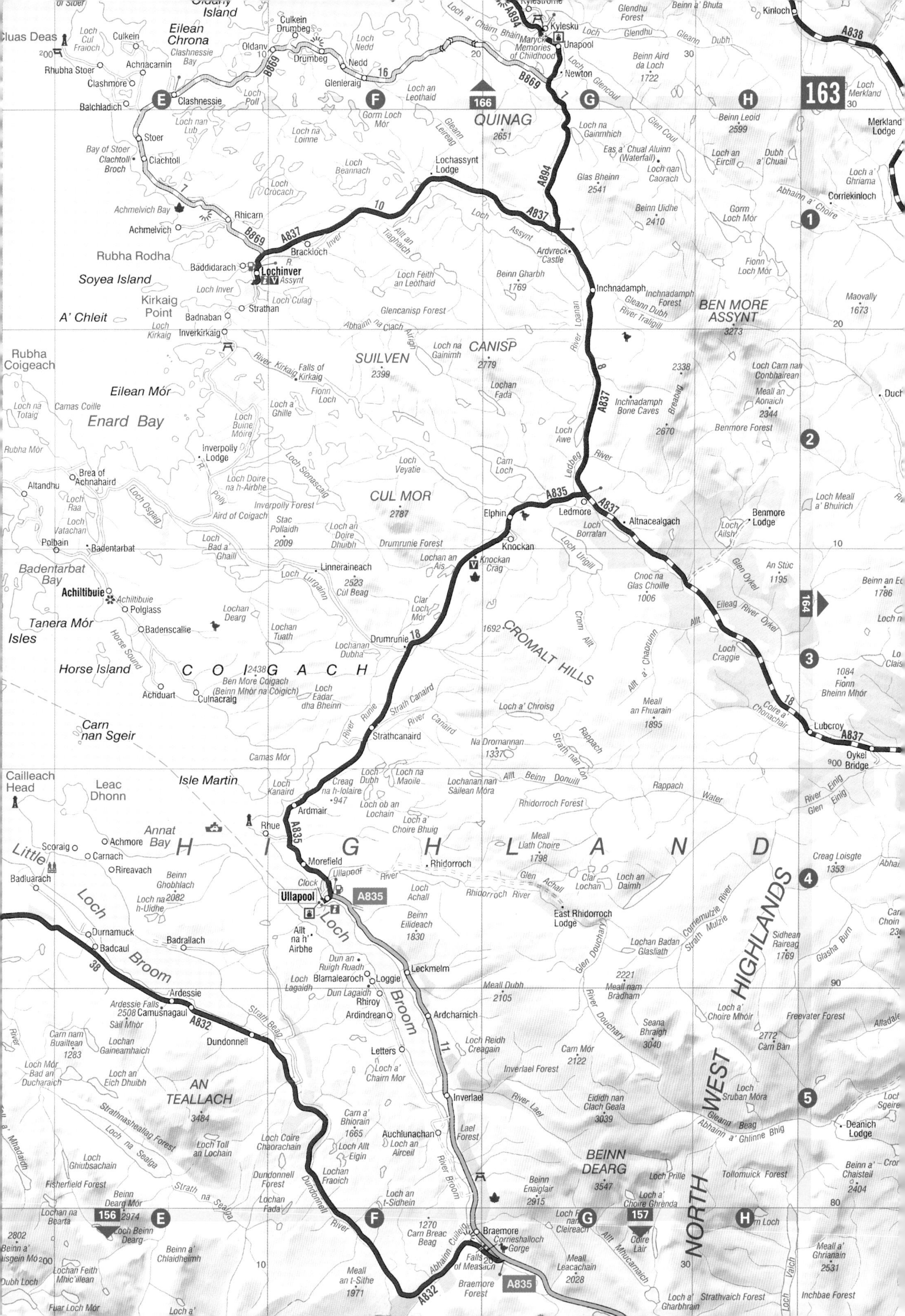

Oldany Island
Eilean Chrona
Culkein Drumbeg
Kylestrome
Kinloch
A838
Cluas Deas
Loch Cul Fraioch
Culkein
Oldany
Clashnessie Bay
Drumbeg
Loch Nedd
Nedd
Loch a' Chàirn Bhàin
Kylesku
Maryck Memories of Childhood
Unapool
Loch Glendhu
Glendhu Forest
Glendhu
Beinn a' Bhuta
Gleann Dubh
Rhubha Stoer
Achnacarnin
Clashmore
Balchladich
Clashnessie
B869
Glenleraig
Loch Poll
Loch an Leothaid
166
QUINAG
2651
Newton
Loch Glencoul
Beinn Aird da Loch
1722
163
Loch Merkland
Merkland Lodge
Stoer
Loch nan Lub
Loch na Loinne
Gorm Loch Mór
Gleann Leireag
Loch na Gainmhich
Glen Coul
Beinn Leoid
2599
Bay of Stoer
Clachtoll Broch
Clachtoll
Loch Beannach
Lochassynt Lodge
Eas a' Chual Aluinn (Waterfall)
Loch nan Caorach
Loch an Eircill
Dubh a' Chuail
Loch a' Ghriama
Loch Crocach
Glas Bheinn
2541
A894
Corriekinloch
Abhainn a' Choire
Achmelvich Bay
Rhicarn
A837
Beinn Uidhe
2410
Gorm Loch Mór
Achmelvich
Loch Assynt
Allt an Tiaghaich
Rubha Rodha
Brackloch
Inver
Ardvreck Castle
Baddidarach
Lochinver
Assynt
Loch Fèith an Leòthaid
Beinn Gharbh
1769
Fionn Loch Mór
Soyea Island
Loch Inver
Loch Culag
Inchnadamph
Inchnadamph Forest
Gleann Dubh
River Traligill
Maovally
1673
Kirkaig Point
Strathan
Glencanisp Forest
BEN MORE ASSYNT
3273
A' Chleit
Badnaban
Loch Kirkaig
Inverkirkaig
Abhainn na Clach Airigh
Loch na Gainimh
CANISP
2779
River Loanan
Rubha Coigeach
River Kirkaig
Falls of Kirkaig
SUILVEN
2399
2338
Loch Carn nan Conbhairean
Fionn Loch
Lochan Fada
Meall an Aonaich
2344
Duch
Eilean Mór
Loch na Totaig
Camas Coille
Loch a' Ghille
Inchnadamph Bone Caves
Breabag
Enard Bay
Loch Buine Mòire
Loch Awe
2670
Benmore Forest
Rubha Mór
Inverpolly Lodge
Loch Sionascaig
Loch Veyatie
Ledbeg River
Cam Loch
Brea of Achnahaird
Altandhu
Loch Doire na h-Airbhe
CUL MOR
2787
A835
Loch Meall a' Bhuirich
Loch Raa
Loch Osgaig
Polly
Inverpolly Forest
Ledmore
Loch Vatachan
Aird of Coigach
Elphin
Altnacealgach
Benmore Lodge
Stac Pollaidh
2009
Loch an Doire Dhuibh
Drumrunie Forest
Loch Borralan
Loch Ailsh
Polbain
Badentarbat
Loch Bad a' Ghaill
Knockan
Loch Urigill
Badentarbat Bay
Linneraineach
Lochan an Ais
Knockan Crag
Glen Oykel
An Stùc
1195
Beinn an Eoin
1786
Loch Lurgainn
2523
Cùl Beag
Cnoc na Glas Choille
1006
164
Achiltibuie
Polglass
Clar Loch Mór
Eileag
River Oykel
Loch n
Tanera Mór
Lochan Dearg
Crom Allt
Isles
Badenscallie
Lochan Tuath
1692
CROMALT HILLS
Allt
Horse Sound
Drumrunie
18
Loch Craggie
Loch Claise
Lochanan Dubha
Allt a' Chaoruinn
1084
Horse Island
2438
C O I G A C H
Fionn Bheinn Mhòr
Ben More Coigach (Beinn Mhòr na Coigich)
Achduart
Culnacraig
Loch Eadar dha Bheinn
Strath Canaird
Meall an Fhuarain
1895
Coire a' Chonachair
Loch a' Chroisg
Lubcroy
Carn nan Sgeir
River Runie
River Canaird
Strathcanaird
Rappach
Strath nan Lon
Na Dromannan
1337
Oykel Bridge
Camas Mór
Cailleach Head
Leac Dhonn
Isle Martin
Loch Kanaird
Creag na h-Iolaire
947
Loch Dubh
Loch na Maoile
Lochanan Sàilean Mòra
Allt Beinn Donuill
Rappach Water
River Einig
Glen Einig
Ardmair
Loch ob an Lochain
Rhidorroch Forest
Annat Bay
Rhue
Loch a' Choire Bhuig
Meall Liath Choire
1798
Creag Loisgte
1353
Little
Scoraig
Achmore
Carnach
H I G H L A N D
Morefield
Rhidorroch
Clar Lochan
Loch an Daimh
Rireavach
Ullapool River
Glen Achall
Badluarach
Beinn Ghobhlach
Clock
Ullapool
Loch Achall
Rhidorroch River
Corriemulzie River
Loch na h-Uidhe
2082
Loch
Beinn Eilideach
1830
East Rhidorroch Lodge
NORTH WEST HIGHLANDS
Sidhean Raireag
1769
Glasha Burn
Dunramuck
Allt na h' Airbhe
Glen Douchary
Lochan Badan Glasliath
Strath Mulzie
Badcaul
Badrallach
Broom
Dun an Ruigh Ruadh
Leckmelm
38
Loch Lagaidh
Blarnalearoch
Loggie
Dun Lagaidh
Rhiroy
Meall Dubh
2105
2221
Meall nam Bràdham
Ardessie
Ardessie Falls
2508
Camusnagaul
Sàil Mhòr
A832
Strath Beag
Ardindrean
Ardcharnich
Broom
River Douchary
Loch a' Choire Mhòir
Freevater Forest
Alladale
Carn nam Buailtean
1283
Lochan Gaineamhaich
Dundonnell
Seana Bhraigh
3040
2772
Càm Bàn
Letters
Loch Reidh Creagain
Carn Mór
2122
Loch Mór Bad an Ducharaich
Loch an Eich Dhuibh
AN TEALLACH
Loch a' Chairn Mor
Inverlael Forest
11
Loch Sruban Mòra
Loch Sgeire
Inverlael
River Lael
Eididh nan Clach Geala
3039
Strathnasheallag Forest
3484
Carn a' Bhiorain
1665
Auchlunachan
Lael Forest
Gleann Beag
Abhainn a' Ghlinne Bhig
Deanich Lodge
Loch na Sealga
Loch Toll an Lochain
Loch Coire Chaorachain
Loch Allt Eigin
Loch an Airceil
BEINN DEARG
Loch Ghiubsachain
Dundonnell Forest
Lochan Fraoich
River Broom
Beinn Enaiglair
2915
3547
Loch Prille
Tollomuick Forest
Beinn a' Chaisteil
2404
Fisherfield Forest
Strath na Sealga
Beinn Dearg Mór
2974
Dundonnell River
Lochan Fada
Loch an t-Sidhein
Loch a' Choire Ghrenda
Lochan na Bearta
156
Loch Beinn Dearg
1270
Carn Breac Beag
Braemore
Corrieshalloch Gorge
Loch nan Cleireach
157
Coire Lair
Loch
Meall a' Ghrianain
2531
2802
Beinn a' Chlaidheimh
Abhainn Cuileig
Falls of Measach
Allt Mhucarnaich
Meall Leacachain
2028
Lochan Feith Mhic'illean
Meall an t-Sithe
1971
Braemore Forest
Dubh Loch
Fuar Loch Mór
Loch a'
Loch a' Gharbhrain
Strathvaich Forest
Inchbae Forest
Loch Vaich

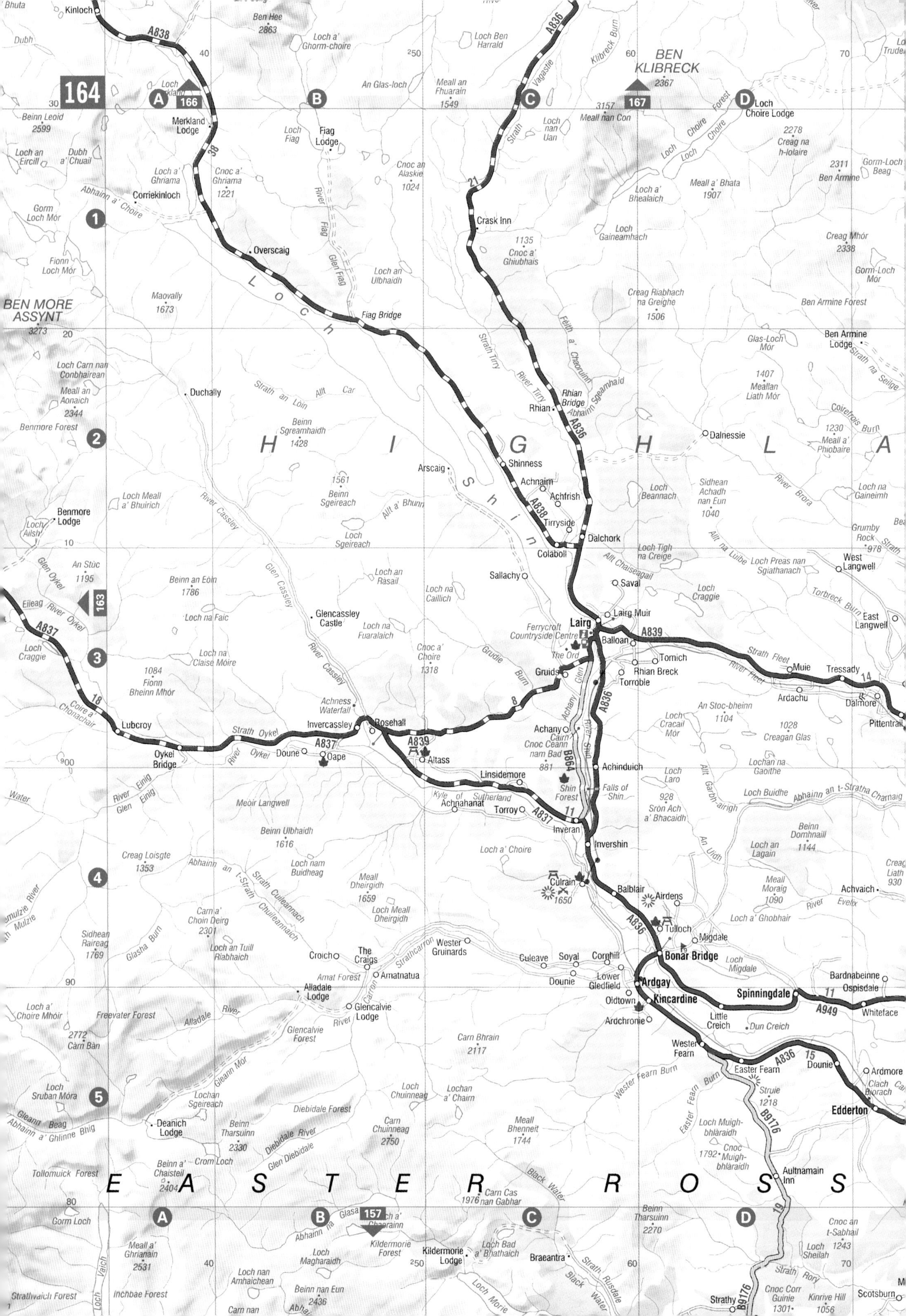

Bhuta
Kinloch
A838
Ben Hee
2863
Loch a' Ghorm-choire
Loch Ben Harrald
A836
Klibreck Burn
Dubh
40
250
60
BEN KLIBRECK
2367
70
Loch Truderscaig
164
A
166
B
An Glas-loch
Meall an Fhuarain
1549
C
Vagastie
3157
Meall nan Con
167
D
Loch Choire Lodge
30
Beinn Leoid
2599
Merkland Lodge
Loch Fiag
Fiag Lodge
Strath
Loch nan Uan
Loch Choire
Forest
2278
Creag na h-Iolaire
Loch an Eircill
Dubh a' Chuail
38
Loch a' Ghriama
Cnoc a' Ghriama
1221
Cnoc an Alaskie
1024
River Fiag
21
Loch a' Bhealaich
Meall a' Bhata
1907
2311
Ben Armine
Gorm-Loch Beag
Abhainn a' Choire
Corriekinloch
Gorm Loch Mór
1
Crask Inn
Loch Gaineamhach
Creag Mhór
2338
Overscaig
Glen Fiag
1135
Cnoc a' Ghiubhais
Fionn Loch Mór
Loch an Ulbhaidh
Gorm-Loch Mór
Loch
Creag Riabhach na Greighe
1506
Maovally
1673
Ben Armine Forest
BEN MORE ASSYNT
3273
Fiag Bridge
20
Glas-Loch Mór
Ben Armine Lodge
Strath na Seilge
Strath Tirry
Féith a' Chaoruinn
Loch Carn nan Conbhairean
Meall an Aonaich
2344
Duchally
Strath an Lòin
Allt Car
River Tirry
Rhian Bridge
Abhainn Sgeamhaid
1407
Meallan Liath Mór
Rhian
A836
Coirefrois Burn
Benmore Forest
2
Beinn Sgreamhaidh
1428
1230
Meall a' Phiobaire
Dalnessie
H I G H L A
Arscaig
Shinness
Achnairn
Achfrish
1561
Beinn Sgeireach
Loch Beannach
Sidhean Achadh nan Eun
1040
River Brora
Loch na Gaineimh
Loch Meall a' Bhuirich
River Cassley
Allt a' Bhunn
A838
Benmore Lodge
Loch Ailsh
Tirryside
Loch Sgeireach
Dalchork
Grumby Rock
978
10
Colaboll
Loch Tigh na Creige
Allt na Luibe
Loch Preas nan Sgiathanach
West Langwell
Glen Oykel
An Stùc
1195
Beinn an Eòin
1786
Loch an Ràsail
Sallachy
Allt Chaiseagail
Saval
Loch na Caillich
Loch Craggie
Torbreck Burn
163
Eileag
River Oykel
Loch na Faic
Glen Cassley
Glencassley Castle
Loch na Fuaralaich
Lairg
Lairg Muir
East Langwell
A837
Ferrycroft Countryside Centre
A839
Balloan
Loch Craggie
3
Loch na Claise Móire
Cnoc a' Choire
1318
The Ord
Tomich
Strath Fleet
Muie
Tressady
1084
Fionn Bheinn Mhór
River Cassley
Grudie Burn
Gruids
Rhian Breck
River Fleet
Torroble
14
18
Coire a' Chonachair
Achness Waterfall
Ardachu
Dalmore
Pittentrail
8
Glen Achany
A836
Loch Cracail Mór
An Stoc-bheinn
1104
Lubcroy
Invercassley
Rosehall
Achany
Cairn
1028
Creagan Glas
Strath Oykel
A837
A839
Cnoc Ceann nam Bad
881
Oykel Bridge
River Oykel
Doune
Oape
Altass
B864
River Shin
Achinduich
Lochan na Gaoithe
900
Linsidemore
Loch Laro
Allt Garbh-airigh
Water
River Einig
Glen Einig
Shin Forest
Falls of Shin
Loch Buidhe
Abhainn an t-Stratha Charnaig
Meòir Langwell
Kyle of Sutherland
Achnahanat
Torroy
A837
11
928
Sròn Ach a' Bhacaidh
Beinn Domhnaill
1144
Inveran
Beinn Ulbhaidh
1616
Invershin
Loch an Lagain
Creag Liath
930
Creag Loisgte
1353
Abhainn an t-Strath
Loch nam Buidheag
Loch a' Choire
An Uidh
4
Strath Cuileannach
Meall Dheirgidh
1659
Culrain
1650
Balblair
Meall Moraig
1090
Achvaich
Airdens
River Evelix
Carn a' Choin Deirg
2301
Loch Meall Dheirgidh
A836
Loch a' Ghobhair
Sidhean Raireag
1769
Glasha Burn
Loch an Tuill Riabhaich
Strathcarron
Wester Gruinards
Tulloch
Migdale
Croich
The Craigs
Culeave
Soyal
Cornhill
Bonar Bridge
Loch Migdale
90
Amat Forest
Amatnatua
Lower Gledfield
Dounie
Ardgay
Bardnabeinne
Ospisdale
Alladale Lodge
Oldtown
Kincardine
Spinningdale
11
Loch a' Choire Mhóir
Freevater Forest
Alladale
River
Glencalvie Lodge
River
A949
Whiteface
Little Creich
Dun Creich
Ardchronie
Glencalvie Forest
2772
Carn Bàn
Carn Bhrain
2117
Wester Fearn
Easter Fearn
A836
15
Dounie
Ardmore
Loch Sruban Móra
5
Gleann Mór
Lochan Sgeireach
Loch Chuinneag
Lochan a' Chairn
Wester Fearn Burn
Struie
1218
Clach Biorach
Diebidale Forest
Easter Fearn Burn
Edderton
Gleann Beag
Deanich Lodge
Beinn Tharsuinn
2330
Carn Chuinneag
2750
Meall Bhenneit
1744
Loch Muigh-bhlàraidh
B9176
Abhainn a' Ghlinne Bhig
Diebidale River
Glen Diebidale
1792
Cnoc Muigh-bhlàraidh
Crom Loch
Beinn a' Chaisteil
2404
Tollomuick Forest
Black Water
Aultnamain Inn
E A S T E R R O S S
Carn Cas nan Gabhar
1976
80
A
B
157
Loch a' Chaorainn
C
Beinn Tharsuinn
2270
D
19
Gorm Loch
Abhainn na Glasa
Kildermorie Forest
Loch Bad a' Bhathaich
Cnoc an t-Sabhail
1243
Meall a' Ghrianain
2531
Loch Magharaidh
Kildermorie Lodge
Braeantra
Strath Rusdale
Loch Sheilah
40
250
60
70
Loch nan Amhaichean
Strath Rory
Black Water
Loch Vaich
Inchbae Forest
Beinn nan Eun
2436
Loch Morie
Strathy
B9176
Cnoc Corr Guinie
1301
Kinrive Hill
1056
Scotsburn
Strathvaich Forest
Carn nan

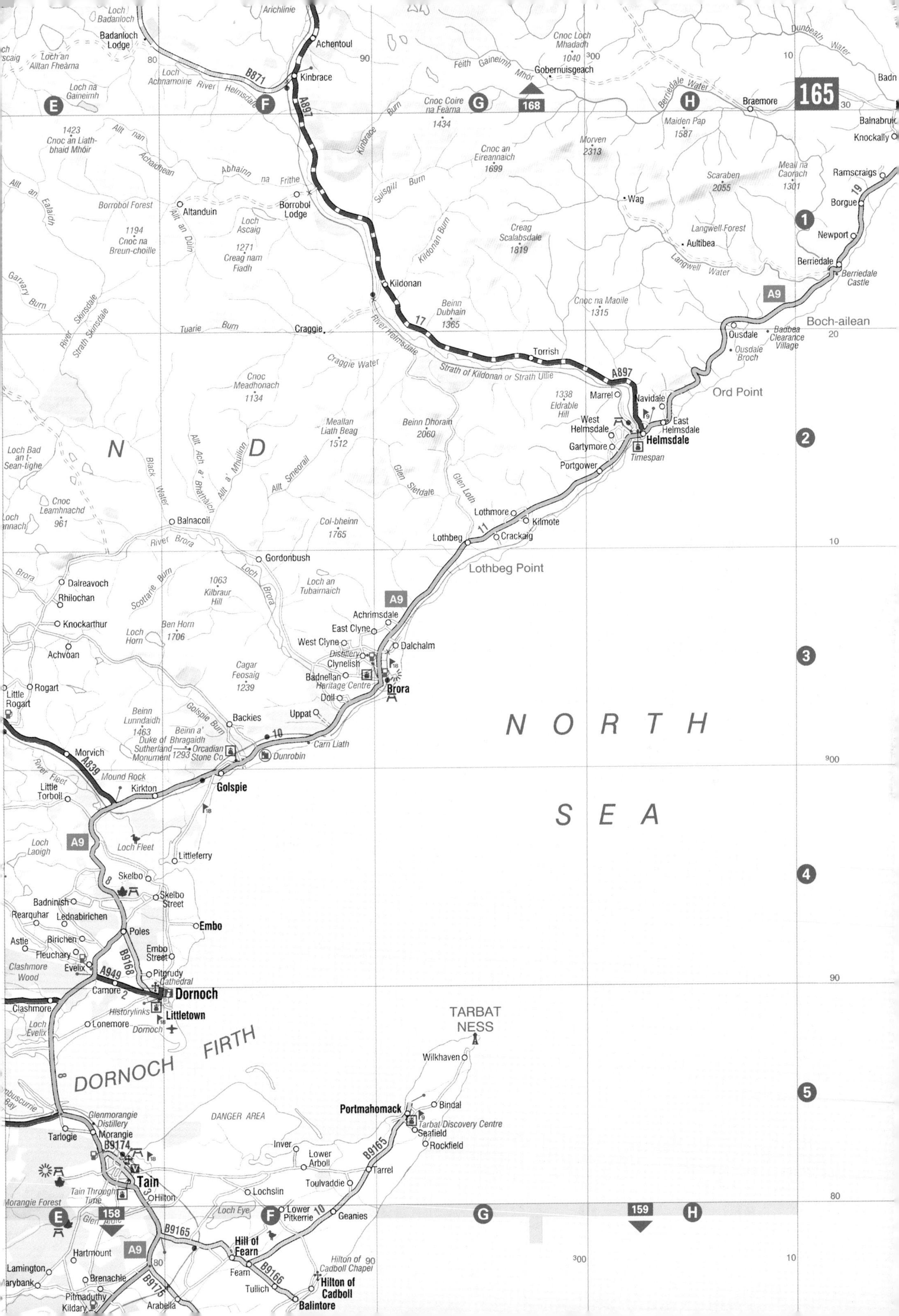
165
Loch Badanloch
Arichlinie
Badanloch Lodge
Achentoul
Loch an Alltan Fhearna
Loch Achnamoine
River Helmsdale
B871
Kinbrace
Loch na Gaineimh
E
F
A897
Cnoc Coire na Fearna
1434
G
168
Cnoc Loch Mhadadh
1040
Feith Gaineimh Mhor
Gobernuisgeach
Berriedale Water
H
Braemore
Dunbeath Water
Badn
Balnabruic
Knockally
1423
Cnoc an Liath-bhaid Mhòir
Allt nan Achaidhean
Abhainn na Frithe
Kinbrace Burn
Cnoc an Eireannaich
1699
Morven
2313
Maiden Pap
1587
Scaraben
2055
Meall na Caorach
1301
Ramscraigs
Borgue
Allt an Ealaidh
Borrobol Forest
Altanduin
Allt an Dùin
Borrobol Lodge
Suisgill Burn
Wag
1
Newport
Loch Ascaig
1194
Cnoc na Breun-choille
1271
Creag nam Fiadh
Kildonan Burn
Creag Scalabsdale
1819
Langwell Forest
Aultibea
Langwell Water
Berriedale
Berriedale Castle
Garvary Burn
Kildonan
Beinn Dubhain
1365
Cnoc na Maoile
1315
A9
River Skinsdale
Strath Skinsdale
Tuarie Burn
Craggie
River Helmsdale
17
Boch-ailean
Ousdale
Badbea Clearance Village
Ousdale Broch
Craggie Water
Torrish
Strath of Kildonan or Strath Ullie
A897
Cnoc Meadhonach
1134
1338
Eldrable Hill
Marrel
Navidale
Ord Point
Meallan Liath Beag
1512
Beinn Dhorain
2060
West Helmsdale
East Helmsdale
Helmsdale
Timespan
Gartymore
Loch Bad an t-Sean-tighe
N
D
Black Water
Allt Ach a' Bhathaich
Allt a' Mhuilinn
Allt Smeorail
Glen Sletdale
Glen Loth
Portgower
2
Cnoc Leamhnachd
961
Balnacoil
Col-bheinn
1765
Lothmore
Kilmote
Lothbeg
11
Crackaig
River Brora
Gordonbush
Loch Brora
Lothbeg Point
Brora
Dalreavoch
Rhilochan
Scottarie Burn
1063
Kilbraur Hill
Loch an Tubairnaich
A9
Knockarthur
Loch Horn
Ben Horn
1706
Achrimsdale
East Clyne
Achvoan
West Clyne
Dalchalm
Distillery
Clynelish
Cagar Feosaig
1239
Badnellan
Heritage Centre
Brora
3
Little Rogart
Rogart
Doll
Beinn Lunndaidh
1463
Golspie Burn
Backies
Uppat
N O R T H
Beinn a' Bhragaidh
Duke of Sutherland Monument
1293
Orcadian Stone Co
10
Carn Liath
Dunrobin
Morvich
A839
River Fleet
Mound Rock
Little Torboll
Kirkton
Golspie
S E A
Loch Laoigh
A9
Loch Fleet
Littleferry
8
Skelbo
4
Skelbo Street
Badninish
Rearquhar
Lednabirichen
Embo
Poles
Astle
Birichen
Embo Street
Fleuchary
Clashmore Wood
Evelix
A949
B9168
Pitgrudy
Cathedral
Camore
2
Dornoch
Clashmore
Historylinks
Littletown
Loch Evelix
Lonemore
Dornoch
TARBAT NESS
DORNOCH FIRTH
Wilkhaven
8
Cambuscurrie Bay
DANGER AREA
Portmahomack
Bindal
5
Glenmorangie Distillery
Morangie
Tarlogie
Tarbat Discovery Centre
Seafield
Rockfield
B9174
Inver
Lower Arboll
B9165
Tarrel
Tain
Toulvaddie
Morangie Forest
Tain Through Time
Hilton
3
Lochslin
Loch Eye
Lower Pitkerrie
10
Geanies
E
158
F
G
159
H
Glen Aldie
B9165
Hill of Fearn
Hartmount
A9
Lamington
80
Fearn
B9166
Hilton of Cadboll Chapel
Hilton of Cadboll
Brenachie
Marybank
Pitmaduthy
Tullich
Kildary
B9175
Arabella
Balintore
80
90
300
10
30
20
10
900
90
80
300
10

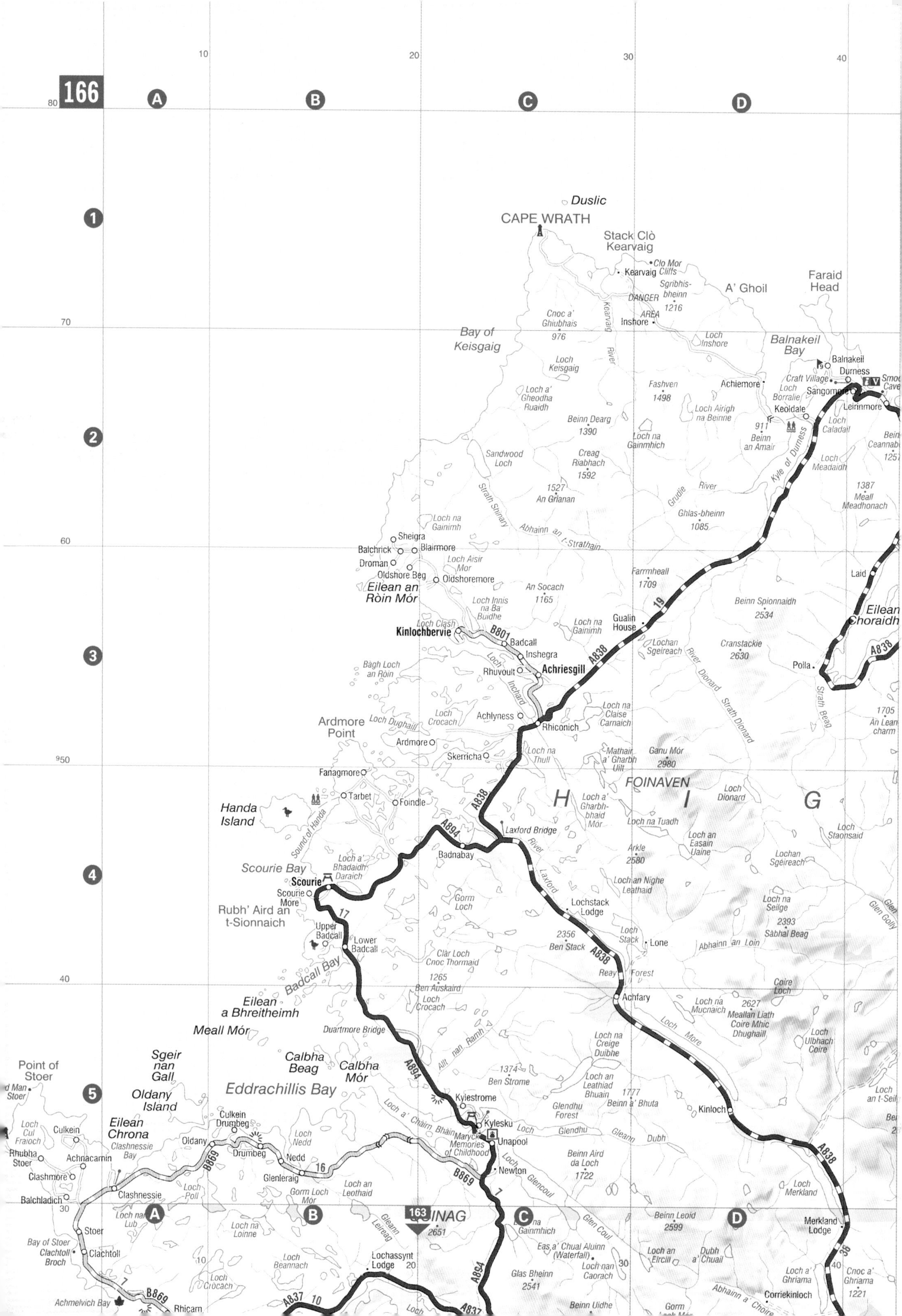

A
B
C
D
CAPE WRATH
Duslic
Stack Clò Kearvaig
Clo Mor Cliffs
Kearvaig
Sgribhis-bheinn 1216
DANGER AREA
Inshore
A' Ghoil
Faraid Head
Bay of Keisgaig
Cnoc a' Ghiubhais 976
Loch Keisgaig
Loch Inshore
Balnakeil Bay
Balnakeil
Craft Village
Durness
Smoo Cave
Sangomore
Achiemore
Loch Borralie
Leirinmore
Fashven 1498
Loch a' Gheodha Ruaidh
Loch Airigh na Beinne
Keoldale
Beinn Dearg 1390
Loch na Gainmhich
911 Beinn an Amair
Loch Caladail
Kyle of Durness
Sandwood Loch
Creag Riabhach 1592
Loch Meadaidh
1527 An Grianan
Strath Shinary
Grudie River
1387 Meall Meadhonach
Ghlas-bheinn 1085
Loch na Gainimh
Abhainn an t-Strathain
Sheigra
Balchrick
Blairmore
Droman
Loch Aisir Mor
Oldshore Beg
Oldshoremore
Eilean an Ròin Mór
Farrmheall 1709
An Socach 1165
Laid
Loch Innis na Ba Buidhe
Beinn Spionnaidh 2534
Eilean Choraidh
Loch Clash
Kinlochbervie
B801
Badcall
Loch na Gainimh
Gualin House
19
Inshegra
Lochan Sgeireach
Cranstackie 2630
A838
Bàgh Loch an Ròin
Loch Inchard
Rhuvoult
Achriesgill
River Dionard
Polla
Strath Dionard
Strath Beag
Loch Crocach
Achlyness
Loch na Claise Carnaich
1705 An Leam charm
Ardmore Point
Loch Dughaill
Rhiconich
Ardmore
Loch na Thull
Mathair a' Gharbh Uilt
Ganu Mór 2980
Skerricha
Fanagmore
FOINAVEN
Loch Dionard
H
I
G
Tarbet
Foindle
Handa Island
Sound of Handa
Loch a' Gharbh-bhaid Mór
Laxford Bridge
Loch na Tuadh
Loch Staonsaid
A894
River Laxford
Badnabay
Arkle 2580
Loch an Easain Uaine
Lochan Sgeireach
Scourie Bay
Loch a' Bhadaidh Daraich
Loch an Nighe Leathaid
Scourie
Scourie More
Gorm Loch
Rubh' Aird an t-Sionnaich
17
Lochstack Lodge
Loch na Seilge
Glen Golly
2393 Sàbhal Beag
Upper Badcall
2356 Ben Stack
Loch Stack
Lone
Lower Badcall
Clàr Loch
Cnoc Thormaid
Abhainn an Loin
1265 Ben Auskaird
Reay Forest
Coire Loch
Badcall Bay
Loch Crocach
Achfary
Eilean a Bhreitheimh
Loch na Mucnaich
2627 Meallan Liath Coire Mhic Dhughaill
Loch More
Meall Mór
Duartmore Bridge
Allt nan Ramh
Loch Ulbhach Coire
Loch na Creige Duibhe
Point of Stoer
Sgeir nan Gall
Calbha Beag
Calbha Mór
1374 Ben Strome
Loch an Leathiad Bhuain
Old Man of Stoer
Oldany Island
Eddrachillis Bay
Kylestrome
1777 Beinn a' Bhuta
Kinloch
Loch an t-Seil
Loch Cul Fraioch
Culkein
Eilean Chrona
Culkein Drumbeg
Loch Nedd
Loch a' Chàirn Bhàin
Glendhu Forest
Kylesku
Clashnessie Bay
Oldany
Marycks Memories of Childhood
Unapool
Loch Glendhu
Gleann Dubh
Rhubha Stoer
Achnacarnin
B869
Drumbeg
Nedd
Beinn Aird da Loch 1722
A838
16
Loch Glencoul
Clashmore
Glenleraig
Newton
Loch Poll
Gorm Loch Mor
Loch an Leothaid
Loch Merkland
Clashnessie
Balchladich
Loch nan Lub
163
QUINAG 2651
Gleann Leireag
Loch na Gainmhich
Glen Coul
Beinn Leoid 2599
Merkland Lodge
Stoer
Loch na Loinne
Bay of Stoer
Clachtoll Broch
Clachtoll
Loch Beannach
Lochassynt Lodge
Eas a' Chual Aluinn (Waterfall)
Loch nan Caorach
Loch an Eircill
Dubh a' Chuail
Loch a' Ghriama
Cnoc a' Ghriama 1221
Loch Crocach
Glas Bheinn 2541
Corriekinloch
Abhainn a' Choire
Achmelvich Bay
B869
Rhicarn
A837
Beinn Uidhe
Gorm

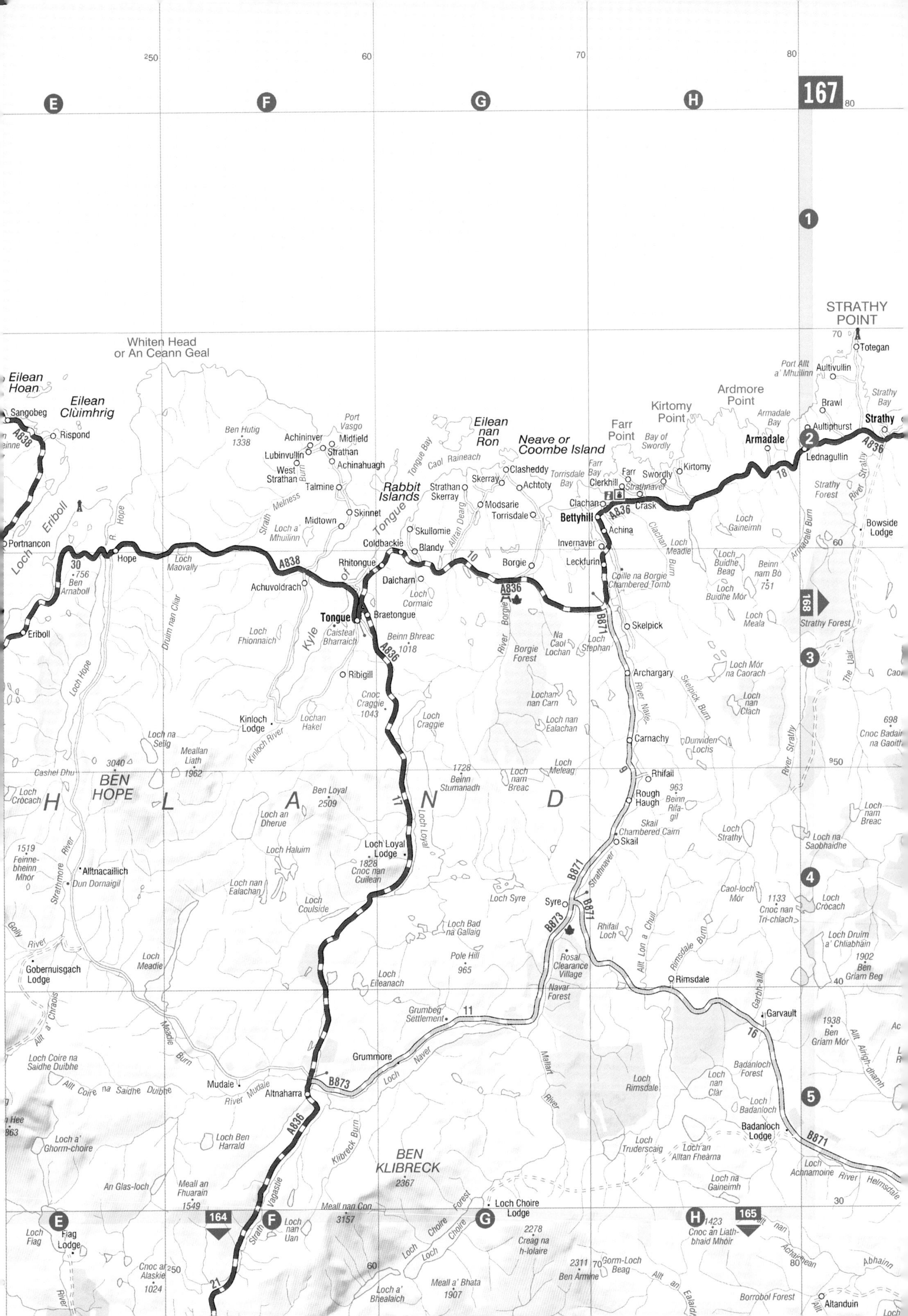
167
STRATHY POINT
Totegan
Aultivullin
Port Allt a' Mhuilinn
Strathy Bay
Brawl
Aultiphurst
Strathy
Ardmore Point
Armadale Bay
Armadale
Lednagullin
A836
Kirtomy Point
Kirtomy
Farr Point
Bay of Swordly
Swordly
Farr
Farr Bay
Clerkhill
Strathnaver
Clachan
Crask
Bettyhill
Achina
Invernaver
Leckfurin
Torrisdale Bay
Torrisdale
Neave or Coombe Island
Eilean nan Ron
Clasheddy
Skerray
Achtoty
Strathan Skerray
Modsarie
Borgie
Caol Raineach
Rabbit Islands
Tongue Bay
Kyle of Tongue
Skullomie
Coldbackie
Blandy
Rhitongue
Dalcharn
Loch Cormaic
Tongue
Braetongue
Caisteal Bharraich
Beinn Bhreac 1018
Ribigill
Cnoc Craggie 1043
Loch Craggie
Port Vasgo
Achininver
Midfield
Strathan
Lubinvullin
Achinahuagh
West Strathan
Talmine
Skinnet
Midtown
Strath Melness
Loch a' Mhuilinn
Ben Hutig 1338
Whiten Head or An Ceann Geal
Eilean Hoan
Eilean Clùimhrig
Sangobeg
Rispond
A838
Loch Eriboll
Portnancon
Eriboll
Hope
R. Hope
Ben Arnaboll 756
Loch Maovally
Achuvoldrach
Loch Fhionnaich
Loch Hope
Druim nan Cliar
Kinloch Lodge
Kinloch River
Lochan Hakel
Loch na Seilg
Meallan Liath 1962
BEN HOPE 3040
Cashel Dhu
Loch Cròcach
H L A N D
Ben Loyal 2509
Loch an Dherue
Loch Haluim
Loch Loyal Lodge
Loch Loyal
1828 Cnoc nan Cuilean
1519 Feinne-bheinn Mhòr
Strathmore River
Alltnacaillich
Dun Dornaigil
Loch nan Ealachan
Loch Coulside
Golly River
Gobernuisgach Lodge
Loch Meadie
Meadie Burn
Loch Coire na Saidhe Duibhe
Allt Coire na Saidhe Duibhe
Allt a' Chraois
Mudale
River Mudale
Altnaharra
Grummore
B873
Loch Naver
Grumbeg Settlement
Loch Eileanach
Loch Ben Harrald
Loch a' Ghorm-choire
Hee 863
An Glas-loch
Meall an Fhuarain 1549
Strath Vagastie
A836
Loch nan Uan
Loch Fiag
Fiag Lodge
Cnoc an Alaskie 1024
River
BEN KLIBRECK 2367
Klibreck Burn
Meall nan Con 3157
Loch Choire Forest
Loch Choire Lodge
Loch Choire
Loch a' Bhealaich
Meall a' Bhata 1907
Creag na h-Iolaire 2278
Ben Armine 2311
Gorm-Loch Beag
Allt an Ealaidh
Borrobol Forest
Altanduin
Abhainn
Achaineran
Cnoc an Liath-bhaid Mhòir 1423
Loch na Gaineimh
Loch an Alltan Fhearna
Loch Truderscaig
Loch Achnamoine
River Helmsdale
Badanloch Lodge
B871
Loch Badanloch
Loch nan Clàr
Badanloch Forest
Loch Rimsdale
Mallart River
Garvault
Garbh-allt
Ben Griam Mòr 1938
Allt Airigh-dhamh
Ben Griam Beg 1902
Loch Druim a' Chliabhain
Loch Cròcach
Cnoc nan Tri-chlach 1133
Caol-loch Mòr
Loch na Saobhaidhe
Loch nam Breac
Loch Strathy
River Strathy
Cnoc Badaidh na Gaoithe 698
The Uair
Strathy Forest
168
Loch Mòr na Caorach
Loch nan Clach
Loch Meala
Loch Buidhe Mòr
Beinn nam Bò 751
Loch Buidhe Beag
Loch Gaineimh
Loch Meadie
Armadale Burn
Strathy Forest
Bowside Lodge
Strathy River
Clachan Burn
Coille na Borgie Chambered Tomb
B871
Skelpick
Skelpick Burn
Loch Stephan
Na Caol Lochan
Borgie Forest
River Borgie
Archargary
River Naver
Lochan nan Carn
Loch nan Ealachan
Carnachy
Dunviden Lochs
Loch Meleag
Loch nam Breac
1728 Beinn Stumanadh
Rhifail
Rough Haugh
Beinn Rifa-gil 963
Skail Chambered Cairn
Skail
Strathnaver
Loch Syre
Syre
Loch Bad na Gallaig
Rhifail Loch
Allt Lon a Chuil
Rimsdale Burn
Rimsdale
Pole Hill 965
Rosal Clearance Village
Navar Forest
Allt an Alltan
164
165
E F G H
1 2 3 4 5

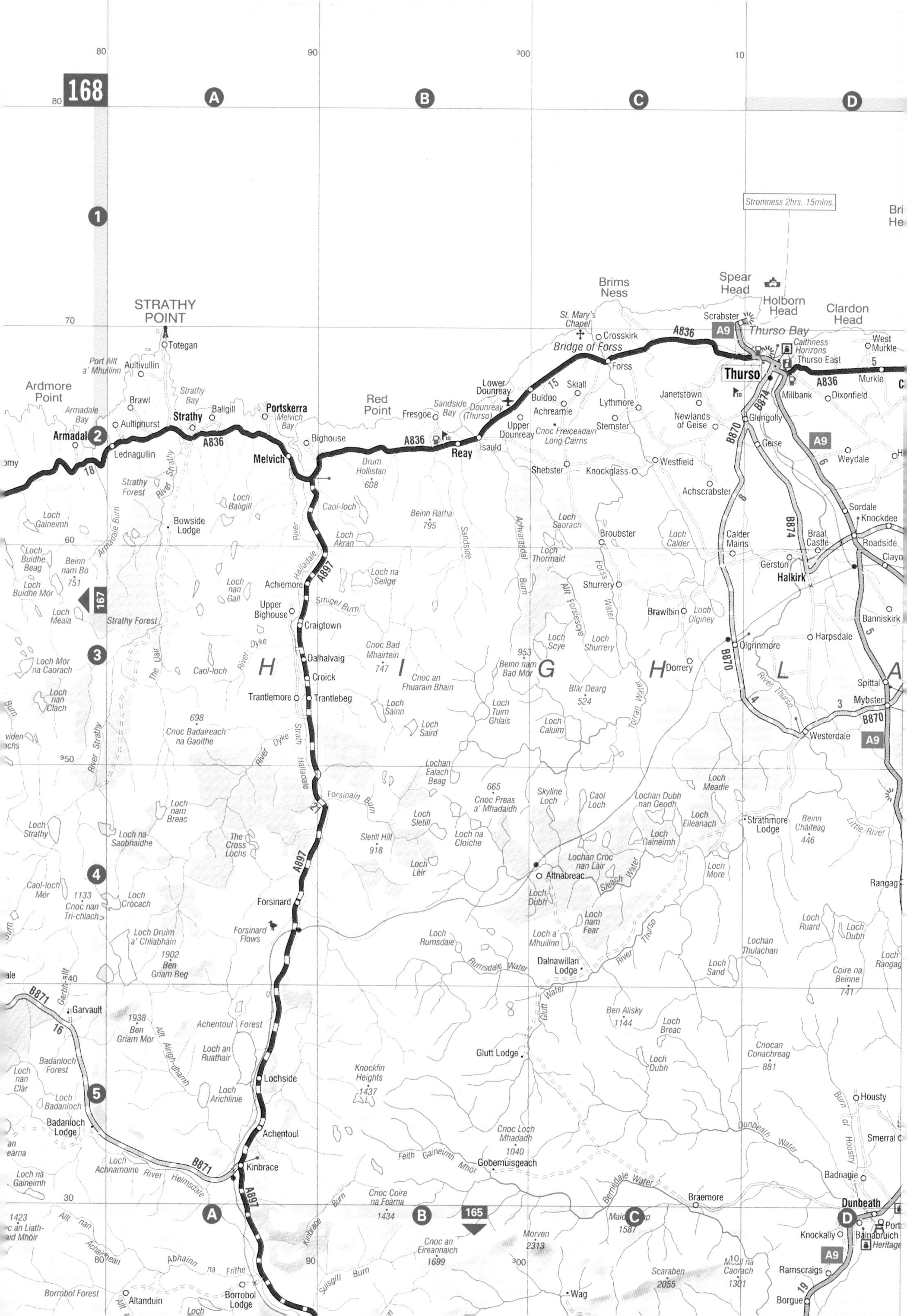

168
A
B
C
D
1
2
3
4
5
167
165
STRATHY POINT
Totegan
Ardmore Point
Armadale Bay
Armadale
Port Allt a' Mhuilinn
Aultivullin
Strathy Bay
Brawl
Aultiphurst
Strathy
Baligill
Portskerra
Melvich Bay
Lednagullin
A836
Melvich
Bighouse
Red Point
Fresgoe
Sandside Bay
Reay
Lower Dounreay
Dounreay (Thurso)
Upper Dounreay
Isauld
Buldoo
Achreamie
Skiall
Brims Ness
St. Mary's Chapel
Crosskirk
Bridge of Forss
Forss
Lythmore
Stemster
Cnoc Freiceadain Long Cairns
Spear Head
Scrabster
Holborn Head
Thurso Bay
Clardon Head
Caithness Horizons
Thurso East
West Murkle
Murkle
Thurso
Millbank
Dixonfield
Janetstown
Newlands of Geise
Glengolly
Geise
Weydale
Stromness 2hrs. 15mins.
A9
B874
B870
Westfield
Knockglass
Shebster
Achscrabster
Sordale
Knockdee
Braal Castle
Roadside
Calder Mains
Gerston
Halkirk
Loch Calder
Broubster
Loch Saorach
Loch Thormaid
Shurrery
Brawlbin
Loch Olginey
Banniskirk
Harpsdale
Olgrinmore
Dorrery
Spittal
Mybster
Westerdale
River Thurso
Drum Hollistan 608
Caol-loch
Beinn Ratha 795
Loch Akran
Loch na Seilge
Achiemore
Upper Bighouse
Craigtown
Dalhalvaig
Croick
Trantlemore
Trantlebeg
Smigel Burn
Halladale
A897
Strathy Forest
Loch Baligill
Bowside Lodge
Loch Gaineimh
Loch Buidhe Beag
Beinn nam Bò 751
Loch Buidhe Mòr
Loch Meala
Loch nan Gall
Loch Mòr na Caorach
Loch nan Clach
Caol-loch
698 Cnoc Badaireach na Gaoithe
HIGHLAND
Cnoc Bad Mhairtein 747
Cnoc an Fhuarain Bhain
953 Beinn nam Bad Mòr
Loch Scye
Loch Shurrery
Blàr Dearg 524
Loch Tuim Ghlais
Loch Calium
Loch Sàinn
Loch Saird
Lochan Ealach Beag
665 Cnoc Preas a' Mhadaidh
Skyline Loch
Caol Loch
Lochan Dubh nan Geodh
Loch Meadie
Strathmore Lodge
Beinn Chàiteag 446
Loch Eileanach
Loch Gaineimh
Loch Sletill
Sletill Hill 918
Loch na Cloiche
Loch Lèir
Lochan Cròc nan Lair
Altnabreac
Loch Dubh
Loch More
Rangag
Forsinain Burn
Loch nam Breac
Loch Strathy
Loch na Saobhaidhe
The Cross Lochs
Caol-loch Mòr
1133 Cnoc nan Tri-chlach
Loch Cròcach
Forsinard
Forsinard Flows
Loch Druim a' Chliabhain
1902 Ben Griam Beg
Loch nam Fear
Loch a' Mhuilinn
Loch Rumsdale
Rumsdale Water
Dalnawillan Lodge
Loch Sand
Lochan Thulachan
Loch Ruard
Loch Dubh
Coire na Beinne 741
B871
Garvault
1938 Ben Griam Mòr
Achentoul Forest
Loch an Ruathair
Ben Alisky 1144
Loch Breac
Glutt Lodge
Glutt Water
Cnocan Conachreag 881
Badanloch Forest
Loch nan Clàr
Loch Badanloch
Badanloch Lodge
Lochside
Loch Arichlinie
Knockfin Heights 1437
Loch Dubh
Achentoul
Cnoc Loch Mhadadh 1040
Gobernuisgeach
Fèith Gaineimh Mhòr
Kinbrace
Loch Achnamoine
River Helmsdale
Loch na Gaineimh
Berriedale Water
Braemore
Dunbeath Water
Housty
Smerral
Badnagie
Dunbeath
Knockally
Balnabruich
Heritage
Ramscraigs
Borgue
Cnoc Coire na Feàrna 1434
Maiden Pap 1587
Morven 2313
Cnoc an Eireannaich 1699
Scaraben 2055
Meall na Caorach 1301
Wag
Suisgill Burn
Abhainn na Frithe
Borrobol Lodge
Borrobol Forest
Altanduin
1423

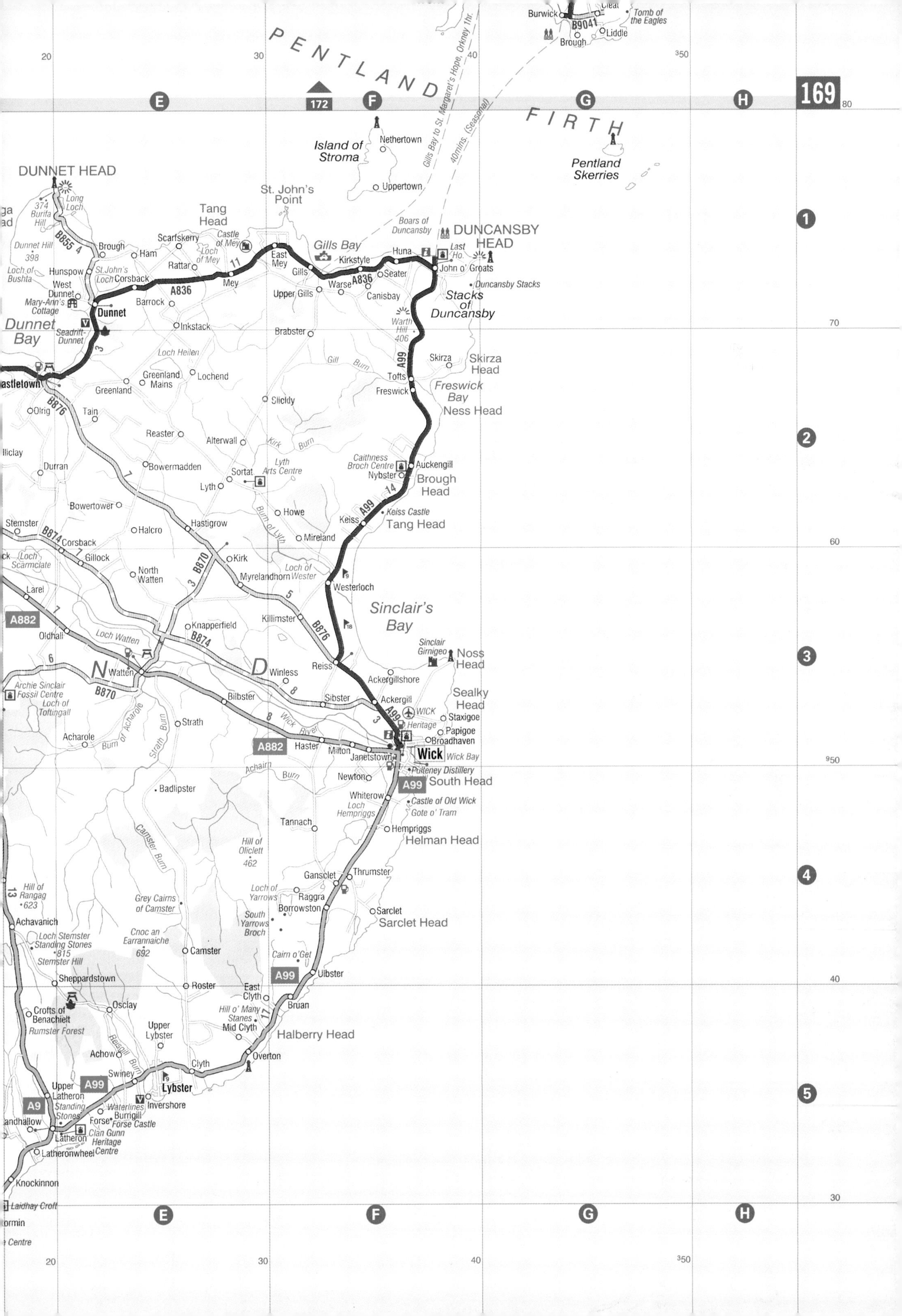
PENTLAND FIRTH
172
Island of Stroma
Nethertown
Uppertown
Gills Bay to St. Margaret's Hope, Orkney 1hr.
40mins. (Seasonal)
Pentland Skerries
Burwick
B9041
Brough
Liddle
Tomb of the Eagles
DUNNET HEAD
Long Loch
374 Burifa Hill
Dunnet Hill 398
Loch of Bushta
B855
Brough
Ham
Scarfskerry
Tang Head
Castle of Mey
Loch of Mey
St. John's Point
East Mey
Gills Bay
Huna
Last Ho.
Boars of Duncansby
DUNCANSBY HEAD
John o' Groats
Duncansby Stacks
Stacks of Duncansby
Hunspow
St.John's Loch
Corsback
Rattar
Mey
Gills
Kirkstyle
Seater
Warse
A836
Canisbay
Upper Gills
West Dunnet
Mary-Ann's Cottage
Dunnet
Barrock
Dunnet Bay
Seadrift-Dunnet
Inkstack
Brabster
Warth Hill 406
Loch Heilen
Gill Burn
Skirza
Skirza Head
A99
Tofts
Freswick
Freswick Bay
Ness Head
Greenland Mains
Greenland
Lochend
Castletown
Olrig
B876
Tain
Slickly
Reaster
Alterwall
Kirk Burn
Caithness Broch Centre
Auckengill
Nybster
Brough Head
Durran
Bowermadden
Sortat
Lyth Arts Centre
Lyth
Bowertower
Howe
Keiss
Keiss Castle
Tang Head
Stemster
Halcro
Hastigrow
Mireland
B874
Corsback
Gillock
Loch Scarmclate
North Watten
Kirk
B870
Burn of Lyth
Loch of Wester
Myrelandhorn
Westerloch
Sinclair's Bay
Larel
A882
Oldhall
Knapperfield
Killimster
Loch Watten
Watten
Winless
Reiss
Sinclair Girnigoe
Noss Head
Ackergillshore
Archie Sinclair Fossil Centre
Loch of Toftingall
Bilbster
Sibster
Ackergill
Sealky Head
WICK
Heritage
Staxigoe
Papigoe
Broadhaven
Strath
Acharole
Burn of Acharole
Strath Burn
Wick River
Haster
Milton
Janetstown
Wick
Wick Bay
Achairn Burn
Newton
Pulteney Distillery
South Head
Badlipster
Whiterow
Loch Hempriggs
Castle of Old Wick
Gote o' Tram
Tannach
Hempriggs
Helman Head
Camster Burn
Hill of Oliclett 462
Gansclet
Thrumster
Hill of Rangag 623
Grey Cairns of Camster
Loch of Yarrows
Raggra
Borrowston
Sarclet
Sarclet Head
South Yarrows Broch
Achavanich
Loch Stemster Standing Stones
815 Stemster Hill
Cnoc an Earrannaiche 692
Camster
Cairn o'Get
Ulbster
Sheppardstown
Roster
East Clyth
Bruan
Crofts of Benachielt
Oscley
Hill o' Many Stanes
Mid Clyth
Halberry Head
Rumster Forest
Upper Lybster
Achow
Reisgill Burn
Overton
Clyth
Swiney
Lybster
Upper Latheron
Standing Stones
Waterlines
Invershore
Burrigill
Forse
Forse Castle
A9
Landhallow
Latheron
Clan Gunn Heritage Centre
Latheronwheel
Knockinnon
Laidhay Croft
Dormin
E
F
G
H
1
2
3
4
5
20
30
40
350
80
70
60
950
40
30

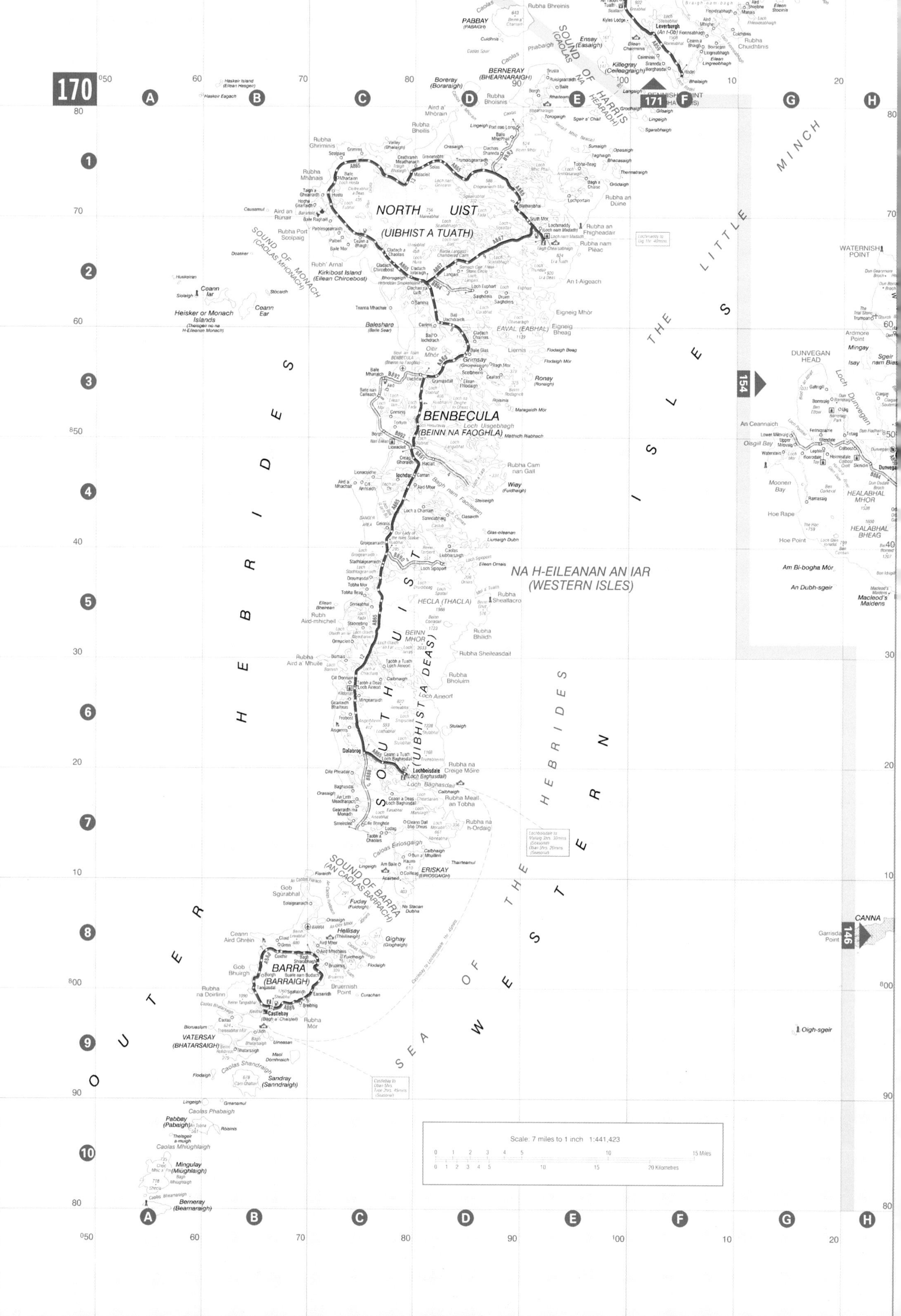
PABBAY
(PABAIGH)
Rubha Bhreinis
SOUND OF HARRIS
(CAOLAS NA HEARADH)
Ensay
(Easaigh)
Leverburgh
(An t-Ob)
Rubha Chuidhtinis
Killegray
(Ceileagraigh)
BERNERAY
(BHEARNARAIGH)
Boreray
(Boraraigh)
Rubha Bhoisnis
171
RENISH POINT
Aird a' Mhòrain
Rubha Bheilis
Rubha Ghriminis
Rubha Mhànais
THE LITTLE MINCH
NORTH UIST
(UIBHIST A TUATH)
Lochmaddy
Rubha an Fhigheadair
Rubha nam Pleac
Rubha Port Scolpaig
SOUND OF MONACH
(CAOLAS MHONACH)
Rubh' Arnal
Kirkibost Island
(Eilean Chircebost)
An t-Aigeach
Ceann Iar
Ceann Ear
Heisker or Monach Islands
Baleshare
(Baile Sear)
Eigneig Mhòr
EAVAL (EABHAL)
Eigneig Bheag
Grimsay
Ronay
(Ronaigh)
BENBECULA
(BEINN NA FAOGHLA)
Loch Uisgebhagh
Rubha Cam nan Gall
Wiay
(Fuidhaigh)
Iochdar
WATERNISH POINT
DUNVEGAN HEAD
154
Loch Dunvegan
An Ceannaich
Oisgill Bay
Moonen Bay
Hoe Rape
Hoe Point
HEALABHAL MHOR
HEALABHAL BHEAG
Am Bi-bogha Mór
An Dubh-sgeir
Macleod's Maidens
NA H-EILEANAN AN IAR
(WESTERN ISLES)
HECLA (THACLA)
Rubha Sheallacro
Rubha Bhìlidh
BEINN MHÒR
Rubha Sheileasdair
Rubha Bholuim
Loch Aineort
SOUTH UIST
(UIBHIST A DEAS)
Dalabrog
Lochboisdale
(Loch Baghasdail)
Rubha na Creige Mòire
Rubha Meall an Tobha
Rubha na h-Ordaig
OUTER HEBRIDES
THE HEBRIDES
SEA OF THE HEBRIDES
Caolas Eiriosgaigh
ERISKAY
(EIRIOSGAIGH)
SOUND OF BARRA
(AN CAOLAS BARRACH)
Gob Sgùrabhal
Fuday
(Fuideigh)
Hellisay
(Theiliseigh)
Gighay
(Giogha)
Ceann Aird Ghrèin
Gob Bhuirgh
BARRA
(BARRAIGH)
Bruernish Point
Rubha na Doirlinn
Castlebay
(Bàgh a' Chaisteil)
Rubha Mòr
VATERSAY
(BHATARSAIGH)
Caolas Shandraigh
Sandray
(Sanndraigh)
Caolas Phabaigh
Pabbay
(Pabaigh)
Caolas Mhiughlaigh
Mingulay
(Miùghlaigh)
Berneray
(Beàrnaraigh)
CANNA
Garrisdale Point
146
Oigh-sgeir
Scale: 7 miles to 1 inch 1:441,423
0 1 2 3 4 5 10 15 Miles
0 1 2 3 4 5 10 15 20 Kilometres
A B C D E F G H
1 2 3 4 5 6 7 8 9 10

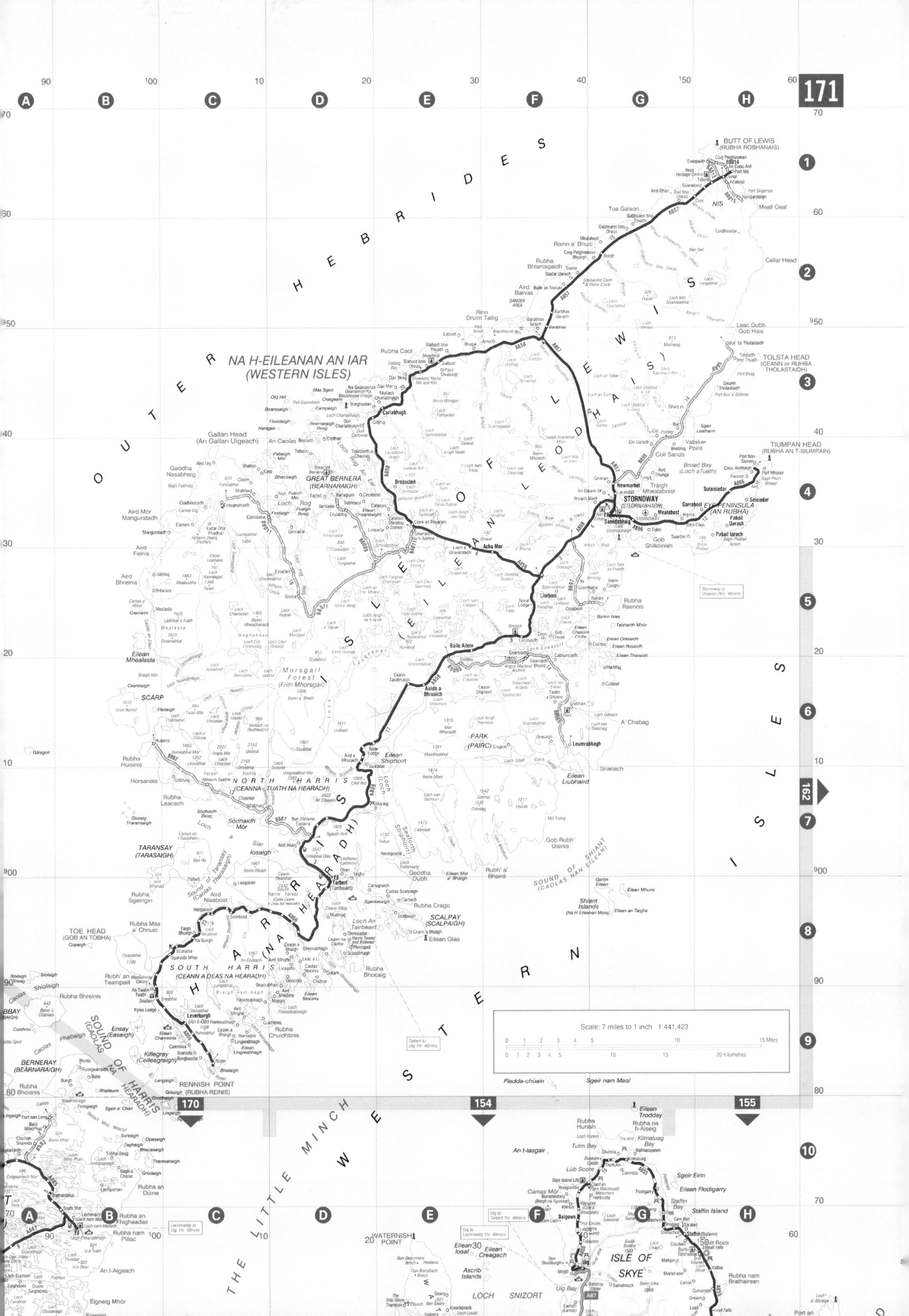
OUTER HEBRIDES
NA H-EILEANAN AN IAR
(WESTERN ISLES)
BUTT OF LEWIS
(RUBHA ROBHANAIS)
ISLE OF LEWIS
(EILEAN LEODHAIS)
STORNOWAY
(STEÒRNABHAGH)
TOLSTA HEAD
(CEANN or RUBHA THOLASTAIDH)
TIUMPAN HEAD
(RUBHA AN T-SIUMPAIN)
EYE PENINSULA
(AN RUBHA)
GREAT BERNERA
(BEARNARAIGH)
Gallan Head
(An Gallan Uigeach)
NORTH HARRIS
(CEANNA TUATH NA HEARADH)
SOUTH HARRIS
(CEANN A DEAS NA HEARADH)
HARRIS (NA HEARADH)
Tarbert
(Tairbeart)
Leverburgh
(An t-Ob)
TARANSAY
(TARASAIGH)
SCALPAY
(SCALPAIGH)
PARK
(PAIRC)
SCARP
TOE HEAD
(GOB AN TOBHA)
RENNISH POINT
(RUBHA REINIS)
SOUND OF HARRIS
(CAOLAS NA HEARADH)
BERNERAY
(BEÀRNARAIGH)
SOUND OF SHIANT
(CAOLAS NAN EILEAN)
Shiant Islands
(Na H Eileanan Mora)
NORTH MINCH
THE LITTLE MINCH
WESTERN ISLES
ISLE OF SKYE
LOCH SNIZORT
WATERNISH POINT
Ascrib Islands
Uig
Staffin
Scale: 7 miles to 1 inch 1:441,423
0 1 2 3 4 5 10 15 Miles
0 1 2 3 4 5 10 15 20 Kilometres
Stornoway to Ullapool 2hrs 40mins
Tarbert to Uig 1hr 40mins
Uig to Tarbert 1hr 40mins
Uig to Lochmaddy 1hr 40mins
Lochmaddy to Uig 1hr 40mins
170
154
155
162
A B C D E F G H
1 2 3 4 5 6 7 8 9 10

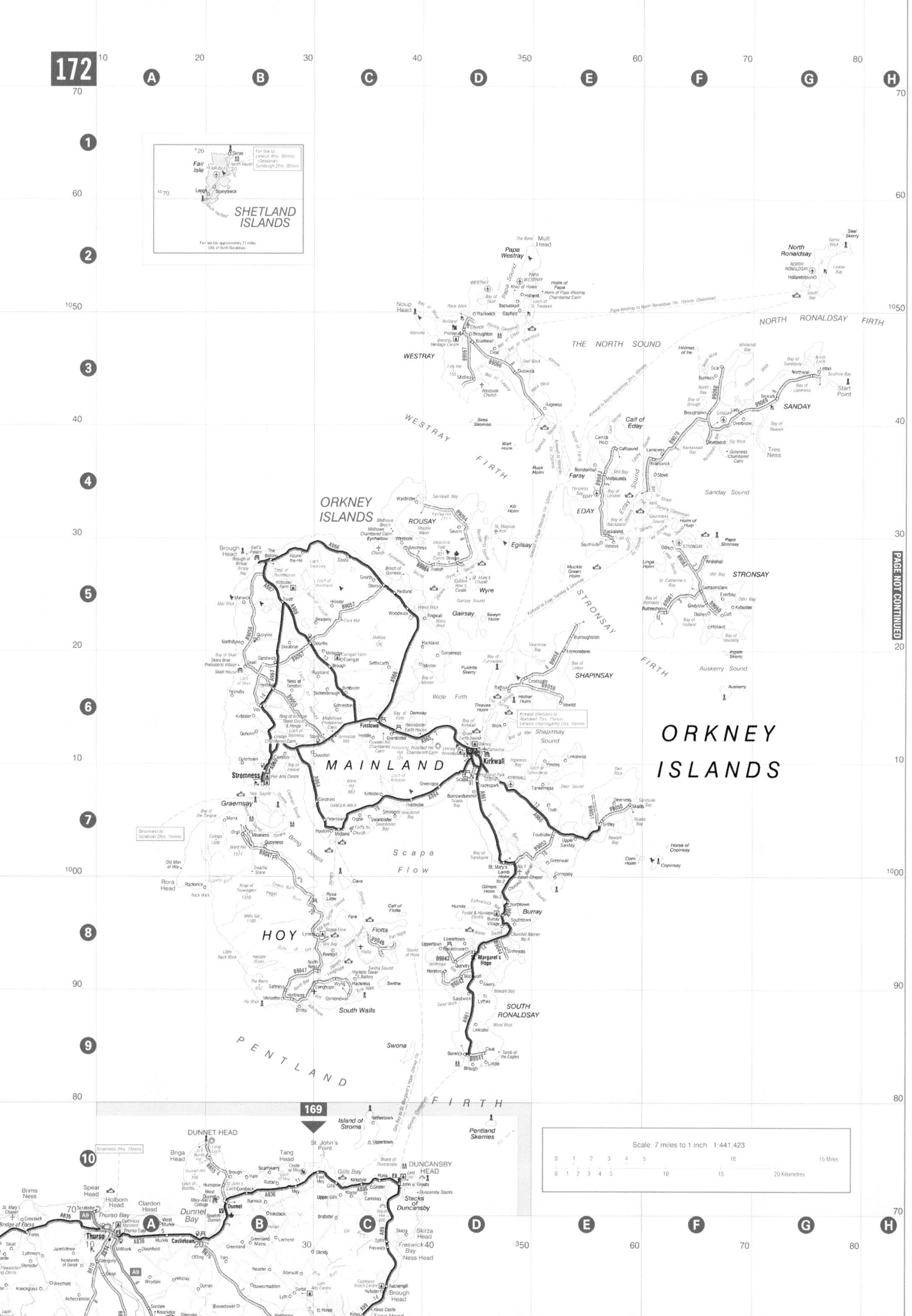

SHETLAND ISLANDS
Fair Isle
Skroo
Stonybreck
ORKNEY ISLANDS
MAINLAND
HOY
South Walls
Flotta
Scapa Flow
Kirkwall
Stromness
Finstown
St. Margaret's Hope
Burray
SOUTH RONALDSAY
ROUSAY
Egilsay
Wyre
Gairsay
SHAPINSAY
STRONSAY
EDAY
Calf of Eday
SANDAY
North Ronaldsay
NORTH RONALDSAY FIRTH
Papa Westray
WESTRAY
THE NORTH SOUND
WESTRAY FIRTH
STRONSAY FIRTH
PENTLAND FIRTH
Swona
Island of Stroma
Pentland Skerries
Graemsay
Copinsay
Mull Head
Noup Head
Brough Head
Rora Head
DUNNET HEAD
Dunnet Bay
Thurso
Castletown
Dunnet
John o' Groats
DUNCANSBY HEAD
Stacks of Duncansby
Freswick Bay
Tang Head
Skirza Head
Brough Head
Holborn Head
Clardon Head
Spear Head
Brims Ness
Thurso Bay
Gills Bay
St. John's Point
PAGE NOT CONTINUED
169
Scale: 7 miles to 1 inch 1:441,423
15 Miles
20 Kilometres

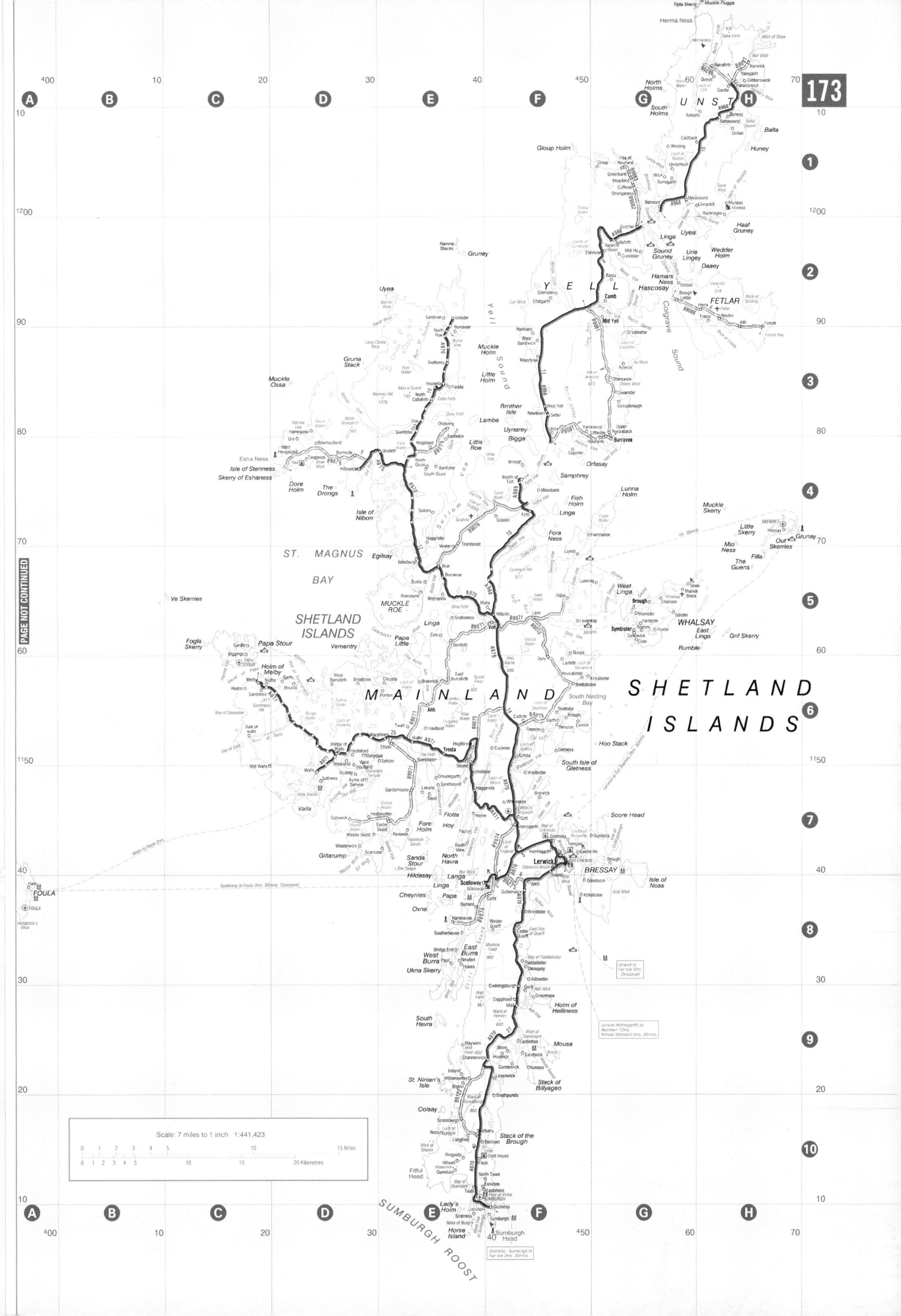
SHETLAND ISLANDS
MAINLAND
SHETLAND ISLANDS
ST. MAGNUS BAY
UNST
YELL
FETLAR
WHALSAY
BRESSAY
FOULA
PAPA STOUR
Yell Sound
Colgrave Sound
Sullom Voe
SUMBURGH ROOST
Herma Ness
Muckle Flugga
Balta
Huney
Uyea
Linga
Haaf Gruney
Wedder Holm
Urie Lingey
Daaey
Sound Gruney
Hamars Ness
Hascosay
Gloup Holm
Gruney
Ramna Stacks
Muckle Holm
Little Holm
Brother Isle
Lamba
Uynarey
Bigga
Little Roe
Samphrey
Orfasay
Fish Holm
Linga
Fora Ness
Lunna Holm
Muckle Skerry
Little Skerry
Out Skerries
Grunay
Mio Ness
The Guens
Muckle Ossa
Gruna Stack
Esha Ness
Isle of Stenness
Skerry of Eshaness
Dore Holm
The Drongs
Isle of Nibon
Egilsay
MUCKLE ROE
Linga
Papa Little
Vementry
Ve Skerries
Fogla Skerry
Holm of Melby
West Linga
East Linga
Rumble
Grif Skerry
Hoo Stack
South Isle of Gletness
Score Head
Isle of Noss
Vaila
Flotta
Hoy
Fore Holm
Giltarump
Sanda Stour
North Havra
Hildasay
Langa
Linga
Cheynies
Papa
Oxna
East Burra
West Burra
Ukna Skerry
South Havra
Holm of Helliness
Mousa
Stack of Billyageo
St. Ninian's Isle
Colsay
Stack of the Brough
Fitful Head
Lady's Holm
Horse Island
Sumburgh Head
Lerwick
Scalloway
Mid Yell
Burravoe
Voe
Aith
Tresta
Symbister
Scale: 7 miles to 1 inch 1:441,423
15 Miles
20 Kilometres
PAGE NOT CONTINUED

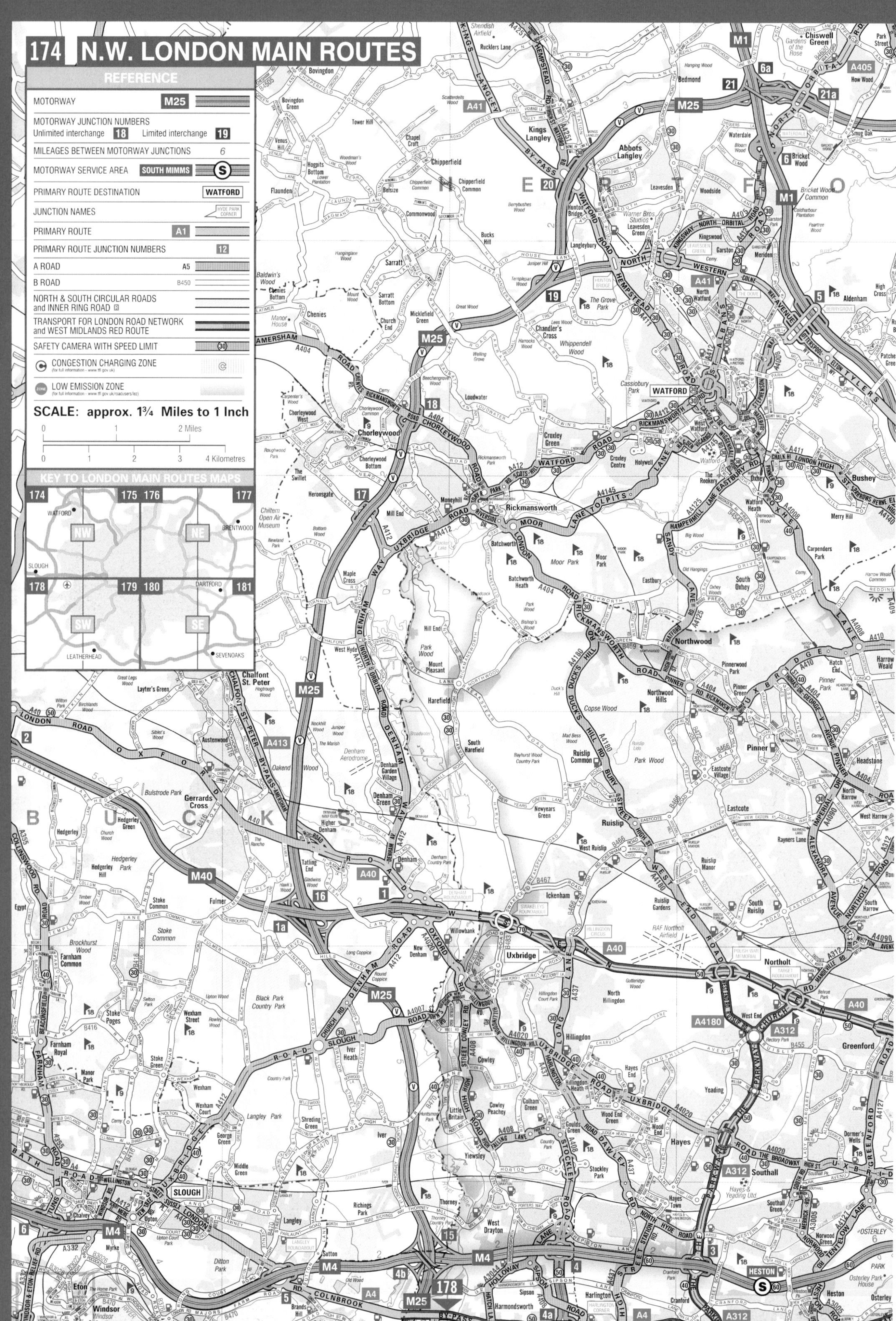
REFERENCE
MOTORWAY M25
MOTORWAY JUNCTION NUMBERS
Unlimited interchange 18 Limited interchange 19
MILEAGES BETWEEN MOTORWAY JUNCTIONS 6
MOTORWAY SERVICE AREA SOUTH MIMMS S
PRIMARY ROUTE DESTINATION WATFORD
JUNCTION NAMES HYDE PARK CORNER
PRIMARY ROUTE A1
PRIMARY ROUTE JUNCTION NUMBERS 12
A ROAD A5
B ROAD B450
NORTH & SOUTH CIRCULAR ROADS and INNER RING ROAD R
TRANSPORT FOR LONDON ROAD NETWORK and WEST MIDLANDS RED ROUTE
SAFETY CAMERA WITH SPEED LIMIT 30
CONGESTION CHARGING ZONE
(for full information - www.tfl.gov.uk)
LOW EMISSION ZONE
(for full information - www.tfl.gov.uk/roadusers/lez)
SCALE: approx. 1¾ Miles to 1 Inch
0 1 2 Miles
0 1 2 3 4 Kilometres
KEY TO LONDON MAIN ROUTES MAPS
174 175 176 177
WATFORD NW NE BRENTWOOD
SLOUGH
178 179 180 181
DARTFORD
SW SE
LEATHERHEAD SEVENOAKS

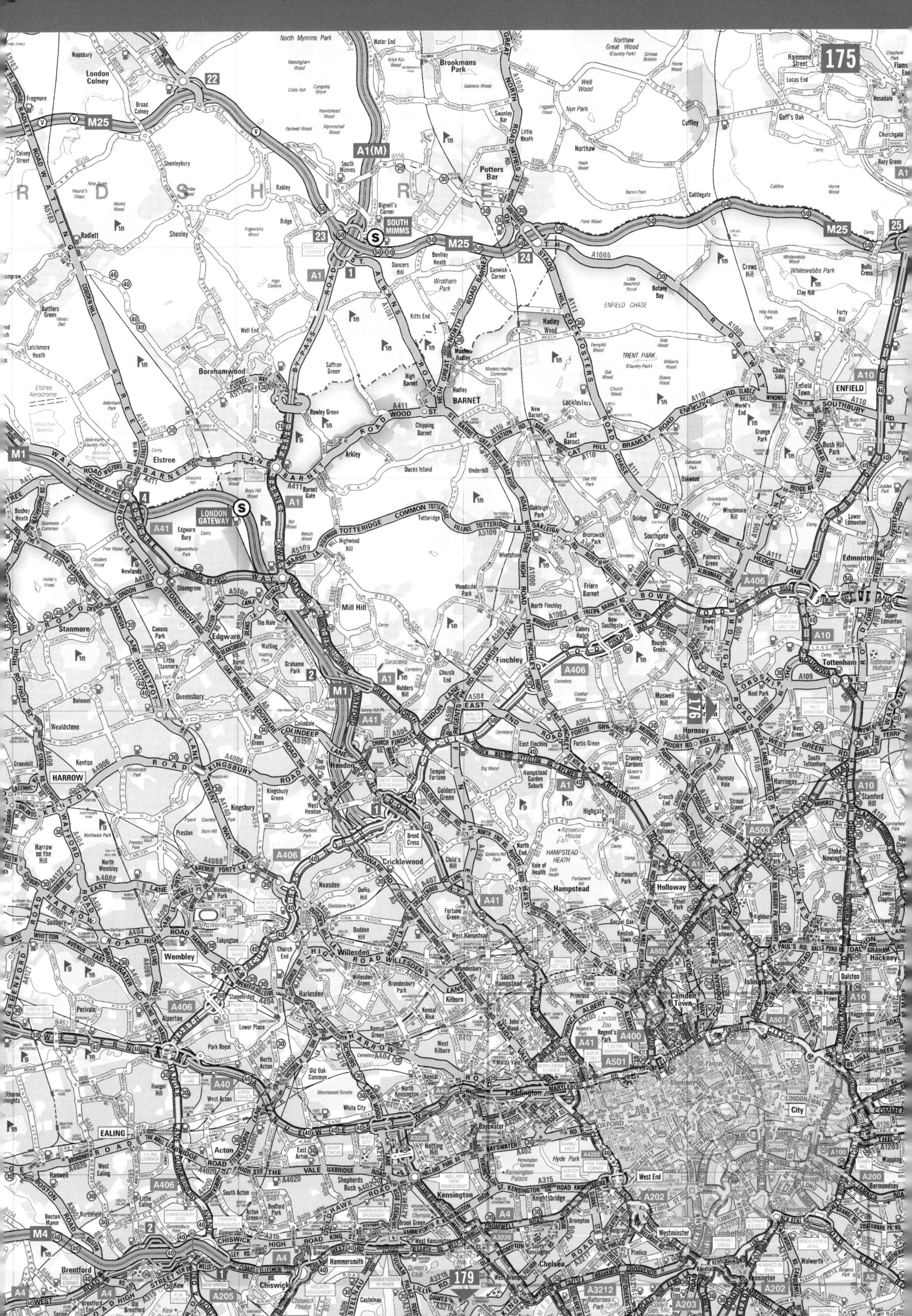
175
North Mymms Park
Water End
Brookmans Park
Northaw Great Wood (Country Park)
Hammond Street
Napsbury
London Colney
Frogmore
Broad Colney
M25
A1(M)
South Mimms
Potters Bar
Little Heath
Northaw
Cuffley
Goff's Oak
Lucas End
Rosedale
Churchgate
Bury Green
Colney Street
Shenleybury
Rabley
Ridge
Bignell's Corner
SOUTH MIMMS
Cattlegate
Radlett
Shenley
Bentley Heath
Dancers Hill
Wrotham Park
Ganwick Corner
Crews Hill
Whitewebbs Park
Bulls Cross
Botany Bay
ENFIELD CHASE
Clay Hill
Forty Hill
Battlers Green
Letchmore Heath
Well End
Kitts End
Saffron Green
Hadley Wood
TRENT PARK (Country Park)
Elstree Aerodrome
Borehamwood
High Barnet
Monken Hadley
Hadley
BARNET
Cockfosters
New Barnet
Chase Side
Enfield Town
ENFIELD
Southbury
World's End
Grange Park
Bush Hill Park
Rowley Green
Chipping Barnet
Arkley
East Barnet
M1
Elstree
Ducks Island
Underhill
Oakwood
Winchmore Hill
Lower Edmonton
Bushey Heath
Barnet Gate
LONDON GATEWAY
Edgware Bury
Totteridge
Oakleigh Park
Osidge
Southgate
Edmonton
Highwood Hill
Brunswick Park
Palmers Green
Newlands
Stonegrove
Whetstone
Friern Barnet
Upper Edmonton
Stanmore
Canons Park
Edgware
The Hale
Mill Hill
Woodside Park
North Finchley
New Southgate
Colney Hatch
Bounds Green
Bowes Park
Tottenham
Little Stanmore
Burnt Oak
Watling Park
Grahame Park
Saracens
Finchley
Belmont
Queensbury
Holders Hill
Church End
Muswell Hill
Noel Park
Wealdstone
Colindale
Roe Green
Hornsey
West Green
Harringay
South Tottenham
Kenton
HARROW
Kingsbury
The Hyde
Hendon
East Finchley
Fortis Green
Temple Fortune
Golders Green
Hampstead Garden Suburb
Highgate
Crouch End
Hornsey Vale
Stroud Green
Stamford Hill
Harrow on the Hill
Preston
West Hendon
Upper Holloway
Finsbury Park
Stoke Newington
North Wembley
Brent Cross
Cricklewood
Child's Hill
HAMPSTEAD HEATH
Vale of Health
Hampstead
Dartmouth Park
Holloway
Highbury
Upper Clapton
Sudbury
Wembley Park
Neasden
Dollis Hill
Fortune Green
West Hampstead
Gospel Oak
Kentish Town
Tufnell Park
Kingsland
Hackney
Wembley
Tokyngton
Church End
Willesden
Dudden Hill
Brondesbury
South Hampstead
Chalk Farm
Primrose Hill
Camden Town
Islington
Dalston
Perivale
Alperton
Stonebridge
Harlesden
Willesden Green
Brondesbury Park
Kilburn
Kensal Rise
London Zoo
Regent's Park
Hoxton
Haggerston
Lower Place
Park Royal
North Acton
Kensal Green
West Kilburn
St John's Wood
Maida Vale
Shoreditch
Hanger Hill
West Acton
Old Oak Common
Wormwood Scrubs
North Kensington
Paddington
MARYLEBONE
St Pancras
City
EALING
Acton
East Acton
White City
Notting Hill
Bayswater
Hyde Park
Kensington Palace
West End
Wapping
Hanwell
West Ealing
Little Ealing
South Acton
Bedford Park
Shepherds Bush
Kensington
Knightsbridge
Brompton
Westminster
Bermondsey
Northfields
Boston Manor
Gunnersbury
Brook Green
Olympia
West Kensington
Belgravia
Pimlico
Lambeth
Walworth
M4
Brentford
Chiswick
Turnham Green
Hammersmith
Chelsea
Kennington
Old Brentford
Kew
Castelnau
West Brompton
Battersea Park
Nine Elms
179
176

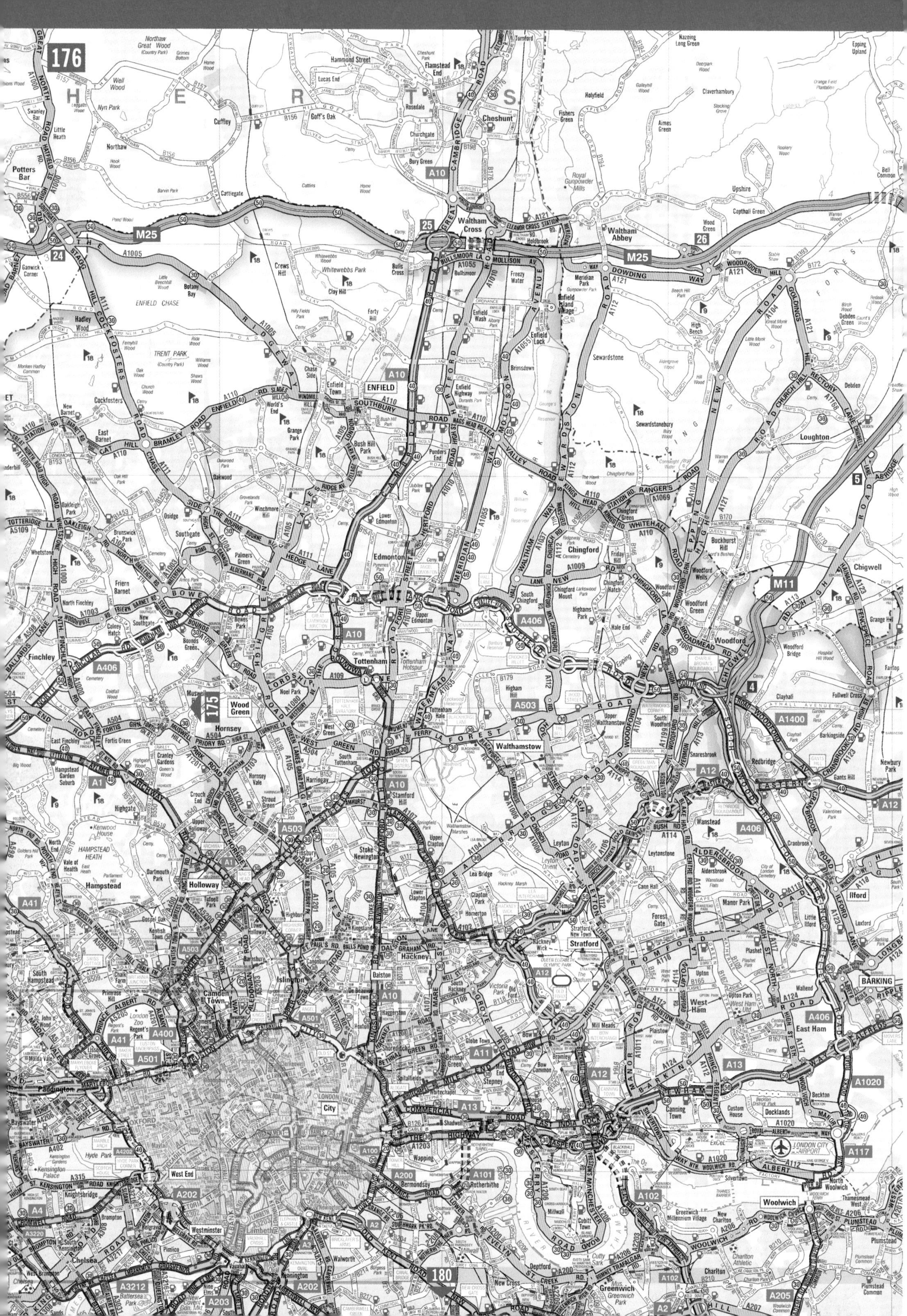
176
HERTS
Potters Bar
Northaw
Cuffley
Goff's Oak
Hammond Street
Flamstead End
Rosedale
Churchgate
Bury Green
Cheshunt
Turnford
Nazeing Long Green
Holyfield
Claverhambury
Fishers Green
Royal Gunpowder Mills
Upshire
Epping Upland
Bell Common
Copthall Green
Waltham Cross
Waltham Abbey
M25
Crews Hill
Bulls Cross
Whitewebbs Park
Clay Hill
Forty Hill
Bullsmoor
Freezy Water
Enfield Island Village
Enfield Wash
Enfield Lock
Hadley Wood
Enfield Chase
Trent Park
Cockfosters
Chase Side
Enfield Town
ENFIELD
Southbury
Brimsdown
Sewardstone
High Beech
Debden Green
Debden
Loughton
New Barnet
East Barnet
World's End
Grange Park
Bush Hill Park
Ponders End
Oakwood
Winchmore Hill
Southgate
Osidge
Oakleigh Park
Whetstone
Brunswick Park
Palmers Green
Friern Barnet
North Finchley
New Southgate
Colney Hatch
Bowes Park
Bounds Green
Finchley
Lower Edmonton
Edmonton
Upper Edmonton
Tottenham
Chingford
Chingford Hatch
Chingford Mount
Friday Hill
South Chingford
Highams Park
Hale End
Woodford Wells
Woodford Green
Woodford
Woodford Bridge
Buckhurst Hill
Chigwell
M11
Grange Hill
Fairlop
Clayhall
Fullwell Cross
Barkingside
Newbury Park
Gants Hill
Redbridge
Wood Green
Hornsey
Muswell Hill
East Finchley
Fortis Green
Highgate
Crouch End
Stroud Green
Harringay
West Green
South Tottenham
Tottenham Hale
Higham Hill
Walthamstow
Upper Walthamstow
South Woodford
Snaresbrook
Wanstead
Leytonstone
Aldersbrook
Hampstead Garden Suburb
Hampstead
Upper Holloway
Holloway
Finsbury Park
Stoke Newington
Stamford Hill
Upper Clapton
Lower Clapton
Clapton Park
Lea Bridge
Leyton
Homerton
Hackney Wick
Stratford
Forest Gate
Manor Park
Ilford
Little Ilford
Cranbrook
Valentines Park
Kentish Town
Gospel Oak
Tufnell Park
Highbury
Dalston
Hackney
South Hackney
Victoria Park
Old Ford
Chalk Farm
Camden Town
Islington
Hoxton
Haggerston
South Hampstead
Primrose Hill
Regent's Park
St. John's Wood
Maida Vale
Paddington
Marylebone
Bayswater
Hyde Park
Kensington
Knightsbridge
Brompton
Chelsea
Battersea Park
West End
Westminster
Lambeth
Pimlico
Vauxhall
Kennington
Walworth
City
Shoreditch
Bethnal Green
Globe Town
Spitalfields
Whitechapel
Stepney
Mile End
Bow
Bow Common
Bromley
Poplar
Shadwell
Wapping
Limehouse
Bermondsey
Rotherhithe
Millwall
Cubitt Town
Greenwich
Deptford
New Cross
Mill Meads
Plaistow
West Ham
East Ham
Upton Park
Upton
Plashet
Wallend
Beckton
BARKING
Canning Town
Custom House
Docklands
Silvertown
London City Airport
North Woolwich
Woolwich
Charlton
New Charlton
Greenwich Millennium Village
Plumstead
Plumstead Common
Thamesmead West
175
180

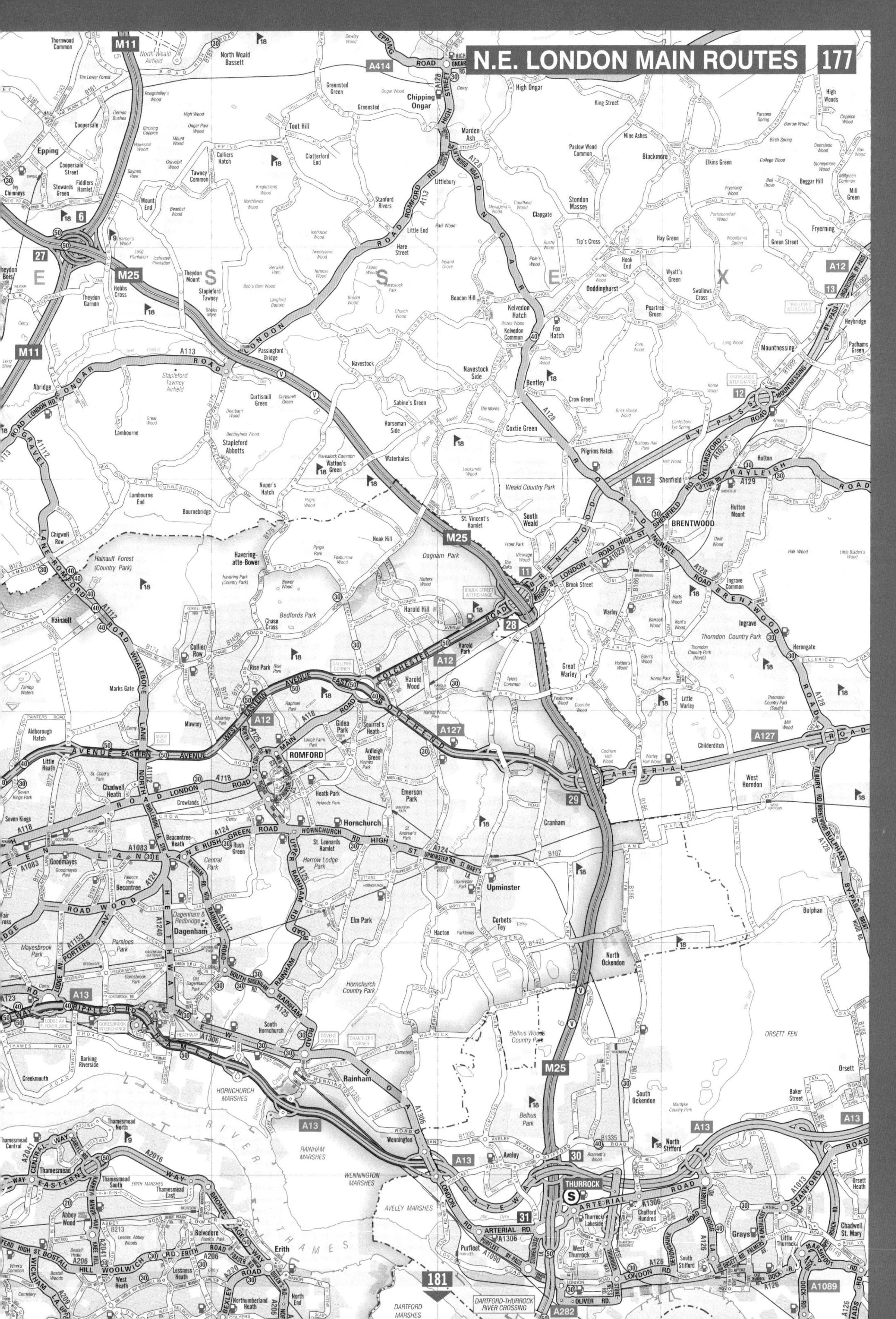
M11
M25
A414
A12
A127
A13
A128
A113
A1112
A118
A124
A125
A1306
A282
A1089
North Weald Bassett
High Ongar
Chipping Ongar
Greensted
Toot Hill
Epping
Coopersale
Thornwood Common
Theydon Bois
Theydon Mount
Theydon Garnon
Hobbs Cross
Stapleford Tawney
Stapleford Abbotts
Abridge
Lambourne
Lambourne End
Bournebridge
Passingford Bridge
Navestock
Navestock Side
Kelvedon Hatch
Kelvedon Common
Doddinghurst
Blackmore
Stondon Massey
Mountnessing
Ingatestone By-Pass
Shenfield
BRENTWOOD
Pilgrims Hatch
Bentley
Coxtie Green
South Weald
Brook Street
Warley
Great Warley
Little Warley
Herongate
Ingrave
Hutton
Hutton Mount
Childerditch
West Horndon
Bulphan
Havering-atte-Bower
Chigwell Row
Hainault
Harold Hill
Harold Wood
Harold Park
Noak Hill
Collier Row
Rise Park
Marks Gate
Mawney
Gidea Park
ROMFORD
Squirrel's Heath
Ardleigh Green
Emerson Park
Hornchurch
Upminster
Cranham
Chadwell Heath
Seven Kings
Goodmayes
Becontree
Dagenham
Rush Green
St. Leonards Hamlet
Harrow Lodge Park
Elm Park
Corbets Tey
Hacton
North Ockendon
South Ockendon
Aveley
Belhus Park
Wennington
Rainham
South Hornchurch
Barking Riverside
Creekmouth
RAINHAM MARSHES
WENNINGTON MARSHES
AVELEY MARSHES
Thamesmead
Thamesmead Central
Thamesmead North
Thamesmead South
Thamesmead East
Abbey Wood
Belvedere
Erith
West Heath
Northumberland Heath
North End
RIVER THAMES
THURROCK
West Thurrock
Purfleet
Chafford Hundred
South Stifford
North Stifford
Grays
Little Thurrock
Chadwell St. Mary
Orsett
Orsett Heath
Baker Street
ORSETT FEN
DARTFORD-THURROCK RIVER CROSSING
DARTFORD MARSHES
181

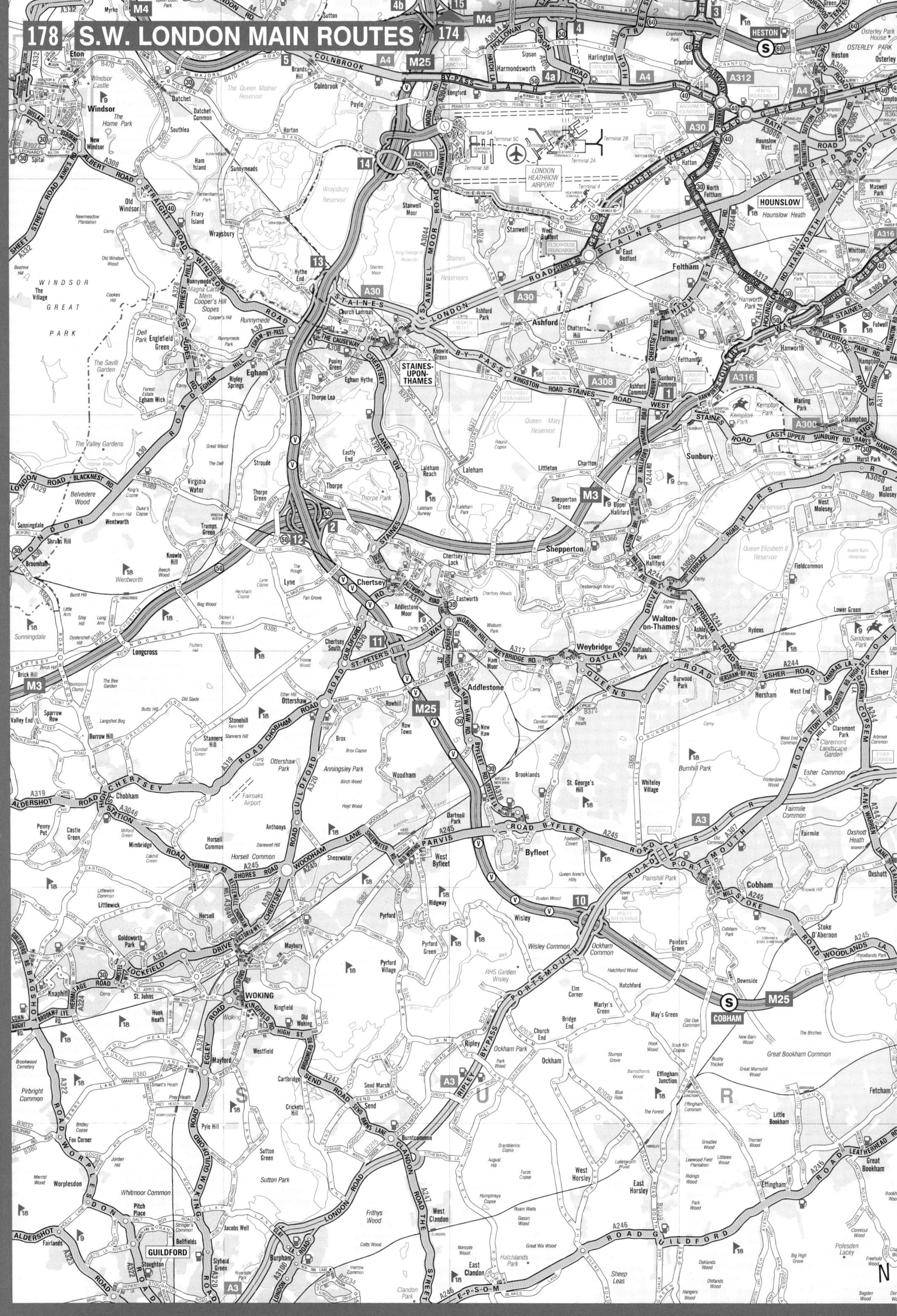
174
M4
M25
M3
A30
A308
A3
A4
A312
A316
A320
Eton
Windsor
Datchet
Colnbrook
Poyle
Harmondsworth
Sipson
Harlington
Cranford
HESTON
Heston
Osterley
LONDON HEATHROW AIRPORT
Stanwell
Stanwell Moor
HOUNSLOW
Hounslow Heath
Feltham
Hanworth
Ashford
STAINES-UPON-THAMES
Egham
Runnymede
Wraysbury
Old Windsor
Englefield Green
Virginia Water
Sunningdale
Wentworth
Thorpe
Chertsey
Laleham
Littleton
Shepperton
Sunbury
Hampton
Lower Halliford
Walton-on-Thames
Weybridge
Addlestone
Ottershaw
Longcross
Chobham
Byfleet
West Byfleet
Woodham
Hersham
Esher
Cobham
COBHAM
Oxshott
Stoke D'Abernon
Wisley
Ockham
Ripley
Send
Pyrford
WOKING
Knaphill
St. Johns
Mayford
Westfield
Worplesdon
GUILDFORD
Burpham
West Clandon
East Clandon
West Horsley
East Horsley
Effingham
Great Bookham
Fetcham
Brookwood
Pirbright Common
Bisley
Horsell
Mimbridge
Sheerwater
Fairmile
Claremont Landscape Garden
Queen Mary Reservoir
Queen Elizabeth II Reservoir
Wraysbury Reservoir
The Queen Mother Reservoir
WINDSOR GREAT PARK
The Valley Gardens
The Savill Garden
Thorpe Park
Brooklands
Sandown Park
Kempton Park
RHS Garden Wisley

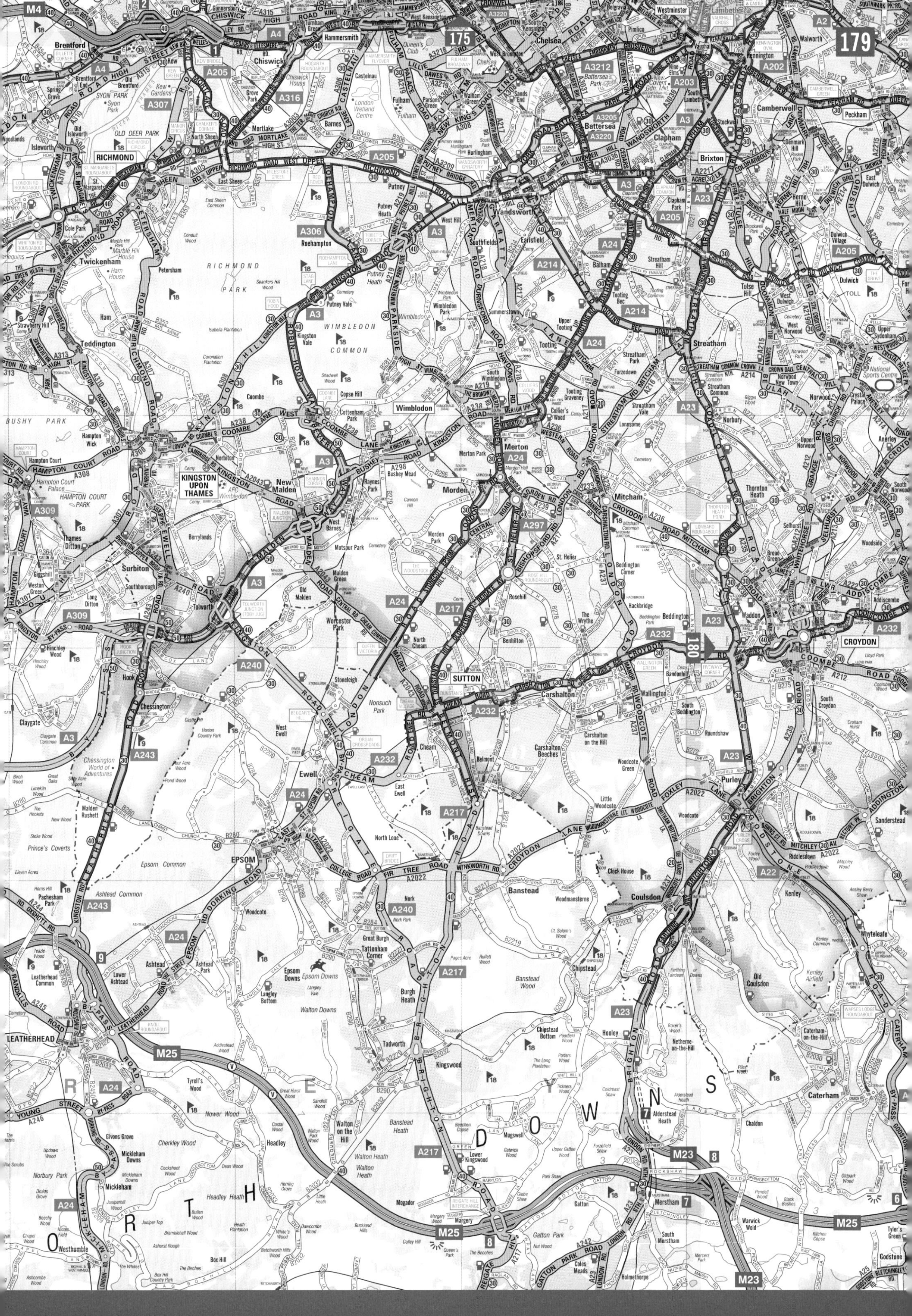

175
179
180
Brentford
Chiswick
Hammersmith
Fulham
Chelsea
Westminster
Walworth
Kennington
Camberwell
Peckham
Mortlake
Barnes
Putney
Battersea
Clapham
Brixton
RICHMOND
Twickenham
Petersham
RICHMOND PARK
Roehampton
Wandsworth
Earlsfield
Balham
Streatham
Dulwich
Teddington
Ham
WIMBLEDON COMMON
Wimbledon
Tooting
Merton
Mitcham
Norbury
Norwood
Crystal Palace
BUSHY PARK
Hampton Court
KINGSTON UPON THAMES
New Malden
Morden
Thornton Heath
Surbiton
Tolworth
Worcester Park
Sutton
Carshalton
Wallington
Beddington
CROYDON
Hook
Chessington
Claygate
Ewell
Cheam
Purley
EPSOM
Epsom Common
Banstead
Coulsdon
Kenley
Ashtead
Epsom Downs
Tattenham Corner
Whyteleafe
LEATHERHEAD
Tadworth
Kingswood
Chipstead
Hooley
Caterham
Headley
Mickleham
Merstham
Westhumble
Box Hill
Gatton
NORTH DOWNS
M25
M23
M4

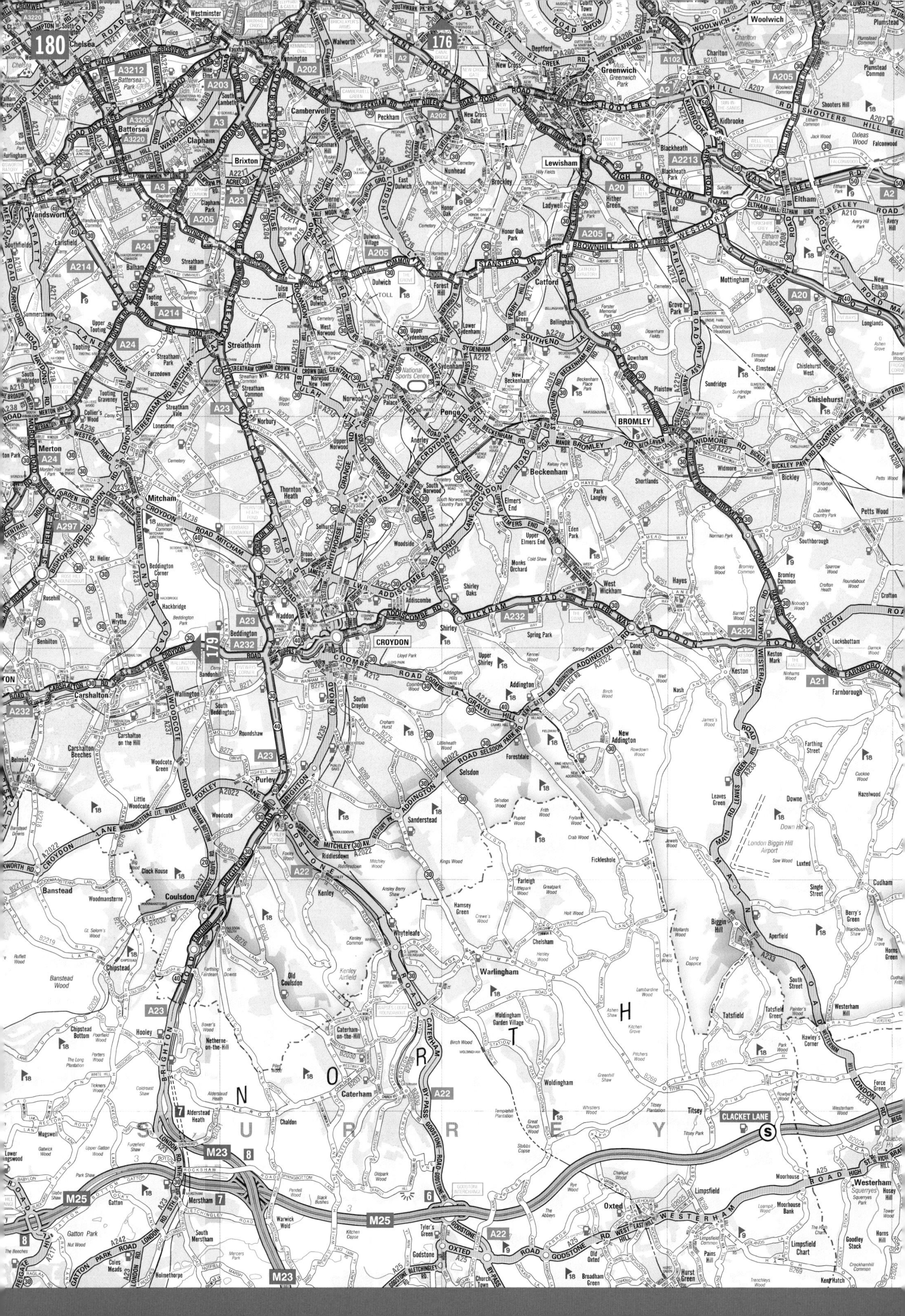
180
176
179
Westminster
Chelsea
Pimlico
Vauxhall
Kennington
Walworth
Deptford
Woolwich
Plumstead
New Cross
Greenwich
Charlton
Battersea
Clapham
Camberwell
Peckham
Brixton
Wandsworth
Lewisham
Blackheath
Kidbrooke
Shooters Hill
Eltham
Earlsfield
Balham
Streatham Hill
Tooting Bec
Dulwich
Forest Hill
Catford
Brockley
Nunhead
Honor Oak
Ladywell
Hither Green
Lee
Mottingham
Grove Park
Tooting
Streatham
Sydenham
Bellingham
Downham
Plaistow
Sundridge
Chislehurst
Merton
Mitcham
Norbury
Norwood
Crystal Palace
National Sports Centre
Penge
Anerley
Beckenham
BROMLEY
Shortlands
Widmore
Bickley
Petts Wood
Thornton Heath
Selhurst
Woodside
Elmers End
Eden Park
Park Langley
Hayes
Bromley Common
Southborough
Crofton
St. Helier
Rosehill
Beddington
Hackbridge
Waddon
Addiscombe
Shirley
West Wickham
Coney Hall
Keston
Locksbottom
Farnborough
CROYDON
Carshalton
Wallington
Bandonhill
South Croydon
Addington
New Addington
Selsdon
Forestdale
Sanderstead
Purley
Woodcote
Riddlesdown
Kenley
Coulsdon
Banstead
Chipstead
Whyteleafe
Warlingham
Hamsey Green
Farleigh
Chelsham
Fickleshole
Biggin Hill
Downe
Cudham
Leaves Green
Aperfield
Tatsfield
Westerham Hill
Old Coulsdon
Caterham
Caterham-on-the-Hill
Woldingham
Hooley
Netherne-on-the-Hill
Chaldon
Titsey
Limpsfield
Oxted
Westerham
Merstham
South Merstham
Gatton
Godstone
Tyler's Green
Hurst Green
Holmethorpe
CLACKET LANE
N O R T H
S U R R E Y
M25
M23
A23
A22
A21
A20
A232
A2
A205
A3
A24

177

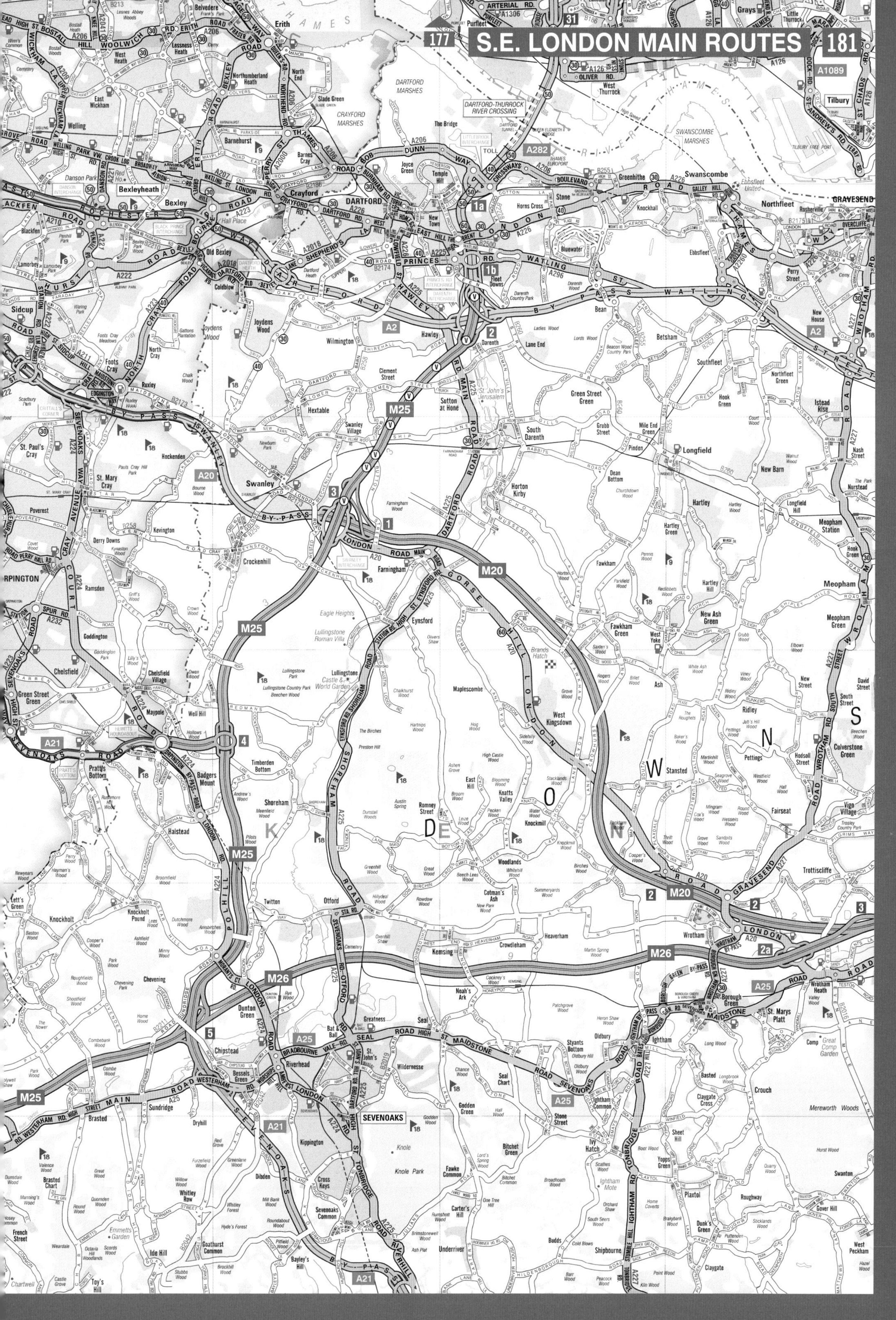

Erith
Belvedere
Purfleet
Grays
West Thurrock
Tilbury
Welling
East Wickham
Barnehurst
Northumberland Heath
North End
Slade Green
Dartford Marshes
Crayford Marshes
Dartford-Thurrock River Crossing
The Bridge
Swanscombe Marshes
Barnes Cray
Joyce Green
Temple Hill
Danson Park
Bexleyheath
Bexley
Crayford
Dartford
Stone
Greenhithe
Swanscombe
Northfleet
Gravesend
Horns Cross
Knockhall
Ebbsfleet
Bluewater
Old Bexley
Blackfen
Lamorbey
Coldblow
Fleet Downs
Perry Street
Sidcup
Joydens Wood
Wilmington
Hawley
Darenth
Lane End
Betsham
Southfleet
Bean
Foots Cray
North Cray
Ruxley
Clement Street
Hextable
Sutton at Hone
Green Street Green
Northfleet Green
Istead Rise
Swanley Village
South Darenth
Grubb Street
Mile End Green
Pinden
Longfield
Nash Street
St. Paul's Cray
Hockenden
Swanley
St. Mary Cray
Horton Kirby
Dean Bottom
New Barn
Nurstead
Hartley
Longfield Hill
Poverest
Kevington
Derry Downs
Crockenhill
Farningham
Hartley Green
Meopham Station
Orpington
Ramsden
Fawkham
Hartley Hill
Meopham
Eagle Heights
Eynsford
New Ash Green
Fawkham Green
West Yoke
Meopham Green
Goddington
Lullingstone Roman Villa
Brands Hatch
Lullingstone Castle & World Garden
Chelsfield
Chelsfield Village
Green Street Green
Maplescombe
Ash
New Street
West Kingsdown
Ridley
David Street
South Street
Maypole
Well Hill
Culverstone Green
Timberden Bottom
Pratts Bottom
Badgers Mount
Stansted
Pettings
Hodsoll Street
Shoreham
East Hill
Knatts Valley
Romney Street
Vigo Village
Halstead
Knockmill
Fairseat
Trottiscliffe
Woodlands
Cotman's Ash
Knockholt Pound
Knockholt
Twitton
Otford
Kemsing
Crowdleham
Heaverham
Wrotham
Wrotham Heath
Borough Green
Noah's Ark
Platt
St. Marys Platt
Chevening
Dunton Green
Greatness
Seal
Bat & Ball
Chipstead
Riverhead
Bessels Green
Ightham
Basted
Wildernesse
Seal Chart
Crouch
Sundridge
Brasted
Dryhill
Sevenoaks
Godden Green
Ightham Common
Claygate Cross
Stone Street
Sheet Hill
Kippington
Knole
Knole Park
Fawke Common
Bitchet Green
Ivy Hatch
Yopps Green
Mereworth Woods
Dibden
Cross Keys
Carter's Hill
Ightham Mote
Plaxtol
Roughway
Swanton
Brasted Chart
Whitley Row
Sevenoaks Common
Underriver
Dunk's Green
Gover Hill
French Street
Emmetts Garden
Ide Hill
Goathurst Common
Bayley's Hill
Budds
Shipbourne
Claygate
West Peckham
Toy's Hill
Chartwell
KENT
DOWNS
M25
M20
M26
A20
A21
A25
A2
A282
A1089

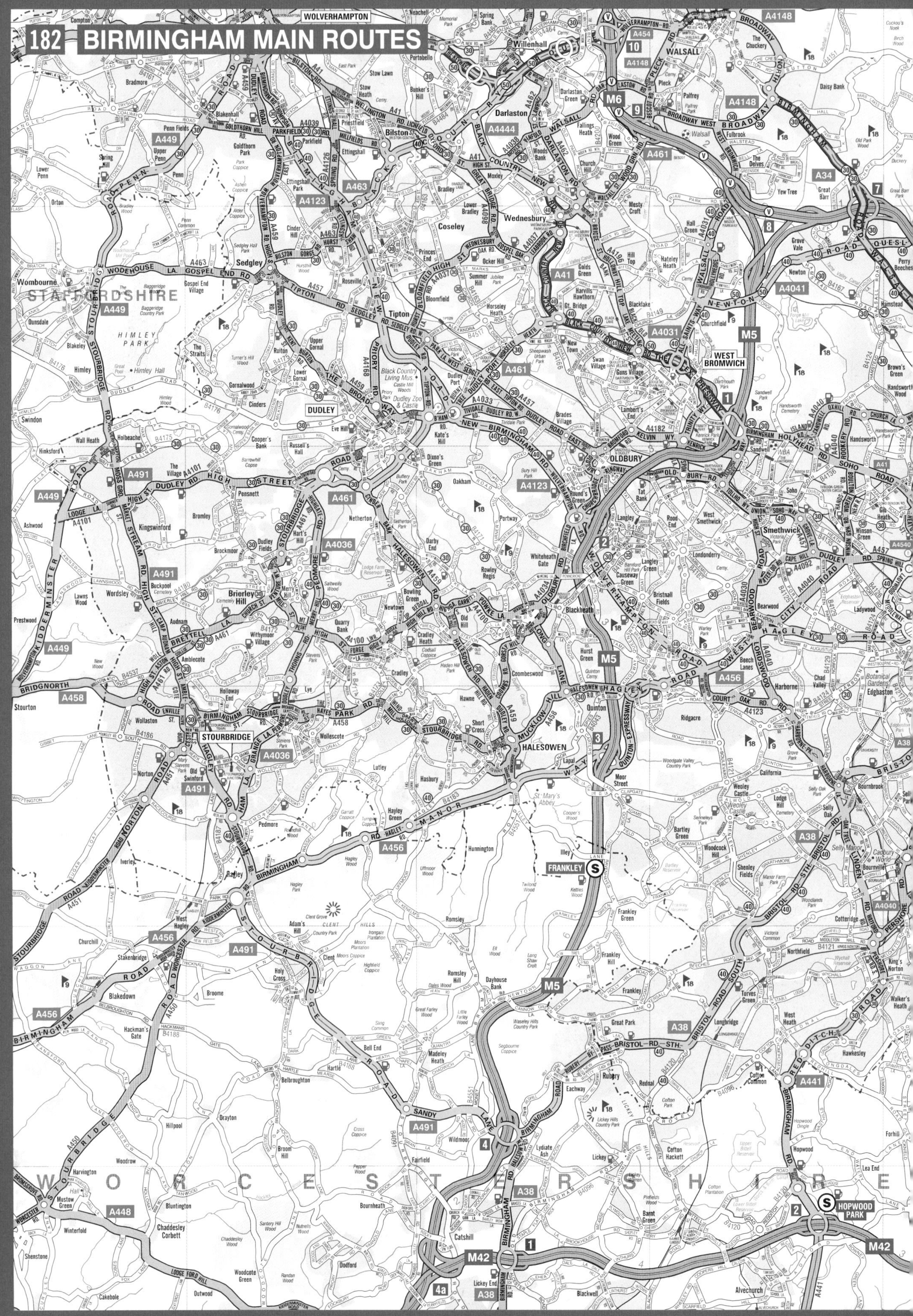
WOLVERHAMPTON
Willenhall
WALSALL
Darlaston
Bilston
Coseley
Wednesbury
Sedgley
Tipton
DUDLEY
WEST BROMWICH
OLDBURY
Smethwick
Harborne
Edgbaston
Brierley Hill
STOURBRIDGE
HALESOWEN
Quinton
Northfield
Rubery
Hagley
Clent
Romsley
Belbroughton
Wombourne
STAFFORDSHIRE
WORCESTERSHIRE
FRANKLEY
HOPWOOD PARK
Alvechurch
Kingswinford
Cradley Heath
Rowley Regis
Blackheath
Bartley Green
Selly Oak
Bournville
Kings Norton
Hollywood
Great Barr
Amblecote
Wollaston
Pedmore
Lye
Netherton
Quarry Bank
Wordsley
Himley
Stourton
Churchill
Blakedown
Chaddesley Corbett
Hopwood
Cofton Hackett
Rednal
Lickey
M5
M6
M42
A449
A491
A456
A458
A461
A4123
A38
A441
A34
A41
A457
A4036
A4040

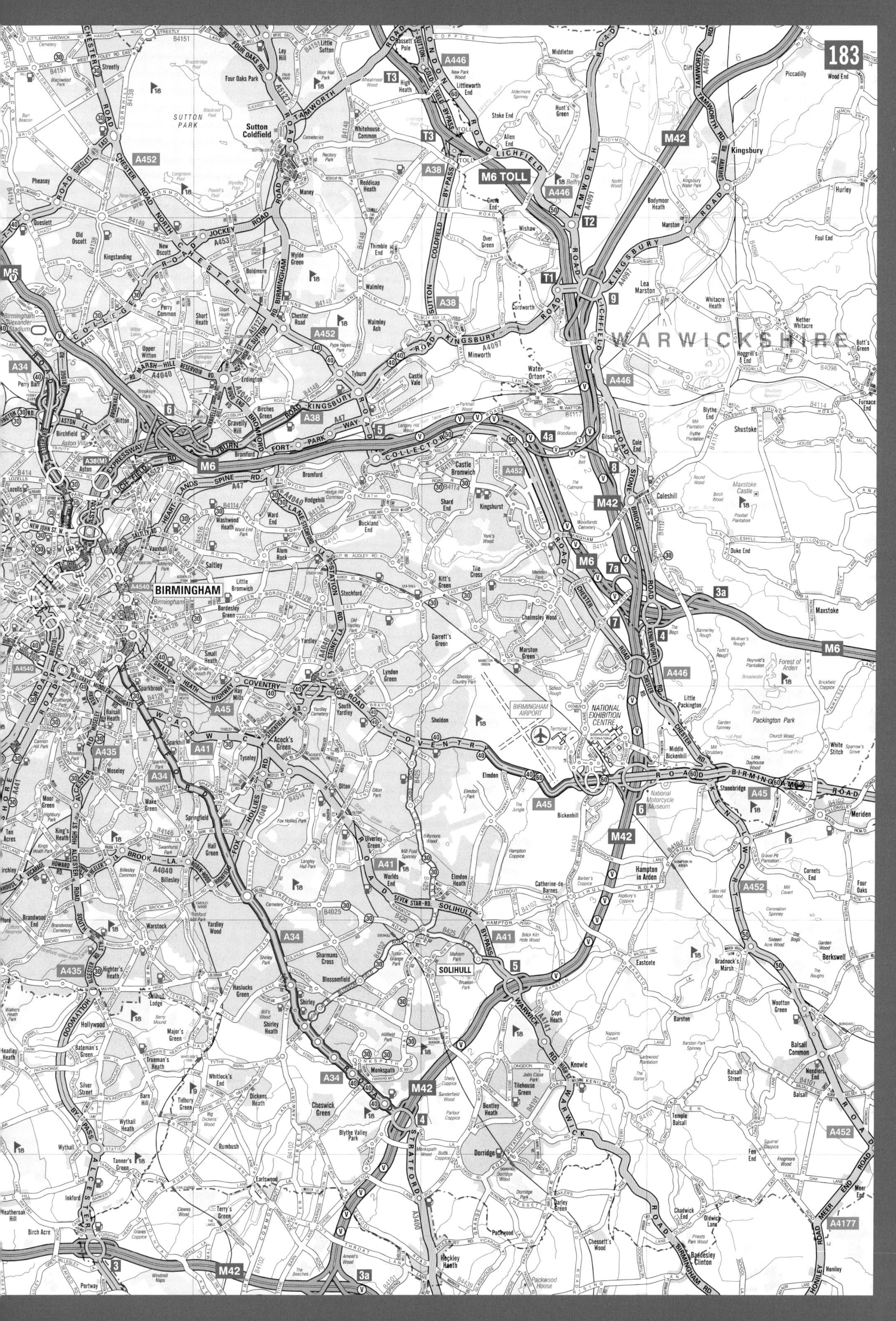

183
BIRMINGHAM
WARWICKSHIRE
SUTTON PARK
Sutton Coldfield
Four Oaks Park
Little Sutton
Streetly
Pheasey
Queslett
Old Oscott
Kingstanding
New Oscott
Boldmere
Wylde Green
Maney
Walmley
Walmley Ash
Minworth
Water Orton
Curdworth
Wishaw
Middleton
Kingsbury
Piccadilly
Wood End
Hurley
Foul End
Marston
Bodymoor Heath
Lea Marston
Whitacre Heath
Nether Whitacre
Bott's Green
Furnace End
Shustoke
Coleshill
Maxstoke Castle
Maxstoke
Packington Park
Forest of Arden
White Stitch
Meriden
Four Oaks
Cornets End
Berkswell
Balsall Common
Balsall
Balsall Street
Temple Balsall
Fen End
Honiley
Chadwick End
Oldwich Lane
Baddesley Clinton
Knowle
Dorridge
Bentley Heath
Tilehouse Green
Copt Heath
Barston
Eastcote
Hampton in Arden
Bickenhill
Catherine-de-Barnes
Elmdon
Elmdon Heath
NATIONAL EXHIBITION CENTRE
BIRMINGHAM AIRPORT
National Motorcycle Museum
Stonebridge
Little Packington
Middle Bickenhill
Marston Green
Chelmsley Wood
Kingshurst
Castle Bromwich
Castle Vale
Tyburn
Erdington
Gravelly Hill
Bromford
Hodgehill
Ward End
Washwood Heath
Saltley
Alum Rock
Stechford
Little Bromwich
Bordesley Green
Yardley
Kitt's Green
Tile Cross
Shard End
Garrett's Green
Lyndon Green
Sheldon
South Yardley
Acock's Green
Tyseley
Small Heath
Sparkbrook
Sparkhill
Hay Mills
Balsall Heath
Moseley
Springfield
Hall Green
Olton
Ulverley Green
Worlds End
Solihull
Sharmans Cross
Blossomfield
Shirley
Shirley Heath
Monkspath
Cheswick Green
Blyth Valley Park
Dickens Heath
Tidbury Green
Whitlock's End
Major's Green
Hasluck's Green
Yardley Wood
Billesley
Warstock
Brandwood End
Kings Heath
Moor Green
Highter's Heath
Trueman's Heath
Bateman's Green
Hollywood
Silver Street
Wythall
Wythall Heath
Tanner's Green
Rumbush
Earlswood
Terry's Green
Inkford
Birch Acre
Portway
Packwood
Hockley Heath
Chessett's Wood
Darley Green
Aston
Aston Villa
Witton
Perry Barr
Birchfield
Lozells
Nechells
Vauxhall
Perry Common
Short Heath
Upper Witton
Chester Road
Reddicap Heath
Thimble End
Whitehouse Common
Stoke End
Allen End
Hunt's Green
Over Green
Grove End
M6 TOLL
M6
M42
A38
A446
A452
A45
A41
A34
A435
A4177
A4040
A47
A452

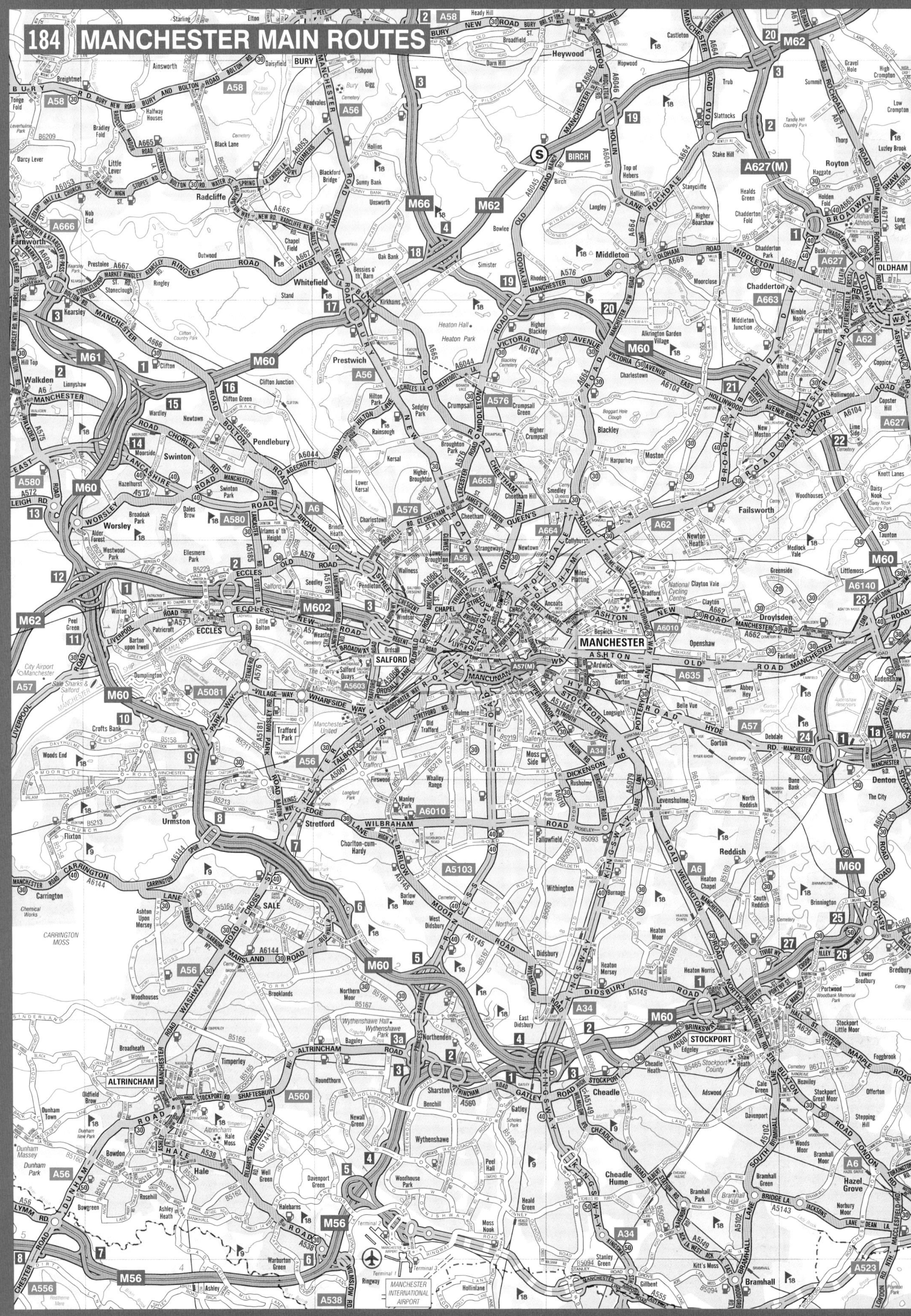
BURY
Heywood
Castleton
Radcliffe
Farnworth
Whitefield
Prestwich
Middleton
Chadderton
OLDHAM
Royton
Walkden
Swinton
Pendlebury
Worsley
ECCLES
SALFORD
MANCHESTER
Failsworth
Droylsden
Openshaw
Gorton
Denton
Urmston
Stretford
Chorlton-cum-Hardy
Withington
Didsbury
Reddish
STOCKPORT
SALE
ALTRINCHAM
Timperley
Hale
Bowdon
Northenden
Wythenshawe
Gatley
Cheadle
Cheadle Hulme
Bramhall
Hazel Grove
Heald Green
MANCHESTER INTERNATIONAL AIRPORT
M60
M62
M61
M66
M602
M56
A627(M)
A57(M)
M67

Town Plans

Port Plans

Airport Plans

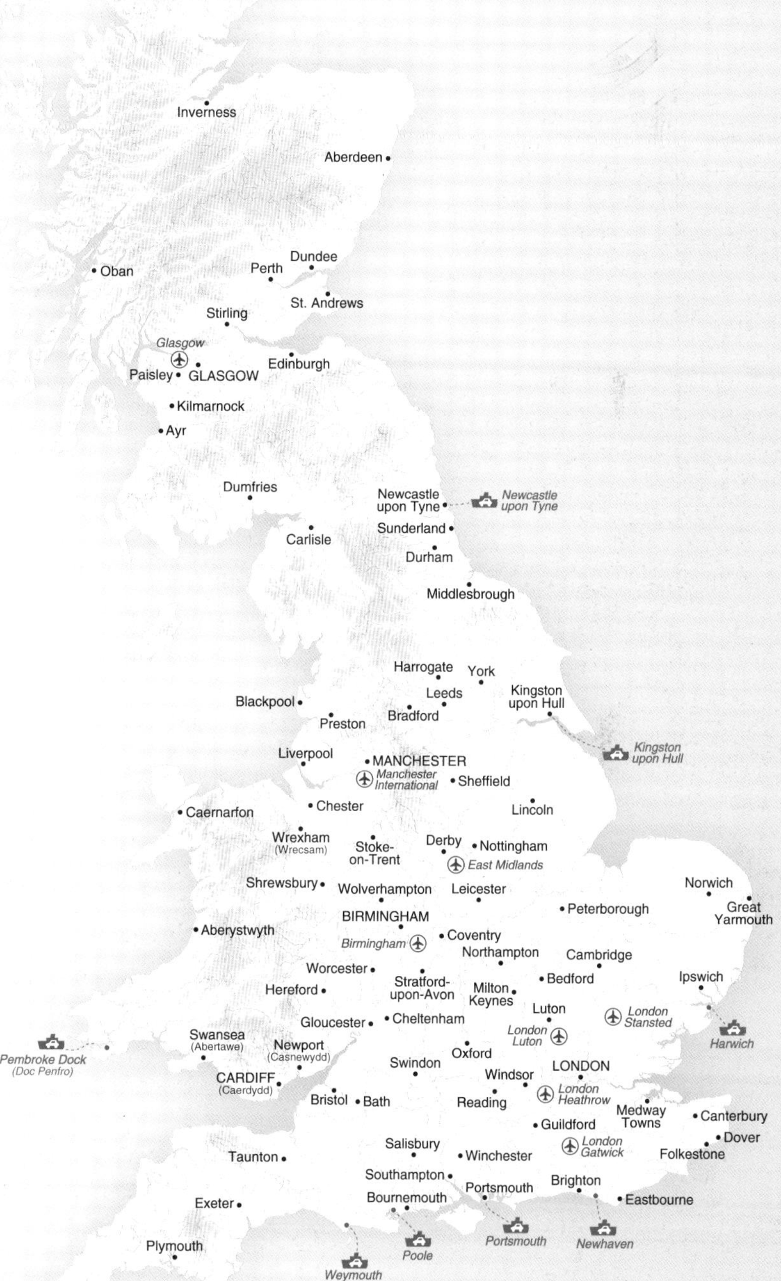

Motorway
Autoroute
Autobahn

Motorway Under Construction
Autoroute en construction
Autobahn im Bau

Motorway Proposed
Autoroute prévue
Geplante Autobahn

Motorway Junctions with Numbers
Unlimited Interchange
Limited Interchange

Autoroute échangeur numéroté
Echangeur complet
Echangeur partiel

Autobahnanschlußstelle mit Nummer
Unbeschränkter Fahrtrichtungswechsel
Beschränkter Fahrtrichtungswechsel

Primary Route
Route à grande circulation
Hauptverkehrsstraße

Dual Carriageways (A & B roads)
Route à double chaussées séparées (route A & B)
Zweispurige Schnellstraße (A- und B- Straßen)

Class A Road
Route de type A
A-Straße

Class B Road
Route de type B
B-Straße

Major Roads Under Construction
Route prioritaire en construction
Hauptverkehrsstaße im Bau

Major Roads Proposed
Route prioritaire prévue
Geplante Hauptverkehrsstaße

Minor Roads
Route secondaire
Nebenstraße

Safety Camera
Radars de contrôle de vitesse
Sicherheitskamera

Restricted Access
Accès réglementé
Beschränkte Zufahrt

Pedestrianized Road & Main Footway
Rue piétonne et chemin réservé aux piétons
Fußgängerstraße und Fußweg

One Way Streets
Sens unique
Einbahnstraße

Fuel Station
Station service
Tankstelle

Toll
Barrière de péage
Gebührenpflichtig

Railway & Station
Voie ferrée et gare
Eisenbahnlinie und Bahnhof

Underground / Metro & DLR Station
Station de métro et DLR
U-Bahnstation und DLR-Station

Level Crossing & Tunnel
Passage à niveau et tunnel
Bahnübergang und Tunnel

Tram Stop & One Way Tram Stop
Arrêt de tramway
Straßenbahnhaltestelle

Built-up Area
Agglomération
Geschlossene Ortschaft

Abbey, Cathedral, Priory etc
Abbaye, cathédrale, prieuré etc
Abtei, Kathedrale, Kloster usw

Airport
Aéroport
Flughafen

Bus Station
Gare routière
Bushaltestelle

Car Park (selection of)
Sélection de parkings
Auswahl von Parkplatz

Church
Eglise
Kirche

City Wall
Murs d'enceinte
Stadtmauer

Congestion Charging Zone
Zone de péage urbain
City-Maut Zone

Ferry (vehicular)
    (foot only)

Bac (véhicules)
    (piétons)

Fähre (autos)
    (nur für Personen)

Golf Course
Terrain de golf
Golfplatz

Heliport
Héliport
Hubschrauberlandeplatz

Hospital
Hôpital
Krankenhaus

Lighthouse
Phare
Leuchtturm

Market
Marché
Markt

National Trust Property
    (open)
    (restricted opening)
    (National Trust for Scotland)
National Trust Property
    (ouvert)
    (heures d'ouverture)
    (National Trust for Scotland)
National Trust- Eigentum
    (geöffnet)
    (beschränkte Öffnungszeit)
    (National Trust for Scotland)

NT
NT
NTS   NTS

Park & Ride
Parking relais
Auswahl von Parkplatz

Place of Interest
Curiosité
Sehenswürdigkeit

Police Station
Commissariat de police
Polizeirevier

Post Office
Bureau de poste
Postamt

Shopping Area (main street & precinct)
Quartier commerçant (rue et zone principales)
Einkaufsviertel (hauptgeschäftsstraße, fußgängerzone)

Shopmobility
Shopmobility
Shopmobility

Toilet
Toilettes
Toilette

Tourist Information Centre
Syndicat d'initiative
Information

Viewpoint
Vue panoramique
Aussichtspunkt

Visitor Information Centre
Centre d'information touristique
Besucherzentrum

Please note: symbols have been enlarged for clarity

ABERDEEN

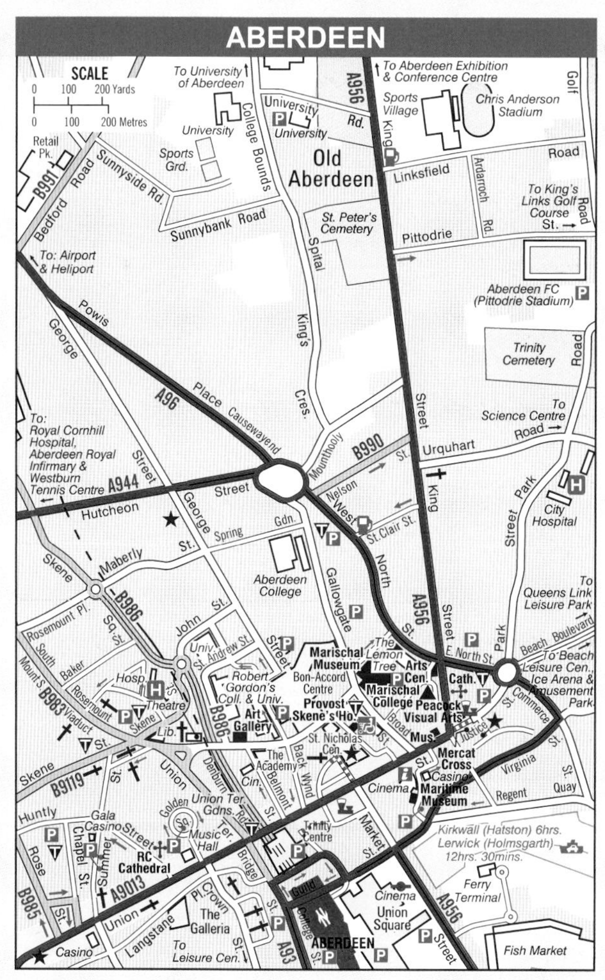
SCALE
0 100 200 Yards
0 100 200 Metres
To University of Aberdeen
To Aberdeen Exhibition & Conference Centre
Sports Village
Chris Anderson Stadium
Golf
University
University Rd.
University
College Bounds
A956
King
Retail Pk.
B991
Bedford Road
Sunnyside Rd.
Sports Grd.
Old Aberdeen
Linksfield
Road
Ardarroch Rd.
To King's Links Golf Course
St.
Sunnybank Road
Spital
St. Peter's Cemetery
Pittodrie
To: Airport & Heliport
Aberdeen FC (Pittodrie Stadium)
Powis
George
King's Cres.
Trinity Cemetery
Road
A96
Place
Causewayend
Street
To Science Centre
Road
To: Royal Cornhill Hospital, Aberdeen Royal Infirmary & Westburn Tennis Centre
A944
Hutcheon
Street
Mounthooly
B990
Urquhart
Nelson St.
Park
Street
City Hospital
Skene
Maberly
George St.
Spring Gdn.
West North
St. Clair St.
Aberdeen College
Gallowgate
A956
Street
Queens Link Leisure Park
Rosemount Pl.
B986
Sq.
St.
John St.
Univ.
St. Andrew St.
Street
Marischal Museum
The Lemon Tree
Arts Cen.
E. North St.
Beach Boulevard
To Beach Leisure Cen., Ice Arena & Amusement Park
South
Baker
Hosp.
Robert Gordon's Coll. & Univ.
Bon-Accord Centre
Marischal College
Cath.
Commerce
Mount St.
Rosemount Viaduct
Theatre
B983
Skene
Art Gallery
Provost Skene's Ho.
Peacock Visual Arts
Justice
St.
Lib.
B986
Denburn
The Academy
Back Wynd
St. Nicholas Cen.
Mus.
Mercat Cross
Casino
St.
Virginia
St.
Skene
B9119
Union
Belmont
Cin.
Cinema
Maritime Museum
Regent
Quay
Huntly
Golden
Union Ter. Gdns.
Gala Casino
Street
Music Hall
Trinity Centre
Market
Kirkwall (Hatston) 6hrs.
Lerwick (Holmsgarth) 12hrs. 30mins.
Rose
Chapel St.
Summer
RC Cathedral
Bridge
Guild
Ferry Terminal
A9013
St.
Crown
Cinema
Union Square
A956
B985
Union
Langstane Pl.
The Galleria
St.
Street
Casino
To Leisure Cen.
A93
ABERDEEN
Fish Market

ABERYSTWYTH

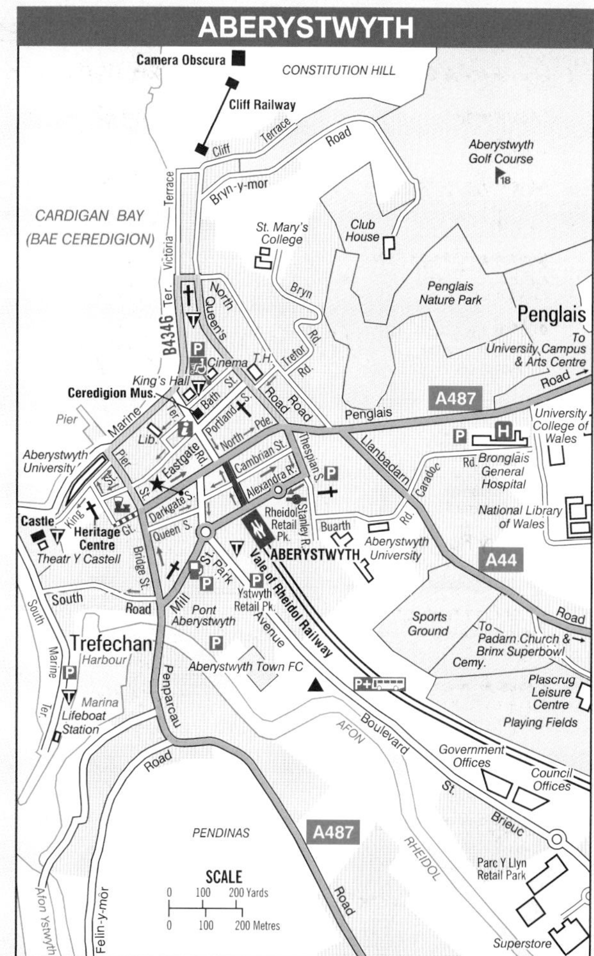
Camera Obscura
CONSTITUTION HILL
Cliff Railway
Cliff
Terrace
Road
Aberystwyth Golf Course
Bryn-y-mor
CARDIGAN BAY
(BAE CEREDIGION)
Victoria Terrace
St. Mary's College
Club House
Bryn
Penglais Nature Park
Penglais
To University Campus & Arts Centre
B4346
Ter.
North
Queen's
Cinema
T.H.
Trefor Rd.
Road
King's Hall
Ceredigion Mus.
Bath St.
Portland St.
North Pde.
Road
A487
Penglais
Pier
Marine
Ter.
Lib.
University College of Wales
Aberystwyth University
Pier St.
Eastgate
Cambrian St.
Thespian S.
Llanbadarn
Caradoc Rd.
Bronglais General Hospital
Alexandra R.
Castle
King St.
Heritage Centre
Darkgate S.
Rheidol Retail Pk.
Stanley R.
Buarth
Rd.
National Library of Wales
Theatr Y Castell
Queen S.
Bridge St.
Vale of Rheidol Railway
ABERYSTWYTH
Aberystwyth University
A44
South
Road
Mill St.
Park
Ystwyth Retail Pk.
Avenue
Road
Sports Ground
To Padarn Church & Brinx Superbowl
Cemy.
Trefechan
Pont Aberystwyth
Harbour
Aberystwyth Town FC
Plascrug Leisure Centre
Playing Fields
South Marine Ter.
Marina
Lifeboat Station
Penparcau
AFON
Boulevard
Government Offices
Council Offices
Road
St.
Brieuc
PENDINAS
A487
RHEIDOL
Parc Y Llyn Retail Park
SCALE
0 100 200 Yards
0 100 200 Metres
Road
Afon Ystwyth
Felin-y-mor
Superstore

AYR

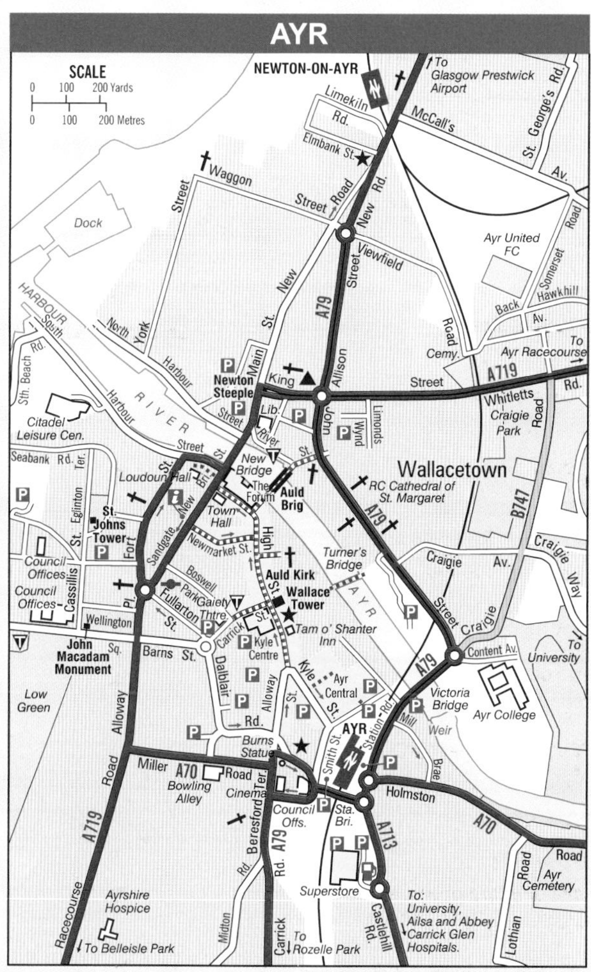
SCALE
0 100 200 Yards
0 100 200 Metres
NEWTON-ON-AYR
To Glasgow Prestwick Airport
Limekiln Rd.
McCall's
St. George's Rd.
Elmbank St.
Av.
Waggon
Street
Street Road
New Rd.
Dock
Road
Ayr United FC
Viewfield
Street
Somerset
Hawkhill
Back Av.
HARBOUR
South
North York
Harbour
New St.
A79
Road
Cemy.
Ayr Racecourse
To
Sth. Beach Rd.
Main St.
King
Allison
A719
Street
Rd.
Newton Steeple
Street
Whitletts
Harbour
RIVER
Craigie Park
Citadel Leisure Cen.
Lib.
River
John
Wynd
Limonds
Road
Seabank Rd.
Ter.
Street
St.
New Bridge
Wallacetown
Loudoun Hall
Auld Brig
RC Cathedral of St. Margaret
B747
St. Eglinton
The Forum
A79
Craigie Way
St. Johns Tower
Fort
Sandgate
New
Town Hall
Newmarket St.
High
Turner's Bridge
Craigie
Av.
Council Offices
Cassillis
Council Offices
Boswell
Park
Auld Kirk
Wallace Tower
AYR
Gaiety Thtre
Fullarton St.
Pl.
Wellington
Tam o' Shanter Inn
Street
Craigie
John Macadam Monument
Sq.
Barns St.
Carrick
Kyle Centre
Content Av.
To University
Dalblair
Kyle
Ayr Central
St.
Victoria Bridge
Ayr College
Low Green
Alloway
Rd.
Alloway
A79
Mill
Weir
AYR
Station Rd.
Burns Statue
Smith St.
Brae
Miller
A70
Road
Bowling Alley
Cinema
Holmston
Ter.
Council Offs.
Sta. Bri.
A70
Road
A719
Beresford
A713
Road
Ayr Cemetery
Carrick Rd.
Superstore
Castlehill Rd.
To: University, Ailsa and Abbey Carrick Glen Hospitals.
Racecourse
Ayrshire Hospice
Midton
To Rozelle Park
Lothian
To Belleisle Park

BATH

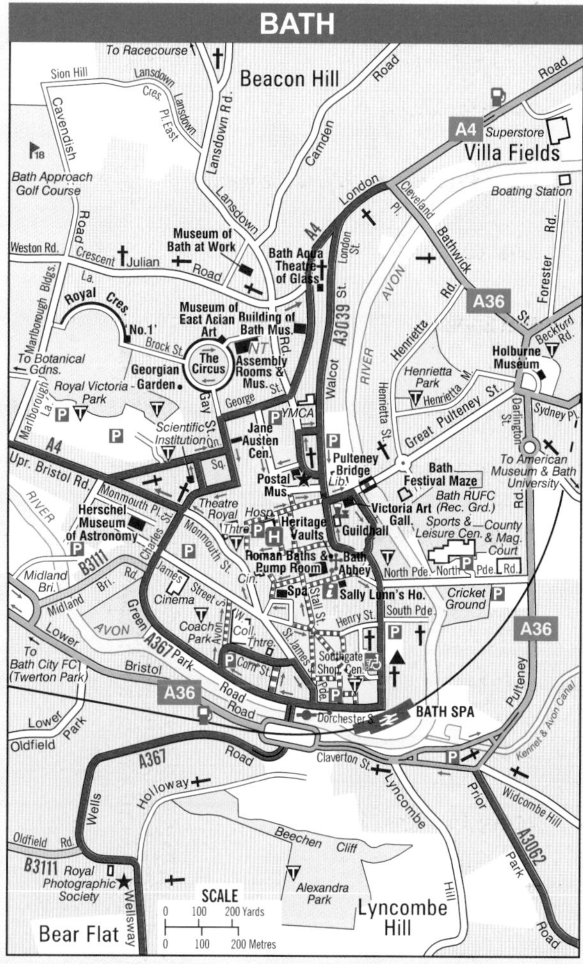
To Racecourse
Sion Hill
Lansdown Cres.
Lansdown Pl. East
Beacon Hill
Road
Lansdown Rd.
Camden
Road
Cavendish
Bath Approach Golf Course
A4
Superstore
Villa Fields
Road
Lansdown
London
Boating Station
Weston Rd.
Crescent
Julian
La.
Museum of Bath at Work
Road
A4
Bath Aqua Theatre of Glass
London St.
Cleveland Pl.
Bathwick
Rd.
Forester
Marlborough Bldgs.
Royal Cres.
No.1
Museum of East Asian Art
Building of Bath Mus.
A3039
St.
AVON
RIVER
Walcot
Henrietta
Rd.
A36
St.
Beckford Rd.
Brock St.
To Botanical Gdns.
Georgian Garden
The Circus
Assembly Rooms & Mus.
Henrietta Park
Holburne Museum
Marlborough La.
Royal Victoria Park
St.
George
YMCA
Henrietta St.
Henrietta M.
Great Pulteney St.
Darlington St.
Sydney Pl.
Scientific Institution
Gay
A4
Upr. Bristol Rd.
Sq.
Qn.
Jane Austen Cen.
Pulteney Bridge
Bath Festival Maze
To American Museum & Bath University
Monmouth Pl.
St.
Postal Mus.
Lib.
RIVER
Herschel Museum of Astronomy
Theatre Royal
Hosp.
Thtre.
Heritage Vaults
Guildhall
Victoria Art Gall.
Bath RUFC (Rec. Grd.)
Sports & Leisure Cen.
County & Mag. Court
Rd.
B3111
Chapel
Monmouth St.
Roman Baths & Pump Room
Bath Abbey
North Pde.
North Pde.
Midland Bri.
Rd.
Bri.
James Street W.
Spa
Sally Lunn's Ho.
Cricket Ground
Midland
Cinema
South Pde.
Henry St.
AVON
Green Park
A367
Coach Park
Avon St.
Coll. Thtre.
St. James Pde.
Stall St.
A36
Lower
Bristol
SouthGate Shop. Cen.
To Bath City FC (Twerton Park)
Road
Corn St.
Pulteney
A36
Road
Dorchester S.
BATH SPA
Lower Oldfield Park
Road
Claverton St.
Kennet & Avon Canal
A367
Holloway
Lyncombe
Widcombe Hill
Prior
Wells
Beechen Cliff
Oldfield Rd.
A3062
Park
Hill
B3111
Royal Photographic Society
Alexandra Park
SCALE
0 100 200 Yards
0 100 200 Metres
Lyncombe Hill
Road
Bear Flat
Wellsway

BEDFORD

BLACKPOOL

BIRMINGHAM (CITY CENTRE)

SCALE
0 100 200 Yards ¼ Mile
0 100 200 300 400 Metres

JEWELLERY QUARTER, Branston St., Mus. of the Jewellery Quarter, Vyse St., Gt. Hampton St., Hampton St., B4100, Buckingham St., Smith St., Hospital St., Rec. Grd., New Summer St., Lane, To: Alexander Stadium & Aston Villa FC, New Town Row, B4114, A38(M), 13, Canal, Dartmouth, Lord St., Sports Centre, St. Rupert St., Lister St., 14 Great, A4540, Parkway, A47, Nechells Green

Pitsford St., Camden St., New Spring St., A4540, 8, Cemetery, School of Jewellery (University), Hockley Centre, Augusta St., Spencer St., Lane, Mott St., Howard St., Constitution Hill, 30, Henrietta St., Hanley St., Clive St., Birmingham Canal, Bagot St., Stamford St., Moland St., Aston Rd., A38, Holt St., Art & Design Institute, Digbeth Branch Canal, Lister, Woodcock St., Middleway, Brookfields, Warstone, Vittoria St., Carver St., Tenby St. N., Frederick St., Caroline St., Northwood St., Cox St., Livery St., St. Pauls, Summer St., Lwr. Loveday St., Princip St., Price St., Council Offs., Aston University, Nechells, 15, Lawley Middleway

Spring Hill, Ellen St., Icknield St., Pope St., Tenby St., Legge La., Regent Pl., St. Paul's Sq., James St., RBSA Gall., Water St., Shadwell St., RC Cathedral, Dental Hosp., Children's Hosp., Aston Student Village, Sports Centre, Aston St., Cardigan St., To City Hospital, A457, Lib., 7, Camden St., Albion St., Graham St., Sikh Temple, Newhall St., Ludgate Hill, Telecom Tower, Snow Hill, Police H.Q., Whittall St., Weaman St., Mag. Cts., Corporation St., Central Hall, College, B4114, The Giant-Millennium Point, Thinktank, Jennens Rd., B4132, Vauxhall Rd., 16, A4540

Middleway, B4284, Summer Hill Rd., Powell St., Sand Pits, Parade, George St., Charlotte St., Chest Clinic, Fleet St., Lionel St., Edmund St., Church St., SNOW HILL, Bull St., Justice Cen., The Priory Queensway, Crown Ct., City Park, Curzon St., Ladywood, Nelson St., Clement St., Edward St., Summer Hill, Livery St., Street, Museum & Art Gallery, Colmore Row, Cathedral, City Plaza, Martineau Pl., Priory Sq., Fazeley St., B4100, Grand Union Canal, Montague, Barr St.

National Indoor Arena, King Edwards Rd., Cambridge St., Liby., Hall of Memory, Birmingham Canal, St. Vincent St., ICC and Symphony Hall, National Sea Life Cen., Gt. Tindal St., Browning St., Sheepcote St., Adrian Boult Hall, Theatre, Town Hall, New St., Grand Central, Temple St., Corporation St., Pavilions, BIRMINGHAM NEW ST., MOOR ST., Bordesley St., New Canal St., The Bond Gallery, Ledsam St., St. Vincent St. W., Brindley Place, Ikon Gallery, Crescent Theatre, Gas St. Basin, Bridge St., A38, Hill St., Gala Casino, The Pallasades, Bullring Shop Cen., Park St., Meriden St., Fazeley Studios, Liverpool St., Mill La.

Ladywood Middleway, Morville St., Ryland St., Grosvenor St. W., Broad St., Berkley St., Granville St., ITV Central, Mailbox, BBC Birmingham Public Space, Severn St., Theatres, Dean St., Moat La., Digbeth, Oxford St., Digbeth College, Bordesley, A4540, Tennant St., Register Office, Holliday St., Commercial St., Gough St., Syn., Ellis St., Hippodrome, Arcadian Cen., Back to Backs, The Leisurebox, Coach Station, B4100, Heath Mill La., Bowlplex, Cinema, Bishopsgate St., Marshall St., Hurst St., Pershore St., Wholesale Market, Rea St., High St. Deritend, Bradford St., Deritend, Adderley St., To Birmingham City FC

A456, 5, Cinema, Five Ways Shopping Centre, Islington Row, 4, Bath Row, Holloway Head, Sutton St., Sports Ground, Irving St., Bromsgrove St., Kent St., Essex St., Gooch St. N., Sherlock St., Barford St., River Rea, Cheapside, Alcester St., High St. Bordesley, BORDESLEY, Superstore, B4284, Harborne Rd., Five Ways, To Botanical Gardens, FIVE WAYS, Wheeleys Rd., Lee Bank, A4540, Cregoe St., Great Colmore Street, A38, Wrentham St., To Edgbaston Cricket Ground, Macdonald St., B4100, Camp Hill

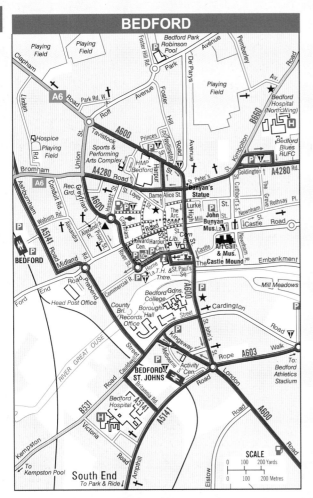

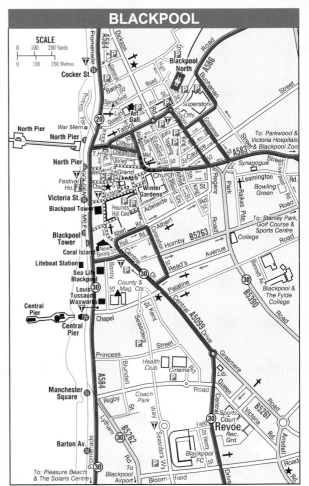

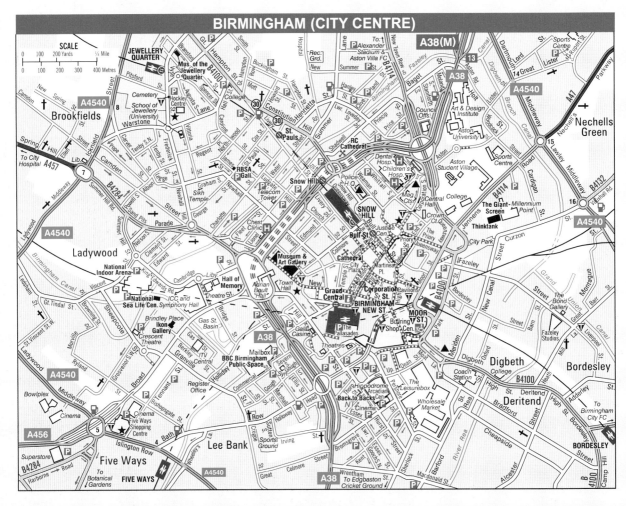

BRIGHTON and HOVE

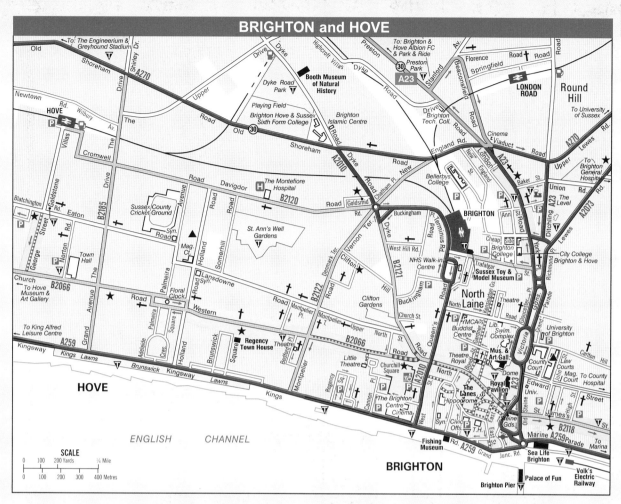

SCALE

0 100 200 Yards ¼ Mile
0 100 200 300 400 Metres

ENGLISH CHANNEL

HOVE

BRIGHTON

BRISTOL

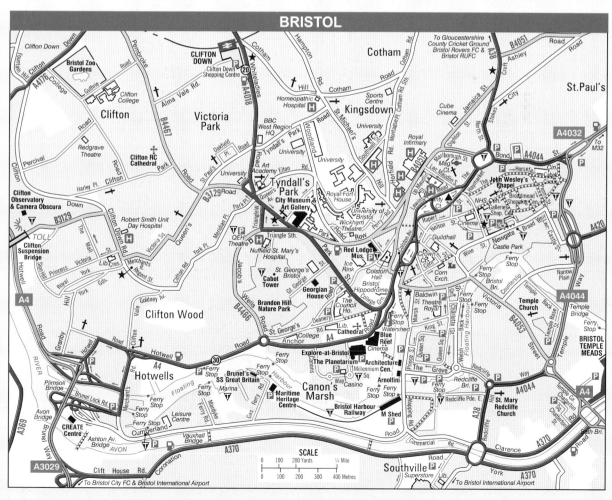

SCALE

0 100 200 Yards ¼ Mile
0 100 200 300 400 Metres

BOURNEMOUTH

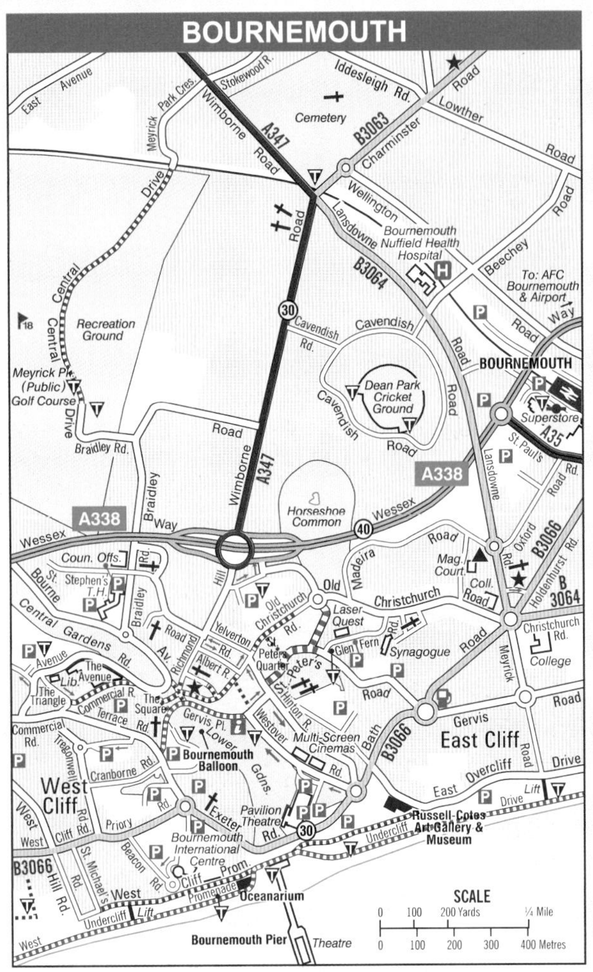
East Avenue
Stokewood R.
Iddesleigh Rd.
Meyrick Park Cres.
Wimborne Road
A347
Cemetery
B3063
Charminster Road
Lowther Road
Wellington
Lansdowne
Bournemouth Nuffield Health Hospital
B3064
Beechey Road
To: AFC Bournemouth & Airport
Central Drive
Recreation Ground
Meyrick Pk (Public) Golf Course
Cavendish Rd.
Cavendish Road
Dean Park Cricket Ground
BOURNEMOUTH
Superstore
A35
St. Paul's Rd.
Braidley Rd.
Bradley Road
Wimborne Road
A347
Horseshoe Common
A338
Wessex Way
Coun. Offs.
St. Stephen's T.H.
Bourne
Central Gardens
Old Christchurch Rd.
Madeira Road
Christchurch Road
Mag. Court
Coll. Road
Oxford Rd.
B3066
Holdenhurst Rd.
B 3064
Christchurch Rd.
College
Laser Quest
Glen Fern Rd.
Synagogue
Yelverton
Richmond
Albert R.
The Avenue
Lib.
The Triangle
Commercial R.
The Square
Terrace
Commercial Rd.
Gervis Pl.
Lower Gdns.
Westover
Hinton R.
Multi-Screen Cinemas
Bath
B3066
Gervis Road
East Cliff
Meyrick Road
Overcliff Drive
East Drive
Lift
Bournemouth Balloon
Cranborne Rd.
West Cliff
Priory
Exeter Rd.
Pavilion Theatre
Russell-Cotes Art Gallery & Museum
Undercliff
Bournemouth International Centre
B3066
West Hill Rd.
St. Michael's Rd.
Beacon Rd.
West Promenade
Undercliff
Oceanarium
Bournemouth Pier
Theatre
SCALE
0 100 200 Yards ¼ Mile
0 100 200 300 400 Metres

BRADFORD

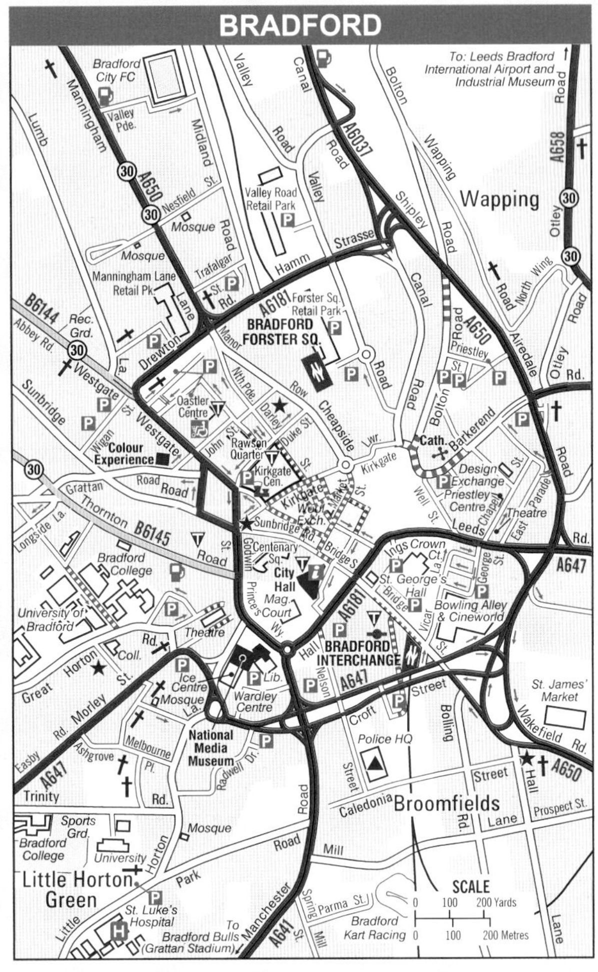
Bradford City FC
Manningham
Lumb
Valley Pde.
Valley Road
Canal Road
Midland Road
A6037
Bolton
To: Leeds Bradford International Airport and Industrial Museum
Otley Road
A658
Wapping
A650
Nesfield St.
Mosque
Valley Road Retail Park
Hamm Strasse
Shipley
Canal Road
Manningham Lane Retail Pk.
Trafalgar
St. Mary's Rd.
Forster Sq. Retail Park
B6144
Rec. Grd.
Abbey Rd.
A6181
BRADFORD FORSTER SQ.
Drewton
Lane
Manor
North Wing
Airedale Road
Westgate
Sunbridge
Oastler Centre
Darley
Cheapside
Priestley
Bolton Road
Barkerend
Cath.
Wigan
Colour Experience
John St.
Rawson Quarter
Kirkgate Cen.
Duke St.
Kirkgate
Design Exchange
Priestley Centre
Theatre
Grattan Road
Thornton B6145 Road
Wool Exch.
Market
Sunbridge Rd.
Godwin St.
Centenary Sq.
City Hall
Mag. Court
Ings Crown Ct.
St. George's Hall
Bowling Alley & Cineworld
Leeds Rd.
A647
Longside La.
Bradford College
University of Bradford
Great Horton Rd.
Coll.
Theatre
Ice Centre
Mosque
Lib.
Wardley Centre
BRADFORD INTERCHANGE
Nelson
A647
Street
St. James' Market
Morley St.
Melbourne Pl.
National Media Museum
Croft
Police HQ
Bolling Road
Wakefield Rd.
Easby Rd.
Ashgrove
A647
Trinity
Manchester Road
Caledonia
Broomfields
Street
Hall Lane
Prospect St.
A650
Sports Grd.
Bradford College
University
Horton
Mosque
Mill Lane
Little Horton Green
Park
St. Luke's Hospital
To Bradford Bulls (Grattan Stadium)
A641
Spring Mill
Parma St.
Bradford Kart Racing
SCALE
0 100 200 Yards
0 100 200 Metres

CAERNARFON

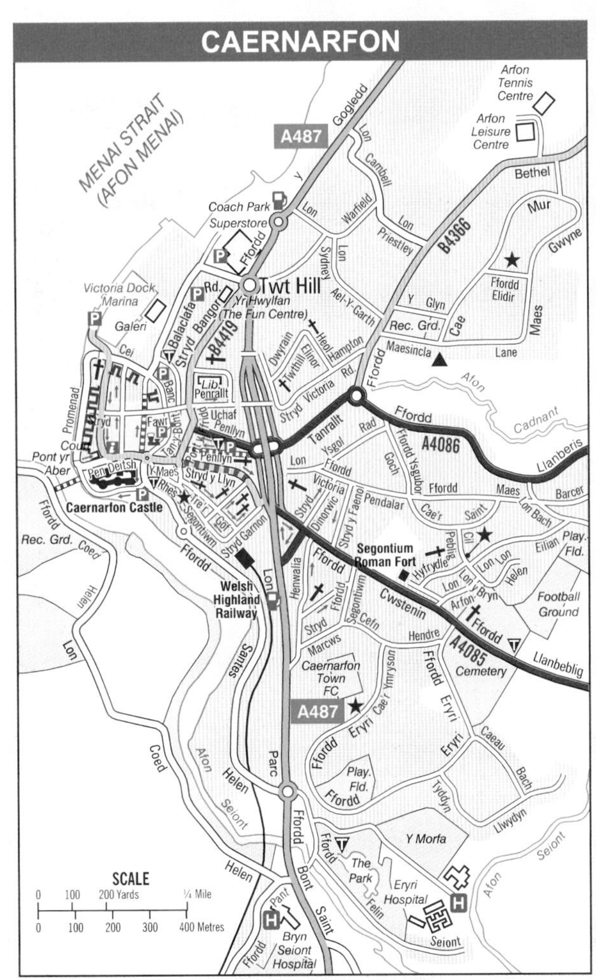
MENAI STRAIT (AFON MENAI)
A487
Gogledd
Lon Cambell
Arfon Tennis Centre
Arfon Leisure Centre
Bethel
Mur Gwyne
Coach Park
Superstore
Lon Warfield
Sydney
Lon Priestley
B4366
Victoria Dock Marina
Balaclava Rd.
Twt Hill
Yr Hwylfan (The Fun Centre)
Galeri
Bangor
B4419
Y Glyn
Rec. Grd.
Ffordd Elidir
Maes
Cei
Lib.
Pencraig
Maesincla
Lane
Afon Cadnant
Promenade
Penllyn
Dwyrain
Hampton
Stryd Victoria Rd.
Ffordd
A4086
Llanberis
Pont yr Aber
Tanrallt
Ysgol
Goch
Ffordd Ysgubor
Pendalar
Barcer
Caernarfon Castle
Segontium Terrace
Stryd y Llyn
Victoria
Lon Bach
Play. Fld.
Rec. Grd.
Segontium Roman Fort
Hyfrydle
Eilian
Welsh Highland Railway
Cwstenin
Football Ground
Hendre
A4085
Cemetery
Llanbeblig
Caernarfon Town FC
A487
Eryri
Caeau Bach
Coed Helen
Lon
Afon Seiont
Parc
Play. Fld.
Llwydyn
Y Morfa
The Park
Eryri Hospital
Bont Saint
Bryn Seiont Hospital
Seiont
SCALE
0 100 200 Yards ¼ Mile
0 100 200 300 400 Metres

CANTERBURY

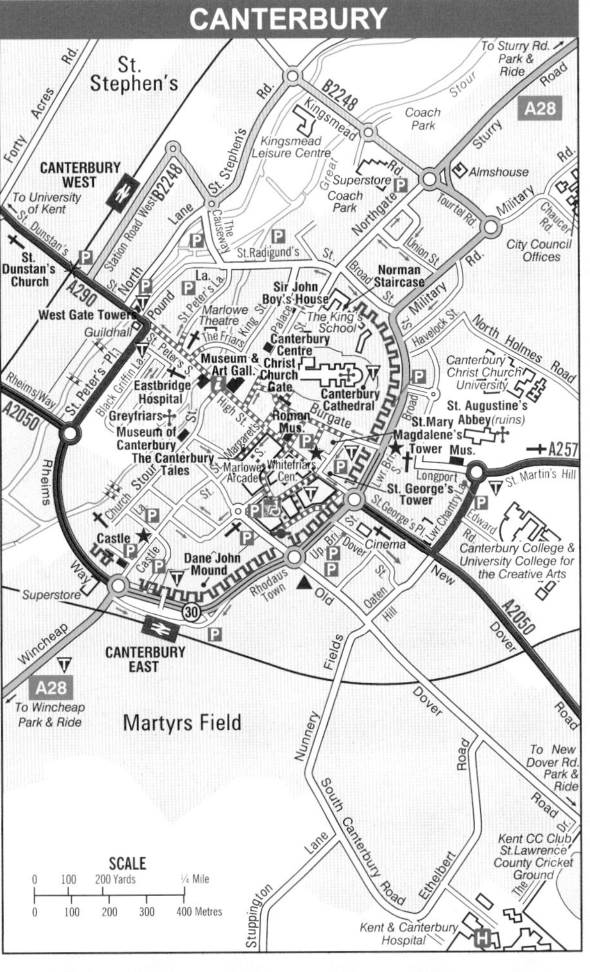
St. Stephen's
Forty Acres Rd.
To Sturry Rd. Park & Ride
B2248
Kingsmead
Coach Park
Stour
A28
Sturry Road
CANTERBURY WEST
To University of Kent
Station Road West
B2248
Kingsmead Leisure Centre
Superstore
Coach Park
Northgate
Almshouse
Tourtel Rd.
Military Rd.
Chaucer Rd.
St. Dunstan's Church
St. Radigund's St.
Union St.
City Council Offices
A290
West Gate Towers
Guildhall
Marlowe Theatre
The Friars
Sir John Boys's House
The King's School
Norman Staircase
Canterbury Centre
Museum & Art Gall.
Christ Church Gate
Canterbury Cathedral
Havelock St.
North Holmes Road
Canterbury Christ Church University
Rheims Way
A2050
St. Peter's Pl.
Eastbridge Hospital
Greyfriars
Museum of Canterbury
The Canterbury Tales
Roman Mus.
Burgate
St. Augustine's Abbey (ruins)
St. Mary Magdalene's Tower
Mus.
A257
Longport
St. Martin's Hill
St. George's Tower
Marlowe Arcade
Whitefriars Cen.
Castle
Dane John Mound
Rhodaus Town
Cinema
Dover St.
Oaten Hill
New Dover Road
Canterbury College & University College for the Creative Arts
A2050
Superstore
Wincheap
CANTERBURY EAST
A28
To Wincheap Park & Ride
Martyrs Field
Fields
Nunnery
Dover
To New Dover Rd. Park & Ride
South Canterbury Road
Ethelbert Road
Kent CC Club/ St.Lawrence County Cricket Ground
Stuppington Lane
Kent & Canterbury Hospital
SCALE
0 100 200 Yards ¼ Mile
0 100 200 300 400 Metres

CAMBRIDGE

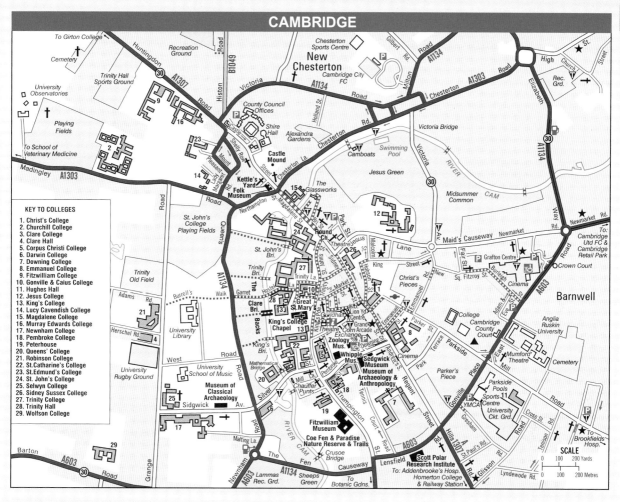

KEY TO COLLEGES
1. Christ's College
2. Churchill College
3. Clare College
4. Clare Hall
5. Corpus Christi College
6. Darwin College
7. Downing College
8. Emmanuel College
9. Fitzwilliam College
10. Gonville & Caius College
11. Hughes Hall
12. Jesus College
13. King's College
14. Lucy Cavendish College
15. Magdalene College
16. Murray Edwards College
17. Newnham College
18. Pembroke College
19. Peterhouse
20. Queens' College
21. Robinson College
22. St.Catharine's College
23. St.Edmund's College
24. St. John's College
25. Selwyn College
26. Sidney Sussex College
27. Trinity College
28. Trinity Hall
29. Wolfson College

CARDIFF (CAERDYDD)

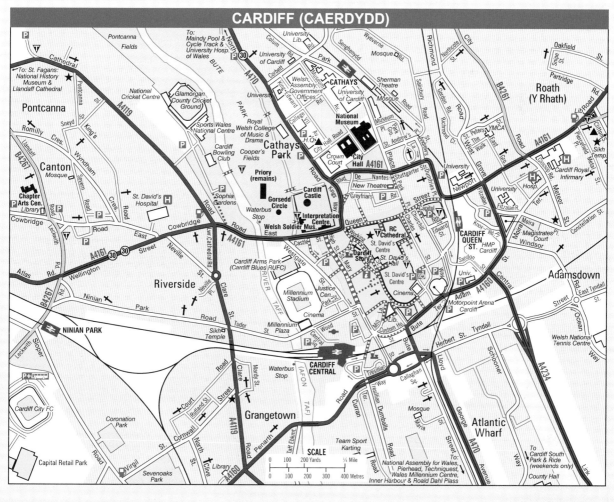

CARLISLE

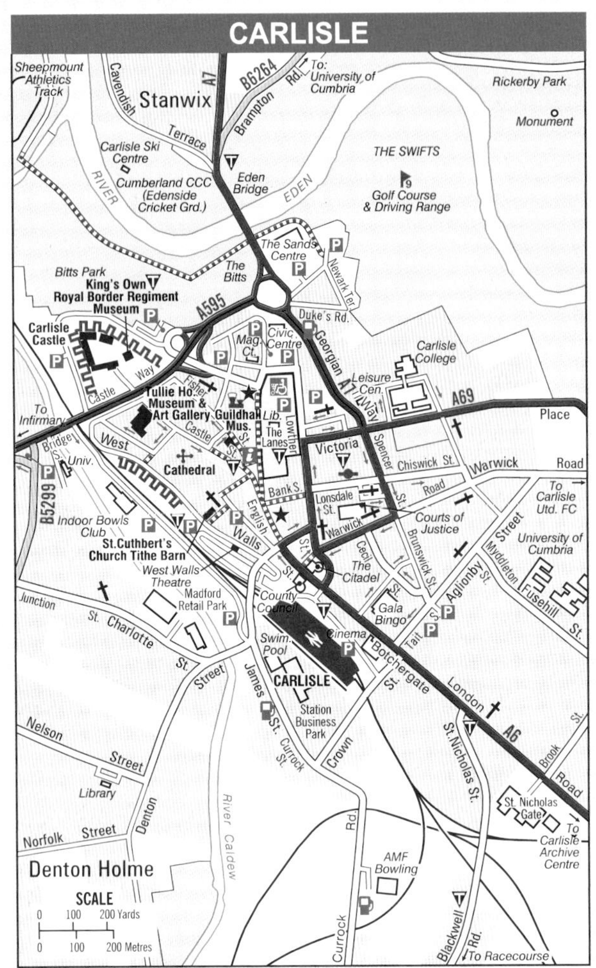
Sheepmount Athletics Track
Stanwix
Cavendish
Terrace
B6264
Brampton Rd.
To: University of Cumbria
Rickerby Park
Monument
Carlisle Ski Centre
THE SWIFTS
Golf Course & Driving Range
RIVER
EDEN
Eden Bridge
Cumberland CCC (Edenside Cricket Grd.)
The Sands Centre
Newark Ter.
The Bitts
Bitts Park
King's Own Royal Border Regiment Museum
A595
Duke's Rd.
Carlisle Castle
Civic Centre
Mag. Ct.
Georgian Way
Carlisle College
Leisure Cen.
A69
Castle Way
Tullie Ho. Museum & Art Gallery
Guildhall Mus.
Lib.
Lowther St.
The Lanes
Place
To Infirmary
West
Castle St.
Cathedral
Victoria
Spencer St.
Chiswick St.
Warwick
Road
Bridge St.
Univ.
B5299
Bank St.
Lonsdale St.
Warwick Rd.
Courts of Justice
To Carlisle Utd. FC
Indoor Bowls Club
English St.
Walls
Cecil St.
The Citadel
Brunswick St.
Aglionby St.
Street
University of Cumbria
St.Cuthbert's Church Tithe Barn
West Walls Theatre
Madford Retail Park
County Council
Gala Bingo
Middleton St.
Fusehill St.
Junction St.
Charlotte St.
Swim. Pool
Cinema
Tait St.
Botchergate
London
A6
CARLISLE
Station Business Park
James St.
Currock St.
Crown
St.Nicholas St.
Brook St.
Road
Nelson
Street
Library
Denton
River Caldew
St. Nicholas Gate
To Carlisle Archive Centre
Norfolk Street
Denton Holme
AMF Bowling
Rd.
Currock
Blackwell Rd.
To Racecourse
SCALE
0 100 200 Yards
0 100 200 Metres

CHELTENHAM

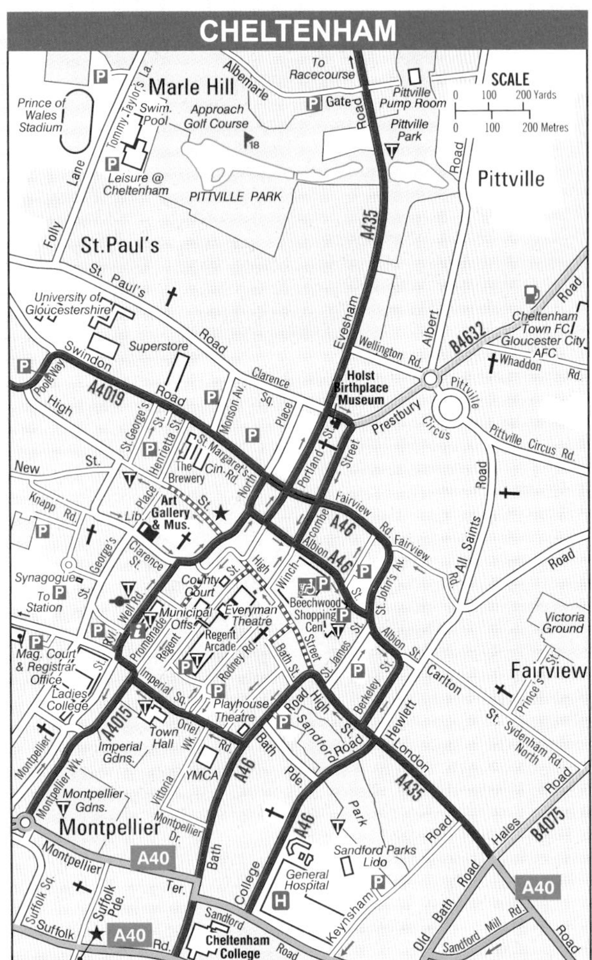
Prince of Wales Stadium
Marle Hill
Tommy Taylor's La.
Albemarle
Swim. Pool
Approach Golf Course
To Racecourse
Gate
Pittville Pump Room
Pittville Park
SCALE
0 100 200 Yards
0 100 200 Metres
Leisure @ Cheltenham
PITTVILLE PARK
Road
Pittville
Folly Lane
St.Paul's
A435
St. Paul's
Evesham
University of Gloucestershire
Superstore
Swindon
Road
Albert
Wellington Rd.
B4632
Cheltenham Town FC/ Gloucester City AFC
Whaddon Rd.
Clarence Sq.
Holst Birthplace Museum
Prestbury
Pittville Circus
Pittville Circus Rd.
Poole Way
A4019
High
St. George's St.
Henrietta St.
Monson Av.
Place
New
St.
The Brewery
St. Margaret's Rd.
North
Portland St.
Street
Knapp Rd.
Lib.
Place
Art Gallery & Mus.
Fairview
Rd.
Fairview
All Saints Road
Synagogue
To Station
St. George's
Clarence St.
County Court
Winch.
Albion
A46
Beechwood Shopping Cen.
St. John's Av.
Rd.
Road
Victoria Ground
Mag. Court & Registrar Office
Ladies College
Promenade
Municipal Offs.
Regent
Everyman Theatre
Regent Arcade
Rodney Rd.
Bath St.
St. James St.
Albion St.
Berkeley St.
Carlton
Fairview
Prince's St.
Imperial Sq.
Playhouse Theatre
Sandford Road
Hewlett
St. Sydenham Rd. North
Town Hall
A4015
Oriel
Imperial Gdns.
YMCA
A46
Bath Pde.
London
A435
Road
Montpellier Wk.
Montpellier Gdns.
Montpellier
Victoria
Montpellier Dr.
A46
Park
Sandford Parks Lido
Road
Hales
B4075
Montpellier
A40
Bath
College
General Hospital
Keynsham
Road
A40
Suffolk Sq.
Suffolk Pde.
Ter.
Old Bath Road
Sandford Mill Rd.
Suffolk
A40
Rd.
Sandford
Cheltenham College
Road

CHESTER

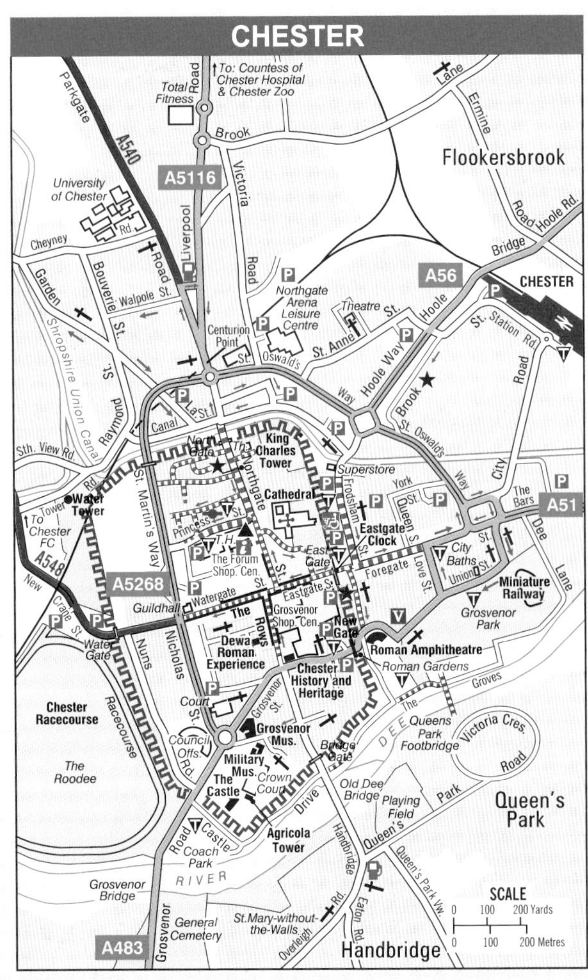
Parkgate
Total Fitness
Road
To: Countess of Chester Hospital & Chester Zoo
Lane
Ermine
Brook
A540
A5116
Victoria
Flookersbrook
University of Chester
Hoole Rd.
Cheyney
Bouverie
Liverpool
Road
Road
Bridge
A56
CHESTER
Garden
Walpole St.
Northgate Arena Leisure Centre
Theatre St.
Hoole Way
St. Station Rd.
Road
Shropshire Union Canal
St.
Centurion Point
St. Oswald's
St. Anne
Way
Brook St.
Raymond St.
Canal St.
Sth. View Rd.
North Gate
King Charles Tower
Superstore
St. Oswald's Way
City
The Bars
A51
Water Tower
St. Martin's Way
Northgate
Cathedral
Frodsham St.
York St.
Queen St.
Tower
To Chester FC
Princess St.
T.H.
The Forum Shop. Cen.
Eastgate Clock
City Baths
St.
Dee
Lane
A548
New
A5268
East Gate
Foregate
Love St.
Union St.
Miniature Railway
Watergate
Eastgate St.
Guildhall
The Rows
Grosvenor Shop. Cen.
Grosvenor Park
Crane St.
Water Gate
Nuns
Nicholas St.
Dewa Roman Experience
Roman Amphitheatre
New Gate
Roman Gardens
Chester History and Heritage
Court
Grovenor St.
Groves
Chester Racecourse
Racecourse
Queens Park Footbridge
Victoria Cres.
Council Offs.
Grosvenor Mus.
Bridge Gate
DEE
Road
The Roodee
Military Mus.
The Castle
Crown Court
Drive
Old Dee Bridge
Playing Field
Park
Queen's Park
Road
Castle
Agricola Tower
Handbridge
Queen's Park Vw.
Coach Park
RIVER
Grosvenor Bridge
Grosvenor Road
General Cemetery
St.Mary-without-the-Walls
Overleigh Rd.
Eaton Rd.
SCALE
0 100 200 Yards
0 100 200 Metres
Handbridge
A483

COVENTRY

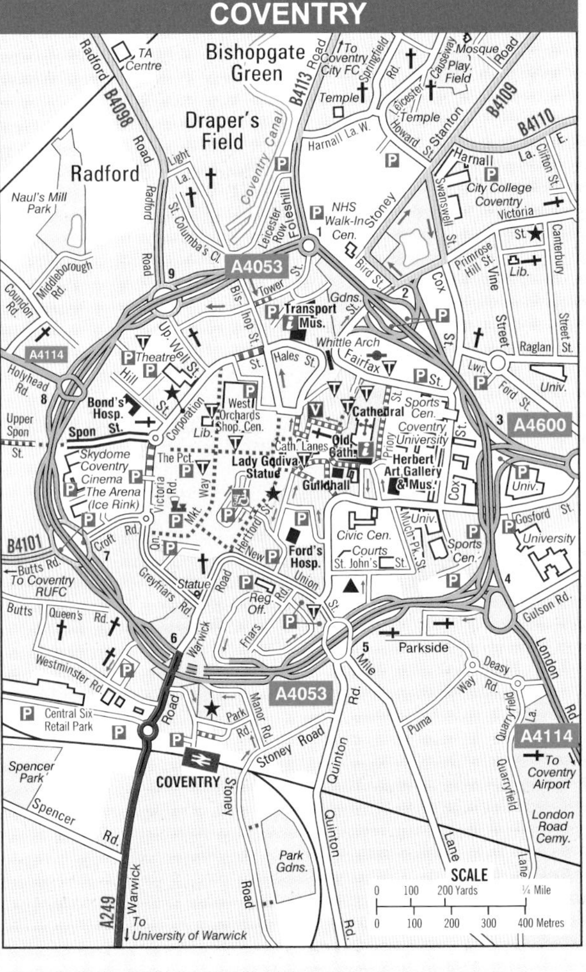
Radford
TA Centre
Bishopgate Green
To Coventry City FC
Springfield Rd.
Mosque
Road
Causeway
Play. Field
B4098
B4113
Temple
Leicester
Temple
Howard St.
Stanton
B4109
B4110
Draper's Field
Road
Coventry Canal
Harnall La. W.
Harnall La.
Clifton St.
Radford
Light
Foleshill
Swanswell
City College Coventry
Naul's Mill Park
La.
St. Columba's Cl.
Leicester Row
Stoney
NHS Walk-In Cen.
Victoria St.
Canterbury
Radford Road
Road
1
A4053
Bird St.
Primrose Hill St.
Vine
Lib.
Middleborough Rd.
9
Tower
Bishop St.
Transport Mus.
Gdns.
2
Cox
Street
Coundon Rd.
Whittle Arch
Raglan St.
A4114
Up. Well St.
Theatre
Hales St.
Fairfax
St.
Lwr. Ford St.
Holyhead Rd.
8
Hill
West Orchards Shop. Cen.
Cathedral
Sports Cen.
Univ.
Bond's Hosp.
Corporation
Coventry University
3
A4600
Upper Spon St.
Spon St.
Lib.
Cath. Lanes
Old Bath
Priory
Skydome Coventry Cinema
The Pct.
Lady Godiva Statue
Herbert Art Gallery & Mus.
Univ.
The Arena (Ice Rink)
Way
Guildhall
Cox
Victoria
Mkt.
Univ.
Gosford St.
University
Croft Rd.
Civic Cen.
Much Pk. St.
Sports Cen.
B4101
7
Hertford St.
New
Ford's Hosp.
Courts
St. John's St.
Butts Rd.
To Coventry RUFC
Statue
Union
4
Greyfriars Rd.
Road
Reg. Off.
Gulson Rd.
Butts
Queen's Rd.
Warwick
Friars
5
Parkside
6
Mile
Deasy
Westminster Rd.
Manor Rd.
Way
Rd.
London
A4053
Road
Park
Rd.
Quarryfield La.
Central Six Retail Park
Puma
A4114
Stoney Road
To Coventry Airport
Spencer Park
COVENTRY
Quinton
Quarryfield
Stoney
London Road Cemy.
Spencer
Rd.
Quinton
Lane
Park Gdns.
Lane
Road
SCALE
0 100 200 Yards ¼ Mile
0 100 200 300 400 Metres
A249
Warwick
Road
To University of Warwick
Rd.

DERBY

DUMFRIES

DOVER

To: Buckland Hospital & Dover Ath FC

Superstores

Connaught Park

Langdon Cliffs Picnic Site

Gateway to the White Cliffs

Bleriot Memorial

A2

Langdon Cliffs NT

TOLL

Castleton Retail Cen.

Charlton Centre

Tower Hamlets

Maison Dieu (Town Hall)

Dover Castle

PWRR & Queen's Regt. Mus.

Hellfire Corner & Underground Hospital

The Pharos

St. Mary-in-Castro Saxon Church

Car Ferry Terminal

Mag. Court

Dover College

Pencester Gds.

Old St. James Church Ruins

Secret Wartime Tunnels

DOVER PRIORY

Moat's Bulwark

Dover Leisure Centre

EASTERN DOCKS

To The Women's Land Army Musem

Roman Painted House

Dover Mus.

Bureau de Change

Dover Discovery Centre & Lib.

Captain Webb Memorial

Clarendon

Drop Redoubt

C S Rolls Statue

Western Heights

Dunkirk Memorial

Sea Sports Centre

De Bradelei Wharf

Wellington Dock

Grand Shaft

Calais 1hr. 30mins. Dunkirk 2hrs.

OUTER HARBOUR

Knights Templar Church (remains of)

Lifeboat Station

WESTERN DOCKS

Prince of Wales Pier

Southern Breakwater

Viaduct

Aycliff

To Shakespeare Cliff

A20

INNER HARBOUR

Cruise Liner Terminal

Admiralty Pier

A256

A258

B2011

SCALE

0 100 200 Yards ¼ Mile

0 100 200 300 400 Metres

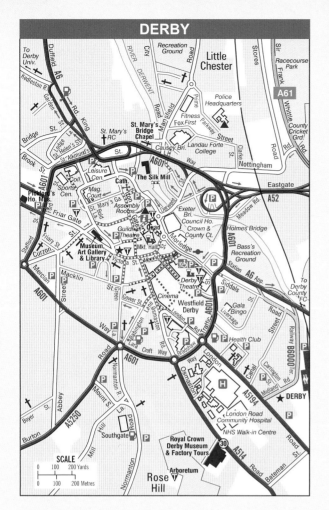

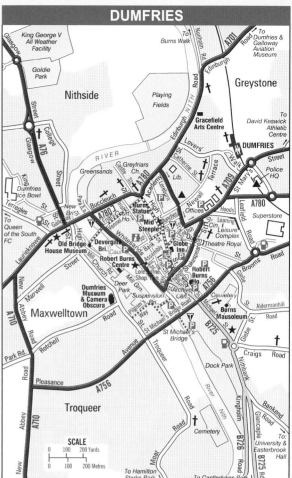

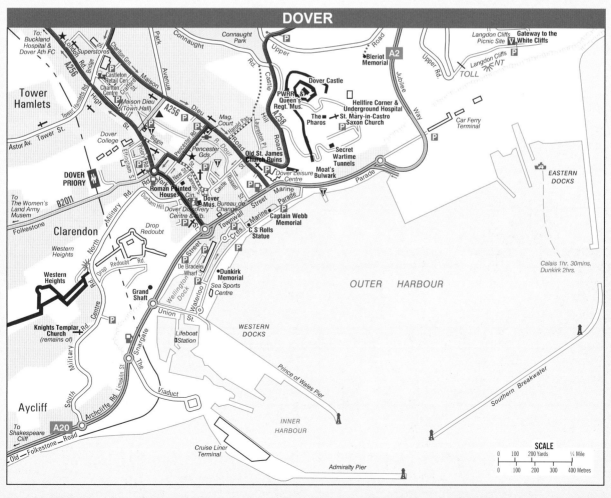

DUNDEE

DURHAM

EDINBURGH

Football Ground
Cricket Ground
Stockbridge
To Royal Botanic Garden
B901
Broughton
Mosque
Annandale St.
Walk
A900
SCALE
0 100 200 Yards ¼ Mile
0 100 200 300 400 Metres
Hibernian FC
Albion Rd.
B900
Henderson Row
Eyre Pl.
Bellevue
St.
Raeburn Pl.
Patriothall Gallery
Dundas
London St.
East London St.
Gayfield Sq.
B900
Hamilton Pl.
St. Stephen St.
Deanhaugh
Drummond Place
Street
Broughton
Union
Montgomery
Street
Norton Park
Gall.
Elm Row
Dean Park Cres.
Circus Lane
Great King
Dublin
London
B1350
Easter Road
To Meadowbank Sports Centre
Ann St.
Dean Ter.
Leith
Circus Pl.
New Town
Street
Abercromby Pl.
York Pl.
Leith
London Road Gardens
Howe St.
The Scottish Gallery
Open Eye Gallery
St. Mary's RC Cathedral
Omni Centre
Edinburgh Playhouse
Terrace
A1
Abbeyhill
Scottish National Portrait Gallery
Row
Vue Cinema
To Scottish National Gallery of Modern Art
Gloucester La.
Heriot Row
Gds.
Street
York Pl.
Casino
St. James Centre
Calton Hill
Regent Gardens
Abbeymount
Spring Gdns.
Queensferry
A90
Moray Place
Queen Street
St. Andrew Sq.
Scotlands People Centre
National Monument
Calton
City Observatory
Water
Hanover
Andrew Mon. Square
Greenside
Regent
A1
Nelson Monument
Frederick
Thistle
Street
Dean Bri.
Ainslie Pl.
A8
The Georgian House
Queen
Young St.
Hill St.
Assembly Rooms
Street
Rose
Street
St. Andrew's House
Calton
Burns Monument
Rd.
Holyrood Abbey (remains)
The Queen's Gall.
Palace of Holyroodhouse
NTS
West Register House
Charlotte Sq.
George
Princes
Scott Mon.
Princes Mall
EDINBURGH WAVERLEY
North Bri.
City Council
New St.
Canongate Kirk
Scottish Parliament
Rd.
Queensferry
No. 28 Charlotte Square
Princes St.
Floral Clock
The Mound
Academy
National Gallery
Waverley Bri.
Fruitmarket Gall.
Dungeon
Stills Gallery
E. Market St.
People's Story
Storytelling Centre
Lib.
Museum of Edinburgh
Drive
West Princes Street Gardens
Open Air Theatre
Mus. on the Mound
Festival Office
City Art Centre
City Chambers
Canongate
Our Dynamic Earth
St. Mary's Episcopal Cathedral
Place
Camera Obscura
NTS
Writers' Mus.
St.
Museum of Childhood
Canongate
Holyrood
St.
Lothian
King's
Tartan Weaving Mill & Exhibition
Gladstone's Land
High St.
Police Info. Cen.
South Bri.
University
William St.
A8
Shandwick Pl.
Edinburgh Castle
War Mem.
Esplanade
Ter.
National Library
St. Giles Cathedral
Museum
Queen's
Manor Pl.
Shandwick Pl.
Traverse Theatre
Museums
Scotch Whisky Experience
The Hub
Central Library
Cowgate
Adam Ho.
Gallery
Univ.
St.
University
Road
Stables
Court
Drummond St.
Torphichen St.
Canning St.
Usher Hall
Ryl. Lyceum Theatre
Johnston Ter.
Grassmarket
Greyfriars Bobby
Pleasance Theatre
Holyrood Park
Conference Centre
Cinema
Lady
Greyfriars Tolbooth & Highland Kirk
National Museum of Scotland
University
Festival Theatre
Univ.
Morrison St.
Bread St.
A702
West Port
Old Town
Surgeons' Hall Mus.
To: Murrayfield Rugby Ground & Airport
Grove
Approach
B700
Cin.
Rd.
Lawson
Museum of Fire
George Heriot's Coll. School
Place
Forrest R.
Theatre
Music Lib.
Nicolson
Pleasance
Salisbury Crags
Gardner's Cr.
Semple St.
Earl Grey St.
Lauriston
McEwan Hall
Potterrow
Mosque
Lauriston Gdns.
Lauriston
Lauriston Building
Reid Concert Hall
Mus. of Instruments
St.
A7
The Crags Community Sports Cen.
Queen's
Arthur's Seat
West
A702
Brougham St.
Princess Alexandra Eye Pavilion
South Side
George Sq.
To Heart of Midlothian FC
Street
Fountainbridge
Cameo Cinema
Home St.
Edinburgh University
George Sq. Theatre
Buccleuch St.
Clerk
St. Leonard's
Dundee St.
Union
Canal
Place
Meadow Walk
North
Meadow La.
St. Leonards
Drive
King's Theatre
Meadow
West Meadow Park
Meadows Tennis Complex
The Queen's Hall
St.
Viewforth
Gilmore
A702
Leven St.
Melville
Middle Meadow
East Meadow Park
Walk
Bernard T.
To Royal Infirmary
To Royal Commonwealth Pool
Holyrood Pk. R.
Drive
A700
A700

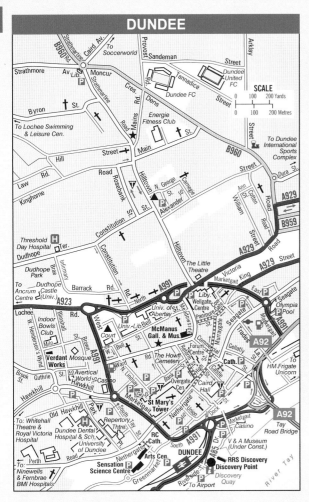

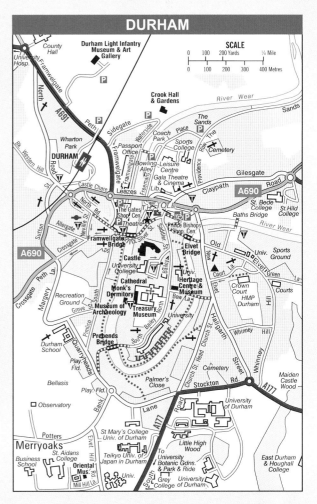

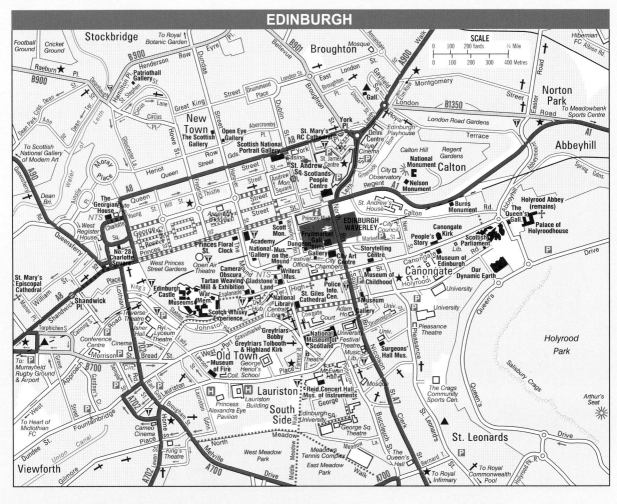

EXETER

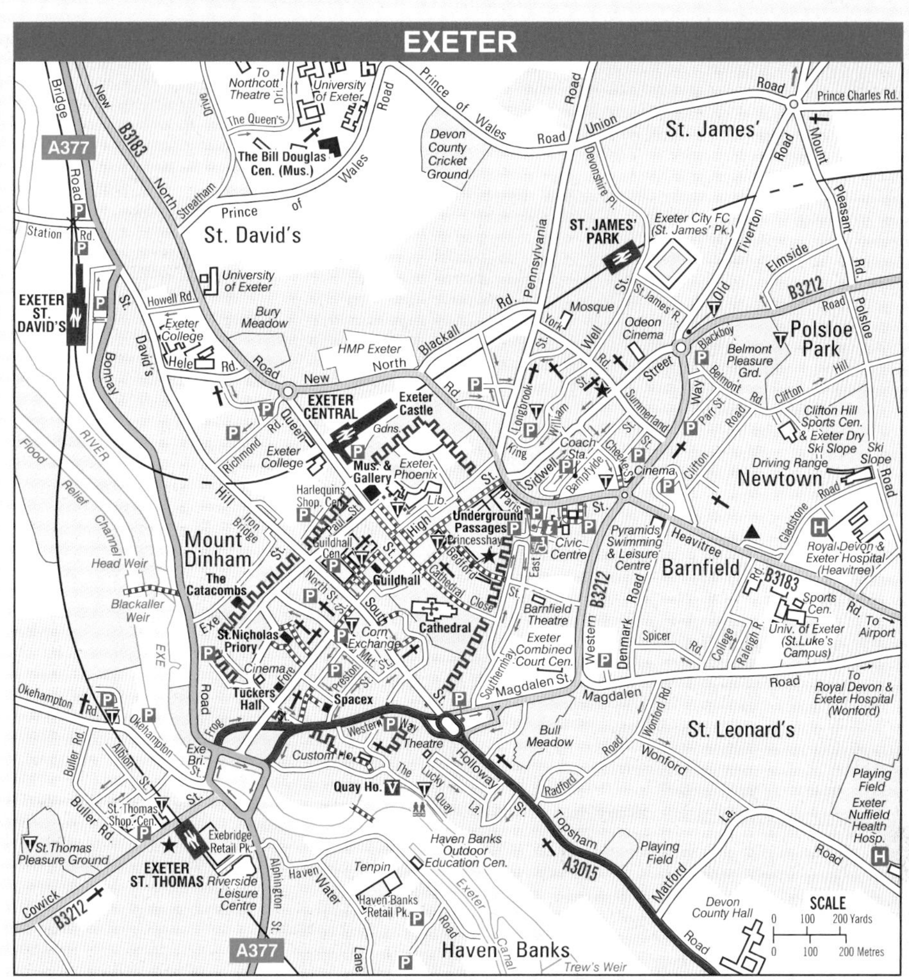

To Northcott Theatre
University of Exeter
The Queen's Dr.
The Bill Douglas Cen. (Mus.)
Prince of Wales Road
Devon County Cricket Ground
Union Road
St. James'
Prince Charles Rd.
Mount Pleasant Rd.
A377
B3183
New North Road
Streatham
St. David's
Station Rd.
EXETER ST. DAVID'S
University of Exeter
ST. JAMES' PARK
Exeter City FC (St. James' Pk.)
Pennsylvania Rd.
Old Tiverton Rd.
Elmside
B3212
Polsloe Park
Polsloe Rd.
Howell Rd.
Exeter College
Hele Rd.
Bury Meadow
HMP Exeter
Blackall Rd.
Mosque
Odeon Cinema
Belmont Pleasure Grd.
Blackboy Rd.
Clifton Hill
Clifton Hill Sports Cen. & Exeter Dry Ski Slope
Ski Slope
Driving Range
Newtown
EXETER CENTRAL
Exeter Castle
Gdns.
Queen St.
Richmond Rd.
Exeter College
Mus. & Gallery
Exeter Phoenix
Coach Sta.
Sidwell St.
Cinema
Harlequins Shop. Cen.
Underground Passages
Princesshay
Civic Centre
Pyramids Swimming & Leisure Centre
Heavitree Rd.
Gladstone Road
Royal Devon & Exeter Hospital (Heavitree)
Mount Dinham
Iron Bridge
Guildhall
The Catacombs
Cathedral
Barnfield Theatre
Barnfield
B3183
Sports Cen.
Univ. of Exeter (St.Luke's Campus)
To Airport
Head Weir
Blackaller Weir
River Exe
Flood Relief Channel
St.Nicholas Priory
Corn Exchange
Exeter Combined Court Cen.
Western Way
Denmark Road
Spicer Rd.
College Rd.
Raleigh R.
Magdalen St.
Magdalen Road
Royal Devon & Exeter Hospital (Wonford)
Cinema
Tuckers Hall
Spacex
Fore St.
Okehampton Rd.
Frog St.
Exe Bri.
Western Way
Theatre
Custom Ho.
Quay Ho.
Holloway St.
Bull Meadow
St. Leonard's
Wonford Rd.
Buller Rd.
Albion St.
St. Thomas Shop. Cen.
Exebridge Retail Pk.
The Lucky Quay
Haven Banks Outdoor Education Cen.
Topsham Rd.
A3015
Playing Field
Exeter Nuffield Health Hosp.
St.Thomas Pleasure Ground
EXETER ST. THOMAS
Riverside Leisure Centre
Alphington St.
Haven Rd.
Tenpin
Haven Banks Retail Pk.
Exeter Canal
Matford La.
Devon County Hall
Cowick St.
B3212
A377
Water Lane
Haven Banks
Trew's Weir
SCALE
0 100 200 Yards
0 100 200 Metres

EASTBOURNE

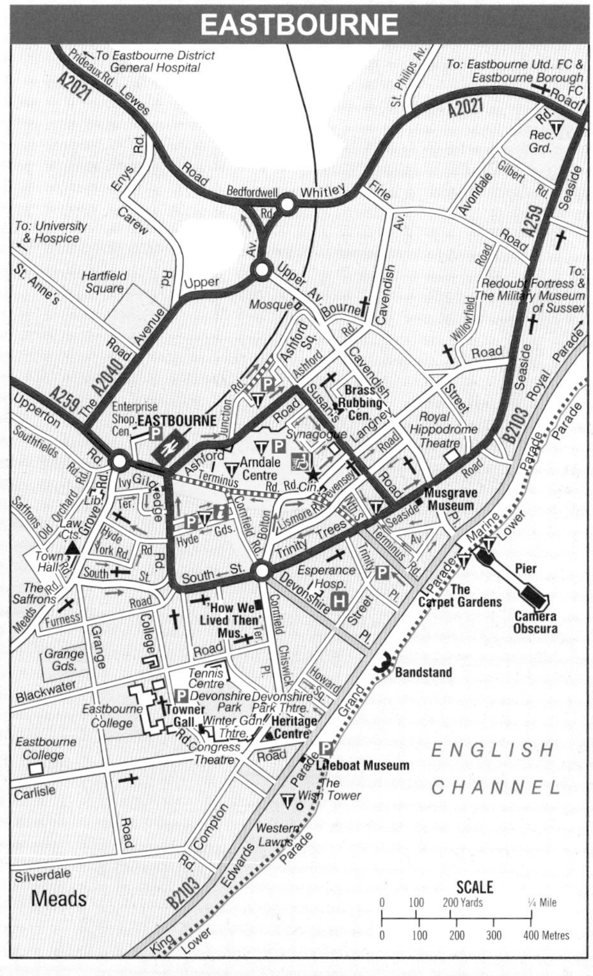

To Eastbourne District General Hospital
Prideaux Rd.
A2021
To: Eastbourne Utd. FC & Eastbourne Borough FC
St. Philips Av.
Lewes Road
Enys Rd.
Bedfordwell Rd.
Whitley Road
Rec. Grd.
Gilbert Rd.
Avondale Road
Seaside
A259
To: University & Hospice
Carew Rd.
Firle Rd.
Hartfield Square
St. Anne's Rd.
Upper Av.
Mosque
Bourne St.
Cavendish Pl.
To: Redoubt Fortress & The Military Museum of Sussex
Willowfield Road
A2040
The Avenue
Upperton Rd.
Southfields Rd.
Enterprise Shop. Cen.
EASTBOURNE
Ashford Rd.
Arndale Centre
Terminus Rd.
Brass Rubbing Cen.
Langney Road
Royal Hippodrome Theatre
B2103
Royal Parade
Synagogue
Musgrave Museum
Marine Pde.
Pier
Camera Obscura
Old Orchard Rd.
Grove Rd.
Hyde Gds.
Law Cts.
Town Hall
The Saffrons
Meads Rd.
South St.
Trinity Trees
Esperance Hosp.
The Carpet Gardens
Furness Road
Grange Rd.
College Rd.
How We Lived Then' Mus.
Cornfield Rd.
Devonshire Pl.
Grange Gds.
Blackwater Rd.
Tennis Centre
Devonshire Park
Bandstand
Eastbourne College
Towner Gall.
Winter Gdn.
Devonshire Park Thtre.
Heritage Centre
Congress Theatre
Lifeboat Museum
The Wish Tower
ENGLISH CHANNEL
Carlisle Rd.
Compton St.
Western Lawns
Grand Parade
Silverdale Rd.
Meads
B2103
Edwards Rd.
King Edwards Parade
Lower
SCALE
0 100 200 Yards ¼ Mile
0 100 200 300 400 Metres

FOLKESTONE

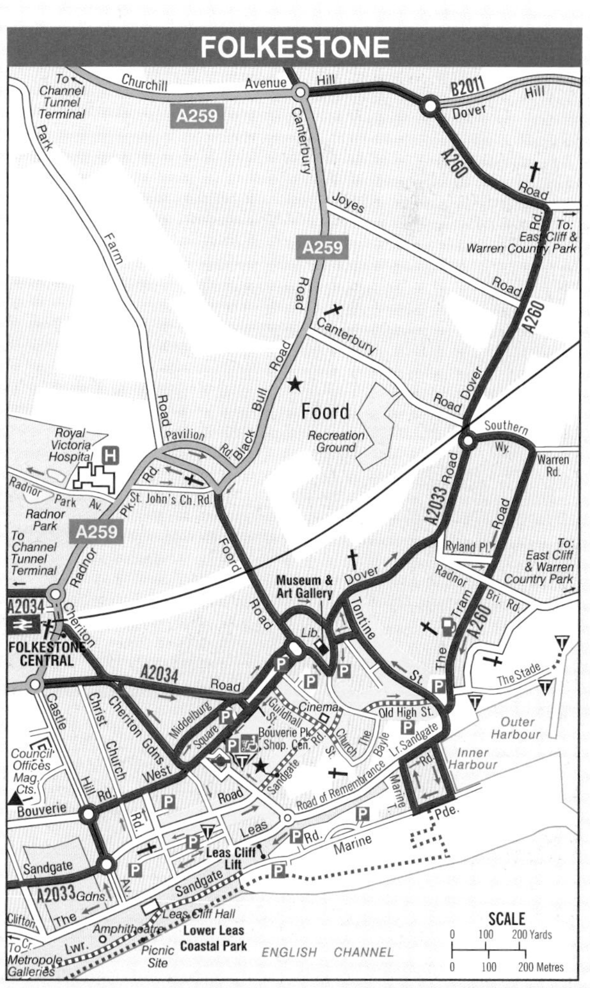

To Channel Tunnel Terminal
Churchill Avenue
Hill
B2011
Dover Hill
A259
Park Farm Road
Canterbury Road
Joyes Rd.
A260
To: East Cliff & Warren Country Park
Canterbury Rd.
Foord
Recreation Ground
Bull Road
Black Bull Road
Royal Victoria Hospital
Pavilion Rd.
Radnor Park Av.
Radnor Park
St. John's Ch. Rd.
A259
To Channel Tunnel Terminal
Radnor Pk. Rd.
Southern Wy.
Warren Rd.
A2033 Road
Foord Road
Ryland Pl.
To: East Cliff & Warren Country Park
Museum & Art Gallery
Dover Rd.
Radnor Bri. Rd.
A2034
Cheriton Rd.
FOLKESTONE CENTRAL
Tontine St.
The Tram Rd.
The Stade
A2034 Road
Lib.
Castle Hill Av.
Christ Church Rd.
Cheriton Gdns.
West Terrace
Middelburg Square
Cinema
Old High St.
Outer Harbour
Inner Harbour
Council Offices
Mag. Cts.
Bouverie Pl. Shop. Cen.
Bouverie Rd.
Guildhall St.
Church St.
The Bayle
Lr. Sandgate Rd.
Road of Remembrance
Marine Pde.
Sandgate Rd.
Leas Cliff Lift
Leas Rd.
Marine
A2033 Gdns.
Leas Cliff Hall
Amphitheatre
Lower Leas Coastal Park
Clifton
To Metropole Galleries
Lwr.
Picnic Site
ENGLISH CHANNEL
SCALE
0 100 200 Yards
0 100 200 Metres

GLASGOW

SCALE
0 100 200 Yards ¼ Mile
0 100 200 300 400 Metres

To: Hunterian Mus., Art Gallery & Univ. of Glasgow
ST. GEORGE'S CROSS
To Partick Thistle FC
North Woodside Leis. Cen.
Sighthill Park
Kelvingrove Park
M8
Tenement House NTS
COWCADDENS
Royal Highland Fusiliers Museum
Garnethill
Mus. of Piping
Passport Office
Glasgow Caledonian University
Royal Scottish Academy
Theatre Royal
Arts Centre
School of Art
Film Theatre
Henry Wood Hall
CHARING CROSS
Buchanan Galleries
Royal Concert Hall
College University
Royal Infirmary
St. Mungo's Cathedral
Glasgow Necropolis
Provand's Lordship
St. Mungo Museum
BUCHANAN ST.
QUEEN ST.
Scott's Statue
University of Strathclyde
Collins Gallery
Cranston Hill
Anderston
To Riverside Museum
ANDERSTON
Stock Exch.
Gallery of Modern Art
City Chambers
Greens Health & Fitness
To Scottish Exhibition & Conference Centre
The Lighthouse
Trades Hall
Hutchesons' Hall NTS
City Halls
HIGH STREET
Princes Sq. Shop. Cen.
GLASGOW CENTRAL
The Arches
Police Mus.
Tolbooth Steeple
ST. ENOCH
St. Enoch Shop. Cen.
ARGYLE ST.
Trongate 103
Tron Theatre
St. Andrew's RC Cathedral
The Merchant's Steeple
To: Glasgow Science Cen., Imax Cinema & Glasgow Tower
Odeon Cinema
Mecca Bingo
Glasgow's Grand Ole Opry
AMF Bowling
Kingston
Kingston Bridge
Tradeston Bridge
George V Bridge
Glasgow Bridge
Suspension Bridge
Hospice
Glasgow Sheriff Court
The Briggait
Victoria Bridge
Mosque
College of Nautical Studies
High Court
Albert Bridge
Glasgow Green
People's Palace
Calton
To Celtic FC
To Southern General Hospital & Rangers FC
Tradeston
BRIDGE ST.
To Hampden Park (Queens Park FC)
M74

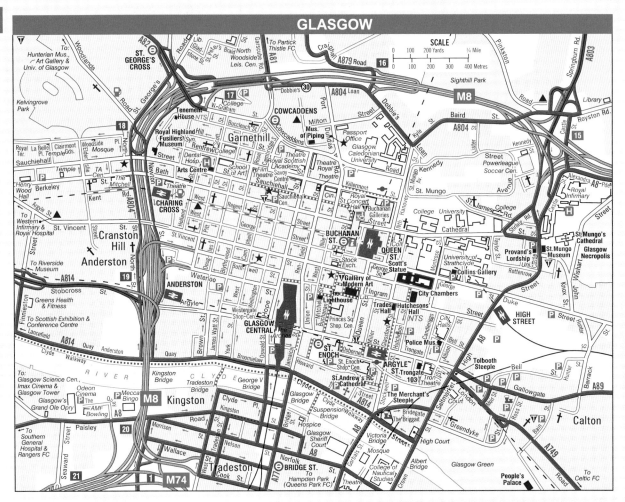

GLOUCESTER

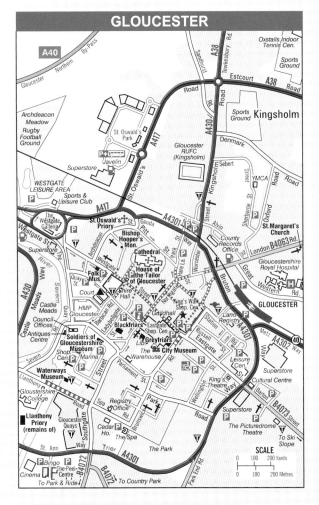

GREAT YARMOUTH

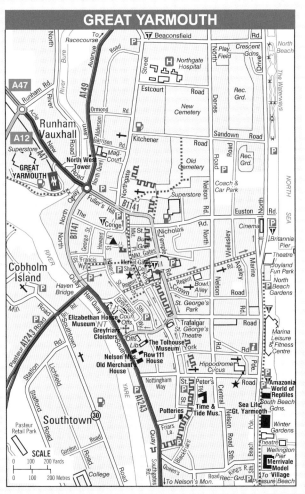

GUILDFORD

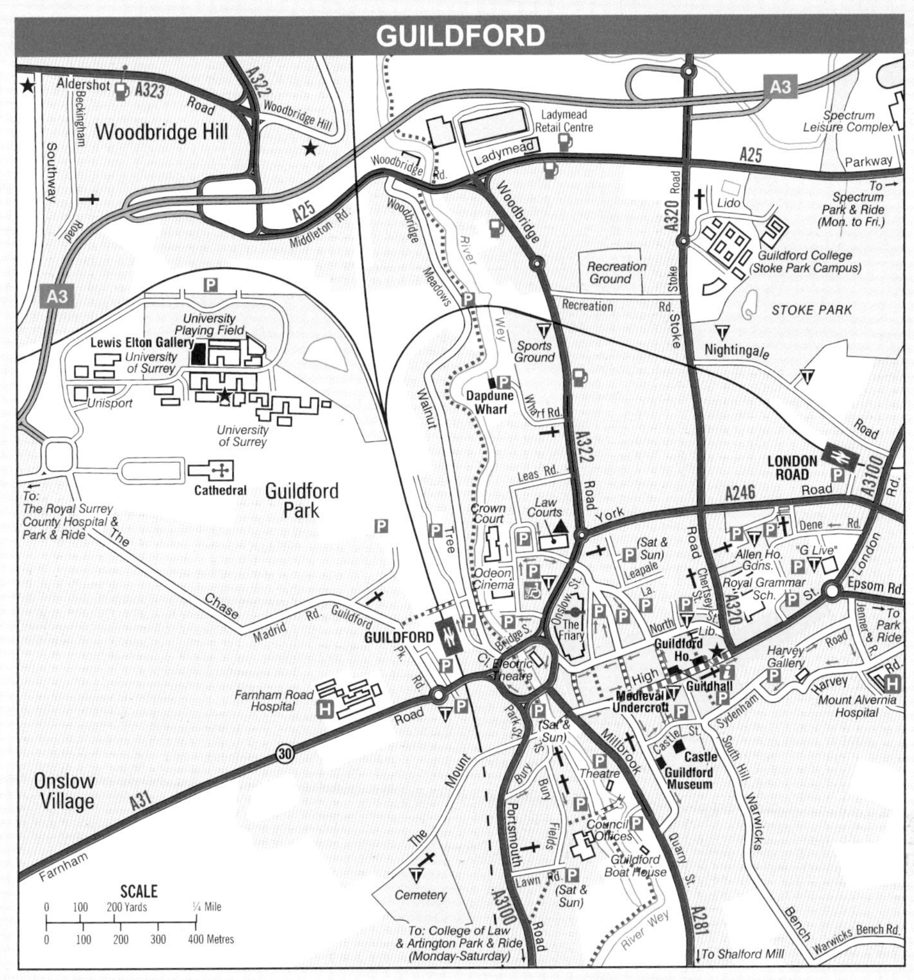

Aldershot
A323
Road
A322
Woodbridge Hill
Beckingham
Southway
Road
A3
A25
Middleton Rd.
Woodbridge Rd.
Ladymead
Ladymead Retail Centre
Woodbridge Meadows
River Wey
Woodbridge
A320
Stoke Road
Lido
Spectrum Leisure Complex
Parkway
To Spectrum Park & Ride (Mon. to Fri.)
Guildford College (Stoke Park Campus)
STOKE PARK
Recreation Ground
Recreation Rd.
Nightingale
Sports Ground
University Playing Field
Lewis Elton Gallery
University of Surrey
Unisport
University of Surrey
Cathedral
Guildford Park
To: The Royal Surrey County Hospital & Park & Ride
The Chase
Madrid Rd.
Guildford Pk. Rd.
GUILDFORD
Walnut Tree
Dapdune Wharf
Wharf Rd.
A322
Leas Rd.
Crown Court
Law Courts
Odeon Cinema
York Road
A246
LONDON ROAD
London Road
A3100
Dene Rd.
"G Live"
Allen Ho. Gdns.
Royal Grammar Sch.
Epsom Rd.
To Park & Ride
Jenner Rd.
Harvey Road
Harvey Gallery
Mount Alvernia Hospital
Onslow St.
The Friary
Leapale
(Sat & Sun)
Chertsey St.
Lib.
Guildford Ho.
Guildhall
High St.
Medieval Undercroft
Bridge St.
Electric Theatre
Farnham Road Hospital
Farnham Road
30
Onslow Village
A31
Farnham
The Mount
Park St.
(Sat & Sun)
Millbrook
Castle St.
Castle
Guildford Museum
Sydenham
South Hill
Warwicks
Bury Fields
Theatre
Council Offices
Guildford Boat House
Quarry St.
Portsmouth Road
A3100
Lawn Rd.
(Sat & Sun)
Cemetery
To: College of Law & Artington Park & Ride (Monday-Saturday)
River Wey
A281
To Shalford Mill
Warwicks Bench Rd.
SCALE
0 100 200 Yards ¼ Mile
0 100 200 300 400 Metres

HARROGATE

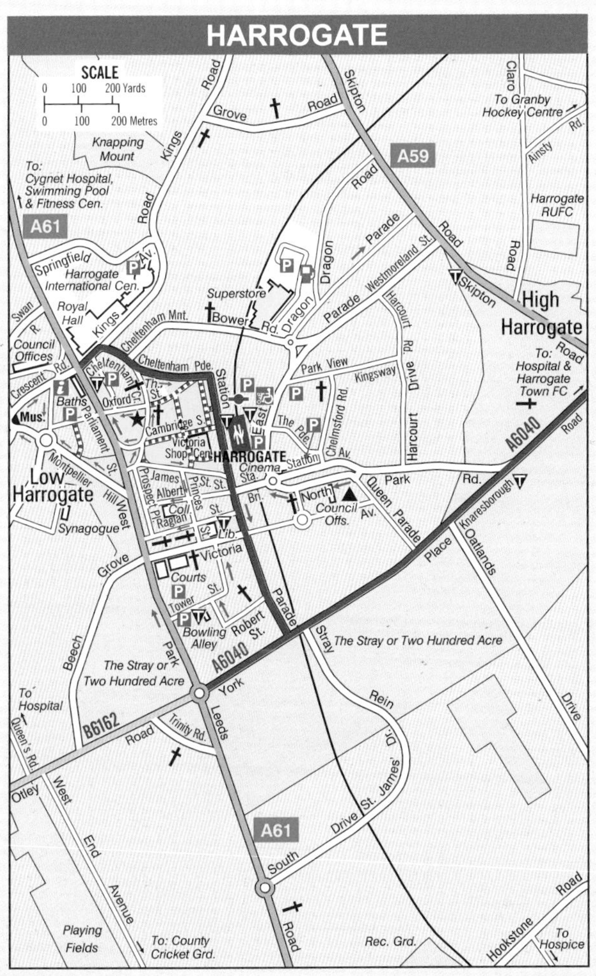

SCALE
0 100 200 Yards
0 100 200 Metres
Grove Road
Skipton
Claro
To Granby Hockey Centre
Knapping Mount
To: Cygnet Hospital, Swimming Pool & Fitness Cen.
Kings Road
A59
Ainsty Rd.
Harrogate RUFC
A61
Springfield Av.
Harrogate International Cen.
Royal Hall
Swan Rd.
Council Offices
Dragon Parade
Westmoreland St.
Superstore
Bower Rd.
Cheltenham Mnt.
Cheltenham Pde.
Skipton Road
High Harrogate
To: Hospital & Harrogate Town FC
Park View
Kingsway
Harcourt Drive
Chelmsford Rd.
Crescent Rd.
Baths
Mus.
Oxford St.
Parliament St.
Cambridge St.
Victoria Shop. Cen.
Station
HARROGATE
Cinema
Station Av.
East Parade
Park Rd.
A6040
Knaresborough Rd.
Low Harrogate
Montpellier Hill
Prospect Pl.
James St.
Albert St.
Princes St.
Raglan St.
Lib.
North Council Offs.
Queen Parade
Synagogue
West Grove
Victoria Av.
Courts
Tower St.
Bowling Alley
Robert St.
Parade
Oatlands
Beech Grove
The Stray or Two Hundred Acre
Park
A6040
York Place
Stray Rein
The Stray or Two Hundred Acre
To Hospital
B6162
Otley Road
Trinity Rd.
Leeds Road
St. James' Dr.
Drive
Queen's Rd.
West End Avenue
A61
South Drive
Hookstone Road
Playing Fields
To: County Cricket Grd.
Rec. Grd.
To Hospice

HEREFORD

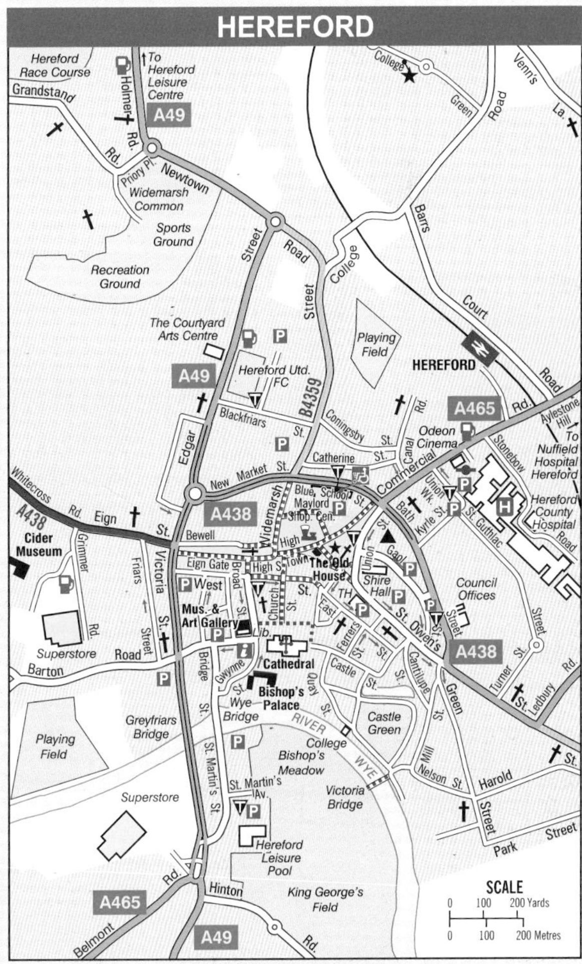

Hereford Race Course
To Hereford Leisure Centre
Grandstand Rd.
Holmer Rd.
A49
College
Venn's La.
Green
Priory Pl.
Newtown Road
Widemarsh Common
Sports Ground
Recreation Ground
Street
Road
College Road
Barrs Court Road
Playing Field
The Courtyard Arts Centre
Hereford Utd. FC
HEREFORD
A49
A465
B4359
Blackfriars St.
Coningsby St.
Catherine St.
Canal Rd.
Odeon Cinema
Aylestone Hill
To Nuffield Hospital Hereford
Edgar St.
New Market St.
Commercial Rd.
Whitecross Rd.
A438
Eign St.
A438
Widemarsh St.
Blue School St.
Maylord Shop. Cen.
Bath St.
Kyrle St.
Stonebow Rd.
St. Guthlac
Hereford County Hospital
Cider Museum
Grimmer Rd.
Friars St.
Victoria St.
Bewell
Eign Gate
High Town
The Old House
Union St.
Gaol St.
Shire Hall
Council Offices
Turner St.
Ledbury Rd.
West St.
Mus. & Art Gallery
Church St.
East St.
Lib.
Cathedral
Ferrers St.
St. Owen's Street
Superstore Road
Barton
Bishop's Palace
Castle St.
Cantilupe St.
Green
Castle Green
Greyfriars Bridge
Wye Bridge
RIVER WYE
Quay St.
College
Bishop's Meadow
Gwynne St.
Bridge St.
Playing Field
St. Martin's St.
St. Martin's Av.
Victoria Bridge
Mill St.
Nelson St.
Harold Street
Superstore
Hereford Leisure Pool
Park Street
Hinton Rd.
A465
King George's Field
Belmont Rd.
A49
SCALE
0 100 200 Yards
0 100 200 Metres

INVERNESS

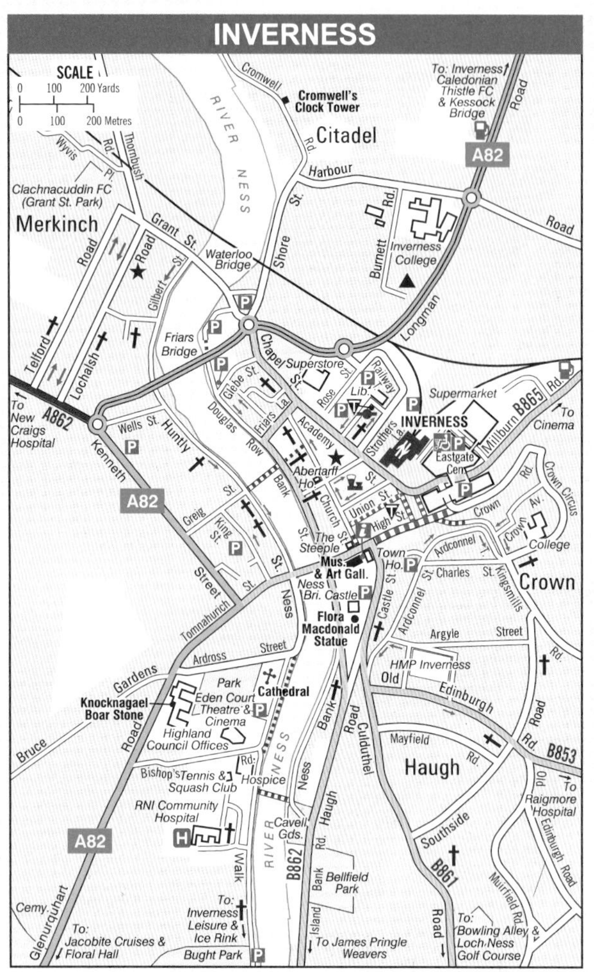
SCALE
0 100 200 Yards
0 100 200 Metres
Cromwell's Clock Tower
To: Inverness Caledonian Thistle FC & Kessock Bridge
Citadel
A82
Harbour
Clachnacuddin FC (Grant St. Park)
Merkinch
Grant St.
Waterloo Bridge
Shore St.
Burnett Rd.
Inverness College
Longman
Road
Telford
Lochalsh
Gilbert
Friars Bridge
Chapel St.
Superstore
Supermarket
To New Craigs Hospital
A862
Kenneth
Wells St.
Huntly
Academy
Strothers
INVERNESS
Eastgate Cen.
Millburn
B865
To Cinema
Crown Circus
A82
Greig St.
King St.
Abertarff Ho.
Church St.
Union St.
High St.
The Steeple
Mus. & Art Gall.
Town Ho.
Ness Bri.
Castle
Crown
College
Ardconnel St.
Charles St.
Kingsmills
Flora Macdonald Statue
Argyle
Street
Tomnahurich
Ardross
Street
Gardens
Park
Eden Court Theatre & Cinema
Cathedral
Knocknagael Boar Stone
HMP Inverness
Old Edinburgh
Road
Highland Council Offices
Bruce
Culduthel
Mayfield
Haugh
B853
Bishop's Tennis & Squash Club
Hospice
RNI Community Hospital
River Ness
Cavell Gds.
B862
Southside
To Raigmore Hospital
A82
Walk
Bellfield Park
B861
To: Inverness Leisure & Ice Rink
Cemy.
Glenurquhart
To: Jacobite Cruises & Floral Hall
Bught Park
Island Bank
To James Pringle Weavers
To: Bowling Alley & Loch Ness Golf Course

IPSWICH

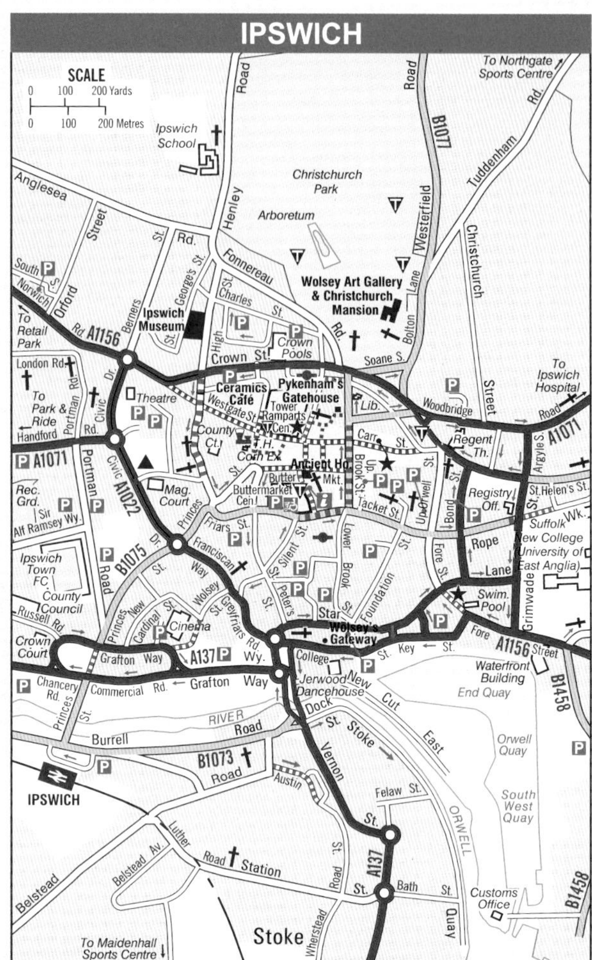
SCALE
0 100 200 Yards
0 100 200 Metres
Ipswich School
To Northgate Sports Centre
B1077
Tuddenham Rd.
Christchurch Park
Arboretum
Anglesea
Henley Road
Westerfield
Christchurch
Fonnereau
Wolsey Art Gallery & Christchurch Mansion
Ipswich Museum
To Retail Park
A1156
Crown St.
Crown Pools
Soane St.
Bolton Lane
Street
To Ipswich Hospital
London Rd.
Theatre
Ceramics Café
Pykenham's Gatehouse
Woodbridge Road
To Park & Ride Handford
A1071
Tower Ramparts
Carr St.
Regent Th.
Argyle St.
A1071
Rec. Grd.
Sir Alf Ramsey Wy.
Civic Dr.
Mag. Court
Ancient Ho.
Buttermarket
Mkt.
Tacket St.
St. Helen's St.
Registry Off.
Suffolk New College University of East Anglia
Rope Lane
Ipswich Town FC
County Council
Portman Road
Franciscan Way
Friars St.
Silent St.
Lower Brook
Foundation
Swim. Pool
Russell Rd.
Cinema
St. Peter's
Star Lane
Wolsey's Gateway
Fore St.
A1156
Grimwade Street
Crown Court
Grafton Way
A137
College
St. Key St.
Waterfront Building
End Quay
B1458
Chancery Rd.
Commercial Rd.
Grafton Way
Jerwood Dancehouse
New Cut East
Dock St.
River
Burrell Road
Orwell Quay
IPSWICH
B1073
Austin
Vernon
Stoke St.
Felaw St.
Orwell
South West Quay
Belstead Av.
Luther Road
Station
A137
Bath St.
Customs Office
Belstead
Quay
B1458
To Maidenhall Sports Centre
Stoke
Wherstead Road

KILMARNOCK

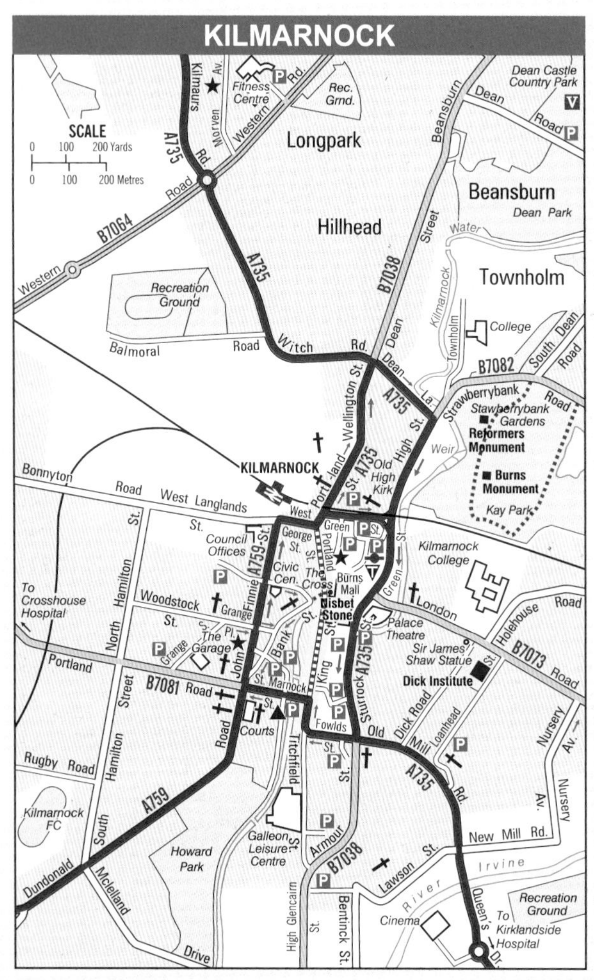
Kilmaurs
Morven Av.
Fitness Centre
Western
Rec. Grnd.
Dean Castle Country Park
Dean Road
SCALE
0 100 200 Yards
0 100 200 Metres
A735
Longpark
Beansburn
Road
Beansburn
Dean Park
B7064
Hillhead
Street
Western
Townholm
Water
Recreation Ground
A735
B7038
Kilmarnock
Townholm
College
Balmoral
Road
Witch Rd.
Dean St.
B7082
South Dean Road
Wellington St.
A735
Strawberrybank
Strawberrybank Gardens
Reformers Monument
Burns Monument
Kay Park
KILMARNOCK
Bonnyton
Road
West Langlands
Portland
Old High Kirk
High St.
West
Green
Council Offices
Kilmarnock College
Civic Cen.
The Cross
Burns Mall
To Crosshouse Hospital
Woodstock
Hamilton
Grange
London Road
Nisbet Stone
Palace Theatre
Holehouse Road
The Garage
Sir James Shaw Statue
Dick Institute
B7073
Portland
B7081 Road
John Finnie St.
Bank St.
King St.
St. Marnock St.
Sturrock St.
A735
Courts
Fowlds
Dick Road
Nursery Av.
Rugby Road
A759
Hamilton
Old Mill Rd.
Loanhead
Street
Kilmarnock FC
Titchfield
Nursery Av.
South
Howard Park
Galleon Leisure Centre
Armour St.
New Mill Rd.
Dundonald
Mcelland
B7038
Lawson St.
Irvine
River
High Glencairn St.
Bentinck St.
Cinema
Queen's Dr.
To Kirklandside Hospital
Recreation Ground
Drive

LINCOLN

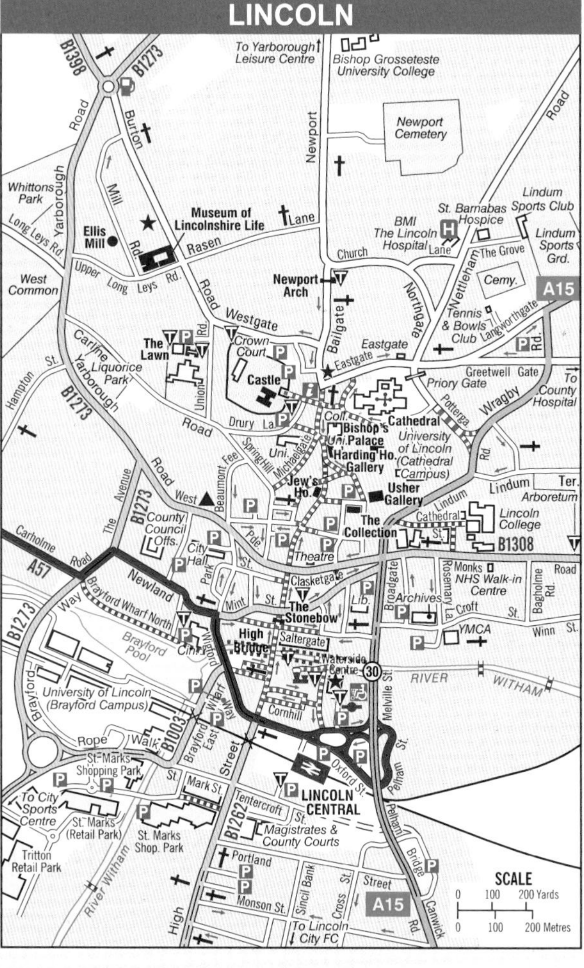
B1398
B1273
To Yarborough Leisure Centre
Bishop Grosseteste University College
Burton Rd.
Road
Newport
Road
Newport Cemetery
Whittons Park
Yarborough
Mill
Museum of Lincolnshire Life
Lane
Lindum Sports Club
St. Barnabas Hospice
BMI The Lincoln Hospital
Lindum Sports Grd.
Ellis Mill
Rasen
Long Leys Rd.
Upper Long Leys Rd.
Church
Lane
Nettleham
The Grove
Cemy.
West Common
Newport Arch
A15
Tennis & Bowls Club
Langworthgate
Westgate
Northgate
Eastgate
Bailgate
Carline
Yarborough
The Lawn
Crown Court
Liquorice Park
Castle
Greetwell Gate
Priory Gate
To County Hospital
Wragby Road
Hampton St.
B1273
Union Rd.
Cathedral
Pottergate
Drury La.
Bishop's Palace
Uni.
University of Lincoln (Cathedral Campus)
Harding Ho. Gallery
Spring Hill
Michaelgate
Jew's Ho.
Beaumont Fee
Lindum Ter.
Arboretum
Usher Gallery
West
The Avenue
B1273
County Council Offs.
The Collection
Lincoln College
B1308
City Hall
Carholme Road
A57
Newland
Theatre
Clasketgate
Monks Rd.
NHS Walk-in Centre
Rosemary La.
Broadgate
Baggholme Rd.
Brayford Wharf North
Mint St.
The Stonebow
Lib.
Archives
Croft St.
Winn St.
YMCA
Brayford Way
Brayford Pool
High Bridge
Saltergate
Waterside Centre
River Witham
B1273
University of Lincoln (Brayford Campus)
Brayford Wharf East
Melville St.
Cornhill
Rope Walk
B1003
St. Marks Shopping Park
Street
Pelham Bri.
Oxford St.
Mark St.
LINCOLN CENTRAL
To City Sports Centre
St. Marks (Retail Park)
St. Marks Shop. Park
Tentercroft St.
Magistrates & County Courts
B1262
Portland St.
Tritton Retail Park
River Witham
Sincil Bank
Monson St.
Cross St.
Street
A15
To Lincoln City FC
High
SCALE
0 100 200 Yards
0 100 200 Metres
Canwick Rd.

KINGSTON upon HULL

LEEDS

SCALE
0 100 200 Yards ¼ Mile
0 100 200 300 400 Metres

Yorkshire Television Studios
Burley Rd.
Kirkstall Rd.
Studio Rd.
To Yorkshire County Cricket Grd. (Headingley), Leeds RLFC & RUFC
A65
University of Leeds
A58(M)
Clarendon Rd.
Hyde Ter.
St. John's Rd.
Kendal Lane
Clarendon Road
Hosp.
Clarendon Way
Dental Hosp.
General Infirmary (Clarendon Wing)
Little Woodhouse
Leeds City College
Hanover Wy.
Park Lane
Cavendish St.
Road
Marlborough St.
West St.
Gala Casino
Leeds & Liverpool Canal
River Aire
Wellington St.
Armley Road
A647
Canal St.
A58
Wellington Road
New Wortley
Wellington Rd.
B6154
Whitehall
Holbeck La.
Water La.
Sydenham St.
Domestic St.
A58
Gelderd Rd.
A62
Domestic Road
A643
To Leeds United FC (Elland Road)
Woodhouse La.
Univ.
Little London
A58
Clay Pit La.
Metropolitan University
Calverley St.
Civic Hall
General Infirmary
Portland Cres.
Leeds Arena
Merrion Way
Leeds City Museum
Merrion Cen.
Millennium Sq.
Theatre
Gt. George St.
Courts
Mag. Ct.
Oxford Row
Oxford Pl.
Town Hall
Lib. City Art Gal.
RC Cathedral
The Light
St. John's Centre
Headrow
Merrion St.
Belgrave St.
Wade La.
Bowl. Alley
Park Sq. W.
Park Sq.
Park Sq. E.
East Pde.
Cts.
Bedford St.
Greek St.
St. Paul's St.
Park Place
York Place
Infirmary St.
Quebec St.
City Sq.
Park Row
Albion St.
Bond St.
The Core
City Varieties
Albion Pl.
Commercial St.
Kirkgate
Trinity Leeds
Briggate
Vicar La.
Northern St.
Aire St.
Boar La.
LEEDS
Open University
Swinegate
Corn Exchange
Kirkgate
Calls
Granary Wharf
Globe Road
Neville St.
Sovereign St.
Victoria Bridge
Dock St.
Bowman La.
Kendell St.
Waterloo St.
Meadow La.
Crown Point
Camp Field
David St.
Marshall St.
Road
Great Wilson St.
Victoria Road
Meadow Road
Dewsbury Rd.
Manor Road
Sweet Street West
Sweet Street
Bath Road
Bridge Rd.
Holbeck
Bowling Alley
Nineveh Road
Jack La.
Meadow Rd.
A653
Crown Point Retail Park
Kidacre St.
Hunslet La.
Hunslet Road
Butterley St.
Leathley Road
Pottery Field
M621
St. Matthew's St.
Street
Sheepscar St. Sth.
Street
Park La.
Grafton St.
Lovell Park
Byron St.
Leeds College
North St.
Trafalgar St.
Skinner Lane
Regent St.
A61
Rosevile Rd.
St. James's University Hospital
New Town
Cherry Rw.
Lincoln Rd.
Lincoln Green Road
To St. James's University Hospital & Thackray Medical Museum
Leeds College
Mabgate
Beckett St.
Burmantofts St.
Nippet La.
A64(M)
A64
Templar St.
Lady La.
Bridge
Govt. Offices
West Yorkshire Playhouse
BBC Studio
Northern Ballet
Union St.
Shannon St.
St. Peter's St.
George St.
Kirkgate Market
Duke St.
Marsh Lane
York St.
The Calls
A653
Crown Point Rd.
Richmond St.
Rec. Grd.
Ellerby La.
Recreation Ground
Accommodation Road
Upper St.
Cavalier Hill
Ellerby Rd.
Armouries Way
Royal Armouries Museum
A61
Clarence Dock
Armouries Dr.
Clarence Rd.
Black Bull St.
Chadwick St.
Carlisle Rd.
Sayner Rd.
Sayner Lane
Leeds Museum Discovery Centre
Indoor Karting
Sth. Accomodation Rd.
Road
Atkinson St.
A639
RIVER AIRE
A61

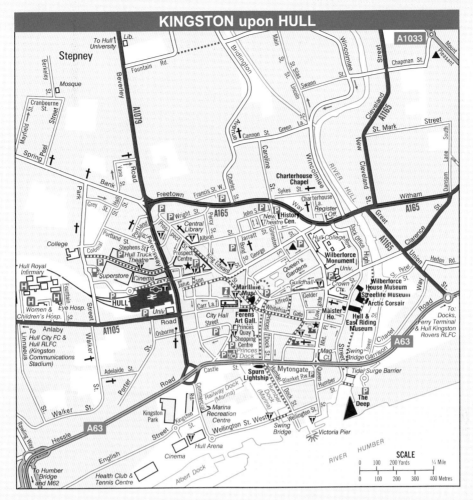

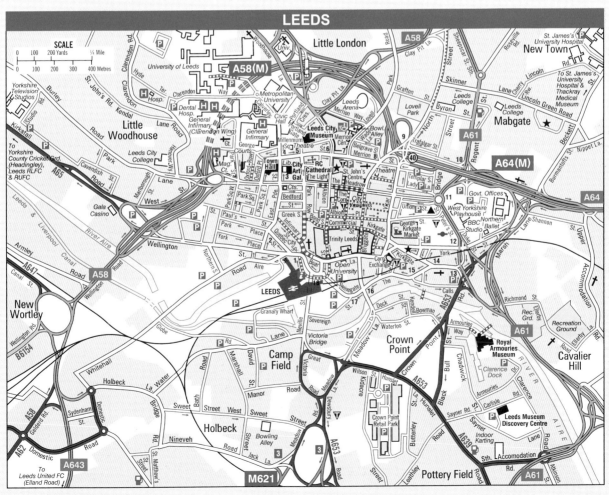

LEICESTER

LIVERPOOL

Elaine Norris Sports Centre
Recreation Ground
To Liverpool FC & Everton FC
Prince Rupert's Tower
A565
A5036
A5038
A59
A580
Vauxhall
Liverpool Community College
Kingsway (Mersey Tunnel) TOLL
Superstore
NHS Walk-in Centre
Grant Gardens
Whitley Gardens
Princes Half Tide Dock
A5053
Thurston Billiard & Snooker Mus.
Football Pitch
Liverpool John Moores University
University College
Islington
Douglas I.O.M. 2hrs. 30mins. (Fast Ferry)
Passport Off.
MOORFIELDS
Mag. Court
Walker Art Gallery
St. George's Hall
Royal Liverpool University Hospital
Liverpool University Dental Hospital
A57
A5047
A5048
Cruise Terminal
Western Approaches
Town Hall
Municipal Offs.
Theatre
LIME ST.
University of Liverpool
Victoria Gallery & Museum
Royal Ct. Theatre
St. John's Cen.
Royal Liver Bldg.
Cavern Club
Liverpool Playhouse
Clayton Sq. Shop. Cen.
Central Shop. Cen.
Seacombe Ferry 7-8mins.
RIVER MERSEY
Ferry Terminal & Fab4D
JAMES ST.
Cinema
The Bluecoat
CENTRAL
University Liverpool Metropolitan Cathedral
University of Liverpool Sports Cen.
Open Eye Gallery
City Law Courts
Liverpool One
Chavasse Park
FACT
YMCA
John Moores University
Everyman Playhouse
University Art Gallery
Museum of Liverpool
International Slavery Museum
Queensway (Mersey Tunnel) TOLL
Woodside Ferry
Mersey Railway Tunnel
Merseyside Maritime Museum
Tate Liverpool
Albert Dock
Salthouse Dock
The Colonnades
The Beatles Story
Philharmonic Hall
Unity Theatre
Uni.
A5039
Liverpool Community College
TV Studio
Wapping Basin
Echo Arena & Convention Centre
Duke's Dock
A5036
A561
Cathedral
Liverpool Women's Hosp.

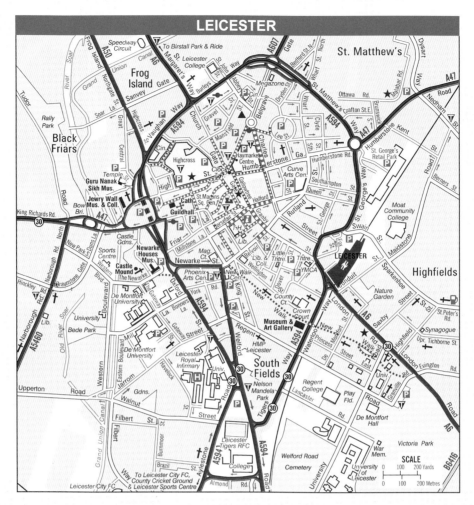

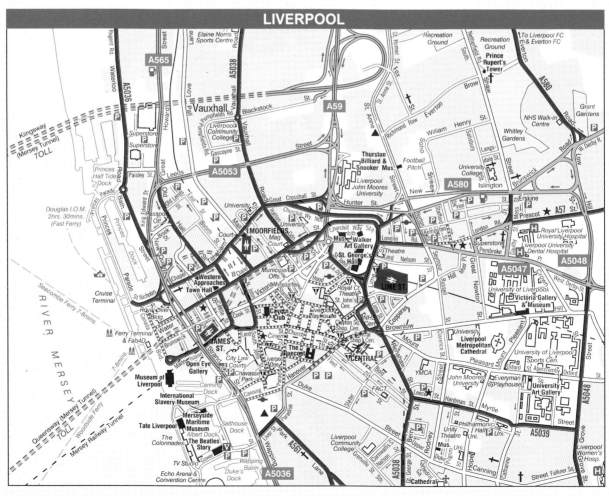

LUTON

To Wardown Park Museum
Wardown Park
People's Park
Popes's Meadow
New Bedford Rd.
Old Bedford Road
Talbot Rd.
Biscot Rd.
Cromwell Rd.
Clarendon Road
Reginald Street
Frederick Street
Havelock Road
North St.
Ridgway
High Town
Hart Hill
Barnfield College
York St.
Sports & Arts Cen.
Wenlock St.
Dudley St.
North St.
Brunswick St.
High Town Road
Back St.
Burr St.
Midland Rd.
Hitchin Road
Crawley Road
To Luton Town FC
Waldeck Rd.
Bury Park
Superstores
Mill St.
Dunstable Rd.
LUTON
(Buses only)
Crescent
A6
A505
Hatters Way
Telford Way
Liverpool Rd.
Dallow Rd.
Rec. Grd.
Inkerman St.
Cinema
Guildford St.
Lib.
Thtre.
County Court
T.H.
Bute St.
John St.
Church St.
St. Mary's Rd.
George St.
The Mall
Stuart St.
Cardiff Rd.
Grove Rd.
Magistrates Court
King St.
NHS Walk-in Centre
Church Park
Park Sq.
Crown Court
University
Vicarage St.
Crawley Green Rd.
Windmill Rd.
Napier Rd.
Cemetery
Buxton Rd.
Dumfries St.
Regent St.
Chapel St.
Casino
Cumberland St.
Viaduct
Manor Road
Rec. Grd.
To London Luton Airport
Park Town
Salisbury Rd.
Stanley St.
Park Street
Chequer St.
Superstore
Meyrick Av.
Russell Street
Hibbert St.
Latimer Rd.
B4540
Castle St.
New Town St.
Strathmore Av.
Seymour Rd.
Farley Hill
London Road
New Town
To Stockwood Park
SCALE
0 100 200 Yards
0 100 200 Metres

MIDDLESBROUGH

SCALE
0 100 200 Yards ¼ Mile
0 100 200 300 400 Metres
To Teessaurus Park
TOLL
Transporter Bridge
Ferry Rd.
Durham St.
Cleveland St.
A178
Forty Foot Road
North Road
Snowdon Road
Bridge Street West
Queens Sq.
East Dock St.
Middlesbrough College
Station Street
MIDDLESBROUGH
Middlesbrough By-Pass
A66
Archives
Windward Way
To Middlesbrough FC (Riverside Stadium)
Metz Bri. Rd.
Superstore
Wilson St.
Hill Street Shopping Centre
Dundas Arcade
Newport Rd.
Corporation Rd.
Cinema
To Teesside Retail & Leisure Park
Cannon Park Way
Cannon Park Ind. Est.
Gilkes St.
Crafts Centre
Captain Cook Sq.
Grange Rd.
The Cleveland Cen.
T.H.
Government Offs.
Register Offs.
Law Courts
Marton Rd.
Russell Sq.
Centre Lib.
Bottle of Notes
MIMA
Central Gardens
Grange Rd.
Mag. Courts
Newport Road
B6541
Hartington Rd.
B1272
Linthorpe Rd.
Albert Rd.
Bright St.
Borough Road
St. Paul's Rd.
Community Cen.
Library
Melrose St.
Abingdon Rd.
University of Teesside
Southfield Road
Mosque
To The James Cook University Hospital
Union St.
Princes Road
Glebe Rd.
Gresham Road
Mosque
Parliament Road
University
Victoria Road
Waterloo Road
Woodlands Road
Middletown Park
Park Lane
Crescent Road
Albert Ter.
North Road
Ayresome Gardens
Mosque
Park Rd.
NHS Treatment Centre
Clairville Rd.
Vale
Ayresome Street
ALBERT PARK
Rec. Grd.
Clairville Sports Stadium
Dorman Museum
Linthorpe Road
Park Road South

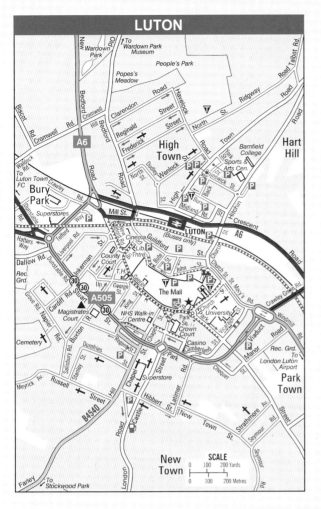

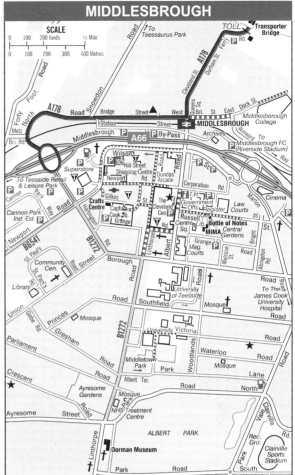

MANCHESTER (CITY CENTRE)

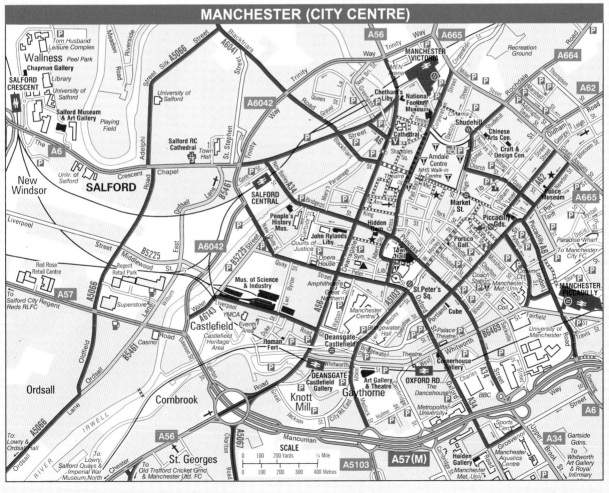

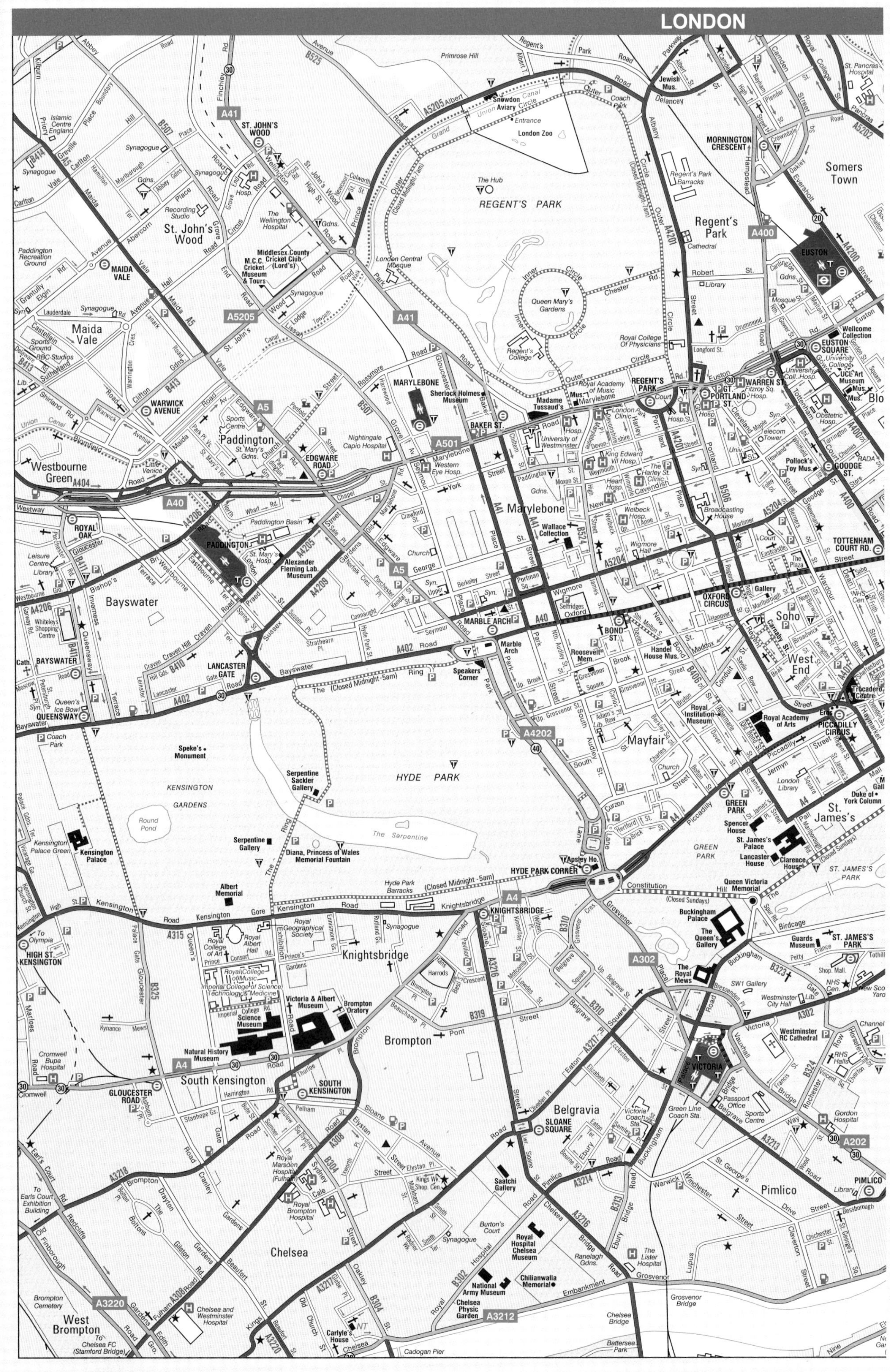
Primrose Hill
REGENT'S PARK
London Zoo
Snowdon Aviary
The Hub
Queen Mary's Gardens
Regent's College
Royal College Of Physicians
Regent's Park
Somers Town
EUSTON
EUSTON SQUARE
MORNINGTON CRESCENT
Jewish Mus.
Regent's Park Barracks
Cathedral
Wellcome Collection
UCL Art Museum
University Coll. Hosp.
WARREN ST.
GT. PORTLAND ST.
REGENT'S PARK
Madame Tussaud's
Royal Academy of Music Mus.
Sherlock Holmes Museum
BAKER ST.
MARYLEBONE
St. John's Wood
ST. JOHN'S WOOD
Lord's
M.C.C. Cricket Museum & Tours
Middlesex County Cricket Club
The Wellington Hospital
London Central Mosque
Maida Vale
MAIDA VALE
WARWICK AVENUE
Paddington
Paddington Recreation Ground
Sports Ground
BBC Studios
Little Venice
Westbourne Green
Westway
ROYAL OAK
PADDINGTON
Paddington Basin
St. Mary's Hosp.
Alexander Fleming Lab. Museum
EDGWARE ROAD
Nightingale Capio Hospital
Western Eye Hosp.
Marylebone
University of Westminster
King Edward VII Hosp.
The Harley St. Clinic
London Clinic
Wallace Collection
Wigmore Hall
Broadcasting House
Pollock's Toy Mus.
GOODGE ST.
Telecom Tower
TOTTENHAM COURT RD.
OXFORD CIRCUS
BOND ST.
MARBLE ARCH
Selfridges
Soho
West End
Carnaby St.
Gallery
Trocadero Centre
PICCADILLY CIRCUS
Eros
Royal Academy of Arts
Royal Institution Museum
Handel House Mus.
Roosevelt Mem.
Mayfair
Bayswater
BAYSWATER
QUEENSWAY
Queen's Ice Bowl
Whiteleys Shopping Centre
Leisure Centre Library
LANCASTER GATE
Speakers' Corner
Marble Arch
HYDE PARK
KENSINGTON GARDENS
Speke's Monument
Round Pond
The Serpentine
Serpentine Sackler Gallery
Serpentine Gallery
Diana, Princess of Wales Memorial Fountain
Kensington Palace
Albert Memorial
Hyde Park Barracks
HYDE PARK CORNER
Apsley Ho.
GREEN PARK
Spencer House
St. James's Palace
Lancaster House
Clarence House
St. James's
London Library
Duke of York Column
ST. JAMES'S PARK
Queen Victoria Memorial
Buckingham Palace
The Queen's Gallery
The Royal Mews
Guards Museum
ST. JAMES'S PARK
KNIGHTSBRIDGE
Knightsbridge
Harrods
Royal Albert Hall
Royal College of Art
Royal Geographical Society
Royal College of Music
Imperial College of Science Technology & Medicine
Victoria & Albert Museum
Brompton Oratory
Science Museum
Natural History Museum
Brompton
HIGH ST. KENSINGTON
GLOUCESTER ROAD
South Kensington
SOUTH KENSINGTON
Cromwell Bupa Hospital
Belgravia
SLOANE SQUARE
VICTORIA
Victoria Coach Sta.
Green Line Coach Sta.
Westminster City Hall
Westminster RC Cathedral
Gordon Hospital
PIMLICO
Pimlico
Saatchi Gallery
Royal Marsden Hospital
Royal Brompton Hospital
Chelsea
Burton's Court
Royal Hospital Chelsea Museum
National Army Museum
Chelsea Physic Garden
Chilianwalla Memorial
Ranelagh Gdns.
The Lister Hospital
Grosvenor Bridge
Chelsea Bridge
Battersea Park
Carlyle's House
Cadogan Pier
Chelsea and Westminster Hospital
Brompton Cemetery
West Brompton
To Chelsea FC (Stamford Bridge)
To Earls Court Exhibition Building
To Olympia
Earl's Court
A41
A5205
A5
A501
A40
A404
A4206
A402
A4202
A4
A315
A3216
A302
A3217
A3213
A202
A3218
A3220
A308
A3212
A400
A4200
A4201
A5204
A3214
B507
B413
B410
B411
B525
B310
B319
B325
B302
B304
B313
B324
B323
B506
B406
B414

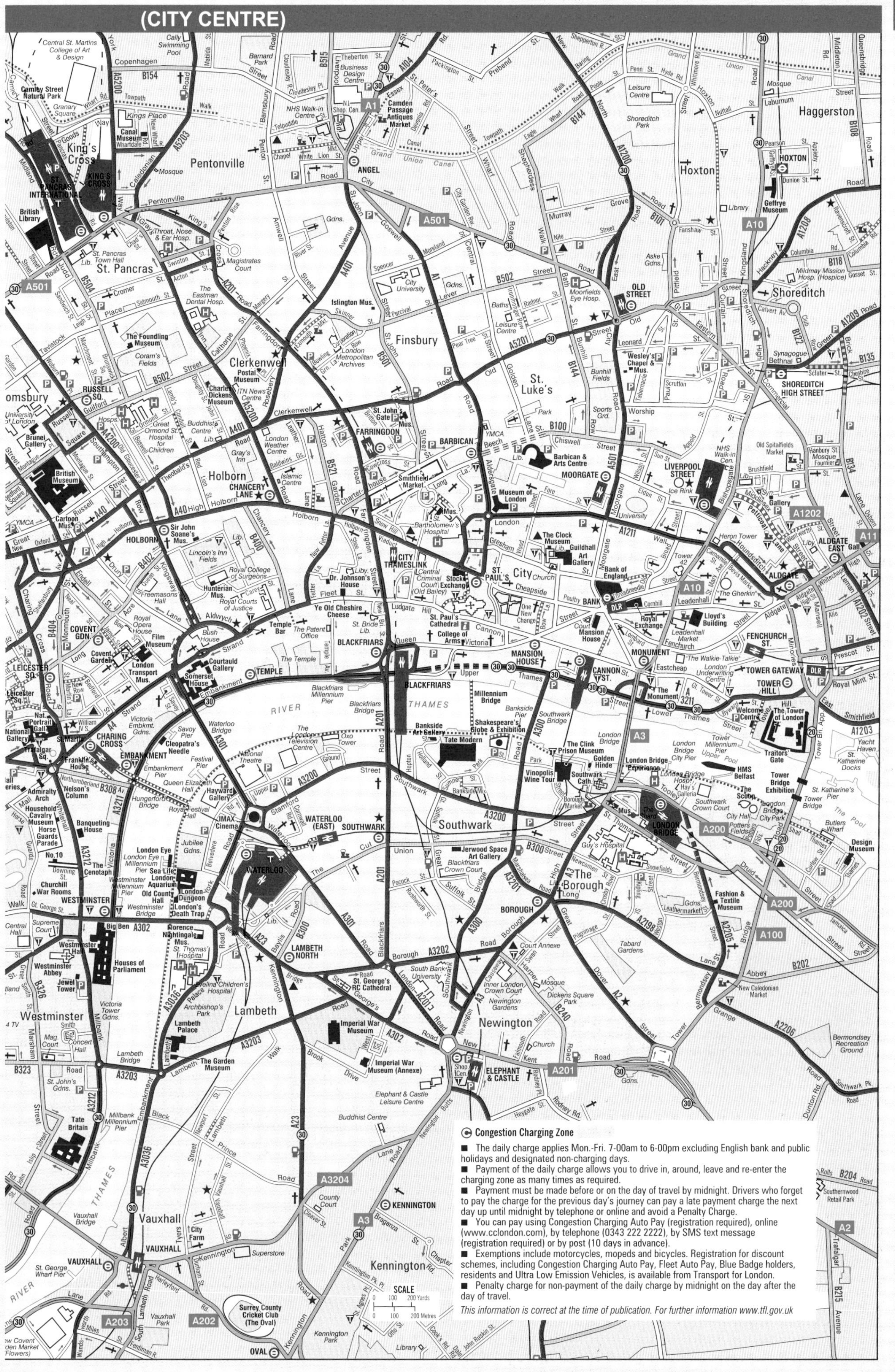

Congestion Charging Zone

■ The daily charge applies Mon.-Fri. 7-00am to 6-00pm excluding English bank and public holidays and designated non-charging days.

■ Payment of the daily charge allows you to drive in, around, leave and re-enter the charging zone as many times as required.

■ Payment must be made before or on the day of travel by midnight. Drivers who forget to pay the charge for the previous day's journey can pay a late payment charge the next day up until midnight by telephone or online and avoid a Penalty Charge.

■ You can pay using Congestion Charging Auto Pay (registration required), online (www.cclondon.com), by telephone (0343 222 2222), by SMS text message (registration required) or by post (10 days in advance).

■ Exemptions include motorcycles, mopeds and bicycles. Registration for discount schemes, including Congestion Charging Auto Pay, Fleet Auto Pay, Blue Badge holders, residents and Ultra Low Emission Vehicles, is available from Transport for London.

■ Penalty charge for non-payment of the daily charge by midnight on the day after the day of travel.

This information is correct at the time of publication. For further information www.tfl.gov.uk

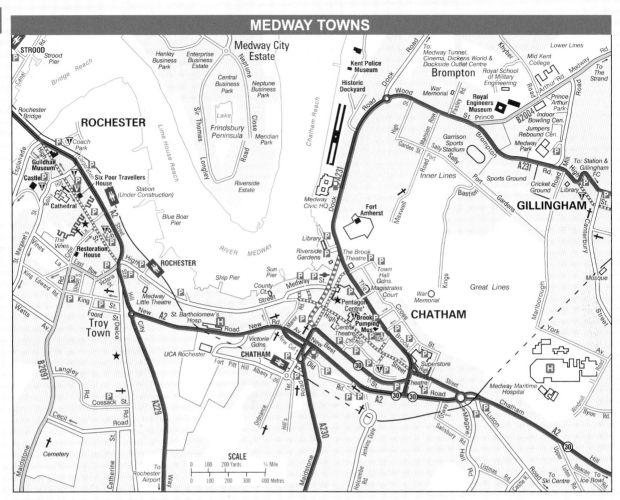

SCALE

| 0 | 100 | 200 Yards | ¼ Mile |
| 0 | 100 | 200 | 300 | 400 Metres |

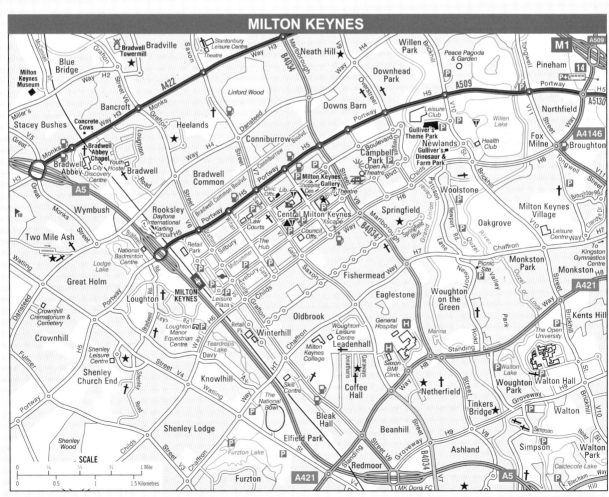

SCALE

| 0 | ¼ | ½ | ¾ | 1 Mile |
| 0 | 0.5 | 1 | 1.5 Kilometres |

NORWICH

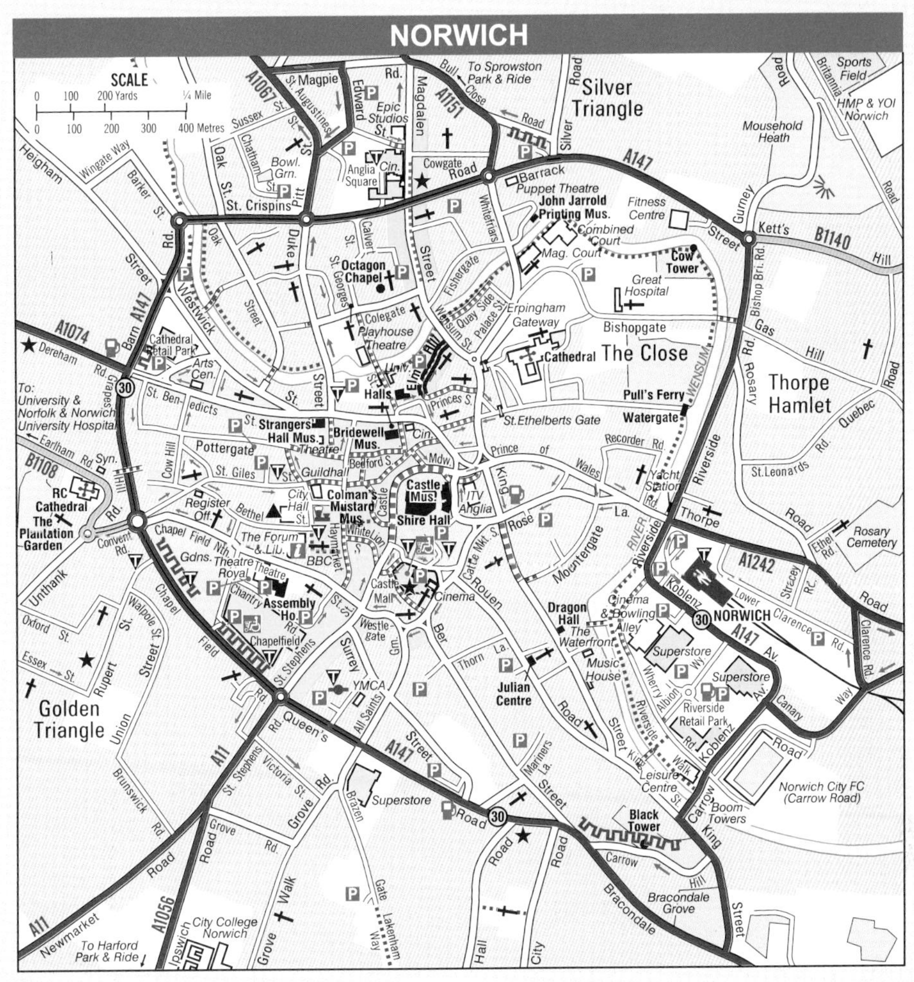
SCALE
200 Yards
¼ Mile
400 Metres
Silver Triangle
To Sprowston Park & Ride
Sports Field
HMP & YOI Norwich
Mousehold Heath
St. Magpie
St. Augustines
Epic Studios
Bowl. Grn.
Anglia Square
Cowgate
Barrack
Puppet Theatre
John Jarrold Printing Mus.
Fitness Centre
Combined Court
Mag. Court
Cow Tower
Kett's
B1140
Hill
St. Crispins
Octagon Chapel
Great Hospital
Colegate
Playhouse Theatre
Erpingham Gateway
Bishopgate
Cathedral
The Close
Thorpe Hamlet
Dereham
Cathedral Retail Park
Arts Cen.
To: University & Norfolk & Norwich University Hospital
Halls
Pull's Ferry
Strangers Hall Mus.
Bridewell Mus.
St.Ethelberts Gate
Watergate
Pottergate
Recorder Rd.
Riverside
St.Leonards Rd.
Guildhall
RC Cathedral
The Plantation Garden
Castle Mus.
City Hall
Colman's Mustard Mus.
Shire Hall
ITV Anglia
Yacht Station
Thorpe
Rosary Cemetery
Register Off.
The Forum & Lib.
BBC
Theatre Royal
Assembly Ho.
Castle Mall
Cinema
Rouen
Dragon Hall
The Waterfront
Cinema & Bowling Alley
NORWICH
A1242
A147
Superstore
Chapelfield
St.Stephens
YMCA
Music House
Julian Centre
Riverside Retail Park
Golden Triangle
Queen's
Superstore
Black Tower
Leisure Centre
Boom Towers
Norwich City FC (Carrow Road)
Carrow
Bracondale Grove
City College Norwich
To Harford Park & Ride
Newmarket
A11
A1056
A1074

NEWCASTLE UPON TYNE

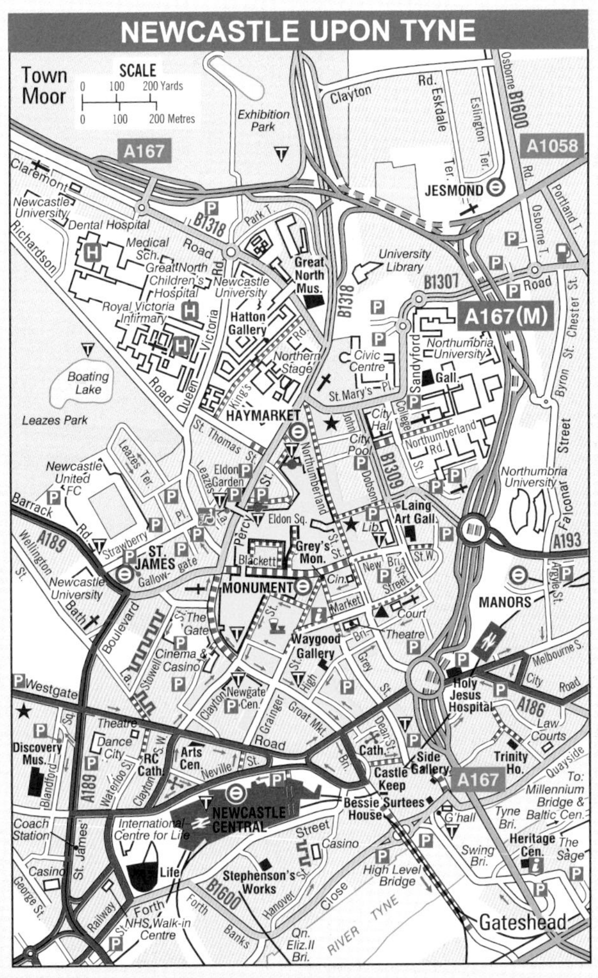
Town Moor
SCALE
200 Yards
200 Metres
A167
Exhibition Park
Clayton
Eskdale
Osborne
B1600
A1058
JESMOND
Claremont
Newcastle University
Dental Hospital
B1318
Medical Sch.
Great North Children's Hospital
Newcastle University
Great North Mus.
University Library
B1307
A167(M)
Royal Victoria Infirmary
Hatton Gallery
Northern Stage
Civic Centre
Northumbria University
Gall.
Boating Lake
Leazes Park
HAYMARKET
St. Mary's Pl.
Northumberland Rd.
Newcastle United FC
Eldon Garden
Northumbria University
Barrack
A189
Eldon Sq.
Laing Art Gall.
ST. JAMES
Grey's Mon.
MONUMENT
A193
Newcastle University
Blackett
MANORS
The Gate
Waygood Gallery
Theatre
Cinema & Casino
Holy Jesus Hospital
Westgate
Newgate Cen.
A186
Theatre
Discovery Mus.
Dance City
RC Cath.
Arts Cen.
Cath.
Law Courts
Trinity Ho.
Side Gallery
A167
Castle Keep
NEWCASTLE CENTRAL
Bessie Surtees House
To: Millennium Bridge & Baltic Cen.
Coach Station
International Centre for Life
Casino
Tyne Bri.
Heritage Cen.
The Sage
Life
Stephenson's Works
Swing Bri.
High Level Bridge
B1600
Gateshead
NHS Walk-in Centre
Qn. Eliz.II Bri.
RIVER TYNE

NEWPORT (CASNEWYDD)

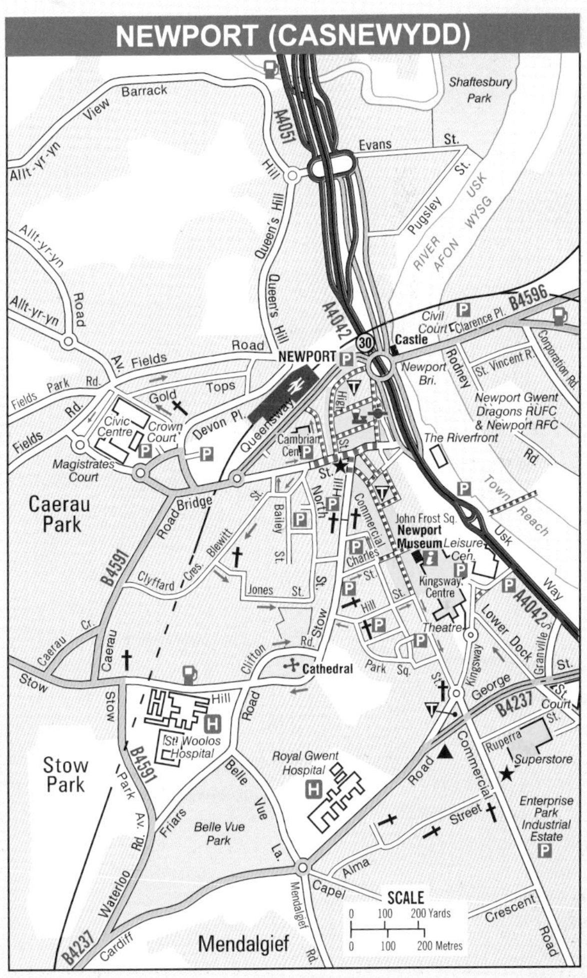
Barrack
View
Shaftesbury Park
A4051
Evans St.
Allt-yr-yn
Queen's Hill
Pugsley St.
RIVER USK
AFON WYSG
Civil Court
Clarence Pl.
B4596
A4042
Castle
Fields
NEWPORT
Newport Bri.
St. Vincent Rd.
Gold Tops
Civic Centre
Crown Court
Devon Pl.
Newport Gwent Dragons RUFC & Newport RFC
The Riverfront
Magistrates Court
Cambrian Cen.
Caerau Park
Bridge
Town Reach
B4591
Clyffard Cres.
John Frost Sq.
Newport Museum
Leisure Cen.
Kingsway Centre
Jones St.
Theatre
Cathedral
Park Sq.
Lower Dock
Stow Hill
St. Woolos Hospital
George
B4237
Royal Gwent Hospital
Superstore
Stow Park
Belle Vue Park
Commercial
Enterprise Park Industrial Estate
Alma
Capel
SCALE
200 Yards
200 Metres
Crescent
Mendalgief
Cardiff
B4237

NOTTINGHAM

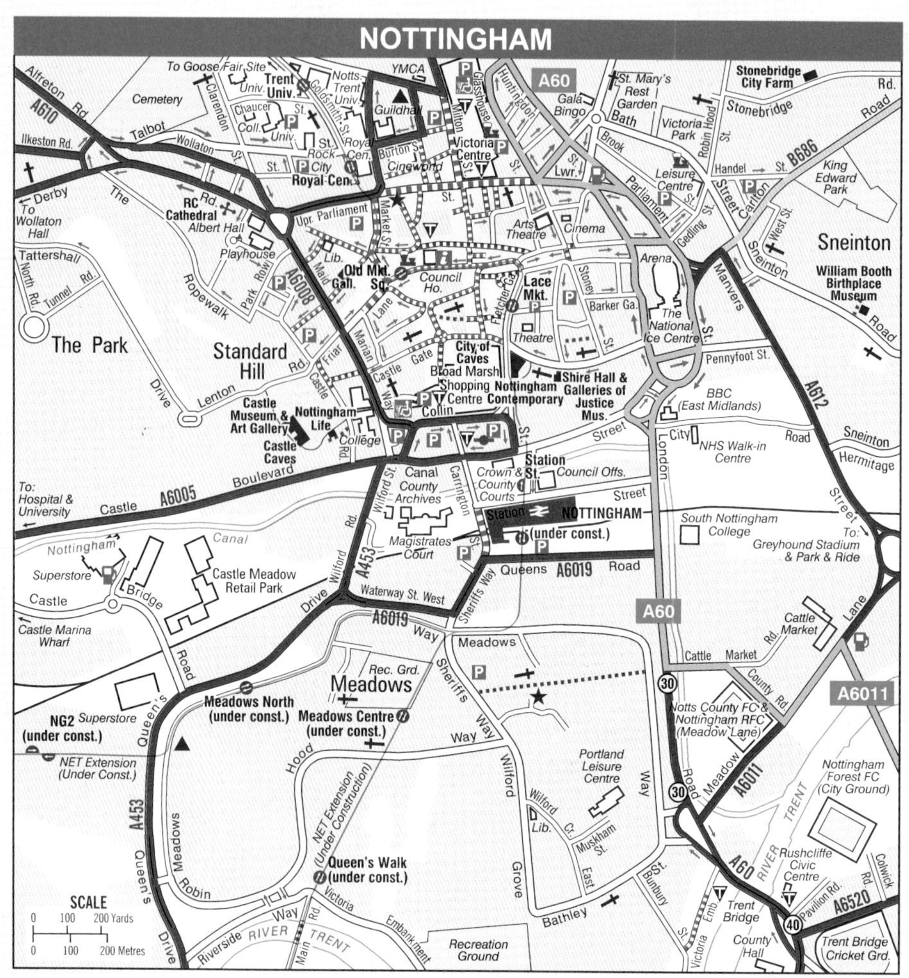

To Goose Fair Site
Trent Univ.
Notts. Trent Univ.
YMCA
Guildhall
A60
St. Mary's Rest Garden
Gala Bingo
Stonebridge City Farm
Rd.
Stonebridge
Road
Cemetery
Alfreton Rd.
A610
Ilkeston Rd.
Talbot
Wollaton St.
Chaucer St.
Coll.
Univ.
Royal Cen.
City
Royal Cen.
Burton St.
Cineworld
Victoria Centre
Milton St.
Glasshouse St.
Huntingdon St.
Bath St.
Victoria Park
Robin Hood St.
Brook St.
Lwr. Parliament St.
Leisure Centre
Handel St.
B686
King Edward Park
Derby Rd.
The Ropewalk
To Wollaton Hall
RC Cathedral
Albert Hall
Upr. Parliament St.
Arts Theatre
Cinema
Carlton St.
West St.
Sneinton Rd.
Sneinton
William Booth Birthplace Museum
Tattershall
North Rd.
Tunnel Rd.
Playhouse
Park Row
A6008
Maid Marian Way
Lib.
Old Mkt. Sq.
Gall.
Council Ho.
Lace Mkt.
Stoney St.
Barker Ga.
Arena
Gedling St.
Manvers St.
The National Ice Centre
Road
The Park
Standard Hill
Friar Lane
Castle Gate
Theatre
City of Caves
Broad Marsh
Shopping Centre
Nottingham Contemporary
Shire Hall & Galleries of Justice Mus.
Pennyfoot St.
A612
Lenton Rd.
Castle Museum & Art Gallery
Nottingham Life
Castle Caves
College
Collin St.
Fletcher Gate
Station St.
Street
City
NHS Walk-in Centre
BBC (East Midlands)
Sneinton Hermitage
To: Hospital & University
Castle Boulevard
A6005
Canal County Archives
Carrington St.
Crown & County Courts
Council Offs.
Station NOTTINGHAM
(under const.)
Street
London Road
South Nottingham College
To: Greyhound Stadium & Park & Ride
Nottingham Canal
Superstore
Castle Meadow Retail Park
Magistrates Court
Wilford St.
Wilford Rd.
A453
Queens A6019 Road
Castle Bridge
Castle Marina Wharf
Waterway St. West
Sheriffs Way
A6019 Way
Drive
A60
Cattle Market
Cattle Market Rd.
County Rd.
Lane
Meadows
Rec. Grd.
Meadows
A6011
Queen's Road
Meadows North (under const.)
Meadows Centre (under const.)
NG2 Superstore (under const.)
NET Extension (Under Const.)
Notts County FC & Nottingham RFC (Meadow Lane)
Meadow Lane
30
Portland Leisure Centre
Wilford Grove
Hood
NET Extension (Under Construction)
Nottingham Forest FC (City Ground)
Wilford Ct.
Lib.
Muskham St.
East St.
Way
A601
River Trent
A453
Queen's Drive
Robin Hood Meadows
SCALE
0 100 200 Yards
0 100 200 Metres
Queen's Walk (under const.)
St. Bunbury
Rushcliffe Civic Centre
Colwick Rd.
A60
Trent Bridge
Pavilion Rd.
A6520
40
Victoria Emb.
Riverside Way
River Trent
Main Rd.
Embankment
Bathley
Recreation Ground
County Hall
Trent Bridge Cricket Grd.

NORTHAMPTON

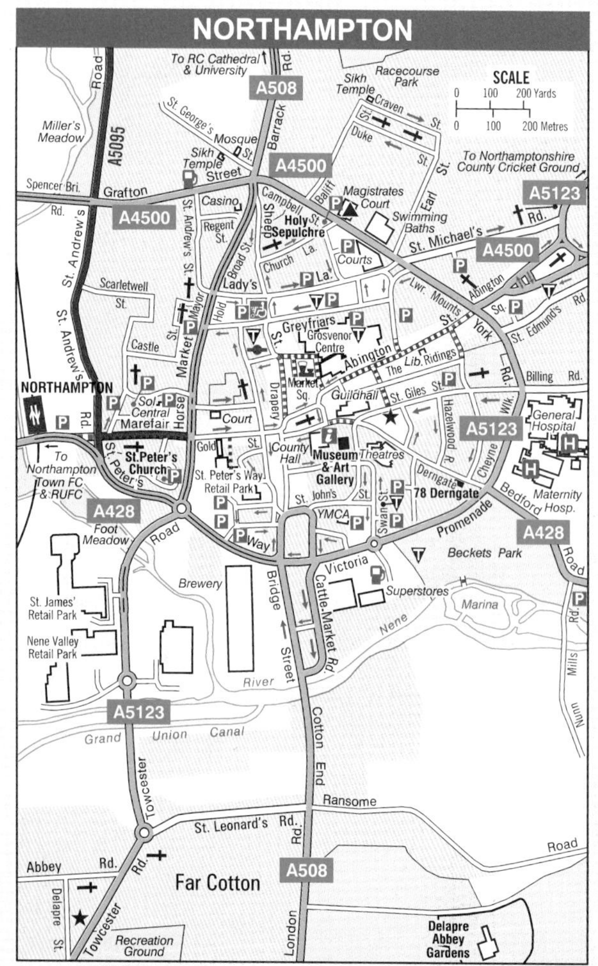

To RC Cathedral & University
Racecourse Park
A508
Sikh Temple
SCALE
0 100 200 Yards
0 100 200 Metres
Road
Miller's Meadow
A5095
St. George's St.
Mosque
Barrack Rd.
Craven St.
Duke St.
Sikh Temple
A4500
To Northamptonshire County Cricket Ground
Spencer Bri. Rd.
Grafton Street
A5123
Casino
Campbell St.
Magistrates Court
Earl St.
A4500
Regent St.
St. Andrew's St.
Sheep St.
Holy Sepulchre
Swimming Baths
St. Michael's Rd.
Bailiff St.
Church La.
Courts
A4500
St. Andrew's Rd.
Scarletwell St.
Broad St.
Lady's La.
Abington
Lwr. Mounts
Sq.
St. Edmund's Rd.
Mayor Hold
Greyfriars
Grosvenor Centre
York Rd.
Castle St.
Market Sq.
Abington St.
The Lib. Ridings
Billing Rd.
NORTHAMPTON
Sol Central
Horse Market
Drapery
Guildhall
St. Giles St.
Wlk.
Marefair
Court
Hazelwood R.
A5123
General Hospital
To Northampton Town FC & RUFC
St. Peter's Church
Gold St.
County Hall
Museum & Art Gallery
Theatres
Cheyne
St. Peter's Way Retail Park
Derngate
78 Derngate
Bedford Rd.
Maternity Hosp.
A428
St. John's St.
YMCA
Swan St.
Promenade
A428
Foot Meadow
Road
Way
Beckets Park
Road
Brewery
Victoria
Superstores
Bridge Street
St. James' Retail Park
Cattle Market Rd.
Marina
Nene
Nene Valley Retail Park
River
Mills Rd.
A5123
Grand Union Canal
Towcester Rd.
Cotton End
Ransome
St. Leonard's Rd.
Road
Abbey Rd.
A508
Far Cotton
Delapre St.
Towcester Rd.
London Rd.
Recreation Ground
Delapre Abbey Gardens

OBAN

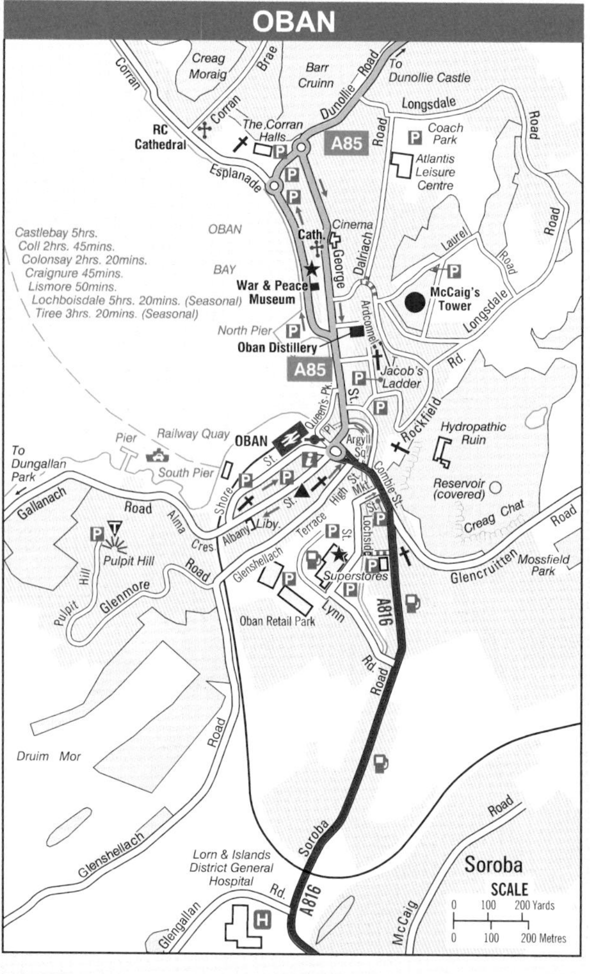

Creag Moraig
Brae
Barr Cruinn
To Dunollie Castle
Corran
Dunollie Road
Longsdale
Road
RC Cathedral
Corran
The Corran Halls
A85
Coach Park
Atlantis Leisure Centre
Esplanade
Cinema
Road
Castlebay 5hrs.
Coll 2hrs. 45mins.
Colonsay 2hrs. 20mins.
Craignure 45mins.
Lismore 50mins.
Lochboisdale 5hrs. 20mins. (Seasonal)
Tiree 3hrs. 20mins. (Seasonal)
OBAN
BAY
Cath.
War & Peace Museum
George St.
Dalriach
Laurel
Road
McCaig's Tower
Longsdale
North Pier
Oban Distillery
Ardconnel
Jacob's Ladder
Rd.
A85
Rockfield
Hydropathic Ruin
To Dungallan Park
Pier
Railway Quay
OBAN
South Pier
Queen's Pk. Pl.
Argyll Sq.
Combie St.
Reservoir (covered)
Gallanach Road
Shore St.
Stevenson St.
Albany St.
Liby.
High St.
Creag Chat
Road
Alma Cres.
Pulpit Hill
Road
Glenshellach Terrace
Lochside St.
Superstores
Mossfield Park
Glencruitten Road
Pulpit Hill
Glenmore
Lynn
Oban Retail Park
A816
Rd.
Road
Druim Mor
Road
Road
Glenshellach
Soroba
Lorn & Islands District General Hospital
Rd.
A816
Soroba
SCALE
0 100 200 Yards
0 100 200 Metres
Glengallan
McCaig

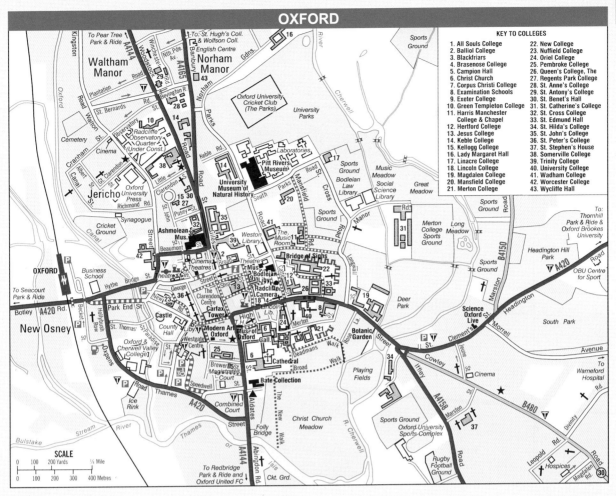

KEY TO COLLEGES

1. All Souls College	22. New College
2. Balliol College	23. Nuffield College
3. Blackfriars	24. Oriel College
4. Brasenose College	25. Pembroke College
5. Campion Hall	26. Queen's College, The
6. Christ Church	27. Regents Park College
7. Corpus Christi College	28. St. Anne's College
8. Examination Schools	29. St. Antony's College
9. Exeter College	30. St. Benet's Hall
10. Green Templeton College	31. St. Catherine's College
11. Harris Manchester College & Chapel	32. St. Cross College
12. Hertford College	33. St. Edmund Hall
13. Jesus College	34. St. Hilda's College
14. Keble College	35. St. John's College
15. Kellogg College	36. St. Peter's College
16. Lady Margaret Hall	37. St. Stephen's House
17. Linacre College	38. Somerville College
18. Lincoln College	39. Trinity College
19. Magdalen College	40. University College
20. Mansfield College	41. Wadham College
21. Merton College	42. Worcester College
	43. Wycliffe Hall

PAISLEY

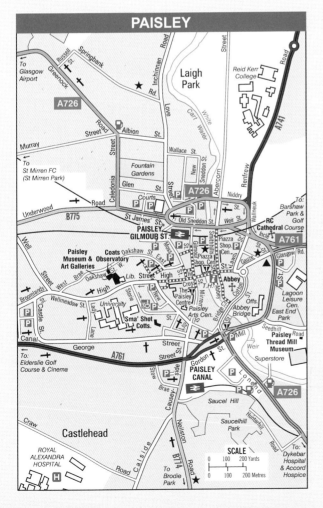

PERTH

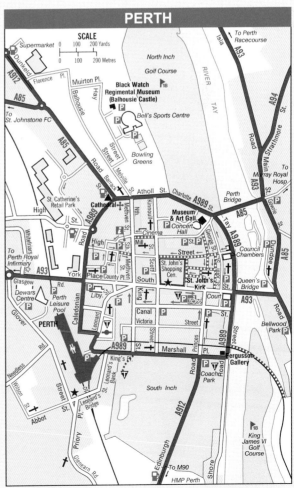

PLYMOUTH

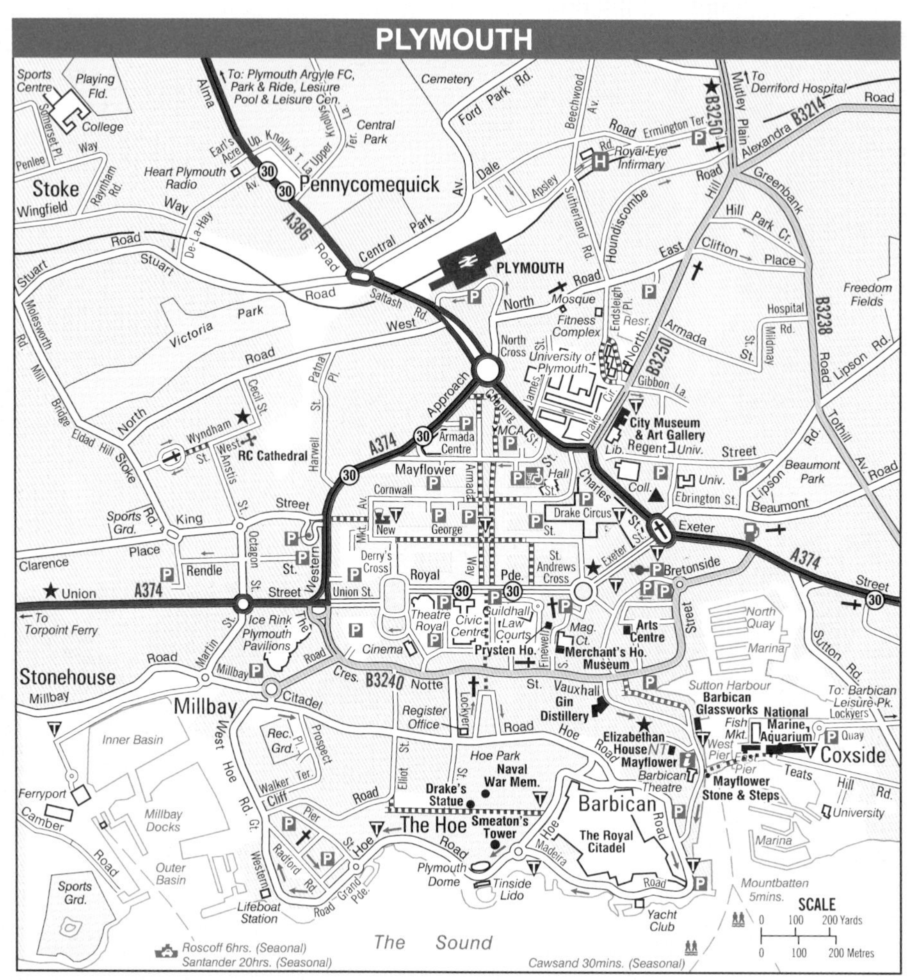
To: Plymouth Argyle FC, Park & Ride, Lesiure Pool & Leisure Cen.
Cemetery
To Derriford Hospital
Sports Centre
Playing Fld.
College
Central Park
Pennycomequick
Stoke
Wingfield
Heart Plymouth Radio
Royal Eye Infirmary
Mutley Plain
Alexandra Road
Greenbank
Hill Park Cr.
Clifton Place
Freedom Fields
PLYMOUTH
Mosque
Fitness Complex
University of Plymouth
North Cross
Victoria Park
City Museum & Art Gallery
RC Cathedral
Armada Centre
Mayflower
Drake Circus
Beaumont Park
Exeter St.
Bretonside
Sports Grd.
Clarence Place
Union
To Torpoint Ferry
Ice Rink Plymouth Pavilions
Derry's Cross
Royal Pde.
St. Andrews Cross
Theatre Royal
Civic Centre
Guildhall
Law Courts
Mag. Ct.
Arts Centre
Cinema
Prysten Ho.
Merchant's Ho. Museum
North Quay
Marina
Stonehouse
Millbay
Citadel
Notte St.
Vauxhall
Gin Distillery
Sutton Harbour
Barbican Glassworks
National Marine Aquarium
To: Barbican Leisure Pk.
Lockyers Quay
Inner Basin
Register Office
Elizabethan House
Fish Mkt.
Mayflower
Coxside
Hoe Park
Naval War Mem.
Barbican Theatre
Mayflower Stone & Steps
Teats Hill Rd.
Ferryport
Millbay Docks
Drake's Statue
Barbican
University
The Hoe
Smeaton's Tower
The Royal Citadel
Marina
Outer Basin
Plymouth Dome
Tinside Lido
Mountbatten 5mins.
Sports Grd.
Lifeboat Station
Yacht Club
Roscoff 6hrs. (Seasonal)
Santander 20hrs. (Seasonal)
The Sound
Cawsand 30mins. (Seasonal)
SCALE
0 100 200 Yards
0 100 200 Metres

PETERBOROUGH

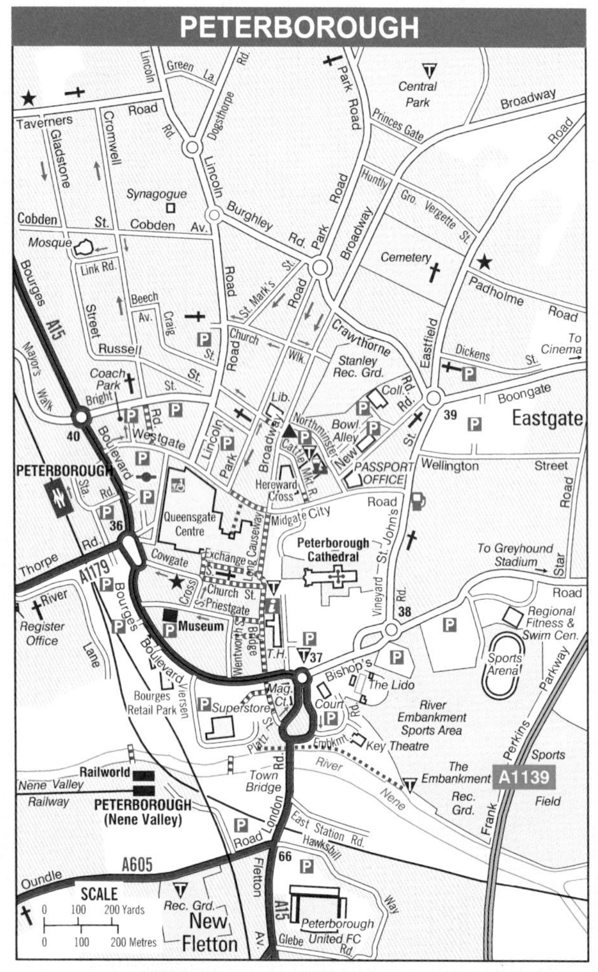
Central Park
Broadway
Taverners
Synagogue
Cobden Av.
Mosque
Cemetery
Padholme Road
To Cinema
Stanley Rec. Grd.
Coach Park
Eastgate
Boongate
Bowl Alley
PASSPORT OFFICE
Wellington Street
PETERBOROUGH
Queensgate Centre
Hereward Cross
City
Peterborough Cathedral
To Greyhound Stadium
Museum
Regional Fitness & Swim Cen.
Register Office
Sports Arena
The Lido
Bourges Retail Park
Superstore
River Embankment Sports Area
Key Theatre
The Embankment
A1139
Railworld
Nene Valley Railway
PETERBOROUGH (Nene Valley)
Town Bridge
Rec. Grd.
Sports Field
A605
Oundle
Rec. Grd.
New Fletton
Peterborough United FC
SCALE
0 100 200 Yards
0 100 200 Metres

PRESTON

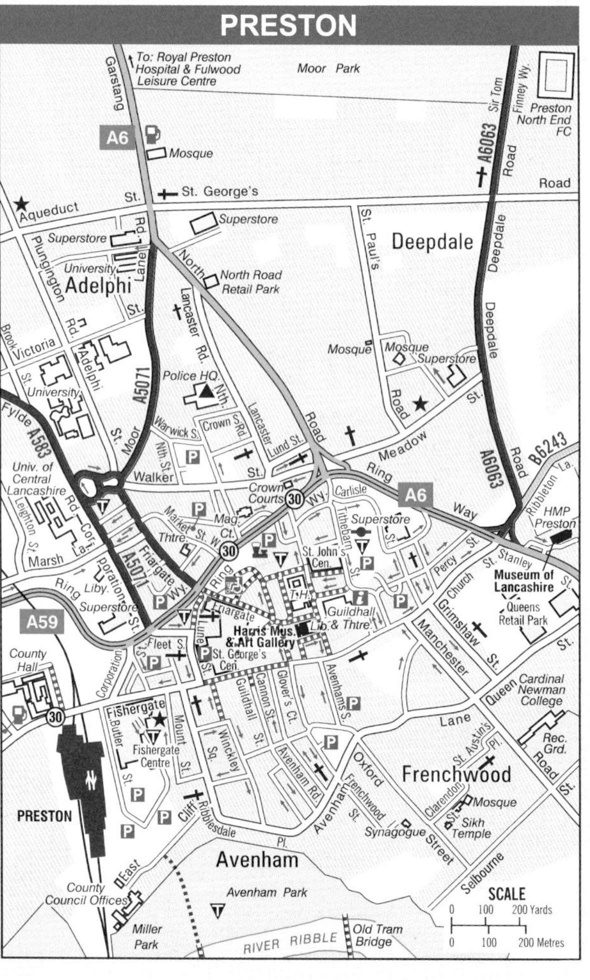
To: Royal Preston Hospital & Fulwood Leisure Centre
Moor Park
Preston North End FC
A6
Mosque
St. George's
Aqueduct
Superstore
Deepdale
Adelphi
University
North Road Retail Park
Mosque
Superstore
Police HQ
Univ. of Central Lancashire
Walker
Crown Courts
Ring Way
A6
HMP Preston
Museum of Lancashire
Queens Retail Park
Marsh
Mag. Ct.
Superstore
St. John Cen.
Guildhall & Thtre
Harris Mus. & Art Gallery
St. George's Cen.
A59
County Hall
Cardinal Newman College
Rec. Grd.
Fishergate Centre
Frenchwood
Mosque
Sikh Temple
Synagogue
PRESTON
Avenham
Avenham Park
County Council Offices
Miller Park
RIVER RIBBLE
Old Tram Bridge
SCALE
0 100 200 Yards
0 100 200 Metres

PORTSMOUTH

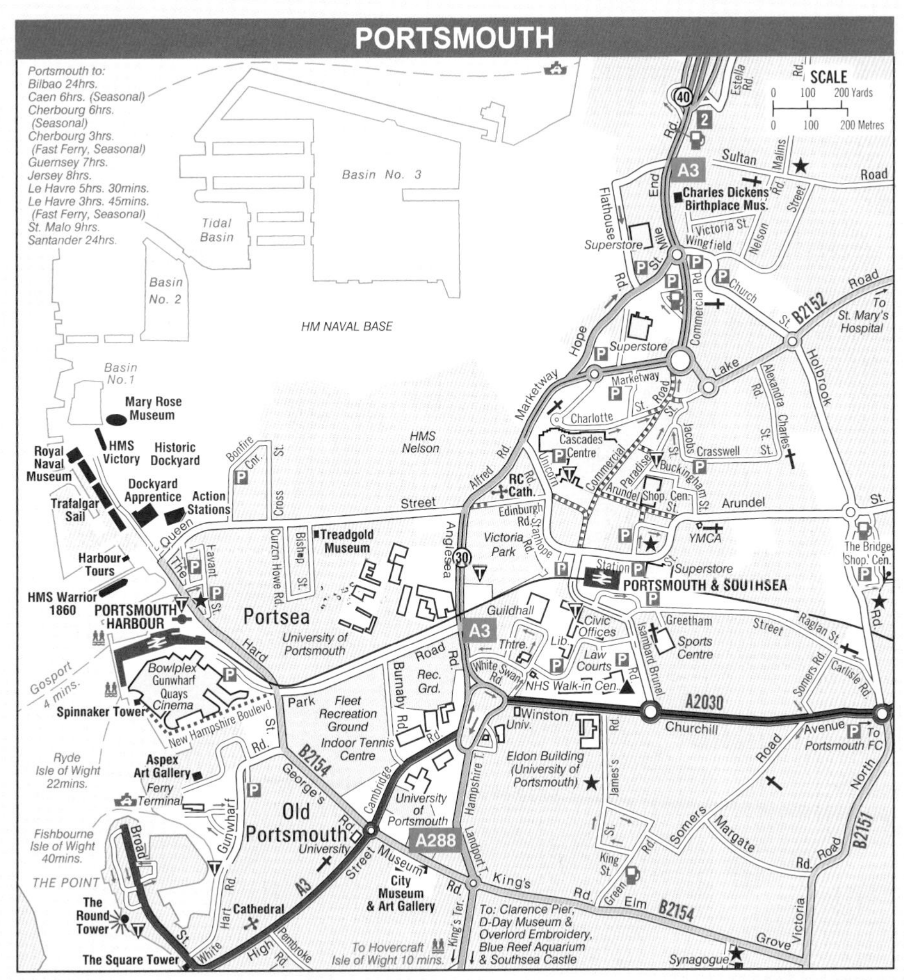

Portsmouth to:
Bilbao 24hrs.
Caen 6hrs. (Seasonal)
Cherbourg 6hrs.
(Seasonal)
Cherbourg 3hrs.
(Fast Ferry, Seasonal)
Guernsey 7hrs.
Jersey 8hrs.
Le Havre 5hrs. 30mins.
Le Havre 3hrs. 45mins.
(Fast Ferry, Seasonal)
St. Malo 9hrs.
Santander 24hrs.

SCALE

Basin No. 3

Tidal Basin

HM NAVAL BASE

Basin No. 2

Basin No. 1

Mary Rose Museum
Royal Naval Museum
HMS Victory
Historic Dockyard
Dockyard Apprentice
Trafalgar Sail
Action Stations
Harbour Tours
HMS Warrior 1860
PORTSMOUTH HARBOUR
Gosport 4 mins.
Spinnaker Tower
Ryde Isle of Wight 22mins.
Aspex Art Gallery
Ferry Terminal
Fishbourne Isle of Wight 40mins.
THE POINT
The Round Tower
The Square Tower

Charles Dickens Birthplace Mus.
Superstore
Victoria St.
Wingfield
Superstore
Marketway
Cascades Centre
RC Cath.
Edinburgh Rd.
Victoria Park
YMCA
The Bridge Shop' Cen.
Treadgold Museum
Portsea
University of Portsmouth
Guildhall
Civic Offices
Law Courts
NHS Walk-in Cen
Greetham Sports Centre
Station
PORTSMOUTH & SOUTHSEA
Superstore
White Swan
Winston Univ.
Churchill
To Portsmouth FC
Eldon Building (University of Portsmouth)
Bowlplex Gunwharf Quays Cinema
New Hampshire Boulevd.
Fleet Recreation Ground Indoor Tennis Centre
Old Portsmouth
University
University of Portsmouth
City Museum & Art Gallery
Cathedral
To: Clarence Pier, D-Day Museum & Overlord Embroidery, Blue Reef Aquarium & Southsea Castle
To Hovercraft Isle of Wight 10 mins.
Synagogue

READING

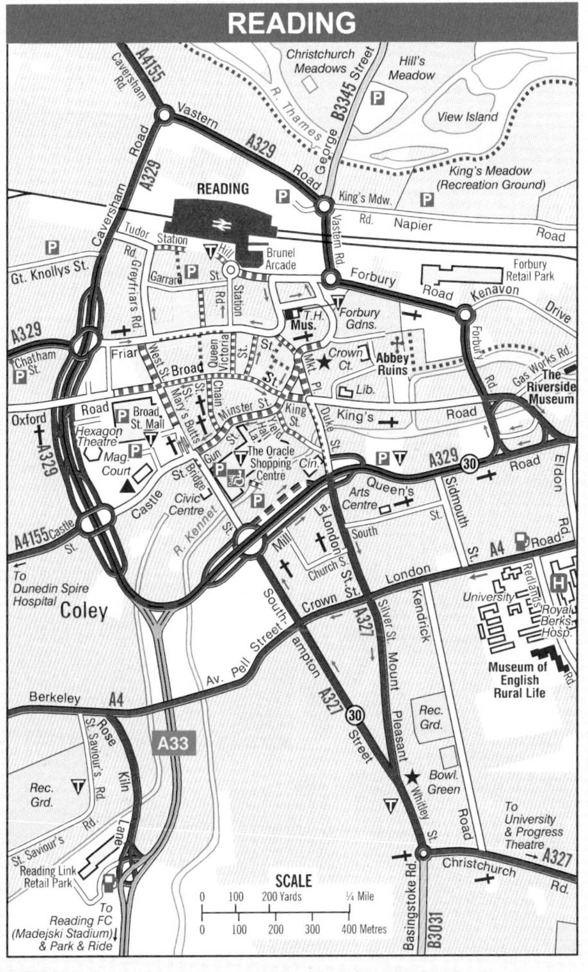

Christchurch Meadows
Hill's Meadow
View Island
King's Meadow (Recreation Ground)
READING
Station
Brunel Arcade
Napier
Forbury Retail Park
Forbury Gdns.
T.H. Mus.
Crown Ct.
Abbey Ruins
Lib.
The Riverside Museum
Gt. Knollys St.
Hexagon Theatre
Civic Centre
The Oracle Shopping Centre
Arts Centre
Queen's
Coley
Museum of English Rural Life
Royal Berks Hosp.
To Dunedin Spire Hospital
Berkeley
Rec. Grd.
Bowl Green
To University & Progress Theatre
Reading Link Retail Park
To Reading FC (Madejski Stadium) & Park & Ride

SCALE

ST ANDREWS

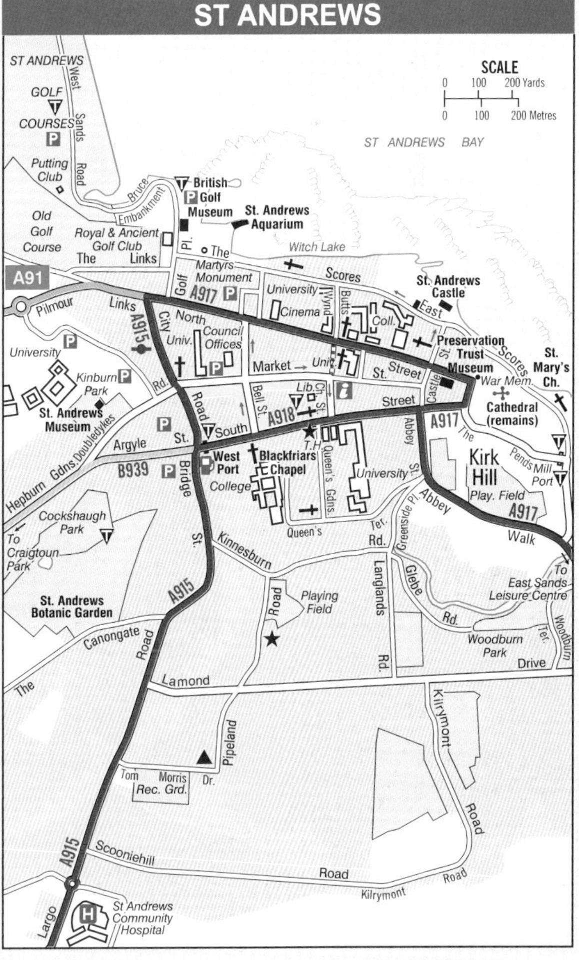

ST ANDREWS
GOLF COURSES
Putting Club
Old Golf Course
British Golf Museum
St. Andrews Aquarium
Royal & Ancient Golf Club
The Links
Witch Lake
ST ANDREWS BAY
St. Andrews Castle
Preservation Trust Museum
St. Mary's Ch.
Pilmour
North Univ.
Council Offices
Cinema
University
Kinburn Park
St. Andrews Museum
Cathedral (remains)
Market
University
War Mem.
Kirk Hill
Play. Field
West Port
Blackfriars Chapel
College
Queen's
Cockshaugh Park
To Craigtoun Park
St. Andrews Botanic Garden
Playing Field
Tom Morris Rec. Grd.
To East Sands Leisure Centre
Woodburn Park
Lamond
Kinnessburn
Langlands
Kilrymont
St Andrews Community Hospital
Largo
Scooniehill

SCALE

SALISBURY

SHREWSBURY

SHEFFIELD

SCALE
0 100 200 Yards
0 100 200 Metres

Infirmary Rd. · To Sheffield Wednesday FC · To Concord Sports Centre · Howard Rd. · Lib. · Albert Ter. Rd. · Healthy Living Centre · Upperthorpe · Kelham Island Museum · Mowbray · B6074 · Pitsmoor Rd. · Chatham St. · A6135 · Spital · Carlisle St. · A6109 · Savile · Street · A6178 · Attercliffe · To Don Valley Stadium & Meadowhall Shop. Cen. · Rd. · A61 · Green · Lane · Alma St. · Shalesmoor · Russell St. · Nursery · Johnson St. · Stanley St. · B6073 · DON · Effingham St. · Sussex · Effingham Rd. · Addy · Road · Watery St. · Meadow · Hoyle St. · A61 · Bridge · RIVER · Wicker · Sheffield & Tinsley Canal · Barber · Rd. · Road · Recreation Ground · Bellefield St. · Road · Shalesmoor · Gibraltar · Corporation · Law Courts · St. · Derek Dooley Way · A61 · Crookesmoor · Fawcett St. · St. Philip's Rd. · Street · Scotland · Fire, Police Museum · Blonk St. · Bernard Rd. · Crookesmoor · Road · Crookes Valley Rd. · Street · Netherthorpe Rd. · Street · Mag. Ct. · Bank St. · Furnival · Parkway · 40 · A61 · Hyde Park · A57 · Crookes Valley Park · University of Sheffield · Winter St. · Weston · Hollis Croft · Tenter St. · Hawley St. · Castle Sq. · Fitzalan Sq./Ponds Forge · Broad St. · Street · Harcourt · Mushroom La. · University of Sheffield · Bolsover St. · Research Centre · NHS Walk-in Centre · Lane · Cath. La. · Park Hill · Solly · Broad · B6539 · Rockingham · Bailey St. · Campo · Church · Cathedral · RC Cath. · High St. · Gate · Bingo Hall · Ponds Forge International Sports Cen. · Duke St. · B6071 · Northumberland · Weston Park · Weston Park Museum · Netherthorpe · Brook · Hill · Turner Museum of Glass · Trippet La. · University of Sheffield · Shop Cen. · Cutlers' Hall · The Crucible · Bank · St. · City Hall · Fountain Prect. · Thtre. · Pond Hill · B6070 · Western Bank · Univ. Road · Portobello · Regent St. · Cinema · Children's Hosp. · Clarkson · Octagon Cen. · Univ. of Sheffield · West · West St. · Carver St. · City Hall · Surrey St. · Winter Gdn. · Theatre · Pond · Archway Centre · A61 · A57 · Rd. · Brunswick · Glossop Rd. · Upr. Hanover St. · Fitzwilliam · Eldon · Graves Gallery · Sheffield Station/Sheffield Hallam University · Playing Fields · Whitham · Weston Park Hospital · Dental Hosp. · Road · Drama Studio · Wilkinson St. · Devonshire St. · The Forum · Victoria Hall · Cambridge St. · Millennium Gallery · Millennium Sq. · Pinstone · Hallam University · Sheaf St. · SHEFFIELD · Talbot St. · Library · Royal Hallamshire Hospital · Broomspring · La. · Wellington · Street · Union St. · Arundel Gate · Arundel · Street · Charles St. · Cinema · Shrewsbury Rd. · Norfolk · Street · Univ. · Dorset St. · Street · Moor · Furnival · Site Gallery · Suffolk · B6071 · City Rd. · Glossop · B6547 · Road · Broomfield · Cres. · Hanover · Charter Rw. · The · Matilda St. · Monument Grounds · Swimming Pool · B6069 · Collegiate · Street · The Moor · Eyre · Arundel · Sidney St. · Street · Rd · Clay Wood · Newbould La. · Clarkegrove Rd. · Broomsgrove · Road · Broomhall · William St. · A61 · Way · Moore · Young St. · La. · Jessop St. · Granville Rd./The Sheffield College · A6135 · Road · Clarkehouse · Broomhall · Sunnybank Nature Reserve · St. Mary's · South La. · Retail Park Gate · Road · Granville · Sheffield City College · Goals Soccer Centre · Road · Road · Collegiate Cres. · Road · Superstore · Rd. · St. Mary's · Rd. · Skate Central · Farm · Park · Sheffield Botanical Gardens · Southgrove · Sheffield Hallam University · A625 · Summerfield St. · Highfield · London Rd. · B6388 · Bramall La. · A621 · Clough · Sheffield United FC · Shoreham · Charlotte · A61 · Queens Rd. · Norfolk · Rd. · Ecclesall · Rd. · Cemetery Rd. · Superstore · East Bank Rd. · Norfolk Park

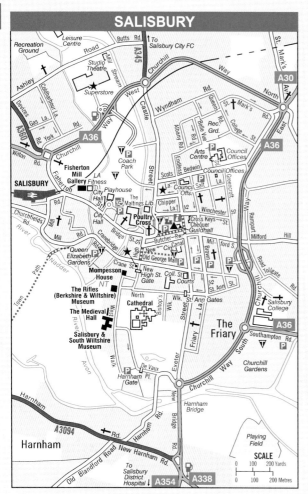

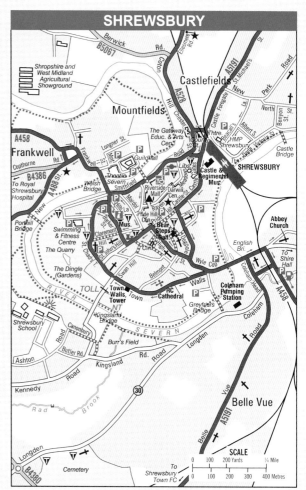

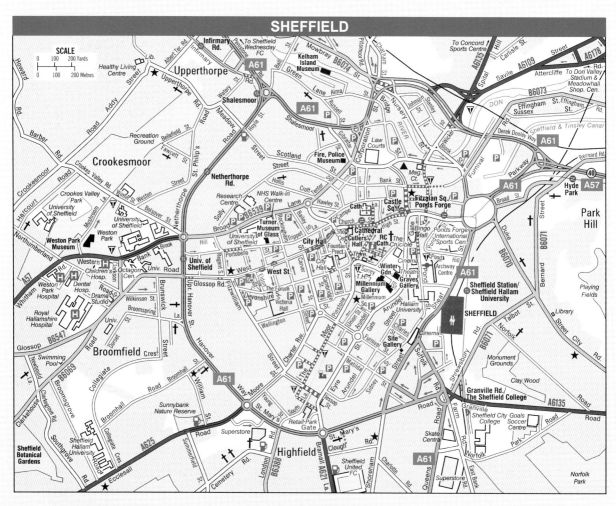

SOUTHAMPTON

SCALE
0 100 200 Yards ¼ Mile
0 100 200 300 400 Metres

To: University
To: County Cricket Ground
Newtown
Mount Pleasant
Gurdwara Lyon
YMCA
Law Courts
Royal South Hants Hospital
Hill
Polygon
Bedford Place
Fourposts
Howard Road
Milton Rd.
Wilton Avenue
Carlton Cr.
Devonshire Rd.
Bedford Pl.
Cumberland Pl.
London Rd.
Dorset St.
Onslow Rd.
A33
A335
St. Mary's
Graham Rd.
Leisure Cen.
Mosque
Northam
Millbank
Coalporters Rowing Club
Temple
Union Rd.
Princes St.
Radcliffe Rd.
Northam Bridge
Shamrock Quay
River Itchen
Shirley Road
A3057
Commercial Rd.
Mayflower Theatre
Cenotaph
West (Watts) Park
Titanic Memorial
Andrews Park
Solent University
City Art Gall.
SeaCity Mus.
Guildhall
Civic Cen.
Arts Complex
Nichols Town
Solent University
Six Dials
SOUTHAMPTON
BBC Hampshire
A3024
A33
Western Esplanade
Coach Station
Mountbatten Retail Park
Marlands Shopping Cen.
New Road
Palmerston Park
South Front
Kingsway
Northam Rd.
Southampton FC (St. Mary's Stadium)
Belvidere
Britannia Road
Peartree Green
Pound Tree Rd.
Ogle Rd.
West Quay Retail Park
West Quay Shopping Centre
Houndwell Park
Hoglands Park
James St.
Southampton City College
Hanover Bgs.
Bargate
East St.
Chapel
Chapel Rd.
Marine Parade
B3038
Western Docks
Leisure World & Cinema
Herbert Walker Av.
City Cruise Terminal
Back of the Walls
High St.
Orchard La.
Threefield Lane
Marsh La.
Central Rd.
Albert Rd. North
Crosshouse
Itchen
Itchen Bridge
Radstock Rd.
WOOLSTON
TOLL
City College
A3025
The Quays
West Gate
St. Michael's Church
Tudor Ho. Mus.
Bernard St.
Medieval Merchant's House
Queen's Way
Queens Terrace
Queens Park
Latimer St.
Oxford St.
Terminus Ter.
Canute Rd.
Aviation Museum
Southampton Water Activities Centre
Portsmouth Rd.
Lib.
Mayflower Park
Town Quay
River Test
Royal Pier (Closed)
Platform Rd.
Ocean Village
Cinema
Royal Southampton Yacht Club
Ocean Village Marina
Harbour Lights Picturehouse
Obelisk Road
Woolston
Victoria Rd.
John Thornycroft Way
Woodley Rd.
Hythe 12mins. West Cowes 22mins. (Fast Ferry)
East Cowes 55mins.
To QEII Cruise Terminal
To National Oceanography Centre

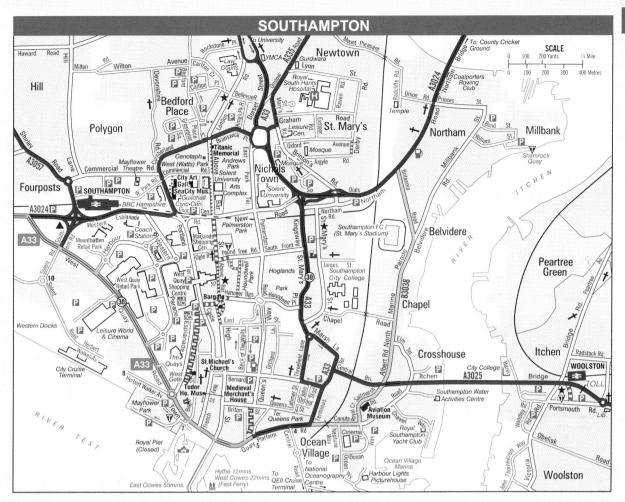

STIRLING

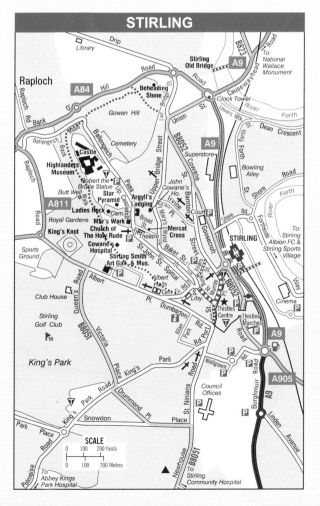

STOKE-ON-TRENT

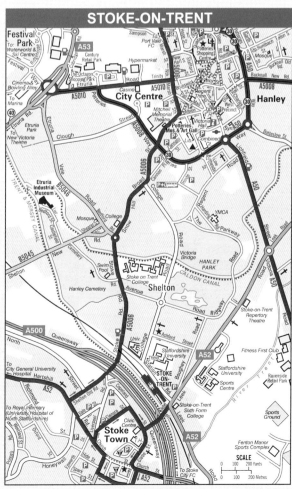

STRATFORD upon AVON

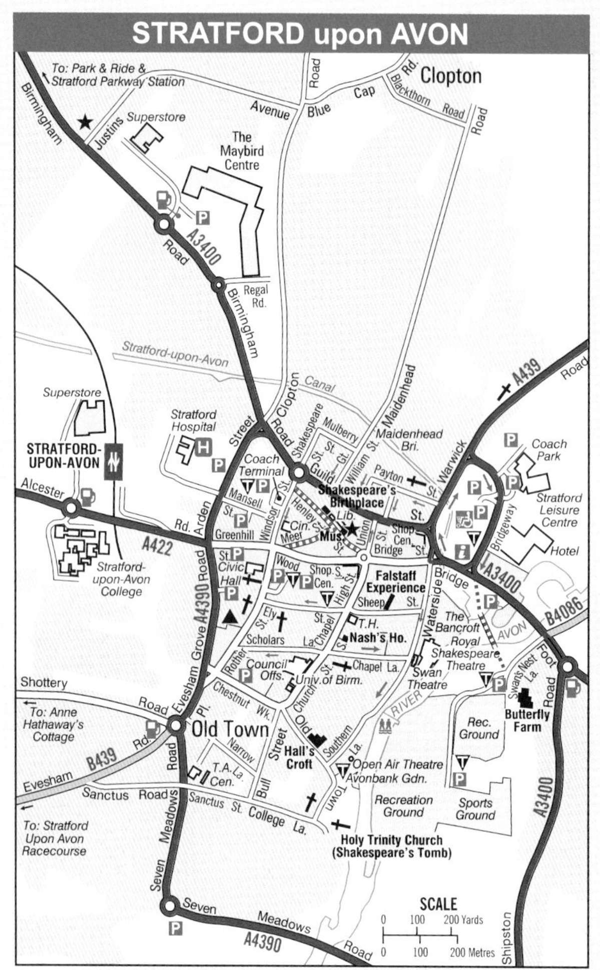

SUNDERLAND

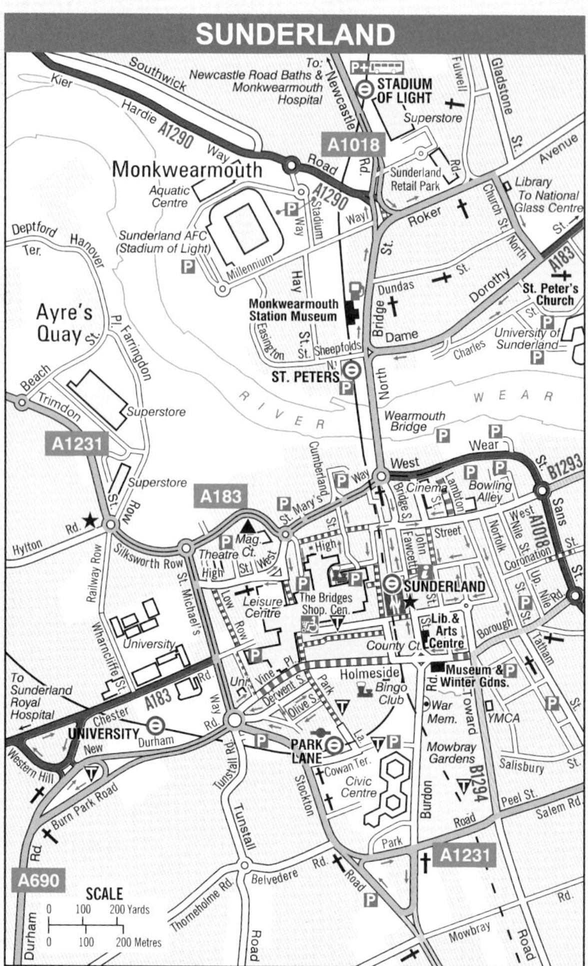

SWANSEA (ABERTAWE)

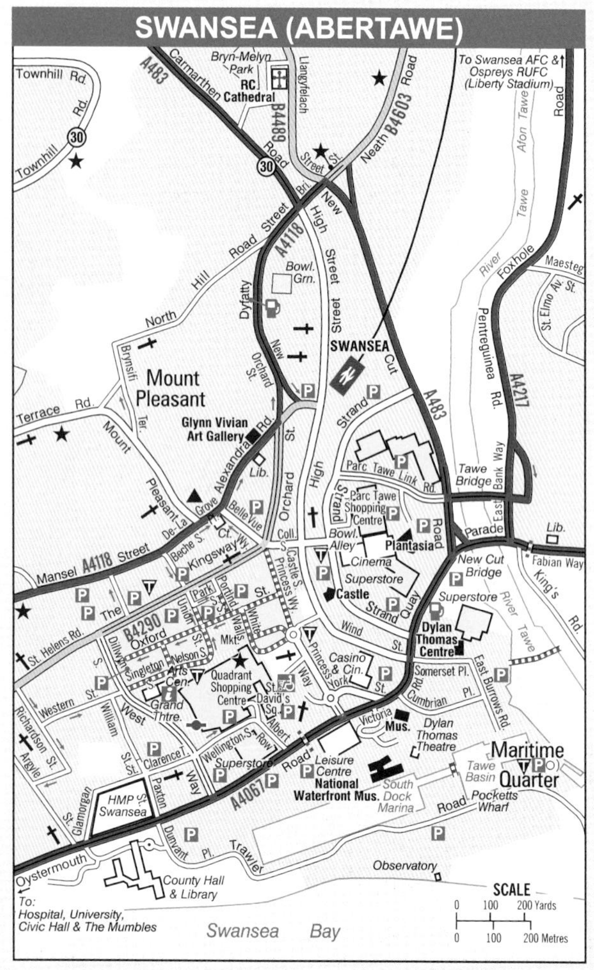

SWINDON

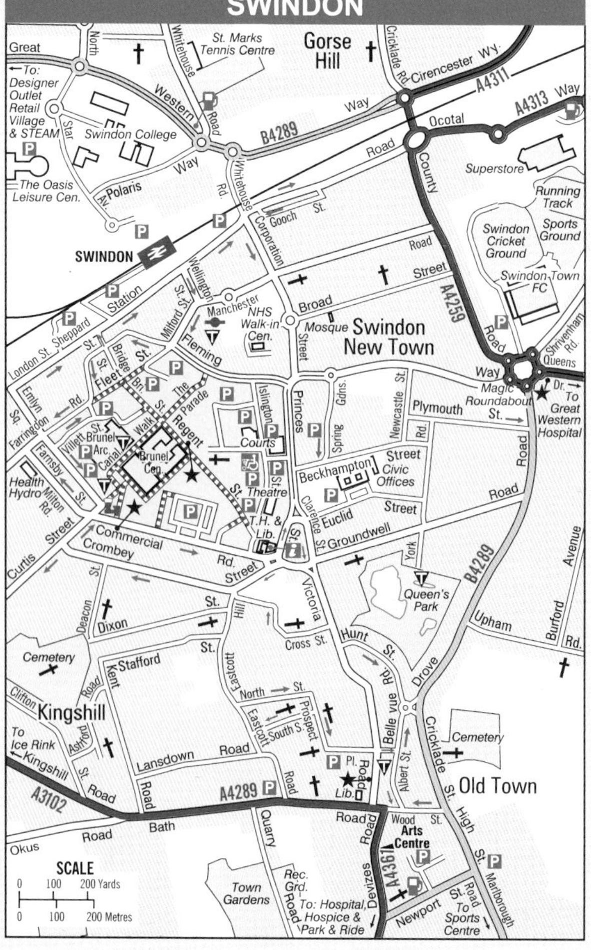

TAUNTON

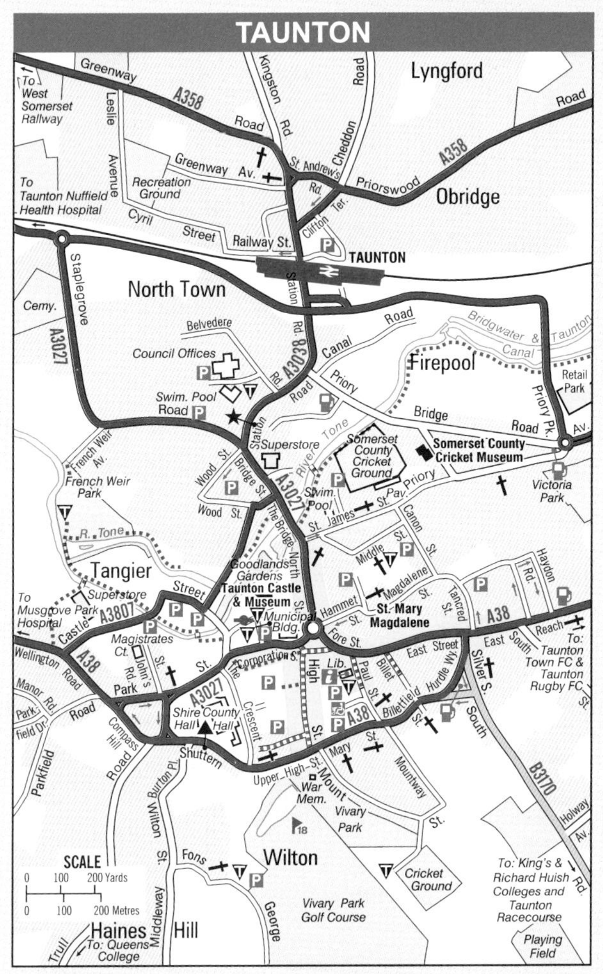
Lyngford
Obridge
TAUNTON
North Town
Firepool
Tangier
Wilton
Haines
Hill
To West Somerset Railway
To Taunton Nuffield Health Hospital
Greenway
Greenway Av.
Leslie Avenue
Recreation Ground
Cyril Street
Railway St.
Kingston Rd
Cheddon Road
Priorswood Road
Staplegrove Road
Cemy.
Belvedere
Council Offices
Swim. Pool Road
Superstore
Somerset County Cricket Ground
Somerset County Cricket Museum
Bridgwater & Taunton Canal
Priory Bridge Road
Priory Pk.
Retail Park
Victoria Park
French Weir Av.
French Weir Park
Wood St.
R. Tone
Goodlands Gardens
Taunton Castle & Museum
Municipal Bldg.
St. Mary Magdalene
To Musgrove Park Hospital
Castle
Magistrates Ct.
Wellington Road
Shire County Hall
Corporation St.
East Street
South Rd.
To: Taunton Town FC & Taunton Rugby FC
Shuttern
Upper High St.
War Mem.
Vivary Park
Mount
Cricket Ground
Vivary Park Golf Course
To: King's & Richard Huish Colleges and Taunton Racecourse
Playing Field
To: Queens College
Trull
Middleway
Parkfield
Fons George
SCALE
0 100 200 Yards
0 100 200 Metres

WINCHESTER

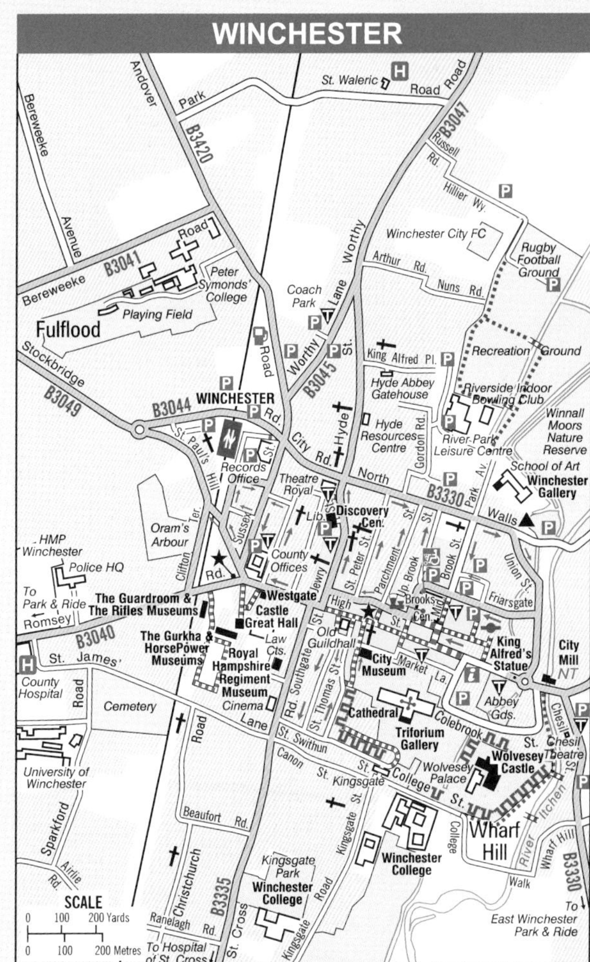
St. Waleric
Andover Road
Bereweeke Avenue
Park Road
B3420
B3041
Peter Symonds' College
Playing Field
Fulflood
Winchester City FC
Rugby Football Ground
Coach Park
Worthy Lane
Hyde Abbey Gatehouse
Hyde Resources Centre
Riverside Indoor Bowling Club
River Park Leisure Centre
Recreation Ground
Winnall Moors Nature Reserve
School of Art
Winchester Gallery
WINCHESTER
Stockbridge
B3049
B3044
Records Office
Theatre Royal
Discovery Cen.
HMP Winchester
Police HQ
Oram's Arbour
To Park & Ride
Romsey
The Guardroom & The Rifles Museums
Westgate
Castle Great Hall
The Gurkha & HorsePower Museums
Royal Hampshire Regiment Museum
Law Cts.
Old Guildhall
City Museum
King Alfred's Statue
City Mill
Abbey Gds.
Cathedral
Triforium Gallery
Wolvesey Castle
Wolvesey Palace
Theatre
County Hospital
Cemetery
University of Winchester
Sparkford
Christchurch
Kingsgate Park
Winchester College
Wharf Hill
B3335
B3330
East Winchester Park & Ride
To Hospital of St. Cross
SCALE
0 100 200 Yards
0 100 200 Metres

WINDSOR

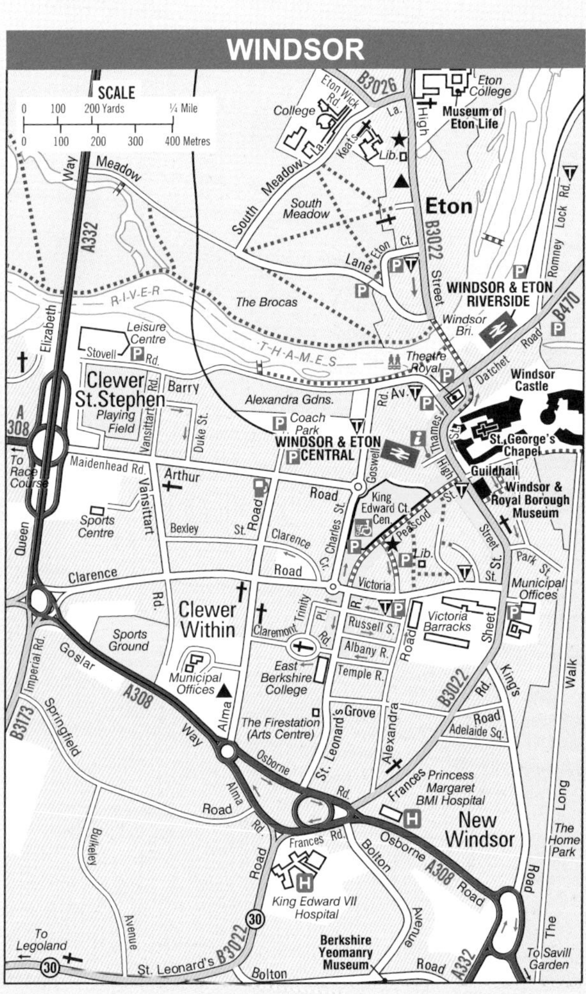
SCALE
0 100 200 Yards ¼ Mile
0 100 200 300 400 Metres
Eton College
Museum of Eton Life
Eton
B3026
B3022
South Meadow
The Brocas
R-I-V-E-R T-H-A-M-E-S
WINDSOR & ETON RIVERSIDE
Windsor Bri.
Theatre Royal
Leisure Centre
Clewer St.Stephen
Playing Field
Alexandra Gdns.
Coach Park
WINDSOR & ETON CENTRAL
Windsor Castle
St. George's Chapel
Guildhall
Windsor & Royal Borough Museum
King Edward Ct. Cen.
Sports Centre
Victoria Barracks
Municipal Offices
Clewer Within
Sports Ground
East Berkshire College
The Firestation (Arts Centre)
A332
A308
Goslar Way
Princess Margaret BMI Hospital
New Windsor
King Edward VII Hospital
Berkshire Yeomanry Museum
To Legoland
To Savill Garden
The Long Walk
To Race Course

WOLVERHAMPTON

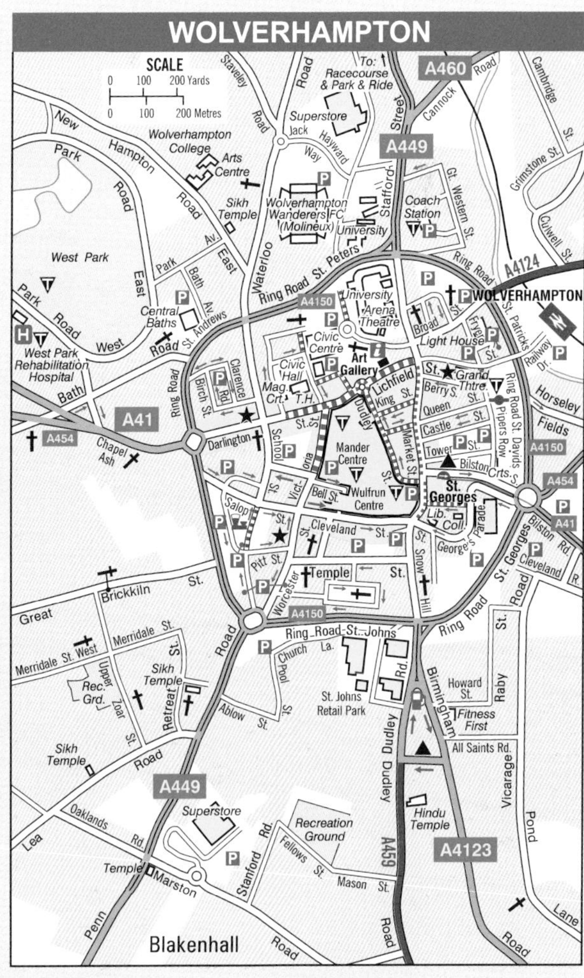
SCALE
0 100 200 Yards
0 100 200 Metres
To: Racecourse & Park & Ride
A460
A449
Superstore
Wolverhampton College
Arts Centre
Sikh Temple
Wolverhampton Wanderers FC (Molineux)
University
Coach Station
West Park
A4124
A4150
University Arena Theatre
WOLVERHAMPTON
West Park Rehabilitation Hospital
Central Baths
Civic Centre
Art Gallery
Light House
Grand Thtre
A41
A454
Mander Centre
Wulfrun Centre
St. Georges
Brickkiln St.
Rec. Grd.
St. Johns Retail Park
Howard
Fitness First
Sikh Temple
Hindu Temple
Superstore
Recreation Ground
A459
A4123
Blakenhall
Penn Road
Temple

WORCESTER

WREXHAM (WRECSAM)

YORK

To Rawcliffe Bar Park & Ride
York City FC Kitkat Crescent
York Hospital
To York Nuffield Health Hospital
To: Monks Cross Park & Ride & York City Knights RLFC
Clifton
Hewarth Golf Course
Clifton Bridge
Bootham Park Hospital
Haxby Rd.
Huntington Rd.
Dodsworth Av.
Malton Rd.
Stockton La.
Heworth Green
Lowther Street
A1036
Sports Ground
Coach Park
Play. Field
B1363
Townend St.
Penley's Grove Street
York St. John University
Lord Mayor's Wk.
Parade
Sports Ground
Bootham
Gillygate
NHS Walk-In Centre
Monkgate
Heworth
Glen Gardens
Melrosegate
Treasurer's House
York Minster
Richard III Mus.
Superstore
Layerthorpe
York Art Gallery
Purey Cust Nuffield Hosp.
St. William's Coll.
Hallfield Rd.
Marygate
King's Manor
Monk Bar
Leeman Road
Yorkshire Museum Gardens
Theatre Royal
Merchant Taylors Hall
Barley Hall
Quilt Museum & Gallery
Play. Fields
National Railway Museum
Lendal Bridge
Baths
Superstore
Foss Islands
Guildhall
Shambles
DIG
St. Nicholas Fields
Cinema
Merchant Adventurers' Hall
Foss Islands Retail Park
YORK
Jorvik Viking Centre
Red Tower
Brewery
Opera Ho.
Dungeon
Fairfax House
Walmgate
Micklegate Bar Museum
Mag. Courts
Reg. Mus.
Clifford's Tower
Walmgate Bar
To Poppleton Park & Ride
Brass Rubbing Cen.
Castle Museum
Raindale Watermill
Fishergate Tower
Lawrence Street
A1079
Hull Rd.
To Grimston Bar Park & Ride
Holgate Road
Cinema
Bar Convent Museum
Baile Hill
Skeldergate Bridge
Paragon St.
York Barbican Centre
A59
Nunnery Lane
Clementhorpe
Kent St.
Heslington Road
Scarcroft Road
Coach Park
Play. Fields
Vine St.
Caravan Park
Clementhorpe
A19
Cemetery Road
Cemetery
A1036
The Mount
Rowntree Park
To Askham Bar Park & Ride
Racecourse
To McArthur Glen Park & Ride
To University
SCALE
0 100 200 Yards ¼ Mile
0 100 200 300 400 Metres

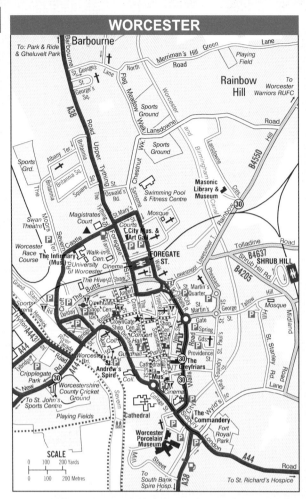

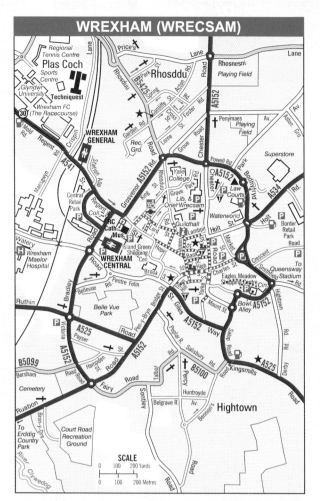

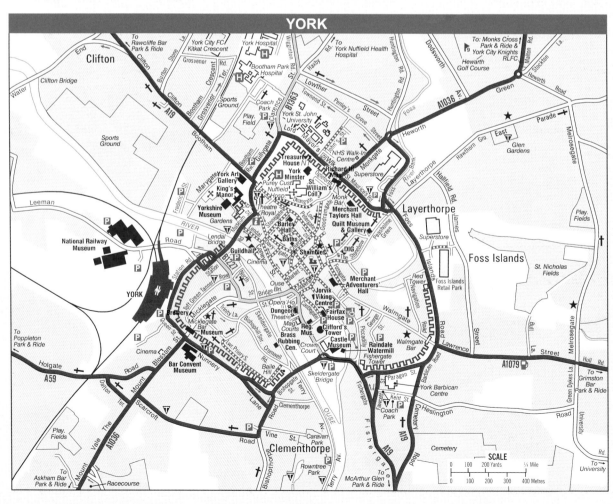

HARWICH

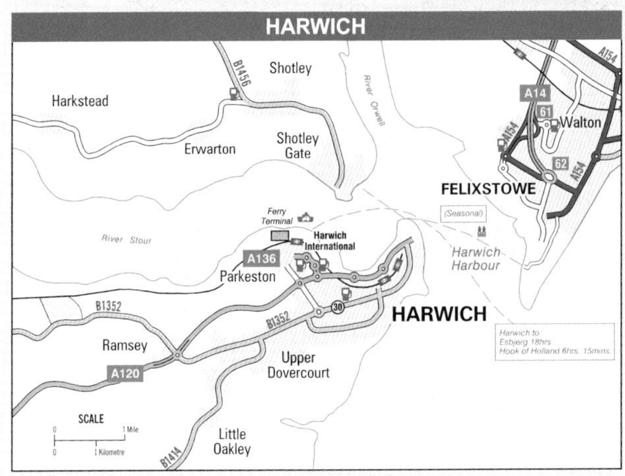

KINGSTON UPON HULL

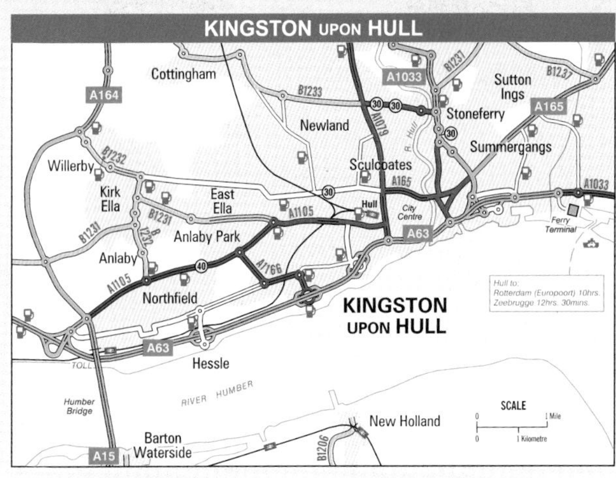

NEWCASTLE UPON TYNE

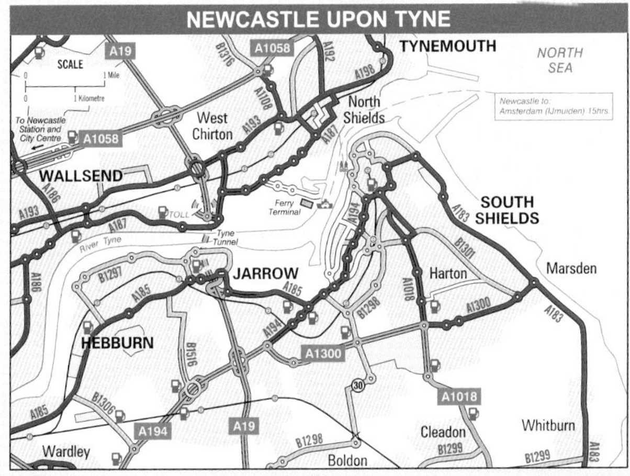

NEWHAVEN

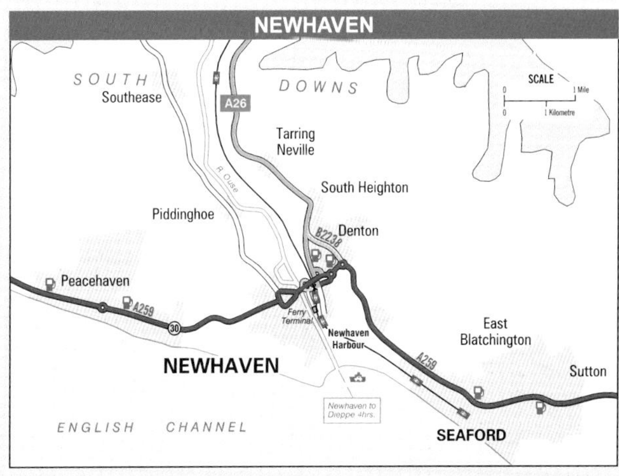

PEMBROKE DOCK (DOC PENFRO)

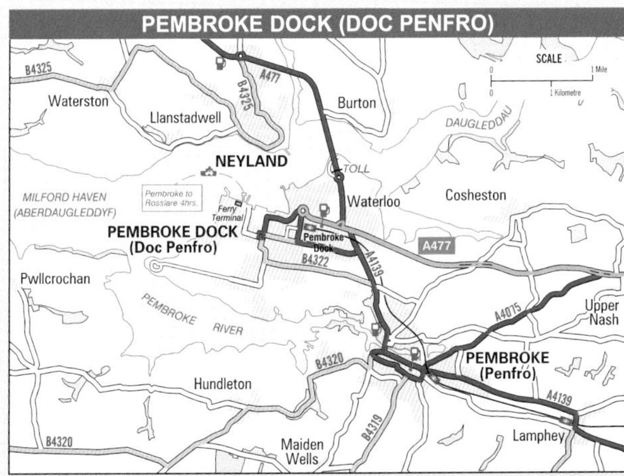

POOLE

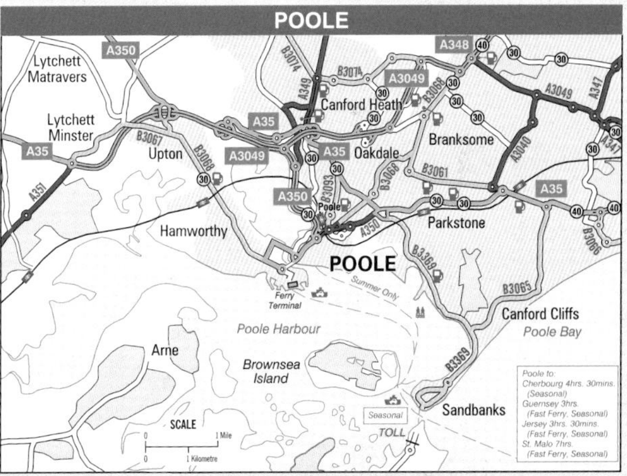

PORTSMOUTH

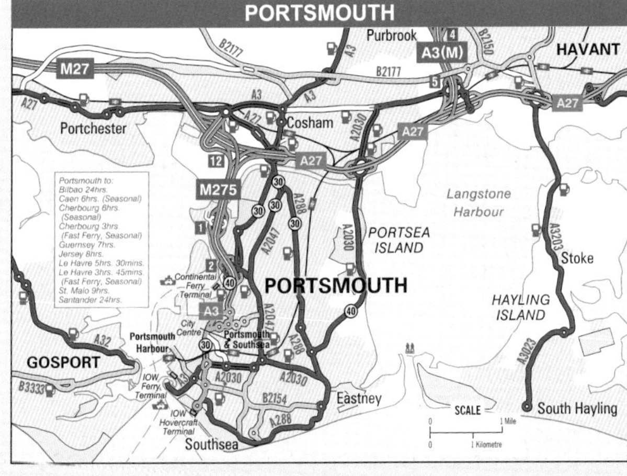

WEYMOUTH

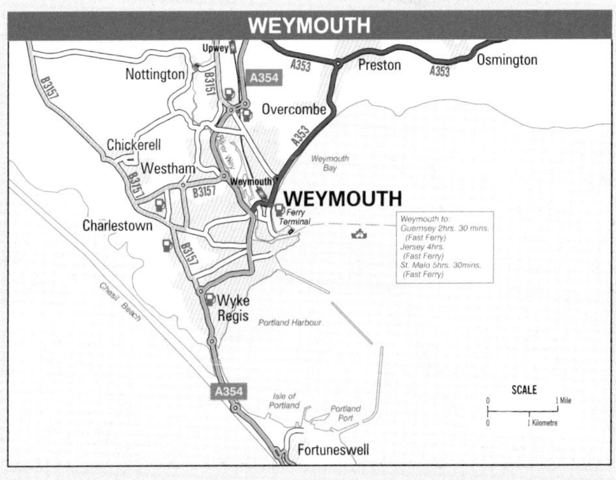

BIRMINGHAM

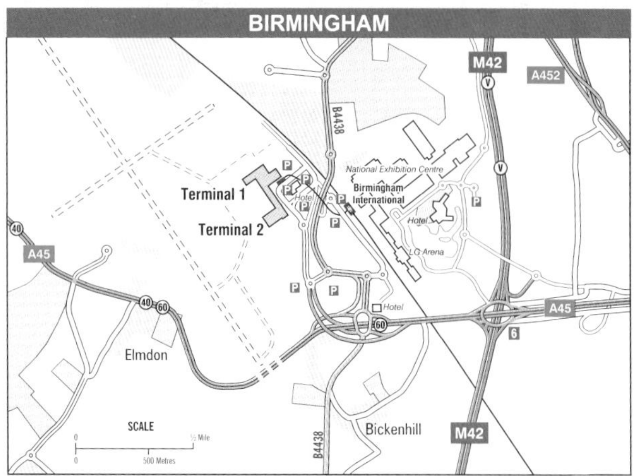

EAST MIDLANDS

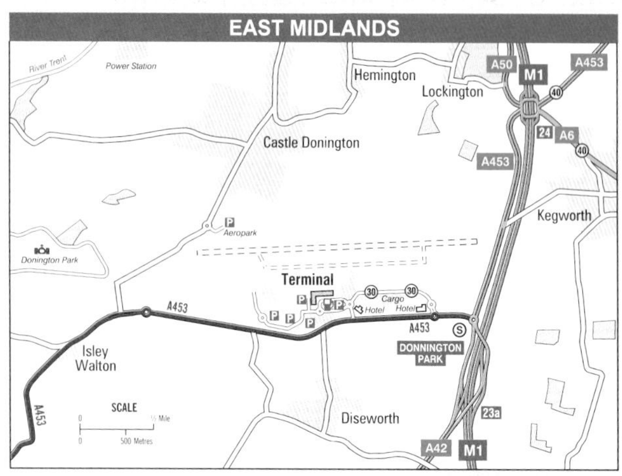

GLASGOW

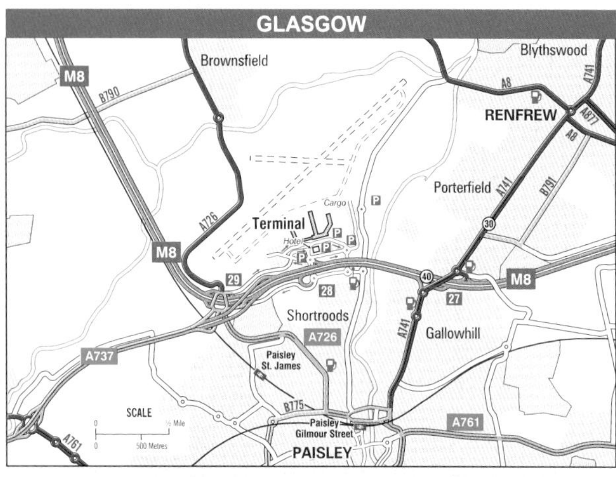

LONDON GATWICK

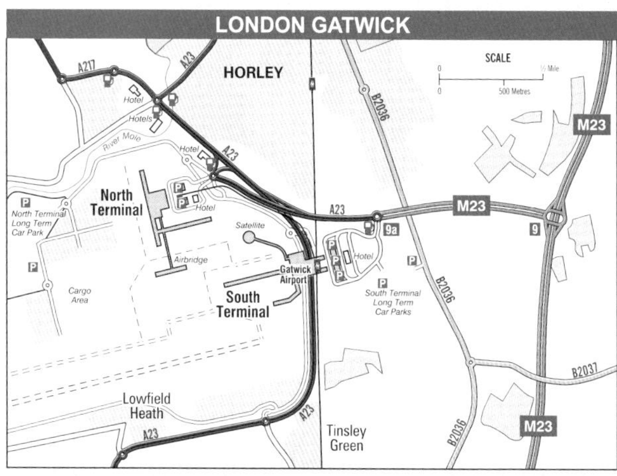

LONDON HEATHROW

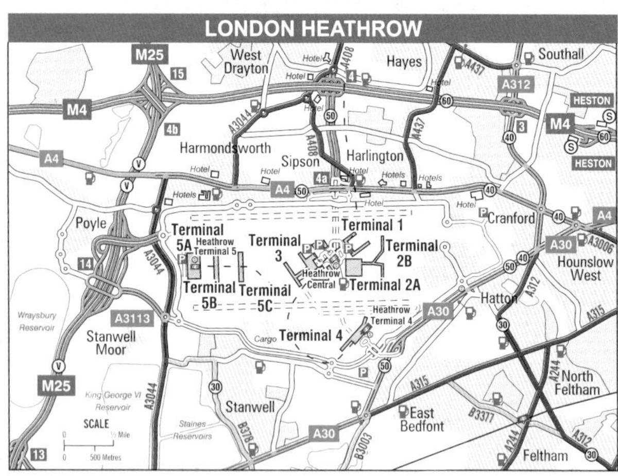

LONDON LUTON

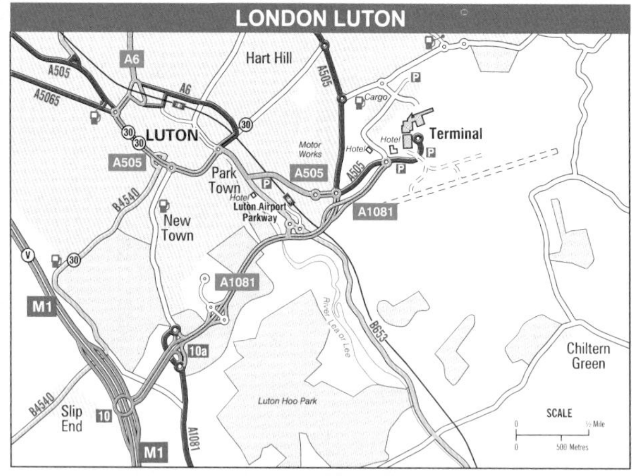

LONDON STANSTED

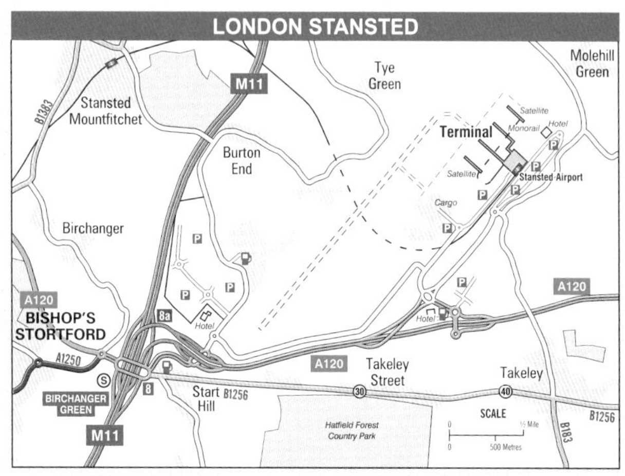

MANCHESTER INTERNATIONAL

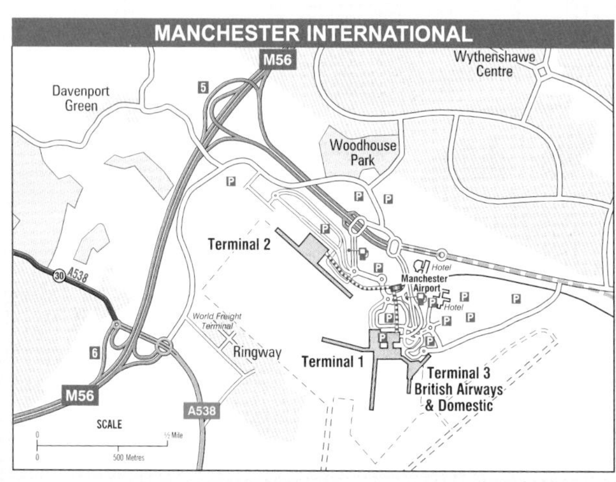

INDEX TO CITIES, TOWNS, VILLAGES, HAMLETS, LOCATIONS, AIRPORTS & PORTS

(1) A strict alphabetical order is used e.g. An Dùnan follows Andreas but precedes Andwell.

(2) The map reference given refers to the actual map square in which the town spot or built-up area is located and not to the place name.

(3) Major towns and destinations are shown in bold, i.e. **Aberdeen.** *Aber* . . . .3G **153** & **187**
Where they appear on a Town Plan a second page reference is given.

(4) Where two or more places of the same name occur in the same County or Unitary Authority, the nearest large town is also given; e.g. Achiemore. *High* . . . .2D **166** (nr. Durness) indicates that Achiemore is located in square 2D on page **166** and is situated near Durness in the Unitary Authority of Highland.

(5) Only one reference is given although due to page overlaps the place may appear on more than one page.

COUNTIES and UNITARY AUTHORITIES with the abbreviations used in this index

Aberdeen : *Aber*
Aberdeenshire : *Abers*
Angus : *Ang*
Argyll & Bute : *Arg*
Bath & N E Somerset : *Bath*
Bedford : *Bed*
Blackburn with Darwen : *Bkbn*
Blackpool : *Bkpl*
Blaenau Gwent : *Blae*
Bournemouth : *Bour*
Bracknell Forest : *Brac*
Bridgend : *B'end*
Brighton & Hove : *Brig*
Bristol : *Bris*
Buckinghamshire : *Buck*
Caerphilly : *Cphy*
Cambridgeshire : *Cambs*
Cardiff : *Card*
Carmarthenshire : *Carm*
Central Bedfordshire : *C Beds*
Ceredigion : *Cdgn*
Cheshire East : *Ches E*
Cheshire West & Chester : *Ches W*
Clackmannanshire : *Clac*
Conwy : *Cnwy*
Cornwall : *Corn*
Cumbria : *Cumb*
Darlington : *Darl*
Denbighshire : *Den*

Derby : *Derb*
Derbyshire : *Derbs*
Devon : *Devn*
Dorset : *Dors*
Dumfries & Galloway : *Dum*
Dundee : *D'dee*
Durham : *Dur*
East Ayrshire : *E Ayr*
East Dunbartonshire : *E Dun*
East Lothian : *E Lot*
East Renfrewshire : *E Ren*
East Riding of Yorkshire : *E Yor*
East Sussex : *E Sus*
Edinburgh : *Edin*
Essex : *Essx*
Falkirk : *Falk*
Fife : *Fife*
Flintshire : *Flin*
Glasgow : *Glas*
Gloucestershire : *Glos*
Greater London : *G Lon*
Greater Manchester : *G Man*
Gwynedd : *Gwyn*
Halton : *Hal*
Hampshire : *Hants*
Hartlepool : *Hart*
Herefordshire : *Here*
Hertfordshire : *Herts*
Highland : *High*

Inverclyde : *Inv*
Isle of Anglesey : *IOA*
Isle of Man : *IOM*
Isle of Wight : *IOW*
Isles of Scilly : *IOS*
Kent : *Kent*
Kingston upon Hull : *Hull*
Lancashire : *Lanc*
Leicester : *Leic*
Leicestershire : *Leics*
Lincolnshire : *Linc*
Luton : *Lutn*
Medway : *Medw*
Merseyside : *Mers*
Merthyr Tydfil : *Mer T*
Middlesbrough : *Midd*
Midlothian : *Midl*
Milton Keynes : *Mil*
Monmouthshire : *Mon*
Moray : *Mor*
Neath Port Talbot : *Neat*
Newport : *Newp*
Norfolk : *Norf*
Northamptonshire : *Nptn*
North Ayrshire : *N Ayr*
North East Lincolnshire : *NE Lin*
North Lanarkshire : *N Lan*
North Lincolnshire : *N Lin*
North Somerset : *N Som*

Northumberland : *Nmbd*
North Yorkshire : *N Yor*
Nottingham : *Nott*
Nottinghamshire : *Notts*
Orkney : *Orkn*
Oxfordshire : *Oxon*
Pembrokeshire : *Pemb*
Perth & Kinross : *Per*
Peterborough : *Pet*
Plymouth : *Plym*
Poole : *Pool*
Portsmouth : *Port*
Powys : *Powy*
Reading : *Read*
Redcar & Cleveland : *Red C*
Renfrewshire : *Ren*
Rhondda Cynon Taff : *Rhon*
Rutland : *Rut*
Scottish Borders : *Bord*
Shetland : *Shet*
Shropshire : *Shrp*
Slough : *Slo*
Somerset : *Som*
Southampton : *Sotn*
South Ayrshire : *S Ayr*
Southend-on-Sea : *S'end*
South Gloucestershire : *S Glo*
South Lanarkshire : *S Lan*
South Yorkshire : *S Yor*

Staffordshire : *Staf*
Stirling : *Stir*
Stockton-on-Tees : *Stoc T*
Stoke-on-Trent : *Stoke*
Suffolk : *Suff*
Surrey : *Surr*
Swansea : *Swan*
Swindon : *Swin*
Telford & Wrekin : *Telf*
Thurrock : *Thur*
Torbay : *Torb*
Torfaen : *Torf*
Tyne & Wear : *Tyne*
Vale of Glamorgan, The : *V Glam*
Warrington : *Warr*
Warwickshire : *Warw*
West Berkshire : *W Ber*
West Dunbartonshire : *W Dun*
Western Isles : *W Isl*
West Lothian : *W Lot*
West Midlands : *W Mid*
West Sussex : *W Sus*
West Yorkshire : *W Yor*
Wiltshire : *Wilts*
Windsor & Maidenhead : *Wind*
Wokingham : *Wok*
Worcestershire : *Worc*
Wrexham : *Wrex*
York : *York*

INDEX

Aith—Ashby

Aith. Shet 2H 173 (on Fetlar)
Aith. Shet 6E 173 (on Mainland)
Aithsetter. Shet 8F 173
Akeld. Nmbd 2D 120
Akeley. Buck 2F 51
Akenham. Suff 1E 55
Albaston. Corn 5E 11
Alberbury. Shrp 4F 71
Albert Town. Pemb 3D 42
Albert Village. Leics 4H 73
Albourne. W Sus 4D 26
Albrighton. Shrp 4G 71 (nr. Shrewsbury)
Albrighton. Shrp 5C 72 (nr. Telford)
Alburgh. Norf 2E 67
Albury. Herts 3E 53
Albury. Surr 1B 26
Albyfield. Cumb 4G 113
Alby Hill. Norf 2D 78
Alcaig. High 3H 157
Alcaston. Shrp 2G 59
Alcester. Warw 5E 61
Alciston. E Sus 5G 27
Alcombe. Som 2C 20
Alconbury. Cambs 3A 64
Alconbury Weston. Cambs 3A 64
Aldborough. Norf 2D 78
Aldborough. N Yor 3G 99
Aldbourne. Wilts 4A 36
Aldbrough. E Yor 1F 95
Aldbrough St John. N Yor 3F 105
Aldbury. Herts 4H 51
Aldcliffe. Lanc 3D 96
Aldclune. Per 2G 143
Aldeburgh. Suff 5G 67
Aldeby. Norf 1G 67
Aldenham. Herts 1C 38
Alderbury. Wilts 4G 23
Aldercar. Derbs 1B 74
Alderford. Norf 4D 78
Alderholt. Dors 1G 15
Alderley. Glos 2C 34
Alderley Edge. Ches E 3C 84
Aldermaston. W Ber 5D 36
Aldermaston Soke. W Ber 5E 36
Aldermaston Wharf. W Ber 5E 36
Alderminster. Warw 1H 49
Alder Moor. Staf 3G 73
Aldersey Green. Ches W 5G 83
Aldershot. Hants 1G 25
Alderton. Glos 2E 49
Alderton. Nptn 1F 51
Alderton. Shrp 3G 71
Alderton. Suff 1G 55
Alderton. Wilts 3D 34
Alderton Fields. Glos 2F 49
Alderwasley. Derbs 5H 85
Aldfield. N Yor 3E 99
Aldford. Ches W 5G 83
Aldgate. Rut 5G 75
Aldham. Essx 3C 54
Aldham. Suff 1D 54
Aldingbourne. W Sus 5A 26
Aldingham. Cumb 2B 96
Aldington. Kent 2E 29
Aldington. Worc 1F 49
Aldington Frith. Kent 2E 29
Aldochlay. Arg 4C 134
Aldon. Shrp 3G 59
Aldoth. Cumb 5C 112
Aldreth. Cambs 3D 64
Aldridge. W Mid 5E 73
Aldringham. Suff 4G 67
Aldsworth. Glos 4G 49
Aldsworth. W Sus 2F 17
Aldwark. Derbs 5G 85
Aldwark. N Yor 3G 99
Aldwick. W Sus 3H 17
Aldwincle. Nptn 2H 63
Aldworth. W Ber 4D 36
Alexandria. W Dun 1E 127
Aley. Som 3E 21
Aley Green. C Beds 4A 52
Alfardisworthy. Devn 1C 10
Alfington. Devn 3E 12
Alfold. Surr 2B 26
Alfold Bars. W Sus 2B 26
Alfold Crossways. Surr 2B 26
Alford. Abers 2C 152
Alford. Linc 3D 88
Alford. Som 3B 22
Alfreton. Derbs 5B 86
Alfrick. Worc 5B 60
Alfrick Pound. Worc 5B 60
Alfriston. E Sus 5G 27
Algarkirk. Linc 2B 76
Alhampton. Som 3B 22
Aline Lodge. W Isl 6D 171
Alkborough. N Lin 2B 94
Alkerton. Oxon 1B 50
Alkham. Kent 1G 29
Alkington. Shrp 2H 71
Alkmonton. Derbs 2F 73
Alladale Lodge. High 5B 164
Allaleigh. Devn 3E 9
Allanbank. N Lan 4B 128
Allanton. N Lan 4B 128
Allanton. Bord 4E 131
Allaston. Glos 5B 48
Allbrook. Hants 4C 24
All Cannings. Wilts 5F 35
Allendale Town. Nmbd 4B 114
Allen End. Warw 1F 61
Allenheads. Nmbd 5B 114
Allensford. Dur 5D 115
Allen's Green. Herts 4E 53
Allensmore. Here 2H 47
Allenton. Derb 2A 74
Aller. Som 4H 21
Allerby. Cumb 1B 102
Allercombe. Devn 3D 12
Allerford. Som 2C 20
Allerston. N Yor 1C 100
Allerthorpe. E Yor 5B 100
Allerton. Mers 2G 83
Allerton. W Yor 1B 92
Allerton Bywater. W Yor 2E 93
Allerton Mauleverer. N Yor 4G 99
Allesley. W Mid 2G 61
Allestree. Derb 2H 73
Allet. Corn 4B 6
Allexton. Leics 5F 75
Allgreave. Ches E 4D 84
Allhallows. Medw 3C 40
Allhallows-on-Sea. Medw 3C 40
Alligin Shuas. High 3H 155
Allimore Green. Staf 4C 72
Allington. Kent 5B 40
Allington. Linc 1F 75
Allington. Wilts 3H 23 (nr. Amesbury)
Allington. Wilts 5F 35 (nr. Devizes)
Allithwaite. Cumb 2C 96
Alloa. Clac 4A 136
Allonby. Cumb 5B 112
Allostock. Ches W 3B 84
Alloway. S Ayr 3C 116
Allowenshay. Som 1G 13
All Saints South Elmham. Suff 2F 67
Allscott. Shrp 1B 60
Allscott. Telf 4A 72
All Stretton. Shrp 1G 59
Allt. Carm 5F 45
Alltami. Flin 4E 83
Alltgobhlach. N Ayr 5G 125
Alltmawr. Powy 1D 46
Alltnacaillich. High 4E 167
Allt na h' Airbhe. High 4F 163
Alltour. High 5E 148
Alltsigh. High 2G 149
Alltwalis. Carm 2E 45
Alltwen. Neat 5H 45
Alltyblacca. Cdgn 1F 45
Allt-y-goed. Pemb 1B 44
Almeley. Here 5F 59
Almeley Wooton. Here 5F 59
Almer. Dors 3E 15
Almholme. S Yor 4F 93
Almington. Staf 2B 72
Alminstone Cross. Devn 4D 18
Almodington. W Sus 3G 17
Almondbank. Per 1C 136
Almondbury. W Yor 3B 92
Almondsbury. S Glo 3B 34
Alne. N Yor 3G 99
Alness. High 2A 158
Alnessferry. High 2A 158
Alnham. Nmbd 3D 121
Alnmouth. Nmbd 3G 121
Alnwick. Nmbd 3F 121
Alphamstone. Essx 2B 54
Alpheton. Suff 5A 66
Alphington. Devn 3C 12
Alpington. Norf 5E 79
Alport. Derbs 4G 85
Alport. Powy 1E 59
Alpraham. Ches E 5H 83
Alresford. Essx 3D 54
Alrewas. Staf 4F 73
Alsager. Ches E 5B 84
Alsagers Bank. Staf 1C 72
Alsop en le Dale. Derbs 5F 85
Alston. Cumb 5A 114
Alston. Devn 2G 13
Alstone. Glos 2E 49
Alstone. Som 2G 21
Alstonefield. Staf 5F 85
Alston Sutton. Som 1H 21
Alswear. Devn 4H 19
Altandhu. High 2D 163
Altanduin. High 1F 165
Altarnun. Corn 4C 10
Altass. High 3B 164
Alterwall. High 2E 169
Altgaltraig. Arg 2B 126
Altham. Lanc 1F 91
Althorne. Essx 1D 40
Althorpe. N Lin 4B 94
Altnabreac. High 4C 168
Altnacealgach. High 2G 163
Altnafeadh. High 3G 141
Altnaharra. High 5F 167
Altofts. W Yor 2D 92
Alton. Derbs 4A 86
Alton. Hants 3F 25
Alton. Staf 1E 73
Alton Barnes. Wilts 5G 35
Altonhill. E Ayr 1D 116
Alton Pancras. Dors 2C 14
Alton Priors. Wilts 5G 35
Altrincham. G Man 2B 84
Altrua. High 4E 149
Alva. Clac 4A 136
Alvanley. Ches W 3G 83
Alvaston. Derb 2A 74
Alvechurch. Worc 3E 61
Alvecote. Warw 5G 73
Alvediston. Wilts 4E 23
Alveley. Shrp 2B 60
Alverdiscott. Devn 4F 19
Alverstoke. Hants 3D 16
Alverstone. IOW 4D 16
Alverthorpe. W Yor 2D 92
Alverton. Notts 1E 75
Alves. Mor 2F 159
Alvescot. Oxon 5A 50
Alveston. S Glo 3B 34
Alveston. Warw 5G 61
Alvie. High 3C 150
Alvingham. Linc 1C 88
Alvington. Glos 5B 48
Alwalton. Cambs 1A 64
Alweston. Dors 1B 14
Alwington. Devn 4E 19
Alwinton. Nmbd 4D 120
Alwoodley. W Yor 5E 99
Alyth. Per 4B 144
Amatnatua. High 4B 164
Am Baile. W Isl 7C 170
Ambaston. Derbs 2B 74
Ambergate. Derbs 5H 85
Amber Hill. Linc 1B 76
Amberley. Glos 5D 48
Amberley. W Sus 4B 26
Amble. Nmbd 4G 121
Amblecote. W Mid 2C 60
Ambler Thorn. W Yor 2A 92
Ambleside. Cumb 4E 103
Ambleston. Pemb 2E 43
Ambrosden. Oxon 4E 50
Amcotts. N Lin 3B 94
Amersham. Buck 1A 38
Amerton. Staf 3D 73
Amesbury. Wilts 2G 23
Amisfield. Dum 1B 112
Amlwch. IOA 1D 80
Amlwch Port. IOA 1D 80
Ammanford. Carm 4G 45
Amotherby. N Yor 2B 100
Ampfield. Hants 4B 24
Ampleforth. N Yor 2H 99
Ampleforth College. N Yor 2H 99
Ampney Crucis. Glos 5F 49
Ampney St Mary. Glos 5F 49
Ampney St Peter. Glos 5F 49
Amport. Hants 2A 24
Ampthill. C Beds 2A 52
Ampton. Suff 3A 66
Amroth. Pemb 4F 43
Amulree. Per 5G 143
Amwell. Herts 4B 52
Anaheilt. High 2C 140
An Àird. High 3D 147
An Camus Darach. High 4E 147
Ancaster. Linc 1G 75
Anchor. Shrp 2D 58
Anchorsholme. Bkpl 5C 96
Anchor Street. Norf 3F 79
An Cnoc. W Isl 4G 171
An Cnoc Ard. W Isl 1H 171
An Coroghon. High 3A 146
Ancroft. Nmbd 5G 131
Ancrum. Bord 2A 120
Ancton. W Sus 5A 26
Anderby. Linc 3E 89
Anderby Creek. Linc 3E 89
Anderson. Dors 3D 15
Anderton. Ches W 3A 84
Andertons Mill. Lanc 3D 90
Andover. Hants 2B 24
Andover Down. Hants 2B 24
Andoversford. Glos 4F 49
Andreas. IOM 2D 108
An Dùnan. High 1D 147
Andwell. Hants 1E 25
Anelog. Gwyn 3A 68
Anfield. Mers 1F 83
Angarrack. Corn 3C 4
Angelbank. Shrp 3H 59
Angersleigh. Som 1F 13
Angerton. Cumb 4D 112
Angle. Pemb 4C 42
An Gleann Ur. W Isl 4G 171
Angmering. W Sus 5B 26
Angmering-on-Sea. W Sus 5B 26
Angram. N Yor 5B 104 (nr. Keld)
Angram. N Yor 5H 99 (nr. York)
Anick. Nmbd 3C 114
Ankerbold. Derbs 4A 86
Ankerville. High 1C 158
Anlaby. E Yor 2D 94
Anlaby Park. Hull 2D 94
An Leth Meadhanach. W Isl 7C 170
Anmer. Norf 3G 77
Anmore. Hants 1E 17
Annan. Dum 3D 112
Annaside. Cumb 1A 96
Annat. Arg 1H 133
Annat. High 3A 156
Annathill. N Lan 2A 128
Anna Valley. Hants 2B 24
Annbank. S Ayr 2D 116
Annesley. Notts 5C 86
Annesley Woodhouse. Notts 5C 86
Annfield Plain. Dur 4E 115
Annscroft. Shrp 5G 71
An Sailean. High 2A 140
Ansdell. Lanc 2B 90
Ansford. Som 3B 22
Ansley. Warw 1G 61
Anslow. Staf 3G 73
Anslow Gate. Staf 3F 73
Ansteadbrook. Surr 2A 26
Anstey. Herts 2E 53
Anstey. Leics 5C 74
Anston. S Lan 5D 128
Anstruther Easter. Fife 3H 137
Anstruther Wester. Fife 3H 137
Ansty. Warw 2A 62
Ansty. W Sus 3D 27
Ansty. Wilts 4E 23
An Taobh Tuath. W Isl 9B 171
An t-Aodann Ban. High 3C 154
An t Ath Leathann. High 1E 147
An Teanga. High 3E 147
Anthill Common. Hants 1E 17
Anthorn. Cumb 4C 112
Antingham. Norf 2E 79
An t-Ob. W Isl 9C 171
Anton's Gowt. Linc 1B 76
Antony. Corn 3A 8
An t-Ord. High 2E 147
Antrobus. Ches W 3A 84
Anvil Corner. Devn 2D 10
Anwick. Linc 5A 88
Anwoth. Dum 4C 110
Apethorpe. Nptn 1H 63
Apeton. Staf 4C 72
Apley. Linc 3A 88
Apperknowle. Derbs 3A 86
Apperley. Glos 3D 48
Apperley Dene. Nmbd 4D 114
Appersett. N Yor 5B 104
Appin. Arg 4D 140
Appleby. N Lin 3C 94
Appleby-in-Westmorland. Cumb 2H 103
Appleby Magna. Leics 5H 73
Appleby Parva. Leics 5H 73
Applecross. High 4G 155
Appledore. Devn 3E 19 (nr. Bideford)
Appledore. Devn 1D 12 (nr. Tiverton)
Appledore. Kent 3D 28
Appledore Heath. Kent 2D 28
Appleford. Oxon 2D 36
Applegarthtown. Dum 1C 112
Applemore. Hants 2B 16
Appleshaw. Hants 2B 24
Applethwaite. Cumb 2D 102
Appleton. Hal 2H 83
Appleton. Oxon 5C 50
Appleton-le-Moors. N Yor 1B 100
Appleton-le-Street. N Yor 2B 100
Appleton Roebuck. N Yor 5H 99
Appleton Thorn. Warr 2A 84
Appleton Wiske. N Yor 4A 106
Appletree. Nptn 1C 50
Appletreehall. Bord 3H 119
Appletreewick. N Yor 3C 98
Appley. Som 4D 20
Appley Bridge. Lanc 4D 90
Apse Heath. IOW 4D 16
Apsley End. C Beds 2B 52
Apuldram. W Sus 2G 17
Arabella. High 1C 158
Arasaig. High 5E 147
Arbeadie. Abers 4D 152
Arberth. Pemb 3F 43
Arbirlot. Ang 4F 145
Arborfield. Wok 5F 37
Arborfield Cross. Wok 5F 37
Arborfield Garrison. Wok 5F 37
Arbourthorne. S Yor 2A 86
Arbroath. Ang 4F 145
Arbuthnott. Abers 1H 145
Arcan. High 3H 157
Archargary. High 3H 167
Archdeacon Newton. Darl 3F 105
Archiestown. Mor 4G 159
Arclid. Ches E 4B 84
Arclid Green. Ches E 4B 84
Ardachu. High 3D 164
Ardalanish. Arg 2A 132
Ardaneaskan. High 5H 155
Ardarroch. High 5H 155
Ardbeg. Arg 1C 126 (nr. Dunoon)
Ardbeg. Arg 5C 124 (on Islay)
Ardbeg. Arg 3B 126 (on Isle of Bute)
Ardcharnich. High 5F 163
Ardchiavaig. Arg 2A 132
Ardchonnell. Arg 2G 133
Ardchrishnish. Arg 1B 132
Ardchronie. High 5D 164
Ardchullarie. Stir 2E 135
Ardchyle. Stir 1E 135
Ard-dhubh. High 4G 155
Arddleen. Powy 4E 71
Arddlîn. Powy 4E 71
Ardechive. High 4D 148
Ardeley. Herts 3D 52
Ardelve. High 1A 148
Arden. Arg 1E 127
Ardendrain. High 5H 157
Arden Hall. N Yor 5C 106
Ardens Grafton. Warw 5F 61
Ardentinny. Arg 1C 126
Ardeonaig. Stir 5D 142
Ardersier. High 3B 158
Ardery. High 2B 140
Ardessie. High 5E 163
Ardfern. Arg 3F 133
Ardfernal. Arg 2D 124
Ardfin. Arg 3C 124
Ardgartan. Arg 3B 134
Ardgay. High 4C 164
Ardgour. High 2E 141
Ardheslaig. High 3G 155
Ardindrean. High 5F 163
Ardingly. W Sus 3E 27
Ardington. Oxon 3C 36
Ardlamont House. Arg 3A 126
Ardleigh. Essx 3D 54
Ardler. Per 4B 144
Ardley. Oxon 3D 50
Ardlui. Arg 2C 134
Ardlussa. Arg 1E 125
Ardmair. High 4F 163
Ardmay. Arg 3B 134
Ardminish. Arg 5E 125
Ardmolich. High 1B 140
Ardmore. High 3C 166 (nr. Kinlochbervie)
Ardmore. High 5E 164 (nr. Tain)
Ardnacross. Arg 4G 139
Ardnadam. Arg 1C 126
Ardnagrask. High 4H 157
Ardnamurach. High 4G 147
Ardnarff. High 5A 156
Ardnastang. High 2C 140
Ardoch. Per 5H 143
Ardochy House. High 3E 148
Ardpatrick. Arg 3F 125
Ardrishaig. Arg 1G 125
Ardroag. High 4B 154
Ardross. High 1A 158
Ardrossan. N Ayr 5D 126
Ardshealach. High 2A 140
Ardsley. S Yor 4D 93
Ardslignish. High 2G 139
Ardtalla. Arg 4C 124
Ardtalnaig. Per 5E 142
Ardtoe. High 1A 140
Arduaine. Arg 2E 133
Ardullie. High 2H 157
Ardvasar. High 3E 147
Ardvorlich. Per 1F 135
Ardwell. Dum 5G 109
Ardwell. Mor 5A 160
Arean. High 1A 140
Areley Common. Worc 3C 60
Areley Kings. Worc 3B 60
Arford. Hants 3G 25
Argoed. Cphy 2E 33
Argoed Mill. Powy 4B 58
Aridhglas. Arg 2B 132
Arinacrinachd. High 3G 155
Arinagour. Arg 3D 138
Arisaig. High 5E 147
Ariundle. High 2C 140
Arivegaig. High 2A 140
Arkendale. N Yor 3F 99
Arkesden. Essx 2E 53
Arkholme. Lanc 2E 97
Arkle Town. N Yor 4D 104
Arkley. G Lon 1D 38
Arksey. S Yor 4F 93
Arkwright Town. Derbs 3B 86
Arlecdon. Cumb 3B 102
Arlescote. Warw 1B 50
Arlesey. C Beds 2B 52
Arleston. Telf 4A 72
Arley. Ches E 2A 84
Arlingham. Glos 4C 48
Arlington. Devn 2G 19
Arlington. E Sus 5G 27
Arlington. Glos 5G 49
Arlington Beccott. Devn 2G 19
Armadail. High 3E 147
Armadale. High 3E 147 (nr. Isleornsay)
Armadale. High 2H 167 (nr. Strathy)
Armadale. W Lot 3C 128
Armathwaite. Cumb 5G 113
Arminghall. Norf 5E 79
Armitage. Staf 4E 73
Armitage Bridge. W Yor 3B 92
Armley. W Yor 1C 92
Armscote. Warw 1H 49
Arms, The. Norf 1A 66
Armston. Nptn 2H 63
Armthorpe. S Yor 4G 93
Arncliffe. N Yor 2B 98
Arncliffe Cote. N Yor 2B 98
Arncroach. Fife 3H 137
Arne. Dors 4E 15
Arnesby. Leics 1D 62
Arnicle. Arg 2B 122
Arnisdale. High 2G 147
Arnish. High 4E 155
Arniston. Midl 3G 129
Arnol. W Isl 3F 171
Arnold. E Yor 5F 101
Arnold. Notts 1C 74
Arnprior. Stir 4F 135
Arnside. Cumb 2D 96
Aros Mains. Arg 4G 139
Arpafeelie. High 3A 158
Arrad Foot. Cumb 1C 96
Arram. E Yor 5E 101
Arras. E Yor 5D 100
Arrathorne. N Yor 5E 105
Arreton. IOW 4D 16
Arrington. Cambs 5C 64
Arrochar. Arg 3B 134
Arrow. Warw 5E 61
Arscaig. High 2C 164
Artafallie. High 4A 158
Arthington. W Yor 5E 99
Arthingworth. Nptn 2E 63
Arthog. Gwyn 4F 69
Arthrath. Abers 5G 161
Arthurstone. Per 4B 144
Artington. Surr 1A 26
Arundel. W Sus 5B 26
Asby. Cumb 2B 102
Ascog. Arg 3C 126
Ascot. Wind 4A 38
Ascott-under-Wychwood. Oxon 4B 50
Asenby. N Yor 2F 99
Asfordby. Leics 4E 74
Asfordby Hill. Leics 4E 74
Asgarby. Linc 4C 88 (nr. Horncastle)
Asgarby. Linc 1A 76 (nr. Sleaford)
Ash. Devn 4E 9
Ash. Dors 1D 14
Ash. Kent 5G 41 (nr. Sandwich)
Ash. Kent 4H 39 (nr. Swanley)
Ash. Som 4H 21
Ash. Surr 1G 25
Ashampstead. W Ber 4D 36
Ashbocking. Suff 5D 66
Ashbourne. Derbs 1F 73
Ashbrittle. Som 4D 20
Ashbrook. Shrp 1G 59
Ashburton. Devn 2D 8
Ashbury. Devn 3F 11
Ashbury. Oxon 3A 36
Ashby. N Lin 4B 94

Ashby by Partney—Ballochan

Ashby by Partney. Linc 4D 88
Ashby cum Fenby. NE Lin 4F 95
Ashby de la Launde. Linc 5H 87
Ashby-de-la-Zouch. Leics 4A 74
Ashby Folville. Leics 4E 74
Ashby Magna. Leics 1C 62
Ashby Parva. Leics 2C 62
Ashby Puerorum. Linc 3C 88
Ashby St Ledgars. Nptn 4C 62
Ashby St Mary. Norf 5F 79
Ashchurch. Glos 2E 49
Ashcombe. Devn 5C 12
Ashcott. Som 3H 21
Ashdon. Essx 1F 53
Ashe. Hants 1D 24
Asheldham. Essx 5C 54
Ashen. Essx 1H 53
Ashendon. Buck 4F 51
Ashey. IOW 4D 16
Ashfield. Hants 1B 16
Ashfield. Here 3A 48
Ashfield. Shrp 2H 59
Ashfield. Stir 3G 135
Ashfield. Suff 4E 66
Ashfield Green. Suff 3E 67
Ashfold Crossways. W Sus 3D 26
Ashford. Devn 3F 19
(nr. Barnstaple)
Ashford. Devn 4C 8
(nr. Kingsbridge)
Ashford. Hants 1G 15
Ashford. Kent 1E 28
Ashford. Surr 3B 38
Ashford Bowdler. Shrp 3H 59
Ashford Carbonel. Shrp 3H 59
Ashford Hill. Hants 5D 36
Ashford in the Water. Derbs 4F 85
Ashgill. S Lan 5A 128
Ash Green. Warw 2H 61
Ashgrove. Mor 2G 159
Ashill. Devn 1D 12
Ashill. Norf 5A 78
Ashill. Som 1G 13
Ashingdon. Essx 1C 40
Ashington. Nmbd 1F 115
Ashington. W Sus 4C 26
Ashkirk. Bord 2G 119
Ashlett. Hants 2C 16
Ashleworth. Glos 3D 48
Ashley. Cambs 4F 65
Ashley. Ches E 2B 84
Ashley. Dors 2G 15
Ashley. Glos 2E 35
Ashley. Hants 3A 16
(nr. New Milton)
Ashley. Hants 3B 24
(nr. Winchester)
Ashley. Kent 1H 29
Ashley. Nptn 1E 63
Ashley. Staf 2B 72
Ashley. Wilts 5D 34
Ashley Green. Buck 5H 51
Ashley Heath. Dors 2G 15
Ashley Heath. Staf 2B 72
Ashley Moor. Here 4G 59
Ash Magna. Shrp 2H 71
Ashmanhaugh. Norf 3F 79
Ashmansworth. Hants 1C 24
Ashmansworthy. Devn 1D 10
Ashmead Green. Glos 2C 34
Ashmill. Devn 3D 11
(nr. Holsworthy)
Ash Mill. Devn 4A 20
(nr. South Molton)
Ashmore. Dors 1E 15
Ashmore Green. W Ber 5D 36
Ashorne. Warw 5H 61
Ashover. Derbs 4A 86
Ashow. Warw 3H 61
Ash Parva. Shrp 2H 71
Ashperton. Here 1B 48
Ashprington. Devn 3E 9
Ash Priors. Som 4E 21
Ashreigney. Devn 1G 11
Ash Street. Suff 1D 54
Ashtead. Surr 5C 38
Ash Thomas. Devn 1D 12
Ashton. Corn 4D 4
Ashton. Here 4H 59
Ashton. Inv 2D 126
Ashton. Nptn 2H 63
(nr. Oundle)
Ashton. Nptn 1F 51
(nr. Roade)
Ashton. Pet 5A 76
Ashton Common. Wilts 1E 23
Ashton Hayes. Ches W 4H 83
Ashton-in-Makerfield. G Man 4D 90
Ashton Keynes. Wilts 2F 35
Ashton under Hill. Worc 2E 49
Ashton-under-Lyne. G Man 1D 84
Ashton upon Mersey. G Man 1B 84
Ashurst. Hants 1B 16
Ashurst. Kent 2G 27
Ashurst. Lanc 4C 90
Ashurst. W Sus 4C 26
Ashurst Wood. W Sus 2F 27
Ash Vale. Surr 1G 25
Ashwater. Devn 3D 11
Ashwell. Herts 2C 52
Ashwell. Rut 4F 75
Ashwellthorpe. Norf 1D 66
Ashwick. Som 2B 22
Ashwicken. Norf 4G 77
Ashwood. Staf 2C 60
Askam in Furness. Cumb 2B 96
Askern. S Yor 3F 93
Askerswell. Dors 3A 14
Askett. Buck 5G 51
Askham. Cumb 2G 103
Askham. Notts 3E 87
Askham Bryan. York 5H 99
Askham Richard. York 5H 99
Askrigg. N Yor 5C 104
Askwith. N Yor 5D 98
Aslackby. Linc 2H 75
Aslacton. Norf 1D 66
Aslockton. Notts 1E 75
Aspatria. Cumb 5C 112
Aspenden. Herts 3D 52
Asperton. Linc 2B 76
Aspley Guise. C Beds 2H 51
Aspley Heath. C Beds 2H 51
Aspull. G Man 4E 90
Asselby. E Yor 2H 93
Assington. Suff 2C 54
Assington Green. Suff 5G 65
Astbury. Ches E 4C 84
Astcote. Nptn 5D 62
Asterby. Linc 3B 88
Asterley. Shrp 5F 71
Asterton. Shrp 1F 59
Asthall. Oxon 4A 50
Asthall Leigh. Oxon 4B 50
Astle. High 4E 165
Astley. G Man 4F 91
Astley. Shrp 4H 71
Astley. Warw 2H 61
Astley. Worc 4B 60
Astley Abbotts. Shrp 1B 60
Astley Bridge. G Man 3F 91
Astley Cross. Worc 4C 60
Aston. Ches E 1A 72
Aston. Ches W 3H 83
Aston. Derbs 2F 85
(nr. Hope)
Aston. Derbs 2F 73
(nr. Sudbury)
Aston. Flin 4F 83
Aston. Here 4G 59
Aston. Herts 3C 52
Aston. Oxon 5B 50
Aston. Shrp 1C 60
(nr. Bridgnorth)
Aston. Shrp 3H 71
(nr. Wem)
Aston. S Yor 2B 86
Aston. Staf 1B 72
Aston. Telf 5A 72
Aston. W Mid 1E 61
Aston. Wok 3F 37
Aston Abbotts. Buck 3G 51
Aston Botterell. Shrp 2A 60
Aston-by-Stone. Staf 2D 72
Aston Cantlow. Warw 5F 61
Aston Clinton. Buck 4G 51
Aston Crews. Here 3B 48
Aston Cross. Glos 2E 49
Aston End. Herts 3C 52
Aston Eyre. Shrp 1A 60
Aston Fields. Worc 4D 60
Aston Flamville. Leics 1B 62
Aston Ingham. Here 3B 48
Aston juxta Mondrum. Ches E 5A 84
Astonlane. Shrp 1A 60
Aston le Walls. Nptn 5B 62
Aston Magna. Glos 2G 49
Aston Munslow. Shrp 2H 59
Aston on Carrant. Glos 2E 49
Aston on Clun. Shrp 2F 59
Aston-on-Trent. Derbs 3B 74
Aston Pigott. Shrp 5F 71
Aston Rogers. Shrp 5F 71
Aston Rowant. Oxon 2F 37
Aston Sandford. Buck 5F 51
Aston Somerville. Worc 2F 49
Aston Subedge. Glos 1G 49
Aston Tirrold. Oxon 3D 36
Aston Upthorpe. Oxon 3D 36
Astrop. Nptn 2D 50
Astwick. C Beds 2C 52
Astwood. Mil 1H 51
Astwood Bank. Worc 4E 61
Aswarby. Linc 2H 75
Aswardby. Linc 3C 88
Atcham. Shrp 5H 71
Atch Lench. Worc 5E 61
Athelhampton. Dors 3C 14
Athelington. Suff 3E 66
Athelney. Som 4G 21
Athelstaneford. E Lot 2B 130
Atherfield Green. IOW 5C 16
Atherington. Devn 4F 19
Atherington. W Sus 5B 26
Athersley. S Yor 4D 92
Atherstone. Warw 1H 61
Atherstone on Stour. Warw 5G 61
Atherton. G Man 4E 91
Ath-Tharracail. High 2A 140
Atlow. Derbs 1G 73
Attadale. High 5B 156
Attenborough. Notts 2C 74
Atterby. Linc 1G 87
Atterley. Shrp 1A 60
Atterton. Leics 1A 62
Attleborough. Norf 1C 66
Attleborough. Warw 1A 62
Attlebridge. Norf 4D 78
Atwick. E Yor 4F 101
Atworth. Wilts 5D 34
Auberrow. Here 1H 47
Aubourn. Linc 4G 87
Aucharnie. Abers 4D 160
Auchattie. Abers 4D 152
Auchavan. Ang 2A 144
Auchbreck. Mor 1G 151
Auchenback. E Ren 4G 127
Auchenblae. Abers 1G 145
Auchenbrack. Dum 5G 117
Auchenbreck. Arg 1B 126
Auchencairn. Dum 4E 111
(nr. Dalbeattie)
Auchencairn. Dum 1A 112
(nr. Dumfries)
Auchencarroch. W Dun 1F 127
Auchencrow. Bord 3E 131
Auchendennan. W Dun 1E 127
Auchendinny. Midl 3F 129
Auchengray. S Lan 4C 128
Auchenhalrig. Mor 2A 160
Auchenheath. S Lan 5B 128
Auchenlochan. Arg 2A 126
Auchenmade. N Ayr 5E 127
Auchenmalg. Dum 4H 109
Auchentiber. N Ayr 5E 127
Auchenvennel. Arg 1D 126
Auchindrain. Arg 3H 133
Auchininna. Abers 4D 160
Auchinleck. Dum 2B 110
Auchinleck. E Ayr 2E 117
Auchinloch. N Lan 2H 127
Auchinstarry. N Lan 2A 128
Auchleven. Abers 1D 152
Auchlochan. S Lan 1H 117
Auchlunachan. High 5F 163
Auchmillan. E Ayr 2E 117
Auchmithie. Ang 4F 145
Auchmuirbridge. Per 3E 136
Auchmull. Ang 1E 145
Auchnacree. Ang 2D 144
Auchnafree. Per 5F 143
Auchnagallin. High 5E 159
Auchnagatt. Abers 4G 161
Aucholzie. Abers 4H 151
Auchreddie. Abers 4F 161
Auchterarder. Per 2B 136
Auchteraw. High 3F 149
Auchterderran. Fife 4E 136
Auchterhouse. Ang 5C 144
Auchtermuchty. Fife 2E 137
Auchterneed. High 3G 157
Auchtertool. Fife 4E 136
Auchtertyre. High 1G 147
Auchtubh. Stir 1E 135
Auckengill. High 2F 169
Auckley. S Yor 4G 93
Audenshaw. G Man 1D 84
Audlem. Ches E 1A 72
Audley. Staf 5B 84
Audley End. Essx 2F 53
Audmore. Staf 3C 72
Auds. Abers 2D 160
Aughertree. Cumb 1D 102
Aughton. E Yor 1H 93
Aughton. Lanc 3E 97
(nr. Lancaster)
Aughton. Lanc 4B 90
(nr. Ormskirk)
Aughton. S Yor 2B 86
Aughton. Wilts 1H 23
Aughton Park. Lanc 4C 90
Auldearn. High 3D 158
Aulden. Here 5G 59
Auldgirth. Dum 1G 111
Auldhouse. S Lan 4H 127
Ault a' chruinn. High 1B 148
Aultbea. High 5C 162
Aultdearg. High 2E 157
Aultgrishan. High 5B 162
Aultguish Inn. High 1F 157
Ault Hucknall. Derbs 4B 86
Aultibea. High 1H 165
Aultiphurst. High 2A 168
Aultivullin. High 2A 168
Aultmore. Mor 3B 160
Aultnamain Inn. High 5D 164
Aunby. Linc 4H 75
Aunsby. Linc 2H 75
Aust. S Glo 3A 34
Austerfield. S Yor 1D 86
Austin Fen. Linc 1C 88
Austrey. Warw 5G 73
Austwick. N Yor 3G 97
Authorpe. Linc 2D 88
Authorpe Row. Linc 3E 89
Avebury. Wilts 5G 35
Avebury Trusloe. Wilts 5F 35
Aveley. Thur 2G 39
Avening. Glos 2D 35
Averham. Notts 5E 87
Aveton Gifford. Devn 4C 8
Avielochan. High 2D 150
Aviemore. High 2C 150
Avington. Hants 3D 24
Avoch. High 3B 158
Avon. Hants 3G 15
Avonbridge. Falk 2C 128
Avon Dassett. Warw 5B 62
Avonmouth. Bris 4A 34
Avonwick. Devn 3D 8
Awbridge. Hants 4B 24
Awliscombe. Devn 2E 13
Awre. Glos 5C 48
Awsworth. Notts 1B 74
Axbridge. Som 1H 21
Axford. Hants 2E 24
Axford. Wilts 5H 35
Axminster. Devn 3F 13
Axmouth. Devn 3F 13
Aycliffe Village. Dur 2F 105
Aydon. Nmbd 3D 114
Aykley Heads. Dur 5F 115
Aylburton. Glos 5B 48
Aylburton Common. Glos 5B 48
Ayle. Nmbd 5A 114
Aylesbeare. Devn 3D 12
Aylesbury. Buck 4G 51
Aylesby. NE Lin 4F 95
Aylescott. Devn 1G 11
Aylesford. Kent 5B 40
Aylesham. Kent 5G 41
Aylestone. Leic 5C 74
Aylmerton. Norf 2D 78
Aylsham. Norf 3D 78
Aylton. Here 2B 48
Aylworth. Glos 3G 49
Aymestrey. Here 4G 59
Aynho. Nptn 2D 50
Ayot Green. Herts 4C 52
Ayot St Lawrence. Herts 4B 52
Ayot St Peter. Herts 4C 52
Ayr. S Ayr 2C 116 & 187
Ayres of Selivoe. Shet 7D 173
Ayreville. Torb 2E 9
Aysgarth. N Yor 1C 98
Ayshford. Devn 1D 12
Ayside. Cumb 1C 96
Ayston. Rut 5F 75
Ayton. Bord 3F 131
Aywick. Shet 3G 173
Azerley. N Yor 2E 99

B

Babbacombe. Torb 2F 9
Babbinswood. Shrp 3F 71
Babb's Green. Herts 4D 53
Babcary. Som 4A 22
Babel. Carm 2B 46
Babell. Flin 3D 82
Babingley. Norf 3F 77
Bablock Hythe. Oxon 5C 50
Babraham. Cambs 5E 65
Babworth. Notts 2D 86
Bac. W Isl 3G 171
Bachau. IOA 2D 80
Bacheldre. Powy 1E 59
Bachymbyd Fawr. Den 4C 82
Backaland. Orkn 4E 172
Backaskaill. Orkn 2D 172
Backbarrow. Cumb 1C 96
Backe. Carm 3G 43
Backfolds. Abers 3H 161
Backford. Ches W 3G 83
Backhill. Abers 5E 161
Backhill of Clackriach. Abers 4G 161
Backies. High 3F 165
Backmuir of New Gilston. Fife 3G 137
Back of Keppoch. High 5E 147
Back Street. Suff 5G 65
Backwell. N Som 5H 33
Backworth. Tyne 2G 115
Bacon End. Essx 4G 53
Baconsthorpe. Norf 2D 78
Bacton. Here 2G 47
Bacton. Norf 2F 79
Bacton. Suff 4C 66
Bacton Green. Norf 2F 79
Bacup. Lanc 2G 91
Badachonacher. High 1A 158
Badachro. High 1G 155
Badanloch Lodge. High 5H 167
Badavanich. High 3D 156
Badbury. Swin 3G 35
Badby. Nptn 5C 62
Badcall. High 3C 166
Badcaul. High 4E 163
Baddeley Green. Stoke 5D 84
Baddesley Clinton. W Mid 3G 61
Baddesley Ensor. Warw 1G 61
Baddidarach. High 1E 163
Baddoch. Abers 5F 151
Badenscallie. High 3E 163
Badenscoth. Abers 5E 160
Badentarbat. High 2E 163
Badgall. Corn 4C 10
Badgers Mount. Kent 4F 39
Badgeworth. Glos 4E 49
Badgworth. Som 1G 21
Badicaul. High 1F 147
Badingham. Suff 4F 67
Badlesmere. Kent 5E 40
Badlipster. High 4E 169
Badluarach. High 4D 163
Badminton. S Glo 3D 34
Badnaban. High 1E 163
Badnabay. High 4C 166
Badnagie. High 5D 168
Badnellan. High 3F 165
Badninish. High 4E 165
Badrallach. High 4E 163
Badsey. Worc 1F 49
Badshot Lea. Surr 2G 25
Badsworth. W Yor 3E 93
Badwell Ash. Suff 4B 66
Bae Cinmel. Cnwy 2B 82
Bae Colwyn. Cnwy 3A 82
Bae Penrhyn. Cnwy 2H 81
Bagby. N Yor 1G 99
Bag Enderby. Linc 3C 88
Bagendon. Glos 5F 49
Bagginswood. Shrp 2A 60
Bàgh a Chàise. W Isl 1E 170
Bàgh a' Chaisteil. W Isl 9B 170
Bagham. Kent 5E 41
Baghasdal. W Isl 7C 170
Bagh Mor. W Isl 3D 170
Bagh Shiarabhagh. W Isl 8C 170
Bagillt. Flin 3E 83
Baginton. Warw 3H 61
Baglan. Neat 2A 32
Bagley. Shrp 3G 71
Bagley. Som 2H 21
Bagnall. Staf 5D 84
Bagnor. W Ber 5C 36
Bagshot. Surr 4A 38
Bagshot. Wilts 5B 36
Bagstone. S Glo 3B 34
Bagthorpe. Norf 2G 77
Bagthorpe. Notts 5B 86
Bagworth. Leics 5B 74
Bagwy Llydiart. Here 3H 47
Baildon. W Yor 1B 92
Baildon Green. W Yor 1B 92
Baile. W Isl 1E 170
Baile Ailein. W Isl 5E 171
Baile an Truiseil. W Isl 2F 171
Baile Boidheach. Arg 2F 125
Baile Glas. W Isl 3D 170
Bailemeonach. Arg 4A 140
Baile Mhanaich. W Isl 3C 170
Baile Mhartainn. W Isl 1C 170
Baile MhicPhail. W Isl 1D 170
Baile Mòr. Arg 2A 132
Baile Mor. W Isl 2C 170
Baile nan Cailleach. W Isl 3C 170
Baile Raghaill. W Isl 2C 170
Bailey Green. Hants 4E 25
Baileyhead. Cumb 1G 113
Bailiesward. Abers 5B 160
Bail' Iochdrach. W Isl 3D 170
Baillieston. Glas 3H 127
Bailrigg. Lanc 4D 97
Bail Uachdraich. W Isl 2D 170
Bail' Ur Tholastaidh. W Isl 3H 171
Bainbridge. N Yor 5C 104
Bainsford. Falk 1B 128
Bainshole. Abers 5D 160
Bainton. E Yor 4D 100
Bainton. Oxon 3D 50
Bainton. Pet 5H 75
Baintown. Fife 3F 137
Baker Street. Thur 2H 39
Bakewell. Derbs 4G 85
Bala. Gwyn 2B 70
Balachuirn. High 4E 155
Balbeg. High 5G 157
(nr. Cannich)
Balbeg. High 1G 149
(nr. Loch Ness)
Balbeggie. Per 1D 136
Balblair. High 4C 164
(nr. Bonar Bridge)
Balblair. High 2B 158
(nr. Invergordon)
Balblair. High 4H 157
(nr. Inverness)
Balby. S Yor 4F 93
Balcathie. Ang 5F 145
Balchladich. High 1E 163
Balchraggan. High 4H 157
Balchrick. High 3B 166
Balcombe. W Sus 2E 27
Balcombe Lane. W Sus 2E 27
Balcurvie. Fife 3F 137
Baldersby. N Yor 2F 99
Baldersby St James. N Yor 2F 99
Balderstone. Lanc 1E 91
Balderton. Ches W 4F 83
Balderton. Notts 5F 87
Baldinnie. Fife 2G 137
Baldock. Herts 2C 52
Baldrine. IOM 3D 108
Baldslow. E Sus 4C 28
Baldwin. IOM 3C 108
Baldwinholme. Cumb 4E 113
Baldwin's Gate. Staf 2B 72
Bale. Norf 2C 78
Balearn. Abers 3H 161
Balemartine. Arg 4A 138
Balephetrish. Arg 4B 138
Balephuil. Arg 4A 138
Balerno. Edin 3E 129
Balevullin. Arg 4A 138
Balfield. Ang 2E 145
Balfour. Orkn 6D 172
Balfron. Stir 1G 127
Balgaveny. Abers 4D 160
Balgonar. Fife 4C 136
Balgowan. High 4A 150
Balgown. High 2C 154
Balgrochan. E Dun 2H 127
Balgy. High 3H 155
Balhalgardy. Abers 1E 153
Baliasta. Shet 1H 173
Baligill. High 2A 168
Balintore. Ang 3B 144
Balintore. High 1C 158
Balintraid. High 1B 158
Balk. N Yor 1G 99
Balkeerie. Ang 4C 144
Balkholme. E Yor 2A 94
Ball. Shrp 3F 71
Ballabeg. IOM 4B 108
Ballacannell. IOM 3D 108
Ballacarnane Beg. IOM 3C 108
Ballachulish. High 3E 141
Ballagyr. IOM 3B 108
Ballajora. IOM 2D 108
Ballaleigh. IOM 3C 108
Ballamodha. IOM 4B 108
Ballantrae. S Ayr 1F 109
Ballards Gore. Essx 1D 40
Ballasalla. IOM 4B 108
(nr. Castletown)
Ballasalla. IOM 2C 108
(nr. Kirk Michael)
Ballater. Abers 4A 152
Ballaugh. IOM 2C 108
Ballencrieff. E Lot 2A 130
Ballencrieff Toll. W Lot 2C 128
Ballentoul. Per 2F 143
Ball Hill. Hants 5C 36
Ballidon. Derbs 5G 85
Balliemore. Arg 1B 126
(nr. Dunoon)
Balliemore. Arg 1F 133
(nr. Oban)
Ballieward. High 5E 159
Ballig. IOM 3B 108
Ballimore. Stir 2E 135
Ballingdon. Suff 1B 54
Ballinger Common. Buck 5H 51
Ballingham. Here 2A 48
Ballingry. Fife 4D 136
Ballinluig. Per 3G 143
Ballintuim. Per 3A 144
Balliveolan. Arg 4C 140
Balloan. High 3C 164
Balloch. High 4B 158
Balloch. N Lan 2A 128
Balloch. Per 2H 135
Balloch. W Dun 1E 127
Ballochan. Abers 4C 152

Ballochgoy—Bellerby Camp

Ballochgoy. Arg 3B 126
Ballochmyle. E Ayr 2E 117
Ballochroy. Arg 4F 125
Balls Cross. W Sus 3A 26
Ball's Green. E Sus 2F 27
Ballygown. Arg 4F 139
Ballygrant. Arg 3B 124
Ballymichael. N Ayr 2D 122
Balmacara. High 1G 147
Balmaclellan. Dum 2D 110
Balmacqueen. High 1D 154
Balmaha. Stir 4D 134
Balmalcolm. Fife 3F 137
Balmalloch. N Lan 2A 128
Balmeanach. High 5E 155
Balmedie. Abers 2G 153
Balmerino. Fife 1F 137
Balmerlawn. Hants 2B 16
Balmore. E Dun 2H 127
Balmore. High 4B 154
Balmuir. Ang 5D 144
Balmullo. Fife 1G 137
Balmurrie. Dum 3H 109
Balnaboth. Ang 2C 144
Balnabruaich. High 1B 158
Balnabruich. High 5D 168
Balnacoil. High 2F 165
Balnacra. High 4B 156
Balnacroft. Abers 4G 151
Balnageith. Mor 3E 159
Balnaglaic. High 5G 157
Balnagrantach. High 5G 157
Balnaguard. Per 3G 143
Balnahard. Arg 4B 132
Balnain. High 5G 157
Balnakeil. High 2D 166
Balnaknock. High 2D 154
Balnamoon. Abers 3G 161
Balnamoon. Ang 2E 145
Balnapaling. High 2B 158
Balornock. Glas 3H 127
Balquhidder. Stir 1E 135
Balsall. W Mid 3G 61
Balsall Common. W Mid 3G 61
Balscote. Oxon 1B 50
Balsham. Cambs 5E 65
Balstonia. Thur 2A 40
Baltasound. Shet 1H 173
Balterley. Staf 5B 84
Baltersan. Dum 3B 110
Balthangie. Abers 3F 161
Baltonsborough. Som 3A 22
Balvaird. High 3H 157
Balvaird. Per 2D 136
Balvenie. Mor 4H 159
Balvicar. Arg 2E 133
Balvraid. High 2G 147
Balvraid Lodge. High 5C 158
Bamber Bridge. Lanc 2D 90
Bamber's Green. Essx 3F 53
Bamburgh. Nmbd 1F 121
Bamford. Derbs 2G 85
Bamfurlong. G Man 4D 90
Bampton. Cumb 3G 103
Bampton. Devn 4C 20
Bampton. Oxon 5B 50
Bampton Grange. Cumb 3G 103
Banavie. High 1F 141
Banbury. Oxon 1C 50
Bancffosfelen. Carm 4E 45
Banchory. Abers 4D 152
Banchory-Devenick. Abers 3G 153
Bancycapel. Carm 4E 45
Bancyfelin. Carm 3H 43
Banc-y-ffordd. Carm 2E 45
Banff. Abers 2D 160
Bangor. Gwyn 3E 81
Bangor-is-y-coed. Wrex 1F 71
Bangors. Corn 3C 10
Bangor's Green. Lanc 4B 90
Banham. Norf 2C 66
Bank. Hants 2A 16
Bankend. Dum 3B 112
Bankfoot. Per 5H 143
Bankglen. E Ayr 3E 117
Bankhead. Aber 2F 153
Bankhead. Abers 3D 152
Bankhead. S Lan 5B 128
Bankland. Som 4G 21
Bank Newton. N Yor 4B 98
Banknock. Falk 2A 128
Banks. Cumb 3G 113
Banks. Lanc 2B 90
Bankshill. Dum 1C 112
Bank Street. Worc 4A 60
Bank, The. Ches E 5C 84
Bank, The. Shrp 1A 60
Bank Top. Lanc 4D 90
Banners Gate. W Mid 1E 61
Banningham. Norf 3E 78
Banniskirk. High 3D 168
Bannister Green. Essx 3G 53
Bannockburn. Stir 4H 135
Banstead. Surr 5D 38
Bantham. Devn 4C 8
Banton. N Lan 2A 128
Banwell. N Som 1G 21
Banyard's Green. Suff 3F 67
Bapchild. Kent 4D 40
Bapton. Wilts 3E 23
Barabhas. W Isl 2F 171
Barabhas Iarach. W Isl 3F 171
Baramore. High 1A 140
Barassie. S Ayr 1C 116
Baravullin. Arg 4D 140
Barbaraville. High 1B 158
Barber Booth. Derbs 2F 85
Barber Green. Cumb 1C 96
Barbhas Uarach. W Isl 2F 171
Barbieston. S Ayr 3D 116
Barbon. Cumb 1F 97
Barbourne. Worc 5C 60
Barbridge. Ches E 5A 84
Barbrook. Devn 2H 19
Barby. Nptn 3C 62
Barby Nortoft. Nptn 3C 62
Barcaldine. Arg 4D 140
Barcheston. Warw 1A 50
Barclose. Cumb 3F 113
Barcombe. E Sus 4F 27
Barcombe Cross. E Sus 4F 27
Barden. N Yor 5E 105
Barden Scale. N Yor 4C 98
Bardfield End Green. Essx 2G 53
Bardfield Saling. Essx 3G 53
Bardister. Shet 4E 173
Bardnabeinne. High 4E 164
Bardney. Linc 4A 88
Bardon. Leics 4B 74
Bardon Mill. Nmbd 3A 114
Bardowie. E Dun 2G 127
Bardrainney. Inv 2E 127
Bardsea. Cumb 2C 96
Bardsey. W Yor 5F 99
Bardsley. G Man 4H 91
Bardwell. Suff 3B 66
Bare. Lanc 3D 96
Barelees. Nmbd 1C 120
Barewood. Here 5F 59
Barford. Hants 3G 25
Barford. Norf 5D 78
Barford. Warw 4G 61
Barford St John. Oxon 2C 50
Barford St Martin. Wilts 3F 23
Barford St Michael. Oxon 2C 50
Barfrestone. Kent 5G 41
Bargeddie. N Lan 3A 128
Bargod. Cphy 2E 33
Bargoed. Cphy 2E 33
Bargrennan. Dum 2A 110
Barham. Cambs 3A 64
Barham. Kent 5G 41
Barham. Suff 5D 66
Barharrow. Dum 4D 110
Bar Hill. Cambs 4C 64
Barholm. Linc 4H 75
Barkby. Leics 4D 74
Barkestone-le-Vale. Leics 2E 75
Barkham. Wok 5F 37
Barking. G Lon 2F 39
Barking. Suff 5C 66
Barkingside. G Lon 2F 39
Barking Tye. Suff 5C 66
Barkisland. W Yor 3A 92
Barkston. Linc 1G 75
Barkston Ash. N Yor 1E 93
Barkway. Herts 2D 53
Barlanark. Glas 3H 127
Barlaston. Staf 2C 72
Barlavington. W Sus 4A 26
Barlborough. Derbs 3B 86
Barlby. N Yor 1G 93
Barlestone. Leics 5B 74
Barley. Herts 2D 53
Barley. Lanc 5H 97
Barley Mow. Tyne 4F 115
Barleythorpe. Rut 5F 75
Barling. Essx 2D 40
Barlings. Linc 3H 87
Barlow. Derbs 3H 85
Barlow. N Yor 2G 93
Barlow. Tyne 3E 115
Barmby Moor. E Yor 5B 100
Barmby on the Marsh. E Yor 2G 93
Barmer. Norf 2H 77
Barming. Kent 5B 40
Barming Heath. Kent 5B 40
Barmoor. Nmbd 1E 121
Barmouth. Gwyn 4F 69
Barmpton. Darl 3A 106
Barmston. E Yor 4F 101
Barmulloch. Glas 3H 127
Barnack. Pet 5H 75
Barnacle. Warw 2A 62
Barnard Castle. Dur 3D 104
Barnard Gate. Oxon 4C 50
Barnardiston. Suff 1H 53
Barnbarroch. Dum 4F 111
Barnburgh. S Yor 4E 93
Barnby. Suff 2G 67
Barnby Dun. S Yor 4G 93
Barnby in the Willows. Notts 5F 87
Barnby Moor. Notts 2D 86
Barnes. G Lon 3D 38
Barnes Street. Kent 1H 27
Barnet. G Lon 1D 38
Barnetby le Wold. N Lin 4D 94
Barney. Norf 2B 78
Barnham. Suff 3A 66
Barnham. W Sus 5A 26
Barnham Broom. Norf 5C 78
Barnhead. Ang 3F 145
Barnhill. D'dee 5D 145
Barnhill. Mor 3F 159
Barnhill. Per 1D 136
Barnhills. Dum 2E 109
Barningham. Dur 3D 105
Barningham. Suff 3B 66
Barnoldby le Beck. NE Lin 4F 95
Barnoldswick. Lanc 5A 98
Barns Green. W Sus 3C 26
Barnsley. Glos 5F 49
Barnsley. Shrp 1B 60
Barnsley. S Yor 4D 92
Barnstaple. Devn 3F 19
Barnston. Essx 4G 53
Barnston. Mers 2E 83
Barnstone. Notts 2E 75
Barnt Green. Worc 3E 61
Barnton. Ches W 3A 84
Barnwell. Cambs 5D 64
Barnwell. Nptn 2H 63
Barnwood. Glos 4D 48
Barons Cross. Here 5G 59
Barony, The. Orkn 5B 172
Barr. Dum 4G 117
Barr. S Ayr 5B 116
Barra Airport. W Isl 8C 170
Barrachan. Dum 5A 110
Barraglom. W Isl 4D 171
Barrahormid. Arg 1F 125
Barrapol. Arg 4A 138
Barrasford. Nmbd 2C 114
Barravullin. Arg 3F 133
Barregarrow. IOM 3C 108
Barrhead. E Ren 4G 127
Barrhill. S Ayr 1H 109
Barri. V Glam 5E 32
Barrington. Cambs 1D 53
Barrington. Som 1G 13
Barripper. Corn 3D 4
Barrmill. N Ayr 4E 127
Barrock. High 1E 169
Barrow. Lanc 1F 91
Barrow. Rut 4F 75
Barrow. Shrp 5A 72
Barrow. Som 3C 22
Barrow. Suff 4G 65
Barroway Drove. Norf 5E 77
Barrow Bridge. G Man 3E 91
Barrowburn. Nmbd 3C 120
Barrowby. Linc 2F 75
Barrowcliff. N Yor 1E 101
Barrow Common. N Som 5A 34
Barrowden. Rut 5G 75
Barrowford. Lanc 1G 91
Barrow Gurney. N Som 5A 34
Barrow Haven. N Lin 2D 94
Barrow Hill. Derbs 3B 86
Barrow-in-Furness. Cumb 3B 96
Barrow Nook. Lanc 4C 90
Barrows Green. Cumb 1E 97
Barrow's Green. Hal 2H 83
Barrow Street. Wilts 3D 22
Barrow upon Humber. N Lin 2D 94
Barrow upon Soar. Leics 4C 74
Barrow upon Trent. Derbs 3A 74
Barry. Ang 5E 145
Barry. V Glam 5E 32
Barry Island. V Glam 5E 32
Barsby. Leics 4D 74
Barsham. Suff 2F 67
Barston. W Mid 3G 61
Bartestree. Here 1A 48
Barthol Chapel. Abers 5F 161
Bartholomew Green. Essx 3H 53
Barthomley. Ches E 5B 84
Bartley. Hants 1B 16
Bartley Green. W Mid 2E 61
Bartlow. Cambs 1F 53
Barton. Cambs 5D 64
Barton. Ches W 5G 83
Barton. Cumb 2F 103
Barton. Glos 3F 49
Barton. IOW 4D 16
Barton. Lanc 4B 90
(nr. Ormskirk)
Barton. Lanc 1D 90
(nr. Preston)
Barton. N Som 1G 21
Barton. N Yor 4F 105
Barton. Oxon 5D 50
Barton. Torb 2F 9
Barton. Warw 5F 61
Barton Bendish. Norf 5G 77
Barton Gate. Staf 4F 73
Barton Green. Staf 4F 73
Barton Hartsthorn. Buck 2E 51
Barton Hill. N Yor 3B 100
Barton in Fabis. Notts 2C 74
Barton in the Beans. Leics 5A 74
Barton-le-Clay. C Beds 2A 52
Barton-le-Street. N Yor 2B 100
Barton-le-Willows. N Yor 3B 100
Barton Mills. Suff 3G 65
Barton on Sea. Hants 3H 15
Barton-on-the-Heath. Warw 2A 50
Barton St David. Som 3A 22
Barton Seagrave. Nptn 3F 63
Barton Stacey. Hants 2C 24
Barton Town. Devn 2G 19
Barton Turf. Norf 3F 79
Barton-under-Needwood. Staf 4F 73
Barton-upon-Humber. N Lin 2D 94
Barton Waterside. N Lin 2D 94
Barugh Green. S Yor 4D 92
Barway. Cambs 3E 65
Barwell. Leics 1B 62
Barwick. Herts 4D 53
Barwick. Som 1A 14
Barwick in Elmet. W Yor 1D 93
Baschurch. Shrp 3G 71
Bascote. Warw 4B 62
Basford Green. Staf 5D 85
Bashall Eaves. Lanc 5F 97
Bashall Town. Lanc 5G 97
Bashley. Hants 3H 15
Basildon. Essx 2B 40
Basingstoke. Hants 1E 25
Baslow. Derbs 3G 85
Bason Bridge. Som 2G 21
Bassaleg. Newp 3F 33
Bassendean. Bord 5C 130
Bassenthwaite. Cumb 1D 102
Bassett. Sotn 1C 16
Bassingbourn. Cambs 1D 52
Bassingfield. Notts 2D 74
Bassingham. Linc 4G 87
Bassingthorpe. Linc 3G 75
Bassus Green. Herts 3D 52
Basta. Shet 2G 173
Baston. Linc 4A 76
Bastonford. Worc 5C 60
Bastwick. Norf 4G 79
Batchley. Worc 4E 61
Batchworth. Herts 1B 38
Batcombe. Dors 2B 14
Batcombe. Som 3B 22
Bate Heath. Ches E 3A 84
Bath. Bath 5C 34 & 187
Bathampton. Bath 5C 34
Bathealton. Som 4D 20
Batheaston. Bath 5C 34
Bathford. Bath 5C 34
Bathgate. W Lot 3C 128
Bathley. Notts 5E 87
Bathpool. Corn 5C 10
Bathpool. Som 4F 21
Bathville. W Lot 3C 128
Bathway. Som 1A 22
Batley. W Yor 2C 92
Batsford. Glos 2G 49
Batson. Devn 5D 8
Battersby. N Yor 4C 106
Battersea. G Lon 3D 39
Battisborough Cross. Devn 4C 8
Battisford. Suff 5C 66
Battisford Tye. Suff 5C 66
Battle. E Sus 4B 28
Battle. Powy 2D 46
Battleborough. Som 1G 21
Battledown. Glos 3E 49
Battlefield. Shrp 4H 71
Battlesbridge. Essx 1B 40
Battlesden. C Beds 3H 51
Battlesea Green. Suff 3E 66
Battleton. Som 4C 20
Battram. Leics 5B 74
Battramsley. Hants 3B 16
Batt's Corner. Surr 2G 25
Bauds of Cullen. Mor 2B 160
Baugh. Arg 4B 138
Baughton. Worc 1D 49
Baughurst. Hants 5D 36
Baulking. Oxon 2B 36
Baumber. Linc 3B 88
Baunton. Glos 5F 49
Baverstock. Wilts 3F 23
Bawburgh. Norf 5D 78
Bawdeswell. Norf 3C 78
Bawdrip. Som 3G 21
Bawdsey. Suff 1G 55
Bawdsey Manor. Suff 2G 55
Bawsey. Norf 4F 77
Bawtry. S Yor 1D 86
Baxenden. Lanc 2F 91
Baxterley. Warw 1G 61
Baxter's Green. Suff 5G 65
Bay. High 3B 154
Baybridge. Hants 4D 24
Baybridge. Nmbd 4C 114
Baycliff. Cumb 2B 96
Baydon. Wilts 4A 36
Bayford. Herts 5D 52
Bayford. Som 4C 22
Bayles. Cumb 5A 114
Baylham. Suff 5D 66
Baynard's Green. Oxon 3D 50
Bayston Hill. Shrp 5G 71
Baythorn End. Essx 1H 53
Baythorpe. Linc 1B 76
Bayton. Worc 3A 60
Bayton Common. Worc 3B 60
Bayworth. Oxon 5D 50
Beach. S Glo 4C 34
Beachampton. Buck 2F 51
Beachamwell. Norf 5G 77
Beachley. Glos 2A 34
Beacon. Devn 2E 13
Beacon End. Essx 3C 54
Beacon Hill. Surr 3G 25
Beacon's Bottom. Buck 2F 37
Beaconsfield. Buck 1A 38
Beacrabhaic. W Isl 8D 171
Beadlam. N Yor 1A 100
Beadnell. Nmbd 2G 121
Beaford. Devn 1F 11
Beal. Nmbd 5G 131
Beal. N Yor 2F 93
Bealsmill. Corn 5D 10
Beam Hill. Staf 3G 73
Beamhurst. Staf 2E 73
Beaminster. Dors 2H 13
Beamish. Dur 4F 115
Beamond End. Buck 1A 38
Beamsley. N Yor 4C 98
Bean. Kent 3G 39
Beanacre. Wilts 5E 35
Beanley. Nmbd 3E 121
Beaquoy. Orkn 5C 172
Beardwood. Bkbn 2E 91
Beare Green. Surr 1C 26
Bearley. Warw 4F 61
Bearpark. Dur 5F 115
Bearsbridge. Nmbd 4A 114
Bearsden. E Dun 2G 127
Bearsted. Kent 5B 40
Bearstone. Shrp 2B 72
Bearwood. Pool 3F 15
Bearwood. W Mid 2E 61
Beattock. Dum 4C 118
Beauchamp Roding. Essx 5F 53
Beauchief. S Yor 2H 85
Beaufort. Blae 4E 47
Beaulieu. Hants 2B 16
Beauly. High 4H 157
Beaumaris. IOA 3F 81
Beaumont. Cumb 4E 113
Beaumont. Essx 3E 55
Beaumont Hill. Darl 3F 105
Beaumont Leys. Leic 5C 74
Beausale. Warw 3G 61
Beauvale. Notts 1B 74
Beauworth. Hants 4D 24
Beaworthy. Devn 3E 11
Beazley End. Essx 3H 53
Bebington. Mers 2F 83
Bebside. Nmbd 1F 115
Beccles. Suff 2G 67
Becconsall. Lanc 2C 90
Beckbury. Shrp 5B 72
Beckenham. G Lon 4E 39
Beckermet. Cumb 4B 102
Beckett End. Norf 1G 65
Beckfoot. Cumb 1A 96
(nr. Broughton in Furness)
Beck Foot. Cumb 5H 103
(nr. Kendal)
Beckfoot. Cumb 4C 102
(nr. Seascale)
Beckfoot. Cumb 5B 112
(nr. Silloth)
Beckford. Worc 2E 49
Beckhampton. Wilts 5F 35
Beck Hole. N Yor 4F 107
Beckingham. Linc 5F 87
Beckingham. Notts 1E 87
Beckington. Som 1D 22
Beckley. E Sus 3C 28
Beckley. Hants 3H 15
Beckley. Oxon 4D 50
Beck Row. Suff 3F 65
Beck Side. Cumb 1C 96
(nr. Cartmel)
Beckside. Cumb 1F 97
(nr. Sedbergh)
Beck Side. Cumb 1B 96
(nr. Ulverston)
Beckton. G Lon 2F 39
Beckwithshaw. N Yor 4E 99
Becontree. G Lon 2F 39
Bedale. N Yor 1E 99
Bedburn. Dur 1E 105
Bedchester. Dors 1D 14
Beddau. Rhon 3D 32
Beddgelert. Gwyn 1E 69
Beddingham. E Sus 5F 27
Beddington. G Lon 4D 39
Bedfield. Suff 4E 66
Bedford. Bed 1A 52 & 188
Bedford. G Man 4E 91
Bedham. W Sus 3B 26
Bedhampton. Hants 2F 17
Bedingfield. Suff 4D 66
Bedingham Green. Norf 1E 67
Bedlam. N Yor 3E 99
Bedlar's Green. Essx 4F 53
Bedlington. Nmbd 1F 115
Bedlinog. Mer T 5D 46
Bedminster. Bris 4A 34
Bedmond. Herts 5A 52
Bednall. Staf 4D 72
Bedrule. Bord 3A 120
Bedstone. Shrp 3F 59
Bedwas. Cphy 3E 33
Bedwellty. Cphy 5E 47
Bedworth. Warw 2A 62
Beeby. Leics 5D 74
Beech. Hants 3E 25
Beech. Staf 2C 72
Beechcliffe. W Yor 5C 98
Beech Hill. W Ber 5E 37
Beechingstoke. Wilts 1F 23
Beedon. W Ber 4C 36
Beeford. E Yor 4F 101
Beeley. Derbs 4G 85
Beelsby. NE Lin 4F 95
Beenham. W Ber 5D 36
Beeny. Corn 3B 10
Beer. Devn 4F 13
Beer. Som 3H 21
Beercrocombe. Som 4G 21
Beer Hackett. Dors 1B 14
Beesands. Devn 4E 9
Beesby. Linc 2D 88
Beeson. Devn 4E 9
Beeston. C Beds 1B 52
Beeston. Ches W 5H 83
Beeston. Norf 4B 78
Beeston. Notts 2C 74
Beeston. W Yor 1C 92
Beeston Regis. Norf 1D 78
Beeswing. Dum 3F 111
Beetham. Cumb 2D 97
Beetham. Som 1F 13
Beetley. Norf 4B 78
Beffcote. Staf 4C 72
Began. Card 3F 33
Begbroke. Oxon 4C 50
Begdale. Cambs 5D 76
Begelly. Pemb 4F 43
Beggar Hill. Essx 5G 53
Beggar's Bush. Powy 4E 59
Beggearn Huish. Som 3D 20
Beguildy. Powy 3D 58
Beighton. Norf 5F 79
Beighton. S Yor 2B 86
Beighton Hill. Derbs 5G 85
Beinn Casgro. W Isl 5G 171
Beith. N Ayr 4E 127
Bekesbourne. Kent 5F 41
Belaugh. Norf 4E 79
Belbroughton. Worc 3D 60
Belchalwell. Dors 2C 14
Belchalwell Street. Dors 2C 14
Belchamp Otten. Essx 1B 54
Belchamp St Paul. Essx 1A 54
Belchamp Walter. Essx 1B 54
Belchford. Linc 3B 88
Belfatton. Abers 3H 161
Belford. Nmbd 1F 121
Belgrano. Cnwy 3B 82
Belhaven. E Lot 2C 130
Belhelvie. Abers 2G 153
Belhinnie. Abers 1B 152
Bellabeg. Abers 2A 152
Belladrum. High 4H 157
Bellamore. S Ayr 1H 109
Bellanoch. Arg 4F 133
Bell Busk. N Yor 4B 98
Belleau. Linc 3D 88
Belleheiglash. Mor 5F 159
Bell End. Worc 3D 60
Bellerby. N Yor 5E 105
Bellerby Camp. N Yor 5D 105

Bradford Leigh—Brome

Bradford Leigh. Wilts 5D 34
Bradford-on-Avon. Wilts 5D 34
Bradford-on-Tone. Som 4E 21
Bradford Peverell. Dors 3B 14
Bradiford. Devn 3F 19
Brading. IOW 4E 16
Bradley. Ches W 3H 83
Bradley. Derbs 1G 73
Bradley. Glos 2C 34
Bradley. Hants 2E 25
Bradley. NE Lin 4F 95
Bradley. N Yor 1C 98
Bradley. Staf 4C 72
Bradley. W Mid 1D 60
Bradley. W Yor 2B 92
Bradley. Wrex 5F 83
Bradley Cross. Som 1H 21
Bradley Green. Ches W 1H 71
Bradley Green. Som 3F 21
Bradley Green. Warw 5G 73
Bradley Green. Worc 4D 61
Bradley in the Moors. Staf 1E 73
Bradley Mount. Ches E 3D 84
Bradley Stoke. S Glo 3B 34
Bradlow. Here 2C 48
Bradmore. Notts 2C 74
Bradmore. W Mid 1C 60
Bradninch. Devn 2D 12
Bradnop. Staf 5E 85
Bradpole. Dors 3H 13
Bradshaw. G Man 3F 91
Bradstone. Devn 4D 11
Bradwall Green. Ches E 4B 84
Bradway. S Yor 2H 85
Bradwell. Derbs 2F 85
Bradwell. Essx 3B 54
Bradwell. Mil 2G 51
Bradwell. Norf 5H 79
Bradwell-on-Sea. Essx 5D 54
Bradwell Waterside. Essx 5C 54
Bradworthy. Devn 1D 10
Brae. High 5C 162
Brae. Shet 5E 173
Braeantra. High 1H 157
Braefield. High 5G 157
Braefindon. High 3A 158
Braegrum. Per 1C 136
Braehead. Ang 3F 145
Braehead. Dum 4B 110
Braehead. Mor 4G 159
Braehead. Orkn 3D 172
Braehead. S Lan 1H 117
(nr. Coalburn)
Braehead. S Lan 4C 128
(nr. Forth)
Braehoulland. Shet 4D 173
Braemar. Abers 4F 151
Braemore. High 5C 168
(nr. Dunbeath)
Braemore. High 1D 156
(nr. Ullapool)
Brae of Achnahaird. High 2E 163
Brae Roy Lodge. High 4F 149
Braeside. Abers 5G 161
Braeside. Inv 2D 126
Braes of Coul. Ang 3B 144
Braeswick. Orkn 4F 172
Braetongue. High 3F 167
Braeval. Stir 3E 135
Braevallich. Arg 3G 133
Braewick. Shet 6E 173
Brafferton. Darl 2F 105
Brafferton. N Yor 2G 99
Brafield-on-the-Green. Nptn 5F 63
Bragar. W Isl 3E 171
Bragbury End. Herts 3C 52
Bragleenbeg. Arg 1G 133
Braichmelyn. Gwyn 4F 81
Braides. Lanc 4D 96
Braidwood. S Lan 5B 128
Braigo. Arg 3A 124
Brailsford. Derbs 1G 73
Braintree. Essx 3A 54
Braiseworth. Suff 3D 66
Braishfield. Hants 4B 24
Braithwaite. Cumb 2D 102
Braithwaite. S Yor 3G 93
Braithwaite. W Yor 5C 98
Braithwell. S Yor 1C 86
Brakefield Green. Norf 5C 78
Bramber. W Sus 4C 26
Brambledown. Kent 3D 40
Brambridge. Hants 4C 24
Bramcote. Notts 2C 74
Bramcote. Warw 2B 62
Bramdean. Hants 4E 24
Bramerton. Norf 5E 79
Bramfield. Herts 4C 52
Bramfield. Suff 3F 67
Bramford. Suff 1E 54
Bramhall. G Man 2C 84
Bramham. W Yor 5G 99
Bramhope. W Yor 5E 99
Bramley. Hants 1E 25
Bramley. S Yor 1B 86
Bramley. Surr 1B 26
Bramley. W Yor 1C 92
Bramley Green. Hants 1E 25
Bramley Head. N Yor 4D 98
Bramley Vale. Derbs 4B 86
Bramling. Kent 5G 41
Brampford Speke. Devn 3C 12
Brampton. Cambs 3B 64
Brampton. Cumb 2H 103
(nr. Appleby-in-Westmorland)
Brampton. Cumb 3G 113
(nr. Carlisle)
Brampton. Linc 3F 87
Brampton. Norf 3E 78
Brampton. S Yor 4E 93
Brampton. Suff 2G 67
Brampton Abbotts. Here 3B 48
Brampton Ash. Nptn 2E 63
Brampton Bryan. Here 3F 59
Brampton en le Morthen. S Yor 2B 86
Bramshall. Staf 2E 73
Bramshaw. Hants 1A 16
Bramshill. Hants 5F 37
Bramshott. Hants 3G 25
Branault. High 2G 139
Brancaster. Norf 1G 77
Brancaster Staithe. Norf 1G 77
Brancepeth. Dur 1F 105
Branch End. Nmbd 3D 114
Branchill. Mor 3E 159
Brand End. Linc 1C 76
Branderburgh. Mor 1G 159
Brandesburton. E Yor 5F 101
Brandeston. Suff 4E 67
Brand Green. Glos 3C 48
Brandhill. Shrp 3G 59
Brandis Corner. Devn 2E 11
Brandish Street. Som 2C 20
Brandiston. Norf 3D 78
Brandon. Dur 1F 105
Brandon. Linc 1G 75
Brandon. Nmbd 3E 121
Brandon. Suff 2G 65
Brandon. Warw 3B 62
Brandon Bank. Cambs 2F 65
Brandon Creek. Norf 1F 65
Brandon Parva. Norf 5C 78
Brandsby. N Yor 2H 99
Brandy Wharf. Linc 1H 87
Brane. Corn 4B 4
Bran End. Essx 3G 53
Branksome. Pool 3F 15
Bransbury. Hants 2C 24
Bransby. Linc 3F 87
Branscombe. Devn 4E 13
Bransford. Worc 5B 60
Bransgore. Hants 3G 15
Bransholme. Hull 1D 94
Bransley. Shrp 3A 60
Branston. Leics 3F 75
Branston. Linc 4H 87
Branston. Staf 3G 73
Branston Booths. Linc 4H 87
Branstone. IOW 4D 16
Bransty. Cumb 3A 102
Brant Broughton. Linc 5G 87
Brantham. Suff 2E 54
Branthwaite. Cumb 1D 102
(nr. Caldbeck)
Branthwaite. Cumb 2B 102
(nr. Workington)
Brantingham. E Yor 2C 94
Branton. Nmbd 3E 121
Branton. S Yor 4G 93
Branton Green. N Yor 3G 99
Branxholme. Bord 3G 119
Branxton. Nmbd 1C 120
Brassington. Derbs 5G 85
Brasted. Kent 5F 39
Brasted Chart. Kent 5F 39
Bratch, The. Staf 1C 60
Brathens. Abers 4D 152
Bratoft. Linc 4D 88
Brattleby. Linc 2G 87
Bratton. Som 2C 20
Bratton. Telf 4A 72
Bratton. Wilts 1E 23
Bratton Clovelly. Devn 3E 11
Bratton Fleming. Devn 3G 19
Bratton Seymour. Som 4B 22
Braughing. Herts 3D 53
Braulen Lodge. High 5E 157
Braunston. Nptn 4C 62
Braunstone Town. Leic 5C 74
Braunston-in-Rutland. Rut 5F 75
Braunton. Devn 3E 19
Brawby. N Yor 2B 100
Brawl. High 2A 168
Brawlbin. High 3C 168
Bray. Wind 3A 38
Braybrooke. Nptn 2E 63
Brayford. Devn 3G 19
Bray Shop. Corn 5D 10
Braystones. Cumb 4B 102
Brayton. N Yor 1G 93
Bray Wick. Wind 4G 37
Brazacott. Corn 3C 10
Brea. Corn 4A 6
Breach. W Sus 2F 17
Breachwood Green. Herts 3B 52
Breacleit. W Isl 4D 171
Breaden Heath. Shrp 2G 71
Breadsall. Derbs 1A 74
Breadstone. Glos 5C 48
Breage. Corn 4D 4
Breakachy. High 4G 157
Breakish. High 1E 147
Bream. Glos 5B 48
Breamore. Hants 1G 15
Bream's Meend. Glos 5B 48
Brean. Som 1F 21
Breanais. W Isl 5B 171
Brearton. N Yor 3F 99
Breascleit. W Isl 4E 171
Breaston. Derbs 2B 74
Brecais Ard. High 1E 147
Brecais Iosal. High 1E 147
Brechfa. Carm 2F 45
Brechin. Ang 3F 145
Breckles. Norf 1B 66
Brecon. Powy 3D 46
Brecon Beacons. Powy 3C 46
Bredbury. G Man 1D 84
Brede. E Sus 4C 28
Bredenbury. Here 5A 60
Bredfield. Suff 5E 67
Bredgar. Kent 4C 40
Bredhurst. Kent 4B 40
Bredicot. Worc 5D 60
Bredon. Worc 2E 49
Bredon's Norton. Worc 2E 49
Bredwardine. Here 1G 47
Breedon on the Hill. Leics 3B 74
Breibhig. W Isl 9B 170
(on Barra)
Breibhig. W Isl 4G 171
(on Isle of Lewis)
Breich. W Lot 3C 128
Breightmet. G Man 3F 91
Breighton. E Yor 1H 93
Breinton. Here 2H 47
Breinton Common. Here 2H 47
Breiwick. Shet 7F 173
Brelston Green. Here 3A 48
Bremhill. Wilts 4E 35
Brenachie. High 1B 158
Brenchley. Kent 1A 28
Brendon. Devn 2A 20
Brent Cross. G Lon 2D 38
Brent Eleigh. Suff 1C 54
Brentford. G Lon 3C 38
Brentingby. Leics 4E 75
Brent Knoll. Som 1G 21
Brent Pelham. Herts 2E 53
Brentwood. Essx 1H 39
Brenzett. Kent 3E 28
Brereton. Staf 4E 73
Brereton Cross. Staf 4E 73
Brereton Green. Ches E 4B 84
Brereton Heath. Ches E 4C 84
Bressingham. Norf 2C 66
Bretby. Derbs 3G 73
Bretford. Warw 3B 62
Bretforton. Worc 1F 49
Bretherdale Head. Cumb 4G 103
Bretherton. Lanc 2C 90
Brettabister. Shet 6F 173
Brettenham. Norf 2B 66
Brettenham. Suff 5B 66
Bretton. Flin 4F 83
Bretton. Pet 5A 76
Brewer Street. Surr 5E 39
Brewlands Bridge. Ang 2A 144
Brewood. Staf 5C 72
Briantspuddle. Dors 3D 14
Bricket Wood. Herts 5B 52
Bricklehampton. Worc 1E 49
Bride. IOM 1D 108
Bridekirk. Cumb 1C 102
Bridell. Pemb 1B 44
Bridestowe. Devn 4F 11
Brideswell. Abers 5C 160
Bridford. Devn 4B 12
Bridge. Corn 4A 6
Bridge. Kent 5F 41
Bridge. Som 2G 13
Bridge End. Bed 5H 63
Bridge End. Cumb 5D 102
(nr. Broughton in Furness)
Bridge End. Cumb 5E 113
(nr. Dalston)
Bridge End. Linc 2A 76
Bridge End. Shet 8E 173
Bridgefoot. Ang 5C 144
Bridgefoot. Cumb 2B 102
Bridge Green. Essx 2E 53
Bridgehampton. Som 4A 22
Bridge Hewick. N Yor 2F 99
Bridgehill. Dur 4D 115
Bridgemary. Hants 2D 16
Bridgemere. Ches E 1B 72
Bridgemont. Derbs 2E 85
Bridgend. Abers 5C 160
(nr. Huntly)
Bridgend. Abers 5H 161
(nr. Peterhead)
Bridgend. Ang 2E 145
(nr. Brechin)
Bridgend. Ang 4C 144
(nr. Kirriemuir)
Bridgend. Arg 4F 133
(nr. Lochgilphead)
Bridgend. Arg 3B 124
(on Islay)
Bridgend. B'end 3C 32
Bridgend. Cumb 3F 103
Bridgend. Devn 4B 8
Bridgend. Fife 2F 137
Bridgend. High 3F 157
Bridgend. Mor 5A 160
Bridgend. Per 1D 136
Bridgend. W Lot 2D 128
Bridgend of Lintrathen. Ang 3B 144
Bridgeness. Falk 1D 128
Bridge of Alford. Abers 2C 152
Bridge of Allan. Stir 4G 135
Bridge of Avon. Mor 5F 159
Bridge of Awe. Arg 1H 133
Bridge of Balgie. Per 4C 142
Bridge of Brown. High 1F 151
Bridge of Cally. Per 3A 144
Bridge of Canny. Abers 4D 152
Bridge of Dee. Dum 3E 111
Bridge of Don. Aber 2G 153
Bridge of Dun. Ang 3F 145
Bridge of Dye. Abers 5D 152
Bridge of Earn. Per 2D 136
Bridge of Ericht. Per 3C 142
Bridge of Feugh. Abers 4E 152
Bridge of Gairn. Abers 4A 152
Bridge of Gaur. Per 3C 142
Bridge of Muchalls.
Abers 4F 153
Bridge of Oich. High 3F 149
Bridge of Orchy. Arg 5H 141
Bridge of Walls. Shet 6D 173
Bridge of Weir. Ren 3E 127
Bridge Reeve. Devn 1G 11
Bridgerule. Devn 2C 10
Bridge Sollers. Here 1H 47
Bridge Street. Suff 1B 54
Bridgetown. Devn 2E 9
Bridgetown. Som 3C 20
Bridge Town. Warw 5G 61
Bridge Trafford. Ches W 3G 83
Bridgeyate. S Glo 4B 34
Bridgham. Norf 2B 66
Bridgnorth. Shrp 1B 60
Bridgtown. Staf 5D 73
Bridgwater. Som 3G 21
Bridlington. E Yor 3F 101
Bridport. Dors 3H 13
Bridstow. Here 3A 48
Brierfield. Lanc 1G 91
Brierley. Glos 4B 48
Brierley. Here 5G 59
Brierley. S Yor 3E 93
Brierley Hill. W Mid 2D 60
Brierton. Hart 1B 106
Briestfield. W Yor 3C 92
Brigg. N Lin 4D 94
Briggate. Norf 3F 79
Briggswath. N Yor 4F 107
Brigham. Cumb 1B 102
Brigham. E Yor 4E 101
Brighouse. W Yor 2B 92
Brighstone. IOW 4C 16
Brightgate. Derbs 5G 85
Brighthampton. Oxon 5B 50
Brightholmlee. S Yor 1G 85
Brightley. Devn 3G 11
Brightling. E Sus 3A 28
Brightlingsea. Essx 4D 54
Brighton. Brig 5E 27 & 189
Brighton. Corn 3D 6
Brighton Hill. Hants 2E 24
Brightons. Falk 2C 128
Brightwalton. W Ber 4C 36
Brightwalton Green. W Ber 4C 36
Brightwell. Suff 1F 55
Brightwell Baldwin. Oxon 2E 37
Brightwell-cum-Sotwell. Oxon 2D 36
Brigmerston. Wilts 2G 23
Brignall. Dur 3D 104
Brig o' Turk. Stir 3E 135
Brigsley. NE Lin 4F 95
Brigsteer. Cumb 1D 97
Brigstock. Nptn 2G 63
Brill. Buck 4E 51
Brill. Corn 4E 5
Brilley. Here 1F 47
Brimaston. Pemb 2D 42
Brimfield. Here 4H 59
Brimington. Derbs 3B 86
Brimley. Devn 5B 12
Brimpsfield. Glos 4E 49
Brimpton. W Ber 5D 36
Brims. Orkn 9B 172
Brimscombe. Glos 5D 48
Brimstage. Mers 2F 83
Brincliffe. S Yor 2H 85
Brind. E Yor 1H 93
Brindister. Shet 6D 173
(nr. West Burrafirth)
Brindister. Shet 8F 173
(nr. West Lerwick)
Brindle. Lanc 2E 90
Brindley. Ches E 5H 83
Brindley Ford. Stoke 5C 84
Brineton. Staf 4C 72
Bringhurst. Leics 1F 63
Bringsty Common. Here 5A 60
Brington. Cambs 3H 63
Brinian. Orkn 5D 172
Briningham. Norf 2C 78
Brinkhill. Linc 3C 88
Brinkley. Cambs 5F 65
Brinklow. Warw 3B 62
Brinkworth. Wilts 3F 35
Brinscall. Lanc 2E 91
Brinscombe. Som 1H 21
Brinsley. Notts 1B 74
Brinsworth. S Yor 2B 86
Brinton. Norf 2C 78
Brisco. Cumb 4F 113
Brisley. Norf 3B 78
Brislington. Bris 4B 34
Brissenden Green. Kent 2D 28
Bristol. Bris 4A 34 & 189
Bristol International Airport.
N Som 5A 34
Briston. Norf 2C 78
Britannia. Lanc 2G 91
Britford. Wilts 4G 23
Brithdir. Cphy 5E 47
Brithdir. Cdgn 1D 44
Brithdir. Gwyn 4G 69
Briton Ferry. Neat 3G 31
Britwell Salome. Oxon 2E 37
Brixham. Torb 3F 9
Brixton. Devn 3B 8
Brixton. G Lon 3E 39
Brixton Deverill. Wilts 3D 22
Brixworth. Nptn 3E 63
Brize Norton. Oxon 5B 50
Broad Alley. Worc 4C 60
Broad Blunsdon. Swin 2G 35
Broadbottom. G Man 1D 85
Broadbridge. W Sus 2G 17
Broadbridge Heath. W Sus 2C 26
Broad Campden. Glos 2G 49
Broad Chalke. Wilts 4F 23
Broadclyst. Devn 3C 12
Broadfield. Inv 2E 127
Broadfield. Pemb 4F 43
Broadfield. W Sus 2D 26
Broadford. High 1E 147
Broadford Bridge. W Sus 3B 26
Broadgate. Cumb 1A 96
Broad Green. Cambs 5F 65
Broad Green. C Beds 1H 51
Broad Green. Worc 3D 61
(nr. Bromsgrove)
Broad Green. Worc 5B 60
(nr. Worcester)
Broadhaven. High 3F 169
Broad Haven. Pemb 3C 42
Broadheath. G Man 2B 84
Broad Heath. Staf 3C 72
Broadheath. Worc 4A 60
Broadhembury. Devn 2E 12
Broadhempston. Devn 2E 9
Broad Hill. Cambs 3E 65
Broad Hinton. Wilts 4G 35
Broadholm. Derbs 1A 74
Broadholme. Linc 3F 87
Broadlay. Carm 5D 44
Broad Laying. Hants 5C 36
Broadley. Lanc 3G 91
Broadley. Mor 2A 160
Broadley Common. Essx 5E 53
Broad Marston. Worc 1G 49
Broadmayne. Dors 4C 14
Broadmere. Hants 2E 24
Broadmoor. Pemb 4E 43
Broad Oak. Carm 3F 45
Broad Oak. Cumb 5C 102
Broad Oak. Devn 3D 12
Broadoak. Dors 3H 13
(nr. Bridport)
Broad Oak. Dors 1C 14
(nr. Sturminster Newton)
Broad Oak. E Sus 4C 28
(nr. Hastings)
Broad Oak. E Sus 3H 27
(nr. Heathfield)
Broadoak. Glos 4B 48
Broadoak. Hants 1C 16
Broad Oak. Here 3H 47
Broad Oak. Kent 4F 41
Broadrashes. Mor 3B 160
Broads. Norf 5G 79
Broadsea. Abers 2G 161
Broad's Green. Essx 4G 53
Broadshard. Som 1H 13
Broadstairs. Kent 4H 41
Broadstone. Pool 3F 15
Broadstone. Shrp 2H 59
Broad Street. E Sus 4C 28
Broad Street. Kent 1F 29
(nr. Ashford)
Broad Street. Kent 5C 40
(nr. Maidstone)
Broad Street Green. Essx 5B 54
Broad, The. Here 4G 59
Broad Town. Wilts 4F 35
Broadwas. Worc 5B 60
Broadwath. Cumb 4F 113
Broadway. Carm 5D 45
(nr. Kidwelly)
Broadway. Carm 3G 43
(nr. Laugharne)
Broadway. Pemb 3C 42
Broadway. Som 1G 13
Broadway. Suff 3F 67
Broadway. Worc 2G 49
Broadwell. Glos 4A 48
(nr. Cinderford)
Broadwell. Glos 3H 49
(nr. Stow-on-the-Wold)
Broadwell. Oxon 5A 50
Broadwell. Warw 4B 62
Broadwell House. Nmbd 4C 114
Broadwey. Dors 4B 14
Broadwindsor. Dors 2H 13
Broadwoodkelly. Devn 2G 11
Broadwoodwidger. Devn 4E 11
Broallan. High 4G 157
Brobury. Here 1G 47
Brochel. High 4E 155
Brockamin. Worc 5B 60
Brockbridge. Hants 1E 16
Brockdish. Norf 3E 66
Brockencote. Worc 3C 60
Brockenhurst. Hants 2A 16
Brocketsbrae. S Lan 1H 117
Brockford Street. Suff 4D 66
Brockhall. Nptn 4D 62
Brockham. Surr 1C 26
Brockhampton. Glos 3E 49
(nr. Bishop's Cleeve)
Brockhampton. Glos 3F 49
(nr. Sevenhampton)
Brockhampton. Here 2A 48
Brockhill. Bord 2F 119
Brockholes. W Yor 3B 92
Brockhurst. Hants 2D 16
Brocklesby. Linc 3E 95
Brockley. N Som 5H 33
Brockley Corner. Suff 3H 65
Brockley Green. Suff 1H 53
(nr. Bury St Edmunds)
Brockley Green. Suff 5H 65
(nr. Haverhill)
Brockleymoor. Cumb 1F 103
Brockmoor. W Mid 2C 60
Brockton. Shrp 2F 59
(nr. Bishop's Castle)
Brockton. Shrp 5B 72
(nr. Madeley)
Brockton. Shrp 1H 59
(nr. Much Wenlock)
Brockton. Shrp 5F 71
(nr. Pontesbury)
Brockton. Staf 2C 72
Brockton. Telf 4B 72
Brockweir. Glos 5A 48
Brockworth. Glos 4D 49
Brocton. Staf 4D 72
Brodick. N Ayr 2E 123
Brodie. Mor 3D 159
Brodiesord. Abers 3C 160
Brodsworth. S Yor 4F 93
Brogaig. High 2D 154
Brogborough. C Beds 2H 51
Brokenborough. Wilts 3E 35
Broken Cross. Ches E 3C 84
Bromborough. Mers 2F 83
Bromdon. Shrp 2A 60
Brome. Suff 3D 66

Chevithorne—Clwt-y-bont

Chevithorne. Devn 1C 12
Chew Magna. Bath 5A 34
Chew Moor. G Man 4E 91
Chew Stoke. Bath 5A 34
Chewton Keynsham. Bath 5B 34
Chewton Mendip. Som 1A 22
Chichacott. Devn 3G 11
Chicheley. Mil 1H 51
Chichester. W Sus 2G 17
Chickerell. Dors 4B 14
Chickering. Suff 3E 66
Chicklade. Wilts 3E 23
Chicksands. C Beds 2B 52
Chickward. Here 5E 59
Chidden. Hants 1E 17
Chiddingfold. Surr 2A 26
Chiddingly. E Sus 4G 27
Chiddingstone. Kent 1G 27
Chiddingstone Causeway. Kent 1G 27
Chiddingstone Hoath. Kent 1F 27
Chideock. Dors 3H 13
Chidgley. Som 3D 20
Chidham. W Sus 2F 17
Chieveley. W Ber 4C 36
Chignall St James. Essx 5G 53
Chignall Smealy. Essx 4G 53
Chigwell. Essx 1F 39
Chigwell Row. Essx 1F 39
Chilbolton. Hants 2B 24
Chilcomb. Hants 4D 24
Chilcombe. Dors 3A 14
Chilcompton. Som 1B 22
Chilcote. Leics 4G 73
Childer Thornton. Ches W 3F 83
Child Okeford. Dors 1D 14
Childrey. Oxon 3B 36
Child's Ercall. Shrp 3A 72
Childswickham. Worc 2F 49
Childwall. Mers 2G 83
Childwick Green. Herts 4B 52
Chilfrome. Dors 3A 14
Chilgrove. W Sus 1G 17
Chilham. Kent 5E 41
Chilhampton. Wilts 3F 23
Chilla. Devn 2E 11
Chilland. Hants 3D 24
Chillaton. Devn 4E 11
Chillenden. Kent 5G 41
Chillerton. IOW 4C 16
Chillesford. Suff 5F 67
Chillingham. Nmbd 2E 121
Chillington. Devn 4D 9
Chillington. Som 1G 13
Chilmark. Wilts 3E 23
Chilmington Green. Kent 1D 28
Chilson. Oxon 4B 50
Chilsworthy. Corn 5E 11
Chilsworthy. Devn 2D 10
Chiltern Green. C Beds 4B 52
Chilthorne Domer. Som 1A 14
Chilton. Buck 4E 51
Chilton. Devn 2B 12
Chilton. Dur 2F 105
Chilton. Oxon 3C 36
Chilton Candover. Hants 2D 24
Chilton Cantelo. Som 4A 22
Chilton Foliat. Wilts 4B 36
Chilton Lane. Dur 1A 106
Chilton Polden. Som 3G 21
Chilton Street. Suff 1A 54
Chilton Trinity. Som 3F 21
Chilwell. Notts 2C 74
Chilworth. Hants 1C 16
Chilworth. Surr 1B 26
Chimney. Oxon 5B 50
Chimney Street. Suff 1H 53
Chineham. Hants 1E 25
Chingford. G Lon 1E 39
Chinley. Derbs 2E 85
Chinnor. Oxon 5F 51
Chipley. Som 4E 20
Chipnall. Shrp 2B 72
Chippenham. Cambs 4F 65
Chippenham. Wilts 4E 35
Chipperfield. Herts 5A 52
Chipping. Herts 2D 52
Chipping. Lanc 5F 97
Chipping Campden. Glos 2G 49
Chipping Hill. Essx 4B 54
Chipping Norton. Oxon 3B 50
Chipping Ongar. Essx 5F 53
Chipping Sodbury. S Glo 3C 34
Chipping Warden. Nptn 1C 50
Chipstable. Som 4D 20
Chipstead. Kent 5G 39
Chipstead. Surr 5D 38
Chirbury. Shrp 1E 59
Chirk. Wrex 2E 71
Chirmorie. S Ayr 2H 109
Chirnside. Bord 4E 131
Chirnsidebridge. Bord 4E 131
Chirton. Wilts 1F 23
Chisbridge Cross. Buck 3G 37
Chisbury. Wilts 5A 36
Chiselborough. Som 1H 13
Chiseldon. Swin 4G 35
Chiselhampton. Oxon 2D 36
Chiserley. W Yor 2A 92
Chislehurst. G Lon 4F 39
Chislet. Kent 4G 41
Chiswell. Dors 5B 14
Chiswell Green. Herts 5B 52
Chiswick. G Lon 3D 38
Chisworth. Derbs 1D 85
Chitcombe. E Sus 3C 28
Chithurst. W Sus 4G 25
Chittering. Cambs 4D 65
Chitterley. Devn 2C 12
Chitterne. Wilts 2E 23
Chittlehamholt. Devn 4G 19
Chittlehampton. Devn 4G 19
Chittoe. Wilts 5E 35
Chivelstone. Devn 5D 9
Chivenor. Devn 3F 19
Chobham. Surr 4A 38
Cholderton. Wilts 2H 23
Cholesbury. Buck 5H 51
Chollerford. Nmbd 2C 114
Chollerton. Nmbd 2C 114
Cholsey. Oxon 3D 36
Cholstrey. Here 5G 59
Chop Gate. N Yor 5C 106
Choppington. Nmbd 1F 115
Chopwell. Tyne 4E 115
Chorley. Ches E 5H 83
Chorley. Lanc 3D 90
Chorley. Shrp 2A 60
Chorley. Staf 4E 73
Chorleywood. Herts 1B 38
Chorlton. Ches E 5B 84
Chorlton-cum-Hardy. G Man 1C 84
Chorlton Lane. Ches W 1G 71
Choulton. Shrp 2F 59
Chrishall. Essx 2E 53
Christchurch. Cambs 1D 65
Christchurch. Dors 3G 15
Christchurch. Glos 4A 48
Christian Malford. Wilts 4E 35
Christleton. Ches W 4G 83
Christmas Common. Oxon 2F 37
Christon. N Som 1G 21
Christon Bank. Nmbd 2G 121
Christow. Devn 4B 12
Chryston. N Lan 2H 127
Chuck Hatch. E Sus 2F 27
Chudleigh. Devn 5B 12
Chudleigh Knighton. Devn 5B 12
Chulmleigh. Devn 1G 11
Chunal. Derbs 1E 85
Church. Lanc 2F 91
Churcham. Glos 4C 48
Church Aston. Telf 4B 72
Church Brampton. Nptn 4E 62
Church Brough. Cumb 3A 104
Church Broughton. Derbs 2G 73
Church Corner. Suff 2G 67
Church Crookham. Hants 1G 25
Churchdown. Glos 4D 48
Church Eaton. Staf 4C 72
Church End. Cambs 5D 65
(nr. Cambridge)
Church End. Cambs 2B 64
(nr. Sawtry)
Church End. Cambs 3C 64
(nr. Willingham)
Church End. Cambs 5C 76
(nr. Wisbech)
Church End. C Beds 3H 51
(nr. Dunstable)
Church End. C Beds 2B 52
(nr. Stotfold)
Church End. E Yor 4E 101
Church End. Essx 3H 53
(nr. Braintree)
Churchend. Essx 3G 53
(nr. Great Dunmow)
Church End. Essx 1F 53
(nr. Saffron Walden)
Churchend. Essx 1E 40
(nr. Southend-on-Sea)
Church End. Glos 5C 48
Church End. Hants 1E 25
Church End. Linc 2B 76
(nr. Donington)
Church End. Linc 1D 88
(nr. North Somercotes)
Church End. Norf 4E 77
Church End. Warw 1G 61
(nr. Coleshill)
Church End. Warw 1G 61
(nr. Nuneaton)
Church End. Wilts 4F 35
Church Enstone. Oxon 3B 50
Church Fenton. N Yor 1F 93
Church Green. Devn 3E 13
Church Gresley. Derbs 4G 73
Church Hanborough. Oxon 4C 50
Church Hill. Ches W 4A 84
Church Hill. Worc 4E 61
Church Hougham. Kent 1G 29
Church Houses. N Yor 5D 106
Churchill. Devn 2G 13
(nr. Axminster)
Churchill. Devn 2F 19
(nr. Barnstaple)
Churchill. N Som 1H 21
Churchill. Oxon 3A 50
Churchill. Worc 3C 60
(nr. Kidderminster)
Churchill. Worc 5D 60
(nr. Worcester)
Churchinford. Som 1F 13
Church Knowle. Dors 4E 15
Church Laneham. Notts 3F 87
Church Langley. Essx 5E 53
Church Langton. Leics 1E 62
Church Lawford. Warw 3B 62
Church Lawton. Ches E 5C 84
Church Leigh. Staf 2E 73
Church Lench. Worc 5E 61
Church Mayfield. Staf 1F 73
Church Minshull. Ches E 4A 84
Church Norton. W Sus 3G 17
Churchover. Warw 2C 62
Church Preen. Shrp 1H 59
Church Pulverbatch. Shrp 5G 71
Churchstanton. Som 1E 13
Church Stoke. Powy 1E 59
Churchstow. Devn 4D 8
Church Stowe. Nptn 5D 62
Church Street. Kent 3B 40
Church Stretton. Shrp 1G 59
Churchthorpe. Linc 1C 88
Churchtown. Cumb 5E 113
Churchtown. Derbs 4G 85
Churchtown. Devn 2G 19
Churchtown. IOM 2D 108
Churchtown. Lanc 5D 97
Church Town. Leics 4A 74
Churchtown. Mers 3B 90
Church Town. N Lin 4A 94
Churchtown. Shrp 2E 59
Church Village. Rhon 3D 32
Church Warsop. Notts 4C 86
Church Westcote. Glos 3H 49
Church Wilne. Derbs 2B 74
Churnsike Lodge. Nmbd 2H 113
Churston Ferrers. Torb 3F 9
Churt. Surr 3G 25
Churton. Ches W 5G 83
Churwell. W Yor 2C 92
Chute Standen. Wilts 1B 24
Chwilog. Gwyn 2D 68
Chwittfordd. Flin 3D 82
Chyandour. Corn 3B 4
Cilan Uchaf. Gwyn 3B 68
Cilcain. Flin 4D 82
Cilcennin. Cdgn 4E 57
Cilfrew. Neat 5A 46
Cilfynydd. Rhon 2D 32
Cilgerran. Pemb 1B 44
Cilgeti. Pemb 4F 43
Cilgwyn. Carm 3H 45
Cilgwyn. Pemb 1E 43
Ciliau Aeron. Cdgn 5D 57
Cill Amhlaidh. W Isl 4C 170
Cill Donnain. W Isl 6C 170
Cille a' Bhacstair. High 2C 154
Cille Bhrighde. W Isl 7C 170
Cille Pheadair. W Isl 7C 170
Cilmaengwyn. Neat 5H 45
Cilmeri. Powy 5C 58
Cilmery. Powy 5C 58
Cilrhedyn. Pemb 1G 43
Cilsan. Carm 3F 45
Ciltalgarth. Gwyn 1A 70
Ciltwrch. Powy 1E 47
Cilybebyll. Neat 5H 45
Cilycwm. Carm 2A 46
Cimla. Neat 2A 32
Cinderford. Glos 4B 48
Cinderhill. Derbs 1A 74
Cippenham. Slo 2A 38
Cippyn. Pemb 1B 44
Cirbhig. W Isl 3D 171
Circebost. W Isl 4D 171
Cirencester. Glos 5F 49
City. Powy 1E 58
City. V Glam 4C 32
City Centre. Stoke 1C 72 & Stoke 211
City Dulas. IOA 2D 80
City (London) Airport. G Lon 2F 39
City of London. G Lon 2E 39
City, The. Buck 2F 37
Clabhach. Arg 3C 138
Clachaig. Arg 1C 126
Clachaig. High 3F 141
(nr. Kinlochleven)
Clachaig. High 2E 151
(nr. Nethy Bridge)
Clachamish. High 3C 154
Clachan. Arg 4F 125
(on Kintyre)
Clachan. Arg 4C 140
(on Lismore)
Clachan. High 2H 167
(nr. Bettyhill)
Clachan. High 2D 155
(nr. Staffin)
Clachan. High 1C 154
(nr. Uig)
Clachan. High 5E 155
(on Raasay)
Clachan Farm. Arg 2A 134
Clachan na Luib. W Isl 2D 170
Clachan of Campsie. E Dun 2H 127
Clachan of Glendaruel. Arg 1A 126
Clachan-Seil. Arg 2E 133
Clachan Shannda. W Isl 1D 170
Clachan Strachur. Arg 3H 133
Clachbreck. Arg 2F 125
Clachnaharry. High 4A 158
Clachtoll. High 1E 163
Clackmannan. Clac 4B 136
Clackmannanshire Bridge. Falk 1C 128
Clackmarras. Mor 3G 159
Clacton-on-Sea. Essx 4E 55
Cladach a Chaolais. W Isl 2C 170
Cladach Chairinis. W Isl 3D 170
Cladach Chirceboist. W Isl 2C 170
Cladach Iolaraigh. W Isl 2C 170
Cladich. Arg 1H 133
Cladswell. Worc 5E 61
Claggan. High 1F 141
(nr. Fort William)
Claggan. High 4A 140
(nr. Lochaline)
Claigan. High 3B 154
Clandown. Bath 1B 22
Clanfield. Hants 1E 17
Clanfield. Oxon 5A 50
Clanville. Hants 2B 24
Clanville. Som 3B 22
Claonaig. Arg 4G 125
Clapgate. Dors 2F 15
Clapgate. Herts 3E 53
Clapham. Bed 5H 63
Clapham. Devn 4B 12
Clapham. G Lon 3D 39
Clapham. N Yor 3G 97
Clapham. W Sus 5B 26
Clap Hill. Kent 2E 29
Clappers. Bord 4F 131
Clappersgate. Cumb 4E 103
Clapphoull. Shet 9F 173
Clapton. Som 2H 13
(nr. Crewkerne)
Clapton. Som 1B 22
(nr. Radstock)
Clapton-in-Gordano. N Som 4H 33
Clapton-on-the-Hill. Glos 4G 49
Clapworthy. Devn 4G 19
Clara Vale. Tyne 3E 115
Clarbeston. Pemb 2E 43
Clarbeston Road. Pemb 2E 43
Clarborough. Notts 2E 87
Clare. Suff 1A 54
Clarebrand. Dum 3E 111
Clarencefield. Dum 3B 112
Clarilaw. Bord 3H 119
Clark's Green. Surr 2C 26
Clark's Hill. Linc 3C 76
Clarkston. E Ren 4G 127
Clasheddy. High 2G 167
Clashindarroch. Abers 5B 160
Clashmore. High 5E 165
(nr. Dornoch)
Clashmore. High 1E 163
(nr. Stoer)
Clashnessie. High 5A 166
Clashnoir. Mor 1G 151
Clate. Shet 5G 173
Clathick. Per 1H 135
Clathy. Per 2B 136
Clatt. Abers 1C 152
Clatter. Powy 1B 58
Clatterford. IOW 4C 16
Clatworthy. Som 3D 20
Claughton. Lanc 3E 97
(nr. Caton)
Claughton. Lanc 5E 97
(nr. Garstang)
Claughton. Mers 2F 83
Claverdon. Warw 4F 61
Claverham. N Som 5H 33
Clavering. Essx 2E 53
Claverley. Shrp 1B 60
Claverton. Bath 5C 34
Clawdd-coch. V Glam 4D 32
Clawdd-newydd. Den 5C 82
Clawson Hill. Leics 3E 75
Clawton. Devn 3D 10
Claxby. Linc 3D 88
(nr. Alford)
Claxby. Linc 1A 88
(nr. Market Rasen)
Claxton. Norf 5F 79
Claxton. N Yor 4A 100
Claybrooke Magna. Leics 2B 62
Claybrooke Parva. Leics 2B 62
Clay Common. Suff 2G 67
Clay Coton. Nptn 3C 62
Clay Cross. Derbs 4A 86
Claydon. Oxon 5B 62
Claydon. Suff 5D 66
Clay End. Herts 3D 52
Claygate. Dum 2E 113
Claygate. Kent 1B 28
Claygate. Surr 4C 38
Claygate Cross. Kent 5H 39
Clayhall. Hants 3E 16
Clayhanger. Devn 4D 20
Clayhanger. W Mid 5E 73
Clayhidon. Devn 1E 13
Clay Hill. Bris 4B 34
Clayhill. E Sus 3C 28
Clayhill. Hants 2B 16
Clayhithe. Cambs 4E 65
Clayholes. Ang 5E 145
Clay Lake. Linc 3B 76
Clayock. High 3D 168
Claypits. Glos 5C 48
Claypole. Linc 1F 75
Claythorpe. Linc 3D 88
Clayton. G Man 1C 84
Clayton. S Yor 4E 93
Clayton. Staf 1C 72
Clayton. W Sus 4E 27
Clayton. W Yor 1B 92
Clayton Green. Lanc 2D 90
Clayton-le-Moors. Lanc 1F 91
Clayton-le-Woods. Lanc 2D 90
Clayton West. W Yor 3C 92
Clayworth. Notts 2E 87
Cleadale. High 5C 146
Cleadon. Tyne 3G 115
Clearbrook. Devn 2B 8
Clearwell. Glos 5A 48
Cleasby. N Yor 3F 105
Cleat. Orkn 3D 172
(nr. Braehead)
Cleat. Orkn 9D 172
(nr. St Margaret's Hope)
Cleatlam. Dur 3E 105
Cleator. Cumb 3B 102
Cleator Moor. Cumb 3B 102
Cleckheaton. W Yor 2B 92
Cleedownton. Shrp 2H 59
Cleehill. Shrp 3H 59
Cleekhimin. N Lan 4A 128
Clee St Margaret. Shrp 2H 59
Cleestanton. Shrp 3H 59
Cleethorpes. NE Lin 4G 95
Cleeton St Mary. Shrp 3A 60
Cleeve. N Som 5H 33
Cleeve. Oxon 3E 36
Cleeve Hill. Glos 3E 49
Cleeve Prior. Worc 1F 49
Clehonger. Here 2H 47
Cleigh. Arg 1F 133
Cleish. Per 4C 136
Cleland. N Lan 4B 128
Clench Common. Wilts 5G 35
Clenchwarton. Norf 3E 77
Clennell. Nmbd 4D 120
Clent. Worc 3D 60
Cleobury Mortimer. Shrp 3A 60
Cleobury North. Shrp 2A 60
Clephanton. High 3C 158
Clerkhill. High 2H 167
Clestrain. Orkn 7C 172
Clevancy. Wilts 4F 35
Clevedon. N Som 4H 33
Cleveley. Oxon 3B 50
Cleveleys. Lanc 5C 96
Clevelode. Worc 1D 48
Cleverton. Wilts 3E 35
Clewer. Som 1H 21
Cley next the Sea. Norf 1C 78
Cliaid. W Isl 8B 170
Cliasmol. W Isl 7C 171
Clibberswick. Shet 1H 173
Cliburn. Cumb 2G 103
Cliddesden. Hants 2E 25
Clieves Hills. Lanc 4B 90
Cliff. Warw 1G 61
Cliffburn. Ang 4F 145
Cliffe. Medw 3B 40
Cliffe. N Yor 3F 105
(nr. Darlington)
Cliffe. N Yor 1G 93
(nr. Selby)
Cliff End. E Sus 4C 28
Cliffe Woods. Medw 3B 40
Clifford. Here 1F 47
Clifford. W Yor 5G 99
Clifford Chambers. Warw 5F 61
Clifford's Mesne. Glos 3B 48
Cliffsend. Kent 4H 41
Clifton. Bris 4A 34
Clifton. C Beds 2B 52
Clifton. Cumb 2G 103
Clifton. Derbs 1F 73
Clifton. Devn 2G 19
Clifton. G Man 4F 91
Clifton. Lanc 1C 90
Clifton. Nmbd 1F 115
Clifton. N Yor 5D 98
Clifton. Nott 2C 74
Clifton. Oxon 2C 50
Clifton. S Yor 1C 86
Clifton. Stir 5H 141
Clifton. W Yor 2B 92
Clifton. Worc 1D 48
Clifton. York 4H 99
Clifton Campville. Staf 4G 73
Clifton Hampden. Oxon 2D 36
Clifton Hill. Worc 4B 60
Clifton Reynes. Mil 5G 63
Clifton upon Dunsmore. Warw 3C 62
Clifton upon Teme. Worc 4B 60
Cliftonville. Kent 3H 41
Cliftonville. Norf 2F 79
Climping. W Sus 5A 26
Climpy. S Lan 4C 128
Clint. N Yor 4E 99
Clint Green. Norf 4C 78
Clintmains. Bord 1A 120
Cliobh. W Isl 4C 171
Clipiau. Gwyn 4H 69
Clippesby. Norf 4G 79
Clippings Green. Norf 4C 78
Clipsham. Rut 4G 75
Clipston. Nptn 2E 62
Clipston. Notts 2D 74
Clipstone. Notts 4C 86
Clitheroe. Lanc 5G 97
Cliuthar. W Isl 8D 171
Clive. Shrp 3H 71
Clivocast. Shet 1H 173
Clixby. Linc 4D 94
Clocaenog. Den 5C 82
Clochan. Mor 2B 160
Clochforbie. Abers 3F 161
Clock Face. Mers 1H 83
Cloddiau. Powy 5E 70
Cloddymoss. Mor 2D 159
Clodock. Here 3G 47
Cloford. Som 2C 22
Clola. Abers 4H 161
Clophill. C Beds 2A 52
Clopton. Nptn 2H 63
Clopton Corner. Suff 5E 66
Clopton Green. Suff 5G 65
Closeburn. Dum 5A 118
Close Clark. IOM 4B 108
Closworth. Som 1A 14
Clothall. Herts 2C 52
Clotton. Ches W 4H 83
Clough. G Man 3H 91
Clough. W Yor 3A 92
Clough Foot. W Yor 2H 91
Cloughton. N Yor 5H 107
Cloughton Newlands. N Yor 5H 107
Clousta. Shet 6E 173
Clouston. Orkn 6B 172
Clova. Abers 1B 152
Clova. Ang 1C 144
Clovelly. Devn 4D 18
Clovenfords. Bord 1G 119
Clovenstone. Abers 2E 153
Clovullin. High 2E 141
Clowne. Derbs 3B 86
Clows Top. Worc 3B 60
Cloy. Wrex 1F 71
Cluanie Inn. High 2C 148
Cluanie Lodge. High 2C 148
Cluddley. Telf 5A 72
Clun. Shrp 2F 59
Clunas. High 4C 158
Clunbury. Shrp 2F 59
Clunderwen. Pemb 3F 43
Clune. High 1B 150
Clunes. High 5E 148
Clungunford. Shrp 3F 59
Clunie. Per 4A 144
Clunton. Shrp 2F 59
Cluny. Fife 4E 137
Clutton. Bath 1B 22
Clutton. Ches W 5G 83
Clwt-y-bont. Gwyn 4E 81

Crowhurst Lane End—Denton

Crowhurst Lane End. *Surr* 1E **27**
Crowland. *Linc* 4B **76**
Crowland. *Suff* 3C **66**
Crowlas. *Corn* 3C **4**
Crowle. *N Lin* 3A **94**
Crowle. *Worc* 5D **60**
Crowle Green. *Worc* 5D **60**
Crowmarsh Gifford. *Oxon* 3E **36**
Crown Corner. *Suff* 3E **67**
Crownthorpe. *Norf* 5C **78**
Crowntown. *Corn* 3D **4**
Crows-an-wra. *Corn* 4A **4**
Crowshill. *Norf* 5B **78**
Crowthorne. *Brac* 5G **37**
Crowton. *Ches W* 3H **83**
Croxall. *Staf* 4F **73**
Croxby. *Linc* 1A **88**
Croxdale. *Dur* 1F **105**
Croxden. *Staf* 2E **73**
Croxley Green. *Herts* 1B **38**
Croxton. *Cambs* 4B **64**
Croxton. *Norf* 2B **78**
(nr. Fakenham)
Croxton. *Norf* 2A **66**
(nr. Thetford)
Croxton. *N Lin* 3D **94**
Croxton. *Staf* 2B **72**
Croxtonbank. *Staf* 2B **72**
Croxton Green. *Ches E* 5H **83**
Croxton Kerrial. *Leics* 3F **75**
Croy. *High* 4B **158**
Croy. *N Lan* 2A **128**
Croyde. *Devn* 3E **19**
Croydon. *Cambs* 1D **52**
Croydon. *G Lon* 4E **39**
Crubenbeg. *High* 4A **150**
Crubenmore Lodge. *High* 4A **150**
Cruckmeole. *Shrp* 5G **71**
Cruckton. *Shrp* 4G **71**
Cruden Bay. *Abers* 5H **161**
Crudgington. *Telf* 4A **72**
Crudie. *Abers* 3E **161**
Crudwell. *Wilts* 2E **35**
Cruft. *Devn* 3E **11**
Crug. *Powy* 3D **58**
Crughywel. *Powy* 4F **47**
Crugmeer. *Corn* 1D **6**
Crugybar. *Carm* 2G **45**
Crug-y-byddar. *Powy* 2D **58**
Crulabhig. *W Isl* 4D **171**
Crumlin. *Cphy* 2F **33**
Crumpsall. *G Man* 4G **91**
Crumpsbrook. *Shrp* 3A **60**
Crundale. *Kent* 1E **29**
Crundale. *Pemb* 3D **42**
Cruwys Morchard. *Devn* 1B **12**
Crux Easton. *Hants* 1C **24**
Cruxton. *Dors* 3B **14**
Crwbin. *Carm* 4E **45**
Cryers Hill. *Buck* 2G **37**
Crymych. *Pemb* 1F **43**
Crynant. *Neat* 5A **46**
Crystal Palace. *G Lon* 3E **39**
Cuaich. *High* 5A **150**
Cuaig. *High* 3G **155**
Cuan. *Arg* 2E **133**
Cubbington. *Warw* 4H **61**
Cubert. *Corn* 3B **6**
Cubley. *S Yor* 4C **92**
Cubley Common. *Derbs* 2F **73**
Cublington. *Buck* 3G **51**
Cublington. *Here* 2H **47**
Cuckfield. *W Sus* 3E **27**
Cucklington. *Som* 4C **22**
Cuckney. *Notts* 3C **86**
Cuckron. *Shet* 6F **173**
Cuddesdon. *Oxon* 5E **50**
Cuddington. *Buck* 4F **51**
Cuddington. *Ches W* 3A **84**
Cuddington Heath. *Ches W* 1G **71**
Cuddy Hill. *Lanc* 1C **90**
Cudham. *G Lon* 5F **39**
Cudlipptown. *Devn* 5F **11**
Cudworth. *Som* 1G **13**
Cudworth. *S Yor* 4D **93**
Cudworth. *Surr* 1D **26**
Cuerdley Cross. *Warr* 2H **83**
Cuffley. *Herts* 5D **52**
Cuidhir. *W Isl* 8B **170**
Cuidhsiadar. *W Isl* 2H **171**
Cuidhtinis. *W Isl* 9C **171**
Culbo. *High* 2A **158**
Culbokie. *High* 3A **158**
Culburnie. *High* 4G **157**
Culcabock. *High* 4A **158**
Culcharry. *High* 3C **158**
Culcheth. *Warr* 1A **84**
Culduie. *High* 4G **155**
Culeave. *High* 4C **164**
Culford. *Suff* 4H **65**
Culgaith. *Cumb* 2H **103**
Culham. *Oxon* 2D **36**
Culkein. *High* 1E **163**
Culkein Drumbeg. *High* 5B **166**
Culkerton. *Glos* 2E **35**
Cullen. *Mor* 2C **160**
Cullercoats. *Tyne* 2G **115**
Cullicudden. *High* 2A **158**
Cullingworth. *W Yor* 1A **92**
Cullipool. *Arg* 2E **133**
Cullivoe. *Shet* 1G **173**
Culloch. *Per* 2G **135**
Culloden. *High* 4B **158**
Cullompton. *Devn* 2D **12**
Culm Davy. *Devn* 1E **13**
Culmington. *Shrp* 2G **59**
Culmstock. *Devn* 1E **12**
Cul na Caepaich. *High* 5E **147**
Culnacnoc. *High* 2E **155**
Culnacraig. *High* 3E **163**
Culrain. *High* 4C **164**
Culross. *Fife* 1C **128**
Culroy. *S Ayr* 3C **116**
Culswick. *Shet* 7D **173**
Cults. *Aber* 3F **153**
Cults. *Abers* 5C **160**
Cults. *Fife* 3F **137**
Cultybraggan Camp.
Per 1G **135**
Culver. *Devn* 3B **12**
Culverlane. *Devn* 2D **8**
Culverstone Green. *Kent* 4H **39**
Culverthorpe. *Linc* 1H **75**
Culworth. *Nptn* 1D **50**
Culzie Lodge. *High* 1H **157**
Cumberlow Green. *Herts* 2D **52**
Cumbernauld. *N Lan* 2A **128**
Cumbernauld Village.
N Lan 2A **128**
Cumberworth. *Linc* 3E **89**
Cumdivock. *Cumb* 5E **113**
Cuminestown. *Abers* 3F **161**
Cumledge Mill. *Bord* 4D **130**
Cumlewick. *Shet* 9F **173**
Cummersdale. *Cumb* 4E **113**
Cummertrees. *Dum* 3C **112**
Cummingstown. *Mor* 2F **159**
Cumnock. *E Ayr* 3E **117**
Cumnor. *Oxon* 5C **50**
Cumrew. *Cumb* 4G **113**
Cumwhinton. *Cumb* 4F **113**
Cumwhitton. *Cumb* 4G **113**
Cundall. *N Yor* 2G **99**
Cunninghamhead. *N Ayr* 5E **127**
Cunning Park. *S Ayr* 3C **116**
Cunningsburgh. *Shet* 9F **173**
Cunnister. *Shet* 2G **173**
Cupar. *Fife* 2F **137**
Cupar Muir. *Fife* 2F **137**
Cupernham. *Hants* 4B **24**
Curbar. *Derbs* 3G **85**
Curborough. *Staf* 4F **73**
Curbridge. *Hants* 1D **16**
Curbridge. *Oxon* 5B **50**
Curdridge. *Hants* 1D **16**
Curdworth. *Warw* 1F **61**
Curland. *Som* 1F **13**
Curland Common. *Som* 1F **13**
Curridge. *W Ber* 4C **36**
Currie. *Edin* 3E **129**
Curry Mallet. *Som* 4G **21**
Curry Rivel. *Som* 4G **21**
Curtisden Green. *Kent* 1B **28**
Curtisknowle. *Devn* 3D **8**
Cury. *Corn* 4D **5**
Cusgarne. *Corn* 4B **6**
Cusop. *Here* 1F **47**
Cusworth. *S Yor* 4F **93**
Cutcombe. *Som* 3C **20**
Cuthill. *E Lot* 2G **129**
Cutiau. *Gwyn* 4F **69**
Cutlers Green. *Essx* 2F **53**
Cutmadoc. *Corn* 2E **7**
Cutnall Green. *Worc* 4C **60**
Cutsdean. *Glos* 2F **49**
Cutthorpe. *Derbs* 3H **85**
Cuttiford's Door. *Som* 1G **13**
Cuttivett. *Corn* 2H **7**
Cutts. *Shet* 8F **173**
Cuttybridge. *Pemb* 3D **42**
Cuttyhill. *Abers* 3H **161**
Cuxham. *Oxon* 2E **37**
Cuxton. *Medw* 4B **40**
Cuxwold. *Linc* 4E **95**
Cwm. *Blae* 5E **47**
Cwm. *Den* 3C **82**
Cwm. *Powy* 1E **59**
Cwmafan. *Neat* 2A **32**
Cwmaman. *Rhon* 2C **32**
Cwmann. *Carm* 1F **45**
Cwmbach. *Carm* 2G **43**
Cwmbach. *Powy* 2E **47**
Cwmbach. *Rhon* 5D **46**
Cwmbach Llechrhyd. *Powy* 5C **58**
Cwmbelan. *Powy* 2B **58**
Cwmbran. *Torf* 2F **33**
Cwmbrwyno. *Cdgn* 2G **57**
Cwm Capel. *Carm* 5E **45**
Cwmcarn. *Cphy* 2F **33**
Cwmcarvan. *Mon* 5H **47**
Cwm-celyn. *Blae* 5F **47**
Cwmcerdinen. *Swan* 5G **45**
Cwm-Cewydd. *Gwyn* 4A **70**
Cwm-cou. *Cdgn* 1C **44**
Cwmcych. *Pemb* 1G **43**
Cwmdare. *Rhon* 5C **46**
Cwmdu. *Carm* 2G **45**
Cwmdu. *Powy* 3E **47**
Cwmduad. *Carm* 2D **45**
Cwm Dulais. *Swan* 5G **45**
Cwmerfyn. *Cdgn* 2F **57**
Cwmfelin. *B'end* 3B **32**
Cwmfelin Boeth. *Carm* 3F **43**
Cwmfelinfach. *Cphy* 2E **33**
Cwmfelin Mynach. *Carm* 2G **43**
Cwmffrwd. *Carm* 4E **45**
Cwmgiedd. *Powy* 4A **46**
Cwmgors. *Neat* 4H **45**
Cwmgwili. *Carm* 4F **45**
Cwmgwrach. *Neat* 5B **46**
Cwmhiraeth. *Carm* 1H **43**
Cwmifor. *Carm* 3G **45**
Cwmisfael. *Carm* 4E **45**
Cwm-Llinau. *Powy* 5H **69**
Cwmllynfell. *Neat* 4H **45**
Cwm-mawr. *Carm* 4F **45**
Cwm-miles. *Carm* 2F **43**
Cwmorgan. *Carm* 1G **43**
Cwmparc. *Rhon* 2C **32**
Cwm Penmachno. *Cnwy* 1G **69**
Cwmpennar. *Rhon* 5D **46**
Cwm Plysgog. *Pemb* 1B **44**
Cwmrhos. *Powy* 3E **47**
Cwmsychpant. *Cdgn* 1E **45**
Cwmsyfiog. *Cphy* 5E **47**
Cwmsymlog. *Cdgn* 2F **57**
Cwmtillery. *Blae* 5F **47**
Cwm-twrch Isaf. *Powy* 5A **46**
Cwm-twrch Uchaf. *Powy* 4A **46**
Cwmwysg. *Powy* 3B **46**
Cwm-y-glo. *Gwyn* 4E **81**
Cwmyoy. *Mon* 3G **47**
Cwmystwyth. *Cdgn* 3G **57**
Cwrt. *Gwyn* 1F **57**
Cwrtnewydd. *Cdgn* 1E **45**
Cwrt-y-Cadno. *Carm* 1G **45**
Cydweli. *Carm* 5E **45**
Cyffylliog. *Den* 5C **82**
Cymau. *Flin* 5E **83**
Cymer. *Neat* 2B **32**
Cymmer. *Neat* 2B **32**
Cymmer. *Rhon* 2D **32**
Cyncoed. *Card* 3E **33**
Cynghordy. *Carm* 2B **46**
Cynghordy. *Swan* 5G **45**
Cynheidre. *Carm* 5E **45**
Cynonville. *Neat* 2B **32**
Cynwyd. *Den* 1C **70**
Cynwyl Elfed. *Carm* 3D **44**
Cywarch. *Gwyn* 4A **70**

D

Dacre. *Cumb* 2F **103**
Dacre. *N Yor* 3D **98**
Dacre Banks. *N Yor* 3D **98**
Daddry Shield. *Dur* 1B **104**
Dadford. *Buck* 2E **51**
Dadlington. *Leics* 1B **62**
Dafen. *Carm* 5F **45**
Daffy Green. *Norf* 5B **78**
Dagdale. *Staf* 2E **73**
Dagenham. *G Lon* 2F **39**
Daggons. *Dors* 1G **15**
Daglingworth. *Glos* 5E **49**
Dagnall. *Buck* 4H **51**
Dagtail End. *Worc* 4E **61**
Dail. *Arg* 5E **141**
Dail Beag. *W Isl* 3E **171**
Dail bho Dheas. *W Isl* 1G **171**
Dailly. *S Ayr* 4B **116**
Dail Mor. *W Isl* 3E **171**
Dairsie. *Fife* 2G **137**
Daisy Bank. *W Mid* 1E **61**
Daisy Hill. *G Man* 4E **91**
Daisy Hill. *W Yor* 1B **92**
Dalabrog. *W Isl* 6C **170**
Dalavich. *Arg* 2G **133**
Dalbeattie. *Dum* 3F **111**
Dalblair. *E Ayr* 3F **117**
Dalbury. *Derbs* 2G **73**
Dalby. *IOM* 4B **108**
Dalby Wolds. *Leics* 3D **74**
Dalchalm. *High* 3G **165**
Dalcharn. *High* 3G **167**
Dalchork. *High* 2C **164**
Dalchreichart. *High* 2E **149**
Dalchruin. *Per* 2G **135**
Dalcross. *High* 4B **158**
Dalderby. *Linc* 4B **88**
Dale. *Cumb* 5G **113**
Dale. *Pemb* 4C **42**
Dale Abbey. *Derbs* 2B **74**
Dalebank. *Derbs* 4A **86**
Dale Bottom. *Cumb* 2D **102**
Dale Head. *Cumb* 3F **103**
Dalehouse. *N Yor* 3E **107**
Dalelia. *High* 2B **140**
Dale of Walls. *Shet* 6C **173**
Dalgarven. *N Ayr* 5D **126**
Dalgety Bay. *Fife* 1E **129**
Dalginross. *Per* 1G **135**
Dalguise. *Per* 4G **143**
Dalhalvaig. *High* 3A **168**
Dalham. *Suff* 4G **65**
Dalintart. *Arg* 1F **133**
Dalkeith. *Midl* 3G **129**
Dallas. *Mor* 3F **159**
Dalleagles. *E Ayr* 3E **117**
Dall House. *Per* 3C **142**
Dallinghoo. *Suff* 5E **67**
Dallington. *E Sus* 4A **28**
Dallow. *N Yor* 2D **98**
Dalmally. *Arg* 1A **134**
Dalmarnock. *Glas* 3H **127**
Dalmellington. *E Ayr* 4D **117**
Dalmeny. *Edin* 2E **129**
Dalmigavie. *High* 2B **150**
Dalmilling. *S Ayr* 2C **116**
Dalmore. *High* 2A **158**
(nr. Alness)
Dalmore. *High* 3E **164**
(nr. Rogart)
Dalmuir. *W Dun* 2F **127**
Dalmunach. *Mor* 4G **159**
Dalnabreck. *High* 2B **140**
Dalnacardoch Lodge. *Per* 1E **142**
Dalnamein Lodge. *Per* 2E **143**
Dalnaspidal Lodge. *Per* 1D **142**
Dalnatrat. *High* 3D **140**
Dalnavie. *High* 1A **158**
Dalnawillan Lodge. *High* 4C **168**
Dalness. *High* 3F **141**
Dalnessie. *High* 2D **164**
Dalqueich. *Per* 3C **136**
Dalquhairn. *S Ayr* 5C **116**
Dalreavoch. *High* 3E **165**
Dalreoch. *Per* 2C **136**
Dalry. *Edin* 2F **129**
Dalry. *N Ayr* 5D **126**
Dalrymple. *E Ayr* 3C **116**
Dalscote. *Nptn* 5D **62**
Dalserf. *S Lan* 4B **128**
Dalsmirren. *Arg* 4A **122**
Dalston. *Cumb* 4E **113**
Dalswinton. *Dum* 1G **111**
Dalton. *Dum* 2C **112**
Dalton. *Lanc* 4C **90**
Dalton. *Nmbd* 4C **114**
(nr. Hexham)
Dalton. *Nmbd* 2E **115**
(nr. Ponteland)
Dalton. *N Yor* 4E **105**
(nr. Richmond)
Dalton. *N Yor* 2G **99**
(nr. Thirsk)
Dalton. *S Lan* 4H **127**
Dalton. *S Yor* 1B **86**
Dalton-in-Furness. *Cumb* 2B **96**
Dalton-le-Dale. *Dur* 5H **115**
Dalton Magna. *S Yor* 1B **86**
Dalton-on-Tees. *N Yor* 4F **105**
Dalton Piercy. *Hart* 1B **106**
Daltot. *Arg* 1F **125**
Dalvey. *High* 5F **159**
Dalwhinnie. *High* 5A **150**
Dalwood. *Devn* 2F **13**
Damerham. *Hants* 1G **15**
Damgate. *Norf* 5G **79**
(nr. Acle)
Damgate. *Norf* 4G **79**
(nr. Martham)
Dam Green. *Norf* 2C **66**
Damhead. *Mor* 3E **159**
Danaway. *Kent* 4C **40**
Danbury. *Essx* 5A **54**
Danby. *N Yor* 4E **107**
Danby Botton. *N Yor* 4D **107**
Danby Wiske. *N Yor* 5A **106**
Danderhall. *Midl* 3G **129**
Danebank. *Ches E* 2D **85**
Danebridge. *Ches E* 4D **84**
Dane End. *Herts* 3D **52**
Danehill. *E Sus* 3F **27**
Danesford. *Shrp* 1B **60**
Daneshill. *Hants* 1E **25**
Danesmoor. *Derbs* 4A **86**
Danestone. *Aber* 2G **153**
Dangerous Corner. *Lanc* 3D **90**
Daniel's Water. *Kent* 1D **28**
Dan's Castle. *Dur* 1E **105**
Danzey Green. *Warw* 4F **61**
Dapple Heath. *Staf* 3E **73**
Daren. *Powy* 4F **47**
Darenth. *Kent* 3G **39**
Daresbury. *Hal* 2H **83**
Darfield. *S Yor* 4E **93**
Dargate. *Kent* 4E **41**
Dargill. *Per* 2A **136**
Darite. *Corn* 2G **7**
Darlaston. *W Mid* 1D **60**
Darley. *N Yor* 4E **98**
Darley Abbey. *Derb* 2A **74**
Darley Bridge. *Derbs* 4G **85**
Darley Dale. *Derbs* 4G **85**
Darley Head. *N Yor* 4D **98**
Darlingscott. *Warw* 1H **49**
Darlington. *Darl* 3F **105**
Darliston. *Shrp* 2H **71**
Darlton. *Notts* 3E **87**
Darmsden. *Suff* 5C **66**
Darnall. *S Yor* 2A **86**
Darnford. *Abers* 4E **153**
Darnford. *Staf* 5F **73**
Darnhall. *Ches W* 4A **84**
Darnick. *Bord* 1H **119**
Darowen. *Powy* 5H **69**
Darra. *Abers* 4E **161**
Darracott. *Devn* 3E **19**
Darras Hall. *Nmbd* 2E **115**
Darrington. *W Yor* 3E **93**
Darrow Green. *Norf* 2E **67**
Darsham. *Suff* 4G **67**
Dartfield. *Abers* 3H **161**
Dartford. *Kent* 3G **39**
Dartford-Thurrock River Crossing.
Kent 3G **39**
Dartington. *Devn* 2D **9**
Dartmeet. *Devn* 5G **11**
Dartmoor. *Devn* 4F **11**
Dartmouth. *Devn* 3E **9**
Darton. *S Yor* 3D **92**
Darvel. *E Ayr* 1E **117**
Darwen. *Bkbn* 2E **91**
Dassels. *Herts* 3D **53**
Datchet. *Wind* 3A **38**
Datchworth. *Herts* 4C **52**
Datchworth Green. *Herts* 4C **52**
Daubhill. *G Man* 4F **91**
Dauntsey. *Wilts* 3E **35**
Dauntsey Green. *Wilts* 3E **35**
Dauntsey Lock. *Wilts* 3E **35**
Dava. *Mor* 5E **159**
Davenham. *Ches W* 3A **84**
Daventry. *Nptn* 4C **62**
Davidson's Mains. *Edin* 2F **129**
Davidston. *High* 2B **158**
Davidstow. *Corn* 4B **10**
David's Well. *Powy* 3C **58**
Davington. *Dum* 4E **119**
Daviot. *Abers* 1E **153**
Daviot. *High* 5B **158**
Davyhulme. *G Man* 1B **84**
Daw Cross. *N Yor* 4E **99**
Dawdon. *Dur* 5H **115**
Dawesgreen. *Surr* 1D **26**
Dawley. *Telf* 5A **72**
Dawlish. *Devn* 5C **12**
Dawlish Warren. *Devn* 5C **12**
Dawn. *Cnwy* 3A **82**
Daws Heath. *Essx* 2C **40**
Dawshill. *Worc* 5C **60**
Daw's House. *Corn* 4D **10**
Dawsmere. *Linc* 2D **76**
Dayhills. *Staf* 2D **72**
Dayhouse Bank. *Worc* 3D **60**
Daylesford. *Glos* 3H **49**
Daywall. *Shrp* 2E **71**
Ddol. *Flin* 3D **82**
Ddol Cownwy. *Powy* 4C **70**
Deadman's Cross. *C Beds* 1B **52**
Deadwater. *Nmbd* 5A **120**
Deaf Hill. *Dur* 1A **106**
Deal. *Kent* 5H **41**
Dean. *Cumb* 2B **102**
Dean. *Devn* 2G **19**
(nr. Combe Martin)
Dean. *Devn* 2H **19**
(nr. Lynton)
Dean. *Dors* 1E **15**
Dean. *Hants* 1D **16**
(nr. Bishop's Waltham)
Dean. *Hants* 3C **24**
(nr. Winchester)
Dean. *Oxon* 3B **50**
Dean. *Som* 2B **22**
Dean Bank. *Dur* 1F **105**
Deanburnhaugh. *Bord* 3F **119**
Dean Cross. *Devn* 2F **19**
Deane. *Hants* 1D **24**
Deanich Lodge. *High* 5A **164**
Deanland. *Dors* 1E **15**
Deanlane End. *W Sus* 1F **17**
Dean Park. *Shrp* 4H **59**
Dean Prior. *Devn* 2D **8**
Dean Row. *Ches E* 2C **84**
Deans. *W Lot* 3D **128**
Deanscales. *Cumb* 2B **102**
Deanshanger. *Nptn* 2F **51**
Deanston. *Stir* 3G **135**
Dearham. *Cumb* 1B **102**
Dearne. *S Yor* 4E **93**
Dearne Valley. *S Yor* 4D **93**
Debach. *Suff* 5E **67**
Debden. *Essx* 2F **53**
Debden Green. *Essx* 1F **39**
(nr. Loughton)
Debden Green. *Essx* 2F **53**
(nr. Saffron Walden)
Debenham. *Suff* 4D **66**
Dechmont. *W Lot* 2D **128**
Deddington. *Oxon* 2C **50**
Dedham. *Essx* 2D **54**
Dedham Heath. *Essx* 2D **54**
Deebank. *Abers* 4D **152**
Deene. *Nptn* 1G **63**
Deenethorpe. *Nptn* 1G **63**
Deepcar. *S Yor* 1G **85**
Deepcut. *Surr* 5A **38**
Deepdale. *Cumb* 1G **97**
Deepdale. *N Lin* 3D **94**
Deepdale. *N Yor* 2A **98**
Deeping Gate. *Pet* 5A **76**
Deeping St James. *Linc* 5A **76**
Deeping St Nicholas. *Linc* 4B **76**
Deerhill. *Mor* 3B **160**
Deerhurst. *Glos* 3D **48**
Deerhurst Walton. *Glos* 3D **49**
Deerness. *Orkn* 7E **172**
Defford. *Worc* 1E **49**
Defynnog. *Powy* 3C **46**
Deganwy. *Cnwy* 3G **81**
Deighton. *N Yor* 4A **106**
Deighton. *W Yor* 3B **92**
Deighton. *York* 5A **100**
Deiniolen. *Gwyn* 4E **81**
Delabole. *Corn* 4A **10**
Delamere. *Ches W* 4H **83**
Delfour. *High* 3C **150**
Delliefure. *High* 5E **159**
Dell, The. *Suff* 1G **67**
Delly End. *Oxon* 4B **50**
Delny. *High* 1B **158**
Delph. *G Man* 4H **91**
Delves. *Dur* 5E **115**
Delves, The. *W Mid* 1E **61**
Delvin End. *Essx* 2A **54**
Dembleby. *Linc* 2H **75**
Demelza. *Corn* 2D **6**
Denaby Main. *S Yor* 1B **86**
Denbeath. *Fife* 4F **137**
Denbigh. *Den* 4C **82**
Denbury. *Devn* 2E **9**
Denby. *Derbs* 1A **74**
Denby Common. *Derbs* 1B **74**
Denby Dale. *W Yor* 4C **92**
Denchworth. *Oxon* 2B **36**
Dendron. *Cumb* 2B **96**
Deneside. *Dur* 5H **115**
Denford. *Nptn* 3G **63**
Dengie. *Essx* 5C **54**
Denham. *Buck* 2B **38**
Denham. *Suff* 4G **65**
(nr. Bury St Edmunds)
Denham. *Suff* 3D **66**
(nr. Eye)
Denham Green. *Buck* 2B **38**
Denham Street. *Suff* 3D **66**
Denhead. *Abers* 5G **161**
(nr. Ellon)
Denhead. *Abers* 3G **161**
(nr. Strichen)
Denhead. *Fife* 2G **137**
Denholm. *Bord* 3H **119**
Denholme. *W Yor* 1A **92**
Denholme Clough. *W Yor* 1A **92**
Denholme Gate. *W Yor* 1A **92**
Denio. *Gwyn* 2C **68**
Denmead. *Hants* 1E **17**
Dennington. *Suff* 4E **67**
Denny. *Falk* 1B **128**
Denny End. *Cambs* 4D **65**
Dennyloanhead. *Falk* 1B **128**
Den of Lindores. *Fife* 2E **137**
Denshaw. *G Man* 3H **91**
Denside. *Abers* 4F **153**
Densole. *Kent* 1G **29**
Denston. *Suff* 5G **65**
Denstone. *Staf* 1F **73**
Denstroude. *Kent* 4F **41**
Dent. *Cumb* 1G **97**
Den, The. *N Ayr* 4E **127**
Denton. *Cambs* 2A **64**
Denton. *Darl* 3F **105**

Denton—Dunlop

Denton. E Sus 5F 27
Denton. G Man 1D 84
Denton. Kent 1G 29
Denton. Linc 2F 75
Denton. Norf 2E 67
Denton. Nptn 5F 63
Denton. N Yor 5D 98
Denton. Oxon 5D 50
Denver. Norf 5F 77
Denwick. Nmbd 3G 121
Deopham. Norf 5C 78
Deopham Green. Norf 1C 66
Depden. Suff 5G 65
Depden Green. Suff 5G 65
Deptford. G Lon 3E 39
Deptford. Wilts 3F 23
Derby. Derb . . . . 2A 74 & 193
Derbyhaven. IOM 5B 108
Derculich. Per 3F 143
Dereham. Norf 4B 78
Deri. Cphy 5E 47
Derril. Devn 2D 10
Derringstone. Kent 1G 29
Derrington. Shrp 1A 60
Derrington. Staf 3C 72
Derriton. Devn 2D 10
Derryguaig. Arg 5F 139
Derry Hill. Wilts 4E 35
Derrythorpe. N Lin 4B 94
Dersingham. Norf 2F 77
Dervaig. Arg 3F 139
Derwen. Den 5C 82
Derwen Gam. Cdgn 5D 56
Derwenlas. Powy 1G 57
Desborough. Nptn 2F 63
Desford. Leics 5B 74
Detchant. Nmbd 1E 121
Dethick. Derbs 5H 85
Detling. Kent 5B 40
Deuchar. Ang 2D 144
Deuddwr. Powy 4E 71
Devauden. Mon 2H 33
Devil's Bridge. Cdgn 3G 57
Devitts Green. Warw 1G 61
Devizes. Wilts 5F 35
Devonport. Plym 3A 8
Devonside. Clac 4B 136
Devoran. Corn 5B 6
Dewartown. Midl 3G 129
Dewlish. Dors 3C 14
Dewsall Court. Here 2H 47
Dewsbury. W Yor 2C 92
Dexbeer. Devn 2C 10
Dhoon. IOM 3D 108
Dhoor. IOM 2D 108
Dhowin. IOM 1D 108
Dial Green. W Sus 3A 26
Dial Post. W Sus 4C 26
Dibberford. Dors 2H 13
Dibden. Hants 2C 16
Dibden Purlieu. Hants 2C 16
Dickleburgh. Norf 2D 66
Didbrook. Glos 2F 49
Didcot. Oxon 2D 36
Diddington. Cambs 4A 64
Diddlebury. Shrp 2H 59
Didley. Here 2H 47
Didling. W Sus 1G 17
Didmarton. Glos 3D 34
Didsbury. G Man 1C 84
Didworthy. Devn 2C 8
Digby. Linc 5H 87
Digg. High 2D 154
Diggle. G Man 4A 92
Digmoor. Lanc 4C 90
Digswell. Herts 4C 52
Dihewyd. Cdgn 5D 57
Dilham. Norf 3F 79
Dilhorne. Staf 1D 72
Dillarburn. S Lan 5B 128
Dillington. Cambs 4A 64
Dilston. Nmbd 3C 114
Dilton Marsh. Wilts 2D 22
Dilwyn. Here 5G 59
Dimmer. Som 3B 22
Dimple. G Man 3F 91
Dinas. Carm 1G 43
Dinas. Gwyn 5D 81
(nr. Caernarfon)
Dinas. Gwyn 2B 68
(nr. Tudweiliog)
Dinas Cross. Pemb 1E 43
Dinas Dinlle. Gwyn 5D 80
Dinas Mawddwy. Gwyn 4A 70
Dinas Powys. V Glam 4E 33
Dinbych. Den 4C 82
Dinbych-y-Pysgod. Pemb 4F 43
Dinckley. Lanc 1E 91
Dinder. Som 2A 22
Dinedor. Here 2A 48
Dinedor Cross. Here 2A 48
Dingestow. Mon 4H 47
Dingle. Mers 2F 83
Dingleden. Kent 2C 28
Dingleton. Bord 1H 119
Dingley. Nptn 2E 63
Dingwall. High 3H 157
Dinmael. Cnwy 1C 70
Dinnet. Abers 4B 152
Dinnington. Som 1H 13
Dinnington. S Yor 2C 86
Dinnington. Tyne 2F 115
Dinorwig. Gwyn 4E 81
Dinton. Buck 4F 51
Dinton. Wilts 3F 23
Dinworthy. Devn 1D 10
Dipley. Hants 1F 25
Dippen. Arg 2B 122
Dippenhall. Surr 2G 25
Dippertown. Devn 4E 11
Dippin. N Ayr 3E 123
Dipple. S Ayr 4B 116
Diptford. Devn 3D 8
Dipton. Dur 4E 115
Dirleton. E Lot 1B 130
Dirt Pot. Nmbd 5B 114
Discoed. Powy 4E 59
Diseworth. Leics 3B 74
Dishes. Orkn 5F 172
Dishforth. N Yor 2F 99
Disley. Ches E 2D 85
Diss. Norf 3D 66
Disserth. Powy 5C 58
Distington. Cumb 2B 102
Ditchampton. Wilts 3F 23
Ditcheat. Som 3B 22
Ditchingham. Norf 1F 67
Ditchling. E Sus 4E 27
Ditteridge. Wilts 5D 34
Dittisham. Devn 3E 9
Ditton. Hal 2G 83
Ditton. Kent 5B 40
Ditton Green. Cambs 5F 65
Ditton Priors. Shrp 2A 60
Divach. High 1G 149
Dixonfield. High 2D 168
Dixton. Glos 2E 49
Dixton. Mon 4A 48
Dizzard. Corn 3B 10
Dobcross. G Man 4H 91
Dobs Hill. Flin 4F 83
Dobson's Bridge. Shrp 2G 71
Dobwalls. Corn 2G 7
Doccombe. Devn 4A 12
Dochgarroch. High 4A 158
Docking. Norf 2G 77
Docklow. Here 5H 59
Dockray. Cumb 2E 103
Doc Penfro. Pemb . . . . 4D 42 & 215
Dodbrooke. Devn 4D 8
Doddenham. Worc 5B 60
Doddinghurst. Essx 1G 39
Doddington. Cambs 1C 64
Doddington. Kent 5D 40
Doddington. Linc 4G 87
Doddington. Nmbd 1D 121
Doddington. Shrp 3A 60
Doddiscombsleigh. Devn 4B 12
Doddshill. Norf 2G 77
Dodford. Nptn 4D 62
Dodford. Worc 3D 60
Dodington. Som 2E 21
Dodington. S Glo 4C 34
Dodleston. Ches W 4F 83
Dods Leigh. Staf 2E 73
Dodworth. S Yor 4D 92
Doe Lea. Derbs 4B 86
Dogdyke. Linc 5B 88
Dogmersfield. Hants 1F 25
Dogsthorpe. Pet 5B 76
Dog Village. Devn 3C 12
Dolanog. Powy 4C 70
Dolau. Powy 4D 58
Dolau. Rhon 3D 32
Dolbenmaen. Gwyn 1E 69
Doley. Staf 3B 72
Dol-fâch. Powy 5B 70
(nr. Llanbrynmair)
Dolfach. Powy 3B 58
(nr. Llanidloes)
Dolfor. Powy 2D 58
Dolgarrog. Cnwy 4G 81
Dolgellau. Gwyn 4G 69
Dolgoch. Gwyn 5F 69
Dol-gran. Carm 2E 45
Dolhelfa. Powy 3B 58
Doll. High 3F 165
Dollar. Clac 4B 136
Dolley Green. Powy 4E 59
Dollwen. Cdgn 2F 57
Dolphin. Flin 3D 82
Dolphingstone. E Lot 2G 129
Dolphinholme. Lanc 4E 97
Dolphinton. S Lan 5E 129
Dolton. Devn 1F 11
Dolwen. Cnwy 3A 82
Dolwyddelan. Cnwy 5G 81
Dol-y-Bont. Cdgn 2F 57
Dolyhir. Powy 5E 59
Domgay. Powy 4E 71
Doncaster. S Yor 4F 93
Donhead St Andrew. Wilts 4E 23
Donhead St Mary. Wilts 4E 23
Doniford. Som 2D 20
Donington. Linc 2B 76
Donington. Shrp 5C 72
Donington Eaudike. Linc 2B 76
Donington le Heath. Leics 4B 74
Donington on Bain. Linc 2B 88
Donington South Ing. Linc 2B 76
Donisthorpe. Leics 4H 73
Donkey Street. Kent 2F 29
Donkey Town. Surr 4A 38
Donna Nook. Linc 1D 88
Donnington. Glos 3G 49
Donnington. Here 2C 48
Donnington. Shrp 5H 71
Donnington. Telf 4B 72
Donnington. W Ber 5C 36
Donnington. W Sus 2G 17
Donyatt. Som 1G 13
Doomsday Green. W Sus 2C 26
Doonfoot. S Ayr 3C 116
Doonholm. S Ayr 3C 116
Dorback Lodge. High 2E 151
Dorchester. Dors 3B 14
Dorchester on Thames. Oxon 2D 36
Dordon. Warw 5G 73
Dore. S Yor 2H 85
Dores. High 5H 157
Dorking. Surr 1C 26
Dorking Tye. Suff 2C 54
Dormansland. Surr 1F 27
Dormans Park. Surr 1E 27
Dormanstown. Red C 2C 106
Dormington. Here 1A 48
Dormston. Worc 5D 61
Dorn. Glos 2H 49
Dorney. Buck 3A 38
Dornie. High 1A 148
Dornoch. High 5E 165
Dornock. Dum 3D 112
Dorrery. High 3C 168
Dorridge. W Mid 3F 61
Dorrington. Linc 5H 87
Dorrington. Shrp 5G 71
Dorsington. Warw 1G 49
Dorstone. Here 1G 47
Dorton. Buck 4E 51
Dosthill. Staf 5G 73
Dotham. IOA 3C 80
Dottery. Dors 3H 13
Doublebois. Corn 2F 7
Dougarie. N Ayr 2C 122
Doughton. Glos 2D 35
Douglas. IOM 4C 108
Douglas. S Lan 1H 117
Douglastown. Ang 4D 144
Douglas Water. S Lan 1A 118
Doulting. Som 2B 22
Dounby. Orkn 5B 172
Doune. High 3C 150
(nr. Kingussie)
Doune. High 3B 164
(nr. Lairg)
Doune. Stir 3G 135
Dounie. High 4C 164
(nr. Bonar Bridge)
Dounie. High 5D 164
(nr. Tain)
Dounreay. High 2B 168
Doura. N Ayr 5E 127
Dousland. Devn 2B 8
Dovaston. Shrp 3F 71
Dove Holes. Derbs 3E 85
Dovenby. Cumb 1B 102
Dover. Kent . . . . 1H 29 & 193
Dovercourt. Essx 2F 55
Doverdale. Worc 4C 60
Doveridge. Derbs 2F 73
Doversgreen. Surr 1D 26
Dowally. Per 4H 143
Dowbridge. Lanc 1C 90
Dowdeswell. Glos 4F 49
Dowlais. Mer T 5D 46
Dowland. Devn 1F 11
Dowlands. Devn 3F 13
Dowles. Worc 3B 60
Dowlesgreen. Wok 5G 37
Dowlish Wake. Som 1G 13
Downall Green. Mers 4D 90
Down Ampney. Glos 2F 35
Downderry. Corn 3H 7
(nr. Looe)
Downderry. Corn 3D 6
(nr. St Austell)
Downe. G Lon 4F 39
Downend. IOW 4D 16
Downend. S Glo 4B 34
Downend. W Ber 4C 36
Down Field. Cambs 3F 65
Downfield. D'dee 5C 144
Downgate. Corn 5D 10
(nr. Kelly Bray)
Downgate. Corn 5C 10
(nr. Upton Cross)
Downham. Essx 1B 40
Downham. Lanc 5G 97
Downham. Nmbd 1C 120
Downham Market. Norf 5F 77
Down Hatherley. Glos 3D 48
Downhead. Som 2B 22
(nr. Frome)
Downhead. Som 4A 22
(nr. Yeovil)
Downholland Cross. Lanc 4B 90
Downholme. N Yor 5E 105
Downies. Abers 4G 153
Downley. Buck 2G 37
Down St Mary. Devn 2H 11
Downside. Som 1B 22
(nr. Chilcompton)
Downside. Som 2B 22
(nr. Shepton Mallet)
Downside. Surr 5C 38
Down, The. Shrp 1A 60
Down Thomas. Devn 3B 8
Downton. Hants 3A 16
Downton. Wilts 4G 23
Downton on the Rock. Here 3G 59
Dowsby. Linc 3A 76
Dowsdale. Linc 4B 76
Dowthwaitehead. Cumb 2E 103
Doxey. Staf 3D 72
Doxford. Nmbd 2F 121
Doynton. S Glo 4C 34
Drabblegate. Norf 3E 78
Draethen. Cphy 3F 33
Draffan. S Lan 5A 128
Dragonby. N Lin 3C 94
Dragons Green. W Sus 3C 26
Drakelow. Worc 2C 60
Drakemyre. N Ayr 4D 126
Drakes Broughton. Worc 1E 49
Drakes Cross. Worc 3E 61
Drakewalls. Corn 5E 11
Draughton. Nptn 3E 63
Draughton. N Yor 4C 98
Drax. N Yor 2G 93
Draycot. Oxon 5E 51
Draycote. Warw 4B 62
Draycot Foliat. Swin 4G 35
Draycott. Derbs 2B 74
Draycott. Glos 2G 49
Draycott. Shrp 1C 60
Draycott. Som 1H 21
(nr. Cheddar)
Draycott. Som 4A 22
(nr. Yeovil)
Draycott. Worc 1D 48
Draycott in the Clay. Staf 3F 73
Draycott in the Moors. Staf 1D 73
Drayford. Devn 1A 12
Drayton. Leics 1F 63
Drayton. Linc 2B 76
Drayton. Norf 4D 78
Drayton. Nptn 4C 62
Drayton. Oxon 2C 36
(nr. Abingdon)
Drayton. Oxon 1C 50
(nr. Banbury)
Drayton. Port 2E 17
Drayton. Som 4H 21
Drayton. Warw 5F 61
Drayton. Worc 3D 60
Drayton Bassett. Staf 5F 73
Drayton Beauchamp. Buck 4H 51
Drayton Parslow. Buck 3G 51
Drayton St Leonard. Oxon 2D 36
Drebley. N Yor 4C 98
Dreenhill. Pemb 3D 42
Drefach. Carm 4F 45
(nr. Meidrim)
Drefach. Carm 2D 44
(nr. Newcastle Emlyn)
Drefach. Carm 2G 43
(nr. Tumble)
Drefach. Cdgn 1E 45
Dreghorn. N Ayr 1C 116
Drellingore. Kent 1G 29
Drem. E Lot 2B 130
Dreumasdal. W Isl 5C 170
Drewsteignton. Devn 3H 11
Driby. Linc 3C 88
Driffield. E Yor 4E 101
Driffield. Glos 2F 35
Drift. Corn 4B 4
Drigg. Cumb 5B 102
Drighlington. W Yor 2C 92
Drimnin. High 3G 139
Drimpton. Dors 2H 13
Dringhoe. E Yor 4F 101
Drinisiadar. W Isl 8D 171
Drinkstone. Suff 4B 66
Drinkstone Green. Suff 4B 66
Drointon. Staf 3E 73
Droitwich Spa. Worc 4C 60
Droman. High 3B 166
Dron. Per 2D 136
Dronfield. Derbs 3A 86
Dronfield Woodhouse. Derbs 3H 85
Drongan. E Ayr 3D 116
Dronley. Ang 5C 144
Droop. Dors 2C 14
Drope. V Glam 4E 32
Droxford. Hants 1E 16
Droylsden. G Man 1C 84
Druggers End. Worc 2C 48
Druid. Den 1C 70
Druid's Heath. W Mid 5E 73
Druidston. Pemb 3C 42
Druim. High 3D 158
Druimarbin. High 1E 141
Druim Fhearna. High 2E 147
Druimindarroch. High 5E 147
Druim Saighdinis. W Isl 2D 170
Drum. Per 3C 136
Drumbeg. High 5B 166
Drumblade. Abers 4C 160
Drumbuie. Dum 1C 110
Drumbuie. High 5G 155
Drumburgh. Cumb 4D 112
Drumburn. Dum 3A 112
Drumchapel. Glas 2G 127
Drumchardine. High 4H 157
Drumchork. High 5C 162
Drumclog. S Lan 1F 117
Drumeldrie. Fife 3G 137
Drumelzier. Bord 1D 118
Drumfearn. High 2E 147
Drumgask. High 4A 150
Drumgelloch. N Lan 3A 128
Drumgley. Ang 3D 144
Drumguish. High 4B 150
Drumin. Mor 5F 159
Drumindorsair. High 4G 157
Drumlamford House. S Ayr 2H 109
Drumlasie. Abers 3D 152
Drumlemble. Arg 4A 122
Drumlithie. Abers 5E 153
Drummoddie. Dum 5A 110
Drummond. High 2A 158
Drummore. Dum 5E 109
Drummuir. Mor 4A 160
Drumnadrochit. High 5H 157
Drumnagorrach. Mor 3C 160
Drumoak. Abers 4E 153
Drumrunie. High 3F 163
Drumry. W Dun 2G 127
Drums. Abers 1G 153
Drumsleet. Dum 2G 111
Drumsmittal. High 4A 158
Drums of Park. Abers 3C 160
Drumsturdy. Ang 5D 145
Drumtochty Castle. Abers 5D 152
Drumuie. High 4D 154
Drumuillie. High 1D 150
Drumvaich. Stir 3F 135
Drumwhindle. Abers 5G 161
Drunkendub. Ang 4F 145
Drury. Flin 4E 83
Drury Square. Norf 4B 78
Drybeck. Cumb 3H 103
Drybridge. Mor 2B 160
Drybridge. N Ayr 1C 116
Drybrook. Glos 4B 48
Drybrook. Here 4A 48
Dryburgh. Bord 1H 119
Dry Doddington. Linc 1F 75
Dry Drayton. Cambs 4C 64
Drym. Corn 3D 4
Drymen. Stir 1F 127
Drymuir. Abers 4G 161
Drynachan Lodge. High 5C 158
Drynie Park. High 3H 157
Drynoch. High 5D 154
Dry Sandford. Oxon 5C 50
Dryslwyn. Carm 3F 45
Dry Street. Essx 2A 40
Dryton. Shrp 5H 71
Dubford. Abers 2E 161
Dubiton. Abers 3D 160
Dubton. Ang 3E 145
Duchally. High 2A 164
Duck End. Essx 3G 53
Duckington. Ches W 5G 83
Ducklington. Oxon 5B 50
Duckmanton. Derbs 3B 86
Duck Street. Hants 2B 24
Dudbridge. Glos 5D 48
Duddenhoe End. Essx 2E 53
Duddingston. Edin 2F 129
Duddington. Nptn 5G 75
Duddleswell. E Sus 3F 27
Duddo. Nmbd 5F 131
Duddon. Ches W 4H 83
Duddon Bridge. Cumb 1A 96
Dudleston. Shrp 2F 71
Dudleston Heath. Shrp 2F 71
Dudley. Tyne 2F 115
Dudley. W Mid 2D 60
Dudston. Shrp 1E 59
Dudwells. Pemb 2D 42
Duffield. Derbs 1H 73
Duffryn. Neat 2B 32
Dufftown. Mor 4H 159
Duffus. Mor 2F 159
Dufton. Cumb 2H 103
Duggleby. N Yor 3C 100
Duirinish. High 5G 155
Duisdalemore. High 2E 147
Duisdeil Mòr. High 2E 147
Duisky. High 1E 141
Dukesfield. Nmbd 4C 114
Dukestown. Blae 5E 47
Dukinfield. G Man 1D 84
Dulas. IOA 2D 81
Dulcote. Som 2A 22
Dulford. Devn 2D 12
Dull. Per 4F 143
Dullatur. N Lan 2A 128
Dullingham. Cambs 5F 65
Dullingham Ley. Cambs 5F 65
Dulnain Bridge. High 1D 151
Duloe. Bed 4A 64
Duloe. Corn 3G 7
Dulverton. Som 4C 20
Dulwich. G Lon 3E 39
Dumbarton. W Dun 2F 127
Dumbleton. Glos 2F 49
Dumfin. Arg 1E 127
Dumfries. Dum . . . . 2A 112 & 193
Dumgoyne. Stir 1G 127
Dummer. Hants 2D 24
Dumpford. W Sus 4G 25
Dun. Ang 2F 145
Dunagoil. Arg 4B 126
Dunalastair. Per 3E 142
Dunan. High 1D 147
Dunball. Som 2G 21
Dunbar. E Lot 2C 130
Dunbeath. High 5D 168
Dunbeg. Arg 5C 140
Dunblane. Stir 3G 135
Dunbog. Fife 2E 137
Dunbridge. Hants 4B 24
Duncanston. Abers 1C 152
Duncanston. High 3H 157
Dun Charlabhaigh. W Isl 3D 171
Dunchideock. Devn 4B 12
Dunchurch. Warw 3B 62
Duncote. Nptn 5D 62
Duncow. Dum 1A 112
Duncrievie. Per 3D 136
Duncton. W Sus 4A 26
Dundee. D'dee . . . . 5D 144 & 194
Dundee Airport. D'dee 1F 137
Dundon. Som 3H 21
Dundonald. S Ayr 1C 116
Dundonnell. High 5E 163
Dundraw. Cumb 5D 112
Dundreggan. High 2F 149
Dundrennan. Dum 5E 111
Dundridge. Hants 1D 16
Dundry. N Som 5A 34
Dunecht. Abers 3E 153
Dunfermline. Fife 1D 129
Dunford Bridge. S Yor 4B 92
Dungate. Kent 5D 40
Dunge. Wilts 1D 23
Dungeness. Kent 4E 29
Dungworth. S Yor 2G 85
Dunham-on-the-Hill. Ches W 3G 83
Dunham-on-Trent. Notts 3F 87
Dunhampton. Worc 4C 60
Dunham Town. G Man 2B 84
Dunham Woodhouses. G Man 2B 84
Dunholme. Linc 3H 87
Dunino. Fife 2H 137
Dunipace. Falk 1B 128
Dunira. Per 1G 135
Dunkeld. Per 4H 143
Dunkerton. Bath 1C 22
Dunkeswell. Devn 2E 13
Dunkeswick. N Yor 5F 99
Dunkirk. Kent 5E 41
Dunkirk. S Glo 3C 34
Dunkirk. Staf 5C 84
Dunkirk. Wilts 5E 35
Dunk's Green. Kent 5H 39
Dunlappie. Ang 2E 145
Dunley. Hants 1C 24
Dunley. Worc 4B 60
Dunlichity Lodge. High 5A 158
Dunlop. E Ayr 5F 127

Dunmaglass Lodge—Ebernoe

Dunmaglass Lodge. *High* 1H 149
Dunmore. *Arg* 3F 125
Dunmore. *Falk* 1B 128
Dunmore. *High* 4H 157
Dunnet. *High* 1E 169
Dunnichen. *Ang* 4E 145
Dunning. *Per* 2C 136
Dunnington. *E Yor* 4F 101
Dunnington. *Warw* 5E 61
Dunnington. *York* 4A 100
Dunningwell. *Cumb* 1A 96
Dunnockshaw. *Lanc* 2G 91
Dunoon. *Arg* 2C 126
Dunphail. *Mor* 4E 159
Dunragit. *Dum* 4G 109
Dunrostan. *Arg* 1F 125
Duns. *Bord* 4D 130
Dunsby. *Linc* 3A 76
Dunscar. *G Man* 3F 91
Dunscore. *Dum* 1F 111
Dunscroft. *S Yor* 4G 93
Dunsdale. *Red C* 3D 106
Dunsden Green. *Oxon* 4F 37
Dunsfold. *Surr* 2B 26
Dunsford. *Devn* 4B 12
Dunshalt. *Fife* 2E 137
Dunshillock. *Abers* 4G 161
Dunsley. *N Yor* 3F 107
Dunsley. *Staf* 2C 60
Dunsmore. *Buck* 5G 51
Dunsop Bridge. *Lanc* 4F 97
Dunstable. *C Beds* 3A 52
Dunstal. *Staf* 3E 73
Dunstall. *Staf* 3F 73
Dunstall Green. *Suff* 4G 65
Dunstall Hill. *W Mid* 1D 60
Dunstan. *Nmbd* 3G 121
Dunster. *Som* 2C 20
Duns Tew. *Oxon* 3C 50
Dunston. *Linc* 4H 87
Dunston. *Norf* 5E 79
Dunston. *Staf* 4D 72
Dunston. *Tyne* 3F 115
Dunstone. *Devn* 3B 8
Dunston Heath. *Staf* 4D 72
Dunsville. *S Yor* 4G 93
Dunswell. *E Yor* 1D 94
Dunsyre. *S Lan* 5D 128
Dunterton. *Devn* 5D 11
Duntisbourne Abbots. *Glos* 5E 49
Duntisbourne Leer. *Glos* 5E 49
Duntisbourne Rouse. *Glos* 5E 49
Duntish. *Dors* 2B 14
Duntocher. *W Dun* 2F 127
Dunton. *Buck* 3G 51
Dunton. *C Beds* 1C 52
Dunton. *Norf* 2A 78
Dunton Bassett. *Leics* 1C 62
Dunton Green. *Kent* 5G 39
Dunton Patch. *Norf* 2A 78
Duntulm. *High* 1D 154
Dunure. *S Ayr* 3B 116
Dunvant. *Swan* 3E 31
Dunvegan. *High* 4B 154
Dunwich. *Suff* 3G 67
Dunwood. *Staf* 5D 84
Durdar. *Cumb* 4F 113
Durgates. *E Sus* 2H 27
Durham. *Dur* 5F 115 & 194
Durham Tees Valley Airport. *Darl* 3A 106
Durisdeer. *Dum* 4A 118
Durisdeermill. *Dum* 4A 118
Durkar. *W Yor* 3D 92
Durleigh. *Som* 3F 21
Durley. *Hants* 1D 16
Durley. *Wilts* 5H 35
Durley Street. *Hants* 1D 16
Durlow Common. *Here* 2B 48
Durnamuck. *High* 4E 163
Durness. *High* 2E 166
Durno. *Abers* 1E 152
Durns Town. *Hants* 3A 16
Duror. *High* 3D 141
Durran. *Arg* 3G 133
Durran. *High* 2D 169
Durrant Green. *Kent* 2C 28
Durrants. *Hants* 1F 17
Durrington. *W Sus* 5C 26
Durrington. *Wilts* 2G 23
Dursley. *Glos* 2C 34
Dursley Cross. *Glos* 4B 48
Durston. *Som* 4F 21
Durweston. *Dors* 2D 14
Dury. *Shet* 6F 173
Duston. *Nptn* 4E 62
Duthil. *High* 1D 150
Dutlas. *Powy* 3E 58
Duton Hill. *Essx* 3G 53
Dutson. *Corn* 4D 10
Dutton. *Ches W* 3H 83
Duxford. *Cambs* 1E 53
Duxford. *Oxon* 2B 36
Dwygyfylchi. *Cnwy* 3G 81
Dwyran. *IOA* 4D 80
Dyce. *Aber* 2F 153
Dyffryn. *B'end* 2B 32
Dyffryn. *Carm* 2H 43
Dyffryn. *Pemb* 1D 42
Dyffryn. *V Glam* 4D 32
Dyffryn Ardudwy. *Gwyn* 3E 69
Dyffryn Castell. *Cdgn* 2G 57
Dyffryn Ceidrych. *Carm* 3H 45
Dyffryn Cellwen. *Neat* 5B 46
Dyke. *Linc* 3A 76
Dyke. *Mor* 3D 159
Dykehead. *Ang* 2C 144
Dykehead. *N Lan* 3B 128
Dykehead. *Stir* 4E 135
Dykend. *Ang* 3B 144
Dykesfield. *Cumb* 4E 112
Dylife. *Powy* 1A 58
Dymchurch. *Kent* 3F 29
Dymock. *Glos* 2C 48
Dyrham. *S Glo* 4C 34
Dysart. *Fife* 4F 137
Dyserth. *Den* 3C 82

E

Eachwick. *Nmbd* 2E 115
Eadar Dha Fhadhail. *W Isl* 4C 171
Eagland Hill. *Lanc* 5D 96
Eagle. *Linc* 4F 87
Eagle Barnsdale. *Linc* 4F 87
Eagle Moor. *Linc* 4F 87
Eaglescliffe. *Stoc T* 3B 106
Eaglesfield. *Cumb* 2B 102
Eaglesfield. *Dum* 2D 112
Eaglesham. *E Ren* 4G 127
Eaglethorpe. *Nptn* 1H 63
Eagley. *G Man* 3F 91
Eairy. *IOM* 4B 108
Eakley Lanes. *Mil* 5F 63
Eakring. *Notts* 4D 86
Ealand. *N Lin* 3A 94
Ealing. *G Lon* 2C 38
Eallabus. *Arg* 3B 124
Eals. *Nmbd* 4H 113
Eamont Bridge. *Cumb* 2G 103
Earby. *Lanc* 5B 98
Earcroft. *Bkbn* 2E 91
Eardington. *Shrp* 1B 60
Eardisland. *Here* 5G 59
Eardisley. *Here* 1G 47
Eardiston. *Shrp* 3F 71
Eardiston. *Worc* 4A 60
Earith. *Cambs* 3C 64
Earlais. *High* 2C 154
Earle. *Nmbd* 2D 121
Earlesfield. *Linc* 2G 75
Earlestown. *Mers* 1H 83
Earley. *Wok* 4F 37
Earlham. *Norf* 5D 78
Earlish. *High* 2C 154
Earls Barton. *Nptn* 4F 63
Earls Colne. *Essx* 3B 54
Earls Common. *Worc* 5D 60
Earl's Croome. *Worc* 1D 48
Earlsdon. *W Mid* 3H 61
Earlsferry. *Fife* 3G 137
Earlsford. *Abers* 5F 161
Earl's Green. *Suff* 4C 66
Earlsheaton. *W Yor* 2C 92
Earl Shilton. *Leics* 1B 62
Earl Soham. *Suff* 4E 67
Earl Sterndale. *Derbs* 4E 85
Earlston. *E Ayr* 1D 116
Earlston. *Bord* 1H 119
Earl Stonham. *Suff* 5D 66
Earlstoun. *Dum* 1D 110
Earlswood. *Mon* 2H 33
Earlswood. *Warw* 3F 61
Earlyvale. *Bord* 4F 129
Earnley. *W Sus* 3G 17
Earsairidh. *W Isl* 9C 170
Earsdon. *Tyne* 2G 115
Earsham. *Norf* 2F 67
Earsham Street. *Suff* 3E 67
Earswick. *York* 4A 100
Eartham. *W Sus* 5A 26
Earthcott Green. *S Glo* 3B 34
Easby. *N Yor* 4C 106 (nr. Great Ayton)
Easby. *N Yor* 4E 105 (nr. Richmond)
Easdale. *Arg* 2E 133
Easebourne. *W Sus* 4G 25
Easenhall. *Warw* 3B 62
Eashing. *Surr* 1A 26
Easington. *Buck* 4E 51
Easington. *Dur* 5H 115
Easington. *E Yor* 3G 95
Easington. *Nmbd* 1F 121
Easington. *Oxon* 2C 50 (nr. Banbury)
Easington. *Oxon* 2E 37 (nr. Watlington)
Easington. *Red C* 3E 107
Easington Colliery. *Dur* 5H 115
Easington Lane. *Tyne* 5G 115
Easingwold. *N Yor* 3H 99
Eassie. *Ang* 4C 144
Eassie and Nevay. *Ang* 4C 144
East Aberthaw. *V Glam* 5D 32
Eastacombe. *Devn* 4F 19
Eastacott. *Devn* 4G 19
East Allington. *Devn* 4D 8
East Anstey. *Devn* 4B 20
East Anton. *Hants* 2B 24
East Appleton. *N Yor* 5F 105
East Ardsley. *W Yor* 2D 92
East Ashley. *Devn* 1G 11
East Ashling. *W Sus* 2G 17
East Aston. *Hants* 2C 24
East Ayton. *N Yor* 1D 101
East Barkwith. *Linc* 2A 88
East Barnby. *N Yor* 3F 107
East Barnet. *G Lon* 1D 39
East Barns. *E Lot* 2D 130
East Barsham. *Norf* 2B 78
East Beach. *W Sus* 3G 17
East Beckham. *Norf* 1D 78
East Bedfont. *G Lon* 3B 38
East Bennan. *N Ayr* 3D 123
East Bergholt. *Suff* 2D 54
East Bierley. *W Yor* 2B 92
East Bilney. *Norf* 4B 78
East Blatchington. *E Sus* 5F 27
East Bloxworth. *Dors* 3D 15
East Boldre. *Hants* 2B 16
East Bolton. *Nmbd* 3F 121
Eastbourne. *Darl* 3F 105
Eastbourne. *E Sus* 5H 27 & 195
East Brent. *Som* 1G 21
East Bridge. *Suff* 4G 67
East Bridgford. *Notts* 1D 74
East Briscoe. *Dur* 3C 104
East Buckland. *Devn* 3G 19 (nr. Barnstaple)
East Buckland. *Devn* 4C 8 (nr. Thurlestone)
East Budleigh. *Devn* 4D 12
Eastburn. *W Yor* 5C 98
East Burnham. *Buck* 2A 38
East Burrafirth. *Shet* 6E 173
East Burton. *Dors* 4D 14
Eastbury. *Herts* 1B 38
Eastbury. *W Ber* 4B 36
East Butsfield. *Dur* 5E 115
East Butterleigh. *Devn* 2C 12
East Butterwick. *N Lin* 4B 94
Eastby. *N Yor* 4C 98
East Calder. *W Lot* 3D 129
East Carleton. *Norf* 5D 78
East Carlton. *Nptn* 2F 63
East Carlton. *W Yor* 5E 98
East Chaldon. *Dors* 4C 14
East Challow. *Oxon* 3B 36
East Charleton. *Devn* 4D 8
East Chelborough. *Dors* 2A 14
East Chiltington. *E Sus* 4E 27
East Chinnock. *Som* 1H 13
East Chisenbury. *Wilts* 1G 23
Eastchurch. *Kent* 3D 40
East Clandon. *Surr* 5B 38
East Claydon. *Buck* 3F 51
East Clevedon. *N Som* 4H 33
East Clyne. *High* 3F 165
East Clyth. *High* 5E 169
East Coker. *Som* 1A 14
Eastcombe. *Glos* 5D 49
East Combe. *Som* 3E 21
East Common. *N Yor* 1G 93
East Compton. *Som* 2B 22
East Cornworthy. *Devn* 3E 9
Eastcote. *G Lon* 2C 38
Eastcote. *Nptn* 5D 62
Eastcote. *W Mid* 3F 61
Eastcott. *Corn* 1C 10
Eastcott. *Wilts* 1F 23
East Cottingwith. *E Yor* 5B 100
Eastcourt. *Wilts* 5H 35 (nr. Pewsey)
Eastcourt. *Wilts* 2E 35 (nr. Tetbury)
East Cowes. *IOW* 3D 16
East Cowick. *E Yor* 2G 93
East Cowton. *N Yor* 4A 106
East Cramlington. *Nmbd* 2F 115
East Cranmore. *Som* 2B 22
East Creech. *Dors* 4E 15
East Croachy. *High* 1A 150
East Dean. *E Sus* 5G 27
East Dean. *Glos* 3B 48
East Dean. *Hants* 4A 24
East Dean. *W Sus* 4A 26
East Down. *Devn* 2G 19
East Drayton. *Notts* 3E 87
East Dundry. *N Som* 5A 34
East Ella. *Hull* 2D 94
East End. *Cambs* 3C 64
East End. *Dors* 3E 15
East End. *E Yor* 4F 101 (nr. Ulrome)
East End. *E Yor* 2F 95 (nr. Withernsea)
East End. *Hants* 3B 16 (nr. Lymington)
East End. *Hants* 5C 36 (nr. Newbury)
East End. *Herts* 3E 53
East End. *Kent* 3D 40 (nr. Minster)
East End. *Kent* 2C 28 (nr. Tenterden)
East End. *N Som* 4H 33
East End. *Oxon* 4B 50
East End. *Som* 1A 22
East End. *Suff* 2E 54
Easter Ardross. *High* 1A 158
Easter Balgedie. *Per* 3D 136
Easter Balmoral. *Abers* 4G 151
Easter Brae. *High* 2A 158
Easter Buckieburn. *Stir* 1A 128
Easter Bush. *Midl* 3F 129
Easter Compton. *S Glo* 3A 34
Easter Fearn. *High* 5D 164
Easter Galcantray. *High* 4C 158
Eastergate. *W Sus* 5A 26
Easterhouse. *Glas* 3H 127
Easter Howgate. *Midl* 3F 129
Easter Kinkell. *High* 3H 157
Easter Lednathie. *Ang* 2C 144
Easter Ogil. *Ang* 2D 144
Easter Ord. *Abers* 3F 153
Easter Quarff. *Shet* 8F 173
Easter Rhynd. *Per* 2D 136
Easter Skeld. *Shet* 7E 173
Easter Suddie. *High* 3A 158
Easterton. *Wilts* 1F 23
Eastertown. *Som* 1G 21
Easter Tulloch. *Abers* 1G 145
East Everleigh. *Wilts* 1H 23
East Farleigh. *Kent* 5B 40
East Farndon. *Nptn* 2E 62
East Ferry. *Linc* 1F 87
Eastfield. *N Lan* 3B 128 (nr. Caldercruix)
Eastfield. *N Lan* 3B 128 (nr. Harthill)
Eastfield. *N Yor* 1E 101
Eastfield. *S Lan* 3H 127
Eastfield Hall. *Nmbd* 4G 121
East Fortune. *E Lot* 2B 130
East Garforth. *W Yor* 1E 93
East Garston. *W Ber* 4B 36
Eastgate. *Dur* 1C 104
Eastgate. *Norf* 3D 78
East Ginge. *Oxon* 3C 36
East Gores. *Essx* 3B 54
East Goscote. *Leics* 4D 74
East Grafton. *Wilts* 5A 36
East Green. *Suff* 5F 65
East Grimstead. *Wilts* 4H 23
East Grinstead. *W Sus* 2E 27
East Guldeford. *E Sus* 3D 28
East Haddon. *Nptn* 4D 62
East Hagbourne. *Oxon* 3D 36
East Halton. *N Lin* 2E 95
East Ham. *G Lon* 2F 39
Eastham. *Mers* 2F 83
Eastham. *Worc* 4A 60
Eastham Ferry. *Mers* 2F 83
Easthampstead. *Brac* 5G 37
Easthampton. *Here* 4G 59
East Hanney. *Oxon* 2C 36
East Hanningfield. *Essx* 5A 54
East Hardwick. *W Yor* 3E 93
East Harling. *Norf* 2B 66
East Harlsey. *N Yor* 5B 106
East Harnham. *Wilts* 4G 23
East Harptree. *Bath* 1A 22
East Hartford. *Nmbd* 2F 115
East Harting. *W Sus* 1G 17
East Hatch. *Wilts* 4E 23
East Hatley. *Cambs* 5B 64
Easthaugh. *Norf* 4C 78
East Hauxwell. *N Yor* 5E 105
East Haven. *Ang* 5E 145
Eastheath. *Wok* 5G 37
East Heckington. *Linc* 1A 76
East Hedleyhope. *Dur* 5E 115
East Helmsdale. *High* 2H 165
East Hendred. *Oxon* 3C 36
East Heslerton. *N Yor* 2D 100
East Hoathly. *E Sus* 4G 27
East Holme. *Dors* 4D 15
Easthope. *Shrp* 1H 59
Easthorpe. *Essx* 3C 54
Easthorpe. *Leics* 2F 75
East Horrington. *Som* 2A 22
East Horsley. *Surr* 5B 38
East Horton. *Nmbd* 1E 121
Easthouses. *Midl* 3G 129
East Howe. *Bour* 3F 15
East Huntspill. *Som* 2G 21
East Hyde. *C Beds* 4B 52
East Ilsley. *W Ber* 3C 36
Eastington. *Devn* 2H 11
Eastington. *Glos* 4G 49 (nr. Northleach)
Eastington. *Glos* 5C 48 (nr. Stonehouse)
East Keal. *Linc* 4C 88
East Kennett. *Wilts* 5G 35
East Keswick. *W Yor* 5F 99
East Kilbride. *S Lan* 4H 127
East Kirkby. *Linc* 4C 88
East Knapton. *N Yor* 2C 100
East Knighton. *Dors* 4D 14
East Knowstone. *Devn* 4B 20
East Knoyle. *Wilts* 3D 23
East Kyloe. *Nmbd* 1E 121
East Lambrook. *Som* 1H 13
East Langdon. *Kent* 1H 29
East Langton. *Leics* 1E 63
East Langwell. *High* 3E 164
East Lavant. *W Sus* 2G 17
East Lavington. *W Sus* 4A 26
East Layton. *N Yor* 4E 105
Eastleach Martin. *Glos* 5H 49
Eastleach Turville. *Glos* 5G 49
East Leake. *Notts* 3C 74
East Learmouth. *Nmbd* 1C 120
Eastleigh. *Devn* 4E 19 (nr. Bideford)
East Leigh. *Devn* 2H 11 (nr. Crediton)
East Leigh. *Devn* 3C 8 (nr. Modbury)
Eastleigh. *Hants* 1C 16
East Lexham. *Norf* 4A 78
East Lilburn. *Nmbd* 2E 121
Eastling. *Kent* 5D 40
East Linton. *E Lot* 2B 130
East Liss. *Hants* 4F 25
East Lockinge. *Oxon* 3C 36
East Looe. *Corn* 3G 7
East Lound. *N Lin* 1E 87
East Lulworth. *Dors* 4D 14
East Lutton. *N Yor* 3D 100
East Lydford. *Som* 3A 22
East Lyng. *Som* 4G 21
East Mains. *Abers* 4D 152
East Malling. *Kent* 5B 40
East Marden. *W Sus* 1G 17
East Markham. *Notts* 3E 87
East Marton. *N Yor* 4B 98
East Meon. *Hants* 4E 25
East Mersea. *Essx* 4D 54
East Mey. *High* 1F 169
East Midlands Airport. *Leics* 3B 74 & 216
East Molesey. *Surr* 4C 38
Eastmoor. *Norf* 5G 77
East Morden. *Dors* 3E 15
East Morton. *W Yor* 5D 98
East Ness. *N Yor* 2A 100
East Newton. *E Yor* 1F 95
East Newton. *N Yor* 2A 100
Eastney. *Port* 3E 17
Eastnor. *Here* 2C 48
East Norton. *Leics* 5E 75
East Nynehead. *Som* 4E 21
East Oakley. *Hants* 1D 24
Eastoft. *N Lin* 3B 94
East Ogwell. *Devn* 5B 12
Easton. *Cambs* 3A 64
Easton. *Cumb* 4D 112 (nr. Burgh by Sands)
Easton. *Cumb* 2F 113 (nr. Longtown)
Easton. *Devn* 4H 11
Easton. *Dors* 5B 14
Easton. *Hants* 3D 24
Easton. *Linc* 3G 75
Easton. *Norf* 4D 78
Easton. *Som* 2A 22
Easton. *Suff* 5E 67
Easton. *Wilts* 4D 35
Easton Grey. *Wilts* 3D 35
Easton-in-Gordano. *N Som* 4A 34
Easton Maudit. *Nptn* 5F 63
Easton on the Hill. *Nptn* 5H 75
Easton Royal. *Wilts* 5H 35
East Orchard. *Dors* 1D 14
East Ord. *Nmbd* 4F 131
East Panson. *Devn* 3D 10
East Peckham. *Kent* 1A 28
East Pennard. *Som* 3A 22
East Perry. *Cambs* 4A 64
East Pitcorthie. *Fife* 3H 137
East Portlemouth. *Devn* 5D 8
East Prawle. *Devn* 5D 9
East Preston. *W Sus* 5B 26
East Putford. *Devn* 1D 10
East Quantoxhead. *Som* 2E 21
East Rainton. *Tyne* 5G 115
East Ravendale. *NE Lin* 1B 88
East Raynham. *Norf* 3A 78
Eastrea. *Cambs* 1B 64
East Rhidorroch Lodge. *High* 4G 163
Eastriggs. *Dum* 3D 112
East Rigton. *W Yor* 5F 99
Eastrington. *E Yor* 1A 94
East Rounton. *N Yor* 4B 106
East Row. *N Yor* 3F 107
East Rudham. *Norf* 3H 77
East Runton. *Norf* 1D 78
East Ruston. *Norf* 3F 79
Eastry. *Kent* 5H 41
East Saltoun. *E Lot* 3A 130
East Shaws. *Dur* 3D 105
East Shefford. *W Ber* 4B 36
Eastshore. *Shet* 10E 173
East Sleekburn. *Nmbd* 1F 115
East Somerton. *Norf* 4G 79
East Stockwith. *Linc* 1E 87
East Stoke. *Dors* 4D 14
East Stoke. *Notts* 1E 75
East Stoke. *Som* 1H 13
East Stour. *Dors* 4D 22
East Stourmouth. *Kent* 4G 41
East Stowford. *Devn* 4G 19
East Stratton. *Hants* 2D 24
East Studdal. *Kent* 1H 29
East Taphouse. *Corn* 2F 7
East-the-Water. *Devn* 4E 19
East Thirston. *Nmbd* 5F 121
East Tilbury. *Thur* 3A 40
East Tisted. *Hants* 3F 25
East Torrington. *Linc* 2A 88
East Tuddenham. *Norf* 4C 78
East Tytherley. *Hants* 4A 24
East Tytherton. *Wilts* 4E 35
East Village. *Devn* 2B 12
Eastville. *Linc* 5D 88
East Wall. *Shrp* 1H 59
East Walton. *Norf* 4G 77
East Week. *Devn* 3G 11
Eastwell. *Leics* 3E 75
East Wellow. *Hants* 4B 24
East Wemyss. *Fife* 4F 137
East Whitburn. *W Lot* 3C 128
Eastwick. *Herts* 4E 53
Eastwick. *Shet* 4E 173
East Williamston. *Pemb* 4E 43
East Winch. *Norf* 4F 77
East Winterslow. *Wilts* 3H 23
East Wittering. *W Sus* 3F 17
East Witton. *N Yor* 1D 98
Eastwood. *Notts* 1B 74
Eastwood. *S'end* 2C 40
East Woodburn. *Nmbd* 1C 114
Eastwood End. *Cambs* 1D 64
East Woodhay. *Hants* 5C 36
East Woodlands. *Som* 2C 22
East Worldham. *Hants* 3F 25
East Worlington. *Devn* 1A 12
East Wretham. *Norf* 1B 66
East Youlstone. *Devn* 1C 10
Eathorpe. *Warw* 4A 62
Eaton. *Ches E* 4C 84
Eaton. *Ches W* 4H 83
Eaton. *Leics* 3E 75
Eaton. *Norf* 2F 77 (nr. Heacham)
Eaton. *Norf* 5E 78 (nr. Norwich)
Eaton. *Notts* 3E 86
Eaton. *Oxon* 5C 50
Eaton. *Shrp* 2F 59 (nr. Bishop's Castle)
Eaton. *Shrp* 1H 59 (nr. Church Stretton)
Eaton Bishop. *Here* 2H 47
Eaton Bray. *C Beds* 3H 51
Eaton Constantine. *Shrp* 5H 71
Eaton Hastings. *Oxon* 2A 36
Eaton Socon. *Cambs* 5A 64
Eaton upon Tern. *Shrp* 3A 72
Eau Brink. *Norf* 4E 77
Eaves Green. *W Mid* 2G 61
Ebberley Hill. *Devn* 1F 11
Ebberston. *N Yor* 1C 100
Ebbesbourne Wake. *Wilts* 4E 23
Ebblake. *Dors* 2G 15
Ebbsfleet. *Kent* 3H 39
Ebbw Vale. *Blae* 5E 47
Ebchester. *Dur* 4E 115
Ebernoe. *W Sus* 3A 26

Ebford—Falkland

Ebford. Devn 4C 12
Ebley. Glos 5D 48
Ebnal. Ches W 1G 71
Ebrington. Glos 1G 49
Ecchinswell. Hants 1D 24
Ecclefechan. Dum 2C 112
Eccles. G Man 1B 84
Eccles. Kent 4B 40
Eccles. Bord 5D 130
Ecclesall. S Yor 2H 85
Ecclesfield. S Yor 1A 86
Eccles Green. Here 1G 47
Eccleshall. Staf 3C 72
Eccleshill. W Yor 1B 92
Ecclesmachan. W Lot 2D 128
Eccles on Sea. Norf 3G 79
Eccles Road. Norf 1C 66
Eccleston. Ches W 4G 83
Eccleston. Lanc 3D 90
Eccleston. Mers 1G 83
Eccup. W Yor 5E 99
Echt. Abers 3E 153
Eckford. Bord 2B 120
Eckington. Derbs 3B 86
Eckington. Worc 1E 49
Ecton. Nptn 4F 63
Edale. Derbs 2F 85
Eday Airport. Orkn 4E 172
Edburton. W Sus 4D 26
Edderside. Cumb 5C 112
Edderton. High 5E 164
Eddington. Kent 4F 41
Eddington. W Ber 5B 36
Eddleston. Bord 5F 129
Eddlewood. S Lan 4A 128
Edenbridge. Kent 1F 27
Edendonich. Arg 1A 134
Edenfield. Lanc 3G 91
Edenhall. Cumb 1G 103
Edenham. Linc 3H 75
Edensor. Derbs 4G 85
Edentaggart. Arg 4C 134
Edenthorpe. S Yor 4G 93
Eden Vale. Dur 1B 106
Edern. Gwyn 2B 68
Edgarley. Som 3A 22
Edgbaston. W Mid 2E 61
Edgcott. Buck 3E 51
Edgcott. Som 3B 20
Edge. Glos 5D 48
Edge. Shrp 5F 71
Edgebolton. Shrp 3H 71
Edge End. Glos 4A 48
Edgefield. Norf 2C 78
Edgefield Street. Norf 2C 78
Edge Green. Ches W 5G 83
Edgehead. Midl 3G 129
Edgeley. Shrp 1H 71
Edgeside. Lanc 2G 91
Edgeworth. Glos 5E 49
Edgiock. Worc 4E 61
Edgmond. Telf 4B 72
Edgmond Marsh. Telf 3B 72
Edgton. Shrp 2F 59
Edgware. G Lon 1C 38
Edgworth. Bkbn 3F 91
Edinbane. High 3C 154
Edinburgh. Edin 2F 129 & 194
Edinburgh Airport. Edin 2E 129
Edingale. Staf 4G 73
Edingley. Notts 5D 86
Edingthorpe. Norf 2F 79
Edington. Som 3G 21
Edington. Wilts 1E 23
Edingworth. Som 1G 21
Edistone. Devn 4C 18
Edithmead. Som 2G 21
Edith Weston. Rut 5G 75
Edlaston. Derbs 1F 73
Edlesborough. Buck 4H 51
Edlingham. Nmbd 4F 121
Edlington. Linc 3B 88
Edmondsham. Dors 1F 15
Edmondsley. Dur 5F 115
Edmondthorpe. Leics 4F 75
Edmonstone. Orkn 5E 172
Edmonton. Corn 1D 6
Edmonton. G Lon 1E 39
Edmundbyers. Dur 4D 114
Ednam. Bord 1B 120
Ednaston. Derbs 1G 73
Edney Common. Essx 5G 53
Edrom. Bord 4E 131
Edstaston. Shrp 2H 71
Edstone. Warw 4F 61
Edwalton. Notts 2D 74
Edwardstone. Suff 1C 54
Edwardsville. Mer T 2D 32
Edwinsford. Carm 2G 45
Edwinstowe. Notts 4D 86
Edworth. C Beds 1C 52
Edwyn Ralph. Here 5A 60
Edzell. Ang 2F 145
Efail-fach. Neat 2A 32
Efail Isaf. Rhon 3D 32
Efailnewydd. Gwyn 2C 68
Efail-rhyd. Powy 3D 70
Efailwen. Carm 2F 43
Efenechtyd. Den 5D 82
Effingham. Surr 5C 38
Effingham Common. Surr 5C 38
Effirth. Shet 6E 173
Efflinch. Staf 4F 73
Efford. Devn 2B 12
Efstigarth. Shet 2F 173
Egbury. Hants 1C 24
Egdon. Worc 5D 60
Egerton. G Man 3F 91
Egerton. Kent 1D 28
Egerton Forstal. Kent 1C 28
Eggborough. N Yor 2F 93
Eggbuckland. Plym 3A 8
Eggesford. Devn 1G 11
Eggington. C Beds 3H 51
Egginton. Derbs 3G 73
Egglescliffe. Stoc T 3B 106
Eggleston. Dur 2C 104
Egham. Surr 3B 38
Egham Hythe. Surr 3B 38
Egleton. Rut 5F 75
Eglingham. Nmbd 3F 121
Egloshayle. Corn 5A 10
Egloskerry. Corn 4C 10
Eglwysbach. Cnwy 3H 81
Eglwys-Brewis. V Glam 5D 32
Eglwys Fach. Cdgn 1F 57
Eglwyswrw. Pemb 1F 43
Egmanton. Notts 4E 87
Egmere. Norf 2B 78
Egremont. Cumb 3B 102
Egremont. Mers 1F 83
Egton. N Yor 4F 107
Egton Bridge. N Yor 4F 107
Egypt. Buck 2A 38
Egypt. Hants 2C 24
Eight Ash Green. Essx 3C 54
Eight Mile Burn. Midl 4E 129
Eignaig. High 4B 140
Eilanreach. High 2G 147
Eildon. Bord 1H 119
Eileanach Lodge. High 2H 157
Eilean Fhlodaigh. W Isl 3D 170
Eilean Iarmain. High 2F 147
Einacleit. W Isl 5D 171
Eisgein. W Isl 6F 171
Eisingrug. Gwyn 2F 69
Elan Village. Powy 4B 58
Elberton. S Glo 3B 34
Elbridge. W Sus 5A 26
Elburton. Plym 3B 8
Elcho. Per 1D 136
Elcombe. Swin 3G 35
Elcot. W Ber 5B 36
Eldernell. Cambs 1C 64
Eldersfield. Worc 2D 48
Elderslie. Ren 3F 127
Elder Street. Essx 2F 53
Eldon. Dur 2F 105
Eldroth. N Yor 3G 97
Eldwick. W Yor 5D 98
Elfhowe. Cumb 5F 103
Elford. Nmbd 1F 121
Elford. Staf 4F 73
Elford Closes. Cambs 3D 65
Elgin. Mor 2G 159
Elgol. High 2D 146
Elham. Kent 1F 29
Elie. Fife 3G 137
Eling. Hants 1B 16
Eling. W Ber 4D 36
Elishaw. Nmbd 5C 120
Elizafield. Dum 2B 112
Elkesley. Notts 3D 86
Elkington. Nptn 3D 62
Elkins Green. Essx 5G 53
Elkstone. Glos 4E 49
Ellan. High 1C 150
Elland. W Yor 2B 92
Ellary. Arg 2F 125
Ellastone. Staf 1F 73
Ellbridge. Corn 2A 8
Ellel. Lanc 4D 97
Ellemford. Bord 3D 130
Ellenabeich. Arg 2E 133
Ellenborough. Cumb 1B 102
Ellenbrook. Herts 5C 52
Ellenhall. Staf 3C 72
Ellen's Green. Surr 2B 26
Ellerbeck. N Yor 5B 106
Ellerburn. N Yor 1C 100
Ellerby. N Yor 3E 107
Ellerdine. Telf 3A 72
Ellerdine Heath. Telf 3A 72
Ellerhayes. Devn 2C 12
Elleric. Arg 4E 141
Ellerker. E Yor 2C 94
Ellerton. E Yor 1H 93
Ellerton. N Yor 5F 105
Ellerton. Shrp 3B 72
Ellesborough. Buck 5G 51
Ellesmere. Shrp 2F 71
Ellesmere Port. Ches W 3G 83
Ellingham. Hants 2G 15
Ellingham. Norf 1F 67
Ellingham. Nmbd 2F 121
Ellingstring. N Yor 1D 98
Ellington. Cambs 3A 64
Ellington. Nmbd 5G 121
Ellington Thorpe. Cambs 3A 64
Elliot. Ang 5F 145
Ellisfield. Hants 2E 25
Ellishadder. High 2E 155
Ellistown. Leics 4B 74
Ellon. Abers 5G 161
Ellonby. Cumb 1F 103
Ellough. Suff 2G 67
Elloughton. E Yor 2C 94
Ellwood. Glos 5A 48
Elm. Cambs 5D 76
Elmbridge. Glos 4D 48
Elmbridge. Worc 4D 60
Elmdon. Essx 2E 53
Elmdon. W Mid 2F 61
Elmdon Heath. W Mid 2F 61
Elmesthorpe. Leics 1B 62
Elmfield. IOW 3D 16
Elm Hill. Dors 4D 22
Elmhurst. Staf 4F 73
Elmley Castle. Worc 1E 49
Elmley Lovett. Worc 4C 60
Elmore. Glos 4C 48
Elmore Back. Glos 4C 48
Elm Park. G Lon 2G 39
Elmscott. Devn 4C 18
Elmsett. Suff 1D 54
Elmstead. Essx 3D 54
Elmstead Heath. Essx 3D 54
Elmstead Market. Essx 3D 54
Elmsted. Kent 1F 29
Elmstone. Kent 4G 41
Elmstone Hardwicke. Glos 3E 49
Elmswell. E Yor 4D 101
Elmswell. Suff 4B 66
Elmton. Derbs 3C 86
Elphin. High 2G 163
Elphinstone. E Lot 2G 129
Elrick. Abers 3F 153
Elrick. Mor 1B 152
Elrig. Dum 5A 110
Elsdon. Nmbd 5D 120
Elsecar. S Yor 1A 86
Elsenham. Essx 3F 53
Elsfield. Oxon 4D 50
Elsham. N Lin 3D 94
Elsing. Norf 4C 78
Elslack. N Yor 5B 98
Elsrickle. S Lan 5D 128
Elstead. Surr 1A 26
Elsted. W Sus 1G 17
Elsted Marsh. W Sus 4G 25
Elsthorpe. Linc 3H 75
Elstob. Dur 2A 106
Elston. Devn 2A 12
Elston. Lanc 1E 90
Elston. Notts 1E 75
Elston. Wilts 2F 23
Elstone. Devn 1G 11
Elstow. Bed 1A 52
Elstree. Herts 1C 38
Elstronwick. E Yor 1F 95
Elswick. Lanc 1C 90
Elswick. Tyne 3F 115
Elsworth. Cambs 4C 64
Elterwater. Cumb 4E 103
Eltham. G Lon 3F 39
Eltisley. Cambs 5B 64
Elton. Cambs 1H 63
Elton. Ches W 3G 83
Elton. Derbs 4G 85
Elton. Glos 4C 48
Elton. G Man 3F 91
Elton. Here 3G 59
Elton. Notts 2E 75
Elton. Stoc T 3B 106
Elton Green. Ches W 3G 83
Eltringham. Nmbd 3D 115
Elvanfoot. S Lan 3B 118
Elvaston. Derbs 2B 74
Elveden. Suff 3H 65
Elvetham Heath. Hants 1F 25
Elvingston. E Lot 2A 130
Elvington. Kent 5G 41
Elvington. York 5B 100
Elwick. Hart 1B 106
Elwick. Nmbd 1F 121
Elworth. Ches E 4B 84
Elworth. Dors 4A 14
Elworthy. Som 3D 20
Ely. Cambs 2E 65
Ely. Card 4E 33
Emberton. Mil 1G 51
Embleton. Cumb 1C 102
Embleton. Dur 2B 106
Embleton. Nmbd 2G 121
Embo. High 4F 165
Emborough. Som 1B 22
Embo Street. High 4F 165
Embsay. N Yor 4C 98
Emery Down. Hants 2A 16
Emley. W Yor 3C 92
Emmbrook. Wok 5F 37
Emmer Green. Read 4F 37
Emmington. Oxon 5F 51
Emneth. Norf 5D 77
Emneth Hungate. Norf 5E 77
Empingham. Rut 5G 75
Empshott. Hants 3F 25
Emsworth. Hants 2F 17
Enborne. W Ber 5C 36
Enborne Row. W Ber 5C 36
Enchmarsh. Shrp 1H 59
Enderby. Leics 1C 62
Endmoor. Cumb 1E 97
Endon. Staf 5D 84
Endon Bank. Staf 5D 84
Enfield. G Lon 1E 39
Enfield Wash. G Lon 1E 39
Enford. Wilts 1G 23
Engine Common. S Glo 3B 34
Englefield. W Ber 4E 36
Englefield Green. Surr 3A 38
Englesea-brook. Ches E 5B 84
English Bicknor. Glos 4A 48
Englishcombe. Bath 5C 34
English Frankton. Shrp 3G 71
Enham Alamein. Hants 2B 24
Enmore. Som 3F 21
Ennerdale Bridge. Cumb 3B 102
Enniscaven. Corn 3D 6
Enoch. Dum 4A 118
Enochdhu. Per 2H 143
Ensay. Arg 4E 139
Ensbury. Bour 3F 15
Ensdon. Shrp 4G 71
Ensis. Devn 4F 19
Enson. Staf 3D 72
Enstone. Oxon 3B 50
Enterkinfoot. Dum 4A 118
Enville. Staf 2C 60
Eolaigearraidh. W Isl 8C 170
Eorabus. Arg 1A 132
Eoropaidh. W Isl 1H 171
Epney. Glos 4C 48
Epperstone. Notts 1D 74
Epping. Essx 5E 53
Epping Green. Essx 5E 53
Epping Green. Herts 5C 52
Epping Upland. Essx 5E 53
Eppleby. N Yor 3E 105
Eppleworth. E Yor 1D 94
Epsom. Surr 4D 38
Epwell. Oxon 1B 50
Epworth. N Lin 4A 94
Epworth Turbary. N Lin 4A 94
Erbistock. Wrex 1F 71
Erbusaig. High 1F 147
Erchless Castle. High 4G 157
Erdington. W Mid 1F 61
Eredine. Arg 3G 133
Eriboll. High 3E 167
Ericstane. Dum 3C 118
Eridge Green. E Sus 2G 27
Erines. Arg 2G 125
Eriswell. Suff 3G 65
Erith. G Lon 3G 39
Erlestoke. Wilts 1E 23
Ermine. Linc 3G 87
Ermington. Devn 3C 8
Ernesettle. Plym 3A 8
Erpingham. Norf 2D 78
Erriottwood. Kent 5D 40
Errogie. High 1H 149
Errol. Per 1E 137
Errol Station. Per 1E 137
Erskine. Ren 2F 127
Erskine Bridge. Ren 2F 127
Ervie. Dum 3F 109
Erwarton. Suff 2F 55
Erwood. Powy 1D 46
Eryholme. N Yor 4A 106
Eryrys. Den 5E 82
Escalls. Corn 4A 4
Escomb. Dur 1E 105
Escrick. N Yor 5A 100
Esgair. Carm 3D 45
(nr. Carmarthen)
Esgair. Carm 3G 43
(nr. St Clears)
Esgairgeiliog. Powy 5G 69
Esh. Dur 5E 115
Esher. Surr 4C 38
Esholt. W Yor 5D 98
Eshott. Nmbd 5G 121
Eshton. N Yor 4B 98
Esh Winning. Dur 5E 115
Eskadale. High 5G 157
Eskbank. Midl 3G 129
Eskdale Green. Cumb 4C 102
Eskdalemuir. Dum 5E 119
Eskham. Linc 1C 88
Esknish. Arg 3B 124
Esk Valley. N Yor 4F 107
Eslington Hall. Nmbd 3E 121
Espley Hall. Nmbd 5F 121
Esprick. Lanc 1C 90
Essendine. Rut 4H 75
Essendon. Herts 5C 52
Essich. High 5A 158
Essington. Staf 5D 72
Eston. Red C 3C 106
Estover. Plym 3B 8
Eswick. Shet 6F 173
Etal. Nmbd 1D 120
Etchilhampton. Wilts 5F 35
Etchingham. E Sus 3B 28
Etchinghill. Kent 2F 29
Etchinghill. Staf 4E 73
Etherley Dene. Dur 2E 105
Ethie Haven. Ang 4F 145
Etling Green. Norf 4C 78
Etloe. Glos 5B 48
Eton. Wind 3A 38
Eton Wick. Wind 3A 38
Etteridge. High 4A 150
Ettersgill. Dur 2B 104
Ettiley Heath. Ches E 4B 84
Ettington. Warw 1A 50
Etton. E Yor 5D 101
Etton. Pet 5A 76
Ettrick. Bord 3E 119
Ettrickbridge. Bord 2F 119
Etwall. Derbs 2G 73
Eudon Burnell. Shrp 2B 60
Eudon George. Shrp 2A 60
Euston. Suff 3A 66
Euxton. Lanc 3D 90
Evanstown. B'end 3C 32
Evanton. High 2A 158
Evedon. Linc 1H 75
Evelix. High 4E 165
Evendine. Here 1C 48
Evenjobb. Powy 4E 59
Evenley. Nptn 2D 50
Evenlode. Glos 3H 49
Even Swindon. Swin 3G 35
Evenwood. Dur 2E 105
Evenwood Gate. Dur 2E 105
Everbay. Orkn 5F 172
Evercreech. Som 3B 22
Everdon. Nptn 5C 62
Everingham. E Yor 5C 100
Everleigh. Wilts 1H 23
Everley. N Yor 1D 100
Eversholt. C Beds 2H 51
Evershot. Dors 2A 14
Eversley. Hants 5F 37
Eversley Centre. Hants 5F 37
Eversley Cross. Hants 5F 37
Everthorpe. E Yor 1C 94
Everton. C Beds 5B 64
Everton. Hants 3A 16
Everton. Mers 1F 83
Everton. Notts 1D 86
Evertown. Dum 2E 113
Evesbatch. Here 1B 48
Evesham. Worc 1F 49
Evington. Leic 5D 74
Ewden Village. S Yor 1G 85
Ewdness. Shrp 1B 60
Ewell. Surr 4D 38
Ewell Minnis. Kent 1G 29
Ewelme. Oxon 2E 37
Ewen. Glos 2F 35
Ewenny. V Glam 4C 32
Ewerby. Linc 1A 76
Ewes. Dum 5F 119
Ewesley. Nmbd 5E 121
Ewhurst. Surr 1B 26
Ewhurst Green. E Sus 3B 28
Ewhurst Green. Surr 2B 26
Ewlo. Flin 4F 83
Ewloe. Flin 4F 83
Ewood Bridge. Lanc 2F 91
Eworthy. Devn 3E 11
Ewshot. Hants 1G 25
Ewyas Harold. Here 3G 47
Exbourne. Devn 2G 11
Exbury. Hants 2C 16
Exceat. E Sus 5G 27
Exebridge. Som 4C 20
Exelby. N Yor 1E 99
Exeter. Devn 3C 12 & 195
Exeter International Airport. Devn 3D 12
Exford. Som 3B 20
Exfords Green. Shrp 5G 71
Exhall. Warw 5F 61
Exlade Street. Oxon 3E 37
Exminster. Devn 4C 12
Exmoor. Som 3B 20
Exmouth. Devn 4D 12
Exnaboe. Shet 10E 173
Exning. Suff 4F 65
Exton. Devn 4C 12
Exton. Hants 4E 24
Exton. Rut 4G 75
Exton. Som 3C 20
Exwick. Devn 3C 12
Eyam. Derbs 3G 85
Eydon. Nptn 5C 62
Eye. Here 4G 59
Eye. Pet 5B 76
Eye. Suff 3D 66
Eye Green. Pet 5B 76
Eyemouth. Bord 3F 131
Eyeworth. C Beds 1C 52
Eyhorne Street. Kent 5C 40
Eyke. Suff 5F 67
Eynesbury. Cambs 5A 64
Eynort. High 1B 146
Eynsford. Kent 4G 39
Eynsham. Oxon 5C 50
Eyre. High 3D 154
(on Isle of Skye)
Eyre. High 5E 155
(on Raasay)
Eythorne. Kent 1G 29
Eyton. Here 4G 59
Eyton. Shrp 2F 59
(nr. Bishop's Castle)
Eyton. Shrp 4F 71
(nr. Shrewsbury)
Eyton. Wrex 1F 71
Eyton on Severn. Shrp 5H 71
Eyton upon the Weald Moors. Telf 4A 72

F

Faccombe. Hants 1B 24
Faceby. N Yor 4B 106
Faddiley. Ches E 5H 83
Fadmoor. N Yor 1A 100
Fagwyr. Swan 5G 45
Faichem. High 3E 149
Faifley. W Dun 2G 127
Fail. S Ayr 2D 116
Failand. N Som 4A 34
Failford. S Ayr 2D 116
Failsworth. G Man 4H 91
Fairbourne. Gwyn 4F 69
Fairbourne Heath. Kent 5C 40
Fairburn. N Yor 2E 93
Fairfield. Derbs 3E 85
Fairfield. Kent 3D 28
Fairfield. Worc 3D 60
(nr. Bromsgrove)
Fairfield. Worc 1F 49
(nr. Evesham)
Fairford. Glos 5G 49
Fair Green. Norf 4F 77
Fair Hill. Cumb 1G 103
Fairhill. S Lan 4A 128
Fair Isle Airport. Shet 1B 172
Fairlands. Surr 5A 38
Fairlie. N Ayr 4D 126
Fairlight. E Sus 4C 28
Fairlight Cove. E Sus 4C 28
Fairmile. Devn 3D 12
Fairmile. Surr 4C 38
Fairmilehead. Edin 3F 129
Fair Oak. Devn 1D 12
Fair Oak. Hants 1C 16
(nr. Eastleigh)
Fair Oak. Hants 5D 36
(nr. Kingsclere)
Fairoak. Staf 2B 72
Fair Oak Green. Hants 5E 37
Fairseat. Kent 4H 39
Fairstead. Essx 4A 54
Fairstead. Norf 4F 77
Fairwarp. E Sus 3F 27
Fairwater. Card 4E 33
Fairy Cross. Devn 4E 19
Fakenham. Norf 3B 78
Fakenham Magna. Suff 3B 66
Fala. Midl 3H 129
Fala Dam. Midl 3H 129
Falcon. Here 2B 48
Faldingworth. Linc 2H 87
Falfield. S Glo 2B 34
Falkenham. Suff 2F 55
Falkirk. Falk 2B 128
Falkland. Fife 3E 137

Forneth—Germansweek

Forneth. Per 4H 143
Fornham All Saints. Suff 4H 65
Fornham St Martin. Suff 4A 66
Forres. Mor 3E 159
Forrestfield. N Lan 3B 128
Forrest Lodge. Dum 1C 110
Forsbrook. Staf 1D 72
Forse. High 5E 169
Forsinard. High 4A 168
Forss. High 2C 168
Forstal, The. Kent 2E 29
Forston. Dors 3B 14
Fort Augustus. High 3F 149
Forteviot. Per 2C 136
Fort George. High 3B 158
Forth. S Lan 4C 128
Forthampton. Glos 2D 48
Forthay. Glos 2C 34
Forth Road Bridge. Fife 2E 129
Fortingall. Per 4E 143
Fort Matilda. Inv 2D 126
Forton. Hants 2C 24
Forton. Lanc 4D 97
Forton. Shrp 4G 71
Forton. Som 2G 13
Forton. Staf 3B 72
Forton Heath. Shrp 4G 71
Fortrie. Abers 4D 160
Fortrose. High 3B 158
Fortuneswell. Dors 5B 14
Fort William. High 1F 141
Forty Green. Buck 1A 38
Forty Hill. G Lon 1E 39
Forward Green. Suff 5C 66
Fosbury. Wilts 1B 24
Foscot. Oxon 3H 49
Fosdyke. Linc 2C 76
Foss. Per 3E 143
Fossebridge. Glos 4F 49
Foster Street. Essx 5E 53
Foston. Derbs 2F 73
Foston. Leics 1D 62
Foston. Linc 1F 75
Foston. N Yor 3A 100
Foston on the Wolds. E Yor 4F 101
Fotherby. Linc 1C 88
Fothergill. Cumb 1B 102
Fotheringhay. Nptn 1H 63
Foubister. Orkn 7E 172
Foula Airport. Shet 8A 173
Foul Anchor. Cambs 4D 76
Foulbridge. Cumb 5F 113
Foulden. Norf 1G 65
Foulden. Bord 4F 131
Foul Mile. E Sus 4H 27
Foulridge. Lanc 5A 98
Foulsham. Norf 3C 78
Fountainhall. Bord 5H 129
Four Alls, The. Shrp 2A 72
Four Ashes. Staf 5D 72
(nr. Cannock)
Four Ashes. Staf 2C 60
(nr. Kinver)
Four Ashes. Suff 3C 66
Four Crosses. Powy 5C 70
(nr. Llanerfyl)
Four Crosses. Powy 4E 71
(nr. Llanymynech)
Four Crosses. Staf 5D 72
Four Elms. Kent 1F 27
Four Forks. Som 3F 21
Four Gotes. Cambs 4D 76
Four Lane End. S Yor 4C 92
Four Lane Ends. Lanc 4E 97
Four Lanes. Corn 5A 6
Fourlanes End. Ches E 5B 84
Four Marks. Hants 3E 25
Four Mile Bridge. IOA 3B 80
Four Oaks. E Sus 3C 28
Four Oaks. Glos 3B 48
Four Oaks. W Mid 2G 61
Four Roads. Carm 5E 45
Four Roads. IOM 5B 108
Fourstones. Nmbd 3B 114
Four Throws. Kent 3B 28
Fovant. Wilts 4F 23
Foveran. Abers 1G 153
Fowey. Corn 3F 7
Fowlershill. Abers 2G 153
Fowley Common. Warr 1A 84
Fowlis. Ang 5C 144
Fowlis Wester. Per 1B 136
Fowlmere. Cambs 1E 53
Fownhope. Here 2A 48
Foxcombe Hill. Oxon 5C 50
Fox Corner. Surr 5A 38
Foxcote. Glos 4F 49
Foxcote. Som 1C 22
Foxdale. IOM 4B 108
Foxearth. Essx 1B 54
Foxfield. Cumb 1B 96
Foxham. Wilts 4E 35
Fox Hatch. Essx 1G 39
Foxhole. Corn 3D 6
Foxholes. N Yor 2E 101
Foxhunt Green. E Sus 4G 27
Fox Lane. Hants 1G 25
Foxley. Norf 3C 78
Foxley. Nptn 5D 62
Foxley. Wilts 3D 35
Foxlydiate. Worc 4E 61
Fox Street. Essx 3D 54
Foxt. Staf 1E 73
Foxton. Cambs 1E 53
Foxton. Dur 2A 106
Foxton. Leics 2D 62
Foxton. N Yor 5B 106
Foxup. N Yor 2A 98
Foxwist Green. Ches W 4A 84
Foxwood. Shrp 3A 60
Foy. Here 3A 48
Foyers. High 1G 149
Foynesfield. High 3C 158
Fraddam. Corn 3C 4
Fraddon. Corn 3D 6
Fradley. Staf 4F 73
Fradley South. Staf 4F 73
Fradswell. Staf 2D 73
Fraisthorpe. E Yor 3F 101
Framfield. E Sus 3F 27
Framingham Earl. Norf 5E 79
Framingham Pigot. Norf 5E 79
Framlingham. Suff 4E 67
Frampton. Dors 3B 14
Frampton. Linc 2C 76
Frampton Cotterell. S Glo 3B 34
Frampton Mansell. Glos 5E 49
Frampton on Severn. Glos 5C 48
Frampton West End. Linc 1B 76
Framsden. Suff 5D 66
Framwellgate Moor. Dur 5F 115
Franche. Worc 3C 60
Frandley. Ches W 3A 84
Frankby. Mers 2E 83
Frankfort. Norf 3F 79
Frankley. Worc 2D 61
Frank's Bridge. Powy 5D 58
Frankton. Warw 3B 62
Frankwell. Shrp 4G 71
Frant. E Sus 2G 27
Fraserburgh. Abers 2G 161
Frating Green. Essx 3D 54
Fratton. Port 2E 17
Freathy. Corn 3A 8
Freckenham. Suff 3F 65
Freckleton. Lanc 2C 90
Freeby. Leics 3F 75
Freefolk Priors. Hants 2C 24
Freehay. Staf 1E 73
Freeland. Oxon 4C 50
Freester. Shet 6F 173
Freethorpe. Norf 5G 79
Freiston. Linc 1C 76
Freiston Shore. Linc 1C 76
Fremington. Devn 3F 19
Fremington. N Yor 5D 104
Frenchay. Bris 4B 34
Frenchbeer. Devn 4G 11
French Street. Kent 5F 39
Frenich. Stir 3D 134
Frensham. Surr 2G 25
Frenze. Norf 2D 66
Fresgoe. High 2B 168
Freshfield. Mers 4A 90
Freshford. Bath 5C 34
Freshwater. IOW 4B 16
Freshwater Bay. IOW 4B 16
Freshwater East. Pemb 5E 43
Fressingfield. Suff 3E 67
Freston. Suff 2E 55
Freswick. High 2F 169
Fretherne. Glos 5C 48
Frettenham. Norf 4E 79
Freuchie. Fife 3E 137
Freystrop. Pemb 3D 42
Friar's Gate. E Sus 2F 27
Friar Waddon. Dors 4B 14
Friday Bridge. Cambs 5D 76
Friday Street. E Sus 5H 27
Friday Street. Surr 1C 26
Fridaythorpe. E Yor 4C 100
Friden. Derbs 4F 85
Friern Barnet. G Lon 1D 39
Friesthorpe. Linc 2H 87
Frieston. Linc 1G 75
Frieth. Buck 2F 37
Friezeland. Notts 5B 86
Frilford. Oxon 2C 36
Frilsham. W Ber 4D 36
Frimley. Surr 1G 25
Frimley Green. Surr 1G 25
Frindsbury. Medw 4B 40
Fring. Norf 2G 77
Fringford. Oxon 3E 50
Frinsted. Kent 5C 40
Frinton-on-Sea. Essx 4F 55
Friockheim. Ang 4E 145
Friog. Gwyn 4F 69
Frisby. Leics 5E 74
Frisby on the Wreake. Leics 4D 74
Friskney. Linc 5D 88
Friskney Eaudyke. Linc 5D 88
Friston. E Sus 5G 27
Friston. Suff 4G 67
Fritchley. Derbs 5A 86
Fritham. Hants 1H 15
Frith Bank. Linc 1C 76
Frith Common. Worc 4A 60
Frithelstock. Devn 1E 11
Frithelstock Stone. Devn 1E 11
Frithsden. Herts 5A 52
Frithville. Linc 5C 88
Frittenden. Kent 1C 28
Frittiscombe. Devn 4E 9
Fritton. Norf 5G 79
(nr. Great Yarmouth)
Fritton. Norf 1E 67
(nr. Long Stratton)
Fritwell. Oxon 3D 50
Frizinghall. W Yor 1B 92
Frizington. Cumb 3B 102
Frobost. W Isl 6C 170
Frocester. Glos 5C 48
Frochas. Powy 5D 70
Frodesley. Shrp 5H 71
Frodingham. N Lin 3C 94
Frodsham. Ches W 3H 83
Froggatt. Derbs 3G 85
Froghall. Staf 1E 73
Frogham. Hants 1G 15
Frogham. Kent 5G 41
Frogmore. Devn 4D 8
Frogmore. Hants 5G 37
Frogmore. Herts 5B 52
Frognall. Linc 4A 76
Frogshall. Norf 2E 79
Frogwell. Corn 2H 7
Frolesworth. Leics 1C 62
Frome. Som 2C 22
Fromefield. Som 2C 22
Frome St Quintin. Dors 2A 14
Fromes Hill. Here 1B 48
Fron. Gwyn 2C 68
Fron. Powy 4C 58
(nr. Llandrindod Wells)
Fron. Powy 1D 58
(nr. Newtown)
Fron. Powy 5E 71
(nr. Welshpool)
Froncysyllte. Wrex 1E 71
Frongoch. Gwyn 2B 70
Fronoleu. Gwyn 2G 69
Fron Isaf. Wrex 1E 71
Frosterley. Dur 1D 104
Frotoft. Orkn 5D 172
Froxfield. C Beds 2H 51
Froxfield. Wilts 5A 36
Froxfield Green. Hants 4F 25
Fryern Hill. Hants 4C 24
Fryerning. Essx 5G 53
Fryton. N Yor 2A 100
Fugglestone St Peter. Wilts 3G 23
Fulbeck. Linc 5G 87
Fulbourn. Cambs 5E 65
Fulbrook. Oxon 4A 50
Fulflood. Hants 3C 24
Fulford. Som 4F 21
Fulford. Staf 2D 72
Fulford. York 5A 100
Fulham. G Lon 3D 38
Fulking. W Sus 4D 26
Fuller's Moor. Ches W 5G 83
Fuller Street. Essx 4H 53
Fullerton. Hants 3B 24
Fulletby. Linc 3B 88
Full Sutton. E Yor 4B 100
Fullwood. E Ayr 4F 127
Fulmer. Buck 2A 38
Fulmodestone. Norf 2B 78
Fulnetby. Linc 3H 87
Fulney. Linc 3B 76
Fulstow. Linc 1C 88
Fulthorpe. Stoc T 2B 106
Fulwell. Tyne 4G 115
Fulwood. Lanc 1D 90
Fulwood. Notts 5B 86
Fulwood. Som 1F 13
Fulwood. S Yor 2G 85
Fundenhall. Norf 1D 66
Funtington. W Sus 2G 17
Funtley. Hants 2D 16
Funzie. Shet 2H 173
Furley. Devn 2F 13
Furnace. Arg 3H 133
Furnace. Carm 5F 45
Furnace. Cdgn 1F 57
Furner's Green. E Sus 3F 27
Furness Vale. Derbs 2E 85
Furneux Pelham. Herts 3E 53
Furzebrook. Dors 4E 15
Furzehill. Devn 2H 19
Furzehill. Dors 2F 15
Furzeley Corner. Hants 1E 17
Furzey Lodge. Hants 2B 16
Furzley. Hants 1A 16
Fyfield. Essx 5F 53
Fyfield. Glos 5H 49
Fyfield. Hants 2A 24
Fyfield. Oxon 2C 36
Fyfield. Wilts 5G 35
Fylde, The. Lanc 1B 90
Fylingthorpe. N Yor 4G 107
Fyning. W Sus 4G 25
Fyvie. Abers 5E 161

G

Gabhsann bho Dheas. W Isl 2G 171
Gabhsann bho Thuath. W Isl 2G 171
Gabroc Hill. E Ayr 4F 127
Gadbrook. Surr 1D 26
Gaddesby. Leics 4D 74
Gadfa. IOA 2D 80
Gadgirth. S Ayr 2D 116
Gaer. Powy 3E 47
Gaerwen. IOA 3D 81
Gagingwell. Oxon 3C 50
Gaick Lodge. High 5B 150
Gailey. Staf 4D 72
Gainford. Dur 3E 105
Gainsborough. Linc 1F 87
Gainsborough. Suff 1E 55
Gainsford End. Essx 2H 53
Gairletter. Arg 1C 126
Gairloch. Abers 3E 153
Gairloch. High 1H 155
Gairlochy. High 5D 148
Gairney Bank. Per 4D 136
Gairnshiel Lodge. Abers 3G 151
Gaisgill. Cumb 4H 103
Gaitsgill. Cumb 5E 113
Galashiels. Bord 1G 119
Galgate. Lanc 4D 97
Galhampton. Som 4B 22
Gallatown. Fife 4E 137
Galley Common. Warw 1H 61
Galleyend. Essx 5H 53
Galleywood. Essx 5H 53
Gallin. Per 4C 142
Gallowfauld. Ang 4D 144
Gallowhill. E Dun 2H 127
Gallowhill. Per 5A 144
Gallowhill. Ren 3F 127
Gallowhills. Abers 3H 161
Gallows Green. Staf 1E 73
Gallows Green. Worc 4D 60
Gallowstree Common. Oxon 3E 37
Galltair. High 1G 147
Gallt Melyd. Den 2C 82
Galmington. Som 4F 21
Galmisdale. High 5C 146
Galmpton. Devn 4C 8
Galmpton. Torb 3E 9
Galmpton Warborough. Torb 3E 9
Galphay. N Yor 2E 99
Galston. E Ayr 1D 117
Galton. Dors 4C 14
Galtrigill. High 3A 154
Gamblesby. Cumb 1H 103
Gamelsby. Cumb 4D 112
Gamesley. Derbs 1E 85
Gamlingay. Cambs 5B 64
Gamlingay Cinques. Cambs 5B 64
Gamlingay Great Heath. C Beds 5B 64
Gammaton. Devn 4E 19
Gammersgill. N Yor 1C 98
Gamston. Notts 2D 74
(nr. Nottingham)
Gamston. Notts 3E 86
(nr. Retford)
Ganarew. Here 4A 48
Ganavan. Arg 5C 140
Ganborough. Glos 3G 49
Gang. Corn 2H 7
Ganllwyd. Gwyn 3G 69
Gannochy. Ang 1E 145
Gannochy. Per 1D 136
Gansclet. High 4F 169
Ganstead. E Yor 1E 95
Ganthorpe. N Yor 2A 100
Ganton. N Yor 2D 101
Gants Hill. G Lon 2F 39
Gappah. Devn 5B 12
Garafad. High 2D 155
Garboldisham. Norf 2C 66
Garden City. Flin 4F 83
Gardeners Green. Wok 5G 37
Gardenstown. Abers 2F 161
Garden Village. S Yor 1G 85
Garden Village. Swan 3E 31
Garderhouse. Shet 7E 173
Gardham. E Yor 5D 100
Gardie. Shet 5C 173
(on Papa Stour)
Gardie. Shet 1H 173
(on Unst)
Gardie Ho. Shet 7F 173
Gare Hill. Som 2C 22
Garelochhead. Arg 4B 134
Garford. Oxon 2C 36
Garforth. W Yor 1E 93
Gargrave. N Yor 4B 98
Gargunnock. Stir 4G 135
Garleffin. S Ayr 1F 109
Garlieston. Dum 5B 110
Garlinge Green. Kent 5F 41
Garlogie. Abers 3E 153
Garmelow. Staf 3B 72
Garmond. Abers 3F 161
Garmondsway. Dur 1A 106
Garmony. Arg 4A 140
Garmouth. Mor 2H 159
Garmston. Shrp 5A 72
Garnant. Carm 4G 45
Garndiffaith. Torf 5F 47
Garndolbenmaen. Gwyn 1D 69
Garnett Bridge. Cumb 5G 103
Garnfadryn. Gwyn 2B 68
Garnkirk. N Lan 3H 127
Garnlydan. Blae 4E 47
Garnsgate. Linc 3D 76
Garnswllt. Swan 5G 45
Garn-yr-erw. Torf 4F 47
Garrabost. W Isl 4H 171
Garrallan. E Ayr 3E 117
Garras. Corn 4E 5
Garreg. Gwyn 1F 69
Garrigill. Cumb 5A 114
Garriston. N Yor 5E 105
Garrogie Lodge. High 2H 149
Garros. High 2D 155
Garrow. Per 4F 143
Garsdale. Cumb 1G 97
Garsdale Head. Cumb 5A 104
Garsdon. Wilts 3E 35
Garshall Green. Staf 2D 72
Garsington. Oxon 5D 50
Garstang. Lanc 5D 97
Garston. Mers 2G 83
Garswood. Mers 1H 83
Gartcosh. N Lan 3H 127
Garth. B'end 2B 32
Garth. Cdgn 2F 57
Garth. Gwyn 2E 69
Garth. IOM 4C 108
Garth. Powy 1C 46
(nr. Builth Wells)
Garth. Powy 3E 59
(nr. Knighton)
Garth. Shet 6D 173
(nr. Sandness)
Garth. Shet 6F 173
(nr. Skellister)
Garth. Wrex 1E 71
Garthamlock. Glas 3H 127
Garthbrengy. Powy 2D 46
Gartheli. Cdgn 5E 57
Garthmyl. Powy 1D 58
Garthorpe. Leics 3F 75
Garthorpe. N Lin 3B 94
Garth Owen. Powy 1D 58
Garth Row. Cumb 5G 103
Gartly. Abers 5C 160
Gartmore. Stir 4E 135
Gartness. N Lan 3A 128
Gartness. Stir 1G 127
Gartocharn. W Dun 1F 127
Garton. E Yor 1F 95
Garton-on-the-Wolds. E Yor 4D 101
Gartsherrie. N Lan 3A 128
Gartymore. High 2H 165
Garvald. E Lot 2B 130
Garvamore. High 4H 149
Garvard. Arg 4A 132
Garvault. High 5H 167
Garve. High 2F 157
Garvestone. Norf 5C 78
Garvie. Arg 4H 133
Garvock. Abers 1G 145
Garvock. Inv 2D 126
Garway. Here 3H 47
Garway Common. Here 3H 47
Garway Hill. Here 3H 47
Garwick. Linc 1A 76
Gaskan. High 1C 140
Gasper. Wilts 3C 22
Gastard. Wilts 5D 35
Gasthorpe. Norf 2B 66
Gatcombe. IOW 4C 16
Gateacre. Mers 2G 83
Gatebeck. Cumb 1E 97
Gate Burton. Linc 2F 87
Gateforth. N Yor 2F 93
Gatehead. E Ayr 1C 116
Gate Helmsley. N Yor 4A 100
Gatehouse. Nmbd 1A 114
Gatehouse of Fleet. Dum 4D 110
Gatelawbridge. Dum 5B 118
Gateley. Norf 3B 78
Gatenby. N Yor 1F 99
Gatesgarth. Cumb 3C 102
Gateshead. Tyne 3F 115
Gatesheath. Ches W 4G 83
Gateside. Ang 4D 144
(nr. Forfar)
Gateside. Ang 4C 144
(nr. Kirriemuir)
Gateside. Fife 3D 136
Gateside. N Ayr 4E 127
Gathurst. G Man 4D 90
Gatley. G Man 2C 84
Gatton. Surr 5D 39
Gattonside. Bord 1H 119
Gatwick (London) Airport. W Sus 1D 27 & 216
Gaufron. Powy 4B 58
Gaulby. Leics 5D 74
Gauldry. Fife 1F 137
Gaultree. Norf 5D 77
Gaunt's Common. Dors 2F 15
Gaunt's Earthcott. S Glo 3B 34
Gautby. Linc 3A 88
Gavinton. Bord 4D 130
Gawber. S Yor 4D 92
Gawcott. Buck 2E 51
Gawsworth. Ches E 4C 84
Gawthorpe. W Yor 2C 92
Gawthrop. Cumb 1F 97
Gawthwaite. Cumb 1B 96
Gay Bowers. Essx 5A 54
Gaydon. Warw 5A 62
Gayfield. Orkn 2D 172
Gayhurst. Mil 1G 51
Gayle. N Yor 1A 98
Gayles. N Yor 4E 105
Gay Street. W Sus 3B 26
Gayton. Mers 2E 83
Gayton. Norf 4G 77
Gayton. Nptn 5E 62
Gayton. Staf 3D 73
Gayton le Marsh. Linc 2D 88
Gayton le Wold. Linc 2B 88
Gayton Thorpe. Norf 4G 77
Gaywood. Norf 3F 77
Gazeley. Suff 4G 65
Geanies. High 1C 158
Gearraidh Bhailteas. W Isl 6C 170
Gearraidh Bhaird. W Isl 6F 171
Gearraidh ma Monadh. W Isl 7C 170
Gearraidh na h-Aibhne. W Isl 4E 171
Geary. High 2B 154
Geddes. High 3C 158
Gedding. Suff 5B 66
Geddington. Nptn 2F 63
Gedintailor. High 5E 155
Gedling. Notts 1D 74
Gedney. Linc 3D 76
Gedney Broadgate. Linc 3D 76
Gedney Drove End. Linc 3D 76
Gedney Dyke. Linc 3D 76
Gedney Hill. Linc 4C 76
Gee Cross. G Man 1D 84
Geeston. Rut 5G 75
Geilston. Arg 2E 127
Geirinis. W Isl 4C 170
Geise. High 2D 168
Geisiadar. W Isl 4D 171
Gelder Shiel. Abers 5G 151
Geldeston. Norf 1F 67
Gell. Cnwy 4A 82
Gelli. Pemb 3E 43
Gelli. Rhon 2C 32
Gellifor. Den 4D 82
Gelligaer. Cphy 2E 33
Gellilydan. Gwyn 2F 69
Gellinudd. Neat 5H 45
Gellyburn. Per 5H 143
Gellywen. Carm 2G 43
Gelston. Dum 4E 111
Gelston. Linc 1G 75
Gembling. E Yor 4F 101
Geneva. Cdgn 5D 56
Gentleshaw. Staf 4E 73
Geocrab. W Isl 8D 171
George Green. Buck 2A 38
Georgeham. Devn 3E 19
George Nympton. Devn 4H 19
Georgetown. Blae 5E 47
Georgetown. Ren 3F 127
Georth. Orkn 5C 172
Gerlan. Gwyn 4F 81
Germansweek. Devn 3E 11

Germoe—Great Brington

Germoe. *Corn* 4C 4
Gerrans. *Corn* 5C 6
Gerrard's Bromley. *Staf* 2B 72
Gerrards Cross. *Buck* 2A 38
Gerston. *High* 3D 168
Gestingthorpe. *Essx* 2B 54
Gethsemane. *Pemb* 1A 44
Geuffordd. *Powy* 4E 70
Gibraltar. *Buck* 4F 51
Gibraltar. *Linc* 5E 89
Gibraltar. *Suff* 5D 66
Gibsmere. *Notts* 1E 74
Giddeahall. *Wilts* 4D 34
Gidea Park. *G Lon* 2G 39
Gidleigh. *Devn* 4G 11
Giffnock. *E Ren* 4G 127
Gifford. *E Lot* 3B 130
Giffordtown. *Fife* 2E 137
Giggetty. *Staf* 1C 60
Giggleswick. *N Yor* 3H 97
Gignog. *Pemb* 2C 42
Gilberdyke. *E Yor* 2B 94
Gilbert's End. *Worc* 1D 48
Gilbert's Green. *Warw* 3F 61
Gilchriston. *E Lot* 3A 130
Gilcrux. *Cumb* 1C 102
Gildersome. *W Yor* 2C 92
Gildingwells. *S Yor* 2C 86
Gilesgate Moor. *Dur* 5F 115
Gileston. *V Glam* 5D 32
Gilfach. *Cphy* 2E 33
Gilfach Goch. *Rhon* 2C 32
Gilfachreda. *Cdgn* 5D 56
Gilgarran. *Cumb* 2B 102
Gillamoor. *N Yor* 5D 107
Gillan. *Corn* 4E 5
Gillar's Green. *Mers* 1G 83
Gillen. *High* 3B 154
Gilling East. *N Yor* 2A 100
Gillingham. *Dors* 4D 22
Gillingham. *Medw* 4B 40 & **Medway 204**
Gillingham. *Norf* 1G 67
Gilling West. *N Yor* 4E 105
Gillock. *High* 3E 169
Gillow Heath. *Staf* 5C 84
Gills. *High* 1F 169
Gill's Green. *Kent* 2B 28
Gilmanscleuch. *Bord* 2F 119
Gilmerton. *Edin* 3F 129
Gilmerton. *Per* 1A 136
Gilmonby. *Dur* 3C 104
Gilmorton. *Leics* 2C 62
Gilsland. *Nmbd* 3H 113
Gilsland Spa. *Cumb* 3H 113
Gilston. *Midl* 4H 129
Giltbrook. *Notts* 1B 74
Gilwern. *Mon* 4F 47
Gimingham. *Norf* 2E 79
Giosla. *W Isl* 5D 171
Gipping. *Suff* 4C 66
Gipsey Bridge. *Linc* 1B 76
Gipton. *W Yor* 1D 92
Girdle Toll. *N Ayr* 5E 127
Girlsta. *Shet* 6F 173
Girsby. *N Yor* 4A 106
Girthon. *Dum* 4D 110
Girton. *Cambs* 4D 64
Girton. *Notts* 4F 87
Girvan. *S Ayr* 5A 116
Gisburn. *Lanc* 5H 97
Gisleham. *Suff* 2H 67
Gislingham. *Suff* 3C 66
Gissing. *Norf* 2D 66
Gittisham. *Devn* 3E 13
Gladestry. *Powy* 5E 59
Gladsmuir. *E Lot* 2A 130
Glaichbea. *High* 5H 157
Glais. *Swan* 5H 45
Glaisdale. *N Yor* 4E 107
Glame. *High* 4E 155
Glamis. *Ang* 4C 144
Glanaman. *Carm* 4G 45
Glan-Conwy. *Cnwy* 5H 81
Glandford. *Norf* 1C 78
Glan Duar. *Carm* 1F 45
Glandwr. *Blae* 5F 47
Glandwr. *Pemb* 2F 43
Glan-Dwyfach. *Gwyn* 1D 69
Glandy Cross. *Carm* 2F 43
Glandyfi. *Cdgn* 1F 57
Glangrwyney. *Powy* 4F 47
Glanmule. *Powy* 1D 58
Glanrhyd. *Gwyn* 2B 68
Glanrhyd. *Pemb* 1B 44
(nr. Cardigan)
Glan-rhyd. *Pemb* 1F 43
(nr. Crymych)
Glan-rhyd. *Powy* 5A 46
Glanton. *Nmbd* 3E 121
Glanton Pyke. *Nmbd* 3E 121
Glanvilles Wootton. *Dors* 2B 14
Glan-y-don. *Flin* 3D 82
Glan-y-nant. *Powy* 2B 58
Glan-yr-afon. *Gwyn* 1C 70
Glan-yr-afon. *IOA* 2F 81
Glan-yr-afon. *Powy* 5C 70
Glan-y-wern. *Gwyn* 2F 69
Glapthorn. *Nptn* 1H 63
Glapwell. *Derbs* 4B 86
Glas Aird. *Arg* 4A 132
Glas-allt Shiel. *Abers* 5G 151
Glasbury. *Powy* 2E 47
Glaschoil. *High* 5E 159
Glascoed. *Den* 3B 82
Glascoed. *Mon* 5G 47
Glascote. *Staf* 5G 73
Glascwm. *Powy* 5D 58
Glasfryn. *Cnwy* 5B 82
Glasgow. *Glas* 3G 127 & 196
Glasgow Airport. *Ren* 3F 127 & 216
Glasgow Prestwick Airport. *S Ayr* 2C 116
Glashvin. *High* 2D 154
Glasinfryn. *Gwyn* 4E 81
Glas na Cardaich. *High* 4E 147
Glasnacardoch. *High* 4E 147
Glasnakille. *High* 2D 146
Glaspwll. *Cdgn* 1G 57
Glassburn. *High* 5F 157
Glassenbury. *Kent* 2B 28
Glasserton. *Dum* 5B 110
Glassford. *S Lan* 5A 128
Glassgreen. *Mor* 2G 159
Glasshouse. *Glos* 3C 48
Glasshouses. *N Yor* 3D 98
Glasson. *Cumb* 3D 112
Glasson. *Lanc* 4D 96
Glassonby. *Cumb* 1G 103
Glasterlaw. *Ang* 3E 145
Glaston. *Rut* 5F 75
Glastonbury. *Som* 3H 21
Glatton. *Cambs* 2A 64
Glazebrook. *Warr* 1A 84
Glazebury. *Warr* 1A 84
Glazeley. *Shrp* 2B 60
Gleadless. *S Yor* 2A 86
Gleadsmoss. *Ches E* 4C 84
Gleann Dail bho Dheas. *W Isl* 7C 170
Gleann Tholastaidh. *W Isl* 3H 171
Gleann Uige. *High* 1A 140
Gleaston. *Cumb* 2B 96
Glecknabae. *Arg* 3B 126
Gledrid. *Shrp* 2E 71
Gleiniant. *Powy* 1B 58
Glemsford. *Suff* 1B 54
Glen. *Dum* 4C 110
Glenancross. *High* 4E 147
Glen Auldyn. *IOM* 2D 108
Glenbarr. *Arg* 2A 122
Glenbeg. *High* 2G 139
Glen Bernisdale. *High* 4D 154
Glenbervie. *Abers* 5E 153
Glenboig. *N Lan* 3A 128
Glenborrodale. *High* 2A 140
Glenbranter. *Arg* 4A 134
Glenbreck. *Bord* 2C 118
Glenbrein Lodge. *High* 2G 149
Glenbrittle. *High* 1C 146
Glenbuchat Lodge. *Abers* 2H 151
Glenbuck. *E Ayr* 2G 117
Glenburn. *Ren* 3F 127
Glencalvie Lodge. *High* 5B 164
Glencaple. *Dum* 3A 112
Glencarron Lodge. *High* 3C 156
Glencarse. *Per* 1D 136
Glencassley Castle. *High* 3B 164
Glencat. *Abers* 4C 152
Glencoe. *High* 3F 141
Glen Cottage. *High* 5E 147
Glencraig. *Fife* 4D 136
Glendale. *High* 4A 154
Glendevon. *Per* 3B 136
Glendoebeg. *High* 3G 149
Glendoick. *Per* 1E 136
Glendoune. *S Ayr* 5A 116
Glenduckie. *Fife* 2E 137
Gleneagles. *Per* 3B 136
Glenegedale. *Arg* 4B 124
Glenegedale Lots. *Arg* 4B 124
Glenelg. *High* 2G 147
Glenernie. *Mor* 4E 159
Glenesslin. *Dum* 1F 111
Glenfarg. *Per* 2D 136
Glenfarquhar Lodge. *Abers* 5E 152
Glenferness Mains. *High* 4D 158
Glenfeshie Lodge. *High* 4C 150
Glenfiddich Lodge. *Mor* 5H 159
Glenfield. *Leics* 5C 74
Glenfinnan. *High* 5B 148
Glenfintaig Lodge. *High* 5E 149
Glenfoot. *Per* 2D 136
Glenfyne Lodge. *Arg* 2B 134
Glengap. *Dum* 4D 110
Glengarnock. *N Ayr* 4E 126
Glengolly. *High* 2D 168
Glengorm Castle. *Arg* 3F 139
Glengrasco. *High* 4D 154
Glenhead Farm. *Ang* 2B 144
Glenholm. *Bord* 1D 118
Glen House. *Bord* 1E 119
Glenhurich. *High* 2C 140
Glenkerry. *Bord* 3E 119
Glenkiln. *Dum* 2F 111
Glenkindie. *Abers* 2B 152
Glenkinglass Lodge. *Arg* 5F 141
Glenkirk. *Bord* 2C 118
Glenlean. *Arg* 1B 126
Glenlee. *Dum* 1D 110
Glenleraig. *High* 5B 166
Glenlichorn. *Per* 2G 135
Glenlivet. *Mor* 1F 151
Glenlochar. *Dum* 3E 111
Glenlochsie Lodge. *Per* 1H 143
Glenluce. *Dum* 4G 109
Glenmarksie. *High* 3F 157
Glenmassan. *Arg* 1C 126
Glenmavis. *N Lan* 3A 128
Glen Maye. *IOM* 4B 108
Glenmazeran Lodge. *High* 1B 150
Glenmidge. *Dum* 1F 111
Glen Mona. *IOM* 3D 108
Glenmore. *High* 2G 139
(nr. Glenborrodale)
Glenmore. *High* 3D 151
(nr. Kingussie)
Glenmore. *High* 4D 154
(on Isle of Skye)
Glenmoy. *Ang* 2D 144
Glennoe. *Arg* 5E 141
Glen of Coachford. *Abers* 4B 160
Glenogil. *Ang* 2D 144
Glen Parva. *Leics* 1C 62
Glenprosen Village. *Ang* 2C 144
Glenree. *N Ayr* 3D 122
Glenridding. *Cumb* 3E 103
Glenrosa. *N Ayr* 2E 123
Glenrothes. *Fife* 3E 137
Glensanda. *High* 4C 140
Glensaugh. *Abers* 1F 145
Glenshero Lodge. *High* 4H 149
Glensluain. *Arg* 4H 133
Glenstockadale. *Dum* 3F 109
Glenstriven. *Arg* 2B 126
Glen Tanar House. *Abers* 4B 152
Glentham. *Linc* 1H 87
Glenton. *Abers* 1D 152
Glentress. *Bord* 1E 119
Glentromie Lodge. *High* 4B 150
Glentrool Lodge. *Dum* 1B 110
Glentrool Village. *Dum* 2A 110
Glentruim House. *High* 4A 150
Glentworth. *Linc* 2G 87
Glenuig. *High* 1A 140
Glen Village. *Falk* 2B 128
Glen Vine. *IOM* 4C 108
Glenwhilly. *Dum* 2G 109
Glenzierfoot. *Dum* 2E 113
Glespin. *S Lan* 2H 117
Gletness. *Shet* 6F 173
Glewstone. *Here* 3A 48
Glib Cheois. *W Isl* 5F 171
Glinton. *Pet* 5A 76
Glooston. *Leics* 1E 63
Glossop. *Derbs* 1E 85
Gloster Hill. *Nmbd* 4G 121
Gloucester. *Glos* 4D 48 & 196
Gloucestershire Airport. *Glos* 3D 49
Gloup. *Shet* 1G 173
Glusburn. *N Yor* 5C 98
Glutt Lodge. *High* 5B 168
Glutton Bridge. *Staf* 4E 85
Gluvian. *Corn* 2D 6
Glympton. *Oxon* 3C 50
Glyn. *Cnwy* 3A 82
Glynarthen. *Cdgn* 1D 44
Glynbrochan. *Powy* 2B 58
Glyn Ceiriog. *Wrex* 2E 70
Glyncoch. *Rhon* 2D 32
Glyncorrwg. *Neat* 2B 32
Glynde. *E Sus* 5F 27
Glyndebourne. *E Sus* 4F 27
Glyndyfrdwy. *Den* 1D 70
Glyn Ebwy. *Blae* 5E 47
Glynllan. *B'end* 3C 32
Glyn-neath. *Neat* 5B 46
Glynogwr. *B'end* 3C 32
Glyntaff. *Rhon* 3D 32
Glyntawe. *Powy* 4B 46
Glynteg. *Carm* 2D 44
Gnosall. *Staf* 3C 72
Gnosall Heath. *Staf* 3C 72
Goadby. *Leics* 1E 63
Goadby Marwood. *Leics* 3E 75
Goatacre. *Wilts* 4F 35
Goathill. *Dors* 1B 14
Goathland. *N Yor* 4F 107
Goathurst. *Som* 3F 21
Goathurst Common. *Kent* 5F 39
Goat Lees. *Kent* 1E 28
Gobernuisgach Lodge. *High* 4E 167
Gobernuisgeach. *High* 5B 168
Gobhaig. *W Isl* 7C 171
Gobowen. *Shrp* 2F 71
Godalming. *Surr* 1A 26
Goddard's Corner. *Suff* 4E 67
Goddard's Green. *Kent* 2C 28
(nr. Benenden)
Goddard's Green. *Kent* 2B 28
(nr. Cranbrook)
Goddards Green. *W Sus* 3D 27
Godford Cross. *Devn* 2E 13
Godleybrook. *Staf* 1D 73
Godmanchester. *Cambs* 3B 64
Godmanstone. *Dors* 3B 14
Godmersham. *Kent* 5E 41
Godolphin Cross. *Corn* 3D 4
Godre'r-graig. *Neat* 5A 46
Godshill. *Hants* 1G 15
Godshill. *IOW* 4D 16
Godstone. *Staf* 2E 73
Godstone. *Surr* 5E 39
Goetre. *Mon* 5G 47
Goff's Oak. *Herts* 5D 52
Gogar. *Edin* 2E 129
Goginan. *Cdgn* 2F 57
Golan. *Gwyn* 1E 69
Golant. *Corn* 3F 7
Golberdon. *Corn* 5D 10
Golborne. *G Man* 1A 84
Golcar. *W Yor* 3A 92
Goldcliff. *Newp* 3G 33
Golden Cross. *E Sus* 4G 27
Golden Green. *Kent* 1H 27
Golden Grove. *Carm* 4F 45
Golden Grove. *N Yor* 4F 107
Golden Hill. *Pemb* 2D 43
Goldenhill. *Stoke* 5C 84
Golden Pot. *Hants* 2F 25
Golden Valley. *Glos* 3E 49
Golders Green. *G Lon* 2D 38
Goldhanger. *Essx* 5C 54
Gold Hill. *Norf* 1E 65
Golding. *Shrp* 5H 71
Goldington. *Bed* 5H 63
Goldsborough. *N Yor* 4F 99
(nr. Harrogate)
Goldsborough. *N Yor* 3F 107
(nr. Whitby)
Goldsithney. *Corn* 3C 4
Goldstone. *Kent* 4G 41
Goldstone. *Shrp* 3B 72
Goldthorpe. *S Yor* 4E 93
Goldworthy. *Devn* 4D 19
Golfa. *Powy* 3D 70
Gollanfield. *High* 3C 158
Gollinglith Foot. *N Yor* 1D 98
Golsoncott. *Som* 3D 20
Golspie. *High* 4F 165
Gomeldon. *Wilts* 3G 23
Gomersal. *W Yor* 2C 92
Gometra House. *Arg* 4E 139
Gomshall. *Surr* 1B 26
Gonalston. *Notts* 1D 74
Gonerby Hill Foot. *Linc* 2G 75
Gonfirth. *Shet* 5E 173
Good Easter. *Essx* 4G 53
Gooderstone. *Norf* 5G 77
Goodleigh. *Devn* 3G 19
Goodmanham. *E Yor* 5C 100
Goodmayes. *G Lon* 2F 39
Goodnestone. *Kent* 5G 41
(nr. Aylesham)
Goodnestone. *Kent* 4E 41
(nr. Faversham)
Goodrich. *Here* 4A 48
Goodrington. *Torb* 3E 9
Goodshaw. *Lanc* 2G 91
Goodshaw Fold. *Lanc* 2G 91
Goodstone. *Devn* 5A 12
Goodwick. *Pemb* 1D 42
Goodworth Clatford. *Hants* 2B 24
Goole. *E Yor* 2H 93
Goom's Hill. *Worc* 5E 61
Goonabarn. *Corn* 3D 6
Goonbell. *Corn* 4B 6
Goonhavern. *Corn* 3B 6
Goonvrea. *Corn* 4B 6
Goose Green. *Cumb* 1E 97
Goose Green. *S Glo* 3C 34
Gooseham. *Corn* 1C 10
Goosewell. *Plym* 3B 8
Goosey. *Oxon* 2B 36
Goosnargh. *Lanc* 1D 90
Goostrey. *Ches E* 3B 84
Gorcott Hill. *Warw* 4E 61
Gord. *Shet* 9F 173
Gordon. *Bord* 5C 130
Gordonbush. *High* 3F 165
Gordonstown. *Abers* 3C 160
(nr. Cornhill)
Gordonstown. *Abers* 5E 160
(nr. Fyvie)
Gorebridge. *Midl* 3G 129
Gorefield. *Cambs* 4D 76
Gores. *Wilts* 1G 23
Gorgie. *Edin* 2F 129
Goring. *Oxon* 3E 36
Goring-by-Sea. *W Sus* 5C 26
Goring Heath. *Oxon* 4E 37
Gorleston-on-Sea. *Norf* 5H 79
Gornalwood. *W Mid* 1D 60
Gorran Churchtown. *Corn* 4D 6
Gorran Haven. *Corn* 4E 6
Gorran High Lanes. *Corn* 4D 6
Gors. *Cdgn* 3F 57
Gorsedd. *Flin* 3D 82
Gorseinon. *Swan* 3E 31
Gorseness. *Orkn* 6D 172
Gorseybank. *Derbs* 5G 85
Gorsgoch. *Cdgn* 5D 57
Gorslas. *Carm* 4F 45
Gorsley. *Glos* 3B 48
Gorsley Common. *Here* 3B 48
Gorstan. *High* 2F 157
Gorstella. *Ches W* 4F 83
Gorsty Common. *Here* 2H 47
Gorsty Hill. *Staf* 3E 73
Gortantaoid. *Arg* 2B 124
Gorteneorn. *High* 2A 140
Gortenfern. *High* 2A 140
Gorton. *G Man* 1C 84
Gosbeck. *Suff* 5D 66
Gosberton. *Linc* 2B 76
Gosberton Cheal. *Linc* 3B 76
Gosberton Clough. *Linc* 3A 76
Goseley Dale. *Derbs* 3H 73
Gosfield. *Essx* 3A 54
Gosford. *Oxon* 4D 50
Gosforth. *Cumb* 4B 102
Gosforth. *Tyne* 3F 115
Gosmore. *Herts* 3B 52
Gospel End Village. *Staf* 1C 60
Gosport. *Hants* 2E 16
Gossabrough. *Shet* 3G 173
Gossington. *Glos* 5C 48
Gossops Green. *W Sus* 2D 26
Goswick. *Nmbd* 5G 131
Gotham. *Notts* 2C 74
Gotherington. *Glos* 3E 49
Gott. *Arg* 4B 138
Gott. *Shet* 7F 173
Goudhurst. *Kent* 2B 28
Goulceby. *Linc* 3B 88
Gourdon. *Abers* 1H 145
Gourock. *Inv* 2D 126
Govan. *Glas* 3G 127
Govanhill. *Glas* 3G 127
Goverton. *Notts* 1E 74
Goveton. *Devn* 4D 8
Govilon. *Mon* 4F 47
Gowanhill. *Abers* 2H 161
Gowdall. *E Yor* 2G 93
Gowerton. *Swan* 3E 31
Gowkhall. *Fife* 1D 128
Gowthorpe. *E Yor* 4B 100
Goxhill. *E Yor* 5F 101
Goxhill. *N Lin* 2E 94
Goxhill Haven. *N Lin* 2E 94
Goytre. *Neat* 3A 32
Grabhair. *W Isl* 6F 171
Graby. *Linc* 3H 75
Graffham. *W Sus* 4A 26
Grafham. *Cambs* 4A 64
Grafham. *Surr* 1B 26
Grafton. *Here* 2H 47
Grafton. *N Yor* 3G 99
Grafton. *Oxon* 5A 50
Grafton. *Shrp* 4G 71
Grafton. *Worc* 2E 49
(nr. Evesham)
Grafton. *Worc* 4H 59
(nr. Leominster)
Grafton Flyford. *Worc* 5D 60
Grafton Regis. *Nptn* 1F 51
Grafton Underwood. *Nptn* 2G 63
Grafty Green. *Kent* 1C 28
Graianrhyd. *Den* 5E 82
Graig. *Carm* 5E 45
Graig. *Cnwy* 3H 81
Graig. *Den* 3C 82
Graig-fechan. *Den* 5D 82
Graig Penllyn. *V Glam* 4C 32
Grain. *Medw* 3C 40
Grainsby. *Linc* 1B 88
Grainthorpe. *Linc* 1C 88
Grainthorpe Fen. *Linc* 1C 88
Graiselound. *N Lin* 1E 87
Gramasdail. *W Isl* 3D 170
Grampound. *Corn* 4D 6
Grampound Road. *Corn* 3D 6
Granborough. *Buck* 3F 51
Granby. *Notts* 2E 75
Grandborough. *Warw* 4B 62
Grandpont. *Oxon* 5D 50
Grandtully. *Per* 3G 143
Grange. *Cumb* 3D 102
Grange. *E Ayr* 1D 116
Grange. *Here* 3G 59
Grange. *Mers* 2E 83
Grange. *Per* 1E 137
Grange Crossroads. *Mor* 3B 160
Grange Hill. *G Lon* 1F 39
Grangemill. *Derbs* 5G 85
Grange Moor. *W Yor* 3C 92
Grangemouth. *Falk* 1C 128
Grange of Lindores. *Fife* 2E 137
Grange-over-Sands. *Cumb* 2D 96
Grangepans. *Falk* 1D 128
Grange, The. *N Yor* 5C 106
Grangetown. *Card* 4E 33
Grangetown. *Red C* 2C 106
Grange Villa. *Dur* 4F 115
Granish. *High* 2C 150
Gransmoor. *E Yor* 4F 101
Granston. *Pemb* 1C 42
Grantchester. *Cambs* 5D 64
Grantham. *Linc* 2G 75
Grantley. *N Yor* 3E 99
Grantlodge. *Abers* 2E 152
Granton. *Edin* 2F 129
Grantown-on-Spey. *High* 1E 151
Grantshouse. *Bord* 3E 130
Grappenhall. *Warr* 2A 84
Grasby. *Linc* 4D 94
Grasmere. *Cumb* 4E 103
Grasscroft. *G Man* 4H 91
Grassendale. *Mers* 2F 83
Grassgarth. *Cumb* 5E 113
Grassholme. *Dur* 2C 104
Grassington. *N Yor* 3C 98
Grassmoor. *Derbs* 4B 86
Grassthorpe. *Notts* 4E 87
Grateley. *Hants* 2A 24
Gratton. *Devn* 1D 11
Gratton. *Staf* 5D 84
Gratwich. *Staf* 2E 73
Graveley. *Cambs* 4B 64
Graveley. *Herts* 3C 52
Gravelhill. *Shrp* 4G 71
Gravel Hole. *G Man* 4H 91
Gravelly Hill. *W Mid* 1F 61
Graven. *Shet* 4F 173
Graveney. *Kent* 4E 41
Gravesend. *Kent* 3H 39
Grayingham. *Linc* 1G 87
Grayrigg. *Cumb* 5G 103
Grays. *Thur* 3H 39
Grayshott. *Hants* 3G 25
Grayson Green. *Cumb* 2A 102
Grayswood. *Surr* 2A 26
Graythorp. *Hart* 2C 106
Grazeley. *Wok* 5E 37
Grealin. *High* 2E 155
Greasbrough. *S Yor* 1B 86
Greasby. *Mers* 2E 83
Great Abington. *Cambs* 1F 53
Great Addington. *Nptn* 3G 63
Great Alne. *Warw* 5F 61
Great Altcar. *Lanc* 4B 90
Great Amwell. *Herts* 4D 52
Great Asby. *Cumb* 3H 103
Great Ashfield. *Suff* 4B 66
Great Ayton. *N Yor* 3C 106
Great Baddow. *Essx* 5H 53
Great Bardfield. *Essx* 2G 53
Great Barford. *Bed* 5A 64
Great Barr. *W Mid* 1E 61
Great Barrington. *Glos* 4H 49
Great Barrow. *Ches W* 4G 83
Great Barton. *Suff* 4A 66
Great Barugh. *N Yor* 2B 100
Great Bavington. *Nmbd* 1C 114
Great Bealings. *Suff* 1F 55
Great Bedwyn. *Wilts* 5A 36
Great Bentley. *Essx* 3E 54
Great Billing. *Nptn* 4F 63
Great Bircham. *Norf* 2G 77
Great Blakenham. *Suff* 5D 66
Great Blencow. *Cumb* 1F 103
Great Bolas. *Telf* 3A 72
Great Bookham. *Surr* 5C 38
Great Bosullow. *Corn* 3B 4
Great Bourton. *Oxon* 1C 50
Great Bowden. *Leics* 2E 63
Great Bradley. *Suff* 5F 65
Great Braxted. *Essx* 4B 54
Great Bricett. *Suff* 5C 66
Great Brickhill. *Buck* 2H 51
Great Bridgeford. *Staf* 3C 72
Great Brington. *Nptn* 4D 62

Great Bromley—Halfway

Great Bromley. *Essx* 3D **54**
Great Broughton. *Cumb* 1B **102**
Great Broughton. *N Yor* 4C **106**
Great Budworth. *Ches W* 3A **84**
Great Burdon. *Darl* 3A **106**
Great Burstead. *Essx* 1A **40**
Great Busby. *N Yor* 4C **106**
Great Canfield. *Essx* 4F **53**
Great Carlton. *Linc* 2D **88**
Great Casterton. *Rut* 5H **75**
Great Chalfield. *Wilts* 5D **34**
Great Chart. *Kent* 1D **28**
Great Chatwell. *Staf* 4B **72**
Great Chesterford. *Essx* 1F **53**
Great Cheverell. *Wilts* 1E **23**
Great Chilton. *Dur* 1F **105**
Great Chishill. *Cambs* 2E **53**
Great Clacton. *Essx* 4E **55**
Great Cliff. *W Yor* 3D **92**
Great Clifton. *Cumb* 2B **102**
Great Coates. *NE Lin* 3F **95**
Great Comberton. *Worc* 1E **49**
Great Corby. *Cumb* 4F **113**
Great Cornard. *Suff* 1B **54**
Great Cowden. *E Yor* 5G **101**
Great Coxwell. *Oxon* 2A **36**
Great Crakehall. *N Yor* 1E **99**
Great Cransley. *Nptn* 3F **63**
Great Cressingham. *Norf* 5H **77**
Great Crosby. *Mers* 1F **83**
Great Cubley. *Derbs* 2F **73**
Great Dalby. *Leics* 4E **75**
Great Doddington. *Nptn* 4F **63**
Great Doward. *Here* 4A **48**
Great Dunham. *Norf* 4A **78**
Great Dunmow. *Essx* 3G **53**
Great Durnford. *Wilts* 3G **23**
Great Easton. *Essx* 3G **53**
Great Easton. *Leics* 1F **63**
Great Eccleston. *Lanc* 5D **96**
Great Edstone. *N Yor* 1B **100**
Great Ellingham. *Norf* 1C **66**
Great Elm. *Som* 2C **22**
Great Eppleton. *Tyne* 5G **115**
Great Eversden. *Cambs* 5C **64**
Great Fencote. *N Yor* 5F **105**
Great Finborough. *Suff* 5C **66**
Greatford. *Linc* 4H **75**
Great Fransham. *Norf* 4A **78**
Great Gaddesden. *Herts* 4A **52**
Great Gate. *Staf* 1E **73**
Great Gidding. *Cambs* 2A **64**
Great Givendale. *E Yor* 4C **100**
Great Glemham. *Suff* 4F **67**
Great Glen. *Leics* 1D **62**
Great Gonerby. *Linc* 2G **75**
Great Gransden. *Cambs* 5B **64**
Great Green. *Norf* 2E **67**
Great Green. *Suff* 5B **66** (nr. Lavenham)
Great Green. *Suff* 3D **66** (nr. Palgrave)
Great Habton. *N Yor* 2B **100**
Great Hale. *Linc* 1A **76**
Great Hallingbury. *Essx* 4F **53**
Greatham. *Hants* 3F **25**
Greatham. *Hart* 2B **106**
Greatham. *W Sus* 4B **26**
Great Hampden. *Buck* 5G **51**
Great Harrowden. *Nptn* 3F **63**
Great Harwood. *Lanc* 1F **91**
Great Haseley. *Oxon* 5E **51**
Great Hatfield. *E Yor* 5F **101**
Great Haywood. *Staf* 3D **73**
Great Heath. *W Mid* 2H **61**
Great Heck. *N Yor* 2F **93**
Great Henny. *Essx* 2B **54**
Great Hinton. *Wilts* 1E **23**
Great Hockham. *Norf* 1B **66**
Great Holland. *Essx* 4F **55**
Great Horkesley. *Essx* 2C **54**
Great Hormead. *Herts* 2E **53**
Great Horton. *W Yor* 1B **92**
Great Horwood. *Buck* 2F **51**
Great Houghton. *Nptn* 5E **63**
Great Houghton. *S Yor* 4E **93**
Great Hucklow. *Derbs* 3F **85**
Great Kelk. *E Yor* 4F **101**
Great Kendale. *E Yor* 3E **101**
Great Kimble. *Buck* 5G **51**
Great Kingshill. *Buck* 2G **37**
Great Langdale. *Cumb* 4D **102**
Great Langton. *N Yor* 5F **105**
Great Leighs. *Essx* 4H **53**
Great Limber. *Linc* 4E **95**
Great Linford. *Mil* 1G **51**
Great Livermere. *Suff* 3A **66**
Great Longstone. *Derbs* 3G **85**
Great Lumley. *Dur* 5F **115**
Great Lyth. *Shrp* 5G **71**
Great Malvern. *Worc* 1C **48**
Great Maplestead. *Essx* 2B **54**
Great Marton. *Bkpl* 1B **90**
Great Massingham. *Norf* 3G **77**
Great Melton. *Norf* 5D **78**
Great Milton. *Oxon* 5E **51**
Great Missenden. *Buck* 5G **51**
Great Mitton. *Lanc* 1F **91**
Great Mongeham. *Kent* 5H **41**
Great Moulton. *Norf* 1D **66**
Great Munden. *Herts* 3D **52**
Great Musgrave. *Cumb* 3A **104**
Great Ness. *Shrp* 4F **71**
Great Notley. *Essx* 3H **53**
Great Oak. *Mon* 5G **47**
Great Oakley. *Essx* 3E **55**
Great Oakley. *Nptn* 2F **63**
Great Offley. *Herts* 3B **52**
Great Ormside. *Cumb* 3A **104**
Great Orton. *Cumb* 4E **113**
Great Ouseburn. *N Yor* 3G **99**
Great Oxendon. *Nptn* 2E **63**
Great Oxney Green. *Essx* 5G **53**
Great Parndon. *Essx* 5E **53**
Great Paxton. *Cambs* 4B **64**
Great Plumpton. *Lanc* 1B **90**
Great Plumstead. *Norf* 4F **79**
Great Ponton. *Linc* 2G **75**
Great Potheridge. *Devn* 1F **11**
Great Preston. *W Yor* 2E **93**
Great Raveley. *Cambs* 2B **64**
Great Rissington. *Glos* 4G **49**
Great Rollright. *Oxon* 2B **50**
Great Ryburgh. *Norf* 3B **78**
Great Ryle. *Nmbd* 3E **121**
Great Ryton. *Shrp* 5G **71**
Great Saling. *Essx* 3G **53**
Great Salkeld. *Cumb* 1G **103**
Great Sampford. *Essx* 2G **53**
Great Sankey. *Warr* 2H **83**
Great Saredon. *Staf* 5D **72**
Great Saxham. *Suff* 4G **65**
Great Shefford. *W Ber* 4B **36**
Great Shelford. *Cambs* 5D **64**
Great Shoddesden. *Hants* 2A **24**
Great Smeaton. *N Yor* 4A **106**
Great Snoring. *Norf* 2B **78**
Great Somerford. *Wilts* 3E **35**
Great Stainton. *Darl* 2A **106**
Great Stambridge. *Essx* 1C **40**
Great Staughton. *Cambs* 4A **64**
Great Steeping. *Linc* 4D **88**
Great Stonar. *Kent* 5H **41**
Greatstone-on-Sea. *Kent* 3E **29**
Great Strickland. *Cumb* 2G **103**
Great Stukeley. *Cambs* 3B **64**
Great Sturton. *Linc* 3B **88**
Great Sutton. *Ches W* 3F **83**
Great Sutton. *Shrp* 2H **59**
Great Swinburne. *Nmbd* 2C **114**
Great Tew. *Oxon* 3B **50**
Great Tey. *Essx* 3B **54**
Great Thirkleby. *N Yor* 2G **99**
Great Thorness. *IOW* 3C **16**
Great Thurlow. *Suff* 5F **65**
Great Torr. *Devn* 4C **8**
Great Torrington. *Devn* 1E **11**
Great Tosson. *Nmbd* 4E **121**
Great Totham North. *Essx* 4B **54**
Great Totham South. *Essx* 4B **54**
Great Tows. *Linc* 1B **88**
Great Urswick. *Cumb* 2B **96**
Great Wakering. *Essx* 2D **40**
Great Waldingfield. *Suff* 1C **54**
Great Walsingham. *Norf* 2B **78**
Great Waltham. *Essx* 4G **53**
Great Warley. *Essx* 1G **39**
Great Washbourne. *Glos* 2E **49**
Great Wenham. *Suff* 2D **54**
Great Whelnetham. *Suff* 5A **66**
Great Whittington. *Nmbd* 2D **114**
Great Wigborough. *Essx* 4C **54**
Great Wilbraham. *Cambs* 5E **65**
Great Wilne. *Derbs* 2B **74**
Great Wishford. *Wilts* 3F **23**
Great Witchingham. *Norf* 3D **78**
Great Witcombe. *Glos* 4E **49**
Great Witley. *Worc* 4B **60**
Great Wolford. *Warw* 2H **49**
Greatworth. *Nptn* 1D **50**
Great Wratting. *Suff* 1G **53**
Great Wymondley. *Herts* 3C **52**
Great Wyrley. *Staf* 5D **73**
Great Wytheford. *Shrp* 4H **71**
Great Yarmouth. *Norf* 5H **79** & **196**
Great Yeldham. *Essx* 2A **54**
Grebby. *Linc* 4D **88**
Greeba Castle. *IOM* 3C **108**
Greenbank. *Shet* 1G **173**
Greenbottom. *Corn* 4B **6**
Greenburn. *W Lot* 3C **128**
Greencroft. *Dur* 4E **115**
Greencroft Park. *Dur* 5F **115**
Greendown. *Som* 1A **22**
Greendykes. *Nmbd* 2E **121**
Green End. *Bed* 1A **52** (nr. Bedford)
Green End. *Bed* 4A **64** (nr. St Neots)
Green End. *Herts* 2D **52** (nr. Buntingford)
Green End. *Herts* 3D **52** (nr. Stevenage)
Green End. *N Yor* 4F **107**
Green End. *Warw* 2G **61**
Greenfield. *Arg* 4B **134**
Greenfield. *C Beds* 2A **52**
Greenfield. *Flin* 3D **82**
Greenfield. *G Man* 4H **91**
Greenfield. *Oxon* 2F **37**
Greenfoot. *N Lan* 3A **128**
Greenford. *G Lon* 2C **38**
Greengairs. *N Lan* 2A **128**
Greengate. *Norf* 4C **78**
Greengill. *Cumb* 1C **102**
Greenhalgh. *Lanc* 1C **90**
Greenham. *Dors* 2H **13**
Greenham. *Som* 4D **20**
Greenham. *W Ber* 5C **36**
Green Hammerton. *N Yor* 4G **99**
Greenhaugh. *Nmbd* 1A **114**
Greenhead. *Nmbd* 3H **113**
Green Heath. *Staf* 4D **73**
Greenhill. *Dum* 2C **112**
Greenhill. *Falk* 2B **128**
Greenhill. *Kent* 4F **41**
Greenhill. *S Yor* 2H **85**
Greenhill. *Worc* 3C **60**
Greenhills. *N Ayr* 4E **127**
Greenhithe. *Kent* 3G **39**
Greenholm. *E Ayr* 1E **117**
Greenhow Hill. *N Yor* 3D **98**
Greenigoe. *Orkn* 7D **172**
Greenland. *High* 2E **169**
Greenland Mains. *High* 2E **169**
Greenlands. *Worc* 4E **61**
Green Lane. *Shrp* 3A **72**
Green Lane. *Warw* 4E **61**
Greenlaw. *Bord* 5D **130**
Greenlea. *Dum* 2B **112**
Greenloaning. *Per* 3H **135**
Greenmount. *G Man* 3F **91**
Greenmow. *Shet* 9F **173**
Greenock. *Inv* 2D **126**
Greenock Mains. *E Ayr* 2F **117**
Greenodd. *Cumb* 1C **96**
Green Ore. *Som* 1A **22**
Greenrow. *Cumb* 4C **112**
Greens. *Abers* 4F **161**
Greensgate. *Norf* 4D **78**
Greenside. *Tyne* 3E **115**
Greensidehill. *Nmbd* 3D **121**
Greens Norton. *Nptn* 1E **51**
Greenstead Green. *Essx* 3B **54**
Greensted Green. *Essx* 5F **53**
Green Street. *Herts* 1C **38**
Green Street. *Suff* 3D **66**
Green Street Green. *G Lon* 4F **39**
Green Street Green. *Kent* 3G **39**
Greenstreet Green. *Suff* 1D **54**
Green, The. *Cumb* 1A **96**
Green, The. *Wilts* 3D **22**
Green Tye. *Herts* 4E **53**
Greenwall. *Orkn* 7E **172**
Greenway. *Pemb* 2E **43**
Greenway. *V Glam* 4D **32**
Greenwell. *Cumb* 4G **113**
Greenwich. *G Lon* 3E **39**
Greet. *Glos* 2F **49**
Greete. *Shrp* 3H **59**
Greetham. *Linc* 3C **88**
Greetham. *Rut* 4G **75**
Greetland. *W Yor* 2A **92**
Gregson Lane. *Lanc* 2D **90**
Grein. *W Isl* 8B **170**
Greinetobht. *W Isl* 1D **170**
Greinton. *Som* 3H **21**
Gremista. *Shet* 7F **173**
Grenaby. *IOM* 4B **108**
Grendon. *Nptn* 4F **63**
Grendon. *Warw* 1G **61**
Grendon Common. *Warw* 1G **61**
Grendon Green. *Here* 5H **59**
Grendon Underwood. *Buck* 3E **51**
Grenofen. *Devn* 5E **11**
Grenoside. *S Yor* 1H **85**
Greosabhagh. *W Isl* 8D **171**
Gresford. *Wrex* 5F **83**
Gresham. *Norf* 2D **78**
Greshornish. *High* 3C **154**
Gressenhall. *Norf* 4B **78**
Gressingham. *Lanc* 2E **97**
Greta Bridge. *Dur* 3D **105**
Gretna. *Dum* 3E **112**
Gretna Green. *Dum* 3E **112**
Gretton. *Glos* 2F **49**
Gretton. *Nptn* 1G **63**
Gretton. *Shrp* 1H **59**
Grewelthorpe. *N Yor* 2E **99**
Greygarth. *N Yor* 2D **98**
Grey Green. *N Lin* 4A **94**
Greylake. *Som* 3G **21**
Greysouthen. *Cumb* 2B **102**
Greystoke. *Cumb* 1F **103**
Greystoke Gill. *Cumb* 2F **103**
Greystone. *Ang* 4E **145**
Greystones. *S Yor* 2H **85**
Greywell. *Hants* 1F **25**
Griais. *W Isl* 3G **171**
Grianan. *W Isl* 4G **171**
Gribthorpe. *E Yor* 1A **94**
Gribun. *Arg* 5F **139**
Griff. *Warw* 2A **62**
Griffithstown. *Torf* 2F **33**
Griffydam. *Leics* 4B **74**
Griggs Green. *Hants* 3G **25**
Grimbister. *Orkn* 6C **172**
Grimeford Village. *Lanc* 3E **90**
Grimeston. *Orkn* 6C **172**
Grimethorpe. *S Yor* 4E **93**
Griminis. *W Isl* 3C **170** (on Benbecula)
Griminis. *W Isl* 1C **170** (on North Uist)
Grimister. *Shet* 2F **173**
Grimley. *Worc* 4C **60**
Grimness. *Orkn* 8D **172**
Grimoldby. *Linc* 2C **88**
Grimpo. *Shrp* 3F **71**
Grimsargh. *Lanc* 1D **90**
Grimsbury. *Oxon* 1C **50**
Grimsby. *NE Lin* 3F **95**
Grimscote. *Nptn* 5D **62**
Grimscott. *Corn* 2C **10**
Grimshaw. *Bkbn* 2F **91**
Grimshaw Green. *Lanc* 3C **90**
Grimsthorpe. *Linc* 3H **75**
Grimston. *E Yor* 1F **95**
Grimston. *Leics* 3D **74**
Grimston. *Norf* 3G **77**
Grimston. *York* 4A **100**
Grimstone. *Dors* 3B **14**
Grimstone End. *Suff* 4B **66**
Grinacombe Moor. *Devn* 3E **11**
Grindale. *E Yor* 2F **101**
Grindhill. *Devn* 3E **11**
Grindiscol. *Shet* 8F **173**
Grindle. *Shrp* 5B **72**
Grindleford. *Derbs* 3G **85**
Grindleton. *Lanc* 5G **97**
Grindley. *Staf* 3E **73**
Grindley Brook. *Shrp* 1H **71**
Grindlow. *Derbs* 3F **85**
Grindon. *Nmbd* 5F **131**
Grindon. *Staf* 5E **85**
Gringley on the Hill. *Notts* 1E **87**
Grinsdale. *Cumb* 4E **113**
Grinshill. *Shrp* 3H **71**
Grinton. *N Yor* 5D **104**
Griomsidar. *W Isl* 5G **171**
Grishipoll. *Arg* 3C **138**
Grisling Common. *E Sus* 3F **27**
Gristhorpe. *N Yor* 1E **101**
Griston. *Norf* 1B **66**
Gritley. *Orkn* 7E **172**
Grittenham. *Wilts* 3F **35**
Grittleton. *Wilts* 4D **34**
Grizebeck. *Cumb* 1B **96**
Grizedale. *Cumb* 5E **103**
Grobister. *Orkn* 5F **172**
Grobsness. *Shet* 5E **173**
Groby. *Leics* 5C **74**
Groes. *Cnwy* 4C **82**
Groes. *Neat* 3A **32**
Groes-faen. *Rhon* 3D **32**
Groesffordd. *Gwyn* 2B **68**
Groesffordd. *Powy* 3D **46**
Groeslon. *Gwyn* 5D **81**
Groes-lwyd. *Powy* 4E **70**
Groes-wen. *Cphy* 3E **33**
Grogport. *Arg* 5G **125**
Groigearraidh. *W Isl* 4C **170**
Gromford. *Suff* 5F **67**
Gronant. *Flin* 2C **82**
Groombridge. *E Sus* 2G **27**
Grosmont. *Mon* 3H **47**
Grosmont. *N Yor* 4F **107**
Groton. *Suff* 1C **54**
Grove. *Dors* 5C **14**
Grove. *Kent* 4G **41**
Grove. *Notts* 3E **87**
Grove. *Oxon* 2B **36**
Grovehill. *E Yor* 1D **94**
Grove Park. *G Lon* 3F **39**
Grovesend. *Swan* 5F **45**
Grove, The. *Dum* 2A **112**
Grove, The. *Worc* 1D **48**
Grub Street. *Staf* 3B **72**
Grudie. *High* 2F **157**
Gruids. *High* 3C **164**
Gruinard House. *High* 4D **162**
Gruinart. *Arg* 3A **124**
Grulinbeg. *Arg* 3A **124**
Gruline. *Arg* 4G **139**
Grummore. *High* 5G **167**
Grundisburgh. *Suff* 5E **66**
Gruting. *Shet* 7D **173**
Grutness. *Shet* 10F **173**
Gualachulain. *High* 4F **141**
Gualin House. *High* 3D **166**
Guardbridge. *Fife* 2G **137**
Guarlford. *Worc* 1D **48**
Guay. *Per* 4H **143**
Gubblecote. *Herts* 4H **51**
Guestling Green. *E Sus* 4C **28**
Guestling Thorn. *E Sus* 4C **28**
Guestwick. *Norf* 3C **78**
Guestwick Green. *Norf* 3C **78**
Guide. *Bkbn* 2F **91**
Guide Post. *Nmbd* 1F **115**
Guilden Down. *Shrp* 2F **59**
Guilden Morden. *Cambs* 1C **52**
Guilden Sutton. *Ches W* 4G **83**
Guildford. *Surr* 1A **26** & **197**
Guildtown. *Per* 5A **144**
Guilsborough. *Nptn* 3D **62**
Guilsfield. *Powy* 4E **70**
Guineaford. *Devn* 3F **19**
Guisborough. *Red C* 3D **106**
Guiseley. *W Yor* 5D **98**
Guist. *Norf* 3B **78**
Guiting Power. *Glos* 3F **49**
Gulberwick. *Shet* 8F **173**
Gullane. *E Lot* 1A **130**
Gulling Green. *Suff* 5H **65**
Gulval. *Corn* 3B **4**
Gumfreston. *Pemb* 4F **43**
Gumley. *Leics* 1D **62**
Gunby. *E Yor* 1H **93**
Gunby. *Linc* 3G **75**
Gundleton. *Hants* 3E **24**
Gun Green. *Kent* 2B **28**
Gun Hill. *E Sus* 4G **27**
Gunn. *Devn* 3G **19**
Gunnerside. *N Yor* 5C **104**
Gunnerton. *Nmbd* 2C **114**
Gunness. *N Lin* 3B **94**
Gunnislake. *Corn* 5E **11**
Gunnista. *Shet* 7F **173**
Gunsgreenhill. *Bord* 3F **131**
Gunstone. *Staf* 5C **72**
Gunthorpe. *Norf* 2C **78**
Gunthorpe. *N Lin* 1F **87**
Gunthorpe. *Notts* 1D **74**
Gunthorpe. *Pet* 5A **76**
Gunville. *IOW* 4C **16**
Gupworthy. *Som* 3C **20**
Gurnard. *IOW* 3C **16**
Gurney Slade. *Som* 2B **22**
Gurnos. *Powy* 5A **46**
Gussage All Saints. *Dors* 1F **15**
Gussage St Andrew. *Dors* 1E **15**
Gussage St Michael. *Dors* 1E **15**
Guston. *Kent* 1H **29**
Gutcher. *Shet* 2G **173**
Guthram Gowt. *Linc* 3A **76**
Guthrie. *Ang* 3E **145**
Guyhirn. *Cambs* 5D **76**
Guyhirn Gull. *Cambs* 5C **76**
Guy's Head. *Linc* 3D **77**
Guy's Marsh. *Dors* 4D **22**
Guyzance. *Nmbd* 4G **121**
Gwaelod-y-garth. *Card* 3E **32**
Gwaenynog Bach. *Den* 4C **82**
Gwaenysgor. *Flin* 2C **82**
Gwalchmai. *IOA* 3C **80**
Gwastad. *Pemb* 2E **43**
Gwaun-Cae-Gurwen. *Neat* 4H **45**
Gwaun-y-bara. *Cphy* 3E **33**
Gwbert. *Cdgn* 1B **44**
Gweek. *Corn* 4E **5**
Gwehelog. *Mon* 5G **47**
Gwenddwr. *Powy* 1D **46**
Gwennap. *Corn* 4B **6**
Gwenter. *Corn* 5E **5**
Gwernaffield. *Flin* 4E **82**
Gwernesney. *Mon* 5H **47**
Gwernogle. *Carm* 2F **45**
Gwern-y-go. *Powy* 1E **58**
Gwernymynydd. *Flin* 4E **82**
Gwersyllt. *Wrex* 5F **83**
Gwespyr. *Flin* 2D **82**
Gwinear. *Corn* 3C **4**
Gwithian. *Corn* 2C **4**
Gwredog. *IOA* 2D **80**
Gwyddelwern. *Den* 1C **70**
Gwyddgrug. *Carm* 2E **45**
Gwynfryn. *Wrex* 5E **83**
Gwystre. *Powy* 4C **58**
Gwytherin. *Cnwy* 4A **82**
Gyfelia. *Wrex* 1F **71**
Gyffin. *Cnwy* 3G **81**

H

Haa of Houlland. *Shet* 1G **173**
Habberley. *Shrp* 5F **71**
Habblesthorpe. *Notts* 2E **87**
Habergham. *Lanc* 1G **91**
Habin. *W Sus* 4G **25**
Habrough. *NE Lin* 3E **95**
Haceby. *Linc* 2H **75**
Hacheston. *Suff* 5F **67**
Hackenthorpe. *S Yor* 2B **86**
Hackford. *Norf* 5C **78**
Hackforth. *N Yor* 5F **105**
Hackland. *Orkn* 5C **172**
Hackleton. *Nptn* 5F **63**
Hackman's Gate. *Worc* 3C **60**
Hackness. *N Yor* 5G **107**
Hackness. *Orkn* 8C **172**
Hackney. *G Lon* 2E **39**
Hackthorn. *Linc* 2G **87**
Hackthorpe. *Cumb* 2G **103**
Haclait. *W Isl* 4D **170**
Haconby. *Linc* 3A **76**
Hadden. *Bord* 1B **120**
Haddenham. *Buck* 5F **51**
Haddenham. *Cambs* 3D **64**
Haddenham End. *Cambs* 3D **64**
Haddington. *E Lot* 2B **130**
Haddington. *Linc* 4G **87**
Haddiscoe. *Norf* 1G **67**
Haddo. *Abers* 5F **161**
Haddon. *Cambs* 1A **64**
Hademore. *Staf* 5F **73**
Hadfield. *Derbs* 1E **85**
Hadham Cross. *Herts* 4E **53**
Hadham Ford. *Herts* 3E **53**
Hadleigh. *Essx* 2C **40**
Hadleigh. *Suff* 1D **54**
Hadleigh Heath. *Suff* 1C **54**
Hadley. *Telf* 4A **72**
Hadley. *Worc* 4C **60**
Hadley End. *Staf* 3F **73**
Hadley Wood. *G Lon* 1D **38**
Hadlow. *Kent* 1H **27**
Hadlow Down. *E Sus* 3G **27**
Hadnall. *Shrp* 3H **71**
Hadstock. *Essx* 1F **53**
Hadston. *Nmbd* 5G **121**
Hady. *Derbs* 3A **86**
Hadzor. *Worc* 4D **60**
Haffenden Quarter. *Kent* 1C **28**
Haggate. *Lanc* 1G **91**
Haggbeck. *Cumb* 2F **113**
Haggersta. *Shet* 7E **173**
Haggerston. *Nmbd* 5G **131**
Haggrister. *Shet* 4E **173**
Hagley. *Here* 1A **48**
Hagley. *Worc* 2D **60**
Hagnaby. *Linc* 4C **88**
Hagworthingham. *Linc* 4C **88**
Haigh. *G Man* 4E **90**
Haigh Moor. *W Yor* 2C **92**
Haighton Green. *Lanc* 1D **90**
Haile. *Cumb* 4B **102**
Hailes. *Glos* 2F **49**
Hailey. *Herts* 4D **52**
Hailey. *Oxon* 4B **50**
Hailsham. *E Sus* 5G **27**
Hail Weston. *Cambs* 4A **64**
Hainault. *G Lon* 1F **39**
Hainford. *Norf* 4E **78**
Hainton. *Linc* 2A **88**
Hainworth. *W Yor* 1A **92**
Haisthorpe. *E Yor* 3F **101**
Hakin. *Pemb* 4C **42**
Halam. *Notts* 5D **86**
Halbeath. *Fife* 1E **129**
Halberton. *Devn* 1D **12**
Halcro. *High* 2E **169**
Hale. *Cumb* 2E **97**
Hale. *G Man* 2B **84**
Hale. *Hal* 2G **83**
Hale. *Hants* 1G **15**
Hale. *Surr* 2G **25**
Hale Bank. *Hal* 2G **83**
Halebarns. *G Man* 2B **84**
Hales. *Norf* 1F **67**
Hales. *Staf* 2B **72**
Halesgate. *Linc* 3C **76**
Hales Green. *Derbs* 1F **73**
Halesowen. *W Mid* 2D **60**
Hale Street. *Kent* 1A **28**
Halesworth. *Suff* 3F **67**
Halewood. *Mers* 2G **83**
Halford. *Shrp* 2G **59**
Halford. *Warw* 1A **50**
Halfpenny. *Cumb* 1E **97**
Halfpenny Furze. *Carm* 3G **43**
Halfpenny Green. *Shrp* 1C **60**
Halfway. *Carm* 2G **45**
Halfway. *Powy* 2B **46**

Halfway—Haye

Halfway. *S Yor* 2B **86**
Halfway. *W Ber* 5C **36**
Halfway House. *Shrp* 4F **71**
Halfway Houses. *Kent* 3D **40**
Halgabron. *Corn* 4A **10**
Halifax. *W Yor* 2A **92**
Halistra. *High* 3B **154**
Halket. *E Ayr* 4F **127**
Halkirk. *High* 3D **168**
Halkyn. *Flin* 3E **82**
Hall. *E Ren* 4F **127**
Hallam Fields. *Derbs* 1B **74**
Halland. *E Sus* 4G **27**
Hallands, The. *N Lin* 2D **94**
Hallaton. *Leics* 1E **63**
Hallatrow. *Bath* 1B **22**
Hallbank. *Cumb* 5H **103**
Hallbankgate. *Cumb* 4G **113**
Hall Dunnerdale. *Cumb* 5D **102**
Hallen. *S Glo* 3A **34**
Hall End. *Bed* 1A **52**
Hallgarth. *Dur* 5G **115**
Hall Green. *Ches E* 5C **84**
Hall Green. *Norf* 2D **66**
Hall Green. *W Mid* 2F **61**
Hall Green. *W Yor* 3D **92**
Hall Green. *Wrex* 1G **71**
Halliburton. *Bord* 5C **130**
Hallin. *High* 3B **154**
Halling. *Medw* 4B **40**
Hallington. *Linc* 2C **88**
Hallington. *Nmbd* 2C **114**
Halloughton. *Notts* 5D **86**
Hallow. *Worc* 5C **60**
Hallow Heath. *Worc* 5C **60**
Hallowsgate. *Ches W* 4H **83**
Hallsands. *Devn* 5E **9**
Hall's Green. *Herts* 3C **52**
Hallspill. *Devn* 4E **19**
Hallthwaites. *Cumb* 1A **96**
Hall Waberthwaite. *Cumb* 5C **102**
Hallwood Green. *Glos* 2B **48**
Hallworthy. *Corn* 4B **10**
Hallyne. *Bord* 5E **129**
Halmer End. *Staf* 1C **72**
Halmond's Frome. *Here* 1B **48**
Halmore. *Glos* 5B **48**
Halnaker. *W Sus* 5A **26**
Halsall. *Lanc* 3B **90**
Halse. *Nptn* 1D **50**
Halse. *Som* 4E **21**
Halsetown. *Corn* 3C **4**
Halsham. *E Yor* 2F **95**
Halsinger. *Devn* 3F **19**
Halstead. *Essx* 2B **54**
Halstead. *Kent* 4F **39**
Halstead. *Leics* 5E **75**
Halstock. *Dors* 2A **14**
Halsway. *Som* 3E **21**
Haltcliff Bridge. *Cumb* 1E **103**
Haltham. *Linc* 4B **88**
Haltoft End. *Linc* 1C **76**
Halton. *Buck* 5G **51**
Halton. *Hal* 2H **83**
Halton. *Lanc* 3E **97**
Halton. *Nmbd* 3C **114**
Halton. *W Yor* 1D **92**
Halton. *Wrex* 2F **71**
Halton East. *N Yor* 4C **98**
Halton Fenside. *Linc* 4D **88**
Halton Gill. *N Yor* 2A **98**
Halton Holegate. *Linc* 4D **88**
Halton Lea Gate. *Nmbd* 4H **113**
Halton Moor. *W Yor* 1D **92**
Halton Shields. *Nmbd* 3D **114**
Halton West. *N Yor* 4H **97**
Haltwhistle. *Nmbd* 3A **114**
Halvergate. *Norf* 5G **79**
Halwell. *Devn* 3D **9**
Halwill. *Devn* 3E **11**
Halwill Junction. *Devn* 3E **11**
Ham. *Devn* 2F **13**
Ham. *Glos* 2B **34**
Ham. *G Lon* 3C **38**
Ham. *High* 1E **169**
Ham. *Kent* 5H **41**
Ham. *Plym* 3A **8**
Ham. *Shet* 8A **173**
Ham. *Som* 1F **13** (nr. Ilminster)
Ham. *Som* 4F **21** (nr. Taunton)
Ham. *Som* 4E **21** (nr. Wellington)
Ham. *Wilts* 5B **36**
Hambleden. *Buck* 3F **37**
Hambledon. *Hants* 1E **17**
Hambledon. *Surr* 2A **26**
Hamble-le-Rice. *Hants* 2C **16**
Hambleton. *Lanc* 5C **96**
Hambleton. *N Yor* 1F **93**
Hambridge. *Som* 4G **21**
Hambrook. *S Glo* 4B **34**
Hambrook. *W Sus* 2F **17**
Ham Common. *Dors* 4D **22**
Hameringham. *Linc* 4C **88**
Hamerton. *Cambs* 3A **64**
Ham Green. *Here* 1C **48**
Ham Green. *Kent* 4C **40**
Ham Green. *N Som* 4A **34**
Ham Green. *Worc* 4E **61**
Ham Hill. *Kent* 4A **40**
Hamilton. *Leics* 5D **74**
Hamilton. *S Lan* 4A **128**
Hamister. *Shet* 5G **173**
Hammer. *W Sus* 3G **25**
Hammersmith. *G Lon* 3D **38**
Hammerwich. *Staf* 5E **73**
Hammerwood. *E Sus* 2F **27**
Hammill. *Kent* 5G **41**
Hammond Street. *Herts* 5D **52**
Hammoon. *Dors* 1D **14**
Hamnavoe. *Shet* 3D **173** (nr. Braehoulland)
Hamnavoe. *Shet* 8E **173** (nr. Burland)
Hamnavoe. *Shet* 4F **173** (nr. Lunna)
Hamnavoe. *Shet* 3F **173** (on Yell)
Hamp. *Som* 3G **21**
Hampden Park. *E Sus* 5H **27**
Hampen. *Glos* 3F **49**
Hamperden End. *Essx* 2F **53**
Hamperley. *Shrp* 2G **59**
Hampnett. *Glos* 4F **49**
Hampole. *S Yor* 3F **93**
Hampreston. *Dors* 3F **15**
Hampstead. *G Lon* 2D **38**
Hampstead Norreys. *W Ber* 4D **36**
Hampsthwaite. *N Yor* 4E **99**
Hampton. *Devn* 3F **13**
Hampton. *G Lon* 3C **38**
Hampton. *Kent* 4F **41**
Hampton. *Shrp* 2B **60**
Hampton. *Swin* 2G **35**
Hampton. *Worc* 1F **49**
Hampton Bishop. *Here* 2A **48**
Hampton Fields. *Glos* 2D **35**
Hampton Hargate. *Pet* 1A **64**
Hampton Heath. *Ches W* 1H **71**
Hampton in Arden. *W Mid* 2G **61**
Hampton Loade. *Shrp* 2B **60**
Hampton Lovett. *Worc* 4C **60**
Hampton Lucy. *Warw* 5G **61**
Hampton Magna. *Warw* 4G **61**
Hampton on the Hill. *Warw* 4G **61**
Hampton Poyle. *Oxon* 4D **50**
Hampton Wick. *G Lon* 4C **38**
Hamptworth. *Wilts* 1H **15**
Hamrow. *Norf* 3B **78**
Hamsey. *E Sus* 4F **27**
Hamsey Green. *Surr* 5E **39**
Hamstall Ridware. *Staf* 4F **73**
Hamstead. *IOW* 3C **16**
Hamstead. *W Mid* 1E **61**
Hamstead Marshall. *W Ber* 5C **36**
Hamsterley. *Dur* 4E **115** (nr. Consett)
Hamsterley. *Dur* 1E **105** (nr. Wolsingham)
Hamsterley Mill. *Dur* 4E **115**
Hamstreet. *Kent* 2E **28**
Ham Street. *Som* 3A **22**
Hamworthy. *Pool* 3E **15**
Hanbury. *Staf* 3F **73**
Hanbury. *Worc* 4D **60**
Hanbury Woodend. *Staf* 3F **73**
Hanby. *Linc* 2H **75**
Hanchurch. *Staf* 1C **72**
Hand and Pen. *Devn* 3D **12**
Handbridge. *Ches W* 4G **83**
Handcross. *W Sus* 3D **26**
Handforth. *Ches E* 2C **84**
Handley. *Ches W* 5G **83**
Handley. *Derbs* 4A **86**
Handsacre. *Staf* 4E **73**
Handsworth. *S Yor* 2B **86**
Handsworth. *W Mid* 1E **61**
Handy Cross. *Buck* 2G **37**
Hanford. *Dors* 1D **14**
Hanford. *Stoke* 1C **72**
Hangersley. *Hants* 2G **15**
Hanging Houghton. *Nptn* 3E **63**
Hanging Langford. *Wilts* 3F **23**
Hangleton. *Brig* 5D **26**
Hangleton. *W Sus* 5B **26**
Hanham. *S Glo* 4B **34**
Hanham Green. *S Glo* 4B **34**
Hankelow. *Ches E* 1A **72**
Hankerton. *Wilts* 2E **35**
Hankham. *E Sus* 5H **27**
Hanley. *Stoke* 1C **72** & **Stoke 211**
Hanley Castle. *Worc* 1D **48**
Hanley Childe. *Worc* 4A **60**
Hanley Swan. *Worc* 1D **48**
Hanley William. *Worc* 4A **60**
Hanlith. *N Yor* 3B **98**
Hanmer. *Wrex* 2G **71**
Hannaborough. *Devn* 2F **11**
Hannaford. *Devn* 4G **19**
Hannah. *Linc* 3E **89**
Hannington. *Hants* 1D **24**
Hannington. *Nptn* 3F **63**
Hannington. *Swin* 2G **35**
Hannington Wick. *Swin* 2G **35**
Hanscombe End. *C Beds* 2B **52**
Hanslope. *Mil* 1G **51**
Hanthorpe. *Linc* 3H **75**
Hanwell. *G Lon* 2C **38**
Hanwell. *Oxon* 1C **50**
Hanwood. *Shrp* 5G **71**
Hanworth. *G Lon* 3C **38**
Hanworth. *Norf* 2D **78**
Happas. *Ang* 4D **144**
Happendon. *S Lan* 1A **118**
Happisburgh. *Norf* 2F **79**
Happisburgh Common. *Norf* 3F **79**
Hapsford. *Ches W* 3G **83**
Hapton. *Lanc* 1F **91**
Hapton. *Norf* 1D **66**
Harberton. *Devn* 3D **9**
Harbertonford. *Devn* 3D **9**
Harbledown. *Kent* 5F **41**
Harborne. *W Mid* 2E **61**
Harborough Magna. *Warw* 3B **62**
Harbottle. *Nmbd* 4D **120**
Harbourneford. *Devn* 2D **8**
Harbours Hill. *Worc* 4D **60**
Harbridge. *Hants* 1G **15**
Harbury. *Warw* 4A **62**
Harby. *Leics* 2E **75**
Harby. *Notts* 3F **87**
Harcombe. *Devn* 3E **13**
Harcombe Bottom. *Devn* 3G **13**
Harcourt. *Corn* 5C **6**
Harden. *W Yor* 1A **92**
Hardenhuish. *Wilts* 4E **35**
Hardgate. *Abers* 3E **153**
Hardgate. *Dum* 3F **111**
Hardham. *W Sus* 4B **26**
Hardingham. *Norf* 5C **78**
Hardingstone. *Nptn* 5E **63**
Hardings Wood. *Ches E* 5C **84**
Hardington. *Som* 1C **22**
Hardington Mandeville. *Som* 1A **14**
Hardington Marsh. *Som* 2A **14**
Hardington Moor. *Som* 1A **14**
Hardley. *Hants* 2C **16**
Hardley Street. *Norf* 5F **79**
Hardmead. *Mil* 1H **51**
Hardraw. *N Yor* 5B **104**
Hardstoft. *Derbs* 4B **86**
Hardway. *Hants* 2E **16**
Hardway. *Som* 3C **22**
Hardwick. *Buck* 4G **51**
Hardwick. *Cambs* 5C **64**
Hardwick. *Norf* 2E **66**
Hardwick. *Nptn* 4F **63**
Hardwick. *Oxon* 3D **50** (nr. Bicester)
Hardwick. *Oxon* 5B **50** (nr. Witney)
Hardwick. *Shrp* 1F **59**
Hardwick. *S Yor* 2B **86**
Hardwick. *Stoc T* 2B **106**
Hardwick. *W Mid* 1E **61**
Hardwicke. *Glos* 3E **49** (nr. Cheltenham)
Hardwicke. *Glos* 4C **48** (nr. Gloucester)
Hardwicke. *Here* 1F **47**
Hardwick Village. *Notts* 3D **86**
Hardy's Green. *Essx* 3C **54**
Hare. *Som* 1F **13**
Hareby. *Linc* 4C **88**
Hareden. *Lanc* 4F **97**
Harefield. *G Lon* 1B **38**
Hare Green. *Essx* 3D **54**
Hare Hatch. *Wok* 4G **37**
Harehill. *Derbs* 2F **73**
Harehills. *W Yor* 1D **92**
Harehope. *Nmbd* 2E **121**
Harelaw. *Dum* 2F **113**
Harelaw. *Dur* 4E **115**
Hareplain. *Kent* 2C **28**
Haresceugh. *Cumb* 5H **113**
Harescombe. *Glos* 4D **48**
Haresfield. *Glos* 4D **48**
Haresfinch. *Mers* 1H **83**
Hareshaw. *N Lan* 3B **128**
Hare Street. *Essx* 5E **53**
Hare Street. *Herts* 3D **53**
Harewood. *W Yor* 5F **99**
Harewood End. *Here* 3A **48**
Harford. *Devn* 3C **8**
Hargate. *Norf* 1D **66**
Hargatewall. *Derbs* 3F **85**
Hargrave. *Ches W* 4G **83**
Hargrave. *Nptn* 3H **63**
Hargrave. *Suff* 5G **65**
Harker. *Cumb* 3E **113**
Harkland. *Shet* 3F **173**
Harkstead. *Suff* 2E **55**
Harlaston. *Staf* 4G **73**
Harlaxton. *Linc* 2F **75**
Harlech. *Gwyn* 2E **69**
Harlequin. *Notts* 2D **74**
Harlescott. *Shrp* 4H **71**
Harleston. *Devn* 4D **9**
Harleston. *Norf* 2E **67**
Harleston. *Suff* 4C **66**
Harlestone. *Nptn* 4E **62**
Harley. *Shrp* 5H **71**
Harley. *S Yor* 1A **86**
Harling Road. *Norf* 2B **66**
Harlington. *C Beds* 2A **52**
Harlington. *G Lon* 3B **38**
Harlington. *S Yor* 4E **93**
Harlosh. *High* 4B **154**
Harlow. *Essx* 4E **53**
Harlow Hill. *Nmbd* 3D **115**
Harlsey Castle. *N Yor* 5B **106**
Harlthorpe. *E Yor* 1H **93**
Harlton. *Cambs* 5C **64**
Harlyn Bay. *Corn* 1C **6**
Harman's Cross. *Dors* 4E **15**
Harmby. *N Yor* 1D **98**
Harmer Green. *Herts* 4C **52**
Harmer Hill. *Shrp* 3G **71**
Harmondsworth. *G Lon* 3B **38**
Harmston. *Linc* 4G **87**
Harnage. *Shrp* 5H **71**
Harnham. *Nmbd* 1D **115**
Harnhill. *Glos* 5F **49**
Harold Hill. *G Lon* 1G **39**
Haroldston West. *Pemb* 3C **42**
Haroldswick. *Shet* 1H **173**
Harold Wood. *G Lon* 1G **39**
Harome. *N Yor* 1A **100**
Harpenden. *Herts* 4B **52**
Harpford. *Devn* 3D **12**
Harpham. *E Yor* 3E **101**
Harpley. *Norf* 3G **77**
Harpley. *Worc* 4A **60**
Harpole. *Nptn* 4D **62**
Harpsdale. *High* 3D **168**
Harpsden. *Oxon* 3F **37**
Harpswell. *Linc* 2G **87**
Harpurhey. *G Man* 4G **91**
Harpur Hill. *Derbs* 3E **85**
Harraby. *Cumb* 4F **113**
Harracott. *Devn* 4F **19**
Harrapool. *High* 1E **147**
Harrapul. *High* 1E **147**
Harrietfield. *Per* 1B **136**
Harrietsham. *Kent* 5C **40**
Harrington. *Cumb* 2A **102**
Harrington. *Linc* 3C **88**
Harrington. *Nptn* 2E **63**
Harringworth. *Nptn* 1G **63**
Harriseahead. *Staf* 5C **84**
Harriston. *Cumb* 5C **112**
Harrogate. *N Yor* 4F **99** & **197**
Harrold. *Bed* 5G **63**
Harrop Dale. *G Man* 4A **92**
Harrow. *G Lon* 2C **38**
Harrowbarrow. *Corn* 2H **7**
Harrowden. *Bed* 1A **52**
Harrowgate Hill. *Darl* 3F **105**
Harrow on the Hill. *G Lon* 2C **38**
Harrow Weald. *G Lon* 1C **38**
Harry Stoke. *S Glo* 4B **34**
Harston. *Cambs* 5D **64**
Harston. *Leics* 2F **75**
Harswell. *E Yor* 5C **100**
Hart. *Hart* 1B **106**
Hartburn. *Nmbd* 1D **115**
Hartburn. *Stoc T* 3B **106**
Hartest. *Suff* 5H **65**
Hartfield. *E Sus* 2F **27**
Hartford. *Cambs* 3B **64**
Hartford. *Ches W* 3A **84**
Hartford. *Som* 4C **20**
Hartfordbridge. *Hants* 1F **25**
Hartford End. *Essx* 4G **53**
Harthill. *Ches W* 5H **83**
Harthill. *N Lan* 3C **128**
Harthill. *S Yor* 2B **86**
Hartington. *Derbs* 4F **85**
Hartland. *Devn* 4C **18**
Hartland Quay. *Devn* 4C **18**
Hartle. *Worc* 3D **60**
Hartlebury. *Worc* 3C **60**
Hartlepool. *Hart* 1C **106**
Hartley. *Cumb* 4A **104**
Hartley. *Kent* 2B **28** (nr. Cranbrook)
Hartley. *Kent* 4H **39** (nr. Dartford)
Hartley. *Nmbd* 2G **115**
Hartley Green. *Staf* 2D **73**
Hartley Mauditt. *Hants* 3F **25**
Hartley Wespall. *Hants* 1E **25**
Hartley Wintney. *Hants* 1F **25**
Hartlip. *Kent* 4C **40**
Hartmount. *High* 1B **158**
Hartoft End. *N Yor* 5E **107**
Harton. *N Yor* 3B **100**
Harton. *Shrp* 2G **59**
Harton. *Tyne* 3G **115**
Hartpury. *Glos* 3C **48**
Hartshead. *W Yor* 2B **92**
Hartshill. *Warw* 1H **61**
Hartshorne. *Derbs* 3H **73**
Hartsop. *Cumb* 3F **103**
Hart Station. *Hart* 1B **106**
Hartswell. *Som* 4D **20**
Hartwell. *Nptn* 5E **63**
Hartwood. *Lanc* 3D **90**
Hartwood. *N Lan* 4B **128**
Harvel. *Kent* 4A **40**
Harvington. *Worc* 1F **49** (nr. Evesham)
Harvington. *Worc* 3C **60** (nr. Kidderminster)
Harwell. *Oxon* 3C **36**
Harwich. *Essx* 2F **55** & **215**
Harwood. *Dur* 1B **104**
Harwood. *G Man* 3F **91**
Harwood Dale. *N Yor* 5G **107**
Harworth. *Notts* 1D **86**
Hascombe. *Surr* 2A **26**
Haselbech. *Nptn* 3E **62**
Haselbury Plucknett. *Som* 1H **13**
Haseley. *Warw* 4G **61**
Haselor. *Warw* 5F **61**
Hasfield. *Glos* 3D **48**
Hasguard. *Pemb* 4C **42**
Haskayne. *Lanc* 4B **90**
Hasketon. *Suff* 5E **67**
Hasland. *Derbs* 4A **86**
Haslemere. *Surr* 2A **26**
Haslingden. *Lanc* 2F **91**
Haslingden Grane. *Lanc* 2F **91**
Haslingfield. *Cambs* 5D **64**
Haslington. *Ches E* 5B **84**
Hassall. *Ches E* 5B **84**
Hassall Green. *Ches E* 5B **84**
Hassell Street. *Kent* 1E **29**
Hassendean. *Bord* 2H **119**
Hassingham. *Norf* 5F **79**
Hassocks. *W Sus* 4E **27**
Hassop. *Derbs* 3G **85**
Haster. *High* 3F **169**
Hasthorpe. *Linc* 4D **89**
Hastigrow. *High* 2E **169**
Hastingleigh. *Kent* 1E **29**
Hastings. *E Sus* 5C **28**
Hastingwood. *Essx* 5E **53**
Hastoe. *Herts* 5H **51**
Haston. *Shrp* 3H **71**
Haswell. *Dur* 5G **115**
Haswell Plough. *Dur* 5G **115**
Hatch. *C Beds* 1B **52**
Hatch Beauchamp. *Som* 4G **21**
Hatch End. *G Lon* 1C **38**
Hatch Green. *Som* 1G **13**
Hatching Green. *Herts* 4B **52**
Hatchmere. *Ches W* 3H **83**
Hatch Warren. *Hants* 2E **24**
Hatcliffe. *NE Lin* 4F **95**
Hatfield. *Here* 5H **59**
Hatfield. *Herts* 5C **52**
Hatfield. *S Yor* 4G **93**
Hatfield. *Worc* 5C **60**
Hatfield Broad Oak. *Essx* 4F **53**
Hatfield Garden Village. *Herts* 5C **52**
Hatfield Heath. *Essx* 4F **53**
Hatfield Hyde. *Herts* 4C **52**
Hatfield Peverel. *Essx* 4A **54**
Hatfield Woodhouse. *S Yor* 4G **93**
Hatford. *Oxon* 2B **36**
Hatherden. *Hants* 1B **24**
Hatherleigh. *Devn* 2F **11**
Hathern. *Leics* 3C **74**
Hatherop. *Glos* 5G **49**
Hathersage. *Derbs* 2G **85**
Hathersage Booths. *Derbs* 2G **85**
Hatherton. *Ches E* 1A **72**
Hatherton. *Staf* 4D **72**
Hatley St George. *Cambs* 5B **64**
Hatt. *Corn* 2H **7**
Hattersley. *G Man* 1D **85**
Hattingley. *Hants* 3E **25**
Hatton. *Abers* 5H **161**
Hatton. *Derbs* 2G **73**
Hatton. *G Lon* 3B **38**
Hatton. *Linc* 3A **88**
Hatton. *Shrp* 1G **59**
Hatton. *Warr* 2H **83**
Hatton. *Warw* 4G **61**
Hattoncrook. *Abers* 1F **153**
Hatton Heath. *Ches W* 4G **83**
Hatton of Fintray. *Abers* 2F **153**
Haugh. *E Ayr* 2D **117**
Haugh. *Linc* 3D **88**
Haugham. *Linc* 2C **88**
Haugh Head. *Nmbd* 2E **121**
Haughley. *Suff* 4C **66**
Haughley Green. *Suff* 4C **66**
Haugh of Ballechin. *Per* 3G **143**
Haugh of Glass. *Mor* 5B **160**
Haugh of Urr. *Dum* 3F **111**
Haughton. *Ches E* 5H **83**
Haughton. *Notts* 3D **86**
Haughton. *Shrp* 1A **60** (nr. Bridgnorth)
Haughton. *Shrp* 3F **71** (nr. Oswestry)
Haughton. *Shrp* 5B **72** (nr. Shifnal)
Haughton. *Shrp* 4H **71** (nr. Shrewsbury)
Haughton. *Staf* 3C **72**
Haughton Green. *G Man* 1D **84**
Haughton le Skerne. *Darl* 3A **106**
Haultwick. *Herts* 3D **52**
Haunn. *Arg* 4E **139**
Haunn. *W Isl* 7C **170**
Haunton. *Staf* 4G **73**
Hauxton. *Cambs* 5D **64**
Havannah. *Ches E* 4C **84**
Havant. *Hants* 2F **17**
Haven. *Here* 5G **59**
Haven Bank. *Linc* 5B **88**
Havenside. *E Yor* 2E **95**
Havenstreet. *IOW* 3D **16**
Haven, The. *W Sus* 2B **26**
Havercroft. *W Yor* 3D **93**
Haverfordwest. *Pemb* 3D **42**
Haverhill. *Suff* 1G **53**
Haverigg. *Cumb* 2A **96**
Havering-atte-Bower. *G Lon* 1G **39**
Havering's Grove. *Essx* 1A **40**
Haversham. *Mil* 1G **51**
Haverthwaite. *Cumb* 1C **96**
Haverton Hill. *Stoc T* 2B **106**
Havyatt. *Som* 3A **22**
Hawarden. *Flin* 4F **83**
Hawbridge. *Worc* 1E **49**
Hawcoat. *Cumb* 2B **96**
Hawcross. *Glos* 2C **48**
Hawen. *Cdgn* 1D **44**
Hawes. *N Yor* 1A **98**
Hawes Green. *Norf* 1E **67**
Hawick. *Bord* 3H **119**
Hawkchurch. *Devn* 2G **13**
Hawkedon. *Suff* 5G **65**
Hawkenbury. *Kent* 1C **28**
Hawkeridge. *Wilts* 1D **22**
Hawkerland. *Devn* 4D **12**
Hawkesbury. *S Glo* 3C **34**
Hawkesbury. *W Mid* 2A **62**
Hawkesbury Upton. *S Glo* 3C **34**
Hawkes End. *W Mid* 2G **61**
Hawk Green. *G Man* 2D **84**
Hawkhurst. *Kent* 2B **28**
Hawkhurst Common. *E Sus* 4G **27**
Hawkinge. *Kent* 1G **29**
Hawkley. *Hants* 4F **25**
Hawkridge. *Som* 3B **20**
Hawksdale. *Cumb* 5E **113**
Hawkshaw. *G Man* 3F **91**
Hawkshead. *Cumb* 5E **103**
Hawkshead Hill. *Cumb* 5E **103**
Hawkswick. *N Yor* 2B **98**
Hawksworth. *Notts* 1E **75**
Hawksworth. *W Yor* 5D **98**
Hawkwell. *Essx* 1C **40**
Hawley. *Hants* 1G **25**
Hawley. *Kent* 3G **39**
Hawling. *Glos* 3F **49**
Hawnby. *N Yor* 1H **99**
Haworth. *W Yor* 1A **92**
Hawstead. *Suff* 5A **66**
Hawthorn. *Dur* 5H **115**
Hawthorn Hill. *Brac* 4G **37**
Hawthorn Hill. *Linc* 5B **88**
Hawthorpe. *Linc* 3H **75**
Hawton. *Notts* 5E **87**
Haxby. *York* 4A **100**
Haxey. *N Lin* 1E **87**
Haybridge. *Shrp* 3A **60**
Haybridge. *Som* 2A **22**
Haydock. *Mers* 1H **83**
Haydon. *Bath* 1B **22**
Haydon. *Dors* 1B **14**
Haydon. *Som* 4F **21**
Haydon Bridge. *Nmbd* 3B **114**
Haydon Wick. *Swin* 3G **35**
Haye. *Corn* 2H **7**

Hightae—Horton Cross

Hightae. *Dum* 2B 112
High Throston. *Hart* 1B 106
Hightown. *Ches E* 4C 84
Hightown. *Mers* 4A 90
High Town. *Staf* 4D 73
Hightown Green. *Suff* 5B 66
High Toynton. *Linc* 4B 88
High Trewhitt. *Nmbd* 4E 121
High Valleyfield. *Fife* 1D 128
Highway. *Here* 1H 47
Highweek. *Devn* 5B 12
High Westwood. *Dur* 4E 115
Highwood. *Staf* 2E 73
Highwood. *Worc* 4A 60
High Worsall. *N Yor* 4A 106
Highworth. *Swin* 2H 35
High Wray. *Cumb* 5E 103
High Wych. *Herts* 4E 53
High Wycombe. *Buck* 2G 37
Hilborough. *Norf* 5H 77
Hilcott. *Wilts* 1G 23
Hildenborough. *Kent* 1G 27
Hildersham. *Cambs* 1F 53
Hilderstone. *Staf* 2D 72
Hilderthorpe. *E Yor* 3F 101
Hilfield. *Dors* 2B 14
Hilgay. *Norf* 1F 65
Hill. *S Glo* 2B 34
Hill. *Warw* 4B 62
Hill. *Worc* 1E 49
Hillam. *N Yor* 2F 93
Hillbeck. *Cumb* 3A 104
Hillberry. *IOM* 4C 108
Hillborough. *Kent* 4G 41
Hillbourne. *Pool* 3F 15
Hillbrae. *Abers* 4D 160 (nr. Aberchirder)
Hillbrae. *Abers* 1E 153 (nr. Inverurie)
Hillbrae. *Abers* 5F 161 (nr. Methlick)
Hill Brow. *Hants* 4F 25
Hillbutts. *Dors* 2E 15
Hillcliffane. *Derbs* 1G 73
Hillcommon. *Som* 4E 21
Hill Deverill. *Wilts* 2D 22
Hilldyke. *Linc* 1C 76
Hill End. *Dur* 1D 104
Hillend. *Fife* 1E 129 (nr. Inverkeithing)
Hill End. *Fife* 4C 136 (nr. Saline)
Hillend. *N Lan* 3B 128
Hill End. *N Yor* 4C 98
Hillend. *Shrp* 1C 60
Hillend. *Swan* 3D 30
Hillersland. *Glos* 4A 48
Hillerton. *Devn* 3H 11
Hillesden. *Buck* 3E 51
Hillesley. *Glos* 3C 34
Hillfarrance. *Som* 4E 21
Hill Furze. *Worc* 1E 49
Hill Gate. *Here* 3H 47
Hill Green. *Essx* 2E 53
Hillgreen. *W Ber* 4C 36
Hillhead. *Abers* 5C 160
Hill Head. *Hants* 2D 16
Hillhead. *S Ayr* 3D 116
Hillhead. *Torb* 3F 9
Hillhead of Auchentumb. *Abers* 3G 161
Hilliard's Cross. *Staf* 4F 73
Hilliclay. *High* 2D 168
Hillingdon. *G Lon* 2B 38
Hillington. *Norf* 3G 77
Hillington. *Ren* 3G 127
Hillmorton. *Warw* 3C 62
Hill of Beath. *Fife* 4D 136
Hill of Fearn. *High* 1C 158
Hill of Fiddes. *Abers* 1G 153
Hill of Keillor. *Ang* 4B 144
Hill of Overbrae. *Abers* 2F 161
Hill Ridware. *Staf* 4E 73
Hillsborough. *S Yor* 1H 85
Hillside. *Abers* 4G 153
Hillside. *Ang* 2G 145
Hillside. *Devn* 2D 8
Hillside. *Mers* 3B 90
Hillside. *Orkn* 5C 172
Hillside. *Shet* 5F 173
Hillside. *Shrp* 2A 60
Hill Side. *W Yor* 3B 92
Hillside. *Worc* 4B 60
Hillside of Prieston. *Ang* 5C 144
Hill Somersal. *Derbs* 2F 73
Hillstown. *Derbs* 4B 86
Hillstreet. *Hants* 1B 16
Hillswick. *Shet* 4D 173
Hill, The. *Cumb* 1A 96
Hill Top. *Dur* 2C 104 (nr. Barnard Castle)
Hill Top. *Dur* 5F 115 (nr. Durham)
Hill Top. *Dur* 4E 115 (nr. Stanley)
Hill View. *Dors* 3E 15
Hillwell. *Shet* 10E 173
Hill Wootton. *Warw* 4H 61
Hillyland. *Per* 1C 136
Hilmarton. *Wilts* 4F 35
Hilperton. *Wilts* 1D 22
Hilperton Marsh. *Wilts* 1D 22
Hilsea. *Port* 2E 17
Hilston. *E Yor* 1F 95
Hiltingbury. *Hants* 4C 24
Hilton. *Cambs* 4B 64
Hilton. *Cumb* 2A 104
Hilton. *Derbs* 2G 73
Hilton. *Dors* 2C 14
Hilton. *Dur* 2E 105
Hilton. *High* 5E 165
Hilton. *Shrp* 1B 60
Hilton. *Staf* 5E 73
Hilton. *Stoc T* 3B 106
Hilton of Cadboll. *High* 1C 158
Himbleton. *Worc* 5D 60
Himley. *Staf* 1C 60
Hincaster. *Cumb* 1E 97
Hinchcliffe Mill. *W Yor* 4B 92
Hinchwick. *Glos* 2G 49
Hinckley. *Leics* 1B 62
Hinderclay. *Suff* 3C 66
Hinderwell. *N Yor* 3E 107
Hindford. *Shrp* 2F 71
Hindhead. *Surr* 3G 25
Hindley. *G Man* 4E 90
Hindley. *Nmbd* 4D 114
Hindley Green. *G Man* 4E 91
Hindlip. *Worc* 5C 60
Hindolveston. *Norf* 3C 78
Hindon. *Wilts* 3E 23
Hindringham. *Norf* 2B 78
Hingham. *Norf* 5C 78
Hinksford. *Staf* 2C 60
Hinstock. *Shrp* 3A 72
Hintlesham. *Suff* 1D 54
Hinton. *Hants* 3H 15
Hinton. *Here* 2G 47
Hinton. *Nptn* 5C 62
Hinton. *Shrp* 5G 71
Hinton. *S Glo* 4C 34
Hinton Ampner. *Hants* 4D 24
Hinton Blewett. *Bath* 1A 22
Hinton Charterhouse. *Bath* 1C 22
Hinton-in-the-Hedges. *Nptn* 2D 50
Hinton Martell. *Dors* 2F 15
Hinton on the Green. *Worc* 1F 49
Hinton Parva. *Swin* 3H 35
Hinton St George. *Som* 1H 13
Hinton St Mary. *Dors* 1C 14
Hinton Waldrist. *Oxon* 2B 36
Hints. *Shrp* 3A 60
Hints. *Staf* 5F 73
Hinwick. *Bed* 4G 63
Hinxhill. *Kent* 1E 29
Hinxton. *Cambs* 1E 53
Hinxworth. *Herts* 1C 52
Hipley. *Hants* 1E 16
Hipperholme. *W Yor* 2B 92
Hipsburn. *Nmbd* 3G 121
Hipswell. *N Yor* 5E 105
Hiraeth. *Carm* 2F 43
Hirn. *Abers* 3E 153
Hirnant. *Powy* 3C 70
Hirst. *N Lan* 3B 128
Hirst. *Nmbd* 1F 115
Hirst Courtney. *N Yor* 2G 93
Hirwaen. *Den* 4D 82
Hirwaun. *Rhon* 5C 46
Hiscott. *Devn* 4F 19
Histon. *Cambs* 4D 64
Hitcham. *Suff* 5B 66
Hitchin. *Herts* 3B 52
Hittisleigh. *Devn* 3H 11
Hittisleigh Barton. *Devn* 3H 11
Hive. *E Yor* 1B 94
Hixon. *Staf* 3E 73
Hoaden. *Kent* 5G 41
Hoar Cross. *Staf* 3F 73
Hoarwithy. *Here* 3A 48
Hoath. *Kent* 4G 41
Hobarris. *Shrp* 3F 59
Hobbister. *Orkn* 7C 172
Hobbles Green. *Suff* 5G 65
Hobbs Cross. *Essx* 1F 39
Hobkirk. *Bord* 3H 119
Hobson. *Dur* 4E 115
Hoby. *Leics* 4D 74
Hockering. *Norf* 4C 78
Hockering Heath. *Norf* 4C 78
Hockerton. *Notts* 5E 86
Hockley. *Essx* 1C 40
Hockley. *Staf* 5G 73
Hockley. *W Mid* 3G 61
Hockley Heath. *W Mid* 3F 61
Hockliffe. *C Beds* 3H 51
Hockwold cum Wilton. *Norf* 2G 65
Hockworthy. *Devn* 1D 12
Hoddesdon. *Herts* 5D 52
Hoddlesden. *Bkbn* 2F 91
Hoddomcross. *Dum* 2C 112
Hodgeston. *Pemb* 5E 43
Hodley. *Powy* 1D 58
Hodnet. *Shrp* 3A 72
Hodsoll Street. *Kent* 4H 39
Hodson. *Swin* 3G 35
Hodthorpe. *Derbs* 3C 86
Hoe. *Norf* 4B 78
Hoe Gate. *Hants* 1E 17
Hoe, The. *Plym* 3A 8
Hoff. *Cumb* 3H 103
Hoffleet Stow. *Linc* 2B 76
Hogaland. *Shet* 4E 173
Hogben's Hill. *Kent* 5E 41
Hoggard's Green. *Suff* 5A 66
Hoggeston. *Buck* 3G 51
Hoggrill's End. *Warw* 1G 61
Hogha Gearraidh. *W Isl* 1C 170
Hoghton. *Lanc* 2E 90
Hoghton Bottoms. *Lanc* 2E 91
Hognaston. *Derbs* 5G 85
Hogsthorpe. *Linc* 3E 89
Hogstock. *Dors* 2E 15
Holbeach. *Linc* 3C 76
Holbeach Bank. *Linc* 3C 76
Holbeach Clough. *Linc* 3C 76
Holbeach Drove. *Linc* 4C 76
Holbeach Hurn. *Linc* 3C 76
Holbeach St Johns. *Linc* 4C 76
Holbeach St Marks. *Linc* 2C 76
Holbeach St Matthew. *Linc* 2D 76
Holbeck. *Notts* 3C 86
Holbeck. *W Yor* 1C 92
Holbeck Woodhouse. *Notts* 3C 86
Holberrow Green. *Worc* 5E 61
Holbeton. *Devn* 3C 8
Holborn. *G Lon* 2E 39
Holbrook. *Derbs* 1A 74
Holbrook. *S Yor* 2B 86
Holbrook. *Suff* 2E 55
Holburn. *Nmbd* 1E 121
Holbury. *Hants* 2C 16
Holcombe. *Devn* 5C 12
Holcombe. *G Man* 3F 91
Holcombe. *Som* 2B 22
Holcombe Brook. *G Man* 3F 91
Holcombe Rogus. *Devn* 1D 12
Holcot. *Nptn* 4E 63
Holden. *Lanc* 5G 97
Holdenby. *Nptn* 4D 62
Holder's Green. *Essx* 3G 53
Holdgate. *Shrp* 2H 59
Holdingham. *Linc* 1H 75
Holditch. *Dors* 2G 13
Holemoor. *Devn* 2E 11
Hole Street. *W Sus* 4C 26
Holford. *Som* 2E 21
Holker. *Cumb* 2C 96
Holkham. *Norf* 1A 78
Hollacombe. *Devn* 2D 11
Holland. *Orkn* 2D 172 (on Papa Westray)
Holland. *Orkn* 5F 172 (on Stronsay)
Holland Fen. *Linc* 1B 76
Holland Lees. *Lanc* 4D 90
Holland-on-Sea. *Essx* 4F 55
Holland Park. *W Mid* 5E 73
Hollandstoun. *Orkn* 2G 172
Hollesley. *Suff* 1G 55
Hollinfare. *Warr* 1A 84
Hollingbourne. *Kent* 5C 40
Hollingbury. *Brig* 5E 27
Hollingdon. *Buck* 3G 51
Hollingrove. *E Sus* 3A 28
Hollington. *Derbs* 1G 73
Hollington. *E Sus* 4B 28
Hollington. *Staf* 2E 73
Hollington Grove. *Derbs* 2G 73
Hollingworth. *G Man* 1E 85
Hollins. *Derbs* 3H 85
Hollins. *G Man* 4G 91 (nr. Bury)
Hollins. *G Man* 4G 91 (nr. Middleton)
Hollinsclough. *Staf* 4E 85
Hollinswood. *Telf* 5A 72
Hollinthorpe. *W Yor* 1D 93
Hollinwood. *G Man* 4H 91
Hollinwood. *Shrp* 2H 71
Hollocombe. *Devn* 1G 11
Holloway. *Derbs* 5H 85
Hollow Court. *Worc* 5D 61
Hollowell. *Nptn* 3D 62
Hollow Meadows. *S Yor* 2G 85
Hollows. *Dum* 2E 113
Hollybush. *Cphy* 5E 47
Hollybush. *E Ayr* 3C 116
Hollybush. *Worc* 2C 48
Holly End. *Norf* 5D 77
Holly Hill. *N Yor* 4E 105
Hollyhurst. *Ches E* 1H 71
Hollym. *E Yor* 2G 95
Hollywood. *Worc* 3E 61
Holmacott. *Devn* 4F 19
Holmbridge. *W Yor* 4B 92
Holmbury St Mary. *Surr* 1C 26
Holmbush. *Corn* 3E 7
Holmcroft. *Staf* 3D 72
Holme. *Cambs* 2A 64
Holme. *Cumb* 2E 97
Holme. *N Lin* 4C 94
Holme. *N Yor* 1F 99
Holme. *Notts* 5F 87
Holme. *W Yor* 4B 92
Holmebridge. *Dors* 4D 15
Holme Chapel. *Lanc* 2G 91
Holme Hale. *Norf* 5A 78
Holme Lacy. *Here* 2A 48
Holme Marsh. *Here* 5F 59
Holmend. *Dum* 4C 118
Holme next the Sea. *Norf* 1G 77
Holme-on-Spalding-Moor. *E Yor* 1B 94
Holme on the Wolds. *E Yor* 5D 100
Holme Pierrepont. *Notts* 2D 74
Holmer. *Here* 1A 48
Holmer Green. *Buck* 1A 38
Holmes. *Lanc* 3C 90
Holme St Cuthbert. *Cumb* 5C 112
Holmes Chapel. *Ches E* 4B 84
Holmesfield. *Derbs* 3H 85
Holmeswood. *Lanc* 3C 90
Holmewood. *Derbs* 4B 86
Holmfirth. *W Yor* 4B 92
Holmhead. *E Ayr* 2E 117
Holmisdale. *High* 4A 154
Holm of Drumlanrig. *Dum* 5H 117
Holmpton. *E Yor* 2G 95
Holmrook. *Cumb* 5B 102
Holmsgarth. *Shet* 7F 173
Holmside. *Dur* 5F 115
Holmwrangle. *Cumb* 5G 113
Holne. *Devn* 2D 8
Holsworthy. *Devn* 2D 10
Holsworthy Beacon. *Devn* 2D 10
Holt. *Dors* 2F 15
Holt. *Norf* 2C 78
Holt. *Wilts* 5D 34
Holt. *Worc* 4C 60
Holt. *Wrex* 5G 83
Holtby. *York* 4A 100
Holt End. *Hants* 3E 25
Holt End. *Worc* 4E 61
Holt Fleet. *Worc* 4C 60
Holt Green. *Lanc* 4B 90
Holt Heath. *Dors* 2F 15
Holt Heath. *Worc* 4C 60
Holton. *Oxon* 5E 50
Holton. *Som* 4B 22
Holton. *Suff* 3F 67
Holton cum Beckering. *Linc* 2A 88
Holton Heath. *Dors* 3E 15
Holton le Clay. *Linc* 4F 95
Holton le Moor. *Linc* 1H 87
Holton St Mary. *Suff* 2D 54
Holt Pound. *Hants* 2G 25
Holtsmere End. *Herts* 4A 52
Holtye. *E Sus* 2F 27
Holwell. *Dors* 1C 14
Holwell. *Herts* 2B 52
Holwell. *Leics* 3E 75
Holwell. *Oxon* 5H 49
Holwell. *Som* 2C 22
Holwick. *Dur* 2C 104
Holworth. *Dors* 4C 14
Holybourne. *Hants* 2F 25
Holy City. *Devn* 2G 13
Holy Cross. *Worc* 3D 60
Holyfield. *Essx* 5D 53
Holyhead. *IOA* 2B 80
Holy Island. *Nmbd* 5H 131
Holymoorside. *Derbs* 4H 85
Holyport. *Wind* 4G 37
Holystone. *Nmbd* 4D 120
Holytown. *N Lan* 3A 128
Holywell. *Cambs* 3C 64
Holywell. *Corn* 3B 6
Holywell. *Dors* 2A 14
Holywell. *Flin* 3D 82
Holywell. *Glos* 2C 34
Holywell. *Nmbd* 2G 115
Holywell. *Warw* 4F 61
Holywell Bay. *Corn* 3B 6
Holywell Green. *W Yor* 3A 92
Holywell Lake. *Som* 4E 20
Holywell Row. *Suff* 3G 65
Holywood. *Dum* 1G 111
Homer. *Shrp* 5A 72
Homer Green. *Mers* 4B 90
Homersfield. *Suff* 2E 67
Hom Green. *Here* 3A 48
Homington. *Wilts* 4G 23
Honeyborough. *Pemb* 4D 42
Honeybourne. *Worc* 1G 49
Honeychurch. *Devn* 2G 11
Honeydon. *Bed* 5A 64
Honey Hill. *Kent* 4F 41
Honey Street. *Wilts* 5G 35
Honey Tye. *Suff* 2C 54
Honeywick. *C Beds* 3H 51
Honiley. *Warw* 3G 61
Honing. *Norf* 3F 79
Honingham. *Norf* 4D 78
Honington. *Linc* 1G 75
Honington. *Suff* 3B 66
Honington. *Warw* 1A 50
Honiton. *Devn* 2E 13
Honley. *W Yor* 3B 92
Honnington. *Telf* 4B 72
Hoo. *Suff* 5E 67
Hoobrook. *Worc* 3C 60
Hood Green. *S Yor* 4D 92
Hooe. *E Sus* 5A 28
Hooe. *Plym* 3B 8
Hooe Common. *E Sus* 4A 28
Hoo Green. *Ches E* 2B 84
Hoohill. *Bkpl* 1B 90
Hook. *Cambs* 1D 64
Hook. *E Yor* 2A 94
Hook. *G Lon* 4C 38
Hook. *Hants* 1F 25 (nr. Basingstoke)
Hook. *Hants* 2D 16 (nr. Fareham)
Hook. *Pemb* 3D 43
Hook. *Wilts* 3F 35
Hook-a-Gate. *Shrp* 5G 71
Hook Bank. *Worc* 1D 48
Hooke. *Dors* 2A 14
Hooker Gate. *Tyne* 4E 115
Hookgate. *Staf* 2B 72
Hook Green. *Kent* 2A 28 (nr. Lamberhurst)
Hook Green. *Kent* 3H 39 (nr. Longfield)
Hook Green. *Kent* 4H 39 (nr. Meopham)
Hook Norton. *Oxon* 2B 50
Hook's Cross. *Herts* 3C 52
Hook Street. *Glos* 2B 34
Hookway. *Devn* 3B 12
Hookwood. *Surr* 1D 26
Hoole. *Ches W* 4G 83
Hooley. *Surr* 5D 39
Hooley Bridge. *G Man* 3G 91
Hooley Brow. *G Man* 3G 91
Hoo St Werburgh. *Medw* 3B 40
Hooton. *Ches W* 3F 83
Hooton Levitt. *S Yor* 1C 86
Hooton Pagnell. *S Yor* 4E 93
Hooton Roberts. *S Yor* 1B 86
Hoove. *Shet* 7E 173
Hope. *Derbs* 2F 85
Hope. *Flin* 5F 83
Hope. *High* 2E 167
Hope. *Powy* 5E 71
Hope. *Shrp* 5F 71
Hope. *Staf* 5F 85
Hope Bagot. *Shrp* 3H 59
Hope Bowdler. *Shrp* 1G 59
Hopedale. *Staf* 5F 85
Hope Green. *Ches E* 2D 84
Hopeman. *Mor* 2F 159
Hope Mansell. *Here* 4B 48
Hopesay. *Shrp* 2F 59
Hope's Green. *Essx* 2B 40
Hopetown. *W Yor* 2D 93
Hope under Dinmore. *Here* 5H 59
Hopley's Green. *Here* 5F 59
Hopperton. *N Yor* 4G 99
Hop Pole. *Linc* 4A 76
Hopstone. *Shrp* 1B 60
Hopton. *Derbs* 5G 85
Hopton. *Powy* 1E 59
Hopton. *Shrp* 3F 71 (nr. Oswestry)
Hopton. *Shrp* 3H 71 (nr. Wem)
Hopton. *Staf* 3D 72
Hopton. *Suff* 3B 66
Hopton Cangeford. *Shrp* 2H 59
Hopton Castle. *Shrp* 3F 59
Hoptonheath. *Shrp* 3F 59
Hopton Heath. *Staf* 3D 72
Hopton on Sea. *Norf* 5H 79
Hopton Wafers. *Shrp* 3A 60
Hopwas. *Staf* 5F 73
Hopwood. *Worc* 3E 61
Horam. *E Sus* 4G 27
Horbling. *Linc* 2A 76
Horbury. *W Yor* 3C 92
Horcott. *Glos* 5G 49
Horden. *Dur* 5H 115
Horderley. *Shrp* 2G 59
Hordle. *Hants* 3A 16
Hordley. *Shrp* 2F 71
Horeb. *Carm* 3F 45 (nr. Brechfa)
Horeb. *Carm* 5E 45 (nr. Llanelli)
Horeb. *Cdgn* 1D 45
Horfield. *Bris* 4B 34
Horgabost. *W Isl* 8C 171
Horham. *Suff* 3E 66
Horkesley Heath. *Essx* 3C 54
Horkstow. *N Lin* 3C 94
Horley. *Oxon* 1C 50
Horley. *Surr* 1D 27
Horn Ash. *Dors* 2G 13
Hornblotton Green. *Som* 3A 22
Hornby. *Lanc* 3E 97
Hornby. *N Yor* 4A 106 (nr. Appleton Wiske)
Hornby. *N Yor* 5F 105 (nr. Catterick Garrison)
Horncastle. *Linc* 4B 88
Hornchurch. *G Lon* 2G 39
Horncliffe. *Nmbd* 5F 131
Horndean. *Hants* 1E 17
Horndean. *Bord* 5E 131
Horndon. *Devn* 4F 11
Horndon on the Hill. *Thur* 2A 40
Horne. *Surr* 1E 27
Horner. *Som* 2C 20
Horning. *Norf* 4F 79
Horninghold. *Leics* 1F 63
Horninglow. *Staf* 3G 73
Horningsea. *Cambs* 4D 65
Horningsham. *Wilts* 2D 22
Horningtoft. *Norf* 3B 78
Hornsbury. *Som* 1G 13
Hornsby. *Cumb* 4G 113
Hornsbygate. *Cumb* 4G 113
Horns Corner. *Kent* 3B 28
Horns Cross. *Devn* 4D 19
Hornsea. *E Yor* 5G 101
Hornsea Burton. *E Yor* 5G 101
Hornsey. *G Lon* 2E 39
Hornton. *Oxon* 1B 50
Horpit. *Swin* 3H 35
Horrabridge. *Devn* 2B 8
Horringer. *Suff* 4H 65
Horringford. *IOW* 4D 16
Horrocks Fold. *G Man* 3F 91
Horrocksford. *Lanc* 5G 97
Horsbrugh Ford. *Bord* 1E 119
Horsebridge. *Devn* 5E 11
Horsebridge. *E Sus* 4G 27
Horsebridge. *Hants* 3B 24
Horse Bridge. *Staf* 5D 84
Horsebrook. *Staf* 4C 72
Horsecastle. *N Som* 5H 33
Horsehay. *Telf* 5A 72
Horseheath. *Cambs* 1G 53
Horsehouse. *N Yor* 1C 98
Horsell. *Surr* 5A 38
Horseman's Green. *Wrex* 1G 71
Horsenden. *Buck* 5F 51
Horseway. *Cambs* 2D 64
Horsey. *Norf* 3G 79
Horsey. *Som* 3G 21
Horsford. *Norf* 4D 78
Horsforth. *W Yor* 1C 92
Horsham. *W Sus* 2C 26
Horsham. *Worc* 5B 60
Horsham St Faith. *Norf* 4E 78
Horsington. *Linc* 4A 88
Horsington. *Som* 4C 22
Horsley. *Derbs* 1A 74
Horsley. *Glos* 2D 34
Horsley. *Nmbd* 3D 115 (nr. Prudhoe)
Horsley. *Nmbd* 5C 120 (nr. Rochester)
Horsley Cross. *Essx* 3E 54
Horsleycross Street. *Essx* 3E 54
Horsleyhill. *Bord* 3H 119
Horsleyhope. *Dur* 5D 114
Horsley Woodhouse. *Derbs* 1A 74
Horsmonden. *Kent* 1A 28
Horspath. *Oxon* 5D 50
Horstead. *Norf* 4E 79
Horsted Keynes. *W Sus* 3E 27
Horton. *Buck* 4H 51
Horton. *Dors* 2F 15
Horton. *Lanc* 4A 98
Horton. *Nptn* 5F 63
Horton. *Shrp* 2G 71
Horton. *Som* 1G 13
Horton. *S Glo* 3C 34
Horton. *Staf* 5D 84
Horton. *Swan* 4D 30
Horton. *Wilts* 5F 35
Horton. *Wind* 3B 38
Horton Cross. *Som* 1G 13

Horton-cum-Studley—Islibhig

Horton-cum-Studley. *Oxon* 4D **50**
Horton Grange. *Nmbd* 2F **115**
Horton Green. *Ches W* 1G **71**
Horton Heath. *Hants* 1C **16**
Horton in Ribblesdale. *N Yor* 2H **97**
Horton Kirby. *Kent* 4G **39**
Hortonwood. *Telf* 4A **72**
Horwich. *G Man* 3E **91**
Horwich End. *Derbs* 2E **85**
Horwood. *Devn* 4F **19**
Hoscar. *Lanc* 3C **90**
Hose. *Leics* 3E **75**
Hosh. *Per* 1A **136**
Hosta. *W Isl* 1C **170**
Hoswick. *Shet* 9F **173**
Hotham. *E Yor* 1B **94**
Hothfield. *Kent* 1D **28**
Hoton. *Leics* 3C **74**
Houbie. *Shet* 2H **173**
Hough. *Arg* 4A **138**
Hough. *Ches E* 5B **84**
(nr. Crewe)
Hough. *Ches E* 3C **84**
(nr. Wilmslow)
Hougham. *Linc* 1F **75**
Hough Green. *Hal* 2G **83**
Hough-on-the-Hill. *Linc* 1G **75**
Houghton. *Cambs* 3B **64**
Houghton. *Cumb* 4F **113**
Houghton. *Hants* 3B **24**
Houghton. *Nmbd* 3E **115**
Houghton. *Pemb* 4D **43**
Houghton. *W Sus* 4B **26**
Houghton Bank. *Darl* 2F **105**
Houghton Conquest. *C Beds* 1A **52**
Houghton Green. *E Sus* 3D **28**
Houghton-le-Side. *Darl* 2F **105**
Houghton-le-Spring. *Tyne* 5G **115**
Houghton on the Hill. *Leics* 5D **74**
Houghton Regis. *C Beds* 3A **52**
Houghton St Giles. *Norf* 2B **78**
Houlland. *Shet* 6E **173**
(on Mainland)
Houlland. *Shet* 4G **173**
(on Yell)
Houlsyke. *N Yor* 4E **107**
Hound. *Hants* 2C **16**
Hound Green. *Hants* 1F **25**
Houndslow. *Bord* 5C **130**
Houndsmoor. *Som* 4E **21**
Houndwood. *Bord* 3E **131**
Hounsdown. *Hants* 1B **16**
Hounslow. *G Lon* 3C **38**
Housabister. *Shet* 6F **173**
Housay. *Shet* 4H **173**
Househill. *High* 3C **158**
Housetter. *Shet* 3E **173**
Houss. *Shet* 8E **173**
Houston. *Ren* 3F **127**
Housty. *High* 5D **168**
Houton. *Orkn* 7C **172**
Hove. *Brig* 5D **27** & **189**
Hoveringham. *Notts* 1E **74**
Hoveton. *Norf* 4F **79**
Hovingham. *N Yor* 2A **100**
How. *Cumb* 4G **113**
How Caple. *Here* 2B **48**
Howden. *E Yor* 2H **93**
Howden-le-Wear. *Dur* 1E **105**
Howe. *High* 2F **169**
Howe. *Norf* 5E **79**
Howe. *N Yor* 1F **99**
Howe Green. *Essx* 5H **53**
(nr. Chelmsford)
Howegreen. *Essx* 5B **54**
(nr. Maldon)
Howe Green. *Warw* 2H **61**
Howell. *Linc* 1A **76**
How End. *C Beds* 1A **52**
Howe of Teuchar. *Abers* 4E **161**
Howes. *Dum* 3C **112**
Howe Street. *Essx* 4G **53**
(nr. Chelmsford)
Howe Street. *Essx* 2G **53**
(nr. Finchingfield)
Howe, The. *Cumb* 1D **96**
Howe, The. *IOM* 5A **108**
Howey. *Powy* 5C **58**
Howgate. *Midl* 4F **129**
Howgill. *Lanc* 5H **97**
Howgill. *N Yor* 4C **98**
How Green. *Kent* 1F **27**
How Hill. *Norf* 4F **79**
Howick. *Nmbd* 3G **121**
Howle. *Telf* 3A **72**
Howle Hill. *Here* 3B **48**
Howleigh. *Som* 1F **13**
Howlett End. *Essx* 2F **53**
Howley. *Som* 2F **13**
Howley. *Warr* 2A **84**
Hownam. *Bord* 3B **120**
Howsham. *N Lin* 4D **94**
Howsham. *N Yor* 3B **100**
Howtel. *Nmbd* 1C **120**
Howt Green. *Kent* 4C **40**
Howton. *Here* 3H **47**
Howwood. *Ren* 3E **127**
Hoxne. *Suff* 3D **66**
Hoylake. *Mers* 2E **82**
Hoyland. *S Yor* 4D **92**
Hoylandswaine. *S Yor* 4C **92**
Hoyle. *W Sus* 4A **26**
Hubberholme. *N Yor* 2B **98**
Hubberston. *Pemb* 4C **42**
Hubbert's Bridge. *Linc* 1B **76**
Huby. *N Yor* 5E **99**
(nr. Harrogate)
Huby. *N Yor* 3H **99**
(nr. York)
Hucclecote. *Glos* 4D **48**
Hucking. *Kent* 5C **40**
Hucknall. *Notts* 1C **74**
Huddersfield. *W Yor* 3B **92**
Huddington. *Worc* 5D **60**
Huddlesford. *Staf* 5F **73**
Hudswell. *N Yor* 4E **105**
Huggate. *E Yor* 4C **100**
Hugglescote. *Leics* 4B **74**
Hughenden Valley. *Buck* 2G **37**
Hughley. *Shrp* 1H **59**
Hughton. *High* 4G **157**
Hugh Town. *IOS* 1B **4**
Hugus. *Corn* 4B **6**
Huish. *Devn* 1F **11**
Huish. *Wilts* 5G **35**
Huish Champflower. *Som* 4D **20**
Huish Episcopi. *Som* 4H **21**
Huisinis. *W Isl* 6B **171**
Hulcote. *Nptn* 5E **62**
Hulcott. *Buck* 4G **51**
Hulham. *Devn* 4D **12**
Hull. *Hull* 2D **94** & **199**
Hulland. *Derbs* 1G **73**
Hulland Moss. *Derbs* 1G **73**
Hulland Ward. *Derbs* 1G **73**
Hullavington. *Wilts* 3D **35**
Hullbridge. *Essx* 1C **40**
Hulme. *G Man* 1C **84**
Hulme. *Staf* 1D **72**
Hulme End. *Staf* 5F **85**
Hulme Walfield. *Ches E* 4C **84**
Hulverstone. *IOW* 4B **16**
Hulver Street. *Suff* 2G **67**
Humber. *Devn* 5C **12**
Humber. *Here* 5H **59**
Humber Bridge. *N Lin* 2D **94**
Humberside International Airport.
N Lin 3D **94**
Humberston. *NE Lin* 4G **95**
Humberstone. *Leic* 5D **74**
Humbie. *E Lot* 3A **130**
Humbleton. *E Yor* 1F **95**
Humbleton. *Nmbd* 2D **121**
Humby. *Linc* 2H **75**
Hume. *Bord* 5D **130**
Humshaugh. *Nmbd* 2C **114**
Huna. *High* 1F **169**
Huncoat. *Lanc* 1F **91**
Huncote. *Leics* 1C **62**
Hundall. *Derbs* 3A **86**
Hunderthwaite. *Dur* 2C **104**
Hundleby. *Linc* 4C **88**
Hundle Houses. *Linc* 5B **88**
Hundleton. *Pemb* 4D **42**
Hundon. *Suff* 1H **53**
Hundred Acres. *Hants* 1D **16**
Hundred House. *Powy* 5D **58**
Hundred, The. *Here* 4H **59**
Hungarton. *Leics* 5D **74**
Hungerford. *Hants* 1G **15**
Hungerford. *Shrp* 2H **59**
Hungerford. *Som* 2D **20**
Hungerford. *W Ber* 5B **36**
Hungerford Newtown.
W Ber 4B **36**
Hunger Hill. *G Man* 4E **91**
Hungerton. *Linc* 2F **75**
Hungladder. *High* 1C **154**
Hungryhatton. *Shrp* 3A **72**
Hunmanby. *N Yor* 2E **101**
Hunmanby Sands. *N Yor* 2F **101**
Hunningham. *Warw* 4A **62**
Hunnington. *Worc* 2D **60**
Hunny Hill. *IOW* 4C **16**
Hunsdon. *Herts* 4E **53**
Hunsdonbury. *Herts* 4E **53**
Hunsingore. *N Yor* 4G **99**
Hunslet. *W Yor* 1D **92**
Hunslet Carr. *W Yor* 2D **92**
Hunsonby. *Cumb* 1G **103**
Hunspow. *High* 1E **169**
Hunstanton. *Norf* 1F **77**
Hunstanworth. *Dur* 5C **114**
Hunston. *Suff* 4B **66**
Hunston. *W Sus* 2G **17**
Hunstrete. *Bath* 5B **34**
Hunt End. *Worc* 4E **61**
Hunterfield. *Midl* 3G **129**
Hunters Forstal. *Kent* 4F **41**
Hunter's Quay. *Arg* 2C **126**
Huntham. *Som* 4G **21**
Hunthill Lodge. *Ang* 1D **144**
Huntingdon. *Cambs* 3B **64**
Huntingfield. *Suff* 3F **67**
Huntingford. *Wilts* 3D **22**
Huntington. *Ches W* 4G **83**
Huntington. *E Lot* 2A **130**
Huntington. *Here* 5E **59**
Huntington. *Staf* 4D **72**
Huntington. *Telf* 5A **72**
Huntington. *York* 4A **100**
Huntingtower. *Per* 1C **136**
Huntley. *Glos* 4C **48**
Huntley. *Staf* 1E **73**
Huntly. *Abers* 4C **160**
Huntlywood. *Bord* 5C **130**
Hunton. *Hants* 3C **24**
Hunton. *Kent* 1B **28**
Hunton. *N Yor* 5E **105**
Hunton Bridge. *Herts* 5A **52**
Hunt's Corner. *Norf* 2C **66**
Huntscott. *Som* 2C **20**
Hunt's Cross. *Mers* 2G **83**
Hunts Green. *Warw* 1F **61**
Huntsham. *Devn* 4D **20**
Huntshaw. *Devn* 4F **19**
Huntspill. *Som* 2G **21**
Huntstile. *Som* 3F **21**
Huntworth. *Som* 3G **21**
Hunwick. *Dur* 1E **105**
Hunworth. *Norf* 2C **78**
Hurcott. *Som* 1G **13**
(nr. Ilminster)
Hurcott. *Som* 4A **22**
(nr. Somerton)
Hurdcott. *Wilts* 3G **23**
Hurdley. *Powy* 1E **59**
Hurdsfield. *Ches E* 3D **84**
Hurlet. *Glas* 3G **127**
Hurley. *Warw* 1G **61**
Hurley. *Wind* 3G **37**
Hurlford. *E Ayr* 1D **116**
Hurliness. *Orkn* 9B **172**
Hurlston Green. *Lanc* 3B **90**
Hurn. *Dors* 3G **15**
Hursey. *Dors* 2H **13**
Hursley. *Hants* 4C **24**
Hurst. *G Man* 4H **91**
Hurst. *N Yor* 4D **104**
Hurst. *Som* 1H **13**
Hurst. *Wok* 4F **37**
Hurstbourne Priors. *Hants* 2C **24**
Hurstbourne Tarrant. *Hants* 1B **24**
Hurst Green. *Ches E* 1H **71**
Hurst Green. *E Sus* 3B **28**
Hurst Green. *Essx* 4D **54**
Hurst Green. *Lanc* 1E **91**
Hurst Green. *Surr* 5E **39**
Hurstley. *Here* 1G **47**
Hurstpierpoint. *W Sus* 4D **27**
Hurstway Common. *Here* 1F **47**
Hurst Wickham. *W Sus* 4D **27**
Hurstwood. *Lanc* 1G **91**
Hurtmore. *Surr* 1A **26**
Hurworth-on-Tees. *Darl* 3A **106**
Hurworth Place. *Darl* 3F **105**
Hury. *Dur* 3C **104**
Husbands Bosworth. *Leics* 2D **62**
Husborne Crawley. *C Beds* 2H **51**
Husthwaite. *N Yor* 2H **99**
Hutcherleigh. *Devn* 3D **9**
Hut Green. *N Yor* 2F **93**
Huthwaite. *Notts* 5B **86**
Huttoft. *Linc* 3E **89**
Hutton. *Cumb* 2F **103**
Hutton. *E Yor* 4E **101**
Hutton. *Essx* 1H **39**
Hutton. *Lanc* 2C **90**
Hutton. *N Som* 1G **21**
Hutton. *Bord* 4F **131**
Hutton Bonville. *N Yor* 4A **106**
Hutton Buscel. *N Yor* 1D **100**
Hutton Conyers. *N Yor* 2F **99**
Hutton Cranswick. *E Yor* 4E **101**
Hutton End. *Cumb* 1F **103**
Hutton Gate. *Red C* 3C **106**
Hutton Henry. *Dur* 1B **106**
Hutton-le-Hole. *N Yor* 1B **100**
Hutton Magna. *Dur* 3E **105**
Hutton Mulgrave. *N Yor* 4F **107**
Hutton Roof. *Cumb* 2E **97**
(nr. Kirkby Lonsdale)
Hutton Roof. *Cumb* 1E **103**
(nr. Penrith)
Hutton Rudby. *N Yor* 4B **106**
Huttons Ambo. *N Yor* 3B **100**
Hutton Sessay. *N Yor* 2G **99**
Hutton Village. *Red C* 3D **106**
Hutton Wandesley. *N Yor* 4H **99**
Huxham. *Devn* 3C **12**
Huxham Green. *Som* 3A **22**
Huxley. *Ches W* 4H **83**
Huxter. *Shet* 6C **173**
(on Mainland)
Huxter. *Shet* 5G **173**
(on Whalsay)
Huyton. *Mers* 1G **83**
Hwlffordd. *Pemb* 3D **42**
Hycemoor. *Cumb* 1A **96**
Hyde. *Glos* 5D **49**
(nr. Stroud)
Hyde. *Glos* 3F **49**
(nr. Winchcombe)
Hyde. *G Man* 1D **84**
Hyde Heath. *Buck* 5H **51**
Hyde Lea. *Staf* 3D **72**
Hyde Park. *S Yor* 4F **93**
Hydestile. *Surr* 1A **26**
Hyndford Bridge. *S Lan* 5C **128**
Hynish. *Arg* 5A **138**
Hyssington. *Powy* 1F **59**
Hythe. *Hants* 2C **16**
Hythe. *Kent* 2F **29**
Hythe End. *Wind* 3B **38**
Hythie. *Abers* 3H **161**
Hyton. *Cumb* 1A **96**

I

Ianstown. *Mor* 2B **160**
Iarsiadar. *W Isl* 4D **171**
Ibberton. *Dors* 2C **14**
Ible. *Derbs* 5G **85**
Ibrox. *Glas* 3G **127**
Ibsley. *Hants* 2G **15**
Ibstock. *Leics* 4B **74**
Ibstone. *Buck* 2F **37**
Ibthorpe. *Hants* 1B **24**
Iburndale. *N Yor* 4F **107**
Ibworth. *Hants* 1D **24**
Icelton. *N Som* 5G **33**
Ichrachan. *Arg* 5E **141**
Ickburgh. *Norf* 1H **65**
Ickenham. *G Lon* 2B **38**
Ickenthwaite. *Cumb* 1C **96**
Ickford. *Buck* 5E **51**
Ickham. *Kent* 5G **41**
Ickleford. *Herts* 2B **52**
Icklesham. *E Sus* 4C **28**
Ickleton. *Cambs* 1E **53**
Icklingham. *Suff* 3G **65**
Ickwell. *C Beds* 1B **52**
Icomb. *Glos* 3H **49**
Idbury. *Oxon* 3H **49**
Iddesleigh. *Devn* 2F **11**
Ide. *Devn* 3B **12**
Ideford. *Devn* 5B **12**
Ide Hill. *Kent* 5F **39**
Iden. *E Sus* 3D **28**
Iden Green. *Kent* 2C **28**
(nr. Benenden)
Iden Green. *Kent* 2B **28**
(nr. Goudhurst)
Idle. *W Yor* 1B **92**
Idless. *Corn* 4C **6**
Idlicote. *Warw* 1A **50**
Idmiston. *Wilts* 3G **23**
Idole. *Carm* 4E **45**
Idridgehay. *Derbs* 1G **73**
Idrigill. *High* 2C **154**
Idstone. *Oxon* 3A **36**
Iffley. *Oxon* 5D **50**
Ifield. *W Sus* 2D **26**
Ifieldwood. *W Sus* 2D **26**
Ifold. *W Sus* 2B **26**
Iford. *E Sus* 5F **27**
Ifton Heath. *Shrp* 2F **71**
Ightfield. *Shrp* 2H **71**
Ightham. *Kent* 5G **39**
Iken. *Suff* 5G **67**
Ilam. *Staf* 5F **85**
Ilchester. *Som* 4A **22**
Ilderton. *Nmbd* 2E **121**
Ilford. *G Lon* 2F **39**
Ilford. *Som* 1G **13**
Ilfracombe. *Devn* 2F **19**
Ilkeston. *Derbs* 1B **74**
Ilketshall St Andrew. *Suff* 2F **67**
Ilketshall St Lawrence. *Suff* 2F **67**
Ilketshall St Margaret. *Suff* 2F **67**
Ilkley. *W Yor* 5D **98**
Illand. *Corn* 5C **10**
Illey. *W Mid* 2D **61**
Illidge Green. *Ches E* 4B **84**
Illington. *Norf* 2B **66**
Illingworth. *W Yor* 2A **92**
Illogan. *Corn* 4A **6**
Illogan Highway. *Corn* 4A **6**
Illston on the Hill. *Leics* 1E **62**
Ilmer. *Buck* 5F **51**
Ilmington. *Warw* 1H **49**
Ilminster. *Som* 1G **13**
Ilsington. *Devn* 5A **12**
Ilsington. *Dors* 3C **14**
Ilston. *Swan* 3E **31**
Ilton. *N Yor* 2D **98**
Ilton. *Som* 1G **13**
Imachar. *N Ayr* 5G **125**
Imber. *Wilts* 2E **23**
Immingham. *NE Lin* 3E **95**
Immingham Dock. *NE Lin* 3E **95**
Impington. *Cambs* 4D **64**
Ince. *Ches W* 3G **83**
Ince Blundell. *Mers* 4B **90**
Ince-in-Makerfield. *G Man* 4D **90**
Inchbae Lodge. *High* 2G **157**
Inchbare. *Ang* 2F **145**
Inchberry. *Mor* 3H **159**
Inchbraoch. *Ang* 3G **145**
Inchbrook. *Glos* 5D **48**
Incheril. *High* 2C **156**
Inchinnan. *Ren* 3F **127**
Inchlaggan. *High* 3D **148**
Inchmichael. *Per* 1E **137**
Inchnadamph. *High* 1G **163**
Inchree. *High* 2E **141**
Inchture. *Per* 1E **137**
Inchyra. *Per* 1D **136**
Indian Queens. *Corn* 3D **6**
Ingatestone. *Essx* 1H **39**
Ingbirchworth. *S Yor* 4C **92**
Ingestre. *Staf* 3D **73**
Ingham. *Linc* 2G **87**
Ingham. *Norf* 3F **79**
Ingham. *Suff* 3A **66**
Ingham Corner. *Norf* 3F **79**
Ingleborough. *Norf* 4D **76**
Ingleby. *Derbs* 3H **73**
Ingleby Arncliffe. *N Yor* 4B **106**
Ingleby Barwick. *Stoc T* 3B **106**
Ingleby Greenhow. *N Yor* 4C **106**
Ingleigh Green. *Devn* 2G **11**
Inglemire. *Hull* 1D **94**
Inglesbatch. *Bath* 5C **34**
Ingleton. *Dur* 2E **105**
Ingleton. *N Yor* 2F **97**
Inglewhite. *Lanc* 5E **97**
Ingoe. *Nmbd* 2D **114**
Ingol. *Lanc* 1D **90**
Ingoldisthorpe. *Norf* 2F **77**
Ingoldmells. *Linc* 4E **89**
Ingoldsby. *Linc* 2H **75**
Ingon. *Warw* 5G **61**
Ingram. *Nmbd* 3E **121**
Ingrave. *Essx* 1H **39**
Ingrow. *W Yor* 1A **92**
Ings. *Cumb* 5F **103**
Ingst. *S Glo* 3A **34**
Ingthorpe. *Rut* 5G **75**
Ingworth. *Norf* 3D **78**
Inkberrow. *Worc* 5E **61**
Inkford. *Worc* 3E **61**
Inkpen. *W Ber* 5B **36**
Inkstack. *High* 1E **169**
Innellan. *Arg* 3C **126**
Inner Hope. *Devn* 5C **8**
Innerleith. *Fife* 2E **137**
Innerleithen. *Bord* 1F **119**
Innerleven. *Fife* 3F **137**
Innermessan. *Dum* 3F **109**
Innerwick. *E Lot* 2D **130**
Innerwick. *Per* 4C **142**
Innsworth. *Glos* 3D **48**
Insch. *Abers* 1D **152**
Insh. *High* 3C **150**
Inshegra. *High* 3C **166**
Inshore. *High* 1D **166**
Inskip. *Lanc* 1C **90**
Instow. *Devn* 3E **19**
Intwood. *Norf* 5D **78**
Inver. *Abers* 4G **151**
Inver. *High* 5F **165**
Inver. *Per* 4H **143**
Inverailort. *High* 5F **147**
Inveralligin. *High* 3H **155**
Inverallochy. *Abers* 2H **161**
Inveramsay. *Abers* 1E **153**
Inveran. *High* 4C **164**
Inveraray. *Arg* 3H **133**
Inverarish. *High* 5E **155**
Inverarity. *Ang* 4D **144**
Inverarnan. *Arg* 2C **134**
Inverarnie. *High* 5A **158**
Inverbeg. *Arg* 4C **134**
Inverbervie. *Abers* 1H **145**
Inverboyndie. *Abers* 2D **160**
Invercassley. *High* 3B **164**
Invercharnan. *High* 4F **141**
Inverchoran. *High* 3E **157**
Invercreran. *Arg* 4E **141**
Inverdruie. *High* 2D **150**
Inverebrie. *Abers* 5G **161**
Invereck. *Arg* 1C **126**
Inveresk. *E Lot* 2G **129**
Inveresragan. *Arg* 5D **141**
Inverey. *Abers* 5E **151**
Inverfarigaig. *High* 1H **149**
Invergarry. *High* 3F **149**
Invergeldie. *Per* 1G **135**
Invergordon. *High* 2B **158**
Invergowrie. *Per* 5C **144**
Inverguseran. *High* 3F **147**
Inverharroch. *Mor* 5A **160**
Inverie. *High* 3F **147**
Inverinan. *Arg* 2G **133**
Inverinate. *High* 1B **148**
Inverkeilor. *Ang* 4F **145**
Inverkeithing. *Fife* 1E **129**
Inverkeithny. *Abers* 4D **160**
Inverkip. *Inv* 2D **126**
Inverkirkaig. *High* 2E **163**
Inverlael. *High* 5F **163**
Inverliever Lodge. *Arg* 3F **133**
Inverliver. *Arg* 5E **141**
Inverlochlarig. *Stir* 2D **134**
Inverlochy. *High* 1F **141**
Inverlussa. *Arg* 1E **125**
Inver Mallie. *High* 5D **148**
Invermarkie. *Abers* 5B **160**
Invermoriston. *High* 2G **149**
Invernaver. *High* 2H **167**
Inverneil House. *Arg* 1G **125**
Inverness. *High* 4A **158** & **198**
Inverness Airport. *High* 3B **158**
Invernettie. *Abers* 4H **161**
Inverpolly Lodge. *High* 2E **163**
Inverquhomery. *Abers* 4H **161**
Inverroy. *High* 5E **149**
Inversanda. *High* 3D **140**
Invershiel. *High* 2B **148**
Invershin. *High* 4C **164**
Invershore. *High* 5E **169**
Inversnaid. *Stir* 3C **134**
Inverugie. *Abers* 4H **161**
Inveruglas. *Arg* 3C **134**
Inverurie. *Abers* 1E **153**
Invervar. *Per* 4D **142**
Inverythan. *Abers* 4E **161**
Inwardleigh. *Devn* 3F **11**
Inworth. *Essx* 4B **54**
Iochdar. *W Isl* 4C **170**
Iping. *W Sus* 4G **25**
Ipplepen. *Devn* 2E **9**
Ipsden. *Oxon* 3E **37**
Ipstones. *Staf* 1E **73**
Ipswich. *Suff* 1E **55** & **198**
Irby. *Mers* 2E **83**
Irby in the Marsh. *Linc* 4D **88**
Irby upon Humber. *NE Lin* 4E **95**
Irchester. *Nptn* 4G **63**
Ireby. *Cumb* 1D **102**
Ireby. *Lanc* 2F **97**
Ireland. *Shet* 9E **173**
Ireleth. *Cumb* 2B **96**
Ireshopeburn. *Dur* 1B **104**
Ireton Wood. *Derbs* 1G **73**
Irlam. *G Man* 1B **84**
Irnham. *Linc* 3H **75**
Iron Acton. *S Glo* 3B **34**
Iron Bridge. *Cambs* 1D **65**
Ironbridge. *Telf* 5A **72**
Iron Cross. *Warw* 5E **61**
Ironville. *Derbs* 5B **86**
Irstead. *Norf* 3F **79**
Irthington. *Cumb* 3F **113**
Irthlingborough. *Nptn* 3G **63**
Irton. *N Yor* 1E **101**
Irvine. *N Ayr* 1C **116**
Irvine Mains. *N Ayr* 1C **116**
Isabella Pit. *Nmbd* 1G **115**
Isauld. *High* 2B **168**
Isbister. *Orkn* 6C **172**
Isbister. *Shet* 2E **173**
(on Mainland)
Isbister. *Shet* 5G **173**
(on Whalsay)
Isfield. *E Sus* 4F **27**
Isham. *Nptn* 3F **63**
Island Carr. *N Lin* 4C **94**
Islay Airport. *Arg* 4B **124**
Isle Abbotts. *Som* 4G **21**
Isle Brewers. *Som* 4G **21**
Isleham. *Cambs* 3F **65**
Isle of Man Airport. *IOM* 5B **108**
Isle of Thanet. *Kent* 4H **41**
Isle of Whithorn. *Dum* 5B **110**
Isleornsay. *High* 2F **147**
Islesburgh. *Shet* 5E **173**
Isles of Scilly (St Mary's) Airport.
IOS 1B **4**
Islesteps. *Dum* 2A **112**
Isleworth. *G Lon* 3C **38**
Isley Walton. *Leics* 3B **74**
Islibhig. *W Isl* 5B **171**

Kingston—Laneham

Kingston. E Lot 1B 130
Kingston. Hants 2G 15
Kingston. IOW 4C 16
Kingston. Kent 5F 41
Kingston. Mor 2H 159
Kingston. W Sus 5B 26
Kingston Bagpuize. Oxon 2C 36
Kingston Blount. Oxon 2F 37
Kingston by Sea. W Sus 5D 26
Kingston Deverill. Wilts 3D 22
Kingstone. Here 2H 47
Kingstone. Som 1G 13
Kingstone. Staf 3E 73
Kingston Lisle. Oxon 3B 36
Kingston Maurward. Dors 3C 14
Kingston near Lewes. E Sus 5E 27
Kingston on Soar. Notts 3C 74
Kingston Russell. Dors 3A 14
Kingston St Mary. Som 4F 21
Kingston Seymour. N Som 5H 33
Kingston Stert. Oxon 5F 51
Kingston upon Hull. Hull 2D 94 & 199
Kingston upon Thames. G Lon 4C 38
King's Walden. Herts 3B 52
Kingswear. Devn 3E 9
Kingswells. Aber 3F 153
Kingswinford. W Mid 2C 60
Kingswood. Buck 4E 51
Kingswood. Glos 2C 34
Kingswood. Here 5E 59
Kingswood. Kent 5C 40
Kingswood. Per 5H 143
Kingswood. Powy 5E 71
Kingswood. Som 3E 20
Kingswood. S Glo 4B 34
Kingswood. Surr 5D 38
Kingswood. Warw 3F 61
Kingswood Common. Staf 5C 72
Kings Worthy. Hants 3C 24
Kingthorpe. Linc 3A 88
Kington. Here 5F 59
Kington. S Glo 2B 34
Kington. Worc 5D 61
Kington Langley. Wilts 4E 35
Kington Magna. Dors 4C 22
Kington St Michael. Wilts 4E 35
Kingussie. High 3B 150
Kingweston. Som 3A 22
Kinharrachie. Abers 5G 161
Kinhrive. High 1B 158
Kinkell Bridge. Per 2B 136
Kinknockie. Abers 4H 161
Kinkry Hill. Cumb 2G 113
Kinlet. Shrp 2B 60
Kinloch. High 5D 166
(nr. Loch More)
Kinloch. High 3A 140
(nr. Lochaline)
Kinloch. High 4C 146
(on Rùm)
Kinloch. Per 4A 144
Kinlochard. Stir 3D 134
Kinlochbervie. High 3C 166
Kinlocheil. High 1D 141
Kinlochewe. High 2C 156
Kinloch Hourn. High 3B 148
Kinloch Laggan. High 5H 149
Kinlochleven. High 2F 141
Kinloch Lodge. High 3F 167
Kinlochmoidart. High 1B 140
Kinlochmore. High 2F 141
Kinloch Rannoch. Per 3D 142
Kinlochspelve. Arg 1D 132
Kinloid. High 5E 147
Kinloss. Mor 2E 159
Kinmel Bay. Cnwy 2B 82
Kinmuck. Abers 2F 153
Kinnadie. Abers 4G 161
Kinnaird. Per 1E 137
Kinneff. Abers 1H 145
Kinnelhead. Dum 4C 118
Kinnell. Ang 3F 145
Kinnerley. Shrp 3F 71
Kinnernie. Abers 2E 152
Kinnersley. Here 1G 47
Kinnersley. Worc 1D 48
Kinnerton. Powy 4E 59
Kinnerton. Shrp 1F 59
Kinnesswood. Per 3D 136
Kinninvie. Dur 2D 104
Kinnordy. Ang 3C 144
Kinoulton. Notts 2D 74
Kinross. Per 3D 136
Kinrossie. Per 5A 144
Kinsbourne Green. Herts 4B 52
Kinsey Heath. Ches E 1A 72
Kinsham. Here 4F 59
Kinsham. Worc 2E 49
Kinsley. W Yor 3E 93
Kinson. Bour 3F 15
Kintbury. W Ber 5B 36
Kintessack. Mor 2E 159
Kintillo. Per 2D 136
Kinton. Here 3G 59
Kinton. Shrp 4F 71
Kintore. Abers 2E 153
Kintour. Arg 4C 124
Kintra. Arg 2B 132
Kintraw. Arg 3F 133
Kinveachy. High 2D 150
Kinver. Staf 2C 60
Kinwarton. Warw 5F 61
Kiplingcotes. E Yor 5D 100
Kippax. W Yor 1E 93
Kippen. Stir 4F 135
Kippford. Dum 4F 111
Kipping's Cross. Kent 1H 27
Kirbister. Orkn 7C 172
(nr. Hobbister)
Kirbister. Orkn 6B 172
(nr. Quholm)
Kirbuster. Orkn 5F 172
Kirby Bedon. Norf 5E 79
Kirby Bellars. Leics 4E 74
Kirby Cane. Norf 1F 67
Kirby Cross. Essx 3F 55
Kirby Fields. Leics 5C 74
Kirby Green. Norf 1F 67
Kirby Grindalythe. N Yor 3D 100
Kirby Hill. N Yor 4E 105
(nr. Richmond)
Kirby Hill. N Yor 3F 99
(nr. Ripon)
Kirby Knowle. N Yor 1G 99
Kirby-le-Soken. Essx 3F 55
Kirby Misperton. N Yor 2B 100
Kirby Muxloe. Leics 5C 74
Kirby Sigston. N Yor 5B 106
Kirby Underdale. E Yor 4C 100
Kirby Wiske. N Yor 1F 99
Kirdford. W Sus 3B 26
Kirk. High 3E 169
Kirkabister. Shet 8F 173
(on Bressay)
Kirkabister. Shet 6F 173
(on Mainland)
Kirkandrews. Dum 5D 110
Kirkandrews-on-Eden. Cumb 4E 113
Kirkapol. Arg 4B 138
Kirkbampton. Cumb 4E 112
Kirkbean. Dum 4A 112
Kirk Bramwith. S Yor 3G 93
Kirkbride. Cumb 4D 112
Kirkbridge. N Yor 5F 105
Kirkbuddo. Ang 4E 145
Kirkburn. E Yor 4D 101
Kirkburton. W Yor 3B 92
Kirkby. Linc 1H 87
Kirkby. Mers 1G 83
Kirkby. N Yor 4C 106
Kirkby Fenside. Linc 4C 88
Kirkby Fleetham. N Yor 5F 105
Kirkby Green. Linc 5H 87
Kirkby-in-Ashfield. Notts 5C 86
Kirkby-in-Furness. Cumb 1B 96
Kirkby la Thorpe. Linc 1A 76
Kirkby Lonsdale. Cumb 2F 97
Kirkby Malham. N Yor 3A 98
Kirkby Mallory. Leics 5B 74
Kirkby Malzeard. N Yor 2E 99
Kirkby Mills. N Yor 1B 100
Kirkbymoorside. N Yor 1A 100
Kirkby on Bain. Linc 4B 88
Kirkby Overblow. N Yor 5F 99
Kirkby Stephen. Cumb 4A 104
Kirkby Thore. Cumb 2H 103
Kirkby Underwood. Linc 3H 75
Kirkby Wharfe. N Yor 5H 99
Kirkcaldy. Fife 4E 137
Kirkcambeck. Cumb 3G 113
Kirkcolm. Dum 3F 109
Kirkconnel. Dum 3G 117
Kirkconnell. Dum 3A 112
Kirkcowan. Dum 3A 110
Kirkcudbright. Dum 4D 111
Kirkdale. Mers 1F 83
Kirk Deighton. N Yor 4F 99
Kirk Ella. E Yor 2D 94
Kirkfieldbank. S Lan 5B 128
Kirkforthar Feus. Fife 3E 137
Kirkgunzeon. Dum 3F 111
Kirk Hallam. Derbs 1B 74
Kirkham. Lanc 1C 90
Kirkham. N Yor 3B 100
Kirkhamgate. W Yor 2C 92
Kirk Hammerton. N Yor 4G 99
Kirkharle. Nmbd 1D 114
Kirkheaton. Nmbd 2D 114
Kirkheaton. W Yor 3B 92
Kirkhill. Ang 2F 145
Kirkhill. High 4H 157
Kirkhope. S Lan 4B 118
Kirkhouse. Bord 1F 119
Kirkibost. High 2D 146
Kirkinch. Ang 4C 144
Kirkinner. Dum 4B 110
Kirkintilloch. E Dun 2H 127
Kirk Ireton. Derbs 5G 85
Kirkland. Cumb 3B 102
(nr. Cleator Moor)
Kirkland. Cumb 1H 103
(nr. Penrith)
Kirkland. Cumb 5D 112
(nr. Wigton)
Kirkland. Dum 3G 117
(nr. Kirkconnel)
Kirkland. Dum 5H 117
(nr. Moniaive)
Kirkland Guards. Cumb 5C 112
Kirk Langley. Derbs 2G 73
Kirklauchline. Dum 4F 109
Kirkleatham. Red C 2C 106
Kirklevington. Stoc T 4B 106
Kirkley. Suff 1H 67
Kirklington. N Yor 1F 99
Kirklington. Notts 5D 86
Kirklinton. Cumb 3F 113
Kirkliston. Edin 2E 129
Kirkmabreck. Dum 4B 110
Kirkmaiden. Dum 5E 109
Kirk Merrington. Dur 1F 105
Kirk Michael. IOM 2C 108
Kirkmichael. Per 2H 143
Kirkmichael. S Ayr 4C 116
Kirkmuirhill. S Lan 5A 128
Kirknewton. Nmbd 1D 120
Kirknewton. W Lot 3E 129
Kirkney. Abers 5C 160
Kirk of Shotts. N Lan 3B 128
Kirkoswald. Cumb 5G 113
Kirkoswald. S Ayr 4B 116
Kirkpatrick. Dum 5B 118
Kirkpatrick Durham. Dum 2E 111
Kirkpatrick-Fleming. Dum 2D 112
Kirk Sandall. S Yor 4G 93
Kirksanton. Cumb 1A 96
Kirk Smeaton. N Yor 3F 93
Kirkstall. W Yor 1C 92
Kirkstile. Dum 5F 119
Kirkstyle. High 1F 169
Kirkthorpe. W Yor 2D 92
Kirkton. Abers 2D 152
(nr. Alford)
Kirkton. Abers 1D 152
(nr. Insch)
Kirkton. Abers 4F 161
(nr. Turriff)
Kirkton. Ang 5D 144
(nr. Dundee)
Kirkton. Ang 4D 144
(nr. Forfar)
Kirkton. Ang 5B 152
(nr. Tarfside)
Kirkton. Dum 1A 112
Kirkton. Fife 1F 137
Kirkton. High 4E 165
(nr. Golspie)
Kirkton. High 1G 147
(nr. Kyle of Lochalsh)
Kirkton. High 4B 156
(nr. Lochcarron)
Kirkton. Bord 3H 119
Kirkton. S Lan 2B 118
Kirktonhill. W Dun 2E 127
Kirkton Manor. Bord 1E 118
Kirkton of Airlie. Ang 3C 144
Kirkton of Auchterhouse. Ang 5C 144
Kirkton of Bourtie. Abers 1F 153
Kirkton of Collace. Per 5A 144
Kirkton of Craig. Ang 3G 145
Kirkton of Culsalmond. Abers 5D 160
Kirkton of Durris. Abers 4E 153
Kirkton of Glenbuchat. Abers 2A 152
Kirkton of Glenisla. Ang 2B 144
Kirkton of Kingoldrum. Ang 3C 144
Kirkton of Largo. Fife 3G 137
Kirkton of Lethendy. Per 4A 144
Kirkton of Logie Buchan. Abers 1G 153
Kirkton of Maryculter. Abers 4F 153
Kirkton of Menmuir. Ang 2E 145
Kirkton of Monikie. Ang 5E 145
Kirkton of Oyne. Abers 1D 152
Kirkton of Rayne. Abers 5D 160
Kirkton of Skene. Abers 3F 153
Kirktown. Abers 2G 161
(nr. Fraserburgh)
Kirktown. Abers 3H 161
(nr. Peterhead)
Kirktown of Alvah. Abers 2D 160
Kirktown of Auchterless. Abers 4E 160
Kirktown of Deskford. Mor 2C 160
Kirktown of Fetteresso. Abers 5F 153
Kirktown of Mortlach. Mor 5H 159
Kirktown of Slains. Abers 1H 153
Kirkurd. Bord 5E 129
Kirkwall. Orkn 6D 172
Kirkwall Airport. Orkn 7D 172
Kirkwhelpington. Nmbd 1C 114
Kirk Yetholm. Bord 2C 120
Kirmington. N Lin 3E 94
Kirmond le Mire. Linc 1A 88
Kirn. Arg 2C 126
Kirriemuir. Ang 3C 144
Kirstead Green. Norf 1E 67
Kirtlebridge. Dum 2D 112
Kirtleton. Dum 2D 112
Kirtling. Cambs 5F 65
Kirtling Green. Cambs 5F 65
Kirtlington. Oxon 4D 50
Kirtomy. High 2H 167
Kirton. Linc 2C 76
Kirton. Notts 4D 86
Kirton. Suff 2F 55
Kirton End. Linc 1B 76
Kirton Holme. Linc 1B 76
Kirton in Lindsey. N Lin 1G 87
Kishorn. High 4H 155
Kislingbury. Nptn 5D 62
Kites Hardwick. Warw 4B 62
Kittisford. Som 4D 20
Kittle. Swan 4E 31
Kittybrewster. Aber 3G 153
Kitwood. Hants 3E 25
Kivernoll. Here 2H 47
Kiveton Park. S Yor 2B 86
Knaith. Linc 2F 87
Knaith Park. Linc 2F 87
Knaphill. Surr 5A 38
Knapp. Hants 4C 24
Knapp. Per 5B 144
Knapp. Som 4G 21
Knapperfield. High 3E 169
Knapton. Norf 2F 79
Knapton. York 4H 99
Knapton Green. Here 5G 59
Knapwell. Cambs 4C 64
Knaresborough. N Yor 4F 99
Knarsdale. Nmbd 4H 113
Knatts Valley. Kent 4G 39
Knaven. Abers 4F 161
Knayton. N Yor 1G 99
Knebworth. Herts 3C 52
Knedlington. E Yor 2H 93
Kneesall. Notts 4E 86
Kneesworth. Cambs 1D 52
Kneeton. Notts 1E 74
Knelston. Swan 4D 30
Knenhall. Staf 2D 72
Knightacott. Devn 3G 19
Knightcote. Warw 5B 62
Knightcott. N Som 1G 21
Knightley. Staf 3C 72
Knightley Dale. Staf 3C 72
Knightlow Hill. Warw 3B 62
Knighton. Devn 4B 8
Knighton. Dors 1B 14
Knighton. Leic 5D 74
Knighton. Powy 3E 59
Knighton. Som 2E 21
Knighton. Staf 3B 72
(nr. Eccleshall)
Knighton. Staf 1B 72
(nr. Woore)
Knighton. Wilts 4A 36
Knighton. Worc 5E 61
Knighton Common. Worc 3A 60
Knight's End. Cambs 1D 64
Knightswood. Glas 3G 127
Knightwick. Worc 5B 60
Knill. Here 4E 59
Knipton. Leics 2F 75
Knitsley. Dur 5E 115
Kniveton. Derbs 5G 85
Knock. Arg 5G 139
Knock. Cumb 2H 103
Knock. Mor 3C 160
Knockally. High 5D 168
Knockan. Arg 1B 132
Knockan. High 2G 163
Knockandhu. Mor 1G 151
Knockando. Mor 4F 159
Knockarthur. High 3E 165
Knockbain. High 3A 158
Knockbreck. High 2B 154
Knockdee. High 2D 168
Knockdolian. S Ayr 1G 109
Knockdon. S Ayr 3C 116
Knockdown. Glos 3D 34
Knockenbaird. Abers 1D 152
Knockenkelly. N Ayr 3E 123
Knockentiber. E Ayr 1C 116
Knockfarrel. High 3H 157
Knockglass. High 2C 168
Knockholt. Kent 5F 39
Knockholt Pound. Kent 5F 39
Knockie Lodge. High 2G 149
Knockin. Shrp 3F 71
Knockinlaw. E Ayr 1D 116
Knockinnon. High 5D 169
Knockrome. Arg 2D 124
Knocksharry. IOM 3B 108
Knockshinnoch. E Ayr 3D 116
Knockvennie. Dum 2E 111
Knockvologan. Arg 3B 132
Knodishall. Suff 4G 67
Knole. Som 4H 21
Knollbury. Mon 3H 33
Knolls Green. Ches E 3C 84
Knolton. Wrex 2F 71
Knook. Wilts 2E 23
Knossington. Leics 5F 75
Knott. High 3C 154
Knott End-on-Sea. Lanc 5C 96
Knotting. Bed 4H 63
Knotting Green. Bed 4H 63
Knottingley. W Yor 2E 93
Knotts. Cumb 2F 103
Knotty Ash. Mers 1G 83
Knotty Green. Buck 1A 38
Knowbury. Shrp 3H 59
Knowe. Dum 2A 110
Knowefield. Cumb 4F 113
Knowehead. Dum 5F 117
Knowes. E Lot 2C 130
Knowesgate. Nmbd 1C 114
Knoweside. S Ayr 3B 116
Knowes of Elrick. Abers 3D 160
Knowle. Bris 4A 34
Knowle. Devn 3E 19
(nr. Braunton)
Knowle. Devn 4D 12
(nr. Budleigh Salterton)
Knowle. Devn 2A 12
(nr. Crediton)
Knowle. Shrp 3H 59
Knowle. W Mid 3F 61
Knowle Green. Lanc 1E 91
Knowle St Giles. Som 1G 13
Knowlesands. Shrp 1B 60
Knowle Village. Hants 2D 16
Knowl Hill. Wind 4G 37
Knowlton. Kent 5G 41
Knowsley. Mers 1G 83
Knowstone. Devn 4B 20
Knucklas. Powy 3E 59
Knuston. Nptn 4G 63
Knutsford. Ches E 3B 84
Knypersley. Staf 5C 84
Krumlin. W Yor 3A 92
Kuggar. Corn 5E 5
Kyleakin. High 1F 147
Kyle of Lochalsh. High 1F 147
Kylerhea. High 1F 147
Kylesku. High 5C 166
Kyles Lodge. W Isl 9B 171
Kylesmorar. High 4G 147
Kylestrome. High 5C 166
Kymin. Mon 4A 48
Kynaston. Here 2B 48
Kynaston. Shrp 3F 71
Kynnersley. Telf 4A 72
Kyre Green. Worc 4A 60
Kyre Park. Worc 4A 60
Kyrewood. Worc 4A 60

L

Labost. W Isl 3E 171
Lacasaidh. W Isl 5F 171
Lacasdail. W Isl 4G 171
Laceby. NE Lin 4F 95
Lacey Green. Buck 5G 51
Lach Dennis. Ches W 3B 84
Lache. Ches W 4F 83
Lackford. Suff 3G 65
Lacock. Wilts 5E 35
Ladbroke. Warw 5B 62
Laddingford. Kent 1A 28
Lade Bank. Linc 5C 88
Ladock. Corn 3C 6
Lady. Orkn 3F 172
Ladybank. Fife 2F 137
Ladycross. Corn 4D 10
Lady Green. Mers 4B 90
Lady Hall. Cumb 1A 96
Ladykirk. Bord 5E 131
Ladysford. Abers 2G 161
Ladywood. W Mid 2E 61
Ladywood. Worc 4C 60
Laga. High 2A 140
Lagavulin. Arg 5C 124
Lagg. Arg 2D 125
Lagg. N Ayr 3D 122
Laggan. Arg 4A 124
Laggan. High 4E 149
(nr. Fort Augustus)
Laggan. High 4A 150
(nr. Newtonmore)
Laggan. Mor 5H 159
Lagganlia. High 3C 150
Lagganulva. Arg 4F 139
Laglingarten. Arg 3A 134
Lagness. W Sus 2G 17
Laid. High 3E 166
Laide. High 4D 162
Laigh Fenwick. E Ayr 5F 127
Laindon. Essx 2A 40
Lairg. High 3C 164
Lairg Muir. High 3C 164
Laithes. Cumb 1F 103
Laithkirk. Dur 2C 104
Lake. Devn 3F 19
Lake. IOW 4D 16
Lake. Wilts 3G 23
Lake District. Cumb 3E 103
Lakenham. Norf 5E 79
Lakenheath. Suff 2G 65
Lakesend. Norf 1E 65
Lakeside. Cumb 1C 96
Laleham. Surr 4B 38
Laleston. B'end 3B 32
Lamancha. Bord 4F 129
Lamarsh. Essx 2B 54
Lamas. Norf 3E 79
Lamb Corner. Essx 2D 54
Lambden. Bord 5D 130
Lamberhead Green. G Man 4D 90
Lamberhurst. Kent 2A 28
Lamberhurst Quarter. Kent 2A 28
Lamberton. Bord 4F 131
Lambeth. G Lon 3E 39
Lambfell Moar. IOM 3B 108
Lambhill. Glas 3G 127
Lambley. Nmbd 4H 113
Lambley. Notts 1D 74
Lambourn. W Ber 4B 36
Lambourne End. Essx 1F 39
Lambourn Woodlands. W Ber 4B 36
Lambrook. Som 4F 21
Lambs Green. Dors 3E 15
Lambs Green. W Sus 2D 26
Lambston. Pemb 3D 42
Lamellion. Corn 2G 7
Lamerton. Devn 5E 11
Lamesley. Tyne 4F 115
Laminess. Orkn 4F 172
Lamington. High 1B 158
Lamington. S Lan 1B 118
Lamlash. N Ayr 2E 123
Lamonby. Cumb 1F 103
Lamorick. Corn 2E 7
Lamorna. Corn 4B 4
Lamorran. Corn 4C 6
Lampeter. Cdgn 1F 45
Lampeter Velfrey. Pemb 3F 43
Lamphey. Pemb 4E 43
Lamplugh. Cumb 2B 102
Lamport. Nptn 3E 63
Lamyatt. Som 3B 22
Lana. Devn 3D 10
(nr. Ashwater)
Lana. Devn 2D 10
(nr. Holsworthy)
Lanark. S Lan 5B 128
Lanarth. Corn 4E 5
Lancaster. Lanc 3D 97
Lanchester. Dur 5E 115
Lancing. W Sus 5C 26
Landbeach. Cambs 4D 64
Landcross. Devn 4E 19
Landerberry. Abers 3E 153
Landford. Wilts 1A 16
Land Gate. G Man 4D 90
Landhallow. High 5D 169
Landimore. Swan 3D 30
Landkey. Devn 3F 19
Landkey Newland. Devn 3F 19
Landore. Swan 3F 31
Landport. Port 2E 17
Landrake. Corn 2H 7
Landscove. Devn 2D 9
Land's End (St Just) Airport. Corn 4A 4
Landshipping. Pemb 3E 43
Landulph. Corn 2A 8
Landywood. Staf 5D 73
Lane. Corn 2C 6
Laneast. Corn 4C 10
Lane Bottom. Lanc 1G 91
Lane End. Buck 2G 37
Lane End. Hants 4D 24
Lane End. IOW 4E 17
Lane End. Wilts 2D 22
Lane Ends. Derbs 2G 73
Lane Ends. Dur 1E 105
Lane Ends. Lanc 4G 97
Laneham. Notts 3F 87

Lanehead—Lintmill

Lanehead. Dur 5B 114
(nr. Cowshill)
Lane Head. Dur 3E 105
(nr. Hutton Magna)
Lane Head. Dur 2D 105
(nr. Woodland)
Lane Head. G Man 1A 84
Lanehead. Nmbd 1A 114
Lane Head. W Yor 4B 92
Lane Heads. Lanc 1C 90
Lanercost. Cumb 3G 113
Laneshaw Bridge. Lanc 5B 98
Laney Green. Staf 5D 72
Langais. W Isl 2D 170
Langal. High 2B 140
Langar. Notts 2E 74
Langbank. Ren 2E 127
Langbar. N Yor 4C 98
Langburnshiels. Bord 4H 119
Langcliffe. N Yor 3H 97
Langdale End. N Yor 5G 107
Langdon. Corn 3C 10
Langdon Beck. Dur 1B 104
Langdon Cross. Corn 4D 10
Langdon Hills. Essx 2A 40
Langdown. Hants 2C 16
Langdyke. Fife 3F 137
Langenhoe. Essx 4D 54
Langford. C Beds 1B 52
Langford. Devn 2D 12
Langford. Essx 5B 54
Langford. Notts 5F 87
Langford. Oxon 5H 49
Langford. Som 4F 21
Langford Budville. Som 4E 20
Langham. Dors 4C 22
Langham. Essx 2D 54
Langham. Norf 1C 78
Langham. Rut 4F 75
Langham. Suff 4B 66
Langho. Lanc 1F 91
Langholm. Dum 1E 113
Langland. Swan 4F 31
Langleeford. Nmbd 2D 120
Langley. Ches E 3D 84
Langley. Derbs 1B 74
Langley. Essx 2E 53
Langley. Glos 3F 49
Langley. Hants 2C 16
Langley. Herts 3C 52
Langley. Kent 5C 40
Langley. Nmbd 3B 114
Langley. Slo 3B 38
Langley. Som 4D 20
Langley. Warw 4F 61
Langley. W Sus 4G 25
Langley Burrell. Wilts 4E 35
Langleybury. Herts 5A 52
Langley Common. Derbs 2G 73
Langley Green. Derbs 2G 73
Langley Green. Norf 5F 79
Langley Green. Warw 4F 61
Langley Green. W Sus 2D 26
Langley Heath. Kent 5C 40
Langley Marsh. Som 4D 20
Langley Moor. Dur 5F 115
Langley Park. Dur 5F 115
Langley Street. Norf 5F 79
Langney. E Sus 5H 27
Langold. Notts 2C 86
Langore. Corn 4D 10
Langport. Som 4H 21
Langrick. Linc 1B 76
Langridge. Bath 5C 34
Langridgeford. Devn 4F 19
Langrigg. Cumb 5C 112
Langrish. Hants 4F 25
Langsett. S Yor 4C 92
Langshaw. Bord 1H 119
Langstone. Hants 2F 17
Langthorne. N Yor 5F 105
Langthorpe. N Yor 3F 99
Langthwaite. N Yor 4D 104
Langtoft. E Yor 3E 101
Langtoft. Linc 4A 76
Langton. Dur 3E 105
Langton. Linc 4B 88
(nr. Horncastle)
Langton. Linc 3C 88
(nr. Spilsby)
Langton. N Yor 3B 100
Langton by Wragby. Linc 3A 88
Langton Green. Kent 2G 27
Langton Herring. Dors 4B 14
Langton Long Blandford. Dors 2E 15
Langton Matravers. Dors 5F 15
Langtree. Devn 1E 11
Langwathby. Cumb 1G 103
Langwith. Derbs 4C 86
Langworth. Linc 3H 87
Lanivet. Corn 2E 7
Lanjeth. Corn 3D 6
Lank. Corn 5A 10
Lanlivery. Corn 3E 7
Lanner. Corn 5B 6
Lanreath. Corn 3F 7
Lansallos. Corn 3F 7
Lansdown. Bath 5C 34
Lansdown. Glos 3E 49
Lanteglos Highway. Corn 3F 7
Lanton. Nmbd 1D 120
Lanton. Bord 2A 120
Lapford. Devn 2H 11
Lapford Cross. Devn 2H 11
Laphroaig. Arg 5B 124
Lapley. Staf 4C 72
Lapworth. Warw 3F 61
Larachbeg. High 4A 140
Larbert. Falk 1B 128
Larden Green. Ches E 5H 83
Larel. High 3D 169
Largie. Abers 5D 160
Largiemore. Arg 1H 125
Largoward. Fife 3G 137
Largs. N Ayr 4D 126
Largue. Abers 4D 160
Largybeg. N Ayr 3E 123
Largymeanoch. N Ayr 3E 123
Largymore. N Ayr 3E 123
Larkfield. Inv 2D 126
Larkfield. Kent 5A 40
Larkhall. Bath 5C 34
Larkhall. S Lan 4A 128
Larkhill. Wilts 2G 23
Larling. Norf 2B 66
Larport. Here 2A 48
Lartington. Dur 3D 104
Lary. Abers 3H 151
Lasham. Hants 2E 25
Lashenden. Kent 1C 28
Lassodie. Fife 4D 136
Lasswade. Midl 3G 129
Lastingham. N Yor 5E 107
Latchford. Herts 3D 53
Latchford. Oxon 5E 51
Latchingdon. Essx 5B 54
Latchley. Corn 5E 11
Latchmere Green. Hants 5E 37
Lathbury. Mil 1G 51
Latheron. High 5D 169
Latheronwheel. High 5D 169
Lathom. Lanc 4C 90
Lathones. Fife 3G 137
Latimer. Buck 1B 38
Latteridge. S Glo 3B 34
Lattiford. Som 4B 22
Latton. Wilts 2F 35
Laudale House. High 3B 140
Lauder. Bord 5B 130
Laugharne. Carm 3H 43
Laughterton. Linc 3F 87
Laughton. E Sus 4G 27
Laughton. Leics 2D 62
Laughton. Linc 1F 87
(nr. Gainsborough)
Laughton. Linc 2H 75
(nr. Grantham)
Laughton Common. S Yor 2C 86
Laughton en le Morthen. S Yor 2C 86
Launcells. Corn 2C 10
Launceston. Corn 4D 10
Launcherley. Som 2A 22
Launton. Oxon 3E 50
Laurencekirk. Abers 1G 145
Laurieston. Dum 3D 111
Laurieston. Falk 2C 128
Lavendon. Mil 5G 63
Lavenham. Suff 1C 54
Laverhay. Dum 5D 118
Laversdale. Cumb 3F 113
Laverstock. Wilts 3G 23
Laverstoke. Hants 2C 24
Laverton. Glos 2F 49
Laverton. N Yor 2E 99
Laverton. Som 1C 22
Lavister. Wrex 5F 83
Law. S Lan 4B 128
Lawers. Per 5D 142
Lawford. Essx 2D 54
Lawhitton. Corn 4D 10
Lawkland. N Yor 3G 97
Lawley. Telf 5A 72
Lawnhead. Staf 3C 72
Lawrenny. Pemb 4E 43
Lawshall. Suff 5A 66
Lawton. Here 5G 59
Laxey. IOM 3D 108
Laxfield. Suff 3E 67
Laxfirth. Shet 6F 173
Laxo. Shet 5F 173
Laxton. E Yor 2A 94
Laxton. Nptn 1G 63
Laxton. Notts 4E 86
Laycock. W Yor 5C 98
Layer Breton. Essx 4C 54
Layer-de-la-Haye. Essx 3C 54
Layer Marney. Essx 4C 54
Layland's Green. W Ber 5B 36
Laymore. Dors 2G 13
Laysters Pole. Here 4H 59
Layter's Green. Buck 1A 38
Laytham. E Yor 1H 93
Lazenby. Red C 3C 106
Lazonby. Cumb 1G 103
Lea. Derbs 5H 85
Lea. Here 3B 48
Lea. Linc 2F 87
Lea. Shrp 2F 59
(nr. Bishop's Castle)
Lea. Shrp 5G 71
(nr. Shrewsbury)
Lea. Wilts 3E 35
Leabrooks. Derbs 5B 86
Leac a Li. W Isl 8D 171
Leachd. Arg 4H 133
Leachkin. High 4A 158
Leachpool. Pemb 3D 42
Leadburn. Midl 4F 129
Leadenham. Linc 5G 87
Leaden Roding. Essx 4F 53
Leaderfoot. Bord 1H 119
Leadgate. Cumb 5A 114
Leadgate. Dur 4E 115
Leadgate. Nmbd 4E 115
Leadhills. S Lan 3A 118
Leadingcross Green. Kent 5C 40
Lea End. Worc 3E 61
Leafield. Oxon 4B 50
Leagrave. Lutn 3A 52
Lea Hall. W Mid 2F 61
Lea Heath. Staf 3E 73
Leake. N Yor 5B 106
Leake Common Side. Linc 5C 88
Leake Fold Hill. Linc 5D 88
Leake Hurn's End. Linc 1D 76
Lealholm. N Yor 4E 107
Lealt. Arg 4D 132
Lealt. High 2E 155
Leam. Derbs 3G 85
Lea Marston. Warw 1G 61
Leamington Hastings. Warw 4B 62
Leamington Spa, Royal. Warw 4H 61
Leamonsley. Staf 5F 73
Leamside. Dur 5G 115
Leargybreck. Arg 2D 124
Lease Rigg. N Yor 4F 107
Leasgill. Cumb 1D 97
Leasingham. Linc 1H 75
Leasingthorne. Dur 1F 105
Leasowe. Mers 1E 83
Leatherhead. Surr 5C 38
Leathley. N Yor 5E 99
Leaths. Dum 3E 111
Leaton. Shrp 4G 71
Leaton. Telf 4A 72
Lea Town. Lanc 1C 90
Leaveland. Kent 5E 40
Leavenheath. Suff 2C 54
Leavening. N Yor 3B 100
Leaves Green. G Lon 4F 39
Lea Yeat. Cumb 1G 97
Leazes. Dur 4E 115
Lebberston. N Yor 1E 101
Lechlade on Thames. Glos 2H 35
Leck. Lanc 2F 97
Leckford. Hants 3B 24
Leckfurin. High 3H 167
Leckgruinart. Arg 3A 124
Leckhampstead. Buck 2F 51
Leckhampstead. W Ber 4C 36
Leckhampstead Street. W Ber 4C 36
Leckhampton. Glos 4E 49
Leckmelm. High 4F 163
Leckwith. V Glam 4E 33
Leconfield. E Yor 5E 101
Ledaig. Arg 5D 140
Ledburn. Buck 3H 51
Ledbury. Here 2C 48
Ledgemoor. Here 5G 59
Ledgowan. High 3D 156
Ledicot. Here 4G 59
Ledmore. High 2G 163
Lednabirichen. High 4E 165
Lednagullin. High 2A 168
Ledsham. Ches W 3F 83
Ledsham. W Yor 2E 93
Ledston. W Yor 2E 93
Ledstone. Devn 4D 8
Ledwell. Oxon 3C 50
Lee. Devn 2E 19
(nr. Ilfracombe)
Lee. Devn 4B 20
(nr. South Molton)
Lee. G Lon 3F 39
Lee. Hants 1B 16
Lee. Lanc 4E 97
Lee. Shrp 2G 71
Leeans. Shet 7E 173
Leebotten. Shet 9F 173
Leebotwood. Shrp 1G 59
Lee Brockhurst. Shrp 3H 71
Leece. Cumb 3B 96
Leechpool. Mon 3A 34
Lee Clump. Buck 5H 51
Leeds. Kent 5C 40
Leeds. W Yor 1C 92 & 199
Leeds Bradford International Airport.
W Yor 5E 98
Leedstown. Corn 3D 4
Leegomery. Telf 4A 72
Lee Head. Derbs 1E 85
Leek. Staf 5D 85
Leekbrook. Staf 5D 85
Leek Wootton. Warw 4G 61
Lee Mill. Devn 3B 8
Leeming. N Yor 1E 99
Leeming Bar. N Yor 5F 105
Lee Moor. Devn 2B 8
Lee Moor. W Yor 2D 92
Lee-on-the-Solent. Hants 2D 16
Lees. Derbs 2G 73
Lees. G Man 4H 91
Lees. W Yor 1A 92
Lees, The. Kent 5E 40
Leeswood. Flin 4E 83
Lee, The. Buck 5H 51
Leetown. Per 1E 136
Leftwich. Ches W 3A 84
Legbourne. Linc 2C 88
Legburthwaite. Cumb 3E 102
Legerwood. Bord 5B 130
Legsby. Linc 2A 88
Leicester. Leic 5C 74 & 200
Leicester Forest East. Leics 5C 74
Leigh. Dors 2B 14
Leigh. G Man 4E 91
Leigh. Kent 1G 27
Leigh. Shrp 5F 71
Leigh. Surr 1D 26
Leigh. Wilts 2F 35
Leigh. Worc 5B 60
Leigham. Plym 3B 8
Leigh Beck. Essx 2C 40
Leigh Common. Som 4C 22
Leigh Delamere. Wilts 4D 35
Leigh Green. Kent 2D 28
Leighland Chapel. Som 3D 20
Leigh-on-Sea. S'end 2C 40
Leigh Park. Hants 2F 17
Leigh Sinton. Worc 5B 60
Leighterton. Glos 2D 34
Leigh, The. Glos 3D 48
Leighton. N Yor 2D 98
Leighton. Powy 5E 71
Leighton. Shrp 5A 72
Leighton. Som 2C 22
Leighton Bromswold. Cambs 3A 64
Leighton Buzzard. C Beds 3H 51
Leigh-upon-Mendip. Som 2B 22
Leinthall Earls. Here 4G 59
Leinthall Starkes. Here 4G 59
Leintwardine. Here 3G 59
Leire. Leics 1C 62
Leirinmore. High 2E 166
Leishmore. High 4G 157
Leiston. Suff 4G 67
Leitfie. Per 4B 144
Leith. Edin 2F 129
Leitholm. Bord 5D 130
Lelant. Corn 3C 4
Lelant Downs. Corn 3C 4
Lelley. E Yor 1F 95
Lem Hill. Worc 3B 60
Lemington. Tyne 3E 115
Lemmington Hall. Nmbd 3F 121
Lempitlaw. Bord 1B 120
Lemsford. Herts 4C 52
Lenacre. Cumb 1F 97
Lenchie. Abers 5C 160
Lenchwick. Worc 1F 49
Lendalfoot. S Ayr 5A 116
Lendrick. Stir 3E 135
Lenham. Kent 5C 40
Lenham Heath. Kent 1D 28
Lenimore. N Ayr 5G 125
Lennel. Bord 5E 131
Lennoxtown. E Dun 2H 127
Lenton. Linc 2H 75
Lentran. High 4H 157
Lenwade. Norf 4C 78
Lenzie. E Dun 2H 127
Leochel Cushnie. Abers 2C 152
Leogh. Shet 1B 172
Leominster. Here 5G 59
Leonard Stanley. Glos 5D 48
Lepe. Hants 3C 16
Lephenstrath. Arg 5A 122
Lephin. High 4A 154
Lephinchapel. Arg 4G 133
Lephinmore. Arg 4G 133
Leppington. N Yor 3B 100
Lepton. W Yor 3C 92
Lerryn. Corn 3F 7
Lerwick. Shet 7F 173
Lerwick (Tingwall) Airport.
Shet 7F 173
Lesbury. Nmbd 3G 121
Leslie. Abers 1C 152
Leslie. Fife 3E 137
Lesmahagow. S Lan 1H 117
Lesnewth. Corn 3B 10
Lessingham. Norf 3F 79
Lessonhall. Cumb 4D 112
Leswalt. Dum 3F 109
Letchmore Heath. Herts 1C 38
Letchworth Garden City. Herts 2C 52
Letcombe Bassett. Oxon 3B 36
Letcombe Regis. Oxon 3B 36
Letham. Ang 4E 145
Letham. Falk 1B 128
Letham. Fife 2F 137
Lethanhill. E Ayr 3D 116
Lethenty. Abers 4F 161
Letheringham. Suff 5E 67
Letheringsett. Norf 2C 78
Lettaford. Devn 4H 11
Lettan. Orkn 3G 172
Letter. Abers 2E 153
Letterewe. High 1B 156
Letterfearn. High 1A 148
Lettermore. Arg 4F 139
Letters. High 5F 163
Letterston. Pemb 2D 42
Letton. Here 1G 47
(nr. Kington)
Letton. Here 3F 59
(nr. Leintwardine)
Letty Green. Herts 4C 52
Letwell. S Yor 2C 86
Leuchars. Fife 1G 137
Leumrabhagh. W Isl 6F 171
Leusdon. Devn 5H 11
Levaneap. Shet 5F 173
Levedale. Staf 4C 72
Leven. E Yor 5F 101
Leven. Fife 3F 137
Levencorroch. N Ayr 3E 123
Levenhall. E Lot 2G 129
Levens. Cumb 1D 97
Levens Green. Herts 3D 52
Levenshulme. G Man 1C 84
Levenwick. Shet 9F 173
Leverburgh. W Isl 9C 171
Leverington. Cambs 4D 76
Leverton. Linc 1C 76
Leverton. W Ber 4B 36
Leverton Lucasgate. Linc 1D 76
Leverton Outgate. Linc 1D 76
Levington. Suff 2F 55
Levisham. N Yor 5F 107
Levishie. High 2G 149
Lew. Oxon 5B 50
Lewaigue. IOM 2D 108
Lewannick. Corn 4C 10
Lewdown. Devn 4E 11
Lewes. E Sus 4F 27
Leweston. Pemb 2D 42
Lewisham. G Lon 3E 39
Lewiston. High 1H 149
Lewistown. B'end 3C 32
Lewknor. Oxon 2F 37
Leworthy. Devn 3G 19
(nr. Barnstaple)
Leworthy. Devn 2D 10
(nr. Holsworthy)
Lewson Street. Kent 4D 40
Lewthorn Cross. Devn 5A 12
Lewtrenchard. Devn 4E 11
Ley. Corn 2F 7
Leybourne. Kent 5A 40
Leyburn. N Yor 5E 105
Leycett. Staf 1B 72
Leyfields. Staf 5G 73
Ley Green. Herts 3B 52
Ley Hill. Buck 5H 51
Leyland. Lanc 2D 90
Leylodge. Abers 2E 153
Leymoor. W Yor 3B 92
Leys. Per 5B 144
Leysdown-on-Sea. Kent 3E 41
Leysmill. Ang 4F 145
Leyton. G Lon 2E 39
Leytonstone. G Lon 2F 39
Lezant. Corn 5D 10
Leziate. Norf 4F 77
Lhanbryde. Mor 2G 159
Lhen, The. IOM 1C 108
Liatrie. High 5E 157
Libanus. Powy 3C 46
Libberton. S Lan 5C 128
Libbery. Worc 5D 60
Liberton. Edin 3F 129
Liceasto. W Isl 8D 171
Lichfield. Staf 5F 73
Lickey. Worc 3D 61
Lickey End. Worc 3D 61
Lickfold. W Sus 3A 26
Liddaton. Devn 4E 11
Liddington. Swin 3H 35
Liddle. Orkn 9D 172
Lidgate. Suff 5G 65
Lidgett. Notts 4D 86
Lidham Hill. E Sus 4C 28
Lidlington. C Beds 2H 51
Lidsey. W Sus 5A 26
Lidstone. Oxon 3B 50
Lienassie. High 1B 148
Liff. Ang 5C 144
Lifford. W Mid 2E 61
Lifton. Devn 4D 11
Liftondown. Devn 4D 10
Lighthorne. Warw 5H 61
Light Oaks. Staf 5D 84
Lightwater. Surr 4A 38
Lightwood. Staf 1E 73
Lightwood. Stoke 1D 72
Lightwood Green. Ches E 1A 72
Lightwood Green. Wrex 1F 71
Lilbourne. Nptn 3C 62
Lilburn Tower. Nmbd 2E 121
Lillesdon. Som 4G 21
Lilleshall. Telf 4B 72
Lilley. Herts 3B 52
Lilliesleaf. Bord 2H 119
Lillingstone Dayrell.
Buck 2F 51
Lillingstone Lovell. Buck 1F 51
Lillington. Dors 1B 14
Lilstock. Som 2E 21
Lilybank. Inv 2E 126
Lilyhurst. Shrp 4B 72
Limbrick. Lanc 3E 90
Limbury. Lutn 3A 52
Limekilnburn. S Lan 4A 128
Limekilns. Fife 1D 129
Limerigg. Falk 2B 128
Limestone Brae. Nmbd 5A 114
Lime Street. Worc 2D 48
Limington. Som 4A 22
Limpenhoe. Norf 5F 79
Limpley Stoke. Wilts 5C 34
Limpsfield. Surr 5E 39
Limpsfield Chart. Surr 5F 39
Linburn. W Lot 3E 129
Linby. Notts 5C 86
Linchmere. W Sus 3G 25
Lincluden. Dum 2A 112
Lincoln. Linc 3G 87 & 198
Lincomb. Worc 4C 60
Lindale. Cumb 1D 96
Lindal in Furness. Cumb 2B 96
Lindean. Bord 1G 119
Linden. Glos 4D 48
Lindfield. W Sus 3E 27
Lindford. Hants 3G 25
Lindores. Fife 2E 137
Lindridge. Worc 4A 60
Lindsell. Essx 3G 53
Lindsey. Suff 1C 54
Lindsey Tye. Suff 1C 54
Linford. Hants 2G 15
Linford. Thur 3A 40
Lingague. IOM 4B 108
Lingdale. Red C 3D 106
Lingen. Here 4F 59
Lingfield. Surr 1E 27
Lingreabhagh. W Isl 9C 171
Ling, The. Norf 1F 67
Lingwood. Norf 5F 79
Lingy Close. Cumb 4E 113
Linicro. High 2C 154
Linkend. Worc 2D 48
Linkenholt. Hants 1B 24
Linkinhorne. Corn 5D 10
Linklater. Orkn 9D 172
Linksness. Orkn 6E 172
Linktown. Fife 4E 137
Linkwood. Mor 2G 159
Linley. Shrp 1F 59
(nr. Bishop's Castle)
Linley. Shrp 1A 60
(nr. Bridgnorth)
Linley Green. Here 5A 60
Linlithgow. W Lot 2C 128
Linlithgow Bridge. Falk 2C 128
Linneraineach. High 3F 163
Linshiels. Nmbd 4C 120
Linsiadar. W Isl 4E 171
Linsidemore. High 4C 164
Linslade. C Beds 3H 51
Linstead Parva. Suff 3F 67
Linstock. Cumb 4F 113
Linthwaite. W Yor 3B 92
Lintlaw. Bord 4E 131
Lintmill. Mor 2C 160

Midge Hall—Moulsoe

Midge Hall. Lanc 2D 90
Midgeholme. Cumb 4H 113
Midgham. W Ber 5D 36
Midgley. W Yor 2A 92
(nr. Halifax)
Midgley. W Yor 3C 92
(nr. Horbury)
Mid Ho. Shet 2G 173
Midhopestones. S Yor 1G 85
Midhurst. W Sus 4G 25
Mid Kirkton. N Ayr 4C 126
Mid Lambrook. Som 1H 13
Midland. Orkn 7C 172
Mid Lavant. W Sus 2G 17
Midlem. Bord 2H 119
Midney. Som 4A 22
Midsomer Norton. Bath 1B 22
Midton. Inv 2D 126
Midtown. High 5C 162
(nr. Poolewe)
Midtown. High 2F 167
(nr. Tongue)
Midville. Linc 5C 88
Mid Walls. Shet 7C 173
Mid Yell. Shet 2G 173
Migdale. High 4D 164
Migvie. Abers 3B 152
Milborne Port. Som 1B 14
Milborne St Andrew. Dors 3D 14
Milborne Wick. Som 4B 22
Milbourne. Nmbd 2E 115
Milbourne. Wilts 3E 35
Milburn. Cumb 2H 103
Milbury Heath. S Glo 2B 34
Milby. N Yor 3G 99
Milcombe. Oxon 2C 50
Milden. Suff 1C 54
Mildenhall. Suff 3G 65
Mildenhall. Wilts 5H 35
Milebrook. Powy 3F 59
Milebush. Kent 1B 28
Mile End. Cambs 2F 65
Mile End. Essx 3C 54
Mileham. Norf 4B 78
Mile Oak. Brig 5D 26
Miles Green. Staf 5C 84
Miles Hope. Here 4H 59
Milesmark. Fife 1D 128
Mile Town. Kent 3D 40
Milfield. Nmbd 1D 120
Milford. Derbs 1A 74
Milford. Devn 4C 18
Milford. Powy 1C 58
Milford. Staf 3D 72
Milford. Surr 1A 26
Milford Haven. Pemb 4D 42
Milford on Sea. Hants 3A 16
Milkwall. Glos 5A 48
Milkwell. Wilts 4E 23
Milland. W Sus 4G 25
Millbank. High 2D 168
Mill Bank. W Yor 2A 92
Millbeck. Cumb 2D 102
Millbounds. Orkn 4E 172
Millbreck. Abers 4H 161
Millbridge. Surr 2G 25
Millbrook. C Beds 2A 52
Millbrook. Corn 3A 8
Millbrook. G Man 1D 85
Millbrook. Sotn 1B 16
Mill Common. Suff 2G 67
Mill Corner. E Sus 3C 28
Milldale. Staf 5F 85
Millden Lodge. Ang 1E 145
Milldens. Ang 3E 145
Millearn. Per 2B 136
Mill End. Buck 3F 37
Mill End. Cambs 5F 65
Millend. Glos 2C 34
(nr. Dursley)
Mill End. Glos 4G 49
(nr. Northleach)
Mill End. Herts 2D 52
Millerhill. Midl 3G 129
Miller's Dale. Derbs 3F 85
Millers Green. Derbs 5G 85
Millerston. N Lan 3H 127
Millfield. Abers 4B 152
Millfield. Pet 1A 64
Millgate. Lanc 3G 91
Mill Green. Essx 5G 53
Mill Green. Norf 2D 66
Mill Green. Shrp 3A 72
Mill Green. Staf 3E 73
Mill Green. Suff 1C 54
Millhalf. Here 1F 47
Millhall. E Ren 4G 127
Millhayes. Devn 2F 13
(nr. Honiton)
Millhayes. Devn 1E 13
(nr. Wellington)
Millhead. Lanc 2D 97
Millheugh. S Lan 4A 128
Mill Hill. Bkbn 2E 91
Mill Hill. G Lon 1D 38
Millholme. Cumb 5G 103
Millhouse. Arg 2A 126
Millhouse. Cumb 1E 103
Millhousebridge. Dum 1C 112
Millhouses. S Yor 2H 85
Millikenpark. Ren 3F 127
Millington. E Yor 4C 100
Millington Green. Derbs 1G 73
Mill Knowe. Arg 3B 122
Mill Lane. Hants 1F 25
Millmeece. Staf 2C 72
Mill of Craigievar. Abers 2C 152
Mill of Fintray. Abers 2F 153
Mill of Haldane. W Dun 1F 127
Millom. Cumb 1A 96
Millow. C Beds 1C 52
Millpool. Corn 5B 10
Millport. N Ayr 4C 126
Mill Side. Cumb 1D 96
Mill Street. Norf 4C 78
(nr. Lyng)
Mill Street. Norf 4C 78
(nr. Swanton Morley)
Millthorpe. Derbs 3H 85
Millthorpe. Linc 2A 76
Millthrop. Cumb 5H 103
Milltimber. Aber 3F 153
Milltown. Abers 3G 151
(nr. Corgarff)
Milltown. Abers 2B 152
(nr. Lumsden)
Milltown. Corn 3F 7
Milltown. Derbs 4A 86
Milltown. Devn 3F 19
Milltown. Dum 2E 113
Milltown of Aberdalgie. Per 1C 136
Milltown of Auchindoun. Mor 4A 160
Milltown of Campfield. Abers 3D 152
Milltown of Edinvillie. Mor 4G 159
Milltown of Rothiemay. Mor 4C 160
Milltown of Towie. Abers 2B 152
Milnacraig. Ang 3B 144
Milnathort. Per 3D 136
Milngavie. E Dun 2G 127
Milnholm. Stir 1A 128
Milnrow. G Man 3H 91
Milnthorpe. Cumb 1D 97
Milnthorpe. W Yor 3D 92
Milson. Shrp 3A 60
Milstead. Kent 5D 40
Milston. Wilts 2G 23
Milthorpe. Nptn 1D 50
Milton. Ang 4C 144
Milton. Cambs 4D 65
Milton. Cumb 3G 113
(nr. Brampton)
Milton. Cumb 1E 97
(nr. Crooklands)
Milton. Derbs 3H 73
Milton. Dum 2F 111
(nr. Crocketford)
Milton. Dum 4H 109
(nr. Glenluce)
Milton. E Ayr 2D 116
Milton. Glas 2G 127
Milton. High 3F 157
(nr. Achnasheen)
Milton. High 4G 155
(nr. Applecross)
Milton. High 5G 157
(nr. Drumnadrochit)
Milton. High 1B 158
(nr. Invergordon)
Milton. High 4H 157
(nr. Inverness)
Milton. High 3F 169
(nr. Wick)
Milton. Mor 2C 160
(nr. Cullen)
Milton. Mor 2F 151
(nr. Tomintoul)
Milton. N Som 5G 33
Milton. Notts 3E 86
Milton. Oxon 2C 50
(nr. Bloxham)
Milton. Oxon 2C 36
(nr. Didcot)
Milton. Pemb 4E 43
Milton. Port 3E 17
Milton. Som 4H 21
Milton. Stir 3E 135
(nr. Aberfoyle)
Milton. Stir 4D 134
(nr. Drymen)
Milton. Stoke 5D 84
Milton. W Dun 2F 127
Milton Abbas. Dors 2D 14
Milton Abbot. Devn 5E 11
Milton Auchlossan. Abers 3C 152
Milton Bridge. Midl 3F 129
Milton Bryan. C Beds 2H 51
Milton Clevedon. Som 3B 22
Milton Coldwells. Abers 5G 161
Milton Combe. Devn 2A 8
Milton Common. Oxon 5E 51
Milton Damerel. Devn 1D 11
Miltonduff. Mor 2F 159
Milton End. Glos 5G 49
Milton Ernest. Bed 5H 63
Milton Green. Ches W 5G 83
Milton Hill. Devn 5C 12
Milton Hill. Oxon 2C 36
Milton Keynes. Mil 2G 51 & 204
Milton Keynes Village. Mil 2G 51
Milton Lilbourne. Wilts 5G 35
Milton Malsor. Nptn 5E 63
Milton Morenish. Per 5D 142
Milton of Auchinhove. Abers 3C 152
Milton of Balgonie. Fife 3F 137
Milton of Barras. Abers 1H 145
Milton of Campsie. E Dun 2H 127
Milton of Cultoquhey. Per 1A 136
Milton of Cushnie. Abers 2C 152
Milton of Finavon. Ang 3D 145
Milton of Gollanfield. High 3B 158
Milton of Lesmore. Abers 1B 152
Milton of Leys. High 4A 158
Milton of Tullich. Abers 4A 152
Milton on Stour. Dors 4C 22
Milton Regis. Kent 4C 40
Milton Street. E Sus 5G 27
Milton-under-Wychwood. Oxon 4A 50
Milverton. Som 4E 20
Milverton. Warw 4H 61
Milwich. Staf 2D 72
Mimbridge. Surr 4A 38
Minard. Arg 4G 133
Minchington. Dors 1E 15
Minchinhampton. Glos 5D 49
Mindrum. Nmbd 1C 120
Minehead. Som 2C 20
Minera. Wrex 5E 83
Minety. Wilts 2F 35
Minffordd. Gwyn 2E 69
Mingarrypark. High 2A 140
Mingary. High 2G 139
Mingearraidh. W Isl 6C 170
Miningsby. Linc 4C 88
Minions. Corn 5C 10
Minishant. S Ayr 3C 116
Minllyn. Gwyn 4A 70
Minnigaff. Dum 3B 110
Minorca. IOM 3D 108
Minskip. N Yor 3F 99
Minstead. Hants 1A 16
Minsted. W Sus 4G 25
Minster. Kent 4H 41
(nr. Ramsgate)
Minster. Kent 3D 40
(nr. Sheerness)
Minsteracres. Nmbd 4D 114
Minsterley. Shrp 5F 71
Minster Lovell. Oxon 4B 50
Minsterworth. Glos 4C 48
Minterne Magna. Dors 2B 14
Minterne Parva. Dors 2B 14
Minting. Linc 3A 88
Mintlaw. Abers 4H 161
Minto. Bord 2H 119
Minton. Shrp 1G 59
Minwear. Pemb 3E 43
Minworth. W Mid 1F 61
Miodar. Arg 4B 138
Mirbister. Orkn 5C 172
Mirehouse. Cumb 3A 102
Mireland. High 2F 169
Mirfield. W Yor 3C 92
Miserden. Glos 5E 49
Miskin. Rhon 3D 32
Misson. Notts 1D 86
Misterton. Leics 2C 62
Misterton. Notts 1E 87
Misterton. Som 2H 13
Mistley. Essx 2E 54
Mistley Heath. Essx 2E 55
Mitcham. G Lon 4D 39
Mitcheldean. Glos 4B 48
Mitchell. Corn 3C 6
Mitchel Troy. Mon 4H 47
Mitcheltroy Common. Mon 5H 47
Mitford. Nmbd 1E 115
Mithian. Corn 3B 6
Mitton. Staf 4C 72
Mixbury. Oxon 2E 50
Mixenden. W Yor 2A 92
Mixon. Staf 5E 85
Moaness. Orkn 7B 172
Moarfield. Shet 1G 173
Moat. Cumb 2F 113
Moats Tye. Suff 5C 66
Mobberley. Ches E 3B 84
Mobberley. Staf 1E 73
Moccas. Here 1G 47
Mochdre. Cnwy 3H 81
Mochdre. Powy 2C 58
Mochrum. Dum 5A 110
Mockbeggar. Hants 2G 15
Mockerkin. Cumb 2B 102
Modbury. Devn 3C 8
Moddershall. Staf 2D 72
Modsarie. High 2G 167
Moelfre. Cnwy 3B 82
Moelfre. IOA 2E 81
Moelfre. Powy 3D 70
Moffat. Dum 4C 118
Moggerhanger. C Beds 1B 52
Mogworthy. Devn 1B 12
Moira. Leics 4H 73
Molash. Kent 5E 41
Mol-chlach. High 2C 146
Mold. Flin 4E 83
Molehill Green. Essx 3F 53
Molescroft. E Yor 5E 101
Molesden. Nmbd 1E 115
Molesworth. Cambs 3H 63
Moll. High 5E 155
Molland. Devn 4B 20
Mollington. Ches W 3F 83
Mollington. Oxon 1C 50
Mollinsburn. N Lan 2A 128
Monachty. Cdgn 4E 57
Monachyle. Stir 2D 134
Monar Lodge. High 4E 156
Monaughty. Powy 4E 59
Monewden. Suff 5E 67
Moneydie. Per 1C 136
Moneyrow Green. Wind 4G 37
Moniaive. Dum 5G 117
Monifieth. Ang 5E 145
Monikie. Ang 5E 145
Monimail. Fife 2E 137
Monington. Pemb 1B 44
Monk Bretton. S Yor 4D 92
Monken Hadley. G Lon 1D 38
Monk Fryston. N Yor 2F 93
Monk Hesleden. Dur 1B 106
Monkhide. Here 1B 48
Monkhill. Cumb 4E 113
Monkhopton. Shrp 1A 60
Monkland. Here 5G 59
Monkleigh. Devn 4E 19
Monknash. V Glam 4C 32
Monkokehampton. Devn 2F 11
Monkseaton. Tyne 2G 115
Monks Eleigh. Suff 1C 54
Monk's Gate. W Sus 3D 26
Monk's Heath. Ches E 3C 84
Monk Sherborne. Hants 1E 24
Monkshill. Abers 4E 161
Monksilver. Som 3D 20
Monks Kirby. Warw 2B 62
Monk Soham. Suff 4E 66
Monk Soham Green. Suff 4E 66
Monkspath. W Mid 3F 61
Monks Risborough. Buck 5G 51
Monksthorpe. Linc 4D 88
Monk Street. Essx 3G 53
Monkswood. Mon 5G 47
Monkton. Devn 2E 13
Monkton. Kent 4G 41
Monkton. Pemb 4D 42
Monkton. S Ayr 2C 116
Monkton Combe. Bath 5C 34
Monkton Deverill. Wilts 3D 22
Monkton Farleigh. Wilts 5D 34
Monkton Heathfield. Som 4F 21
Monktonhill. S Ayr 2C 116
Monkton Up Wimborne. Dors 1F 15
Monkton Wyld. Dors 3G 13
Monkwearmouth. Tyne 4H 115
Monkwood. Dors 3H 13
Monkwood. Hants 3E 25
Monmarsh. Here 1A 48
Monmouth. Mon 4A 48
Monnington on Wye. Here 1G 47
Monreith. Dum 5A 110
Montacute. Som 1H 13
Montford. Arg 3C 126
Montford. Shrp 4G 71
Montford Bridge. Shrp 4G 71
Montgarrie. Abers 2C 152
Montgarswood. E Ayr 2E 117
Montgomery. Powy 1E 58
Montgreenan. N Ayr 5E 127
Montrave. Fife 3F 137
Montrose. Ang 3G 145
Monxton. Hants 2B 24
Monyach. Derbs 4F 85
Monymusk. Abers 2D 152
Monzie. Per 1A 136
Moodiesburn. N Lan 2H 127
Moon's Green. Kent 3C 28
Moonzie. Fife 2F 137
Moor. Som 1H 13
Moor Allerton. W Yor 1C 92
Moorbath. Dors 3H 13
Moorbrae. Shet 3F 173
Moorby. Linc 4B 88
Moorcot. Here 5F 59
Moor Crichel. Dors 2E 15
Moor Cross. Devn 3C 8
Moordown. Bour 3F 15
Moore. Hal 2H 83
Moorend. Dum 2D 112
Moor End. E Yor 1B 94
Moorend. Glos 5C 48
(nr. Dursley)
Moorend. Glos 4D 48
(nr. Gloucester)
Moorends. S Yor 3G 93
Moorgate. S Yor 1B 86
Moorgreen. Hants 1C 16
Moorgreen. Notts 1B 74
Moor Green. Wilts 5D 34
Moorhaigh. Notts 4C 86
Moorhall. Derbs 3H 85
Moorhampton. Here 1G 47
Moorhouse. Cumb 4E 113
(nr. Carlisle)
Moorhouse. Cumb 4D 112
(nr. Wigton)
Moorhouse. Notts 4E 87
Moorhouse. Surr 5F 39
Moorhouses. Linc 5B 88
Moorland. Som 3G 21
Moorlinch. Som 3H 21
Moor Monkton. N Yor 4H 99
Moor of Granary. Mor 3E 159
Moor Row. Cumb 3B 102
(nr. Whitehaven)
Moor Row. Cumb 5D 112
(nr. Wigton)
Moorsholm. Red C 3D 107
Moorside. Dors 1C 14
Moorside. G Man 4H 91
Moor, The. Kent 3B 28
Moortown. Devn 3D 10
Moortown. Hants 2G 15
Moortown. IOW 4C 16
Moortown. Linc 1H 87
Moortown. Telf 4A 72
Moortown. W Yor 1D 92
Morangie. High 5E 165
Morar. High 4E 147
Morborne. Cambs 1A 64
Morchard Bishop. Devn 2A 12
Morcombelake. Dors 3H 13
Morcott. Rut 5G 75
Morda. Shrp 3E 71
Morden. G Lon 4D 38
Mordiford. Here 2A 48
Mordon. Dur 2A 106
More. Shrp 1F 59
Morebath. Devn 4C 20
Morebattle. Bord 2B 120
Morecambe. Lanc 3D 96
Morefield. High 4F 163
Moreleigh. Devn 3D 8
Morenish. Per 5C 142
Moresby Parks. Cumb 3A 102
Morestead. Hants 4D 24
Moreton. Dors 4D 14
Moreton. Essx 5F 53
Moreton. Here 4H 59
Moreton. Mers 1E 83
Moreton. Oxon 5E 51
Moreton. Staf 4B 72
Moreton Corbet. Shrp 3H 71
Moretonhampstead. Devn 4A 12
Moreton-in-Marsh. Glos 2H 49
Moreton Jeffries. Here 1B 48
Moreton Morrell. Warw 5H 61
Moreton on Lugg. Here 1A 48
Moreton Pinkney. Nptn 1D 50
Moreton Say. Shrp 2A 72
Moreton Valence. Glos 5C 48
Morfa. Cdgn 5C 56
Morfa Bach. Carm 4D 44
Morfa Bychan. Gwyn 2E 69
Morfa Glas. Neat 5B 46
Morfa Nefyn. Gwyn 1B 68
Morganstown. Card 3E 33
Morgan's Vale. Wilts 4G 23
Morham. E Lot 2B 130
Moriah. Cdgn 3F 57
Morland. Cumb 2G 103
Morley. Ches E 2C 84
Morley. Derbs 1A 74
Morley. Dur 2E 105
Morley. W Yor 2C 92
Morley St Botolph. Norf 1C 66
Morningside. Edin 2F 129
Morningside. N Lan 4B 128
Morningthorpe. Norf 1E 66
Morpeth. Nmbd 1F 115
Morrey. Staf 4F 73
Morridge Side. Staf 5E 85
Morridge Top. Staf 4E 85
Morrington. Dum 1F 111
Morris Green. Essx 2H 53
Morriston. Swan 3F 31
Morston. Norf 1C 78
Mortehoe. Devn 2E 19
Morthen. S Yor 2B 86
Mortimer. W Ber 5E 37
Mortimer's Cross. Here 4G 59
Mortimer West End. Hants 5E 37
Mortomley. S Yor 1H 85
Morton. Cumb 1F 103
(nr. Calthwaite)
Morton. Cumb 4E 113
(nr. Carlisle)
Morton. Derbs 4B 86
Morton. Linc 3H 75
(nr. Bourne)
Morton. Linc 1F 87
(nr. Gainsborough)
Morton. Linc 4F 87
(nr. Lincoln)
Morton. Norf 4D 78
Morton. Notts 5E 87
Morton. Shrp 3E 71
Morton. S Glo 2B 34
Morton Bagot. Warw 4F 61
Morton Mill. Shrp 3H 71
Morton-on-Swale. N Yor 5A 106
Morton Tinmouth. Dur 2E 105
Morvah. Corn 3B 4
Morval. Corn 3G 7
Morvich. High 3E 165
(nr. Golspie)
Morvich. High 1B 148
(nr. Shiel Bridge)
Morvil. Pemb 1E 43
Morville. Shrp 1A 60
Morwenstow. Corn 1C 10
Morwick Hall. Nmbd 4G 121
Mosborough. S Yor 2B 86
Moscow. E Ayr 5F 127
Mose. Shrp 1B 60
Mosedale. Cumb 1E 103
Moseley. W Mid 2E 61
(nr. Birmingham)
Moseley. W Mid 5D 72
(nr. Wolverhampton)
Moseley. Worc 5C 60
Moss. Arg 4A 138
Moss. High 2A 140
Moss. S Yor 3F 93
Moss. Wrex 5F 83
Mossatt. Abers 2B 152
Moss Bank. Mers 1H 83
Mossbank. Shet 4F 173
Mossblown. S Ayr 2D 116
Mossbrow. G Man 2B 84
Mossburnford. Bord 3A 120
Mossdale. Dum 2D 110
Mossedge. Cumb 3F 113
Mossend. N Lan 3A 128
Mossgate. Staf 2D 72
Moss Lane. Ches E 3D 84
Mossley. Ches E 4C 84
Mossley. G Man 4H 91
Mossley Hill. Mers 2F 83
Moss of Barmuckity. Mor 2G 159
Mosspark. Glas 3G 127
Mosspaul. Bord 5G 119
Moss Side. Cumb 4C 112
Moss Side. G Man 1C 84
Moss-side. High 3C 158
Moss Side. Lanc 1B 90
(nr. Blackpool)
Moss Side. Lanc 2D 90
(nr. Preston)
Moss Side. Mers 4B 90
Moss-side of Cairness. Abers 2H 161
Mosstodloch. Mor 2H 159
Mosswood. Nmbd 4D 114
Mossy Lea. Lanc 3D 90
Mosterton. Dors 2H 13
Moston. Shrp 3H 71
Moston Green. Ches E 4B 84
Mostyn. Flin 2D 82
Mostyn Quay. Flin 2D 82
Motcombe. Dors 4D 22
Mothecombe. Devn 4C 8
Motherby. Cumb 2F 103
Motherwell. N Lan 4A 128
Mottingham. G Lon 3F 39
Mottisfont. Hants 4B 24
Mottistone. IOW 4C 16
Mottram in Longdendale.
G Man 1D 85
Mottram St Andrew. Ches E 3C 84
Mott's Mill. E Sus 2G 27
Mouldsworth. Ches W 3H 83
Moulin. Per 3G 143
Moulsecoomb. Brig 5E 27
Moulsford. Oxon 3D 36
Moulsoe. Mil 1H 51

Moulton—Newholm

Moulton. *Ches W* 4A **84**
Moulton. *Linc* 3C **76**
Moulton. *Nptn* 4E **63**
Moulton. *N Yor* 4F **105**
Moulton. *Suff* 4F **65**
Moulton. *V Glam* 4D **32**
Moulton Chapel. *Linc* 4B **76**
Moulton Eaugate. *Linc* 4B **76**
Moulton St Mary. *Norf* 5F **79**
Moulton Seas End. *Linc* 3C **76**
Mount. *Corn* 2F **7**
(nr. Bodmin)
Mount. *Corn* 3B **6**
(nr. Newquay)
Mountain Ash. *Rhon* 2D **32**
Mountain Cross. *Bord* 5E **129**
Mountain Street. *Kent* 5E **41**
Mountain Water. *Pemb* 2D **42**
Mount Ambrose. *Corn* 4B **6**
Mountbenger. *Bord* 2F **119**
Mountblow. *W Dun* 2F **127**
Mount Bures. *Essx* 2C **54**
Mountfield. *E Sus* 3B **28**
Mountgerald. *High* 2H **157**
Mount Hawke. *Corn* 4B **6**
Mount High. *High* 2A **158**
Mountjoy. *Corn* 2C **6**
Mount Lothian. *Midl* 4F **129**
Mountnessing. *Essx* 1H **39**
Mounton. *Mon* 2A **34**
Mount Pleasant. *Buck* 2E **51**
Mount Pleasant. *Ches E* 5C **84**
Mount Pleasant. *Derbs* 1H **73**
(nr. Derby)
Mount Pleasant. *Derbs* 4G **73**
(nr. Swadlincote)
Mount Pleasant. *E Sus* 4F **27**
Mount Pleasant. *Fife* 2E **137**
Mount Pleasant. *Hants* 3A **16**
Mount Pleasant. *Norf* 1B **66**
Mount Skippett. *Oxon* 4B **50**
Mountsorrel. *Leics* 4C **74**
Mount Stuart. *Arg* 4C **126**
Mousehole. *Corn* 4B **4**
Mouswald. *Dum* 2B **112**
Mow Cop. *Ches E* 5C **84**
Mowden. *Darl* 3F **105**
Mowhaugh. *Bord* 2C **120**
Mowmacre Hill. *Leic* 5C **74**
Mowsley. *Leics* 2D **62**
Moy. *High* 5B **158**
Moylgrove. *Pemb* 1B **44**
Moy Lodge. *High* 5G **149**
Muasdale. *Arg* 5E **125**
Muchalls. *Abers* 4G **153**
Much Birch. *Here* 2A **48**
Much Cowarne. *Here* 1B **48**
Much Dewchurch. *Here* 2H **47**
Muchelney. *Som* 4H **21**
Muchelney Ham. *Som* 4H **21**
Much Hadham. *Herts* 4E **53**
Much Hoole. *Lanc* 2C **90**
Muchlarnick. *Corn* 3G **7**
Much Marcle. *Here* 2B **48**
Muchrachd. *High* 5E **157**
Much Wenlock. *Shrp* 1A **60**
Mucking. *Thur* 2A **40**
Muckle Breck. *Shet* 5G **173**
Muckleford. *Dors* 3B **14**
Mucklestone. *Staf* 2B **72**
Muckleton. *Norf* 2H **77**
Muckleton. *Shrp* 3H **71**
Muckley. *Shrp* 1A **60**
Muckley Corner. *Staf* 5E **73**
Muckton. *Linc* 2C **88**
Mudale. *High* 5F **167**
Muddiford. *Devn* 3F **19**
Mudeford. *Dors* 3G **15**
Mudford. *Som* 1A **14**
Mudgley. *Som* 2H **21**
Mugdock. *Stir* 2G **127**
Mugeary. *High* 5D **154**
Muggington. *Derbs* 1G **73**
Muggintonlane End. *Derbs* 1G **73**
Muggleswick. *Dur* 4D **114**
Mugswell. *Surr* 5D **38**
Muie. *High* 3D **164**
Muirden. *Abers* 3E **160**
Muirdrum. *Ang* 5E **145**
Muiredge. *Per* 1E **137**
Muirend. *Glas* 3G **127**
Muirhead. *Ang* 5C **144**
Muirhead. *Fife* 3E **137**
Muirhead. *N Lan* 3H **127**
Muirhouses. *Falk* 1D **128**
Muirkirk. *E Ayr* 2F **117**
Muir of Alford. *Abers* 2C **152**
Muir of Fairburn. *High* 3G **157**
Muir of Fowlis. *Abers* 2C **152**
Muir of Miltonduff. *Mor* 3F **159**
Muir of Ord. *High* 3H **157**
Muir of Tarradale. *High* 3H **157**
Muirshearlich. *High* 5D **148**
Muirtack. *Abers* 5G **161**
Muirton. *High* 2B **158**
Muirton. *Per* 1D **136**
Muirton of Ardblair. *Per* 4A **144**
Muirtown. *Per* 2B **136**
Muiryfold. *Abers* 3E **161**
Muker. *N Yor* 5C **104**
Mulbarton. *Norf* 5D **78**
Mulben. *Mor* 3A **160**
Mulindry. *Arg* 4B **124**
Mulla. *Shet* 5F **173**
Mullach Charlabhaigh. *W Isl* 3E **171**
Mullacott. *Devn* 2F **19**
Mullion. *Corn* 5D **5**
Mullion Cove. *Corn* 5D **4**
Mumbles. *Swan* 4F **31**
Mumby. *Linc* 3E **89**
Munderfield Row. *Here* 5A **60**
Munderfield Stocks. *Here* 5A **60**
Mundesley. *Norf* 2F **79**
Mundford. *Norf* 1H **65**
Mundham. *Norf* 1F **67**
Mundon. *Essx* 5B **54**
Munerigie. *High* 3E **149**
Muness. *Shet* 1H **173**
Mungasdale. *High* 4D **162**
Mungrisdale. *Cumb* 1E **103**
Munlochy. *High* 3A **158**
Munsley. *Here* 1B **48**
Munslow. *Shrp* 2H **59**
Murchington. *Devn* 4G **11**
Murcot. *Worc* 1F **49**
Murcott. *Oxon* 4D **50**
Murdishaw. *Hal* 2H **83**
Murieston. *W Lot* 3D **128**
Murkle. *High* 2D **168**
Murlaggan. *High* 4C **148**
Murra. *Orkn* 7B **172**
Murrayfield. *Edin* 2F **129**
Murray, The. *S Lan* 4H **127**
Murrell Green. *Hants* 1F **25**
Murroes. *Ang* 5D **144**
Murrow. *Cambs* 5C **76**
Mursley. *Buck* 3G **51**
Murthly. *Per* 5H **143**
Murton. *Cumb* 2A **104**
Murton. *Dur* 5G **115**
Murton. *Nmbd* 5F **131**
Murton. *Swan* 4E **31**
Murton. *York* 4A **100**
Musbury. *Devn* 3F **13**
Muscoates. *N Yor* 1A **100**
Muscott. *Nptn* 4D **62**
Musselburgh. *E Lot* 2G **129**
Muston. *Leics* 2F **75**
Muston. *N Yor* 2E **101**
Mustow Green. *Worc* 3C **60**
Muswell Hill. *G Lon* 2D **39**
Mutehill. *Dum* 5D **111**
Mutford. *Suff* 2G **67**
Muthill. *Per* 2A **136**
Mutterton. *Devn* 2D **12**
Muxton. *Telf* 4B **72**
Mwmbwls. *Swan* 4F **31**
Mybster. *High* 3D **168**
Myddfai. *Carm* 2A **46**
Myddle. *Shrp* 3G **71**
Mydroilyn. *Cdgn* 5D **56**
Myerscough. *Lanc* 1C **90**
Mylor Bridge. *Corn* 5C **6**
Mylor Churchtown. *Corn* 5C **6**
Mynachlog-ddu. *Pemb* 1F **43**
Mynydd-bach. *Mon* 2H **33**
Mynydd Isa. *Flin* 4E **83**
Mynyddislwyn. *Cphy* 2E **33**
Mynydd Llandegai. *Gwyn* 4F **81**
Mynydd Mechell. *IOA* 1C **80**
Mynydd-y-briw. *Powy* 3D **70**
Mynyddygarreg. *Carm* 5E **45**
Mynytho. *Gwyn* 2C **68**
Myrebird. *Abers* 4E **153**
Myrelandhorn. *High* 3E **169**
Mytchett. *Surr* 1G **25**
Mythe, The. *Glos* 2D **49**
Mytholmroyd. *W Yor* 2A **92**
Myton-on-Swale. *N Yor* 3G **99**
Mytton. *Shrp* 4G **71**

N

Naast. *High* 5C **162**
Na Buirgh. *W Isl* 8C **171**
Naburn. *York* 5H **99**
Nab Wood. *W Yor* 1B **92**
Nackington. *Kent* 5F **41**
Nacton. *Suff* 1F **55**
Nafferton. *E Yor* 4E **101**
Na Gearrannan. *W Isl* 3D **171**
Nailbridge. *Glos* 4B **48**
Nailsbourne. *Som* 4F **21**
Nailsea. *N Som* 4H **33**
Nailstone. *Leics* 5B **74**
Nailsworth. *Glos* 2D **34**
Nairn. *High* 3C **158**
Nalderswood. *Surr* 1D **26**
Nancegollan. *Corn* 3D **4**
Nancledra. *Corn* 3B **4**
Nangreaves. *G Man* 3G **91**
Nanhyfer. *Pemb* 1A **44**
Nannerch. *Flin* 4D **82**
Nanpantan. *Leics* 4C **74**
Nanpean. *Corn* 3D **6**
Nanstallon. *Corn* 2E **7**
Nant-ddu. *Powy* 4D **46**
Nanternis. *Cdgn* 5C **56**
Nantgaredig. *Carm* 3E **45**
Nantgarw. *Rhon* 3E **33**
Nant Glas. *Powy* 4B **58**
Nantglyn. *Den* 4C **82**
Nantgwyn. *Powy* 3B **58**
Nantlle. *Gwyn* 5E **81**
Nantmawr. *Shrp* 3E **71**
Nantmel. *Powy* 4C **58**
Nantmor. *Gwyn* 1F **69**
Nant Peris. *Gwyn* 5F **81**
Nantwich. *Ches E* 5A **84**
Nant-y-bai. *Carm* 1A **46**
Nant-y-bwch. *Blae* 4E **47**
Nant-y-Derry. *Mon* 5G **47**
Nant-y-dugoed. *Powy* 4B **70**
Nant-y-felin. *Cnwy* 3F **81**
Nantyffyllon. *B'end* 2B **32**
Nantyglo. *Blae* 4E **47**
Nant-y-meichiaid. *Powy* 4D **70**
Nant-y-moel. *B'end* 2C **32**
Nant-y-Pandy. *Cnwy* 3F **81**
Naphill. *Buck* 2G **37**
Nappa. *Lanc* 4A **98**
Napton on the Hill. *Warw* 4B **62**
Narberth. *Pemb* 3F **43**
Narberth Bridge. *Pemb* 3F **43**
Narborough. *Leics* 1C **62**
Narborough. *Norf* 4G **77**
Narkurs. *Corn* 3H **7**
Narth, The. *Mon* 5A **48**
Narthwaite. *Cumb* 5A **104**
Nasareth. *Gwyn* 1D **68**
Naseby. *Nptn* 3D **62**
Nash. *Buck* 2F **51**
Nash. *Here* 4F **59**
Nash. *Kent* 5G **41**
Nash. *Newp* 3G **33**
Nash. *Shrp* 3A **60**
Nash Lee. *Buck* 5G **51**
Nassington. *Nptn* 1H **63**
Nasty. *Herts* 3D **52**
Natcott. *Devn* 4C **18**
Nateby. *Cumb* 4A **104**
Nateby. *Lanc* 5D **96**
Nately Scures. *Hants* 1F **25**
Natland. *Cumb* 1E **97**
Naughton. *Suff* 1D **54**
Naunton. *Glos* 3G **49**
Naunton. *Worc* 2D **49**
Naunton Beauchamp. *Worc* 5D **60**
Navenby. *Linc* 5G **87**
Navestock. *Essx* 1G **39**
Navestock Side. *Essx* 1G **39**
Navidale. *High* 2H **165**
Nawton. *N Yor* 1A **100**
Nayland. *Suff* 2C **54**
Nazeing. *Essx* 5E **53**
Neacroft. *Hants* 3G **15**
Nealhouse. *Cumb* 4E **113**
Neal's Green. *W Mid* 2H **61**
Neap House. *N Lin* 3B **94**
Near Sawrey. *Cumb* 5E **103**
Neasden. *G Lon* 2D **38**
Neasham. *Darl* 3A **106**
Neath. *Neat* 2A **32**
Neath Abbey. *Neat* 3G **31**
Neatishead. *Norf* 3F **79**
Neaton. *Norf* 5B **78**
Nebo. *Cdgn* 4E **57**
Nebo. *Cnwy* 5H **81**
Nebo. *Gwyn* 5D **81**
Nebo. *IOA* 1D **80**
Necton. *Norf* 5A **78**
Nedd. *High* 5B **166**
Nedderton. *Nmbd* 1F **115**
Nedging. *Suff* 1D **54**
Nedging Tye. *Suff* 1D **54**
Needham. *Norf* 2E **67**
Needham Market. *Suff* 5C **66**
Needham Street. *Suff* 4G **65**
Needingworth. *Cambs* 3C **64**
Needwood. *Staf* 3F **73**
Neen Savage. *Shrp* 3A **60**
Neen Sollars. *Shrp* 3A **60**
Neenton. *Shrp* 2A **60**
Nefyn. *Gwyn* 1C **68**
Neilston. *E Ren* 4F **127**
Neithrop. *Oxon* 1C **50**
Nelly Andrews Green. *Powy* 5E **71**
Nelson. *Cphy* 2E **32**
Nelson. *Lanc* 1G **91**
Nelson Village. *Nmbd* 2F **115**
Nemphlar. *S Lan* 5B **128**
Nempnett Thrubwell. *Bath* 5A **34**
Nene Terrace. *Linc* 5B **76**
Nenthall. *Cumb* 5A **114**
Nenthead. *Cumb* 5A **114**
Nenthorn. *Bord* 1A **120**
Nercwys. *Flin* 4E **83**
Neribus. *Arg* 4A **124**
Nerston. *S Lan* 4H **127**
Nesbit. *Nmbd* 1D **121**
Nesfield. *N Yor* 5C **98**
Ness. *Ches W* 3F **83**
Nesscliffe. *Shrp* 4F **71**
Ness of Tenston. *Orkn* 6B **172**
Neston. *Ches W* 3E **83**
Neston. *Wilts* 5D **34**
Nethanfoot. *S Lan* 5B **128**
Nether Alderley. *Ches E* 3C **84**
Netheravon. *Wilts* 2G **23**
Nether Blainslie. *Bord* 5B **130**
Netherbrae. *Abers* 3E **161**
Netherbrough. *Orkn* 6C **172**
Nether Broughton. *Leics* 3D **74**
Netherburn. *S Lan* 5B **128**
Nether Burrow. *Lanc* 2F **97**
Netherbury. *Dors* 3H **13**
Netherby. *Cumb* 2E **113**
Nether Careston. *Ang* 3E **145**
Nether Cerne. *Dors* 3B **14**
Nether Compton. *Dors* 1A **14**
Nethercote. *Glos* 3G **49**
Nethercote. *Warw* 4C **62**
Nethercott. *Devn* 3E **19**
Nethercott. *Oxon* 3C **50**
Nether Dallachy. *Mor* 2A **160**
Nether Durdie. *Per* 1E **136**
Nether End. *Derbs* 3G **85**
Netherend. *Glos* 5A **48**
Nether Exe. *Devn* 2C **12**
Netherfield. *E Sus* 4B **28**
Netherfield. *Notts* 1D **74**
Nethergate. *Norf* 3C **78**
Netherhampton. *Wilts* 4G **23**
Nether Handley. *Derbs* 3B **86**
Nether Haugh. *S Yor* 1B **86**
Nether Heage. *Derbs* 5A **86**
Nether Heyford. *Nptn* 5D **62**
Netherhouses. *Cumb* 1B **96**
Nether Howcleugh. *Dum* 3C **118**
Nether Kellet. *Lanc* 3E **97**
Nether Kinmundy. *Abers* 4H **161**
Netherland Green. *Staf* 2F **73**
Nether Langwith. *Notts* 3C **86**
Netherlaw. *Dum* 5E **111**
Netherley. *Abers* 4F **153**
Nethermill. *Dum* 1B **112**
Nethermills. *Mor* 3C **160**
Nether Moor. *Derbs* 4A **86**
Nether Padley. *Derbs* 3G **85**
Netherplace. *E Ren* 4G **127**
Nether Poppleton. *York* 4H **99**
Netherseal. *Derbs* 4G **73**
Nether Silton. *N Yor* 5B **106**
Nether Stowey. *Som* 3E **21**
Nether Street. *Essx* 4F **53**
Netherstreet. *Wilts* 5E **35**
Netherthird. *E Ayr* 3E **117**
Netherthong. *W Yor* 4B **92**
Netherton. *Ang* 3E **145**
Netherton. *Cumb* 1B **102**
Netherton. *Devn* 5B **12**
Netherton. *Hants* 1B **24**
Netherton. *Here* 3A **48**
Netherton. *Mers* 1F **83**
Netherton. *N Lan* 4A **128**
Netherton. *Nmbd* 4D **121**
Netherton. *Per* 3A **144**
Netherton. *Shrp* 2B **60**
Netherton. *Stir* 2G **127**
Netherton. *W Mid* 2D **60**
Netherton. *W Yor* 3C **92**
(nr. Horbury)
Netherton. *W Yor* 3B **92**
(nr. Huddersfield)
Netherton. *Worc* 1E **49**
Nethertown. *Cumb* 4A **102**
Nethertown. *High* 1F **169**
Nethertown. *Staf* 4F **73**
Nether Urquhart. *Fife* 3D **136**
Nether Wallop. *Hants* 3B **24**
Nether Wasdale. *Cumb* 4C **102**
Nether Welton. *Cumb* 5E **113**
Nether Westcote. *Glos* 3H **49**
Nether Whitacre. *Warw* 1G **61**
Nether Winchendon.
Buck 4F **51**
Netherwitton. *Nmbd* 5F **121**
Nether Worton. *Oxon* 2C **50**
Nethy Bridge. *High* 1E **151**
Netley. *Hants* 2C **16**
Netley. *Shrp* 5G **71**
Netley Marsh. *Hants* 1B **16**
Nettlebed. *Oxon* 3F **37**
Nettlebridge. *Som* 2B **22**
Nettlecombe. *Dors* 3A **14**
Nettlecombe. *IOW* 5D **16**
Nettleden. *Herts* 4A **52**
Nettleham. *Linc* 3H **87**
Nettlestead. *Kent* 5A **40**
Nettlestead Green. *Kent* 5A **40**
Nettlestone. *IOW* 3E **16**
Nettlesworth. *Dur* 5F **115**
Nettleton. *Linc* 4E **94**
Nettleton. *Wilts* 4D **34**
Netton. *Devn* 4B **8**
Netton. *Wilts* 3G **23**
Neuadd. *Powy* 5C **70**
Neuk, The. *Abers* 4E **153**
Nevendon. *Essx* 1B **40**
Nevern. *Pemb* 1A **44**
New Abbey. *Dum* 3A **112**
New Aberdour. *Abers* 2F **161**
New Addington. *G Lon* 4E **39**
Newall. *W Yor* 5D **98**
New Alresford. *Hants* 3D **24**
New Alyth. *Per* 4B **144**
Newark. *Orkn* 3G **172**
Newark. *Pet* 5B **76**
Newark-on-Trent. *Notts* 5E **87**
New Arley. *Warw* 2G **61**
Newarthill. *N Lan* 4A **128**
New Ash Green. *Kent* 4H **39**
New Balderton. *Notts* 5F **87**
New Barn. *Kent* 4H **39**
New Barnetby. *N Lin* 3D **94**
Newbattle. *Midl* 3G **129**
New Bewick. *Nmbd* 2E **121**
Newbie. *Dum* 3C **112**
Newbiggin. *Cumb* 2H **103**
(nr. Appleby)
Newbiggin. *Cumb* 3B **96**
(nr. Barrow-in-Furness)
Newbiggin. *Cumb* 5G **113**
(nr. Cumrew)
Newbiggin. *Cumb* 2F **103**
(nr. Penrith)
Newbiggin. *Cumb* 5B **102**
(nr. Seascale)
Newbiggin. *Dur* 5E **115**
(nr. Consett)
Newbiggin. *Dur* 2C **104**
(nr. Holwick)
Newbiggin. *Nmbd* 5C **114**
Newbiggin. *N Yor* 5C **104**
(nr. Askrigg)
Newbiggin. *N Yor* 1F **101**
(nr. Filey)
Newbiggin. *N Yor* 1B **98**
(nr. Thoralby)
Newbiggin-by-the-Sea. *Nmbd* 1G **115**
Newbigging. *Ang* 5D **145**
(nr. Monikie)
Newbigging. *Ang* 4B **144**
(nr. Newtyle)
Newbigging. *Ang* 5D **144**
(nr. Tealing)
Newbigging. *Edin* 2E **129**
Newbigging. *S Lan* 5D **128**
Newbiggin-on-Lune. *Cumb* 4A **104**
Newbold. *Derbs* 3A **86**
Newbold. *Leics* 4B **74**
Newbold on Avon. *Warw* 3B **62**
Newbold on Stour. *Warw* 1H **49**
Newbold Pacey. *Warw* 5G **61**
Newbold Verdon. *Leics* 5B **74**
New Bolingbroke. *Linc* 5C **88**
Newborough. *IOA* 4D **80**
Newborough. *Pet* 5B **76**
Newborough. *Staf* 3F **73**
Newbottle. *Nptn* 2D **50**
Newbottle. *Tyne* 4G **115**
New Boultham. *Linc* 3G **87**
Newbourne. *Suff* 1F **55**
New Brancepeth. *Dur* 5F **115**
Newbridge. *Cphy* 2F **33**
Newbridge. *Cdgn* 5E **57**
Newbridge. *Corn* 3B **4**
New Bridge. *Dum* 2G **111**
Newbridge. *Edin* 2E **129**
Newbridge. *Hants* 1A **16**
Newbridge. *IOW* 4C **16**
Newbridge. *N Yor* 1C **100**
Newbridge. *Pemb* 1D **42**
Newbridge. *Wrex* 1E **71**
Newbridge Green. *Worc* 2D **48**
Newbridge-on-Usk. *Mon* 2G **33**
Newbridge on Wye. *Powy* 5C **58**
New Brighton. *Flin* 4E **83**
New Brighton. *Hants* 2F **17**
New Brighton. *Mers* 1F **83**
New Brinsley. *Notts* 5B **86**
Newbrough. *Nmbd* 3B **114**
New Broughton. *Wrex* 5F **83**
New Buckenham. *Norf* 1C **66**
Newbuildings. *Devn* 2A **12**
Newburgh. *Abers* 1G **153**
Newburgh. *Fife* 2E **137**
Newburgh. *Lanc* 3C **90**
Newburn. *Tyne* 3E **115**
Newbury. *W Ber* 5C **36**
Newbury. *Wilts* 2D **22**
Newby. *Cumb* 2G **103**
Newby. *N Yor* 2G **97**
(nr. Ingleton)
Newby. *N Yor* 1E **101**
(nr. Scarborough)
Newby. *N Yor* 3C **106**
(nr. Stokesley)
Newby Bridge. *Cumb* 1C **96**
Newby Cote. *N Yor* 2G **97**
Newby East. *Cumb* 4F **113**
Newby Head. *Cumb* 2G **103**
New Byth. *Abers* 3F **161**
Newby West. *Cumb* 4E **113**
Newby Wiske. *N Yor* 1F **99**
Newcastle. *B'end* 3B **32**
Newcastle. *Mon* 4H **47**
Newcastle. *Shrp* 2E **59**
Newcastle Emlyn. *Carm* 1D **44**
Newcastle International Airport.
Tyne 2E **115**
Newcastleton. *Bord* 1F **113**
Newcastle-under-Lyme. *Staf* 1C **72**
Newcastle Upon Tyne.
Tyne 3F **115** & **205**
Newchapel. *Pemb* 1G **43**
Newchapel. *Powy* 2B **58**
Newchapel. *Staf* 5C **84**
Newchapel. *Surr* 1E **27**
New Cheriton. *Hants* 4D **24**
Newchurch. *Carm* 3D **45**
Newchurch. *Here* 5F **59**
Newchurch. *IOW* 4D **16**
Newchurch. *Kent* 2E **29**
Newchurch. *Lanc* 1G **91**
(nr. Nelson)
Newchurch. *Lanc* 2G **91**
(nr. Rawtenstall)
Newchurch. *Mon* 2H **33**
Newchurch. *Powy* 5E **58**
Newchurch. *Staf* 3F **73**
New Costessey. *Norf* 4D **78**
Newcott. *Devn* 2F **13**
New Cowper. *Cumb* 5C **112**
Newcraighall. *Edin* 2G **129**
New Crofton. *W Yor* 3D **93**
New Cross. *Cdgn* 3F **57**
New Cross. *Som* 1H **13**
New Cumnock. *E Ayr* 3F **117**
New Deer. *Abers* 4F **161**
New Denham. *Buck* 2B **38**
Newdigate. *Surr* 1C **26**
New Duston. *Nptn* 4E **62**
New Earswick. *York* 4A **100**
New Edlington. *S Yor* 1C **86**
New Elgin. *Mor* 2G **159**
New Ellerby. *E Yor* 1E **95**
Newell Green. *Brac* 4G **37**
New Eltham. *G Lon* 3F **39**
New End. *Warw* 4F **61**
New End. *Worc* 5E **61**
Newenden. *Kent* 3C **28**
New England. *Essx* 1H **53**
New England. *Pet* 5A **76**
Newent. *Glos* 3C **48**
New Ferry. *Mers* 2F **83**
Newfield. *Dur* 4F **115**
(nr. Chester-le-Street)
Newfield. *Dur* 1F **105**
(nr. Willington)
New Forest. *Hants* 1H **15**
Newfound. *Hants* 1D **24**
New Fryston. *W Yor* 2E **93**
Newgale. *Pemb* 2C **42**
New Galloway. *Dum* 2D **110**
Newgate. *Norf* 1C **78**
Newgate Street. *Herts* 5D **52**
New Greens. *Herts* 5B **52**
New Grimsby. *IOS* 1A **4**
New Hainford. *Norf* 4E **78**
Newhall. *Ches E* 1A **72**
Newhall. *Staf* 3G **73**
Newham. *Nmbd* 2F **121**
New Hartley. *Nmbd* 2G **115**
Newhaven. *Derbs* 4F **85**
Newhaven. *E Sus* 5F **27** & **215**
Newhaven. *Edin* 2F **129**
New Haw. *Surr* 4B **38**
New Hedges. *Pemb* 4F **43**
New Herrington. *Tyne* 4G **115**
Newhey. *G Man* 3H **91**
New Holkham. *Norf* 2A **78**
New Holland. *N Lin* 2D **94**
Newholm. *N Yor* 3F **107**

New Houghton—North Ormesby

New Houghton. Derbs 4C 86
New Houghton. Norf 3G 77
Newhouse. N Lan 3A 128
New Houses. N Yor 2H 97
New Hutton. Cumb 5G 103
New Hythe. Kent 5B 40
Newick. E Sus 3F 27
Newingreen. Kent 2F 29
Newington. Edin 2F 129
Newington. Kent 2F 29
(nr. Folkestone)
Newington. Kent 4C 40
(nr. Sittingbourne)
Newington. Notts 1D 86
Newington. Oxon 2E 36
Newington Bagpath. Glos 2D 34
New Inn. Carm 2E 45
New Inn. Mon 5H 47
New Inn. N Yor 2H 97
New Inn. Torf 5G 47
New Invention. Shrp 3E 59
New Kelso. High 4B 156
New Lanark. S Lan 5B 128
Newland. Glos 5A 48
Newland. Hull 1D 94
Newland. N Yor 2G 93
Newland. Som 3B 20
Newland. Worc 1C 48
Newlandrig. Midl 3G 129
Newlands. Cumb 1E 103
Newlands. Essx 2C 40
Newlands. High 4B 158
Newlands. Nmbd 4D 115
Newlands. Staf 3E 73
Newlands of Geise. High 2C 168
Newlands of Tynet. Mor 2A 160
Newlands Park. IOA 2B 80
New Lane. Lanc 3C 90
New Lane End. Warr 1A 84
New Langholm. Dum 1E 113
New Leake. Linc 5D 88
New Leeds. Abers 3G 161
New Lenton. Nott 2C 74
New Longton. Lanc 2D 90
Newlot. Orkn 6E 172
New Luce. Dum 3G 109
Newlyn. Corn 4B 4
Newmachar. Abers 2F 153
Newmains. N Lan 4B 128
New Mains of Ury. Abers 5F 153
New Malden. G Lon 4D 38
Newman's Green. Suff 1B 54
Newmarket. Suff 4F 65
Newmarket. W Isl 4G 171
New Marske. Red C 2D 106
New Marton. Shrp 2F 71
New Micklefield. W Yor 1E 93
New Mill. Abers 4E 160
New Mill. Corn 3B 4
New Mill. Herts 4H 51
Newmill. Mor 3B 160
Newmill. Bord 3G 119
New Mill. W Yor 4B 92
New Mill. Wilts 5G 35
Newmillerdam. W Yor 3D 92
New Mills. Corn 3C 6
New Mills. Derbs 2E 85
Newmills. Fife 1D 128
Newmills. High 2A 158
New Mills. Mon 5A 48
New Mills. Powy 5C 70
Newmiln. Per 5A 144
Newmilns. E Ayr 1E 117
New Milton. Hants 3H 15
New Mistley. Essx 2E 54
New Moat. Pemb 2E 43
Newmore. High 3H 157
(nr. Dingwall)
Newmore. High 1A 158
(nr. Invergordon)
Newnham. Cambs 5D 64
Newnham. Glos 4B 48
Newnham. Hants 1F 25
Newnham. Herts 2C 52
Newnham. Kent 5D 40
Newnham. Nptn 5C 62
Newnham. Warw 4F 61
Newnham Bridge. Worc 4A 60
New Ollerton. Notts 4D 86
New Oscott. W Mid 1F 61
Newpark. Fife 2G 137
New Park. N Yor 4E 99
New Pitsligo. Abers 3F 161
New Polzeath. Corn 1D 6
Newport. Corn 4D 10
Newport. Devn 3F 19
Newport. E Yor 1B 94
Newport. Essx 2F 53
Newport. Glos 2B 34
Newport. High 1H 165
Newport. IOW 4D 16
Newport. Newp 3G 33 & 205
Newport. Norf 4H 79
Newport. Pemb 1E 43
Newport. Som 4G 21
Newport. Telf 4B 72
Newport-on-Tay. Fife 1G 137
Newport Pagnell. Mil 1G 51
Newpound Common. W Sus 3B 26
New Prestwick. S Ayr 2C 116
New Quay. Cdgn 5C 56
Newquay. Corn 2C 6
Newquay Cornwall Airport. Corn 2C 6
New Rackheath. Norf 4E 79
New Radnor. Powy 4E 58
New Rent. Cumb 1F 103
New Ridley. Nmbd 4D 114
New Romney. Kent 3E 29
New Rossington. S Yor 1D 86
New Row. Cdgn 3G 57
New Row. Lanc 1E 91
New Sauchie. Clac 4A 136
Newsbank. Ches E 4C 84
Newseat. Abers 5E 160
Newsham. Lanc 1D 90
Newsham. Nmbd 2G 115
Newsham. N Yor 3E 105
(nr. Richmond)
Newsham. N Yor 1F 99
(nr. Thirsk)
New Sharlston. W Yor 3D 93
Newsholme. E Yor 2H 93
Newsholme. Lanc 4H 97
New Shoreston. Nmbd 1F 121
New Springs. G Man 4D 90
Newstead. Notts 5C 86
Newstead. Bord 1H 119
New Stevenston. N Lan 4A 128
New Street. Here 5F 59
Newstreet Lane. Shrp 2A 72
New Swanage. Dors 4F 15
New Swannington. Leics 4B 74
Newthorpe. N Yor 1E 93
Newthorpe. Notts 1B 74
Newton. Arg 4H 133
Newton. B'end 4B 32
Newton. Cambs 1E 53
(nr. Cambridge)
Newton. Cambs 4D 76
(nr. Wisbech)
Newton. Ches W 4G 83
(nr. Chester)
Newton. Ches W 5H 83
(nr. Tattenhall)
Newton. Cumb 2B 96
Newton. Derbs 5B 86
Newton. Dors 1C 14
Newton. Dum 2D 112
(nr. Annan)
Newton. Dum 5D 118
(nr. Moffat)
Newton. G Man 1D 84
Newton. Here 2G 47
(nr. Ewyas Harold)
Newton. Here 5H 59
(nr. Leominster)
Newton. High 2B 158
(nr. Cromarty)
Newton. High 4B 158
(nr. Inverness)
Newton. High 5C 166
(nr. Kylestrome)
Newton. High 4F 169
(nr. Wick)
Newton. Lanc 1B 90
(nr. Blackpool)
Newton. Lanc 2E 97
(nr. Carnforth)
Newton. Lanc 4F 97
(nr. Clitheroe)
Newton. Linc 2H 75
Newton. Mers 2E 83
Newton. Mor 2F 159
Newton. Norf 4H 77
Newton. Nptn 2F 63
Newton. Nmbd 3D 114
Newton. Notts 1D 74
Newton. Bord 2A 120
Newton. Shet 8E 173
Newton. Shrp 1B 60
(nr. Bridgnorth)
Newton. Shrp 2G 71
(nr. Wem)
Newton. Som 3E 20
Newton. S Lan 3H 127
(nr. Glasgow)
Newton. S Lan 1B 118
(nr. Lanark)
Newton. Staf 3E 73
Newton. Suff 1C 54
Newton. Swan 4F 31
Newton. Warw 3C 62
Newton. W Lot 2D 129
Newton. Wilts 4H 23
Newton Abbot. Devn 5B 12
Newtonairds. Dum 1F 111
Newton Arlosh. Cumb 4D 112
Newton Aycliffe. Dur 2F 105
Newton Bewley. Hart 2B 106
Newton Blossomville. Mil 5G 63
Newton Bromswold. Bed 4G 63
Newton Burgoland. Leics 5A 74
Newton by Toft. Linc 2H 87
Newton Ferrers. Devn 4B 8
Newton Flotman. Norf 1E 66
Newtongrange. Midl 3G 129
Newton Green. Mon 2A 34
Newton Hall. Dur 5F 115
Newton Hall. Nmbd 3D 114
Newton Harcourt. Leics 1D 62
Newton Heath. G Man 4G 91
Newtonhill. Abers 4G 153
Newtonhill. High 4H 157
Newton Hill. W Yor 2D 92
Newton Ketton. Darl 2A 106
Newton Kyme. N Yor 5G 99
Newton-le-Willows. Mers 1H 83
Newton-le-Willows. N Yor 1E 98
Newton Longville. Buck 2G 51
Newton Mearns. E Ren 4G 127
Newtonmore. High 4B 150
Newton Morrell. N Yor 4F 105
Newton Mulgrave. N Yor 3E 107
Newton of Ardtoe. High 1A 140
Newton of Balcanquhal. Per 2D 136
Newton of Beltrees. Ren 4E 127
Newton of Falkland. Fife 3E 137
Newton of Mountblairy. Abers 3E 160
Newton of Pitcairns. Per 2C 136
Newton-on-Ouse. N Yor 4H 99
Newton-on-Rawcliffe. N Yor 5F 107
Newton on the Hill. Shrp 3G 71
Newton-on-the-Moor. Nmbd 4F 121
Newton on Trent. Linc 3F 87
Newton Poppleford. Devn 4D 12
Newton Purcell. Oxon 2E 51
Newton Regis. Warw 5G 73
Newton Reigny. Cumb 1F 103
Newton Rigg. Cumb 1F 103
Newton St Cyres. Devn 3B 12
Newton St Faith. Norf 4E 78
Newton St Loe. Bath 5C 34
Newton St Petrock. Devn 1E 11
Newton Solney. Derbs 3G 73
Newton Stacey. Hants 2C 24
Newton Stewart. Dum 3B 110
Newton Toney. Wilts 2H 23
Newton Tony. Wilts 2H 23
Newton Tracey. Devn 4F 19
Newton under Roseberry. Red C 3C 106
Newton Unthank. Leics 5B 74
Newton upon Ayr. S Ayr 2C 116
Newton upon Derwent. E Yor 5B 100
Newton Valence. Hants 3F 25
Newton-with-Scales. Lanc 1C 90
Newtown. Abers 2E 160
Newtown. Cambs 4H 63
Newtown. Corn 5C 10
Newtown. Cumb 5B 112
(nr. Aspatria)
Newtown. Cumb 3G 113
(nr. Brampton)
Newtown. Cumb 2G 103
(nr. Penrith)
Newtown. Derbs 2D 85
Newtown. Devn 4A 20
Newtown. Dors 2H 13
(nr. Beaminster)
New Town. Dors 1E 15
(nr. Sixpenny Handley)
New Town. E Lot 2H 129
Newtown. Falk 1C 128
Newtown. Glos 5B 48
(nr. Lydney)
Newtown. Glos 2E 49
(nr. Tewkesbury)
Newtown. Hants 1D 16
(nr. Bishop's Waltham)
Newtown. Hants 3G 25
(nr. Liphook)
Newtown. Hants 1A 16
(nr. Lyndhurst)
Newtown. Hants 5C 36
(nr. Newbury)
Newtown. Hants 4B 24
(nr. Romsey)
Newtown. Hants 2C 16
(nr. Warsash)
Newtown. Hants 1E 16
(nr. Wickham)
Newtown. Here 2A 48
(nr. Little Dewchurch)
Newtown. Here 1B 48
(nr. Stretton Grandison)
Newtown. High 3F 149
Newtown. IOM 4C 108
Newtown. IOW 3C 16
Newtown. Lanc 3D 90
New Town. Lutn 3A 52
Newtown. Nmbd 4E 121
(nr. Rothbury)
Newtown. Nmbd 2E 121
(nr. Wooler)
Newtown. Pool 3F 15
Newtown. Powy 1D 58
Newtown. Rhon 2D 32
Newtown. Shet 3F 173
Newtown. Shrp 2G 71
Newtown. Som 1F 13
Newtown. Staf 4D 84
(nr. Biddulph)
Newtown. Staf 5D 73
(nr. Cannock)
Newtown. Staf 4E 85
(nr. Longnor)
New Town. W Yor 2E 93
Newtown. Wilts 4E 23
Newtown-in-St Martin. Corn 4E 5
Newtown Linford. Leics 4C 74
Newtown St Boswells. Bord 1H 119
New Tredegar. Cphy 5E 47
Newtyle. Ang 4B 144
New Village. E Yor 1D 94
New Village. S Yor 4F 93
New Walsoken. Cambs 5D 76
New Waltham. NE Lin 4F 95
New Winton. E Lot 2H 129
New World. Cambs 1C 64
New Yatt. Oxon 4B 50
Newyears Green. G Lon 2B 38
New York. Linc 5B 88
New York. Tyne 2G 115
Nextend. Here 5F 59
Neyland. Pemb 4D 42
Nib Heath. Shrp 4G 71
Nicholashayne. Devn 1E 12
Nicholaston. Swan 4E 31
Nidd. N Yor 3F 99
Niddrie. Edin 2F 129
Niddry. Edin 2D 129
Nigg. Aber 3G 153
Nigg. High 1C 158
Nigg Ferry. High 2B 158
Nightcott. Som 4B 20
Nimmer. Som 1G 13
Nine Ashes. Essx 5F 53
Ninebanks. Nmbd 4A 114
Nine Elms. Swin 3G 35
Ninemile Bar. Dum 2F 111
Nine Mile Burn. Midl 4E 129
Ninfield. E Sus 4B 28
Ningwood. IOW 4C 16
Nisbet. Bord 2A 120
Nisbet Hill. Bord 4D 130
Niton. IOW 5D 16
Nitshill. E Ren 4G 127
Niwbwrch. IOA 4D 80
Noak Hill. G Lon 1G 39
Nobold. Shrp 4G 71
Nobottle. Nptn 4D 62
Nocton. Linc 4H 87
Nogdam End. Norf 5F 79
Noke. Oxon 4D 50
Nolton. Pemb 3C 42
Nolton Haven. Pemb 3C 42
No Man's Heath. Ches W 1H 71
No Man's Heath. Warw 5G 73
Nomansland. Devn 1B 12
Nomansland. Wilts 1A 16
Noneley. Shrp 3G 71
Noness. Shet 9F 173
Nonikiln. High 1A 158
Nonington. Kent 5G 41
Nook. Cumb 2F 113
(nr. Longtown)
Nook. Cumb 1E 97
(nr. Milnthorpe)
Noranside. Ang 2D 144
Norbreck. Bkpl 5C 96
Norbridge. Here 1C 48
Norbury. Ches E 1H 71
Norbury. Derbs 1F 73
Norbury. Shrp 1F 59
Norbury. Staf 3B 72
Norby. N Yor 1G 99
Norby. Shet 6C 173
Norcross. Lanc 5C 96
Nordelph. Norf 5E 77
Norden. G Man 3G 91
Nordley. Shrp 1A 60
Norfolk Broads. Norf 5G 79
Norham. Nmbd 5F 131
Norland Town. W Yor 2A 92
Norley. Ches W 3H 83
Norleywood. Hants 3B 16
Normanby. N Lin 3B 94
Normanby. N Yor 1B 100
Normanby. Red C 3C 106
Normanby-by-Spital. Linc 2H 87
Normanby le Wold. Linc 1A 88
Norman Cross. Cambs 1A 64
Normandy. Surr 5A 38
Norman's Bay. E Sus 5A 28
Norman's Green. Devn 2D 12
Normanton. Derb 2H 73
Normanton. Leics 1F 75
Normanton. Linc 1G 75
Normanton. Notts 5E 86
Normanton. W Yor 2D 93
Normanton le Heath. Leics 4A 74
Normanton on Soar. Notts 3C 74
Normanton-on-the-Wolds. Notts 2D 74
Normanton on Trent. Notts 4E 87
Normoss. Lanc 1B 90
Norrington Common. Wilts 5D 35
Norris Green. Mers 1F 83
Norris Hill. Leics 4H 73
Norristhorpe. W Yor 2C 92
Northacre. Norf 1B 66
Northall. Buck 3H 51
Northallerton. N Yor 5A 106
Northam. Devn 4E 19
Northam. Sotn 1C 16
Northampton. Nptn 4E 63 & 206
North Anston. S Yor 2C 86
North Ascot. Brac 4A 38
North Aston. Oxon 3C 50
Northaw. Herts 5C 52
Northay. Som 1F 13
North Baddesley. Hants 4B 24
North Balfern. Dum 4B 110
North Ballachulish. High 2E 141
North Barrow. Som 4B 22
North Barsham. Norf 2B 78
Northbeck. Linc 1H 75
North Benfleet. Essx 2B 40
North Bersted. W Sus 5A 26
North Berwick. E Lot 1B 130
North Bitchburn. Dur 1E 105
North Blyth. Nmbd 1G 115
North Boarhunt. Hants 1E 16
North Bockhampton. Dors 3G 15
Northborough. Pet 5A 76
Northbourne. Kent 5H 41
Northbourne. Oxon 3D 36
North Bovey. Devn 4H 11
North Bowood. Dors 3H 13
North Bradley. Wilts 1D 22
North Brentor. Devn 4E 11
North Brewham. Som 3C 22
Northbrook. Oxon 3C 50
North Brook End. Cambs 1C 52
North Broomhill. Nmbd 4G 121
North Buckland. Devn 2E 19
North Burlingham. Norf 4F 79
North Cadbury. Som 4B 22
North Carlton. Linc 3G 87
North Cave. E Yor 1B 94
North Cerney. Glos 5F 49
North Chailey. E Sus 3E 27
Northchapel. W Sus 3A 26
North Charford. Hants 1G 15
North Charlton. Nmbd 2F 121
North Cheriton. Som 4B 22
North Chideock. Dors 3H 13
Northchurch. Herts 5H 51
North Cliffe. E Yor 1B 94
North Clifton. Notts 3F 87
North Close. Dur 1F 105
North Cockerington. Linc 1C 88
North Coker. Som 1A 14
North Collafirth. Shet 3E 173
North Common. E Sus 3E 27
North Commonty. Abers 4F 161
North Coombe. Devn 1B 12
North Cornelly. B'end 3B 32
North Cotes. Linc 4G 95
Northcott. Devn 3D 10
(nr. Boyton)
Northcott. Devn 1D 12
(nr. Culmstock)
Northcourt. Oxon 2D 36
North Cove. Suff 2G 67
North Cowton. N Yor 4F 105
North Craigo. Ang 2F 145
North Crawley. Mil 1H 51
North Cray. G Lon 3F 39
North Creake. Norf 2A 78
North Curry. Som 4G 21
North Dalton. E Yor 4D 100
North Deighton. N Yor 4F 99
North Dronley. Ang 5C 144
North Duffield. N Yor 1G 93
Northdyke. Orkn 5B 172
Northedge. Derbs 4A 86
North Elkington. Linc 1B 88
North Elmham. Norf 3B 78
North Elmsall. W Yor 3E 93
Northend. Buck 2F 37
North End. E Yor 1F 95
North End. Essx 4G 53
(nr. Great Dunmow)
North End. Essx 2A 54
(nr. Great Yeldham)
North End. Hants 5C 36
North End. Leics 4C 74
North End. Linc 1B 76
North End. Norf 1B 66
North End. N Som 5H 33
North End. Port 2E 17
Northend. Warw 5A 62
North End. W Sus 5C 26
North End. Wilts 2F 35
North Erradale. High 5B 162
North Evington. Leic 5D 74
North Fambridge. Essx 1C 40
North Fearns. High 5E 155
North Featherstone. W Yor 2E 93
North Feorline. N Ayr 3D 122
North Ferriby. E Yor 2C 94
Northfield. Aber 3F 153
Northfield. Hull 2D 94
Northfield. Som 3F 21
Northfield. W Mid 3E 61
Northfleet. Kent 3H 39
North Frodingham. E Yor 4F 101
Northgate. Linc 3A 76
North Gluss. Shet 4E 173
North Gorley. Hants 1G 15
North Green. Norf 2E 66
North Green. Suff 4F 67
(nr. Framlingham)
North Green. Suff 3F 67
(nr. Halesworth)
North Green. Suff 4F 67
(nr. Saxmundham)
North Greetwell. Linc 3H 87
North Grimston. N Yor 3C 100
North Halling. Medw 4B 40
North Hayling. Hants 2F 17
North Hazelrigg. Nmbd 1E 121
North Heasley. Devn 3H 19
North Heath. W Sus 3B 26
North Hill. Corn 5C 10
North Hinksey Village. Oxon 5C 50
North Holmwood. Surr 1C 26
North Huish. Devn 3D 8
North Hykeham. Linc 4G 87
Northiam. E Sus 3C 28
Northill. C Beds 1B 52
Northington. Hants 3D 24
North Kelsey. Linc 4D 94
North Kelsey Moor. Linc 4D 94
North Kessock. High 4A 158
North Killingholme. N Lin 3E 95
North Kilvington. N Yor 1G 99
North Kilworth. Leics 2D 62
North Kyme. Linc 5A 88
North Lancing. W Sus 5C 26
Northlands. Linc 5C 88
Northleach. Glos 4G 49
North Lee. Buck 5G 51
North Lees. N Yor 2E 99
Northleigh. Devn 3G 19
(nr. Barnstaple)
Northleigh. Devn 3E 13
(nr. Honiton)
North Leigh. Kent 1F 29
North Leigh. Oxon 4B 50
North Leverton. Notts 2E 87
Northlew. Devn 3F 11
North Littleton. Worc 1F 49
North Lopham. Norf 2C 66
North Luffenham. Rut 5G 75
North Marden. W Sus 1G 17
North Marston. Buck 3F 51
North Middleton. Midl 4G 129
North Middleton. Nmbd 2E 121
North Molton. Devn 4H 19
North Moor. N Yor 1D 100
Northmoor. Oxon 5C 50
Northmoor Green. Som 3G 21
North Moreton. Oxon 3D 36
Northmuir. Ang 3C 144
North Mundham. W Sus 2G 17
North Murie. Per 1E 137
North Muskham. Notts 5E 87
North Ness. Orkn 8C 172
North Newbald. E Yor 1C 94
North Newington. Oxon 2C 50
North Newnton. Wilts 1G 23
North Newton. Som 3F 21
Northney. Hants 2F 17
North Nibley. Glos 2C 34
North Oakley. Hants 1D 24
North Ockendon. G Lon 2G 39
Northolt. G Lon 2C 38
Northop. Flin 4E 83
Northop Hall. Flin 4E 83
North Ormesby. Midd 3C 106

Pensford. Bath 5B 34
Pensham. Worc 1E 49
Penshaw. Tyne 4G 115
Penshurst. Kent 1G 27
Pensilva. Corn 2G 7
Pensnett. W Mid 2D 60
Penston. E Lot 2H 129
Penstone. Devn 2A 12
Pente-tafarn-y-fedw. Cnwy 4H 81
Pentewan. Corn 4E 6
Pentir. Gwyn 4E 81
Pentire. Corn 2B 6
Pentlepoir. Pemb 4F 43
Pentlow. Essx 1B 54
Pentney. Norf 4G 77
Penton Mewsey. Hants 2B 24
Pentraeth. IOA 3E 81
Pentre. Powy 1E 59
(nr. Church Stoke)
Pentre. Powy 2D 58
(nr. Kerry)
Pentre. Powy 2C 58
(nr. Mochdre)
Pentre. Rhon 2C 32
Pentre. Shrp 4F 71
Pentre. Wrex 2D 70
(nr. Llanfyllin)
Pentre. Wrex 1E 71
(nr. Rhosllanerchrugog)
Pentrebach. Carm 2B 46
Pentre-bach. Cdgn 1F 45
Pentrebach. Mer T 5D 46
Pentre-bach. Powy 2C 46
Pentrebach. Swan 5G 45
Pentre Berw. IOA 3D 80
Pentre-bont. Cnwy 5G 81
Pentrecagal. Carm 1D 44
Pentre-celyn. Den 5D 82
Pentre-clawdd. Shrp 2E 71
Pentreclwydau. Neat 5B 46
Pentre-cwrt. Carm 2D 45
Pentre Dolau Honddu. Powy 1C 46
Pentre-dwr. Swan 3F 31
Pentrefelin. Carm 3F 45
Pentrefelin. Cdgn 1G 45
Pentrefelin. Cnwy 3H 81
Pentrefelin. Gwyn 2E 69
Pentrefoelas. Cnwy 5A 82
Pentre Galar. Pemb 1F 43
Pentregat. Cdgn 5C 56
Pentre Gwenlais. Carm 4G 45
Pentre Gwynfryn. Gwyn 3E 69
Pentre Halkyn. Flin 3E 82
Pentre Hodre. Shrp 3F 59
Pentre-Llanrhaeadr. Den 4C 82
Pentre Llifior. Powy 1D 58
Pentrellwyn. IOA 2E 81
Pentre-llwyn-llwyd. Powy 5B 58
Pentre-llyn-cymmer. Cnwy 5B 82
Pentre Meyrick. V Glam 4C 32
Pentre-piod. Gwyn 2A 70
Pentre-poeth. Newp 3F 33
Pentre'r beirdd. Powy 4D 70
Pentre'r-felin. Powy 2C 46
Pentre-ty-gwyn. Carm 2B 46
Pentre-uchaf. Gwyn 2C 68
Pentrich. Derbs 5A 86
Pentridge. Dors 1F 15
Pen-twyn. Cphy 5F 47
(nr. Oakdale)
Pentwyn. Cphy 5E 46
(nr. Rhymney)
Pentwyn. Card 3F 33
Pentyrch. Card 3E 32
Pentywyn. Carm 4G 43
Penuwch. Cdgn 4E 57
Penwithick. Corn 3E 7
Penwyllt. Powy 4B 46
Penybanc. Carm 4G 45
(nr. Ammanford)
Pen-y-banc. Carm 3G 45
(nr. Llandeilo)
Pen-y-bont. Carm 2H 43
Penybont. Powy 4D 58
(nr. Llandrindod Wells)
Pen-y-bont. Powy 3E 70
(nr. Llanfyllin)
Pen-y-Bont Ar Ogwr. B'end 3C 32
Penybontfawr. Powy 3C 70
Penybryn. Cphy 2E 33
Pen-y-bryn. Pemb 1B 44
Pen-y-bryn. Wrex 1E 71
Pen-y-cae. Powy 4B 46
Penycae. Wrex 1E 71
Pen-y-cae mawr. Mon 2H 33
Penycaerau. Gwyn 3A 68
Pen-y-cefn. Flin 3D 82
Pen-y-clawdd. Mon 5H 47
Pen-y-coedcae. Rhon 3D 32
Penycwm. Pemb 2C 42
Pen-y-Darren. Mer T 5D 46
Pen-y-fai. B'end 3B 32
Penyffordd. Flin 4F 83
(nr. Mold)
Pen-y-ffordd. Flin 2D 82
(nr. Prestatyn)
Penyffridd. Gwyn 5E 81
Pen-y-garn. Cdgn 2F 57
Pen-y-garnedd. IOA 3E 81
Penygarnedd. Powy 3D 70
Pen-y-graig. Gwyn 2B 68
Penygraig. Rhon 2C 32
Penygraigwen. IOA 2D 80
Pen-y-groes. Carm 4F 45
Penygroes. Gwyn 5D 80
Penygroes. Pemb 1F 43
Pen-y-Mynydd. Carm 5E 45
Penymynydd. Flin 4F 83
Penyrheol. Cphy 3E 33
Pen-yr-heol. Mon 4H 47
Penyrheol. Swan 3E 31
Pen-yr-Heolgerrig. Mer T 5D 46
Penysarn. IOA 1D 80
Pen-y-stryt. Den 5E 82
Penywaun. Rhon 5C 46
Penzance. Corn 3B 4
Peopleton. Worc 5D 60
Peover Heath. Ches E 3B 84
Peper Harow. Surr 1A 26
Peplow. Shrp 3A 72
Pepper Arden. N Yor 4F 105
Perceton. N Ayr 5E 127
Percyhorner. Abers 2G 161
Perham Down. Wilts 2A 24
Periton. Som 2C 20
Perkinsville. Dur 4F 115
Perlethorpe. Notts 3D 86
Perranarworthal. Corn 5B 6
Perranporth. Corn 3B 6
Perranuthnoe. Corn 4C 4
Perranwell. Corn 5B 6
Perranzabuloe. Corn 3B 6
Perrott's Brook. Glos 5F 49
Perry. W Mid 1E 61
Perry Barr. W Mid 1E 61
Perry Crofts. Staf 5G 73
Perry Green. Essx 3B 54
Perry Green. Herts 4E 53
Perry Green. Wilts 3E 35
Perry Street. Kent 3H 39
Perry Street. Som 2G 13
Perrywood. Kent 5E 41
Pershall. Staf 3C 72
Pershore. Worc 1E 49
Pertenhall. Bed 4H 63
Perth. Per 1D 136 & 207
Perthy. Shrp 2F 71
Perton. Staf 1C 60
Pertwood. Wilts 3D 23
Peterborough. Pet 1A 64 & 208
Peterburn. High 5B 162
Peterchurch. Here 2G 47
Peterculter. Aber 3F 153
Peterhead. Abers 4H 161
Peterlee. Dur 5H 115
Petersfield. Hants 4F 25
Petersfinger. Wilts 4G 23
Peter's Green. Herts 4B 52
Peters Marland. Devn 1E 11
Peterstone Wentlooge. Newp 3F 33
Peterston-super-Ely. V Glam 4D 32
Peterstow. Here 3A 48
Peter Tavy. Devn 5F 11
Petertown. Orkn 7C 172
Petham. Kent 5F 41
Petherwin Gate. Corn 4C 10
Petrockstowe. Devn 2F 11
Petsoe End. Mil 1G 51
Pett. E Sus 4C 28
Pettaugh. Suff 5D 66
Pett Bottom. Kent 5F 41
Petteridge. Kent 1A 28
Pettinain. S Lan 5C 128
Pettistree. Suff 5E 67
Petton. Devn 4D 20
Petton. Shrp 3G 71
Petts Wood. G Lon 4F 39
Pettycur. Fife 1F 129
Pettywell. Norf 3C 78
Petworth. W Sus 3A 26
Pevensey. E Sus 5A 28
Pevensey Bay. E Sus 5A 28
Pewsey. Wilts 5G 35
Pheasants Hill. Buck 3F 37
Philadelphia. Tyne 4G 115
Philham. Devn 4C 18
Philiphaugh. Bord 2G 119
Phillack. Corn 3C 4
Philleigh. Corn 5C 6
Philpstoun. W Lot 2D 128
Phocle Green. Here 3B 48
Phoenix Green. Hants 1F 25
Pibsbury. Som 4H 21
Pibwrlwyd. Carm 4E 45
Pica. Cumb 2B 102
Piccadilly. Warw 1G 61
Piccadilly Corner. Norf 2E 67
Piccotts End. Herts 5A 52
Pickering. N Yor 1B 100
Picket Piece. Hants 2B 24
Picket Post. Hants 2G 15
Pickford. W Mid 2G 61
Pickhill. N Yor 1F 99
Picklenash. Glos 3C 48
Picklescott. Shrp 1G 59
Pickletillem. Fife 1G 137
Pickmere. Ches E 3A 84
Pickstock. Telf 3B 72
Pickwell. Devn 2E 19
Pickwell. Leics 4E 75
Pickworth. Linc 2H 75
Pickworth. Rut 4G 75
Picton. Ches W 3G 83
Picton. Flin 2D 82
Picton. N Yor 4B 106
Pict's Hill. Som 4H 21
Piddinghoe. E Sus 5F 27
Piddington. Buck 2G 37
Piddington. Nptn 5F 63
Piddington. Oxon 4E 51
Piddlehinton. Dors 3C 14
Piddletrenthide. Dors 2C 14
Pidley. Cambs 3C 64
Pidney. Dors 2C 14
Pie Corner. Here 4A 60
Piercebridge. Darl 3F 105
Pierowall. Orkn 3D 172
Pigdon. Nmbd 1E 115
Pightley. Som 3F 21
Pikehall. Derbs 5F 85
Pikeshill. Hants 2A 16
Pilford. Dors 2F 15
Pilgrims Hatch. Essx 1G 39
Pilham. Linc 1F 87
Pill. N Som 4A 34
Pillaton. Corn 2H 7
Pillaton. Staf 4D 72
Pillerton Hersey. Warw 1A 50
Pillerton Priors. Warw 1A 50
Pilleth. Powy 4E 59
Pilley. Hants 3B 16
Pilley. S Yor 4D 92
Pillgwenlly. Newp 3G 33
Pilling. Lanc 5D 96
Pilling Lane. Lanc 5C 96
Pillowell. Glos 5B 48
Pill, The. Mon 3H 33
Pillwell. Dors 1C 14
Pilning. S Glo 3A 34
Pilsbury. Derbs 4F 85
Pilsdon. Dors 3H 13
Pilsgate. Pet 5H 75
Pilsley. Derbs 3G 85
(nr. Bakewell)
Pilsley. Derbs 4B 86
(nr. Clay Cross)
Pilson Green. Norf 4F 79
Piltdown. E Sus 3F 27
Pilton. Edin 2F 129
Pilton. Nptn 2H 63
Pilton. Rut 5G 75
Pilton. Som 2A 22
Pilton Green. Swan 4D 30
Pimperne. Dors 2E 15
Pinchbeck. Linc 3B 76
Pinchbeck Bars. Linc 3A 76
Pinchbeck West. Linc 3B 76
Pinfold. Lanc 3B 90
Pinford End. Suff 5H 65
Pinged. Carm 5E 45
Pinhoe. Devn 3C 12
Pinkerton. E Lot 2D 130
Pinkneys Green. Wind 3G 37
Pinley. W Mid 3A 62
Pinley Green. Warw 4G 61
Pinmill. Suff 2F 55
Pinmore. S Ayr 5B 116
Pinner. G Lon 2C 38
Pins Green. Worc 1C 48
Pinsley Green. Ches E 1H 71
Pinvin. Worc 1E 49
Pinwherry. S Ayr 1G 109
Pinxton. Derbs 5B 86
Pipe and Lyde. Here 1A 48
Pipe Aston. Here 3G 59
Pipe Gate. Shrp 1B 72
Pipehill. Staf 5E 73
Piperhill. High 3C 158
Pipe Ridware. Staf 4E 73
Pipers Pool. Corn 4C 10
Pipewell. Nptn 2F 63
Pippacott. Devn 3F 19
Pipton. Powy 2E 47
Pirbright. Surr 5A 38
Pirnmill. N Ayr 5G 125
Pirton. Herts 2B 52
Pirton. Worc 1D 49
Pisgah. Stir 3G 135
Pishill. Oxon 3F 37
Pistyll. Gwyn 1C 68
Pitagowan. Per 2F 143
Pitcairn. Per 3F 143
Pitcairngreen. Per 1C 136
Pitcalnie. High 1C 158
Pitcaple. Abers 1E 152
Pitchcombe. Glos 5D 48
Pitchcott. Buck 3F 51
Pitchford. Shrp 5H 71
Pitch Green. Buck 5F 51
Pitch Place. Surr 5A 38
Pitcombe. Som 3B 22
Pitcox. E Lot 2C 130
Pitcur. Per 5B 144
Pitfichie. Abers 2D 152
Pitgrudy. High 4E 165
Pitkennedy. Ang 3E 145
Pitlessie. Fife 3F 137
Pitlochry. Per 3G 143
Pitmachie. Abers 1D 152
Pitmaduthy. High 1B 158
Pitmedden. Abers 1F 153
Pitminster. Som 1F 13
Pitnacree. Per 3G 143
Pitney. Som 4H 21
Pitroddie. Per 1E 136
Pitscottie. Fife 2G 137
Pitsea. Essx 2B 40
Pitsford. Nptn 4E 63
Pitsford Hill. Som 3E 20
Pitsmoor. S Yor 2A 86
Pitstone. Buck 4H 51
Pitt. Hants 4C 24
Pitt Court. Glos 2C 34
Pittentrail. High 3E 164
Pittenweem. Fife 3H 137
Pittington. Dur 5G 115
Pitton. Swan 4D 30
Pitton. Wilts 3H 23
Pittswood. Kent 1H 27
Pittulie. Abers 2G 161
Pittville. Glos 3E 49
Pitversie. Per 2D 136
Pityme. Corn 1D 6
Pity Me. Dur 5F 115
Pixey Green. Suff 3E 67
Pixley. Here 2B 48
Place Newton. N Yor 2C 100
Plaidy. Abers 3E 161
Plaidy. Corn 3G 7
Plain Dealings. Pemb 3E 43
Plains. N Lan 3A 128
Plainsfield. Som 3E 21
Plaish. Shrp 1H 59
Plaistow. Here 2B 48
Plaistow. W Sus 2B 26
Plaitford. Wilts 1A 16
Plas Llwyd. Cnwy 3B 82
Plastow Green. Hants 5D 36
Plas yn Cefn. Den 3C 82
Platt. Kent 5H 39
Platt Bridge. G Man 4E 90
Platt Lane. Shrp 2H 71
Platts Common. S Yor 4D 92
Platt's Heath. Kent 5C 40
Platt, The. E Sus 2G 27
Plawsworth. Dur 5F 115
Plaxtol. Kent 5H 39
Playden. E Sus 3D 28
Playford. Suff 1F 55
Play Hatch. Oxon 4F 37
Playing Place. Corn 4C 6
Playley Green. Glos 2C 48
Plealey. Shrp 5G 71
Plean. Stir 1B 128
Pleasington. Bkbn 2E 91
Pleasley. Derbs 4C 86
Pledgdon Green. Essx 3F 53
Plenmeller. Nmbd 3A 114
Pleshey. Essx 4G 53
Plockton. High 5H 155
Plocrapol. W Isl 8D 171
Ploughfield. Here 1G 47
Plowden. Shrp 2F 59
Ploxgreen. Shrp 5F 71
Pluckley. Kent 1D 28
Plucks Gutter. Kent 4G 41
Plumbland. Cumb 1C 102
Plumgarths. Cumb 5F 103
Plumley. Ches E 3B 84
Plummers Plain. W Sus 3D 26
Plumpton. Cumb 1F 103
Plumpton. E Sus 4E 27
Plumpton. Nptn 1D 50
Plumpton Foot. Cumb 1F 103
Plumpton Green. E Sus 4E 27
Plumpton Head. Cumb 1G 103
Plumstead. G Lon 3F 39
Plumstead. Norf 2D 78
Plumtree. Notts 2D 74
Plumtree Park. Notts 2D 74
Plungar. Leics 2E 75
Plush. Dors 2C 14
Plushabridge. Corn 5D 10
Plwmp. Cdgn 5C 56
Plymouth. Plym 3A 8 & 208
Plympton. Plym 3B 8
Plymstock. Plym 3B 8
Plymtree. Devn 2D 12
Pockley. N Yor 1A 100
Pocklington. E Yor 5C 100
Pode Hole. Linc 3B 76
Podimore. Som 4A 22
Podington. Bed 4G 63
Podmore. Staf 2B 72
Poffley End. Oxon 4B 50
Point Clear. Essx 4D 54
Pointon. Linc 2A 76
Pokesdown. Bour 3G 15
Polbae. Dum 2H 109
Polbain. High 3E 163
Polbathic. Corn 3H 7
Polbeth. W Lot 3D 128
Polbrock. Corn 2E 6
Polchar. High 3C 150
Polebrook. Nptn 2H 63
Pole Elm. Worc 1D 48
Polegate. E Sus 5G 27
Pole Moor. W Yor 3A 92
Poles. High 4E 165
Polesworth. Warw 5G 73
Polglass. High 3E 163
Polgooth. Corn 3D 6
Poling. W Sus 5B 26
Poling Corner. W Sus 5B 26
Polio. High 1B 158
Polkerris. Corn 3E 7
Polla. High 3D 166
Pollard Street. Norf 2F 79
Pollicott. Buck 4F 51
Pollington. E Yor 3G 93
Polloch. High 2B 140
Pollok. Glas 3G 127
Pollokshaws. Glas 3G 127
Pollokshields. Glas 3G 127
Polmaily. High 5G 157
Polmassick. Corn 4D 6
Polmont. Falk 2C 128
Polnessan. E Ayr 3D 116
Polnish. High 5F 147
Polperro. Corn 3G 7
Polruan. Corn 3F 7
Polscoe. Corn 2F 7
Polsham. Som 2A 22
Polskeoch. Dum 4F 117
Polstead. Suff 2C 54
Polstead Heath. Suff 1C 54
Poltesco. Corn 5E 5
Poltimore. Devn 3C 12
Polton. Midl 3G 129
Polwarth. Bord 4D 130
Polyphant. Corn 4C 10
Polzeath. Corn 1D 6
Ponde. Powy 2E 46
Pondersbridge. Cambs 1B 64
Ponders End. G Lon 1E 39
Pond Street. Essx 2E 53
Pondtail. Hants 1G 25
Ponsanooth. Corn 5B 6
Ponsongath. Corn 5E 5
Ponsworthy. Devn 5H 11
Pontamman. Carm 4G 45
Pontantwn. Carm 4E 45
Pontardawe. Neat 5H 45
Pontarddulais. Swan 5F 45
Pontarfynach. Cdgn 3G 57
Pont-ar-gothi. Carm 3F 45
Pont ar Hydfer. Powy 3B 46
Pontarllechau. Carm 3H 45
Pontarsais. Carm 3E 45
Pontblyddyn. Flin 4E 83
Pontbren Llwyd. Rhon 5C 46
Pont Cyfyng. Cnwy 5G 81
Pontdolgoch. Powy 1C 58
Pontefract. W Yor 2E 93
Ponteland. Nmbd 2E 115
Ponterwyd. Cdgn 2G 57
Pontesbury. Shrp 5G 71
Pontesford. Shrp 5G 71
Pontfadog. Wrex 2E 71
Pontfaen. Pemb 1E 43
Pont-faen. Powy 2C 46
Pont-Faen. Shrp 2E 71
Pontgarreg. Cdgn 5C 56
Pont-Henri. Carm 5E 45
Ponthir. Torf 2G 33
Ponthirwaun. Cdgn 1C 44
Pont-iets. Carm 5E 45
Pontllanfraith. Cphy 2E 33
Pontlliw. Swan 5G 45
Pont Llogel. Powy 4C 70
Pontllyfni. Gwyn 5D 80
Pontlottyn. Cphy 5E 46
Pontneddfechan. Neat 5C 46
Pont-newydd. Carm 5E 45
Pont-newydd. Flin 4D 82
Pontnewydd. Torf 2F 33
Ponton. Shet 6E 173
Pont Pen-y-benglog. Gwyn 4F 81
Pontrhydfendigaid. Cdgn 4G 57
Pont Rhyd-y-cyff. B'end 3B 32
Pontrhydyfen. Neat 2A 32
Pont-rhyd-y-groes. Cdgn 3G 57
Pontrhydyrun. Torf 2F 33
Pont-Rhythallt. Gwyn 4E 81
Pontrilas. Here 3G 47
Pontrilas Road. Here 3G 47
Pontrobert. Powy 4D 70
Pont-rug. Gwyn 4E 81
Ponts Green. E Sus 4A 28
Pontshill. Here 3B 48
Pont-Sian. Cdgn 1E 45
Pontsticill. Mer T 4D 46
Pont-Walby. Neat 5B 46
Pontwelly. Carm 2E 45
Pontwgan. Cnwy 3G 81
Pontyates. Carm 5E 45
Pontyberem. Carm 4F 45
Pontybodkin. Flin 5E 83
Pontyclun. Rhon 3D 32
Pontycymer. B'end 2C 32
Pontyglazier. Pemb 1F 43
Pontygwaith. Rhon 2D 32
Pont-y-pant. Cnwy 5G 81
Pontypool. Torf 2G 33
Pontypridd. Rhon 2D 32
Pontypwl. Torf 2G 33
Pontywaun. Cphy 2F 33
Pooksgreen. Hants 1B 16
Pool. Corn 4A 6
Pool. W Yor 5E 99
Poole. N Yor 2E 93
Poole. Pool 3F 15 & 215
Poole. Som 4E 21
Poole Keynes. Glos 2E 35
Poolend. Staf 5D 84
Poolewe. High 5C 162
Pooley Bridge. Cumb 2F 103
Poolfold. Staf 5C 84
Pool Head. Here 5H 59
Pool Hey. Lanc 3B 90
Poolhill. Glos 3C 48
Poolmill. Here 3A 48
Pool o' Muckhart. Clac 3C 136
Pool Quay. Powy 4E 71
Poolsbrook. Derbs 3B 86
Pool Street. Essx 2A 54
Pootings. Kent 1F 27
Pope Hill. Pemb 3D 42
Pope's Hill. Glos 4B 48
Popeswood. Brac 5G 37
Popham. Hants 2D 24
Poplar. G Lon 2E 39
Popley. Hants 1E 25
Porchfield. IOW 3C 16
Porin. High 3F 157
Poringland. Norf 5E 79
Porkellis. Corn 5A 6
Porlock. Som 2B 20
Porlock Weir. Som 2B 20
Portachoillan. Arg 4F 125
Port Adhair Bheinn na Faoghla. W Isl 3C 170
Port Adhair Thirlodh. Arg 4B 138
Port Ann. Arg 1H 125
Port Appin. Arg 4D 140
Port Asgaig. Arg 3C 124
Port Askaig. Arg 3C 124
Portavadie. Arg 3H 125
Port Bannatyne. Arg 3B 126
Portbury. N Som 4A 34
Port Carlisle. Cumb 3D 112
Port Charlotte. Arg 4A 124
Portchester. Hants 2E 16
Port Clarence. Stoc T 2B 106
Port Dinorwig. Gwyn 4E 81
Port Driseach. Arg 2A 126
Port Dundas. Glas 3H 127
Port Ellen. Arg 5B 124
Port Elphinstone. Abers 1E 153
Portencalzie. Dum 2F 109
Portencross. N Ayr 5C 126
Port Erin. IOM 5A 108
Port Erroll. Abers 5H 161
Porter's Fen Corner. Norf 5E 77
Portesham. Dors 4B 14
Portessie. Mor 2B 160
Port e Vullen. IOM 2D 108
Port-Eynon. Swan 4D 30
Portfield. Som 4H 21
Portfield Gate. Pemb 3D 42
Portgate. Devn 4E 11
Port Gaverne. Corn 4A 10
Port Glasgow. Inv 2E 127
Portgordon. Mor 2A 160
Portgower. High 2H 165

Q

R

Rostherne—Sandford

Rostherne. Ches E 2B 84
Rostholme. S Yor 4F 93
Rosthwaite. Cumb 3D 102
Roston. Derbs 1F 73
Rosudgeon. Corn 4C 4
Rosyth. Fife 1E 129
Rothbury. Nmbd 4E 121
Rotherby. Leics 4D 74
Rotherfield. E Sus 3G 27
Rotherfield Greys. Oxon 3F 37
Rotherfield Peppard. Oxon 3F 37
Rotherham. S Yor 1B 86
Rothersthorpe. Nptn 5E 62
Rotherwick. Hants 1F 25
Rothes. Mor 4G 159
Rothesay. Arg 3B 126
Rothienorman. Abers 5E 160
Rothiesholm. Orkn 5F 172
Rothley. Leics 4C 74
Rothley. Nmbd 1D 114
Rothwell. Linc 1A 88
Rothwell. Nptn 2F 63
Rothwell. W Yor 2D 92
Rotsea. E Yor 4E 101
Rottal. Ang 2C 144
Rotten End. Suff 4F 67
Rotten Row. Norf 4C 78
Rotten Row. W Ber 4D 36
Rotten Row. W Mid 3F 61
Rottingdean. Brig 5E 27
Rottington. Cumb 3A 102
Roud. IOW 4D 16
Rougham. Norf 3H 77
Rougham. Suff 4B 66
Rough Close. Staf 2D 72
Rough Common. Kent 5F 41
Roughcote. Staf 1D 72
Rough Haugh. High 4H 167
Rough Hay. Staf 3G 73
Roughlee. Lanc 5H 97
Roughley. W Mid 1F 61
Roughsike. Cumb 2G 113
Roughton. Linc 4B 88
Roughton. Norf 2E 78
Roughton. Shrp 1B 60
Roundbush Green. Essx 4F 53
Roundham. Som 2H 13
Roundhay. W Yor 1D 92
Round Hill. Torb 2F 9
Roundhurst. W Sus 2A 26
Round Maple. Suff 1C 54
Round Oak. Shrp 2F 59
Roundstreet Common. W Sus 3B 26
Roundthwaite. Cumb 4H 103
Roundway. Wilts 5F 35
Roundyhill. Ang 3C 144
Rousdon. Devn 3F 13
Rousham. Oxon 3C 50
Rous Lench. Worc 5E 61
Routh. E Yor 5E 101
Rout's Green. Buck 2F 37
Row. Corn 5A 10
Row. Cumb 1D 96 (nr. Kendal)
Row. Cumb 1H 103 (nr. Penrith)
Rowanburn. Dum 2F 113
Rowanhill. Abers 3H 161
Rowardennan. Stir 4C 134
Rowarth. Derbs 2E 85
Row Ash. Hants 1D 16
Rowberrow. Som 1H 21
Rowde. Wilts 5E 35
Rowden. Devn 3G 11
Rowen. Cnwy 3G 81
Rowfoot. Nmbd 3H 113
Row Green. Essx 3H 53
Row Heath. Essx 4E 55
Rowhedge. Essx 3D 54
Rowhook. W Sus 2C 26
Rowington. Warw 4G 61
Rowland. Derbs 3G 85
Rowland's Castle. Hants 1F 17
Rowlands Gill. Tyne 4E 115
Rowledge. Surr 2G 25
Rowley. Dur 5D 115
Rowley. E Yor 1C 94
Rowley. Shrp 5F 71
Rowley Hill. W Yor 3B 92
Rowley Regis. W Mid 2D 60
Rowlstone. Here 3G 47
Rowly. Surr 1B 26
Rowner. Hants 2D 16
Rowney Green. Worc 3E 61
Rownhams. Hants 1B 16
Rowrah. Cumb 3B 102
Rowsham. Buck 4G 51
Rowsley. Derbs 4G 85
Rowstock. Oxon 3C 36
Rowston. Linc 5H 87
Row, The. Lanc 2D 96
Rowthorne. Derbs 4B 86
Rowton. Ches W 4G 83
Rowton. Shrp 2G 59 (nr. Ludlow)
Rowton. Shrp 4F 71 (nr. Shrewsbury)
Rowton. Telf 4A 72
Row Town. Surr 4B 38
Roxburgh. Bord 1B 120
Roxby. N Lin 3C 94
Roxby. N Yor 3E 107
Roxton. Bed 5A 64
Roxwell. Essx 5G 53
Royal Leamington Spa. Warw 4H 61
Royal Oak. Darl 2F 105
Royal Oak. Lanc 4C 90
Royal Oak. N Yor 2F 101
Royal's Green. Ches E 1A 72
Royal Tunbridge Wells. Kent 2G 27
Royal Wootton Bassett. Wilts 3F 35
Roybridge. High 5E 149
Roydon. Essx 4E 53
Roydon. Norf 2C 66 (nr. Diss)
Roydon. Norf 3G 77 (nr. King's Lynn)
Roydon Hamlet. Essx 5E 53
Royston. Herts 1D 52
Royston. S Yor 3D 92
Royston Water. Som 1F 13
Royton. G Man 4H 91
Ruabon. Wrex 1F 71
Ruaig. Arg 4B 138
Ruan High Lanes. Corn 5D 6
Ruan Lanihorne. Corn 4C 6
Ruan Major. Corn 5E 5
Ruan Minor. Corn 5E 5
Ruarach. High 1B 148
Ruardean. Glos 4B 48
Ruardean Hill. Glos 4B 48
Ruardean Woodside. Glos 4B 48
Rubery. W Mid 3D 61
Ruchazie. Glas 3H 127
Ruckcroft. Cumb 5G 113
Ruckinge. Kent 2E 29
Ruckland. Linc 3C 88
Rucklers Lane. Herts 5A 52
Ruckley. Shrp 5H 71
Rudbaxton. Pemb 2D 42
Rudby. N Yor 4B 106
Ruddington. Notts 2C 74
Rudford. Glos 3C 48
Rudge. Shrp 1C 60
Rudge. Wilts 1D 22
Rudge Heath. Shrp 1B 60
Rudgeway. S Glo 3B 34
Rudgwick. W Sus 2B 26
Rudhall. Here 3B 48
Rudheath. Ches W 3A 84
Rudley Green. Essx 5B 54
Rudloe. Wilts 4D 34
Rudry. Cphy 3E 33
Rudston. E Yor 3E 101
Rudyard. Staf 5D 84
Rufford. Lanc 3C 90
Rufforth. York 4H 99
Rugby. Warw 3C 62
Rugeley. Staf 4E 73
Ruglen. S Ayr 4B 116
Ruilick. High 4H 157
Ruisaurie. High 4G 157
Ruishton. Som 4F 21
Ruisigearraidh. W Isl 1E 170
Ruislip. G Lon 2B 38
Ruislip Common. G Lon 2B 38
Rumbling Bridge. Per 4C 136
Rumburgh. Suff 2F 67
Rumford. Corn 1C 6
Rumford. Falk 2C 128
Rumney. Card 4F 33
Rumwell. Som 4E 21
Runcorn. Hal 2H 83
Runcton. W Sus 2G 17
Runcton Holme. Norf 5F 77
Rundlestone. Devn 5F 11
Runfold. Surr 2G 25
Runhall. Norf 5C 78
Runham. Norf 4G 79
Runnington. Som 4E 20
Runshaw Moor. Lanc 3D 90
Runswick. N Yor 3F 107
Runtaleave. Ang 2B 144
Runwell. Essx 1B 40
Ruscombe. Wok 4F 37
Rushall. Here 2B 48
Rushall. Norf 2D 66
Rushall. W Mid 5E 73
Rushall. Wilts 1G 23
Rushbrooke. Suff 4A 66
Rushbury. Shrp 1H 59
Rushden. Herts 2D 52
Rushden. Nptn 4G 63
Rushenden. Kent 3D 40
Rushford. Devn 5E 11
Rushford. Suff 2B 66
Rush Green. Herts 3C 52
Rushlake Green. E Sus 4H 27
Rushmere. Suff 2G 67
Rushmere St Andrew. Suff 1E 55
Rushmoor. Surr 2G 25
Rushock. Worc 3C 60
Rusholme. G Man 1C 84
Rushton. Ches W 4H 83
Rushton. Nptn 2F 63
Rushton. Shrp 5A 72
Rushton Spencer. Staf 4D 84
Rushwick. Worc 5C 60
Rushyford. Dur 2F 105
Ruskie. Stir 3F 135
Ruskington. Linc 5H 87
Rusland. Cumb 1C 96
Rusper. W Sus 2D 26
Ruspidge. Glos 4B 48
Russell's Water. Oxon 3F 37
Russel's Green. Suff 3E 67
Russ Hill. Surr 1D 26
Russland. Orkn 6C 172
Rusthall. Kent 2G 27
Rustington. W Sus 5B 26
Ruston. N Yor 1D 100
Ruston Parva. E Yor 3E 101
Ruswarp. N Yor 4F 107
Rutherglen. S Lan 3H 127
Ruthernbridge. Corn 2E 6
Ruthin. Den 5D 82
Ruthin. V Glam 4C 32
Ruthrieston. Aber 3G 153
Ruthven. Abers 4C 160
Ruthven. Ang 4B 144
Ruthven. High 5C 158 (nr. Inverness)
Ruthven. High 4B 150 (nr. Kingussie)
Ruthvoes. Corn 2D 6
Ruthwaite. Cumb 1D 102
Ruthwell. Dum 3C 112
Ruxton Green. Here 4A 48
Ruyton-XI-Towns. Shrp 3F 71
Ryal. Nmbd 2D 114
Ryall. Dors 3H 13
Ryall. Worc 1D 48
Ryarsh. Kent 5A 40
Rychraggan. High 5G 157
Rydal. Cumb 4E 103
Ryde. IOW 3D 16
Rye. E Sus 3D 28
Ryecroft Gate. Staf 4D 84
Ryeford. Here 3B 48
Rye Foreign. E Sus 3D 28
Rye Harbour. E Sus 4D 28
Ryehill. E Yor 2F 95
Rye Street. Worc 2C 48
Ryhall. Rut 4H 75
Ryhill. W Yor 3D 93
Ryhope. Tyne 4H 115
Ryhope Colliery. Tyne 4H 115
Rylands. Notts 2C 74
Rylstone. N Yor 4B 98
Ryme Intrinseca. Dors 1A 14
Ryther. N Yor 1F 93
Ryton. Glos 2C 48
Ryton. N Yor 2B 100
Ryton. Shrp 5B 72
Ryton. Tyne 3E 115
Ryton. Warw 2A 62
Ryton-on-Dunsmore. Warw 3A 62
Ryton Woodside. Tyne 3E 115

S

Saasaig. High 3E 147
Sabden. Lanc 1F 91
Sacombe. Herts 4D 52
Sacriston. Dur 5F 115
Sadberge. Darl 3A 106
Saddell. Arg 2B 122
Saddington. Leics 1D 62
Saddle Bow. Norf 4F 77
Saddlescombe. W Sus 4D 26
Saddleworth. G Man 4H 91
Sadgill. Cumb 4F 103
Saffron Walden. Essx 2F 53
Sageston. Pemb 4E 43
Saham Hills. Norf 5B 78
Saham Toney. Norf 5A 78
Saighdinis. W Isl 2D 170
Saighton. Ches W 4G 83
Sain Dunwyd. V Glam 5C 32
Sain Hilari. V Glam 4D 32
St Abbs. Bord 3F 131
St Agnes. Corn 3B 6
St Albans. Herts 5B 52
St Allen. Corn 3C 6
St Andrews. Fife 2H 137 & 209
St Andrews Major. V Glam 4E 33
St Anne's. Lanc 2B 90
St Ann's. Dum 5C 118
St Ann's Chapel. Corn 5E 11
St Ann's Chapel. Devn 4C 8
St Anthony. Corn 5C 6
St Anthony-in-Meneage. Corn 4E 5
St Arvans. Mon 2A 34
St Asaph. Den 3C 82
St Athan. V Glam 5D 32
Sain Tathan. V Glam 5D 32
St Austell. Corn 3E 6
St Bartholomew's Hill. Wilts 4E 23
St Bees. Cumb 3A 102
St Blazey. Corn 3E 7
St Blazey Gate. Corn 3E 7
St Boswells. Bord 1A 120
St Breock. Corn 1D 6
St Breward. Corn 5A 10
St Briavels. Glos 5A 48
St Brides. Pemb 3B 42
St Bride's Major. V Glam 4B 32
St Bride's Netherwent. Mon 3H 33
St Bride's-super-Ely. V Glam 4D 32
St Brides Wentlooge. Newp 3F 33
St Budeaux. Plym 3A 8
Saintbury. Glos 2G 49
St Buryan. Corn 4B 4
St Catherine. Bath 4C 34
St Catherines. Arg 3A 134
St Clears. Carm 3G 43
St Cleer. Corn 2G 7
St Clement. Corn 4C 6
St Clether. Corn 4C 10
St Colmac. Arg 3B 126
St Columb Major. Corn 2D 6
St Columb Minor. Corn 2C 6
St Columb Road. Corn 3D 6
St Combs. Abers 2H 161
St Cross. Hants 4C 24
St Cross South Elmham. Suff 2E 67
St Cyrus. Abers 2G 145
St Davids. Pemb 2B 42
St David's. Per 1B 136
St Day. Corn 4B 6
St Dennis. Corn 3D 6
St Dogmaels. Pemb 1B 44
St Dominick. Corn 2H 7
St Donat's. V Glam 5C 32
St Edith's Marsh. Wilts 5E 35
St Endellion. Corn 1D 6
St Enoder. Corn 3C 6
St Erme. Corn 4C 6
St Erney. Corn 3H 7
St Erth. Corn 3C 4
St Erth Praze. Corn 3C 4
St Ervan. Corn 1C 6
St Eval. Corn 2C 6
St Ewe. Corn 4D 6
St Fagans. Card 4E 32
St Fergus. Abers 3H 161
St Fillans. Per 1F 135
St Florence. Pemb 4E 43
St Gennys. Corn 3B 10
St George. Cnwy 3B 82
St Georges. N Som 5G 33
St Georges. V Glam 4D 32
St George's Hill. Surr 4B 38
St Germans. Corn 3H 7
St Giles in the Wood. Devn 1F 11
St Giles on the Heath. Devn 3D 10
St Giles's Hill. Hants 4C 24
St Gluvias. Corn 5B 6
St Harmon. Powy 3B 58
St Helena. Warw 5G 73
St Helen Auckland. Dur 2E 105
St Helens. Cumb 1B 102
St Helen's. E Sus 4C 28
St Helens. IOW 4E 17
St Helens. Mers 1G 83
St Hilary. Corn 3C 4
St Hilary. V Glam 4D 32
Saint Hill. Devn 2D 12
Saint Hill. W Sus 2E 27
St Illtyd. Blae 5F 47
St Ippolyts. Herts 3B 52
St Ishmael. Carm 5D 44
St Ishmael's. Pemb 4C 42
St Issey. Corn 1D 6
St Ive. Corn 2H 7
St Ives. Cambs 3C 64
St Ives. Corn 2C 4
St Ives. Dors 2G 15
St James' End. Nptn 4E 63
St James South Elmham. Suff 2F 67
St Jidgey. Corn 2D 6
St John. Corn 3A 8
St John's. IOM 3B 108
St Johns. Worc 5C 60
St John's Chapel. Devn 4F 19
St John's Chapel. Dur 1B 104
St John's Fen End. Norf 4E 77
St John's Hall. Dur 1D 104
St John's Town of Dalry. Dum 1D 110
St Judes. IOM 2C 108
St Just. Corn 5C 6 (nr. Falmouth)
St Just. Corn 3A 4 (nr. Penzance)
St Just in Roseland. Corn 5C 6
St Katherines. Abers 5E 161
St Keverne. Corn 4E 5
St Kew. Corn 5A 10
St Kew Highway. Corn 5A 10
St Keyne. Corn 2G 7
St Lawrence. Corn 2E 7
St Lawrence. Essx 5C 54
St Lawrence. IOW 5D 16
St Leonards. Buck 5H 51
St Leonards. Dors 2G 15
St Leonards. E Sus 5B 28
St Levan. Corn 4A 4
St Lythans. V Glam 4E 32
St Mabyn. Corn 5A 10
St Madoes. Per 1D 136
St Margarets. Here 2G 47
St Margaret's. Herts 4A 52 (nr. Hemel Hempstead)
St Margarets. Herts 4D 53 (nr. Hoddesdon)
St Margaret's. Wilts 5G 35
St Margaret's at Cliffe. Kent 1H 29
St Margaret's Hope. Orkn 8D 172
St Margaret South Elmham. Suff 2F 67
St Mark's. IOM 4B 108
St Martin. Corn 4E 5 (nr. Helston)
St Martin. Corn 3G 7 (nr. Looe)
St Martins. Per 5A 144
St Martin's. Shrp 2F 71
St Mary Bourne. Hants 1C 24
St Marychurch. Torb 2F 9
St Mary Church. V Glam 4D 32
St Mary Cray. G Lon 4F 39
St Mary Hill. V Glam 4C 32
St Mary Hoo. Medw 3C 40
St Mary in the Marsh. Kent 3E 29
St Mary's. Orkn 7D 172
St Mary's Bay. Kent 3E 29
St Maughan's Green. Mon 4H 47
St Mawes. Corn 5C 6
St Mawgan. Corn 2C 6
St Mellion. Corn 2H 7
St Mellons. Card 3F 33
St Merryn. Corn 1C 6
St Mewan. Corn 3D 6
St Michael Caerhays. Corn 4D 6
St Michael Penkevil. Corn 4C 6
St Michaels. Kent 2C 28
St Michaels. Torb 3E 9
St Michaels. Worc 4H 59
St Michael's on Wyre. Lanc 5D 96
St Michael South Elmham. Suff 2F 67
St Minver. Corn 1D 6
St Monans. Fife 3H 137
St Neot. Corn 2F 7
St Neots. Cambs 4A 64
St Newlyn East. Corn 3C 6
St Nicholas. Pemb 1D 42
St Nicholas. V Glam 4D 32
St Nicholas at Wade. Kent 4G 41
St Nicholas South Elmham. Suff 2F 67
St Ninians. Stir 4H 135
St Olaves. Norf 1G 67
St Osyth. Essx 4E 54
St Osyth Heath. Essx 4E 55
St Owen's Cross. Here 3A 48
St Paul's Cray. G Lon 4F 39
St Paul's Walden. Herts 3B 52
St Peter's. Kent 4H 41
St Peter The Great. Worc 5C 60
St Petrox. Pemb 5D 42
St Pinnock. Corn 2G 7
St Quivox. S Ayr 2C 116
St Ruan. Corn 5E 5
St Stephen. Corn 3D 6
St Stephens. Corn 4D 10 (nr. Launceston)
St Stephens. Corn 3A 8 (nr. Saltash)
St Teath. Corn 4A 10
St Thomas. Devn 3C 12
St Thomas. Swan 3F 31
St Tudy. Corn 5A 10
St Twynnells. Pemb 5D 42
St Veep. Corn 3F 7
St Vigeans. Ang 4F 145
St Wenn. Corn 2D 6
St Weonards. Here 3H 47
St Winnolls. Corn 3H 7
St Winnow. Corn 3F 7
Salcombe. Devn 5D 8
Salcombe Regis. Devn 4E 13
Salcott. Essx 4C 54
Sale. G Man 1B 84
Saleby. Linc 3D 88
Sale Green. Worc 5D 60
Salehurst. E Sus 3B 28
Salem. Carm 3G 45
Salem. Cdgn 2F 57
Salen. Arg 4G 139
Salen. High 2A 140
Salesbury. Lanc 1E 91
Saleway. Worc 5D 60
Salford. C Beds 2H 51
Salford. G Man 1C 84 & **Manchester 201**
Salford. Oxon 3A 50
Salford Priors. Warw 5E 61
Salfords. Surr 1D 27
Salhouse. Norf 4F 79
Saligo. Arg 3A 124
Saline. Fife 4C 136
Salisbury. Wilts 3G 23 & 210
Salkeld Dykes. Cumb 1G 103
Sallachan. High 2D 141
Sallachy. High 3C 164 (nr. Lairg)
Sallachy. High 5B 156 (nr. Stromeferry)
Salle. Norf 3D 78
Salmonby. Linc 3C 88
Salmond's Muir. Ang 5E 145
Salperton. Glos 3F 49
Salph End. Bed 5H 63
Salsburgh. N Lan 3B 128
Salt. Staf 3D 72
Salta. Cumb 5B 112
Saltaire. W Yor 1B 92
Saltash. Corn 3A 8
Saltburn. High 2B 158
Saltburn-by-the-Sea. Red C 2D 106
Saltby. Leics 3F 75
Saltcoats. Cumb 5B 102
Saltcoats. N Ayr 5D 126
Saltdean. Brig 5E 27
Salt End. E Yor 2E 95
Salter. Lanc 3F 97
Salterforth. Lanc 5A 98
Salters Lode. Norf 5E 77
Salterswall. Ches W 4A 84
Salterton. Wilts 3G 23
Saltfleet. Linc 1D 88
Saltfleetby All Saints. Linc 1D 88
Saltfleetby St Clements. Linc 1D 88
Saltfleetby St Peter. Linc 2D 88
Saltford. Bath 5B 34
Salthouse. Norf 1C 78
Saltmarshe. E Yor 2A 94
Saltmead. Card 4E 33
Saltness. Orkn 9B 172
Saltness. Shet 7D 173
Saltney. Flin 4F 83
Salton. N Yor 2B 100
Saltrens. Devn 4E 19
Saltwick. Nmbd 2E 115
Saltwood. Kent 2F 29
Salum. Arg 4B 138
Salwarpe. Worc 4C 60
Salwayash. Dors 3H 13
Samalaman. High 1A 140
Sambourne. Warw 4E 61
Sambourne. Wilts 2D 22
Sambrook. Telf 3B 72
Samhia. W Isl 2C 170
Samlesbury. Lanc 1D 90
Samlesbury Bottoms. Lanc 2E 90
Sampford Arundel. Som 1E 12
Sampford Brett. Som 2D 20
Sampford Courtenay. Devn 2G 11
Sampford Peverell. Devn 1D 12
Sampford Spiney. Devn 5F 11
Samsonslane. Orkn 5F 172
Samuelston. E Lot 2A 130
Sanaigmore. Arg 2A 124
Sancreed. Corn 4B 4
Sancton. E Yor 1C 94
Sand. High 4D 162
Sand. Shet 7E 173
Sand. Som 2H 21
Sandaig. Arg 4A 138
Sandaig. High 3F 147
Sandale. Cumb 5D 112
Sandal Magna. W Yor 3D 92
Sandavore. High 5C 146
Sanday Airport. Orkn 3F 172
Sandbach. Ches E 4B 84
Sandbank. Arg 1C 126
Sandbanks. Pool 4F 15
Sandend. Abers 2C 160
Sanderstead. G Lon 4E 39
Sandfields. Neat 3G 31
Sandford. Cumb 3A 104
Sandford. Devn 2B 12
Sandford. Dors 4E 15

Sandford—Shenleybury

Sandford. *Hants* 2G 15
Sandford. *IOW* 4D 16
Sandford. *N Som* 1H 21
Sandford. *Shrp* 3F 71 (nr. Oswestry)
Sandford. *Shrp* 2H 71 (nr. Whitchurch)
Sandford. *S Lan* 5A 128
Sandfordhill. *Abers* 4H 161
Sandford-on-Thames. *Oxon* 5D 50
Sandford Orcas. *Dors* 4B 22
Sandford St Martin. *Oxon* 3C 50
Sandgate. *Kent* 2F 29
Sandgreen. *Dum* 4C 110
Sandhaven. *Abers* 2G 161
Sandhead. *Dum* 4F 109
Sandhill. *Cambs* 2E 65
Sandhills. *Dors* 1B 14
Sandhills. *Oxon* 5D 50
Sandhills. *Surr* 2A 26
Sandhoe. *Nmbd* 3C 114
Sand Hole. *E Yor* 1B 94
Sandholme. *E Yor* 1B 94
Sandholme. *Linc* 2C 76
Sandhurst. *Brac* 5G 37
Sandhurst. *Glos* 3D 48
Sandhurst. *Kent* 3B 28
Sandhurst Cross. *Kent* 3B 28
Sandhutton. *N Yor* 1F 99 (nr. Thirsk)
Sand Hutton. *N Yor* 4A 100 (nr. York)
Sandiacre. *Derbs* 2B 74
Sandilands. *Linc* 2E 89
Sandiway. *Ches W* 3A 84
Sandleheath. *Hants* 1G 15
Sandling. *Kent* 5B 40
Sandlow Green. *Ches E* 4B 84
Sandness. *Shet* 6C 173
Sandon. *Essx* 5H 53
Sandon. *Herts* 2D 52
Sandon. *Staf* 3D 72
Sandonbank. *Staf* 3D 72
Sandown. *IOW* 4D 16
Sandplace. *Corn* 3G 7
Sandridge. *Herts* 4B 52
Sandringham. *Norf* 3F 77
Sandsend. *N Yor* 3F 107
Sandside. *Cumb* 2C 96
Sandsound. *Shet* 7E 173
Sands, The. *Surr* 2G 25
Sandtoft. *N Lin* 4H 93
Sandvoe. *Shet* 2E 173
Sandway. *Kent* 5C 40
Sandwich. *Kent* 5H 41
Sandwick. *Cumb* 3F 103
Sandwick. *Orkn* 6B 172 (on Mainland)
Sandwick. *Orkn* 9D 172 (on South Ronaldsay)
Sandwick. *Shet* 9F 173 (on Mainland)
Sandwick. *Shet* 5G 173 (on Whalsay)
Sandwith. *Cumb* 3A 102
Sandy. *Carm* 5E 45
Sandy. *C Beds* 1B 52
Sandy Bank. *Linc* 5B 88
Sandycroft. *Flin* 4F 83
Sandy Cross. *Here* 5A 60
Sandygate. *Devn* 5B 12
Sandygate. *IOM* 2C 108
Sandy Haven. *Pemb* 4C 42
Sandyhills. *Dum* 4F 111
Sandylands. *Lanc* 3D 96
Sandylane. *Swan* 4E 31
Sandy Lane. *Wilts* 5E 35
Sandystones. *Bord* 2H 119
Sandyway. *Here* 3H 47
Sangobeg. *High* 2E 167
Sangomore. *High* 2E 166
Sankyn's Green. *Worc* 4B 60
Sanna. *High* 2F 139
Sanndabhaig. *W Isl* 4G 171 (on Isle of Lewis)
Sanndabhaig. *W Isl* 4D 170 (on South Uist)
Sannox. *N Ayr* 5B 126
Sanquhar. *Dum* 3G 117
Santon. *Cumb* 4B 102
Santon Bridge. *Cumb* 4C 102
Santon Downham. *Suff* 2H 65
Sapcote. *Leics* 1B 62
Sapey Common. *Here* 4B 60
Sapiston. *Suff* 3B 66
Sapley. *Cambs* 3B 64
Sapperton. *Derbs* 2F 73
Sapperton. *Glos* 5E 49
Sapperton. *Linc* 2H 75
Saracen's Head. *Linc* 3C 76
Sarclet. *High* 4F 169
Sardis. *Carm* 5F 45
Sardis. *Pemb* 4D 42 (nr. Milford Haven)
Sardis. *Pemb* 4F 43 (nr. Tenby)
Sarisbury. *Hants* 2D 16
Sarn. *B'end* 3C 32
Sarn. *Powy* 1E 58
Sarnau. *Carm* 3E 45
Sarnau. *Cdgn* 5C 56
Sarnau. *Gwyn* 2B 70
Sarnau. *Powy* 2D 46 (nr. Brecon)
Sarnau. *Powy* 4E 71 (nr. Welshpool)
Sarn Bach. *Gwyn* 3C 68
Sarnesfield. *Here* 5F 59
Sarn Meyllteyrn. *Gwyn* 2B 68
Saron. *Carm* 4G 45 (nr. Ammanford)
Saron. *Carm* 2D 45 (nr. Newcastle Emlyn)
Saron. *Gwyn* 4E 81 (nr. Bethel)
Saron. *Gwyn* 5D 80 (nr. Bontnewydd)
Sarratt. *Herts* 1B 38
Sarre. *Kent* 4G 41
Sarsden. *Oxon* 3A 50
Satley. *Dur* 5E 115
Satron. *N Yor* 5C 104
Satterleigh. *Devn* 4G 19
Satterthwaite. *Cumb* 5E 103
Satwell. *Oxon* 3F 37
Sauchen. *Abers* 2D 152
Saucher. *Per* 5A 144
Saughall. *Ches W* 3F 83
Saughtree. *Bord* 5H 119
Saul. *Glos* 5C 48
Saundby. *Notts* 2E 87
Saundersfoot. *Pemb* 4F 43
Saunderton. *Buck* 5F 51
Saunderton Lee. *Buck* 2G 37
Saunton. *Devn* 3E 19
Sausthorpe. *Linc* 4C 88
Saval. *High* 3C 164
Saverley Green. *Staf* 2D 72
Sawbridge. *Warw* 4C 62
Sawbridgeworth. *Herts* 4E 53
Sawdon. *N Yor* 1D 100
Sawley. *Derbs* 2B 74
Sawley. *Lanc* 5G 97
Sawley. *N Yor* 3E 99
Sawston. *Cambs* 1E 53
Sawtry. *Cambs* 2A 64
Saxby. *Leics* 3F 75
Saxby. *Linc* 2H 87
Saxby All Saints. *N Lin* 3C 94
Saxelby. *Leics* 3D 74
Saxelbye. *Leics* 3D 74
Saxham Street. *Suff* 4C 66
Saxilby. *Linc* 3F 87
Saxlingham. *Norf* 2C 78
Saxlingham Green. *Norf* 1E 67
Saxlingham Nethergate. *Norf* 1E 67
Saxlingham Thorpe. *Norf* 1E 66
Saxmundham. *Suff* 4F 67
Saxondale. *Notts* 1D 74
Saxon Street. *Cambs* 5F 65
Saxtead. *Suff* 4E 67
Saxtead Green. *Suff* 4E 67
Saxthorpe. *Norf* 2D 78
Saxton. *N Yor* 1E 93
Sayers Common. *W Sus* 4D 26
Scackleton. *N Yor* 2A 100
Scadabhagh. *W Isl* 8D 171
Scaftworth. *Notts* 1D 86
Scagglethorpe. *N Yor* 2C 100
Scaitcliffe. *Lanc* 2F 91
Scaladal. *W Isl* 6D 171
Scalasaig. *Arg* 4A 132
Scalby. *E Yor* 2B 94
Scalby. *N Yor* 5H 107
Scalby Mills. *N Yor* 5H 107
Scaldwell. *Nptn* 3E 63
Scaleby. *Cumb* 3F 113
Scaleby Hill. *Cumb* 3F 113
Scale Houses. *Cumb* 5G 113
Scales. *Cumb* 2B 96 (nr. Barrow-in-Furness)
Scales. *Cumb* 2E 103 (nr. Keswick)
Scalford. *Leics* 3E 75
Scaling. *Red C* 3E 107
Scaling Dam. *Red C* 3E 107
Scalloway. *Shet* 8E 173
Scalpaigh. *W Isl* 8E 171
Scalpay House. *High* 1E 147
Scamblesby. *Linc* 3B 88
Scamodale. *High* 1C 140
Scampston. *N Yor* 2C 100
Scampton. *Linc* 3G 87
Scaniport. *High* 5A 158
Scapa. *Orkn* 7D 172
Scapegoat Hill. *W Yor* 3A 92
Scar. *Orkn* 3F 172
Scarasta. *W Isl* 8C 171
Scarborough. *N Yor* 1E 101
Scarcliffe. *Derbs* 4B 86
Scarcroft. *W Yor* 5F 99
Scardroy. *High* 3E 156
Scarfskerry. *High* 1E 169
Scargill. *Dur* 3D 104
Scarinish. *Arg* 4B 138
Scarisbrick. *Lanc* 3B 90
Scarning. *Norf* 4B 78
Scarrington. *Notts* 1E 75
Scarth Hill. *Lanc* 4C 90
Scartho. *NE Lin* 4F 95
Scarvister. *Shet* 7E 173
Scatness. *Shet* 10E 173
Scatwell. *High* 3F 157
Scaur. *Dum* 4F 111
Scawby. *N Lin* 4C 94
Scawby Brook. *N Lin* 4C 94
Scawsby. *S Yor* 4F 93
Scawton. *N Yor* 1H 99
Scayne's Hill. *W Sus* 3E 27
Scethrog. *Powy* 3E 46
Scholar Green. *Ches E* 5C 84
Scholes. *G Man* 4D 90
Scholes. *W Yor* 2B 92 (nr. Bradford)
Scholes. *W Yor* 4B 92 (nr. Holmfirth)
Scholes. *W Yor* 1D 93 (nr. Leeds)
Scholey Hill. *W Yor* 2D 93
School Aycliffe. *Dur* 2F 105
School Green. *Ches W* 4A 84
School Green. *Essx* 2H 53
Scissett. *W Yor* 3C 92
Scleddau. *Pemb* 1D 42
Scofton. *Notts* 2D 86
Scole. *Norf* 3D 66
Scolpaig. *W Isl* 1C 170
Scolton. *Pemb* 2D 43
Scone. *Per* 1D 136
Sconser. *High* 5E 155
Scoonie. *Fife* 3F 137
Scopwick. *Linc* 5H 87
Scoraig. *High* 4E 163
Scorborough. *E Yor* 5E 101
Scorrier. *Corn* 4B 6
Scorriton. *Devn* 2D 8
Scorton. *Lanc* 5E 97
Scorton. *N Yor* 4F 105
Sco Ruston. *Norf* 3E 79
Scotbheinn. *W Isl* 3D 170
Scotby. *Cumb* 4F 113
Scotch Corner. *N Yor* 4F 105
Scotforth. *Lanc* 3D 97
Scot Hay. *Staf* 1C 72
Scothern. *Linc* 3H 87
Scotland End. *Oxon* 2B 50
Scotlandwell. *Per* 3D 136
Scot Lane End. *G Man* 4E 91
Scotsburn. *High* 1B 158
Scotsburn. *Mor* 2G 159
Scotsdike. *Cumb* 2E 113
Scot's Gap. *Nmbd* 1D 114
Scotstoun. *Glas* 3G 127
Scotstown. *High* 2C 140
Scotswood. *Tyne* 3F 115
Scottas. *High* 3F 147
Scotter. *Linc* 4B 94
Scotterthorpe. *Linc* 4B 94
Scottlethorpe. *Linc* 3H 75
Scotton. *Linc* 1F 87
Scotton. *N Yor* 5E 105 (nr. Catterick Garrison)
Scotton. *N Yor* 4F 99 (nr. Harrogate)
Scottow. *Norf* 3E 79
Scoulton. *Norf* 5B 78
Scounslow Green. *Staf* 3E 73
Scourie. *High* 4B 166
Scourie More. *High* 4B 166
Scousburgh. *Shet* 10E 173
Scout Green. *Cumb* 4G 103
Scouthead. *G Man* 4H 91
Scrabster. *High* 1C 168
Scrafield. *Linc* 4C 88
Scrainwood. *Nmbd* 4D 121
Scrane End. *Linc* 1C 76
Scraptoft. *Leic* 5D 74
Scratby. *Norf* 4H 79
Scrayingham. *N Yor* 3B 100
Scredington. *Linc* 1H 75
Scremby. *Linc* 4D 88
Scremerston. *Nmbd* 5G 131
Screveton. *Notts* 1E 75
Scrivelsby. *Linc* 4B 88
Scriven. *N Yor* 4F 99
Scronkey. *Lanc* 5D 96
Scrooby. *Notts* 1D 86
Scropton. *Derbs* 2F 73
Scrub Hill. *Linc* 5B 88
Scruton. *N Yor* 5F 105
Scuggate. *Cumb* 2F 113
Sculamus. *High* 1E 147
Sculcoates. *Hull* 1D 94
Sculthorpe. *Norf* 2A 78
Scunthorpe. *N Lin* 3B 94
Scurlage. *Swan* 4D 30
Sea. *Som* 1G 13
Seaborough. *Dors* 2H 13
Seabridge. *Staf* 1C 72
Seabrook. *Kent* 2F 29
Seaburn. *Tyne* 3H 115
Seacombe. *Mers* 1F 83
Seacroft. *Linc* 4E 89
Seacroft. *W Yor* 1D 92
Seadyke. *Linc* 2C 76
Seafield. *High* 5G 165
Seafield. *Midl* 3F 129
Seafield. *S Ayr* 2C 116
Seafield. *W Lot* 3D 128
Seaford. *E Sus* 5F 27
Seaforth. *Mers* 1F 83
Seagrave. *Leics* 4D 74
Seaham. *Dur* 5H 115
Seahouses. *Nmbd* 1G 121
Seal. *Kent* 5G 39
Sealand. *Flin* 4F 83
Seale. *Surr* 2G 25
Seamer. *N Yor* 1E 101 (nr. Scarborough)
Seamer. *N Yor* 3B 106 (nr. Stokesley)
Seamill. *N Ayr* 5C 126
Sea Mills. *Bris* 4A 34
Sea Palling. *Norf* 3G 79
Searby. *Linc* 4D 94
Seasalter. *Kent* 4E 41
Seascale. *Cumb* 4B 102
Seaside. *Per* 1E 137
Seater. *High* 1F 169
Seathorne. *Linc* 4E 89
Seathwaite. *Cumb* 3D 102 (nr. Buttermere)
Seathwaite. *Cumb* 5D 102 (nr. Ulpha)
Seatle. *Cumb* 1C 96
Seatoller. *Cumb* 3D 102
Seaton. *Corn* 3H 7
Seaton. *Cumb* 1B 102
Seaton. *Devn* 3F 13
Seaton. *Dur* 4G 115
Seaton. *E Yor* 5F 101
Seaton. *Nmbd* 2G 115
Seaton. *Rut* 1G 63
Seaton Burn. *Tyne* 2F 115
Seaton Carew. *Hart* 2C 106
Seaton Delaval. *Nmbd* 2G 115
Seaton Junction. *Devn* 3F 13
Seaton Ross. *E Yor* 5B 100
Seaton Sluice. *Nmbd* 2G 115
Seatown. *Abers* 2C 160
Seatown. *Dors* 3H 13
Seatown. *Mor* 2C 160 (nr. Cullen)
Seatown. *Mor* 1G 159 (nr. Lossiemouth)
Seave Green. *N Yor* 4C 106
Seaview. *IOW* 3E 17
Seaville. *Cumb* 4C 112
Seavington St Mary. *Som* 1H 13
Seavington St Michael. *Som* 1H 13
Seawick. *Essx* 4E 55
Sebastopol. *Torf* 2F 33
Sebergham. *Cumb* 5E 113
Seckington. *Warw* 5G 73
Second Coast. *High* 4D 162
Sedbergh. *Cumb* 5H 103
Sedbury. *Glos* 2A 34
Sedbusk. *N Yor* 5B 104
Sedgeberrow. *Worc* 2F 49
Sedgebrook. *Linc* 2F 75
Sedgefield. *Dur* 2A 106
Sedgeford. *Norf* 2G 77
Sedgehill. *Wilts* 4D 22
Sedgley. *W Mid* 1D 60
Sedgwick. *Cumb* 1E 97
Sedlescombe. *E Sus* 4B 28
Seend. *Wilts* 5E 35
Seend Cleeve. *Wilts* 5E 35
Seer Green. *Buck* 1A 38
Seething. *Norf* 1F 67
Sefster. *Shet* 6E 173
Sefton. *Mers* 4B 90
Sefton Park. *Mers* 2F 83
Segensworth. *Hants* 2D 16
Seggat. *Abers* 4E 161
Seghill. *Nmbd* 2F 115
Seifton. *Shrp* 2G 59
Seighford. *Staf* 3C 72
Seilebost. *W Isl* 8C 171
Seisdon. *Staf* 1C 60
Seisiadar. *W Isl* 4H 171
Selattyn. *Shrp* 2E 71
Selborne. *Hants* 3F 25
Selby. *N Yor* 1G 93
Selham. *W Sus* 3A 26
Selkirk. *Bord* 2G 119
Sellack. *Here* 3A 48
Sellafirth. *Shet* 2G 173
Sellick's Green. *Som* 1F 13
Sellindge. *Kent* 2F 29
Selling. *Kent* 5E 41
Sells Green. *Wilts* 5E 35
Selly Oak. *W Mid* 2E 61
Selmeston. *E Sus* 5G 27
Selsdon. *G Lon* 4E 39
Selsey. *W Sus* 3G 17
Selsfield Common. *W Sus* 2E 27
Selside. *Cumb* 5G 103
Selside. *N Yor* 2G 97
Selsley. *Glos* 5D 48
Selsted. *Kent* 1G 29
Selston. *Notts* 5B 86
Selworthy. *Som* 2C 20
Semblister. *Shet* 6E 173
Semer. *Suff* 1D 54
Semington. *Wilts* 5D 35
Semley. *Wilts* 4D 23
Sempringham. *Linc* 2A 76
Send. *Surr* 5B 38
Send Marsh. *Surr* 5B 38
Senghenydd. *Cphy* 2E 32
Sennen. *Corn* 4A 4
Sennen Cove. *Corn* 4A 4
Sennicotts. *W Sus* 2G 17
Sennybridge. *Powy* 3C 46
Serlby. *Notts* 2D 86
Sessay. *N Yor* 2G 99
Setchey. *Norf* 4F 77
Setley. *Hants* 2B 16
Setter. *Shet* 3F 173
Settiscarth. *Orkn* 6C 172
Settle. *N Yor* 3H 97
Settrington. *N Yor* 2C 100
Seven Ash. *Som* 3E 21
Sevenhampton. *Glos* 3F 49
Sevenhampton. *Swin* 2H 35
Sevenoaks. *Kent* 5G 39
Sevenoaks Weald. *Kent* 5G 39
Seven Sisters. *Neat* 5B 46
Seven Springs. *Glos* 4E 49
Severn Beach. *S Glo* 3A 34
Severn Stoke. *Worc* 1D 48
Sevington. *Kent* 1E 29
Sewards End. *Essx* 2F 53
Sewardstone. *Essx* 1E 39
Sewell. *C Beds* 3H 51
Sewerby. *E Yor* 3G 101
Seworgan. *Corn* 5B 6
Sewstern. *Leics* 3F 75
Sgallairidh. *W Isl* 9B 170
Sgarasta Mhor. *W Isl* 8C 171
Sgiogarstaigh. *W Isl* 1H 171
Sgreadan. *Arg* 4A 132
Shabbington. *Buck* 5E 51
Shackerley. *Shrp* 5C 72
Shackerstone. *Leics* 5A 74
Shackleford. *Surr* 1A 26
Shadforth. *Dur* 5G 115
Shadingfield. *Suff* 2G 67
Shadoxhurst. *Kent* 2D 28
Shadsworth. *Bkbn* 2E 91
Shadwell. *Norf* 2B 66
Shadwell. *W Yor* 1D 92
Shaftesbury. *Dors* 4D 22
Shafton. *S Yor* 3D 93
Shafton Two Gates. *S Yor* 3D 93
Shaggs. *Dors* 4D 14
Shakesfield. *Glos* 2B 48
Shalbourne. *Wilts* 5B 36
Shalcombe. *IOW* 4B 16
Shalden. *Hants* 2E 25
Shaldon. *Devn* 5C 12
Shalfleet. *IOW* 4C 16
Shalford. *Essx* 3H 53
Shalford. *Surr* 1B 26
Shalford Green. *Essx* 3H 53
Shallowford. *Devn* 2H 19
Shallowford. *Staf* 3C 72
Shalmsford Street. *Kent* 5E 41
Shalstone. *Buck* 2E 51
Shamley Green. *Surr* 1B 26
Shandon. *Arg* 1D 126
Shandwick. *High* 1C 158
Shangton. *Leics* 1E 62
Shankhouse. *Nmbd* 2F 115
Shanklin. *IOW* 4D 16
Shannochie. *N Ayr* 3D 122
Shap. *Cumb* 3G 103
Shapwick. *Dors* 2E 15
Shapwick. *Som* 3H 21
Sharcott. *Wilts* 1G 23
Shardlow. *Derbs* 2B 74
Shareshill. *Staf* 5D 72
Sharlston. *W Yor* 3D 93
Sharlston Common. *W Yor* 3D 93
Sharnal Street. *Medw* 3B 40
Sharnbrook. *Bed* 5G 63
Sharneyford. *Lanc* 2G 91
Sharnford. *Leics* 1B 62
Sharnhill Green. *Dors* 2C 14
Sharoe Green. *Lanc* 1D 90
Sharow. *N Yor* 2F 99
Sharpenhoe. *C Beds* 2A 52
Sharperton. *Nmbd* 4D 120
Sharpness. *Glos* 5B 48
Sharp Street. *Norf* 3F 79
Sharpthorne. *W Sus* 2E 27
Sharrington. *Norf* 2C 78
Shatterford. *Worc* 2B 60
Shatton. *Derbs* 2G 85
Shaugh Prior. *Devn* 2B 8
Shavington. *Ches E* 5B 84
Shaw. *G Man* 4H 91
Shaw. *W Ber* 5C 36
Shaw. *Wilts* 5D 35
Shawbirch. *Telf* 4A 72
Shawbury. *Shrp* 3H 71
Shawdon Hall. *Nmbd* 3E 121
Shawell. *Leics* 2C 62
Shawford. *Hants* 4C 24
Shawforth. *Lanc* 2G 91
Shaw Green. *Lanc* 3D 90
Shawhead. *Dum* 2F 111
Shaw Mills. *N Yor* 3E 99
Shawwood. *E Ayr* 2E 117
Shearington. *Dum* 3B 112
Shearsby. *Leics* 1D 62
Shearston. *Som* 3F 21
Shebbear. *Devn* 2E 11
Shebdon. *Staf* 3B 72
Shebster. *High* 2C 168
Sheddocksley. *Aber* 3F 153
Shedfield. *Hants* 1D 16
Shedog. *N Ayr* 2D 122
Sheen. *Staf* 4F 85
Sheepbridge. *Derbs* 3A 86
Sheep Hill. *Tyne* 4E 115
Sheepscar. *W Yor* 1D 92
Sheepscombe. *Glos* 4D 49
Sheepstor. *Devn* 2B 8
Sheepwash. *Devn* 2E 11
Sheepwash. *Nmbd* 1F 115
Sheepway. *N Som* 4H 33
Sheepy Magna. *Leics* 5H 73
Sheepy Parva. *Leics* 5H 73
Sheering. *Essx* 4F 53
Sheerness. *Kent* 3D 40
Sheerwater. *Surr* 4B 38
Sheet. *Hants* 4F 25
Sheffield. *S Yor* 2H 85 & 210
Sheffield Bottom. *W Ber* 5E 37
Sheffield Green. *E Sus* 3F 27
Shefford. *C Beds* 2B 52
Shefford Woodlands. *W Ber* 4B 36
Sheigra. *High* 2B 166
Sheinton. *Shrp* 5A 72
Shelderton. *Shrp* 3G 59
Sheldon. *Derbs* 4F 85
Sheldon. *Devn* 2E 12
Sheldon. *W Mid* 2F 61
Sheldwich. *Kent* 5E 40
Sheldwich Lees. *Kent* 5E 40
Shelf. *W Yor* 2B 92
Shelfanger. *Norf* 2D 66
Shelfield. *Warw* 4F 61
Shelfield. *W Mid* 5E 73
Shelford. *Notts* 1D 74
Shelford. *Warw* 2B 62
Shell. *Worc* 5D 60
Shelley. *Suff* 2D 54
Shelley. *W Yor* 3C 92
Shell Green. *Hal* 2H 83
Shellingford. *Oxon* 2B 36
Shellow Bowells. *Essx* 5G 53
Shelsley Beauchamp. *Worc* 4B 60
Shelsley Walsh. *Worc* 4B 60
Shelthorpe. *Leics* 4C 74
Shelton. *Bed* 4H 63
Shelton. *Norf* 1E 67
Shelton. *Notts* 1E 75
Shelton. *Shrp* 4G 71
Shelton Green. *Norf* 1E 67
Shelton Lock. *Derb* 2A 74
Shelve. *Shrp* 1F 59
Shelwick. *Here* 1A 48
Shelwick Green. *Here* 1A 48
Shenfield. *Essx* 1H 39
Shenington. *Oxon* 1B 50
Shenley. *Herts* 5B 52
Shenley Brook End. *Mil* 2G 51
Shenleybury. *Herts* 5B 52

T

Theakston—Tottenhill

Theakston. N Yor 1F 99
Thealby. N Lin 3B 94
Theale. Som 2H 21
Theale. W Ber 4E 37
Thearne. E Yor 1D 94
Theberton. Suff 4G 67
Theddingworth. Leics 2D 62
Theddlethorpe All Saints. Linc 2D 88
Theddlethorpe St Helen. Linc 2D 89
Thelbridge Barton. Devn 1A 12
Thelnetham. Suff 3C 66
Thelveton. Norf 2D 66
Thelwall. Warr 2A 84
Themelthorpe. Norf 3C 78
Thenford. Nptn 1D 50
Therfield. Herts 2D 52
Thetford. Linc 4A 76
Thetford. Norf 2A 66
Thethwaite. Cumb 5E 113
Theydon Bois. Essx 1F 39
Thick Hollins. W Yor 3B 92
Thickwood. Wilts 4D 34
Thimbleby. Linc 3B 88
Thimbleby. N Yor 5B 106
Thingwall. Mers 2E 83
Thirlby. N Yor 1G 99
Thirlestane. Bord 5B 130
Thirn. N Yor 1E 98
Thirsk. N Yor 1G 99
Thirtleby. E Yor 1E 95
Thistleton. Lanc 1C 90
Thistleton. Rut 4G 75
Thistley Green. Suff 3F 65
Thixendale. N Yor 3C 100
Thockrington. Nmbd 2C 114
Tholomas Drove. Cambs 5D 76
Tholthorpe. N Yor 3G 99
Thomas Chapel. Pemb 4F 43
Thomas Close. Cumb 5F 113
Thomastown. Abers 4E 160
Thomastown. Rhon 3D 32
Thompson. Norf 1B 66
Thomshill. Mor 3G 159
Thong. Kent 3A 40
Thongsbridge. W Yor 4B 92
Thoralby. N Yor 1C 98
Thoresby. Notts 3D 86
Thoresway. Linc 1A 88
Thorganby. Linc 1B 88
Thorganby. N Yor 5A 100
Thorgill. N Yor 5E 107
Thorington. Suff 3G 67
Thorington Street. Suff 2D 54
Thorlby. N Yor 4B 98
Thorley. Herts 4E 53
Thorley Street. Herts 4E 53
Thorley Street. IOW 4B 16
Thormanby. N Yor 2G 99
Thorn. Powy 4E 59
Thornaby-on-Tees. Stoc T 3B 106
Thornage. Norf 2C 78
Thornborough. Buck 2F 51
Thornborough. N Yor 2E 99
Thornbury. Devn 2E 11
Thornbury. Here 5A 60
Thornbury. S Glo 3B 34
Thornby. Cumb 4D 112
Thornby. Nptn 3D 62
Thorncliffe. Staf 5E 85
Thorncombe. Dors 2G 13
Thorncombe Street. Surr 1A 26
Thorncote Green. C Beds 1B 52
Thorndon. Suff 4D 66
Thorndon Cross. Devn 3F 11
Thorne. S Yor 3G 93
Thornehillhead. Devn 1E 11
Thorner. W Yor 5F 99
Thorne St Margaret. Som 4D 20
Thorney. Notts 3F 87
Thorney. Pet 5B 76
Thorney. Som 4H 21
Thorney Hill. Hants 3G 15
Thorney Toll. Cambs 5C 76
Thornfalcon. Som 4F 21
Thornford. Dors 1B 14
Thorngrafton. Nmbd 3A 114
Thorngrove. Som 3G 21
Thorngumbald. E Yor 2F 95
Thornham. Norf 1G 77
Thornham Magna. Suff 3D 66
Thornham Parva. Suff 3D 66
Thornhaugh. Pet 5H 75
Thornhill. Cphy 3E 33
Thornhill. Cumb 4B 102
Thornhill. Derbs 2G 85
Thornhill. Dum 5A 118
Thornhill. Sotn 1C 16
Thornhill. Stir 4F 135
Thornhill. W Yor 3C 92
Thornhill Lees. W Yor 3C 92
Thornhills. W Yor 2B 92
Thornholme. E Yor 3F 101
Thornicombe. Dors 2D 14
Thornington. Nmbd 1C 120
Thornley. Dur 1A 106
(nr. Durham)
Thornley. Dur 1E 105
(nr. Tow Law)
Thornley Gate. Nmbd 4B 114
Thornliebank. E Ren 4G 127
Thornroan. Abers 5F 161
Thorns. Suff 5G 65
Thornsett. Derbs 2E 85
Thornthwaite. Cumb 2D 102
Thornthwaite. N Yor 4D 98
Thornton. Ang 4C 144
Thornton. Buck 2F 51
Thornton. E Yor 5B 100
Thornton. Fife 4E 137
Thornton. Lanc 5C 96
Thornton. Leics 5B 74
Thornton. Linc 4B 88
Thornton. Mers 4B 90
Thornton. Midd 3B 106
Thornton. Nmbd 5F 131
Thornton. Pemb 4D 42
Thornton. W Yor 1A 92
Thornton Curtis. N Lin 3D 94
Thorntonhall. S Lan 4G 127
Thornton Heath. G Lon 4E 39
Thornton Hough. Mers 2F 83
Thornton in Craven. N Yor 5B 98
Thornton in Lonsdale. N Yor 2F 97
Thornton-le-Beans. N Yor 5A 106
Thornton-le-Clay. N Yor 3A 100
Thornton-le-Dale. N Yor 1C 100
Thornton le Moor. Linc 1H 87
Thornton-le-Moor. N Yor 1F 99
Thornton-le-Moors. Ches W 3G 83
Thornton-le-Street. N Yor 1G 99
Thorntonloch. E Lot 2D 130
Thornton Rust. N Yor 1B 98
Thornton Steward. N Yor 1D 98
Thornton Watlass. N Yor 1E 99
Thornwood Common. Essx 5E 53
Thornythwaite. Cumb 2E 103
Thoroton. Notts 1E 75
Thorp Arch. W Yor 5G 99
Thorpe. Derbs 5F 85
Thorpe. E Yor 5D 101
Thorpe. Linc 2D 89
Thorpe. Norf 1G 67
Thorpe. N Yor 3C 98
Thorpe. Notts 1E 75
Thorpe. Surr 4B 38
Thorpe Abbotts. Norf 3D 66
Thorpe Acre. Leics 3C 74
Thorpe Arnold. Leics 3E 75
Thorpe Audlin. W Yor 3E 93
Thorpe Bassett. N Yor 2C 100
Thorpe Bay. S'end 2D 40
Thorpe by Water. Rut 1F 63
Thorpe Common. S Yor 1A 86
Thorpe Common. Suff 2F 55
Thorpe Constantine. Staf 5G 73
Thorpe End. Norf 4E 79
Thorpe Fendike. Linc 4D 88
Thorpe Green. Essx 3E 55
Thorpe Green. Suff 5B 66
Thorpe Hall. N Yor 2H 99
Thorpe Hamlet. Norf 5E 79
Thorpe Hesley. S Yor 1A 86
Thorpe in Balne. S Yor 3F 93
Thorpe in the Fallows. Linc 2G 87
Thorpe Langton. Leics 1E 63
Thorpe Larches. Dur 2A 106
Thorpe Latimer. Linc 1A 76
Thorpe-le-Soken. Essx 3E 55
Thorpe le Street. E Yor 5C 100
Thorpe Malsor. Nptn 3F 63
Thorpe Mandeville. Nptn 1D 50
Thorpe Market. Norf 2E 79
Thorpe Marriott. Norf 4D 78
Thorpe Morieux. Suff 5B 66
Thorpeness. Suff 4G 67
Thorpe on the Hill. Linc 4G 87
Thorpe on the Hill. W Yor 2D 92
Thorpe St Andrew. Norf 5E 79
Thorpe St Peter. Linc 4D 89
Thorpe Salvin. S Yor 2C 86
Thorpe Satchville. Leics 4E 75
Thorpe Thewles. Stoc T 2B 106
Thorpe Tilney. Linc 5A 88
Thorpe Underwood. N Yor 4G 99
Thorpe Waterville. Nptn 2H 63
Thorpe Willoughby. N Yor 1F 93
Thorpland. Norf 5F 77
Thorrington. Essx 3D 54
Thorverton. Devn 2C 12
Thrandeston. Suff 3D 66
Thrapston. Nptn 3G 63
Thrashbush. N Lan 3A 128
Threapland. Cumb 1C 102
Threapland. N Yor 3B 98
Threapwood. Ches W 1G 71
Threapwood. Staf 1E 73
Three Ashes. Here 3A 48
Three Bridges. Linc 2D 88
Three Bridges. W Sus 2D 27
Three Burrows. Corn 4B 6
Three Chimneys. Kent 2C 28
Three Cocks. Powy 2E 47
Three Crosses. Swan 3E 31
Three Cups Corner. E Sus 3H 27
Threehammer Common. Norf 3F 79
Three Holes. Norf 5E 77
Threekingham. Linc 2H 75
Three Leg Cross. E Sus 2A 28
Three Legged Cross. Dors 2F 15
Three Mile Cross. Wok 5F 37
Threemilestone. Corn 4B 6
Three Oaks. E Sus 4C 28
Threlkeld. Cumb 2E 102
Threshfield. N Yor 3B 98
Thrigby. Norf 4G 79
Thringarth. Dur 2C 104
Thringstone. Leics 4B 74
Thrintoft. N Yor 5A 106
Thriplow. Cambs 1E 53
Throckenholt. Linc 5C 76
Throcking. Herts 2D 52
Throckley. Tyne 3E 115
Throckmorton. Worc 1E 49
Throop. Bour 3G 15
Throphill. Nmbd 1E 115
Thropton. Nmbd 4E 121
Throsk. Stir 4A 136
Througham. Glos 5E 49
Throughgate. Dum 1F 111
Throwleigh. Devn 3G 11
Throwley. Kent 5D 40
Throwley Forstal. Kent 5D 40
Throxenby. N Yor 1E 101
Thrumpton. Notts 2C 74
Thrumster. High 4F 169
Thrunton. Nmbd 3E 121
Thrupp. Glos 5D 48
Thrupp. Oxon 4C 50
Thrushelton. Devn 4E 11
Thrushgill. Lanc 3F 97
Thrussington. Leics 4D 74
Thruxton. Hants 2A 24
Thruxton. Here 2H 47
Thrybergh. S Yor 1B 86
Thulston. Derbs 2B 74
Thundergay. N Ayr 5G 125
Thundersley. Essx 2B 40
Thundridge. Herts 4D 52
Thurcaston. Leics 4C 74
Thurcroft. S Yor 2B 86
Thurdon. Corn 1C 10
Thurgarton. Norf 2D 78
Thurgarton. Notts 1D 74
Thurgoland. S Yor 4C 92
Thurlaston. Leics 1C 62
Thurlaston. Warw 3B 62
Thurlbear. Som 4F 21
Thurlby. Linc 3D 89
(nr. Alford)
Thurlby. Linc 4A 76
(nr. Baston)
Thurlby. Linc 4G 87
(nr. Lincoln)
Thurleigh. Bed 5H 63
Thurlestone. Devn 4C 8
Thurloxton. Som 3F 21
Thurlstone. S Yor 4C 92
Thurlton. Norf 1G 67
Thurmaston. Leics 5D 74
Thurnby. Leics 5D 74
Thurne. Norf 4G 79
Thurnham. Kent 5C 40
Thurning. Norf 3C 78
Thurning. Nptn 2H 63
Thurnscoe. S Yor 4E 93
Thursby. Cumb 4E 113
Thursford. Norf 2B 78
Thursford Green. Norf 2B 78
Thursley. Surr 2A 26
Thurso. High 2D 168
Thurso East. High 2D 168
Thurstaston. Mers 2E 83
Thurston. Suff 4B 66
Thurston End. Suff 5G 65
Thurstonfield. Cumb 4E 112
Thurstonland. W Yor 3B 92
Thurton. Norf 5F 79
Thurvaston. Derbs 2F 73
(nr. Ashbourne)
Thurvaston. Derbs 2G 73
(nr. Derby)
Thuxton. Norf 5C 78
Thwaite. Dur 3D 104
Thwaite. N Yor 5B 104
Thwaite. Suff 4D 66
Thwaite Head. Cumb 5E 103
Thwaites. W Yor 5C 98
Thwaite St Mary. Norf 1F 67
Thwing. E Yor 2E 101
Tibbermore. Per 1C 136
Tibberton. Glos 3C 48
Tibberton. Telf 3A 72
Tibberton. Worc 5D 60
Tibenham. Norf 2D 66
Tibshelf. Derbs 4B 86
Tibthorpe. E Yor 4D 100
Ticehurst. E Sus 2A 28
Tichborne. Hants 3D 24
Tickencote. Rut 5G 75
Tickenham. N Som 4H 33
Tickhill. S Yor 1C 86
Ticklerton. Shrp 1G 59
Ticknall. Derbs 3H 73
Tickton. E Yor 5E 101
Tidbury Green. W Mid 3F 61
Tidcombe. Wilts 1A 24
Tiddington. Oxon 5E 51
Tiddington. Warw 5G 61
Tiddleywink. Wilts 4D 34
Tidebrook. E Sus 3H 27
Tideford. Corn 3H 7
Tideford Cross. Corn 2H 7
Tidenham. Glos 2A 34
Tideswell. Derbs 3F 85
Tidmarsh. W Ber 4E 37
Tidmington. Warw 2A 50
Tidpit. Hants 1F 15
Tidworth. Wilts 2H 23
Tidworth Camp. Wilts 2H 23
Tiers Cross. Pemb 3D 42
Tiffield. Nptn 5D 62
Tifty. Abers 4E 161
Tigerton. Ang 2E 145
Tighnabruaich. Arg 2A 126
Tigley. Devn 2D 8
Tilbrook. Cambs 4H 63
Tilbury. Thur 3H 39
Tilbury Green. Essx 1H 53
Tilbury Juxta Clare. Essx 1A 54
Tile Hill. W Mid 3G 61
Tilehurst. Read 4E 37
Tilford. Surr 2G 25
Tilgate Forest Row. W Sus 2D 26
Tillathrowie. Abers 5B 160
Tillers Green. Glos 2B 48
Tillery. Abers 1G 153
Tilley. Shrp 3H 71
Tillicoultry. Clac 4B 136
Tillingham. Essx 5C 54
Tillington. Here 1H 47
Tillington. W Sus 3A 26
Tillington Common. Here 1H 47
Tillybirloch. Abers 3D 152
Tillyfourie. Abers 2D 152
Tilmanstone. Kent 5H 41
Tilney All Saints. Norf 4E 77
Tilney Fen End. Norf 4E 77
Tilney High End. Norf 4E 77
Tilney St Lawrence. Norf 4E 77
Tilshead. Wilts 2F 23
Tilstock. Shrp 2H 71
Tilston. Ches W 5G 83
Tilstone Fearnall. Ches W 4H 83
Tilsworth. C Beds 3H 51
Tilton on the Hill. Leics 5E 75
Tiltups End. Glos 2D 34
Timberland. Linc 5A 88
Timbersbrook. Ches E 4C 84
Timberscombe. Som 2C 20
Timble. N Yor 4D 98
Timperley. G Man 2B 84
Timsbury. Bath 1B 22
Timsbury. Hants 4B 24
Timsgearraidh. W Isl 4C 171
Timworth Green. Suff 4A 66
Tincleton. Dors 3C 14
Tindale. Cumb 4H 113
Tindale Crescent. Dur 2F 105
Tingewick. Buck 2E 51
Tingrith. C Beds 2A 52
Tingwall. Orkn 5D 172
Tinhay. Devn 4D 11
Tinshill. W Yor 1C 92
Tinsley. S Yor 1B 86
Tinsley Green. W Sus 2D 27
Tintagel. Corn 4A 10
Tintern. Mon 5A 48
Tintinhull. Som 1A 14
Tintwistle. Derbs 1E 85
Tinwald. Dum 1B 112
Tinwell. Rut 5H 75
Tippacott. Devn 2A 20
Tipperty. Abers 1G 153
Tipps End. Cambs 1E 65
Tiptoe. Hants 3A 16
Tipton. W Mid 1D 60
Tipton St John. Devn 3D 12
Tiptree. Essx 4B 54
Tiptree Heath. Essx 4B 54
Tirabad. Powy 1B 46
Tircoed. Swan 5G 45
Tiree Airport. Arg 4B 138
Tirinie. Per 2F 143
Tirley. Glos 3D 48
Tirnewydd. Flin 3D 82
Tiroran. Arg 1B 132
Tirphil. Cphy 5E 47
Tirril. Cumb 2G 103
Tirryside. High 2C 164
Tir-y-dail. Carm 4G 45
Tisbury. Wilts 4E 23
Tisman's Common. W Sus 2B 26
Tissington. Derbs 5F 85
Titchberry. Devn 4C 18
Titchfield. Hants 2D 16
Titchmarsh. Nptn 3H 63
Titchwell. Norf 1G 77
Tithby. Notts 2D 74
Titley. Here 5F 59
Titlington. Nmbd 3F 121
Titsey. Surr 5F 39
Titson. Corn 2C 10
Tittensor. Staf 2C 72
Tittleshall. Norf 3A 78
Titton. Worc 4C 60
Tiverton. Ches W 4H 83
Tiverton. Devn 1C 12
Tivetshall St Margaret. Norf 2D 66
Tivetshall St Mary. Norf 2D 66
Tivington. Som 2C 20
Tixall. Staf 3D 73
Tixover. Rut 5G 75
Toab. Orkn 7E 172
Toab. Shet 10E 173
Toadmoor. Derbs 5H 85
Tobermory. Arg 3G 139
Toberonochy. Arg 3E 133
Tobha-Beag. W Isl 1E 170
(on North Uist)
Tobha Beag. W Isl 5C 170
(on South Uist)
Tobha Mor. W Isl 5C 170
Tobhtarol. W Isl 4D 171
Tobson. W Isl 4D 171
Tocabhaig. High 2E 147
Tocher. Abers 5D 160
Tockenham. Wilts 4F 35
Tockenham Wick. Wilts 3F 35
Tockholes. Bkbn 2E 91
Tockington. S Glo 3B 34
Tockwith. N Yor 4G 99
Todber. Dors 4D 22
Todding. Here 3G 59
Toddington. C Beds 3A 52
Toddington. Glos 2F 49
Todenham. Glos 2H 49
Todhills. Cumb 3E 113
Todmorden. W Yor 2H 91
Todwick. S Yor 2B 86
Toft. Cambs 5C 64
Toft. Linc 4H 75
Toft Hill. Dur 2E 105
Toft Monks. Norf 1G 67
Toft next Newton. Linc 2H 87
Toftrees. Norf 3A 78
Tofts. High 2F 169
Toftwood. Norf 4B 78
Togston. Nmbd 4G 121
Tokavaig. High 2E 147
Tokers Green. Oxon 4F 37
Tolastadh a Chaolais. W Isl 4D 171
Tolladine. Worc 5C 60
Tolland. Som 3E 20
Tollard Farnham. Dors 1E 15
Tollard Royal. Wilts 1E 15
Toll Bar. S Yor 4F 93
Toller Fratrum. Dors 3A 14
Toller Porcorum. Dors 3A 14
Tollerton. N Yor 3H 99
Tollerton. Notts 2D 74
Toller Whelme. Dors 2A 14
Tollesbury. Essx 4C 54
Tolleshunt D'Arcy. Essx 4C 54
Tolleshunt Knights. Essx 4C 54
Tolleshunt Major. Essx 4C 54
Tollie. High 3H 157
Tollie Farm. High 1A 156
Tolm. W Isl 4G 171
Tolpuddle. Dors 3C 14
Tolstadh bho Thuath. W Isl 3H 171
Tolworth. G Lon 4C 38
Tomachlaggan. Mor 1F 151
Tomaknock. Per 1A 136
Tomatin. High 1C 150
Tombuidhe. Arg 3H 133
Tomdoun. High 3D 148
Tomich. High 1F 149
(nr. Cannich)
Tomich. High 1B 158
(nr. Invergordon)
Tomich. High 3D 164
(nr. Lairg)
Tomintoul. Mor 2F 151
Tomnavoulin. Mor 1G 151
Tomsléibhe. Arg 5A 140
Ton. Mon 2G 33
Tonbridge. Kent 1G 27
Tondu. B'end 3B 32
Tonedale. Som 4E 21
Tonfanau. Gwyn 5E 69
Tong. Shrp 5B 72
Tonge. Leics 3B 74
Tong Forge. Shrp 5B 72
Tongham. Surr 2G 25
Tongland. Dum 4D 111
Tong Norton. Shrp 5B 72
Tongue. High 3F 167
Tongue End. Linc 4A 76
Tongwynlais. Card 3E 33
Tonmawr. Neat 2B 32
Tonna. Neat 2A 32
Tonnau. Neat 2A 32
Ton-Pentre. Rhon 2C 32
Ton-Teg. Rhon 3D 32
Tonwell. Herts 4D 52
Tonypandy. Rhon 2C 32
Tonyrefail. Rhon 3D 32
Toot Baldon. Oxon 5D 50
Toot Hill. Essx 5F 53
Toot Hill. Hants 1B 16
Topcliffe. N Yor 2G 99
Topcliffe. W Yor 2C 92
Topcroft. Norf 1E 67
Topcroft Street. Norf 1E 67
Toppesfield. Essx 2H 53
Toppings. G Man 3F 91
Toprow. Norf 1D 66
Topsham. Devn 4C 12
Torbay. Torb 2F 9
Torbeg. N Ayr 3C 122
Torbothie. N Lan 3B 128
Torbryan. Devn 2E 9
Torcross. Devn 4E 9
Tore. High 3A 158
Torgyle. High 2F 149
Torinturk. Arg 3G 125
Torksey. Linc 3F 87
Torlum. W Isl 3C 170
Torlundy. High 1F 141
Tormarton. S Glo 4C 34
Tormitchell. S Ayr 5B 116
Tormore. High 3E 147
Tormore. N Ayr 2C 122
Tornagrain. High 4B 158
Tornaveen. Abers 3D 152
Torness. High 1H 149
Toronto. Dur 1E 105
Torpenhow. Cumb 1D 102
Torphichen. W Lot 2C 128
Torphins. Abers 3D 152
Torpoint. Corn 3A 8
Torquay. Torb 2F 9
Torr. Devn 3B 8
Torra. Arg 4B 124
Torran. High 4E 155
Torrance. E Dun 2H 127
Torrans. Arg 1B 132
Torranyard. E Ayr 5E 127
Torre. Som 3D 20
Torre. Torb 2E 9
Torridon. High 3B 156
Torrin. High 1D 147
Torrisdale. Arg 2B 122
Torrisdale. High 2G 167
Torrish. High 2G 165
Torrisholme. Lanc 3D 96
Torroble. High 3C 164
Torroy. High 4C 164
Torry. Aber 3G 153
Torryburn. Fife 1D 128
Torthorwald. Dum 2B 112
Tortington. W Sus 5B 26
Tortworth. S Glo 2C 34
Torvaig. High 4D 155
Torver. Cumb 5D 102
Torwood. Falk 1B 128
Torworth. Notts 2D 86
Toscaig. High 5G 155
Toseland. Cambs 4B 64
Tosside. Lanc 4G 97
Tostock. Suff 4B 66
Totaig. High 3B 154
Totardor. High 5C 154
Tote. High 4D 154
Totegan. High 2A 168
Tothill. Linc 2D 88
Totland. IOW 4B 16
Totley. S Yor 3H 85
Totnell. Dors 2B 14
Totnes. Devn 2E 9
Toton. Derbs 2B 74
Totronald. Arg 3C 138
Totscore. High 2C 154
Tottenham. G Lon 1E 39
Tottenhill. Norf 4F 77

Tottenhill Row—Uig

Tottenhill Row. Norf 4F 77
Totteridge. G Lon 1D 38
Totternhoe. C Beds 3H 51
Tottington. G Man 3F 91
Totton. Hants 1B 16
Touchen-end. Wind 4G 37
Toulvaddie. High 5F 165
Towans, The. Corn 3C 4
Toward. Arg 3C 126
Towcester. Nptn 1E 51
Towednack. Corn 3B 4
Tower End. Norf 4F 77
Tower Hill. Mers 4C 90
Tower Hill. W Sus 3C 26
Towersey. Oxon 5F 51
Towie. Abers 2B 152
Towiemore. Mor 4A 160
Tow Law. Dur 1E 105
Town End. Cambs 1D 64
Town End. Cumb 4F 103 (nr. Ambleside)
Town End. Cumb 2H 103 (nr. Kirkby Thore)
Town End. Cumb 1D 96 (nr. Lindale)
Town End. Cumb 1C 96 (nr. Newby Bridge)
Town End. Mers 2G 83
Townend. W Dun 2F 127
Townfield. Dur 5C 114
Towngate. Cumb 5G 113
Towngate. Linc 4A 76
Town Green. Lanc 4B 90
Town Head. Cumb 4E 103 (nr. Grasmere)
Town Head. Cumb 3H 103 (nr. Great Asby)
Townhead. Cumb 1G 103 (nr. Lazonby)
Townhead. Cumb 1B 102 (nr. Maryport)
Townhead. Cumb 1H 103 (nr. Ousby)
Townhead. Dum 5D 111
Townhead of Greenlaw. Dum 3E 111
Townhill. Fife 1E 129
Townhill. Swan 3F 31
Town Kelloe. Dur 1A 106
Town Littleworth. E Sus 4F 27
Town Row. E Sus 2G 27
Towns End. Hants 1D 24
Townsend. Herts 5B 52
Townshend. Corn 3C 4
Town Street. Suff 2G 65
Town, The. IOS 1A 4
Town Yetholm. Bord 2C 120
Towthorpe. E Yor 3C 100
Towthorpe. York 4A 100
Towton. N Yor 1E 93
Towyn. Cnwy 3B 82
Toxteth. Mers 2F 83
Toynton All Saints. Linc 4C 88
Toynton Fen Side. Linc 4C 88
Toynton St Peter. Linc 4D 88
Toy's Hill. Kent 5F 39
Trabboch. E Ayr 2D 116
Traboe. Corn 4E 5
Tradespark. High 3C 158
Tradespark. Orkn 7D 172
Trafford Park. G Man 1B 84
Trallong. Powy 3C 46
Tranent. E Lot 2H 129
Tranmere. Mers 2F 83
Trantlebeg. High 3A 168
Trantlemore. High 3A 168
Tranwell. Nmbd 1E 115
Trapp. Carm 4G 45
Traquair. Bord 1F 119
Trash Green. W Ber 5E 37
Trawden. Lanc 1H 91
Trawscoed. Powy 2D 46
Trawsfynydd. Gwyn 2G 69
Trawsgoed. Cdgn 3F 57
Treaddow. Here 3A 48
Trealaw. Rhon 2D 32
Treales. Lanc 1C 90
Trearddur. IOA 3B 80
Treaslane. High 3C 154
Treator. Corn 1D 6
Trebanog. Rhon 2D 32
Trebanos. Neat 5H 45
Trebarber. Corn 2C 6
Trebartha. Corn 5C 10
Trebarwith. Corn 4A 10
Trebetherick. Corn 1D 6
Treborough. Som 3D 20
Trebudannon. Corn 2C 6
Trebullett. Corn 5D 10
Treburley. Corn 5D 10
Treburrick. Corn 1C 6
Trebyan. Corn 2E 7
Trecastle. Powy 3B 46
Trecenydd. Cphy 3E 33
Trecott. Devn 2G 11
Trecwn. Pemb 1D 42
Trecynon. Rhon 5C 46
Tredaule. Corn 4C 10
Tredavoe. Corn 4B 4
Tredegar. Blae 5E 47
Trederwen. Powy 4E 71
Tredington. Glos 3E 49
Tredington. Warw 1A 50
Tredinnick. Corn 2F 7 (nr. Bodmin)
Tredinnick. Corn 3G 7 (nr. Looe)
Tredinnick. Corn 1D 6 (nr. Padstow)
Tredogan. V Glam 5D 32
Tredomen. Powy 2E 46
Tredunnock. Mon 2G 33
Tredustan. Powy 2E 47
Treen. Corn 4A 4 (nr. Land's End)
Treen. Corn 3B 4 (nr. St Ives)
Treeton. S Yor 2B 86
Trefaldwyn. Powy 1E 58
Trefasser. Pemb 1C 42
Trefdraeth. IOA 3D 80
Trefdraeth. Pemb 1E 43
Trefecca. Powy 2E 47
Trefechan. Mer T 5D 46
Trefeglwys. Powy 1B 58
Trefenter. Cdgn 4F 57
Treffgarne. Pemb 2D 42
Treffynnon. Flin 3D 82
Treffynnon. Pemb 2C 42
Trefil. Blae 4E 46
Trefilan. Cdgn 5E 57
Trefin. Pemb 1C 42
Treflach. Shrp 3E 71
Trefnant. Den 3C 82
Trefonen. Shrp 3E 71
Trefor. Gwyn 1C 68
Trefor. IOA 2C 80
Treforest. Rhon 3D 32
Trefrew. Corn 4B 10
Trefriw. Cnwy 4G 81
Tref-y-Clawdd. Powy 3E 59
Trefynwy. Mon 4A 48
Tregada. Corn 4D 10
Tregadillett. Corn 4D 10
Tregare. Mon 4H 47
Tregarne. Corn 4E 5
Tregaron. Cdgn 5F 57
Tregarth. Gwyn 4F 81
Tregear. Corn 3C 6
Tregeare. Corn 4C 10
Tregeiriog. Wrex 2D 70
Tregele. IOA 1C 80
Tregeseal. Corn 3A 4
Tregiskey. Corn 4E 6
Tregole. Corn 3B 10
Tregolwyn. V Glam 4C 32
Tregonetha. Corn 2D 6
Tregonhawke. Corn 3A 8
Tregony. Corn 4D 6
Tregoodwell. Corn 4B 10
Tregorrick. Corn 3E 6
Tregoss. Corn 2D 6
Tregowris. Corn 4E 5
Tregoyd. Powy 2E 47
Tregrehan Mills. Corn 3E 7
Tre-groes. Cdgn 1E 45
Tregullon. Corn 2E 7
Tregurrian. Corn 2C 6
Tregynon. Powy 1C 58
Trehafod. Rhon 2D 32
Trehan. Corn 3A 8
Treharris. Mer T 2E 32
Treherbert. Rhon 2C 32
Trehunist. Corn 2H 7
Trekenner. Corn 5D 10
Trekenning. Corn 2D 6
Treknow. Corn 4A 10
Trelales. B'end 3B 32
Trelan. Corn 5E 5
Trelash. Corn 3B 10
Trelassick. Corn 3C 6
Trelawnyd. Flin 3C 82
Trelech. Carm 1G 43
Treleddyd-fawr. Pemb 2B 42
Trelewis. Mer T 2E 32
Treligga. Corn 4A 10
Trelights. Corn 1D 6
Trelill. Corn 5A 10
Trelissick. Corn 5C 6
Trellech. Mon 5A 48
Trelleck Grange. Mon 5H 47
Trelogan. Flin 2D 82
Trelystan. Powy 5E 71
Tremadog. Gwyn 1E 69
Tremail. Corn 4B 10
Tremain. Cdgn 1C 44
Tremaine. Corn 4C 10
Tremar. Corn 2G 7
Trematon. Corn 3H 7
Tremeirchion. Den 3C 82
Tremore. Corn 2E 6
Tremorfa. Card 4F 33
Trenance. Corn 2C 6 (nr. Newquay)
Trenance. Corn 1D 6 (nr. Padstow)
Trenarren. Corn 4E 7
Trench. Telf 4A 72
Trencreek. Corn 2C 6
Trendeal. Corn 3C 6
Trenear. Corn 5A 6
Treneglos. Corn 4C 10
Trenewan. Corn 3F 7
Trengune. Corn 3B 10
Trent. Dors 1A 14
Trentham. Stoke 1C 72
Trentishoe. Devn 2G 19
Trentlock. Derbs 2B 74
Treoes. V Glam 4C 32
Treorchy. Rhon 2C 32
Treorci. Rhon 2C 32
Tre'r-ddol. Cdgn 1F 57
Tre'r llai. Powy 5E 71
Trerulefoot. Corn 3H 7
Tresaith. Cdgn 5B 56
Trescott. Staf 1C 60
Trescowe. Corn 3C 4
Tresham. Glos 2C 34
Tresigin. V Glam 4C 32
Tresillian. Corn 4C 6
Tresimwn. V Glam 4D 32
Tresinney. Corn 4B 10
Treskillard. Corn 5A 6
Treskinnick Cross. Corn 3C 10
Tresmeer. Corn 4C 10
Tresparrett. Corn 3B 10
Tresparrett Posts. Corn 3B 10
Tressady. High 3D 164
Tressait. Per 2F 143
Tresta. Shet 2H 173 (on Fetlar)
Tresta. Shet 6E 173 (on Mainland)
Treswell. Notts 3E 87
Treswithian. Corn 3D 4
Tre Taliesin. Cdgn 1F 57
Trethomas. Cphy 3E 33
Trethosa. Corn 3D 6
Trethurgy. Corn 3E 7
Tretio. Pemb 2B 42
Tretire. Here 3A 48
Tretower. Powy 3E 47
Treuddyn. Flin 5E 83
Trevadlock. Corn 5C 10
Trevalga. Corn 3A 10
Trevalyn. Wrex 5F 83
Trevance. Corn 1D 6
Trevanger. Corn 1D 6
Trevanson. Corn 1D 6
Trevarrack. Corn 3B 4
Trevarren. Corn 2D 6
Trevarrian. Corn 2C 6
Trevarrick. Corn 4D 6
Tre-vaughan. Carm 3E 45 (nr. Carmarthen)
Trevaughan. Carm 3F 43 (nr. Whitland)
Treveighan. Corn 5A 10
Trevellas. Corn 3B 6
Trevelmond. Corn 2G 7
Treverva. Corn 5B 6
Trevescan. Corn 4A 4
Trevethin. Torf 5F 47
Trevia. Corn 4A 10
Trevigro. Corn 2H 7
Trevilley. Corn 4A 4
Treviscoe. Corn 3D 6
Trevivian. Corn 4B 10
Trevone. Corn 1C 6
Trevor. Wrex 1E 71
Trevor Uchaf. Den 1E 71
Trew. Corn 4D 4
Trewalder. Corn 4A 10
Trewarlett. Corn 4D 10
Trewarmett. Corn 4A 10
Trewassa. Corn 4B 10
Treween. Corn 4C 10
Trewellard. Corn 3A 4
Trewen. Corn 4C 10
Trewennack. Corn 4D 5
Trewern. Powy 4E 71
Trewetha. Corn 5A 10
Trewidland. Corn 2G 7
Trewint. Corn 3B 10
Trewithian. Corn 5C 6
Trewoofe. Corn 4B 4
Trewoon. Corn 3D 6
Treworthal. Corn 5C 6
Trewyddel. Pemb 1B 44
Treyarnon. Corn 1C 6
Treyford. W Sus 1G 17
Triangle. Staf 5E 73
Triangle. W Yor 2A 92
Trickett's Cross. Dors 2F 15
Trimdon. Dur 1A 106
Trimdon Colliery. Dur 1A 106
Trimdon Grange. Dur 1A 106
Trimingham. Norf 2E 79
Trimley Lower Street. Suff 2F 55
Trimley St Martin. Suff 2F 55
Trimley St Mary. Suff 2F 55
Trimpley. Worc 3B 60
Trimsaran. Carm 5E 45
Trimstone. Devn 2F 19
Trinafour. Per 2E 142
Trinant. Cphy 2F 33
Tring. Herts 4H 51
Trinity. Ang 2F 145
Trinity. Edin 2F 129
Trisant. Cdgn 3G 57
Triscombe. Som 3E 21
Trislaig. High 1E 141
Trispen. Corn 3C 6
Tritlington. Nmbd 5G 121
Trochry. Per 4G 143
Troedrhiwdalar. Powy 5B 58
Troedrhiwfuwch. Cphy 5E 47
Troedrhiwgwair. Blae 5E 47
Troedyraur. Cdgn 1D 44
Troedyrhiw. Mer T 5D 46
Trondavoe. Shet 4E 173
Troon. Corn 5A 6
Troon. S Ayr 1C 116
Troqueer. Dum 2A 112
Troston. Suff 3A 66
Trottiscliffe. Kent 4H 39
Trotton. W Sus 4G 25
Troutbeck. Cumb 4F 103 (nr. Ambleside)
Troutbeck. Cumb 2E 103 (nr. Penrith)
Troutbeck Bridge. Cumb 4F 103
Troway. Derbs 3A 86
Trowbridge. Wilts 1D 22
Trowell. Notts 2B 74
Trowle Common. Wilts 1D 22
Trowley Bottom. Herts 4A 52
Trowse Newton. Norf 5E 79
Trudoxhill. Som 2C 22
Trull. Som 4F 21
Trumaisgearraidh. W Isl 1D 170
Trumpan. High 2B 154
Trumpet. Here 2B 48
Trumpington. Cambs 5D 64
Trumps Green. Surr 4A 38
Trunch. Norf 2E 79
Trunnah. Lanc 5C 96
Truro. Corn 4C 6
Trusham. Devn 4B 12
Trusley. Derbs 2G 73
Trusthorpe. Linc 2E 89
Tryfil. IOA 2D 80
Trysull. Staf 1C 60
Tubney. Oxon 2C 36
Tuckenhay. Devn 3E 9
Tuckhill. Staf 2B 60
Tuckingmill. Corn 4A 6
Tuckton. Bour 3G 15
Tuddenham. Suff 3G 65
Tuddenham St Martin. Suff 1E 55
Tudeley. Kent 1H 27
Tudhoe. Dur 1F 105
Tudhoe Grange. Dur 1F 105
Tudorville. Here 3A 48
Tudweiliog. Gwyn 2B 68
Tuesley. Surr 1A 26
Tufton. Hants 2C 24
Tufton. Pemb 2E 43
Tugby. Leics 5E 75
Tugford. Shrp 2H 59
Tughall. Nmbd 2G 121
Tulchan. Per 1B 136
Tullibardine. Per 2B 136
Tullibody. Clac 4A 136
Tullich. Arg 2H 133
Tullich. High 4B 156 (nr. Lochcarron)
Tullich. High 1C 158 (nr. Tain)
Tullich. Mor 4H 159
Tullich Muir. High 1B 158
Tulliemet. Per 3G 143
Tulloch. Abers 5F 161
Tulloch. High 4D 164 (nr. Bonar Bridge)
Tulloch. High 5F 149 (nr. Fort William)
Tulloch. High 2D 151 (nr. Grantown-on-Spey)
Tulloch. Per 1C 136
Tullochgorm. Arg 4G 133
Tullybeagles Lodge. Per 5H 143
Tullymurdoch. Per 3A 144
Tullynessle. Abers 2C 152
Tumble. Carm 4F 45
Tumbler's Green. Essx 3B 54
Tumby. Linc 4B 88
Tumby Woodside. Linc 5B 88
Tummel Bridge. Per 3E 143
Tunbridge Wells, Royal. Kent 2G 27
Tunga. W Isl 4G 171
Tungate. Norf 3E 79
Tunley. Bath 1B 22
Tunstall. E Yor 1G 95
Tunstall. Kent 4C 40
Tunstall. Lanc 2F 97
Tunstall. Norf 5G 79
Tunstall. N Yor 5F 105
Tunstall. Staf 3B 72
Tunstall. Stoke 5C 84
Tunstall. Suff 5F 67
Tunstall. Tyne 4G 115
Tunstead. Derbs 3F 85
Tunstead. Norf 3E 79
Tunstead Milton. Derbs 2E 85
Tunworth. Hants 2E 25
Tupsley. Here 1A 48
Tupton. Derbs 4A 86
Turfholm. S Lan 1H 117
Turfmoor. Devn 2F 13
Turgis Green. Hants 1E 25
Turkdean. Glos 4G 49
Turkey Island. Hants 1D 16
Tur Langton. Leics 1E 62
Turleigh. Wilts 5D 34
Turlin Moor. Pool 3E 15
Turnastone. Here 2G 47
Turnberry. S Ayr 4B 116
Turnchapel. Plym 3A 8
Turnditch. Derbs 1G 73
Turners Hill. W Sus 2E 27
Turners Puddle. Dors 3D 14
Turnford. Herts 5D 52
Turnhouse. Edin 2E 129
Turnworth. Dors 2D 14
Turriff. Abers 4E 161
Tursdale. Dur 1A 106
Turton Bottoms. Bkbn 3F 91
Turtory. Mor 4C 160
Turves Green. W Mid 3E 61
Turvey. Bed 5G 63
Turville. Buck 2F 37
Turville Heath. Buck 2F 37
Turweston. Buck 2E 50
Tushielaw. Bord 3F 119
Tutbury. Staf 3G 73
Tutnall. Worc 3D 61
Tutshill. Glos 2A 34
Tuttington. Norf 3E 79
Tutts Clump. W Ber 4D 36
Tutwell. Corn 5D 11
Tuxford. Notts 3E 87
Twatt. Orkn 5B 172
Twatt. Shet 6E 173
Twechar. E Dun 2A 128
Tweedale. Telf 5B 72
Tweedmouth. Nmbd 4F 131
Tweedsmuir. Bord 2C 118
Twelveheads. Corn 4B 6
Twemlow Green. Ches E 4B 84
Twenty. Linc 3A 76
Twerton. Bath 5C 34
Twickenham. G Lon 3C 38
Twigworth. Glos 3D 48
Twineham. W Sus 3D 26
Twinhoe. Bath 1C 22
Twinstead. Essx 2B 54
Twinstead Green. Essx 2B 54
Twiss Green. Warr 1A 84
Twiston. Lanc 5H 97
Twitchen. Devn 3A 20
Twitchen. Shrp 3F 59
Two Bridges. Devn 5G 11
Two Bridges. Glos 5B 48
Two Dales. Derbs 4G 85
Two Gates. Staf 5G 73
Two Mile Oak. Devn 2E 9
Twycross. Leics 5H 73
Twyford. Buck 3E 51
Twyford. Derbs 3H 73
Twyford. Dors 1D 14
Twyford. Hants 4C 24
Twyford. Leics 4E 75
Twyford. Norf 3C 78
Twyford. Wok 4F 37
Twyford Common. Here 2A 48
Twyncarno. Cphy 5E 46
Twynholm. Dum 4D 110
Twyning. Glos 2D 49
Twyning Green. Glos 2E 49
Twynllanan. Carm 3A 46
Twyn-y-Sheriff. Mon 5H 47
Twywell. Nptn 3G 63
Tyberton. Here 2G 47
Tyburn. W Mid 1F 61
Tyby. Norf 3C 78
Tycroes. Carm 4G 45
Tycrwyn. Powy 4D 70
Tyddewi. Pemb 2B 42
Tydd Gote. Linc 4D 76
Tydd St Giles. Cambs 4D 76
Tydd St Mary. Linc 4D 76
Tye. Hants 2F 17
Tye Green. Essx 3F 53 (nr. Bishop's Stortford)
Tye Green. Essx 3A 54 (nr. Braintree)
Tye Green. Essx 2F 53 (nr. Saffron Walden)
Tyersal. W Yor 1B 92
Ty Issa. Powy 3D 70
Tyldesley. G Man 4E 91
Tyler Hill. Kent 4F 41
Tylers Green. Buck 2G 37
Tyler's Green. Essx 5F 53
Tylorstown. Rhon 2D 32
Tylwch. Powy 2B 58
Ty-nant. Cnwy 1B 70
Tyndrum. Stir 5H 141
Tyneham. Dors 4D 15
Tynehead. Midl 4G 129
Tynemouth. Tyne 3G 115
Tyneside. Tyne 3F 115
Tyne Tunnel. Tyne 3G 115
Tynewydd. Rhon 2C 32
Tyninghame. E Lot 2C 130
Tynron. Dum 5H 117
Ty'n-y-bryn. Rhon 3D 32
Tyn-y-celyn. Wrex 2D 70
Tyn-y-cwm. Swan 5G 45
Tyn-y-ffridd. Powy 2D 70
Tynygongl. IOA 2E 81
Tynygraig. Cdgn 4F 57
Tyn-y-groes. Cnwy 3G 81
Ty'n-yr-eithin. Cdgn 4F 57
Tyn-y-rhyd. Powy 4C 70
Tyn-y-wern. Powy 3C 70
Tyrie. Abers 2G 161
Tyringham. Mil 1G 51
Tythecott. Devn 1E 11
Tythegston. B'end 4B 32
Tytherington. Ches E 3D 84
Tytherington. Som 2C 22
Tytherington. S Glo 3B 34
Tytherington. Wilts 2E 23
Tytherleigh. Devn 2G 13
Tywardreath. Corn 3E 7
Tywardreath Highway. Corn 3E 7
Tywyn. Cnwy 3G 81
Tywyn. Gwyn 5E 69

U

Uachdar. W Isl 3D 170
Uags. High 5G 155
Ubbeston Green. Suff 3F 67
Ubley. Bath 1A 22
Uckerby. N Yor 4F 105
Uckfield. E Sus 3F 27
Uckinghall. Worc 2D 48
Uckington. Glos 3E 49
Uckington. Shrp 5H 71
Uddingston. S Lan 3H 127
Uddington. S Lan 1A 118
Udimore. E Sus 4C 28
Udny Green. Abers 1F 153
Udny Station. Abers 1G 153
Udston. S Lan 4A 128
Udstonhead. S Lan 5A 128
Uffcott. Wilts 4G 35
Uffculme. Devn 1D 12
Uffington. Linc 5H 75
Uffington. Oxon 3B 36
Uffington. Shrp 4H 71
Ufford. Pet 5H 75
Ufford. Suff 5E 67
Ufton. Warw 4A 62
Ufton Nervet. W Ber 5E 37
Ugadale. Arg 3B 122
Ugborough. Devn 3C 8
Ugford. Wilts 3F 23
Uggeshall. Suff 2G 67
Ugglebarnby. N Yor 4F 107
Ugley. Essx 3F 53
Ugley Green. Essx 3F 53
Ugthorpe. N Yor 3E 107
Uidh. W Isl 9B 170
Uig. Arg 3C 138

Walton—Wester Quarff

Walton. *Derbs* 4A 86
Walton. *Leics* 2C 62
Walton. *Mers* 1F 83
Walton. *Mil* 2G 51
Walton. *Pet* 5A 76
Walton. *Powy* 5E 59
Walton. *Som* 3H 21
Walton. *Staf* 3C 72 (nr. Eccleshall)
Walton. *Staf* 2C 72 (nr. Stone)
Walton. *Suff* 2F 55
Walton. *Telf* 4H 71
Walton. *Warw* 5G 61
Walton. *W Yor* 3D 92 (nr. Wakefield)
Walton. *W Yor* 5G 99 (nr. Wetherby)
Walton Cardiff. *Glos* 2E 49
Walton East. *Pemb* 2E 43
Walton Elm. *Dors* 1C 14
Walton Highway. *Norf* 4D 77
Walton-in-Gordano. *N Som* 4H 33
Walton-le-Dale. *Lanc* 2D 90
Walton-on-Thames. *Surr* 4C 38
Walton-on-the-Hill. *Staf* 3D 72
Walton on the Hill. *Surr* 5D 38
Walton-on-the-Naze. *Essx* 3F 55
Walton on the Wolds. *Leics* 4C 74
Walton-on-Trent. *Derbs* 4G 73
Walton West. *Pemb* 3C 42
Walwick. *Nmbd* 2C 114
Walworth. *Darl* 3F 105
Walworth Gate. *Darl* 2F 105
Walwyn's Castle. *Pemb* 3C 42
Wambrook. *Som* 2F 13
Wampool. *Cumb* 4D 112
Wanborough. *Surr* 1A 26
Wanborough. *Swin* 3H 35
Wandel. *S Lan* 2B 118
Wandsworth. *G Lon* 3D 38
Wangford. *Suff* 2G 65 (nr. Lakenheath)
Wangford. *Suff* 3G 67 (nr. Southwold)
Wanlip. *Leics* 4D 74
Wanlockhead. *Dum* 3A 118
Wannock. *E Sus* 5G 27
Wansford. *E Yor* 4E 101
Wansford. *Pet* 1H 63
Wanshurst Green. *Kent* 1B 28
Wanstead. *G Lon* 2F 39
Wanstrow. *Som* 2C 22
Wanswell. *Glos* 5B 48
Wantage. *Oxon* 3C 36
Wapley. *S Glo* 4C 34
Wappenbury. *Warw* 4A 62
Wappenham. *Nptn* 1E 51
Warbleton. *E Sus* 4H 27
Warblington. *Hants* 2F 17
Warborough. *Oxon* 2D 36
Warboys. *Cambs* 2C 64
Warbreck. *Bkpl* 1B 90
Warbstow. *Corn* 3C 10
Warburton. *G Man* 2A 84
Warcop. *Cumb* 3A 104
Warden. *Kent* 3E 40
Warden. *Nmbd* 3C 114
Ward End. *W Mid* 2F 61
Ward Green. *Suff* 4C 66
Ward Green Cross. *Lanc* 1E 91
Wardhedges. *C Beds* 2A 52
Wardhouse. *Abers* 5C 160
Wardington. *Oxon* 1C 50
Wardle. *Ches E* 5A 84
Wardle. *G Man* 3H 91
Wardley. *Rut* 5F 75
Wardley. *W Sus* 4G 25
Wardlow. *Derbs* 3F 85
Wardsend. *Ches E* 2D 84
Wardy Hill. *Cambs* 2D 64
Ware. *Herts* 4D 52
Ware. *Kent* 4G 41
Wareham. *Dors* 4E 15
Warehorne. *Kent* 2D 28
Warenford. *Nmbd* 2F 121
Waren Mill. *Nmbd* 1F 121
Warenton. *Nmbd* 1F 121
Wareside. *Herts* 4D 53
Waresley. *Cambs* 5B 64
Waresley. *Worc* 4C 60
Warfield. *Brac* 4G 37
Warfleet. *Devn* 3E 9
Wargate. *Linc* 2B 76
Wargrave. *Wok* 4F 37
Warham. *Norf* 1B 78
Wark. *Nmbd* 1C 120 (nr. Coldstream)
Wark. *Nmbd* 2B 114 (nr. Hexham)
Warkleigh. *Devn* 4G 19
Warkton. *Nptn* 3F 63
Warkworth. *Nptn* 1C 50
Warkworth. *Nmbd* 4G 121
Warlaby. *N Yor* 5A 106
Warland. *W Yor* 2H 91
Warleggan. *Corn* 2F 7
Warlingham. *Surr* 5E 39
Warmanbie. *Dum* 3C 112
Warmfield. *W Yor* 2D 93
Warmingham. *Ches E* 4B 84
Warminghurst. *W Sus* 4C 26
Warmington. *Nptn* 1H 63
Warmington. *Warw* 1C 50
Warminster. *Wilts* 2D 23
Warmley. *S Glo* 4B 34
Warmsworth. *S Yor* 4F 93
Warmwell. *Dors* 4C 14
Warndon. *Worc* 5C 60
Warners End. *Herts* 5A 52
Warnford. *Hants* 4E 24
Warnham. *W Sus* 2C 26
Warningcamp. *W Sus* 5B 26
Warninglid. *W Sus* 3D 26
Warren. *Ches E* 3C 84
Warren. *Pemb* 5D 42
Warrenby. *Red C* 2C 106
Warren Corner. *Hants* 2G 25 (nr. Aldershot)
Warren Corner. *Hants* 4F 25 (nr. Petersfield)
Warren Row. *Wind* 3G 37
Warren Street. *Kent* 5D 40
Warrington. *Mil* 5F 63
Warrington. *Warr* 2A 84
Warsash. *Hants* 2C 16
Warse. *High* 1F 169
Warslow. *Staf* 5E 85
Warsop. *Notts* 4C 86
Warsop Vale. *Notts* 4C 86
Warter. *E Yor* 4C 100
Warthermarske. *N Yor* 2E 98
Warthill. *N Yor* 4A 100
Wartling. *E Sus* 5A 28
Wartnaby. *Leics* 3E 74
Warton. *Lanc* 2D 97 (nr. Carnforth)
Warton. *Lanc* 2C 90 (nr. Freckleton)
Warton. *Nmbd* 4E 121
Warton. *Warw* 5G 73
Warwick. *Warw* 4G 61
Warwick Bridge. *Cumb* 4F 113
Warwick-on-Eden. *Cumb* 4F 113
Warwick Wold. *Surr* 5E 39
Wasbister. *Orkn* 4C 172
Wasdale Head. *Cumb* 4C 102
Wash. *Derbs* 2E 85
Washaway. *Corn* 2E 7
Washbourne. *Devn* 3E 9
Washbrook. *Suff* 1E 54
Wash Common. *W Ber* 5C 36
Washerwall. *Staf* 1D 72
Washfield. *Devn* 1C 12
Washfold. *N Yor* 4D 104
Washford. *Som* 2D 20
Washford Pyne. *Devn* 1B 12
Washingborough. *Linc* 3H 87
Washington. *Tyne* 4G 115
Washington. *W Sus* 4C 26
Washington Village. *Tyne* 4G 115
Waskerley. *Dur* 5D 114
Wasperton. *Warw* 5G 61
Wasp Green. *Surr* 1E 27
Wasps Nest. *Linc* 4H 87
Wass. *N Yor* 2H 99
Watchet. *Som* 2D 20
Watchfield. *Oxon* 2H 35
Watchgate. *Cumb* 5G 103
Watchhill. *Cumb* 5C 112
Watcombe. *Torb* 2F 9
Watendlath. *Cumb* 3D 102
Water. *Devn* 4A 12
Water. *Lanc* 2G 91
Waterbeach. *Cambs* 4D 65
Waterbeach. *W Sus* 2G 17
Waterbeck. *Dum* 2D 112
Waterditch. *Hants* 3G 15
Water End. *C Beds* 2A 52
Water End. *E Yor* 1A 94
Water End. *Essx* 1F 53
Water End. *Herts* 5C 52 (nr. Hatfield)
Water End. *Herts* 4A 52 (nr. Hemel Hempstead)
Waterfall. *Staf* 5E 85
Waterfoot. *E Ren* 4G 127
Waterfoot. *Lanc* 2G 91
Waterford. *Herts* 4D 52
Water Fryston. *W Yor* 2E 93
Waterhead. *Cumb* 4E 103
Waterhead. *E Ayr* 3E 117
Waterhead. *S Ayr* 5C 116
Waterheads. *Bord* 4F 129
Waterhouses. *Dur* 5E 115
Waterhouses. *Staf* 5E 85
Wateringbury. *Kent* 5A 40
Waterlane. *Glos* 5E 49
Waterlip. *Som* 2B 22
Waterloo. *Cphy* 3E 33
Waterloo. *Corn* 5B 10
Waterloo. *Here* 1G 47
Waterloo. *High* 1E 147
Waterloo. *Mers* 1F 83
Waterloo. *Norf* 4E 78
Waterloo. *N Lan* 4B 128
Waterloo. *Pemb* 4D 42
Waterloo. *Per* 5H 143
Waterloo. *Pool* 3F 15
Waterloo. *Shrp* 2G 71
Waterlooville. *Hants* 2E 17
Watermead. *Buck* 4G 51
Watermillock. *Cumb* 2F 103
Water Newton. *Cambs* 1A 64
Water Orton. *Warw* 1F 61
Waterperry. *Oxon* 5E 51
Waterrow. *Som* 4D 20
Watersfield. *W Sus* 4B 26
Waterside. *Buck* 5H 51
Waterside. *Cambs* 3F 65
Waterside. *Cumb* 5D 112
Waterside. *E Ayr* 4D 116 (nr. Ayr)
Waterside. *E Ayr* 5F 127 (nr. Kilmarnock)
Waterside. *E Dun* 2H 127
Waterstein. *High* 4A 154
Waterstock. *Oxon* 5E 51
Waterston. *Pemb* 4D 42
Water Stratford. *Buck* 2E 51
Waters Upton. *Telf* 4A 72
Water Yeat. *Cumb* 1B 96
Watford. *Herts* 1B 38
Watford. *Nptn* 4D 62
Wath. *Cumb* 4H 103
Wath. *N Yor* 3D 98 (nr. Pateley Bridge)
Wath. *N Yor* 2F 99 (nr. Ripon)
Wath Brow. *Cumb* 3B 102
Wath upon Dearne. *S Yor* 1B 86
Watlington. *Norf* 4F 77
Watlington. *Oxon* 2E 37
Watten. *High* 3E 169
Wattisfield. *Suff* 3C 66
Wattisham. *Suff* 5C 66
Wattlesborough Heath. *Shrp* 4F 71
Watton. *Dors* 3H 13
Watton. *E Yor* 4E 101
Watton. *Norf* 5B 78
Watton at Stone. *Herts* 4C 52
Wattston. *N Lan* 2A 128
Wattstown. *Rhon* 2D 32
Wattsville. *Cphy* 2F 33
Wauldby. *E Yor* 2C 94
Waulkmill. *Abers* 4D 152
Waun. *Powy* 4E 71
Waunarlwydd. *Swan* 3F 31
Waun Fawr. *Cdgn* 2F 57
Waunfawr. *Gwyn* 5E 81
Waungilwen. *Carm* 1H 43
Waunlwyd. *Blae* 5E 47
Waun-y-Clyn. *Carm* 5E 45
Wavendon. *Mil* 2H 51
Waverbridge. *Cumb* 5D 112
Waverley. *Surr* 2G 25
Waverton. *Ches W* 4G 83
Waverton. *Cumb* 5D 112
Wavertree. *Mers* 2F 83
Wawne. *E Yor* 1D 94
Waxham. *Norf* 3G 79
Waxholme. *E Yor* 2G 95
Wayford. *Som* 2H 13
Way Head. *Cambs* 2D 65
Waytown. *Dors* 3H 13
Way Village. *Devn* 1B 12
Wdig. *Pemb* 1D 42
Wealdstone. *G Lon* 2C 38
Weardley. *W Yor* 5E 99
Weare. *Som* 1H 21
Weare Giffard. *Devn* 4E 19
Wearhead. *Dur* 1B 104
Wearne. *Som* 4H 21
Weasdale. *Cumb* 4H 103
Weasenham All Saints. *Norf* 3H 77
Weasenham St Peter. *Norf* 3A 78
Weaverham. *Ches W* 3A 84
Weaverthorpe. *N Yor* 2D 100
Webheath. *Worc* 4E 61
Webton. *Here* 2H 47
Wedderlairs. *Abers* 5F 161
Weddington. *Warw* 1A 62
Wedhampton. *Wilts* 1F 23
Wedmore. *Som* 2H 21
Wednesbury. *W Mid* 1D 61
Wednesfield. *W Mid* 5D 72
Weecar. *Notts* 4F 87
Weedon. *Buck* 4G 51
Weedon Bec. *Nptn* 5D 62
Weedon Lois. *Nptn* 1E 50
Weeford. *Staf* 5F 73
Week. *Devn* 4F 19 (nr. Barnstaple)
Week. *Devn* 2G 11 (nr. Okehampton)
Week. *Devn* 1H 11 (nr. South Molton)
Week. *Devn* 2D 9 (nr. Totnes)
Week. *Som* 3C 20
Weeke. *Devn* 2A 12
Weeke. *Hants* 3C 24
Week Green. *Corn* 3C 10
Weekley. *Nptn* 2F 63
Week St Mary. *Corn* 3C 10
Weel. *E Yor* 1D 94
Weeley. *Essx* 3E 55
Weeley Heath. *Essx* 3E 55
Weem. *Per* 4F 143
Weeping Cross. *Staf* 3D 72
Weethly. *Warw* 5E 61
Weeting. *Norf* 2G 65
Weeton. *E Yor* 2G 95
Weeton. *Lanc* 1B 90
Weeton. *N Yor* 5E 99
Weetwood Hall. *Nmbd* 2E 121
Weir. *Lanc* 2G 91
Welborne. *Norf* 4C 78
Welbourn. *Linc* 5G 87
Welburn. *N Yor* 1A 100 (nr. Kirkbymoorside)
Welburn. *N Yor* 3B 100 (nr. Malton)
Welbury. *N Yor* 4A 106
Welby. *Linc* 2G 75
Welches Dam. *Cambs* 2D 64
Welcombe. *Devn* 1C 10
Weld Bank. *Lanc* 3D 90
Weldon. *Nptn* 2G 63
Weldon. *Nmbd* 5F 121
Welford. *Nptn* 2D 62
Welford. *W Ber* 4C 36
Welford-on-Avon. *Warw* 5F 61
Welham. *Leics* 1E 63
Welham. *Notts* 2E 87
Welham Green. *Herts* 5C 52
Well. *Hants* 2F 25
Well. *Linc* 3D 88
Well. *N Yor* 1E 99
Welland. *Worc* 1C 48
Wellbank. *Ang* 5D 144
Well Bottom. *Dors* 1E 15
Welldale. *Dum* 3C 112
Wellesbourne. *Warw* 5G 61
Well Hill. *Kent* 4F 39
Wellhouse. *W Ber* 4D 36
Welling. *G Lon* 3F 39
Wellingborough. *Nptn* 4F 63
Wellingham. *Norf* 3A 78
Wellingore. *Linc* 5G 87
Wellington. *Cumb* 4B 102
Wellington. *Here* 1H 47
Wellington. *Som* 4E 21
Wellington. *Telf* 4A 72
Wellington Heath. *Here* 1C 48
Wellow. *Bath* 1C 22
Wellow. *IOW* 4B 16
Wellow. *Notts* 4D 86
Wellpond Green. *Herts* 3E 53
Wells. *Som* 2A 22
Wellsborough. *Leics* 5A 74
Wells Green. *Ches E* 5A 84
Wells-next-the-Sea. *Norf* 1B 78
Wellswood. *Torb* 2F 9
Wellwood. *Fife* 1D 129
Welney. *Norf* 1E 65
Welsford. *Devn* 4C 18
Welshampton. *Shrp* 2G 71
Welsh End. *Shrp* 2H 71
Welsh Frankton. *Shrp* 2F 71
Welsh Hook. *Pemb* 2D 42
Welsh Newton. *Here* 4H 47
Welsh Newton Common. *Here* 4A 48
Welshpool. *Powy* 5E 70
Welsh St Donats. *V Glam* 4D 32
Welton. *Bath* 1B 22
Welton. *Cumb* 5E 113
Welton. *E Yor* 2C 94
Welton. *Linc* 2H 87
Welton. *Nptn* 4C 62
Welton Hill. *Linc* 2H 87
Welton le Marsh. *Linc* 4D 88
Welton le Wold. *Linc* 2B 88
Welwick. *E Yor* 2G 95
Welwyn. *Herts* 4C 52
Welwyn Garden City. *Herts* 4C 52
Wem. *Shrp* 3H 71
Wembdon. *Som* 3F 21
Wembley. *G Lon* 2C 38
Wembury. *Devn* 4B 8
Wembworthy. *Devn* 2G 11
Wemyss Bay. *Inv* 2C 126
Wenallt. *Cdgn* 3F 57
Wenallt. *Gwyn* 1B 70
Wendens Ambo. *Essx* 2F 53
Wendlebury. *Oxon* 4D 50
Wendling. *Norf* 4B 78
Wendover. *Buck* 5G 51
Wendron. *Corn* 5A 6
Wendy. *Cambs* 1D 52
Wenfordbridge. *Corn* 5A 10
Wenhaston. *Suff* 3G 67
Wennington. *Cambs* 3B 64
Wennington. *G Lon* 2G 39
Wennington. *Lanc* 2F 97
Wensley. *Derbs* 4G 85
Wensley. *N Yor* 1C 98
Wentbridge. *W Yor* 3E 93
Wentnor. *Shrp* 1F 59
Wentworth. *Cambs* 3D 65
Wentworth. *S Yor* 1A 86
Wenvoe. *V Glam* 4E 32
Weobley. *Here* 5G 59
Weobley Marsh. *Here* 5G 59
Wepham. *W Sus* 5B 26
Wereham. *Norf* 5F 77
Wergs. *W Mid* 5C 72
Wern. *Gwyn* 1E 69
Wern. *Powy* 4E 46 (nr. Brecon)
Wern. *Powy* 4E 71 (nr. Guilsfield)
Wern. *Powy* 4B 70 (nr. Llangadfan)
Wern. *Powy* 3E 71 (nr. Llanymynech)
Wernffrwd. *Swan* 3E 31
Wernyrheolydd. *Mon* 4G 47
Werrington. *Corn* 4D 10
Werrington. *Pet* 5A 76
Werrington. *Staf* 1D 72
Wervin. *Ches W* 3G 83
Wesham. *Lanc* 1C 90
Wessington. *Derbs* 5A 86
West Aberthaw. *V Glam* 5D 32
West Acre. *Norf* 4G 77
West Allerdean. *Nmbd* 5F 131
West Alvington. *Devn* 4D 8
West Amesbury. *Wilts* 2G 23
West Anstey. *Devn* 4B 20
West Appleton. *N Yor* 5F 105
West Ardsley. *W Yor* 2C 92
West Arthurlie. *E Ren* 4F 127
West Ashby. *Linc* 3B 88
West Ashling. *W Sus* 2G 17
West Ashton. *Wilts* 1D 23
West Auckland. *Dur* 2E 105
West Ayton. *N Yor* 1D 101
West Bagborough. *Som* 3E 21
West Bank. *Hal* 2H 83
West Barkwith. *Linc* 2A 88
West Barnby. *N Yor* 3F 107
West Barns. *E Lot* 2C 130
West Barsham. *Norf* 2B 78
West Bay. *Dors* 3H 13
West Beckham. *Norf* 2D 78
West Bennan. *N Ayr* 3D 123
Westbere. *Kent* 4F 41
West Bergholt. *Essx* 3C 54
West Bexington. *Dors* 4A 14
West Bilney. *Norf* 4G 77
West Blackdene. *Dur* 1B 104
West Blatchington. *Brig* 5D 27
Westborough. *Linc* 1F 75
Westbourne. *Bour* 3F 15
Westbourne. *W Sus* 2F 17
West Bowling. *W Yor* 1B 92
West Brabourne. *Kent* 1E 29
West Bradford. *Lanc* 5G 97
West Bradley. *Som* 3A 22
West Bretton. *W Yor* 3C 92
West Bridgford. *Notts* 2C 74
West Briggs. *Norf* 4F 77
West Bromwich. *W Mid* 1D 61
Westbrook. *Here* 1F 47
Westbrook. *Kent* 3H 41
Westbrook. *Wilts* 5E 35
West Buckland. *Devn* 3G 19 (nr. Barnstaple)
West Buckland. *Devn* 4C 8 (nr. Thurlestone)
West Buckland. *Som* 4E 21
West Burnside. *Abers* 1G 145
West Burrafirth. *Shet* 6D 173
West Burton. *N Yor* 1C 98
West Burton. *W Sus* 4B 26
Westbury. *Buck* 2E 50
Westbury. *Shrp* 5F 71
Westbury. *Wilts* 1D 22
Westbury Leigh. *Wilts* 2D 22
Westbury-on-Severn. *Glos* 4C 48
Westbury on Trym. *Bris* 4A 34
Westbury-sub-Mendip. *Som* 2A 22
West Butsfield. *Dur* 5E 115
West Butterwick. *N Lin* 4B 94
Westby. *Linc* 3G 75
West Byfleet. *Surr* 4B 38
West Caister. *Norf* 4H 79
West Calder. *W Lot* 3D 128
West Camel. *Som* 4A 22
West Carr. *N Lin* 4H 93
West Chaldon. *Dors* 4C 14
West Challow. *Oxon* 3B 36
West Charleton. *Devn* 4D 8
West Chelborough. *Dors* 2A 14
West Chevington. *Nmbd* 5G 121
West Chiltington. *W Sus* 4B 26
West Chiltington Common. *W Sus* 4B 26
West Chinnock. *Som* 1H 13
West Chisenbury. *Wilts* 1G 23
West Clandon. *Surr* 5B 38
West Cliffe. *Kent* 1H 29
Westcliff-on-Sea. *S'end* 2C 40
West Clyne. *High* 3F 165
West Coker. *Som* 1A 14
Westcombe. *Som* 3B 22 (nr. Evercreech)
Westcombe. *Som* 4H 21 (nr. Somerton)
West Compton. *Dors* 3A 14
West Compton. *Som* 2A 22
West Cornforth. *Dur* 1A 106
Westcot. *Oxon* 3B 36
Westcott. *Buck* 4F 51
Westcott. *Devn* 2D 12
Westcott. *Surr* 1C 26
Westcott Barton. *Oxon* 3C 50
West Cowick. *E Yor* 2G 93
West Cranmore. *Som* 2B 22
West Croftmore. *High* 2D 150
West Cross. *Swan* 4F 31
West Cullerlie. *Abers* 3E 153
West Culvennan. *Dum* 3H 109
West Curry. *Corn* 3C 10
West Curthwaite. *Cumb* 5E 113
Westdean. *E Sus* 5G 27
West Dean. *W Sus* 1G 17
West Dean. *Wilts* 4A 24
West Deeping. *Linc* 5A 76
West Derby. *Mers* 1F 83
West Dereham. *Norf* 5F 77
West Down. *Devn* 2F 19
Westdowns. *Corn* 4A 10
West Drayton. *G Lon* 3B 38
West Drayton. *Notts* 3E 86
West Dunnet. *High* 1E 169
West Ella. *E Yor* 2D 94
West End. *Bed* 5G 63
West End. *Cambs* 1D 64
West End. *Dors* 2E 15
West End. *E Yor* 3E 101 (nr. Kilham)
West End. *E Yor* 1E 95 (nr. Preston)
West End. *E Yor* 1C 94 (nr. South Cove)
West End. *E Yor* 4F 101 (nr. Ulrome)
West End. *G Lon* 2D 39
West End. *Hants* 1C 16
West End. *Herts* 5C 52
West End. *Kent* 4F 41
West End. *Lanc* 3D 96
West End. *Linc* 1C 76
West End. *Norf* 4G 79
West End. *N Som* 5H 33
West End. *N Yor* 4D 98
West End. *S Glo* 3C 34
West End. *S Lan* 5C 128
West End. *Surr* 4A 38
West End. *Wilts* 4E 23
West End. *Wind* 4G 37
West End. *Worc* 2F 49
West End Green. *Hants* 5E 37
Westenhanger. *Kent* 2F 29
Wester Aberchalder. *High* 2H 149
Wester Balgedie. *Per* 3D 136
Wester Brae. *High* 2A 158
Wester Culbeuchly. *Abers* 2D 160
Westerdale. *High* 3D 168
Westerdale. *N Yor* 4D 106
Wester Dechmont. *W Lot* 2D 128
Wester Fearn. *High* 5D 164
Westerfield. *Suff* 1E 55
Wester Galcantray. *High* 4C 158
Westergate. *W Sus* 5A 26
Wester Gruinards. *High* 4C 164
Westerham. *Kent* 5F 39
Westerleigh. *S Glo* 4B 34
Westerloch. *High* 3F 169
Wester Mandally. *High* 3E 149
Wester Quarff. *Shet* 8F 173

Whitson—Woodland

Whitson. *Newp* 3G **33**
Whitstable. *Kent* 4F **41**
Whitstone. *Corn* 3C **10**
Whittingham. *Nmbd* 3E **121**
Whittingslow. *Shrp* 2G **59**
Whittington. *Derbs* 3B **86**
Whittington. *Glos* 3F **49**
Whittington. *Lanc* 2F **97**
Whittington. *Shrp* 2F **71**
Whittington. *Staf* 2C **60**
(nr. Kinver)
Whittington. *Staf* 5F **73**
(nr. Lichfield)
Whittington. *Warw* 1G **61**
Whittington. *Worc* 5C **60**
Whittington Barracks. *Staf* 5F **73**
Whittlebury. *Nptn* 1E **51**
Whittleford. *Warw* 1H **61**
Whittle-le-Woods. *Lanc* 2D **90**
Whittlesey. *Cambs* 1B **64**
Whittlesford. *Cambs* 1E **53**
Whittlestone Head. *Bkbn* 3F **91**
Whitton. *N Lin* 2C **94**
Whitton. *Nmbd* 4E **121**
Whitton. *Powy* 4E **59**
Whitton. *Bord* 2B **120**
Whitton. *Shrp* 3H **59**
Whitton. *Stoc T* 2A **106**
Whittonditch. *Wilts* 4A **36**
Whittonstall. *Nmbd* 4D **114**
Whitway. *Hants* 1C **24**
Whitwell. *Derbs* 3C **86**
Whitwell. *Herts* 3B **52**
Whitwell. *IOW* 5D **16**
Whitwell. *N Yor* 5F **105**
Whitwell. *Rut* 5G **75**
Whitwell-on-the-Hill. *N Yor* 3B **100**
Whitwick. *Leics* 4B **74**
Whitwood. *W Yor* 2E **93**
Whitworth. *Lanc* 3G **91**
Whixall. *Shrp* 2H **71**
Whixley. *N Yor* 4G **99**
Whoberley. *W Mid* 3G **61**
Whorlton. *Dur* 3E **105**
Whorlton. *N Yor* 4B **106**
Whygate. *Nmbd* 2A **114**
Whyle. *Here* 4H **59**
Whyteleafe. *Surr* 5E **39**
Wibdon. *Glos* 2A **34**
Wibtoft. *Warw* 2B **62**
Wichenford. *Worc* 4B **60**
Wichling. *Kent* 5D **40**
Wick. *Bour* 3G **15**
Wick. *Devn* 2E **13**
Wick. *High* 3F **169**
Wick. *Shet* 8F **173**
(on Mainland)
Wick. *Shet* 1G **173**
(on Unst)
Wick. *Som* 2F **21**
(nr. Bridgwater)
Wick. *Som* 1G **21**
(nr. Burnham-on-Sea)
Wick. *Som* 4H **21**
(nr. Somerton)
Wick. *S Glo* 4C **34**
Wick. *V Glam* 4C **32**
Wick. *W Sus* 5B **26**
Wick. *Wilts* 4G **23**
Wick. *Worc* 1E **49**
Wick Airport. *High* 3F **169**
Wicken. *Cambs* 3E **65**
Wicken. *Nptn* 2F **51**
Wicken Bonhunt. *Essx* 2E **53**
Wickenby. *Linc* 2H **87**
Wicken Green Village. *Norf* 2H **77**
Wickersley. *S Yor* 1B **86**
Wicker Street Green. *Suff* 1C **54**
Wickford. *Essx* 1B **40**
Wickham. *Hants* 1D **16**
Wickham. *W Ber* 4B **36**
Wickham Bishops. *Essx* 4B **54**
Wickhambreaux. *Kent* 5G **41**
Wickhambrook. *Suff* 5G **65**
Wickhamford. *Worc* 1F **49**
Wickham Green. *Suff* 4C **66**
Wickham Heath. *W Ber* 5C **36**
Wickham Market. *Suff* 5F **67**
Wickhampton. *Norf* 5G **79**
Wickham St Paul. *Essx* 2B **54**
Wickham Skeith. *Suff* 4C **66**
Wickham Street. *Suff* 4C **66**
Wick Hill. *Wok* 5F **37**
Wicklewood. *Norf* 5C **78**
Wickmere. *Norf* 2D **78**
Wick St Lawrence. *N Som* 5G **33**
Wickwar. *S Glo* 3C **34**
Widdington. *Essx* 2F **53**
Widdrington. *Nmbd* 5G **121**
Widdrington Station. *Nmbd* 5G **121**
Widecombe in the Moor. *Devn* 5H **11**
Widegates. *Corn* 3G **7**
Widemouth Bay. *Corn* 2C **10**
Wide Open. *Tyne* 2F **115**
Widewall. *Orkn* 8D **172**
Widford. *Essx* 5G **53**
Widford. *Herts* 4E **53**
Widham. *Wilts* 3F **35**
Widmer End. *Buck* 2G **37**
Widmerpool. *Notts* 3D **74**
Widnes. *Hal* 2H **83**
Widworthy. *Devn* 3F **13**
Wigan. *G Man* 4D **90**
Wigbeth. *Dors* 2F **15**
Wigborough. *Som* 1H **13**
Wiggaton. *Devn* 3E **12**
Wiggenhall St Germans. *Norf* 4E **77**
Wiggenhall St Mary Magdalen.
Norf 4E **77**
Wiggenhall St Mary the Virgin.
Norf 4E **77**
Wiggenhall St Peter. *Norf* 4F **77**
Wiggens Green. *Essx* 1G **53**
Wigginton. *Herts* 4H **51**
Wigginton. *Oxon* 2B **50**
Wigginton. *Staf* 5G **73**
Wigginton. *York* 4H **99**
Wigglesworth. *N Yor* 4H **97**
Wiggonby. *Cumb* 4D **112**
Wiggonholt. *W Sus* 4B **26**
Wighill. *N Yor* 5G **99**
Wighton. *Norf* 1B **78**
Wightwick. *Staf* 1C **60**
Wigley. *Hants* 1B **16**
Wigmore. *Here* 4G **59**
Wigmore. *Medw* 4C **40**
Wigsley. *Notts* 3F **87**
Wigsthorpe. *Nptn* 2H **63**
Wigston. *Leics* 1D **62**
Wigtoft. *Linc* 2B **76**
Wigton. *Cumb* 5D **112**
Wigtown. *Dum* 4B **110**
Wigtwizzle. *S Yor* 1G **85**
Wike. *W Yor* 5F **99**
Wilbarston. *Nptn* 2F **63**
Wilberfoss. *E Yor* 4B **100**
Wilburton. *Cambs* 3D **65**
Wilby. *Norf* 2C **66**
Wilby. *Nptn* 4F **63**
Wilby. *Suff* 3E **67**
Wilcot. *Wilts* 5G **35**
Wilcott. *Shrp* 4F **71**
Wilcove. *Corn* 3A **8**
Wildboarclough. *Ches E* 4D **85**
Wilden. *Bed* 5H **63**
Wilden. *Worc* 3C **60**
Wildern. *Hants* 1C **16**
Wilderspool. *Warr* 2A **84**
Wilde Street. *Suff* 3G **65**
Wildhern. *Hants* 1B **24**
Wildmanbridge. *S Lan* 4B **128**
Wildmoor. *Worc* 3D **60**
Wildsworth. *Linc* 1F **87**
Wildwood. *Staf* 3D **72**
Wilford. *Nott* 2C **74**
Wilkesley. *Ches E* 1A **72**
Wilkhaven. *High* 5G **165**
Wilkieston. *W Lot* 3E **129**
Wilksby. *Linc* 4B **88**
Willand. *Devn* 1D **12**
Willaston. *Ches E* 5A **84**
Willaston. *Ches W* 3F **83**
Willaston. *IOM* 4C **108**
Willen. *Mil* 1G **51**
Willenhall. *W Mid* 3A **62**
(nr. Coventry)
Willenhall. *W Mid* 1D **60**
(nr. Wolverhampton)
Willerby. *E Yor* 1D **94**
Willerby. *N Yor* 2E **101**
Willersey. *Glos* 2G **49**
Willersley. *Here* 1G **47**
Willesborough. *Kent* 1E **28**
Willesborough Lees. *Kent* 1E **29**
Willesden. *G Lon* 2D **38**
Willesley. *Wilts* 3D **34**
Willett. *Som* 3E **20**
Willey. *Shrp* 1A **60**
Willey. *Warw* 2B **62**
Willey Green. *Surr* 5A **38**
Williamscot. *Oxon* 1C **50**
Williamsetter. *Shet* 9E **173**
Willian. *Herts* 2C **52**
Willingale. *Essx* 5F **53**
Willingdon. *E Sus* 5G **27**
Willingham. *Cambs* 3D **64**
Willingham by Stow. *Linc* 2F **87**
Willingham Green. *Cambs* 5F **65**
Willington. *Bed* 1B **52**
Willington. *Derbs* 3G **73**
Willington. *Dur* 1E **105**
Willington. *Tyne* 3G **115**
Willington. *Warw* 2A **50**
Willington Corner. *Ches W* 4H **83**
Willisham Tye. *Suff* 5C **66**
Willitoft. *E Yor* 1H **93**
Williton. *Som* 2D **20**
Willoughbridge. *Staf* 1B **72**
Willoughby. *Linc* 3D **88**
Willoughby. *Warw* 4C **62**
Willoughby-on-the-Wolds.
Notts 3D **74**
Willoughby Waterleys. *Leics* 1C **62**
Willoughton. *Linc* 1G **87**
Willow Green. *Worc* 5B **60**
Willows Green. *Essx* 4H **53**
Willsbridge. *S Glo* 4B **34**
Willslock. *Staf* 2E **73**
Wilmcote. *Warw* 5F **61**
Wilmington. *Bath* 5B **34**
Wilmington. *Devn* 3F **13**
Wilmington. *E Sus* 5G **27**
Wilmington. *Kent* 3G **39**
Wilmslow. *Ches E* 2C **84**
Wilnecote. *Staf* 5G **73**
Wilney Green. *Norf* 2C **66**
Wilpshire. *Lanc* 1E **91**
Wilsden. *W Yor* 1A **92**
Wilsford. *Linc* 1H **75**
Wilsford. *Wilts* 3G **23**
(nr. Amesbury)
Wilsford. *Wilts* 1G **23**
(nr. Devizes)
Wilsill. *N Yor* 3D **98**
Wilsley Green. *Kent* 2B **28**
Wilson. *Here* 3A **48**
Wilson. *Leics* 3B **74**
Wilsontown. *S Lan* 4C **128**
Wilstead. *Bed* 1A **52**
Wilsthorpe. *E Yor* 3F **101**
Wilsthorpe. *Linc* 4H **75**
Wilstone. *Herts* 4H **51**
Wilton. *Cumb* 3B **102**
Wilton. *N Yor* 1C **100**
Wilton. *Red C* 3C **106**
Wilton. *Bord* 3H **119**
Wilton. *Wilts* 5A **36**
(nr. Marlborough)
Wilton. *Wilts* 3F **23**
(nr. Salisbury)
Wimbish. *Essx* 2F **53**
Wimbish Green. *Essx* 2G **53**
Wimblebury. *Staf* 4E **73**
Wimbledon. *G Lon* 3D **38**
Wimblington. *Cambs* 1D **64**
Wimboldsley. *Ches W* 4A **84**
Wimborne Minster. *Dors* 2F **15**
Wimborne St Giles. *Dors* 1F **15**
Wimbotsham. *Norf* 5F **77**
Wimpole. *Cambs* 1D **52**
Wimpstone. *Warw* 1H **49**
Wincanton. *Som* 4C **22**
Winceby. *Linc* 4C **88**
Wincham. *Ches W* 3A **84**
Winchburgh. *W Lot* 2D **129**
Winchcombe. *Glos* 3F **49**
Winchelsea. *E Sus* 4D **28**
Winchelsea Beach. *E Sus* 4D **28**
Winchester. *Hants* 4C **24** & **213**
Winchet Hill. *Kent* 1B **28**
Winchfield. *Hants* 1F **25**
Winchmore Hill. *Buck* 1A **38**
Winchmore Hill. *G Lon* 1E **39**
Wincle. *Ches E* 4D **84**
Windermere. *Cumb* 5F **103**
Winderton. *Warw* 1B **50**
Windhill. *High* 4H **157**
Windle Hill. *Ches W* 3F **83**
Windlesham. *Surr* 4A **38**
Windley. *Derbs* 1H **73**
Windmill. *Derbs* 3F **85**
Windmill Hill. *E Sus* 4H **27**
Windmill Hill. *Som* 1G **13**
Windrush. *Glos* 4G **49**
Windsor. *Wind* 3A **38** & **213**
Windsor Green. *Suff* 5A **66**
Windyedge. *Abers* 4G **153**
Windygates. *Fife* 3F **137**
Windyharbour. *Ches E* 3C **84**
Windyknowe. *W Lot* 3C **128**
Wineham. *W Sus* 3D **26**
Winestead. *E Yor* 2G **95**
Winfarthing. *Norf* 2D **66**
Winford. *IOW* 4D **16**
Winford. *N Som* 5A **34**
Winforton. *Here* 1F **47**
Winfrith Newburgh. *Dors* 4D **14**
Wing. *Buck* 3G **51**
Wing. *Rut* 5F **75**
Wingate. *Dur* 1A **106**
Wingates. *G Man* 4E **91**
Wingates. *Nmbd* 5F **121**
Wingerworth. *Derbs* 4A **86**
Wingfield. *C Beds* 3A **52**
Wingfield. *Suff* 3E **67**
Wingfield. *Wilts* 1D **22**
Wingfield Park. *Derbs* 5A **86**
Wingham. *Kent* 5G **41**
Wingmore. *Kent* 1F **29**
Wingrave. *Buck* 4G **51**
Winkburn. *Notts* 5E **86**
Winkfield. *Brac* 3A **38**
Winkfield Row. *Brac* 4G **37**
Winkhill. *Staf* 5E **85**
Winklebury. *Hants* 1E **24**
Winkleigh. *Devn* 2G **11**
Winksley. *N Yor* 2E **99**
Winkton. *Dors* 3G **15**
Winlaton. *Tyne* 3E **115**
Winlaton Mill. *Tyne* 3E **115**
Winless. *High* 3F **169**
Winmarleigh. *Lanc* 5D **96**
Winnal Common. *Here* 2H **47**
Winnard's Perch. *Corn* 2D **6**
Winnersh. *Wok* 4F **37**
Winnington. *Ches W* 3A **84**
Winnington. *Staf* 2B **72**
Winnothdale. *Staf* 1E **73**
Winscales. *Cumb* 2B **102**
Winscombe. *N Som* 1H **21**
Winsford. *Ches W* 4A **84**
Winsford. *Som* 3C **20**
Winsham. *Devn* 3F **19**
Winsham. *Som* 2G **13**
Winshill. *Staf* 3G **73**
Winsh-wen. *Swan* 3F **31**
Winskill. *Cumb* 1G **103**
Winslade. *Hants* 2E **25**
Winsley. *Wilts* 5C **34**
Winslow. *Buck* 3F **51**
Winson. *Glos* 5F **49**
Winson Green. *W Mid* 2E **61**
Winsor. *Hants* 1B **16**
Winster. *Cumb* 5F **103**
Winster. *Derbs* 4G **85**
Winston. *Dur* 3E **105**
Winston. *Suff* 4D **66**
Winstone. *Glos* 5E **49**
Winswell. *Devn* 1E **11**
Winterborne Clenston. *Dors* 2D **14**
Winterborne Herringston. *Dors* 4B **14**
Winterborne Houghton. *Dors* 2D **14**
Winterborne Kingston. *Dors* 3D **14**
Winterborne Monkton. *Dors* 4B **14**
Winterborne St Martin. *Dors* 4B **14**
Winterborne Stickland. *Dors* 2D **14**
Winterborne Whitechurch. *Dors* 2D **14**
Winterborne Zelston. *Dors* 3E **15**
Winterbourne. *S Glo* 3B **34**
Winterbourne. *W Ber* 4C **36**
Winterbourne Abbas. *Dors* 3B **14**
Winterbourne Bassett. *Wilts* 4G **35**
Winterbourne Dauntsey. *Wilts* 3G **23**
Winterbourne Earls. *Wilts* 3G **23**
Winterbourne Gunner. *Wilts* 3G **23**
Winterbourne Monkton. *Wilts* 4F **35**
Winterbourne Steepleton. *Dors* 4B **14**
Winterbourne Stoke. *Wilts* 2F **23**
Winterbrook. *Oxon* 3E **36**
Winterburn. *N Yor* 4B **98**
Winter Gardens. *Essx* 2B **40**
Winterhay Green. *Som* 1G **13**
Winteringham. *N Lin* 2C **94**
Winterley. *Ches E* 5B **84**
Wintersett. *W Yor* 3D **93**
Winterton. *N Lin* 3C **94**
Winterton-on-Sea. *Norf* 4G **79**
Winthorpe. *Linc* 4E **89**
Winthorpe. *Notts* 5F **87**
Winton. *Bour* 3F **15**
Winton. *Cumb* 3A **104**
Winton. *E Sus* 5G **27**
Wintringham. *N Yor* 2C **100**
Winwick. *Cambs* 2A **64**
Winwick. *Nptn* 3D **62**
Winwick. *Warr* 1A **84**
Wirksworth. *Derbs* 5G **85**
Wirswall. *Ches E* 1H **71**
Wisbech. *Cambs* 4D **76**
Wisbech St Mary. *Cambs* 5D **76**
Wisborough Green. *W Sus* 3B **26**
Wiseton. *Notts* 2E **86**
Wishaw. *N Lan* 4B **128**
Wishaw. *Warw* 1F **61**
Wisley. *Surr* 5B **38**
Wispington. *Linc* 3B **88**
Wissenden. *Kent* 1D **28**
Wissett. *Suff* 3F **67**
Wistanstow. *Shrp* 2G **59**
Wistanswick. *Shrp* 3A **72**
Wistaston. *Ches E* 5A **84**
Wiston. *Pemb* 3E **43**
Wiston. *S Lan* 1B **118**
Wiston. *W Sus* 4C **26**
Wistow. *Cambs* 2B **64**
Wistow. *N Yor* 1F **93**
Wiswell. *Lanc* 1F **91**
Witcham. *Cambs* 2D **64**
Witchampton. *Dors* 2E **15**
Witchford. *Cambs* 3E **65**
Witham. *Essx* 4B **54**
Witham Friary. *Som* 2C **22**
Witham on the Hill. *Linc* 4H **75**
Witham St Hughs. *Linc* 4F **87**
Withcall. *Linc* 2B **88**
Witherenden Hill. *E Sus* 3H **27**
Withergate. *Norf* 3E **79**
Witheridge. *Devn* 1B **12**
Witheridge Hill. *Oxon* 3E **37**
Witherley. *Leics* 1H **61**
Withermarsh Green. *Suff* 2D **54**
Withern. *Linc* 2D **88**
Withernsea. *E Yor* 2G **95**
Withernwick. *E Yor* 5F **101**
Withersdale Street. *Suff* 2E **67**
Withersfield. *Suff* 1G **53**
Witherslack. *Cumb* 1D **96**
Withiel. *Corn* 2D **6**
Withiel Florey. *Som* 3C **20**
Withington. *Glos* 4F **49**
Withington. *G Man* 1C **84**
Withington. *Here* 1A **48**
Withington. *Shrp* 4H **71**
Withington. *Staf* 2E **73**
Withington Green. *Ches E* 3C **84**
Withington Marsh. *Here* 1A **48**
Withleigh. *Devn* 1C **12**
Withnell. *Lanc* 2E **91**
Withnell Fold. *Lanc* 2E **90**
Withybrook. *Warw* 2B **62**
Withycombe. *Som* 2D **20**
Withycombe Raleigh. *Devn* 4D **12**
Withyham. *E Sus* 2F **27**
Withypool. *Som* 3B **20**
Witley. *Surr* 1A **26**
Witnesham. *Suff* 5D **66**
Witney. *Oxon* 4B **50**
Wittering. *Pet* 5H **75**
Wittersham. *Kent* 3D **28**
Witton. *Norf* 5F **79**
Witton. *Worc* 4D **60**
Witton Bridge. *Norf* 2F **79**
Witton Gilbert. *Dur* 5F **115**
Witton-le-Wear. *Dur* 1E **105**
Witton Park. *Dur* 1E **105**
Wiveliscombe. *Som* 4D **20**
Wivelrod. *Hants* 3E **25**
Wivelsfield. *E Sus* 3E **27**
Wivelsfield Green. *E Sus* 4E **27**
Wivenhoe. *Essx* 3D **54**
Wiveton. *Norf* 1C **78**
Wix. *Essx* 3E **55**
Wixford. *Warw* 5E **61**
Wixhill. *Shrp* 3H **71**
Wixoe. *Suff* 1H **53**
Woburn. *C Beds* 2H **51**
Woburn Sands. *Mil* 2H **51**
Woking. *Surr* 5B **38**
Wokingham. *Wok* 5G **37**
Wolborough. *Devn* 5B **12**
Woldingham. *Surr* 5E **39**
Wold Newton. *E Yor* 2E **101**
Wold Newton. *NE Lin* 1B **88**
Wolferlow. *Here* 4A **60**
Wolferton. *Norf* 3F **77**
Wolfhill. *Per* 5A **144**
Wolf's Castle. *Pemb* 2D **42**
Wolfsdale. *Pemb* 2D **42**
Wolgarston. *Staf* 4D **72**
Wollaston. *Nptn* 4G **63**
Wollaston. *Shrp* 4F **71**
Wollaston. *W Mid* 2C **60**
Wollaton. *Nott* 1C **74**
Wollerton. *Shrp* 2A **72**
Wollescote. *W Mid* 2D **60**
Wolseley Bridge. *Staf* 3E **73**
Wolsingham. *Dur* 1D **105**
Wolstanton. *Staf* 1C **72**
Wolston. *Warw* 3B **62**
Wolsty. *Cumb* 4C **112**
Wolterton. *Norf* 2D **78**
Wolvercote. *Oxon* 5C **50**
Wolverhampton. *W Mid* 1D **60** & **213**
Wolverley. *Shrp* 2G **71**
Wolverley. *Worc* 3C **60**
Wolverton. *Hants* 1D **24**
Wolverton. *Mil* 1G **51**
Wolverton. *Warw* 4G **61**
Wolverton. *Wilts* 3C **22**
Wolverton Common. *Hants* 1D **24**
Wolvesnewton. *Mon* 2H **33**
Wolvey. *Warw* 2B **62**
Wolvey Heath. *Warw* 2B **62**
Wolviston. *Stoc T* 2B **106**
Womaston. *Powy* 4E **59**
Wombleton. *N Yor* 1A **100**
Wombourne. *Staf* 1C **60**
Wombwell. *S Yor* 4D **93**
Womenswold. *Kent* 5G **41**
Womersley. *N Yor* 3F **93**
Wonersh. *Surr* 1B **26**
Wonson. *Devn* 4G **11**
Wonston. *Dors* 2C **14**
Wonston. *Hants* 3C **24**
Wooburn. *Buck* 2A **38**
Wooburn Green. *Buck* 2A **38**
Wood. *Pemb* 2C **42**
Woodacott. *Devn* 2D **11**
Woodale. *N Yor* 2C **98**
Woodall. *S Yor* 2B **86**
Woodbank. *Ches W* 3F **83**
Woodbastwick. *Norf* 4F **79**
Woodbeck. *Notts* 3E **87**
Woodborough. *Notts* 1D **74**
Woodborough. *Wilts* 1G **23**
Woodbridge. *Devn* 3E **13**
Woodbridge. *Dors* 1C **14**
Woodbridge. *Suff* 1F **55**
Wood Burcote. *Nptn* 1E **51**
Woodbury. *Devn* 4D **12**
Woodbury Salterton. *Devn* 4D **12**
Woodchester. *Glos* 5D **48**
Woodchurch. *Kent* 2D **28**
Woodchurch. *Mers* 2E **83**
Woodcock Heath. *Staf* 3E **73**
Woodcombe. *Som* 2C **20**
Woodcote. *Oxon* 3E **37**
Woodcote Green. *Worc* 3D **60**
Woodcott. *Hants* 1C **24**
Woodcroft. *Glos* 2A **34**
Woodcutts. *Dors* 1E **15**
Wood Dalling. *Norf* 3C **78**
Woodditton. *Cambs* 5F **65**
Woodeaton. *Oxon* 4D **50**
Wood Eaton. *Staf* 4C **72**
Wood End. *Bed* 4H **63**
Woodend. *Cumb* 5C **102**
Wood End. *Herts* 3D **52**
Woodend. *Nptn* 1E **50**
Woodend. *Staf* 3F **73**
Wood End. *Warw* 2G **61**
(nr. Bedworth)
Wood End. *Warw* 1G **61**
(nr. Dordon)
Wood End. *Warw* 3F **61**
(nr. Tanworth-in-Arden)
Woodend. *W Sus* 2G **17**
Wood Enderby. *Linc* 4B **88**
Woodend Green. *Essx* 3F **53**
Woodfalls. *Wilts* 4G **23**
Woodfield. *Oxon* 3D **50**
Woodfields. *Lanc* 1E **91**
Woodford. *Corn* 1C **10**
Woodford. *Devn* 3D **9**
Woodford. *Glos* 2B **34**
Woodford. *G Lon* 1E **39**
Woodford. *G Man* 2C **84**
Woodford. *Nptn* 3G **63**
Woodford. *Plym* 3B **8**
Woodford Green. *G Lon* 1F **39**
Woodford Halse. *Nptn* 5C **62**
Woodgate. *Norf* 4C **78**
Woodgate. *W Mid* 2D **61**
Woodgate. *W Sus* 5A **26**
Woodgate. *Worc* 4D **60**
Wood Green. *G Lon* 1D **39**
Woodgreen. *Hants* 1G **15**
Woodgreen. *Oxon* 4B **50**
Wood Hall. *E Yor* 1E **95**
Woodhall. *Inv* 2E **127**
Woodhall. *Linc* 4B **88**
Woodhall. *N Yor* 5C **104**
Woodhall Spa. *Linc* 4A **88**
Woodham. *Surr* 4B **38**
Woodham Ferrers. *Essx* 1B **40**
Woodham Mortimer. *Essx* 5B **54**
Woodham Walter. *Essx* 5B **54**
Woodhaven. *Fife* 1G **137**
Wood Hayes. *W Mid* 5D **72**
Woodhead. *Abers* 2G **161**
(nr. Fraserburgh)
Woodhead. *Abers* 5E **161**
(nr. Fyvie)
Woodhill. *N Som* 4H **33**
Woodhill. *Shrp* 2B **60**
Woodhill. *Som* 4G **21**
Woodhorn. *Nmbd* 1G **115**
Woodhouse. *Leics* 4C **74**
Woodhouse. *S Yor* 2B **86**
Woodhouse. *W Yor* 1C **92**
(nr. Leeds)
Woodhouse. *W Yor* 2D **93**
(nr. Normanton)
Woodhouse Eaves. *Leics* 4C **74**
Woodhouses. *Ches W* 3H **83**
Woodhouses. *G Man* 4H **91**
(nr. Failsworth)
Woodhouses. *G Man* 1B **84**
(nr. Sale)
Woodhouses. *Staf* 4F **73**
Woodhuish. *Devn* 3F **9**
Woodhurst. *Cambs* 3C **64**
Woodingdean. *Brig* 5E **27**
Woodland. *Devn* 2D **9**
Woodland. *Dur* 2D **104**

Woodland Head—Zouch

Woodland Head. *Devn* 3A **12**
Woodlands. *Abers* 4E **153**
Woodlands. *Dors* 2F **15**
Woodlands. *Hants* 1B **16**
Woodlands. *Kent* 4G **39**
Woodlands. *N Yor* 4F **99**
Woodlands. *S Yor* 4F **93**
Woodlands Park. *Wind* 4G **37**
Woodlands St Mary. *W Ber* 4B **36**
Woodlane. *Shrp* 3A **72**
Woodlane. *Staf* 3F **73**
Woodleigh. *Devn* 4D **8**
Woodlesford. *W Yor* 2D **92**
Woodley. *G Man* 1D **84**
Woodley. *Wok* 4F **37**
Woodmancote. *Glos* 3E **49** (nr. Cheltenham)
Woodmancote. *Glos* 5F **49** (nr. Cirencester)
Woodmancote. *W Sus* 2F **17** (nr. Chichester)
Woodmancote. *W Sus* 4D **26** (nr. Henfield)
Woodmancote. *Worc* 1E **49**
Woodmancott. *Hants* 2D **24**
Woodmansey. *E Yor* 1D **94**
Woodmansgreen. *W Sus* 4G **25**
Woodmansterne. *Surr* 5D **39**
Woodmanton. *Devn* 4D **12**
Woodmill. *Staf* 3F **73**
Woodminton. *Wilts* 4F **23**
Woodnesborough. *Kent* 5H **41**
Woodnewton. *Nptn* 1H **63**
Woodnook. *Linc* 2G **75**
Wood Norton. *Norf* 3C **78**
Woodplumpton. *Lanc* 1D **90**
Woodrising. *Norf* 5B **78**
Woodrow. *Cumb* 5D **112**
Woodrow. *Dors* 1C **14** (nr. Fifehead Neville)
Woodrow. *Dors* 2C **14** (nr. Hazelbury Bryan)
Wood Row. *W Yor* 2D **93**
Woods Eaves. *Here* 1F **47**
Woodseaves. *Shrp* 2A **72**
Woodseaves. *Staf* 3B **72**
Woodsend. *Wilts* 4H **35**
Woodsetts. *S Yor* 2C **86**
Woodsford. *Dors* 3C **14**
Wood's Green. *E Sus* 2H **27**
Woodshaw. *Wilts* 3F **35**
Woodside. *Aber* 3G **153**
Woodside. *Brac* 3A **38**
Woodside. *Derbs* 1A **74**
Woodside. *Dum* 2B **112**
Woodside. *Dur* 2E **105**
Woodside. *Fife* 3G **137**
Woodside. *Herts* 5C **52**
Woodside. *Per* 5B **144**
Wood Stanway. *Glos* 2F **49**
Woodstock. *Oxon* 4C **50**
Woodstock Slop. *Pemb* 2E **43**
Woodston. *Pet* 1A **64**
Wood Street. *Norf* 3F **79**
Wood Street Village. *Surr* 5A **38**
Woodthorpe. *Derbs* 3B **86**
Woodthorpe. *Leics* 4C **74**
Woodthorpe. *Linc* 2D **88**
Woodthorpe. *Notts* 1C **74**
Woodthorpe. *York* 5H **99**
Woodton. *Norf* 1E **67**
Woodtown. *Devn* 4E **19** (nr. Bideford)
Woodtown. *Devn* 4E **19** (nr. Littleham)
Woodvale. *Mers* 3B **90**
Woodville. *Derbs* 4H **73**
Woodwalton. *Cambs* 2B **64**
Woodwick. *Orkn* 5C **172**
Woodyates. *Dors* 1F **15**
Woody Bay. *Devn* 2G **19**
Woofferton. *Shrp* 4H **59**
Wookey. *Som* 2A **22**
Wookey Hole. *Som* 2A **22**
Wool. *Dors* 4D **14**
Woolacombe. *Devn* 2E **19**
Woolage Green. *Kent* 1G **29**
Woolage Village. *Kent* 5G **41**
Woolaston. *Glos* 2A **34**
Woolavington. *Som* 2G **21**
Woolbeding. *W Sus* 4G **25**
Woolcotts. *Som* 3C **20**
Wooldale. *W Yor* 4B **92**
Wooler. *Nmbd* 2D **121**
Woolfardisworthy. *Devn* 4D **18** (nr. Bideford)
Woolfardisworthy. *Devn* 2B **12** (nr. Crediton)
Woolfords. *S Lan* 4D **128**
Woolgarston. *Dors* 4E **15**
Woolhampton. *W Ber* 5D **36**
Woolhope. *Here* 2B **48**
Woolland. *Dors* 2C **14**
Woollard. *Bath* 5B **34**
Woolley. *Bath* 5C **34**
Woolley. *Cambs* 3A **64**
Woolley. *Corn* 1C **10**
Woolley. *Derbs* 4A **86**
Woolley. *W Yor* 3D **92**
Woolley Green. *Wilts* 5D **34**
Woolmere Green. *Worc* 4D **60**
Woolmer Green. *Herts* 4C **52**
Woolminstone. *Som* 2H **13**
Woolpit. *Suff* 4B **66**
Woolridge. *Glos* 3D **48**
Woolscott. *Warw* 4B **62**
Woolsery. *Devn* 4D **18**
Woolsington. *Tyne* 3E **115**
Woolstaston. *Shrp* 1G **59**
Woolsthorpe By Belvoir. *Linc* 2F **75**
Woolsthorpe-by-Colsterworth. *Linc* 3G **75**
Woolston. *Devn* 4D **8**
Woolston. *Shrp* 2G **59** (nr. Church Stretton)
Woolston. *Shrp* 3F **71** (nr. Oswestry)
Woolston. *Som* 4B **22**
Woolston. *Sotn* 1C **16**
Woolston. *Warr* 1A **84**
Woolstone. *Glos* 2E **49**
Woolstone. *Oxon* 3A **36**
Woolston Green. *Devn* 2D **9**
Woolton. *Mers* 2G **83**
Woolton Hill. *Hants* 5C **36**
Woolverstone. *Suff* 2E **55**
Woolverton. *Som* 1C **22**
Woolwell. *Devn* 2B **8**
Woolwich. *G Lon* 3F **39**
Woonton. *Here* 5F **59** (nr. Kington)
Woonton. *Here* 4H **59** (nr. Leominster)
Wooperton. *Nmbd* 2E **121**
Woore. *Shrp* 1B **72**
Wooth. *Dors* 3H **13**
Wooton. *Shrp* 2B **60**
Wootton. *Bed* 1A **52**
Wootton. *Hants* 3H **15**
Wootton. *IOW* 3D **16**
Wootton. *Kent* 1G **29**
Wootton. *Nptn* 5E **63**
Wootton. *N Lin* 3D **94**
Wootton. *Oxon* 5C **50** (nr. Abingdon)
Wootton. *Oxon* 4C **50** (nr. Woodstock)
Wootton. *Shrp* 3G **59** (nr. Ludlow)
Wootton. *Shrp* 3F **71** (nr. Oswestry)
Wootton. *Staf* 3C **72** (nr. Eccleshall)
Wootton. *Staf* 1F **73** (nr. Ellastone)
Wootton Bridge. *IOW* 3D **16**
Wootton Common. *IOW* 3D **16**
Wootton Courtenay. *Som* 2C **20**
Wootton Fitzpaine. *Dors* 3G **13**
Wootton Rivers. *Wilts* 5G **35**
Wootton St Lawrence. *Hants* 1D **24**
Wootton Wawen. *Warw* 4F **61**
Worcester. *Worc* 5C **60** & **214**
Worcester Park. *G Lon* 4D **38**
Wordsley. *W Mid* 2C **60**
Worfield. *Shrp* 1B **60**
Work. *Orkn* 6D **172**
Workhouse Green. *Suff* 2C **54**
Workington. *Cumb* 2A **102**
Worksop. *Notts* 3C **86**
Worlaby. *N Lin* 3D **94**
Worlds End. *Hants* 1E **17**
Worldsend. *Shrp* 1G **59**
World's End. *W Ber* 4C **36**
Worlds End. *W Mid* 2F **61**
Worlds End. *W Sus* 4E **27**
Worle. *N Som* 5G **33**
Worleston. *Ches E* 5A **84**
Worlingham. *Suff* 1G **67**
Worlington. *Suff* 3F **65**
Worlingworth. *Suff* 4E **67**
Wormbridge. *Here* 2H **47**
Wormegay. *Norf* 4F **77**
Wormelow Tump. *Here* 2H **47**
Wormhill. *Derbs* 3F **85**
Wormingford. *Essx* 2C **54**
Worminghall. *Buck* 5E **51**
Wormington. *Glos* 2F **49**
Worminster. *Som* 2A **22**
Wormit. *Fife* 1F **137**
Wormleighton. *Warw* 5B **62**
Wormley. *Herts* 5D **52**
Wormley. *Surr* 2A **26**
Wormshill. *Kent* 5C **40**
Wormsley. *Here* 1H **47**
Worplesdon. *Surr* 5A **38**
Worrall. *S Yor* 1H **85**
Worsbrough. *S Yor* 4D **92**
Worsley. *G Man* 4F **91**
Worstead. *Norf* 3F **79**
Worsthorne. *Lanc* 1G **91**
Worston. *Lanc* 5G **97**
Worth. *Kent* 5H **41**
Worth. *W Sus* 2E **27**
Wortham. *Suff* 3C **66**
Worthen. *Shrp* 5F **71**
Worthenbury. *Wrex* 1G **71**
Worthing. *Norf* 4B **78**
Worthing. *W Sus* 5C **26**
Worthington. *Leics* 3B **74**
Worth Matravers. *Dors* 5E **15**
Worting. *Hants* 1E **24**
Wortley. *Glos* 2C **34**
Wortley. *S Yor* 1H **85**
Wortley. *W Yor* 1C **92**
Worton. *N Yor* 5C **104**
Worton. *Wilts* 1E **23**
Wortwell. *Norf* 2E **67**
Wotherton. *Shrp* 5E **71**
Wothorpe. *Nptn* 5H **75**
Wotter. *Devn* 2B **8**
Wotton. *Glos* 4D **48**
Wotton. *Surr* 1C **26**
Wotton-under-Edge. *Glos* 2C **34**
Wotton Underwood. *Buck* 4E **51**
Wouldham. *Kent* 4B **40**
Wrabness. *Essx* 2E **55**
Wrafton. *Devn* 3E **19**
Wragby. *Linc* 3A **88**
Wragby. *W Yor* 3E **93**
Wramplingham. *Norf* 5D **78**
Wrangbrook. *W Yor* 3E **93**
Wrangle. *Linc* 5D **88**
Wrangle Lowgate. *Linc* 5D **88**
Wrangway. *Som* 1E **13**
Wrantage. *Som* 4G **21**
Wrawby. *N Lin* 4D **94**
Wraxall. *N Som* 4H **33**
Wraxall. *Som* 3B **22**
Wray. *Lanc* 3F **97**
Wraysbury. *Wind* 3B **38**
Wrayton. *Lanc* 2F **97**
Wrea Green. *Lanc* 1B **90**
Wreay. *Cumb* 5F **113** (nr. Carlisle)
Wreay. *Cumb* 2F **103** (nr. Penrith)
Wrecclesham. *Surr* 2G **25**
Wrecsam. *Wrex* 5F **83** & **Wrexham 214**
Wrekenton. *Tyne* 4F **115**
Wrelton. *N Yor* 1B **100**
Wrenbury. *Ches E* 1H **71**
Wreningham. *Norf* 1D **66**
Wrentham. *Suff* 2G **67**
Wrenthorpe. *W Yor* 2D **92**
Wrentnall. *Shrp* 5G **71**
Wressle. *E Yor* 1H **93**
Wressle. *N Lin* 4C **94**
Wrestlingworth. *C Beds* 1C **52**
Wretton. *Norf* 1F **65**
Wrexham. *Wrex* 5F **83** & **214**
Wreyland. *Devn* 4A **12**
Wrickton. *Shrp* 2A **60**
Wrightington Bar. *Lanc* 3D **90**
Wright's Green. *Essx* 4F **53**
Wrinehill. *Staf* 1B **72**
Wrington. *N Som* 5H **33**
Writtle. *Essx* 5G **53**
Wrockwardine. *Telf* 4A **72**
Wroot. *N Lin* 4H **93**
Wrotham. *Kent* 5H **39**
Wrotham Heath. *Kent* 5H **39**
Wroughton. *Swin* 3G **35**
Wroxall. *IOW* 4D **16**
Wroxall. *Warw* 3G **61**
Wroxeter. *Shrp* 5H **71**
Wroxham. *Norf* 4F **79**
Wroxton. *Oxon* 1C **50**
Wyaston. *Derbs* 1F **73**
Wyatt's Green. *Essx* 1G **39**
Wybers Wood. *NE Lin* 4F **95**
Wyberton. *Linc* 1C **76**
Wyboston. *Bed* 5A **64**
Wybunbury. *Ches E* 1A **72**
Wychbold. *Worc* 4D **60**
Wych Cross. *E Sus* 2F **27**
Wychnor. *Staf* 4F **73**
Wychnor Bridges. *Staf* 4F **73**
Wyck. *Hants* 3F **25**
Wyck Hill. *Glos* 3G **49**
Wyck Rissington. *Glos* 3G **49**
Wycliffe. *Dur* 3E **105**
Wycombe Marsh. *Buck* 2G **37**
Wyddial. *Herts* 2D **52**
Wye. *Kent* 1E **29**
Wyesham. *Mon* 4A **48**
Wyfold Grange. *Oxon* 3E **37**
Wyfordby. *Leics* 4E **75**
Wyke. *Devn* 3B **12**
Wyke. *Dors* 4C **22**
Wyke. *Shrp* 5A **72**
Wyke. *Surr* 5A **38**
Wyke. *W Yor* 2B **92**
Wyke Champflower. *Som* 3B **22**
Wykeham. *Linc* 3B **76**
Wykeham. *N Yor* 2C **100** (nr. Malton)
Wykeham. *N Yor* 1D **100** (nr. Scarborough)
Wyken. *Shrp* 1B **60**
Wyken. *W Mid* 2A **62**
Wyke Regis. *Dors* 5B **14**
Wyke, The. *Shrp* 5B **72**
Wykey. *Shrp* 3F **71**
Wykin. *Leics* 1B **62**
Wylam. *Nmbd* 3E **115**
Wylde Green. *W Mid* 1F **61**
Wylye. *Wilts* 3F **23**
Wymering. *Port* 2E **17**
Wymeswold. *Leics* 3D **74**
Wymington. *Bed* 4G **63**
Wymondham. *Leics* 4F **75**
Wymondham. *Norf* 5D **78**
Wyndham. *B'end* 2C **32**
Wynford Eagle. *Dors* 3A **14**
Wyng. *Orkn* 8C **172**
Wynyard Village. *Stoc T* 2B **106**
Wyre Piddle. *Worc* 1E **49**
Wysall. *Notts* 3D **74**
Wyson. *Here* 4H **59**
Wythall. *Worc* 3E **61**
Wytham. *Oxon* 5C **50**
Wythenshawe. *G Man* 2C **84**
Wythop Mill. *Cumb* 2C **102**
Wyton. *Cambs* 3B **64**
Wyton. *E Yor* 1E **95**
Wyverstone. *Suff* 4C **66**
Wyverstone Street. *Suff* 4C **66**
Wyville. *Linc* 3F **75**
Wyvis Lodge. *High* 1G **157**

Y

Yaddlethorpe. *N Lin* 4B **94**
Yafford. *IOW* 4C **16**
Yafforth. *N Yor* 5A **106**
Yalding. *Kent* 5A **40**
Yanley. *N Som* 5A **34**
Yanwath. *Cumb* 2G **103**
Yanworth. *Glos* 4F **49**
Yapham. *E Yor* 4B **100**
Yapton. *W Sus* 5A **26**
Yarburgh. *Linc* 1C **88**
Yarcombe. *Devn* 2F **13**
Yarde. *Som* 3D **20**
Yardley. *W Mid* 2F **61**
Yardley Gobion. *Nptn* 1F **51**
Yardley Hastings. *Nptn* 5F **63**
Yardley Wood. *W Mid* 2F **61**
Yardro. *Powy* 5E **58**
Yarhampton. *Worc* 4B **60**
Yarkhill. *Here* 1B **48**
Yarlet. *Staf* 3D **72**
Yarley. *Som* 2A **22**
Yarlington. *Som* 4B **22**
Yarm. *Stoc T* 3B **106**
Yarmouth. *IOW* 4B **16**
Yarnbrook. *Wilts* 1D **22**
Yarnfield. *Staf* 2C **72**
Yarnscombe. *Devn* 4F **19**
Yarnton. *Oxon* 4C **50**
Yarpole. *Here* 4G **59**
Yarrow. *Nmbd* 1A **114**
Yarrow. *Bord* 2F **119**
Yarrow. *Som* 2G **21**
Yarrow Feus. *Bord* 2F **119**
Yarrow Ford. *Bord* 1G **119**
Yarsop. *Here* 1H **47**
Yarwell. *Nptn* 1H **63**
Yate. *S Glo* 3C **34**
Yateley. *Hants* 5G **37**
Yatesbury. *Wilts* 4F **35**
Yattendon. *W Ber* 4D **36**
Yatton. *Here* 4G **59** (nr. Leominster)
Yatton. *Here* 2B **48** (nr. Ross-on-Wye)
Yatton. *N Som* 5H **33**
Yatton Keynell. *Wilts* 4D **34**
Yaverland. *IOW* 4E **16**
Yawl. *Devn* 3G **13**
Yaxham. *Norf* 4C **78**
Yaxley. *Cambs* 1A **64**
Yaxley. *Suff* 3D **66**
Yazor. *Here* 1H **47**
Y Bala. *Gwyn* 2B **70**
Y Bont-Faen. *V Glam* 4C **32**
Y Clun. *Neat* 5B **46**
Y Dref. *Gwyn* 2D **69**
Y Drenewydd. *Powy* 1D **58**
Yeading. *G Lon* 2C **38**
Yeadon. *W Yor* 5E **98**
Yealand Conyers. *Lanc* 2E **97**
Yealand Redmayne. *Lanc* 2E **97**
Yealand Storrs. *Lanc* 2D **97**
Yealmpton. *Devn* 3B **8**
Yearby. *Red C* 2D **106**
Yearngill. *Cumb* 5C **112**
Yearsett. *Here* 5B **60**
Yearsley. *N Yor* 2H **99**
Yeaton. *Shrp* 4G **71**
Yeaveley. *Derbs* 1F **73**
Yeavering. *Nmbd* 1D **120**
Yedingham. *N Yor* 2C **100**
Yeldersley Hollies. *Derbs* 1G **73**
Yelford. *Oxon* 5B **50**
Yelland. *Devn* 3E **19**
Yelling. *Cambs* 4B **64**
Yelsted. *Kent* 4C **40**
Yelvertoft. *Nptn* 3C **62**
Yelverton. *Devn* 2B **8**
Yelverton. *Norf* 5E **79**
Yenston. *Som* 4C **22**
Yeoford. *Devn* 3A **12**
Yeolmbridge. *Corn* 4D **10**
Yeo Mill. *Devn* 4B **20**
Yeovil. *Som* 1A **14**
Yeovil Marsh. *Som* 1A **14**
Yeovilton. *Som* 4A **22**
Yerbeston. *Pemb* 4E **43**
Yesnaby. *Orkn* 6B **172**
Yetlington. *Nmbd* 4E **121**
Yetminster. *Dors* 1A **14**
Yett. *N Lan* 4A **128**
Yett. *S Ayr* 2D **116**
Yettington. *Devn* 4D **12**
Yetts o' Muckhart. *Clac* 3C **136**
Y Fali. *IOA* 3B **80**
Y Felinheli. *Gwyn* 4E **81**
Y Fenni. *Mon* 4G **47**
Y Ferwig. *Cdgn* 1B **44**
Y Fflint. *Flin* 3E **83**
Y Ffor. *Gwyn* 2C **68**
Y Fron. *Gwyn* 5E **81**
Y Gelli Gandryll. *Powy* 1F **47**
Yielden. *Bed* 4H **63**
Yieldshields. *S Lan* 4B **128**
Yiewsley. *G Lon* 2B **38**
Yinstay. *Orkn* 6E **172**
Ynysboeth. *Rhon* 2D **32**
Ynysddu. *Cphy* 2E **33**
Ynysforgan. *Swan* 3F **31**
Ynyshir. *Rhon* 2D **32**
Ynyslas. *Cdgn* 1F **57**
Ynysmaerdy. *Rhon* 3D **32**
Ynysmeudwy. *Neat* 5H **45**
Ynystawe. *Swan* 5G **45**
Ynyswen. *Powy* 4B **46**
Ynys-wen. *Rhon* 2C **32**
Ynys y Barri. *V Glam* 5E **32**
Ynysybwl. *Rhon* 2D **32**
Ynysymaerdy. *Neat* 3G **31**
Yockenthwaite. *N Yor* 2B **98**
Yockleton. *Shrp* 4G **71**
Yokefleet. *E Yor* 2B **94**
Yoker. *Glas* 3G **127**
Yonder Bognie. *Abers* 4C **160**
Yonderton. *Abers* 5G **161**
York. *York* 4A **100** & **214**
Yorkletts. *Kent* 4E **41**
Yorkley. *Glos* 5B **48**
Yorkshire Dales. *N Yor* 2H **97**
Yorton. *Shrp* 3H **71**
Yorton Heath. *Shrp* 3H **71**
Youlgreave. *Derbs* 4G **85**
Youlthorpe. *E Yor* 4B **100**
Youlton. *N Yor* 3G **99**
Young's End. *Essx* 4H **53**
Young Wood. *Linc* 3A **88**
Yoxall. *Staf* 4F **73**
Yoxford. *Suff* 4F **67**
Yr Hob. *Flin* 5F **83**
Y Rhws. *V Glam* 5D **32**
Yr Wyddgrug. *Flin* 4E **83**
Ysbyty Cynfyn. *Cdgn* 3G **57**
Ysbyty Ifan. *Cnwy* 1H **69**
Ysbyty Ystwyth. *Cdgn* 3G **57**
Ysceifiog. *Flin* 3D **82**
Yspitty. *Carm* 3E **31**
Ystalyfera. *Neat* 5A **46**
Ystrad. *Rhon* 2C **32**
Ystrad Aeron. *Cdgn* 5E **57**
Ystradfellte. *Powy* 4C **46**
Ystradffin. *Carm* 1A **46**
Ystradgynlais. *Powy* 4A **46**
Ystradmeurig. *Cdgn* 4G **57**
Ystrad Mynach. *Cphy* 2E **33**
Ystradowen. *Carm* 4A **46**
Ystradowen. *V Glam* 4D **32**
Ystumtuen. *Cdgn* 3G **57**
Ythanbank. *Abers* 5G **161**
Ythanwells. *Abers* 5D **160**
Y Trallwng. *Powy* 5E **70**
Y Tymbl. *Carm* 4F **45**
Y Waun. *Wrex* 2E **71**

Z

Zeal Monachorum. *Devn* 2H **11**
Zeals. *Wilts* 3C **22**
Zelah. *Corn* 3C **6**
Zennor. *Corn* 3B **4**
Zouch. *Notts* 3C **74**

(1) A strict alphabetical order is used e.g. Benmore Botanic Gdn. follows Ben Macdui but precedes Ben Nevis.

(2) Entries shown without a main map index reference have the name of the appropriate Town Plan and its page number; e.g. Ashmolean Mus. of Art & Archaeology (OX1 2PH) .... **Oxford 207**
The Town Plan title is not given when this is included in the name of the Place of Interest.

(3) Entries in italics are not named on the map but are shown with a symbol only.
Entries in Italics and enclosed in brackets are not shown on the map.
Where this occurs the nearest town or village may also be given, unless that name is already included in the name of the Place of Interest.

SAT NAV POSTCODES

Postcodes (in brackets) are included as a navigation aid to assist Sat Nav users and are supplied on this basis. It should be noted that postcodes have been selected by their proximity to the Place of Interest and that they may not form part of the actual postal address.
Drivers should follow the Tourist Brown Signs when available.

ABBREVIATIONS USED IN THIS INDEX

Garden : Gdn.	National : Nat
Gardens : Gdns.	Park : Pk.
Museum : Mus.	

INDEX

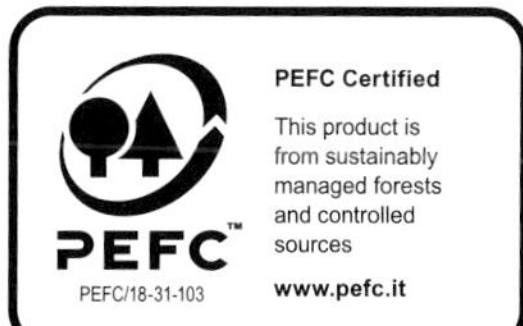

Limited Interchange Motorway Junctions are shown on the maps by RED junction indicators

M1

Junction 2
Northbound: No exit, access from A1 only
Southbound: No access, exit to A1 only

Junction 4
Northbound: No exit, access from A41 only
Southbound: No access, exit to A41 only

Junction 6a
Northbound: No exit, access from M25 only
Southbound: No access, exit to M25 only

Junction 17
Northbound: No access, exit to M45 only
Southbound: No exit, access from M45 only

Junction 19
Northbound: Exit to M6 only,
access from A14 only
Southbound: Access from M6 only,
exit to A14 only

Junction 21a
Northbound: No access, exit to A46 only
Southbound: No exit, access from A46 only

Junction 24a
Northbound: Access from A50 only
Southbound: Exit to A50 only

Junction 35a
Northbound: No access, exit to A616 only
Southbound: No exit, access from A616 only

Junction 43
Northbound: Exit to M621 only
Southbound: Access from M621 only

Junction 48
Eastbound: Exit to A1(M)
Northbound only
Westbound: Access from A1(M) Southbound
only

M2

Junction 1
Eastbound: Access from A2 Eastbound only
Westbound: Exit to A2 Westbound only

M3

Junction 8
Westbound: No access, exit to A303 only
Eastbound: No exit, access from A303 only

Junction 10
Northbound: No access from A31
Southbound: No exit to A31

Junction 13
Southbound: No access from A335 to M3
leading to M27 Eastbound

M4

Junction 1
Westbound: Access from A4 Westbound only
Eastbound: Exit to A4 Eastbound only

Junction 21
Westbound: No access from M48
Eastbound: No exit to M48

Junction 23
Westbound: No exit to M48
Eastbound: No access from M48

Junction 25
Westbound: No access
Eastbound: No exit

Junction 25a
Westbound: No access
Eastbound: No exit

Junction 29
Westbound: No access, exit to A48(M) only
Eastbound: No exit, access from A48(M) only

Junction 38
Westbound: No access, exit to A48 only

Junction 39
Westbound: No exit, access from A48 only
Eastbound: No access or exit

Junction 42
Westbound: No exit to A48
Eastbound: No access from A48

M5

Junction 10
Southbound: No access, exit to A4019 only
Northbound: No exit, access from A4019 only

Junction 11a
Southbound: No exit to A417 Westbound

Junction 18a
Southbound: No exit to M49
Northbound: No access from M49

M6

Junction 3a
Eastbound: No exit to M6 TOLL
Westbound: No access from M6 TOLL

Junction 4
Northbound: No exit to M42 Northbound
No access from M42 Southbound
Southbound: No exit to M42
No access from M42 Southbound

Junction 4a
Northbound: No exit, access from M42
Southbound only
Southbound: No access, exit to M42 only

Junction 5
Northbound: No access, exit to A452 only
Southbound: No exit, access from A452 only

Junction 10a
Northbound: No access, exit to M54 only
Southbound: No exit, access from M54 only

Junction 11a
Northbound: No exit to M6 TOLL
Southbound: No access from M6 TOLL

Junction 20
Northbound: No exit to M56 Eastbound
Southbound: No access from M56 Westbound

Junction 24
Northbound: No exit, access from A58 only
Southbound: No access, exit to A58 only

Junction 25
Northbound: No access, exit to A49 only
Southbound: No exit, access from A49 only

Junction 30
Northbound: No exit, access from M61
Northbound only
Southbound: No access, exit to M61
Southbound only

Junction 31a
Northbound: No access, exit to B6242 only
Southbound: No exit, access from B6242 only

Junction 45
Northbound: No access onto A74(M)
Southbound: No exit from A74(M)

M6 TOLL

Junction 11
Northbound: No exit
Southbound: No access

Junction 12
Northbound: No access or exit
Southbound: No access

Junction 15
Northbound: No exit
Southbound: No access

Junction 17
Northbound: No access from A5
Southbound: No exit

Junction 18
Northbound: No exit to A460 Northbound
Southbound: No exit

M8

Junction 8
Westbound: No access from M73 Southbound
Eastbound: No exit to M73 Northbound

Junction 9
Westbound: No exit, access only
Eastbound: No access, exit only

Junction 13
Westbound: No exit to M80 Northbound
Eastbound: No access from M80 Southbound

Junction 14
Westbound: No exit, access only
Eastbound: No access, exit only

Junction 16
Westbound: No exit, access only
Eastbound: No access, exit only

Junction 17
Westbound: No exit, access to A82 only
Eastbound: No access, exit from A82 only

Junction 18
Westbound: No exit, access only

Junction 19
Westbound: No access from A814 Westbound
Eastbound: No exit to A814 Eastbound

Junction 20
Westbound: No exit, access only
Eastbound: No access, exit only

Junction 21
Westbound: No exit, access only
Eastbound: No access, exit only

Junction 22
Westbound: No access, exit to M77 only
Eastbound: No exit, access from M77 only

Junction 23
Westbound: No access, exit to B768 only
Eastbound: No exit, access from B768 only

Junction 25
Westbound and Eastbound:
Exit to A739 Northbound only
Access from A739 Southbound only

Junction 25a
Eastbound: Access only
Westbound: Exit only

Junction 28
Westbound: no access, exit to airport only
Eastbound: no exit, access from airport only

M9

Junction 2
Northbound: No exit, access from B8046 only
Southbound: No access, exit to B8046 only

Junction 3
Northbound: No access, exit to A803 only
Southbound: No exit, access from A803 only

Junction 6
Northbound: No exit, access only
Southbound: No access, exit to A905 only

Junction 8
Northbound: No access, exit to M876 only
Southbound: No exit, access from M876 only

Junction with A90
Northbound: Exit onto A90 westbound only
Southbound: Access from A90 eastbound only

M11

Junction 4
Northbound: No exit, access from A406
Eastbound only
Southbound: No access, exit to A406
Westbound only

Junction 5
Northbound: No access, exit to A1168 only
Southbound: No exit, access from A1168 only

Junction 8a
Northbound: No access, exit only
Southbound: No exit, access only

Junction 9
Northbound: No access, exit only
Southbound: No exit, access only

Junction 13
Northbound: No access, exit only
Southbound: No exit, access only

Junction 14
Northbound: No access from A428 Eastbound
No exit to A428 Westbound
Southbound: No exit, access from A428
Eastbound only

M20

Junction 2
Eastbound: No access, exit to A20 only
(access via M26 Junction 2a)
Westbound: No exit, access only
(exit via M26 Junction 2a)

Junction 3
Eastbound: No exit, access from M26
Eastbound only
Westbound: No access, exit to M26
Westbound only

Junction 11a
Westbound: No exit to Channel Tunnel
Eastbound: No access from Channel Tunnel

M23

Junction 7
Southbound: No access from A23 Northbound
Northbound: No exit to A23 Southbound

Junction 10a
Northbound: No exit, access only
Southbound: No access, exit only

M25

Junction 5
Clockwise: No exit to M26 Eastbound
Anti-clockwise: No access from M26
Westbound

Spur to A21
Southbound: No access from M26 Westbound
Northbound: No exit to M26 Eastbound

Junction 19
Clockwise: No access exit only
Anti-clockwise: No exit access only

Junction 21
Clockwise and Anti-clockwise:
No exit to M1 Southbound
No access from M1 Northbound

Junction 31
Southbound: No exit access only
(exit via Junction 30)
Northbound: No access exit only
(access via Junction 30)

M26

Junction with M25 (M25 Junc. 5)
Westbound: No exit to M25 anti-clockwise
or spur to A21 Southbound
Eastbound: No access from M25 clockwise
or spur from A21 Northbound

Junction with M20 (M20 Junc. 3)
Eastbound: No exit to M20 Westbound
Westbound: No access from M20 Eastbound

M27

Junction 4
Eastbound and Westbound: No exit to A33
Southbound (Southampton)
No access from A33 Northbound

Junction 10
Eastbound: No exit, access from A32 only
Westbound: No access, exit to A32 only

M40

Junction 3
North-Westbound: No access,
exit to A40 only
South-Eastbound: No exit,
access from A40 only

Junction 7
South-Eastbound: No access, exit only
North-Westbound: No exit, access only

Junction 13
South-Eastbound: No access, exit only
North-Westbound: No exit, access only

Junction 14
South-Eastbound: No access, exit only
North-Westbound: No exit, access only

Junction 16
South-Eastbound: No access, exit only
North-Westbound: No exit, access only

M42

Junction 1
Eastbound: No exit
Westbound: No access

Junction 7
Northbound: No access, exit to M6 only
Southbound: No exit, access from M6
Northbound only

Junction 8
Northbound: No access, exit to M6
Southbound only
Southbound: Exit to M6 Northbound only
Access from M6 Southbound only

M45

Junction with M1 (M1 Junc. 17)
Eastbound: No exit to M1 Northbound
Westbound: No access from M1 Southbound

**Junction with A45 east
of Dunchurch**
Eastbound: No access, exit to A45 only
Westbound: No exit, access from A45
Northbound only

M48

Junction with M4 (M4 Junc. 21)
Westbound: No access from M4 Eastbound
Eastbound: No exit to M4 Westbound

Junction with M4 (M4 Junc. 23)
Westbound: No exit to M4 Eastbound
Eastbound: No access from M4 Westbound

M53

Junction 11
Southbound and Northbound: No access from
M56 Eastbound, no exit to M56 Westbound

M56

Junction 1
Westbound: No access from M60
South-Eastbound
No access from A34 Northbound
Eastbound: No exit to M60 North-Westbound
No exit to A34 Southbound

Junction 2
Westbound: No access, exit to A560 only
Eastbound: No exit, access from A560 only

Junction 3
Westbound: No exit, access only
Eastbound: No access, exit only

Junction 4
Westbound: No access, exit only
Eastbound: No exit, access only

Junction 7
Westbound: No access, exit only

Junction 8
Westbound: No exit, access from A556 only
Eastbound: No access or exit

Junction 9
Westbound: No exit to M6 Southbound
Eastbound: No access from M6 Northbound

Junction 15
Westbound: No access from M53
Eastbound: No exit to M53

M57

Junction 3
Northbound: No exit, access only
Southbound: No access, exit only

Junction 5
Northbound: No exit, access from A580
Westbound only
Southbound: No access, exit to A580
Eastbound only

M58

Junction 1
Eastbound: No exit, access from A506 only
Westbound: No access, exit to A506 only

M60

Junction 2
Nth.-Eastbound: No access, exit to A560 only
Sth.-Westbound: No exit,
access from A560 only

Junction 3
Westbound: No exit to A34 Northbound
Eastbound: No access from A34 Southbound

Junction 4
Westbound: No access from A34 Southbound
No access from M56 Eastbound
Eastbound: No exit to M56 South-Westbound
No exit to A34 Northbound

Junction 5
South-Eastbound: No access from or exit to
A5103 Northbound
North-Westbound: No access from or exit to
A5103 Southbound

Junction 14
Eastbound: No exit to A580
No access from A580 Westbound
Westbound: No exit to A580 Eastbound
No access from A580

Junction 16
Eastbound: No exit, access from A666 only
Westbound: No access, exit to A666 only

Junction 20
Eastbound: No access from A664
Westbound: No exit to A664

Junction 22
Westbound: No access from A62

Junction 25
South-Westbound:
No access from A560/A6017

Junction 26
North-Eastbound: No access or exit

Junction 27
North-Eastbound: No access, exit only
South-Westbound: No exit, access only

M61

Junctions 2 and 3
North-Westbound:
No access from A580 Eastbound
Sth.-Eastbound: No exit to A580 Westbound
Junction with M6 (M6 Junc. 30)
North-Westbound:
No exit to M6 Southbound
South-Eastbound:
No access from M6 Northbound

M62

Junction 23
Eastbound: No access, exit to A640 only
Westbound: No exit, access from A640 only

M65

Junction 9
Nth.-Eastbound: No access, exit to A679 only
Sth.-Westbound:
No exit, access from A679 only

Junction 11
North-Eastbound: No exit, access only
South-Westbound: No access, exit only

M66

Junction 1
Southbound: No exit, access from A56 only
Northbound: No access, exit to A56 only

M67

Junction 1
Eastbound: Access from A57 Eastbound only
Westbound: Exit to A57 Westbound only

Junction 1a
Fastbound: No access, exit to A6017 only
Westbound: No exit, access from A6017 only

Junction 2
Eastbound: No exit, access from A57 only
Westbound: No access, exit to A57 only

M69

Junction 2
North-Eastbound:
No exit, access from B4669 only
South-Westbound:
No access, exit to B4669 only

M73

Junction 1
Southbound: No exit to A74 Eastbound

Junction 2
Northbound: No access from M8 Eastbound
No exit to A89 Eastbound
Southbound: No exit to M8 Westbound
No access from A89 Westbound

Junction 3
Northbound: No exit to A80 South-Westbound
Southbound:
No access from A80 North-Eastbound

M74

Junction 1
Eastbound: No access from M8 Westbound
Westbound: No exit to M8 Westbound

Junction 3
Eastbound: No exit
Westbound: No access

Junction 3a
Eastbound: No access
Westbound: No exit

Junction 7
Southbound: No access, exit to A72 only
Northbound: No exit, access from A72 only

Junction 9
Southbound: No access, exit to B7078 only
Northbound: No access or exit

Junction 10
Southbound: No exit, access from B7078 only

Junction 11
Southbound: No access, exit to B7078 only
Northbound: No exit, access from B7078 only

Junction 12
Southbound: No exit, access from A70 only
Northbound: No access, exit to A70 only

M77

Junction with M8 (M8 Junc. 22)
Southbound: No access from M8 Eastbound
Northbound: No exit to M8 Westbound

Junction 4
Southbound: No access
Northbound: No exit

Junction 6
Southbound: No access from A77
Northbound: No exit to A77

Junction 7
Northbound: No access from A77
No exit to A77

M80

Junction 1
Northbound: No access from M8 Westbound
Southbound: No exit to M8 Eastbound

M90 (right column continues)

Junction 4a
Northbound: No access
Southbound: No exit

Junction 6a
Northbound: No exit
Southbound: No access

Junction 8
Northbound: No access from M876
Southbound: No exit to M876

M90

Junction 2a
Northbound: No access, exit to A92 only
Southbound: No exit, access from A92 only

Junction 7
Northbound: No exit, access from A91 only
Southbound: No access, exit to A91 only

Junction 8
Northbound: No exit, access from A91 only
Southbound: No access, exit to A91 only

Junction 10
Northbound: No access from A912
Exit to A912 Northbound only
Southbound: No exit to A912
Access from A912 Southbound only

M180

Junction 1
Eastbound: No access, exit only
Westbound: No exit, access from A18 only

M606

Junction 2
Northbound: No access, exit only

M621

Junction 2a
Eastbound: No exit, access only
Westbound: No access, exit only

Junction 4
Southbound: No exit

Junction 5
Northbound: No access, exit to A61 only
Southbound: No exit, access from A61 only

Junction 6
Northbound: No exit, access only
Southbound: No access, exit only

Junction 7
Westbound: No exit, access only
Eastbound: No access, exit only

Junction 8
Northbound: No access, exit only
Southbound: No exit, access only

M876

Junction with M80 (M80 Junc. 5)
North-Eastbound:
No access from M80 Southbound
South-Westbound: No exit to M80 Northbound
Junction with M9 (M9 Junc. 8)
North-Eastbound: No exit to M9 Northbound
South-Westbound:
No access from M9 Southbound

A1(M) (Hertfordshire Section)

Junction 2
Southbound: No exit, access from A1001 only
Northbound: No access, exit only

Junction 3
Southbound: No access, exit only

Junction 5
Northbound: No exit, access only
Southbound: No access or exit

A1(M) (Cambridgeshire Section)

Junction 14
Northbound: No exit, access only
Southbound: No access, exit only

A1(M) (Leeds Section)

Junction 40
bound: Exit to A1 Southbound only
on 43
nd: Access from M1 Eastbound only
nd: Exit to M1 Westbound only

A1(M) (Durham Section)

Junction 57
Northbound: No access,
exit to A66(M) only
Southbound: No exit, access from A66(M)

Junction 65
Northbound: Exit to A1 North-Westbound,
and to A194(M) only
Southbound: Access from A1 South-Eastbound,
and from A194(M) only

A3(M)

Junction 4
Northbound: No access, exit only
Southbound: No access, exit only

A38(M) Aston Expressway

**Junction with Victoria Road,
Aston**
Northbound: No exit, access only
Southbound: No access, exit only

A48(M)

**Junction with M4
(M4 Junc. 29)**
South-Westbound: access from M4 Westbound
North-Eastbound: exit to M4 Eastbound only

Junction 29a
South-Westbound: Exit to A48 Westbound only.
North-Eastbound:
Access from A48 Eastbound only

A57(M) Mancunian Way

**Junction with A34 Brook Street,
Manchester**
Eastbound: No access, exit to A34 Brook Street
Southbound
Westbound: No exit, access only

A58(M) Leeds Inner Ring Road

**Junction with Park Lane/
Westgate**
Southbound: No access, exit only

A64(M) Leeds Inner Ring Road
(Continuation of A58(M))

Junction with A58 Clay Pit Lane
Eastbound: No Access
Westbound: No exit

A66(M)

**Junction with A1(M)
(A1(M) Junc. 57)**
South-Westbound:
Exit to A1(M) Southbound only
North-Eastbound:
Access from A1(M) Northbound only

A74(M)

Junction 18
Northbound: No access
Southbound: No exit

A167(M) Newcastle Central Motorway

Junction with Camden Street
Northbound: No exit, access only
Southbound: No access or exit

A194(M)

**Junction with A1(M)
(A1(M) Junc. 65) and
A1 Gateshead Western By-Pass**
Southbound: Exit to A1(M) only
Northbound: Access from A1(M) only

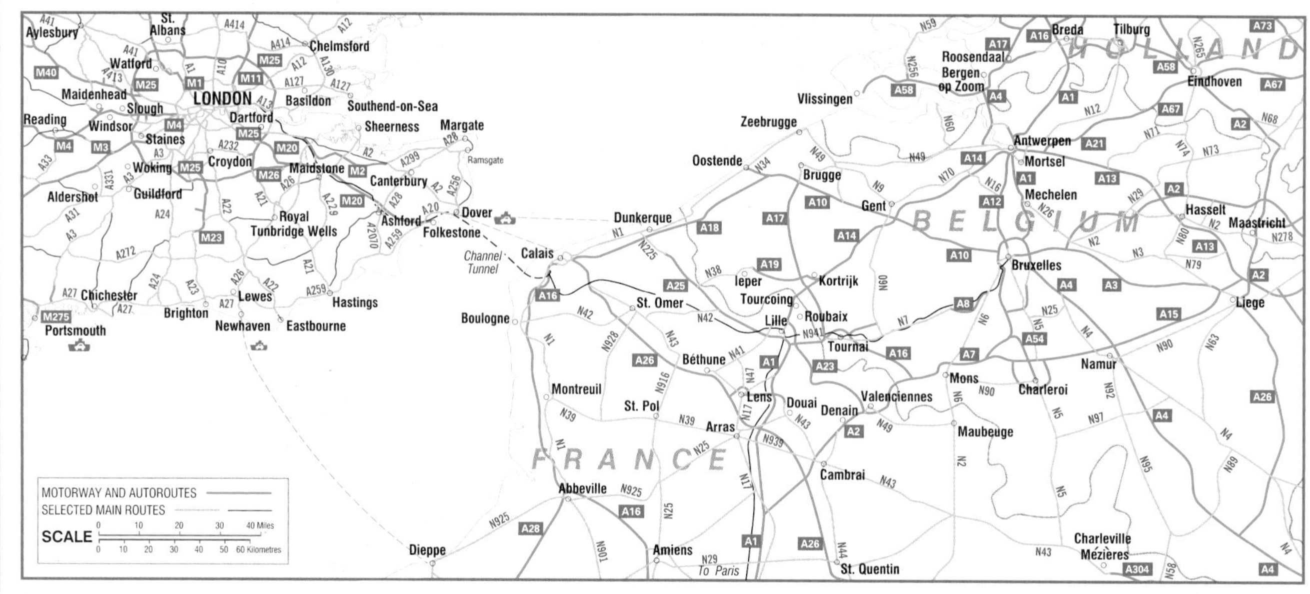

LONDON
Aylesbury
St. Albans
Watford
Chelmsford
Maidenhead
Slough
Reading
Windsor
Staines
Dartford
Basildon
Southend-on-Sea
Sheerness
Margate
Woking
Croydon
Maidstone
Canterbury
Aldershot
Guildford
Royal Tunbridge Wells
Ashford
Dover
Folkestone
Channel Tunnel
Calais
Chichester
Lewes
Hastings
Brighton
Newhaven
Eastbourne
Portsmouth
Dunkerque
Boulogne
St. Omer
Ieper
Tourcoing
Lille
Roubaix
Kortrijk
Tournai
Béthune
Montreuil
St. Pol
Lens
Douai
Denain
Valenciennes
Arras
Cambrai
Abbeville
Amiens
To Paris
St. Quentin
Dieppe
FRANCE
Zeebrugge
Oostende
Brugge
Gent
Vlissingen
Roosendaal
Bergen op Zoom
Breda
Tilburg
Eindhoven
HOLLAND
Antwerpen
Mortsel
Mechelen
Hasselt
Maastricht
BELGIUM
Bruxelles
Liège
Mons
Charleroi
Namur
Maubeuge
Charleville Mézières
MOTORWAY AND AUTOROUTES
SELECTED MAIN ROUTES
SCALE
0 10 20 30 40 Miles
0 10 20 30 40 50 60 Kilometres

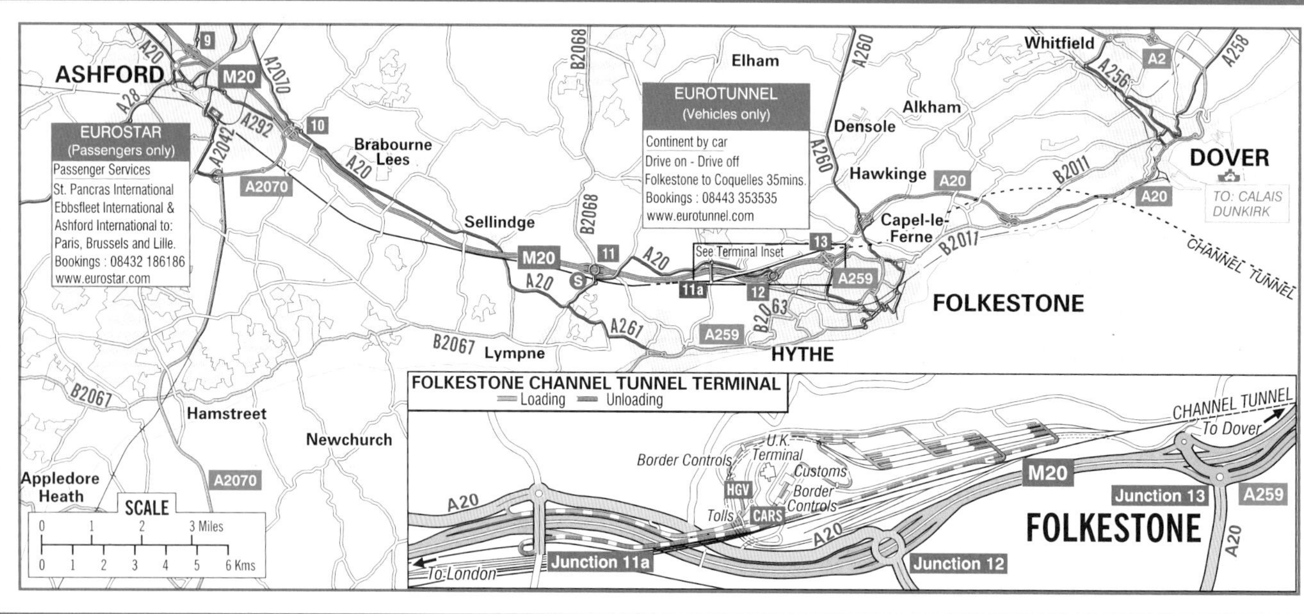

ASHFORD
EUROSTAR
(Passengers only)
Passenger Services
St. Pancras International
Ebbsfleet International &
Ashford International to:
Paris, Brussels and Lille.
Bookings : 08432 186186
www.eurostar.com
Brabourne Lees
Sellindge
Elham
EUROTUNNEL
(Vehicles only)
Continent by car
Drive on - Drive off
Folkestone to Coquelles 35mins.
Bookings : 08443 353535
www.eurotunnel.com
Whitfield
Alkham
Densole
Hawkinge
Capel-le-Ferne
DOVER
TO: CALAIS
DUNKIRK
CHANNEL TUNNEL
See Terminal Inset
FOLKESTONE
Lympne
HYTHE
Hamstreet
Newchurch
Appledore Heath
SCALE
0 1 2 3 Miles
0 1 2 3 4 5 6 Kms
FOLKESTONE CHANNEL TUNNEL TERMINAL
Loading
Unloading
Border Controls
U.K. Terminal
Customs
Border Controls
Tolls
HGV
CARS
To Dover
To London
Junction 11a
Junction 12
Junction 13
FOLKESTONE

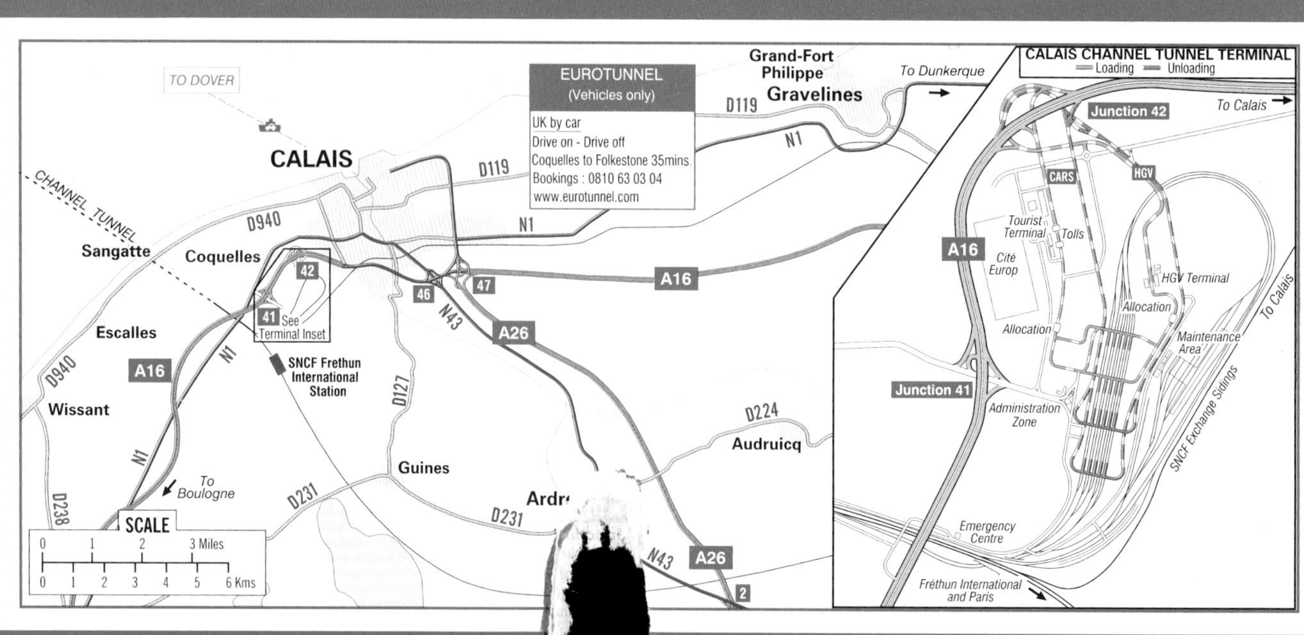

TO DOVER
CALAIS
CHANNEL TUNNEL
Sangatte
Coquelles
Escalles
Wissant
See Terminal Inset
SNCF Frethun International Station
To Boulogne
Grand-Fort Philippe
Gravelines
To Dunkerque
EUROTUNNEL
(Vehicles only)
UK by car
Drive on - Drive off
Coquelles to Folkestone 35mins.
Bookings : 0810 63 03 04
www.eurotunnel.com
Guines
Audruicq
SCALE
0 1 2 3 Miles
0 1 2 3 4 5 6 Kms
CALAIS CHANNEL TUNNEL TERMINAL
Loading
Unloading
Junction 42
To Calais
CARS
HGV
Tourist Terminal
Tolls
Cité Europ
HGV Terminal
Allocation
Maintenance Area
Junction 41
Administration Zone
SNCF Exchange Sidings
Emergency Centre
Fréthun International and Paris